NEVADA CIVIL PRACTICE MANUAL

Third Edition

CONTINUING LEGAL EDUCATION COMMITTEE
OF
STATE BAR OF NEVADA

THE MICHIE COMPANY
Law Publishers
CHARLOTTESVILLE, VIRGINIA

Janice J. Brown	Las Vegas
Sara Beth Brown	Reno
Henry W. Cavallera	Reno
E. Leslie Combs, Jr.	Las Vegas
Curtis B. Coulter	Reno
Craig R. Delk	Las Vegas
Craig Demetris	Reno
Jeffrey A. Dickerson	Reno
Mary Phelps Dugan	Reno
Allan R. Earl	Las Vegas
Douglas A. Emerick	Reno
Suellen Fulstone	Reno
Steven B. Glade	Las Vegas
Elizabeth Goff Gonzales	Las Vegas
Rew R. Goodenow	Reno
David R. Grundy	Reno
Salvatore C. Gugino	Las Vegas
John R. Hawley	Carson City
Katherine Henderson	Las Vegas
Ginger R. James	Las Vegas
Rex A. Jemison	Las Vegas
Lynne K. Jones	Reno
Bruce M. Judd	Las Vegas
Brent A. Larsen	Las Vegas
Kirk B. Lenhard	Las Vegas
Pat Lundvall	Reno
Arthur E. Mallory	Reno
James N. Mancuso	Incline Village
A. William Maupin	Las Vegas
B. Alan McKissick	Reno
Ann Morgan	Reno
James P. Pace	Reno
Jean Parraguirre	Reno
Stanley W. Parry	Las Vegas
Michael E. Pavlakis	Carson City
Bridget Robb Peck	Reno
John R. Petty	Reno
Marc Picker	Reno
Joseph R. Plater	Reno
Pamela G. Roberts	Las Vegas
Kent R. Robison	Reno
Cecilia L. Rosenauer	Reno
Michael A. Rosenauer	Reno
Susan Ball Rothe	Reno

Margaret M. Springgate	Reno
Don Springmeyer	Reno
Todd Touton	Las Vegas
Richard M. Trachok, II	Reno
Patricia A. Trent	Las Vegas
Evan J. Wallach	Las Vegas

TABLE OF CONTENTS

CHAPTER 5

PARTIES

CHAPTER 6

VENUE

CHAPTER 7

REMOVAL

CHAPTER 10

DEFAULTS AND DEFAULT JUDGMENTS

CHAPTER 11

MOTIONS, AFFIDAVITS, STIPULATIONS AND ORDERS

CHAPTER 12

DEFENSIVE MOTIONS

CHAPTER 13

ANSWERS AND REPLIES

CHAPTER 14

COUNTERCLAIMS AND CROSS-CLAIMS

CHAPTER 15

THIRD-PARTY PRACTICE

CHAPTER 16

DEPOSITIONS AND DISCOVERY

E. Procedural Requirements

CHAPTER 19

CONSOLIDATION AND SEVERANCE

CHAPTER 20

DISMISSAL OF ACTIONS

CHAPTER 21

ALTERNATIVE DISPUTE RESOLUTION (ADR)

CHAPTER 22

TRIALS

CHAPTER 23

THE JURY TRIAL

CHAPTER 24

JUDGMENTS

CHAPTER 26

PRE-JUDGMENT REMEDIES

CHAPTER 27

ENFORCEMENT OF JUDGMENTS

CHAPTER 28

INJUNCTIVE RELIEF

CHAPTER 29

A PRACTICAL GUIDE TO JUDICIAL DISCRETION

CHAPTER 30

RECEIVERS

CHAPTER 31

DECLARATORY JUDGMENTS

CHAPTER 32

NEVADA BOND AND LIEN LAW

CHAPTER 33

GUARDIANSHIPS

CHAPTER 34

ESTATES OF DECEASED PERSONS

CHAPTER 35

EXTRAORDINARY WRITS

TABLE OF CONTENTS

INTRODUCTION TO THE THIRD EDITION

The Nevada Civil Practice Manual was envisioned by Robert C. Anderson and realized by District Judge J. Charles Thompson, editor-in-chief of the 1986 and 1988 editions. This edition continues that project.

The editors and authors of all the editions received no compensation for the contributions of time and skill reflected in these pages. Their unselfish devotion to the development of the law is gratefully acknowledged.

The assistance of Pamela Gullihur, Pat Brackett-Wright, Sherry A. Stagnaro and Lorain T. Wilson was invaluable in preparation of the manuscript for publication.

This manual is intended to be a handy reference tool, not an exhaustive statement of Nevada law. It should be the beginning, not the end of legal research.

The observation of Oliver Wendell Holmes, Jr., in the 1881 edition of *The Common Law* is equally true today: "The life of the law has not been logic; it has been experience."

Brent T. Adams
District Judge

CHAPTER 1

SOURCES OF NEVADA LAW

Authors: Katherine Henderson
            Pamela G. Roberts

§ 101. Introduction and scope.

Nevada law springs from a rich heritage rooted in the English common law and Spanish-Mexican civil law traditions embodied in the territorial laws and early California constitutional provisions and statutes Nevada adopted upon statehood. Sources are examined against this backdrop to provide the historical context essential to a clear understanding of the diverse strands woven into the fabric of Nevada law. Emphasis has been placed upon the discussion of primary and secondary authorities from a practical viewpoint to enhance civil practice research strategy.

§ 102. Primary sources.

§ 103. — English and American common law.

The oldest source of Nevada law is the English common law as it existed at the time of the American Revolution in 1776. *Hamilton v. Kneeland*, 1 Nev. 40 (1865). When the "Battle Born" State of Nevada joined the Union in 1864 during the Civil War, the application of common law in the courts already had been established by the Territorial Legislature. As presently codified under *NRS* 1.030, "the common law of England, so far as it is not repugnant to or in conflict with the Constitution and laws of the United States, or the Constitution and laws of this state, shall be the rule of decision in all courts of this state." From the very beginning of statehood the Nevada Supreme Court proclaimed that common law also governed judicial authority and procedure. *Burling v. Goodman*, 1 Nev. 314 (1865).

1

American common law is another source of Nevada law. The *Restatement of the Law*, promulgated by the American Law Institute organized in 1923, provides statements of the general common law of the United States, including law developed by judicial decision after American independence and law that has grown from the application of long standing statutes. Since 1966, the ALI also has allowed prediction of the developing law as well as restatement to reflect current circumstances.

The *Restatement* is a fruitful source of Nevada law for those subjects covered which include agency, conflict of laws, contracts, foreign relations, judgments, property (landlord/tenant and donative transfers), restitution, security, torts, and trusts. The Nevada Supreme Court has expressly adopted several sections of the *Restatement* in its opinions, and cited many others as supporting authority. Moreover, the *Restatement* provides a body of generally accepted common law on issues which the Court may not as yet have had the opportunity to address. *Restatement in the Courts* reports decisions citing the *Restatement* by subject and jurisdiction, providing the *Restatement* section cited and description of law the *Restatement* applied in the case.

§ 104. — Territorial laws and constitution.

The Act of Congress Organizing the Territory of Nevada is the earliest source of Nevada statutory law. The Act created territorial boundaries and set up the governmental structure. Moreover, it established Nevada's first court system with "chancery as well as common-law jurisdiction; and authority for redress of all wrongs committed against the Constitution or laws of the United States, or of the Territory, affecting persons or property." 12 *United States Statutes at Large* 209-14 (1863).

The Territory of Nevada was created on March 2, 1861, two days before President Abraham Lincoln took office. After his inauguration, Lincoln wasted no time in appointing James W. Nye of New York as governor to organize the new territory. Upon his arrival in Carson City in July, 1861, Nye issued a proclamation organizing the Territory of Nevada and summoned the first Territorial Legislature to meet in Carson City to begin the law making process for the newly formed Territory of Nevada. The *Territorial Laws of Nevada* subsequently enacted during the territorial period from 1861-1864 constitute the roots of Nevada statutory law and as such are still cited in the opinions of the Nevada Supreme Court. *Paradise Homes, Inc. v. Central Surety & Insurance Corporation*, 84 Nev. 109, 437 P.2d 78 (1968). The *Territorial Laws* are published in three volumes as follows:

Laws of the Territory of Nevada Passed at the First Regular Session (1861)

Laws of the Territory of Nevada Passed at the Second Regular Session (1862)

Laws of the Territory of Nevada Passed at the Third Regular Session (1864)

Nevada had been a territory only four short years when An Act of Congress Enabling the People of Nevada to Form a Constitution and State Government was passed in 1864. 13 *United States Statutes at Large* 30-32 (1864). The Constitutional Convention which convened to carry out this mandate produced the *Constitution of the State of Nevada,* which became the bedrock of Nevada law upon approval of the electorate and Nevada's admission to statehood on October 31, 1864 by presidential proclamation. 13 *Statutes at Large* 749-50 (1864).

The proceedings of the Constitutional Convention were published in *Debates and Proceedings in the Constitutional Convention of the State of Nevada* which is useful in researching legislative intent and understanding the history and background of Nevada law. Annotations to the *Debates* are found exclusively in the *Nevada Revised Statutes.*

Nevada still operates under its original constitution, unlike the majority of other states. Eleanor Bushnell, *The Nevada Constitution: Origin and Growth,* p. 69 (3d ed., Reno: University of Nevada Press, 1972). However, the original text has been amended occasionally throughout the years, and new provisions added. Both the *Nevada Revised Statutes* and the *Nevada Revised Statutes Annotated* indicate the source of the amendment or addition in the history notes immediately following the text of the new or amended section.

§ 105. — Statutory law.

With the publication of the *Statutes of the State of Nevada* Passed at the First Session of the Legislature 1864-1865, statutory law has been an integral part of Nevada law since the Constitutional Convention. Although no provision was made for statutory revision until 1951, the first compilation of Nevada statutes entitled *The Compiled Laws of the State of Nevada* was published in 1873. All told, eight statutory compilations were published during the time period between 1873-1949 as follows:

B	Bonnifield and Healy, *The Compiled Laws of the State of Nevada* (1873)
BH	Baily and Hammond, *The General Statutes of the State of Nevada* (1885)
C	Cutting, *Compiled Laws of Nevada* (1900)
RL	*Revised Laws of Nevada* (1912)
1919 RL	*Revised Laws of Nevada* (1919)
NCL	*Nevada Compiled Laws* (1919)
1931 NCL	*Nevada Compiled Laws 1931-41 Supplement* (1941)

1943 NCL   *Nevada Compiled Laws 1943-49 Supplement* (1949)

In addition, the following Practice Acts were published in the *Revised Laws of Nevada* of 1912.

CPA   *Civil Practice Act of 1911*
C&P   *Crimes and Punishment Act of 1911*
Cr.Prac.   *Criminal Practice Act of 1911*

In 1951, the Legislature authorized a comprehensive revision of the laws of the State of Nevada for the first time in Nevada's history. Revision commenced under the auspices of the newly created Statute Revision Commission to eliminate from the accumulation of 95 years of legislation provisions no longer in force, and to restate and compile the remainder in an understandable form. The *Nevada Revised Statutes*, which the Legislature enacted in their entirety as law of the State of Nevada in 1957, marked the culmination of the Commission's work. Updated every two years since 1957 upon the conclusion of each legislative session, the *Nevada Revised Statutes* are published by the Legislative Counsel Bureau in looseleaf binders.

From 1957 through the 1965 legislative session, the *Nevada Revised Statutes* were published in large post binders designated *Nevada Revised Statutes: Statute Revision Commission*. The first complete reprinting of the *Nevada Revised Statutes* occurred in 1967, along with the adoption of the present looseleaf binder design.

The *Nevada Revised Statutes* are divided into 4 main parts: Remedial, Civil, Penal, and Political. The Civil Practice section deals with limitation of actions, parties, commencement of actions, trials, judgments, costs, fees, enforcement of judgments, and contempts.

In addition to statutory law, the *Nevada Revised Statutes* also contain Nevada Supreme Court Rules, District Court Rules, Justices' Court Rules, Nevada Rules of Civil Procedure, and Nevada Rules of Appellate Procedure, found in the Remedial section dealing with structure and organization of courts and with civil procedure and remedies.

As discussed in the Preface, annotations, historical notes, and other reviser's notes were published separately in *Annotations to Nevada Revised Statutes* from 1965-1985. In 1987, this information was fully integrated into the *Nevada Revised Statutes* with the applicable text and chapters and now includes references to the *Nevada Administrative Code*, reviser's notes, *Nevada Constitutional Debates and Proceedings*, notes of Advisory Committees of the Nevada Supreme Court, Nevada Attorney General opinions, and citations to decisions of the Nevada Supreme Court, federal courts, and courts of other jurisdictions involving provisions of the *Nevada Revised Statutes*.

In 1986, Michie Company launched publication of the *Nevada Revised Statutes Annotated* in collaboration with the Nevada State Bar Committee on Legislative Publications. Michie, a publisher of legal treatises and statutes since 1855, retained the same titling and numbering system utilized in the *Nevada Revised Statutes*. However, from its inception, Michie's *Nevada Revised Statutes Annotated* featured case annotations fully integrated with the statutes to benefit the lawyer user, an enhancement the *Nevada Revised Statutes* did not adopt until later. Case annotations include citations to Nevada Supreme Court and federal decisions which have construed Nevada law. In addition, *NRSA* annotations provide notes taken from applicable opinions of the Nevada Attorney General, and cross-references to related statutory provisions as well as references to relevant legal periodical articles and *American Law Reports*, Third and Fourth Series.

Endorsed by the Nevada State Bar, the *Nevada Revised Statutes Annotated* is published in hard-bound volumes updated biennially with pocket parts and a new index. A soft-bound volume of court rules, updated and revised annually, is also provided which contains Nevada Supreme Court Rules, local practice rules for the U.S. District Court for the District of Nevada, and United States Court of Appeals Rules for the Ninth Circuit. Although the *NRSA* uses the official wording of the statutes throughout, should any textual variance with the *Nevada Revised Statutes* occur, the *NRS* version controls as the Legislative Counsel Bureau publication.

Both the *Nevada Revised Statutes* and *Nevada Revised Statutes Annotated* provide legislative history notes which appear at the end of each section. The history includes reference to section, chapter, and year of the Statutes of Nevada from which the section is derived, subsequent amendments, and section numbers in prior compilations when applicable. In addition, comparative section tables and tables of repealed, expired, and replaced sections are provided at the end of each set.

An excellent source of information for researching Nevada legislative history is "Researching Legislative History in Nevada," a 1989 Forum article written by Susan Southwick and James L. Olmsted which appeared in *Inter Alia*. Coverage includes sections on the treatment of legislative history by the Nevada Supreme Court, types of legislative materials and their persuasive value, and a guide to locating legislative history materials. University of Pacific, McGeorge School of Law's *Pacific Law Journal* in its Silver Sheets also published a "Review of Selected Nevada Legislation" after each legislative session from 1979 through 1987, which provides commentary.

The *Martindale-Hubbell Law Digest* is a handy compendium of Nevada statutory law. The Nevada Law Digest section provides a topical summary of current law, together with applicable citations to statutes, cases, court rules, and uniform laws. Of special benefit to the practitioner are the numerous forms preferred by local usage which appear under the appropriate topic in addition to the Commercial Code forms provided at the end of the section. Helpful also is the Uniform and Model Acts section that contains the text of many of the uniform and model acts (such as the Uniform Commercial Code and the Uniform Partnership Act) which Nevada substantially has incorporated into its statutory law. For the benefit of the Bar, the American Bar Association section includes the Model Rules of Professional Conduct of the American Bar Association, the Code of Judicial Conduct, and the composition, jurisdiction, and rules of procedure of the American Bar Association Standing Committee on Ethics and Professional Responsibility.

The Nevada Legislature meets biennially in the odd-numbered years for an approximately five-month session starting in January. Senate and Assembly bills enacted into law are published in the *Statutes of Nevada* and subsequently codified in *NRS* and *NRSA*. *Advance Sheets of Nevada Statutes* are available within three months of the conclusion of the legislative session. However, since laws enacted may become effective upon passage, it is important to keep abreast of legislative bills as passed by consulting the *Senate History* and *Assembly History*. The Legislative Counsel Bureau also offers NELIS, an online bill tracking information system it makes available by subscription. Lexis and Westlaw Advanced Legislative and Bill Tracking databases are useful, too, as online resources in monitoring the progress of legislation.

§ 106. — Case law.

Nevada has three judicial levels: Supreme Court, District Court, and Justices' Court. Additionally, the Legislature may establish Municipal Courts in incorporated cities and towns. The Legislature also established a Family Court, effective 1993, as a division of the District Court in each judicial district that includes a county whose population is 100,000 or more as specified in *NRS* 3.0105. Although Nevada has no Intermediate Appellate Court, a Senate Joint Resolution was passed during the 1993 Legislative Session proposing to amend the Nevada Constitution to create a Court of Appeals.

Nevada Supreme Court decisions are the only Nevada judicial opinions published. District Court opinions are on file and available in the Clerk's office of the County in which the case was heard. However, Justice Court decisions are on record only if transcribed in a judicial proceeding.

The official Nevada Supreme Court decisions are published in the *Nevada Reports* as reported by the Clerk of the Supreme Court. West Publishing Company's *Pacific Reporter* contains the unofficial version with West's synopses and headnotes. However, the *Pacific Reporter* does *not* contain Nevada Supreme Court cases decided before the *Pacific Reporter* commenced publication in 1882. Thus, *Nevada Reports* Volumes

1-16 are the sole source of Nevada Supreme Court cases decided during the first seventeen years of statehood. The more recent Nevada Supreme Court cases may also be accessed online by means of Lexis and Westlaw.

Bound volumes of the *Nevada Reports* are published annually. In addition to the cases reported, tables list United States and Nevada statutes and constitutional provisions cited, as well as Nevada city and county ordinances. Reference is also made to the *Code of Federal Regulations* and statutes of other states cited. Nevada Court Rules, *Nevada Administrative Code* provisions, and Federal Rules of Civil Procedure cited in the cases are noted, too. A Digest of Headnotes and Words and Phrases Index is included at the back of each volume as well as the listing of unpublished decisions.

The Clerk of the Nevada Supreme Court issues Advance Opinion slipsheets within a few days following a Supreme Court decision. Subsequently, the Clerk publishes the official Advance Opinion in about three weeks. This version contains the text of the decision that eventually will be published in the *Nevada Reports* and *Pacific Reporter*. As a caveat, it is important to remember that the Advance Opinion text may differ slightly from the decision as it first appeared in the slipsheets. This is due to the fact that the initial slipsheet version is not the official report, thus subject to subsequent correction and modification.

Nevada Supreme Court cases are keyed into West's Digest System, utilizing the *Pacific Reporter* citation. In addition, the Legislative Counsel Bureau has published the *Nevada Digest* since 1957 as prescribed by legislative and judicial mandate. Organized according to subject following topical outlines used in Bancroft-Whitney's *California Jurisprudence*, 2d edition (but not subsequently converted to follow *California Jurisprudence*, 3d edition), the *Digest* contains synopses of Nevada, federal, and other cases as well as Nevada Attorney General's opinions. The *Digest* also makes pertinent reference to Lawyers Co-operative's *American Jurisprudence*, 2d series and *American Law Reports*, 1st, 2d, and 3d series. Scope notes are placed at the beginning of each topic outline which contain an analysis of the topic and references to related topics. Like the *Nevada Revised Statutes*, the Legislative Counsel Bureau publishes the *Digest* in loose-leaf binders, with periodic updates. The *Nevada Index*, a monthly publication containing citations to all Nevada Supreme Court decisions by topic is also available to subscribers.

Shepard's Nevada Citations is an excellent finding aid for both case and statutory law. As explained in its preface, *Nevada Shepard's* shows all citations to Nevada cases reported in the *Nevada Reports* or in the *Pacific Reporter*, as cited in the reported decisions of the Nevada Supreme Court and Federal Courts. Citations to Nevada cases appearing in selected law review articles (including *Inter Alia*) and legal texts, are included, too. Shepard's softbound cumulative supplement contains Nevada Advance Opinion citations.

Statutory citations show all citations to the Nevada Constitution, Revised Statutes, codes, statutes (including territorial laws), court rules, and ordinances as cited in the reported decisions of the Nevada and federal courts since 1931. Also included are citations to Nevada statutes cited in the *Statutes of Nevada*, and in selected legal periodicals and texts. Citations by the Nevada Supreme Court and in the *Statutes of Nevada* to the United States Constitution and federal statutes are also shown. Citations to Nevada case and statutory law as appearing in annotations of *United States Supreme Court, Lawyers Edition, American Law Reports,* and *American Law Reports, Federal* are noted, too.

Shepard's Nevada Citations contain two tables which are particularly helpful for research purposes. The Table of Nevada Acts lists Nevada acts by popular names or short titles, and indicates where each act can be located in the *Nevada Revised Statutes/Nevada Revised Statutes Annotated* or the *Statutes of Nevada*. This table also lists the names of principal Nevada cities and indicates where their city charters can be located in the *Statutes of Nevada*. The Ordinances Table provides an alphabetical subject heading listing of cited provisions of Nevada municipal ordinances.

§ 107. — Administrative law.

An important primary source of Nevada law is the body of regulations promulgated by state administrative agencies. In 1977, the Legislature decreed that "permanent regulations be incorporated into an administrative code in accordance with state policy to make agency regulations clear, concise, and easily accessible to the public." *NRS* 233B.062. As a result, the *Nevada Administrative Code* commenced publication in 1984 under the direction of the Legislative Counsel. Prior to 1984, it was necessary to contact the individual agencies for regulations.

The *Nevada Administrative Code*, published in loose-leaf binders, arranges regulations in accordance with numbered chapters corresponding to the numbers of the *NRS* Chapters where the respective subjects are treated. As the Preface explains, each *NAC* section is followed by a source note which shows the name of the agency which adopted the regulation, the effective date of the section, and any amendments. The source note also indicates the origin of regulations which were adopted before codification. The *NAC* tables volume contains a Table of Sections Repealed or Replaced and a listing by agencies of regulations promulgated, along with their effective date and *NAC* number. Tracking of regulations can also be accomplished by utilizing Lexis and Westlaw online services. The Nevada Gaming Commission publishes regulations of the State Gaming Control Board and Nevada Gaming Commission.

§ 108. — Attorney general's opinions.

Heads of state agencies may seek the advice of the Attorney General upon any question of law related to their respective departments. The Attorney General's opinions published in response do not constitute binding legal authority or precedent. *Cannon v. Taylor*, 88 Nev. 89, 493 P.2d 1313 (1972). However, they are entitled to great weight. *Prescott v. United States*, 731 F.2d 1388 (9th Cir. Nev., 1984). Attorney General's opinions are also helpful in determining legislative intent in the enactment of a statute or administrative regulation.

The Attorney General acts as the state's chief legal advisor and as such furnishes opinions in response to inquiries submitted by the governor, state officials, and district and city attorneys. The first published opinions appear in *Report of the Attorney General of the State of Nevada for the Years 1875 and 1876* and subsequent opinions over the next fifteen years were published sporadically. Since 1891, however, opinions have been published without break and appear in the annual *Official Opinions of the Attorney General*. Opinions are arranged in chronological order with a subject index at the end of each volume. Indexed, too, are provisions of the Nevada Constitution, *Nevada Revised Statutes, Statutes of Nevada*, and previous opinions of the Attorney General cited in the opinions published.

To ensure currency, the office of the Attorney General makes available individual copies of each opinion within approximately ten days after it is written. Attorney General's opinions dating back to 1977 are accessible also on Lexis and Westlaw.

§ 109. Secondary sources.

§ 110. —California law.

California law has been a prominent source of Nevada law since the inception of statehood. Most of the framers of Nevada's constitution originally came to Nevada from California and drew heavily upon California's constitution and statutes in devising the framework for Nevada's governmental structure and legal system. Bushnell, *supra*, at 55. As the Nevada Supreme Court observed three years after Nevada was admitted to the Union, "We have copied most of our Constitution and most of our laws from the sister state of California." *State of Nevada v. Milliam*, 3 Nev. 409 (1867). Furthermore, like California, Nevada is a community property state having adopted the Spanish-Mexican civil law as it was administered in California under the early statutes. *Nixon v. Brown*, 46

Nev. 439, 214 P. 524 (1923). From the practice standpoint therefore, the California Continuing Education of the Bar (CEB) publications can be most helpful to the Nevada attorney in researching those areas of the law which Nevada substantially adopted from California.

The Nevada Supreme Court also made it clear early on that "when the legislature of one state adopts the laws of another, it is presumed to know the construction placed upon those laws in the state from which they are adopted, and therefore that it adopts that construction with the law." *McLane v. Abrams*, 2 Nev. 199 (1866). Thus, substantial weight has been given historically to opinions of the California appellate courts in their construction of California statutes subsequently adopted by Nevada.

§ 111. Federal law.

Federal statutory and Ninth Circuit decisional law also constitute fertile sources of Nevada law. Indeed, the Act of Congress organizing the Territory of Nevada in 1861 stated, "That the Constitution and all laws of the United States which are not locally inapplicable shall have the same force and effect within the said Territory of Nevada as elsewhere in the United States." 12 *United States Statutes at Large* 209-14 (1863). Furthermore, the Nevada Supreme Court has concluded that a federal court decision in a case arising within Nevada is persuasive of what the common law is in Nevada. *Carlton v. Manuel*, 64 Nev. 570, 187 P.2d 558 (1947).

Federal cases also offer analyses of Nevada law not found elsewhere. For example, an extensive examination of Nevada case and statutory law regarding the Nevada Wrongful Death Act is provided in *Borrego v. Stauffer Chemical Co.*, 315 F. Supp. 980 (D. Nev. 1970). Moreover, since Nevada substantially has adopted the Federal Rules of Civil Procedure and the Proposed Federal Rules of Evidence, federal court opinions discussing the federal rules are often a productive resource.

Reported decisions of the United States District Court for Nevada (sitting in both Reno and Las Vegas) appear in the *Federal Supplement*. Selected appellate decisions are reported in the *Federal Reporter*. Decisions and rulings involving the federal rules are published in *Federal Rules Decisions*. Of particular help to researchers in the *Federal Supplement*, *Federal Reporter* and *Federal Rules Decisions* are the introductory statutes and rules table in each volume which itemize federal and state statutes referred to in the opinions, as well as rules cited.

§ 112. — Legal periodicals.

Legal Periodical articles can be extremely useful research tools, particularly in the areas of specialized and developing law. Both the *Index to*

Legal Periodicals published by H.W. Wilson Company and Information Access Company's *Current Law Index* provide bibliographic access to law journals of high quality and permanent reference value published in the United States and other English-speaking countries. In addition, *CLI* includes selected journals treating allied disciplines.

The *Index to Legal Periodicals* dates back to 1907 when it was first published by the American Association of Law Libraries "at a time when there was no key of a periodical nature to the extremely important contributions to legal literature contained in the legal periodicals," according to its Preface. Articles published prior to 1980 are accessible through *ILP* only, because the *Current Law Index* did not commence publication until 1980. However, the *CLI* is particularly advantageous to the Nevada researcher because it includes *Inter Alia* among the journals listed, unlike *ILP*. In addition to standard indexing features, both the *ILP* and *CLI* contain tables of cases and statutes cited which can be particularly helpful when pertinent to Nevada or ninth circuit federal law. The LegalTrac database is also a useful tool to access legal publications including law reviews and specialty law publications, bar association journals, and selected legal newspapers.

§ 113. — State Bar of Nevada publications and practice related materials.

State Bar of Nevada publications are an excellent source of information respecting the current state of Nevada law and developing trends. In 1936, the Bar published the first volume of *Nevada State Bar Journal*, changing the *Journal's* name to *Inter Alia* in 1973. Although the editorial format has broadened over the intervening years, the basic character of the publication has remained the same in keeping with its original purpose to make available State Bar information regarding officers, committees and membership, and to provide a forum for "articles, letters, essays and news items contributed by members from all parts of the state," as explained in the first issue.

Bibliographic access to *Inter Alia* articles from 1936-1989 can be obtained through *An Index to the Nevada State Bar Journal and Inter Alia*, 1936-1989, compiled by Larry D. Strate and Janice Loutzenhiser. Strate's *1990-1991 Supplement* Index was published in *Inter Alia's* July, 1992 issue. Since 1980, the *Current Law Index* has indexed the main articles, too.

In 1989, the State Bar also commenced publication of *Bar Letter*, which contains current informational items connected with State Bar business, continuing legal educational opportunities, and practice tips. In 1993, *Inter Alia* and *Bar Letter* were combined and merged into *Nevada Lawyer* as a new publication.

Form books, although rarely a source of Nevada case law, are a useful resource for the new attorney beginning the practice of law in Nevada. The Nevada Trial Lawyers Association's *Personal Injury Form Book* and the Nevada Association of Legal Secretaries' *Official Handbook of Nevada Legal Forms* (which covers topics such as probate, gaming, extraordinary remedies, and more) can be particularly helpful. Naturally, a thorough attorney will always compare the forms with present statutory requirements. For case law and analysis regarding discovery procedures, attorneys in Washoe County can also utilize articles authored by Discovery Master John Petty and published in the *WRIT*, which is the Washoe County Lawyers Association's monthly publication. The Clark County Bar Association's *COMMUNIQUE* provides topical news related to the courts and current legal practice matters, too. Newsletters published by the State Bar sections and Nevada Trial Lawyers Association also offer useful information exchange.

In connection with Continuing Legal Education courses and seminars offered through the State Bar of Nevada, Professional Education Systems Incorporated (PESI) publishes numerous manuals and soft-bound texts that are useful to the general practitioner. Both Clark and Washoe County Law Libraries receive courtesy copies of the various texts and manuals. Other resource books written for the Nevada attorney cover a wide range of topics. The PESI seminar materials, along with other Nevada resource books, are typically shelved in the KFN section of the Library.

CHAPTER 2

JUDGES AND ATTORNEYS

Authors: Salvatore C. Gugino
James N. Mancuso

§ 201. Introduction and scope.

With the adoption of a new Nevada Code of Judicial Conduct and the establishment of a system of alternative dispute resolution under the Nevada Arbitration Rules, the Nevada Supreme Court has significantly altered the authority, duties and responsibilities of judges and attorneys in this state.

While this chapter is not intended to be an exhaustive review of all subjects discussed, it will primarily emphasize topics relating to practice before the local district courts. Various references will also be made regarding the role of judges in general, judicial ethics, the rules of professional conduct, and the role of attorneys as hearing officers or other quasi-judicial triers of fact.

§ 202. Definitions and authority of judges and attorneys.

The judiciary, as a co-equal branch of government, has inherent powers to administer its own affairs. *Goldberg v. Eighth Judicial District Court,* 93 Nev. 614, 572 P.2d 521 (1977). Attorneys being court officers and essential aids in the administration of justice, the government of the legal profession is a judicial function subject to the rules established for it by the Supreme Court. SCR 39.

A judge is a public officer authorized by law to hear and determine causes and to hold court for that purpose. As a judge alone does not constitute a court, with its additional attributes of time, place, and jurisdiction (*see* Chapters 4 and 9, *infra*), one judge may preside over two or more courts. *Ex parte Gardner,* 22 Nev. 280, 39 P. 570 (1895). But note: The district courts of this state have equal and coextensive jurisdiction; therefore, the various district courts lack jurisdiction to review the acts of other district courts. *See* Nev. Const. Art. 6, § 6; NRS 3.220; *Rohlfing v. District Court,* 106 Nev. 902, 803 P.2d 659 (1990); *Murray v. State,* 106 Nev. 907, 803 P.2d 225 (1990); *State Engineer v. Sustacha,* 108 Nev. 223, 826 P.2d 959 (1992). Similarly, lower federal courts have absolutely no authority to sit in review of state court decisions, whether issued by the district trial court or appellate court. *Mirin v. Justices of Supreme Court of Nevada,* 415 F. Supp. 1178 (D. Nev. 1976).

Upon the filing of a timely notice of appeal, a district court loses its authority over a matter and jurisdiction is vested in the Supreme Court. Thus, a district court has no authority to grant a new trial once the notice of appeal has been filed. The court may, however, entertain a motion for new trial and certify that it is inclined to grant it. *See Huneycutt v. Huneycutt,* 94 Nev. 79, 575 P.2d 585 (1978); *Smith v. Emery,* 109 Nev. __, __ P.2d __ (1993).

Only the Supreme Court is given general appellate jurisdiction. *See* Nev. Const. Art. 6, § 6; *State Engineer v. Sustacha,* 108 Nev. 223, 826 P.2d 959 (1992). Supreme Court justices, like district court judges, have the inherent authority to ensure the efficient administration of justice, including the use of effective methods of ensuring court decorum and dignity, and the right to issue reprimands. *See Mirin v. Justices of Supreme Court of Nevada,* 415 F. Supp. 1178 (D. Nev. 1976).

Under the doctrine of judicial immunity, a judge or justice is protected from civil suit when acting in his or her judicial capacity and while carrying out his or her judicial functions. *Mirin, supra,* at 1192.

A hearing officer in an administrative law proceeding has much less authority than a judge or justice. For example, under NRS 616.542, an appeals officer is given quasi-judicial powers to the extent necessary to execute his or her duties, which include accepting and evaluating evidence, and entering final administrative decisions in accordance therewith. *Southwest Gas Corp. v. Woods,* 108 Nev. 11, 823 P.2d 288 (1992).

All persons admitted to practice in any of the courts in this state shall be known as attorneys and counselors at law. SCR 40. With the exception of NRS 4.010 (justices of peace in townships of less than 250,000), only attorneys and counselors at law may serve as supreme court judges

(NRS 2.020(2)), district court judges (NRS 3.060(2)), justices of the peace (NRS 4.101(2)) or special masters (WDCR 26(1); EDCR 1.40(a)).

Pursuant to statutory authority, only licensed and admitted attorneys may serve as elected district attorneys (NRS 252.010(2)), substitute municipal court judges (NRS 5.023(1)(a)), appeals officers with the Department of Industrial Relations (NRS 616.542(2)), Nevada attorneys for injured workers (NRS 616.253(2)(a)), mental commitment hearing masters (EDCR 1.44(b)), paternity hearing masters (EDCR 1.42(a)) or Uniform Reciprocal Support Act masters (EDCR 1.40(a)). Licensed attorneys who have completed a course of instruction in administrative law may be appointed as hearing officers for the State Board of Education (NRS 391.3161(1)).

With regard to attorneys acting as arbitrators pursuant to NRS 38.215 and NRS 38.250, the Nevada Supreme Court has ordered that the State Bar of Nevada shall maintain two (2) panels of arbitrators, one consisting of licensed attorneys and a separate panel of arbitrators qualified to engage in professions other than law. *See* Rule 7(A), as amended, Nevada Arbitration Rules.

Unlicensed attorneys may serve as hearing officers for the county (NRS 244.3525(2)), and law students may be certified for practical training pursuant to NRS 49.5.

Attorneys who are licensed and admitted in other jurisdictions may engage in practice in Nevada under certain limited purposes, such as: associating with local counsel in order to participate in a particular lawsuit (SCR 42.1), representing the United States Government (SCR 43), representing indigents or an organized legal services program (SCR 49.3), or acting as a deputy district attorney in a county whose population is less than 10,000 (SCR 49.4). Pursuant to SCR 49.6, an attorney licensed to practice in any other jurisdiction may be admitted to practice on behalf of the State Bar of Nevada as Bar Counsel or Assistant Bar Counsel.

§ 203. Presiding judge.

The legislature has directed that the Second and Eighth Judicial Districts shall each have a presiding judge. NRS 3.025. Under NRS 3.025, a presiding judge has the duty to assign cases to the judges in the district, prescribe the hours of court and adopt necessary rules and regulations. Case assignment procedure is set forth in § 204, *infra*. By reason of SCR 8, the presiding judge is the district judge member of the regional judicial council. Presiding judges are selected annually (WDCR 2(3)); (EDCR 1.30)(a)) although in the Eighth District the term may be extended for one year.

In both the Second and Eighth Judicial Districts the presiding judge is known as the chief judge and is generally responsible for resolving calendar problems. WDCR 2(3), 3(2), 4(2), 4(11), 4(16); EDCR 1.30. The chief judge in the Eighth Judicial District has special responsibilities in connection with the appointment of masters under the Uniform Reciprocal Support Act, the Uniform Parentage Act and all involuntary mental commitment proceedings.

§ 204. Initial assignment of cases to a judge.

In the Second and Eighth Judicial Districts, all civil and criminal cases are distributed to the judges on a random basis. WDCR 2(1); EDCR 1.60(a), 1.64. If the assignment is made when the initial pleadings are filed, the department number will be noted on the pleading. In all other instances, the district court clerk may be contacted to determine when an assignment has been made. No attorney or party is to directly or indirectly attempt to influence the clerk of the court or the court staff or any officer thereof to assign a case to a particular judge. EDCR 1.60(g).

Rule 1(F)(1) of the FJDCR and the TJDCR require all civil actions to be assigned a department for all further action therein when set for trial or pretrial or when any contested matter has been heard therein. Rule 2(c) of the NJDCR states that all civil and criminal actions shall be assigned by the Court Clerk to a department when filed with the Court Clerk.

In general, once the case is assigned to a department, all matters in connection therewith will be presented to the judge presiding in that department. *See, e.g.,* FJDCR 1(F)(1); TJDCR 1(F)(1); EDCR 7.10. Local rules provide exceptions for having a matter heard by another judge when the assigned judge is unavailable or if the matter is of an emergency nature. WDCR 4(2), 4(8), 4(17); EDCR 7.10; NJDCR 4(d). In the First and Third Judicial Districts, the judges of their courts may "interchange with each other" with regard to assignments. FJDCR 1(E); TJDCR 1(E).

Once the judge has entered an order or decision in any case, no other judge shall do any act or thing in or about such case unless upon the written request of the first judge. DCR 18. *See Collins v. Union Federal Savings & Loan Association,* 97 Nev. 88, 624 P.2d 496 (1981); *State v. Babayan,* 106 Nev. 155, 787 P.2d 805 (1990); *see also* EDCR 7.10(b). This prohibition does not prevent another judge from setting, vacating or resetting a trial. *State ex rel. Marshall v. Eighth Judicial District Court,* 79 Nev. 280, 382 P.2d 214 (1963). *See also* NRS 1.250, and *State ex rel. Stokes v. Second Judicial District Court,* 55 Nev. 115, 27 P.2d 534 (1933). Modifications or exceptions to this rule are contained in the Local Rules. *See, e.g.,* WDCR 4(6); EDCR 1.60; EDCR 7.10.

§ 205. Voluntary recusal.

A judge may voluntarily recuse himself. NRS 1.230(3); DCR 18.1; 18; EDCR 1.60(d); *Jeaness v. Second Judicial District Court*, 97 Nev. 218, 626 P.2d 272 (1981); *but see Ham v. Eighth Judicial District Court*, 93 Nev. 409, 566 P.2d 420 (1977) (where prohibition was granted preventing a District Court Judge who had been handling an active case for three years and who expressly stated he was not biased or prejudiced from voluntarily recusing himself). *See also* Nevada Code of Judicial Conduct, Canon 3(c) (Disqualification) and 3(F) (Remittal of Disqualification).

§ 206. Peremptory challenge.

Peremptory challenges are mechanisms designed to ensure a fair tribunal by allowing a party to disqualify a judge thought to be unfair or biased. A movant may be said to properly take advantage of a peremptory challenge when the litigant is concerned that the judge may be biased or unfair for some real or imagined reason. *State ex rel. Smith v. District Court*, 107 Nev. 674, 818 P.2d 849 (1991). In any civil action originating in a district court, each "side" has one opportunity to change the assigned judge by peremptory challenge. SCR 48.1. For this purpose, an estate or probate matter is a "civil action." *Cord v. Second Judicial District Court*, 91 Nev. 260, 533 P.2d 1355 (1975). Each action is treated as having only two sides. SCR 48.1. If one of two or more parties on one side of an action files a peremptory challenge, no other party on that side may file a separate challenge. SCR 48.1.

Intervenors under NRCP 24 are not considered parties to an action until they have filed a complaint with the court. *State ex rel. Moore v. Fourth Judicial District Court*, 77 Nev. 357, 364 P.2d 1073 (1961); *Aetna Life & Casualty Co. v. Rowan*, 107 Nev. 362, 812 P.2d 350 (1991). Once they have successfully intervened, they are accorded the same status as an original party, and have the same right to file affidavits of prejudice against a district court judge as other original parties. *Moore, supra*, 77 Nev. at 363, 364 P.2d at 1077. *But see also Carr-Bricken v. First Interstate Bank*, 105 Nev. 570, 799 P.2d 967 (1989) (where supreme court refused to renew the time period for filing a peremptory challenge after counterclaim was filed).

Peremptory challenges are permitted to disqualify a judge to whom a matter is reassigned for trial even if a previously assigned judge has already made pretrial rulings. *Tarsey v. Dunes Hotel*, 75 Nev. 364, 343 P.2d 910 (1959). Similarly, if a newly-elected district judge takes the bench during the pendency of a case, any party thereto may legitimately file a peremptory challenge to the successor judge prior to the time he or she has heard any contested matter in the underlying case. *See State ex rel. Smith v. Eighth Judicial District Court,* 107 Nev. 674, 818 P.2d 849 (1991) (where court permitted peremptory challenge to successor judge presiding over post-trial motions).

The party wishing to exercise its right to change the judge shall file a notice entitled "Peremptory Challenge of Judge." The peremptory challenge of the judge must be filed in writing with the clerk of the court in which the case is pending and a copy served on the opposing party. The notice must be signed by a party or by an attorney and must state the name of the judge to be changed. The challenge shall not specify grounds nor be accompanied by an affidavit. The filing shall be accompanied by a filing fee of $200. SCR 48.1.

§ 207. — Time for filing a peremptory challenge.

The peremptory challenge shall be filed within ten days after notification to the parties of a trial or hearing date or not less than three days before the date set for hearing of any contested matter, whichever first occurs. Because NRCP 6 does not expressly apply to supreme court rules, weekends and nonjudicial days may count for purposes of the three-day time limit of SCR 48.1(3)(b). The time set forth in former SCR 48.1(3) has been construed to mean that a challenge filed after a pretrial matter has been determined by the judge but more than thirty days before trial is untimely. *Jeaness v. Second Judicial District Court,* 97 Nev. 218, 626 P.2d 272 (1981).

If a case is not assigned to a judge before the time required for filing the peremptory challenge, the challenge shall be filed within three days after the party or its attorney is notified that the case has been assigned to a judge or before the jury is sworn and evidence taken or any ruling is made in the trial or hearing, whichever occurs first. SCR 48.1(4).

The time limits set forth in Rule 48.1, as well as the rule itself, will be strictly construed. *See United States v. Conforte,* 457 F. Supp. 641, 654 n.7 (D. Nev. 1978), *aff'd,* 624 F.2d 869 (9th Cir.), *cert. denied,* 449 U.S. 1012 (1980); *Nevada Pay TV v. Eighth Judicial District Court,* 102 Nev. 203, 719 P.2d 797 (1986). *See also Carr-Bricken v. First Interstate Bank,* 105 Nev. 570, 799 P.2d 967 (1989) (where supreme court refused to renew the time period for filing a peremptory challenge after counterclaim was filed). The rule is designed to prevent its use as a device for "judge shopping" or the facilitation of dilatory tactics. *Smith v. Eighth Judicial District Court,* 107 Nev. 674, 818 P.2d 849 (1991). Failure to file within the time strictures of the rule results in waiver of the right to make a peremptory challenge. *Smith, supra,* at 678.

§ 208. — Notice of peremptory challenge.

A notice of peremptory challenge (see "Peremptory Challenge of Judge" in § 206 *supra*) may not be filed against any judge who has made any ruling in a contested matter or commenced a contested hearing.

The term "contested matter" has not been specifically defined by the court. *See State ex rel. Marshall v. Eighth Judicial District Court,* 79 Nev. 280, 382 P.2d 214 (1963); and *see Jeaness v. Second Judicial District Court,* 97 Nev. 218, 626 P.2d 272 (1981). However, the Court has noted, in *State ex rel. Moore v. Fourth Judicial District Court,* 77 Nev. 357, 364 P.2d 1073 (1961), that a "contested matter" does not include matters involving the arrangement of the court's calendar or the regulation of the order of the court's business. *See also Nevada Pay TV v. Eight Judicial District Court,* 102 Nev. 203, 719 P.2d 797 (1986), at 205 n.2 (where the court discusses the addition of the term "contested" in the amended rule) and at page 206 (where it states that the phrase "any pretrial matter" must be read literally).

§ 209. — Reassignment.

In order to avoid any potential problems with regard to ex parte communications initiated by a challenged judge, the Nevada Supreme Court has amended SCR 48.1 to provide that the judge against whom a peremptory challenge is filed shall not contact any party or the attorney representing any party, nor shall the judge direct any communication to the clerk of the district court with respect to the reassignment of the case in which the peremptory challenge was filed. SCR 48.1(6).

Instead, the clerk of the court shall randomly reassign the case to another judge within two (2) days of the notice of peremptory challenge having been filed. SCR 48.1(2)(a). In a judicial district having two (2) or less departments, however, the clerk shall assign the case to the remaining judge. Alternatively, the presiding judge in the district may request the chief justice to assign the case to a judge of another district. SCR 48.1(2)(b).

In determining whether the peremptory challenge was timely filed, the original judge retains jurisdiction. *See Nevada Pay TV v. Eighth Judicial District Court,* 102 Nev. 203, 719 P.2d 797 (1986).

§ 210. Disqualification.

A judge has as great an obligation not to disqualify himself, when there is no occasion to do so, as he has to do so in the presence of valid reasons. A judge or justice is presumed not to be biased, and the burden is on the party asserting the challenge to establish sufficient factual grounds warranting disqualification. *Goldman v. Bryan*, 104 Nev. 644, 764 P.2d 1296 (1988).

A supreme court or district court judge may be disqualified for actual or implied bias or prejudice for or against one of the parties to the action. NRS 1.230. Implied bias exists when a judge is a party to or interested in the action or proceeding, when he is related to either party by consanguinity or affinity within the third degree, or when he has been an attorney or counsel for either of the parties in the particular action or proceeding before the court. NRS 1.230(2). Implied bias also exists when the judge is related to the attorney or counselor for either of the parties by consanguinity or affinity within the third degree. This latter ground for disqualification does not apply to the presentation of ex parte or contested matters except when fixing fees for an attorney so related to the judge. NRS 1.230(2).

In adopting the Code of Judicial Conduct promulgated by the American Bar Association in August of 1990, the Supreme Court has also provided that a judge shall disqualify himself or herself in a proceeding in which the judge's impartiality might reasonably be questioned. NCJC 3(E)(1). This would include instances where the judge has a personal bias or prejudice concerning a party or a party's lawyer, or personal knowledge of disputed evidentiary facts concerning the proceeding. NCJC 3(E)(1)(a). It would also include instances where the judge knows that he or she, individually or as a fiduciary, or the judge's spouse, parent, or child wherever residing, or any other member of the judge's family residing in the judge's household, has an economic interest in the subject matter in controversy or in a party to the proceeding or has any other more than de minimis interest that could be substantially affected by the proceeding. NCJC 3(E)(1)(c).

Further, a judge should disqualify himself or herself if the judge, his or her spouse (or relative within the third degree of relationship, or the spouse of such a relative) is a party to the proceeding, or an officer, director, or trustee of a party; is acting as a lawyer in the proceeding; is known by the judge to have more than a de minimis interest that could be substantially affected by the proceeding; or is, to the judge's knowledge, likely to be a material witness in the proceeding. NCJC 3(E)(1)(d).

On the other hand, Supreme Court justices who act in an administrative capacity to reach or make decisions that later become directly implicated in litigation which is reviewed or otherwise acted upon by the same justices as part of the Supreme Court are not disqualified by any form of inherent conflict posed by acting in two different capacities concerning matters that were litigated. *See Goldman v. Bryan,* 104 Nev. 644, 764 P.2d 1296 (1988); *In re Petition to Recall Dunleavy,* 104 Nev. 784, 769 P.2d 1271 (1988); *Kelch v. Director,* 107 Nev. 827, 822 P.2d 1094 (1991).

§ 211. — Procedure.

NRS 1.235 provides that any party to an action sitting in the district court who seeks to disqualify a judge for actual or implied bias or prejudice must file an affidavit specifying the facts upon which the party seeks disqualification. SCR 48.1(7) and *Johnson v. Goldman,* 94 Nev. 6, 575 P.2d 929 (1978) appear to also allow a party who has not filed a peremptory challenge to disqualify a judge by filing an affidavit of bias or prejudice without specifying the facts. The affidavit of a party represented by an attorney must be accompanied by a certificate of the attorney of record that the affidavit is filed in good faith and is not interposed for delay.

The affidavit must be filed not less than twenty days before the date set for the trial or hearing of the case and not less than three days before the date set for the hearing of any pretrial matter. NRS 1.235(1). If a case is not assigned to a judge before this time, the affidavit must be filed within ten days after the party or its attorney is notified that the case has been assigned to a judge, before the hearing of any pretrial matter or before the jury is impaneled, evidence taken or any ruling made in the trial or hearing, whichever occurs first. If the facts upon which disqualification of the judge is sought are not known to the party before he is notified of the assignment of the judge or before any pretrial hearing is held, the affidavit may be filed not later than the commencement of the trial or hearing of the case. NRS 1.235(2).

If a case is reassigned to a new judge and the time for filing the affidavit is expired, the parties have ten days after notice of the new assignment within which to file the affidavit and the trial or hearing of the case must be rescheduled for a date after the expiration of the ten-day period unless the parties stipulate to an earlier date. NRS 1.235(3).

At the time the affidavit is filed, a copy must be served upon the judge sought to be disqualified. Service must be made by delivering a copy to the judge personally or by leaving it at his chambers with some person of suitable age and discretion employed therein. NRS 1.235(4).

NRS 1.235(5)(a), relating to challenges for actual or implied bias, is virtually identical to Rule 48.1(6). *Nevada Pay TV v. Eighth Judicial District Court,* 102 Nev. 203, 719 P.2d 797 (1986). The judge against whom an affidavit alleging bias or prejudice is filed can proceed no further with the matter and must immediately transfer the case to another department of the court if there is more than one department of the court in the district or request the judge of another district court to preside at the trial or hearing of the matter.

The challenged judge, however, is not required to transfer a case to another judge where the affidavit of prejudice is not timely filed. *See State ex rel. Welfare Division v. Eighth Judicial District Court,* 85 Nev.

642, 462 P.2d 37 (1969). *See also Jacobson v. Manfredi,* 100 Nev. 226, 679 P.2d 251 (1984). Failure to comply timely with the requirements for seeking recusal provided in NRS 1.235(1) and (2) results in a waiver of the issue. *Brown v. Federal Savings & Loan Insurance Corp.,* 105 Nev. 409, 777 P.2d 361 (1989).

The challenged judge may also file a written answer with the clerk of the court within two days after the affidavit is filed admitting or denying any or all of the allegations contained in the affidavit and setting forth any additional facts which bear on the question of his disqualification. The question of the judge's disqualification must be heard and determined by another judge agreed upon by the parties or, if they are unable to agree, by a judge appointed by the presiding judge of the district. If a presiding judge in the judicial district is sought to be disqualified, the question of the judge's disqualification must be decided by the judge having the greatest number of years of service. In judicial districts having only one judge, the supreme court appoints a judge to decide the disqualification. NRS 1.235(5).

§ 212. Disability and retirement.

In Nevada, a judge may be disabled from performing his duties for a number of reasons, including: losing a bid for re-election (Nev. Const. Art. 6, § 4); losing a recall election (Art. 3, § 21); impeachment (Art. 7, § 3); removal by the Commission on Judicial Discipline (Art. 6, § 21); and absence from the state for ninety consecutive days (Art. 6, § 17; NRS 3.140). Of course, a judge may retire (NRS 3.092) or become disabled as a result of death, sickness, or other disability (NRCP 63).

There is substantial authority supporting the proposition that even in the absence of a specific constitutional or statutory authorization, under its general power of superintendence, a state supreme court may exercise its administrative authority to conduct an inquiry into a judge's judicial capacity and take such action as is deemed necessary, short of removal of a judge from office. *See Goldman v. Bryan,* 104 Nev. 644, 764 P.2d 1296 (1988); Nev. Const. Art. 6, § 19.

Under SCR 7(6), whenever the Chief Justice of the Supreme Court is absent from the Court, disqualified for any reason, disabled, or otherwise unavailable or precluded from performing his administrative role, the Vice Chief Justice shall assume the duties and responsibilities of that office. Pursuant to SCR 7(10), in the event that the Chief Justice or Vice Chief Justice is temporarily disabled to perform the duties of his office, then as provided in Art. 6, § 19(2) of the Nevada Constitution, the Justice next senior in commission shall act in his place and stead.

If a judge becomes disabled or retires, the cases that were pending before him or her are assigned, of course, to the new judge of the court, or to the department, at whatever state of progression they were in at the time of the disability or retirement. There is normally little if any problem here, as NRS 3.180 requires the retiring judge to decide all matters submitted before retirement. A judgment not entered and filed before the expiration of a term of office is null and void. NRCP 58(c); NRS 3.180; *Osman v. Cobb,* 77 Nev. 133, 360 P.2d 258 (1961); *see also* dissenting opinion, *Ainsworth v. Combined Insurance Co.*, 105 Nev. 237, 774 P.2d 1003 (1989).

If physical or mental disability, bias, peremptory challenge, or calendar conflicts disable a judge from performing duties in a particular case, the case is transferred to another judge as discussed in §211, *supra.*

Regardless of the reason for the disability, a problem may arise if, prior to his disability, the disabled judge heard some part of the case but did not render a decision. Any pre-disability rulings actually made and entered by the disabled judge are binding on the parties and, to the degree that they would have been binding on the disabled judge were he still on the case, on the new judge. NRS 1.260. In this situation the case proceeds in regular fashion, with the succeeding judge deciding all matters not decided by the disabled judge. If, however, the disability postdates the hearing or trial, but predates the judgment, the matter is not as clear. The succeeding judge could not decide a matter that he had not heard. However, if the disabled judge filed findings and conclusions, or if a verdict was rendered before him, the succeeding judge may not have to grant a new trial, even though no judgment was entered by the disabled judge. NRCP 63. Moreover, NRS 3.180(3) provides that if a judge has rendered and filed a decision or caused the same to be entered in the minutes of the court and then died, has been removed, or has retired before he could file the findings or entry of judgment, then the succeeding judge must examine the decision or option of the disabled judge as well as the minutes, pleadings, record and reporter's notes. *Coleman v. Moore & McIntosh,* 49 Nev. 139, 241 P. 217 (1925). The practitioner should note that NRS 175.091 through 175.101 set forth the legislature's view of this problem when the court is trying a criminal case; some analogy to the civil arena may be possible.

§213. The judge in chambers.

A district court judge can do anything in chambers other than conduct a public trial. NRCP 77(b). To protect the record, however, the practitioner should be prepared to call a court reporter into chambers when a case is discussed there. Also, a supreme court justice, who can grant or deny most motions without consultation with the other justices [*see* NRAP 27(c)], will presumably entertain such motions in chambers. Occasionally judges permit attorneys to meet with them in chambers. Most judges normally prefer that the attorney call the judge's secretary and make an appointment. If the matter involves a pending case, attorneys for all sides should be present before any discussions take place. *See Commentary,* NCJC 3(B)(7). A judge is precluded from initiating or considering an ex parte communication concerning a pending or impending proceeding. *See* NCJC 3(B)(7).

Although a district court judge must adhere to the Nevada Rules of Civil Procedure and to the various district court rules, he or she is free to regulate his or her practice in any manner not inconsistent with these rules. NRCP 83. Accordingly, the practitioner is well-advised to become familiar with the manner in which each and every judge goes about conducting the day-to-day affairs of his or her court.

§ 214. — Case pending in another district.

A judge, having heard a case in another district, has jurisdiction after returning to his own district to hear a motion for new trial in chambers. *Roberts Mining & Milling Co. v. Third Judicial District Court,* 56 Nev. 299, 50 P.2d 512 (1935). Generally, each judge has statutory power to hold court in any district and is empowered to transact business which may be done in chambers at any point within the state. NRS 3.220. However, no district court judge has the jurisdiction or authority to review the acts or orders of another district court judge. *Rohlfing v. District Court,* 106 Nev. 902, 803 P.2d 659 (1990).

§ 215. Judicial administration and judicial discipline.

In Nevada, all civil and criminal matters are handled by the same judicial system. A Supreme Court, District Courts, and Justices of the Peace comprise the court system in this state. The Legislature also has the power to establish courts for municipal purposes only in incorporated cities and towns. By amendment, the Nevada Constitution provides that the Chief Justice of the Nevada Supreme Court is the administrative head of the court system, with specified administrative authority over District Judges. (Nev. Const. Art. 6, § 19), and a commission on judicial discipline has been created with the authority to censor, retire or remove District Judges or Supreme Court Justices. (Nev. Const. Art. 6, § 21).

In matters relating to disqualification of a judge, a trial judge may not voluntarily disqualify himself from a proceeding where there is no explanation of the claimed bias or prejudice and where the trial judge has already ruled on certain litigated matters. *Ham v. Eighth Judicial District Court In and For Clark County,* 93 Nev. 409, 566 P.2d 420 (1977); *Goldman v. Bryan,* 104 Nev. 644, 764 P.2d 1296 (1988). An allegation that a judge is biased in favor of or against an attorney for a litigant generally states an insufficient ground for disqualification because it is not indicative of extrajudicial bias against a party. *In re Dunleavy*, 104 Nev. 784, 769 P.2d 1271 (1988).

Although a trial judge has wide discretion in how a trial is conducted, the court does not have jurisdiction to enter judgment for or against one who is not a party to the action. *Young v. Nevada Title Co.*, 103 Nev. 436, 744 P.2d 902 (1987).

The Nevada Supreme Court upheld the findings and judgment of the Nevada Commission on Judicial Discipline to impose discipline against a judge who had voluntarily abandoned and relinquished his office and who had engaged in wilful misconduct and habitual intemperance. *Goldman v. Nevada Commission on Judicial Discipline*, 108 Nev. 251, 831 P.2d 107 (1992).

Supreme Court Rule 203(4) provides that it is professional misconduct for a lawyer to engage in conduct that is prejudicial to the administration of justice. Thus, a trial court has an interest in maintaining the efficient administration of justice by preventing prejudicial interference posed by legal counsel. *In re Discipline of Stuhff*, 108 Nev. 629, 837 P.2d 853 (1992).

A new Nevada Code of Judicial Conduct has been adopted by the Nevada Supreme Court. Judicial Canons 1 through 5 of the Nevada Code of Judicial Conduct are intended to establish standards for ethical conduct of judges. A primary purpose for the establishment and maintenance of ethical standards for judges is the promotion of public confidence in the integrity and impartiality of the judiciary.

§ 216. Attorneys.

Pursuant to the rules of the Nevada Supreme Court, no person may practice law in the State of Nevada unless that person is an active member of the State Bar of Nevada. *See* NRS 7.285; SCR 77; and NRS 199.340(8) (criminal contempt for assuming to be an attorney or acting as such without authority).

Certain exceptions are permitted. Thus, SCR 42 has explicit and detailed provisions related to attorneys not admitted in Nevada or admitted but not maintaining Nevada offices to practice in certain instances. The application required by Rule 42 must be on a form approved by the State Bar of Nevada which is available at the county clerk's offices. SCR 43 permits attorneys employed by or representing the United States Government to appear in cases where the United States Government's interests are involved, upon compliance with the rule, by filing the required affidavit.

SCR 44 specifically provides that nothing in the Supreme Court Rules shall be construed to prevent any person from appearing in that persons' own behalf in any court in the state except the Supreme Court. The exception of the Supreme Court from the operation of the rule has been sustained. *See Mirin v. Justices of Supreme Court,* 415 F. Supp. 1178 (D. Nev. 1976).

The provisions of SCR 77 and NRS 7.285 providing that in a court of law only a licensed attorney may be duly authorized to represent a client have been upheld against a claim that NRS 612.705(2) might allow a nonattorney agent to represent an individual claiming employment security benefits. *Martinez v. Eighth Judicial District Court,* 102 Nev. 561, 729 P.2d 487 (1986).

§ 217. — Ethical standards and discipline.

The rules of professional conduct for lawyers who practice in Nevada have been adopted by SCR 150. That rule adopts both the Model Rules of Professional Conduct, adopted by the House of Delegates of the American Bar Association on August 2, 1983, as amended by the Supreme Court of Nevada, as well as the rules established in SCR 150 through SCR 203.5. Those same rules are substantially incorporated by reference by § 120-8 of the Local Rules of Practice of the United States District Court for the District of Nevada.

The Supreme Court of Nevada has jurisdiction to discipline any attorney, whether admitted to practice in Nevada or not, who practices law in Nevada. *Waters v. Barr,* 103 Nev. 694, 747 P.2d 900 (1987).

The Supreme Court had adopted procedural and substantive rules for dealing with cases of alleged lawyer misconduct. These rules are generally found in Supreme Court Rules 99 through 203.5.

Both the Supreme Court Rules and the ABA's Model Rules of Professional Conduct establish detailed guidelines for attorney conduct and provisions for enforcement of those guidelines. While all of the rules are of importance, certain general principles and specific rules have particular relevance in civil practice.

An attorney's gross misconduct will generally not be imputed to the client to bar relief under the appropriate rule of civil practice. *Staschel v. Weaver Brothers, Ltd.,* 98 Nev. 559, 655 P.2d 518 (1982) (relief from default judgment). However, where prejudice or injustice to an opposing party's rights may result, misconduct of counsel may be imputed to the client. *Still v. Huntley,* 102 Nev. 584, 729 P.2d 489 (1986).

Because an attorney has authority to bind his clients in procedural matters in any of the steps of an action or proceeding, SCR 45 and § 1118, *infra,* and because he has control of the litigation process, an attorney is a principal who is jointly and severally liable with his client for court reporting services rendered. *Molezzo Reporters v. Patt,* 94 Nev. 540, 579 P.2d 1243 (1978).

Because SCR 172's duty of candor toward the tribunal continues to the conclusion of the proceeding, the practitioner should be especially careful in preparing findings and orders. The Supreme Court has recently expressed concern over an attorney's preparation of the court's findings of fact where the same were unsupported or falsely portrayed facts different than the evidence actually established. *See Kobinski v. State, Welfare Division,* 103 Nev. 293, 738 P.2d 895 (1987).

Generally, unethical conduct, even that expressly forbidden by Supreme Court Rules, does not by itself create civil liability. *Eikelberger v. Tolotti,* 96 Nev. 525, 611 P.2d 1086 (1980).

§ 218. — Appearance and withdrawal.

DCR 20 provides that unless the appearance is made by an attorney regularly admitted to practice law in Nevada, no entry of appearance or initial pleading purporting to be signed by any party to an action shall be recognized or given any force or effect unless the same shall be acknowledged by signing the same before a notary public. EDCR 7.42(a) has the same effect. *See* discussion of *Naimo v. Fleming,* 95 Nev. 13, 588 P.2d 1025 (1979) and *Cheek v. Bell,* 80 Nev. 244, 391 P.2d 735 (1964), § 812, *infra.*

A number of Nevada decisions stand for the proposition that courts will presume that counsel who appear in a case are fully empowered to act in that case. *See State v. California Mining Co.,* 13 Nev. 203 (1878); *Deegan v. Deegan,* 22 Nev. 185, 37 P. 360 (1894); and *Stanton-Thompson Co. v. Crane,* 24 Nev. 171, 51 P. 116 (1897).

At least two districts have a special rule that where a party has appeared by counsel, the party cannot thereafter appear on his own behalf in the case without the consent of the court. WDCR 22(1); EDCR 7.40(a). Both rules provide that the court in its discretion may hear a party in open court although the party is represented by counsel.

In a case in which the substantive law would not permit a party to appear, a court may nevertheless allow an attorney to appear as amicus curiae. *See Stephens v. First National Bank,* 64 Nev. 292, 182 P.2d 146 (1947).

Although SCR 44 provides that nothing in the Supreme Court Rules shall be so construed as to prevent any person from appearing on his own behalf in any court in this state (except the Supreme Court), at least two districts specifically provide that a corporation may not appear in proper person. WDCR 22(4); EDCR 7.42(b). *See also* § 216, *supra.*

Under EDCR 7.44, a nonresident attorney may not appear as counsel in any cause without the presence of associating Nevada counsel. Further, all pleadings, motions and other papers are required to be signed by the Nevada counsel who is responsible to the court for the content and such Nevada counsel must be present during oral arguments. While the rule is not uniformly enforced in that district, it has its origin in the court's need to have a single party to whom the court can look for responsibility for actions in the courtroom. *Cf.* NRAP 46.

Note that this section does not attempt to cover the rules relating to appearance through counsel or other agent before administrative agencies. SCR 180 does provide that a lawyer representing a client before a legislative or administrative tribunal in a nonadjudicative proceeding must disclose that the appearance is in a representative capacity and must conform his conduct generally to the duties of candor, fairness and impartiality set out in SCR 172(1)-(3), 173(1)-(3), and 174.

Once an attorney has made an appearance, a number of local rules specifically provide that he remains the attorney who must represent that party in the case until proper withdrawal. *See* FJDCR 19; WDCR 22(1); EDCR 7.40(a). *See also* SCR 48.

The rules governing the legal profession in this state provide that once an attorney has appeared in an action, the attorney may be changed upon the application of the attorney or the client with the consequent order of the court, or by stipulation. *Aldabe v. Aldabe,* 84 Nev. 392, 398, 441 P.2d 691 (1968).

A number of rules today further regulate both the procedure and the basis for withdrawal of counsel. *See* SCR 46; SCR 166; Model Rule 1.16; FJDCR 19; WDCR 22; EDCR 7.40. The specific procedural requirements may vary from district to district and the careful practitioner will conform his conduct to the local rule.

Generally the withdrawal of counsel is ultimately dependent upon an order of the court permitting such withdrawal. *See* rules cited *supra.* An attorney must decline further representation when he has been discharged by his client. SCR 166(1)(c); Model Rule 1.16(a)(3). A client may discharge his attorney with or without cause. *Morse v. Eighth Judicial District Court,* 65 Nev. 275, 195 P.2d 199 (1948); *In re Kaufman,* 93 Nev. 452, 567 P.2d 957 (1977).

WDCR 22 and EDCR 7.44 do provide for substitutions of a new attorney in place of the former attorney simply by written consent of both attorneys and the client, all of which must be embodied in a document filed with the court and served upon all parties to the action. Similarly, SCR 48 provides that where an attorney dies, is removed or suspended, and is therefore changed under the provisions of SCR 47, written notice of the change and substitution of a new attorney or the appearance of the party in person must be given to the adverse party.

Other counsel in an action are required to recognize the originally appearing attorney until the originally appearing attorney withdraws, another attorney is substituted, or he is discharged. *See* SCR 48; FJDCR 19; WDCR 22(1); EDCR 7.40(a).

Although the client may discharge the attorney with or without cause, our court has said that with few limitations the attorney should not withdraw from the case except for good cause. *In re Kaufman*, 93 Nev. 452, 456, 567 P.2d 957 (1977). The justification for the rule is said to be the adversities a client may suffer if the client attempts to conduct his own litigation. *In re Kaufman, supra.*

An attorney is required to withdraw from representation if that representation will result in the violation of the rules of professional conduct or other law, the lawyer's physical or mental condition materially impairs his ability to represent the client or, as indicated above, he is discharged. SCR 166(1); Model Rule 1.16(a).

An attorney may withdraw from representing the client if withdrawal can be accomplished without material adverse effects on the interests of the client or where the client persists in a course of action involving a lawyer's services that the lawyer reasonably believes to be criminal or fraudulent; where the client has used the lawyer's services to perpetrate a crime or fraud; where the client insists upon pursuing an objective that the lawyer considers repugnant or imprudent; where the client fails substantially to fulfill an obligation to the lawyer regarding the lawyer's services after reasonable warning from the lawyer that the lawyer will withdraw unless the obligation is fulfilled; where the representation will result in an unreasonable financial burden on the lawyer or has been rendered unreasonably difficult by the client; or where other good cause for withdrawal exists. SCR 166(1)(a) through (f); Model Rule 1.16(b)(1) through (4).

Generally, withdrawal or a change of attorney requires the consent of the attorney, approved by the client, or the specific order of court. SCR 46. However, after judgment or final determination, an attorney may withdraw as the attorney of record at any time upon the attorney's filing a withdrawal, with or without the client's consent. SCR 46.

Notwithstanding good cause for terminating the representation, an attorney must continue representation when ordered to do so by a tribunal. SCR 166(3); Model Rule 1.16(c).

The procedure for accomplishing the withdrawal or change of attorney is generally regulated by SCR 46 through 48, as well as those principles implicit in the discussion of the rules above. Both the Second and Eighth Judicial Districts have adopted detailed procedures for withdrawal. *See* WDCR 22(2); EDCR 7.40(b).

The Second Judicial District provides that except for good cause shown, no application for withdrawal or substitution shall be granted if a trial or hearing delay would result. WDCR 22(3). Discharge of an attorney may not be a ground to delay a trial or hearing. WDCR 22(3).

The Eighth Judicial District Court Rule provides simply that no application for withdrawal or substitution may be granted if a delay of trial or hearing of any matter in the case would result. EDCR 7.40(c).

§ 219. — Service on attorney.

NRCP 5 generally requires the service upon all parties of all pleadings, papers, motions and orders made or obtained by a party. Where a party is represented by an attorney, such service "shall be made upon the attorney" unless the court orders otherwise. NRCP 5(b).

This rule of service upon the attorney has been extended to service of documents including a motion to hold a party in contempt and an order to show cause. *Caplow v. Eighth Judicial District Court,* 72 Nev. 265, 302 P.2d 755 (1956). *Caplow* specifically found that our NRCP 5(b) was derived from a draft of the federal rules which explicitly considered and rejected excepting contempt proceedings from the rule of service upon the attorney. Accordingly, where the contempt proceedings are not original proceedings but are incidental to a pending cause in which the party has appeared through counsel, service on the attorney is sufficient to give the court jurisdiction in the contempt proceedings over the party himself. The careful practitioner, aware of this aspect of Nevada law, may wish to consider formal withdrawal in all cases where counsel's services have ended.

§ 220. — Rights and duties on withdrawal.

Both Supreme Court Rules and the Model Rules of Professional Responsibility incorporated by the Supreme Court set out general standards regarding an attorney's conduct upon termination of representation.

SCR 166(4) provides that upon such termination of representation, the lawyer must take steps to the extent reasonably practicable to protect a client's interests. The rule includes as suggestions the giving of reasonable notice to the client, allowing time for employment of other counsel, surrendering papers and property to which the client is entitled, and refunding any advance payment of fee that has not been earned. Model Rule 1.16(d) has the same effect. The comment to Model Rule 1.16 makes it clear that even if the lawyer has been unfairly discharged by the client, the lawyer must still take all reasonable steps to mitigate the consequences to the client. That is the same position seemingly adopted by the court in *In re Kaufman,* 93 Nev. 452, 567 P.2d 957 (1977).

§ 221. — Return of files.

Upon termination of representation, whether initiated by counsel or the client, certain duties of the attorney still exist. *See* § 220, *supra.*

Nevertheless, "[t]he lawyer may retain papers relating to the client to the extent permitted by other law." SCR 166(4); Model Rule 1.16(d). *In re Kaufman,* 93 Nev. 452, 457, 567 P.2d 957 (1977), found that it was settled in Nevada that an attorney has the right to retain clients' papers, documents and files as a passive lien for the payment of fees owing as of the attorney's withdrawal.

Nevertheless, the extent of this right is unclear. The right is clearly limited by the stricture that an attorney upon withdrawal must take steps to reasonably protect the client's interests including "surrendering papers and property to which the client is entitled...." SCR 166(4); Model Rule 1.16(d); *cf. In re Kaufman,* 93 Nev. 452, 567 P.2d 957 (1977) (retaining lien may be lost with voluntary withdrawal and quoting former American Bar Association Disciplinary Rules).

NRS 7.055, while it gives a client a specific legal right to obtain a court ordered return of papers, documents and tangible property, does not settle the question. NRS 7.055 does require counsel who has been discharged by his client to immediately deliver to the client all papers, documents, etc. "which belong to or were prepared for" that client but only upon payment of the fee due from the client. Thus, where the fee has been paid, the rule is clear and the attorney must turn over all files and papers forthwith.

The only detailed discussion in Nevada of the situation where an attorney's fees are not paid, or where there is a dispute over the amount of the fee to be paid, is *Morse v. Eighth Judicial District Court,* 65 Nev. 275, 195 P.2d 199 (1948). There the court considered the fact that the very leverage which possession of the papers gives to the attorney depends upon how embarrassing to the client the possession by the attorney is. *Morse, supra,* at 285. Yet that leverage may be related to the prejudice or adverse consequences to the client if the attorney retains possession. The court in *Morse* attempted to resolve the question by finding an inherent right in the court to order possession to be transferred to the client upon the client's posting a bond as security for payment of the fees. *Cf. In re Kaufman,* 93 Nev. 452, 567 P.2d 957 (1977) (problems of apportionment of contingent fee).

The one conclusion that can be drawn is that the practitioner must move with extreme caution in this area.

§ 222. — Attorney's liens.

Nevada law provides for certain attorney's liens for the attorney's fees or costs. The exact extent of the right is in part unclear.

NRS 18.015 specifically gives to an attorney a lien upon any "claim, demand or cause of action, including any claim for unliquidated damages," which has been given to the attorney by the client for suit or collection or upon which a suit has been instituted. NRS 18.015(1). That lien exists for the amount of any fee agreed upon by the attorney and client and, where there is no agreement, for a reasonable fee for the services which the attorney has rendered for the client on account of the suit, claim, demand or action. That lien specifically attaches to any "verdict, judgment or decree entered and any money or property which is recovered on account of the suit or other action."

This section's statutory predecessor has been found to be a charging lien. *Morse v. Eighth Judicial District Court,* 65 Nev. 275, 195 P.2d 199 (1948). Such a charging lien is a lien on the judgment obtained for the client for the attorney's services rendered in obtaining it and is entirely separate and distinct from a retaining lien. *Morse, supra.*

The charging lien established by NRS 18.015 has specific provisions for notice. An attorney perfects such a charging lien by serving notice in writing upon his client and upon the party against whom his client has a cause of action, claiming the lien and stating the interest which he has in any cause of action. NRS 18.015(2). The property, verdict, judgment or decree to which the lien attaches is determined from the time of service of those notices. NRS 18.015(3).

The United States Bankruptcy Court has found that such a lien is perfected only after notice is served. *In re Nicholson,* 57 B.R. 672 (Bankr. D. Nev. 1986). The section does not provide for a relation back of an attorney's lien to a date prior to perfection. *In re Nicholson, supra.*

A retaining lien attaches to all papers, books, documents, securities and money that come to the attorney in the course of his professional employment by the client without any special contract regarding it. *Morse v. Eighth Judicial District,* 65 Nev. 275, 195 P.2d 199 (1948). Such a retaining lien will secure a general balance for professional services performed by the attorney whether in the particular action itself or in prior actions or otherwise. *Morse, supra.* The retaining lien is passive and is not enforceable by proceedings to foreclose. *Morse, supra.* The court's discussion in *Morse v. Eighth Judicial District Court, supra,* should be examined carefully for the distinctions between a retaining and charging lien and the possible remedies relating to each. *See also In re Kaufman,* 93 Nev. 452, 567 P.2d 957 (1977); and see § 221, *supra.*

A retaining lien may clearly be lost by turning over the papers, books, documents or property. Further, the court in *In re Kaufman,* 93 Nev. 452, 567 P.2d 957 (1977), found that a retaining lien was lost by the attorney's voluntary withdrawal in the facts of that case.

In light of the decision of *In re Kaufman,* 93 Nev. 452, 567 P.2d 957 (1977), and the continuing duty of an attorney to the extent reasonably practical to protect his client or former client's interests, it is unlikely that clear delineation of the rights and duties of the attorney in this situation will be forthcoming.

§ 223. — Orders to be filed.

DCR 24 provides that any order, judgment or decree must be filed with the clerk of the court promptly. The rule further provides that no attorney shall withhold or delay the filing of any such order, judgment or decree "for any reason, including the nonpayment of attorney's fees." *See* § 1121, *infra.*

By DCR 5 of the Rules of the District Courts of the State of Nevada, the DCRs apply to the practice and procedure in all districts where no local rule covering the same subject has been approved by the Supreme Court. Only Clark County seems to have adopted a rule on this subject. EDCR 7.24 is identical to DCR 24.

§ 224. — Conflict of interest; disqualification.

The appearance of an attorney in a case is further substantially limited by the rules of conduct relating to conflict of interest. Quite a number of Supreme Court Rules and provisions of the Model Rules of Professional Responsibility relate to the subject. Thus, SCR 157 sets out the general rule that an attorney should not represent a client if the representation of that client is directly adverse to another client unless the attorney reasonably believes the representation will not adversely affect the relationship with the other client and each client consents, preferably in writing, after consultation. SCR 157(1). Similarly, an attorney should not represent a client if the representation of that client may be materially limited by the lawyer's responsibilities to another client, subject to the same exceptions. SCR 157(2). Model Rule 1.7 is to the same effect.

There are also specific rules relating to the conflict of interest arising from certain prohibited transactions (SCR 158; Model Rule 1.8), representing clients with interests adverse to former clients (SCR 159; Model Rule 1.9), specific rules relating to successive government and private employment (SCR 161; Model Rule 1.11), and rules relating to matters involving former judges or arbitrators (SCR 162; Model Rule 1.12). There also are elaborate rules relating to imputed disqualification based upon the relationships between lawyers, including relationships in which one lawyer in an association or firm may have a conflict prohibited by other rules. *See* SCR 160; Model Rule 1.10.

In some cases, full disclosure of the conflict or possible conflict and the consent of the client may preclude the finding of prohibited misconduct. *See Eikelberger v. Tolotti,* 96 Nev. 525, 611 P.2d 1086 (1980).

Where representation of multiple clients in a single matter is undertaken, the consultation should include an explanation of the implications of the common representation and the advantages and risks involved. SCR 157. To date, no rule in civil cases similar to that adopted in criminal cases seems to have developed. *See Harvey v. State,* 96 Nev. 850, 619 P.2d 1214 (1980) (in all criminal cases involving joint representation, the trial court must address each defendant personally, explain the dangers of joint representation, and inquire as to facts which might reveal conflicts; if actual or potential conflicts are found, each defendant must voluntarily, knowingly and understandingly decide on the joint representation).

Careful analysis of the appropriate rules should be made before undertaking representation and, when new parties appear in pending actions, re-examination should be made.

In some instances, specific statutes also result in outright prohibition of representation. Thus, NRS 252.120 prohibits a district attorney or a partner of the district attorney from appearing within his county in any civil action begun or prosecuted during his term on behalf of any person suing or sued by the state or any county thereof.

CHAPTER 3

ACTIONS

Authors: Paul J. Anderson
          Suellen Fulstone
          Lynne K. Jones

§ 301. Introduction and scope.

An action is a judicial proceeding to enforce a claim for relief. *Seaborn v. First Judicial District Court,* 55 Nev. 206, 222, 29 P.2d 500 (1934). This chapter addresses the form and commencement of the civil action, the existence of conditions precedent to the commencement of certain types of actions, and the abatement and survival of actions. Other matters related to actions, including joinder, misjoinder and consolidation, as well as venue and transfer of actions, are discussed in other chapters.

§ 302. Form of action.

Section 14 of Article 6 of the Nevada State Constitution provides that "[t]here shall be but one form of civil action, and law and equity may be administered in the same action." Rule 2 of the Nevada Rules of Civil Procedure likewise provides for one form of action in civil litigation known as a "civil action." *See Hart v. City of Las Vegas,* 73 Nev. 29, 307 P.2d 619 (1957).

At common law there were a number of distinct and technical forms of civil action as well as a separation between actions at law and in equity. Article 6, Section 14 and NRCP 2 effectively abolish, for procedural purposes, the multiple forms of action and eliminate any separate equity practice.

The provision for one form of action does not, however, affect the various remedies that were previously available under the different forms of action. The merger of law and equity and the abolition of the multiple

35

forms of action merely establish a single uniform procedure by which a litigant may present his claims to a court empowered to give him whatever relief is found to be appropriate. The substantive and remedial principles of the common law are not changed. *See, e.g., Cann v. George B. Williams Land & Livestock Co.,* 56 Nev. 242, 48 P.2d 887 (1935).

Even under a "one form of action" rule, the courts occasionally must determine the historical nature or form of a particular civil action. The historical form of action remains important, for example, in determining the appropriate statute of limitations and the right to a jury trial. *See, e.g., Harmon v. Tanner Motor Tours,* 79 Nev. 4, 377 P.2d 622 (1963). The merger of law and equity will never be complete so long as the Constitution requires a jury trial only in actions historically at law.

§ 303. Classification of actions.

Actions are variously classified as legal or equitable, ex contractu or ex delicto, in personam or in rem, and common law or statutory. A civil action may include any of the classes.

Legal actions are those cognizable by common law courts. Ordinarily these actions seek a judgment for money or for the recovery of specific real or personal property. Generally all other actions are equitable, although an equitable action may result in money damages or the recovery of property if incidental to the equitable relief.

The classification of actions as ex contractu or ex delicto refers to common law actions. Included in the common law actions ex contractu are the actions of account, assumpsit, covenant and debt. The common law actions ex delicto are case, detinue, ejectment, replevin, trespass and trover. The common law actions of ejectment and replevin have been replaced by statutory actions in Nevada. NRS 40.240 *et seq.;* NRS 31.840 *et seq.*

An action in personam is one directed against a person as distinguished from one directed against property. An action in rem is directed against property and anyone claiming an interest in property. Some actions are called quasi in rem because they deal with property but operate only between the parties to the action. Whether an action is in rem or in personam may be significant for purposes of service of process, a subject discussed in Chapter 9, *infra.*

Statutory actions are those created by a legislature. A legislature may replace common law forms of action, as the Nevada Legislature did with ejectment and replevin, or it may create entirely new causes of action. The legislature may also abolish causes of action, as it has done with the actions for alienation of affection, breach of promise to marry, and criminal conversation. NRS 41.370 *et seq.*

§ 304. Commencement of a civil action.

Under NRCP 3, a civil action is commenced by filing a complaint with the court. *Cunningham v. Eighth Judicial District Court,* 102 Nev. 551, 729 P.2d 1328 (1986). The complaint must contain for each claim for relief: (1) a short and plain statement of the claim showing that the plaintiff is entitled to relief; and (2) a demand for judgment for the relief to which the plaintiff deems himself entitled. NRCP 8(a). In claims for fraud, the pleadings are required to be stated with particularity in lieu of a short and plain statement. *Brown v. Keller,* 97 Nev. 582, 636 P.2d 874 (1981).

Prior to 1959, an action was not commenced until summons was issued. *See, e.g., Woodstock v. Whitaker,* 62 Nev. 224, 146 P.2d 779 (1944); *Deboer v. Fattor,* 72 Nev. 316, 304 P.2d 958 (1956). Since October 1, 1959, however, by amendment to Rule 3, issuance of summons is no longer a prerequisite to the formal commencement of an action. Under a 1985 amendment to Rule 4, summons must be issued and the summons and complaint served within 120 days after the complaint is filed. NRCP 4(i). *See Moore v. Schreck,* 102 Nev. 163, 717 P.2d 49 (1986) (issued contemporaneously with amendment).

A legal action is a matter of public record and fixing the time the action is commenced is important for a number of purposes. For example, the date of commencement determines whether an action has been brought prematurely or, conversely, whether it is barred by the applicable statute of limitations or by laches. The date of commencement is also important in deciding which of two or more courts in which actions involving the same parties and issues have been brought should retain the matter for disposition, whether after-accruing claims and defenses may be litigated, and whether personal jurisdiction and proper venue exist.

The date of commencement can also be the controlling factor in determining whether an action commenced after the effective date of a statute is governed by the statute provisions even though the claim being sued upon occurred prior to its enactment. The time of commencement under Rule 3 also determines the running of the time periods set forth in many of the other rules including NRCP 4(i), 13(a), 26(a), 33 and 56.

§ 305. — Premature commencement.

Every claim for relief is composed of two or more elements. All of the elements must have occurred and must have been completed before an action can be commenced. If all facts giving rise to a claim for relief do not exist at the time the complaint is filed, it is premature and subject to dismissal. The defect of prematurity cannot be cured by an amended or supplemental complaint; the action must be dismissed. The dismissal is usually without prejudice and a second action may be commenced. *See, e.g., Las Vegas Network, Inc. v. B. Shawcross & Associates,* 80 Nev. 405, 395 P.2d 520 (1964).

§ 306. Conditions precedent.

Contracts, statutes, or the circumstances of a case may impose certain acts or events as "conditions precedent." A condition precedent must be performed or complied with before the action may be commenced unless that performance or compliance has been excused or waived in some manner. *See, e.g. ˉ ˙rberg v. Crockett,* 17 Nev. 409, 30 P. 826 (1883).

A condition precedent is an act or event that must occur before the other party becomes liable. Insurance contracts, for example, may require submission of proof of loss to the insurance company. *See, e.g., Arley v. Liberty Mutual Fire Insurance Co.,* 80 Nev. 5, 388 P.2d 576 (1964). Another example is the statutory requirement that, before an action can be commenced against the personal representative, a claim against a deceased must have been filed in the estate proceedings and notice of its rejection given to the claimant. NRS 147.040(1); NRS 147.130; NRS 147.150. In certain cases, the exhaustion of administrative remedies is another type of condition precedent.

In addition to conditions precedent to the accrual of a cause of action, the legislature has imposed a number of general prerequisites to the commencement, maintenance or defense of certain actions. For example, a contractor must be licensed with the state. NRS 624.320. A person doing business under a fictitious name must have registered that name. NRS 602.070. A foreign corporation doing business in the State of Nevada must have qualified with the state. NRS 80.210(1); *see also Bader Enterprises, Inc. v. Olsen,* 98 Nev. 381, 649 P.2d 1369 (1982).

§ 307. — Notice.

Statutes and contracts may require notice as a condition precedent to bringing an action to enforce certain rights. For example, notice of rejection of a creditor's claim must be given by the decedent's personal representative before the creditor can commence an action. NRS 147.130. Until they were amended in 1981, the Nevada statutes required that a claim against a county be filed with the county before an action could be commenced. The claim had to be filed within six months of the time it became due. NRS 244.245; NRS 244.250.

Although the statute still requires the claim to be filed within six months, the action, in the absence of such a claim, is no longer expressly barred. In *Turner v. Staggs,* 89 Nev. 230, 510 P.2d 879, *cert. denied,* 414 U.S. 1079 (1973), the Nevada Supreme Court held that the statutory claim filing requirement did not apply to bar a tort action against a county because the statute created an arbitrary classification of tort-feasor in violation of the state and federal constitutional guarantees of equal protection. Also, claims statutes do not apply to actions for inverse condemnation, "for to do so would deny due process of a constitutionally guaranteed right." *Alper v. Clark County, Nevada*, 93 Nev. 569, 571 P.2d 810 (1977), *cert. denied*, 436 U.S. 905 (1978). However, the statutory requirement has been enforced in contract actions. *See L-M Architects, Inc. v. City of Sparks*, 100 Nev. 334, 683 P.2d 11 (1984).

§ 308. — Demand.

A demand is not a condition precedent to the commencement of an action unless the other party must be put in default before the action is deemed to arise. For example, in an action for conversion, if the party in possession gained that possession in a lawful manner, a demand for its return is necessary to put him in default. Similarly, before an action for specific performance is commenced, the nondefaulting party must tender performance and demand the return performance unless the tender and demand would be useless. A contract may also expressly require a demand before suit can be brought for its breach.

§ 309. — Excuses for nonperformance.

The nonperformance of a condition precedent is excused where performance would be futile or is prevented by the defendant. Impossibility is not an excuse for nonperformance of a condition precedent.

§ 310. — Pleading performance of conditions precedent.

Under NRCP 9(c), it is sufficient to allege generally that all conditions precedent have been performed or have occurred. A condition precedent which is an element of the claim for relief by statute should be pled separately. Specific statutes may also require that certain conditions or prerequisites to action be pled. *See, e.g.*, NRS 624.320.

A denial of the performance or occurrence of a condition precedent is always required to be pled specifically and with particularity. NRCP 9(c).

§ 311. Nonresident costs bond.

The defendant may require a nonresident or foreign corporation plaintiff to post security for the costs and charges which may be awarded against such plaintiff in the action. NRS 18.130(1). Separate security may be required of each nonresident or foreign corporation plaintiff. *Fourchier v. McNeil Construction Co.*, 68 Nev. 109, 227 P.2d 429 (1951). The requirements of NRS 18.130 are mandatory. Even an impecunious, unemployed plaintiff has been required to file the security required by the statute or establish that he is indigent and should be allowed to proceed in forma pauperis. *Arrambide v. St. Mary's Hospital,* 647 F. Supp. 1148 (D. Nev. 1986).

Nevada follows the general rule that where there are several plaintiffs and some, or even one, is a Nevada resident, the defendant cannot require the giving of security for costs either from the nonresident plaintiffs separately or from all the plaintiffs as a group. *Fourchier, supra,* 68 Nev. at 116-17. An exception to this general rule is recognized, however, where several plaintiffs, each with independent claims, join in prosecuting a single suit. In these circumstances, each claim is deemed a separate action and security for costs accordingly may be demanded from each nonresident or foreign corporation plaintiff. *Fourchier, supra,* 68 Nev. at 117-18.

To invoke the requirement for a nonresident costs bond, the defendant must file and serve on the plaintiff, within the time for answering the complaint, a written demand for such security. NRS 18.130(1). When a timely and otherwise proper demand for security has been made, all proceedings in the action are stayed until an undertaking, executed by two or more persons as sureties, is filed with the clerk to the effect that such persons will pay the costs and charges awarded against the plaintiff by judgment or in the progress of the action not exceeding the sum of $500. NRS 18.130(1). Each of the sureties is required to provide an affidavit to the effect that he is a resident and householder or freeholder within the county in which the action is brought and is worth double the amount specified in the undertaking, over and above all his just debts and liabilities and exclusive of property exempt from execution. NRS 18.130(3).

Other Nevada statutes applying generally to undertakings and bonds permit the substitution of a bond or an undertaking with a surety or bonding company authorized to do business in the State of Nevada in the place of personal sureties. NRS 20.040; NRS 691B.020. The bond or undertaking of a licensed corporate surety or bonding company is deemed by law to be full compliance with the cost bond requirement. NRS 691B.020(3).

In lieu of providing any kind of bond or undertaking, the nonresident or foreign corporation plaintiff may simply deposit $500.00 with the clerk of the court, subject to the same conditions as are required for an undertaking. NRS 18.130(1).

Where there are multiple nonresident plaintiffs, each plaintiff is required to post the statutory $500 security or undertaking for each defendant. *Truck Insurance Exchange v. Tetzlaff,* 683 F. Supp. 223 (D. Nev. 1988). For example, if two nonresident plaintiffs were to sue three resident defendants, the plaintiffs could collectively be required to post $3,000 in security, assuming all defendants made a timely demand.

The plaintiff is obligated to notify the defendant that the undertaking or security has been filed. From receipt of the notice, the defendant has ten days or the time allowed under NRCP 12(a), whichever is longer, in which to answer or otherwise plead to the complaint. NRS 18.130(1). Once posted, the bond must remain for the defendant's benefit until the action is dismissed or judgment is entered. *State ex rel. Hersh v. First Judicial District Court,* 86 Nev. 73, 464 P.2d 783 (1970).

A new or additional undertaking may be ordered by the court upon proof that the original undertaking is insufficient. NRS 18.130(2). In that instance, proceedings in the matter are again stayed until the new or additional security has been furnished and proof thereof filed and served. NRS 18.130(2).

If no undertaking or deposit for security is filed, the court may, upon motion of the defendant and after the lapse of thirty days from service of the written demand for security, order the action dismissed. NRS 18.130(4). The action may similarly be dismissed if any new or additional security is not provided within thirty days from an order thereof. NRS 18.130(4). However, dismissal following lapse of the thirty (30) day statutory period is only proper as to any defendant who has demanded security. *Brion v. Union Plaza Corp.,* 104 Nev. 553, 763 P.2d 64 (1988). Defendants who have not joined in the demand for security cannot, therefore, benefit from the plaintiff's lapse in timely filing of security. *Id.* Dismissal is discretionary with the court. *Borders Electronic Co. v. Quirk,* 97 Nev. 205, 626 P.2d 266 (1981); *Fourchier v. McNeil Construction Co.,* 68 Nev. 109, 227 P.2d 429 (1951).

§ 312. Abatement and survival of actions.

Abatement is the defeat of an action by reason of some defect which does not go to the merits of the claim. Although it is sometimes erroneously used interchangeably with a stay of proceedings, abatement means the action is dismissed. A decision abating an action, however, is not a judgment on the merits and does not bar a future action on the same claim. Any further enforcement of the underlying claim or cause of action does require the commencement of a new action.

Grounds for abatement include absence of jurisdiction, incapacity, misjoinder or the nonjoinder of indispensable parties, the pendency of another action, and the premature commencement of the action. Jurisdiction, capacity and joinder are discussed herein in Chapters 4, 5 and 8, *infra,* respectively. Premature commencement and pendency of another action are discussed below.

41

As a rule, an action cannot be maintained if it is commenced before the accrual of the claim which is sought to be enforced. Premature commencement is a ground for abatement of the action. Likewise, a second action based on the same claim will be abated where there is a prior action pending in a court of competent jurisdiction within the same state or jurisdiction between the same parties and involving the same or substantially the same subject matter and claim and in which prior action the rights of the parties may be adjudicated. *See, e.g., Fitzharris v. Phillips,* 74 Nev. 371, 333 P.2d 721 (1958).

At common law, the death of a party resulted in the absolute abatement of a personal action without a right of substitution of the decedent's personal representative. *See, e.g., Walker v. Burkham,* 68 Nev. 250, 253, 229 P.2d 158 (1951). Actions involving the recovery of real property, however, did not abate upon death. This common law rule has long been replaced by the statute in Nevada providing for the nonabatement of any action by reason of death. NRS 41.100 provides in pertinent part as follows:

> Except as provided in this section, no cause of action is lost by reason of the death of any person, but may be maintained by or against his executor or administrator.

By statute and case law, although the cause of action is not abated, a claim for punitive damages will not survive the death of a tortfeasor. NRS 41.100(2); *Allen v. Anderson,* 93 Nev. 204, 562 P.2d 487 (1977).

"Revival" is the procedure by which the proper party is substituted for the decedent and the action is continued in the name of the substituted party. Rule 25 of the Nevada Rules of Civil Procedure is a necessary procedural device which prevents a party's death from destroying an otherwise valid cause of action. *Lummis v. District Court,* 94 Nev. 114, 115, 576 P.2d 272 (1978). Under Rule 25, if a party dies and the claim is not extinguished by the party's death, the court may order substitution of the proper parties. NRCP 25(a)(1). A motion for substitution may be made by any party. However, the motion must be made no later than ninety (90) days after service of a suggestion of death on the record. NRCP 25(a)(1). If a motion is not made within ninety (90) days, the action will be dismissed as to the deceased party. NRCP 25(a)(1).

§ 313. Splitting causes of action.

A cause of action may not be split and generally all damages accruing to a person as the result of a single wrongful act must be claimed and recovered in one action. *See, e.g., Reno Club, Inc. v. Harrah,* 70 Nev. 125, 260 P.2d 304 (1953). The principal reason for the rule against splitting causes of action exists to protect a party from having to defend a multiplicity of actions arising from a single wrong. *State v. California Mining*

Co., 13 Nev. 289 (1878). The Nevada Supreme Court has recognized the "insurance exception" to the rule against splitting a cause of action in personal injury and property damage cases. *Smith v. Hutchins,* 93 Nev. 431, 566 P.2d 1136 (1977).

The objection to splitting a cause of action is raised by the affirmative defense of res judicata. *See, e.g., Zalk-Josephs Co. v. Wells Cargo, Inc.,* 81 Nev. 163, 400 P.2d 621 (1965).

CHAPTER 4

SUBJECT MATTER JURISDICTION

Author: Ann Morgan

§ 401. Introduction and scope.

The Nevada Constitution, Article 6, Section 1, *et seq.,* and the statutes enacted thereunder establish subject matter jurisdiction in civil actions. This chapter will discuss the limits of the subject matter jurisdiction held by each of Nevada's courts, and referees, emphasizing the jurisdiction of the district courts, and will also consider the procedure for challenging subject matter jurisdiction. Jurisdiction over the parties to an action is discussed in Chapter 5, *infra,* and questions relating to venue are discussed in Chapter 6, *infra.*

Subject matter jurisdiction is the power of the court to hear and determine a particular type of controversy. *Azbarea v. City of North Las Vegas,* 95 Nev. 109, 111, 590 P.2d 161, 162 (1979); *Galloway v. Truesdell,* 83 Nev. 13, 20, 422 P.2d 237, 242 (1967); *Alexander v. Archer,* 21 Nev. 22, 31, 24 P. 373, 376 (1890). Subject matter jurisdiction should be distinguished from in personam jurisdiction, which is the power of the court to determine the rights, obligations or status of a particular person. *See Perry v. Edmonds,* 59 Nev. 60, 84 P.2d 711 (1938). Subject matter jurisdiction should also be distinguished from in rem jurisdiction which is the power of the court to determine the status of particular property. *Perry, supra.* The rules of venue, often confused with subject matter jurisdiction, govern the propriety of hearing a controversy in a particular place rather than the court's power to determine the controversy. *Lamb v. Knox,* 77 Nev. 12, 15, 358 P.2d 994 (1961); *see State ex rel. Elsman v. Second Judicial District Court,* 52 Nev. 379, 397, 287 P. 957 (1930).

§ 402. Nevada's court system.

Article 6, Section 1 of the Nevada Constitution provides that the judicial power of this state shall be vested in a court system comprising a

45

Supreme Court, District Courts, and Justices of the Peace. In addition, the section empowers the legislature to establish Courts for municipal purposes in incorporated towns and cities. *See also* NRS 1.010. The legislature may also provide by law for referees in district courts, Article 6, Section 2(a); and a family court division of any district court, Article 6, Section 2(b).

§ 403. — Municipal courts.

Under the authority of Nevada Constitution, Article 6, Sections 1 and 9, the legislature has created a system of municipal courts. NRS. 5.010 *et seq.*

Pursuant to those statutes, municipal courts have subject matter jurisdiction over:

(a) actions relating to violations of a city ordinance,

(b) actions to prevent or abate a nuisance within a city,

(c) offenses committed within the city which violate the peace and good order of the city or which invade any of the police powers of the city or endanger the health of the inhabitants thereof.NRS 5.050; NRS 266.550; NRS 266.555.

Municipal courts are authorized to hear prosecutions for the collection of city taxes and the enforcement of liens and bonds within the city, recovery of personal property belonging to the city, and the collection of damages by the city. NRS 5.050(3); NRS 266.555(3). In all these civil matters, however, the principal amount in issue may not exceed $2,500, NRS 5.050(3), and the action may not require a determination of the validity of any tax or the title to real property. NRS 5.050(4); NRS 266.555(4).

Municipal courts also have jurisdiction over traffic offenses involving juveniles in counties with a population exceeding 250,000. NRS 62.040(2).

Finally, a municipal court has subject matter jurisdiction to issue warrants, writs and process and to take other actions necessary to the exercise of that jurisdiction, to the protection of that jurisdiction and to the administration of its affairs. NRS 5.060; *City of North Las Vegas ex rel. Arndt v. Daines,* 92 Nev. 292, 295, 550 P.2d 399 (1976).

§ 404. — Justices' courts.

The Nevada legislature sets the subject matter jurisdiction of the justices' courts according to the amount in controversy, the nature of the action, the penalty provided, or any combination of these factors. Nev. Const. Art. 6, § 8. The legislature has set the limits of the amount in controversy in the justices' courts at $5,000, NRS 4.370, and has granted the justices' courts the power to determine matters not exceeding that amount involving:

(a) contracts for the recovery of money, NRS 4.370(1)(a);

(b) injuries to persons or personal property, NRS 4.370(1)(b);

(c) injuries to real property where no issue is raised by the verified answer of the defendant involving the title or boundaries; NRS 4.370(1)(b);

(d) fines or forfeitures provided by statute or ordinance where the answer raises no issue involving the legality of any tax imposed, assessment, toll or municipal fine, NRS 4.370(1)(c);

(e) actions or bonds or undertakings conditioned on the payment of money, NRS 4.370(1)(d);

(f) actions for the recovery of personal property, NRS 4.370(1)(e);

(g) taking and entering judgment on the confession of a defendant, NRS 4.370(1)(f);

(h) actions for the possession of lands and tenements where the relation of the landlord and tenant exists, when damages claimed do not exceed $5,000 or when no damages are claimed. NRS 4.370(1)(g);

(i) actions for damages for unlawfully or fraudulently obtaining or withholding lands and tenements, NRS 4.370(1)(h);

(j) actions for the collection of taxes, NRS 4.370(a)(i) 4.370(1)(i);

(k) actions for the enforcement of mechanics' liens and liens of owners of facilities for storage. NRS 4.370(1)(j); NRS 4.370(1)(k);

(l) actions for a fine imposed for a violation of NRS 484.757; NRS 4.370(1)(l);

(m) small claims actions under the provisions of chapter 73 of the NRS; NRS 4.370(1)(n);

(n) actions to contest the validity of liens on mobile homes or manufactured homes, NRS 4.370(1)(o).

NRS 4.370(1)(g) was amended by the 1991 legislature to include a damage limitation on actions for the possession of land and tenements. The amendment overrules the holding of *K.J.B., Inc. v. Second Judicial District Court,* 103 Nev. 473, 745 P.2d 700 (1987), to the effect that the District Court had no jurisdiction over unlawful detainer actions. Original jurisdiction over such matters is now determined by the amount of damages sought.

The justices' courts also have jurisdiction to issue temporary or extended orders of protection against domestic violence in those counties whose population is under 100,000. NRS 4.370(1)(m); *see* Nev. Const. Art. 6, § 6; NRS 3.0105 and NRS 3.223. This power is concurrent with that of the family court in counties whose population is greater than 100,000. NRS 3.223(2).

For the counties that have more than one justice of the peace, the justices have concurrent and coextensive subject matter jurisdiction. NRS 4.155.

§ 405. — District court.

The district courts of Nevada's nine judicial districts have both original and appellate subject matter jurisdiction. Nev. Const. Art. 6, § 6. Their original jurisdiction is defined by exclusion, *i.e.*, all cases excluded by law from the original jurisdiction of the justices' courts. Nev. Const. Art. 6, § 6. *See also* NRS 3.223, giving the family division of the district court certain exclusive jurisdiction. The district courts have final appellate jurisdiction in cases arising in justices' courts and municipal courts, Nev. Const. Art. 6, § 6; *Cavanaugh v. Wright,* 2 Nev. 166 (1866), and have limited review of arbitration awards. NRS 38.135 *et seq.; New Shy Clown Casino, Inc. v. Baldwin,* 103 Nev. 269, 737 P.2d 524 (1987); *Richardson v. Harris,* 107 Nev. 763, 818 P.2d 1209, 1210 (1991). A district court on appeal has the same jurisdiction as the justices' courts or municipal courts from which the appeal was taken. *State ex rel. Harding v. Moore,* 9 Nev. 355 (1874), citing *Peacock v. Leonard,* 8 Nev. 84 (1872). Therefore, the district court has no authority to render judgment on any matter which is beyond the subject matter jurisdiction of the lower court. *State ex rel. Abel v. Breen,* 41 Nev. 516, 173 P. 555 (1918). The rules of civil procedure do not extend or limit the jurisdiction of the district courts. NRCP 82.

District courts have the power to issue writs of mandamus, Nev. Const. Art. 6, § 6; NRS 34.160; prohibition, Nev. Const. Art. 6, § 6; injunctions, Nev. Const. Art. 6, § 6; NRS 33.010; quo warranto, Nev. Const. Art. 6, § 6; NRS 35.080; certiorari, Nev. Const. Art. 6, § 6, NRS 34.020; habeas corpus, NRS 34.710; and all other writs proper and necessary to the complete exercise of their jurisdiction, Nev. Const. Art. 6, § 6. All district courts, including those not designated family courts, appear to have the power to issue extended and temporary orders in cases of domestic violence pursuant to NRS 33.020; *see* § 406, *infra.*

§ 406. Family court.

The family court is a division of the district court. Nev. Const. Art. 6, § 6. The legislature has granted it original, exclusive jurisdiction in the following matters:

(a) all proceedings within the jurisdiction of the juvenile court. NRS 3.223(1)(a);

(b) proceedings involving domestic relations, including determining the rights of husband and wife, dissolving a marriage, determining

SUBJECT MATTER JURISDICTION

custody and visitation issues, determining support obligations, determining parentage, adoptions, terminating parental rights, determinations regarding a minor's disabilities, and proceedings brought pursuant to the Reciprocal Enforcement Support Act; NRS 3.223(1)(a);

(c) proceedings involving guardianships; NRS 3.223(1)(a);

(d) proceedings involving support of dependent children and protection of children from abuse and neglect; NRS 3.223(1)(a);

(e) proceedings brought to facilitate the collection of an obligation for support under chapter 31A of NRS, although other judicial or administrative procedures may be used to collect the obligation; NRS 3.223(1)(b);

(f) rulings on requests for order authorizing abortions; NRS 3.223(1)(c);

The family court also has original, exclusive jurisdiction to approve the marriage of a minor, NRS 3.223(1)(d); approve the compromise of a claim of a minor, NRS 3.223(1)(f); establish the date and place of birth of a minor, NRS 3.223(1)(g); change the name of a minor, NRS 3.223(1)(h); declare the sanity of a minor, NRS 3.223(1)(i); and approve the withholding and withdrawal of life-sustaining procedures for a person as authorized by law, NRS 3.223(1)(j).

In all other matters, the family court judges share equal coextensive and concurrent jurisdiction and power with all other district court judges. NRS 3.220.

§ 407. — Supreme court.

The subject matter jurisdiction of the supreme court is set forth in Article 6, Section 4 of the Nevada Constitution and NRS 2.090.

In addition to jurisdiction over appeals, the supreme court of Nevada has the power to issue writs of mandamus, NRAP 21, and NRS 34.160; certiorari, NRAP 21; NRS 34.020; prohibition, NRAP 21, NRS 34.330; (as noted above, this statute would seem to be inconsistent with Art. 6, § 6, which also grants district courts jurisdiction to issue writs of prohibition); quo warranto, NRS 35.080; habeas corpus, NRAP 22; and all writs necessary and proper to the complete exercise of its appellate jurisdiction. Nev. Const. Art. 6, § 4. Ancillary to this appellate jurisdiction is the court's power to grant a stay of judgment, order or injunction pending appeal and to approve a supersedeas bond. NRAP 8. The Nevada Rules of Appellate Procedure do not extend or limit the jurisdiction of the supreme court as established by law. NRAP 1(b).

§ 408. Objection to subject matter jurisdiction.

The ability to raise the absence of subject matter jurisdiction is never waived and generally may be brought to the court's attention at any time and in almost any manner. *Meinhold v. Clark County School District,* 89 Nev. 56, 59, 506 P.2d 420, 422 (1973); *S. G. & R. Bank v. Milisich,* 43 Nev. 373, 390, 233 P. 41, 46 (1925).

§ 409. — Time for objection.

An objection based on the absence of subject matter jurisdiction may be raised at any time. NRCP 12(h)(3); NJCRCP 12(h)(3).

§ 410. — Methods of raising objections to subject matter jurisdiction.

It is within the inherent powers of all courts to inquire into their own jurisdiction and to determine if jurisdiction over the subject matter exists. *In re Estate of Singleton,* 26 Nev. 106 (1901). Objections to subject matter jurisdiction may be raised in a pleading allowed by NRCP 12(b), NJCRCP 12(b), NRS 226.555(4), and in a motion, if the defect in jurisdiction is apparent on the face of the pleading. NRCP 12(b)(1); NJCRCP 12(b)(1), *Girola v. Roussille,* 81 Nev. 661, 663, 408 P.2d 918, 919 (1965). The absence of subject matter jurisdiction may also be brought to the court's attention by suggestion of the parties or otherwise. NRCP 12(h)(3); NJCRCP 12(h)(3).

Objection to the subject matter jurisdiction of a lower court may be raised by writ of certiorari in a district court or the supreme court, NRS 34.020; *Jahn v. District Court,* 58 Nev. 204, 213, 73 P.2d 499, 500 (1937); by writ of prohibition in the district court or the supreme court, NRS 34.330; Nev. Const. Art. 6, § 6; or by direct appeal, *Parks v. Garrison,* 57 Nev. 480, 482, 67 P.2d 314 (1937). An objection to subject matter jurisdiction must be supported by competent evidence. *Meinhold v. Clark County School District,* 89 Nev. 56, 506 P.2d 420 (1973).

Where a court believes a doubt exists as to jurisdiction, the court has a duty to raise and decide the issue sua sponte, *Phillips v. Welch,* 11 Nev. 187 (1876), even though the matter of jurisdiction may be conceded by the parties.

§ 411. Waiver of subject matter jurisdiction.

Subject matter jurisdiction is never waived. *Phillips v. Welch,* 11 Nev. 187 (1876). A party may, however, be estopped from challenging the court's jurisdiction. *Morse v. Morse,* 99 Nev. 387, 663 P.2d 349 (1983).

§ 412. Inherent jurisdiction.

Courts have inherent jurisdiction to adopt rules and procedures and to enter orders necessary to the proper administration of justice. *Goldman v. Bryan,* 104 Nev. 644, 654, 764 P.2d 1296, 1302 (1988); *State ex rel.*

Coffin v. County Commissioners, 19 Nev. 332, 10 P. 901 (1986); *Sun Realty v. Eighth Judicial District Court,* 91 Nev. 774, 776, 542 P.2d 1072 (1975); *Galloway v. Truesdell,* 83 Nev. 13, 20, 422 P.2d 237, 242 (1967); *Azbarea v. City of North Las Vegas,* 95 Nev. 109, 111, 590 P.2d 161, 162 (1979). This subject matter jurisdiction exists apart from and in addition to any jurisdiction granted by the constitution or statute, although some of the court's inherent powers have been codified. *See Lindauer v. Allen,* 85 Nev. 430, 456 P.2d 851 (1969).

The inherent powers of the courts include the power to adopt rules, NRS 2.120, NRS 3.020, *Caples v. Central Pacific Railroad,* 6 Nev. 265, 275 (1871); the power to compel expenditures for judicial purposes, *Young v. Board of County Commissioners,* 91 Nev. 52, 530 P.2d 1203 (1975); and the power to amend records and orders to remove ambiguity or correct errors, *Grenz v. Grenz,* 78 Nev. 394, 374 P.2d 891 (1962), *Brockman v. Ullom,* 52 Nev. 267, 286 P. 417 (1930). The courts also have the inherent power to hire or dismiss judicial personnel, *City of North Las Vegas ex rel. Arndt v. Daines,* 92 Nev. 292, 550 P.2d 399 (1976). Judges and justices can also take and certify the acknowledgment of conveyances and the satisfaction of a judgment of any court. NRS 2.190; NRS 3.150; NRS 4.180; NRS 5.040.

Courts have the inherent power to control proceedings before them and to enforce their rulings through the use of contempt proceedings. NRS 22.010; *Lamb v. Lamb,* 83 Nev. 425, 428, 433 P.2d 265 (1967).

CHAPTER 5

PARTIES

Author: Marc Picker
         Joseph R. Plater, III

§ 501. Introduction and scope.

Parties are those who are named as such in the record of an action and who are properly served with process or enter their appearance. A person not served or improperly served is not a party. *State ex rel. Pacific States Securities Co. v. Second Judicial District Court,* 48 Nev. 53, 226 P. 1106 (1924). As a general rule, a stranger to the action cannot appear therein and apply to the court for relief. *State ex rel. Garaventa Land & Livestock Co. v. Second Judicial District Court,* 61 Nev. 350, 128 P.2d 266 (1942). Exceptions have been made, however, where a person not named appears and possesses a beneficial interest. *Electrical Products Corp. v. Second Judicial District Court,* 55 Nev. 8, 23 P.2d 501 (1933). Moreover, a person not made a party is entitled to a writ of certiorari challenging the court's jurisdiction where orders are entered restraining that person. *State ex rel. Garaventa Land & Livestock Co., supra.*

This chapter reviews the rules governing real party in interest, standing, capacity to sue or be sued, compulsory joinder (necessary and indispensable parties), permissive joinder, misjoinder and nonjoinder, interpleader, class actions, derivative actions, intervention and substitution of parties. It does not cover impleader, which is found in Chapter 15, *infra*. In discussing certain of the foregoing topics, this chapter also reviews rules pertinent to assignees, subrogation claims, executors or administrators, wrongful death actions, homeowners' associations, unions, actions by and against partnerships, infants or incompetents, governmental agencies, corporations and/or married persons.

§ 502. Real party in interest.

NRCP 17(a) provides that "every action shall be prosecuted in the name of the real party in interest." The concept "real party in interest" means that an action shall be brought by a party who has a right to enforce the claim and who has a significant interest in the litigation. *Painter v. Anderson,* 96 Nev. 941, 620 P.2d 1254 (1980). *See also Back Streets, Inc. v. Campbell,* 95 Nev. 651, 601 P.2d 54 (1979); *Szilagyi v. Testa,* 99 Nev. 834, 673 P.2d 495 (1983); *Nev-Tex Oil v. Precision Rolled Products,* 105 Nev. 685, 782 P.2d 1311 (1989). The purpose of the rule is to enable a defendant to avail himself of evidence and defenses that the defendant has against the real party in interest, assure the defendant finality of judgment, and assure that the defendant will be protected against another suit brought by the real party in interest in the same matter. *Painter, supra,* at 943.

No action shall be dismissed on the ground that it is not prosecuted in the name of the real party in interest until a reasonable time has been allowed for ratification of commencement of the action by, or joinder or substitution of, the real party in interest; such ratification, joinder or substitution shall have the same effect as if the action had been commenced in the name of the real party in interest. NRCP 17(a). Because of the requirement of an objection to commence the reasonable time for ratification, joinder or substitution, failure to raise a real party in interest objection by pleading or motion is generally held to constitute a waiver. 3A J. Moore & J. Lucas, *Moore's Federal Practice* ¶ 17.15-1 (2d ed. 1987). Because ratification, joinder or substitution relates back to the commencement of the action, a correction in parties will be allowed after the statute of limitations has run despite the failure of the real party in interest to bring the original action. 3A J. Moore & J. Lucas, *supra.* If an objection is timely made, whether a reasonable time to join the real party in interest has elapsed is a determination that lies within the sound discretion of the court. *Lawler v. Ginochio,* 94 Nev. 623, 626, 584 P.2d 667 (1978). *See also In re Hilton Hotel,* 101 Nev. 489, 706 P.2d 137 (1985). The most important question to be resolved in this determination is not the length of delay but the extent of prejudice to existing parties resulting from the delay. 3A J. Moore & J. Lucas, *supra.*

A judge acting on behalf of his court personnel may be a "real party in interest" possessing the capacity to commence an action where he is acting in the interest of discharging the responsibilities of his court, even though the direct result of the action will only benefit his employees and not himself. *Azbarea v. City of North Las Vegas*, 95 Nev. 109, 590 P.2d 161 (1979).

Given the requirement for objection, the relation back to the original filing and the reasonable time allowed for joinder, dismissal for failure to join the real party in interest rarely occurs. This contrasts sharply with the dire consequences for failing to join an indispensable party. *See* §§ 416, 517, *infra*. For special rules regarding real party in interest involving assignees, see § 503, *infra;* for rules regarding subrogation claims, see § 504, *infra;* for rules regarding executors and administrators, see § 505, *infra,* for rules regarding wrongful death actions, see § 506, *infra,* for rules regarding homeowner's associations, see § 507, *infra,* for rules regarding unions, see § 508, *infra*.

§ 503. Assignees.

Generally the assignee of a contractual right is the real party in interest as opposed to the assignor. *Peck v. Dodds,* 10 Nev. 204 (1875). But, assignment of authority to receive payments does not include authority to institute legal proceedings without more. *L & H Builders Supply v. Boyd Co.,* 93 Nev. 610, 571 P.2d 167 (1977), citing Restatement of Agency (Second) § 72, Comment d (1958). The assignee is the real party in interest even if the assignment was for purposes of security. *Thelin v. Intermountain Lumber & Builders Supply, Inc.,* 80 Nev. 285, 392 P.2d 626 (1964). Where the issue is whether the plaintiff is the real party in interest, however, an assignment of a claim to the plaintiff after the filing of an action thereon does not relate back to the date of filing. *Thelin, supra; El Ranco, Inc. v. First National Bank,* 406 F.2d 1205, 1209 (9th Cir. 1968), *cert. denied,* 396 U.S. 875 (1969). The right to prosecute an action typically includes the right to institute and maintain a legal proceeding. *State of Florida ex rel. Shevin v. Exxon Corp.,* 526 F.2d 266 (5th Cir. 1976), citing *Thelin, supra.* A third-party beneficiary is a real party in interest in an action to enforce a contractual obligation against the promisor. *Gibbs v. Giles,* 96 Nev. 243, 607 P.2d 118 (1980).

§ 504. Subrogation claims.

Insurance companies generally prefer to assert subrogation claims through the named insured rather than in their own names to preclude possible jury prejudice against the insurer. If the insurance company makes payment to the insured accompanied by a loan receipt agreement repayable to the insurer only to the extent of recovery by the insured, however, the insured is then the real party in interest and an action can be prosecuted only in the name of the insured, not in the name of the insurance company. *Central National Insurance Co. v. Dixon*, 93 Nev. 86, 559 P.2d 1187 (1977). If the insurance company makes payment to the insured, absent a loan receipt agreement, it is subrogated by operation of law to the rights, if any, of the insured, and the insurer, not the insured, becomes the real party in interest and must sue in its own name. *Duboise v. State Farm Mutual Auto Insurance Co.*, 96 Nev. 877, 619 P.2d 1223 (1980). A loan receipt agreement constitutes a true loan rather than payment of a claim if the obligation or liability of the insurer who advances the money is not absolute but is contingent, conditional, excessive or undetermined. *Duboise, supra.*

§ 505. Executors or administrators.

An executor or administrator may sue in his own name without joining the party for whose benefit the action is brought. NRCP 17(a). Before suing or being sued, the executor or administrator must be appointed by order of a court of competent jurisdiction. NRS 143.060; NRS 143.210. Similarly, an executor or administrator who has not been appointed need not be joined in an action. NRS 143.210. If the order appointing an executor or administrator is vacated, he is not a party pursuant to NRCP 17(a).

With one exception, no cause of action is lost by reason of the death of any person; it ordinarily may be maintained by or against his executor or administrator. NRS 41.100. Punitive damages, however, or other damages imposed primarily for the sake of example or to punish the defendant may not be awarded against an executor or administrator. NRS 41.100(2). The rationale for this rule is that punitive damages and other penalties are inflicted for the purpose of deterring wrongful conduct and imposition for such purposes is impossible if the wrongdoer is deceased. *Allen v. Anderson*, 93 Nev. 204, 562 P.2d 487 (1977). *See also Summa Corp. v. Greenspun*, 96 Nev. 247, 607 P.2d 569 (1980). Conversely, if the person who has a cause of action for punitive damages or other penalties dies before judgment, the executor or administrator may recover all losses or damages which the decedent incurred or sustained before his death, including any penalties which the decedent would have recovered if he had lived. NRS 41.100. Except in cases of claims for wrongful death, the executor or administrator of a claimant dying before judgment may also recover damages for pain, suffering or disfigurement and for loss of probable support, companionship, society, comfort and consortium. As discussed in § 506, *infra*, the heirs possess the foregoing damages claims in wrongful death actions.

§ 506. Wrongful death actions.

The Nevada Wrongful Death Act creates two classes of plaintiffs, the heirs and the estate, and provides that each class of plaintiff may sue for a different type of damages. NRS 41.085(2). As used in NRS 41.085(2), "heir" means a person who, under Nevada law, would be entitled to succeed to the separate property of the decedent if he had died intestate. NRS 41.085(1). The heirs are authorized to pursue a claim for pecuniary damages for "grief or sorrow, loss of probable support, companionship, society, comfort and consortium and damages for pain, suffering or disfigurement of the decedent." NRS 41.085(4). The estate, through the administrator or the executor, is authorized to pursue a claim for special damages (*i.e.,* medical expenses and funeral expenses) and punitive damages. NRS 41.085(5). The estate cannot pursue a claim for damages for pain, suffering or disfigurement. Whether or not the heirs can now maintain an independent action for punitive damages (as they could under former law) is debatable, given that punitive damages are a creature of statute and the statute gives the action for punitive damages to the estate. *See* NRS 41.085(5).

A wrongful death action brought by the heirs may but need not be joined to the action brought by the estate. Since the claims of the heirs and the estate are separate causes of action, they should be subject to permissive joinder (NRCP 20) as opposed to mandatory joinder (NRCP 19). *Rodriguez v. Summa Corp.,* CV-LV-84-467 (5/27/86, unreported decision) (J. McKibben); *cf. Field v. Volkswagenwerk AG,* 626 F.2d 293 (3d Cir. 1980).

Nevada law requires that an administrator of a Nevada estate must be a "resident of the State of Nevada." NRS 139.010. This requirement is not imposed upon executors. The residency requirement creates a significant diversity of citizenship issue in wrongful death actions filed by administrators on behalf of nonresident beneficiaries in federal court. Assuming that the defendant is a citizen of Nevada, diversity is destroyed if the citizenship of the Nevada administrator rather than the citizenship of the nonresident beneficiaries is controlling.

A majority of federal courts and the Supreme Court in particular have long held in cases in which an administrator, trustee or executor has control over the litigation that it is the citizenship of the representative and not the decedent or beneficiaries that is determinative of federal jurisdiction. *Navarro Savings Association v. Lee,* 446 U.S. 458 (1980); *Mecom v. Fitzsimmons Drilling Co.,* 284 U.S. 183 (1980). A narrow exception has been recognized, however, where, as in Nevada, a resident ancillary administrator is required to represent the interests of noncitizen beneficiaries by virtue of the laws of the state in which the claim arose. In that situation, the citizenship of the beneficiary has been

57

held controlling for diversity purposes. *See Miller v. Perry,* 456 F.2d 63, 67 (4th Cir. 1972); *Field v. Volkswagenwerk AG,* 626 F.2d, 293, 303 (3d Cir. 1980).

§ 507. Homeowners' associations.

In the absence of any express statutory grant to bring suit on behalf of the owners or a direct ownership interest, a condominium management association is not the real party in interest and the action must be brought by the individual homeowners. *Deal v. 999 Lakeshore Association,* 94 Nev. 301, 579 P.2d 775 (1978). *See also Schouweiler v. Yancey Co.,* 101 Nev. 827, 712 P.2d 786 (1985). Only the owners of condominiums may sue for construction or design defects in the common areas because the owners eventually must bear the costs of assessments made by the association. Effective January 1, 1992, the Nevada legislature, as part of the common interest ownership (Uniform Act), provided that a homeowners' association may institute, defend or intervene in litigation or administrative proceedings in its own name on behalf of itself or two or more units' owners on matters affecting the common interest of the community. NRS 116.3102(1)(d). If the association is the legal owner of property rights involved in the litigation (*e.g.,* wells, water systems), the association is the real party in interest. *Painter v. Anderson,* 96 Nev. 941, 620 P.2d 1254 (1980). For rules regarding class action suits by individual homeowners, see § 522, *supra.*

§ 508. Unions.

The trustee or trustees, rather than the union trust fund, is the real party in interest and the union trust fund itself does not have the capacity to sue. *Causey v. Carpenters Southern Nevada Vacation Trust,* 95 Nev. 609, 600 P.2d 244 (1979). Similarly, the administrator of union trust funds is not a real party in interest. *L & H Builders Supply v. Boyd Co.,* 93 Nev. 610, 571 P.2d 1167 (1977). The trustees of trust funds designated to receive employer contributions towards health and welfare and pension benefit plans are also real parties in interest as trustees of an express trust which is a third-party beneficiary of a written collective bargaining agreement. *Back Streets, Inc. v. Campbell,* 95 Nev. 651, 601 P.2d 54 (1979). A claim against a voluntary unincorporated labor organization may be brought against its president and secretary and against a number of other members without the necessity of joining all of the members of the organization. *Branson v. Industrial Workers of the World,* 30 Nev. 270, 95 P.2d 354 (1908); NRCP 23.2.

§ 509. Standing.

The question of standing is similar to the issue of real party in interest because it also focuses on the party seeking adjudication rather than on the issues sought to be adjudicated. *Szilagyi v. Testa,* 99 Nev. 834, 673 P.2d 495 (1983). Unfortunately, the distinction between "real party in interest" and "standing" is often ignored or the concepts are referred to interchangeably. *Deal v. 999 Lakeshore Association,* 94 Nev. 301, 579 P.2d 775 (1978).

The traditional two-prong test for standing is that the claimant must allege that the complained of action causes the claimant injury in fact and the claimant's interest must arguably be within the zone of interest protected or regulated by the statute or constitutional guarantee in question. *Association of Data Processing Service Organization, Inc. v. Camp,* 397 U.S. 150 (1970). The "injury-in-fact" inquiry has been divided into two parts: (1) has the action complained of caused or threatened to cause injury in fact; and (2) will the relief sought remedy the injury. *Simon v. Eastern Kentucky Welfare Rights Organization,* 426 U.S. 26 (1976). *See also Asarco, Inc. v. Kadish,* 490 U.S. 605, 109 S. Ct. 2037, 104 L. Ed. 696 (1989); *Dellums v. Smith,* 797 F.2d 817 (9th Cir. 1986), *Renne v. Geary,* __ U.S. __ , 111 S. Ct. 2331 (1991). The inquiry of standing is separate from and preliminary to a decision on the merits. *Association of Data Processing Service Organization, Inc., supra;* San Francisco County Democratic Central Committee v. Eu, 826 F.2d 814 (9th Cir. 1987).

§ 510. Capacity to sue or be sued.

The phrase "capacity to sue" means that the plaintiff must be free from general disability, such as infancy or insanity, or, if he sues as a representative, that he possesses the character in which he sues. *Withers v. Rockland Mines Co.,* 58 Nev. 98, 71 P.2d 156 (1937). There is a decided difference between capacity to sue and the right to maintain an action. *Withers, supra.* The capacity to sue is the right to come into court and differs from the cause of action, which is the right to relief in court. *Withers, supra.* The want of capacity to sue pertains to the person of the party — a personal incapacity — and not to the cause or right of action. *Withers, supra.* A plaintiff having a right of action may not have the capacity to sue; a plaintiff with capacity to sue may have no right of action. *Withers, supra.*

The question of whether or not an individual, including one acting in a representative capacity, has the capacity to sue or be sued is determined by Nevada law. NRCP 17(b). *See also Bader Enterprises v. Olsen,* 98 Nev. 381, 649 P.2d 1369 (1982); *Shaw v. Stuchman,* 105 Nev. 128, 771 P.2d 156 (1989). However, the capacity of a foreign corporation to sue or be sued is determined under the laws of the state or country under which it was organized unless a Nevada statute provides to the contrary. NRCP 17(b).

§ 511. Infants or incompetents.

At common law, infants and incompetents lacked the capacity to sue or be sued. The capacity to sue or be sued or have access to the court must be distinguished from an individual's right of action or liability under the substantive law. *Withers v. Rockland Mines Co.,* 58 Nev. 98, 71 P.2d 156 (1937). Nevada statutes and rules provide in various ways for the protection of the interests of minors and incompetents when they become involved in court actions and proceedings.

Chapter 159 of the NRS provides for the appointment of a guardian of the estate and the person of a minor or incompetent. When such a guardian has been appointed, the guardian may sue or defend on behalf of the minor or incompetent, NRCP 17(c), and is obligated to do so unless a guardian ad litem has been appointed. NRS 159.095; *cf. Bourne v. Walker,* 74 Nev. 230, 327 P.2d 344 (1958) ("friend" of minor, not appointed guardian ad litem, has no standing to challenge accounts of guardian of estate of minor).

In the case of actions for the injury of a minor child caused by the wrongful act or neglect of another, the father or the mother, without preference to either, has a statutory cause of action for the benefit of the minor, based on the injury. NRS 12.080. An identical rule applies to causes of actions by guardians for the benefit of wards. NRS 12.080. In other cases, when a minor or incompetent is named as a plaintiff or defendant in an action, NRCP 17(c) provides that the court must either appoint a guardian ad litem or make some other provision "as it deems proper for the protection of the infant or incompetent person." The procedure for the appointment of a guardian ad litem is outlined in NRS 12.050. In the case of a minor plaintiff, the request must come from the minor if he or she is fourteen or over, or from a "relative or friend" if the minor is under fourteen. NRS 12.050(1). In the Eighth Judicial District, the practice is for the attorney to file an application with the clerk of the court and then seek an ex parte order appointing such a guardian before filing the complaint. The complaint would then name the guardian ad litem and allege standing or capacity to present the interest of the infant.

NRS 65.010(1) provides that, in justice court, the appointment of the guardian ad litem must be made before the summons is issued, upon application of the minor if he or she is fourteen or older, or if under fourteen and incompetent, then upon the application of a relative or friend.

Whenever a minor has a disputed claim for money against a third party, a parent or general guardian has the right to compromise the claim, but only with the approval of the district court where the minor resides or where the claim was incurred if the minor is not a Nevada resident. NRS 41.200.

When the minor is a defendant, application for appointment of a guardian ad litem may be made by the minor if fourteen or older, or by a "relative or friend of the infant" or "any other party to the action" if the minor is under fourteen, or has not made application within ten days of service of summons and complaint. NRS 12.050(2). In a justice court action, the appointment must be made at the time the summons is returned or before the answer. NRS 65.010(2). Practitioners should note that summons and complaint must be served both upon a minor personally and upon his or her parent or guardian, if living within the state, and, if not, then upon the minor's employer or person having care and control of the minor. NRCP 4(d)(3). A similar rule applies to incompetents and their guardians. NRCP 4(d)(5).

Whenever an incompetent is a party, application for appointment of a guardian ad litem may be by a relative, friend or any other party to the litigation. NRS 12.050(3). If a person becomes incompetent during the course of litigation, the action may be continued by or against the incompetent's representative. NRCP 25(b).

Default judgment may not be taken against a minor or an incompetent, unless the minor or incompetent is represented in the action by a general guardian, guardian ad litem or other such representative. NRCP 55(b)(2).

§ 512. Governmental agencies.

NRS 12.105 provides that any political subdivision, public corporation, special district or other agency of the state or local government which is capable of being sued in its own name may be sued by naming it as a party, without naming the individual members of its governing board as defendants. Service of the complaint in such an action may be made upon either "the clerk or the secretary of the political subdivision, corporation or agency" being sued. NRS 12.105. That method of service would be cumulative with any other method of service provided by statute or rule. For example, in an action against the state or any agency of the state, service also may be made upon the secretary of state. NRS 41.031. *See also* NRCP 4(d)(5) and discussion dealing with service of process in Chapter 9, *infra.*

In an action upon a claim against the state for services or advances or refund of an overpayment after an adverse ruling by the state board of examiners or the state controller, the State of Nevada must be named as a defendant and the summons served upon the state controller. NRS 41.010. In an action brought against the state under the waiver of sovereign immunity, the State of Nevada must be named as defendant in an action against the state or any agency of the state and summons served upon the secretary of state. NRS 41.031(2). The state or appropriate political subdivision must be named as a party in any tort action brought against an officer or employee of the state, or a political subdivision of the state, or a state legislator under NRS 41.031 and NRS 41.0337, and must be instituted in accord with statutory claim procedures. *See Jiminez v. State Department of Prisons,* 98 Nev. 204, 664 P.2d 1023 (1982).

§ 513. Corporations.

The Nevada Constitution provides that a "corporation may sue and be sued in all courts, in like manner as individuals." Nev. Const. Art. 8, § 6(b).

The capacity of a corporation, whether Nevada or foreign, to sue and be sued shall be determined by the law under which it was organized, unless, in the case of foreign corporations, a Nevada statute provides to the contrary. NRCP 17(b); NRJCP 17(b). Of primary concern is NRS 80.210 which provides that if a corporation fails to qualify to do business as required by NRS 80.010 through 80.040, it may be precluded from bringing, maintaining or defending an action in Nevada courts during the period of its noncompliance. *See Bader Enterprises, Inc. v. Olsen,* 98 Nev. 381, 649 P.2d 1369 (1982). But a plaintiff waives its right to question capacity to defend under NRS 80.210 when it sues such a corporation and compels it to appear and answer. *Marshall Earth Resources v. Parks,* 99 Nev. 251, 252, 661 P.2d 875 (1983); *Walker Bank & Trust Co. v. Smith,* 88 Nev. 502, 501 P.2d 639 (1972). Nonetheless, that corporation has not established residency in any particular county for venue purposes. *Marshall Earth Resources v. Parks, supra,* at 252. A foreign corporation will be precluded from maintaining an action in Nevada even though it commenced the action while it was qualified to do business here, if it subsequently becomes unqualified due to its failure to comply with the continuing statutory requirements. *League to Save Lake Tahoe v. Tahoe Regional Planning Agency,* 93 Nev. 270, 273, 563 P.2d 582 (1977). Moreover, a foreign corporation not qualified to do business in the State of Nevada at the time the action was commenced cannot "maintain" that action, even if it subsequently qualifies to do business in the state. *League to Save Lake Tahoe, supra,* at 273. *Pettit v. Management Guidance, Inc.,* 95 Nev. 834, 603 P.2d 697 (1979). However, in *Lawler v. Ginochio,* 94 Nev. 623, 625, 584 P.2d 667 (1978), a foreign corporation was allowed to intervene in an action where it was not qualified to do business within the State of Nevada at the time the suit was commenced, as it had qualified to do business within the state at the time it brought its motion to intervene.

NRS 80.210 also does not limit the rights of corporate parties beyond the plain language of the statute. Thus, any dismissal of an action pursuant to NRS 80.210 must be without prejudice if the relevant statute of limitations has not run and the corporation is in the process of complying with Nevada's qualifying statutes. *Atlantic Commercial v. Boyles,* 103 Nev. 35, 37-38, 732 P.2d 1360 (1987); *Lake at Las Vegas Investors v. Pacific Malibu Dev.,* 933 F.2d 724 (9th Cir. 1991).

The test of whether a corporation is in fact "doing business in Nevada" and subject to NRS 80.210 is two-pronged — looking first at the nature of the business functions within the forum state and then to the quantity of business conducted within the forum state. *Sierra Glass & Mirror v. Viking Industries,* 107 Nev. Adv. Op. 21 (1991), citing *Eli Lilly & Co. v. Say-On Drugs,* 366 U.S. 276 (1961).

In 1991, the Nevada legislature amended NRS 80.015 to affirm that maintaining, defending or settling any proceeding; holding meetings of the board of directors or stockholders or carrying on other activities concerning internal corporate affairs; maintaining bank accounts; and maintaining offices for specified purposes with respect to the corporation's own securities did not constitute doing business within the state. The prior statutory exclusions remain unchanged, namely: Making sales through independent contractors, soliciting or receiving orders by letters or advertisements in state; acquiring indebtedness, mortgages and security interests; securing or collecting debts enforcing mortgages and security interests; securing or collecting debts or personal property; isolated transactions; production of motion pictures; and transacting business in interstate commerce.

Failure to file a fictitious name certificate as required by NRS 602.010 through 602.020 also precludes a business from commencing or maintaining an action in this state. NRS 602.070.

For actions brought by shareholders on behalf of their corporation, see § 520, *infra.*

§ 514. Limited liability companies.

In 1991, the Nevada legislature created a new type of legal entity (NRS Chapter 86), the limited liability company which may sue and be sued in its name. NRS 86.281. A member of a limited liability company is not a proper party to proceedings by or against the company, except where the object is to enforce the member's right against or liability to the company.

§ 515. Partnerships.

When two or more persons associated in any business transact such business under a common name, whether it comprises the names of such persons or not, the associates may be sued by such common name. NRS 12.110. The summons and complaint need only be served upon one of the associates and the judgment, if any, shall bind the joint property of all associates. NRS 12.110. To bind the separate property of a particular associate, however, that associate must be served individually with process. *Diamond National Corp. v. Thunderbird Hotel, Inc.*, 85 Nev. 271, 454 P.2d 13 (1969). Because each associate is a "necessary" but not an "indispensable" party, see § 517, *infra,* the better practice would be to sue and serve each particular associate, even if some discovery is required before filing an amended pleading. *Diamond National Corp., supra; Smart v. Valencia,* 50 Nev. 359, 261 P. 655 (1927).

NRS 88.270 had modified the foregoing rule when a limited partnership is being sued by providing that a limited partner was not a proper party to proceedings, unless the object of the suit was to enforce a limited partner's right against or liability to the partnership. With adoption of the Limited Partnership Act, NRS 88.270 was repealed. NRS 88.330(1)(b) requires that each limited partnership maintain a resident agent for service of process. Presumably, service upon the resident agent would bind the property of the limited partnership just as service upon the general partner did under former law. Unless the limited partnership is sued in its common name and service is made upon it as a partnership, a claim for relief will not be deemed to have been made against the partnership, despite the fact that one of the partners is involved in the action in an individual capacity. *See Richard Matthews, Jr., Inc. v. Vaughn,* 91 Nev. 583, 540 P.2d 1062 (1975). However, there is no indication in the revised NRS Chapter 88 as to when limited partners are proper parties to a proceeding. Given that the intent of revised NRS 88.430 is to provide a "safe harbor" for certain activities of limited partners (*see* Comment to § 303 of the 1985 Amendments to the Uniform Limited Partnership Act), a limited partner should not be named as a party unless the object of the suit is to impose liability as to the separate property of that limited partner under the theory that the limited partner participated in the control of the business. NRS 88.430. In addition, in the event that a limited partner is liable to partnership creditors for unpaid (but agreed to) capital contributions (NRS 88.475) or for returned capital contributions (NRS 88.525) and the creditor seeks to bind that limited partner's separate property, the limited partners should be joined as parties. In other cases, it should not be necessary to join limited partners individually.

A different rule applies with regard to actions that are commenced by a partnership. A partnership does not have the capacity to commence suit in its own name. *Proprietors of the Mexican Mill v. Yellow Jacket Silver Mining Co.*, 4 Nev. 40 (1868). Partners not joined in the suit as plaintiffs may be joined by the court as involuntary plaintiffs under NRCP 19(a).

An action commenced by a limited partnership must usually be instituted by the general partner. However, a limited partner may bring a derivative action on behalf of the partnership under certain limited circumstances. NRS 88.610; NRS 88.615. The complaint in such an action must set forth with particularity the effort of the plaintiff to secure initiation of the action by a general partner or the reasons for not making such an effort. NRS 88.620.

§516. Married persons.

A husband and wife may sue jointly on the causes of action belonging to both or either of them. NRS 12.020. When the action is for personal injuries or for compensation for services rendered, the spouse suffering the injuries or rendering the service is a necessary party. NRS 12.020(1) and (2).

When a husband and wife are sued together, either may defend on behalf of both. NRS 12.030. When a spouse has deserted the family, the other spouse may prosecute or defend any action in the name and on behalf of the deserting spouse. NRS 12.040.

§517. Necessary and indispensable parties.

Principles governing compulsory joinder of parties were a part of equity practice. The early case of *Robinson v. Kind*, 23 Nev. 330, 47 P. 977 (1896), required that all persons materially interested in the subject matter of the suit be made parties so that there may be a complete decree to bind them all. *Robinson, supra*, at 335. If the interest of absent parties may be affected or bound by the decree, they must be brought before the court or it will not proceed to decree. *Robinson, supra.* If the parties before the court may be subjected to undue inconvenience or potential loss, liability or litigation without joinder, the absent person should be made a party. *Robinson, supra*, at 335, 336. *University of Nevada v. Tarkanian*, 95 Nev. 389, 594 P.2d 1159 (1979).

Consistent with these principles, NRCP 19(a) provides for the joinder of persons needed for just adjudication, *i.e.*, "necessary parties." It requires that "necessary parties" shall be joined if subject to service of process and if joinder will not deprive the court of jurisdiction over the subject matter of the action. A party must be joined under NRCP 19(a) only if complete relief cannot be accorded in his absence or if he claims an interest in the subject of the action. *Lewis v. Smart,* 96 Nev. 846, 849, 619 P.2d 1212 (1980).

A person is an "indispensable party" if (1) the person is a necessary party" under NRCP 19(a); (2) the person cannot be made a party; and (3) the court determines under the factors enumerated in NRCP 19(b) that the action should not proceed among the parties before it without the absent person. If in equity and good conscience a court cannot proceed with an action without an absent party, that party is "indispensable" and the case must be dismissed. NRCP 19(b). *Potts v. Vokits,* 101 Nev. 90, 692 P.2d 1304 (1985). Failure to join an "indispensable party" requires dismissal of the action. *Potts, supra;* NRCP 19(b). Because the failure to join an "indispensable party" may be raised by a party at any time, including on appeal, prudence (as well as the express mandate of NRCP 19(a)) cautions joinder of all "necessary parties." *See Schwob v. Hemsath,* 98 Nev. 293, 646 P.2d 1212 (1982). Failure to join an "indispensable party" cannot be waived and may be raised by either a trial or an appellate court sua sponte. *University of Nevada v. Tarkanian,* 95 Nev. 389, 594 P.2d 1159 (1979).

Pursuant to NRCP 19, a person who is subject to process must be joined if:

> (1) in his absence complete relief cannot be accorded among those already parties, or (2) he claims an interest relating to the subject of the action and is so situated that the disposition of the action in his absence may (i) as a practical matter impair or impede his ability to protect that interest or (ii) leave any of the persons already parties subject to a substantial risk of incurring double, multiple, or otherwise inconsistent obligations by reason of his claimed interest.

The determination of whether a person is an "indispensable" party is only required when the person "cannot be made a party." NRCP 19(b). A person cannot be made a party if he is not subject to service of process or if joinder of that person will deprive the court of jurisdiction over the subject matter of the action. Unlike situations arising in federal court involving diversity of citizenship considerations, joinder of a "necessary party" in state court will rarely deprive the court of jurisdiction over the subject matter.

NRCP 19(b) enumerates four factors to be considered by the court in determining whether an absent person should be regarded as "indispensable":

> first, to what extent a judgment rendered in the person's absence might be prejudicial to him or those already parties; second, the extent to which, by protective provisions in the judgment, by the shaping of relief, or other measures, the prejudice can be lessened or avoided; third, whether a judgment rendered in the person's absence will be adequate; fourth, whether the plaintiff will have an adequate remedy if the action is dismissed for nonjoinder.

§518. — Nevada cases regarding necessary and indispensable parties.

The following list of Nevada cases is designed to aid counsel's search in locating authority for or against the proposition that certain parties are necessary or indispensable. The cases are listed by subject matter.

1. Assignments of Contractual, Tort or Fraud Claims.

Skyrme v. Occidental Mill & Mining Co., 8 Nev. 219 (1873) (assignor of mechanics' lien claim not indispensable party); *Volpert v. Papagna,* 83 Nev. 429, 433 P.2d 533 (1967) (assignor of lease not indispensable party in a wrongful detainer action but tenant in possession and subtenant were indispensable); *Smith v. Mayberry,* 13 Nev. 427 (1878) (assignee of subcontractor can sue contractor); *Castleman v. Redford,* 61 Nev. 259, 124 P.2d 293 (1942) (assignor of fraud claim indispensable because claim not assignable).

2. Spouses.

Slack v. Schwartz, 63 Nev. 47, 161 P.2d 345 (1945) (husband not indispensable party to wife's action for personal injuries); *Johnson v. Johnson,* 93 Nev. 655, 572 P.2d 925 (1977) (present wife indispensable party where transfer to her by husband attacked as fraudulent conveyance by former wife); *Rhodes v. Williams,* 12 Nev. 20 (1877) (wife necessary party where husband's partner claimed partnership money was used to build spouses' house).

3. Real Property.

Paso Builders, Inc. v. Hebard, 83 Nev. 165, 426 P.2d 731 (1967) (holder and beneficiary under deed of trust were both indispensable parties in suit requesting constructive trust on property); *Robinson v. Kind,* 23 Nev. 330, 47 P. 1 (1896), *reh'g denied,* 47 P. 977 (1897) (all parties who executed deed of trust were necessary in action to cancel it); *Schwob v. Hemsath,* 98 Nev. 293, 646 P.2d 1212 (1982) (corporation holding legal title to property in controversy was an indispensable party to quiet title action).

4. Governmental Officers and Entities.

Hawkins v. Eighth Judicial District Court, 67 Nev. 248, 216 P.2d 601 (1950) (state is necessary party in action for removal of public officers); *Rice v. Clark County,* 79 Nev. 253, 382 P.2d 605 (1963) (board of county highway commission not indispensable party where members were named in another capacity).

§ 519. Permissive joinder.

NRCP 20(a) imposes two requirements for permissive joinder. First, the persons to be joined must be asserting or defending against joint, several or alternative rights of relief arising out of the same transaction, occurrence or series of transactions or occurrences. NRCP 20(a). Second, there must exist in the action some question of law or fact common to all the joined persons. NRCP 20(a). However, a plaintiff or defendant need not be interested in obtaining or defending against all the relief demanded. NRCP 20(a).

The purpose of the rule is to promote trial convenience and expedite the final determination of disputes to prevent multiple lawsuits. 7 Wright, Miller & Kane, *Federal Practice & Procedure* § 1652, at 372 (2d ed. 1986). Compulsory joinder is not required in cases under NRCP 20, unless it is dictated by NRCP 19.

An insurance company is not subject to permissive joinder in a personal injury action if it is not defending under a reservation of rights and will pay any judgment against its insured according to the terms of the policy. *Roberts v. Farmers Insurance Co.,* 91 Nev. 199, 533 P.2d 158 (1975). The rationale for this rule is that final judgment against the insured is a pre-condition to the right of relief against the insurer. *Roberts, supra.*

NRCP 20(b) authorizes separate trials to prevent a party from being embarrassed, delayed or put to expense by inclusion of a party against which he asserts no claim and who asserts no claim against him. While NRCP 42 adequately addresses this problem, subsection (b) was added to Rule 20 to clarify that permissive joinder is a problem of trial convenience and to do away with practically all conceivable objections that might have been raised against unlimited joinder in appropriate cases. 3A J. Moore & J. Lucas, *Moore's Federal Practice* ¶ 20.08 (2d ed. 1987). For rules regarding permissive joinder of the heirs and the estate claims in wrongful death actions, see § 506, *supra;* for special rules regarding consolidation and separate trials under NRCP 42, see § 1901 *et seq., infra.*

§ 520. Misjoinder and nonjoinder.

NRCP 21 provides that misjoinder of parties is not grounds for dismissal of an action. This rule, which was designed to repudiate the overly technical common law rule under which misjoinder was fatal to a lawsuit, and is primarily concerned with nonjoinder and misjoinder of parties under the principles set forth in NRCP 18, NRCP 19 and NRCP 20. 3A J. Moore & J. Lucas, *Moore's Federal Practice* ¶ 21.03[1] (2d ed. 1987). Parties may be dropped and added on motion of any party or by the court on its own initiative. NRCP 21.

Since misjoinder is not a ground for dismissal, the objection may not be raised by motion to dismiss or by a motion to quash service. 3A J. Moore & J. Lucas, *Moore's Federal Practice* ¶ 21.03[1] (2d ed. 1987). The only ground for dismissal of an action involving joinder is failure to join an indispensable party under NRCP 19. *See* § 416, *supra.* Misjoinder should be addressed by a motion to drop the misjoined party or to sever the misjoined claim. 3A J. Moore & J. Lucas, *Moore's Federal Practice* ¶ 21.03[1] (2d ed. 1987). The Nevada Supreme Court has considered arguments of misjoinder when first raised on appeal. *Gershenhorn v. Walter R. Stutz Enterprises,* 72 Nev. 293, 304 P.2d 395 (1956).

Substitution of a corporation for an individual as the proper party plaintiff has been authorized under NRCP 21 (in conjunction with NRCP 15). *Good v. Second Judicial District Court,* 71 Nev. 38, 279 P.2d 467 (1955). The primary concern expressed in the decisions is prejudice to the movant. *Good, supra; Gershenhorn v. Walter R. Stutz Enterprises,* 72 Nev. 293, 304 P.2d 395 (1956).

§ 521. Interpleader.

Interpleader is an equitable proceeding to determine the rights of rival claimants to property held by a third person or entity. *Farmers Insurance Exchange v. Civil Service Employees Insurance Co.,* 94 Nev. 733, 587 P.2d 420 (1978). NRCP 22(1) provides that persons having claims against the plaintiff may be joined as defendants and required to interplead when their claims are such that the plaintiff is or may be exposed to double or multiple liability. Similarly, a defendant may plead a claim for interpleader as a counterclaim. 3A J. Moore & J. Lucas, *Moore's Federal Practice* ¶ 22.15 (2d ed. 1987). Since other claimants who are not already parties to the action may be brought in as additional parties on the counterclaim (utilizing permissive joinder) or by a third-party complaint, raising the interpleader issues in this manner is a desirable alternative to initiation of an independent interpleader action and consolidation with the pending action. 3A J. Moore & J. Lucas, *supra.*

In comparison, NRCP 20 authorizes the alternative of joinder by the adverse party where there is a doubt by a defendant as to who possesses the right (permissive joinder of plaintiffs) or where there is a doubt by a plaintiff as to who is liable (permissive joinder of defendants). 3A J. Moore & J. Lucas, *Moore's Federal Practice* ¶ 22.04[1] (2d ed. 1987). NRCP 22(1) authorizes joinder in the converse situation, where two or more persons are claiming against a third and allows the third to obtain a binding declaration of whether he is liable and, if so, to whom and to what extent. 3A J. Moore & J. Lucas, *supra.* In this sense, NRCP 22(1) supplements NRCP 20. 3A J. Moore & J. Lucas, *supra.*

The purpose of obtaining interpleader is to protect one from double vexation in respect to one liability. *Rutherford v. Union Land & Cattle Co.,* 47 Nev. 21, 213 P. 1045 (1923). It allows a stakeholder to force claimants to a fund to contest in one forum the merits of their respective claims. 7 Wright, Miller & Kane, *Federal Procedure & Parties* § 1702 (2d ed. 1987). Historically, the following requirements were necessary in a traditional, "strict" bill of interpleader:

1. Two or more persons must have preferred a claim against the plaintiff.
2. They must claim the same thing, whether it be a debt or duty.
3. The plaintiff must have no beneficial interest in the thing claimed.
4. It must appear that he cannot determine, without hazard to himself, to which of the defendants the thing of right belongs.

Orr Water Ditch Co. v. Larcombe, 14 Nev. 53 (1879). The equity of an action in interpleader was said to lie in requiring the conflicting claimants to litigate the matter among themselves, without involving the plaintiff in their dispute, with which he had no interest. *Mooney v. Newton,* 43 Nev. 441, 187 P. 721 (1920).

The statutory precursors to Rule 22, Revised Laws of Nevada § 5005 (1912) and Nevada Compiled Laws § 8562 (Hillyer 1929), permitted a summary proceeding in cases where a bill of interpleader would lie and were governed by the same principles except that the statutes enlarged the scope of the equitable remedy by permitting conflicting claimants whose titles and claims need not be identical or have a common origin but which could be adverse and independent of one another. *Rutherford v. Union Land & Cattle Co.,* 47 Nev. 21, 213 P. 1045 (1923).

When the Nevada Supreme Court superseded Nevada Compiled Laws § 8562 (Hillyer 1929) through enactment of NRCP 22, it adopted the language of the federal rule, providing that "[i]t is not ground for objection to the joinder ... that the plaintiff avers that he is not liable in whole or in part to any or all of the claimants." NRCP 22. Although federal courts have construed this language as no longer requiring that the stakeholder be disinterested, two modern Nevada cases retain this traditional element, despite citations to NRCP 22. *Farmers Insurance Exchange v. Civil Service Employers Insurance Co.,* 94 Nev. 733, 587 P.2d 420 (1978); *Balish v. Farnham,* 92 Nev. 133, 546 P.2d 1297 (1976). Until the Nevada Supreme Court has had an opportunity to resolve this conflict between rule and case law, the careful practitioner will consider the possibility of raising this defense in cases involving an interested stakeholder.

In an interpleader action, each claimant is treated as a plaintiff and must recover on the strength of his own right or title and not upon the weakness of his adversary's right or title. *Balish v. Farnham,* 92 Nev. 133, 546 P.2d 1297 (1976). Consequently, the failure of one claimant to prove his claim does not mean that the other claimant automatically wins. *Balish, supra.*

Traditionally, the stakeholder must deposit the disputed property in court when the defendants have answered the complaint. If the stakeholder is disinterested, he may then withdraw from the action. Rule 22 does not expressly mention deposit with the court or specify the nature of the deposit. Federal interpleader practice permits a surety bond in lieu of actual deposit of the funds.

NRS 31.350 expressly provides for interpleader by a garnishee, where conflicting claims exist to the funds held by the garnishee.

The interpled property need not be limited to money. For example, pursuant to NRS 104.7603, a bailee may interplead goods in his possession.

§ 522. Class actions.

NRCP 23 authorizes one or more persons to sue as representative parties on behalf of a class only if the four prerequisites set forth in NRCP 23(a) are satisfied and, in addition, if at least one of the prerequisites of either NRCP 23(b)(1)(A), NRCP 23(b)(1)(B), NRCP 23(b)(2) or NRCP 23(b)(3) can be satisfied. *Johnson v. Travelers Insurance Co.,* 89 Nev. 467, 471, 515 P.2d 68 (1973). The determination to use the class action is a discretionary function wherein the district court must determine pragmatically whether it is better to proceed as a single action or in many individual actions in order to redress a single fundamental wrong. *Deal v. 999 Lakeshore Association,* 94 Nev. 301, 579 P.2d 775 (1978).

The first of the four prerequisites in NRCP 23(a) is that the class be so numerous that joinder of all members is impracticable. In determining the number of members of the class, persons who fail to present questions of law or fact common to the class are excluded. *Kane v. Sierra Lincoln-Mercury, Inc.,* 91 Nev. 178, 533 P.2d 464 (1975) (excluding thirty-four of thirty-nine potential class members; the remaining five members were held to be insufficient to justify a class action); no error was found in permitting sixty members to constitute a class in *Deal v. 999 Lakeshore Association,* 94 Nev. 301, 579 P.2d 775 (1978).

The second of the four prerequisites in NRCP 23(a) is that there be questions of law or fact common to the class. NRCP 23(a)(2). The reasonableness of medical bills for patients proposed as class members has been held not to be a common question of fact. *Johnson v. Travelers Insurance Co.,* 89 Nev. 467, 515 P.2d 68 (1973). A class action for fraudulent misrepresentation generally does not present a common question of fact or law, given the inherent uniqueness of misrepresentation actions. *Johnson, supra.* However, a representative suit for collective deceit possibly may be maintained when a fraud element exists and pervades the transaction. *Johnson, supra.* Common issues of liability may be adjudicated on a class basis despite the existence of separate issues concerning the damages sustained by various class members. *Johnson, supra.* Similarly, the fact that property of a particular class member is not damaged is not determinative if he is responsible for his pro rata portion of the damages of the class as a whole. *Deal v. 999 Lakeshore Association,* 94 Nev. 301, 579 P.2d 775 (1978). The third of the four prerequisites in NRCP 23(a) is that the claims or defenses of the representative parties be typical of the claims or defenses of the class. NRCP 23(a)(3). An argument that a class action was inappropriate because the defendant had differing defenses as to different class members was rejected on appeal, however, where defendant failed to demonstrate prejudice through showing that the jury determination was not based on a single theory of liability. *Deal v. 999 Lakeshore Association,* 94 Nev. 301, 579 P.2d 775 (1978).

The fourth prerequisite in NRCP 23(a) is that the representative parties adequately protect the interests of the class. The various prerequisites in NRCP 23(b) have not been discussed in Nevada decisions. However, the Nevada cases which consider the propriety of class actions have relied heavily on federal case law interpreting FRCP 23, and counsel is well advised to research and reference these decisions.

§ 523. Shareholders' derivative actions.

A derivative lawsuit is an action brought by a shareholder in a corporation, a partner in a partnership, or a member of some other form of unincorporated association to enforce a right belonging to that corporation, partnership or unincorporated association which the entity failed to pursue itself. A number of different causes of action may be asserted on behalf of the corporation, partnership or unincorporated association in the derivative action, *e.g.,* breach of fiduciary duty, corporate opportunity doctrine or wrongful interference with prospective economic advantage. *Leavitt v. Leisure Sports Incorporation,* 103 Nev. 81, 734 P.2d 1221 (1987). However, the proceeds of a successful derivative action are the property of the corporation, partnership or unincorporated association. NRS 88.625.

NRCP 23.1 (derivative actions by shareholders), NRS 41.520 (derivative actions by shareholders and by members of unincorporated associations) and NRS 88.610 (derivative actions by limited partners), which closely parallel each other, set forth the basic procedural rules for bringing derivative lawsuits.

To bring a derivative lawsuit, the plaintiff must file a verified complaint alleging with particularity all of the efforts that the plaintiff has undertaken to have the board of directors, general partner or trustees of the business entity enforce the rights which are sought to be enforced through the derivative lawsuit. An exception to this requirement is recognized if the demand would be an exercise in futility because the board of directors or trustees are controlled by the principal wrongdoer. *Johnson v. Steel, Inc.,* 100 Nev. 181, 678 P.2d 676 (1984). Both NRCP 23.1 and NRS 41.520(2) require, however, that the verified complaint state with particularity the reasons why a demand would be futile or unnecessary.

The plaintiff shareholder must have been a member of the corporation or business entity at the time of the transaction of which he complains. NRS 41.520(2); NRCP 23.1. Similarly, a limited partner must be a partner at the time of the bringing of the action and at the time of the transaction of which he complains. NRS 88.615. Thus, persons who have purchased an interest in a business after the wrongdoing occurred have no standing to bring a derivative suit. *Keever v. Jewelry Mountain Mines, Inc.,* 100 Nev. 576, 688 P.2d 317 (1984); *Gascue v. Saralegui Land & Livestock Co.,* 70 Nev. 83, 255 P.2d 335 (1953). Conversely, if the plaintiff shareholder does not maintain his ownership interest in the entity throughout the entire period of the litigation, the action is subject to dismissal for the failure of plaintiff to clearly and adequately represent the interests of the corporation. *Keever v. Jewelry Mountain Mines, Inc.,* 100 Nev. 576, 688 P.2d 317 (1984).

§ 524. Intervention.

Intervention is governed by NRCP 24, NRS 12.130 and NRS 65.030. The latter two statutes are identical for all material purposes, with the exception that NRS 12.130 applies to district court proceedings and NRS 65.030 applies to justice court proceedings. NRCP 24 contains language very similar to the two statutes cited above, except that NRCP 24 requires "timely application" to intervene and the statutes merely require intervention "before the trial." The term "before the trial" in the statute has been held to require intervention at the district court level and to prohibit intervention in the supreme court. *Stephens v. First National Bank,* 64 Nev. 292, 182 P.2d 146 (1947). However, *Stephens* predates the promulgation of NRCP 24, and its continuing validity is subject to doubt, given modern federal authority which interprets the identical FRCP 24 as allowing intervention after trial under proper circumstances. 7C Wright, Miller & Kane, *Federal Practice & Procedure* § 1916, at 451 (2d ed. 1986). The holding of *Stephens* is also questionable in light of a recent decision allowing intervention in the middle of trial, despite the apparent prohibition in NRS 12.130. *See Lawler v. Ginochio,* 94 Nev. 623, 584 P.2d 667 (1978).

"Timeliness" is a requirement for intervention. NRCP 24. The key to the timeliness of a motion to intervene is not the length of delay but the prejudice to existing parties. *Lawler v. Ginochio,* 94 Nev. 623, 584 P.2d 667 (1978). The timeliness of a motion to intervene is a matter within the discretion of the district court. *Lawler, supra; Cleland v. Eighth Judicial District Court,* 92 Nev. 454, 552 P.2d 488 (1976). A motion to intervene clearly is not timely when the controversy no longer exists. *Eckerson v. C.E. Rudy, Inc.,* 72 Nev. 97, 295 P.2d 399 (1956) (default judgment already entered).

NRS 12.130(3) provides that intervention may be made as provided by the Nevada Rules of Civil Procedure. Given this mandate and the duplication in the requirements of NRCP 24 and NRS 12.130(3), the subject of intervention is best addressed by focusing primarily upon the prerequisites of NRCP 24. NRCP 24 differentiates between intervention of right (NRCP 24(a)) and permissive intervention (NRCP 24(b)). Under NRCP 24(a), one has a right to intervene upon timely application (1) when a statute confers such a right or (2) when the applicant claims an interest in the property or transaction involved which is not adequately protected by the existing parties and which might be adversely affected by the outcome of the action. Regarding nonstatutory intervention of right, it has been said that NRCP 24(a)(2) imposes four requirements: (1) the application must be timely; (2) it must show an interest in the subject matter of the action; (3) it must show that the protection of the interest may be impaired by the disposition of the action; and (4) it must show that the interest is not adequately represented by an existing party. 3B J. Moore & J. Kennedy, *Moore's Federal Practice* ¶ 24.07[1] (2d ed. 1987). Where the first three requirements are satisfied but the interest is adequately represented by existing parties, intervention of right may be denied. *Lundberg v. Koontz,* 82 Nev. 360, 418 P.2d 808 (1966).

The exact nature of the interest required to sustain a right to intervene has eluded precise and authoritative judicial definition. 3B J. Moore & J. Kennedy, *Moore's Federal Practice* ¶ 24.07[2] (2d ed. 1987). However, the Nevada Supreme Court has held that to intervene as a matter of right a person must have such an interest in the litigation that he would either gain or lose by direct legal operation and effect of the judgment. *Harlan v. Eureka Mining Co.,* 10 Nev. 92 (1875). The United States Supreme Court has required "a significantly protectable interest." *Donaldson v. United States,* 400 U.S. 517, 551 (1971). In this regard, whether a would-be intervenor has the requisite interest in the subject matter of the litigation may, in some cases, involve questions of standing. 3B J. Moore & J. Kennedy, *Moore's Federal Practice* ¶ 24.07[2] (2d ed. 1987).

Intervention of right has been allowed where the applicant claimed ownership in land involved in the action. *Bartlett v. Bishop of Nevada,* 59 Nev. 283, 91 P.2d 828 (1939). It has been denied where the claimant would not gain or lose in a pecuniary sense. *See Stephens v. First National Bank,* 64 Nev. 292, 182 P.2d 146 (1947) (United States had no right to intervene in action between private parties to determine ownership of savings bonds). By contrast, permissive intervention has been allowed, absent a pecuniary interest, when the public interest can be benefitted. *Azbill v. Fisher,* 84 Nev. 414, 442 P.2d 916 (1968) (newspaper reporter allowed to intervene in mandamus proceeding to determine the constitutionality of a statute permitting exclusion from the courtroom of the general public, including reporters, because the "principle involved is in the public interest").

Under NRCP 24(b), permissive intervention is a matter of trial convenience and may be permitted in the court's discretion when a conditional right to intervene is provided by a statute or when the applicant's claim or defense has a question of law or fact in common with the main action. It has been said that the discretionary right to intervene is a corollary of permissive joinder (NRCP 20), the class action based on several rights (NRCP 23(b)(3)), and joint hearing or consolidation (NRCP 42(a)), all of which are predicated upon the theory that, when claims or defenses have a question of law or fact common to each other, a sound administrative scheme of procedure should encourage one action or hearing rather than a multiplicity of actions or hearings. 3B J. Moore & J. Kennedy, *Moore's Federal Practice* ¶ 24.10[1] (2d ed. 1987).

The manner of intervention is by motion, which must be served with a copy of the proposed pleading. NRCP 24(c). Form 23 in the Appendix of Forms to NRCP contains a sample motion. The intervenor does not become a party to the action until the motion is granted. *Cf. State ex rel. Moore v. Fourth Judicial District Court,* 77 Nev. 357, 364 P.2d 1073 (1961) (persons seeking to intervene not barred from filing a statutory affidavit of prejudice by the requirement that such an affidavit be filed prior to a contested hearing).

§ 525. Substitution of parties.

When a party to litigation has died, has been declared incompetent, or has otherwise transferred any property interest that is subject to such litigation, NRCP 25 governs the manner by which a party may be substituted.

If a party to litigation dies and the claim is not thereby extinguished, successors or representatives of the deceased party (such as the executor of the decedent's estate) may be substituted by the court as the proper party to the litigation in the place of the decedent. The motion for substitution may be made by any party or by the successors or representatives of the deceased party. NRCP 25(a)(1). Such a motion must be served on all parties in accordance with NRCP 5, and upon all persons not parties in the manner provided in Rule 4 for the service of a summons.

The practitioner should be mindful of the timetable within which a motion for substitution under NRCP 25(a) must be made. If a defendant dies before judgment, counsel for the defendant should serve and file upon opposing counsel "a suggestion of death upon the record." The service of such a "suggestion of death" places opposing counsel on notice that a motion for substitution must be filed within ninety days after such service. If a motion for substitution is not filed within that time frame, "the action shall be dismissed as to the deceased party." NRCP 25(a)(1). *See Barto v. Weishaar,* 101 Nev. 27, 28, 692 P.2d 498 (1985). While it is proper for the court to dismiss the claims as to the deceased plaintiff when no motion is made within the statutory period, it is improper for the court to dismiss the entire action if remaining plaintiffs have brought separate causes of action. *Bennett v. Topping,* 102 Nev. 151, 717 P.2d 44 (1986).

NRCP 25(d)(1) provides that when a public officer who is a party to litigation dies or ceases to hold office, his successor is automatically substituted as a party. Further, although the proceedings following the substitution shall be in the name of the successors, any misnomer not affecting the parties' substantial rights will be disregarded. An order of such substitution may be entered at any time.

When one of multiple parties plaintiff or defendant dies and the right to be enforced survives only to the surviving plaintiffs or against the surviving defendants, the action does not abate. The death is simply suggested on the record, and the action proceeds in favor of or against the surviving party. NRCP 25(a)(2).

One of the limitations on the right to substitute parties in the event of death is the extinguishment of the underlying claim by death. NRCP 25(a)(1). NRS 41.100 sets forth the statutory criteria for determining whether a claim is extinguished by death.

NRS 12.100 provides that death of a party shall not abate an action after a verdict has been rendered. Such a case proceeds in the same manner as other cases in which the cause of action would otherwise survive by law.

In the case of *Lummis v. Eighth Judicial District Court,* 94 Nev. 114, 576 P.2d 272 (1978), the court utilized NRCP 25(a) to allow the administrators of the Howard Hughes estate to be substituted in litigation in the place of Howard Hughes, even though Howard Hughes was not a party because he was never personally served with process. The court held that NRCP 25(a) was a necessary procedural device in order to prevent a party's death from destroying, for lack of prosecution, a party's valid

cause of action. *Lummis, supra,* at 115. The substitution of a representative for a party who becomes incompetent during the course of litigation
is covered by NRCP 25(b). That section provides that, upon a motion
served or provided in section (a) dealing with death, the court may allow
the action to be continued by or against the incompetent person's representative.

Whenever a party transfers an interest subject to litigation, the action
may still "be continued by or against the original party," unless the
court, on motion, directs the transferee to be substituted or joined in the
action with the original party. NRCP 25(c). Exceptions to this rule are
found in NRCP 23, 23.1 and 23.2. Where there is an assignment or
transfer of an interest subject to the litigation, such an assignment cannot prejudice the claims or defenses of the opposing party. NRS 12.010.
Where a substitution of parties is necessary because of a transfer of
interest, the parties need not file a supplemental complaint or other
pleading. Instead, the substituted party is bound by the original pleadings. *Virgin v. Brubaker,* 4 Nev. 31 (1868).

In the event that property is transferred during the course of litigation
and one party disclaims any interest in the property so transferred, the
disclaiming party will no longer have any standing to maintain an appeal or other action in district court because of such disclaimer. *Leonard
v. Belanger,* 67 Nev. 577, 222 P.2d 193 (1950).

CHAPTER 6

VENUE

Author: Janice J. Brown

§ 601. Introduction and scope.

This chapter describes selection of venue, *i.e.,* the county where an action must be commenced or tried. Inherent in the selection of venue is selection of a court with jurisdiction over the subject matter and parties, subjects covered fully in Chapters 4, 5 and 9. This chapter includes selection of proper venue for causes of action, demands and motions for change of venue, procedure for obtaining a change of venue and forum non conveniens. This chapter does not discuss transfer, removal to, or remand from, a federal court.

79

§ 602. Venue, generally.

Venue statutes are rules regulating the place of trial. Rules of Civil Procedure neither extend nor limit venue. NRCP 82. No special or local law affecting venue is permissible. Nev. Const. Art. 4, § 20.

§ 603. — Demands and motions for change of venue as a matter of right.

A change of venue, if proper demand has been made, must be granted if the county in the complaint is not the proper county. An application for change of venue as a matter of right permits no exercise of discretion. *Halama v. Halama*, 97 Nev. 628, 637 P.2d 1221 (1981). Once a change of venue has been granted as a matter of right, only the transferee court has jurisdiction. *Stocks v. Stocks*, 64 Nev. 431, 183 P.2d 617 (1947). *Damus v. Avis Rent A Car*, 108 Nev. 46, 824 P.2d 283 (1992).

§ 604. — Venue for particular causes of action.

Chapter 13 of Nevada Revised Statutes governs venue in most actions, as follows:

A. *Contracts.*

NRS 13.010(1) governs commencement of actions if a person has contracted to perform in one place but resides in another. It provides:

> 1. When a person has contracted to perform an obligation at a particular place, and resides in another county, *the action must be commenced,* and, subject to the power of the court to change the place of trial as provided in this chapter, must be tried in the county in which such obligation is to be performed or in which he resides; and the county in which the obligation is incurred shall be deemed to be the county in which it is to be performed, unless there is a special contract to the contrary. (Emphasis added.)

Note that the "special contract to the contrary" referenced in NRS 13.010(1) refers to a contract regarding place of performance, not one regarding venue. *Borden v. Silver State Equipment, Inc.*, 100 Nev. 87, 675 P.2d 995 (1984). As to "residence" of a corporation for venue purposes, see § 608, *infra*. Note the distinction between the place of performance of a contract and a statutory right if the action is one brought against a county. *Lyon County v. Washoe Medical Center, Inc.*, 104 Nev. 765, 767 n.4, 766 P.2d 902 (1988). Except when the suit is between counties, such an action must be brought in the district court of the judicial district embracing the county.

B. *Real property.*

NRS 13.010(2) governs actions regarding real property, with particular requirements if plaintiff seeks an injunction:

2. Actions for the following causes shall be *tried* in the county in
which the subject of the action, or some part thereof, is situated, subject to the power of the court to change the place of trial as provided in
this chapter.
   (a) For the recovery of real property, or an estate, or interest
therein, or for the determination in any form of such right or interest, and for injuries to real property.
   (b) For the partition of real property.
   (c) For the foreclosure of all liens and mortgages on real property.
Where the real property is situated partly in one county and partly
in another the plaintiff may select either of the counties, and the
county so selected is the proper county for the trial of such action;
but, in the case mentioned in this paragraph, if the plaintiff prays in
his complaint *for an injunction pending the action, or applies pending action for an injunction, the proper county for the trial shall be
the county in which the defendant resides or a majority of the defendants reside at the commencement of the action. (Emphasis added.)*

C. *Penalties or forfeitures imposed by statute; actions against public
officers.*

NRS 13.020 governs actions for recovery of penalties or forfeitures
imposed by statute, and actions against public officers for acts done by
virtue of his or her office or by persons acting at the officer's command.
Such cases may be tried where the cause of action or some part of the
cause of action rose.

Note: Several statutes specify where the main office will be for a state
agency. Some agencies have taken this to establish "residence" for venue
purposes, although this contention may be questionable.

D. *Actions by or against counties.*

NRS 13.030 governs an action by a county. Such an action must be
brought in the judicial district embracing the county. *Lyon County v.
Washoe Medical Center,* 104 Nev. 765, 766, 766 P.2d 902 (1988). There
are important public interests such as avoiding the costs to taxpayers of
defending actions in other communities, maintaining actions where relevant official records are kept, and reducing forum shopping which are
promoted by requiring actions to be commenced in the judicial district
embracing the defendant county. A discretionary change of venue may
be requested if the convenience of witnesses and the ends of justice would
be better served by changing the place of trial, but the motion must be
brought in the district court embracing the defendant county. *See* NRS

113.050(2)(b), (c). An action between counties must be commenced in a court of competent jurisdiction in any county not a party to the action.

E. *Divorce actions.*

In determining venue for divorce actions, consider NRS 13.040 and NRS 125.020 together. *Duffill v. Bartlett*, 53 Nev. 228, 297 P. 504 (1931). A defendant in a divorce action has an absolute right to a change of venue if statutory requirements have been met. *Stocks v. Stocks*, 64 Nev. 431, 183 P.2d 617 (1947).

F. *Child custody and juvenile matters.*

These matters are often controlled by interstate compact. The discussions in this chapter must be read in light of those compacts. *See* Chapter 125A, Nevada Revised Statutes, particularly NRS 125A.070, and Chapter 130, particularly 130.120.

G. *Miscellaneous provisions.*

Particular actions may be governed by specific statutes. The following is a summary only and is not intended to be exclusive. Consult specific statutes relating to your action.

Adult Adoption: NRS 127.210(1)
Arbitration: NRS 38.195; NRS 38.045(3)
Eminent Domain: NRS 37.060(1)
Guardianship: NRS 159.037, NRS 159.039
Mechanics Liens: NRS 108.239
Parentage: NRS 126.381
Paternity: NRS 126.091
Indigent Care: NRS 450.400
Fines for Violation: Ch. 616 (NIIA); NRS 616.647(88), *cf.* NRS 617.500

§ 605. Venue for actions not otherwise specified.

NRS 13.040 provides that in the absence of a statute specifying venue, an action must be tried where any defendant resides; but if defendants are nonresidents or if their residence is unknown, then the case may be tried in any county which plaintiff designates. If the defendant is about to depart the state, the action may be tried in any county where either party resides or where service may be had. Most tort actions are governed by NRS 13.040.

§ 606. Residence.

Residence is determined as of the time an action is commenced.

§ 607. — Residence and multiple defendants.

If there are multiple defendants to an action, venue cannot be changed to one defendant's county of residence if another defendant resides in the county where plaintiff filed the action. *Hill v. Summa Corp.,* 90 Nev. 79, 518 P.2d 1094 (1974). There is no Nevada case that determines the result if each defendant resides in a county other than the county where the action was brought but none are residents of the *same* county. But see *Marshall Earth Resources, Inc. v. Parks,* 99 Nev. 251, 661 P.2d 875 (1983), wherein the issue was noted but not addressed.

§ 608. — Residence of corporations.

No Nevada statute deals solely with actions against corporations. Designation of a principal place of business in official documents on file in the state, *i.e.,* articles of incorporation filed with the Secretary of State determines venue. *See Flournoy v. McKinnon Ford Sales,* 90 Nev. 119, 520 P.2d 600 (1974). Another party to the action apparently may controvert the facts set out in those documents. *Flournoy, supra,* at 122 n.3. There appear to be further distinctions drawn between defendants depending upon their corporate status. For instance, if a corporation is a foreign corporation qualified to do business in Nevada, the mere fact that it does business in the state does not fix its residence in any particular county for the purposes of venue so as to defeat the right of another resident defendant to change venue. *Byers v. Graton,* 82 Nev. 92, 411 P.2d 480 (1966). *Western Pacific Railroad v. Krom,* 102 Nev. 40, 714 P.2d 182 (1986). A resident or a domestic corporation seemingly has preference over a foreign corporation qualified to do business in Nevada if a change of venue is requested by both defendants. If, however, the defendant is a foreign corporation which has *not* qualified to do business in Nevada, the corporation has not established residence for venue purposes and will be treated as though its residence were unknown. *Marshall Earth Resources, Inc. v. Parks,* 99 Nev. 251, 661 P.2d 875 (1983). Thus, for a foreign corporation not qualified to do business in Nevada, venue would be proper in any county in which plaintiff resides. *See* NRS 13.040.

§ 609. Effect of naming former "Doe" defendants.

Assume that after an otherwise proper demand and motion for change of venue as a matter of right have been filed, the plaintiff substitutes for a "Doe" defendant a resident of the county where suit was brought. May the change of venue still be ordered as a matter or right? No. Venue cannot be changed if *any* defendant's residence is the county where suit was brought. *Hill v. Summa Corp.,* 90 Nev. 79, 518 P.2d 1094 (1974).

That is, for purposes of venue, the substitution "related back." The court, however, allowed a change of venue to a later-identified "Doe" defendant, holding there had been no waiver of the right to demand change of venue when the "Doe" party stipulated to identification of the "Doe" party by name. *Western Pacific Railroad v. Krom*, 102 Nev. 40, 714 P.2d 182 (1986).

§ 610. Effect of multiple claims.

No Nevada case has discussed whether a cross-defendant or third-party defendant has a right to demand a change of venue when brought into a suit. Note that although Rule 19(a) of Federal Rules of Civil Procedure provides that if the joined party objects to venue and the joinder would render the venue improper, the joined party must be dismissed from the action, Rule 19(a) of the Nevada Rules of Civil Procedure has no such provision.

§ 611. Pleading venue.

Plaintiff fixes the venue merely by filing in a particular county. As a matter of practice, plaintiffs' attorneys recite the plaintiffs' and defendants' residences in the complaint. Contrary to federal practice, there appear to be no particular pleading requirements for alleging venue in a State court case. The Nevada statutory scheme and Nevada case law place the burden of determining and challenging venue squarely upon the defendant. Defendant is not required, however, to demonstrate that *no* co-defendant resides in the county where suit was brought. *Compare Hill v. Summa Corp.*, 90 Nev. 79, 518 P.2d 1094 (1974), with *Ash Springs Development Corp. v. Crunk*, 95 Nev. 73, 589 P.2d 1023 (1979).

Parties may *consent* to venue, but a writing is required. NRS 13.050(3) provides:

> 3. When the place of trial is changed, all other proceedings shall be had in the county to which the place of trial is changed, unless otherwise provided by the consent of the parties in writing duly filed, or by order of the court, and the papers shall be filed or transferred accordingly.

§ 612. Effect of change of venue.

Upon change of venue, all other proceedings must take place in the transferee court and papers must be filed or transferred accordingly. NRS 13.050(3). The party commencing the transfer is responsible for payment of any fees upon transfer. NRS 19.013(1). *See Damus v. Avis Rent A Car, supra*, 108 Nev. at __, 824 P.2d at 284.

§ 613. Discretionary changes of venue; grounds.

NRS 13.050 prescribes the grounds for discretionary change of venue. Venue may be changed if the convenience of witnesses and ends of justice would be promoted by the change and good cause exists for change of venue. Some factors to be considered are the possibility of jury view, whether witnesses can be subpoenaed, and whether a speedy trial can be had. In *Fabbi v. First National Bank,* 62 Nev. 405, 153 P.2d 122 (1944), the court balanced all the various factors and refused to change venue. Note that if the venue must be changed *as a matter of right,* the trial court cannot first consider a motion for change of venue on discretionary grounds. The discretionary motion must be addressed to the court where venue was proper after the transfer as a matter of right. *Ash Springs Development Corp. v. Crunk,* 95 Nev. 73, 589 P.2d 1023 (1979). Venue may also be changed if a fair and impartial trial cannot be had where venue is proper. *Cf. In re Wright,* 68 Nev. 324, 232 P.2d 398 (1951) (jealousy and hostility must exist which will effect the outcome). Bias or prejudice of the trial judge, however, will not be a basis for change of venue. *State ex rel. Elsman v. Second Judicial District Court,* 52 Nev. 379, 287 P. 957 (1930). An application for discretionary change of venue is addressed to the sound discretion of the court and the exercise thereof will not be disturbed unless manifestly abused. *Fabbi v. First National Bank,* 62 Nev. 405, 153 P.2d 122 (1944). See § 519, *infra.* In *Public Service Commission v. Southwest Gas Corp.,* 103 Nev. 307, 738 P.2d 890 (1987), it was error to deny a change of venue. The action sought judicial review of a public service commission order. The court held that the original district court that heard the matter had continuing jurisdiction to review other orders in order to effect the purpose of the statute, one of which is conservation of judicial resources. § 621, *infra.*

§ 614. Procedure for obtaining a change of venue.

The procedure for obtaining a change of venue is set forth in NRS 13.050, as follows:

1. If the county designated for that purpose in the complaint be not the proper county, the action may, notwithstanding, be tried therein, unless the defendant before the time for answering expires *demand in writing* that the trial be had in the proper county, and the place of trial be thereupon changed by consent of the parties, or by order of the court, as provided in this section.
2. The court may, *on motion,* change the place of trial in the following cases:
    (a) When the county designated in the complaint is not the proper county.
    (b) When there is reason to believe that an impartial trial cannot be had therein.

(c) When the convenience of the witnesses and the ends of justice would be promoted by the change of venue. (Emphasis added.)

§ 615. — Demand and motion required if demand is made as a matter of right.

A change of venue, if proper demand has been made, must be granted if the county in the complaint is not the proper county. An application for change of venue as a matter of right permits no exercise of discretion. *Halama v. Halama*, 97 Nev. 628, 637 P.2d 1221 (1981). Once a change of venue has been granted as a matter of right, only the court where venue is proper has jurisdiction. *Stocks v. Stocks*, 64 Nev. 431, 183 P.2d 617 (1947).

Both a demand for change of venue and a motion for a mandatory change of venue as a matter of right are required to obtain the change of venue under NRS 13.050(1)(2)(a). *Nevada Transit Co. v. Harris Brothers Lumber Co.*, 80 Nev. 465, 396 P.2d 133 (1964). The demand and motion may be filed simultaneously. *O'Banion v. O'Banion*, 87 Nev. 88, 482 P.2d 313 (1971).

If the demand is made for a discretionary change, a motion is required, but a demand is not. NRS 13.050(2)(b)(c). *Kenning Car Rental, Inc. v. Desert Rent-A-Car*, 105 Nev. 118, 771 P.2d 150 (1989).

§ 616. — Timeliness.

The time within which to demand a change of venue *as a matter of right* commences to run upon service of summons and complaint. *Page v. Walser*, 43 Nev. 422, 187 P. 509 (1920). A demand for mandatory change of venue is waived if it is not filed within the original time to answer the complaint. *Compare Hood v. Kirby*, 99 Nev. 386, 663 P.2d 348 (1983) with *Randono v. Ballow*, 100 Nev. 142, 676 P.2d 807 (1984). *See also Western Pacific v. Krom*, *supra*, wherein a demand within twenty days of the stipulation to substitute a newly identified defendant for a "Doe" was timely because there was no waiver or intentional relinquishment of the right to challenge venue, nor was the opposing party prejudiced by any delay attached to the change of venue.

When, however, the motion for change of venue is for convenience of witnesses or to secure an impartial trial, the motion is addressed to the discretion of the court and may be made at any time prior to trial, absent prejudice to the other party or unjustifiable delay. *Sheckles v. Sheckles*, 3 Nev. 404 (1867).

§ 617. — Effect of extension, time to answer, motion to quash.

Extending the time in which to answer the complaint does *NOT* enlarge the time in which to demand change of venue. *Connolly v.*

Salsberry, 43 Nev. 182, 183 P. 391 (1919). Conversely, filing an answer does not waive the right to make a timely demand and motion for change of venue. *Byers v. Graton,* 82 Nev. 92, 411 P.2d 480 (1966). Nevada has no counterpart to Federal Rule of Civil Procedure 12(b)(3) which allows a defendant to raise improper venue by motion. Therefore, filing a timely demand and motion for change of venue *apparently will not toll the time in which to answer the complaint.* Would filing a demand and motion for change of venue *before or with a motion to quash service* render the defendant's appearance a "general" one? Must defendant "elect" which right is the more important should defendant believe service improper? Seemingly, there is no conflict between NRS 18.030 relating to security for costs and Chapter 13 because there is no obligation to answer a complaint until security is posted pursuant to NRS 18.030. A demand for change of venue could logically follow the posting of the bond. What result, however, if the bond were not posted? Would defendant have to change venue to the proper court to obtain an order of dismissal for failure to post a bond? Probably, as an order entered by a court without jurisdiction is of no effect.

§ 618. Appeal.

Direct appeal must be taken from an order changing or refusing to change venue. NRS 2.090; NRS 2.110; NRAP 3A(b)(2) and (4). *See Verner v. Jouflas,* 95 Nev. 69, 589 P.2d 1025 (1979). The Supreme Court may remand the case to the proper lower court for a fact-finding proceeding.

§ 619. — Time.

The time in which to file a notice of appeal *may run from the date the Order was entered, not from notice of entry of Order. See* NRAP 3A(b)(4); NRS 2.110; and *In re Herrmann,* 100 Nev. 1, 677 P.2d 594 (1984). In civil cases, a judgment or order is "entered" when it is signed by the judge (or the clerk if applicable) and filed with the clerk. NRAP 4(a).

§ 620. — Stay of proceedings.

The party appealing an order changing venue must obtain a stay of proceedings in the trial court to deprive the trial court of jurisdiction to proceed with the action. NRAP 3A(b)(4). *See Paradise Palms Community Association v. Paradise Homes,* 93 Nev. 488, 568 P.2d 577 (1977), *cert. denied,* 435 U.S. 997 (1978).

§ 621. Actions in different states.

No local rule governs actions filed in more than one state court or one which should have been filed in a sister state or country. The local court may dismiss such a complaint if defendant can make a sufficiently strong showing to overcome the traditional preference given plaintiff's choice of forum. The focal points are the interests of justice and the convenience of the court and parties. The court will balance the private and public factors to reach a conclusion in each case. If the complaint is dismissed, the plaintiff is left to litigate in the proper forum. The courts sometimes condition a dismissal upon defendant's waiver of a statute of limitations defense or acceptance of later service. *See Eaton v. District Court,* 96 Nev. 773, 616 P.2d 400 (1980). A non-resident defendant served in this state may have recourse under the doctrine of forum non conveniens where witnesses and the accident locale are outside the State of Nevada. *See Cariaga v. District Court,* 104 Nev. 544, 763 P.2d 59 (1988).

§ 622. — Factors for application of forum non conveniens doctrine.

A defendant has a heavy burden to demonstrate that the present local forum should cede jurisdiction to another state. The court will carefully examine affidavits in support of such motions. The fact that defendant is a Nevada resident or is incorporated in Nevada weighs heavily against the motion. The court must be able to make specific factual findings as to the number of witnesses, the substance of their testimony, the necessity for their presence, hardship in bringing documentary evidence to Nevada, and reasons why the testimony cannot be presented by deposition. The court then balances public and private interests, access to sources of proof, availability of views of the premises, availability of compulsory process for unwilling witnesses, costs of obtaining testimony from willing witnesses, and the enforceability of the judgment. The court deprives the plaintiff of his or her choice of forum only in exceptional cases and only if defendant will be subjected to harassment, oppression, vexation, or the requisite degree of inconvenience. *Eaton v. District Court,* 96 Nev. 773, 616 P.2d 400 (1980).

If neither party is a resident and the action did not arise in the state, the balance may shift towards granting the motion as the court becomes concerned with the case's impact upon the local court and the citizens the local court was designated to protect. A good discussion of the factors considered on such motions appears in *Gulf Oil Corp. v. Gilbert,* 330 U.S. 501, 67 S. Ct. 839, 91 L. Ed. 1055 (1947) and *Cubbage v. Merchent,* 744 F.2d 665 (9th Cir. 1984).

§ 623. — Denial of motion: remedy.

An order dismissing an action on the ground of *forum non conveniens* is subject to a writ of mandamus. If a district court wrongfully or erroneously divests itself of jurisdiction or refuses to assume jurisdiction, mandamus is the proper remedy. *State ex rel. Swisco, Inc. v. Second Judicial District Court,* 79 Nev. 414, 417, 385 P.2d 772 (1963).

§ 624. Motions for injunction.

A party may apply for an injunction prohibiting a state from litigating a suit concerning the same parties and issues while another state considers the matter. The power to enjoin a foreign court is used reluctantly and sparingly. A clear showing is required that restraint is necessary to prevent manifest wrong or injustice. *Walker v. Walker,* 84 Nev. 118, 437 P.2d 91 (1968). The fact that the foreign state possibly would give the forum's resident less favorable consideration was insufficient basis for enjoining prosecution of a transitory action in another state. *See Brunzell Construction Co. v. Harrah's Club,* 81 Nev. 414, 404 P.2d 902 (1965). The court may also decline to exercise jurisdiction on the basis of comity. *See Mianecki v. District Court,* 99 Nev. 93, 658 P.2d 422, *cert. dismissed,* 104 S. Ct. 195 (1983).

NOTE

This Chapter is not directed to criminal cases. *See* Chapter 174, Nevada Revised Statutes. *See* Ford v. State, 102 Nev. 126, 717 P.2d 27 (1986) for a discussion of pretrial publicity as it affects choice of venue.

Form 6A

DEMAND FOR MANDATORY CHANGE OF VENUE

[Caption]

TO: (Name of each Party);

TO: (Attorney of record for each Party)

Demand is hereby made for change of venue in the above entitled action to the _____(Court)_____ of _____(County)_____ , State of Nevada, pursuant to NRS _____, for the reason that [herein set forth in brief the grounds for the change of venue.] For example:

A.

Defendant was not a resident of __(County where filed)__ at the commencement of the action, but instead resides in _____ County.

B.

The real property which is the subject of the action is not located in __(County where filed)__ , but is instead located in _____ County.

C.

Application for Injunction is or will be made and the defendant (or a majority of defendants) reside in _____ County.

D.

The action is against _____(County)_____ and the suit must be tried in that County.

E.

The action is between __(County where filed)__ County and (Second) County and __(Third)__ County is a proper place for trial.

F.

The action is against public officers and for acts done by virtue of office (or at the officer's command) and the action (or some part of it) arose in _____ County.

G.

The action is one for _____(describe)_____ and NRS _____ sets venue in _____ County, the County where (Set forth venue specified in particular statute.)

DATED AND DONE this _____ day of _____, at
_____, Nevada.

                                    _____
                                                [Party]
                                                  OR

                              DEFENDANT CORPORATION

                              By _____
                                            [Title]

Form 6B

MOTION FOR CHANGE OF VENUE

The motion should reflect the specific grounds upon which change of venue is requested. The motion must be supported by affidavit(s) specific as to facts supporting a change of venue and points and authorities. The motion should also identify the court in which trial should be had. *See* §§ 607 and 614, *supra,* which discuss which court may hear a Motion for Change of Venue and the timing thereof.

Follow general rules as to form, notice and supporting points and authorities.

Form 6C

AFFIDAVIT IN SUPPORT OF MOTION FOR CHANGE OF VENUE

(On basis of defendant's residence.)

[Caption]

[Preliminary matters required by affidavits generally].

I am a Defendant in this action.

At the time of the commencement of this action I was a resident of the county of _____, Nevada, residing at _____ in the City of _____.

I request transfer of this action to (Court and County of Residence) pursuant to NRS _____.

_____
[Party]

[Notarization or affirmation on
pains and penalties of perjury]

Form 6D

AFFIDAVIT IN SUPPORT OF MOTION FOR CHANGE OF VENUE AS A
MATTER OF RIGHT

(Corporate Defendant)

[Caption]

[Preliminary Matters]

That affiant is _____ (Title) _____ of the Defen-
dant _____ (name of corporation) _____ and is duly authorized to make this Affidavit in Support of Change of Venue.

[NEVADA CORPORATION

That _____ is a Nevada Corporation, duly li-
censed and authorized to do business in the State of Nevada with articles of
incorporation on file with the Secretary of State. That the principal place of
business of _____ (Name) _____ as shown in the records on file
therein is _____ (Address) _____, in the City of _____,
County of _____, State of Nevada.]

[FOREIGN CORPORATIONS AUTHORIZED TO DO BUSINESS IN
NEVADA]

That _____ is a ___ (State of Incorporation) ___
Corporation duly authorized and qualified to do business in the State of
Nevada. I maintain a principal place of business in the State of Nevada, at
_____ (Address) _____, City of _____
_____, County of _____, as shown
in the official documents on file with the Secretary of State.]

Defendant corporation requests transfer of this action to (Court and County of
principal place of business) pursuant to NRS _____, upon payment of
proper costs.

_____
(Title)

[Notarization or
Affirmation]

NOTE: A foreign corporation which has not qualified to do business in Nevada
is treated as though its residence were unknown and the action may be tried in
any county which Plaintiff designates.

Form 6E

AFFIDAVIT IN SUPPORT OF MOTION FOR CHANGE OF VENUE AS A MATTER OF RIGHT

(Real Property located in County other than County where sued.)

[Caption]

[Preliminary Matters]

I am (a defendant in this action) (the person duly authorized by defendant corporation to make this affidavit in support of change of venue).

(I reside at ＿＿＿＿＿＿＿＿＿＿＿＿＿＿＿.) (The Corporation's principal place of business is ＿＿＿＿＿＿＿＿＿＿＿＿＿＿＿.)

Plaintiff's action is one relating to real property, to wit, an action for ＿＿ (specify nature of the action) ＿.

The real property which is the subject of the action is situated partly in the County of ＿＿＿＿＿＿＿＿＿＿＿＿＿＿, (and partly in the County of ＿＿＿＿＿＿＿＿＿＿＿＿＿), but no part thereof is situated in the County of ＿＿ (where action is brought) ＿.

The Defendant requests a transfer of the action to (Court and County where property is located) or, (if an application for injunction is or will be made, the County where the defendant or the majority of the defendants reside.)

＿＿＿＿＿＿＿＿＿＿＿＿＿＿＿＿＿＿＿＿
                                            [Signature]

[Notarization or
Affirmation]

95

Form 6F

AFFIDAVIT IN SUPPORT OF MOTION FOR DISCRETIONARY CHANGE
OF VENUE

(For Convenience of Witnesses or to Promote the Ends of Justice.)

[Caption]

[Preliminary Matters]

The convenience of witnesses and the ends of justice would be promoted by the change of place of trial of this action from the County of ____(where filed)____ to the County of _____.

The witnesses to be called at trial are: (Name, address, occupation, and place of employment of each).

The nature of the testimony expected from each witness is as follows: (Describe testimony anticipated).

Depositions could not be used in lieu of live testimony without prejudice to Defendant because (describe).

The reasons why the attendance of the witnesses in ___(County where filed)___ for trial would be inconvenient are: (examples)

The expense of bringing in said witness to the City of _____, a distance of approximately _____ miles, for attendance upon trial of this action, will be great and will entail loss of time on the part of said witnesses which cannot be fully compensated by payment of money.

That the costs to the defendant will be unduly increased by requiring it to defend in _____ County because (describe) and will prejudice its defense by (describe).

A Jury view of (describe premises) is required which cannot be adequately accomplished by photograph or description.

(Set forth any other factors supporting change of venue. See *Fabbi v. First National Bank,* 62 Nev. 405, 153 P.2d 122 (1944) and *Eaton v. Second Judicial District Court,* 96 Nev. 773, 616 P.2d 400 (1980).)

The change of place of trial of this action will promote the ends of justice because: (examples)

[Upon the trial of this action it will be necessary for the court to interpret a number of local ordinances of the _____ of _____.]

[The calendar of ___(court where filed)___ is such that the parties may obtain an earlier trial in ___(County of transfer)___ .]

[The interest of citizens of ___(County where filed)___ can more readily be resolved and actions more closely connected to said county can be more quickly heard if transferred to _____(County)_____ is made.]

[The citizens of ___(County where filed)___ have no interest in the outcome of the action; none of the parties reside there; and no part of the action arose there. (Imposition of jury duty on such citizens in such case is unwarranted.)]

_____

[Signature]

[Notarization or
Affirmation]

NOTE: If an impartial trial cannot be had in the county where filed, the reasons must be specifically alleged and proof shown. Bias of the Court or Judge is not a basis for change of venue.

Form 6G

ORDER CHANGING VENUE

A change of venue must be based on a finding of findings of specific statutory grounds. Separate findings by the court in the Order are recommended. The Order also should include the name of the court to which the action will be transferred.

The Order should further direct that the Clerk, upon payment of costs and fees, to forward to the Clerk of the Court to which the action is ordered transferred, all of the pleadings and papers on file relating to the action, together with a copy of the Order Changing Venue.

[Remember that parties may consent to continue in an improper venue. NRS 13.050(3).]

CHAPTER 7

REMOVAL

Author: Suellen Fulstone

§ 701. Introduction and scope.

This Chapter discusses the "removal" of civil actions from state court to federal court under the federal removal statutes. It addresses the removal jurisdiction of the federal court, the factors to consider before removing an action to federal court, the procedure for removal, the procedure after removal, and the remand of removed cases to the state court. This Chapter addresses only the general federal removal statutes and only the removal of civil cases. It does not encompass the removal of criminal prosecutions. Nor does it address any of the special removal statutes, such as 28 U.S.C. § 2679(d) (the removability of an action against a federal employee for injury caused by his operation of a motor vehicle within the scope of his employment); 12 U.S.C. § 1819(a) (removal of actions involving the FDIC); or 12 U.S.C. § 1441a(1)(3) (removal of actions involving the Resolution Trust Corporation, successor to the Federal Savings and Loan Insurance Corporation). The removal of claims related to bankruptcy cases (28 U.S.C. § 1452) is also outside the scope of this Chapter.

§ 702. The removal statutes, 28 U.S.C. §§ 1441-1451.

"Removal" refers to the transfer of an action from state court to a federal court for adjudication. The right to remove a case is purely statutory and subject to the changing sensibilities of the U.S. Congress. The present removal statutes are found generally at 28 U.S.C. §§ 1441-1450.

§ 703. Removable cases.

The federal statute at 28 U.S.C. § 1441 sets forth the requirements that must be met before a state court action is removable. Section 1441 removal is limited to civil "actions" brought in a state "court." Ancillary or supplementary proceedings are generally not removable, nor are actions before administrative tribunals. The "court" requirement, however, is not limited to state courts of general jurisdiction. Actions may be removed from justice courts, municipal courts, or other courts.

An action is removable to federal court only if it could have been brought in federal court originally. This means the case must either meet the requirements of diversity jurisdiction, including satisfying the jurisdictional amount in controversy (28 U.S.C. § 1332), or the claim must arise under the U.S. Constitution, federal treaty, federal statute, or the federal common law. *See Merrill Dow Pharmaceuticals v. Thompson*, 478 U.S. 804 (1986); *Illinois v. City of Milwaukee*, 406 U.S. 91, 99-100 (1972). When an action contains multiple claims for relief, the entire action can be removed if one of the claims is a federal claim. 28 U.S.C. § 1441(c). The federal court has the discretion to determine all the issues, including those raised by the nonfederal claims or to remand to the State court "all matters in which State law predominates." *Id.*

The practitioner may encounter case law describing the removal jurisdiction of the federal courts as "derivative." Before the 1986 amendments to the removal statute, an action brought in state court alleging a federal claim over which the federal courts had been given exclusive jurisdiction could not be removed to the federal court. Although the action could have been brought in federal court originally, it did not satisfy the requirements for removal because the state court lacked subject matter jurisdiction over the claim and the removal jurisdiction of the federal court was held to be "derivative" of the state court's jurisdiction. The action had to be dismissed rather than removed. The notion that removal jurisdiction is "derivative" has been rendered obsolete by the 1986 amendment to the removal statute and the prior case law to that effect has no application. The removal statutes now expressly provide that the federal court on removal may hear and determine a claim otherwise determinable in federal court notwithstanding the lack of subject matter jurisdiction in the state court over such a claim. 28 U.S.C. § 1441(e).

§ 704. Diversity removal.

The requirements of diversity jurisdiction are complete diversity among the parties and more than $50,000 in controversy exclusive of interest and costs. 28 U.S.C. § 1332. Complete diversity among the parties means that all plaintiffs have citizenship diverse from all defendants. The "amount in controversy" requirement has posed a problem in Nevada because of the provision of NRCP Rule 8(a) that prohibits pleading a specific amount when a plaintiff seeks damages of more than $10,000. On removal, the defendant cannot merely allege the satisfaction of the $50,000 jurisdictional amount but must also be prepared to prove that amount if challenged. *See Gaus v. Miles, Inc.*, __ F.2d __ (Docket No. 91-16385) (9th Cir. 1992).

Even if there is complete diversity among the parties and the requisite amount in controversy, there are several special requirements imposed on diversity cases which may defeat removal. For example, a case cannot be removed if any one of the defendants is a citizen of the state in which the plaintiff brought the action. 28 U.S.C. § 1442(b). Furthermore, a case cannot be removed on diversity grounds absent the joinder of all the defendants in the action who have been served. *See Ely Valley Mines, Inc. v. Hartford Accident & Indemnity Co.*, 644 F.2d 1310, 1314 (9th Cir. 1981). Finally, if the case first becomes diverse more than one year after its commencement, it cannot be removed to federal court on diversity grounds. 28 U.S.C. § 1446(b).

§ 705. Federal claim removal.

As a general rule, the plaintiff must plead a federal claim on the face of the complaint or the case is not removable as a case arising under federal law. *See Caterpillar, Inc. v. Williams*, 482 U.S. 386, 392 (1987). This is called the "well-pleaded complaint" rule. Under the well-pleaded complaint rule, the case is not removable if the plaintiff has not pleaded a federal claim on the face of the complaint even if the complaint as drawn necessarily calls forth a federal law defense. *See Garibaldi v. Lucky Food Stores, Inc.*, 726 F.2d 1367 (9th Cir. 1984).

Furthermore, an action is not removable if the plaintiff asserts only state law claims on the face of the complaint even if federal law claims could have been alleged based on the same facts. *See Sullivan v. First Affiliated Securities, Inc.*, 813 F.2d 1368 (9th Cir. 1987). For example, a plaintiff may avoid federal court removal by pleading a claim for relief expressly under state RICO statutes only, although the facts may also support a federal RICO claim.

There are exceptions to the "well-pleaded complaint" rule. For example, a plaintiff cannot avoid removal to federal court by pleading a state law claim in an area that has been completely preempted by federal law. The two areas that are most familiar in this regard are claims arising under the federal Employee Retirement Income Security Act (ERISA) and the Labor Management Relations Act (LMRA). *See Pilot Life Insurance Co. v. Dedeaux*, 481 U.S. 41 (1987); *Young v. Anthony's Fish Grottos, Inc.*, 830 F.2d 993, 997-98 (9th Cir. 1987).

A complaint that does not set forth a federal question on its face may also be removable if the plaintiff has artfully pleaded its claims in order to avoid federal jurisdiction of claims that are federal in nature. Under the "artful pleading" doctrine, the court is authorized to recharacterize the claim as arising under the federal law.

§ 706. Nonremovable cases.

In addition to the instances described above when the specific requirements of removability are not satisfied, certain kinds of cases are expressly made not removable by statute. These include the following:

1. Cases brought under the Federal Employer's Liability Act (FELA) against a railroad or its receivers or trustees. 28 U.S.C. § 1445(a)
2. Cases arising under 49 U.S.C. § 11707 against a common carrier or its receivers or trustees to recover damages for delay, loss or injury of shipments, unless the matter in controversy exceeds $10,000 exclusive of interest and costs. 28 U.S.C. § 1445(b)
3. Cases arising under the workers' compensation laws of the State. 28 U.S.C. § 1445(c)
4. Actions for misrepresentation under the Securities Act of 1933. 15 U.S.C. § 77v.

Actions under the FELA, 49 U.S.C. § 11707, when the matter in controversy is less than $10,000, and 15 U.S.C. § 77v, would ordinarily be removable as arising under federal law. Because of the express statutory prohibition, however, these actions are not removable either as federal question cases or on diversity grounds.

§ 707. The right of removal belongs to the defendant.

The right to remove an action from state to federal court is conferred only upon the defendant. 28 U.S.C. § 1441(a). A plaintiff cannot remove a case even if the defendant asserts a counterclaim arising under federal law. *See American International Underwriters v. Continental Insurance Co.*, 843 F.2d 1253 (9th Cir. 1988). Although the case law is split, the majority of courts prohibit removal of an action to federal court by a third-party defendant. *See, e.g., Lewis v. Windsor Door Co.*, 926 F.2d 729 (8th Cir. 1991).

The federal court may realign the parties in order to determine who is the defendant. This determination is made by a functional test: the party who attempts to achieve a particular result is the "mainspring" of the action and the plaintiff; the party opposing that claim is the defendant. *General Motors Corp. v. Gunn*, 752 F. Supp. 729 (N.D. Miss. 1990).

Unless a defendant is removing the action as a separate and independent removable claim under 28 U.S.C. § 1441(c), all defendants who have been served must join in the removal. *See Ely Valley Mines, Inc. v.*

Hartford Accident & Indemnity Co., 644 F.2d 1310, 1314 (9th Cir. 1981). Unserved, nominal and sham defendants need not join in removal. *See Republic Western Insurance Co. v. International Insurance Co.*, 765 F. Supp. 628 (N.D. Cal. 1991).

In diversity cases, a defendant may remove the action to federal court only if no defendant "properly joined and served" is a citizen of the state in which the action is filed. Thus, in an action filed in Nevada State Court, even if there is complete diversity between plaintiffs and defendants, the action is not removable if any one of the defendants is a citizen of Nevada.

A single defendant in a separate and independent federal cause of action may remove the entire action to federal court even if the co-defendants named in additional, otherwise nonremovable causes of action do not consent. *See Manis v. North American Rockwell Corp.*, 329 F. Supp. 1077, 1078 (C.D. Cal. 1971). Foreign defendants in cases governed by 28 U.S.C. § 1441(d) may also remove without the joinder of co-defendants. In such cases, the foreign defendant has the right to remove the case even over the objection of co-defendants.

Unless there is exclusive subject matter jurisdiction in the federal court, a defendant can waive his right to remove an action to the federal court. Waiver may be express as in a forum selection clause in a contract. Waiver may also be implied but only from clear and unequivocal actions affirmatively invoking the jurisdiction of the state court. The mere filing of a pleading that raises a defense on the merits is not a waiver nor is a motion made only to preserve the status quo. Seeking a continuance of a hearing in state court, however, may be held to be a waiver of the right to remove the matter to federal court. *Chicago Title & Trust Co. v. Whitney Stores*, 583 F. Supp. 575 (N.D. Ill. 1984). The assertion of a permissive counterclaim is another example of an action that may be deemed a waiver. *George v. Al-Saud*, 478 F. Supp. 773 (N.D. Cal. 1979).

§ 708. Factors in determining desirability of removal.

If an action is removable to federal court, the issue becomes whether the federal forum is preferable. There are various factors to consider. For example, federal practice requires unanimous juries in civil cases as compared to the majority verdicts permitted in state court. Federal civil juries, however, usually consist of only six members. The venire from which jurors are selected is also broader in the federal court.

Other factors to consider include the somewhat different discovery, pretrial and calendaring rules and procedures between the state and federal courts. State and federal courts also follow different procedures with respect to the conduct of the trial, including differences in the conduct of voir dire, the preparation and use of jury instructions, the use of exhibits, and the presentation of closing arguments.

An important factor to be considered is the nature of the case and the legal and factual issues presented. Federal courts may have more expertise than state courts in certain areas of federal law such as ERISA, while at the same time they may be less willing to resolve novel issues of state law. Federal courts as well are generally considered to have less stringent standards for the granting of summary judgment motions.

§ 709. Procedure for removal.

The procedure for removing a case from state to federal court is governed by federal statute and not by the Federal Rules of Civil Procedure. Section 1446 of Title 28 of the U.S. Code sets forth the procedure for removal. That procedure was substantially changed by the Judicial Improvements Act of 1988. Prior to 1988, removal was accomplished by the filing of a petition for removal, verified by counsel, in the federal court setting forth the facts supporting removal. The verified petition had to be accompanied by a bond for costs.

As simplified by the 1988 Act, the procedure now requires only the filing of a notice of removal setting forth the grounds for removal together with copies of all process, pleadings and orders served upon the defendant or defendants in the action. The notice must also be accompanied with the standard civil cover sheet and the payment of the usual first pleading filing fee. The notice need not set forth the specific facts which support removal, nor is it required to be verified. The bond requirement has also been eliminated. Two sample notices of removal are included in the forms accompanying this chapter, for diversity and federal question removal respectively.

Promptly after the notice of removal is filed with the federal court, written notice of the filing, together with a copy of the notice of removal, must be filed with the clerk of the State court from which removal is made and served upon all adverse parties. 28 U.S.C. § 1446(d). Although not specifically required, it is good practice to attach a file-marked copy of the notice of removal as filed in the federal court. This provides the plaintiff's counsel with both the case number and the court assignment in the federal action. A sample notice of filing notice of removal is also included in the forms accompanying this chapter. "Promptly" is not defined by the statute or case law. There is, however, no reason for delay and what may be held undue delay can become grounds for a remand.

The removal of an action from state to federal court does not require the approval of either court. In fact, it does not involve any action whatsoever by either court. The removal of the action is completed and effective upon the filing in the State court of notice of the removal accompanied by a copy of the notice of removal as filed in the federal court. The adjudication thereafter proceeds in federal court until and unless it is remanded. The State court can take no further action in the case until and unless the case is remanded to its jurisdiction.

§ 710. The timing of removal.

The notice of removal must be filed in the federal court within thirty days after either (1) the receipt by the defendant, "through service or otherwise," of a copy of the initial pleading upon which removal is based, or (2) the service of summons upon the defendant, if the initial pleading has been filed and is *not* required to be served, whichever event occurs first. 28 U.S.C. § 1446(b). It should be noted that there need not be either service of the initial pleading or of the summons. The receipt of a courtesy copy of a complaint may constitute "receipt" for purposes of triggering the thirty-day removal period. *See Perimeter Lighting, Inc. v. Karlton*, 456 F. Supp. 355 (N.D. Ga. 1978).

If the case as alleged in the initial pleading is not removable, a notice of removal may be filed within thirty days after receipt by the defendant, through service or otherwise, of a copy of an amended pleading, motion, order or other paper from which it may first be determined that the case is one which is or has become removable. 28 U.S.C. § 1446(b). Under this rule, the thirty-day removal period may be triggered in numerous and diverse ways. The plaintiff may file an amended pleading. The plaintiff may reveal certain information on deposition that invokes federal preemption or reveals unknown residence or citizenship resulting in complete diversity. Damages may be accruing to the point where the amount in controversy requirement is satisfied for diversity jurisdiction.

The statute creates one exception to this rule. A diversity case cannot be removed more than one year after its commencement, even if the basis for diversity removal either comes into existence or is revealed only after that time. For example, a diversity case in which damages are continuing to accrue may first satisfy the requisite jurisdictional amount in controversy more than a year after its commencement. In those circumstances, the action is not removable. Likewise, the voluntary dismissal of a nondiverse defendant may create the basis for a diversity removal. But the dismissal must occur within the first year after the case is filed or the case cannot be removed.

The thirty-day time period for filing the notice of removal is mandatory. It is, however, not jurisdictional. Although, if removal is untimely, the plaintiff has the right to have the case remanded to state court, that right may be waived or lost by estoppel. A motion to remand must be made within thirty days. 28 U.S.C. § 1447(c).

§ 711. Procedure after removal.

Generally, once a matter is removed, it proceeds as if it had been originally filed in the federal court. *Chicago, R.I. & P.R. Co. v. Igoe*, 212 F.2d 378 (7th Cir. 1954). Procedural issues are governed by federal law and rules. *Granny Goose, Inc. v. Brotherhood of Teamsters & Auto Truck Drivers*, 415 U.S. 423, 39 L. Ed. 2d 435 (1974). Rule 81(c) of the Federal Rules of Civil Procedure specifically provides that the Federal Rules apply to cases removed from state courts.

After removal, the federal court may issue all necessary orders and process to bring before it all proper parties to the case. 28 U.S.C. § 1447(a). The federal court may also require the removing party to file with it copies of all records and proceedings from the state court. 28 U.S.C. § 1447(b). This authority supplements the requirement of 28 U.S.C. § 1446 that the removing party file with the federal court as part of the notice of removal, copies of all pleadings, process and orders served upon such party in the action.

When an action has been removed, all injunctions, orders and other proceedings had in the action prior to the removal remain in full force and effect until modified by order of the federal court. 28 U.S.C. § 1450. All bonds and undertakings given in the action prior to the removal remain in full force and effect as to any provisions for attachment or sequestration of property. *Id.*

In most removed actions, two issues arise upon removal. The first is the filing of a responsive pleading. Rule 81(c) provides that if the defendant has not filed its answer prior to the removal, it must do so either within twenty days after service of the state court summons and complaint or five days after the filing of the notice of removal, whichever is later.

The second issue involves the making of a jury demand. It is not the practice in state court to make a jury demand with the filing of a complaint. That demand is generally made at the time the case is set for trial. Under FRCP Rule 81(c), however, a party desiring a jury must make a demand in writing within ten days after the notice of removal is filed (or served if the party demanding the jury is not the removing party).

The law which will govern substantive issues in the removed action depends upon the basis for removal. Cases removed on the grounds that they involve a federal question will be governed by federal substantive law. *Adams Stone Corp. v. United Steel Workers*, 367 F. Supp. 956 (E.D. Ky. 1973). Cases removed on the basis of diversity, on the other hand, are governed by the *Erie* doctrine. *Freeman v. Bee Machine Co.*, 319 U.S. 448, 87 L. Ed. 1509 (1943), *reh'g denied*, 320 U.S. 809, 88 L. Ed. 489, *superseded by statute on other grounds,* as stated in *Nordlicht v. New York Telephone Co.,* 799 F.2d 859 (2d Cir. 1986).

§ 712. Remand.

A state court action which has been improperly removed to the federal district court may be remanded to the state court. 28 U.S.C. § 1447(c). The proper method for seeking a remand is by motion in the federal court action. *La Flower v. Merrill,* 28 F.2d 784 (D. Cal. 1928). A motion for remand based upon a procedural irregularity, such as untimeliness or failure to join all defendants, must be filed within thirty days after the filing of the petition for removal. 28 U.S.C. § 1447(c). However, a motion for remand based upon lack of subject matter jurisdiction may be filed at any time. *Id.* This rule follows the general rule that subject matter jurisdiction cannot be conferred upon the court by stipulation of the parties, nor may lack of such jurisdiction be waived by the parties. *Jones v. General Tire & Rubber Co.,* 541 F.2d 660 (7th Cir. 1976). Procedural defects which would otherwise authorize remand, on the other hand, may be waived. *Leininger v. Leininger,* 705 F.2d 727 (5th Cir. 1983).

Generally, once a matter is remanded to the state court from which it was removed, the state court's jurisdiction is revived, and the federal district court is divested of all authority. Furthermore, § 1447(d) specifically provides that other than with respect to certain federal civil rights actions, an order remanding a matter to the state court is not appealable or reviewable in any manner. While apparently absolute on its face, the Ninth Circuit, as well as other federal courts, has held that the prohibition of appeal imposed by § 1447(d) applies only to remands based upon lack of subject matter jurisdiction and that when the remand is based upon some other non-jurisdictional matter, appeal is available. *See generally Hansen v. Blue Cross,* 891 F.2d 1384 (9th Cir. 1989); *Clorox v. United States District Court,* 779 F.2d 517 (9th Cir. 1985); *In re Shell Oil Co.,* 932 F.2d 1523 (5th Cir.), *reh'g denied,* 940 F.2d 1532 (5th Cir. 1991), *cert. denied,* 116 L. Ed. 2d 814 (1992).

Form 7A

[Attorney name and address]
Telephone: [telephone number]

Attorneys for Defendant
[Name of defendant]

IN THE UNITED STATES DISTRICT COURT
FOR THE DISTRICT OF NEVADA

[Name of Plaintiff(s)],	)	Case No. _____
	)	
Plaintiff(s),	)	
	)	
vs.	)	NOTICE OF REMOVAL
	)	
[Name of defendant(s)],	)	
	)	
Defendant(s).	)	
	)	

TO: THE UNITED STATES DISTRICT COURT FOR THE DISTRICT OF NEVADA

Defendant [name of defendant] notices the removal of this action to the United States District Court, and, in support thereof, states as follows:

1. The [name of defendant] is the defendant in the above-entitled action commenced in the [state court venue], in and for the county of [county], Nevada, and now pending in that court.

2. Service of summons and complaint upon [name of defendant] was made by personal service on [date of service].

3. The [name of defendant] is a corporation incorporated in the State of [state of incorporation] with its principal place of business in that State. Plaintiff alleges he/she is a resident and citizen of the State of Nevada.

4. The complaint alleges claims in negligence and willful and/or malicious conduct. Plaintiff prays for the recovery of general damages "in excess of $10,000." Plaintiff also prays for unspecified special damages consisting of past and future medical expenses and past and future wage loss. Finally, plaintiff alleges a right to recover exemplary damages in excess of $10,000 and "commensurate with the defendant's net worth." The sum of these alleged damages necessarily exceeds $50,000 exclusive of interest and costs.

5. This Court has original jurisdiction over the subject matter of this action under the provisions of Section 1332 of Title 28 of the United States Code in that there is complete diversity between the parties and more than $50,000 in controversy exclusive of interest and costs. Pursuant to Section 1441 of Title 28 of the United States Code, [name of defendant] is therefore entitled to remove this action to this Court.

6. Copies of the summons and complaint are attached hereto and marked respectively Exhibits A and B, constituting all of the papers and pleadings served on [name of defendant(s)].

Based on the foregoing, [name of defendant] removes the above action now pending in the [state court venue], in and for the County of [county], as Case No. [case number], to this Court.

DATED this ____ day of _____, 1992.

[Name of firm]

By_____
   [Attorney]
Attorneys for defendant
[Name of defendant]

Form 7B

[Attorney name and address]
Telephone [telephone number]

Attorneys for Defendant
[Name of defendant]

IN THE UNITED STATES DISTRICT COURT
FOR THE DISTRICT OF NEVADA

[Name of plaintiff(s)]	)	Case No. _____
	)	
Plaintiff(s),	)	
vs.	)	NOTICE OF REMOVAL
[Name of defendant(s)]	)	
	)	
Defendant(s).	)	
_____	)	

TO: THE UNITED STATES DISTRICT COURT FOR THE DISTRICT OF NE-
VADA

Defendant [name of defendant] notices the removal of this action to the United
States District Court, and, in support thereof, states as follows:

1. [name of defendant] is a defendant in the above-entitled action commenced
in the [name of judicial venue, county, and state], and now pending in that court.

2. Service of summons and complaint upon [name of defendant] was made on
[date of service].

3. The complaint concerns [nature of action].

4. This Court has original jurisdiction over the subject matter of this action
under the provisions of Section 1331 of Title 28 of the United States Code in that
it is an action arising under [identify federal statute or U.S. Constitutional
ground]. Pursuant to Section 1441 of Title 28 of the United States Code, [name of
defendant] is therefore entitled to remove this action to this Court.

5. Copies of the summons and complaint from the State Court file are attached
and marked respectively Exhibits A and B, constituting all of the papers and
pleadings served on [name of defendant(s)].

Based on the foregoing, [name of defendant] removes the above action now
pending in the [name of judicial venue, county, and state] as Case No. [case
number], to this Court.

DATED this _____ day of _____, 1992.

[Name of firm]

By_____
[Attorney]
Attorneys for Defendant
[Name of defendant]

Form 7C

[Attorney name and address]
Telephone: [telephone number]

Attorneys for defendant
[Name of defendant]

IN THE UNITED STATES DISTRICT COURT
FOR THE DISTRICT OF NEVADA

[Name of plaintiff(s)],	)	Case No. _____
	)	
Plaintiff(s),	)	
	)	
vs.	)	JOINDER IN NOTICE OF
	)	REMOVAL OF CIVIL ACTION
[Name of defendant(s)],	)	
	)	
Defendant(s).	)	
_____	)	

Defendant, [name of defendant], hereby joins in the Notice of Removal of [XYZ defendant] to this Court of the action filed in the [state judicial venue], Case No. _____.

Attached hereto as Exhibits 1 and 2 are true and correct copies of the Summons and Complaint which were served upon [defendant(s)] on [date of service]. Dated this ____ day of [month], 1992.

[Name of firm]

By_____
　　[Attorney]
Attorneys for defendant
[Name of defendant]

111

Form 7D

Case No. [case number]
Dept. [department number]

[state venue]

IN AND FOR THE COUNTY OF [county]

[Plaintiff(s)],	)
	)
Plaintiff(s),	)
	)
vs.	) NOTICE OF REMOVAL
	)
[Defendant(s)],	)
	)
Defendant(s).	)
	)

TO: The [above named court]
AND TO: Plaintiff, [name of plaintiff(s)],
AND TO: [Name of plaintiff(s)' attorney] his/her attorneys of record.

Defendant(s) hereby notices the removal of this action to the United States District Court. Pursuant to Section 1441 of Title 28 of the United States Code, [name of defendant(s)] files herewith a true copy of the Notice of Removal filed in the United States District Court for the District of Nevada at Reno, Nevada.

DATED this ____ day of _____, 1992.

[Name of firm]

By_____
[Attorney]
Attorneys for Defendant
[Name of defendant(s)]

CHAPTER 8

PLEADINGS, AMENDMENTS TO PLEADINGS AND SUPPLEMENTAL PLEADINGS

Author: Bruce M. Judd

§ 801. Introduction and scope.

Pleadings include the following: complaint, answer, reply to counter-claim, answer to a cross-claim, third-party complaint, third-party answer, reply to an answer, and reply to a third-party answer. We look to NRCP 7 through 11, 15 and 18 for rules governing types and forms of pleadings, claims for relief, denials, affirmative defenses, counsel's obligations in signing pleadings, amendments to pleadings (including relation back of amendments), supplemental pleadings and joinder of claims and remedies.

§ 802. Types of pleadings.

Rule 7(a) expressly identifies and limits papers that constitute pleadings. The following constitute pleadings in Nevada:

1. Complaint
2. Answer, including counterclaim and/or cross-claim
3. Reply to a counterclaim
4. Answer to a cross-claim
5. Third-party complaint
6. Third-party answer
7. Reply to an answer (if ordered by the court)
8. Reply to a third-party answer (if ordered by the court)

The Rules do not refer to any other filings as "pleadings." Rather, the Rules refer simply to "other papers." *See, e.g.,* Rule 7(b); *see also Cunningham v. Eighth Judicial District Court,* 102 Nev. 551, 557, 729 P.2d 1328, 1331 (1986) (pleadings do not include "applications" or motions).

A party must file a responsive pleading to: (i) a complaint, (an answer); (ii) a counterclaim, (a reply, not an answer); (iii) a cross-claim (an answer); and (iv) third-party complaint, (a third party answer). Failure to file a timely responsive pleading results in an admission of the truthfulness of the allegations in the pleading not responded to, other than those as to the amount of damage. Rule 8(d); *Bowers v. Edwards,* 79 Nev. 384, 389, 385 P.2d 783, 785 (1963).

In contrast to the rules requiring responsive pleadings, "averments in a pleading to which no responsive pleading is required or permitted shall be taken as denied or avoided." Rule 8(d). Thus, in *Harrison v. Rodriquez,* 101 Nev. 297, 299, 701 P.2d 1015, 1017 (1985), the court held that the complaint need not allege fraud or estoppel as a defense to an affirmative defense premised on the statute of limitations pled in the answer, since no responsive pleading was required.

§ 803. Pleading claims for relief.

Nevada is a notice-pleading jurisdiction, so our courts are directed to construe liberally pleadings to place into issue matters which are fairly noticed to the adverse party. *Nevada State Bank v. Jamison Family Partnership,* 106 Nev. 792, 801, 801 P.2d 1377, 1383 (1990); *Hay v. Hay,* 100 Nev. 196, 198, 678 P.2d 672, 674 (1984); *accord Chavez v. Robberson Steel Co.,* 94 Nev. 597, 599, 584 P.2d 159 (1978).

In order to plead a claim for relief, a party must include (i) a statement of the claim; and (ii) a demand (or prayer) for relief. Rule 8(a). With respect to the first requirement, the "complaint must set forth sufficient facts to establish all necessary elements of a claim for relief ... so that the adverse party has adequate notice of the nature of the claim and relief sought." *Hay v. Hay,* 100 Nev. 196, 198, 678 P.2d 672, 674 (1984). With respect to the second requirement, case law predating adoption of the Nevada Rules of Civil Procedure states: "[A] complaint without a prayer for relief is incomplete. It is true, however, that the prayer for relief forms no part of the statement of the cause of action." *Keyes v. Nevada Gas Co., Ltd.,* 55 Nev. 431, 435, 38 P.2d 661 (1934). *Keyes* seems consistent with the express language of Rule 8(a).

NRCP Rule 8(e)(2) states that a party pleading a claim may "set forth two or more statements of a claim ... alternatively or hypothetically ... in one count." The court in *Chavez v. Robberson Steel Co.,* 94 Nev. 597, 599, 584 P.2d 159 (1978), repeated the rule: "A single count may allege alternative theories of recovery." 94 Nev. at 599. In that case, the alternative theories were negligence and strict liability in tort.

Despite the leeway thus afforded, a carefully drafted claim for relief will set forth each legal theory, or cause of action, separately; that is, each count will plead only one cause of action. This approach is consistent with the last sentence of NRCP 10(b): "Each claim founded upon a separate transaction or occurrence ... shall be stated in a separate count ... whenever a separation facilitates the clear presentation of the matters set forth." Moreover, the better practice encourages describing each count; for example, breach of contract, negligent misrepresentation, deceit, breach of fiduciary duties.

Nevada permits the pleading of conclusions of law or conclusions of fact, but only "so long as the pleading gives fair notice of the nature and basis of the claim." *Crucil v. Carson City,* 95 Nev. 583, 585, 600 P.2d 216, 217 (1979). Rule 8 does not permit pleading of a legal conclusion (such as waiver of sovereign immunity) if the allegation "fails to give notice of the nature of the ... issues which may be involved in its litigation." *Taylor v. State,* 73 Nev. 151, 153, 311 P.2d 733 (1957). The test appears to be whether the statement of the claim is so general that it renders the opposing party "wholly unable to admit or deny it intelligently or conscientiously." *Id.*

Additional, and more rigorous, rules govern the pleading of certain special matters such as fraud, mistake and special damage. These rules are treated in § 808, *infra.* Chapter 14, *infra,* states the relationship of a cross-claim or a counterclaim to the answer.

Finally, forms of various exemplary complaints found at the end of the NRCP (Appendix of Forms 3 through 18) provide helpful guidance regarding both form and content of claims for relief.

§ 804. — Ten-thousand-dollar limitation on prayers for damages.

The last sentence of NRCP 8(a) provides: "Where a claimant seeks damages of more than $10,000, the demand shall be for damages 'in excess of $10,000' without further specification of amount." (There is no comparable provision in the Federal Rules of Civil Procedure.) The logical purpose of Nevada's rule prevents a claimant from attracting publicity to his or her claim by the mere expedient of adding numerous zeros to the alleged damage figure.

NRCP 8(a)'s $10,000 limitation on the prayer for damages, however, does not create a conflict between that limitation and the requirement of Rule 9(g): "When items of special damage are claimed, they shall be specifically stated." Items of special damage (for example, medical expenses and lost wages in a personal injury case and actual damages in a defamation case) often total more than $10,000 and the party must specify those damages in the claim for relief. A conflict does not exist between Rule 8(a) and 9(g) because the first part of Rule 8(a) identifies two parts of a claim for relief: (i) the statement of the claim and (ii) the demand (or prayer) for relief. Rule 9(g) requires the allegation of special damage in the statement of the claim. The $10,000 limitation in the last sentence of Rule 8(a), by contrast, applies by its own terms only to the demand for relief. Accordingly, an allegation of special damage in a sum certain in excess of $10,000 is proper in the statement of the claim, but in the prayer the reference to such special damage must read only "in excess of $10,000." This approach is not nonsensical. Experience indicates that the news media generally do not look beyond the prayer to determine the alleged "size" of the action.

The Rules, however, do not specify a remedy for a violation of the last sentence of Rule 8(a). There is no case law yet on that issue. The common practice, which appears to be correct, is for a court to grant a motion to strike the offending portions of a prayer. Although such a motion to strike may be deemed different than a Rule 12(f) motion to strike, the careful lawyer will file a motion within the time limitations set forth in Rule 12(f): "before responding to [the offending] ... pleading or, if no responsive pleading is permitted by these rules, ... within 20 days after service of the pleading upon him...."

§ 805. Raising defenses by denials.

Rule 8(b) specifies the manner in which a party admits or denies the opposing party's allegations. The Nevada Supreme Court addressed the provisions of Rule 8(b) in *Northern Nevada Association of Injured Workers v. Nevada State Industrial Insurance System,* 107 Nev. 108, 807 P.2d 728, 733 (1991), only to the extent that the court suggested if a party is "truly perplexed by any aspect" of a pleading, the party may "simply deny allegations of uncertain meaning under NRCP 8(b)." *See also Mays v. Eighth Judicial District Court,* 105 Nev. 60, 768 P.2d 877 (1989). To the extent the rule ever becomes important, the law developed under Rule 8(b) of the Federal Rules of Civil Procedure may be helpful.

Rule 11 requires careful consideration of one sentence from Rule 8(b) "When a pleader intends in good faith to deny only a part or a qualification of an averment, he shall specify so much of it as is true and material and shall deny *only* the remainder" (emphasis added). If a party denies all or a portion of a pleading knowing that any part of the allegation is true, the party and/or the party's lawyer risk sanctions. *See* § 809, *infra.* In the event a party does not respond to an allegation in a claim for relief, Rule 8(d) provides that the allegations "are admitted when not denied in the responsive pleading."

§ 806. Affirmative defenses.

Rule 8(c) sets forth the requirements relative to the pleading of affirmative defenses. The Nevada Supreme Court has addressed Rule 8(c) primarily in two contexts: (i) what constitutes an affirmative defense; and (ii) what consequences follow a failure to plead an affirmative defense.

In *Schmidt v. Sadri*, 95 Nev. 702, 601 P.2d 713 (1979), the court considered what constitutes an affirmative defense in the context of a landlord/tenant action. Tenants sued for forcible entry and unlawful detainer, trespass, conversion and infliction of emotional distress after the landlord and his agents entered the premises and removed the tenants' personal property. The trial court permitted the landlord to present evidence of abandonment over the objection that the landlord did not plead abandonment as an affirmative defense. The Nevada Supreme Court upheld the ruling of the trial court in an opinion that analyzed in some length the method by which courts should characterize an issue as an affirmative defense or not.

An affirmative defense raises a matter which is beyond the limits of the plaintiff's prima facie case. Surprise and prejudice may result when evidence is admitted to prove a true affirmative defense that is without the scope of the plaintiff's complaint. If an affirmative defense is not pleaded, it is ordinarily deemed waived, and no evidence can be submitted relevant to that issue.

The procedural list [in Rule 8(c)] is, by its express terms, not exclusive and it requires affirmative pleading for any matter which constitutes an avoidance or affirmative defense. It is true, however, that evidence which merely controverts the plaintiff's prima facie case does not constitute a confession or avoidance. If a particular issue arises by logical inference from the allegation of the plaintiff's complaint, a general denial is treated as being sufficient to put those matters in issue.

Moreover, a defendant is entitled under a general denial, to introduce evidence which controverts any fact the plaintiff must prove in order to recover.

In the instant case then, it is clear that, because adequate proof of possession was a precondition to plaintiff's recovery, the respondents' denial of that allegation allows them to introduce any relevant evidence which might controvert the fact of possession. In addition, the 1951 legislature authorized this court to promulgate rules to regulate civil practice and procedure. The legislature envisioned that such rules would serve to simplify existing judicial procedures and promote the speedy determination of litigation upon its merits. NRS 2.120. On January 1, 1953, this court adopted the Nevada Rules of Civil Procedure, which are based primarily upon the federal rules. Nevada, then, is a notice pleading state, and it is reasonable to assume that a general denial of the plaintiff's alleged right to possession put the claim of abandonment in issue and provided appellants with sufficient notice.

117

95 Nev. at 704-05, 601 P.2d at 714-15 (citations omitted).

The court used the same type of reasoning in *Shaw v. Stutchman*, 105 Nev. 128, 771 P.2d 156 (1989). There the Court stated that Rule "9(a)'s requirement of a 'specific negative averment' is not an affirmative defense governed by Rule 8(c).... When the issue of lack of capacity is properly raised by a specific negative averment, the burden of persuasion rests with the party claiming capacity." 105 Nev. at 133 n.3, 771 P.2d at 159 n.3.

Failure to plead an affirmative defense may affect the admissibility of evidence. The Nevada Supreme Court established guidelines for determining the admissibility of evidence pertaining to an unpleaded affirmative defense in *Chisholm v. Redfield*, 75 Nev. 502, 347 P.2d 523 (1959). The court held that under NRCP 8(c) an affirmative defense (in that case, the statute of frauds) must be specially pleaded and, under NRCP 12(b) and (h), if not so pleaded, it is waived. Any evidence pertaining to the defense is inadmissible. The court continued with its absolutist view of waiver in *Second Baptist Church v. First National Bank*, 89 Nev. 217, 510 P.2d 630 (1973); *Tobler & Oliver Construction Corp. v. Nevada State Bank*, 89 Nev. 269, 510 P.2d 1364 (1973); *Hennessey v. Price*, 96 Nev. 33, 604 P.2d 355 (1980); and *Contrail Leasing Partners v. Executive Service Corp.*, 100 Nev. 545, 549 n.2, 688 P.2d 765 (1984).

In *Williams v. Cottonwood Cove Development Co.*, 96 Nev. 857, 619 P.2d 1219 (1980), however, the court held that failure to timely assert an affirmative defense will not operate as a waiver if the claimant is given reasonable notice of the unpleaded affirmative defense and an opportunity to respond. In *Williams*, the issue arose in the context of a motion for summary judgment. The court specifically noted that "the better practice would have been to amend [the defendant's] answer pursuant to NRCP 15 [to specifically plead the omitted affirmative defense] before moving for summary judgment...." *Williams, supra*, 96 Nev. at 861, 619 P.2d at 1221. (Standards governing amendment of the pleadings are discussed separately in § 813, *infra*.) The risk that a court will not admit evidence of an affirmative defense increases the longer a party waits to assert the affirmative defense.

§ 807. Construction of pleadings.

Rule 8(f) provides: "All pleadings shall be so construed as to do substantial justice." The Nevada Supreme Court in *Chavez v. Robberson Steel Co.*, 94 Nev. 597, 599, 584 P.2d 159 (1978), pronounced that "Nevada is a notice-pleading jurisdiction and liberally construes pleadings to place into issue matter which is fairly noticed to the adverse party...." See also *Hay v. Hay*, 100 Nev. 196, 198, 678 P.2d 672 (1984). Section

1210, *infra,* details the special rules governing construction of a complaint when subjected to a motion to dismiss.

§ 808. Pleading special matters such as fraud.

Rule 9 creates rules governing the pleading of specified matters, including capacity, fraud, mistake, condition of mind, conditions precedent, official document or act, judgment, time and place, and special damage. When these specified matters are material to a pleading, the party must assert in some detail the factual basis of the matter. *See Tobler & Oliver Construction Corp. v. Nevada State Bank,* 89 Nev. 269, 510 P.2d 1364 (1973) (Rule 9(a), capacity of a party); *Savage v. Salzmann,* 88 Nev. 193, 495 P.2d 367 (1972) (Rule 9(b), fraud); *Britz v. Consolidated Casinos Corp.,* 87 Nev. 441, 488 P.2d 911 (1971) (Rule 9(b), fraud); *Fisher v. Executive Fund Life Insurance Co.,* 88 Nev. 704, 504 P.2d 700 (1972) (Rule 9(b), fraud); *Ivory Ranch, Inc. v. Quinn River Ranch, Inc.,* 101 Nev. 471, 705 P.2d 673 (1985) (Rule 9(b), mistake); *Arley v. Liberty Mutual Fire Insurance Co.,* 80 Nev. 5, 388 P.2d 576 (1964) (Rule 9(c), conditions precedent); *Summa Corp. v. Greenspun,* 96 Nev. 247, 607 P.2d 569 (1980), *modified on other grounds on rehearing,* 98 Nev. 528, 655 P.2d 513 (1982) (Rule 9(g), special damage in slander of title case); *Branda v. Sanford,* 97 Nev. 643, 637 P.2d 1223 (1981) (Rule 9(g), special damages in defamation case); *Contrail Leasing Partners v. Executive Service Corp.,* 100 Nev. 545, 549 n.2, 688 P.2d 765 (1984) (Rule 9(a), capacity of a party). *See also Thornton v. Agassiz Construction, Inc.,* 106 Nev. 676, 678, 799 P.2d 1106 (1990) (excuse need not be specifically pleaded while "a denial of performance need to be made specifically and with particularity."); *Forrest v. Forrest,* 99 Nev. 602, 605, 668 P.2d 275 (1983) (alimony need not be specifically pleaded).

The Nevada Supreme Court has addressed on several occasions the consequences of a failure to comply with Rule 9. In *Britz v. Consolidated Casinos Corp.,* 87 Nev. 441, 488 P.2d 911 (1971), the court stated that a complaint which fails to allege fraud with particularity, as required in Rule 9(b), should be subjected to a motion for a more definite statement, "or at the very worst to dismissal with leave to amend." 87 Nev. at 447, 488 P.2d at 916. One year later, the court repeated this view in *Savage v. Salzmann,* 88 Nev. 193, 495 P.2d 367, 368 (1972), where it stated: "A failure to plead [fraud] with sufficient particularity does not warrant a dismissal of the action with prejudice." *Savage, supra,* 88 Nev. at 196, 495 P.2d at 368. *Accord Occhiuto v. Occhiuto,* 97 Nev. 143, 146, 625 P.2d 568, 570 (1981). Shortly thereafter, in *Fisher v. Executive Fund Life Insurance Co.,* 88 Nev. 704, 504 P.2d 700 (1972), the court reviewed the order of the district court dismissing a complaint with prejudice because it failed to satisfy the requirements of Rule 9(b) that fraud be pleaded with particularity. The court reversed the dismissal, holding that "leave to amend should be permitted when no prejudice to the defendant will result and when justice requires it." 88 Nev. at 706, 504 P.2d at 702. The concurring opinion concluded that the complaint's allegations were adequate to satisfy Rule 9(b). *See also Ivory Ranch, Inc. v. Quinn River Ranch, Inc.,* 101 Nev. 471, 705 P.2d 673 (1985). A lawyer may avoid all of the expense of the types of relief the court has permitted, and the risk that the court may not afford any relief, by comparing the Rule 9 list of matters against the proposed pleading and asserting all possible special matters.

Defendants can waive the requirements of Rule 9 by inaction. The Nevada Supreme Court in *Britz v. Consolidated Casinos Corp.,* 87 Nev. 441, 488 P.2d 911 (1971), stated that a defendant's failure to timely raise the Rule 9 issue waives the pleading requirements of that Rule. 87 Nev. at 447, 488 P.2d at 915. Given the other language in *Britz* regarding a motion for a more definite statement or a motion to dismiss, the court's reference to "timely" appears to invoke the time limitations on such motions set forth in Rule 12.

The defendant apparently did not object timely to the plaintiff's failure to comply with Rule 9(g) and specifically state special damage in a slander of title case in *Summa Corp. v. Greenspun,* 96 Nev. 247, 607 P.2d 569 (1980), *modified on other grounds* 98 Nev. 528, 655 P.2d 814 (1982). The trial court awarded the plaintiff attorneys' fees as an item of special damage. On appeal, the defendant argued that the plaintiff did not comply with Rule 9(g). The Nevada Supreme Court held:

> Although NRCP 9(g) requires the specific pleading of special damages, and applies to a disparagement of title case, ... it does not follow that a failure to do so deprives the court of power to award such fees as damages. Indeed, NRCP 54(c) commands the court to "grant the relief to which the party in whose favor it is rendered is entitled, even if the party has not demanded such relief in his pleadings."

96 Nev. at 255, 607 P.2d 574 (citations omitted).

§ 809. Form of pleadings.

NRCP 10 sets forth the general requirements regarding the form of pleadings.

One aspect of NRCP 10(b) merits comment here. Rule 10(b) provides in part: "All averments of claim or defense shall be made in numbered paragraphs, the contents of each of which shall be limited as far as practicable to a statement of a single set of circumstances; and a paragraph may be referred to by number in all succeeding pleadings." It seems that the simplest numbering system uses arabic rather than roman numerals, and numbers all paragraphs in the complaint consecutively from beginning to end rather than starting over at "1" at the beginning of each count.

DCR provides additional details regarding the form of pleadings. DCR 12 (also EDCR 7.20) sets forth in considerable detail requirements regarding the form of pleadings and other papers presented for filing. Generally, failure to comply with such rules can result in the refusal by the clerk to file the offending pleading or other paper. DCR 12(6) provides that: "The Clerk shall not accept for filing any pleadings or documents which ... do not comply with this rule, but for good cause shown, the court may permit the filing of non-complying pleadings and documents." The Nevada Supreme Court in *Bowman v. Eighth Judicial District Court,* 102 Nev. 474, 478, 728 P.2d 433, 435 (1986), stated:

> The clerk has a ministerial duty to accept and file documents.... The clerk does have the right to exercise discretion regarding matters of form .... [I]t is the duty of the court clerk to accept for filing any paper presented to her which is in acceptable form under court rules and is accompanied by the requisite fee unless she has specific instructions from the court to the contrary.

(citations omitted.)

§ 810. — Doe pleadings.

The last sentence of Rule 10(a) is one that has no counterpart in the Federal Rules of Civil Procedure and which often has caused problems for Nevada lawyers, but which may cause less problems because of the Nevada Supreme Court's decision in *Nurenberger Hercules-Werke GMBH v. Virostek,* 107 Nev. 873, 822 P.2d 1100 (1991). The rule provides: "A party whose name is not known may be designated by any name, and when his true name is discovered, the pleading may be amended accordingly." This sentence is known as the "Doe" rule.

The court in *Virostek* backed away from decisions in *Driscoll v. Collins Home Manufacturing Corp.,* 103 Nev. 608, 747 P.2d 888 (1987), and *Lunn v. American Maintenance Corp.,* 96 Nev. 787, 618 P.2d 343 (1980), in which the court had limited the Doe rule to those cases in which (i) the proper defendant had actual notice of the start of the case; (ii) the defendant knew it was the proper defendant; and (iii) the proper defendant suffered no prejudice. *Virostek* changed all of that.

Now, if a party names Doe defendants and (i) describes "a clear correlation between the fictitious defendants and the pleaded factual basis for liability"; (ii) exercises "reasonable diligence in ascertaining the true identity of the intended defendants"; and (iii) promptly moves to substitute the actual defendant for the fictional defendant, the court should permit an amended claim for relief "that relates back to the date of the filing of the original complaint." 107 Nev. at 881, 822 P.2d at 1106. The court expressly retained the rule of *Servatius v. United Resort Hotels, Inc.,* 85 Nev. 371, 455 P.2d 621 (1969), in which the name of a defendant may be added when the true defendant, although unnamed, had actual knowledge of the action, knew it was the proper defendant and was not misled to its prejudice. 822 P.2d at 1104. Moreover, the court stated:

> The right to amend and relate back should rarely be denied plaintiffs irrespective of the extent of the delay whenever the intended defendant has sought in any way to mislead or deceive the complaining party.

822 P.2d at 1105-06.

To draft a proper "Doe" pleading, a lawyer must have in mind the identity or description of the defendant but not the defendant's true name. *See State ex rel. Department of Highways v. Eighth Judicial District Court,* 95 Nev. 715, 601 P.2d 710 (1979); *Hill v. Summa Corp.,* 90 Nev. 79, 82 n.1, 518 P.2d 1094 (1974) (Thompson, C.J., concurring). For example, if a party knows that an agent of a corporation made misrepresentations but does not know the name of that individual, the facts relative to the misrepresentations should be alleged and attributed to a Doe party. After discovery discloses the true name of the agent, pursuant to Rule 10(a) and Rule 13, the attorney may amend the pleading to designate the true name.

A proper Rule 10(a) designation and subsequent amendment to designate the true name of a party does not constitute the addition of parties subject to Rule 21 (discussed in § 518, *supra*). *See Virostek, supra,* 822 P.2d at 1106; *Hill v. Summa Corp.,* 90 Nev. 79, 518 P.2d 1094 (1974). Likewise, Rule 10(a) is not applicable to an attempt to include a claim for wrongful death after the death of the original plaintiff and the substitution of the plaintiff's representative under Rule 25. *See Fernandez v. Kozar,* 107 Nev. 446, 814 P.2d 68, 70 (1991); § 522, *supra.*

Rule 10(a) thus places a premium on the attorney's knowledge of all wrongful conduct and potential defendants and diligence in promptly searching for the identity of all defendants. Dangers still exist for those who delay their search for the true names of defendants after a statute of limitations has run.

Counsel should also be aware that naming Doe defendants has no effect on removal of a state case to federal court. *See* 28 U.S.C. § 1441(a).

§ 811. — Exhibits.

Rule 10(c) states that "A copy of any written instrument which is an exhibit to a pleading is a part thereof for all purposes."

Under some circumstances, an exhibit may be used to force an admission as to the authenticity of the instrument by the opposing party. If that is the intent, the complaint should refer to the exhibit and not recite the terms of the exhibit again in the body of the complaint. Such practice adds nothing to the clarity intended to be part of pleading practice. However, if a party's only exhibit contains markings not found on the original instrument, the opposing party can properly deny the entire substance of the complaint relative to the instrument when the opposing party could not deny that an agreement was entered into by the parties. In such circumstances, it makes sense to allege in the complaint the general terms of the instrument, including the date, and produce copies of the exhibit upon appropriate requests by the opposing party.

The wholesale use of exhibits attached to pleadings is burdensome and not cost-efficient, particularly if multiple parties are involved or amendments are made to the pleadings (but see exception in the Eighth District below). Exhibits may always be presented to the court in appropriate fashion by affidavit when needed for motions or other proceedings.

The exceptions to the above-stated ideas are found in the Appendix of Forms attached to the Rules, particularly when a cause of action is brought on an account. *See* Form 4. Form 4 illustrates that it is good practice either to set out the terms of the instrument in the complaint or attach a copy of the exhibit, but that both should not be used at the same time. *See* Form 3, n.1. *See also* Form 12.

In the Eighth Judicial District, a pleader may upon an *ex parte* application obtain an order from the court directing the clerk to remove exhibits attached to prior pleadings and attach the exhibits to an amended pleading. EDCR 2.30(b).

When attaching exhibits to pleadings filed in the Eighth Judicial District, the plaintiff must number (arabic numerals) each exhibit at the bottom or on the right side of the exhibit; the defendant must alphabetize his or her exhibits. EDCR 7.20(d). Moreover, in all districts the copies must be legible and not unnecessarily voluminous. Moreover, the lawyer must not attach original documents. DCR 12.4.

If a lawyer requires an exhibit previously attached to a pleading, the lawyer must obtain a special written order of the court; that order will specify the exhibit and limits the time the lawyer may retain it. DCR 11.2; EDCR 7.28(b).

§ 812. Signing of pleadings.

An attorney's signature on a pleading is a certification that he or she has read the pleading, made reasonable inquiry into the facts, that the pleading is well grounded in fact, that it is warranted by law and that it is not interposed for any improper purpose. Occasions to consider this provision are not rare. For example, a general denial made when the defending party simply seeks time to negotiate a settlement violates Rule 11. On those rare occasions when the lawyer drafting the pleading is for some reason unable to sign the pleading, the attorney who signs "for" another subjects herself or himself to the requirements of Rule 11.

NRCP 11 now has reference to papers other than pleadings. It applies to all motions. *See* NRCP 7(b)(3). The sanctions against the person who signs the pleading of paper and/or the lawyer's party in violation of the Rule include "an order to pay to the other party or parties the amount of the reasonable expenses incurred because of the filing of the pleading, motion, or other paper, including a reasonable attorney fee."

In the context of evidence, the attorney's signature creates a presumption that good grounds exist and that the pleading is not interposed for delay. *See Gull v. Hoalst,* 77 Nev. 54, 359 P.2d 383 (1961). Nevertheless, NRCP 11 does not mean that a motion signed by an attorney is sufficient for purposes of establishing a meritorious defense in the context of a motion for relief from default or judgment under Rule 55 or 60. *See Kelso v. Kelso,* 78 Nev. 99, 369 P.2d 668 (1962).

There have been several recent decisions by the Nevada Supreme Court addressing Rule 11. The court has held that a trial court has discretion when ruling on a motion to impose sanctions pursuant to Rule 11. The Nevada Supreme Court will only reverse a Rule 11 decision for a trial court's abuse of that discretion. *See State Department of Motor Vehicles v. Clements,* 106 Nev. 516, 519, 796 P.2d 588, 590 (1990); *Marine Midland Bank v. Monroe,* 104 Nev. 307, 308, 756 P.2d 1193, 1195 (1988); *Barr v. Gaines,* 103 Nev. 548, 551, 746 P.2d 634, 637 (1987). The court typically has not favored Rule 11 sanctions. *See K.J.B., Inc. v. Drakulich,* 107 Nev. 367, 811 P.2d 1305 (1991) (no violation for lawyer to file attorney malpractice action prior to conclusion of underlying unlawful detainer lawsuit); *State Department of Motor Vehicles v. Clements,* 106 Nev. 516, 519, 796 P.2d 588, 590 (1990) (district court abused discretion when imposing sanctions against DMV which filed a motion for rehearing); *Works v. Huhn,* 103 Nev. 65, 732 P.2d 1373 (1987) (sanctions unwarranted when defendants consented to a dismissal of counterclaim); *Barr v. Gaines,* 103 Nev. 548, 551, 746 P.2d 634, 637 (1987) (no abuse when trial court did not award fees against plaintiff whose complaint did not withstand a summary judgment motion). One rationale for the court's reluctance to encourage more Rule 11 sanctions appears in a footnote in a criminal proceeding not governed by Rule 11:

> In the civil rule 11 context, such an effect has been a concern to legal commentators who "feared the rule would 'chill' vigorous advocacy especially in 'disfavored' lawsuits." For example, statistics have shown "that there is a higher incidence of sanctioning in civil rights cases than would be warranted strictly on the basis of their percentage of the filings."

Young v. Ninth Judical District Court, 107 Nev. 642, 818 P.2d 844, 849 n.9 (1991) (citations omitted). *But see Marine Midland Bank v. Mon-*

roe, 104 Nev. 307, 308, 756 P.2d 1193, 1195 (1988) (Court reversed the trial court's dismissal because the defendant established none of the criteria for a collateral estoppel defense; court ordered trial court to reconsider its decision not to award Rule 11 sanctions).

Relative to those cases filed by a plaintiff in proper person, or when the defendant answers in proper person Rule 11 provides that the court shall strike a pleading, motion or other paper not signed. The lawyer should note, however, that the failure to acknowledge a proper-person pleading is not jurisdictional. *Cf.* DCR 20 and EDCR 42(a). Any such defect may be waived by receiving the pleading without objection. Even in the face of an objection to the unacknowledged pleading, the court must afford the proper-person pleader an opportunity to supply an acknowledgment before declaring a defective answer a nullity. *Cheek v. Bell,* 80 Nev. 244, 391 P.2d 735 (1964). Likewise, the failure to provide an address on a proper-person pleading is a mere irregularity which may be waived. *Cheek, supra.*

The failure to have an attorney authorized to practice in the State of Nevada sign a pleading arguably is also not jurisdictional. It is, however, within the court's discretion to strike a pleading which a non-Nevada attorney signs, even though subsequent attempts to cure are made after the statute of limitations has run. *See Naimo v. Fleming,* 95 Nev. 13, 588 P.2d 1025 (1979).

Although *Cheek v. Bell,* 80 Nev. 244, 391 P.2d 735 (1964), clearly holds that defects regarding signing, at least in the proper person context, are *not* jurisdictional, the practitioner should be aware of DCR 20:

> Unless appearing by an attorney regularly admitted to practice law in Nevada and in good standing, no entry of appearance or initial pleading purporting to be signed by any party to an action shall be recognized or given any force or effect by any district court unless the same shall be acknowledged by the party signing the same before a notary public or some other officer having a seal and authorized by law to administer oaths. (Also EDCR 7.42(a)).

Neither *Cheek* nor *Naimo* addressed DCR 20; both focused solely on Rule 11.

In the Eighth Judicial District a corporation cannot appear in proper person. *See* EDCR 7.42(b).

NRS 15.010 sets forth the requirements relative to verified pleadings. The lawyer should note carefully subsections 2 and 4 of 15.010 if the lawyer contemplates verifying a pleading. Subsection 2 requires the lawyer to state in an affidavit why the party is not verifying the pleading. Subsection 4 permits the lawyer to verify a pleading on information and belief if the facts are not within the lawyers' knowledge.

The following civil pleadings must be verified:

1. Adverse possession complaint, NRS 40.090;

2. Annulment of marriage complaint, NRS 125.360 (under oath);
3. Divorce complaint, NRS 125.020;
4. Eminent domain complaint, NRS 37.060;
5. Complaint and answer relative to unlawful detention, NRS 40.370;
6. Complaint in shareholders derivative action, NRCP 23.1.

§ 813. Amendments.

Rule 15(a) sets forth three general categories of procedures under which the party may amend a pleading. The first category is one in which a party may amend as a matter of right if the amended pleading is filed within the time specified in the Rule. The second category permits an amendment with the written consent of all parties. The third procedure provides that a party by motion may seek leave of the court to amend.

Generally, motions to amend will be in writing. Nevertheless, a motion to amend may be made orally in open court in the presence of counsel for the adverse party. *See Weiler v. Ross,* 80 Nev. 380, 395 P.2d 323 (1964). An oral motion appears to be acceptable even in a context other than the trial, such as a pre-trial hearing.

Regarding the likelihood of success of a motion to amend, an amendment which does not go to the merits of the controversy is likely to be granted even after the running of the statute of limitations when no prejudice results to the opposing party. *See Tehansky v. Wilson,* 83 Nev. 263, 428 P.2d 375 (1967); *cf. Nelson v. City of Las Vegas,* 99 Nev. 548, 556-57, 665 P.2d 1141, 1146 (1983). The careful lawyer will note that while leave to amend is to be freely given, the freedom is not absolute and is in fact less than that freedom afforded a party who moves to amend pleadings to conform to evidence. The Nevada Supreme Court stated in *Brown v. Capanna,* 105 Nev. 665, 668, 782 P.2d 1299, 1301 (1989): "the requirement that the amending party acquire leave of the court suggests that there are instances in which leave should not be granted." In *Brown,* the court affirmed the trial court's refusal to permit plaintiffs to amend their negligence allegations when the court had already awarded partial summary judgment against the plaintiffs on the negligence issue. *See also Nevada National Bank v. Snyder,* 108 Nev. 151, 26, 826 P.2d 560, 562 (1992) (trial court erred when it permitted individual to substitute himself as the plaintiff in the place of his corporation, which was not permitted to do business in Nevada).

While Rule 15(a) requires in some circumstances leave of court to amend a pleading, that requirement may be waived by failure to raise an appropriate and timely objection to the amended pleading. *See Polk v. Tully,* 97 Nev. 27, 623 P.2d 972 (1981).

In the Eighth District, a copy of the proposed amended pleading shall be attached to "any motion" to amend. Moreover, any allowed amendment must be complete in itself, including exhibits. For further discussion relative to exhibits, see § 811, *supra*.

§ 814. — Amendments to conform to the evidence.

Failure by a lawyer to pay close attention to the content of the pleadings as they relate to the presentation of evidence at trial may result in a judgment based upon an issue not raised in the pleadings and not contemplated by the lawyer. Under NRCP 15(b), a court may render any judgment consistent with the facts presented in the proceedings. Amendments under NRCP 15(b) are allowed with greater liberality than amendments under NRCP 15(a). *See Marschall v. City of Carson*, 86 Nev. 107, 464 P.2d 494 (1970). On the other hand, a lawyer aware of the issues framed by the pleadings will better be able to prevent the application of NRCP 15(b) by objecting during pre-trial discovery, summary judgment proceedings, opening remarks of counsel, or at any time during the examination of witnesses to any reference to issues not raised in the pleadings. *See Schwartz v. Schwartz*, 95 Nev. 202, 591 P.2d 1137 (1979); *Baughman & Turner, Inc. v. Jory*, 102 Nev. 582, 583, 729 P.2d 488, 489 (1986). A diligent counsel may, by proper objection at trial, cause the court to preclude the introduction of evidence on matters outside the scope of the pleadings, this in spite of the broad language in NRCP 15(b) relative to objections and continuances (which purportedly enable the objecting party to meet such new evidence). *See Schwartz; Connell v. Carl's Air Conditioning*, 97 Nev. 436, 634 P.2d 673 (1981); *Ivory Ranch, Inc. v. Quinn River Ranch, Inc.*, 101 Nev. 471, 473, 705 P.2d 673, 675 (1985). The court pointed out in *Sprouse v. Wentz*, 105 Nev. 597, 603, 781 P.2d 1136, 1139 (1989), "However, we have also placed restrictions on finding implied consent [to try issues not raised in the pleadings]. These restrictions are meant to insure procedural due process and a fair trial to parties ...."

§ 815. — Relation back of amendment.

Often the issue arises of whether allegations in an amended pleading are effective from the date of the original pleading. When the court permits the amendment of allegations of facts which existed at the commencement of the action, the amendment "relates back" to the date of the original pleading. The relation-back doctrine has been applied to the acknowledgment required on a pleading filed by a party in proper person. *Tehansky v. Wilson*, 83 Nev. 263, 428 P.2d 375 (1967).

127

An amended pleading should relate back if the amendment fairly touches the facts originally pled so that the opposing party had adequate notice of the general areas of dispute.

The court in *Servatius v. United Resort Hotels, Inc.,* 85 Nev. 371, 455 P.2d 621 (1969), identified three factors necessary to bring in by amendment a proper party-defendant even though the statute of limitations might have run against the proper defendant by the time of the amendment. A proper party-defendant (1) must have had actual notice of the institution of the action; (ii) must have known that it was the proper party-defendant; and (iii) was not in any way misled to its prejudice. *See also Jimenez v. State,* 98 Nev. 204, 644 P.2d 1023 (1982).

The Nevada Supreme Court has held that "[i]f the original pleadings give fair notice of the fact situation from which the new claim for liability arises, the amendment should relate back for limitation purposes." *Nelson v. City of Las Vegas,* 99 Nev. 548, 556, 665 P.2d 1141, 1146 (1983). *See also Deal v. 999 Lakeshore Association,* 94 Nev. 301, 307, 579 P.2d 775 (1978). If, however, the pleading gives absolutely no indication of the new cause of action contained in the amendment, the amendment does not relate back. *Nelson,* 99 Nev. at 556-57. For example, in *Scott v. Department of Commerce,* 104 Nev. 580, 586-87, 763 P.2d 341, 345 (1988), the court affirmed a trial court's refusal to permit an amended complaint which alleged negligence when the original pleading alleged fraud and intentional misrepresentation.

§ 816. Supplemental pleadings.

Rule 15(d) provides the only mechanism by which a party may supplement pleadings to allege facts that arise after the filing of the original pleading. Unlike amendments permitted as a matter of right, all supplemental pleadings must be made upon motion. Moreover, no responsive pleading to the supplemental pleading is permitted unless ordered by the court.

The standard which governs the granting of a motion to supplement pleadings is more strict than the standard governing amendments. The court, under NRCP 15(d), is not required to "freely give" permission to supplement a pleading. *See Madsen Construction Corp. v. Riverside County Mortgage & Loan Co.,* 71 Nev. 356, 291 P.2d 1056 (1955). When considering a motion to supplement pleadings, the court will distinguish between problems of ultimate justice, and the administration of justice. The Nevada Supreme Court's opinion in *Madsen Construction Corp., supra,* implies that great discretion will be given to a court when a court resolves a motion to supplement a pleading based upon the administration of justice or, in other words, the convenience of the parties and the court. This standard likely will be similar to the standard governing decisions relative to permissive counterclaims which mature after the service of the original pleading. *See* Rule 13(a).

A party may file a supplemental pleading even after the Supreme court remands the case with instructions. *Diversified Capital Corp. v. City of North Las Vegas,* 95 Nev. 15, 22, 590 P.2d 146, 150 (1979).

Further, unlike many federal courts' interpretation of Rule 15(d) of the Federal Rules of Civil Procedure, the Nevada Supreme Court has stated: "NRCP 15(d) is intended to promote as complete an adjudication as possible by allowing the addition of claims that arise after the initial pleadings have been filed." *Szilagyi v. Testa,* 99 Nev. 834, 839-40, 673 P.2d 495, 499 (1983). This ruling should permit a party to join all grievances against another party regardless of when the cause of action arises.

Finally, if there are prior superseded pleadings in an action, the court may look to those pleadings to determine whether the allegations sought to be supplemented rest on facts which occurred after the commencement of the action. *See Las Vegas Network, Inc. v. B. Shawcross & Associates,* 80 Nev. 405, 395 P.2d 520 (1964).

§ 817. Joinder of claims.

Rule 18 is straightforward. An attorney may assert as many claims as the client has against an opposing party. *State v. Webster,* 88 Nev. 690, 695, 504 P.2d 1316, 1320 (1972) (claim for wrongful death joined with claim for personal injuries). Practically, however, lawyers may create confusion by alleging distinct claims, for example, an action under UCC Article 9 for the return of personal property and a deficiency judgment joined with an action on a guarantee.

Joinder of claims in *one action,* under Rule 18, should not be confused with consolidation of *multiple actions,* under Rule 42(a). Rule 42(b), however, which involves separate trials "of any claim ... or of any separate issue," is applicable to a single action involving two or more joined claims. *See* the discussion of Rule 42 in Chapter 19, *infra.*

§ 818. Joinder of remedies.

Along with the joinder of claims, a party may assert all remedies available against an opposing party. In addition to the example cited in the Rule (asserting a claim for money and a claim to set aside a conveyance fraudulent as to him without first having obtained a judgment establishing the claim for money), a party may seek recovery on a bond without a judgment as well as allege an action against a principal; or a party may file a claim relative to stockholder status and at the same time bring a Rule 23.1 action on behalf of the corporation.

CHAPTER 9

SERVICE OF PROCESS

Authors: Brent A. Larsen
          Kirk B. Lenhard

§ 901. Introduction.

Scope. Process signifies a writ or summons in the course of judicial proceedings. NRS 10.055; NRS 28-060. This chapter provides a guideline to the various forms of service of process pursuant to Rule 4 of the NRCP as well as various Nevada statutes specifically providing methods of service of process.

§ 902. Issuance of process.

Issuance of process is governed by NRCP 4(a). A civil action is commenced by filing a complaint with the court. NRCP Rule 3. Upon the filing of the complaint, the clerk of the court shall forthwith issue a summons and deliver it to the plaintiff or to the plaintiff's attorney, who shall be responsible for service of the summons and a copy of the complaint. NRCP 4(a).

The plaintiff is required to request separate or additional summons for multiple defendants. NRCP 4(a); *Cardinal v. Zonneveld,* 89 Nev. 403, 514 P.2d 204 (1973); *Doyle v. Jorgensen,* 82 Nev. 196, 414 P.2d 707 (1966). Each defendant is required to be served with a separate copy of the summons. Service of only one copy of a summons for multiple defendants is insufficient even in the event that two or more defendants reside at the same location and are members of the same family. *Doyle, supra,* 414 P.2d at 707. In the case of service of only one summons upon multiple defendants, a judgment will be void as to those defendants not actually served. *Id.*

The form of the summons is governed by NRCP 4(b), which requires the summons to be signed by the clerk of the court, be under the seal of the court (NRS 1.180), contain the name of the court and county and the names of the parties, be directed to the defendant, state the name and address of the plaintiff's attorney or, in the alternative, the plaintiff's address, and the time within which the rules require the defendant to appear and defend (generally twenty days). The summons shall notify the defendant that in case of his failure to answer or defend, judgment by default will be rendered for the relief demanded in the complaint. In certain actions the form of the summons will be slightly modified, extending the time in which to answer the complaint. For example, NRS 14.080 provides a forty-day period to answer in the case of service of process on foreign manufacturers, producers or suppliers of products, and NRS 37.075 provides a thirty-day period to answer service of process in eminent domain actions. Illustrations as to the form of summons are provided in NRCP Forms 1 and 22-A.

§ 903. Timeliness of service.

The once widespread practice of delay in the service of process is no longer permitted. NRCP 4 was amended contemporaneously with the issuance of the decision in *Moore v. Schreck,* 102 Nev. 163, 717 P.2d 49 (1986), where the court sharply criticized a nineteen-month delay in the service of process. NRCP 4(i) requires the service of the summons and complaint upon a defendant within 120 days of the filing of the complaint. In the event service is not completed within the 120 days, the action may be dismissed upon the court's own initiative unless good cause can be demonstrated why service was not completed within the required time. Although good cause must be defined upon a case-by-case basis, a lengthy discussion of conduct and events that constitute good cause is contained in the Supreme Court decision of *Domino v. Gaughan,* 103 Nev. 582, 747 P.2d 236 (1987). *See also Dallman v. Merrell,* 106 Nev. 929, 803 P.2d 232 (1990). The right to seek a dismissal for any unexcused delay in accomplishing service of process may be waived, however, if an objection to the delay is not timely asserted. *Dougan v. Gustaveson,* 108 Nev. 517, 835 P.2d 795 (1992).

§ 904. Authority to serve process.

Once a summons has been issued by a clerk of the court, it may be served by the sheriff of the county where the defendant is found or by any citizen of the United States over eighteen years of age. If the sheriff is delivered the process, he is statutorily required to execute the same with diligence, according to its command or as required by law, and return it without delay to the proper court or officer with his certificate endorsed thereon of the manner of its service or execution or the reasons for the failure of service. NRS 248.130. Public officers are given special police powers to assist in implementation of service of process where resistance to service is met. The extent of these special powers is partially defined in NRS 281.290.

Service of process outside of the United States may be served either by any citizen of the United States over eighteen years of age or by any resident of the host country, territory, colony or province who is over eighteen years of age, after an order of publication. NRCP 4(c).

Service of a foreign national within a foreign jurisdiction is somewhat more complicated. Unless the foreign jurisdiction is a signatory to the Hague Service Convention (the majority of nations are not signatories to this agreement), service of process must generally be effectuated by letters rogatory. In substance, letters rogatory denote a formal request from the court in the United States in which the action is pending to the corresponding judicial authority in the foreign jurisdiction to perform some judicial act including the service of summons or other legal notice. 22 CFR 92.54. The foreign judge reviews the letters submitted by counsel, and exercises his discretion as to whether the United States litigation warrants subjecting the citizen of that foreign jurisdiction to the jurisdiction of the United States court. The letter should contain a summary of the cause of action pending in the United States and clearly describe the specific assistance requested. In the case of acceptance, it would appear the method of service would be under the absolute control of the foreign jurisdiction. For an excellent discussion of issues surrounding service of process pursuant to the Hague Service Convention and letters rogatory, see generally Delk, Service of Process on a Japanese Defendant in Japan Under Article 10(a) of the Hague Service Convention, 48:5 *Inter Alia* f-1 (1983), and Delk & Nelson, Service of Process on Foreign Parties by Letters Rogatory, 52.3 *Inter Alia* f-1 (1987).

Neither the plaintiff nor plaintiff's attorney are permitted to serve initial process. *Nevada Cornell Silver Mines, Inc. v. Hankins,* 51 Nev. 420, 279 P. 27 (1929); *Sawyer v. Sugarless Shops, Inc.,* 106 Nev. 265, 792 P.2d 14 (1990).

§905. Methods of service.

Service pursuant to each statute or rule must be reviewed in conjunction with the limitations of the due process clause of the Fourteenth Amendment. *World-Wide Volkswagen Corp. v. Woodson,* 444 U.S. 286,

100 S. Ct. 559, 62 L. Ed. 2d 490 (1980); *Kulko v. California Superior Court*, 436 U.S. 84, 98 S. Ct. 1690, 56 L. Ed. 2d 1329 (1978); *Shaffer v. Heitner*, 433 U.S. 186, 97 S. Ct. 2569, 53 L. Ed. 2d 683 (1977); *Hanson v. Denckla*, 357 U.S. 235, 78 S. Ct. 1228, 2 L. Ed. 2d 1283 (1958); *McGee v. International Life Insurance Co.*, 355 U.S. 220, 78 S. Ct. 199, 2 L. Ed. 2d 223 (1957); *International Shoe Co. v. Washington*, 326 U.S. 310, 66 S. Ct. 154, 90 L. Ed. 95 (1945); *Pennoyer v. Neff*, 95 U.S. 714, 24 L. Ed. 565 (1877).

The various methods of service are categorized in NRCP 4 according to whether service is personal service, whether service is inside or outside the state, or whether service is by statute or rule. NRCP 4(d) and (e).

Process must be served properly even when defendants have notice of the pending action. Notice is not an effective substitute for service of process. *C.H.A. Venture v. G.C. Wallace Consulting Engineers, Inc.*, 106 Nev. 381, 794 P.2d 707 (1990).

§ 906. Personal service.

Clearly the preferred and most common method of service is personal service. For proper personal service of process, the summons and complaint (or third-party complaint) must be served together. Unless Rule 4(d) provides a specific method of personal service, service is accomplished by serving the defendant or third-party defendant either personally or by leaving copies of the summons and complaint at the party's dwelling house or usual place of abode with some person of suitable age and discretion then residing therein. NRCP 4(d)(6). Similarly, under NRS 14.065, Nevada's long-arm statute, substituted service upon an individual residing at the defendant's residence is proper for personal service outside the state of Nevada where the defendant is not a resident of Nevada or where the action is not a proceeding "in rem" or "affecting specific property or status." *Orme v. Eighth Judicial District Court*, 105 Nev. 712, 782 P.2d 1325 (1989). For actions in rem or for residents of Nevada out of state, personal service must be personal. NRCP 4(e)(2); *Kelley v. Kelley*, 85 Nev. 317, 454 P.2d 85 (1969). Substituted service outside the state in either circumstance would be ineffective. *Moran v. Second Judicial District Court*, 72 Nev. 142, 297 P.2d 261 (1988). It is presumed a party's usual place of abode is not changed by entering into the military service. *Doyle, supra*, 414 P.2d at 707 (1966). Personal service by methods other than the most common method described in NRCP 4(d)(6) are discussed below.

§ 907. Domestic corporations.

Corporations organized and existing pursuant to the laws of the State of Nevada are required to maintain a resident agent, who may be either an individual or a corporation, resident or located in Nevada, to be in charge of the corporation's principal office. NRS 78.090. Legal process may be served upon the resident agent personally or by leaving a true copy thereof with a person of suitable age and discretion at the address shown on the certificate filed with the Secretary of State designating the resident agent. NRS 78.090(4); NRS 14.020(2).

In addition to service upon a resident agent, NRCP 4(d)(1) provides that a domestic corporation may be served with process through its president or other head of the corporation, secretary, cashier, or managing agent. Unlike the case of a resident agent, the remaining corporate representatives may not be served on behalf of the corporation by leaving a true copy of the summons and complaint with a person of suitable age and discretion at the residence or business address. *See Phillips v. Incline Manor Association,* 91 Nev. 69, 530 P.2d 1207 (1975), where the supreme court invalidated service of the summons and complaint upon the corporate president's fourteen-year-old son for failure to comply with the service requirements of NRCP 4(d)(1). Although NRCP 4(d)(1) provides a number of alternatives for service of process upon a domestic corporation, there is no requirement that the remaining officers of the domestic corporation be served when service is effectuated upon the resident agent. *State ex rel. Hersh v. First Judicial District Court,* 86 Nev. 73, 464 P.2d 783 (1970).

In the event service cannot be obtained upon the individuals or entities described in NRCP 4(d)(1), service may be made upon the domestic corporation by delivering to the Secretary of State a copy of the summons and complaint, together with posting a copy of said process in the office of the clerk of the court in which said action is commenced. Prior to the authorization of this substituted service, plaintiff shall cause to be filed an affidavit detailing the reasons why service cannot be accomplished in the usual manner upon the appropriate corporate officer or resident agent. The rule does not mention any requirement for obtaining a court order as a condition to authorizing such substituted service. If there is a last known address of a known officer of the domestic corporation outside the state, plaintiff is required to mail a copy of the summons and complaint to that address in addition to serving the Secretary of State. NRCP 4(d)(1).

A domestic corporation in the process of dissolution continues as a body corporate for the purpose of prosecuting and defending legal actions for a period of two years following the date of dissolution. NRS 78.585. Service of process upon a domestic corporation continued as a body corporate pursuant to NRS 78.585 may be accomplished by mailing copies of the process via certified mail to the Secretary of State, the resident agent of the corporation if any, and each officer and director of the corporation as named in the last list filed with the Secretary of State prior to dissolu-

135

tion, expiration of the corporation or the forfeiture of its charter. NRS 78.750.

§ 908. Foreign corporations.

Every foreign corporation, association, or municipal corporation owning property or doing business in the State of Nevada is required to appoint and keep a resident agent upon whom all legal process may be served. The foreign corporation, association, or municipal corporation is further required to file a certificate of acceptance of appointment with the Secretary of State, specifying the resident agent's full name and address. NRS 14.020(1). Legal process may be served upon the resident agent personally or by leaving a true copy thereof with a person of suitable age and discretion at the address shown on the current certificate on file with the Secretary of State. NRS 14.020(2). NRCP 4(d)(2) expands service of process against a foreign corporation, nonresident partnership, joint stock company, or association doing business in the state to its managing agent, cashier or secretary, in addition to a resident agent designated for service of process. There remain, however, fairly strict limits on persons upon whom process may be served under this section. *See C.H.A. Venture v. G.C. Wallace Consulting Engineers, Inc.,* 106 Nev. 381, 794 P.2d 707 (1990) (holding invalid service of process on wife of individual doing business as a partnership consisting of two foreign corporations). *See also BASF Corporation v. Jafbros, Inc.,* 105 Nev. 142, 771 P.2d 161 (1989), where the court held that substituted service solely on the Secretary of State was insufficient, where no attempt was made to mail a notice of the summons to the corporation.

When an individual lacks actual authority to act on behalf of the corporation, the individual's representation that he is an authorized agent for service of process does not, by itself, establish authorization. The principal, in this case the foreign corporation, must have granted actual authority or knowingly acquiesced in the representations of the proposed agent. Otherwise, service of process upon the unauthorized agent will be invalid. *Orbit Stations, Inc. v. Curtis,* 100 Nev. 205, 678 P.2d 1153 (1984).

In the event that a foreign business entity fails to comply with the requirements of NRS 14.020, said foreign corporation, association, municipal corporation, nonresident partnership, or joint stock company may be served with all legal process by delivering a copy to the Secretary of State. NRS 14.030(1). Service upon the Secretary of State is only authorized where the plaintiff causes to be filed an affidavit demonstrating that due diligence has been utilized to ascertain the whereabouts of an officer of said foreign entity and that personal service was not possible. A copy of the legal process must be mailed to the last known address of the foreign corporation or any known officers. NRS 14.030(3).

The foreign corporation sought to be served must either own property or do business within the State of Nevada for service to be valid pursuant to NRS 14.030(3). Former ownership is not sufficient to impose continuing answerability to jurisdiction absent other circumstances. *McCulloch Corp. v. O'Donnell,* 83 Nev. 396, 433 P.2d 839 (1967). The mere fact that the foreign corporation is a stockholder of another corporation authorized to do business in Nevada is also of no consequence. *Id.*

§ 909. Limited partnerships.

Pursuant to the Uniform Limited Partnership Act, each limited partnership is required to maintain, for service of process on the limited partnership, an agent who is a resident of Nevada, a domestic corporation or a foreign corporation authorized to do business within Nevada. NRS 88.330(1)(b).

A foreign limited partnership, in order to be registered to transact business in the State of Nevada, must also appoint an agent for service of process. The requirements for this agent are the same as those for a domestic limited partnership. NRS 88.575. In the event of the failure of the foreign limited partnership to properly register within the State of Nevada, the Secretary of State is deemed appointed as its agent for service of process with respect to causes of action arising out of the transaction of business within Nevada. NRS 88.600.

§ 910. Limited liability company.

A limited liability company (hereinafter "LLC") is now an authorized way of doing business in the State of Nevada. An LLC is required to designate in the articles of the organization an agent upon whom process may be served. NRS 86.161. That agent may be any natural person who is a resident of the State of Nevada and the address of such agent may be identical with the registered office of the LLC. The agent may also be a domestic or foreign corporation that is authorized to transact business in the State of Nevada. NRS 86.231(1)(b). That agent must file an acceptance of the appointment of resident agent with the Nevada Secretary of State. NRS 86.231(2).

If the LLC fails to appoint or maintain a resident agent for services of process, or if the agent for service of process cannot be found after exercising reasonable diligence, then the Nevada Secretary of State is appointed as the agent of the LLC for the purpose of receiving process, notice, or any other demand. Service on the Nevada Secretary of State is accomplished by delivering duplicate copies of the process on the Nevada Secretary of State. The Nevada Secretary of State is then required to take the duplicate copy and cause it to be forwarded by registered mail to the address of the LLC's registered office. NRS 86.261.

§ 911. Service of minors, incompetent persons and wards.

In the case of a minor under the age of fourteen years and residing within the state, service must be made upon the minor personally as well upon his father, mother, guardian or, if there are no parents or guardians within Nevada, upon any person maintaining custody and control including the minor's employer. NRCP 4(d)(3).

In the case of service on an individual who has been judicially declared to be of unsound mind, both the guardian and incompetent are to be served. NRCP 4(d)(4).

§ 912. Counties and municipalities.

In order to properly serve a county, city or town, the chairman of the board of commissioners, president of the council or trustees, mayor of the city, or other head of the legislative department must be personally served with process. NRCP 4(d)(5).

§ 913. Substituted service: other cases.

As previously noted, the method of personal service described in NRCP 4(d)(6) clearly is the most common method of service. Aside from personal service upon a defendant, NRCP 4(d)(6) also provides for service upon an agent authorized by appointment or by law to receive service of process. As with the service of an agent of a foreign corporation, discussed in § 908, *supra,* the agent must have been authorized by the principal to accept service under NRCP 4(d)(6). The phrase "an agent authorized by appointment to receive service of process" is intended to cover those situations where an individual actually appoints an agent for that purpose. *Foster v. Lewis,* 78 Nev. 330, 372 P.2d 679 (1962). In the absence of an actual specific appointment or authorization, an agency to accept service of process will not be implied. *Id.* As in the case of foreign corporations, service upon an unauthorized agent is ineffective.

1. *Service by publication.*

Service by publication is authorized when the proposed defendant resides outside of the state, has departed from the state, cannot after due diligence be found within the state, or conceals himself to avoid the service of process. Service by publication is appropriate once it has been established to the court by affidavit that the due diligence requirement has been satisfied and a cause of action against the defendant exists. NRCP 4(e)(1)(i).

In the case of service upon a party that resides outside of the State of Nevada or whose present address is unknown, the affidavit of due diligence must contain the following statements:

(a) The last known address and last date the party resided there;
(b) That such address was the last place the defendant resided;
(c) That said defendant no longer resides at said address;
(d) That the present place of residence of the proposed defendant is unknown; and
(e) That affiant has no reason to believe that said defendant resides in the State of Nevada.

NRCP 4(e)(1)(i).

A litigant seeking to complete service by way of publication must strictly follow the standards of due diligence set out in NRCP 4(e)(1)(i). The statutory provisions for acquiring jurisdiction over a defendant by other than personal service are to be strictly construed. *Foster v. Lewis,* 78 Nev. 330, 372 P.2d 679 (1962). The due diligence affidavit must contain a statement of facts, as distinguished from legal conclusions, in order to assist the court in determining whether due diligence has been properly exercised. *Id.* Good faith and due diligence require reasonable investigation and inquiry in an effort to ascertain the location of the proposed defendant by the party seeking publication of the summons. *Id. See also Dobson v. Dobson,* 108 Nev. 346, 830 P.2d 1336 (1992).

An action relating to real or personal property in Nevada in which a proposed defendant claims a lien or interest may be served by publication. NRCP 4(e)(1)(ii).

Publication is accomplished by publishing notice of the complaint in a newspaper designated by the court for a period of four weeks. Publication must be at least once a week during this time. In the event that the residence of the nonresident or absent defendant is known, the court shall also order a copy of the summons and complaint to be deposited in the post office and directed to the person to be serviced at his place of residence. Service is deemed complete upon the expiration of four weeks from the first publication, and in cases when a deposit of a copy of the summons and complaint in the post office is also required, at the expiration of four weeks from the date of deposit. NRCP 4(3)(1)(iii).

Where publication has been ordered by the court, personal service of the summons and complaint outside of Nevada shall be equivalent to completed service by publication, and the defendant served in this fashion has twenty days in which to respond. NRCP 4(e)(1)(iii). *See generally Gambs v. Morgenthaler,* 83 Nev. 90, 423 P.2d 670 (1967), wherein this procedure was approved although limited to the facts of that case. In attempting to serve by publication, a litigant is well advised to take every step possible to provide actual notice of the proceedings to a proposed defendant. As noted in *Continental Insurance Co. v. Moseley,* 100 Nev. 337, 683 P.2d 20 (1984), more than service by publication may be required in order to afford due process. This position is clearly consistent with the United States Supreme Court decisions in this area. *See Mennonite Board of Missions v. Adams,* 462 U.S. 791, 103 S. Ct. 2706, 77 L. Ed. 2d 180 (1983); *Mullane v. Central Hanover Bank & Trust Co.,* 339 U.S. 306, 705 S. Ct. 652, 94 L. Ed. 865 (1950).

2. *Personal service outside the state.*

NRCP 4(e)(2) provides for personal service outside the State of Nevada on a natural person over the age of eighteen years in two situations:

(a) Any action where the person to be served is a resident of Nevada; and

(b) Any action affecting specific property or status or in any other proceeding in rem without regard to the residence of the person to be served.

Once again, as in the case of service by publication, an order that personal service be made outside of Nevada must be based upon an affidavit stating that a cause of action exists against the person to be served and that said person is a necessary and proper party to the pending action. Service under this subsection may not be substituted service (person of suitable age at residence) but must be personal. *Kelley v. Kelley,* 85 Nev. 317, 454 P.2d 85 (1969).

3. *Statutory service.*

Service by process may also be completed in conformity with any statute providing for service. NRCP 4(e)(3). Chapter 14 of the Nevada Revised Statutes, Commencement of Actions, provides a statutory framework for the service of process outside the framework of NRCP 4. Service of process of foreign corporations has been previously discussed in § 908, *supra.* Service of process pursuant to the statutory provisions of NRS 14.065, the long-arm statute, NRS 14.070, the motor vehicle accident statute, and NRS 14.080, the products liability statute, are in §§ 914 through 916, *infra.*

In the case of the unknown heir, service may be completed by publication in the fashion provided in NRCP 4(e)(1). NRS 14.040(1). Prior to final judgment, the plaintiff must file an affidavit with the court stating either that the identity of an unknown heir has been subsequently discovered or that the same remains unknown to plaintiff and through reasonable diligence could not have been discovered. NRS 14.040(3). In the case of unknown parties, an order for publication of summons shall be issued by the court where the plaintiff alleges there are individuals, other than heirs, that are interested in the subject matter of the complaint who are presently unknown. NRS 14.050. Even though NRS 14.050 was drafted prior to the adoption of the Nevada Rules of Civil Procedure, sound practice would dictate that the requirements for publication of summons contained in NRCP 4(e)(1) be strictly followed.

Various statutory provisions for the service of process that might be encountered by the general practitioner are as follows:

(a) State of Nevada, state agencies.

In actions against the state, or any agency of the state, a summons and copy of the complaint must be served upon the Secretary of State who shall then deliver a copy of the complaint to the Risk Management Division of the Department of Administration. NRS 41.031.

(b) State and local governmental agencies.

In addition to any other method which may be provided by statute or rule of court, service upon any political subdivision, political corporation, special district or other agency of state or local government which is capable of being sued in its own name may be made upon the clerk or secretary of the political subdivision, political corporation, special district or other agency. NRS 12.105.

(c) Sheriff.

Service is accomplished by the delivery of the summons and complaint to the sheriff in person or to one of his deputies or to a person belonging to that office, during normal office hours, or if no such person is available, by leaving a summons and complaint in a conspicuous place within the office. NRS 248.190.

(d) State of Nevada Department of Highways.

Personal service is to be made upon both the Director of the Department of Highways and upon the Chairman of the Board of Directors of the Department; in the absence of the director and the chairman, process must be served personally upon the Secretary of State and also upon the deputy director. NRS 408.116.

(e) Foreign insurance companies.

A foreign insurer is required to appoint the insurance commissioner and his successors as its attorney to receive service of process issued against that insurer in this state. Service of process against a foreign insurer must be made only by service upon the commissioner. NRS 680A.250(3). Service is made upon the commissioner by delivering and leaving two copies of the process with the commissioner or his deputy or a person in apparent charge of his office during the commissioner's absence. The commissioner shall send, by certified mail, one of the copies of process with the date and time of service to the person currently designated by the insurer to receive the copy. NRS 680A.260. Service of process is only completed when the copy has been mailed by the commissioner. *Transamerica Insurance Co. v. C.B. Concrete Co.,* 99 Nev. 677, 669 P.2d 246 (1983).

Although service of process is complete when the copy has been mailed, this type of service, by itself, does not "notify" the insurer of the claim until the forwarded process is actually received. *Id.*

The time within which the insurer is required to appear and defend is extended an additional ten days beyond that otherwise allowed by the Nevada Rules of Civil Procedure, if process is served pursuant to NRS 680A.260.

(f) Domestic insurance companies.

Service of process against a domestic insurance company may be completed in any manner provided by the Nevada Rules of Civil Procedure or as provided by NRS 680A.250 and NRS 680A.260.

(g) Landlord/tenant/dwellings.

Service of process upon the manager of the rental property shall be deemed to be service upon the landlord. NRS 118A.260(4).

§ 914. Long-arm statute.

The proper application of the so-called "long-arm statute," NRS 14.065, has been the source of a great deal of litigation. The majority of this litigation has concerned due process claims and minimum contacts with the State of Nevada and not the actual mechanics of service of process under the statute. Issues pertaining to the propriety of the utilization of NRS 14.065 to acquire jurisdiction within Nevada generally must be decided on a case by case basis. The statute provides as follows:

Any person who, in person or through an agent or instrumentality, does any of the acts enumerated in this subsection thereby submits himself and, if a natural person, his personal representative to the jurisdiction of the courts of this state as to any cause of action which arises from:
(a) Transacting any business or negotiating any commercial paper within this state;
(b) Committing a tortious act within this state;
(c) Owning, using or possessing any real property situated in this state;

(d) Contracting to insure any person, property or risk located within this state at the time of contracting;

(e) Living in the marital relationship within this state notwithstanding subsequent departure from this state, as to all obligations arising for alimony, child support or property settlement, if the other party to the marital relationship continues to reside in this state ....

Pursuant to NRS 14.065, a nonresident must do one or more of the enumerated acts to be subject to the jurisdiction of Nevada courts and the cause of action must arise from those acts. *Rigdon v. Bluff City Transfer & Storage Co.,* 649 F. Supp. 263 (D. Nev. 1983). *See also Shapiro v. Pavlikowski,* 91 Nev. 548, 654 P.2d 1030 (1982).

In order to obtain in personam jurisdiction over an out-of-state defendant pursuant to the long-arm statute, such defendant's activities in Nevada must generally fall into one of two categories. In the first instance, a nonresident defendant may be subjected to "general personal jurisdiction" for "any cause of action" where the defendant's activities in Nevada "are so 'substantial' or 'continuous and systematic' that it may be deemed present in the forum." *Budget Rent-A-Car v. District Court,* 108 Nev. 983, 985, 835 P.2d 17, 19 (1992) and *Price & Sons v. District Court,* 108 Nev. 387, 831 P.2d 600, 601 (1992). Mere sales to Nevada customers and other marketing efforts in Nevada, without more, however, are insufficient to establish "general jurisdiction." *Price & Sons, supra,* 831 P.2d at 601-02. Absent "general jurisdiction," the second instance where personal jurisdiction can exist is "only where the cause of action arises from the defendant's contacts with Nevada" or what is referred to as "specific personal jurisdiction." *Budget Rent-A-Car,* 108 Nev. at 486, 835 P.2d at 20. *Price & Sons, supra,* 831 P.2d at 602. Thus, the consequences and purposes of the nonresident defendant's activities must have a substantial enough connection with Nevada before a court may reasonably exercise jurisdiction over the nonresident defendant. *Fallen v. Cervi Livestock Co.,* 581 F. Supp. 885 (D. Nev. 1984); *Sage Computer Technology v. P-Code Distributing Corp.,* 576 F. Supp. 1194 (D. Nev. 1983); *Jarstad v. National Farmers Union Property & Casualty Co.,* 92 Nev. 380, 552 P.2d 49 (1976); *Abbott v. Second Judicial District Court,* 90 Nev. 321, 526 P.2d 75 (1974); *Welburn v. Eighth Judicial District Court,* 107 Nev. 105, 806 P.2d 1045 (1991); *Mirage Casino-Hotel v. Caram,* 762 F. Supp. 286 (D. Nev. 1991); *Hotel Ramada of Nevada v. Estate of Cheek,* 716 F. Supp. 473 (D. Nev. 1989).

In determining whether a proposed defendant meets the foregoing test under NRS 14.065 the "legislative intention to reach the outer limits of federal constitutional due process" must be considered. *Trump v. The Eighth Judicial District Court,* 109 Nev. Adv. Op. __ (1993); *Davis v.*

Eighth Judicial District Court, 97 Nev. 332, 629 P.2d 1209, *cert. denied,* 454 U.S. 1049, 102 S. Ct. 592, 70 L. Ed. 2d 585 (1981); *Certain-Teed Products Corp. v. Second Judicial District Court,* 87 Nev. 18, 479 P.2d 781 (1971). It is the cumulative significance of all activities of a defendant within the state rather than the isolated effect of any single activity that will be determinative of issues of jurisdiction. The criteria for a court exercising "specific in personam jurisdiction" is whether the defendant has purposefully availed itself of the privilege of acting in Nevada or causing important consequences in Nevada. Factors dictated by the United States Supreme Court and approved by the Nevada Supreme Court in determining whether it is reasonable to require the non-resident to come to court in Nevada are as follows:

(1) The interstate judicial system's interest in obtaining the most efficient resolution of controversies;

(2) Nevada's interest in adjudicating the dispute;

(3) The plaintiff's interest in convenient and effective relief; and

(4) The interest of the several states in furthering substantive social policies.

Trump v. The Eighth Judicial District Court, 109 Nev. Adv. Op. __ (1993); *Levinson v. District Court,* 103 Nev. 404, 408, 742 P.2d 1024, 1026 (1987); and *World-Wide Volkswagen Corp.,* 444 U.S. at 292. *Abbott v. Second Judicial District Court,* 90 Nev. 321, 526 P.2d 75 (1974). *See also Abbott-Interfast Corporation v. Eighth Judicial District Court,* 107 Nev. 871, 821 P.2d 1043 (1991); *MGM Grand, Inc., v. Eighth Judicial District Court,* 107 Nev. 65, 807 P.2d 201 (1991). As previously noted, in the final analysis, all issues of personal jurisdiction and ultimately due process must be decided on a case-by-case basis. *Wells Fargo & Co. v. Wells Fargo Express Co.,* 556 F.2d 406 (9th Cir. 1977).

In utilizing the long-arm statute, the practitioner must take care to ensure that service is properly completed upon the out-of-state defendant. NRS 14.065(1) provides that service is sufficient if:

(a) The service is made by delivering a copy of the summons, together with a copy of the complaint, to the party served in the manner provided by statute or rule of court for service upon a person of like kind within this state; and

(b) The party has submitted himself to the jurisdiction of the court of this state in a manner provided by this section.

If the appropriate statute or rule of court is not strictly followed, service will be voided. This potential pitfall was clearly demonstrated in *Certain-Teed Products Corp. v. Second Judicial District Court,* 87 Nev. 18, 79 P.2d 781 (1971). In that action, the plaintiff sought to serve an out-of-state corporate defendant pursuant to the long-arm statute by delivering a copy of the summons and complaint upon the chief legal counselor of the corporate defendant. The supreme court interpreted the phrase "a person of like kind within the state" to require service similar to service of a domestic corporation pursuant to NRCP 4(d)(1). As a consequence, out-of-state service would have only been appropriate upon the president or other head of the corporation, secretary, cashier, managing agent or resident agent. As a result of the faulty service, a motion to quash was granted. The Court did not address whether Certain-Teed — as a foreign corporation doing business within the State of Nevada — could have been served through the Secretary of State pursuant to NRCP 4(d)(2).

Similarly, in *Jarstad v. National Farmers Union Property & Casualty Co.,* 92 Nev. 380, 552 P.2d 49 (1976), service upon a foreign corporation was quashed for failure to deliver a copy of the summons and complaint to the appropriate corporate official or agent.

The problems portrayed in *Certain-Teed* and *Jarstad* clearly could have been prevented through detailed instructions to the out-of-state process server or sheriff. The general practitioner is well advised to carefully word his or her service instructions in order to avoid the delays caused by these service defects. *See also Sawyer v. Sugarless Shops, Inc.,* 106 Nev. 265, 792 P.2d 14 (1990).

§ 915. Motor vehicle operation.

NRS 14.070 provides a method for the service of process upon operators of automobiles involved in accidents over the public roads, streets or highways of Nevada. The operator is deemed to have appointed the Director of the Department of Motor Vehicles and Public Safety as his true and lawful attorney for service of process in any action resulting in damage or loss to person or property. Service is completed through the deposit of a copy of the process and the payment of the statutory fee to the director as well as delivery by registered or certified mail of a copy of the process to the defendant at the address supplied in the accident report or the best available address. NRS 14.070(2). A return receipt signed by the defendant, or a return of the United States Postal Service stating the defendant refused to accept delivery or could not be located, or that the address is insufficient, along with the plaintiff's affidavit of compliance, should be attached to the original process and returned and filed in the action in which it was issued. Personal service of notice and a copy of the process upon the defendant outside the State of Nevada is deemed the equivalent of mailing. NRS 14.070(2).

The affidavit of compliance by plaintiff must state the source of the address relied on by the plaintiff, and the affidavit must be based on facts and not mere conclusions. *Mitchell v. Second Judicial Court,* 82 Nev. 377, 418 P.2d 994 (1966).

The return receipt, pursuant to NRS 14.070(2), must be signed personally by the nonresident defendant or service will be deemed insufficient. *Austin v. C & L Trucking,* 610 F. Supp. 465 (D. Nev. 1985).

§ 916. Products liability.

Those who manufacture, produce, make, market or otherwise supply products for distribution, sale or use in Nevada may be lawfully served with process in any action to recover damages for injury to person or property resulting from such distribution, sale or use in this state. NRS 14.080(1). Service of process may be accomplished by delivering a copy of such process to the Secretary of State and by mailing to the last known address of the company, firm, partnership, corporation or association by registered or certified mail a copy of the summons and complaint. NRS 14.080(2). Under this service scheme the defendant shall have forty days, exclusive of the day of service, within which to answer or otherwise plead.

Pursuant to NRS 14.080, any foreign manufacturer of a product which reasonably may be expected to enter interstate commerce and which does, in fact, enter interstate commerce resulting in injury within the State of Nevada due to an alleged defect, may be subject to the jurisdiction of the Nevada courts. *See Judas Priest v. Second Judicial District Court,* 104 Nev. 424, 760 P.2d 137 (1988). Service of process pursuant to this section is inappropriate unless the complaint contains allegations pertaining to the dangerous or defective nature of the product. *Jacobsen v. Ducommun, Inc.,* 87 Nev. 240, 484 P.2d 1095 (1971); *Drew Rentals v. First Judicial District Court,* 85 Nev. 327, 454 P.2d 892 (1969).

§ 917. Third-party practice.

NRCP 14(a) provides the specific method for service of the summons and complaint in a third-party action. The requirements for valid service of process and acquisition of personal jurisdiction in a third-party action are the same as in any other type of litigation. *See generally* 6 Wright, Miller & Kane, *Federal Practice and Procedure*: Civil 2d § 1445 (1992).

§ 918. Return of service.

Under NRCP 4(g), proof of service of process is completed by any one of the four following methods:

    1. Affidavit of sheriff or his deputy;

    2. Affidavit of any other person serving process;

    3. In the case of publication, the affidavit of the publisher or employee having knowledge of publication, and an affidavit of a deposit of a copy of the summons in the United States mail; or

4. The written admission of the defendant.

The person serving process is required to promptly file with the court proof of service and in any event within the time during which the person served must respond to process. NRCP 4(g). Failure to make proof of service, however, does not affect the validity of the service (NRCP 4(g)), and little can be done to compel a prompt return by the process server except the issuance of a court order. 4A Wright & Miller, *Federal Practice and Procedure*: Civil 2d § 1130 (1987).

Although NRCP 4(g) does not describe the contents of the return of service, it should disclose enough facts to demonstrate the validity of service. At a minimum, the date, manner of service, place of service, and the identity of any other papers served should be contained within the proof of service. 4A Wright & Miller, *Federal Practice and Procedure*: Civil 2d § 1130 (1987).

As a general rule, amendments to process are granted freely since the possibility is remote that an amendment will result in material prejudice to any substantial right of any of the parties. The most common problem is a mistake or technical error in properly identifying the defendant. If the defect is one of form over substance, and the defendant has received the original process and is thus on notice of the pending action, no sound reason exists to refuse to permit the amendment. 4A Wright & Miller, *Federal Practice and Procedure*: Civil 2d § 1131 (1987). The standard for amending proof of service is identical to the standard controlling the amendment of the actual process. 4A Wright & Miller, *Federal Practice and Procedure*: Civil 2d § 1132 (1987).

§919. Service of other pleadings and papers.

After the commencement of the action and the completion of service of original process, the provisions of NRCP 5(a) come into effect. Every pleading subsequent to the complaint, unless otherwise ordered by the court due to numerous defendants, is required to be served upon a party. These pleadings include papers relating to discovery, non-ex-parte motions, notices, appearances, demands, offers of judgment and designations of record on appeal. NRCP 5(a).

Service of these other papers is made by serving the attorney of record for a particular party, unless otherwise ordered by the court. Service upon the attorney or party shall be made by delivering a copy to him or by mailing it to him at his last known address, or, if no address be known, by leaving it with the clerk of the court. Delivery may be accomplished in any one of the following four ways:

1. Handing a copy to the attorney;

2. Leaving a copy at the office of the attorney with a person in charge;
3. Leaving a copy in the office in a conspicuous place when no one is in charge; and
4. Leaving a copy at the attorney's place of abode with someone of suitable age and discretion in the event the office is closed.

NRCP 5(b).

Service by mail is complete upon mailing, but after the initial appearance of a party, service by mail must be made only by mailing from a point within the State of Nevada. NRCP 5(b).

Proof of service may be made by the certificate of an attorney or of his employee, written admission, by affidavit, or other proof satisfactory to the court. Failure to make proof of service shall not affect the validity of the service. In the event of a challenge to proper service, the burden of proof rests upon the party who asserts that a particular notice or motion was properly served. *See Zugel v. Miller,* 99 Nev. 100, 101 n.1, 659 P.2d 296 (1983).

The failure to comply with court rules, *e.g.,* the failure to properly file and serve a notice of motion and motion to dismiss, is a valid ground to vacate an order. *Monroe, Ltd. v. Central Telephone Co., Southern Nevada Division,* 91 Nev. 450, 538 P.2d 152 (1975).

All papers and pleadings are to be filed with the clerk of the court unless otherwise ordered. NRCP 5(d). NRCP 5(d) specifically prohibits the filing with the court of certain papers relating to discovery. As a consequence, the party initiating discovery has the duty to preserve the original discovery for any pretrial hearing or trial.

§ 920. Time.

The computation of time in civil actions is detailed in NRCP 6(a). In computing any period of time prescribed or allowed by the rules of civil procedure, local rules of any district court or any applicable statute, the day of the act, event or default from which the designated period of time begins to run shall not be included. The last day of the period shall be included unless it is a Saturday, Sunday or a nonjudicial day, in which event the period runs until the end of the next day which is not a Saturday, Sunday or nonjudicial day. NRCP 6(a). *Rodgers v. State,* 85 Nev. 61, 445 P.2d 172 (1969). Intermediate Saturdays, Sundays and nonjudicial days shall be excluded in the computation of time if the time period is less than seven days. NRCP 6(a).

NRCP 6(a) has been held to apply to the computation of statute of limitation periods. *Romaine v. State Farm Mutual Automobile Insurance Co.,* 87 Nev. 257, 485 P.2d 102 (1971).

In the event of service by mail, three days are to be added to any prescribed time period. NRCP 6(e). This extension of time has been applied by the court to administrative appeals. *Hardin v. Jones,* 102 Nev. 469, 727 P.2d 551 (1986); *Nyberg v. Nevada Industrial Commission,* 100 Nev. 322, 683 P.2d 3 (1984).

§ 921. Tolling period.

Pursuant to NRS 11.300 the absence of a defendant from the State of Nevada will toll the running of the applicable limitation periods. This statute, however, will not protect a cause of action if the absent defendant was otherwise subject to service of process. *Simmons v. Trivelpiece,* 98 Nev. 167, 643 P.2d 1219 (1982). For example, the temporary absence of a resident defendant from the state does not toll the statute of limitations if, in fact, there is a person of suitable age and discretion residing at this defendant's dwelling house or usual place of abode upon whom service can be made. *See Bank of Nevada v. Friedman,* 82 Nev. 417, 420 P.2d 1 (1966).

A defendant is deemed continuously present in the state for purposes of service pursuant to the motorist statute, NRS 14.070; therefore, his temporary absence does not act to toll the running of the statute of limitations in an action arising out of the use of a motor vehicle within the state.

As long as the foreign manufacturer is subject to service of process pursuant to NRS 14.080, the statute of limitations may not be tolled in a suit concerning the manufacturer's product. *Seely v. Illinois-California Express, Inc.,* 541 F. Supp. 1307 (D. Nev. 1982).

§ 922. Challenging a district court's decision on service of process.

The Nevada Supreme Court has established that a writ of prohibition is the appropriate remedy to challenge a district court's refusal to quash service of process. *Price & Sons v. District Court,* 108 Nev. 387, 831 P.2d 600 (1992); *Abbott-Interfast Corp. v. Eighth Judicial District Court,* 107 Nev. 871, 821 P.2d 1043 (1991); *Judas Priest v. Second Judicial District Court,* 104 Nev. 424, 760 P.2d 137 (1988); *Messner v. Eighth Judicial District Court,* 104 Nev. 759, 766 P.2d 1320 (1988); *Shapiro v. Pavlikowski,* 98 Nev. 548, 654 P.2d 1030 (1982). A writ of prohibition, when issued by the court or clerk, effectively restrains the district court from exercising any jurisdiction on the plaintiff's original complaint. *See Shapiro, supra,* 654 P.2d at 1031.

The court has also established that the appropriate remedy to challenge a district court's order quashing service of process is through a writ of mandamus. *Jarstad v. National Farmers Union Property & Casualty Co.,* 92 Nev. 380, 552 P.2d 49 (1976). Mandamus is an appropriate remedy because orders quashing service are not appealable. *Id.,* 552 P.2d at 51. When a writ of mandamus is granted, it compels the district court to accept jurisdiction over the defendant.

In the interest of judicial economy, the court has occasionally treated petitions mistakenly sought in prohibition as ones in mandamus and vice versa. *See Messner,* 766 P.2d at 1320; *Koza v. Eighth Judicial District Court,* 99 Nev. 535, 665 P.2d 244 (1983). Nevertheless, the prudent general practitioner should not rely on the court's discretion and is well advised to seek the appropriate remedy according to the district court's decision.

CHAPTER 10

DEFAULTS AND DEFAULT JUDGMENTS

Authors: Sara Beth Brown
         Bridget Robb Peck

§ 1001. Introduction and scope.

This Chapter addresses the procedures for obtaining defaults and default judgments and for setting these defaults and default judgments aside. This Chapter also deals with those circumstances in which the taking of either a default or a default judgment is not appropriate.

151

The research in this Chapter is not intended to be exhaustive, but rather to illustrate the interplay between the Nevada Rules of Civil Procedure, Nevada Supreme Court Rules, Nevada case authority, and in limited circumstances, federal law, on defaults and default judgments.

§ 1002. Default.

A defendant (or counter-defendant) who has been properly served with a summons and complaint, and fails within the time permitted to appear and defend (for example by filing an answer, a responsive pleading, or an answer following the denial of a responsive pleading or an amended complaint), is in default. NRCP 4(b).

§ 1003. — Entry of default.

The first step toward a default judgment is the "entry" of default. The requirements for entry of default are contained in NRCP 55(a). A default is entered in the record by the clerk of the court when a party against whom affirmative relief is sought has failed to plead or otherwise defend, or in some cases, as a discovery sanction. See Form 10B, infra. The clerk's authority to act comes from NRCP 77(c), but may be rescinded by the court. The entry of default is not automatic, but requires a request by the party seeking affirmative relief and a ministerial determination by the clerk that the grounds for a taking default are present. Opaco Lumber & Realty Co. v. Phipps, 75 Nev. 312, 340 P.2d 95 (1959). However, the clerk has no authority to pass upon the validity of instruments presented for filing. Bowman v. District Court, 102 Nev. 474, 728 P.2d 433 (1986). The clerk has the right to exercise discretion regarding form, but is not entitled to exercise judicial discretion. Id. at 478. Once the clerk determines that the requirements for entry of a default have been shown, the entry of default is mandatory.

Once the default has been entered, it cuts off the defendant's ability to file an answer or other responsive pleading, unless the default is set aside. See § 1023, infra.

After a default has been taken, the defendant is not entitled to notices of activity in the case and need not be served with subsequent papers filed in the action. However, if an appearance is entered after the entry of default, the defendant is entitled to notice prior to the entry of a default judgment under NRCP 55(b)(2). Havas v. Engebregson, 97 Nev. 408, 633 P.2d 682 (1981).

§ 1004. — Effect of amended complaint upon default.

When a plaintiff materially amends the complaint after default has been entered, the defendant may not have been afforded adequate notice as to the allegations in the amended portion of the complaint. Although the Nevada courts have not addressed the issue, a material amendment which substantially increases the damages prayed for, or adds a cause of action based on a different legal theory, would require a new time period for the defendant to answer.

§ 1005. — Default entered against any party.

A default may be taken against any defending party. Any party seeking affirmative relief, including a counterclaimant, or a cross-claimant, may have a default entered against an adverse party. NRCP 55(d).

§ 1006. — Failure to plead or otherwise defend.

A default may be entered for failure to plead or otherwise defend as required by the procedural rules. *McCulloch v. Washoe County,* 551 F. Supp. 1022 (D. Nev. 1982), *aff'd,* 720 F.2d 1020 (9th Cir. 1983). Failure to do either within the time to answer is one of the grounds for default under Rule 55(a). However, Rule 55(a) is not the only rule for entry of default.

§ 1007. — Entry of default as a sanction.

Failure to comply with discovery rules may lead to entry of a default judgment. Nevada Rule of Civil Procedure 37 generally authorizes discovery sanctions for willful noncompliance with a discovery order of the court. *Young v. Johnny Ribeiro Building, Inc.,* 106 Nev. 88, 92, 787 P.2d 777 (1990), *citing, Fire Insurance Exchange v. Zenith Radio Corp.,* 103 Nev. 648, 651, 747 P.2d 911 (1987).

The court also has inherent equitable powers to dismiss actions or to enter default judgments for abusive litigation practices.

In *Young v. Ribeiro,* the Nevada Supreme Court upheld the dismissal and entry of default judgment against a party who willfully fabricated evidence and, when confronted, refused to recant the fabrication. The Supreme Court noted that when a dismissal with prejudice is ordered as a discovery sanction, the court must enter an express order analyzing the pertinent factors including:

(1) the degree of willfulness of the offending party;
(2) the extent the non-offending party would be prejudiced by a lesser sanction;
(3) the severity of the sanction as compared to the severity of the offense;
(4) whether evidence has been irreparably lost;
(5) the feasibility and fairness of other, less severe sanctions;
(6) the policy favoring adjudication on the merits;

(7) whether sanctions unfairly operate to penalize a party for the misconduct of the party's attorney; and

(8) the need to deter this and future litigants from similar abuses.

See also Stubli v. Big D International Trucks, Inc., 107 Nev. 309, 810 P.2d 785 (1991) (failure to preserve evidence); *Kelly Broadcasting Co. v. Sovereign Broadcast, Inc.,* 96 Nev. 188, 606 P.2d 1089 (1980) (failure to answer interrogatories, providing incomplete or evasive answers, or failure to comply with NRCP 16.1 may result in the entry of a default judgment).

Another discovery sanction, imposed for failure to comply with the requirements of NRCP 16.1, is to strike the defending party's answer. Then a default can be entered. A default judgment may also be entered as a sanction for conduct other than discovery violations. *See* WDCR 22; EDCR 7.60.

§ 1008. — Application for default.

The party seeking entry of default must bring the failure of the defendant to plead or respond to the attention of the clerk. The completion, and presentation to the clerk of the official court form of default should be sufficient to apprise the clerk of the facts of default. This is the practice in some judicial districts. A more conservative practice would be to present to the clerk a written application or an affidavit of counsel, or of a party, in support of entry of the default.

§ 1009. Judgment by default.

If a defendant has entered an appearance (discussed more fully *infra* at § 1013), or if the plaintiff has reason to know the defendant is represented by counsel, the plaintiff must give the defendant notice of the plaintiff's intention to take a default. *See* SCR 175; *Cen Val Leasing Corp. v. Bockman,* 99 Nev. 612, 668 P.2d 1074 (1983) (failure to give notice of intent to take default when plaintiff knew of identity of defendant's attorney, required that default be set aside); *Rowland v. Lepire,* 95 Nev. 639, 600 P.2d 237 (1979) (setting aside entry of default and default judgment when notice of intent to take default was not given).

§ 1010. — Application for default judgment.

The plaintiff's request for a default judgment, together with the reason(s) for it, must be brought to the court's attention. This is done by an application for default judgment (*see* Form 10D), supported by an affidavit of counsel or the plaintiff. *See* Form 10E. The affidavit should show:

(1) that the defendant has not answered or filed a responsive pleading;

(2) that the defendant is not an infant, incompetent or in the military

service; (3) that the defendant owes damages to the plaintiff; and (4) the attorney's fees incurred by the plaintiff if the plaintiff is entitled to recover these fees.

§ 1011. — Default judgment by the clerk.

The clerk may enter judgment when the claim is for a sum certain or for a sum that can be made certain by computation. NRCP 55(b)(1). The judgment may be entered at the request of the plaintiff, or other party, when supported by an affidavit substantiating the amount due.

A default judgment cannot be entered by the clerk where the defendant has "appeared" or where the defendant is an infant or incompetent person. Any judgment that violates this rule may be set aside.

§ 1012. — A sum certain.

The requirement of a sum certain is met where damages are claimed for a liquidated amount that is not subject to discretion. The unpaid principal of a promissory note, or the amount due on a check or an account, is a sum certain or a sum which is capable of being made certain by computation. Claims for personal injury, the converted value of property or declaratory relief are not claims for liquidated sums. *See Contrail Leasing Partners, Ltd. v. Executive Service Corp.,* 100 Nev. 545, 550, 688 P.2d 765 (1984); *Kelly Broadcasting Co. v. Sovereign Broadcast, Inc.,* 96 Nev. 188, 606 P.2d 1089 (1980). The assessment of reasonable attorney's fees is not a liquidated sum. That determination must be made by the court.

Costs of suit are recoverable in a judgment entered by the clerk. Since the amount expended is liquidated, the inclusion of costs in the judgment will not make it uncertain of calculation. A memorandum of costs always should be submitted with the application for default judgment.

§ 1013. — Appearance.

Defining "appearance" has given courts the opportunity to be creative. Negotiations between attorneys for parties can be an appearance by the defendant; so can settlement negotiations and exchange of correspondence between a plaintiff's attorney and an insurance adjuster. A layman's attempt to answer, indicating an intent to respond, such as a letter written by a layman in response to receipt of a Summons, is sufficient as an appearance, even though defective as to legal form. The Nevada Supreme Court defines what constitutes an "appearance" in *Franklin v. Bartsas Realty, Inc.,* 95 Nev. 559, 598 P.2d 1147 (1979). *See also Gazin v. Hoy,* 102 Nev. 621, 730 P.2d 436 (1986); *Cen Val Leasing Corp. v. Bockman,* 99 Nev. 612, 668 P.2d 1074 (1983); *Rowland v. Lepire,*

95 Nev. 639, 600 P.2d 237 (1979); *Christy v. Carlisle,* 94 Nev. 651, 584 P.2d 687 (1978). Counsel should also be aware of Supreme Court Rule 175. Before taking a default, counsel knowing the identity of the lawyer representing the opposing party must first inquire about opposing counsel's intention to proceed with the lawsuit.

The key to determining whether an appearance has been made is whether the defendant could reasonably believe that the pleading has been responded to. The response may not be sufficient, and a default may be taken, but before judgment may be entered, the defendant is entitled to notice and hearing. *See* NRCP 55(b)(2). At the hearing, inquiry should be made by the court as to the defendant's intent to defend or proceed.

When in doubt, give the defaulting party the benefit of a notice and hearing. The client's cause generally will be advanced because giving the defendant the opportunity for a hearing enhances the likelihood that a judgment will not later be set aside on a procedural technicality.

§ 1014. — Default judgment by the court.

All cases in which the clerk is not permitted to enter a default judgment must be brought before the court. NRCP 55(b)(2). However, not all applications to the court must be upon notice and hearing. *See* § 1010, *supra.*

As a matter of practice, the default judgment and supporting affidavits can be sent to the judge's chambers unless a notice of application for judgment must be filed.

The court can then conduct a "prove-up" hearing. Although this hearing will be attended only by the party seeking a default judgment, it is crucial to observe the necessary formalities to ensure the judgment is supported by sufficient evidence. *McKinzie v. Nevada Livestock Production Credit Association,* 107 Nev. 936, 822 P.2d 1113 (1991) (setting aside default judgment because record on appeal did not contain the account of the prove-up hearing).

For a form judgment by the court, see Form 10F, *infra.*

§ 1015. Infants and incompetents, and a defendant in the military service.

The clerk's default judgment (NRCP 55(b)(2)), is not available against certain parties. Unless it can be demonstrated by affidavit that the defendant is not an infant, nor incompetent, default judgment cannot be had without the involvement of the court. Similarly, unless an affidavit is presented indicating that the defaulting party is not in the military service, the Soldier's and Sailor's Civil Relief Act, 50 U.S.C. § 520 (1981), must be followed. *See* § 1017, *infra.*

Additionally, NRCP 55(e) provides that no default judgment may be entered against the state, its agencies and officers unless the claimant has established his legal right to relief by presenting satisfactory evidence to the court. *See* § 1020.

§ 1016. — Infants and incompetents.

A default judgment may be taken against an infant or incompetent person only by application made to the court. Before the judgment may be taken, the infant or incompetent must be represented by a general guardian, a guardian *ad litem,* a conservator, "or such other representative." NRCP 55(b)(2).

The authority to appoint guardians is vested in the district court. NRS 159.035; *see also* NRS 12.050 regarding appointment of a guardian *ad litem,* and NRS 12.080 regarding parents as guardians.

§ 1017. — Soldier's and Sailor's Civil Relief Act.

When a default judgment is sought and no affidavit has been filed indicating that the defendant is not in the military service, the Soldier's and Sailor's Civil Relief Act requires that judgment be made only by application to the court. 50 U.S.C. § 520 (1981).

The Act is not designed to provide a special defense for service personnel, nor does it exempt military parties from civil process. Rather, its purpose is to protect military personnel whose military service might interfere with their ability to attend to their personal affairs.

For example, soldiers on active duty in a hostile action or foreign service have experienced difficulty receiving their mail. Soldiers or sailors in such circumstances would be at a distinct disadvantage if safety procedures were not in place.

If an affidavit showing the defendant is not in the military cannot be given, the court in which the action is pending must appoint an attorney to represent and defend the interests of the defendant. Additionally, the court may require a bond of the plaintiff, conditioned to indemnify the defendant, if in the military service, for any loss or damage suffered by reason of the judgment should it thereafter be set aside.

Note that 50 U.S.C. § 520(4) provides an additional basis upon which military personnel may apply to set aside a default judgment. However, that relief must be sought immediately following discharge from the service.

§ 1018. Application when defaulting party has appeared.

When the defaulting party has appeared in the action the clerk may not enter the judgment and the defaulting party must be served with written notice of the application for judgment at least three days prior to the hearing. NRCP 55(b)(2). The judgment can only be entered by the court. *Id.*

This is one of the few circumstances when the default judgment application must be put on the court's motion calendar, if the court has one. The damages claimed may be proved by competent evidence only. Counsel should be aware that the court may conduct such hearings as it deems necessary on the sufficiency of the proof, or on damages, but that the court generally is not required to conduct such hearings.

Although an "appearance" is generally considered to be a presentation or submission to the court, the Nevada courts, as discussed above, are very liberal in finding that there has been an appearance. *See* § 1013, *supra.*

The application to the court can be very brief, and notice may be served in accordance with NRCP 5. The defendant will probably not respond, but thorough counsel will have eliminated any basis for a claim that the judgment must be set aside because of lack of notice.

§ 1019. The notice and hearing.

Where there has been an appearance, the hearing must be conducted with written notice to the defaulting party. The notice must be given at least three days before the hearing. NRCP 55(b)(2). Service by mail complies with NRCP 5, however, if service is by mail, an additional three days will be required and weekends and non-judicial days must not be counted. NRCP 6(e). To give the defaulting party sufficient opportunity to appear, the notice should contain the date, time and place of the hearing, identifying the department and (if possible) the judge who will hear it.

The failure to give notice and provide a hearing is a fatal procedural error because without proper notice the judgment is void and will be set aside. *Gazin v. Hoy,* 102 Nev. 621, 730 P.2d 436 (1986); *Christy v. Carlisle,* 94 Nev. 651, 584 P.2d 687 (1978).

However, the scope of the hearing is not likely to include testimony on all issues to support entry of a default judgment. If the defendant is in default, then all well-pleaded facts will be deemed admitted, except as to items of damages. Thus, liability will be assumed and the inquiry generally will focus on proof of the amount of damages.

The court has discretion to require the plaintiff to establish the truth of *any* averment in the complaint by evidence, and can undertake such investigation as it deems necessary. NRCP 55(b)(2). The defendant can require the court to conduct a trial by jury on the issue of damages. A demand for a jury must be made in writing before the hearing as provided in NRCP 38(b).

§ 1020. Default judgment against the state.

Pursuant to NRCP 55(e), a default judgment against the State or its officers or agencies, is not permitted "unless the claimant establishes his claim or right to relief by evidence satisfactory to the court." Thus, even though a default judgment is appropriately entered against the state or its agencies, the plaintiff must prove all elements of the case.

§ 1021. Attorney's fees and costs.

Where permitted by law, the court may award attorney's fees and tax costs in the default judgment. The default judgment should contain a blank for the judge to fill in the appropriate amount of attorney's fee.

The amount of these fees should be presented to the court by affidavit. The better procedure is to include a detailed summary of the duties performed and the fees charged as an exhibit to the affidavit, to permit the court to assess the reasonableness of the fees. In circumstances where the amount of fees requested is unusual, an explanation in the affidavit of the reason for this will increase the likelihood that the fee will be deemed reasonable by the court.

As with the default judgment entered by the clerk, a request for the judgment to include costs must be supported by a memorandum of costs and disbursements, which should be submitted with the application for default judgment. *See* Form 10G, *infra.* The award of costs can also be made in a default judgment entered by either the clerk or the court, so a memorandum of costs should always be filed with the court.

§ 1022. Setting aside defaults and default judgments.

Practitioners commonly confuse the standards for setting aside defaults and setting aside default judgments. The confusion is probably due to the fact that the standard for setting aside default judgments fulfills the requirements for setting aside defaults. However, the converse is not true. In order to justify setting aside an entry of default, a showing of "good cause" is required under NRCP 55(c). If a default judgment has been entered, the judgment must be set aside in accordance with NRCP 60.

§ 1023. Setting aside defaults.

NRCP 55(c) provides that, in the court's discretion, an entry of default may be set aside "for good cause shown." The requirement of "good cause" to set aside a default is less stringent than the showing required to set aside a default judgment. *Sealed Unit Parts Co. v. Alpha Gamma Chapter of Gamma Phi Beta Sorority, Inc. of Reno*, 99 Nev. 641, 668 P.2d

288 (1983); *Rae v. All American Life & Casualty Co.,* 95 Nev. 920, 605 P.2d 196 (1979).

The phrase "good cause shown" is broad in scope and includes the mistake, inadvertence, surprise and excusable neglect referred to in NRCP 60(b)(1). *Intermountain Lumber & Builders Supply, Inc. v. Glens Falls Insurance Co.,* 83 Nev. 126, 424 P.2d 884 (1967) (the scope of "good cause" does not include inexcusable neglect). In *Intermountain Lumber,* the Nevada Supreme Court determined that the failure of counsel's inexperienced secretary to transcribe a reply to a counterclaim and counsel's claim to be busy with the press of business, constituted inexcusable neglect. The court held that despite the judicial preference for deciding cases on their merits, this policy alone did not justify setting the default aside. *Id.* at 130.

In *Sealed Unit Parts Co. v. Alpha Gamma Chapter,* 99 Nev. 641, 668 P.2d 288 (1983), the Nevada Supreme Court indicated that a trial court's discretion in setting aside a default should be guided by the following: (1) an excuse must be shown for failure to respond; (2) a meritorious defense must be shown; and (3) recognition should be given to the policy of deciding each case on its merits.

The Nevada cases often do not distinguish between setting aside a default and setting aside a default judgment. As a consequence, it is more difficult to predict what may constitute "good cause" to set aside a default. *Sealed Unit Parts Co.* indicates that good cause "may be broader" than NRCP 60(b), but states that "some excuse" for failure to answer or defend must be shown. In this case the defaulted party had incorrectly believed that its co-defendant would be assuming the defaulted party's defense. *See Banks v. Heater,* 95 Nev. 610, 600 P.2d 245 (1979) (to like effect). As a practice tip, the defaulted party's success was also due to moving quickly to set aside the default and accompanying the motion with a proposed answer setting forth a meritorious defense.

An order setting aside the entry of a default cannot be appealed. Where no statutory authority to appeal is granted, no right to appeal exists. *Long v. A-1 24 Hour Towing, Inc.,* 101 Nev. 682, 707 P.2d 1151 (1985); *Kokkos v. Tsalikis,* 91 Nev. 24, 530 P.2d 756 (1975). Similarly, a court's refusal to set aside a default judgment may not be appealed. *Aetna Life & Casualty Insurance Co. v. Rowan,* 107 Nev. 362, 812 P.2d 350 (1991). However, an order quashing service of process, on grounds the default was procured by fraud, is appealable. *Dobson v. Dobson,* 108 Nev. 346, 830 P.2d 1336 (1992).

§ 1024. The requirement of a meritorious defense.

To set aside the entry of default or default judgment, it is necessary to show a meritorious defense. *Sealed Unit Parts Co. v. Alpha Gamma*

Chapter, 99 Nev. 641, 668 P.2d 288 (1983); *Kelso v. Kelso,* 78 Nev. 99, 369 P.2d 668 (1962).

To meet the requirement of a meritorious defense the Nevada Supreme Court has set forth four alternatives:

(a) admissible testimony or affidavit which, if true, would tend to establish a defense to all or part of the claim for relief asserted;

(b) the opinion of counsel that a meritorious defense exists to all or part of the claim asserted based upon facts related to or otherwise known by counsel;

(c) a responsive pleading tendered in good faith with the motion that, if true, would tend to establish a meritorious defense to all or part of the claim for relief asserted;

(d) any combination of the above.

Minton v. Roliff, 86 Nev. 478, 471 P.2d 209 (1970).

The showing of a meritorious defense is unnecessary when a default or default judgment is entered without any notice to the defendant. *Peralta v. Heights Medical Center, Inc.,* 485 U.S. 80, 108 S. Ct. 896, 99 L. Ed. 2d 75 (1988). (The Due Process Clause of the Fourteenth Amendment requires a judgment taken without any notice to be set aside).

§ 1025. Setting aside default judgments.

NRCP 55(c) indicates that the grounds set forth in NRCP 60 for setting aside a judgment are applicable for setting aside a *default judgment.* See § 1023, *supra.*

The primary purpose of NRCP 60(b) is to redress any injustice that may have resulted because of excusable neglect or the wrongs of an opposing party. The rule should be liberally construed to effectuate that purpose. *Nevada Industrial Development, Inc. v. Benedetti,* 103 Nev. 360, 741 P.2d 802 (1987). NRCP 60(b) provides four grounds for setting aside default judgments:

(1) Mistake, inadvertence, surprise or excusable neglect;

(2) Fraud, misrepresentation, or other misconduct of an adverse party which would be of sufficient nature to sustain a collateral attack;

(3) The judgment is void; and

(4) The judgment has been satisfied, released, or discharged, or a prior judgment upon which it is based, has been reversed or vacated, or that it is no longer equitable that an injunction remain in effect.

Any one of these grounds is sufficient for vacating a default judgment. Grounds (1) and (2) must be advanced within a reasonable time, not exceeding six months after entry of judgment. NRCP 60(b). *See, e.g.,*

Smith v. Smith, 82 Nev. 384, 419 P.2d 295 (1966) (judgment entered by surprise is voidable, not void, and must be set aside within six months).

There is no time limit applicable to ground (3), void judgments. Ground (4) must be advanced within a reasonable time. In addition, NRCP 60(b) confirms the inherent power of a court to entertain an independent action to relieve a party from judgment or to set aside a judgment for mistake or fraud upon the court. *See* § 1031, *infra.*

NRCP 60(c) provides an additional ground for setting aside a default judgment in circumstances where the defendant has not been personally served. It provides relief in very narrow circumstances and applies only if no general appearance has been made in a case where personal service was not obtained. All other applications, with the exception of the Soldier's and Sailor's Civil Relief Act, must fall within NRCP 60(b).

An order granting a motion to set aside a default judgment filed and served within sixty days following the entry of a default judgment may not be appealed. NRAP 3A(b)(2); *Long v. A-1 24 Hour Towing, Inc.,* 101 Nev. 682, 707 P.2d 1151 (1985).

§ 1026. Mistake, inadvertence, surprise or excusable neglect.

The most common ground alleged in an attempt to set aside a default judgment is "mistake, inadvertence, surprise or excusable neglect." Any one of these grounds is sufficient to justify setting aside a default judgment. NRCP 60(b). The motion must be filed within six months after the default judgment has been entered.

Motions made under NRCP 60(b) are to be liberally construed to effectuate purpose of redressing injustices caused by the excusable neglect or wrongs of the opposing party. *Peterson v. Peterson,* 105 Nev. 133, 771 P.2d 159 (1989) (decision upholding default set aside where husband misrepresented community assets to wife and wife moved expeditiously to set default aside, although wife's attorney delayed in preparing the motion).

In setting aside a default judgment for these reasons, the trial court is vested with broad discretion. *Union Petrochemical Corp. of Nevada v. Scott,* 96 Nev. 337, 609 P.2d 323 (1980); *Cicerchia v. Cicerchia,* 77 Nev. 158, 360 P.2d 839 (1961). This discretion may not be exercised in an arbitrary or cavalier manner. *Schulman v. Bongberg-Whitney Electric, Inc.,* 98 Nev. 226, 645 P.2d 434 (1982).

The landmark decision in this area, *Hotel Last Frontier Corp. v. Frontier Properties, Inc.,* 79 Nev. 150, 380 P.2d 293 (1963), catalogued the previous default judgment cases in Nevada and enumerated three guidelines for the exercise of discretion by the trial court. First, there must be the requisite showing of mistake, inadvertence, surprise or excusable neglect. Second, the showing of a meritorious defense must be made.

Third, the trial court must keep in mind the underlying policy that justice is best served by a decision on the merits of each case. The court also listed elements for deciding whether the first guideline has been shown:

(1) Prompt action to remove the judgment;
(2) An absence of intent to delay the proceedings;
(3) Lack of knowledge of a party or counsel of procedural requirements; and
(4) Good faith.

See also Yochum v. Davis, 98 Nev. 484, 653 P.2d 1215 (1982) and cases cited therein.

Hotel Last Frontier Corp. repeated the alternatives for the second guideline of a meritorious defense first expressed in *Minton v. Roliff*, 86 Nev. 478, 471 P.2d 209 (1970). *See* § 1022, *supra*.

Finally, for the third guideline, in *Hotel Last Frontier Corp.* the Nevada Supreme Court noted that it would be more likely to affirm a ruling setting aside a default judgment than to affirm a refusal to do so, since in the former case a trial upon the merits is assured, whereas in the latter it is denied forever.

A contrary result occurred in *Tahoe Village Realty v. DeSmet,* 95 Nev. 131, 590 P.2d 1158 (1979), where the attorney for the defendant withdrew without ever filing a responsive pleading on behalf of the client. In allowing the default to stand, the court noted that no attempt had been made to establish that the failure to file an answer was as a result of counsel's mistake, inadvertence or excusable neglect. The court also supported its decision by noting that, even if excusable neglect was shown, the showing of a meritorious defense was not made. The tacit message implied by this case is that the defaulted party's remedy was against his counsel, rather than in setting the default aside.

It is clear that an attorney's inexcusable neglect may be imputed to his clients. *DeSmet, id.; Intermountain Lumber & Builders Supply, Inc. v. Glens Falls Insurance Co.,* 83 Nev. 126, 424 P.2d 884 (1967); *Guardia v. Guardia,* 48 Nev. 230, 229 P. 386 (1924). Although neglect of an attorney may be chargeable to the client, misconduct of an attorney will not be visited upon the client. In *Staschel v. Weaver Brothers, Ltd.,* 98 Nev. 559, 655 P.2d 518, *vacating,* 98 Nev. 199, 644 P.2d 512 (1982), a default judgment was entered as a sanction for failure to comply with discovery. The defendant, who resided in Montana when the case was filed, returned to Nevada to find that the judgment had been entered. His attorney assured him the judgment would be vacated and his attorney advised that the case was "going smoothly." The Nevada Supreme Court noted that during this period the defendant's attorney had blatantly ignored court orders which led to the entry of a default judgment, and that his dereliction constituted "actual misconduct," which would not be charged to the client. After *Staschel,* the Supreme Court made clear that abandonment of the client by counsel will constitute excusable neglect under NRCP 60(b). *Dagher v. Dagher,* 103 Nev. 26, 731 P.2d 1329 (1987); *Passarelli v. J-Mar Development, Inc.,* 102 Nev. 283, 720 P.2d 1221 (1986). However, if manifest prejudice or injustice will result to the opposing party where attorney misconduct is at issue, a court may refuse to set aside the default judgment. *Still v. Huntley,* 102 Nev. 584, 729 P.2d 489 (1986).

§ 1027. Case developments after *Hotel Last Frontier.*

In *McClellan v. David,* 84 Nev. 283, 439 P.2d 673 (1968), a divided Supreme Court reversed the decision of the trial court finding that "no excusable neglect was shown as a matter of law." The defendant received two telephone calls from the plaintiff before the default was entered urging him to file an answer, which the defendant ignored. The majority held that in these circumstances, the failure to answer was not excusable and that the order setting aside the default was an abuse of discretion.

The following cases affirm the setting aside of a default judgment: *Banks v. Heater,* 95 Nev. 610, 600 P.2d 245 (1979); *Helitzer Advertising, Inc. v. Seven Star Media Corp.,* 89 Nev. 411, 514 P.2d 214 (1973); *Horton v. Pringle,* 88 Nev. 358, 498 P.2d 372 (1972); *Ogle v. Miller,* 87 Nev. 573, 491 P.2d 40 (1971).

The following cases affirm the denial of a motion to set aside a default judgment: *Union Petrochemical Corp. of Nevada v. Scott,* 96 Nev. 337, 609 P.2d 323 (1980); *Tahoe Village Realty v. DeSmet,* 95 Nev. 131, 590 P.2d 1158 (1979); *Molever v. Burton,* 94 Nev. 384, 580 P.2d 124 (1978); *Gemini, Inc. v. Fertil,* 92 Nev. 183, 547 P.2d 687 (1976); *Galardi v. Jonco Corp.,* 92 Nev. 194, 547 P.2d 667 (1976); *Britz v. Consolidated Casinos Corp.,* 87 Nev. 441, 488 P.2d 911 (1971).

In *Schulman v. Bongberg-Whitney Electric, Inc.,* 98 Nev. 226, 645 P.2d 434 (1982), the district court judge *sua sponte* entered a default judgment against the defendant when its counsel failed to appear for trial. The defendant filed for relief from the judgment averring that its counsel believed that the matter had been reset for trial. The plaintiff's attorney did not oppose the motion. Nevertheless, the trial court refused to vacate the judgment. The Nevada Supreme Court noted that although the decision was discretionary, the trial court could not be arbitrary or cavalier. The Court was convinced that the failure to appear constituted an innocent mistake and held that the requirements of NRCP 60(b)(1) had been met and the default judgment should be set aside. *See also Cen Val Leasing Corp. v. Bockman,* 99 Nev. 612, 668 P.2d 1074 (1983) (default judgment set aside on appeal since plaintiff's attorney knew identity of defendant's attorney, but failed to inquire as to attorney's intention to defend); *Gazin v. Hoy,* 102 Nev. 621, 730 P.2d 436 (1986) (defense counsel had requested an open extension of time to answer); *Yochum v. Davis,* 98 Nev. 484, 653 P.2d 1215 (1982) (defendants not on actual notice of proceedings against them); *Bruno v. Schoch,* 94 Nev. 712, 582 P.2d 796 (1978) (defendant surprised by entry of default judgment in paternity case); *Olsan v. Comora,* 91 Nev. 621, 541 P.2d 662 (1975) (mandamus issued to reverse trial court's denial of motion for relief from judgment); *Adams v. Lawson,* 84 Nev. 687, 448 P.2d 695 (1968) (insurance defense counsel's neglect inadvertent when he failed to discover a letter in a claim file terminating open extension of time to answer).

§ 1028. Fraud, misrepresentation, or other misconduct.

The second category for setting aside a default judgment is fraud (whether intrinsic or extrinsic), misrepresentation, or other misconduct of an adverse party which would justify a collateral attack upon the judgment. NRCP 60(b)(2). Extrinsic fraud exists when the defaulted party is kept away from the court by conduct which prevents a trial on the issues involved, or any other act or omission which procures the absence of the defaulted party at trial. *Price v. Dunn,* 106 Nev. 100, 787 P.2d 785 (1990). Further, when this ground is alleged it is not necessary to allege a meritorious defense. *Id.* 106 Nev. at 103.

In *Gilbert v. Warren,* 95 Nev. 296, 594 P.2d 696 (1979), the court noted that NRCP 60(b)(2) contemplated a "fraud upon the court," *citing Manville v. Manville,* 79 Nev. 487, 387 P.2d 661 (1963). Intrinsic fraud would include such actions as perjury, the use of forged documents or concealment of evidence. In *Gilbert,* the court dealt with a former version of NRCP 60(b)(2) which now has been amended to include both intrinsic and extrinsic fraud. Under this rule a motion on the ground of either intrinsic or extrinsic fraud must be made within six months.

The federal courts recognize a distinction between "fraud upon the court" and the fraud contemplated by FRCP 60(b)(2). The importance of the distinction is whether or not the six month time period has lapsed prior to bringing the motion. If Nevada does not make this distinction, then the clause of NRCP 60(b) allowing for an independent action, would be much broader than that authorized by the same language of the federal rule. It appears that Nevada intends to preserve extrinsic fraud as a grounds for collateral attack upon a judgment by independent action or motion. *See Occhiuto v. Occhiuto,* 97 Nev. 143, 625 P.2d 568 (1981); *Savage v. Salzmann,* 88 Nev. 193, 495 P.2d 367 (1972), and cases cited therein; *Murphy v. Murphy,* 103 Nev. 185, 186, 734 P.2d 738 (1987).

§ 1029. The judgment is void.

The third category for relief from judgments under NRCP 60(b) is that the judgment complained of is void. A motion made upon this ground is not limited to six months; the judgment may be challenged at any time. *Foster v. Lewis,* 78 Nev. 330, 372 P.2d 679 (1962). In the case of a void judgment the court has no discretion but must set the judgment aside.

A judgment is void where service of process is not proper or where personal jurisdiction is lacking for some other reason. *Milton v. Gesler,* 107 Nev. 767, 819 P.2d 245 (1991) (default judgment reversed due to lack of personal jurisdiction); *Sawyer v. Sugarless Shops, Inc.,* 106 Nev. 265, 792 P.2d 14 (1990) (no competent evidence of valid service of process); *BASF Corp. v. Jafbros, Inc.,* 105 Nev. 142, 771 P.2d 161 (1989) (default judgment set aside because summons not forwarded by secretary of state to corporation); *Orbit Stations, Inc. v. Curtis,* 100 Nev. 205, 678 P.2d 1153 (1984); *Phillips v. Incline Manor Association,* 91 Nev. 69, 530 P.2d 1207 (1975); *Kelley v. Kelley,* 85 Nev. 317, 454 P.2d 85 (1969); *Doyle v. Jorgensen,* 82 Nev. 196, 414 P.2d 707 (1966). A judgment may also be attacked as void where the court which entered the challenged judgment was previously disqualified from acting in the case, *Osman v. Cobb,* 77 Nev. 133, 360 P.2d 258 (1961), or where the court lacked subject matter jurisdiction. *See Swan v. Swan,* 106 Nev. 464, 796 P.2d 221 (1990). *See also* § 2523, *infra.* A judgment taken without notice to a party who has appeared by requesting an extension of time to answer is void. *Gazin v. Hoy,* 102 Nev. 621, 730 P.2d 436 (1986).

§ 1030. The judgment has been satisfied, released, etc.

NRCP 60(b)(4) provides that a default may be set aside: (1) when the judgment has been satisfied, released, or discharged; (2) in circumstances where the prior judgment upon which it is based has been reversed or otherwise vacated; or (3) in a situation where it is no longer equitable to continue to enforce an injunction. *Grouse Creek Ranches v. Budget Financial Corp.,* 87 Nev. 419, 488 P.2d 917 (1971). A motion based upon this category of relief must be made within a reasonable time. The federal rule, FRCP 60(b)(4), allows relief when "it is no longer equitable that the *judgment* should have prospective application" (emphasis added). The Nevada rule limits the court to a determination that "it is no longer equitable that an *injunction* should have prospective application" (emphasis added).

§ 1031. Independent actions to set aside.

NRCP 60(b) contemplates two distinct procedures for obtaining relief from final judgment — by motion and by independent action. An independent action is considered to be a new civil action, not a motion under NRCP 60(b). When a proceeding is an independent action to obtain equitable relief from a prior judgment, it is not brought under NRCP 60(b), and hence the time limitation contained in the rule has no application. The only time limitations on independent actions under NRCP 60(b) are laches or a relevant statute of limitations. *Nevada Industrial Development, Inc. v. Benedetti,* 103 Nev. 360, 741 P.2d 802 (1987).

In addition to giving the four grounds for setting aside default judgments, NRCP 60(b) also confirms the power of a court to entertain an independent action to relieve a party from a judgment, order, or proceeding or to set aside a judgment for fraud upon the court. This portion of the rule was construed by the Nevada Supreme Court to afford relief upon proof of extrinsic fraud. *Murphy v. Murphy,* 103 Nev. 185, 734 P.2d 738 (1987); *Manville v. Manville,* 79 Nev. 487, 387 P.2d 661 (1963); *Savage v. Salzmann,* 88 Nev. 193, 495 P.2d 367 (1972). Under these cases, the six-month limitation of NRCP 60(b)(2) had no application. *Manville, supra; Savage, supra.* Thus, when the six-month period had run, proof of extrinsic fraud formed a basis for attacking a judgment and the extrinsic versus intrinsic fraud distinction was revitalized.

The Nevada Supreme Court later noted in *Occhiuto v. Occhiuto,* 97 Nev. 143, 625 P.2d 568 (1981), that its interpretation of NRCP 60(b) was "out of step" with the federal rule. Clearly, NRCP 60(b)(2) has, by amendment, now been brought into step with the federal rule. *See* § 1028, *supra.* This leaves open the question whether the court intended to bring the "fraud upon the court" provision into line with the federal rule, which is very limited in application. If the Nevada rule parallels the federal rule, then the interpretations of *Manville* and *Savage* would not be important.

A court, in an independent action, may modify a final judgment in a former proceeding on the ground of mistake as well as fraud, at least where mutual mistake is shown and where the party seeking relief is without fault or negligence. *Nevada Industrial Development, Inc. v. Benedetti,* 103 Nev. 360, 741 P.2d 802 (1987).

§ 1032. Set aside of a default judgment where defendant not personally served: Rule 60(c).

In cases where substituted service is appropriate, a defendant who has not been personally served is nevertheless subject to a valid default judgment. Default judgments taken in this manner may be set aside if the defaulted party moves within six months of the judgment for an order vacating it under NRCP 60(c). This rule is strictly limited to default judgments, and the only requisites are timeliness, lack of personal service, and the existence of a meritorious defense. *BASF Corp. v.*

Jafbros, Inc., 105 Nev. 142, 771 P.2d 161 (1989). *Spinosa v. Rowe,* 87 Nev. 27, 480 P.2d 157 (1971); *Jenkins v. Goldwater,* 84 Nev. 422, 442 P.2d 897 (1968).

§ 1033. Appearances which may inure to the benefit of co-defendants.

The practitioner should be aware of the possibility pointed out in *Paul v. Pool,* 96 Nev. 130, 605 P.2d 635 (1980), of a defaulting defendant being able to set aside the default judgment based on a co-defendant's answer. In *Paul,* the defaulting defendant had statutory vicarious liability for the answering defendant's negligence. The court found that the answer inured to the benefit of the defaulting defendant "where there exists, as here, a common defense as to both of them."

As a result of this decision, if a default judgment is to be taken against co-defendants there must be a determination as to whether or not the answer of one might inure to the benefit of the other. If there is defense common to both, as in the case of vicarious liability, then it would appear under *Paul* that default judgment cannot be taken. *See also Gearhart v. Pierce Enterprises, Inc.,* 105 Nev. 517, 779 P.2d 93 (1989).

Form 10A

CASE NO.
DEPT. NO.

IN THE SECOND JUDICIAL DISTRICT COURT
OF THE STATE OF NEVADA IN AND FOR THE COUNTY OF
WASHOE

* * * * * * * *

Plaintiff,

vs.   **NOTICE OF INTENT**
                                        TO TAKE DEFAULT

Defendant.

_____

TO:

   NOTICE IS HEREBY GIVEN that Plaintiff herein intends to take the default of Defendant, _____, on the _____ day of _____, 19_____, for the failure to file an Answer or otherwise respond to the Complaint on file herein.

   DATED: This _____ day of _____, 19_____.

FIRM:

COUNSEL:

_____

Form 10B

CASE NO.
DEPT. NO.

IN THE SECOND JUDICIAL DISTRICT COURT
OF THE STATE OF NEVADA IN AND FOR THE COUNTY OF
WASHOE

* * * * * * * *

Plaintiff,

vs.

Defendant.

**APPLICATION FOR ENTRY
OF DEFAULT**

TO: _____ CLERK OF THE COURT FOR THE SECOND JUDICIAL DISTRICT COURT OF THE STATE OF NEVADA IN AND FOR THE COUNTY OF WASHOE

Please enter the Default of the Defendant _____ for the failure to plead or otherwise defend the above-entitled action as provided by the Nevada Rules of Civil Procedure, as appears from the Affidavit of _____ (Counsel for Plaintiff) attached hereto.

DATED: This ____ day of _____, 19____.

FIRM:

COUNSEL:

Form 10C

District Court

CLARK COUNTY, NEVADA

Plaintiff,

—vs—

Defendant.

Case No. _____

Dept. No. _____

Docket No. _____

DEFAULT

It appearing from the files and records in the above entitled action that _____

_____

Defendant(s) herein, being duly served with a copy of the Summons and Complaint on the _____

_____ ;

that more than 20 days, exclusive of the day of service, having expired since service upon the Defendant(s); that no answer or

other appearance having been filed and no further time having been granted, the default of the above-named Defendant(s) for

failing to answer or otherwise plead to Plaintiff's Complaint is hereby entered.

The undersigned hereby requests
and directs the entry of default

_____

Attorney for

LORETTA BOWMAN, CLERK OF COURT

By: _____

DEPUTY CLERK   Date

Form 10D

CASE NO.
DEPT. NO.

IN THE SECOND JUDICIAL DISTRICT COURT
OF THE STATE OF NEVADA IN AND FOR THE COUNTY OF
WASHOE

* * * * * * * *

Plaintiff,

vs.   **APPLICATION FOR
                                                      DEFAULT JUDGMENT**

Defendant.

Plaintiff moves the above-entitled Court to enter a Default Judgment in favor of Plaintiff and against Defendant _____, in the principal amount of $_____, together with interest accruing at the rate of _____ % per annum or $_____ per day from _____ (date), until paid in full, plus costs in the amount of $_____ and reasonable attorneys' fees.

This Application is made on the ground that a Default has been entered against said Defendant for failure to answer or otherwise defend as to the Complaint on behalf of Plaintiff and that said Defendant is not in the military service of the United States nor an infant or incompetent person.

In support of this Application, Plaintiff relies on the Affidavit of _____ (Counsel or Plaintiff), attached hereto and incorporated by reference herein, and all records, papers, files and pleadings on file herein.

DATED: This _____ day of _____, 19____.

FIRM:

COUNSEL:

Attorneys for Plaintiff

Form 10E

CASE NO.
DEPT. NO.

IN THE SECOND JUDICIAL DISTRICT COURT
OF THE STATE OF NEVADA IN AND FOR THE COUNTY OF
WASHOE

* * * * * * * *

Plaintiff,

vs.

Defendant.

**AFFIDAVIT IN SUPPORT
OF APPLICATION FOR
DEFAULT JUDGMENT**

STATE OF NEVADA   )
                   : ss.
COUNTY OF WASHOE   )

I, _____ (Counsel), do hereby swear under penalty of perjury that the following assertions are true to the best of my knowledge and belief and as provided to me by my client:

1. Affiant is the attorney for Plaintiff in the above-entitled action and has made careful investigation in the cause, and has been informed and believes that Defendant _____, is not in the military service of the United States nor an infant or incompetent person.

2. Defendant was served (explain manner and date of service of summons), he/she has not answered, and a default has been entered.

3. Affiant is further informed and believes that there is now due and owing from Defendant to Plaintiff the principal sum of $_____, together with interest accruing at the rate of ____% per annum or $_____ per day from _____ (date) until paid in full.

4. Plaintiff has incurred costs in the amount of $_____ and is entitled to reasonable attorneys' fees in the above-entitled matter. Plaintiff has incurred $_____ through the _____ (date) in attorneys' fees in this matter. A copy of the billing history is attached hereto.

_____
(Counsel)

SUBSCRIBED AND SWORN to
before me this _____
day of _____, 19____.

_____
NOTARY PUBLIC

173

Form 10F

CASE NO.
DEPT. NO.

IN THE SECOND JUDICIAL DISTRICT COURT OF THE STATE OF NEVADA IN AND FOR THE COUNTY OF WASHOE

* * * * * * * *

Plaintiff,

vs.   **DEFAULT JUDGMENT**

Defendant.

An Application having been duly made by Plaintiff for judgment against Defendant _____, and the default of said Defendant having been entered for failure to answer or otherwise defend as to the Complaint of Plaintiff, and it appearing that said Defendant is not in the military service of the United States and is not an infant or incompetent person, and good cause appearing therefor,

IT IS ORDERED that Plaintiff recover of and from Defendant _____, as follows:

The principal sum of $_____, accrued interest from _____ (date) to _____ (date) in the amount of $_____, together with interest accruing on the principal amount at the rate of ____ % per annum from _____ (date) until paid in full, costs of suit in the amount of $_____ and attorneys' fees in the amount of $_____.

DATED: This _____ day of _____, 19____.

_____
DISTRICT JUDGE

Form 10G

District Court

CLARK COUNTY, NEVADA

Plaintiff,

—vs—

Case No. _____

Dept. No. _____

Docket No. _____

Defendant.

MEMORANDUM OF COSTS
AND DISBURSEMENTS

Filing	$	_____
Service of Process	$	_____
Jury Fees	$	_____
Witness Fees	$	_____
Sheriff's Fees	$	_____
Record & Certify Judgment	$	_____
Garnishment & Execution Fees	$	_____
_____	$	_____
_____	$	_____
TOTAL	$	_____

STATE OF NEVADA

COUNTY OF CLARK

_____, being duly sworn, states: that affiant is the attorney for the _____ and has personal knowledge of the above costs and disbursements expended; that the items contained in the above memorandum are true and correct to the best of this affiant's knowledge and belief; and that the said disbursements have been necessarily incurred and paid in this action.

SUBSCRIBED AND SWORN to before me this _____ day of _____, 19_____.

_____

Attorney for

_____

NOTARY PUBLIC

175

CHAPTER 11

MOTIONS, AFFIDAVITS, STIPULATIONS AND ORDERS

Author: Evan J. Wallach

§ 1101. Introduction and scope.

A large part of civil practice consists of making or opposing motions. In many cases motions may be dispositive. This chapter describes the procedure for making or opposing a motion or "order to show cause"; the use of affidavits, stipulations and orders; reconsideration of motions; and the authority of the clerk to grant motions.

§ 1102. Motions.

Unless otherwise provided by statute, an applicant must formally move the court for an order. NRCP 7(b)(1). A motion is an application for

177

an order in a proceeding directed to the court's authority to act on a given subject. *Iveson v. Second Judicial District Court,* 66 Nev. 145, 206 P.2d 755 (1949). Where a written notice of the hearing of a motion is also used, the motion may be stated in the notice. *See* Form 11B and § 1105, *infra.*

When a practitioner applies to a court for relief pursuant to a statute specifically authorizing that remedy, the statute should be carefully examined for special requirements. An "order to show cause" procedure is frequently required. *See* § 1125, *infra.* For example, a "summons to show cause" is required to add additional persons as joint debtors upon a judgment already entered. NRS 17.030. A motion is not a "pleading," as defined by NRCP 7(a). *See* § 802.

§ 1103. — Motions required to be in writing.

Unless a motion is made during a hearing or a trial, it must be in writing. NRCP 7(b)(1). While oral motions during trial frequently address the admissibility of evidence, many other requests for court action, such as a motion for involuntary dismissal [NRCP 41(b)] or a motion for a directed verdict [NRCP 50(a)] may also be made orally. Unless plaintiff's counsel makes a timely objection, a co-defendant may orally join in a written motion for summary judgment timely submitted by another co-defendant. *Exber, Inc. v. Sletten Construction Co.,* 92 Nev. 721, 558 P.2d 517 (1976); *Wagner v. Carex Investigations & Security, Inc.,* 93 Nev. 627, 572 P.2d 921 (1977).

§ 1104. — Contents of motions.

A motion must state with particularity its grounds and set forth the relief or order sought. NRCP 7(b)(1); *United Pacific Insurance Co. v. St. Denis,* 81 Nev. 103, 399 P.2d 135 (1965) (A motion to hold the defendant liable "as alleged in the complaint" is fatally defective). *See* Form 11A, *infra.* The requirement of a written motion stating the grounds with particularity is intended to guarantee that the adverse party be informed, not only of the motion's pendency, but also of its basis. *Monroe, Ltd. v. Central Telephone Co.,* 91 Nev. 450, 538 P.2d 152 (1975). However, a party who fails to object to the motion for lack of particularity waives the objection. *Grouse Creek Ranches v. Budget Financial Corp.,* 87 Nev. 419, 488 P.2d 917 (1971).

A written motion must have a caption similar to pleadings and be signed in accordance with Rule 11. *See* Introductory Statement to the Appendix of Forms of NRCP; NRCP 7(b)(2), NRCP 7(b)(3).

§ 1105. — Notice of motion, filing, service.

Unless local rules otherwise provide, all motions must contain or be accompanied by a notice of motion with due proof of service of the same. DCR 13; EDCR 2.20(a); FJDCR 13A; *see* Form 11A, *infra.* Where a written notice of a hearing of the motion is used, the motion may be stated in the notice. NRCP 7(b)(1); Form 11B, *infra.* In practice, the notice of a hearing is only used in the Eighth District.

Filing a motion means filing with the clerk of the court. The judge may permit the papers to be filed with him, in which event he shall note thereon the filing date and forthwith transmit them to the office of the clerk. NRCP 5(e). Filing with the court is designed to avoid delay, for example, in implementing temporary restraining orders or in issuing attachments. It can be done even when the clerk's office is closed. Filing is a prerequisite to effectiveness of the order. *See* NRS 1.130. *See also* § 1121, *infra.*

Service of a motion must be made as required by NRCP 5. *See* the discussion in § 919, *supra,* and Forms 11D, 11E, 11G and 11H, *infra.*

Where contempt proceedings are not original proceedings but are incidental to a pending cause, service upon counsel of record is proper. *Caplow v. Eighth Judicial District Court,* 72 Nev. 265, 302 P.2d 755 (1956).

Motions filed in the Eighth District must not only be noticed but must be set for hearing not less than twenty-one days from the date the motion is served and filed. EDCR 2.20(a). [The twenty-one days is reduced to ten days for domestic matters. EDCR 5.82(a)]. Further, the motion must be set on a day when the judge to which the case is assigned is hearing civil motions. The judges of the Eighth District with odd department numbers hear civil motions on Mondays and Wednesdays. Judges with even numbered departments hear civil motions on Tuesdays and Thursdays. The clerk prefers that the date in a notice of motion be left blank and delivered to the clerk's office before service. The clerk will select a day when the judge is available to hear the matter and then "reserve" that time for the hearing.

The Eighth District maintains lockboxes in the lobby of the court in which courtesy copies of motions, affidavits, points and authorities, or other papers may be deposited. Attorneys are requested to leave courtesy copies for the court of any paper filed within five days of a hearing at which the paper may be considered. Courtesy copies must indicate the date of any hearing to which they pertain. EDCR 7.26(b).

§ 1106. — Points and authorities.

A party filing a motion shall also serve and file with it a memorandum of points and authorities in support of each ground. The absence of such a memorandum may be construed as an admission that the motion is not meritorious, providing cause for its denial or as a waiver of all grounds not supported by points and authorities. DCR 13(2). *See also* FJDCR 13E; WDCR 11(1); DCR 6D; Seventh DCR 10(2); EDCR 2.20(a).

"Points" refers to the propositions or questions of law which pertain to the motion. "Authorities" refers to constitutional, statutory, case or secondary authority which supports the points raised. Therefore, the requirement of "points and authorities" includes both points of law succinctly stated and citations to authority which support those principles. Memoranda which consist of bare citations to statutes, rules or case authority do not comply with the requirements of the rule. In the Eighth and Ninth Districts, the court may decline to consider any motion, response or reply which consists only of bare citations to authority. EDCR 2.20(e); NJDCR 5(1). Such bare citations are bad form in the other districts.

The author of any memorandum of points and authorities should avoid "string" citations. Where available, discussion of a directly relevant controlling authority is far more persuasive than multiple citations for the same proposition. A party may file supporting evidence including affidavits, depositions and discovery responses. NRCP 56(e).

Within ten days after the service of a motion, the opposing party must serve and file a written opposition together with a memorandum of points and authorities and supporting affidavits, if any, stating facts showing why the motion should be denied. Failure to serve and file a written opposition may be construed as an admission that the motion is meritorious and as consent to its being granted. DCR 13(3). *See also* FJDCR 13C and 13E; WDCR 11(2); Third DCR 6B and 60; Seventh DCR 10(2); EDCR 5.82(b). *Cf. Orcutt v. Russell F. Miller, M.D.,* 95 Nev. 408, 595 P.2d 1191 (1979) (estoppel to assert untimeliness of opposition where movant's own procedural derelictions during discovery may have contributed to opponent's inability to timely submit an affidavit).

The moving party may serve and file reply points and authorities within five days after service of the answering points and authorities. DCR 13(4). *See also* FJDCR 13D, which allows ten days; WDCR 11(3), which allows five days; Third DCR 6C, which allows ten days; and EDCR 2.20(d), which permits a reply not later than five days before the matter is set for hearing.

When the time for hearing a motion is shortened, the opposition may not have ten days in which to respond, and counsel will not have the time to comply with rules such as WDCR 11(2) and EDCR 2.20(b). Counsel should file the response as soon as possible or, at the least, bring the response to the hearing. Since the recently filed points and authorities may not be placed in the court's file before the hearing date, counsel should deliver a courtesy copy to the judge's chambers. *See* EDCR

7.26(b). In the Eighth District, a reply memorandum may not be filed in open court without court approval. EDCR 2.20(d).

In the Eighth District, all interested parties to a motion may stipulate to continue the day fixed for the filing of a response or a reply thereto. Such a stipulation is ineffective unless it: (1) is in writing; (2) is filed with the clerk before the day fixed for filing the response or reply; and (3) contains an agreement extending the date for the hearing of the motion not less than the number of days granted as a continuance for the filing of a response or reply. EDCR 2.22(c). Failure to follow this rule may result in the court granting the motion as unopposed prior to the hearing.

§ 1107. Affidavits.

Factual contentions involved in any pre-trial or post-trial motion shall be initially presented and heard upon affidavits. DCR 13(6). *See also* EDCR 2.21(a). They must be filed with the motion or opposition to which they pertain. DCR 13 (2, 3, and 5). *See also* WDCR 11(1) and EDCR 2.21(b). Section 1111 discusses the testimony of live witnesses at the hearing of motions.

§ 1108. — Form of affidavits.

An affidavit to be used by either party must identify the affiant, the party on whose behalf it is submitted, and the motion or application to which it pertains. DCR 13(5). *See also* EDCR 2.21(b).

Affidavits shall contain only factual, evidentiary matter, shall conform with the requirements of NRCP 56(e) and shall avoid mere general conclusions or argument. DCR 13(5). An affidavit may only be made on personal knowledge by a competent witness and set forth facts admissible in evidence. Sworn or certified copies of all papers or parts of papers referred to in an affidavit must be attached to or served with it. NRCP 56(e). *See also* EDCR 2.21(c); *see* Form 11C, *infra,* and § 1771, *infra,* which describe their requirements.

§ 1109. — Defective affidavits.

The court may strike affidavits which do not comply with the requirements set forth in § 1108. DCR 13(5). *See also* EDCR 2.21(c); *see generally State v. Fourth Judicial District Court,* 68 Nev. 527, 238 P.2d 1125 (1951). To have an affidavit stricken, the practitioner may file a motion to strike and obtain an order shortening the time for this motion's hearing or submission to a time at or before the time set for the hearing or submission of the motion to which the defective affidavit pertains. In the

Eighth District, the practitioner should use a countermotion. *See* § 1113, *infra.*

If a party does not object to inadmissible matters in the adverse party's affidavit, the otherwise inadmissible matters may be considered by the district court, and the issue of admissibility may not be raised on appeal. *See Whalen v. State,* 100 Nev. 192, 679 P.2d 248 (1984) (unauthenticated document attached to summary judgment affidavit).

§ 1110. — Hearings on motions.

The practice of hearing motions varies widely throughout Nevada, not only among districts but among the judges in multi-judge courts. Thus, depending upon the local rules of court and the policy of the judge, testimony may or may not be received and oral argument may or may not be allowed. *See* NRCP 43(c).

The presentation of testimony depends largely upon the affidavits. Since factual contentions involved in a motion must be presented and heard upon affidavits, oral testimony may be received at a hearing only with the approval of the judge. The purpose of the testimony, if allowed, is to resolve conflicts in the affidavits — factual issues shown by the affidavits to be in dispute. Where affidavits reveal material conflicts and oral testimony appears to be necessary, counsel should check with the clerk or the judge's secretary to determine whether or not the witnesses should be brought to a scheduled hearing. The court may set the matter for hearing at some time in the future to resolve these factual issues. DCR 13(6). In the Eighth District, oral testimony may not be received at the hearing, except upon the stipulation of the parties and with the approval of the court. EDCR 2.21(a).

Oral argument in a motion is a privilege, not a right. NRCP 78. Most districts require the clerk, upon request of a party, to simply submit the matter to the court for decision. FJDCR 13 (F); WDCR 11(3); Third DCR 6(g)(3). In the Ninth District, the clerk submits motions automatically upon expiration of the time for filing reply points and authorities. The court then renders a decision unless it orders oral argument, in which event the clerk sets a date and time for hearing. NJDCR 5.

In the First, Second, Third and Ninth Districts, motions are decided without oral argument unless argument is ordered by the court *sua sponte* or upon request of a party. In the Third and Ninth Districts such requests must be granted with respect to any motion which would dispose of the case on the merits with prejudice unless the motion is denied. FJDCR 13(I); WDCR 14(4); Third DCR 6(g); NJDCR 5(4).

In the Eighth District, all motions must be noticed for hearing. EDCR 2.22 and 5.82. The judge may decide the motion before the hearing date, in which event it will be removed from the calendar and the clerk will enter an order upon the minutes of the court reflecting the action taken. EDCR 2.23(c). If the motion is not decided before the hearing date, counsel for each party to the motion must appear on the date and at the time set for the hearing. EDCR 2.22(A). A hearing in the Eighth District may be continued by stipulation between all interested parties to a motion; however, a written stipulation must be filed not less than one full judicial day before the hearing date. If the stipulation is not in writing, counsel for the movant must appear at the hearing to present the oral stipulation. If the parties, by stipulation, vacate or continue a hearing, they may reset it only by stipulation or by a new notice of motion. The new hearing date must not be less than seven days from the date that the new notice of stipulation is filed. If the motion's hearing date has been set by the judge, counsel must obtain the judge's approval before the hearing will be continued or vacated. EDCR 2.22(b).

§ 1111. — Submitted causes.

Between the fifth and tenth day of each month, the clerk of each district court must compile (by department in the case of counties having more than one department) and post a list of all motions and other matters submitted for decision and undecided, including date of submission, for a period of sixty days or more. Counsel must examine the list and, before the fifteenth day of each month, notify the clerk and the court by letter of any submitted matters omitted from the list. NRCP 77(e). *Cf.* NRS 3.290 and 3.295.

§ 1112. — Reconsideration of motions.

Unless prohibited from doing so by rule or statute, a court has the power to rehear a motion and reconsider its orders. When a motion has been denied and a further hearing is sought, the proper procedure is to ask leave to renew the motion or to receive a rehearing. *Murphy v. Murphy,* 64 Nev. 440, 183 P.2d 632 (1947).

Reconsideration is proper if upon motion the court consents to the rehearing. *Harvey's Wagonwheel, Inc. v. MacSween,* 96 Nev. 215, 606 P.2d 1095 (1980); DCR 13(7); FJDCR 13 (J) and EDCR 2.24. Rehearings are not granted as a matter of right and are not allowed for the purpose of reargument unless there is a reasonable probability that the court may have arrived at an erroneous conclusion. *Geller v. McCowan,* 64 Nev. 106, 178 P.2d 380 (1947). *See also State ex rel. Copeland v. Woodbury,* 17 Nev. 337, 30 P. 1006 (1883). Of course, a change in circumstances may justify the granting of a second motion for relief identical to one previously denied. *Trail v. Faretto,* 91 Nev. 401, 536 P.2d 1026 (1975).

The primary purpose of a petition for rehearing is to inform the court that it has overlooked an important argument or fact or misread or misunderstood a statute, case or fact in the record. A party may not raise a new point for the first time on rehearing. *See In re Ross*, 99 Nev. 657, 668 P.2d 1089 (1983). Indeed, only in very rare instances in which new issues of fact or law are raised supporting a ruling contrary to the ruling already reached, should a motion for rehearing be granted. *Moore v. City of Las Vegas,* 92 Nev. 402, 551 P.2d 244 (1976). A second motion for rehearing is not favored, and the court abuses its discretion when it entertains a second motion which simply cites additional authorities for the same proposition of law. *Moore v. City of Las Vegas,* 92 Nev. 402, 551 P.2d 244 (1976).

Except in the Eighth District, no statute or rule limits the time within which a motion for reconsideration may be filed. In *Giles v. Gibbs,* 96 Nev. 243, 607 P.2d 118 (1980), the supreme court stated that "unless and until an order is appealed, the district court retains jurisdiction to reconsider the matter." NRCP 54(b) provides that an intermediate order which adjudicates fewer than all the claims or the rights and liabilities of fewer than all the parties "is subject to revision at any time before the entry of judgment." The case of *In re Herrmann,* 100 Nev. 1, 677 P.2d 594 (1984), however, may be read as holding that the trial court lacks jurisdiction to grant rehearing of an appealable order after the time to appeal has expired.

In the Eighth District, a party seeking reconsideration of a ruling of the court, other than an order which may be addressed by motion pursuant to NRCP 50(b), 52(b), 59 or 60, must file a motion for such relief within ten days after service of written notice of the order or judgment unless the time is shortened or enlarged by order. EDCR 2.24(b).

A motion for rehearing does not toll the thirty-day period for filing a notice of appeal from a final order or judgment. *Able Electric, Inc. v. Kaufman,* 104 Nev. 29, 752 P.2d 218 (1988); *Alvis v. State,* 99 Nev. 184, 660 P.2d 980 (1983). Therefore, where counsel wishes the court to reconsider an appealable order, it is imperative that the court decide the motion for rehearing before the thirty days to appeal expires. If the thirty days expires while the motion for rehearing is still pending, the right to appeal is lost. If counsel files the notice of appeal, the trial court is divested of jurisdiction to reconsider that order. *Gibbs v. Giles,* 96 Nev. 243, 607 P.2d 118 (1980); *cf. Wilmurth v. First Judicial District Court,* 80 Nev. 337, 393 P.2d 302 (1964) (attempted appeal from a nonappealable order does not divest trial court of jurisdiction to reconsider).

§ 1113. — Countermotions.

In the Eighth Judicial District only, the court may consider an opposition to a motion to be a countermotion if it contains a motion related to the same subject matter. Without a notice of motion, a countermotion will be heard and decided at the same time set for the hearing of the original motion that it opposed. EDCR 2.20(c).

§ 1114. Stipulations.

A stipulation is an agreement between the parties to a cause or their counsel on their behalf. It may affect the procedural rights of one or both of the parties or it may be substantive in nature.

With few exceptions, the courts encourage both procedural and substantive stipulations. Stipulations are of an inestimable value in the administration of justice. *Second Baptist Church of Reno v. Mount Zion Baptist Church,* 86 Nev. 164, 466 P.2d 212 (1970). *See also Gottwals v. Rencher,* 60 Nev. 47, 98 P.2d 1481 (1940). Agreements to settle all or a portion of a pending case are substantive since they resolve a dispute and terminate litigation. Agreements to extend the time to plead or file points and authorities, to waive an objection to the admissibility of evidence or to admit that certain facts are true and not subject to dispute are generally procedural in nature. While they affect procedural rights of the parties to the cause they have no direct bearing on the eventual outcome of the litigation.

There are, however, a few procedural rights or duties that cannot be altered by stipulation, *e.g.,* counsel may not extend the time to file a motion for judgment n.o.v., motion to amend findings, motion for new trial or motion to set aside an order or judgment. NRCP 6(b). In the First, Eighth and Ninth Districts, trial settings may not be vacated solely by stipulation; a court order is required. FJDCR 4, EDCR 7.30(b) and NJDCR 7(3). This is also true in the Second District where WDCR 12 allows a continuance only upon a showing of good cause, the determination of which requires court action.

All stipulations, whether in court or out of court agreements, must satisfy the requirements of DCR 16. *See Resnick v. Valente,* 97 Nev. 615, 637 P.2d 1205 (1981) and § 1115, *infra.*

§ 1115. — Form of stipulation.

A stipulation requires assent to its terms in order to be valid. *Szilagyi v. Testa,* 99 Nev. 843, 673 P.2d 495 (1983).

DCR 16 provides as follows:

No agreement or stipulation between the parties in a cause or their attorneys, in respect to proceedings therein, will be regarded unless the same shall, by consent, be entered in the minutes in the form of an order, or unless the same shall be in writing subscribed by the party against whom the same shall be alleged, or by his attorney. *See also* EDCR 7.50.

185

It is clear from this rule that oral stipulations are ineffective for any purpose as regards the lawsuit to which they pertain. Even an oral stipulation which settles the case is unenforceable by motion in the pending action. *Casentini v. Hines,* 97 Nev. 186, 625 P.2d 1174 (1981) (an oral stipulation which appeared in the transcript of the proceedings but was not entered in the minutes in the form of an order was unenforceable). *Resnick v. Valente,* 97 Nev. 615, 637 P.2d 1205 (1981) (counsel's acceptance of an oral settlement offer could not be enforced by motion). *Szilagyi v. Testa,* 99 Nev. 843, 673 P.2d 495 (1983) (a stipulation not entered in the minutes was unenforceable).

DCR 16 recognizes only two forms of stipulations as enforceable: (1) a written stipulation, which clearly means a writing signed by the party or his attorney; or (2) a stipulation entered in the court minutes in the form of an order, which clearly means that both the contents of the stipulation and the court's adoption of it as an order must be contained within the minute order. *See Prostack v. Lowden,* 96 Nev. 230, 606 P.2d 1099 (1980) (an oral stipulation extending the five-year period prescribed by NRCP 41(e) to bring a case to trial is the equivalent of a written stipulation if it is "entered into in open court, approved by the judge, and spread upon the minutes"). Careful counsel will check the minute entry to insure that it contains the agreement of the parties and, if not, request the judge to direct a change in the minutes to reflect the correct stipulation along with the court's adoption of the stipulation as an order. Reliance or partial performance will not cure a defective minute entry. *Humana, Inc. v. Nguyen,* 102 Nev. 507, 728 P.2d 816 (1986).

A written stipulation prepared for filing with the court should have a caption similar to that of the summons. *See* paragraph 2 of the Introductory Statement to the Appendix of Forms of NRCP; NRCP 7(b)(2).

§ 1116. — Contents of stipulation.

The difference between procedural and substantive stipulations is discussed in § 1115, *supra,* as are a few of the procedural stipulations which are prohibited.

A stipulation of fact which dispenses with formal proof is common practice and the practice is encouraged by the courts. *Gottwals v. Rencher,* 60 Nev. 47, 98 P.2d 481 (1940). *See also* Chapter 18, *infra.*

While the parties may stipulate to the facts, they may not bind the court with a stipulation regarding the law to be applied. *Cf. Beko v. Kelly,* 78 Nev. 489, 376 P.2d 429 (1962). Nor may they stipulate to the unconstitutionality of a statute, *State ex rel. Bible v. Malone,* 68 Nev. 36, 231 P.2d 599 (1951), or enter into a stipulation which ignores the positive requirements of the law. *April Fool Gold Mining & Milling Co. v. Dula,* 24 Nev. 289, 52 P. 648 (1898). They may, however, stipulate to waive a right otherwise available to them under the law. *Wheeler v. Floral Mill & Mining Co.,* 10 Nev. 200 (1875) (a stipulation waiving a right to appeal is enforceable); *see also Walsh v. Wallace,* 26 Nev. 299, 67 P. 914 (1902) (enforcing a stipulation which was intended to extend the statutory time to file a statement on motion for new trial).

§ 1117. — Construction and enforcement of stipulations.

Stipulations between parties should receive a fair and liberal construction in harmony with the apparent intentions of the parties and the spirit of justice, and in the furtherance of fair trials upon the merits. *Walsh v. Wallace,* 26 Nev. 299, 67 P. 914 (1902).

Generally, a court is free to enforce a valid stipulation. *Conrad v. Sadur,* 83 Nev. 39, 422 P.2d 236 (1967). Indeed, because stipulations are of an inestimable value in the administration of justice they "are controlling and conclusive and both trial and appellate courts are bound to enforce them." *Second Baptist Church of Reno v. Mount Zion Baptist Church,* 86 Nev. 164, 466 P.2d 212 (1970) (stipulation between two factions of the church to be bound by the results of a court-supervised election); *Garaventa v. Gardella,* 63 Nev. 304, 169 P.2d 540 (1946) (stipulation to waive a rule of evidence).

Since the enforcement of a stipulation is by order and an application for an order is by motion, it is proper to enforce the stipulation by noticing a motion for appropriate relief. Unless some rule or statute specifically allows such an application or unless the stipulation itself so provides, the application to enforce the stipulation should not be made ex parte.

An oral stipulation which does not comply with DCR 14 may not be enforced by motion. *Resnick v. Valente,* 97 Nev. 615, 637 P.2d 1205 (1981); *Casentini v. Hines,* 97 Nev. 186, 625 P.2d 1174 (1981).

While an oral stipulation may not be enforced by motion, it may be enforced in some other appropriate fashion. If an independent action on such an oral agreement is prosecuted, the court may consider such issues as "the authority of counsel, the nature of communications between counsel and client, and the existence of a meeting of minds by the parties ...." The court should base any judgment upon the contract of the parties. *Resnick v. Valente,* 97 Nev. 615, 637 P.2d 1205 (1981).

§ 1118. — Relief from stipulations.

A court may set aside a stipulation upon a showing that it was entered into through mistake, fraud, collusion, accident or some ground of like nature. *See Citicorp Services v. Lee,* 99 Nev. 511, 665 P.2d 265 (1983); *Gottwals v. Rencher,* 60 Nev. 47, 98 P.2d 481 (1940). *Cf. Nevada Industrial Commission v. Bibb,* 77 Nev. 8, 358 P.2d 360 (1961).

Whether a court should set aside a stipulation on such grounds is generally left to the discretion of the trial court. *Citicorp Services v. Lee,* 99 Nev. 511, 665 P.2d 265 (1983) (abuse of discretion to relieve a party from an agreement to provide a particular witness for a deposition).

Generally, an attorney has the implied authority to bind his client for the management and conduct of the cause while the cause is pending before the court for determination. *Gottwals v. Rencher,* 60 Nev. 47, 98 P.2d 481 (1940). *See also* SCR 45. The attorney's implied power to bind his client includes the power to make admissions of fact, which admissions dispense the necessity of proof. *Gottwals, supra.*

In *Gottwals v. Rencher,* 60 Nev. 47, 92 P.2d 481 (1940), the supreme court emphasized the importance of upholding stipulations of fact and it seems clear that for the orderly administration of justice, courts should be most reluctant to set them aside.

§ 1119. Orders.

Every direction of a court or judge made or entered in writing (not included in a judgment) is an order. *Iveson v. Second Judicial District Court,* 66 Nev. 145, 206 P.2d 755 (1945). Generally, an order is a direction of the court preliminary and incidental to the final determination of the rights of the parties, the latter being denominated a judgment or decree as the case may be. *Elsman v. Elsman,* 54 Nev. 20, 2 P.2d 139 (1931). Where a minute order and a filed written order conflict, the latter will prevail. *Mortimer v. Pacific States Saving & Loan Co.,* 62 Nev. 147, 145 P.2d 733 (1944).

§ 1120. — Preparation and form of orders.

A written order should have a caption similar to that of the summons. *See* paragraph 2 of the Introductory Statement to the Appendix of Forms of NRCP; NRCP 7(b)(2). In the First, Eighth and Ninth Districts, every order must bear the signature, name and office address of counsel presenting or filing the same. FJDCR 17B. *See also* EDCR 7.23 and NJDCR 13(2).

The practice of preparing orders varies among judges. Some prepare their own orders; some have court staff assist them. Often, the court will direct an attorney to prepare a proposed order, usually the attorney for the prevailing party. In some districts, a proposed order must accompany the moving or opposing papers. This is the requirement in the First Judicial District, Rule 13(G); the Third Judicial District, Rule 6(E); the Seventh Judicial District, Rule 10(3); and the Ninth Judicial District, Rule 5(2). The Eighth Judicial District requires proposed orders in probate and guardianship cases to be delivered to the Probate Office not later than 4:00 p.m. on Wednesday of the week the matter is to be heard. EDCR 4.14(4).

DCR 21 provides: "The counsel obtaining any order, judgment or decree shall furnish the form of the same to the clerk or judge in charge of the court." *See also* EDCR 7.231. In practice, this rule is interpreted to mean that if the court does not otherwise order, the attorney for the party prevailing on a motion is responsible for the preparation of the court's order. Of course, the same attorney is also responsible for presenting the order to the court for signature, filing the signed order with the clerk, serving the order on all parties or their attorneys, and, if appropriate, giving notice of entry.

Some judges require that an order entered pursuant to a stipulation be separately typed for filing; however, many allow "It is so ordered" with space for the judge's signature beneath at the conclusion of the stipulation.

Although no rule precludes it, some judges will refuse to sign an order unless at least part of the text appears on the signature page.

§ 1121. — Entry of orders.

"Entry" of an order means the filing of the written order with the clerk of the court. Entry is important because an order is not effective "for any purpose" until entry of the same. *Fitzharris v. Phillips,* 74 Nev. 371, 333 P.2d 721 (1958); *Tener v. Babcock,* 97 Nev. 369, 632 P.2d 1140 (1981). Accordingly, the court's oral pronouncement from the bench, the clerk's minute order and even an unfiled written order are still ineffective "for any purpose." *Rust v. Clark County School District,* 103 Nev. 686, 747 P.2d 1380 (1987). *See also Musso v. Triplett,* 78 Nev. 355, 372 P.2d 687 (1962) (a minute order is not appealable); *Farnham v. Farnham,* 80 Nev. 180, 391 P.2d 26 (1964) (an "opinion" is not appealable).

Once an order is signed by the judge, it must be filed forthwith. DCR 24 provides: "Any order, judgment or decree which has been signed by a judge must be filed with the clerk of the court promptly. No attorney shall withhold or delay the filing of any such order, judgment or decree for any reason, including the nonpayment of attorney's fees." *See also* EDCR 7.24.

As discussed in § 1105, *supra,* the judge may permit the order to be filed with him. An attorney may use this procedure when the clerk's office is closed and it is important that the order be filed immediately.

§ 1122. — Service of orders.

The party who is required to act or refrain from acting as a result of a court order must receive notice thereof "from the opposing party." DCR 15(2). *See also* EDCR 2.28.

Most orders must be served upon all parties or their attorneys. *See* § 921, *supra.* If the party is represented by an attorney, the service must be made upon the attorney unless the service upon the party himself is ordered by the court. NRCP 5(b); *see* § 919, *supra.* Even an order to show cause re contempt may be served upon the attorney. *Caplow v. Eighth Judicial District Court,* 72 Nev. 265, 302 P.2d 755 (1956).

NRCP prescribes the method of service: "Service upon the attorney or upon a party shall be made by delivering a copy to him or by mailing it to him at his last known address or, if no address is known, by leaving it with the clerk of the court. Delivery of a copy within this rule means: handing it to the attorney or to the party; or leaving it at his office with his clerk or other person in charge thereof." NRCP 5(b). *See also* EDCR 7.26.

Proof of service may be made by certificate of an attorney or of his employee (Forms 11D and 11E), or by written admission (Form 11F), or by affidavit (Forms 11G and 11H), or by other proof satisfactory to the court. NRCP 5(b). *See also* EDCR 7.26.

An ex parte order extending time must be served not later than the end of the next judicial day.

> No order, made on ex parte application and in the absence of the opposing party, provided he has appeared, granting or extending the time to file any paper or do any act shall be valid for any purpose in case of objection, unless written notice thereof is given to such opposing party not later than the end of the next judicial day. DCR 17(1). *See* § 1124, *infra.*

§ 1123. — Nunc pro tunc orders.

The purpose of a nunc pro tunc order is to correct a clerical error in a prior order — to make the record speak the truth as to what was actually determined or done or intended to be determined or done by the court. *Koester v. Administrator of Estate of Koester,* 101 Nev. 68, 693 P.2d 569 (1985). A nunc pro tunc order cannot be used to supply omitted action or enlarge upon the order originally entered. *Finley v. Finley,* 65 Nev. 113, 180 P.2d 334 (1948), *overruled on other grounds, Day v. Day,* 80 Nev. 386, 395 P.2d 321 (1964).

The exercise of a "nunc pro tunc order ... depends on the circumstances of a particular case and it is to be granted or refused as justice may require." *Allen v. Allen,* 70 Nev. 412, 270 P.2d 671 (1954).

Generally, NRCP 60(a) prescribes the procedure to correct a "clerical" rather than a "judicial" error or omission. *In re Humboldt River System,* 77 Nev. 244, 362 P.2d 265 (1961). For a complete discussion, see § 2518, *infra.*

In the Eighth District, EDCR 4.46 governs nunc pro tunc probate and guardianship orders.

§ 1124. — Ex parte orders.

Ex parte orders, that is, orders entered upon the granting of a motion without notice, are discouraged. They are only permissible in procedural matters or in emergency situations such as the application for a temporary restraining order pursuant to NRCP 65(b). *Cf. Farnow v. District Court,* 64 Nev. 109, 178 P.2d 371 (1947). *See also In re Custody of Gulick,* 100 Nev. 125, 676 P.2d 801 (1984).

A "special" motion involving judicial discretion that affects the rights of others as contrasted to a motion "of course" must be made on notice even where no rule expressly requires notice to obtain the particular order sought. *Maheu v. Eighth Judicial District Court,* 88 Nev. 26, 493 P.2d 709 (1972). An ex parte order entered in violation of this principle is invalid. *Cheek v. Bell,* 80 Nev. 244, 391 P.2d 735 (1964); *Maheu v. Eighth Judicial District Court,* 88 Nev. 26, 493 P.2d 709 (1972). Even though the order's subject matter would lie within the court's jurisdiction if properly applied for or concern a matter within the court's discretion, the ex parte order is void if entered without the required notice. *Maheu v. Eighth Judicial District Court,* 88 Nev. 26, 493 P.2d 709 (1972).

Subject to the limitations therein, NRCP 6(b) permits ex parte orders enlarging time and NRCP 6(d) permits ex parte orders shortening time. DCR 17 also pertains to orders enlarging time, and many of the districts have special rules concerning ex parte orders which must be complied with. In the First Judicial District, see Rule 7; in the Second District, see WDCR 10 and WDCR 16; in the Seventh District, see Rule 11; in the Eighth District, see EDCR 2.25, 2.26 and, in domestic matters, EDCR 5.20 and 5.38; in the Ninth District, see Rule 6.

The "cause" or "good cause" frequently required for granting a motion ex parte means, in addition to a meritorious application, a showing that counsel has endeavored to obtain the same relief by stipulation.

No attempt is made here to list all permissible ex parte orders. However, motions that are commonly granted ex parte include: (1) extending the time to answer or otherwise plead to a complaint; (2) shortening the time to answer or otherwise plead to a complaint for forcible entry or unlawful detainer (*see* NRS 40.300); (3) shortening the time for hearing of a motion; (4) extending the time to file points and authorities in opposition to a motion; (5) extending the time to comply with a request for discovery; (6) shortening the time to comply with a request for discovery; (7) extending the time to docket the record before the supreme court; (8) granting leave to take the deposition of a person prior to the expiration of 30 days after service of the summons and complaint (*see* NRCP 30(a)); (9) taking a deposition upon less than fifteen days written notice (*see* NRCP 30(b)(3)); (10) perfecting service by publication pursuant to NRCP

4(e)(1); (11) perfecting personal service outside the state pursuant to NRCP 4(e)(2); (12) correcting a clerical mistake pursuant to NRCP 60(a); (13) staying execution or enforcement of an order or judgment pending appeal (NRCP 62); (14) obtaining temporary restraining orders granted pursuant to NRCP 65(b); (15) and filing discovery. The careful practitioner should check the local rules of the particular district to see which matters may be presented ex parte; and, when in doubt, should not approach a judge without giving opposing counsel an opportunity to be present. *See* SCR 174(2) which authorizes ex parte applications only when permitted by law. WDCR 10(2) permits temporary extensions until opposing counsel can be notified. *NOTE:* The court is powerless to extend the time to file a motion for judgment n.o.v., a motion to amend findings, a motion for a new trial, a motion to alter or amend a judgment and a motion to relieve a party from a final order or judgment. *See* NRCP 6(b). Also, the court may not extend the time prescribed by NRAP 4(a) to file a notice of appeal. *See* Walker v. Scully, 99 Nev. 45, 657 P.2d 94 (1983).

Ex parte orders changing the custody of children are of particular concern. Upon an appropriate showing during the pendency of the original suit for divorce, the court may grant an ex parte motion, which temporarily awards or changes custody. *Whitney v. Second Judicial District Court,* 68 Nev. 176, 227 P.2d 960 (1951). A change of custody after a decree may not be granted ex parte. *Abell v. Second Judicial District Court,* 58 Nev. 89, 71 P.2d 111 (1937). *See also* Uniform Child Custody Jurisdiction Act, NRS Chapter 125A.

An additional requirement must be met before an ex parte order extending time is effective. If the opponent properly objects, written notice of the entry of the order must be given not later than the end of the next judicial day. DCR 17(1). *See also* EDCR 7.25. Failure to comply with this rule renders the order invalid — having no force and effect. *See* § 1122, *supra. Beco v. Tonopah Extension Mining Co.,* 37 Nev. 199, 141 P. 453 (1914); *Portland Cattle Loan Co. v. Wheeler & Stoddard,* 50 Nev. 205, 255 P. 999 (1927).

§ 1125. Orders to show cause.

In some instances, where the legislature has authorized particular relief, an "order to show cause" procedure is required, *e.g.,* contempt, NRS 22.040; writ of possession (personal property) NRS 31.853; and temporary writ of restitution (real property) NRS 40.300. The "order to show cause" procedure may not be used, however, unless it is prescribed by statute. *See* NRCP 7(b)(1).

NRCP, DCR and the local rules of practice have little application to "order to show cause" procedures. Accordingly, unless the order to show cause otherwise requires, no written response (points and authorities, affidavits, etc.) need be filed before the hearing. For this reason, counsel applying for an order to show cause will be wise to include, in the proposed order, dates for required responses and a reply thereto, eliminating surprising contentions, narrowing issues and obviating the necessity for testimony to prove uncontroverted facts.

Much debate exists and frequently considerable confusion arises about the burden and order of proof at a hearing on an order to show cause. The most widely accepted procedure (and that which is herein recommended) is to treat the order to show cause as though it were a motion:

A. The affidavits in support and in opposition to the application should contain only factual, evidentiary matter, should conform with the requirements of NRCP 56(e), and should avoid mere general conclusions or argument. An affidavit upon "information and belief" is not permissible unless specifically authorized by statute, *e.g.*, NRS 31.021(1)(h), DCR 14(2)(c) and EDCR 7.30(b)(3). *Cf. McCormick v. Sixth Judicial District Court,* 67 Nev. 318, 218 P.2d 939 (1950).

B. The court should consider the affidavits filed in support and in opposition to the relief requested and (unless responsible affidavits were not required) should only permit oral testimony of the affiants to resolve factual issues shown by the affidavits to be in dispute. Of course, if the court has not required responsible affidavits and the opponent has orally opposed the application, the court should continue the hearing for a written response and then determine which facts are truly disputed.

C. The party who obtained the order to show cause and is thereby requesting relief retains the burden of proof, despite form orders to show cause which purport to shift the burden to the respondent. Of course, the burden of proving "defense" is always the respondent's obligation. *McCormick v. Sixth Judicial District Court,* 67 Nev. 318, 218 P.2d 939 (1950) (in a contempt proceeding the burden of proving inability to comply is upon the "contemners").

§ 1126. Petitions for judicial review.

In the Eighth District, a petitioner seeking judicial review, outside the Nevada Administrative Procedure Act, must serve and file a memorandum of points and authorities within twenty-one days after the record of the proceeding under review has been filed with the court. The respondent must serve and file a memorandum of points and authorities in opposition within twenty-one days after service of petitioner's points and authorities. Petitioner may serve and file reply points and authorities not later than seven days after service of respondent's opposition. After petitioner's time to reply has expired, either party may then notice the hearing of the petition by serving and filing a notice of hearing setting the petition for hearing on a day when the judge to which the case is assigned is hearing civil motions, not less than seven days from the date the notice is served and filed. EDCR 2.15. *See* § 1105, *supra,* to select the correct day.

§ 1127. Clerk's authority to grant motions.

NRCP 77(c) provides, inter alia:

> All motions and applications in the clerk's office for issuing mesne process, for issuing final process to enforce and execute judgments, for entering defaults or judgments by default, and for other proceedings which do not require allowance or order of the court are grantable of course by the clerk; but his action may be suspended or altered or rescinded by the court upon cause shown.

This rule simply repeats the authority already granted by other rules for the clerk to entertain certain motions. For example, NRCP 4(b) specifically directs the clerk to issue summonses, and NRCP 45(a) directs the clerk to issue subpoenas. Rule 55(A) requires the clerk to grant a plaintiff's application for the entry of a default if proper and, under certain circumstances, a default judgment may be entered by the clerk pursuant to NRCP 55(b)(1). *See* Chapter 10, *supra.*

The clerk's practice in granting motions varies widely throughout Nevada. For example, to obtain the entry of a defendant's default pursuant to NRCP 55(a), the clerks of some districts will enter that default upon oral application therefor. However, the Second Judicial District requires a written application to be prepared by the plaintiff or his attorney.

Clerks in all districts routinely issue writs of execution, subpoenas and summonses without written application therefor. They also issue subpoenas to compel the attendance of witnesses at depositions to be taken in actions pending in other states pursuant to NRS 53.060. In the Eighth District, see EDCR 2.80.

Form 11A

CASE NO.

DEPARTMENT NO.

DOCKET

IN THE _____ JUDICIAL DISTRICT COURT OF THE STATE
OF NEVADA
IN AND FOR THE COUNTY OF _____

AB and CD,
 	
               Plaintiffs,
 	
    v.
 	
EF and GH,
 	
              Defendants.
	)
	)
	)
	)
	) DEFENDANT EF's MOTION TO
	) DISMISS THE COMPLAINT OF
	) PLAINTIFF, AB
	) Date of Hearing:
	) Time of Hearing:
	)
	)
	)

TO: Plaintiff AB and to his Attorney XY

The defendant EF moves to dismiss the action filed by plaintiff AB because the complaint fails to state a claim against this defendant upon which relief can be granted.

Signed _____

Address _____
Attorney for Defendant EF

NOTICE OF MOTION

TO: Plaintiff AB and to his attorney XY

Please take notice that the undersigned will bring the above motion on for hearing before Department _____ of this Court on _____, the _____ day of _____, 19____, at 9:00 A.M., or as soon thereafter as counsel can be heard.

Signed _____

Address _____

195

Note: The "notice of motion" should only be used in the Eighth District. If the motion is to be heard by a judge visiting the Eighth District, the following notice should be used.

Please take notice that the undersigned will bring the above motion on for hearing before a visiting or senior judge at such time as shall be prescribed by the court administrator.

Signed _____

Address _____

Form 11B

CASE NO.

DEPARTMENT NO.

DOCKET

IN THE _____ JUDICIAL DISTRICT COURT OF THE STATE
OF NEVADA
IN AND FOR THE COUNTY OF _____

AB,	)
	)
Plaintiff,	)
	)
v.	) DEFENDANT'S MOTION FOR
	) SUMMARY JUDGMENT
	) Date of Hearing:
EF,	) Time of Hearing:
	)
Defendant.	)
	)

TO: Plaintiff AB and to his Attorney XY

Please take notice that on _____, the _____ day of
_____, 19_____, or as soon thereafter as counsel may
be heard, the undersigned will move this court for summary judgment in favor of
Defendant EF upon the ground that there is no genuine issue as to any material
fact and that Defendant EF is entitled to a judgment as a matter of law.

Signed _____

Address _____

Form 11C

CASE NO.

DEPARTMENT NO.

DOCKET

IN THE _____ JUDICIAL DISTRICT COURT OF THE STATE
OF NEVADA
IN AND FOR THE COUNTY OF _____

AB,	)
	)
Plaintiff,	)
	)
v.	) AFFIDAVIT OF EF IN SUPPORT OF
	) DEFENDANT'S MOTION FOR
	) SUMMARY JUDGMENT
EF,	) Date of Hearing:
	) Time of Hearing:
Defendant.	)
_____	)

STATE OF _____)
                                 : ss.
COUNTY OF _____)

EF, being duly sworn, deposes and states:

1. I am the defendant in this case and make this affidavit in support of my Motion for Summary Judgment. I know the matters set forth herein of my own personal knowledge and am competent to testify thereto.

2.

                                                    _____
                                                        EF

SUBSCRIBED and SWORN to before
me this _____ day of _____, 19_____.

_____
NOTARY PUBLIC in and for said County
and State

Form 11D

CASE NO.

DEPARTMENT NO.

DOCKET

IN THE _____ JUDICIAL DISTRICT COURT OF THE STATE
OF NEVADA
IN AND FOR THE COUNTY OF _____

AB,	)	
	)	
Plaintiff,	)	
	)	
v.	)	CERTIFICATE OF SERVICE
	)	(Personal Service)
	)	
EF,	)	
	)	
Defendant.	)	
	)	

I hereby certify that on the _____ day of _____,
19_____, I personally served a copy of Defendant's Motion to Dismiss upon
attorney(s) XY at _____ (address) _____.

(Signed) _____
An employee of PQ
Attorney for Defendant

Note: Only an attorney or his employee may prove service by certificate.

Form 11E

CASE NO.

DEPARTMENT NO.

DOCKET

IN THE _____ JUDICIAL DISTRICT COURT OF THE STATE
OF NEVADA
IN AND FOR THE COUNTY OF _____

AB,	)	
	)	
Plaintiff,	)	
	)	
v.	)	CERTIFICATE OF SERVICE
	)	(Mailing)
	)	
EF,	)	
	)	
Defendant.	)	
	)	

I hereby certify that on the _____ day of _____,
19_____, I mailed a copy of Defendant's Motion for Summary Judgment to
attorney XY, _____ (address) _____, and that postage was fully prepaid thereon.

(Signed) _____
An employee of PQ
Attorney for Defendant

Form 11F

CASE NO.

DEPARTMENT NO.

DOCKET

IN THE _____ JUDICIAL DISTRICT COURT OF THE STATE
OF NEVADA
IN AND FOR THE COUNTY OF _____

AB,	)	
	)	
Plaintiff,	)	
	)	
v.	)	RECEIPT OF COPY
	)	
	)	
EF,	)	
	)	
Defendant.	)	
_____	)	

Receipt of Copy of the Plaintiff's First Motion to Compel Discovery is hereby
acknowledged this _____ day of _____, 19_____.

_____
An employee of PQ
Attorney for Defendant

Form 11G

CASE NO.

DEPARTMENT NO.

DOCKET

IN THE _____ JUDICIAL DISTRICT COURT OF THE STATE
OF NEVADA
IN AND FOR THE COUNTY OF _____

AB,	)
	)
Plaintiff,	)
	)
v.	) AFFIDAVIT OF SERVICE
	)
	)
EF,	)
	)
Defendant.	)
_____	)

STATE OF NEVADA　　　　　)
　　　　　　　　　　　　　　　:　ss.
COUNTY OF _____)

_____, being first duly sworn, deposes
and says:
　　On the _____ day of _____, 19_____, I person-
ally served a copy of the Defendant's Motion to Dismiss upon attorney(s) XY, at
_____ (address) _____ .

_____

SUBSCRIBED and SWORN to before me
this _____ day of _____, 19_____.

_____
NOTARY PUBLIC

Form 11H

CASE NO.

DEPARTMENT NO.

DOCKET

IN THE _____ JUDICIAL DISTRICT COURT OF THE STATE
OF NEVADA
IN AND FOR THE COUNTY OF _____

AB,   )
)
              Plaintiff,   )
)
      v.   )   AFFIDAVIT OF SERVICE
)   BY MAIL
)   _____
EF,   )
)
              Defendant.   )
_____)

STATE OF NEVADA   )
                            : ss.
COUNTY OF _____)

_____, being first duly sworn, deposes
and says:
    On the _____ day of _____, 19_____, I mailed
a copy of Defendant's Motion for Summary Judgment to attorney(s) XY, at
_____ .
          (address)

                              _____

SUBSCRIBED and SWORN to before me
this _____ day of _____, 19_____.

_____
NOTARY PUBLIC

CHAPTER 12

DEFENSIVE MOTIONS

Authors: William A. Baker
          Don Springmeyer

§ 1201. Introduction and scope.

NRCP 12 prescribes a general method for the presentation of defenses and objections to claims or defenses made by any party. This chapter will discuss the timing and general content of motions raising the defenses explicitly set out in Rule 12(b), motions for more definite statement, and motions to strike founded upon Rule 12(e) and (f). Because Rule 12 has preserved the distinctions between a special appearance and a general appearance and has stringent waiver provisions, particular emphasis will be placed upon the personal jurisdiction motions, and the distinction between special and general appearances and waiver.

Certain "defensive motions" are discussed in more detail in other chapters: objections to subject matter jurisdiction under Rule 12(b)(1) and 12(h)(3) are discussed in Chapter 4, *supra,* and venue motions are discussed in Chapter 6, *supra.* The procedure and timing of a motion for failure to join a party under Rule 19 are discussed in this chapter. The substance of such a motion is found in Chapter 5, *supra.*

§ 1202. Form of motions.

Motions under Rule 12 must generally meet the requirements set out in § 1102, *supra,* for all motions. The special requirements of objections to personal jurisdiction by a motion to quash are set out in § 1204, *infra,* and forms are provided at the conclusion of this chapter.

205

§ 1203. Objections to personal jurisdiction by motion to quash.

Rule 12 specifically provides that certain "defenses" *may,* "at the option of the pleader be made by motion ...." Among those listed are: "(2) lack of jurisdiction over the person, (3) insufficiency of process, [and] (4) insufficiency of service of process ...." NRCP 12(b).

Since these defenses are specifically waived by being joined with one or more other defenses or objections in a responsive pleading or motion (Rule 12(b) and 12(h)(1)) the result is that a party wishing to attack personal jurisdiction must do so by motion to quash service. Indeed, it is now settled law in Nevada that a special appearance through a motion to quash service of summons is the only method of attacking personal jurisdiction *Barnato v. Second Judicial District Court,* 76 Nev. 335, 353 P.2d 1103 (1960). That is, a defense that there are insufficient minimum contacts to allow the exercise of personal jurisdiction over a party, a defense that the process used to secure jurisdiction over a party is insufficient, or that the service of process upon a party is insufficient, must all be raised by a special appearance on a motion to quash service.

In this area, federal practice is not a guide to Nevada practice. The Advisory Committee Note to NRCP 12(b) illustrates Nevada's departure from the federal rule. "The federal rule is further revised ... [and the Nevada rule] ... is intended to retain existing practice on motions to quash, and permits application for a writ of prohibition in lieu of trial and appeal." Advisory Committee Note to NRCP 12(b), *Annotations to Nevada Revised Statutes. See also Benson v. Eighth Judicial District Court,* 85 Nev. 327, 454 P.2d 892 (1969).

The Nevada Supreme Court has recently explained that a general appearance is entered when a person "... comes into court as party to a suit and submits to the jurisdiction of the court." *Milton v. Gesler,* 107 Nev. 767, 819 P.2d 245 (1991). A special appearance, by contrast, "... is entered when a person comes into court to test the court's jurisdiction or the sufficiency of service." *Id.*

§ 1204. — Form, content and procedure on the motion to quash.

The form and content of a particular motion to quash service of process will depend upon the particular defect or defense asserted. The majority of reported Nevada decisions have dealt with service of process under the long-arm statutes, NRS 14.065 and 14.080. From those decisions the procedures and practical content for such a motion may be gleaned.

A motion to quash will normally be filed before the time for answering set out in Rule 12(a) has expired, *i.e.,* within twenty days (or within such longer time as may be provided by a specific statute) of the service of the summons and complaint. An attempt to extend the time to answer or otherwise respond, whether by stipulation, or by stipulation with court approval, should be avoided as it may be construed as a general appearance. *See* § 1206, *infra.*

Unless the defect challenged is obvious from the return of service actually filed with the court, a defendant's motion to quash will usually contain an affidavit by or on behalf of the defendant negating the possible bases of jurisdiction. *See Basic Food Industries v. Eighth Judicial District Court,* 94 Nev. 111, 575 P.2d 934 (1978); *see generally Davis v. Eighth Judicial District Court,* 97 Nev. 332, 629 P.2d 1209, *cert. denied,* 454 U.S. 1049 (1981); *Barnato v. Second Judicial District Court,* 76 Nev. 335, 353 P.2d 1103 (1960).

"When a challenge to personal jurisdiction is made, the plaintiff in the action has the burden of establishing the existence of jurisdiction." *Davis, supra,* at 337. *See also Basic Food Industries v. Eighth Judicial District Court, supra.* "This [plaintiff's] burden is met by introducing competent evidence of essential facts which establishes a prima facie showing of the existence of in personam jurisdiction." *Davis, supra,* at 337; *see Abbott-Interfast Corp. v. Eighth Judicial District Court,* 107 Nev. 871, 821 P.2d 1043 (1991). If the challenge asserts a violation of federal due process, the plaintiff must show that the exercise of jurisdiction would comport with that due process. *Certain-Teed Products v. District Court,* 87 Nev. 19, 479 P.2d 781 (1971). The plaintiff may not rely solely on the allegations of his complaint but must offer evidentiary material through affidavits. *Basic Food Industries, supra.* The plaintiff need only make a prima facie showing of jurisdiction. *Davis, supra.* A defendant's introduction of contrary evidentiary material will not rebut such a prima facie showing because factual disputes must be resolved in favor of the plaintiff. *Levinson v. Second Judicial District Court,* 103 Nev. 404, 742 P.2d 1024 (1987).

Where a second complaint alleged with more specificity the tortious acts which the plaintiff contended occurred in Nevada, the previous order quashing service of process on a previous complaint in the same action was found not to have that degree of finality necessary to invoke the doctrine of res judicata. *Davis, supra,* at 336-37. Thus, in at least some circumstances the grant of a motion to quash may not end efforts to assert jurisdiction, even under the same "long-arm" statute.

A form for possible use in drafting a motion to quash is Form 12A, *infra.* Careful review of the grounds for the motion, and careful drafting of the necessary affidavits, will reduce the chance of an inadvertent general appearance. Note that an order submitted after winning a motion to quash must be drafted with equal care and should not make reference to dismissal of the action. *See Consolidated Casinos Corp. v. L.A. Caunter & Co.,* 89 Nev. 501, 515 P.2d 1025 (1973). *See also* Form 12C.

§ 1205. — Depositions and discovery upon a motion to quash.

The question of what, if any, discovery may be had by the parties, without jeopardizing the position of the defendant attacking jurisdiction, is not clear. In *Gardner v. Associated Contractors,* 72 Nev. 1, 291 P.2d 1051 (1956), the only Nevada decision dealing with the question, the court found that a plaintiff could not compel a defendant to come into Nevada for a deposition to determine if jurisdiction existed. *Chitwood v. County of Los Angeles,* 14 Cal. App. 3d 522, 92 Cal. Rptr. 441 (1971), will give any practitioner pause. The *Chitwood* court found, in part, that a defendant who answers interrogatories has made a general appearance waiving jurisdictional objections.

Despite a great many Nevada decisions delineating the distinctions between a general appearance waiving jurisdictional objections and a special appearance preserving them, there are today no definitive answers to the practical problems facing both plaintiff and defendant when attempting depositions or discovery on a motion to quash.

§ 1206. — Special appearances, general appearances and waiver of objections to personal jurisdiction.

The cases and rules dealing with waiver of the defenses to personal jurisdiction and the conversion of a special appearance limited to asserting these defenses into a general appearance waiving the defenses are complex and constitute a serious trap for the practitioner. *See* P. Bible, Special Appearances: Trap for the Unwary, 43 *Inter Alia* 16 (1978). Because of the complexity, and because no summary of decisional law can be assured to be fully accurate, practice in this area should be approached with great caution.

Rule 12(b) provides in pertinent part:

No defense or objection is waived by being joined with one or more other defenses or objections in a responsive pleading or motion, except defenses numbered (2)-(4) [lack of jurisdiction over the person, insufficiency of process, insufficiency of service of process] are waived if joined with one or more defenses other than defenses (2)-(4), or by further pleading after denial of such defenses.

Rule 12(h)(1) emphasizes the same point:

A defense of lack of jurisdiction over the person, improper venue, insufficiency of process, or insufficiency of service of process is waived if not made under subdivision (b) of this rule.

Thus, a party waives the defenses of lack of personal jurisdiction, insufficiency of process and insufficiency of service of process unless those defenses are appropriately raised in a special appearance. NRCP 12(b);

12(h)(1); *Barnato v. Second Judicial District Court,* 76 Nev. 335, 353 P.2d 1103 (1960).

In *Barnato,* a writ of prohibition was sought to prevent the court from proceeding in a divorce action, claiming that the court had no jurisdiction over the petitioner. After the plaintiff had begun the action, the petitioner made four motions: (1) to *dismiss* the action because of lack of jurisdiction over the person of defendant; (2) to *dismiss* the action because of lack of sufficiency of process; (3) to *dismiss* the action because of insufficiency of service of process; and (4) to quash service made on petitioner at Las Vegas, Nevada. The trial court granted the motion to quash on the ground that petitioner had been fraudulently enticed into the State of Nevada for service and at the same time denied the motions to dismiss the action on the ground that by making these motions the same petitioner had generally appeared in the action. The Nevada Supreme Court denied prohibition and rejected the argument that the adoption of NRCP 12(b) changed the former rule to that of the federal courts where a motion to dismiss does not constitute a general appearance. The court referred to the provisions noted above and declared that Rule 12(b) as adopted in Nevada did not change the general rule in existence at the time of its adoption. "[A] defendant who requests relief additional to that necessary to protect him from defective service of process renders his appearance general." *Barnato v. Second Judicial District Court,* 76 Nev. 335, 340, 353 P.2d 1103 (1960).

Since *Barnato,* several other decisions have also held that the filing of a motion to dismiss renders a special appearance general and waives personal jurisdiction defenses. *Selznick v. Eighth Judicial District Court,* 76 Nev. 386, 355 P.2d 854 (1960); *Benson v. Eighth Judicial District Court,* 85 Nev. 327, 454 P.2d 892 (1969); *Deros v. Stern,* 87 Nev. 148, 483 P.2d 648 (1971); *see also Silver v. Telerent Leasing,* 105 Nev. 30, 768 P.2d 879 (1989).

The Note to Form 19 in the Nevada Rules of Civil Procedure Appendix of Forms states the same principle: "A motion to quash and not a motion to dismiss must be used to raise defenses (2)-(4), Rule 12(b), to avoid making a general appearance."

A properly limited motion to quash, "silently expanded" by the inadvertent submission of an overly broad order for signature by the court after ruling, may convert a motion to quash into a motion to dismiss and thus constitute a general appearance waiving personal jurisdiction defenses. *Consolidated Casinos Corp. v. L.A. Caunter & Co.,* 89 Nev. 501, 515 P.2d 1025 (1973). In *Consolidated Casinos Corp.,* the court not only found a general appearance had been made, waiving personal jurisdiction objections, but also explicitly rejected the argument that inclusion of the "dismissal" language in the order quashing service was a clerical mistake.

Activity other than filing a motion to dismiss may also result in converting a special appearance into a general one and waiving a personal jurisdiction defense.

Thus, one may not, without waiver:

(1) Assert defenses other than lack of personal jurisdiction or insufficiency of process or service of process. NRCP 12(b), 12(h)(1) and cases, *infra.*

(2) File a motion for extension of time for appearance (or answer). *Cf. City of Los Angeles v. Eighth Judicial District Court,* 58 Nev. 1, 67 P.2d 1019 (1937).

(3) File a motion for summary judgment. *Havas v. Long,* 85 Nev. 260, 454 P.2d 30 (1969).

(4) File a motion to set aside a default judgment for mistake, inadvertence, surprise, or excusable neglect under Rule 60(b)(1). *Doyle v. Jorgenson,* 82 Nev. 196, 414 P.2d 707 (1966); *Deros v. Stern,* 87 Nev. 148, 483 P.2d 648 (1971) (a waiver of personal jurisdiction after judgment may not be applied retroactively so as to cure initial defects and render proper an otherwise void judgment); *Milton v. Gesler,* 107 Nev. 767, 819 P.2d 245 (1991). *See* discussion in § 2451, *infra.*

(5) Request dismissal of a complaint in addition to setting aside a [void] judgment. *Deros v. Stern,* 87 Nev. 148, 483 P.2d 648 (1971). *See* discussion in § 2451, *infra.*

(6) File a responsive pleading in aid of a Rule 60(b)(3) motion to set aside a default judgment. *Phillips v. Incline Manor Association,* 91 Nev. 69, 530 P.2d 1207 (1975); *but see Milton v. Gesler,* 107 Nev. 767, 819 P.2d 245 (1991) (the filing of *only* a Rule 60(b)(3) motion which seeks only the relief of challenging personal jurisdiction is *not* a waiver).

(7) Object to a motion for leave to file a second amended complaint and seek attorneys fees as a condition for leave to amend the complaint. *Davis v. Eighth Judicial District Court,* 97 Nev. 332, 629 P.2d 1209 (1981).

(8) Sign a stipulation extending the time within which defendants may answer or otherwise respond to a complaint. *See Rahn v. Searchlight Mercantile Co.,* 56 Nev. 289, 49 P.2d 353 (1935).

A number of Nevada decisions have found no waiver of a party's special appearance and preservation of "personal jurisdiction" objections in different fact situations. Thus, a party does not waive his or her special appearance and make a general appearance by:

(1) Filing a petition for removal to federal court. *Alitalia-Linee Aeree v. Second Judicial District Court,* 92 Nev. 638, 556 P.2d 544 (1976).

(2) Moving to associate counsel. *Sun Valley Ford v. Second Judicial District Court,* 97 Nev. 467, 634 P.2d 464 (1981).

(3) Failing to reply to plaintiff's opposition to a motion to quash. *Sun Valley Ford v. Second Judicial District Court,* 97 Nev. 467, 634 P.2d 464 (1981).

(4) Moving to quash service in a divorce action by a motion which recites the provisions of a prior out-of-state judgment for legal separation. *Simpson v. O'Donnell,* 98 Nev. 516, 654 P.2d 1020 (1982).

(5) Accepting an extension of time not sought by movant but apparently offered by the court. *City of Los Angeles v. Eighth Judicial District Court,* 58 Nev. 1, 67 P.2d 1019 (1937).

(6) Filing a Rule 60(b)(3) motion to set aside a judgment as void for lack of personal jurisdiction, so long as no other relief is requested, or no other responsive pleading is filed. *Milton v. Gesler,* 107 Nev. Adv. Op. 118, 819 P.2d 245 (1991); *see also Sawyer v. Sugarless Shops,* 106 Nev. 265, 792 P.2d 14 (1990).

(7) Negotiating with the opposing attorney. *Milton v. Gesler, supra.*

(8) Participating in a domestic referee hearing. *Id.*

§ 1207. Motion for more definite statement.

NRCP 12(e) provides:

> If a pleading to which a responsive pleading is permitted is so vague or ambiguous that a party cannot reasonably be required to frame a responsive pleading, he may move for a more definite statement before interposing his responsive pleading. The motion shall point out the defects complained of and the details desired.

The motion must be filed before a responsive pleading because, if the movant in fact filed a responsive pleading, it could hardly be claimed that the original pleading was so vague or ambiguous that the responsive pleading could not be filed.

Since the motion will lie only as against "a pleading to which a responsive pleading is permitted" (or required), its use is limited to an attack upon a complaint (or third-party complaint), a counterclaim denominated as such in the answer, or a cross-claim. Where, pursuant to Rule 7(a), the court has ordered a reply to an answer or a third-party answer, this motion may also lie.

While the motion for a more definite statement has not received extensive treatment in the Nevada decisions, it is clear that objections to lack of clarity in a complaint are waived if the motion is not made. *Union Pacific R.R. v. Adams,* 77 Nev. 282, 362 P.2d 450 (1961); *Whiteman v. Brandis,* 78 Nev. 320, 372 P.2d 468 (1962).

If any other motion under Rule 12 is made before serving a responsive pleading, this motion for more definite statement, if it was then available to the movant, must be consolidated with it or it is waived. NRCP 12(g).

> If the motion [for more definite statement] is granted and the order of the court is not obeyed within 10 days after notice of the order or within such other time as the court may fix, the court may strike the pleading to which the motion was directed or make such order as it deems just.

NRCP 12(e).

§ 1208. Motion to strike.

There are two forms of motions to strike which are authorized by the Nevada Rules. Other papers, *e.g.,* affidavits, may be stricken under separate provisions of court rules. *See* § 1109, *supra.* The first is founded upon Rule 11, Signing of Pleadings, and is discussed in Chapter 8, *supra.*

The second is founded upon Rule 12(f). It may be used to eliminate "any insufficient defense or any redundant, immaterial, impertinent, or scandalous matter" from a pleading. NRCP 12(f). The motion shall be made "within 20 days after the service of the pleading upon [the movant]...." NRCP 12(f). The court may also enter an order striking such material, upon its own initiative, at any time.

While no reported decisions under Rule 12(f) may be found, a similar motion has existed under Nevada practice since the earliest days. *See Sankey v. Noyes,* 1 Nev. 68 (1865) (frivolous replication). *Ronnow v. Delmue,* 23 Nev. 29, 41 P. 1074 (1895), suggested that a verification of a complaint, where the complaint was not required to be verified, could be the subject of a motion to strike. Note that the Nevada Supreme Court has repeatedly stated that a motion to strike another motion is bad practice and will not be granted. *Lamb v. Lamb,* 55 Nev. 438, 38 P.2d 659 (1934); *Afriat v. Afriat,* 61 Nev. 321, 117 P.2d 83 (1941).

The motion to strike would seem to be applicable to an allegation of specific monetary damages where the amount stated in the demand for judgment is greater than $10,000, but is not phrased in the terms required by Rule 8(a): damages "in excess of $10,000." *See* § 804, *supra.* Such a motion, like other motions, must state with particularity the grounds therefor and shall set forth the relief or order sought. NRCP 7(b)(1). *See* § 1104, *supra.*

§ 1209. Failure to join a party under Rule 19.

Rule 12(b) allows a party to raise by motion the "failure to join a party under Rule 19." NRCP 12(b)(6). Rule 19, of course, deals with the compulsory joinder of parties whose presence before the court is conditionally necessary or indispensable. The substance of a motion raising such an objection may be found in Chapter 5, *supra.*

Rule 12(b) requires an objection for failure to join a party under Rule 19 to be made in a responsive pleading to any claim for relief, or at the option of the pleader, by motion. Unlike other 12(b) motions, however, waiver of such objection will not occur where the party is indispensable. NRCP 12(h)(2). That section provides in part "a defense of failure to join a party indispensable under Rule 19, ... may be made in any pleading permitted or ordered under Rule 7(a), or by motion for judgment on the pleadings, or at the trial on the merits."

Either the trial or appellate court may also enforce the joinder of parties sua sponte, without the necessity of a Rule 12 motion or a pleading raising the objection. *See University of Nevada v. Tarkanian,* 95 Nev. 389, 594 P.2d 1159 (1979) and discussion in Chapter 5, *supra.*

§ 1210. Failure to state a claim.

NRCP 12(b)(5) specifically provides that the defense of the "failure to state a claim upon which relief can be granted" may be made by motion. *Gull v. Hoalst,* 77 Nev. 54, 359 P.2d 383 (1961).

Such a motion tests the legal sufficiency of the claim set out against the moving party. The statement is often made that such a motion should not be granted unless it appears to a certainty that plaintiff is entitled to no relief under any set of facts which could be proved in support of the claim. *See Zalk-Josephs Co. v. Wells-Cargo, Inc.,* 81 Nev. 163, 400 P.2d 621 (1965); *Edgar v. Wagner,* 101 Nev. 226, 699 P.2d 110 (1985); *see also Tahoe Village Homeowners Association v. Douglas County,* 106 Nev. 660, 799 P.2d 556 (1990).

The success or failure of such a motion will normally depend upon the substantive law involved. For the purpose of considering a Rule 12(b)(5) motion, a court must accept the charge of the complaint as true. *Hansen-Niederhauser v. Nevada Tax Commission,* 81 Nev. 307, 402 P.2d 480 (1965); *Haertel v. Sonshine Carpet Co.,* 102 Nev. 614, 730 P.2d 428 (1986).

Although the granting of such a motion is usually done with leave to amend, such leave to amend is largely a matter of discretion in the trial court and will not be held to be error in the absence of an abuse of discretion. *Nelson v. Sierra Construction Corp.,* 77 Nev. 334, 364 P.2d 402 (1961). *Nelson* found no abuse of discretion where there was no suggestion that plaintiffs could have amended by alleging additional facts to support the cause of action. Where no prejudice to a defendant results and where justice requires it, leave to amend should be granted. *See Fisher v. Executive Fund Life Insurance Co.,* 88 Nev. 704, 504 P.2d 700 (1972) and Chapter 8, *supra.*

When the defense of the statute of limitations appears on the face of the complaint, a motion to dismiss for failure to state a claim is proper.

Kellar v. Snowden, 87 Nev. 488, 489 P.2d 90 (1971); *Paso Builders, Inc. v. Hebard,* 83 Nev. 165, 426 P.2d 731 (1967).

The granting of a motion for dismissal for failure to state a claim, where no leave to file an amended pleading has been given, results in a judgment on the merits. *Zalk-Josephs Co. v. Wells-Cargo, Inc.,* 81 Nev. 163, 400 P.2d 621 (1965).

The motion to dismiss for failure to state a claim may also be raised by a motion for judgment on the pleadings. NRCP 12(h)(2).

Note that because a Rule 12(b) motion is not a "responsive pleading" as that term is used in the Rules, where the defense of failure to state a claim is raised by a 12(b)(5) motion, and the pleader has not previously amended his pleading, the pleader against whom the motion is directed may simply amend his pleading to cure any deficiency. *See* NRCP 15(a) and Chapter 8, *supra.*

Form 19 in the Appendix of Forms to NRCP sets out an appropriate form: "The defendant moves this court as follows: 1. To dismiss the action because the complaint fails to state a claim against defendant upon which relief can be granted."

The form should meet the requirements of particularity in motions. NRCP 7(a); § 1104, *supra.* The required memorandum of points and authorities should articulate the substantive law applicable to the particular claim. *See* § 1106, *supra.*

On a motion to dismiss:

> If ... matters outside the pleading are presented to and not excluded by the court, the motion shall be treated as one for summary judgment and disposed of as provided in Rule 56, and all parties shall be given reasonable opportunity to present all material made pertinent to such a motion by Rule 56.

NRCP 12(b). An order of dismissal entered following such a motion, where matters outside the pleading were offered, will be treated upon appellate review as a grant of a motion for summary judgment unless the trial court has expressly excluded the matters outside the pleading from consideration. *Tahoe Village Homeowners Association v. Douglas County,* 106 Nev. 660, 799 P.2d 556 (1990); *Stevens v. McGimsey,* 99 Nev. 840, 673 P.2d 840 (1983); *Paso Builders, Inc. v. Hebard,* 83 Nev. 165, 426 P.2d 731 (1967). However, where the additional documents offered on such a motion are not properly authenticated, the court may not treat the motion as one for summary judgment. *Buss v. Consolidated Casinos Corp.,* 82 Nev. 355, 418 P.2d 815 (1966).

For a more extensive discussion on summary judgment, see Chapter 17, *infra.*

§ 1211. Motion for judgment on the pleadings.

NRCP 12(c) provides for a motion for judgment on the pleadings: "[a]fter the pleadings are closed but within such time as not to delay the trial, any party may move for judgment on the pleadings." Thus, at any time after the pleadings are closed under Rule 7(a), the motion may be made. The only limitation upon such a motion is that it not delay the trial; the trial court has discretion to defer the hearing or determination of the motion until trial. NRCP 12(d).

The determination of the motion will again depend upon the specific substantive law involved. In the court's determination, all well-pleaded material allegations of the opposing party's pleading are to be taken as true, and all allegations of the moving party which have been denied are taken as false. *See Hospital Building Co. v. Trustees of Rex Hospital,* 425 U.S. 738, 96 S. Ct. 1848, 48 L. Ed. 2d 338 (1976). The 12(c) motion is limited to *all* of the pleadings. The 12(c) motion typically says that, given what is admitted by all of the pleadings, the movant is entitled to judgment under the law. Regardless of the law applicable to the case, a defendant may prevent a 12(c) motion simply by denials in his answer. In deciding the 12(c) motion, the court may not look beyond the face of all of the pleadings. *See Bernard v. Rockhill Development Co.,* 103 Nev. 132, 734 P.2d 1238 (1987).

The motion is similar to the motion to dismiss for failure to state a claim. A motion for judgment on the pleadings is one method of raising the defense of failure to state a claim. NRCP 12(h)(2). Thus, any ground effective for a motion to dismiss for failure to state a claim will be sufficient.

As with the motion to dismiss for failure to state a claim, the motion for judgment on the pleadings also has its "conversion" clause: if matters outside the pleadings are offered and not rejected by the court, the procedure shall be as on a motion for summary judgment under Rule 56. NRCP 12(c). *See* Chapter 17, *infra.*

§ 1212. Waiver and consolidation of defenses.

The general goal of Rules 12(g) and (h) is to prevent repetitive motions asserting different defenses or objections when the same could have been made in one motion. The rule attempts to bring about this result by providing for waiver where all grounds available at a particular point in time are not asserted in one common motion.

As is often the case, however, there are both exceptions and complexities surrounding this general rule.

Rule 12(g) provides:

(g) Consolidation of Defenses in Motion. A party who makes a motion under this rule may join with it the other motions herein provided for and then available to him. If a party makes a motion under this rule but omits therefrom any defense or objection then available to him which this rule permits to be raised by motion, he shall not thereafter make a motion based on the defense or objection so omitted, except a motion as provided in subdivision (h)(2) hereof on any of the grounds there stated.

Discussed in § 1203, *supra* in more specific detail is the question of waiver regarding the defenses or objections of lack of personal jurisdiction, insufficiency of process, or insufficiency of service of process. *See also* Rule 12(h)(1). Despite the permissive language in Rule 12(g) allowing a party making a motion to "join with it other motions herein provided for and then available to him," that general language falls before the specific caveat in Rule 12(b) that the defenses of lack of jurisdiction over the person, insufficiency of process and insufficiency of service of process are waived if joined with one or more other defenses or objections in a responsive pleading or motion or by further pleading after denial of those defenses. *See* § 1203, *supra.*

Rule 12(h)(1) emphasizes that objections to venue are also waived if not raised by motion under Rule 12(b). *See* discussion in §§ 615 and 616, *supra.*

Exceptions to this rule of waiver are set out in NRCP 12(h)(2):

> (2) A defense of failure to state a claim upon which relief can be granted, a defense of failure to join a party indispensable under Rule 19, and an objection of failure to state a legal defense to a claim may be made in any pleading permitted or ordered under Rule 7(a), or by motion for judgment on the pleadings, or at the trial on the merits.

Subject matter jurisdiction of the court may not be waived. NRCP 12(h)(3); *see* Chapter 3, *supra.*

Many of the Nevada decisions touching upon waiver of defenses or objections arose under the former wording of NRCP 12(h): "A party waives all defenses and objections which he does not present either by motion ... or, if he has made no motion, in his answer or reply." *See Second Baptist Church v. First National Bank,* 89 Nev. 217, 220, 510 P.2d 630 (1973). As so worded, former NRCP 12(h) complemented Rule 8(c)'s requirement of asserting affirmative defense in any required or permitted responsive pleading.

Despite the deletion of such wording from Rule 12(h), it is clear that under the rules defenses may still be waived. NRCP 12(b) continues to provide that "[e]very defense, in law or fact, to a claim for relief in a pleading, whether a claim, counterclaim, cross-claim, or third-party claim, shall be asserted in the responsive pleading thereto if one is required ...." *See Williams v. Cottonwood Cove Development Co.,* 96 Nev. 857, 619 P.2d 1219 (1980) and § 805, *supra.*

Accordingly, to avoid waiver the careful practitioner will not only carefully review the defenses or objections available to him at the time of filing an initial responsive pleading or motion, but will do so at the time of filing of each defensive motion in the course of the litigation.

§ 1213. Other defensive motions.

While Rule 12 is a rule of general applicability, prescribing a method for the presentation of defenses and objections by any party to a claim or defense, the Rule is not the only source of motions or relief that may be sought. In one sense, of course, any relief sought by motion may be considered a "defensive" motion. Accordingly, a brief recitation of other common motions for relief and their bases may be helpful.

Rule 4(i) provides the basis for a motion to dismiss without prejudice where a plaintiff has failed to effect service of the summons and complaint within 120 days of the filing of the complaint. *See* § 902, *supra*.

Rule 11 provides the basis for a motion to strike unsigned pleadings or pleadings signed with the intent to defeat the purpose of Rule 11. *See* Chapter 8, *supra*.

Motions raising objections to subject matter jurisdiction under Rule 12(b)(1) and 12(h)(3) are discussed in Chapter 4, *supra*.

Motions based upon Rule 21 for the misjoinder or nonjoinder of parties are discussed in Chapter 5, *supra*.

Motions for summary judgment under Rule 56 are discussed in Chapter 17, *infra*. That Chapter also treats the motion to dismiss for failure to state a claim or for judgment on the pleadings which is converted into a Rule 56 motion by consideration of matters outside the pleadings.

Motions relating to venue are treated in Chapter 6, *supra*.

The foregoing is not an exhaustive list. Motions for stays, motions based upon forum non conveniens and motions based upon any specific statute or provision for relief may be made (*e.g.,* seeking an order of contempt, NRS 22.040; writs of attachment or possession, NRS 31.024, 31.853; temporary restraining orders, NRCP 65(b) (discussed in Chapter 28, *infra*). Such motion for particular relief should be made in the form and under the procedure set out in Rule 7(b) or in accord with the more specific rule or statute upon which it is grounded.

Form 12A

MOTION TO QUASH SERVICE OF PROCESS
(Title of the Court)

A.B., Plaintiff	)	SPECIALLY APPEARING DEFENDANT C.D.'S
	)	MOTION TO QUASH SERVICE OF PROCESS AND
vs.	)	FOR NO OTHER RELIEF
	)	
C.D., Defendant	)	

COMES NOW Defendant C.D., specially appearing through _____
_____, ESQ., and moves this Court for its order quashing service of process as to said specially appearing Defendant and for no other relief.

This motion is brought pursuant to NRCP Rule 12(b) and is made upon the ground and for the reason that this Court lacks jurisdiction over the specially appearing Defendant C.D. because [here state the specific ground or grounds, *e.g.*, there are insufficient minimum contacts to allow the exercise of personal jurisdiction over non-resident defendant, there is insufficient process to secure jurisdiction over defendant, or there is insufficient service of process to secure jurisdiction over defendant.]

This motion is based upon the attached Memorandum of Points and Authorities and affidavit, and the papers and pleadings of record herein.

[Attorney's Signature] _____
Attorney for Specially Appearing
Defendant C.D.

[Follow with the appropriate notice of motion where required, points and authorities, and affidavit.]

Note: An abundance of caution suggests consistent reference to the moving defendant as the "specially appearing defendant." Similarly, stating that the motion is to quash service of process "and for no other relief" should heighten the awareness of both moving counsel and the court of the legal dangers in this area.

Remember that joining a motion asserting any one or more of the three personal jurisdiction defenses with any other Rule 12(b) defense waives the personal jurisdiction defense. NRCP 12(b) and (h)(1). Similarly, a motion raising only lack of jurisdiction over the person may be held to waive any claim of insufficiency of process or insufficiency of service of process. *See* Rule 12(h)(1). Accordingly, movant must consider whether to raise more than one of the three personal jurisdiction defenses or risk waiver. A second or third personal jurisdiction defense may not be raised after denial of the first.

Form 12B

AFFIDAVIT IN SUPPORT OF MOTION TO QUASH SERVICE OF PROCESS

(Title of the Court)

A.B., Plaintiff

vs.

C.D., Defendant

C.D., being first duly sworn under penalty of perjury according to law, deposes and says:

1. I am the specially appearing defendant in this action and make this affidavit in support of my Motion to Quash Service of Process. I know the matters set forth herein of my own personal knowledge and am competent to testify thereof.

2. [Here negate, if the same may truthfully be done, each specific statutory basis of jurisdiction or set out the facts and circumstances which establish that defendant is not subject to personal jurisdiction. The statements which follow are based upon NRS 14.065, Nevada's general "long-arm" jurisdictional statute allowing service out of state upon certain persons.] I have not transacted any business or negotiated any commercial paper within the state of Nevada.

3. I have not committed a tortious act within Nevada.

4. I do not own, use, or possess any real property in Nevada.

5. I have not contracted to insure any person, property or risk located in Nevada at the time of contracting.

6. I have not lived in a marital relationship within Nevada.

Further deponent saith not,

[Signature, notary, etc.]

Note: Careful review of the possible statutory and factual bases for the assertion of jurisdiction must be made before preparing the motion and affidavit. Where it can be truthfully done, an affidavit rejecting each specific statutory basis for assertion of jurisdiction presents the simplest format. The particular facts and circumstances of the individual case remain paramount.

Form 12C

ORDER QUASHING SERVICE

(Title of the Court)

A.B., Plaintiff) ORDER QUASHING SERVICE OF PROCESS AS
) TO SPECIALLY APPEARING DEFENDANT C.D.
vs.) AND GRANTING NO OTHER RELIEF
)
C.D., Defendant)

The Motion to Quash Service of Process and For No Other Relief having come on for hearing ——————————————, 1985, Plaintiff A.B., appearing by and through counsel ——————————————, ESQ., and Defendant C.D. appearing by and through ——————————————, ESQ., and the Court having reviewed the pleadings, papers and exhibits on file herein, and having heard argument of counsel, and good cause appearing,

The Court hereby finds [here insert specific ground or grounds supporting the grant of the motion to quash] and

IT IS HEREBY ORDERED that the Motion to Quash Service of Process is hereby granted as to Specially Appearing Defendant C.D., and the return of service as to Specially Appearing Defendant C.D. upon the Complaint herein filed is quashed.

DATED ——————————————.

——————————————
District Judge

Submitted by:

Attorney for Specially
Appearing Defendant C.D.

CHAPTER 13

ANSWERS AND REPLIES

Author: Phillip W. Bartlett

§ 1301. Introduction and scope.

This chapter deals with responsive pleadings, including answers to plaintiff's complaint, answers to cross-claims and third-party complaints and replies to defendant's counterclaim. General rules of pleadings are discussed in Chapter 8, *supra.* While counterclaims and cross-claims technically are considered part of the answer, they are given their own treatment in Chapter 14, *infra,* since they seek affirmative relief. Defensive motions pursuant to Rule 12, which should be considered prior to answering, are covered in Chapter 12, *supra.*

An answer is a responsive pleading to a complaint. A reply is a responsive pleading to a counterclaim. A response to a third-party complaint or to a cross-claim is considered an answer, while a response to cross-defendant's counterclaim is a reply. NRCP 7(a).

§ 1302. Time to answer or reply.

The failure to file a responsive pleading within the time limits prescribed may lead to a default being taken. NRCP 55(a). *See* Chapter 10, *supra.* The court may not enter judgment by default unless three days' written notice has been given to a party who has appeared in the action. NRCP 55(b)(2). An "appearance" does not require a filing with the court, but may be settlement negotiations with an insurance carrier or even correspondence between the defendant and plaintiff's counsel where defendant indicates a "clear purpose to defend the suit." *Christy v. Carlisle,* 94 Nev. 651, 654, 584 P.2d 687 (1978); *Franklin v. Bartsas Realty, Inc.,* 95 Nev. 559, 564, 598 P.2d 1147 (1979); *Gazin v. Hoy,* 102 Nev. 621, 730 P.2d 436 (1986). The Rules of Professional Conduct state that when a lawyer knows the identity of a lawyer representing an opposing party, he should not cause a default to be taken without "first inquiring about the opposing lawyer's intention to proceed." Rule 175, Nevada Supreme Court Rules and see *Rowland v. Lepire,* 95 Nev. 639, 600 P.2d 237 (1979); *Cen Val Leasing Corp. v. Bockman,* 99 Nev. 612, 668 P.2d 1074 (1983). For further discussion, see Chapter 10, *supra.*

A defendant must serve an answer within twenty days after service of the summons and complaint, unless otherwise provided by statute. NRCP 12(a). For example, the time to answer is extended to forty days when plaintiff has served a foreign manufacturer, producer or supplier pursuant to special statute in a products liability action. NRS 14.080(3). When personal service upon the officers, managing agent or resident agent of a corporation has been unsuccessful, the law provides that twenty days will run from posting and mailing. NRCP 4(d)(1). In the event of an order for service by publication, defendant will have twenty days from the expiration of four weeks from the first publication or twenty days from personal service of a copy of the summons and complaint by mail. NRCP 4(e)(1)(iii).

Within the time limit for answering the complaint, the responding party may make a written demand for security for costs if the plaintiff resides out-of-state. NRS 18.130 provides that where the undertaking is required, all proceedings in the action are stayed until security for costs is filed with the clerk in the sum of $500. Upon service of the notice that security is required, the plaintiff has thirty days to file the same; if not filed, the court has the discretion to dismiss the action. NRS 18.130(4). *Borders Electrical Co. v. Quirk,* 97 Nev. 205, 626 P.2d 266 (1981) (where plaintiff simply neglects to comply with thirty-day limit and does not seek extension of time or leave of court for late filing, dismissal is not an abuse of discretion). Dismissal is not mandatory; the trial court has discretion to require the posting of the undertaking. *See Brion v. Union Plaza,* 104 Nev. 553, 555, 763 P.2d 64 (1988); *Fourchier v. McNeil Construction Co.,* 68 Nev. 109, 227 P.2d 429 (1951). Once the plaintiff files the security, he must notify the defendant of the posting. The defendant has the longer of ten days, or the period allowed under NRCP 12(a), from receipt of notice to answer or otherwise plead to the complaint. NRS 18.130(1). NRS 18.130 allows the plaintiff to concurrently file an answer and a demand for security, if done within the time limit for answering the complaint. This is the recommended procedure when the defendant has some question regarding the plaintiff's residency.

Nevada law requires that a motion and demand to change the venue of the action be made before the time for answering expires. *See* Chapter 6, *supra.* Two separate pleadings, a motion and demand to change venue, must be filed before twenty days expires from the date of service of the summons and complaint. *Nevada Transit Co. v. Harris Brothers Lumber Co.,* 80 Nev. 465, 468, 396 P.2d 133 (1964); *Hood v. Kirby,* 99 Nev. 386, 663 P.2d 348 (1983). Extending the time to answer the complaint does not enlarge the time to demand change of venue. *Connolly v. Salsberry,* 43 Nev. 182, 188-89, 183 P. 391 (1919). A motion and demand to change venue does not stay the requirement that the complaint be answered within twenty days from service. *Byers v. Graton,* 82 Nev. 92, 93, 411

P.2d 480 (1966); *Halama v. Halama,* 97 Nev. 628, 637 P.2d 1221 (1981). *See generally* Chapter 6, *supra.*

Any of the several motions Rule 12 allows to be made prior to an answer extends the time to answer or file a responsive pleading to ten days after notice of the court's action on the motion. NRCP 12(a). *See generally* Chapter 12, *supra.* If the court grants a motion for a more definite statement, the responsive pleading has to be served within ten days after the service of the more definite statement. NRCP 12(a)(2).

If a new defendant has been added by means of a third-party complaint, the time limits of NRCP 12(a)(2) apply to a response to the third-party complaint. NRCP 14(a).

If the defendant desires to remove an action to the federal court, the notice of removal must be filed within thirty days from the defendant's receipt of the initial pleading. *See generally* 28 U.S.C.A. § 1446.

§ 1303. Form of answer.

A form of proposed answer and affirmative defenses is contained in NRCP, Appendix of Forms, Form 20.

NRCP 7 describes the pleadings allowed. The responsive pleading to a complaint or cross-claim must be denominated an "answer"; or if to a counterclaim, a "reply"; or if to a third-party complaint, a "third-party answer." There are no other responsive pleadings allowed, except a court may order a reply to an answer or a third-party answer. NRCP 7(a).

The pleading caption should be "answer" or "answer and counter-claim" or "answer and cross-claim." If the answer to the complaint includes a counterclaim or cross-claim, the claim should follow the body of the answer prior to the prayer.

A defendant who is sued by an incorrect name should answer in his correct name using wording such as "Doe Corporation, incorrectly sued herein as ROE Corporation, answers plaintiff's complaint as follows ...."

The body of an answer should respond to each claim asserted with an admission, denial or a plea of lack of knowledge, stated in short and plain terms. A plea that the party is without knowledge or information sufficient to form a belief as to the truth of an allegation has the effect of a denial. Counsel should frame a responsive pleading in good faith, attempting to fairly respond to the allegations made. NRCP 8(b).

Even if an allegation is not expressly directed toward one's client, it is good practice to deny the allegation upon information and belief. Rule 8(b) requires a pleader to deny only a part of an allegation when he in good faith can admit the remainder. Admissions should be made specifically, as opposed to merely failing to deny an allegation. This practice makes for a clearer presentation and avoids inadvertent admission. Subject to the obligations set forth in Rule 11, NRCP 8(b) allows the pleader to generally deny all of the allegations of the complaint, or to generally deny all of the allegations with the exception of specific designated paragraphs expressly admitted.

An admission in a pleading binds the party admitting an allegation and no further proof is required.

§ 1304. Effect of failure to deny.

Allegations in a pleading to which a responsive pleading is required, other than those as to the amount of damage, are deemed admitted if not denied in the responsive pleading. NRCP 8(d). Allegations in a pleading such as an answer, to which no responsive pleading is required, are deemed automatically denied or avoided pursuant to Rule 8(d).

§ 1305. Special matters.

An exception to the rules stated above regarding general denials exists where the answering party wishes to raise the issue of the legal existence of any party or the capacity of any party to sue. In addition, if the answering party wishes to raise the authority of a party to sue in a representative capacity or to challenge the performance or occurrence of a condition precedent, a general denial is insufficient.

In these instances, NRCP 9(a) requires that the answer deny by specific negative averment with supporting particulars within the pleader's knowledge. Failure to so plead waives the issue. *See Tobler & Oliver Construction Corp. v. Nevada State Bank,* 89 Nev. 269, 271, 510 P.2d 1364 (1973), *Contrail Leasing Partners v. Executive Service Corp.,* 100 Nev. 545, 688 P.2d 765 (1984), and *Shaw v. Stutchman,* 105 Nev. 128, 771 P.2d 156 (1989).

Rule 9(g) requires that special damages, such as lost profits and medical expenses, be precisely stated. *Branda v. Sanford,* 97 Nev. 643, 637 P.2d 1223 (1981). The failure to do so, however, does not deprive the court of the power to award all damages proven. *Summa Corp. v. Greenspun,* 96 Nev. 247, 607 P.2d 569 (1980), *modified,* 98 Nev. 528, 655 P.2d 513 (1982).

§ 1306. Affirmative defenses.

An affirmative defense is one that avoids liability in whole or in part by new allegations that sufficiently excuse, justify or otherwise negate the cause of action. Rule 8(c) lists affirmative defenses including accord and satisfaction, arbitration and award, assumption of risk, contributory negligence, discharge in bankruptcy, duress, estoppel, failure of consideration, fraud, illegality, injury by fellow servant, laches, license, payment, release, res judicata, statute of frauds, statute of limitations and waiver. The defenses are only examples and the rule states that any other matter constituting an avoidance should be set forth affirmatively. *Schmidt v. Sadri,* 95 Nev. 702, 704, 601 P.2d 713 (1979). The defenses listed in Rule 12(b) also may be presented by affirmative defense. NRCP 12(h)(2). The failure to plead an affirmative defense at the time of answering may later bar the defendant from introducing evidence of an avoidance if the opposing party has not been given reasonable notice and an opportunity to respond. *Schwartz v. Schwartz,* 95 Nev. 202, 205, 591 P.2d 1137 (1979). In *Williams v. Cottonwood Cove Development Co.,* 96 Nev. 857, 619 P.2d 1219 (1980), the Nevada Supreme Court found that reasonable notice was given where a defense was raised for the first time in a motion for summary judgment.

For purposes of clarity, each affirmative defense should be separately stated in paragraphs and numbered consecutively. The wording of the affirmative defense should make it clear to which of plaintiff's claims for relief the defense is meant to relate.

When a statute creates a claim for relief and establishes conditions precedent that must be satisfied, the conditions are not affirmative defenses. They are part of the claim for relief and must be pleaded by the plaintiff and a failure to do so will make the complaint subject to dismissal. *White Pine County v. Herrick,* 19 Nev. 34, 37, 5 P. 276 (1885).

Counsel should avoid asserting "standard" affirmative defenses such as "failure to state a claim upon which relief can be granted ..." unless there is a factual and legal basis to support the defense. Some judges have become more aggressive about striking such surplusage and or awarding sanctions. NRCP Rule 11.

CHAPTER 14

COUNTERCLAIMS AND CROSS-CLAIMS

Author: James S. Beasley

§ 1401. Introduction and scope.

Rule 13 of the Nevada Rules of Civil Procedure is composed of various subdivisions. This rule defines cross-demand practice in Nevada courts. Included in this cross-demand practice are counterclaims and cross-claims.

§ 1402. Permissive counterclaims.

Cross-demands against opposing parties are designated as counter-claims. NRCP 13(a) and 13(b). Rule 13(b) reads as follows:

(b) Permissive Counterclaims. A pleading may state as a counter-claim any claim against an opposing party not arising out of the trans-action or occurrence that is the subject matter of the opposing party's claim.

Rule 13(c) provides:

(c) Counterclaim Exceeding Opposing Claim. A counterclaim may or may not diminish or defeat the recovery sought by the opposing party. It may claim relief exceeding in amount or different in kind from that sought in the pleading of the opposing party.

These two sections permit the pleading of all independent, unrelated claims so that all differences between the litigants may be disposed of in one action. The claim need not offset the demand of the opposing party, but may exceed it in amount or be of an entirely different nature. For instance, where A sues B for specific performance of a contract, and B has a personal injury claim against A and C as joint tortfeasors, defen-dant B could counterclaim against A, the plaintiff, to recover for the personal injury suffered at A's hands.

The sole test is whether there exists a claim between opposing parties, other than the claim originally sued on by the plaintiff at the time the counterclaim was pleaded.

§ 1403. Compulsory counterclaims.

Certain counterclaims are compulsory and must be asserted as part of a party's answer or the claim will be barred by the doctrine of res judicata. *Wolford v. Wolford,* 65 Nev. 710, 714, 200 P.2d 988 (1948); *MacDonald v. Krause,* 77 Nev. 312, 317, 362 P.2d 724 (1961). The definition of a compulsory counterclaim can be found at NRCP 13(a) which provides a claim must be pleaded if it arises out of the transaction or occurrence that is the subject matter of the opposing party's claim and exists at the time of serving the pleading, unless additional parties are needed over whom the court cannot get jurisdiction or the claim is already the subject of another pending action. The effect of failure to plead such a claim is res judicata. Therefore, if a party has a claim coming within Rule 13(a) which he does not plead, the party is precluded from raising it in a separate action or using the claim as a defense in another suit. *Hancock Oil Co. v. Universal Oil Products Co.,* 115 F.2d 45 (9th Cir. 1940); *Pennsylvania R.R. v. Musante-Phillips, Inc.,* 42 F. Supp. 340 (N.D. Cal. 1941). The words "transaction or occurrence" are liberally construed. *Lesnik v. Public Industrials Corp.,* 144 F.2d 968 (2d Cir. 1944); *Williams v. Robinson,* 1 F.R.D. 211 (D.D.C. 1940). If a pleader is in doubt whether the counterclaim arises out of the "transaction or occurrence," the pleader would be wise to plead it.

The application of Rule 13(a) is not limited to defendants but applies to all parties to the action. Therefore, in an action by A against B and C, A may be required to counterclaim to B's counterclaim, C may be required to counterclaim to a cross-claim by B, and D, brought in as a third-party defendant by C, may be required to counterclaim against C's third-party complaint. Such a claim, although related to the demands made by the opposing party, will not be res judicata if it comes within one of four exceptions stated in Rule 13(a):

1. The counterclaim does not exist at the time the answer is served. In other words, all elements of the cause of action must have accrued or the counterclaim is not compulsory. *Bennett v. Fidelity & Deposit Co.,* 98 Nev. 449, 453, 652 P.2d 1178 (1982).

2. The pleader need not state the claim if at the time the action was commenced the claim was the subject of another pending action.

3. If the opposing party has brought suit upon its claim by attachment or some process by which the court did not acquire the jurisdiction to render a personal judgment on that claim, the answering party

is not required to counterclaim. Any other rule would require a reluctant party to submit his person to the jurisdiction of the court.

4. A counterclaim that would otherwise be compulsory does not need to be stated if it would require the presence of indispensable third parties over whom the court cannot acquire jurisdiction.

§ 1404. Service of process.

The law does not require that a counterclaim be served with process, although any new parties sued under the counterclaim would be entitled to service of process. NRCP 13(h). No summons is required to be served upon the plaintiff because the plaintiff has submitted his person to the jurisdiction of the court by initiating the action. Wright & Miller, Federal Practice & Procedure § 1416, at 89.

§ 1405. Amendments to add counterclaims.

Where a cause of action supporting a counterclaim matures or is acquired after the answer is served, a motion may be made to amend the answer, seeking leave of court to assert the new counterclaim or file a supplemental pleading. NRCP 13(e); NRCP 15(d). Likewise, if the pleader has failed to set up a counterclaim through oversight, inadvertence, or excusable neglect, when justice requires, the pleader may seek leave of court to set up the counterclaim by amendment. NRCP 13(f); and cases interpreting NRCP 60(b).

The liberal theory of the rules regarding amendments applies to a motion to amend an answer to assert an omitted or late counterclaim. Unless the opposing party can show prejudice, amendment to the answer to allow the counterclaim should be allowed in the interest of justice. *Nevada Bank of Commerce v. Edgewater, Inc.,* 84 Nev. 651, 653, 446 P.2d 990 (1968); *Moll v. Nevada Young American Homes, Inc.,* 93 Nev. 68, 69-70, 560 P.2d 252 (1977).

§ 1406. Who may plead a cross-demand.

Any party who has a claim against an opposing party may plead a cross-demand against that party (NRCP 13(a) and 13(b)). A non-party cannot file a counterclaim. *Pelletier v. Pelletier,* 103 Nev. 408, 742 P.2d 1027 (1987). This leaves no possibility that legitimate cross-demands between the parties will remain unsettled at the termination of the litigation if the parties so desire. Because a counterclaim is not limited to any particular pleading, it is not limited to any particular pleader. Consequently, a counterclaim is available to any party to the action, original or otherwise. This means that, in addition to defendants, plaintiffs, additional parties, intervenors, and third-party defendants, or any combination of these parties, may use a counterclaim. For instance, if A sues B and B counterclaims, A may counterclaim against B on a separate claim.

Also, if A sues B and C, and C cross-claims against B, B may counterclaim against C. Likewise, where defendant B brings C in as a third-party defendant by way of impleader, B is subject to being counterclaimed against by C. Also, any party may be the object of an intervenor's counterclaim, provided the requisite adversary relationship exists.

Rule 13(h), moreover, clearly sanctions the joinder of third parties necessary to the determination of a counterclaim. In other words, if A sues B, B may counterclaim against A for a claim owned jointly by B and C and have C brought in as a co-claimant on the counterclaim. Such third parties become parties to the action and may in turn use the counterclaim device, and even bring in other third parties in the same manner as the original disputants.

§ 1407. Counterclaims against the state.

If the State of Nevada brings a civil action, the defendant's counterclaim may be precluded by the principle of sovereign immunity or subject to the limitations on recovery established by NRS 41.032, *et seq.* The state and its officers and agencies do not waive their statutory protections merely by filing suit. NRCP 13(d).

§ 1408. Cross-claims.

NRCP 13(g) allows a pleader to assert along with an answer any claim that the pleader wishes to assert against a co-party. This section provides for a cross-claim by one party against a co-party where the claim arises "out of the transaction or occurrence that is the subject matter either of the original action or of a counterclaim therein or relating to any property that is the subject matter of the original action." Thus, no claim that is unrelated to the controversy between the parties to the original complaint or to a counterclaim will be injected into the action. However, unlike a compulsory counterclaim, the cross-claim is permissive and need not be pleaded. For example, assume that A sues B and C on a contract claim. B may assert a cross-claim against his co-party, C, by alleging that C is or may be liable to B (cross-complainant) for all or part of the claim asserted against B. The claim is not limited to the original defendants, but may be asserted by any party against a co-party, and that co-party may be required by Rule 13(a) to counterclaim against the cross-claimant.

§ 1409. — Third parties to a cross-claim.

If a party wishes to make a claim against one not already a party, he may, subject to the rules regarding compulsory joinder (NRCP 19) or permissive joinder (NRCP 20). NRCP 13(h). The procedures for adding such a party are covered in Chapter 15, *infra.*

An answer to a cross-claim must be accompanied by a responsive compulsory counterclaim if the party against whom the cross-claim is asserted has a claim for relief against the cross-claiming party arising from the same transaction or occurrence.

An omitted cross-claim may be served upon motion to file an amended answer pursuant to NRCP 15 when the claim has been omitted and justice so requires. *See* § 1405, *supra.*

§ 1410. Separate trials: separate judgments.

In some instances, the desirability of asserting cross-demands may be outweighed by the interest in obtaining an expeditious trial without the interjection of confusing issues. However, if the court permits the introduction of those cross-demands, it may be that fairness requires the plaintiff's claim to be adjudicated before the other claims. For example, where A asserts a simple claim against B for goods sold and delivered and B counterclaims to enjoin A from infringing on B's patent and also brings in additional parties plaintiff and defendant, there is merit in deciding A's claim first. NRCP Rule 13(i), read in conjunction with Rule 42(b), permits the court to try separately the issues raised by a counterclaim. Furthermore, in accordance with Rule 54(b), the court upon determining that there is no just reason for delay, may order a separate judgment entered on one party's claims before the final settlement of issues raised by other parties to the action.

§ 1411. Statute of limitations.

The general rule of common law was that a claim barred by the statute of limitations as the foundation of an independent action was also barred as the subject of a counterclaim. *Rhone v. Keystone Coal Co.,* 250 Pa. 336, 95 A. 530 (1915); *Smith v. Fairbanks, Morse & Co.,* 101 Tex. 24, 102 S.W. 908 (1907); 2 Wood, *Limitation of Actions* 1457 (4th ed. 1916). This rule, though, is not without its exceptions. The first qualification is that the commencement of the action tolls the statute of limitations as to cross-demands in that action which are in the nature of recoupment. *Bull v. United States,* 295 U.S. 247 (1935). Returning once again to the illustrative action of A against B, the exception referred to means that B's counterclaim against A may be successfully pleaded irrespective of the fact that the period of the statute of limitations had run at the time it is pleaded, if the claim related to the plaintiff's claim, is used for defense only, and was not barred by the statute of limitations at the time the plaintiff commenced the principal action. *See generally* 1 A.L.R.2d 630,

"Claim barred by limitation as subject of setoff, counterclaim, recoupment or cross-bill"; 51 Am. Jur. 2d 656-57, *Limitation of Actions* §§ 77-78.

CHAPTER 15

THIRD-PARTY PRACTICE

Author: Elizabeth Goff Gonzales

§ 1501. Introduction and scope.

This chapter discusses Rule 14 of the Nevada Rules of Civil Procedure. The purpose of Rule 14 is to resolve all related disputes in a single action which promotes judicial economy by avoiding multiple lawsuits based on the same or similar set of facts. The practical effect of this rule is to permit all potential responsible parties to have their portion of liability adjudicated in one proceeding. Although Rule 14 is intended to promote judicial efficiency and economy, the provisions of the rule are permissive rather than mandatory, and a defending party may elect to file an independent action rather than to assert a third-party claim.

The third-party practice rule codified in Rule 14(a) is also known as impleader because it permits a defending party to file a third-party complaint against "a person not a party to the action who is or may be liable to him for all or part of the plaintiff's claim against him." Rule 14 is a procedural device. It does not form an independent substantive law basis upon which to bring a nonparty into an action; that is, before a nonparty can properly be named in a third-party complaint, the third-party plaintiff must have a substantive law basis for adding the nonparty to the action.

§ 1502. Time for filing third-party complaint.

Rule 14 permits the filing of a third-party complaint without leave of court within ten (10) days of the filing of the original answer. Filing an amended answer does not reopen or expand the time for filing a third-party complaint. Once this ten-day period has elapsed, a defending party must obtain leave of court to file a third-party complaint. A motion for leave to file a third-party complaint should attach as an exhibit the proposed third-party complaint and summons and in accordance with the provisions of Rule 10(c), the third-party complaint may adopt by refer-

233

ence allegations made in the original complaint. The grant or denial of a motion for leave to assert a third-party complaint is addressed to the sound discretion of the trial court. If leave is granted, the third-party plaintiff should attach a copy of the original complaint as an exhibit to the third-party complaint.

§ 1503. When assertion of a third-party claim is appropriate under Rule 14(a).

A third-party claim is a secondary or derivative claim for relief against a third-party defendant; that is, the third-party defendant will not be liable to the third-party plaintiff unless the third-party plaintiff is found liable to the original plaintiff.

Assertion of a third-party claim is appropriate where:

1. A nonparty is or may be liable to the third-party plaintiff for all or part of the plaintiff's claim;
2. The third-party claim is based on the same or similar evidence, or arises out of the same set of operative facts as the underlying claim;
3. The third-party complaint does not unduly complicate adjudication of the underlying action;
4. The third-party claim does not unduly delay disposition of the underlying action, or otherwise prejudice any party to the action;
5. Assertion of the claim is timely; and,
6. The third-party defendant is subject to the court's jurisdiction.

It is clear that the third-party practice rule embodied in Rule 14(a) may not be used by a defendant in the action for the purposes of offering another defendant to the plaintiff. *Reid v. Royal Insurance Co.*, 80 Nev. 137, 390 P.2d 45 (1964). To assert a claim against a nonparty, the defending party may implead only one who is liable or may be liable to him. Rule 14(a) contemplates an action by a defending party, acting as a third-party plaintiff, the purpose of which is to shift to the third-party defendant all or part of the liability asserted against him by the original plaintiff in the action. Stated in another way, a defending party acting as a third-party plaintiff cannot implead someone solely liable to the original plaintiff, but must have an independent substantive law basis for asserting that the third-party defendant is or may be liable to him.

The issue of whether a proposed third-party complaint is timely is addressed to the trial court's sound discretion. Whether a proposed third-party complaint is timely will often turn on the facts of a particular case.

§ 1504. Substantive law bases for third-party claims.

A third-party defendant may be impleaded in an action only if the third-party plaintiff's right to relief exists under applicable substantive law. Rule 14(a) does not, of itself, create a substantive law basis for asserting a claim against a nonparty. As indicated, a third-party defendant may be named even though his liability is contingent, and will not come into existence unless the defendant/third-party plaintiff is found liable to the plaintiff. The rule's use of the "is or may be liable" language makes it clear that the third-party defendant may be impleaded into an action even though the liability of the third-party defendant is not necessarily automatic if the third-party plaintiff is found liable to the plaintiff.

The legal theories upon which the secondary or derivative liability of a third-party complaint may be based are generally claims for indemnity, contribution, subrogation, or warranty.

In *Reid v. Royal, supra,* the Nevada Supreme Court analyzed the third-party practice rule embodied in Rule 14, stating the rule is based upon the theory of indemnity. The court in *Reid v. Royal* went on to note that the third-party practice rule is not available in a case involving joint or concurrent tortfeasors having no legal relationship to one another, and each owing a duty of care to the injured party. Remarking that a plaintiff has the right to decide who he will sue, the court found that Rule 14 could not be used by a defendant "for the purposes of offering another defendant to the plaintiff."

Rule 14(a) is also the procedural mechanism for asserting a contribution claim against a joint tortfeasor. In Nevada, the right of contribution does not exist until a defendant has paid more than his equitable share of common liability. Although any judgment rendered on a third-party claim for contribution will not be enforceable until after the original defendant/third-party plaintiff has discharged the common liability to the original plaintiff, Rule 14 impleader is an appropriate procedural device to assert a contribution claim because it "merely accelerates the determination of liability and does not have the effect of enlarging any substantive rights." 6 *Wright & Miller,* § 1448, at 389.

A third-party claim may also be based upon subrogation, where, for example, plaintiff has sued an insurance carrier for failing to pay an uninsured motorist claim and, pursuant to the provisions of the insurance contract, the insurer is subrogated to the rights of its insured and pursues a third-party complaint against the uninsured motorist.

§ 1505. Defenses to a third-party claim.

Rule 14(a) requires a third-party defendant to assert any defenses he has to the third-party plaintiff's claim as provided in Rule 12. A third-party defendant may assert any affirmative defenses under Rule 8(c), and may move for a more definite statement if the third-party complaint is so vague or ambiguous that the third-party defendant cannot reasonably be required to frame a responsive pleading. A third-party defendant may also assert any defenses the third-party plaintiff has against the original plaintiff's claim even where the defendant/third-party plaintiff has not timely asserted the affirmative defense against the plaintiff's complaint. Permitting a third-party defendant to assert any defenses the third-party plaintiff has against the original plaintiff's complaint prevents prejudice to the third-party defendant due to the third-party plaintiff's failure to assert an affirmative defense since the third-party defendant will not be able to relitigate the liability of the defendant/third-party plaintiff to the plaintiff. Permitting the third-party defendant to assert any defenses the third-party plaintiff has against the original plaintiff's claim is also a procedural safeguard against collusion between the plaintiff and defendant/third-party plaintiff.

§ 1506. Counterclaims and cross-claims by third-party defendants.

A third-party defendant may counterclaim against the third-party plaintiff who has introduced him into the action, and may cross-claim against other third-party defendants as provided in Rule 13.

§ 1507. Plaintiff's right to assert claims against a third-party defendant.

It is clear under Rule 14(a) when a new party is named in a third-party action, the plaintiff has the option of asserting any claim against a third-party defendant which arises out of the transaction or occurrence that is the subject matter of the plaintiff's complaint against the third-party plaintiff. A plaintiff who desires to assert a claim against a third-party defendant should move to amend the complaint to name the third-party defendant as an additional defendant.

§ 1508. Third-party defendant's right to assert claims against original plaintiff.

A third-party defendant may assert any claim he has against the original plaintiff in the action which arises out of the transaction or occurrence that is the subject matter of the plaintiff's claim against the defendant/third-party plaintiff. In practice, these claims are sometimes called "cross-claims" and sometimes called "counterclaims." Technically, a third-party defendant's claim against the original plaintiff is not appropriately termed a "counterclaim" because at the time the third-party defendant's claim is asserted against the original plaintiff, the original plaintiff and the third-party defendants are not opposing parties. Similarly, such a claim is not appropriately termed a "cross-claim" because under Rule 13, a cross-claim may be asserted only against a co-party. To avoid confusion in terminology, it is suggested that a third-party plain-

236

tiff's assertion of a claim against the original plaintiff be denominated "Third-Party Defendant's Complaint Against Plaintiff."

§ 1509. Third-party defendant's right to assert claims against a nonparty.

The third-party defendant is permitted to join additional parties. The last sentence of Rule 14(a) expressly provides that a third-party defendant "may proceed under this rule against any person not a party to the action who is or may be liable to him for all or part of the claim made in the action against the third-party defendant." Additional parties named by a third-party defendant are known as fourth-party defendants. To avoid confusion in terminology, it is suggested that a third-party defendant's pleading against a nonparty be denominated a "Fourth-Party Complaint." Procedurally, the fourth-party defendant is in the same posture as a third-party defendant.

§ 1510. Motions to dismiss, strike, or sever.

Any party may move to strike or sever the third-party claim, or may move for a separate trial. Grounds for a motion to sever exist where delay in asserting the third-party complaint would result in prejudice to the third-party defendant or to other parties to the litigation, or where issues presented in the third-party complaint would unduly complicate the trial or confuse the jury. Bifurcation of third-party claims (i.e., trying the third-party claim before the same jury which hears the main action in a subsequent proceeding) is also a procedural device which should be considered in complex or multi-party cases which have the potential for complicating the trial unnecessarily and confusing the jury if all claims are tried simultaneously. A motion to dismiss or to strike the third-party complaint may be filed where no substantive law basis exists to assert a third-party complaint against a third-party defendant.

CHAPTER 16

DEPOSITIONS AND DISCOVERY

Authors: Thomas W. Biggar
           Craig R. Delk
           Jeffrey A. Dickerson
           John R. Petty
           Margaret M. Springgate

§ 1601. Introduction and scope.

This chapter covers Rules 16.1, 16.2 and 26 through 37. Scheduling orders are discussed in § 1803, *infra*.

Sections 1602 through 1608 contain an outline and explanation of Nevada's unique mandatory discovery requirements. Additional discovery devices and their uses are detailed in §§ 1609 and 1624 through 1632, along with the scope of permissible discovery (§§ 1610 — 1614), work product and privilege issues (§§ 1615 — 1618), discovery of experts and their materials (§§ 1619 — 1623), protective orders (§ 1633), discovery stipulations (§ 1634), supplementation of discovery responses (§ 1635), filing and use of discovery (§ 1636), and sanctions (§ 1637).

Many of the state and federal rules of discovery are identical and reference to federal cases and treatises construing Federal Rules of Civil Procedure 26 through 37 is encouraged.

In those judicial districts with local district court rules, these must also be reviewed, because they supplement the Nevada Rules of Civil Procedure in many specific respects.

Also, under the Nevada Arbitration Rules, effective July 1, 1992, discovery is discretionary with the arbitrator in the first instance in those cases subject to arbitration. *See* NAR 3 and NAR 11. The arbitration rules also provide for pre-hearing conferences, exchange of witness lists and documents, and related matters. Unless a case is exempted from arbitration, or a petition to remove a case from arbitration is granted by the Discovery Commissioner, the Nevada Arbitration Rules provide for mandatory, non-binding arbitration for all civil cases with a probable jury award value not in excess of $25,000 commenced in judicial districts having a population of at least 100,000. Furthermore, judicial districts having a lesser population are given the option of adopting local rules implementing all or part of the arbitration program as set out by the Nevada Arbitration Rules. These rules should be studied to ensure compliance in appropriate cases.

§ 1602. Mandatory discovery at early case conferences.

NRCP 16.1 establishes an innovative and far-reaching procedure intended to preserve the basic structure and principal objectives of the discovery rules, while significantly streamlining the methods by which these objectives are accomplished in the normal case. As of July 1, 1992, Nevada's mandatory arbitration program has eliminated the requirements of NRCP 16.1 compliance in cases which are concluded in arbitration proceedings. Nevada Arbitration Rule 4(c) provides that cases accepted or remanded into the arbitration program are exempt from NRCP 16.1, so long as they are in the program. Of the remaining (non-arbitrated) cases, the Eighth District has clarified by local rule which ones fall under the NRCP 16.1 umbrella, indicating all cases not commenced by the filing of a complaint are also exempted from the mandatory pretrial discovery requirements of NRCP 16.1. *See* EDCR 2.31.

Unless waived by court order pursuant to NRCP 16.1(f), NRCP 16.1 requires that counsel for the parties (and any party not represented by counsel) meet and confer shortly after issue is joined to exchange all available documents and tangible things then contemplated to be used in support of the pleadings within the scope of NRCP 26(b); make specific requests for discoverable documents and tangible things from opposing parties and respond to such requests; exchange lists of persons (other than expert witnesses and consultants) with knowledge of relevant facts; propose a plan and schedule of discovery and attempt to agree on any conditions or limitations thereon; and, finally, discuss settlement and other means to resolve or dispose of the dispute.

The parties must then file with the court one or more case conference reports containing a brief description of the action, a proposed plan and schedule of additional discovery, a list of all documents exchanged as a result of the conference together with any objections to authenticity or genuineness, a list of all documents not exchanged with an explanation of why each document was not produced, a list of persons with knowledge exchanged at the conference, and an estimate of the time required for discovery. The court may then direct the attorneys and the parties to appear before the court or a discovery commissioner to resolve any disputes resulting from the conference. If such a proceeding is held, the court must thereafter enter an order establishing a plan and schedule for discovery and any appropriate limitations thereon, requiring compliance with the conference requirements, imposing appropriate sanctions if necessary, and determining any other matters, including the allocation of expenses, necessary for proper control of the action.

NRCP 16.1 is intended to accomplish several interrelated objectives. First, NRCP 16.1, together with NRCP 11, is intended to compel counsel and the parties to thoroughly and comprehensively investigate their cases early in preparation for the case conference, so that all parties have an informed basis upon which to meaningfully approach settlement early in the litigation, rather than only after there has been a substantial expenditure of time and resources in discovery and pretrial preparation. Secondly, NRCP 16.1 is intended to compel cooperation among counsel and the parties to accomplish the full disclosure objectives of the discovery rules with a minimum of time and expense consumed in procedural requirements, thereby resulting in the most efficient use of professional and judicial time in analyzing, evaluating, arguing and resolving the legal significance of the evidence disclosed.

NRCP 26(a) has been amended to limit the use of traditional discovery devices to obtain additional discovery not available through NRCP 16.1 and delay the use of these devices until after the filing of the case conference reports or an order waiving such reports. See § 1609, infra. As a result, NRCP 16.1 is also intended to accomplish basic discovery without the necessity of drafting and serving separate interrogatories, requests, responses, and objections thereto, motions to compel and motions for protective orders. NRCP 16.1 thus leaves control of discovery in the hands of the parties and their counsel — unless the complexity of the case requires active court involvement, or the court or a discovery commissioner must intervene to resolve discovery disputes. At the same time the Case Conference Report provides the court with a summary of the case and an outline of discovery, so the court or discovery commissioner can monitor the case to ensure that the parties and their counsel are not abusing the discovery process.

Accomplishing these objectives requires the cooperation of all counsel and the parties along with fair but firm, consistent and predictable judicial action to compel those refusing to cooperate or honor their obligations under NRCP 16.1 to do so by the imposition of substantial and meaningful sanctions. *See* Nevada Supreme Court Rules of Professional Conduct 171 and 173. NRCP 16.1 is thus intended to promote and facilitate prompt investigation, preparation, prosecution, and full disclosure, so that cases can be resolved quickly — whether by settlement or otherwise — thereby minimizing ligation delay and needless expense to all parties and the judicial system.

§ 1603. — Attendance at early case conferences.

NRCP 16.1(a) requires that, within thirty days after the first defendant serves an answer, and thereafter as each defendant answers the original or an amended complaint, counsel for the parties (and any party acting without counsel) meet in person. It has been suggested the "meet in person" requirement should be relaxed in cases where the law offices of opposing counsel are located more than seventy-five miles apart or a party in proper person resides outside Nevada. This minor revision would seem to have merit in those cases where the stakes are not extraordinarily high and the parties are willing to cooperate fully in the timely exchange of information and the preparation of the report. However, until a formal rule change takes effect, counsel should check with the appropriate discovery commissioner for a ruling in a particular case.

The plaintiff's attorney is responsible for designating the time and place of each meeting, so long as it is in the county where the action has been filed, unless the parties agree upon a different location. The rule expressly requires the attorneys participating in any such conference "must possess authority to act and knowledge of the case obtained after reasonable inquiry under the circumstances...." Thus, the attorneys attending the conference must have responsibility for the case, must have investigated the case in preparation for the conference and must have authority to act for their clients at the conference.

The time for any case conference may be continued by agreement for up to an additional ninety days. The court may also continue the time for any such conference for good cause shown. However, unless there are "compelling and extraordinary circumstances," neither the court nor the parties may extend the time for the conference to a day more than 180 days after service of process upon the particular defendant in question. Thus, the clear intent of the rule is that, in all but the most exceptional cases, the attorneys will have investigated the case and case conferences for each defendant will have occurred within six months after service of process upon that defendant. However, the time for holding a case conference with respect to a defendant moving to quash service of process is tolled until entry of an order denying the motion.

NRCP 16.1(e) provides that if a case conference is not held within 180 days after service of process upon a defendant, the case may be dismissed as to that defendant without prejudice, on motion or on the court's own initiative, unless compelling and extraordinary circumstances justify continuing the time for the conference. The rule also provides that the court, on motion or on its own initiative, shall impose upon a party, its attorney, or both, appropriate sanctions if an attorney fails to reasonably comply with any provision of NRCP 16.1. Sanctions for failing to comply with NRCP 16.1 include those available under NRCP 37(b)(2), such as striking pleadings, staying the proceedings, dismissing the action, rendering a judgment by default and/or requiring the payment of reasonable expenses, including attorney's fees, caused by the failure. *Dougan v. Gustaveson,* 108 Nev. 517, 835 P.2d 795 (1992). Thus, the rule requires the imposition of an appropriate sanction if an attorney (or party) fails to cooperate in scheduling a case conference, fails to reasonably investigate the case in preparation for the conference, fails to attend a case conference, or fails to meaningfully participate in the case conference and fulfill the obligations imposed by NRCP 16.1. *Cf. Wilmurth v. First Judicial District Court,* 80 Nev. 337, 341-43, 393 P.2d 302, 303-05 (1964).

§ 1604. — Meet and confer requirements; discovery exchanges.

NRCP 16.1(b) provides that, at each case conference, the attorneys (and any party not represented by an attorney) must:

(1) Exchange all documents then reasonably available to the party which are then contemplated to be used in support of the allegations or denials of that party's pleadings, including rebuttal and impeachment documents. The scope of this document discovery may be broader than the limits of Rule 26(b). *See* § 1610, *infra.* The rule contemplates an objective standard to measure compliance, focusing not on intent, but on the effect a failure to disclose may have on the adverse party. *Cf.* 8 Wright & Miller, *Federal Practice and Procedure* § 2030 (1970). If an attorney (or party) fails to reasonably comply with this obligation, NRCP 16.1(e) requires that the court impose appropriate sanctions which may

include, in addition to the sanctions available under NRCP 37(b)(2), an order prohibiting the use of any documents which should have been disclosed and exchanged pursuant to this rule.

(2) Request "with reasonably specificity" from the opposing parties all other discoverable documents that may support the allegations of the requesting party's pleadings, including rebuttal and impeachment documents. Once such a request is made, the opposing party must: (A) provide the additional documents, (B) agree to provide the additional documents as soon as they are reasonably available, or (C) explain why the documents will not be provided. Such an explanation should include objections based on relevancy, privilege, undue burden or expense, or any other ground that would justify a protective order under NRCP 26(c).

(3) Identify, describe or produce all tangible things that constitute or contain discoverable matter and, upon request, arrange for all other parties to inspect and copy, test or sample such things. Again, NRCP 16.1(e) requires that the court impose appropriate sanctions, which may include the sanctions available under NRCP 37(b)(2) and/or a preclusion order, if there is a failure to comply with this requirement. *See Fire Insurance Exchange v. Zenith Radio Corp.,* 103 Nev. 648, 747 P.2d 911 (1987); *Stubli v. Big D. International Trucks,* 107 Nev. 309, 810 P.2d 785 (1991).

(4) Request to inspect and copy, test or sample any tangible thing that constitutes or contains discoverable matter and which is in the possession, custody or control of another party. Once such a request is made, the party having possession, custody or control of the thing must: (A) provide the discovery requested, or (B) explain why the discovery will not be provided. Such an explanation should include any appropriate objection that would justify a protective order against such discovery.

(5) Exchange written lists of persons (other than expert witnesses or consultants) then known or reasonably believed to have knowledge of any facts relevant to the allegations of any pleadings filed by any party, including persons having knowledge of rebuttal or impeachment evidence. *Cf. Davis v. Marathon Oil Co.,* 528 F.2d 395 (6th Cir. 1975); *Napolitano v. Compania Sud Americana de Vapores,* 421 F.2d 382 (2d Cir. 1970). Each person must be identified by name and location and a general description of the subject matter of the person's testimony must be provided. Each party is under a continual duty to promptly supplement its list of persons. *Cf. Scott & Fetzer Co. v. Dile,* 643 F.2d 670 (9th Cir. 1971); *Smith v. Ford Motor Co.,* 626 F.2d 784 (10th Cir. 1980), *cert. denied,* 450 U.S. 918 (1981). Again, NRCP 16.1(e) requires the court impose appropriate sanctions, which may include any sanction available under NRCP 37(b)(2) and/or a preclusion order, if there is a failure to list any such person or timely supplement a prior list of such persons. *See*

Southern Pacific Co. v. Watkins, 83 Nev. 471, 493, 435 P.2d 498, 512 (1967); *cf. Wickliffe v. Sunrise Hospital,* 101 Nev. 542, 548-49, 706 P.2d 1383, 1388-89 (1985); *Otis Elevator Co. v. Reid,* 101 Nev. 515, 522-23, 706 P.2d 1378, 1382-83 (1985).

(6) Propose a plan and schedule of additional discovery and make a reasonable effort to agree with opposing attorneys to provide all discovery requested, with any conditions or limitations thereon. Examples of such agreements might include those concerning procedural details, such as the time of depositions and other discovery, confidentiality stipulations and any other matters that might properly be the subject of a protective order under NRCP 26(c).

(7) Discuss settlement of the action and the use of extrajudicial procedures or alternative methods of dispute resolution to resolve the controversy.

(8) Discuss any other matters that might aid in the disposition of the action. Examples of such matters might include stipulations of fact that would narrow the issues in controversy; special procedures such as masters or receivers to deal with particularly difficult problems; or the need for, and the proper form of, interim relief during the pendency of the action.

If an attorney (or party acting without an attorney) fails to cooperate in this endeavor, by failing or refusing to reasonably comply with any provision of NRCP 16.1, NRCP 16.1(e)(3) requires that the court impose sanctions, which may include any sanctions available under NRCP 37(b)(2) and/or an order prohibiting the use of any witness, document or tangible thing that should have been disclosed, produced, exhibited, or exchanged pursuant to NRCP 16.1(b). *See Smith v. Rowe,* 761 F.2d 360 (7th Cir. 1985). The sanctions available under NRCP 37(b)(2) include: striking pleadings; staying proceedings; dismissing the action; rendering a judgment by default; taking designated facts as established for the action; refusing to allow a party to support or oppose designated claims or defenses or introduce designated matters in evidence; and/or requiring the payment of reasonable expenses (including attorney's fees) caused by the failure. *See* §1637, *infra.*

It should be emphasized there is an important difference between imposing such sanctions under NRCP 37(b)(2) and under NRCP 16.1(e)(3). Under NRCP 37(b)(2), such sanctions can be imposed only for failing to obey a court order to provide or permit discovery. However, under NRCP 16.1(e)(3), such sanctions can be imposed upon motion or the court's own initiative for failure to reasonably comply with any provision of NRCP 16.1 without the prior entry of a court order compelling the discovery in question. As a result, under NRCP 16.1(e)(3) such sanctions are immediately available. An uncooperative attorney or party does not get a second chance to cure a violation of the discovery disclosure rules since NRCP

16.1(e)(3) does not require the entry and violation of a court order before sanctions can be imposed.

Thus, the intent of NRCP 16.1(b) is to accomplish all initial discovery, establish a plan and schedule for any remaining discovery (including any conditions or limitations thereon), and promote extrajudicial resolution of the controversy early in the litigation. Thereafter, if a party either seeks additional discovery or moves for protection against discovery, the court should consider the party's failure to raise and attempt to resolve the question at the case conference in determining whether such additional discovery should be allowed under NRCP 26(b)(1) and 26(c). See § 1609, infra.

§ 1605. — Case conference reports.

NRCP 16.1(c) requires that within thirty days after each case conference, the parties must file a joint case conference report or, if the parties cannot agree on the contents of a joint report, each party must serve and file an individual case conference report. Each case conference report must contain:

(1) A brief description of the nature of the action and each claim for relief and defense;

(2) A proposed plan and schedule for any additional discovery. If the parties have agreed upon any conditions or limitations on additional discovery, such as subject matter limitations, confidentiality stipulations or other protective order provisions, NRCP 16.1(d)(1) requires that such stipulations be either entered in the court minutes or reduced to writing signed by the parties or their attorneys; consequently such agreements should also be recorded in the case conference report. See Szilagyi v. Testa, 99 Nev. 834, 673 P.2d 495 (1983).

(3) A written list of all documents provided at or as a result of the case conference, together with any objection that the document is not authentic or genuine. The rule expressly provides that the failure to state an objection to the authenticity or genuineness of a document constitutes a waiver of that objection at any subsequent hearing or trial. Cf. Hard v. Stevens, 65 F.R.D. 637 (E.D. Pa. 1975). The purpose of this provision is to minimize the need for custodial depositions and other formal authentication procedures, unless there is a real question as to the authenticity or genuineness of the document, while preserving all other objections such as relevancy, hearsay, etc., for later resolution at pretrial or trial. However, the rule also provides that, for good cause shown, the court may permit the withdrawal of a waiver resulting from the failure to state an objection and the assertion of the objection. Thus, if a party later discovers facts giving rise to an objection based on authenticity or genuineness which could not have been discovered with reasonable diligence

before the filing of the case conference report, the rule provides a means for reviving the objection once these facts become known.

(4) A written list of all documents not provided by the opposing party in response to a request for discoverable documents together with the explanation (*e.g.,* privilege, work product, lack of possession, custody or control, etc.) why each document was not provided. This provision contemplates preparation of a schedule of all withheld documents to facilitate meaningful consideration of privilege, work product and similar objections with respect to each separate document. *See Continental Group, Inc. v. Justice,* 536 F. Supp. 658, 664 (D. Del. 1982).

(5) The written lists of persons (other than expert witnesses or consultants) then known or reasonably believed to have knowledge of any facts relevant to the allegations of any pleading filed by any party to the action (including rebuttal or impeachment evidence) exchanged at the case conference, with a general description of the subject matter of each person's knowledge or testimony.

(6) An estimate of the time required to complete discovery in the case. For trial scheduling purposes the discovery commissioner of the Eighth District also requires an estimate of trial time and an indication whether a jury has been demanded to be set forth in the discovery plan section of the report.

If any other agreements acceptable to all parties have been reached at the case conference, such as stipulations of fact, special procedures for resolving particular problems, or the need for interim relief these agreements should also be recorded in or attached to the case conference report.

Since more than one case conference may occur, the rule expressly requires that after any subsequent case conference, the parties must supplement, but need not repeat, the contents of prior case conference reports.

NRCP 16.1(c) also provides that, within seven days after service of any case conference report, any other party may file a response to the report objecting to all or a portion of the report or adding any other matters which are necessary to properly reflect the proceedings occurring at the case conference.

NRCP 16.1(c) expressly provides that all case conference reports and responses must be signed in accordance with NRCP 11. Thus, each attorney or party must certify that, to the best of his or her knowledge, information and belief formed after reasonable inquiry, the matters stated in the report or response are well grounded in fact and warranted by existing law or a good faith argument for the extension, modification or reversal of existing law, and are not asserted for any improper purpose, such as to harass or to cause unnecessary delay or to needlessly increase the cost of litigation. If a case conference report or response is

247

signed in violation of this requirement, NRCP 11 requires the imposition of an appropriate sanction, which may include reasonable expenses, including a reasonable attorney's fee, resulting from the violation. *See* § 812, *supra.*

NRCP 16.1(e)(2) provides that if the plaintiff does not file a case conference report within 240 days after service of process upon a defendant, the case may be dismissed as to that defendant without prejudice, on motion or on the court's own initiative. *Dougan v. Gustaveson,* 108 Nev. 517, 835 P.2d 795 (1992). Since the plaintiff's attorney is responsible for scheduling the case conference, this provision is intended to insure that the case conference is held and the results of the case conference are memorialized in written form and reported to the court. However, NRCP 16.1(e)(3) provides that if an attorney (or party not represented by an attorney) fails to reasonably comply with any provision of NRCP 16.1, the court shall impose upon the party, the attorney or both, appropriate sanctions, which may include any sanction available under NRCP 37(b)(2) and/or a preclusion order. Consequently, both plaintiffs and defendants must be sanctioned appropriately if they fail to comply with their obligations concerning case conference reports.

NRCP 16.1(e)(4) separately provides that if it appears at any time an objection to the authenticity or genuineness of a document was made in violation of NRCP 11, the court must forthwith order the party, the attorney or both to pay to the other party the reasonable expense caused by the objection, including reasonable attorney's fees. This provision, together with the reasonable inquiry and sanction requirements of NRCP 11, is intended to prevent a party from defeating one of the objectives of NRCP 16.1 — the elimination of needless custodial depositions and other unnecessary authentication procedures — by asserting speculative or unfounded objections to the authenticity or genuineness of a document, when the party has no real basis upon which to question its authenticity or genuineness.

§ 1606. — Case conference disputes.

NRCP 16.1(d) provides that, at any time after the filing of a case conference report, the court, upon motion or on its own initiative, may convene a conference among the attorneys and the parties, before the court or a discovery commissioner, to resolve any disputes arising during or as a result of a case conference. If the parties have resolved discovery disputes by stipulation, the rule requires that the stipulation be entered in the minutes as an order, or reduced to writing and signed by the parties or their attorneys. *See Szilagyi v. Testa,* 99 Nev. 834, 673 P.2d 495 (1983).

It is now the rule in the Second and Eighth Districts to have the discovery commissioner resolve all discovery disputes in the first instance. *See* § 1608, *infra*. Immediate resolution of discovery disputes is encouraged by the commissioners who make it a practice to be available by telephone for rulings on deposition problems. The preferred method of resolving a deposition impasse is first to try and get a ruling from the commissioner, thereby preventing in most instances a costly adjournment of the deposition.

If the discovery dispute conference is before a discovery commissioner, the commissioner must prepare and file a report containing the commissioner's recommendations for resolution of each unresolved dispute. The clerk must forthwith serve a copy of the report on all parties, and any party may serve and file written objections to the commissioner's recommendations within five days after service of the report. *See* § 1608, *infra*.

After the filing of a discovery commissioner's report and any objections thereto, or after a dispute resolution conference before the court, the court must enter an order establishing a plan and schedule for discovery. The order will set any appropriate limitations on discovery, mandate compliance with the meet and confer and exchange requirements of NRCP 16.1(b), impose sanctions pursuant to NRCP 16.1(e), if necessary, and determine any other matters, including the allocation of expenses, necessary for proper control of the action. *See* § 1608, *infra*.

NRCP 16.1(e)(3) provides that if an attorney or a party fails to comply with an order entered pursuant to NRCP 16.1(d), the court, upon motion or its own initiative, must impose appropriate sanctions on the party, the attorney, or both. Such sanctions may include any sanctions available under NRCP 37(b)(2) and/or an order prohibiting the use of any witness, document or tangible thing that should have been disclosed, produced, exhibited or exchanged pursuant to NRCP 16.1(b). The sanctions available under NRCP 37(b)(2) include striking pleadings, staying proceedings, dismissing the action, rendering a judgment by default, treating the failure as a contempt of court, taking designated facts as established for the action, refusing to allow a party to support or oppose designated claims or defenses or introduce designated matters in evidence, and/or requiring the payment of reasonable expenses (including attorney's fees) caused by the failure. *See* § 1637, *infra*.

§ 1607. — Complex litigation.

NRCP 16.1(f) provides that, in a potentially difficult or protracted action that may involve complex issues, multiple parties, difficult legal questions or unusual proof problems, the court may, upon motion and for good cause shown, waive any or all of the requirements of NRCP 16.1. In the absence of a finding that the case is potentially difficult or will be a protracted action that might involve complex issues, multiple parties, difficult legal questions or unusual proof problems, a waiver of NRCP 16.1 is improper. *Mays v. Eighth Judicial District Court*, 105 Nev. 60, 768 P.2d 877 (1989). The operative language of this provision parallels that contained in NRCP 16(c)(10) with respect to adopting special procedures for the management of such actions at a pretrial conference called by the court. NRCP 16.1(f) expressly requires that a showing of good cause be made. If the court is satisfied good cause exists it may waive one, some or all of the requirements of the rule. Consequently, a separate good cause showing must be made — usually by affidavit — with respect to each of the requirements of NRCP 16.1 sought to be waived. The purpose of this provision is to prevent the routine making and granting of such motions in those cases that would benefit by at least some, if not all, of the NRCP 16.1 procedures.

NRCP 16(b) exempts cases that have been "designated as complex litigation pursuant to NRCP 16.1(f)" from the mandatory scheduling order required by NRCP 16(b). However, NRCP 16.1(f) requires that all of the requirements of NRCP 16.1 are waived, the court must order a conference pursuant to NRCP 16. Furthermore, NRCP 26(f) expressly provides that a discovery conference pursuant to that rule may be combined with a pretrial conference pursuant to NRCP 16. Consequently, in the truly exceptional case where none of the NRCP 16.1 procedures are appropriate, the court must take control of the discovery and pretrial proceedings to ensure that the objectives of NRCP 16, 16.1 and the discovery rules are accomplished.

If the court waives some, but not all, of the NRCP 16.1 requirements, the court and the parties are responsible for making certain the scheduling and planning objectives of NRCP 16(b) are accomplished, either in the case conference report(s) filed by the parties or otherwise. Furthermore, if the court waives some, but not all, of the NRCP 16.1 requirements, the court and the parties should make certain the NRCP 16.1 procedures that are followed are memorialized in a case conference report or some other writing signed by the parties or their attorneys, so there is no confusion or controversy with respect to such matters in subsequent proceedings.

§ 1608. Discovery commissioners.

Rule 16.2 permits the employment of discovery commissioners to assist the court in resolving Rule 16.1 case conference disputes, conducting Rule 16 scheduling conferences and entering scheduling orders. Both the Second and Eighth Districts now have full-time discovery commissioners. Their compensation is not taxed against the parties, but is paid out of appropriations made for the expenses of the district court. Rule

16.2(a). In those two Districts it is now the rule to have all discovery disputes (except disputes presented at a pretrial conference or at trial) first heard by the discovery commissioner. *See, e.g.*, EDCR 2.34(a).

Rule 16.2(b) authorizes a discovery commissioner to "preside" at case conferences. Thus, the commissioner may attend a case conference in person or by telephone and control the proceeding as appropriate, making recommendations for resolution of any disputes which arise. The discovery commissioner's attendance at a case conference is an exceptional occurrence. Most often the commissioner does not even learn that a Rule 16.1(b) case conference has occurred until a case conference report, filed as required by Rule 16.1(c), is brought to his attention.

If the commissioner does not attend a case conference, a separate dispute resolution conference will be held to resolve disputes which arose during the early case conference. In most instances the dispute resolution conference will be scheduled at the initiative of the court or commissioner and counsel will receive written notice of a time to appear. While written motions to resolve a discovery dispute are unnecessary in the Second or Eighth Districts, they should be filed in cases pending in the remaining districts as a vehicle for bringing the dispute to the attention of the court. Written motions for resolution of any discovery dispute are noticed, filed and served in accordance with the local rules of court. *See generally* § 1105, *supra*.

The resolution of all discovery disputes by stipulation of the parties must be entered in the minutes in the form of an order or reduced to writing subscribed by the parties or by their attorneys. Rule 16.1(d)(1). *Cf.* DCR 16 and, in the Eighth District, EDCR 7.50. *See also* § 1114 *et seq., supra*.

The commissioner is required to report to the court concerning each unresolved dispute and make recommendations for the court's order for their resolution. Rule 16.1(d)(2). While the commissioner must prepare that report, prevailing counsel are frequently requested to assist in its preparation. After the report is signed and filed, the clerk must serve a copy on all parties. Rule 16.1(d)(2).

A party may object to the commissioner's report and recommendation by serving and filing a written objection thereto within five days after it is served. Rule 16.1(d)(2). Objections are not noticed for hearing. If timely filed, they will be brought to the attention of the court in chambers. In the Eighth District no additional points and authorities or oral argument are permitted when objecting to the commissioner's recommendation, without leave of court. EDCR 2.34(f). The judge may rule without a hearing or direct that a hearing be held with notice to counsel. Pursuant to Rule 16.1(d), the order can:

1. Establish a plan and schedule for discovery [*see* § 1606, *supra*];

2. Set limits on the discovery if appropriate [*see* Rules 26(b)(1) and 26(c)];

3. Require discovery exchanges in accordance with Rule 16.1(b); and,

4. If necessary, impose sanctions [*see* Rule 16.1(e)].

§ 1609. Additional discovery methods.

The traditional methods of discovery include oral depositions (Rule 30), depositions upon written questions (Rule 31), written interrogatories to parties (Rule 33), requests to produce documents and things (Rule 34), requests to permit entry upon land for inspection and other purposes (Rule 34), physical and mental examinations (Rule 35), and requests for admissions (Rule 36). The 1988 amendments to Nevada's discovery rules changed the emphasis from these traditional discovery methods to the simple mandatory requirements of Rule 16.1. Good faith compliance with this new rule should substantially complete discovery in many cases.

Rules 30 through 36, the traditional discovery methods, may only be used to obtain "additional" discovery:

1. At any time after the filing of a joint case conference report; or,

2. Upon the entry of an order waiving compliance with Rule 16.1(c); or,

3. Not sooner than ten (10) days after a party has filed his own case conference report.

See Rule 26(a). It is the clear intent of Rule 26(a) that traditional methods of discovery (depositions, interrogatories, etc.) will not be permitted until Rule 16.1 is complied with or its requirements waived.

"Additional" discovery means discovery that was not obtained after full compliance with Rule 16.1. Thus, if a request to produce documents should have been made pursuant to Rule 16.1(b)(2), it would be improper to make the request pursuant to Rule 34.

A motion for a protective order would be an appropriate response to a request for Rule 30 through 36 discovery by a party not in compliance with Rule 16.1, unless compliance is waived. The "compliance" required includes attendance at the early case conference, the exchange of discovery mandated by Rule 16.1(b)(1), (3) and (5), the filing of a case conference report, attendance at any required dispute resolution conferences, and following any plan or schedule for discovery established by the court pursuant to Rule 16(b) or Rule 16.1(d).

§ 1610. — Purpose and scope of additional discovery.

Discovery is designed to take the "sporting aspect" out of litigation and increase the likelihood that the results of lawsuits are based on the merits of the controversy rather than the ability, skill and cunning of counsel. The combination of mandatory discovery at an early case conference with traditional discovery techniques (depositions, interrogatories, requests, etc.) insures that each side will be fully aware of all the facts involved in the case and the positions of the parties, prior to trial. Also, discovery narrows issues, simplifies proof of uncontested issues and, with regard to depositions, preserves testimony for trial. Indeed, discovery can often result in the settlement of suits, thereby avoiding trial.

The scope of traditional discovery methods (Rules 27 - 36) is limited by Rule 26(b) to "any matter, not privileged, which is relevant to the subject matter in the pending action...." *See State ex rel. Tidvall v. Eighth Judicial District Court,* 91 Nev. 520, 539 P.2d 456 (1975) and *Schlatter v. Eighth Judicial District Court,* 93 Nev. 189, 561 P.2d 1342, 1343 (1977). *Cf. Meyer v. Second Judicial District Court,* 95 Nev. 176, 591 P.2d 259, 261 (1979). It is important to note that these two requirements — "nonprivileged" and "relevant" — are set out in the conjunctive; unless both prongs of the test are satisfied, the information sought is not properly the subject of discovery inquiries as a threshold matter. It should also be noted that the "relevance" for discovery purposes is not synonymous with admissibility in evidence. *See Multi-core, Inc. v. Southern Water Treatment Co.,* 139 F.R.D. 262, 264 n.2 (D. Mass. 1991) ("Relevance encompasses more than admissibility at trial. For purposes of Rule 26, relevant information includes any matter that is or may become an issue in the litigation."). Relevant, nonprivileged matter is discoverable, though not admissible from an evidentiary standpoint, if the information sought is "reasonably calculated to lead to the discovery of admissible evidence." Rule 26(b)(1). *See also Greenspun v. Eighth Judicial District Court,* 91 Nev. 211, 533 P.2d 482, 484 (1975), and Advisory Committee Notes, Fed. R. Civ. P. (1946).

The scope of document discovery at the early case conference required by Rule 16.1 is broader than permitted pursuant to Rule 34. Rule 16.1(b)(1) requires an attorney to disclose "all documents ... which are then contemplated to be used in support of the allegations or denials of the pleading filed by that party...." This would include privileged material and "work product" not otherwise discoverable under Rule 26(b)(3). *See* § 1615. The requirement is clear and simple — all documents which you are going to use at trial must be given to the other side, no exceptions.

Rule 16.1(b) also requires disclosure of documents and the identity of witnesses which may be used for rebuttal or impeachment purposes. Clearly, this includes inconsistent statements, surveillance movies and criminal convictions.

§ 1611. — Sequence, timing, frequency and extent of use.

There is no "priority" rule whereby a party may delay an opponent's discovery requests until his own discovery demands are satisfied. Nor is there a rule requiring discovery to proceed in any particular order. Indeed, Rule 26(d) provides that "methods of discovery may be used in any sequence and the fact that a party is conducting discovery, whether by deposition or otherwise, shall not operate to delay any other party's discovery." Rule 26(d) makes it clear, however, that the court has discretion to enter an order establishing a priority or a sequence of discovery. *See Rebel Oil Co. v. Atlantic Richfield Co.*, 133 F.R.D. 41, 43 (D. Nev. 1990) ("Rule 26(d) allows the Court to issue an Order to control the sequence and timing of discovery 'upon motion, for the convenience of the parties and witnesses and in the interests of justice.'"); *and see Greenspun v. Eighth Judicial District Court*, 91 Nev. 211, 533 P.2d 482 (1975), where the Nevada Supreme Court refused to disturb a district court's order requiring discovery to be first undertaken by written interrogatories rather than by oral deposition, stating that the issue of whether the lower court had abused its discretion was not ripe for review via mandamus. It was not then known whether discovery by way of interrogatories was an inadequate vehicle for obtaining the information sought, and the district court order did not preclude the right to ultimately take discovery by way of oral deposition. The *Greenspun* case notwithstanding, orders altogether prohibiting the taking of depositions are probably reversible as a general matter. *See U.S. v. Miracle Recreation Equipment Co.*, 118 F.R.D. 100, 104 (S.D. Iowa 1987) ("[g]enerally, one is required to show both that there is a likelihood of harassment and that the information sought is fully irrelevant before a party is altogether denied the right to take an individual's deposition").

The court also has authority to regulate over-discovery:

> The frequency or extent of use of the discovery methods set forth in subdivision (a) shall be limited by the court if it determines that: (i) the discovery sought is unreasonably cumulative or duplicative, or is obtainable from some other source that is more convenient, less burdensome, or less expensive; (ii) the party seeking discovery has had ample opportunity by discovery in the action to obtain the information sought; or (iii) the discovery is unduly burdensome or expensive, taking into account the needs of the case, the amount in controversy, limitations of the parties' resources, and the importance of the issues at stake in the litigation. The court may act upon its own initiative after reasonable notice or pursuant to a motion under subdivision (c).

Rule 26(b)(1). This sentence was added to the federal rules in 1983 and to NRCP in 1988. It is explained in the Advisory Committee Notes, Fed. R. Civ. P. (1983) as follows:

The objective is to guard against redundant or disproportionate discovery by giving the court authority to reduce the amount of discovery that may be directed to matters that are otherwise proper subjects of inquiry. The new sentence is intended to encourage judges to be more aggressive in identifying and discouraging discovery overuse. The grounds mentioned in the amended rule for limiting discovery reflect the existing practice of many courts in issuing protective orders under Rule (26)(c).

The first element of the standard, Rule 26(b)(1)(i), is designed to minimize redundancy in discovery and encourage attorneys to be sensitive to the comparative costs of different methods of securing information. Subdivision (b)(1)(ii) also seeks to reduce repetitiveness and to oblige lawyers to think through their discovery activities in advance so that full utilization is made of each deposition, document request, or set of interrogatories. The elements of Rule 26(b)(1)(iii) address the problem of discovery that is disproportionate to the individual lawsuit as measured by such matters as its nature and complexity, the importance of the issues at stake in a case seeking damages, the limitations on a financially weak litigant to withstand extensive opposition to a discovery program or to respond to discovery requests, and the significance of the substantive issues, as measured in philosophic, social, or institutional terms. Thus the rule recognizes that many cases in public policy spheres, such as employment practices, free speech, and other matters, may have importance far beyond the monetary amount involved. The court must apply the standards in an evenhanded manner that will prevent use of discovery to wage a war of attrition or as a device to coerce a party, whether financially weak or affluent.

The rule contemplates greater judicial involvement in the discovery process and thus acknowledges the reality that it cannot always operate on a self-regulating basis. *See* Connolly, Holleman & Kuhlman, *Judicial Controls and the Civil Litigative Process: Discovery 77,* Federal Judicial Center (1978). In an appropriate case the court could restrict the number of depositions, interrogatories, or the scope of a production request. But the court must be careful not to deprive a party of discovery that is reasonably necessary to afford a fair opportunity to develop and prepare the case.

The court may act on motion, or its own initiative. It is entirely appropriate to resort to the amended rule in conjunction with a discovery conference under Rule 26(f) or one of the other pretrial conferences authorized by the rules.

Even though these provisions only expressly address the problem of redundant and excessive use of discovery, courts have also used them as a guide for determining other discovery disputes "such as whether individual discovery requests are sufficiently relevant as contrasted with the burden of producing the information." *Marker v. Union Fidelity Life Insurance Co.,* 125 F.R.D. 121, 124 (M.D.N.C. 1989); *and see Anker v. G.D. Searle & Co.,* 126 F.R.D. 515, 518 (M.D.N.C. 1989) ("[t]he factors set out in Rule 26(b)(1)(i), (ii), (iii) provide some specific considerations for use in applying [a] balancing test" which "weighs the need for discovery by the requesting party and the relevance of the discovery to the case against the harm, prejudice or burden to the other party."). Finally, these provisions have been interpreted as superimposing the concept of proportionality on all behavior in the discovery process. The court in *In re Convergent Technologies Securities Litigation*, 108 F.R.D. 328, 331 (N.D. Cal. 1988), eloquently described *counsel's* obligations imposed by these provisions thus: "It is no longer sufficient, as a precondition for conducting discovery, to show that the information sought 'appears reasonably calculated to lead to the discovery of admissible evidence.' After satisfying this threshold requirement, counsel *also must* make a commonsense determination, taking into account all the circumstances, that the information sought is of sufficient potential significance to justify the burden the discovery probe would impose, that the discovery tool selected is the most efficacious of the means that might be used to acquire the desired information (taking into account cost effectiveness and the nature of the information being sought), and that the timing of the probe is sensible, *i.e.*, that there is no other juncture in the pretrial period when there would be a clearly happier balance between the benefit derived from and the burdens imposed by the particular discovery effort." (emphasis in original).

NRCP 26(f), added in 1986, has had a substantial impact on discovery proceedings in complicated or "complex" cases. The drafters of the Rule "envisioned the discovery conference as a specialized tool, invoked in cases that have or potentially have significant discovery concerns." *Union City Barge Line v. Union Carbide Corp.*, 823 F.2d 129, 134 (5th Cir. 1987). The rule provides for discovery conferences upon motion. Following the discovery conference, the court must enter an order identifying discovery issues, setting plans and schedules, limiting discovery, allocation of expenses, etc. The court is also vested with discretion to combine the discovery conference with a pre-trial conference under Rule 16. *See also* Rule 16(b)(5), which requires a scheduling order within 180 days after filing of the complaint, and Rule 16.1(f), which requires a Rule 16 conference if the court designates a case as complex litigation and waives all mandatory pre-trial discovery requirements.

The Advisory Committee's Notes, Fed. R. Civ. P. (1980) suggest that requests for discovery conferences under Rule 26(f) are neither intended nor expected to become routine, and that "relatively narrow" discovery dispute[s] should be resolved by resort to Rules 26(c) or 37(a) (governing protective orders and motions to compel). Further, because NRCP 26(f) and Fed. R. Civ. P. 26(f) contemplate informal good faith efforts by the parties to frame a discovery plan as a condition precedent to the filing of an application to have the court convene a discovery conference, and because the decision to convene such a conference should be determined on a case-by-case basis depending upon the complexity of a particular matter, the court should not convene discovery conferences or enter orders under NRCP 26(f) and Fed. R. Civ. P. 26(f) in all cases.

Also in 1986, time limits were adopted which restrict the time periods during which a party, as a matter of right, may "complete" discovery or have motions concerning discovery heard by the court, *i.e.,* up and until forty-five days prior to the trial date to complete discovery and up and until thirty days prior to the trial date to have motions heard. *See* NRCP 26(i). The time limits are made subject to applications for leave to move the deadlines closer to trial (considerations for granting such leave are set forth in the rule) and stipulations of the parties. These limits will frequently be altered by scheduling orders issued pursuant to Rule 16. *See* Chapter 18, *infra.* As used in Rule 26(i), discovery is "completed" on the day responses are due or the day a deposition begins. Applications to modify these deadlines should be made on notice and not ex parte.

Newly joined parties may obtain discovery materials generated by existing parties prior to joinder. NRCP 26(h) provides that new parties to litigation may serve a written request on the existing parties for such discovery materials, and further describes the method of response.

§ 1612. — Relevant matters.

As noted in § 1610 above, the term "relevant" in Rule 26(b)(1) is broadly construed and encompasses any matter that could bear on an issue that exists or "might" exist in a case. It is not limited to issues raised in the pleadings because discovery is designed to clarify issues. It is also not limited to the merits of a matter because a variety of fact-oriented issues may arise in any case that are not related to the merits. *See Marker v. Union Fidelity Life Insurance Co.,* 125 F.R.D. 121, 124 (M.D.N.C. 1989).

No Nevada cases specifically address the issue of what is relevant discovery as contemplated by NRCP 26(b)(1). However, for a limited discussion of the scope of allowable discovery regarding medical records and tax returns, see *Schlatter v. Eighth Judicial District Court,* 93 Nev. 189, 561 P.2d 1342 (1977).

There are no Nevada cases defining protocol for the discovery of the financial worth of a defendant in a punitive damage case under NRS 42.005. While a defendant's financial worth is generally not discoverable, it does become relevant in a punitive damage case. In such a case discovery of financial worth should only be allowed when issues of malice, fraud or oppression are raised by competent evidence, *i.e.,* not upon the mere allegations of the pleadings. Therefore, to prevent abuse, the claimed need for such information should always be balanced against the possibility of undue intrusion into the defendant's financial affairs. This "balance" can be achieved by requiring the plaintiff at some pre-trial

conference to establish a "prima facie" case of malice, etc., before allowing discovery of the financial affairs of a defendant over objection. Another alternative would be for the court to permit the discovery, subject
to an order that all such information obtained from the defendant be
sealed and disseminated only to co-counsel and the plaintiff's economic
expert, for purposes of trial preparation. If the evidence adduced at trial
does not warrant an instruction on punitive damages, the discovery
should be returned to the defendant without being introduced into evidence or otherwise commented upon in the presence of the jury. *See*
Wickliffe v. Fletcher Jones of Las Vegas, Inc., 99 Nev. 353, 356, 661 P.2d
1295 (1983) ("It is the responsibility of the trial court to determine
whether, as a matter of law, the plaintiff has offered substantial evidence of malice in fact to support a punitive damage instruction"). Of
course, evidence of a defendant's financial condition is not admissible
until the start of the punitive damage proceeding to determine the
amount of punitive damages as provided in NRS 42.005(4).

§ 1613. — Nonprivileged matters.

"Privilege" in this context includes evidentiary privileges which, in
Nevada, are largely governed by statute. *See generally* NRS 49.015(1);
NRS 49.035 *et seq.* (lawyer-client privilege); NRS 49.125 *et seq.* (accoun-
tant-client privilege); NRS 49.215 *et seq.* (doctor-patient privilege); NRS
49.246 *et seq.* (marriage and family therapist and client privilege); NRS
49.251 *et seq.* (social worker and client privilege); NRS 49.255 (confes-
sor-confessant privilege); NRS 49.275 (news media privilege); NRS
49.290 (counselor-pupil privilege); NRS 49.291 (teacher-pupil privilege);
NRS 49.295 *et seq.* (husband-wife privilege); NRS 49.335 *et seq.* (privilege to refuse disclosure of identity of informer); and NRS 49.385 *et seq.*
(waiver of privilege). The foregoing does not constitute a complete listing.

Nonprivileged information can be placed into several general categories. First, there are those communications which are not and were never
protected by any statutory privilege. There is, for instance, no privilege
protecting confidential communications on the basis that the conver-
sants are neighbors. Any statement made in confidence, in a context
other than those specifically providing statutorily-created privileges,
may be subject to disclosure.

Additionally, there are those communications which are nonprivileged
because they fit into one of the statutorily created exceptions to the
privileges. As an example, confidential communications wherein a client
seeks the aid of his attorney or accountant in enabling or aiding the
client in the commission of a crime, or which the attorney or accountant

knows or reasonably should know to be a crime, may not be protected on the basis of privilege. *See* NRS 49.115(1); NRS 49.205(1).

Also, an otherwise privileged communication may become "nonprivileged" if the holder of the privilege voluntarily waives any significant part of it. NRS 49.385. In *Newburn v. Howard Hughes Medical Institute,* 95 Nev. 368, 594 P.2d 1146 (1979), for instance, a newspaper reporter received numerous communications from one group of individuals and later revealed that information to another group. The court held that by voluntarily revealing the information to the second group, the reporter had waived whatever privilege he might have held pursuant to Nevada's shield law, NRS 49.275. *Newburn, supra,* 95 Nev. at 371-72. The court rejected the reporter's contentions that the communication he had received was absolutely protected and was not capable of being waived. *Newburn, supra,* at 371. In *Las Vegas Sun v. District Court,* 104 Nev. 508, 761 P.2d 849 (1988), the Nevada Supreme Court noted that the waiver statute was intended to apply to all privileges included in Chapter 49, not just "confidential" matters (104 Nev. at 511 n.2) including the news gatherers' privilege. 104 Nev. at 513. Waiver occurs when sources are named and are quoted. However, discovery is narrow and limited to the precise matters disclosed.

However, counsel should be aware that not all waivers of privilege result in "nonprivileged" communications. NRS 49.385(2) provides that a disclosure which is itself a privileged communication does not constitute a waiver. For instance, when an attorney, with the consent of his client, reveals a privileged attorney-client communication to one of his law partners, doing so for the purpose of developing the client's case and intending that the second communication remain confidential, the disclosure to the second attorney is itself a privileged communication and does not constitute a waiver. Also, since every waiver of privilege must be by voluntary disclosure, NRS 49.395 provides that:

> [e]vidence of a statement or other disclosure of privileged matter is inadmissible against the holder of the privilege if the disclosure was:
> 1. Compelled erroneously; or
> 2. Made without opportunity to claim the privilege.

Another waiver issue which may arise in civil actions involves a party who wishes to block disclosure of information on federal Fifth Amendment grounds. In *Meyer v. Second Judicial District Court,* 95 Nev. 176, 591 P.2d 259 (1979), the Nevada Supreme Court affirmed a lower court order precluding in-court testimony by a party unless the self incrimination privilege was waived and the party agreed to answer deposition questions under conditions that would protect against disclosure outside the litigation.

§ 1614. — Discovery of insurance agreements.

The existence and contents of liability insurance which might be the source of complete or partial satisfaction of a judgment are discoverable under NRCP 26(b)(2). *See also* Fed. R. Civ. P. 26(b)(2). Disclosure during discovery does not make such material admissible at trial unless offered for some other relevant purpose. *See* NRS 48.135. While no reported Nevada cases interpret NRCP 26(b)(2), proper inquiry would clearly include: the existence of an insurance policy, the identity of the named insured and others covered under the policy, the vehicle or premises covered, the type of coverage, the extent of coverage, whether coverage is being afforded subject to a reservation of rights, and, if so, the provision or provisions of the policy under which the insurance company is contesting coverage.

Prior to enactment of NRCP 26(b)(2), the Nevada Supreme Court had held that NRCP 26 did not allow discovery of insurance agreements. *Washoe County Board of School Trustees v. Pirhala,* 84 Nev. 1, 435 P.2d 756 (1968). With the adoption of NRCP 26(b)(2), insurance agreements became discoverable in Nevada.

Before Fed. R. Civ. P. 26(b) was amended to include 26(b)(2), both state and federal cases were divided on the question of whether insurance agreements were discoverable. The 1970 amendment to Fed. R. Civ. P. 26(b) resolved the issue by allowing disclosure. Advisory Committee Notes on 1970 Amendments to Federal Rules of Civil Procedure, 48 F.R.D. 487, 498 (1970) are instructive. As the Notes indicate, it is the belief of the advisory committee that allowing discovery of insurance agreements enables "counsel for both sides to make the same realistic appraisal of the case, so that settlement and litigation strategy are based on knowledge and not speculation." Advisory Committee Notes, *supra,* 48 F.R.D. at 499.

The Notes make three additional points which further clarify 26(b)(2). First, the drafters of the amendment contemplated disclosure of insurance coverage but did not mean to imply that further discovery of the defendant's financial condition was proper. Advisory Committee Notes on 1970 Amendments to Federal Rules of Civil Procedure, 48 F.R.D. 487 (1970). Second, the drafters intended the rule to require insurance companies to disclose even when the insurance company contests coverage and even when the agreement provides only for indemnification or reimbursement after a judgment has been paid. Advisory Committee Notes, *supra.* Third, NRCP 26(b)(2) only applies to insurance businesses; it does not apply to other businesses which may have entered into an agreement to indemnify. Advisory Committee Notes, *supra.* Similarly, it does not apply to businesses which have set aside a fund for self-insurance purposes. Advisory Committee Notes, *supra.*

§ 1615. — Trial preparation: attorney work product.

"The work product doctrine reflects an attempt to resolve tensions between important competing values. As originally articulated in *Hickman v. Taylor*, 329 U.S. 495, 67 S. Ct. 385, 91 L. Ed. 451 (1947), the purpose of the work product doctrine was to preserve 'the historical and the necessary way in which lawyers act within the framework of our system of jurisprudence to promote justice and to protect their client's interests.' *Id.* at 511, 67 S. Ct. at 393. In developing the work product doctrine, the *Hickman* court *focused exclusively on* the privacy interests of *lawyers*, on shielding 'the privacy of an attorney's course of preparation.' *Id.* at 512, 67 S. Ct. at 394." *Hewlett-Packard Co. v. Bausch & Lomb, Inc.*, 116 F.R.D. 533, 538 (N.D. Cal. 1987) (emphasis in original). In *Hewlett-Packard*, the court noted that *Hickman* was based on the Supreme Court's assumption that "protecting the case preparation privacy of counsel was necessary to preserve the incentive system on which it assumed the adversary system depends." *Id.* at 538. This incentive system has two dimensions: one is the control of fear and the other is attacking temptation. As the court in *Hewlett-Packard* explains: "[t]he fear that the work product doctrine is designed to cabin is the lawyer's fear that his opponent will gain access to his ideas, his perceptions, his assessments, his plans. The temptation the doctrine is designed to attack is the temptation individual lawyers might feel to be lazy, to let opposing counsel do the investigatory homework, then force him to disgorge it." *Id.* at 538. Since *Hickman*, the work product doctrine has been codified by Rule 26(b)(3).

The first paragraph of NRCP 26(b)(3) invests certain documents and tangible things prepared in anticipation of litigation by or on behalf of a party, and which are otherwise discoverable, with a conditional privilege against disclosure by stating that discovery will be allowed only if the party seeking discovery is able to show that he "has substantial need of the materials in the preparation of his case and that he is unable without undue hardship to obtain the substantial equivalent of the materials by other means." NRCP 26(b)(3). The mental impressions, conclusions, opinions and legal theories of a party's attorney or other representative as may be contained in the request documents or other materials remain absolutely immune from discovery. Discovery under Rule 26(b)(3) does not expand the scope of discovery permitted under Rule 26(b)(1), *i.e.*, nonprivileged and relevant materials.

The party objecting to the discovery on the grounds that it is qualifiedly privileged under NRCP 26(b)(3) has the burden of establishing that the information sought is protected by the rule, *i.e.*, (1) that it constitutes documents and tangible things, (2) that it was prepared in anticipation of litigation or trial, and (3) that it was prepared by or for a party or by or for that party's representative. Furthermore, in Nevada, in order for a document or a statement to be protected under the work product doctrine, that document or statement must have been created or taken "at the request of an attorney." *See Ballard v. District Court*, 106 Nev. 83, 787 P.2d 406 (1990).

Immunity from discovery under NRCP 26(b)(3) does not extend to facts learned by a party or a party's lawyer or other representative, or the identity of the person from whom or the documents from which such facts have been learned, even though the document itself may be qualifiedly privileged under the rule. *See Hewlett-Packard Co. v. Bausch & Lomb, Inc.*, 116 F.R.D. 533, 539 (N.D. Cal. 1987) ("The work product doctrine was designed to protect the lawyering process, not prevent access to the raw evidence or facts on which the lawyering process is supposed to operate.").

To be protected, the matter sought to be discovered must be prepared in anticipation of litigation or trial, rather than routinely prepared documents, such as in-house accident reports prepared by a defendant shortly after an accident, the subject of which later becomes the subject matter of a lawsuit. *Soeder v. General Dynamics Corp.*, 90 F.R.D. 253 (D. Nev. 1980) (report prepared by General Dynamics in the ordinary course of business after every F-111 crash).

Some cases hold that documentary work product which is prepared in anticipation of one lawsuit is not privileged from disclosure in discovery proceedings conducted in connection with another lawsuit. While the majority view is to the contrary and while that majority view is supported by dicta in *F.T.C. v. Grolier, Inc.*, 462 U.S. 19, 25-26, 103 S. Ct. 2209, 76 L. Ed. 2d 387 (1983), there are no Nevada Supreme Court cases so holding or holding that discovery will be allowed when the two cases are unrelated as to both issues and parties.

The documents or other things sought to be discovered under NRCP 26(b)(3) need not have been prepared or obtained by an attorney for the qualified privilege to attach. The rule specifically extends protection to materials prepared by or for a party by "his attorney, consultant, surety, indemnitor, insurer, or agent." But, as noted above, the document or other thing sought to be protected under the work product doctrine must have been prepared at the request of an attorney. *Ballard v. District Court*, 106 Nev. 83, 787 P.2d 406 (1990).

The work-product immunity under Fed. R. Civ. P. 26(b)(3), unlike the attorney-client privilege, has generally been held not to be waived by disclosure to a third person absent specific circumstances. Though the Nevada court has not yet addressed this issue, federal courts have. In *United States v. American Telephone & Telegraph*, 642 F.2d 1285, 1299 (D.C. Cir. 1980), the court observed that the work product doctrine does not exist to protect a confidential relationship, but rather "to promote the adversary system by safeguarding the fruits of an attorney's trial preparation from the discovery attempts of an opponent." Thus waiver of the work product immunity "requires more than the disclosure of confidential information; the disclosure must be inconsistent with the adversary system." *Hartford Fire Insurance Co. v. Garvey*, 109 F.R.D. 323, 328 (N.D. Cal. 1985). *See, e.g., Chubb Integrated Systems v. National Bank of Washington*, 103 F.R.D. 52, 63 (D.D.C. 1984) (voluntary disclosure of work product material to an opponent is "inconsistent" with adversary system); *In re Crazy Eddie Securities Litigation*, 131 F.R.D. 374, 379 (E.D.N.Y. 1990) (counsel may share work product material with those having similar interests in fully preparing for litigation. But if a party discloses for reasons not related to the facilitation of its trial preparation, that party is deemed to have waived the privilege).

A problem may also arise under NRS 50.125(1), which outlines the requirements for using a document to refresh the memory of a witness. Under this statute, if a witness uses a writing to refresh his memory either before or while testifying, the adverse party has the right to production of the writing, to inspect it, to cross-examine the witness on the writing, and to introduce portions of the writing to impeach. Compare the statute's federal counterpart, FRE 612, which does not seem to automatically effect a waiver as a matter of law of the qualified privilege under Rule 26(b)(3). *See Derderian v. Polaroid Corp.*, 121 F.R.D. 13 (D. Mass. 1988); *Baker v. CNA Insurance Co.*, 123 F.R.D. 322 (D. Mont. 1988). The proponent of the witness has a practical choice to make, *i.e.*, disclosing all or part of the qualifiedly privileged writing or taking the chance that his witness cannot be restored to competency through other means.

§ 1616. — Burden of party seeking discovery of work product.

If the court finds that the information sought to be discovered is conditionally privileged under NRCP 26(b)(3), the burden shifts to the party seeking disclosure to establish: (1) that he "has substantial need of the materials in the preparation of his case, and (2) that he is unable without undue hardship to obtain the substantial equivalent of the materials by other means." The purpose and policy behind the requirement for the special showing is to prevent one side in an action from automatic entitlement to the benefit of the preparation work and evaluations of the other side. Advisory Committee Notes on 1970 Amendments to Federal Rules of Civil Procedure, 48 F.R.D. 487 (1970).

In the absence of a showing of "substantial need" for the requested discovery, the request will be denied by the court. While no Nevada cases comprehensively discuss what substantial need means in this context, there is a wealth of federal authority to which resort can be made to

assist in the resolution of discovery disputes. In all probability, a showing that a party simply wants to be satisfied that he has not overlooked
anything in the preparation of his case, or he surmises that the work-
product document in question might turn up relevant information, will
be held insufficient under the rule. *See In re Grand Jury Subpoena
Dated November 8, 1979*, 622 F.2d 933 (6th Cir. 1980).

In actual practice, however, it is rarely difficult for a diligent party or
counsel to meet the substantial need requirements. In this connection,
the importance of the materials to the discovering party's case will be
the central issue. To maximize protection for all concerned parties, a
preliminary in camera review by the court of the materials in question
may be necessary in order to confirm the presence of important or critical materials or statements justifying disclosure. Partial disclosure of a
document with nondiscoverable portions deleted may be required in
some cases. The Advisory Committee Notes, Fed. R. Civ. P. (1970), suggest that such a procedure may be utilized when and if necessary. Advisory Committee Notes, *supra,* 48 F.R.D. at 502.

The more difficult element to satisfy in obtaining disclosure of trial
preparation materials is the inability without undue hardship to obtain
substantial equivalent by other means. The most common situation
arises when a statement of a witness has been obtained by one party
shortly after the event which is the subject of the litigation. The question
will always arise as to whether a deposition will provide the "substantial
equivalent" of the statement. Assuming that the deposition will suffice,
the fact that the witness is out of state, or that taking the deposition will
be expensive or inconvenient, will generally not justify disclosure. This
may be the subject of some judicial discretion where, for example, the
economic burden on one of the parties may be too great.

The contrary result would be obtained if the witness were unavailable
through no fault of the discovering party (*e.g.,* where the person inter-
viewed is now deceased; where the witness has refused to testify absent
immunity from criminal prosecution; or where the witness is in the
armed forces in a location preventing the deposition).

The fact that a witness from whom an earlier statement was taken is
now out of state should not, in and of itself, constitute the requisite
showing of need for the reason that the deposition procedure is still
available to the party seeking his testimony.

Although there is authority outside Nevada to the contrary, it would
appear that statements taken from witnesses at or about the time of the
occurrence described in them are so unique, because they provide an
immediate impression of the facts, that they should be ordered disclosed
even though they would satisfy the definition of trial preparation materials under this rule. Advisory Committee Notes, Fed. R. Civ. P., 48
F.R.D. at 501, *citing Southern Railway v. Lanham,* 403 F.2d 119, 127-28

(5th Cir. 1968). As to statements taken substantially after an event, disclosure will be more strictly guarded because the adverse party can depose the witness or obtain a separate statement on his own account.

The first sentence of the first paragraph of NRCP 26(b)(3) preserves the historic treatment accorded the mental impressions, conclusions, opinions and legal theories of a party's legal counsel, providing that the same are absolutely privileged and shall not be discoverable in any event. True mental impressions, etc., can be protected by partial disclosure, deletions, or by in camera evaluation by the court. Protection under this rule may even extend to the mental impressions of a party where disclosure would of necessity divulge the impressions and thought processes of that party's attorney.

Arguably, the rule does not apply to cases where the mental impressions, etc., of an attorney or a party's other representative are directly at issue in the lawsuit. *See generally Federal Trade Commission v. Grolier, Inc.*, 462 U.S. 19, 26-28, 103 S. Ct. 2209, 76 L. Ed. 387 (1983). For example, in so-called "bad-faith" actions against insurers for alleged wrongful denials of coverage, the grounds for denial may have included a legal opinion. *See,* however, *Popelka, Allard, McCowan & Jones v. Superior Court,* 107 Cal. App. 3d 496, 165 Cal. Rptr. 748 (1980) (wherein a party bringing a malicious prosecution suit against a law firm was denied access to the law firm's interoffice memos from the prior suit). Although there are no Nevada cases on this point, better-reasoned federal cases have concluded that where "advice of counsel" is affirmatively raised as a defense, it effects a waiver of any privilege. *See Trans World Airlines v. Hughes,* 332 F.2d 602 (2d Cir. 1964); *Vicinanzo v. Brunschig & Fils, Inc.,* 739 F. Supp. 891 (S.D.N.Y. 1990); *McLaughlin v. Lunde Truck Sales, Inc.,* 714 F. Supp. 916 (N.D. Ill. 1989); *Handgards, Inc. v. Johnson & Johnson,* 413 F. Supp. 926 (N.D. Cal. 1976).

The second paragraph of NRCP 26(b)(3) makes it clear that any party may obtain his own previous statements concerning the action or its subject matter without making a showing of any kind. Nonparties, upon request, may also obtain their prior statements. Parties are often able to circumvent the "showing" requirements of NRCP and Fed. R. Civ. P. 26(b)(3) by persuading the nonparty witness to request his statement from the party seeking to assert the work product privilege. But *see In re Convergent Technologies Second Half 1984 Security Litigation,* 122 F.R.D. 555 (N.D. Cal. 1988), where the court entered an order allowing a nonparty to obtain a copy of the statement he made for plaintiffs, but prohibited him from disclosing in any manner that statement to defendants until such time as he offered testimony, either at deposition or trial, which was refreshed by review of that statement. The form of statements subject to this absolute right of production are specifically set forth in the rule.

§ 1617.　Method of claiming privilege.

Often, in response to a request for production of documents, the responding party will assert that the documents sought are "privileged." A blanket assertion of privilege is not favored. *See Potts v. Allis-Chalmers Corp.*, 118 F.R.D. 597 (N.D. Ill. 1987). Indeed, an improperly asserted claim of privilege "is no claim of privilege at all." *International Paper Co. v. Fibreboard Corp.*, 63 F.R.D. 88, 94 (D. Del. 1974). The correct method of asserting a privilege is to reasonably identify the document or documents claimed to be privilege by way of "privilege log" or "Vaughn Index" which itemizes each document, provides a factual summary of its content and the justification for withholding it. *Pete Rinaldi's Fast Foods v. Great American Ins.*, 123 F.R.D. 198, 203 (M.D.N.C. 1988). In *Miller v. Pancucci*, 141 F.R.D. 292 (C.D. Cal. 1992), the court set forth guidelines as to the content of the index. The court said that "experience has demonstrated that the following list of items are sufficient to sustain the burden of" asserting a privilege: "(1) Date of document; (2) Author; (3) Primary addressee; (4) Secondary addressee(s); persons copied and recipient (and the relationship of that person(s) to the client and/or author of the documents); (5) Type of document (*e.g.*, internal memo, letter with enclosures, draft affidavit, etc.); (6) Client (*i.e.*, party asserting privilege); (7) Attorneys; (8) Subject matter of document or privileged communication (*i.e.*, legal claim for privilege); and (10) Whether the document or communication is work product or attorney-client privilege." 141 F.R.D. at 302.

Although there are no Nevada cases setting forth a requirement of specific identification of privileged materials, the requirement is well settled in the federal courts. *See Smith v. Logansport Community School Corp.*, 139 F.R.D. 637, 648 (N.D. Ind. 1991). The reason supporting the requirement that one make specific identification of privileged material is well stated in *Eureka Financial v. Hartford Accident & Indemnity*, 136 F.R.D. 179, 183 (E.D. Cal. 1991). There, the court said "[t]he purpose of the specific objection requirement is to provide the party seeking discovery with a basis for determining what documents the party asserting the privilege has withheld. Otherwise, how could this opposing party ever know whether the documents withheld under a blanket privilege objection were withheld correctly, incorrectly, or maliciously?"

§ 1618.　Trial preparation: expert witnesses.

Discovery of expert witnesses is governed by NRCP 26(b)(4). The scope of such discovery depends upon the category into which the particular expert falls. There are four categories of expert witnesses: (1) expert witnesses whom a party expects to call at trial; (2) experts who are retained or employed in anticipation of litigation but who are not expected to testify; (3) experts who are not specially retained or employed but who are informally consulted; and (4) expert witnesses who are neither specially retained nor informally consulted, *e.g.*, a party's regularly employed in-house expert. The following four sections address each category of experts in order.

§ 1619. — Expert witnesses expected to be used at trial.

Subsection (A)(i) limits initial discovery of such experts to interrogatories by which the following may be obtained: (1) identity of the expert; (2) the subject matter on which the expert is expected to testify; (3) the substance of the facts to which the expert is expected to testify; (4) the opinions to which the expert is expected to testify; and (5) a summary of the grounds for each such opinion. Discovery of this information by the interrogatory method should be a priority to any party for several important reasons.

First, technically other methods of discovery of experts are available only to a party who has completed the interrogatory method. Under Rule 26(b)(4)(A)(ii), other methods of discovery, *e.g.*, depositions, can be pursued only by court order. Application for such an order may be made only after utilization of the interrogatory method under Rule 26(b)(4)(A)(i). Of course, the parties may part from this circumscribed procedure. *See* NRCP 29. Ordinarily, this is the case. Traditional practice is to allow depositions of a party's experts without court order and often without prior use of the interrogatory procedure. Hardline departure from this traditional leeway is not likely to achieve any limitation on expert discovery in most cases.

Second, the practitioner should give priority to the interrogatory method because it is enforceable. Failure to respond to the interrogatory can be a basis for exclusion of expert testimony. *See* NRCP 37(b) — NRCP 37(d). Under NRCP 33(b), an evasive or incomplete interrogatory response is to be treated as as failure to answer. Tactically, then, it is always wise to propound such an interrogatory. Likewise, it is always prudent to fully and completely respond, and to supplement prior responses per NRCP 26(e)(1)(B).

Third, information and opinions acquired by the interrogatory method facilitate cross-examination either at trial or during a pretrial deposition, and allow opposing counsel to assess the need for rebuttal witnesses. *See* Advisory Committee Notes, Fed. R. Civ. P. (1970).

Fourth, as a technical matter, the interrogatory method may be argued to be a prerequisite to discovery by exchange of expert witness lists under NRCP 26(b)(5) ("In addition to the discovery allowed by subdivision (b)(4) of this rule..."). As a matter of common practice, however, this available argument is not normally posed.

Beyond the interrogatory method, discovery of trial experts typically involves (1) a demand for exchange of expert witness lists, reports and writings and (2) depositions.

NRCP 26(b)(5) governs the exchange procedure. Its provisions are fairly detailed, and any careful litigator should learn them. Briefly, not later than ninety days before trial, any party may serve a written demand for exchange of lists. The lists are to be exchanged simultaneously seventy days prior to trial. The Rule contemplates an in person exchange, but local practice often dispenses with such formality. Better practice is to insist upon an in person exchange, for one basic reason: to prevent the other party from "sandbagging" your list. Although the same result may be obtained by later supplementing an in person exchange, several "obstacles" must be hurdled in order to successfully supplement a previously exchanged list. See NRCP 26(b)(5)(H).

The list should identify the experts and should provide a statement of qualifications and the *general* substance of the expected testimony. The details of the expected testimony should be pursued by the interrogatory and deposition methods.

By far the most productive method to discover trial experts' opinions and the bases of those opinions is to depose them. A deposition provides a forum in which to explore with the witness all facts known or assumed and all opinions held. In addition, one can elicit other information, such as the expert's background, her qualifications, her assignment, her work done, tests performed by her, texts consulted by her and any additional work required. As stated, local practice is to allow such depositions to go forward routinely. Once trial experts are identified, the onus is upon the discovering party to contact opposing counsel to arrange for the taking of the desired depositions. A customary request is to have the expert bring to the deposition her entire "file" on the case. Any and all writings prepared by and relied upon by the expert are discoverable.

Discussion of local customary practice with respect to discovery of trial experts should always be read with the caveat that departures from such practice can and do occur. Judicial understanding of such practice suggests that "hardball" departures from such practice will not be readily tolerated.

§ 1620. — Expert witnesses not expected to be used at trial.

Discovery of experts who have been specially retained or employed, but who are not expected to be used at trial, is limited by NRCP 26(b)(4)(B). Initially, it is not clear whether one party can find out the names of experts specifically retained by another party who are not to be called at trial. The Rule is silent on this issue. In the federal courts, the authorities are split. *See generally* Note, "Discovery of the Non-testifying Expert Witness' Identity Under the Federal Rules of Civil Procedure: You Can't Tell The Players Without A Program," 37 Hast. L.J. 201 (1985). The Advisory Committee Notes to the identical federal rule state that the identity of non-testifying experts may be obtained upon the "proper showing." A "proper showing" may be "exceptional circumstances" or simply "relevant to the subject matter of the action." *Id.* at n.63 (discussing cases).

Pursuit of discovery of the consultant who is not to be called at trial may be beneficial simply in terms of uncovering helpful expert opinions from the opponent's own camp. Beyond "identity", the discovering party may only obtain further discovery as allowed under NRCP 35(b) (independent medical examination reports and reciprocal production of previous doctor reports), or he must make a showing of *exceptional circumstances* under which it is *impracticable* for the party seeking discovery to obtain facts or opinions on the same subject by other means. The discovering party bears a heavy burden in making the required showing. *Barkwell v. Sturm Ruger Co.*, 79 F.R.D. 444 (D. Alaska 1978). Common circumstances in which such discovery has been allowed include unrepeatable testing or examination of physical evidence by the expert, *e.g.*, destructive testing. *See generally* 8 C. Wright & A. Miller, *Federal Practice & Procedure* § 2032 (1970) (collecting cases). Absent such a circumstance, the limitation exists to avoid the unfairness in allowing easy access to a consultant whose work was generated by the good efforts of opposing counsel. *See Pearl Brewing Co. v. Joseph Schlitz Brewing Co.*, 415 F. Supp. 1122, 1138-40 (S.D. Tex. 1976).

Under NRCP 26(b)(4)(C)(i), the court must, absent manifest injustice, require the party obtaining expert discovery under subsection (4)(B) to pay the expert a reasonable fee for his time spent in responding to such discovery. Also, under subsection (C)(ii) of the rule, the court shall, regardless of possible inequities, require the party obtaining discovery of non-trial expert opinions to pay a fair portion of the fees and expenses reasonably incurred by the other party in procuring the opinions.

§ 1621. — Expert witnesses not specially retained but informally consulted in preparation for trial.

Because discovery of trial preparation experts is only allowed in accordance with NRCP 26(b)(4), neither the names of such witnesses nor facts known by them nor their opinions are discoverable. *See* Adv. Comm. Notes, 1970 Amendment, Fed. R. Civ. P. 26 (the subdivision precludes discovery against experts who were informally consulted in preparation for trial ...."). Criteria for determining who is specially retained rather than informally consulted must be found in cases from other states or from the federal system. *See Ager v. Jane C. Stormont Hospital*, 622 F.2d 496, 501 (10th Cir. 1980) (listing criteria).

§ 1622. — Expert witnesses neither specially retained nor consulted.

Because experts whose information was not acquired in preparation for trial are not addressed in the rule, they will probably be treated as ordinary witnesses.

An example of such an expert witness would be a general employee of a party not retained or consulted, either formally or informally, concerning the pending litigation. The mere possession of special knowledge by an individual concerning the circumstances surrounding any given lawsuit does not immunize that person from discovery of the facts known by him or his opinions concerning those circumstances, *e.g.*, a managing agent of a party may be called upon to testify and give his opinion as to why certain technical procedures in a party's business were not followed. This interpretation of the scope of discovery of experts not formally retained or otherwise consulted would logically extend to a party's in-house expert, and to the party himself in a proper case, *e.g.*, in a medical malpractice case the defendant-doctor would be subject to discovery concerning not only the facts known by him but his opinions as well.

§ 1623. — Expert witness fees.

NRCP 30(h)(1) provides that a party desiring to depose any designated trial expert shall pay the reasonable and customary hourly or daily fee for the actual time consumed in the examination of that expert by the party noticing the deposition. If any other attending party desires to question the witness, that party shall be responsible for the expert's fees for the actual time consumed in that party's examination. Where the expert witness requires advance payment of his fees, the party requesting the deposition must tender the requested fee based on the anticipated length of that party's examination of the witness, subject to the provisions of subparagraph (h)(2) relating to disputes regarding the amount of the fee. Where the deposition of the expert exceeds the anticipated time, the party or parties responsible for the additional time are responsible for the additional fees payable within thirty days of receipt of a statement from the expert. The rule contemplates enforcement of these provisions by the trial court.

Subparagraph (h)(1) further provides that any party identifying an expert expected to testify at trial is responsible for any fee charged by the expert for preparing for the deposition as opposed to his testimony in deposition. The party who retains the expert is also required to pay the expert's fee for traveling to the place of the deposition where such travel can be compelled by court process. Subparagraph (h)(1) does not contain any requirement that the party who retains the expert pay the cost of travel to the place of trial for a pretrial deposition. This would require an agreement of the parties or a conditional order of the court limiting the circumstances under which the expert witness could be called at trial.

Subparagraph (h)(2) of NRCP 30 makes provision for disputes regarding the amount of the expert witness fee. Where the party seeking the deposition of the expert witness deems the fee for the deposition testimony to be unreasonable, the party may move for an order setting the compensation of that expert. Subparagraph (h)(2) requires the motion to be supported by an affidavit stating facts showing a reasonable and good faith attempt at an informal resolution of the fee dispute. Notice of the motion must be given to the expert. The court is authorized to set the expert's fee if the court determines that the fee demanded is unreasonable. The rule contemplates a conditional order that any additional fee over the amount allowed by the court may be paid by the party who retains the expert. The court may also condition the appearance of the expert at trial upon the consent of the expert witness to go forward with the deposition testimony for the fee set by the court whether or not supplemented by the party who retains the expert.

Subparagraph (h)(2) provides that the court may impose a sanction pursuant to Rule 37 against any party who does not prevail and in favor of any party who does prevail on a motion to set expert witness fee, providing the prevailing party has engaged in a reasonable and good faith attempt at an informal resolution of the issues presented by the motion.

§ 1624. — Depositions before trial.

Note: Depositions before action or pending appeal taken pursuant to Rule 27 are discussed in § 1628, *infra*.

Generally, any party may use depositions taken upon oral examination or upon written questions to elicit the testimony of any witness; depositions may be used in any combination with other discovery devices, subject to the exception stated in NRCP 26(b)(4)(A)(ii) regarding experts.

NRCP 28 sets forth the qualifications and duties of persons before whom depositions may be taken. *See Greenspun v. Eighth Judicial District Court,* 91 Nev. 211, 217, 533 P.2d 482 (1975) (prohibition against court reporters being employed by or related to parties or their attorneys). *See also Day v. Cloke,* 47 Nev. 75, 81, 215 P. 386 (1923). NRS 18.005 includes costs of taking depositions within the scope of costs that may be awarded to the prevailing party. Use of the depositions at trial is not a requirement for such an award. *Jones v. Viking Freight System*, 101 Nev. 275, 701 P.2d 745 (1985).

§ 1625. — Oral depositions.

NRCP 16.1 establishes mandatory pretrial discovery requirements. These requirements must be satisfied or waived before any party may resort to additional discovery upon oral examination. NRCP 26(a). *See* § 1609, *supra.*

NRCP 30(a) deals with pretrial depositions upon oral examination. Subject to the case conference requirements of NRCP 16.1 and 26(a), a party may take the oral deposition of any person after an action is commenced, except leave of court must be obtained where the party wishes to take a deposition within thirty days after service of the summons and complaint upon any defendant. Subject to Rule 16.1, leave is not required where the defendant initiates the discovery, or where special notice is given under NRCP 30(b)(2) that the deponent intends to leave the state and will be unavailable if the thirty-day requirement is followed. The rule further provides that the deposition of persons confined in prison may only be taken pursuant to court order. *See* NRS 50.215.

Rule 30(a) also provides for the use of a subpoena to compel the attendance of witnesses. *Cf.* Rule 45. Rule 45(d)(2), which places limitations on the distance which a witness may be required to travel to attend a deposition, applies only to nonparty deponents. *Riverside Casino Corp. v. J.W. Brewer Co.,* 80 Nev. 153, 390 P.2d 232 (1964). Nonparty witnesses may only be compelled to attend deposition proceedings by subpoena, and may only be compelled to bring documents or things by subpoena duces tecum. Subpoenas are not required to compel the attendance of a party deponent, although questions as to compelling parties not residing within the state to attend the proceeding locally may be referred to the court's sound discretion in cases of alleged hardship. In unusual situations, court orders may include, among others, awards of expenses, may require parties to bear their own costs of attending, or may require the deposition proceed outside the state. In the Eighth Judicial District, motions regarding such problems may only be brought after unsuccessfully attempting to resolve the question of attendance informally between or among counsel. EDCR 2.34 (the other judicial districts have no local rule comparable to EDCR 2.34). As a practical matter, out-of-state parties are usually required to attend locally if noticed to do so in a Nevada action, although the practice is slightly more stringent on plaintiffs than defendants. *See also Gardner v. Associated Contractors,* 72 Nev. 1, 291 P.2d 1051 (1956), regarding the special problems of requiring nonresident defendants to attend depositions where personal jurisdiction is being contested.

NRCP 30(b) sets out the requirements for written notice of depositions to other parties. Under this rule, a party must give reasonable notice, not less than fifteen days, in writing to every other party. The rule also specifies the contents for such notices. Notices addressed to a party deponent may be accompanied by a request to produce documents and tangible things, although the time requirements of NRCP 34 will apply. *See* § 1630, *infra*. If documents are sought under a subpoena, the designation of the materials to be produced must be set forth in or attached to the Notice of Deposition. NRCP Rule 30(b)(1).

NRCP 30(b)(6) outlines how depositions of corporations, associations, partnerships and government agencies may be noticed where specific names of natural persons holding discoverable information are not known. It requires the organization named in the notice to produce one or more officers, directors, managing agents or other persons in the knowledge of the subject matter set forth in the notice who consent to testify on behalf of the organization. Rule 30(b6) imposes an obligation on the organization or entity served with a deposition notice under this rule to produce persons to testify as matters known or reasonably available to the organization.

NRCP 30(b)(7) sets forth the procedure for telephonic depositions, subject to court order or stipulation. The rule specifically permits a party to physically attend a telephone deposition at the party's own expense.

When a records deposition is desired, the party requesting the documents must serve all other parties with a notice of deposition and a copy of the subpoena. The notice should state that the only purpose of the deposition is to obtain records.

NRCP 30(c) sets forth the procedures for examining and cross-examining witnesses at depositions. Any objection regarding the deposition, the officer presiding, the conduct of the parties or the manner in which evidence is taken shall be noted by the officer and evidence and testimony shall be taken subject to those objections. Objections to the form of a question are waived unless made at the time of the deposition. Furthermore, a witness may not be instructed to refuse to answer a question, except on the ground of privilege.

Subsection (c) also provides that in lieu of a co-party participating in the oral examination, he may serve written questions in a sealed envelope upon the party taking the deposition, who in turn transmits them to the officer. The officer then asks the deponent the questions submitted and the answers are recorded verbatim.

Rule 30(d) enables a party or deponent to suspend a deposition proceeding at any time during the deposition for the purpose of seeking court relief from examination calculated to annoy, embarrass or oppress the deponent or party. The deposition is automatically halted for a period sufficient to allow the person aggrieved to apply to the court, which may, in turn, deny relief, order the proceedings terminated, or limit the scope and manner of the examination under NRCP 26(c). Because judges are usually not available to take such requests, however, the parties should try to resolve these disputes informally. In the Second and Eighth Districts, discovery commissioners have this authority to resolve discovery disputes which arise during depositions. In these two districts an attempt should be made to contact the discovery commissioner for a resolution of the dispute before the deposition is suspended. *See* Rules 16.1(d)(1) and 16.2(b). If the court is contacted and terminates the deposition, the deposition may only be resumed by court order. Note that this remedy is invoked during the actual examination, rather than as a prior protective order as under NRCP 26(c).

NRCP 30(e) sets forth the procedure which allows the witness to review the transcribed deposition and to make changes before signing it. The witness has thirty days following notice from the officer transcribing the deposition to make deposition changes, sign the deposition or to refuse to approve the deposition by not signing it. However, the rule specifically allows an unsigned deposition to "be used as fully as though signed" unless a motion to suppress is filed pursuant to Rule 30(d)(4) and the court finds the reasons given by the witness for refusing to sign to require rejection of the deposition in whole or in part. Under Rule 30(f), the officer before whom the deposition was taken certifies that the witness was properly sworn and that the deposition is a true record of the testimony. The officer then notifies the parties of any changes made by the witness, and the officer sends the certified transcript to the party who took the deposition. The deposition is not filed unless and until "used" in the proceeding. NRCP 5(d). *See* § 1636, *infra*.

NRCP 30(g) provides for the mandatory award of reasonable expenses, including reasonable attorneys' fees, where the party noticing the deposition fails to attend and properly proceed, or fails to subpoena a nonparty witness.

NRCP 30(h) sets forth the procedure for establishing and paying expert witness fees. The rule also sets forth the basis for obtaining court intervention in disputes concerning expert witness fees. *See* § 1623, *supra*.

§ 1626. — Written depositions.

Under NRCP 31, a party may take a deposition upon written questions, in lieu of oral examination. Attendance of the witness may be compelled by Rule 45 subpoena. Examination of an individual representative of a party which is a corporation, partnership, association, or government agency is treated the same as under Rule 30(b)(6).

Rule 31 depositions are taken by the officer in essentially the same manner as oral depositions under Rule 30, *e.g.,* administration of the oath, recording the examination, submission of transcript to the witness, signing, certification, etc.

Because the procedure is somewhat cumbersome and does not afford the examining party flexibility in asking questions tailored to the deponent's responses, this device is best used to obtain discovery of simple or formal matters such as identifying witnesses or authenticating records.

§ 1627. — Out-of-state depositions.

NRCP 16.1 establishes mandatory pretrial discovery requirements. These requirements must first be either satisfied or waived by the trial court before any party may resort to additional discovery by depositions upon oral examination. NRCP 26(a).

Out-of-state depositions are initiated by the service of the usual notice of taking deposition and issuance by the court clerk of a "Commission to Take Deposition Outside the State of Nevada." It is not required that a party request the Commission through motion, as the Clerk must issue the Commission upon being presented with a proper Notice of Deposition. NRCP 28(a). NRCP 30(b)(1) now requires reasonable notice of taking deposition of not less than fifteen days. In addition, letters rogatory may be required by the foreign jurisdiction. Letters rogatory are a formal communication in writing sent by a court in which a matter is pending to a court of a foreign jurisdiction wherein a witness resides, requesting that the testimony of the witness be taken under oath and made available for use in the pending action. The Commission authorizes the officer in the jurisdiction where the deposition is to be taken to conduct the deposition in accordance with instructions as to time, place and manner as set forth in the notice. Errors in the commission or letters rogatory are waived unless objection is filed and served on or before the time fixed in the notice. NRCP 28(a).

The procedures for compelling attendance of an out-of-state witness through subpoena and for payment of witness fees and court costs are dictated by the foreign jurisdiction, and for this reason it may be advisable to associate local counsel to handle matters dealing with witness attendance. It is preferable to have all formalities resolved by stipulation and, where possible, obtain agreement from the witness to attend voluntarily. However, while obtaining the voluntary agreement of an out-of-state witness to attend the deposition is a practical way of avoiding compliance with cumbersome technical requirements for compelling attendance in a foreign jurisdiction, the practitioner should be mindful of the provisions of Rule 30(g) which mandates the imposition of reasonable expenses incurred by a party and his attorney to attend a deposition at which a witness fails to appear "unless good cause be known."

Subsection (b) of Rule 28 provides for depositions to be taken in foreign countries and, in an attempt to meet unpredictable requirements of other nations, is flexible in the options available to the party giving notice of such a deposition. The form of the notice and of the deposition itself is not as important as the fact that actual notice is given to the opposing party. Practitioners should consult 28 U.S.C. § 1781 and the "Convention on the Taking of Evidence Abroad in Civil or Commercial Matters" if contemplating taking a deposition in a foreign country. A copy of the Convention can be found in VIII Martindale Hubbell Law Directory, Part VII at 12-12 (1987), or is available through the United States Department of State. *See also Societe Nationale Industrielle Aerospatiale v. U.S. District Court*, 482 U.S. 522, 107 S. Ct. 2542 (1987).

§ 1628. Depositions before action or pending appeal.

NRCP 27 provides a procedure for obtaining and preserving testimony and evidence before an action has been commenced, NRCP 27(a), or pending appeal, NRCP 27(b). The purpose of the rule is to prevent a failure or delay of justice by perpetuating testimony and evidence which might otherwise be lost before the matter to which it relates is ripe for judicial determination. *Cardinal v. Zonneveld,* 89 Nev. 403, 405, 514 P.2d 204, 205 (1973). Technically, Rule 27 depositions are not discovery, but merely a procedure for perpetuating evidence already known. Therefore, although there is no Nevada authority on the point, petitions to take such depositions should probably be denied where the purpose is merely to enable a prospective litigant to discover facts on which to draft a complaint.

Rule 27 proceedings are instituted by verified petition, and orders granting or denying such petitions are appealable as final orders.

The contents of a petition to take depositions before commencement of an action are governed by NRCP 27(a)(1); service requirements for notices and copies of the petition are governed by NRCP 27(a)(3). Such orders must designate the name of the deponent, specify the subject matter of the examination, and state whether the examination will be taken orally or by written questions. Additionally, the court may make orders of the character provided for by NRCP 34 (production of documents and things and entry upon land for inspection and other purposes) and NRCP 35 (physical and mental examinations).

Perpetuation before action is most often utilized where the prospective witness is gravely ill, is of advanced age, or where the testimony may be lost because of delay and such loss is imminent. For example, a person who expects to be sued but cannot anticipate when the action will be filed may wish to perpetuate beneficial testimony.

NRCP 27(a)(2) requirements for service are slightly different from those in Fed. R. Civ. P. 27(a)(2). The federal provision allows the court to make orders appointing attorneys to represent expected adverse parties where problems with service arise. Violations of technical requirements for service under NRCP 27(a)(2) have been subject to the doctrine of harmless error in Nevada. *See Cardinal v. Zonneveld, supra,* 89 Nev. 403, 514 P.2d 204 (1973). NRCP 27(a)(4) as amended, effective January 1, 1988, permits the use of Rule 27 depositions in accordance with NRCP 32(a).

Perpetuation of testimony pending appeal under NRCP 27(b) most often occurs after an action is resolved by pretrial motion and the party against whom the order is entered appeals. The petition is made in the district court even though the appeal has previously been initiated. As with perpetuation before action, the court may make orders of the character provided under NRCP 34 and 35.

Unlike Federal Rule 27, the Nevada rule does not contain a subsection (c). Federal Rule of Civil Procedure 27(c) provides: "This rule does not limit the power of a court to entertain an action to perpetuate testimony."

Federal Rule of Civil Procedure 27(c) does not create an ancillary or auxiliary proceeding as does Rule 27(a). Rule 27(c) simply recognizes the power of a federal court to entertain an action equivalent to the former bill in equity to perpetuate testimony.

§ 1629. Interrogatories.

NRCP 16.1 establishes mandatory pretrial discovery requirements. These requirements must first be either satisfied or waived by the trial court before any party may resort to additional discovery by written interrogatories. NRCP 26(a). *See* § 1609, *supra.*

Interrogatories may only be propounded by a party against other parties to the action. While inherently less productive than obtaining live testimony, the device is quite useful for obtaining basic background information and objective facts, or as the primary discovery tool in relatively simple cases.

A party need not submit all of his interrogatories at one time. However, no party is allowed to serve more than forty interrogatories, including subparts, on any other single party to an action, except by stipulation or leave of court on a showing of good cause. A sufficient showing of good cause must include a certification that the parties are unable to stipulate and that there is a need to expand the scope of interrogatory discovery because of a special exigency existing in the particular matter, *e.g.,* that additional interrogatories are needed to effect full and complete discovery, or that expanded interrogatory discovery will simplify a complex case or will render a less serious matter less expensive to litigate. Applications for leave to submit additional interrogatories may be special motions and should thus be regularly noticed, and not determined ex parte. *See Maheu v. Eighth Judicial District Court,* 88 Nev. 26, 493 P.2d 709 (1972).

Although the propounding party frequently inserts a clause in the instructions accompanying the interrogatories which states that the interrogatories are deemed to be continuing, the answering party is independently under an affirmative duty to supplement responses and must do so no later than forty-five days before trial under NRCP 26(e)(4). *See* § 1635, *infra.*

Interrogatories are to be answered by the party himself, not by the party's attorney, and if the party is a corporation, partnership, association or governmental agency, an officer or an agent of that entity shall answer the interrogatories. Objections are to be made by the attorney for the responding party. Written interrogatories under Rule 33 can now be served only after the parties have complied with the new mandatory discovery provisions of NRCP 16.1, and then only to request information which could not have been obtained by compliance with Rule 16.1(b). *See* NRCP 26(a) and § 1609, *supra.* Service of process upon one defendant does not entitle that party or any other party to serve interrogatories on a defendant who has not yet been served with process.

Interrogatories must normally be answered or objected to within thirty days after they are served on the answering party. However, a defendant need not serve answers or objections in less than forty-five days following service upon him of the complaint and summons in the action. If answers are not timely served, and no extension of time has been obtained, objections are waived. When a party wishes to object to certain interrogatories and answer others, the objections and answers must be served within the above time frame.

In answering interrogatories, the answering party must repeat each interrogatory and answer each interrogatory separately. Each interrogatory must be answered in writing unless a written objection is made in its place. *See* NRCP 26(j). Originals of answers to interrogatories shall be served upon the party who propounded the interrogatories and that party shall make such originals available at the time of any pre-trial hearing or at trial for use by any party. NRCP 5(d).

Failure to name a witness in answer to interrogatories, or at a pre-trial conference pursuant to court order, will enable the court to exercise its discretion to disallow the calling of the witness at trial. *Southern Pacific Co. v. Watkins,* 83 Nev. 471, 493, 435 P.2d 498 (1967); NRCP 37(d); *but see Wickliffe v. Sunrise Hospital, Inc.,* 101 Nev. 542, 548-49,

706 P.2d 1383 (1985) (error to exclude witness for purpose of authenticating documents where witness not included in pre-trial witness list). Amended NRCP 26(b)(5)(A) makes it clear to practitioners that compliance with the provisions of NRCP 26(b)(5) for demand and exchange of expert witness lists, reports and writings does not excuse noncompliance with the provisions of NRCP 26(b)(4) for discovery of experts.

Any party may move to compel discovery, including answers to interrogatories. NRCP 37(a)(2).

Answers to interrogatories which have not been timely served may be disregarded by the trial court in the face of unanswered requests for admissions. *See Western Mercury, Inc. v. Rix Co.*, 84 Nev. 218, 222, 438 P.2d 792 (1968) (where summary judgment was entered because requests to admit were deemed admitted for failure to answer; the court could use its discretion not to consider tardy answers to interrogatories). Also, refusal by the trial court to compel answers to interrogatories was upheld in a domestic relations dispute, where the parties had stipulated that the husband did not have to provide the answers if he would testify that his deposition had disclosed all of his property interests, and where he satisfied the condition. *Canul v. Canul,* 93 Nev. 459, 460, 567 P.2d 476 (1977).

Answers to interrogatories may be used in trial to the extent permitted under the Nevada Rules of Evidence. *See* discussion under § 1636, *infra.*

NRCP 33(c) allows a party responding to written interrogatories to specify business records from which the answer may be derived or ascertained in lieu of answering where the records will provide the information sought, and where the burden of deriving the answers is substantially the same for the party serving the interrogatory as for the party served. A reasonable opportunity must be given to the discovering party to examine, audit or inspect the designated records. The specification shall be in sufficient detail to permit the discovering party to locate and identify, as readily as the party served, the records from which the answer may be ascertained.

NRCP 11 imposes a duty of objective good faith upon each party and his attorney with respect to the contents of every pleading, motion or paper of a party signed by that party or his attorney. The discovery rules now contain a specific counterpart to Rule 11 in the form of Rule 26(g). Rule 26(g) makes it clear that the duty of objective good faith applies to discovery requests, responses and objections.

§ 1630. Production of documents and things and entry upon land for inspection.

NRCP 16.1 establishes mandatory pretrial discovery requirements. These requirements must first be either satisfied or waived by the trial court before any party may resort to additional discovery by requests for production of documents or things or permission to enter upon land or other property for inspection and other purposes. NRCP 26(a). *See* § 1609, *supra*.

NRCP 34 provides a self-executing procedure enabling any party to require any other party to produce and permit inspection and copying of designated documents or to inspect, copy, test or sample tangible things. Documents sought to be produced must be described with reasonable particularity and the proposed time, place and manner of making the inspection must be specified in the request. Rule 34 also permits a party to gain entry upon land or other property in the possession or control of the party upon whom the request is served for inspection and measuring, surveying, photographing, testing or sampling the property or any designated object or operation thereon.

The party seeking production need not obtain leave of the court to serve requests to produce. Practitioners should note, however, that the procedures of Rule 34 can now be used only after the parties have complied with the provisions of Rule 16.1, and to request discovery which could not have been obtained pursuant to Rule 16.1(b)(2) and (4). *See* NRCP 26(a) and § 1609, *supra*. The discovery exchanges required by Rule 16.1(b)(1) through (4) require the exchange of certain documents and tangible things at early case conferences.

The party against whom production or inspection is sought must respond to the request for production by either giving his consent or by objecting on stated grounds. A written response of the opposing party must be served within thirty days after the service of the request except that a defendant need not serve a response in less than forty-five days after the service of summons and complaint upon him. NRCP 34(b). Originals of responses to requests for production must be served upon the party who made the request and that party must make such originals available at the time of any pre-trial hearing or at trial for use by any party. NRCP 5(d). In the face of an objection to a request, the requesting party may move for an order compelling production, inspection or entry. The party from whom the discovery is sought has the burden of supporting his objection.

The party requesting that documents be copied must pay the reasonable cost therefor and the court may, upon such terms as are just, direct the respondent to copy the documents. Rule 34(d).

The party from whom production of documents, inspection or entry is sought is entitled to the protection afforded by Rule 26(c), and may apply for a protective order preventing the requesting party from disclosing trade secrets or other confidential research, development or commercial information. In the Eighth District, the practioner seeking a protective order should first attempt to resove the matter with opposing counsel in compliance with EDCR 2.34 before moving for a protective order.

Materials resulting from an insurance company's investigation are not privileged unless done at the express direction of counsel for the insured. *Ballard v. Eighth Judicial District Court (Kolath)*, 106 Nev. 83, 787 P.2d 406 (1990).

It is not necessary that the party against whom discovery is being sought have actual possession or custody of the documents or things to be discovered as long as that party has control of the item. The test generally applied to determine questions of "control" is whether the party has a legal right to control or to obtain possession of the documents. A litigant is under a duty to preserve evidence which it knows or reasonably should know is relevant to the action even if there is only a potential for litigation. Failure to preserve the evidence may result in dismissal of the case. *Stabli v. Big D International Trucks, Inc.*, 107 Nev. 309, 810 P.2d 785 (1991); *Fire Insurance Exchange v. Zenith Radio Corp.*, 103 Nev. 648, 747 P.2d 911 (1987).

A notice for the taking of the deposition of a party may be accompanied by a Rule 34 request for production of documents and tangible things at the taking of the deposition. NRCP 30(b)(5). The procedure of Rule 34 applies to such requests, including the time for response.

NRCP 34(c) does not preclude a party from filing an independent action in the nature of a bill in equity against a nonparty for production of documents and things or for permission to enter upon land.

NRCP 34(b) and Fed. R. Civ. P. 34(b) both require production of documents for inspection as they are kept in the usual course of business, or that the producing party organize and label the documents to correspond with the categories contained in the request to produce. This requirement recognizes the need to prevent parties from deliberately mixing critical documents with insignificant documents to obstruct discovery.

Not later than forty-five days before trial, all responses to requests for production must be supplemented. *See* § 1635, *infra.* All requests and responses must be signed by an individual attorney.

NRCP 11 imposes a duty of objective good faith upon each party and his attorney with respect to the contents of every pleading, motion or paper of a party signed by that party or his attorney. The discovery rules now contain a specific counterpart to Rule 11 in the form of Rule 26(g). Rule 26(g) makes it clear that the duty of objective good faith applies to discovery requests, responses and objections.

§ 1631. Physical and mental examinations.

NRCP 16.1 establishes mandatory pretrial discovery requirements. These requirements must first be either satisfied or waived by the trial court before any party may resort to additional discovery by physical or mental examinations. NRCP 26(a). *See* § 1609, *supra.*

In actions where the mental or physical condition of a party, or a person in the custody or under the legal control of the party, is in controversy, the court, for good cause shown, may order the party or person involved to submit to a physical or mental examination. NRCP 35. The party seeking such an examination must file a motion establishing "good cause" with notice upon the person sought to be examined and all other parties to the action. This rule differs from most of the other discovery devices permitted by the rules in that it requires the filing of a motion, a showing of "good cause," and a court order to obtain the examination. A Rule 35 order must specify the time, place, manner, conditions, and scope of the examination as well as the person or persons who are to conduct the examination.

As a practical matter, this rule is usually applied by stipulation of the parties. In addition, since Rule 35 motion is a "discovery motion," it may be argued, in reference to practice before the Eighth Judicial District, that EDCR 2.34 would require a party seeking the examination to attempt to obtain such a stipulation as a condition precedent to bringing the motion.

Under Rule 35, the party examined, upon request, has a right to a copy of a written report of the examiner setting out his findings, results of tests, diagnoses and conclusions, together with like reports of all earlier examinations for the same condition. Upon delivery of the report to the party examined, the party seeking the examination is correspondingly vested with the right to obtain prior and subsequent reports on the condition for which the examination was made. The rule further provides that by requesting and obtaining a report of the examination, or by taking the deposition of the examiner, the party examined waives any privilege regarding the testimony of every other person who has examined or may thereafter examine him regarding his mental and physical condition in controversy in that action.

Sanctions outlined in NRCP 37(b)(2) are available against a party who refuses to obey an order requiring a mental or physical examination, with the exception that contempt of court is not available as a sanction in such cases. *See* NRCP 37(b)(2)(D).

§ 1632. Requests for admission.

NRCP 16.1 establishes mandatory pretrial discovery requirements. These requirements must first be either satisfied or waived by the trial court before any party may resort to additional discovery by requests for admission. NRCP 26(a). *See* § 1609, *supra.*

NRCP 36 allows a party to serve on any other party a written request for the admission of the genuineness of any exhibited document or of the truth of any relevant matter within the scope of Rule 26(b).

Requests for admission must be served by separate document and may not be combined with interrogatories. NRCP 36(a). *See* NRCP 26(a). The frequency of use of this discovery device is limited by NRCP 36(c), which limits the number of requests that a party may serve on any one party to forty, including subparts, unless by stipulation or court order on a showing of good cause. An exception is made for a request for the admission as to the genuineness of a document, where no limit exists, unless the request is annoying, oppressive, or unduly burdensome or expensive. Applications to expand the permissible scope of this type of discovery should be made on notice to all parties and not ex parte.

Each matter of which an admission is requested will be deemed admitted unless the adversary within thirty days (forty-five days when the request accompanies the summons and complaint) provides a written statement specifically denying it, sets forth in detail the reasons why he cannot truthfully admit or deny the matter, or submits objections to the propriety of the request. NRCP 36(a). *See also Wagner v. Carex Investigations & Security, Inc.*, 93 Nev. 627, 572 P.2d 921 (1977).

An answering party may not use lack of information or knowledge as a reason for failing to admit or deny a request unless he states that he has made a reasonable inquiry but remains unable to admit or deny the matter. When good faith requires that a party qualify his answer, or deny only a part of the matter of which an admission is requested, he shall specify so much of it as true and qualify or deny the remainder. A party cannot avoid responding to a request solely because he believes that the requested admission presents a genuine issue of fact for trial. Sanctions for unreasonably denying a request to admit may not be assessed against a party to whom the request is not addressed, and who does not sign the response, even where that party may be the alter ego of the party to whom the request is actually addressed. *Homewood Investment Co. v. Wilt,* 97 Nev. 378, 383-84, 632 P.2d 1140 (1981).

In answering a request for admissions, the answering party must identify and quote each request for admission in full immediately preceding any answer, denial or objection. Rule 26(j). Denials or objections must be signed by the party or by his attorney. Rule 36(a). Originals of responses to requests for admissions must be served upon the party who made the request and that party must make such originals available at the time of any pre-trial hearing or at trial for use by any party.

If the request is admitted, or deemed admitted as provided in subsection (a) of the rule, the fact is conclusively established for purposes of the pending action, unless relief from the court is obtained. Once the court deems the requests admitted, relief is within the court's sound discretion. *See Wagner v. Carex Investigations & Security, Inc.*, 93 Nev. 627, 572 P.2d 921, 922 (1977) (trial court had discretion to reject tardily filed denials, even where submission of the denial is only several days late and failure to timely deny is due to law office oversight); and *Western Mercury, Inc. v. The Rix Co.*, 84 Nev. 218, 222, 438 P.2d 792 (1968) (trial court had discretion to deny relief from summary judgment based on unanswered requests for admission deemed admitted). The admission may not, however, be used against the admitting party in any other proceeding. NRCP 36(b).

The proponent may move to determine the sufficiency of answers or objections. NRCP 36(a) defines the court's choice of alternatives. *See also* EDCR 2.34.

Because matters admitted for failure to timely respond are conclusively established, such an admission will supersede previously filed answers to interrogatories that may have been relied upon to raise an issue of fact on a motion for summary judgment. *Wagner v. Carex Investigation & Security, Inc.*, 93 Nev. 627, 572 P.2d 921 (1977). *See also Ginnochio v. Cockeye Land & Livestock Co.*, 93 Nev. 304, 565 P.2d 328 (1977) (answers to requests for admissions which are untruthful and not set forth with specificity do not comply with the requirements of NRCP 36 and the court may properly consider the requested matter admitted as true); *Graham v. Carson-Tahoe Hospital*, 91 Nev. 609, 540 P.2d 105 (1975) (summary judgment upheld where plaintiff was late in submitting answers to request for admissions of fact); *Lawrence v. Southwest Gas Corp.*, 89 Nev. 433, 514 P.2d 868 (1973) (dispositive facts deemed admitted where appellant failed to timely answer or timely object to request for admissions); *Western Mercury v. The Rix Co.*, 84 Nev. 218, 438 P.2d 792 (1968), and *Dzack v. Marshall*, 80 Nev. 345, 393 P.2d 610 (1964) (unanswered requests for admissions deemed admitted for purposes of motion for summary judgment). However, see *Morgan v. DeMille*, 106 Nev. 671, 799 P.2d 561 (1990), in which the Court in *dicta* states that NRCP 36 is to be used to obtain admission of facts which are in no real dispute and which the adverse party can admit cleanly, without qualifications. A request which involves both factual issues and legal issues is too broad.

NRCP 11 imposes a duty of objective good faith upon each party and his attorney with respect to the contents of every pleading, motion or paper of a party signed by that party or his attorney. The discovery rules contain a specific counterpart to Rule 11 in the form of Rule 26(g). Rule 26(g) makes it clear that the duty of objective good faith applies to discovery requests, responses and objections.

§ 1633. Protective orders.

NRCP 26(c) provides a mechanism for a party or a person from whom discovery is sought to obtain protection from the court in the form of an order protecting the party or persons from annoyance, embarrassment, oppression, or undue burden or expense. The protective devices set forth in NRCP 26(c) are intended to be illustrative only, as the court has broad discretionary powers in this regard.

To obtain the relief afforded by Rule 26(c) a party or person against whom the discovery is sought must file a motion for protective order and notice a hearing on the motion. *See Maheu v. Eighth Judicial District Court,* 88 Nev. 26, 493 P.2d 709 (1972), where the Supreme Court issued a writ of mandamus vacating an ex parte order of the lower court staying depositions. The *Maheu* court held that such orders violated basic rights to depose witnesses without leave of court, NRCP 30(a), and to have the issues of the propriety of deposition discovery resolved by properly noticed motion for protection under NRCP 26(c).

As of January 1, 1988, the filing and service of a motion for protective order under Rule 26(c) no longer acted as an automatic stay of the discovery sought. The companion federal provision, likewise, contains no provision for automatic stay. Accordingly, the discovery proceeds as scheduled until the court enters a protective order. If an appropriate motion for protective order has been served and filed under Rule 26(c), the court could then be requested to stay the discovery sought until the court has had an opportunity to hear and decide the motion.

A motion for protective order may be used by a party or a person against whom discovery is being sought in a wide variety of contexts, *e.g.,* to limit the scope of deposition testimony, to prevent the taking of duplicative depositions, to prohibit the use of confidential or trade secret information obtained during the course of a deposition or other written discovery, to limit the use of overly broad interrogatories or requests for inspection or to produce documents, etc.

§ 1634. Stipulations regarding discovery.

Rule 29 allows the parties by written stipulation to vary any discovery rule or procedure; however, any stipulation varying the procedures may be superseded by court order. Specifically, the rule states:

> Unless the court orders otherwise, the parties may by written stipulation (1) provide that depositions may be taken before any person, at any time or place, upon any notice, and in any manner and (2) modify the procedures provided by these rules for other methods of discovery.

Cf. F. R. Civ. P. 29, which permits stipulations extending the time for responding to discovery conducted under Rules 33, 34 and 36 only with the approval of the court.

Rule 29 is not without exceptions; it does not permit the parties to modify a scheduling order for the completion of discovery except by leave of court or a discovery commissioner. NRCP 16(b). Also, the time for holding an early case conference may not be continued by stipulation more than ninety days. NRCP 16.1(a). Further, the mandatory discovery requirements of NRCP 16.1 may only be waived by the court upon motion and for good cause shown. See NRCP 16.1(f) and § 1607, *supra.* In all other circumstances, a stipulation varying the discovery procedures need not be approved by the court. It may be enforced like any other stipulation. See §§ 1114 through 1118, *supra,* for the Nevada law governing stipulations generally.

A stipulation to record the testimony at a deposition by other than stenographic means has certain requirements. See NRCP 30(b)(4). Also, telephone depositions may be taken pursuant to the provisions of NRCP 30(b)(7).

§ 1635. Supplementation of discovery responses.

When the parties participate in an early case conference under NRCP 16.1, the parties will exchange written lists of persons with knowledge of relevant facts. Under NRCP 16.1(b)(5), each party is under a continual duty to provide prompt supplementation of that party's witness list. Failure to do so may result in the sanctions specified in NRCP 16(e), including an order prohibiting the use of omitted witnesses.

Furthermore, NRCP 26(e) imposes a mandatory duty to supplement discovery responses under various circumstances. First, parties must supplement responses addressing the identity, location, or other relevant information concerning witnesses, including experts. Second, parties must supplement responses so as to correct mistakes in the earlier responses. Third, parties must supplement responses upon order of the court, agreement of the parties, or another party's request for supplementation.

Finally, all parties must supplement all prior answers to interrogatories and responses to requests for production, and all discovery disclosed pursuant to NRCP 16.1, not later than forty-five days before trial. NRCP 26(e)(4). This supplementation is mandatory, without any court order or request for supplementation.

§ 1636. Filing discovery; use of discovery at the hearing of motions or at trial.

Discovery requests and responses are not routinely filed with the clerk. NRCP 5(d) states:

Filing. All papers after the complaint required to be served upon a party shall be filed with the court either before service or within a reasonable time thereafter, except as otherwise provided in Rule 5(b), but, unless filing is ordered by the court on motion of a party or upon its own motion, depositions upon oral examination and interrogatories, requests for production, requests for admission, and the answers and responses thereto, shall not be filed unless and until they are used in the proceedings. Originals of responses to requests for admissions or production and answers to interrogatories shall be served upon the party who made the request or propounded the interrogatories and that party shall make such originals available at the time of any pretrial hearing or at trial for use by any party.

Prior to 1982, original discovery was filed with the clerk. As amended, the rule now provides that depositions, interrogatories, requests for production and requests for admission and the answers thereto are not to be filed unless and until they are used in the proceedings.

As anticipated by the rule, original discovery may be filed by court order. The need for court-ordered filing could arise at any stage of the case where the original discovery was not otherwise used in the proceedings. For example, in an appeal from an order of dismissal granted under NRCP 37(b) for failure to comply with a discovery order, counsel may want the original discovery at issue to be included as part of the record on appeal, thereby requiring filing with the district court clerk in the first instance. During trial, a request that original discovery be filed may be made orally. A written order may be obtained ex parte for discovery to be filed at any other time. *See* § 1124, *supra.*

Rule 5(d) specifies that the party initiating the discovery shall retain original discovery documents generated under NRCP 33, 34 and 36, copies of which should be served on all parties under NRCP 5(a). Original deposition transcripts are to be retained by the party taking the deposition. NRCP 30(f). *See also* EDCR 7.20(d).

If original discovery documents are required for filing or other appropriate use, a written request, *e.g.,* in letter form, should be made to the person retaining the original materials by the person seeking their production. The request should specify the purpose for which the original discovery is being sought, it should identify each item of original discovery being requested, and it should specify a reasonable time and place for its production. If production of the original discovery is not made as requested (due to willful refusal, excusable neglect or otherwise), copies should be allowed to be substituted for all purposes. *Cf.* NRS 52.245.

Newly joined parties may obtain discovery materials generated by existing parties prior to joinder. NRCP 26(h) provides that new parties to litigation may serve a written request on the existing parties for such discovery materials, and further describes the method of response.

The use of original documents in connection with motion practice in the Eighth District, including original discovery documents, is governed by EDCR 7.20(d): Original documents shall be retained by counsel for introduction as exhibits at the time of a hearing or at the time of trial rather than attached to pleadings.

§ 1637. Failure to make discovery; sanctions.

Nevada rules now contain a number of provisions both permitting and requiring the imposition of sanctions if a party, or the party's attorney, fails to properly cooperate in the discovery process, by misusing, abusing or overusing discovery devices, or by failing to properly respond to discovery initiated by one or more other parties.

As discussed previously, NRCP 11 requires the imposition of an appropriate sanction, which may include reasonable expenses (including a reasonable attorney's fee), if a pleading, motion or other paper is signed in violation of the certification requirements of that rule. *See* § 812, *supra.* NRCP 26(g) requires the imposition of an appropriate sanction, which may include reasonable expenses (including a reasonable attorney's fee), if a request for discovery or response or objection thereto is signed in violation of the certification requirements of that rule. In both instances, the court may act upon motion or upon its own initiative, and the sanctions may be imposed upon the person making the certification, the party on whose behalf the certification is made, or both.

NRCP 16.1(e) permits the imposition of the sanction of dismissal without prejudice, on motion or on the court's own initiative, if the early case conference required by NRCP 16.1(a) is not held within 180 days after service of the summons and complaint upon the defendant in question (unless there are compelling and extraordinary circumstances for a continuance), or if the plaintiff does not file a case conference report required by NRCP 16.1(c) within 240 days after service of the summons and complaint upon the defendant in question. *See* §§ 1603, 1605, *supra.*

NRCP 16.1(e)(3) also requires the imposition of appropriate sanctions upon a party, his attorney, or both, on motion or on the court's own initiative, if an attorney (or a party not represented by an attorney) fails to reasonably comply with any provision of NRCP 16.1 or fails to comply with an order entered after a dispute resolution proceeding under NRCP 16.1(d). Such sanctions may include any sanction available under NRCP 37(b)(2) and/or an order prohibiting the use of any witness, document or tangible thing that should have been disclosed, produced, exhibited or exchanged pursuant to NRCP 16.1(b). *See* §§ 1604, 1605 and 1606, *supra.* However, unlike NRCP 37(b)(2) which requires the entry and violation of a court order to provide or permit discovery, NRCP 16.1(e)(3) permits the imposition of such sanctions (including the sanctions available under NRCP 37(b)(2)) solely for violating the requirements of the rule, without the prior entry and violation of a court order.

NRCP 16.1(e)(4) requires that a party, his attorney, or both, making a NRCP 16.1(c)(3) objection to the genuineness or authenticity of a document in violation of NRCP 11, pay the reasonable expenses caused by the objection, including reasonable attorney's fees. *See* § 1605, *supra.*

NRCP 37 defines four categories of failures to make discovery, requires that the court award an aggrieved party its reasonable expenses (including attorney's fees) resulting from such a failure unless it was substantially justified or an award would be otherwise unjust, and vests the court with broad discretion to fashion other sanctions based on the exigencies of any given situation.

Subdivision (a) of the rule addresses situations where a deponent fails to answer a question at a deposition; a corporation fails to designate a person to testify on its behalf under NRCP 30(b)(6) or 31(a); a party fails to answer an interrogatory; or a party, in his response to a request to inspect, fails to respond that the inspection will be allowed or fails to permit the inspection. In such cases, NRCP 37(a) allows any party to seek an order compelling discovery. Evasive or incomplete answers under NRCP 37(a) are treated as failures to answer. If the court denies such a motion, either in whole or in part, it may make such protective orders as are allowed under NRCP 26(c). An award of attorney's fees and reasonable expenses must be made to the prevailing party seeking or resisting imposition of the order, unless the nonprevailing party's position was substantially justified or other circumstances make an award of expenses unjust. The award may be imposed, after opportunity for hearing, upon the party, the attorney advising the party's or deponent's conduct, or both. *See* NRCP 37(a)(4). Expenses and fees may be apportioned in a just manner where such motions are granted in part and denied in part.

Subdivision (b) of the rule defines the sanctions available when a person or party fails to comply with an order compelling discovery or with an order entered under NRCP 26(f) following a discovery conference. Any deponent who fails to be sworn or answer a question in the face of such an order may be considered in contempt of court. NRCP 37(b)(1). Parties failing to obey discovery orders are subject to the entry of any sanction order the court deems just under the circumstances, including but not limited to the following: that matters relating to the failure or other designated facts be taken as established for the purpose of the action; that the disobedient party be prohibited from introducing designated matters in evidence, or from supporting or opposing designated claims or defenses; that all or portions of pleadings be stricken; that proceedings be stayed until the order is obeyed; that a disobedient plaintiff's complaint be dismissed; that a default judgment be entered against a disobedient defendant; that, except as to orders to submit to NRCP 35 examinations, the party be held in contempt. *See* NRCP 37(b)(2)(A)(B)-(C) and (D). Unless the party failing to comply with a NRCP 35 order to submit to physical or mental examination shows inability to produce the party to be examined for examination, the sanctions enumerated in subparagraphs (A), (B) and (C) are available; that is, all sanctions listed above except contempt. Failure to comply with such orders also requires that the court award the reasonable expenses and attorney's fees caused by the failure against the party, the attorney advising the party, or both, unless substantial justification or other circumstances can be shown making such an award unjust.

NRCP 37(c) requires that reasonable expenses, including attorney's fees, be awarded where a party has denied or otherwise failed to admit a NRCP 36 request for admission, if the requesting party has thereafter proved the truth of the matters or the genuineness of the documents which were the subject of the request, unless there was good reason for the failure to admit.

NRCP 37(d) outlines the sanctions available upon the failure of a party to attend a deposition, serve answers or objections to interrogatories, or respond in writing to a request for inspection. In contrast to situations discussed under NRCP 37(a), sanctions under NRCP 37(d) deal with parties who simply fail to respond in any form to discovery requests under NRCP 30, 31, 33 or 34. Violation of a court order is not a prerequisite under subsection (d) as it is under subsection (b). All sanctions allowed under NRCP 37(b)(2)(A),(B), and (C), among others that are just under the circumstances, are available under 37(d), *i.e.*, refusal to allow parties to introduce evidence, deeming certain facts established, striking all or part of the pleadings, dismissing claims for affirmative relief, entry of judgment by default, refusal to allow disobedient party to oppose or support certain claims, etc. In lieu thereof or in addition thereto, again the court must award expenses and fees against the party, his attorney, or both, unless the failure to respond was substantially justified or an award would be unjust.

Failure to engage in the discovery outlined in subparagraph (d) of the rule may not be excused on the ground that the discovery sought is objectionable, unless the party failing to act has applied for a protective order pursuant to NRCP 26(c).

Under NRCP 37(f), the court may, after opportunity for hearing, award reasonable expenses, including attorney's fees, against a party or its attorney, for failure of a party or its attorney to participate in good faith in the framing of a discovery plan as required by NRCP 26(f).

Obviously, failure to appear at a deposition, to obey an order compelling discovery, or to answer interrogatories leaves the court with clear discretion to dismiss an action or enter a default judgment. *See Schatz v. Devitte*, 75 Nev. 124, 335 P.2d 783 (1959); *Riverside Casino Corp. v. J.M. Brewer Co.*, 80 Nev. 153, 390 P.2d 232 (1964). Generally, however, the sanction of dismissal should only be imposed for failure to obey discovery orders in extreme circumstances of willful noncompliance. *See Tempora Trading Co., Ltd. v. Perry,* 98 Nev. 229, 645 P.2d 436 (1982) (sanction applied for refusal to attend depositions after being ordered to do so, as well as otherwise obstructing discovery); *Finkleman v. Clover Jewelers Boulevard, Inc.,* 91 Nev. 146, 532 P.2d 608 (1975) (striking of answer and entry of default reversed where there was partial compliance with order to produce documents and noncompliance was the result of microfilming difficulties). But, entry of a default judgment has been upheld where a defendant failed to attend his deposition without explanation and his failure to provide discovery halted the normal adversary process. *Skeen v. Valley Bank of Nevada,* 89 Nev. 301, 511 P.2d 1053 (1973), *cert. denied,* 415 U.S. 919 (1974). There the court noted that willfulness had been deleted as an element required for such sanctions as part of the 1971 amendments to the Nevada rules. Although *Skeen* was decided prior to *Finkleman* and *Tempora,* a deliberate refusal to provide discovery is probably not the ultimate test of willfulness, so long as the party is able to comply. *See Havas v. Bank of Nevada,* 96 Nev. 567, 613 P.2d 706 (1980). An unexplained or unjustified failure to provide discovery that serves to halt the adversarial process will in all likelihood constitute willful noncompliance. *See Fire Insurance Exchange v. Zenith Radio Corp.,* 103 Nev. 648, 747 P.2d 911 (1987), *Kelly Broadcasting Co. v. Sovereign Broadcast, Inc.,* 96 Nev. 188, 606 P.2d 1089 (1980). Further, dismissal was held appropriate where counsel was served with a motion to compel production of documents, raised no objection to the validity of the original request, and filed no motion for protective order. *Kerley v. The Aetna Casualty & Surety Co.,* 94 Nev. 710, 585 P.2d 1339 (1978). Finally, even where a party did not obey a court order because his attorney failed to advise him of its entry, dismissal was held appropriate and not an abuse of discretion. *Lange v. Hickman,* 92 Nev. 41, 544 P.2d 1208 (1976).

A trial court decision striking a party's pleading is reviewed under an abuse of discretion standard; however, the Nevada Supreme Court has stated that, "under this standard, we must be mindful of the underlying rights of a party to due process and a trial by jury, as well as the judicial policy favoring the disposition of cases on their merits." *Havas v. Bank of Nevada,* 96 Nev. 567, 570, 613 P.2d 706, 707-08 (1980); *cf. Kelly Broadcasting Co. v. Sovereign Broadcast, Inc.,* 96 Nev. 188, 606 P.2d 1089 (1980). The Nevada Supreme Court has also held that NRCP 37(b) sanctions are available where a party fails to preserve evidence it knows or reasonably should know is relevant before potential litigation is commenced, *Fire Insurance Exchange v. Zenith Radio Corp.,* 103 Nev. 648, 747 P.2d 911 (1987), and that a judgment creditor may pursue the remedies provided by NRCP 37(a) and (b) for discovery relating to execution and in aid of the judgment under NRCP 69, even after an appeal without supersedeas has been taken. *Fishmen v. Las Vegas Sun,* 75 Nev. 13, 333 P.2d 988 (1959).

CHAPTER 17

SUMMARY JUDGMENT

A. Generally.

B. Substantive Requirements.

C. Burden of Proof.

D. Standards for Decision and Review.

Author: Richard G. Barrows

A. Generally.

§ 1701. Introduction and scope.

Summary judgment is a pre-trial procedure for adjudication of all, or part, of the legal issues in a case when their resolution does not depend upon the determination of factual issues. In the language of NRCP 56(C), the court must enter summary judgment when "… there is no genuine issue as to any material fact and … the moving party is entitled to a judgment as a matter of law." In that situation, a trial would serve no purpose. Therefore, the decision to grant or deny a summary judgment — or to reverse or affirm the same on appeal — is a balancing of the policy of a trial on the merits, on the one hand, and the policy of a speedy and inexpensive determination, on the other.

For decades, the published decisions of the Nevada Supreme Court have discouraged summary judgment. However, a 1986 trilogy from the United States Supreme Court signals that the use of summary judgment to resolve litigation should be encouraged. *Anderson v. Liberty Lobby, Inc.*, 477 U.S. 242, 106 S. Ct. 2505, 91 L. Ed. 2d 202 (1986); *Celotex Corp. v. Catrett*, 477 U.S. 317, 106 S. Ct. 2548, 91 L. Ed. 2d 265 (1986); and *Matsushita Electric Industrial Co. v. Zenith Radio Corp.*, 475 U.S. 574, 106 S. Ct. 1348, 89 L. Ed. 2d 538 (1986).

In this Chapter, "Rule 56" will refer to *Nevada* Rule of Civil Procedure 56; "Wright & Miller" will refer to Wright, Miller & Kane, *Federal Practice and Procedure: Civil* (2d ed. 1983); "Fed. Proc. L. Ed." will refer to *Federal Procedure, Lawyers Edition* (1984); and "Moore's" will refer to *Moore's Federal Practice* (2d ed. 1985).

§ 1702. Purpose and function.

The purpose of summary judgment procedure is to obviate trials when they would serve no useful purpose. *Short v. Hotel Riviera, Inc.*, 79 Nev. 94, 378 P.2d 979 (1963); and *Coray v. Hom*, 80 Nev. 39, 389 P.2d 76 (1964). It is not to decide any issue of fact which may be presented, but to discover if any real issue of fact exists. *Daugherty v. Wabash Life Insurance Co.*, 87 Nev. 32, 482 P.2d 814 (1971).

The function of summary judgment proceedings is not to test the legal sufficiency of the complaint to state a claim. *Force v. Peccole*, 74 Nev. 64, 322 P.2d 307 (1958). Rather, it is to pierce the pleadings, *Dredge Corp. v. Husite Co.*, 78 Nev. 69, 369 P.2d 676, *cert. denied*, 371 U.S. 821, 83 S. Ct. 39, 9 L. Ed. 2d 61 (1962), and to test whether, under the uncontroverted facts, one party is entitled to judgment as a matter of law. NRCP 56(c); *Force v. Peccole*, 74 Nev. 64, 322 P.2d 307 (1958). *See also Matsushita Electric Industrial Co. v. Zenith Radio Corp.*, 475 U.S. 574, 106 S. Ct. 1348, 89 L. Ed. 2d 538 (1986).

In 1986, the U.S. Supreme Court — presumably because of the national explosion and congestion of the courts — breathed life into summary judgment practice. *Celotex Corp. v. Catrett*, 477 U.S. 317, 106 S. Ct. 2548, 91 L. Ed. 2d 265 (1986). The High Court said:

Summary judgment procedure is properly regarded not as a disfavored procedural shortcut, but rather as an integral part of the Federal Rules as a whole, which are designed to secure the just, speedy and inexpensive determination of every action.

§ 1703. Other motions compared.

The motion for summary judgment serves the same function as a Rule 12(b)(5) motion to dismiss for failure to state a claim, and a Rule 12(c) motion for judgment on the pleadings. They all are methods for obtaining a speedy determination of the suit and will allow determination of the law of the case. But they differ as to the record for the determination.

The 12(b)(5) motion is limited to the face of the pleading of the party challenged. For example, as to a 12(b)(5) motion directed at a complaint, the motion admits the entire complaint, but says that the defendant is entitled to judgment as a matter of law. In deciding the 12(b)(5) motion, the court may not look beyond the face of the challenged pleading.

The 12(c) motion is limited to *all* of the pleadings. The 12(c) motion typically says that, given what is admitted by all of the pleadings, the movant is entitled to judgment under the law. Regardless of the law applicable to the case, a defendant may prevent a 12(c) motion simply by denials in his answer. In deciding the 12(c) motion, the court may not look beyond the face of all of the pleadings. *See Bernard v. Rockhill Development Co.,* 103 Nev. 132, 734 P.2d 1238 (1987).

In contrast, under a motion for summary judgment, the parties may — and usually are required to — offer evidence outside the pleadings and the court is required to look beyond the pleadings at such evidence. *See* NRCP 12(b) (final sentence); NRCP 12(c); NRCP 56(c); and NRCP 56(e).

§ 1704. Effect on jury trial.

The purpose of a summary judgment is not to deprive litigants of their right of trial by jury if they really have issues to try. *Short v. Hotel Riviera, Inc.,* 79 Nev. 94, 378 P.2d 979 (1963); *Nevada Land & Mortgage Co. v. Hidden Wells Ranch,* 83 Nev. 501, 435 P.2d 198 (1967); *Pine v. Leavitt,* 84 Nev. 507, 445 P.2d 942 (1968); *Old West Enterprises v. Reno Escrow Co.,* 86 Nev. 727, 476 P.2d 1 (1970).

But if there are no genuine issues of material fact, there is nothing for a jury to decide, and the entry of summary judgment does not deprive the opponent of his constitutional right to a jury trial. 28 Fed. Proc. L. Ed. § 62:534 n.29; 10 Wright & Miller, § 2714.

§ 1705. Relationship to Rule 41(e).

A motion for summary judgment which is: (a) filed and submitted before expiration of the five year period of Rule 41(e); and *granted* before or after such expiration, is "bringing the action to trial" within the five year period. It is not when the motion is denied. *United Association of Journeymen v. Manson,* 105 Nev. 816, 783 P.2d 955 (1989).

B. Substantive Requirements.

§ 1706. Generally.

Rule 56(c) establishes two basic substantive requirements for the entry of summary judgment:

> A. There must be no genuine issue as to any material fact; *and*
> B. The moving party must be entitled to judgment as a matter of law.

Shapro v. Forsythe, 103 Nev. 666, 747 P.2d 241 (1987); *Wiltsie v. Baby Grand Corp.,* 105 Nev. 291, 774 P.2d 432 (1989); *Fyssakis v. Knight Equipment Corp.,* 108 Nev. 212, 826 P.2d 570 (1992).

§ 1707. Fact issue.

It is axiomatic that the presence of any "genuine" issue of "material" fact precludes the court from entering summary judgment. In such case, a trial for the determination of that issue by the court or jury is required. NRCP 56(c). That basic principal has been reiterated by the Nevada Supreme Court repeatedly since 1954. Most reported cases were reversals of summary judgment and remands for trial. *See for example*: *Parman v. Petricciani,* 70 Nev. 427, 272 P.2d 492 (1954); *Old West Enterprises v. Reno Escrow Co.,* 86 Nev. 727, 476 P.2d 1 (1970); *Orcutt v. Miller,* 95 Nev. 408, 595 P.2d 1991 (1979); *O'Dell v. Martin,* 101 Nev. 142, 696 P.2d 996 (1985); *Tschabold v. Orlando,* 103 Nev. 224, 737 P.2d 506 (1987), *Charles v. J. Steven Lemons & Associates,* 104 Nev. 388, 760 P.2d 118 (1988).

§ 1708. — Question of fact.

To preclude summary judgment, the issue must be a question of fact rather than a question of law. *Cf. Springer v. Federated Church of Reno,* 71 Nev. 177, 283 P.2d 1071 (1955); *Pine v. Leavitt,* 84 Nev. 507, 445 P.2d 942 (1968) (whether land surveyor was performing "engineering" so as to require an engineer's license); *Mitchell v. Bailey & Selover, Inc.,* 96 Nev. 147, 605 P.2d 1138 (1980) (whether party in "good faith"); *Millspaugh v. Millspaugh,* 96 Nev. 446, 611 P.2d 201 (1980) (when party should have discovered fraud so as to start statute of limitations); *Andolino v. State,* 97 Nev. 53, 624 P.2d 7 (1981) (whether party was negligent); *McPherron v. McAuliffe,* 97 Nev. 78, 624 P.2d 21 (1981) (adverse possession); *Nehls v. Leonard,* 97 Nev. 325, 630 P.2d 258 (1981) (negligence and proximate cause); *Steelman v. Lind,* 97 Nev. 425, 634 P.2d 666 (1981) (assumption of risk); *Engelmann v. Westergard,* 98 Nev. 348, 647 P.2d 385 (1982) (failure to exercise diligence in protection of water rights); *Oak Grove Investors v. Bell & Gossett Co.,* 99 Nev. 616, 668 P.2d 1075 (1983) (when plaintiff should have discovered cause of action for purposes of statute of limitations); *Zugel by Zugel v. Miller,* 100 Nev. 525, 688 P.2d 310 (1984) (negligence); *Epperson v. Roloff,* 102 Nev. 206, 719 P.2d 799 (1986) (discovery of cause of action); *Bernard v. Rockhill Development Co.,* 103 Nev. 132, 734 P.2d 1238 (1987) (party's wrongful intent); *Morrow v. Barger,* 103 Nev. 247, 737 P.2d 1153 (1987) (whether one real estate listing was replaced by a subsequent one); *Barr v. Gaines,* 103 Nev. 548, 746 P.2d 634 (1987).

§ 1709. — Negligence cases.

The courts are reluctant to grant summary judgment in negligence cases because the issues of foreseeability, duty, proximate cause and reasonableness usually present questions of fact for the jury. *Sims v. General Telephone & Electronics,* 107 Nev. 516, 815 P.2d 151 (1991). But when plaintiff, as a matter of law, cannot recover (as where Nevada does not recognize the cause of action), defendant is entitled to a summary judgment in a negligence case. *Lockart v. MacLean,* 77 Nev. 210, 361 P.2d 670 (1961); *Thomas v. Bokelman,* 86 Nev. 10, 462 P.2d 1020 (1970); *Cf. Turney v. Sullivan,* 89 Nev. 554, 516 P.2d 738 (1973); *Bill Stremmel Motors, Inc. v. First National Bank of Nevada,* 94 Nev. 131, 575 P.2d 938 (1978); *Bakerink v. Orthopaedic Associates, Ltd.,* 94 Nev. 428, 581 P.2d 9 (1978); *Andolino v. State,* 97 Nev. 53, 624 P.2d 7 (1981); *Phipps v. City of McGill,* 97 Nev. 233, 627 P.2d 401 (1981); *Van Cleave v. Kietz-Mill Minit Mart,* 97 Nev. 414, 633 P.2d 1220 (1981); *Montgomery v. Royal Motel,* 98 Nev. 240, 645 P.2d 968 (1982); *Smith v. Clough,* 106 Nev. 568, 796 P.2d 592 (1990); *Burnett v. C.B.A. Security Service,* 107 Nev. 787, 820 P.2d 750 (1991).

A party's negligence becomes a question of law only when the evidence will support no other inference. *Shepard v. Harrison,* 100 Nev. 178, 678 P.2d 670 (1984).

§ 1710. — State of mind cases.

Cases in which a particular state of mind of the defendant is a prima facie element of the plaintiff's cause of action are another category not generally suited to disposition by summary judgment. *Millspaugh v. Millspaugh,* 96 Nev. 446, 611 P.2d 201 (1980). Nevertheless, a party against whom summary judgment is sought is not entitled to a trial simply because he has asserted a cause of action to which state of mind is a material element. There must be some indication that he can produce the requisite quantum of evidence to enable him to reach the jury with his claim. *Collins v. Union Federal Savings & Loan Association,* 99 Nev. 284, 662 P.2d 610 (1983); *Anderson v. Liberty Lobby, Inc.,* 477 U.S. 242, 106 S. Ct. 2505, 91 L. Ed. 2d 202, 217 (1986).

§ 1711. — Other issues on which summary judgment generally not available.

Genuine issues of material fact consistently are found in other types of cases which make a motion for summary judgment unsuitable, assuming, of course, that the opponent properly opposes the motion. For example, where there is ambiguity in a written contract or document and extrinsic evidence is required to ascertain the intent of the parties, summary judgment should not be entered in the face of contradictory or conflicting evidence. *Mullis v. Nevada National Bank,* 98 Nev. 510, 654 P.2d 533 (1982); *Ma-Gar Mining & Exploration Corp. v. Comstock Bank,* 100 Nev. 66, 675 P.2d 992 (1984). Where the terms of an oral contract are at issue, summary judgment is precluded and trial is the only remedy. *Old West Enterprises v. Reno Escrow Co.,* 86 Nev. 727, 476 P.2d 1 (1970); *Hoffman v. Eighth Judicial District Court,* 90 Nev. 267, 523 P.2d 848 (1974).

The Nevada Supreme Court has held that what is "reasonable" is a question of fact which "turns on the facts" and should be resolved by a trier of fact. *See Selsnick v. Horton,* 96 Nev. 944, 620 P.2d 1256 (1980) (reasonableness of attorneys' conduct in malpractice case). *Nelson v. City of Las Vegas,* 99 Nev. 548, 665 P.2d 1141 (1983) (reasonableness of police conduct in false arrest case).

Questions of whether equitable relief should apply are often triable facts. *See Johnson v. Steel, Inc.,* 100 Nev. 181, 678 P.2d 676 (1984); *Benetti v. Kishner,* 93 Nev. 1, 558 P.2d 537 (1977); *Copeland v. Desert Inn Hotel,* 99 Nev. 823, 673 P.2d 490 (1983). The characterization of property and the rights of the parties thereto are generally questions of fact. *Hubert v. Werner,* 101 Nev. 193, 698 P.2d 426 (1985) (quiet title and boundary line dispute); *Alper v. State,* 96 Nev. 925, 621 P.2d 492 (1980); *McPherron v. McAuliffe,* 97 Nev. 78, 624 P.2d 21 (1981) (adverse possession); *Arley v. State ex rel. Department of Highways,* 92 Nev. 123, 546 P.2d 1001 (1976) (real property title dispute). The intent of parties is a question of fact. *Parman v. Petricciani,* 70 Nev. 427, 272 P.2d 492 (1954) (intended rights of party under a lease); *Mullis v. Nevada National Bank,* 98 Nev. 510, 654 P.2d 533 (1982) (intention to create a security interest).

The application of a statute of limitations may depend on an issue of fact as to whether a party knew, or in the exercise of proper diligence should have known, of the facts constituting the elements of his cause of action. *Oak Grove Investors v. Bell & Gossett Co.,* 99 Nev. 616, 668 P.2d 1075 (1983); *Millspaugh v. Millspaugh,* 96 Nev. 446, 611 P.2d 201 (1980); *Golden Nugget, Inc. v. Ham,* 95 Nev. 45, 589 P.2d 173 (1979). Trade name infringement cases are *generally* not suitable for summary judgment. *A.L.M.N., Inc. v. Rosoff,* 104 Nev. 274, 757 P.2d 1319 (1988).

§ 1712. — "Genuine" issue.

The United States Supreme Court has recently issued two rulings that should enter Nevada summary judgment law: *Matsushita Electric Industrial Co. v. Zenith Radio Corp.,* 475 U.S. 574, 106 S. Ct. 1348, 89 L. Ed. 2d 538 (1986) and *Anderson v. Liberty Lobby, Inc.,* 477 U.S. 242, 106 S. Ct. 2505, 91 L. Ed. 2d 202 (1986).

Matsushita held that when the moving party has carried its burden under Rule 56(c) (*see infra* §§ 1717 and 1718), the party opposing the motion for summary judgment:

> must do more than simply show that there is some metaphysical doubt as to the material facts.... In the language of the Rule, the non-moving party must come forward with 'specific facts showing that there is a *genuine issue for trial.'*... Where the record taken as a whole could not lead a rational trier of fact to find for the non-moving party, there is no 'genuine issue for trial.' 89 L. Ed. 2d at 552.

Anderson held that a "genuine" issue is more than "some" issue. 92 L. Ed. 2d at 211, 213. The standard for "genuineness" mirrors the standard for a directed verdict under Rule 50(a): that the trial judge must direct a verdict if, under the governing law, there can be but one reasonable conclusion as to the verdict. If reasonable minds could differ as to the import of the evidence, a verdict should *not* be directed. 91 L. Ed. 2d at 213.

In particular, *Anderson* held that an issue of material fact is "genuine" if the evidence is such that a reasonable jury, applying the applicable quantum of proof, could return a verdict for the non-moving party, 91 L. Ed. 2d at 212; or, to put it another way, if a reasonable jury applying the applicable quantum of proof could resolve the issue in favor of either party. 91 L. Ed. 2d at 213. The *Anderson* principle has been adopted in Nevada: *Valley Bank of Nevada v. Marble,* 105 Nev. 366, 775 P.2d 1278 (1989); *Oehler v. Humana, Inc.,* 105 Nev. 348, 775 P.2d 1271 (1989); *Bulbman, Inc. v. Nevada Bell,* 108 Nev. 105, 825 P.2d 588, (1992). *See also Collins v. Union Federal Savings & Loan Association,* 99 Nev. 284, 662 P.2d 610 (1983). An issue is not "genuine" if the evidence presented in the opposing affidavits is of insufficient caliber or quantity to allow a rational factfinder, applying the applicable quantum of proof, to find for the non-moving party. 91 L. Ed. 2d at 215.

Two older Nevada cases have also discussed "genuineness." When Rule 56 speaks of a "genuine" issue of material fact, it does so with the adversary system in mind. The word "genuine" has moral overtones. It does not mean a fabricated issue. Although the summary judgment procedure is not available to test and resolve the credibility of opposing witnesses to a fact issue, it may appropriately be invoked to defeat a lie from the mouth of a party against whom summary judgment is sought, when that lie is claimed to be the source of a "genuine" issue of fact for trial. *Aldabe v. Adams,* 81 Nev. 280, 402 P.2d 34 (1965). Further, if the party moving for summary judgment has supported the motion to the point of showing to the satisfaction of the trial court that the issue raised by the opposing party is a *sham,* the issue is not "genuine" and the motion should be granted. *Dzack v. Marshall,* 80 Nev. 345, 393 P.2d 610 (1964).

§ 1713. — "Material" fact.

Curiously, there have been no reported Nevada case referring to the "materiality" requirement of Rule 56(c). Nevertheless, it is clear that if a fact is not "material," an issue over it must not defeat summary judgment. 28 Fed. Proc. L. Ed. § 62:549.

Materiality is determined by the substantive law. If a dispute over a fact might affect the outcome of the suit, it is a "material" fact; if it would not, it is an immaterial, irrelevant or unnecessary fact. Only "material" facts will properly preclude the entry of summary judgment. *Anderson v. Liberty Lobby, Inc.,* 477 U.S. 242, 106 S. Ct. 2505, 91 L. Ed. 2d 202 (1986).

Similarly, the Nevada evidence code silently defines "materiality" as a fact "that is of consequence to the determination of the action." *See* NRS 48.015 and *McCormick on Evidence* 4th Ed., § 185. McCormick gives an example that the employee's contributory negligence is "immaterial" in a workmen's compensation case. § 185 at n.2.

§ 1714. — Question of fact is a question of law.

The decision as to whether a genuine issue of material fact exists is itself a question of law. *Midland Insurance Co. v. Yanke Plumbing & Heating, Inc.,* 99 Nev. 66, 657 P.2d 1152 (1983).

§ 1715. Matter of law.

Even if there are no genuine issues of material fact, it is axiomatic that a party is not entitled to summary judgment in his favor unless he is, under the undisputed facts, entitled to judgment as a matter of law. *See for example: Short v. Hotel Riviera, Inc.,* 79 Nev. 94, 378 P.2d 979

(1963); *Brunzell v. Woodbury,* 85 Nev. 29, 449 P.2d 158 (1969); *Orcutt v. Miller,* 95 Nev. 408, 595 P.2d 1991 (1979); *O'Dell v. Martin,* 101 Nev. 142, 696 P.2d 996 (1985); *Tschabold v. Orlando,* 103 Nev. 224, 737 P.2d 506 (1987); *Charles v. J. Steven Lemons & Associates,* 104 Nev. 388, 760 P.2d 118 (1988).

§ 1716. — Type of legal issues.

If there are no *fact* issues, the issues of *law* that may be decided by summary judgment proceeding are limited only by the legal issues that an imaginative lawyer may assert under the entire body of law. Any legal issue of substantive law in the case may be decided by summary judgment. Rule 56.

C. Burden of Proof.

§ 1717. Initial burden of proof.

It is axiomatic that the party moving for summary judgment has the burden of demonstrating clearly that there is no genuine issue of any material fact to be determined. *See for example: Short v. Hotel Riviera, Inc.,* 79 Nev. 94, 378 P.2d 979 (1963); *Hoffmeister Cabinets of Nevada, Inc. v. Bivins,* 87 Nev. 282, 486 P.2d 57 (1971); *Weaver v. Shell Oil Co.,* 91 Nev. 324, 535 P.2d 787 (1975); *Oak Grove Investors v. Bell & Gossett Co.,* 99 Nev. 616, 668 P.2d 1075 (1983); *Renaud v. 200 Convention Center, Ltd.,* 102 Nev. 500, 728 P.2d 445 (1986); *Matsushita Electric Industrial Co. v. Zenith Radio Corp.,* 475 U.S. 574, 106 S. Ct. 1348, 89 L. Ed. 2d 538 (1986); *Shapro v. Forsyth,* 103 Nev. 666, 747 P.2d 241 (1987); *City of Boulder City v. State,* 106 Nev. 390, 793 P.2d 845 (1990).

§ 1718. — Lack of claimant's evidence.

The burden on the moving party may be met by "showing" [*see* NRCP 56(c)] — that is pointing out to the trial court — that there is an absence of evidence to support any one or more of the prima facie elements of the non-moving party's case. *Celotex Corp. v. Catrett,* 477 U.S. 317, 106 S. Ct. 2548, 91 L. Ed. 2d 265, 275 (1986).

The moving party himself need not affirmatively produce any evidence by affidavit or otherwise, negating the prima facie elements of his opponent's claim. NRCP 56(a); *Celotex; Tobler & Oliver Construction Co. v. Board of Trustees,* 84 Nev. 438, 442 P.2d 904 (1968). *But see* statement to the contrary in *Ferreira v. P.C.H., Inc.,* 105 Nev. 305, 774 P.2d 1041 (1989) and *Clausen v. Lloyd,* 103 Nev. 432, 743 P.2d 631 (1987) (medical malpractice). He may simply point out the lack of evidence produced by the non-moving claimant on any of the prima facie elements of the claim. Lujan v. National Wildlife Federation, 497 U.S. 871, 111 L. Ed. 2d 695,

110 S. Ct. 3177 (1990). For example, in a products liability case, the defendant may obtain summary judgment by pointing out that the plaintiff has not produced any evidence that it was the defendant's product which caused the injury. *Celotex. See also infra* § 1776.

Thus, the *Celotex* rule is that Rule 56 mandates the entry of summary judgment upon motion, after adequate time for discovery, against a party who fails to make a showing sufficient to establish the existence of an element essential to that party's case, and on which that party will bear the burden of proof at trial. 91 L. Ed. 2d 265, 273 (1986).

Without a citation to *Celotex,* the following Nevada Supreme Court cases have properly applied *Celotex*-type analysis in affirming the lower court's grant of summary judgment, because the claimant had not come forward with any evidence that dispelled the movant's demonstration of the lack of material issues of fact: *Charles v. J. Steven Lemon & Associates,* 104 Nev. 388, 760 P.2d 118 (1988); *Elley v. Stephens,* 104 Nev. 413, 760 P.2d 768 (1988); *Bulbman, Inc. v. Nevada Bell,* 108 Nev. 105, 825 P.2d 588 (1992).

However, one reading of some post-*Clauson* cases is a rejection of *Celotex*-type summary judgment practice in negligence cases and other types of cases not suited to summary judgment. *See Judson v. Camelot Food, Inc.,* 104 Nev. 324, 756 P.2d 1198 (1988) (premises liability case in which it may be inferred from the opinion that the personal injury plaintiff did not come forward with any evidence after the pizza parlor defendant pointed out to the court the *lack* of evidence that the collapsing bench was defective). (*But see* Springer dissent); *Sims v. General Telephone & Electronics,* 107 Nev. 516, 815 P.2d 151 (1991). *Sims* was a death case in which the lower court made a *Celotex*-type ruling that — *after discovery* — the plaintiffs produced no *evidence* of proximate cause. The Nevada Supreme Court reversed because although it did not know what evidence plaintiff may produce at trial, the trial evidence *may* fulfill the elements of negligence. *See* n.1.

§ 1719. Burden shifts to opposing party.

Once the movant has made a *prima facie* demonstration of no issues of fact, the party opposing summary judgment has the burden of coming forward with evidence in the form of specific facts to show the existence of a genuine issue of material fact, or the court is required to enter judgment according to the law. NRCP 56(e). *Dredge Corp. v. Husite Co.,* 78 Nev. 69, 369 P.2d 676, *cert. denied,* 371 U.S. 821, 83 S. Ct. 39, 9 L. Ed. 2d 61 (1962); *Nevada Land & Mortgage Co. v. Hidden Wells Ranch,* 83 Nev. 501, 435 P.2d 198 (1967); *Bakerink v. Orthopaedic Associates, Ltd.,* 94 Nev. 428, 581 P.2d 9 (1978); *Bulbman, Inc. v. Nevada Bell,* 108 Nev. 105, 825 P.2d 588 (1992). *Also see Matsushita Electric Industrial Co. v.*

Zenith Radio Corp., 475 U.S. 574, 106 S. Ct. 1348, 89 L. Ed. 2d 538 (86); *Anderson v. Liberty Lobby, Inc.*, 477 U.S. 242, 106 S. Ct. 2505, 91 L. Ed. 2d 202, 217 (1986); *Celotex Corp. v. Catrett*, 477 U.S. 317, 106 S. Ct. 2548, 91 L. Ed. 2d 265 (1986); and *Lujan v. National Wildlife Federation*, 497 U.S. 871, 110 S. Ct. 3177, 111 L. Ed. 2d 695 (1990).

§ 1720. Cannot rest on pleadings.

A party *opposing* a motion for summary judgment can't rest on his pleadings — even if they are verified. He may *not* assume that the allegations and assertions in his pleadings will be taken as true. A mere pleading cannot create a genuine issue of fact. That party must come forward with *evidence* in the form of affidavits and depositions, etc., which set forth "specific" facts showing that there is a genuine issue of material fact for trial. NRCP 56(e). *Aldabe v. Adams,* 81 Nev. 280, 402 P.2d 34 (1965); *Nevada Land & Mortgage Co. v. Hidden Wells Ranch,* 83 Nev. 501, 435 P.2d 198 (1967); *Tobler & Oliver Construction Co. v. Board of Trustees,* 84 Nev. 438, 442 P.2d 904 (1968) (even if the motion is not *supported* by affidavits); *Adamson v. Bowker,* 85 Nev. 115, 450 P.2d 796 (1969); *Bill Stremmel Motors, Inc. v. First National Bank of Nevada,* 94 Nev. 131, 575 P.2d 938 (1978); *Bird v. Casa Royale West,* 97 Nev. 67, 624 P.2d 17 (1981); *Ferreira v. P.C.H., Inc.,* 105 Nev. 305, 774 P.2d 1041 (1989); *Chambers By Cochran v. Sanderson,* 107 Nev. 84, 822 P.2d 657 (1991). *See also Celotex Corp. v. Catrett,* 477 U.S. 317, 106 S. Ct. 2548, 91 L. Ed. 2d 265 (1986). *But see Clauson v. Lloyd,* 103 Nev. 432, 743 P.2d 631 (1987).

However, Rule 56 does not require the non-moving party to produce evidence in a form that would be admissible at trial in order to avoid summary judgment. The non-moving party is obviously not required to depose his own witnesses. He may oppose the motion by affidavits, etc. Rule 56; *Celotex Corp. v. Catrett,* 477 U.S. 317, 106 S. Ct. 2548, 91 L. Ed. 2d 265, 274, 275 (1986).

§ 1721. — "Specific" facts.

The "specific" fact requirement of Rule 56(e) is not satisfied by a sworn affidavit with conclusory allegations. *See* § 1771. The object of Rule 56(e) is not to replace the conclusory allegations of a pleading claim with conclusory allegations in an affidavit.

Rather, the purpose of Rule 56 is to enable a party who believes there is no genuine dispute as to a specific fact essential to the other side's case to demand at least one sworn averment of that fact before the lengthy process of litigation continues.

Lujan v. National Wildlife Federation, 497 U.S. 871, 110 S. Ct. 3177, 111 L. Ed. 2d 695 (1990).

§ 1722. Quantum of proof.

Whatever quantum of proof would apply at the trial on the merits applies at the summary judgment stage. The mere existence of *some* evidence in support of the non-movant's claim is not enough. *Anderson v. Liberty Lobby, Inc.,* 477 U.S. 242, 106 S. Ct. 2505, 91 L. Ed. 2d 202 (1986). In *Anderson,* the High Court stated that the trial judge must "bear in mind the actual quantum and quality of proof necessary to support liability" when inquiring into the existence of a genuine issue of material fact. 477 U.S. at 252. If, for example, "the evidence presented in the opposing affidavits is of insufficient *caliber* or quantity," then no genuine issue of material fact is raised. 477 U.S. at 254 (*emphasis added*).

Thus, in a run-of-the-mill civil case, the quantum of proof is a preponderance of the evidence and the summary judgment inquiry is: whether a reasonable jury could find — by a preponderance of the evidence — that the party opposing the motion is entitled to a verdict. *Cf. Collins v. Union Federal Savings & Loan Association,* 99 Nev. 284, 662 P.2d 610 (1983). In a fraud case, the summary judgment inquiry is: whether a reasonable jury could find — by clear and convincing evidence — that the party claiming fraud is entitled to a verdict.

D. Standards for Decision and Review.

§ 1723. Generally.

Many standards have been announced for making the decision whether or not a genuine issue of material fact exists. Generally, they apply whether the decision is being made by the trial court or the Nevada Supreme Court. Some of the standards are directly opposed to each other. They may be characterized as either "pro" or "anti" summary judgment rules, and are cited by the parties depending on which side of the motion they are on (and by the Court, depending on which way it has decided to rule).

In Nevada case law, "anti" summary judgment rules dominate and generally proceed on the theme that a trial on the merits is favored. Whether the dominance of the "anti" summary judgment rules will continue in Nevada after the U.S. Supreme Court's invitation to revive summary disposition of cases in the *Celotex* trilogy remains to be seen.

§ 1724. — Opponent's facts plus favorable inferences deemed true.

It is axiomatic that in determining whether there exists a "genuine issue as to any material fact," the trial and reviewing court must accept as true all evidence favorable to the party against whom the summary judgment motion is made and accord such party all favorable inferences that may reasonably be drawn from such evidence, *i.e.,* all evidence must be viewed in the light most favorable to such party. *Parman v. Petricciani,* 70 Nev. 427, 272 P.2d 492 (1954); *Smith v. Gabrielli,* 80 Nev. 390, 395 P.2d 325 (1964); *Polk v. MacMillan,* 87 Nev. 526, 490 P.2d 218 (1971); *Crockett v. Sahara Realty Corp.,* 95 Nev. 197, 591 P.2d 1135 (1979); *Hubert v. Werner,* 101 Nev. 193, 698 P.2d 426 (1985); *Morrow v. Barger,* 103 Nev. 247, 737 P.2d 1153 (1987); *Shapro v. Forsyth,* 103 Nev. 666, 747 P.2d 241 (1987); *Fyssakis v. Knight Equipment Corp.,* 108 Nev. 212, 826 P.2d 570 (1992). *See also Matsushita Electric Industrial Co. v. Zenith Radio Corp.,* 475 U.S. 574, 106 S. Ct. 1348, 89 L. Ed. 2d 538 (1986).

The court is *not* entitled to view the evidence in favor of the party moving for summary judgment. *Charles v. J. Steven Lemons & Associates,* 104 Nev. 388, 760 P.2d 118 (1988).

§ 1725. — Assumptions by court.

The obligation to view all evidence in the light most favorable to the non-moving party does not mean that *general* averments in an opposing affidavit must be *assumed* by the Court to embrace the "specific" facts required by Rule 56(e) to defeat the motion. The opposing party is entitled only to favorable inferences and only from "specific" facts. *Lujan v. National Wildlife Federation,* 497 U.S. 871, 110 S. Ct. 3177, 111 L. Ed. 2d 695 (1990), saying:

In ruling upon a Rule 56 motion, "a District Court must resolve any factual issues of controversy in favor of the non-moving party" only in the sense that, where the facts specifically averred by that party contradict facts specifically averred by the movant, the motion must be denied. That is a world apart from "assuming" that general averments embrace the "specific facts" needed to sustain the complaint.

§ 1726. — Trial judge must exercise great care.

Trial judges should exercise great care in granting motions for summary judgment. *Parman v. Petricciani,* 70 Nev. 427, 272 P.2d 492 (1954); *McColl v. Scherer,* 73 Nev. 226, 315 P.2d 807 (1957); *Short v. Hotel Riviera, Inc.,* 79 Nev. 94, 378 P.2d 979 (1963); *Cardinal v. C.H. Masland & Sons,* 87 Nev. 224, 484 P.2d 1075 (1971); *Golden Nugget, Inc. v. Ham,* 95 Nev. 45, 589 P.2d 173 (1979); *Johnson v. Steel, Inc.,* 100 Nev. 181, 678 P.2d 676 (1984); *Montgomery v. Ponderosa Construction, Inc.,* 101 Nev. 416, 705 P.2d 652 (1985); *Charles v. J. Steven Lemons & Associates,* 104 Nev. 388, 760 P.2d 118 (1988).

§ 1727. — Slightest doubt.

A litigant has a right to a trial where there is the slightest doubt as to the facts. *Parman v. Petricciani,* 70 Nev. 427, 272 P.2d 492 (1954); *McColl v. Scherer,* 73 Nev. 226, 315 P.2d 807 (1957); *Short v. Hotel Riviera, Inc.,* 79 Nev. 94, 378 P.2d 979 (1963); *Pine v. Leavitt,* 84 Nev. 507, 445 P.2d 942 (1968); *Golden Nugget, Inc. v. Ham,* 95 Nev. 45, 589 P.2d 173 (1979); *McDermond v. Siemens,* 96 Nev. 226, 607 P.2d 108 (1980); *Stone v. Mission Bay Mortgage Co.,* 99 Nev. 802, 672 P.2d 629 (1983); *Pacific Pools Construction v. McClain's Concrete, Inc.,* 101 Nev. 557, 706 P.2d 849 (1985); *Shapro v. Forsythe,* 103 Nev. 666, 747 P.2d 241 (1987); *Carr-Bricken v. First Interstate Bank,* 105 Nev. 570, 779 P.2d 967 (1989).

§ 1728. — Drastic remedy.

Summary judgment is a drastic remedy. *Pine v. Leavitt,* 84 Nev. 507, 445 P.2d 942 (1968); *Zuni Construction Co. v. Great American Insurance Co.,* 86 Nev. 364, 468 P.2d 980 (1970); *Ottenheimer v. Real Estate Division of Nevada Department of Commerce,* 91 Nev. 338, 535 P.2d 1284 (1975).

§ 1729. — Quite clear.

Rule 56 authorizes summary judgment only where it is quite clear what the truth is and that no genuine fact issue remains for trial. *Short v. Hotel Riviera, Inc.,* 79 Nev. 94, 378 P.2d 979 (1963); *Nevada Land & Mortgage Co. v. Hidden Wells Ranch, Inc.,* 83 Nev. 501, 435 P.2d 198 (1968); *Pine v. Leavitt,* 84 Nev. 507, 445 P.2d 942 (1968); Olson v. Iacometti, 91 Nev. 241, 533 P.2d 1360 (1975); *Bader Enterprises v. Becker,* 95 Nev. 807, 603 P.2d 268 (1979); *In re Las Vegas Hilton Hotel Fire Litigation,* 101 Nev. 489, 706 P.2d 137 (1985).

§ 1730. — All doubts resolved against moving party.

All doubts must be resolved against the moving party and his supporting affidavits and depositions, if any, must be carefully scrutinized by the court even as to inferences. *Hoffmeister Cabinets of Nevada, Inc. v. Bivins,* 87 Nev. 282, 486 P.2d 57 (1971).

§ 1731. — Review record searchingly.

The trial court should review the record searchingly for material issues of fact, the existence of which eliminate the propriety of summary treatment. *Mullis v. Nevada National Bank,* 98 Nev. 510, 654 P.2d 533

(1982); *Charles v. J. Steven Lemons & Associates,* 104 Nev. 388, 760 P.2d 118 (1988).

§ 1732. — Not a shortcut.

Summary judgment may *not* be used as a shortcut to the resolution of disputes upon facts material to the determination of the legal rights of the parties. *Parman v. Petricciani,* 70 Nev. 427, 272 P.2d 492 (1954); *Perry v. Byrd,* 87 Nev. 431, 488 P.2d 550 (1971); *Mullis v. Nevada National Bank,* 98 Nev. 510, 654 P.2d 533 (1982); *Collins v. Union Federal Savings & Loan Association,* 99 Nev. 284, 662 P.2d 610 (1983).

§ 1733. — Reasonable person test.

In determining whether there exists a "genuine issue as to any material fact," the question is whether no reasonable person could conclude from the facts appearing in the record, and reasonable inferences to be drawn therefrom, that such issue of facts exists. *Short v. Hotel Riviera, Inc.,* 79 Nev. 94, 378 P.2d 979 (1963); *cf. Nehls v. Leonard,* 97 Nev. 325, 630 P.2d 258 (1981).

§ 1734. — No weighing the evidence.

If any genuine issue of material fact exists before the trial court, it is not the function of the trial court to weigh that evidence. Even if the weight or believability of the evidence is clearly in favor of one party, the other party is entitled to a trial by jury to determine the facts. *Parman v. Petricciani,* 70 Nev. 427, 272 P.2d 492 (1954); *Cardinal v. C.H. Masland & Sons,* 87 Nev. 224, 484 P.2d 1075 (1971); *see also Anderson v. Liberty Lobby, Inc.,* 477 U.S. 242, 106 S. Ct. 2505, 91 L. Ed. 2d 202, 212 (1986).

§ 1735. — No weighing credibility of witnesses.

In determining whether there exists a "genuine issue as to any material fact," the trial court should not evaluate the credibility of the witnesses who have given conflicting testimony by affidavit or deposition. In such cases, summary judgment becomes improper and a trial indispensable. The interest and credibility of those witnesses should be tested by cross-examination. *Short v. Hotel Riviera, Inc.,* 79 Nev. 94, 378 P.2d 979 (1963); *Hidden Wells Ranch v. Strip Realty,* 83 Nev. 143, 425 P.2d 599 (1967); *Lincoln Welding Works, Inc. v. Ramirez,* 98 Nev. 342, 647 P.2d 381 (1982); *Nevada State Bank v. Jamison Family Partnership,* 106 Nev. 792, 801 P.2d 1377 (1990).

But, if the evidence tendered by an affidavit is too incredible to be accepted by reasonable minds, the trial court may pass upon its credibility and disregard it. *Short v. Hotel Riviera, Inc.,* 79 Nev. 94, 378 P.2d

979 (1963); *Lincoln Welding Works, Inc. v. Ramirez*, 98 Nev. 342, 647 P.2d 381 (1982). *See also Anderson v. Liberty Lobby, Inc.*, 477 U.S. 242, 106 S. Ct. 2505, 91 L. Ed. 2d 202 (1986). *But see contra, Sawyer v. Sugarless Shops, Inc.*, 106 Nev. 265, 792 P.2d 14 (1990).

§ 1736. — Trial by affidavit.

Rule 56 does *not* authorize "trial by affidavits." *Short v. Hotel Riviera, Inc.*, 79 Nev. 94, 378 P.2d 979 (1963); *Hidden Wells Ranch v. Strip Realty*, 83 Nev. 143, 425 P.2d 599 (1967); *cf. Zuni Construction Co. v. Great American Insurance Co.*, 86 Nev. 364, 468 P.2d 980 (1970); *cf. Renaud v. 200 Convention Center, Ltd.*, 102 Nev. 500, 728 P.2d 445 (1986).

§ 1737. — Clearly established defense.

In the absence of a clearly established defense, summary judgment in favor of the defendant must be denied. *Weaver v. Shell Oil Co.*, 91 Nev. 324, 535 P.2d 787 (1975); *Leslie v. J.A. Tiberti Construction Co.*, 99 Nev. 494, 664 P.2d 963 (1983); *Hampton v. Washoe Co.*, 99 Nev. 819, 672 P.2d 640 (1983); *Montgomery v. Ponderosa Construction, Inc.*, 101 Nev. 416, 705 P.2d 652 (1985).

§ 1738. — Matters peculiarly within a party's knowledge.

If one party pleads that the other party committed an act or omission, and the other party denies it in an affidavit or deposition, it is not the function of a summary judgment procedure to determine those issues. For example, suppose a plaintiff sues a defendant for committing an act with a fraudulent or conspiratorial intent and the defendant denies in an affidavit or deposition under oath that he had such intent. The defendant is not entitled to summary judgment because the plaintiff has no further proof of such wrongful intent. The defendant's testimony need not be accepted as true. In such cases, summary judgment is improper and a trial with cross-examination is indispensable. *Short v. Hotel Riviera, Inc.*, 79 Nev. 94, 378 P.2d 979 (1963). *But see supra* §§ 1710 and 1718.

§ 1739. — Denial of trial on disputed facts worse than delay.

Summary judgment, wisely used, is a praise-worthy, time-saving devise. But, although prompt dispatch of judicial business is a virtue, it is neither the sole nor the primary purpose for which courts have been established. Denial of a trial on disputed facts is worse than delay. *Parman v. Petricciani*, 70 Nev. 427, 272 P.2d 492 (1954); *Cardinal v. C.H. Masland & Sons*, 87 Nev. 224, 484 P.2d 1075 (1971).

309

§ 1740. "Pro" summary judgment standards.

Since you can't appeal from the *denial* of a summary judgment motion and most reported decisions are *reversals* of summary judgments, there aren't many reported standards favoring entry of summary judgment. But there are a few which are discussed in the following sections.

§ 1741. — Mere hope.

The party against whom a summary judgment motion has been filed is *not* entitled to have the motion for summary judgment denied on the mere hope that at trial he will be able to discredit movant's evidence. He must at the hearing be able to point out to the court something indicating the existence of a triable issue of fact. *Thomas v. Bokelman,* 86 Nev. 10, 462 P.2d 1020 (1970); *Bair v. Berry,* 86 Nev. 26, 464 P.2d 469 (1970); *Leggett v. Estate of Leggett,* 88 Nev. 140, 494 P.2d 554 (1972); *Hickman v. Meadow Wood Reno,* 96 Nev. 782, 617 P.2d 871 (1980); *VanCleave v. Kietz-Mill Minit Mart,* 97 Nev. 414, 633 P.2d 1220 (1981). *Collins v. Union Federal Savings & Loan Association,* 99 Nev. 284, 662 P.2d 610 (1983) (the opposing party is not entitled to build a case for trial "on the gossamer threads of whimsy, speculation and conjecture"); *Michaels v. Sudeck,* 107 Nev. 332, 810 P.2d 1212 (1991); *Bulbman, Inc. v. Nevada Bell,* 108 Nev. 105, 825 P.2d 588 (1992).

§ 1742. — Sham issue.

A party can't avoid the entry of summary judgment by fabricating an issue or raising a sham issue. *Aldabe v. Adams,* 81 Nev. 280, 402 P.2d 34 (1965), and *Dzack v. Marshall,* 80 Nev. 345, 393 P.2d 610 (1964), *supra,* at § 1712.

§ 1743. — Merely colorable.

Evidence that is "merely colorable" is not sufficient to preclude summary judgment. This is apparently the mirror image of "genuine issue." If the evidence is not sufficient for a reasonable jury to return a verdict for the non-moving party, it is *"merely colorable."* *Oehler v. Humana, Inc.,* 105 Nev. 348, 775 P.2d 1271 (1989). *See also supra* § 1712.

§ 1744. — Unambiguous written instrument.

When the question before the trial court is the meaning or effect of a written instrument between the parties, if the instrument is unambiguous, it speaks for itself and the "true intent" of the parties cannot be said to constitute a "genuine" issue of fact. *Parman v. Petricciani,* 70 Nev. 427, 272 P.2d 492 (1954). Rather, issues of unambiguous contractual construction present questions of law for the court and are suitable for determination by summary judgment. *Ellison v. California State Auto Association,* 106 Nev. 601, 797 P.2d 975 (1990); *Leven v. Wheatherstone Condominium Corp.,* 106 Nev. 307, 791 P.2d 450 (1990).

But if the written instrument is ambiguous, the court must examine the parties' intentions. That involves weighing the credibility of their statements — and that must be done by the trier of fact at trial. *Agricultural Aviation v. Clark County Commissioners,* 106 Nev. 396, 794 P.2d 710 (1990).

§ 1745. — Unreasonable construction of written instrument.

Where the question before the trial court is the meaning and effect of a written instrument between the parties, a construction by one party which is unreasonable under all of the facts and circumstances of the case, may be disregarded and not create a "genuine" issue of fact. If one construction is reasonable and the other unreasonable, the trial court may enter summary judgment in favor of the reasonable construction. *Parman v. Petricciani,* 70 Nev. 427, 272 P.2d 492 (1954).

§ 1746. — Constitutional issues.

Although it is true that a motion for summary judgment should be denied if the record below is inadequate for consideration of the constitutional issues presented or to determine whether genuine issues of material fact exist, a case may be disposed of by summary judgment if the constitutional question has been foreclosed by previous decisions. *Collins v. Union Federal Savings & Loan Association,* 99 Nev. 284, 662 P.2d 610 (1983).

E. Procedural Requirements.

§ 1747. Time for motion.

The time during which a motion for summary judgment may be brought depends upon the identity of the movant and the stage of the proceedings.

§ 1748. — Premature motions — identity of movant.

The time before which it is too soon to file a motion for summary judgment is:

A. For a plaintiff, or other party making a claim, the expiration of twenty days from the commencement of the action. NRCP 56(a); *County of Clark v. Roosevelt Title Insurance Co.,* 80 Nev. 303, 393 P.2d 136 (1964). But if the twenty days have expired, the plaintiff may file the motion even if the defendant has not yet filed a responsive pleading. *Intermountain Lumber & Builders Supply, Inc. v. Glens Falls Insurance Co.,* 83 Nev. 126, 424 P.2d 884 (1967); and

B. For a defendant, or other party defending against a claim, at any time after commencement of the action. NRCP 56(b); *Cummings v. City of Las Vegas Municipal Corp.,* 88 Nev. 479, 499 P.2d 650 (1972). *But see infra* § 1749.

§ 1749. — Premature motions — stage of proceedings.

Even if a motion is not premature according to the time limits of Rule 56(a), any party defending against a motion for summary judgment should be given an opportunity to complete discovery and show, if he can, that there is a genuine issue of material fact. *See* NRCP 56(f); Ottenheimer v. Real Estate Division of Nevada Department of Commerce, 91 Nev. 338, 535 P.2d 1284 (1975); *Collins v. Union Federal Savings & Loan Association,* 99 Nev. 284, 662 P.2d 610 (1983); Harrison v. Falcon Products, Inc., 103 Nev. 558, 746 P.2d 642 (1987); *Halimi v. Blacketor,* 105 Nev. 696, 770 P.2d 531 (1989); *Ameritrade, Inc. v. FIB,* 105 Nev. 696, 782 P.2d 1318 (1989); *Atwell v. Southwest Securities,* 107 Nev. 820, 820 P.2d 766 (1991).

However, before a court should postpone a summary ruling under Rule 56(f), the party opposing the summary judgment has the burden of affirmatively demonstrating by good faith affidavit, why he cannot respond and what facts he believes will be developed. *Bakerink v. Orthopaedic Associates, Ltd.,* 94 Nev. 428, 581 P.2d 9 (1978); *cf. Hickman v. Meadow Wood Reno,* 96 Nev. 782, 617 P.2d 871 (1980); *Collins v. Union Federal Savings & Loan Association,* 99 Nev. 284, 662 P.2d 610 (1983); *But see supra Halimi,* where the court ignored the *affidavit* requirement of Rule 56(f) and held that opposing memorandum was sufficient!

If the party has had sufficient time and opportunity to conduct discovery, summary judgment may be granted against him even if discovery has not been conducted. *Kitzman v. Bank of Nevada,* 92 Nev. 538, 554 P.2d 262 (1976); *Collins v. Union Federal Savings & Loan Association,* 99 Nev. 284, 662 P.2d 610 (1983).

§ 1750. — Too late.

Unless there is a local district court rule otherwise, the time after which it is too late to file a motion for summary judgment is a reasonable period of time before trial — not during or after trial. *See* for example Second Judicial District Court Rule 12(7). A motion made after such deadline should not be entertained by the trial court. *Coray v. Hom,* 80 Nev. 39, 389 P.2d 76 (1964). *See also* 28 Fed. Proc. L. Ed. § 62:574.

§ 1751. Written or oral.

Except when the court allows oral joinder (*see infra* § 1752), all motions for summary judgment must be in writing and accompanied by points and authorities, affidavits, if any, and attachments, if any. NRCP 7(b); NRCP 56(1); NRCP 56(e); and 28 Fed. Proc. L. Ed. § 62:575.

§ 1752. Oral joinder.

Although Rule 56 motions should ordinarily be made in *writing,* a court may allow a party to orally join in the written motion for summary judgment at the hearing of such motion, if the opposing party is not prejudiced. *Exber, Inc. v. Sletten Construction Co.,* 92 Nev. 721, 558 P.2d 517 (1976); and *Wagner v. Carex Investigations & Security, Inc.,* 93 Nev. 627, 572 P.2d 921 (1977). The facts of these cases are arguably limited to oral joinders of cross-motions, but there is no reason to so limit joinder if the opposing party is not prejudiced.

§ 1753. Notice.

The party against whom the motion for summary judgment is filed must be given notice of such filing at least ten days before the hearing, or such longer period of time as required by local rule. *Western Mercury, Inc. v. Rix Co.,* 84 Nev. 218, 438 P.2d 792 (1968).

§ 1754. Hearing.

Although Rule 56 proceeds on the assumption that a hearing will be had on the motion, NRCP 56(c) & (d), the party opposing a motion for summary judgment is not guaranteed a hearing for oral argument by Rule 56. A hearing is not required by the Rule. If the opposing party fails to request a hearing as required by local rule, the court may rule on the motion without hearing, upon the points and authorities submitted. *Western Mercury, Inc. v. Rix Co.,* 84 Nev. 218, 438 P.2d 792 (1968). *See also Daugherty v. Wabash Life Insurance Co.,* 87 Nev. 32, 482 P.2d 814 (1971).

Further, the hearing should, as a general rule, consist of oral *argument* of the law and the facts shown by the record and not involve oral testimony. Allowing oral testimony to support or oppose a motion for summary judgment undesirably turns the hearing into a "mini trial" and is contrary to the spirit and intent of Rule 56. *See* 53 A.L.R. 4th 527 (1987).

§ 1755. Challenging affidavits.

If a supporting or opposing affidavit does not meet the qualification requirements (*see infra* § 1771), the proper procedure to challenge it is a motion to strike the nonqualifying portions and to decide the motion based upon the remaining portions. 10A Wright & Miller, § 2738 nn.55-64.

Any objections to the affidavit not timely raised by motion to strike or other objection will be waived. *Whalen v. State,* 100 Nev. 192, 679 P.2d 248 (1984); *Exber, Inc. v. Sletten Construction Co.,* 92 Nev. 721, 558 P.2d 517 (1976); 10A Wright & Miller, § 2738 n.56.

§ 1756. Partial summary judgment.

The court may enter a partial summary judgment — interlocutory in character — on any point of law and retain jurisdiction to determine other points of law or make other decisions at a later time. NRCP 56(c) and (d). *City of Reno v. Matley,* 79 Nev. 49, 378 P.2d 256 (1963); *Mullen v. Clark Co.,* 89 Nev. 308, 511 P.2d 1036 (1973). The possibilities are endless. Thus, partial summary judgment may be entered against a party as to liability and a trial held on damages. Or, partial summary judgment may be entered as to a particular cause of action or affirmative defense. *Brown v. Capanna,* 105 Nev. 665, 782 P.2d 1299 (1989).

§ 1757. Cross-motions — current law.

The current (post-1982) law of Nevada is that in all cases where cross-motions for summary judgment are made, the trial court is required to rule separately on each party's motion. If a fact issue exists, both motions must be denied and a trial had — even though both sides allege in their cross-motions that there is no genuine issue as to any material fact. *Midland Insurance Co. v. Yanke Plumbing & Heating,* 99 Nev. 66, 657 P.2d 1152 (1983); *Servaites v. Lowden,* 99 Nev. 240, 660 P.2d 1008 (1983); *Collins v. Union Federal Savings & Loan Association,* 99 Nev. 284, 662 P.2d 610 (1983); *Ardmore Leasing Corp. v. State Farm Mutual Automobile Insurance Co.,* 106 Nev. 513, 796 P.2d 232 (1990).

§ 1758. Outside the pleadings.

If a party files a Rule 12(b)(5) motion to dismiss for failure to state a claim, it may be treated as a motion for summary judgment if:
  A. Matters outside the pleading are presented to the court, and
  B. The matters outside the pleading are not expressly excluded by the court.
NRCP 12(b); *Buss v. Consolidated Casinos Corp.,* 82 Nev. 355, 418 P.2d 815 (1966); *Cummings v. City of Las Vegas Municipal Corp.,* 88 Nev. 479, 499 P.2d 650 (1972); *San Diego Prestressed Concrete Co. v. Chicago Title Insurance Corp.,* 92 Nev. 569, 555 P.2d 484 (1976); Hay v. Hay, 100

Nev. 196, 678 P.2d 672 (1984); *Depner Architects & Planners, Inc. v. Nevada National Bank,* 104 Nev. 560, 763 P.2d 1141 (1988).

§ 1759. — "Outside" matters.

The "outside" matters may be affidavits, or any other evidence not on the face of the pleading. *Montesano v. Donrey Media Group,* 99 Nev. 644, 668 P.2d 1081 (1983). But the matters outside the pleading must be in a form which meets the requirements of Rule 56(e) as to qualification and form. *Buss v. Consolidated Casinos Corp.,* 82 Nev. 355, 418 P.2d 815 (1966).

§ 1760. — "Reliance" by court.

There are two factors that the Nevada Supreme Court looks to in determining whether the trial court did, in fact, rely on matters outside the pleading rather than dismissing for failure to state a claim:
  A. Indications that the trial court affirmatively excluded material outside the pleading; and
  B. Whether the reason for dismissal indicates that the trial court did, in fact, consider outside matters. *Montesano v. Donrey Media Group,* 99 Nev. 644, 668 P.2d 1081 (1983).

§ 1761. Findings and conclusions by court.

In rendering a decision upon a motion for summary judgment, the trial may, but is not required to, make express findings of fact. NRCP 52(a); *Smith v. City of Las Vegas,* 80 Nev. 220, 391 P.2d 505 (1964); or, express conclusions of law. NRCP 52(a); *American Fence, Inc. v. Wham,* 95 Nev. 788, 603 P.2d 274 (1979).

§ 1762. — Uncontroverted fact order.

Rule 56(d) contains very important provisions that for some reason are not routinely utilized in Nevada. If the case is not terminated by the motion (either because only a partial summary judgment is entered or because the motion is denied) and a trial is necessary, the court shall, if practicable, make an order specifying the facts that appear without substantial controversy and the material facts that are actually and in good faith controverted. In order to make the "uncontroverted" vs. "controverted" fact analysis, the Rule provides that the court must examine the record of the motion and interrogate counsel for the parties. At the trial, the uncontroverted facts stated in the order must be deemed established, *i.e.,* they have the same standing as facts stated in a pre-trial order under Rule 16. *See* 28 Fed. Proc. L. Ed. § 62:635. Good motion practice should include the preparation and submission of an Order consistent with this provision of Rule 56. *See* First Judicial District Court Rule 13(H).

§ 1763. Necessity of separate judgment.

Once the court decides to grant the summary judgment at movant's request, the court has four procedural alternatives:

A. Enter an order that merely grants the motion but does not adjudge;
B. Enter an order and a judgment combined in one document;
C. Enter a judgment only; or
D. Enter an order and a judgment in two separate documents.

The two separate document procedure is the "better" practice. *See* 73 Am. Jur. 2d § 37; 49 CJS Judgments § 227; 1 Federal Procedure L. Ed. §§ 1771-1812; *Decker v. Tucson,* 419 P.2d 400 (Ariz. 1966); *Atchison v. McGee,* 296 P.2d 860 (Cal. 1956).

If the court elects the order only alternative (whether by design or not), it must subsequently enter a separate document judgment which adjudges. The order granting a motion for summary judgment is not the summary judgment — which must be entered in addition to the order. The order itself is a nonappealable order. Fitzharris v. Phillips, 74 Nev. 371, 333 P.2d 721 (1958); *Musso v. Triplett,* 78 Nev. 355, 372 P.2d 687 (1962); *cf. County of Clark v. Roosevelt Title Insurance Co.,* 80 Nev. 303, 393 P.2d 136 (1964).

§ 1764. — Entry of the judgment.

Summary judgment is not effective for any purpose unless and until it is entered in the manner provided by NRCP 58, *i.e.,* in writing, signed by the judge and filed with the clerk. So, an oral bench order and a written minute order (unsigned by judge) is not a summary judgment. *Fitzharris v. Phillips,* 74 Nev. 371, 333 P.2d 721 (1958); *Musso v. Triplett,* 78 Nev. 355, 372 P.2d 687 (1962).

§ 1765. Conditional summary judgment.

The trial court has the discretion under NRCP 56(f) to grant summary judgment conditionally by offering the party against whom it is entered the opportunity to bring forward evidence, if it can, showing the existence of a material fact. *Las Vegas Star Taxi v. St. Paul Fire & Marine Insurance Co.,* 102 Nev. 11, 714 P.2d 562 (1986).

§ 1766. *Sua sponte* summary judgment.

Although Rule 56 does not discuss whether a court may enter summary judgment on its own in the absence of a request to do so, the cases have held that it has discretion to do so under limited conditions. The most common situation in which the trial court may do so is when there is no fact issue and the party opposing summary judgment is entitled to judgment as a matter of law, but has not made a cross-motion. *Exber, Inc. v. Sletten Construction Co.*, 92 Nev. 721, 558 P.2d 517 (1976). *See also Celotex Corp. v. Catrett*, 477 U.S. 317, 106 S. Ct. 2548, 91 L. Ed. 2d 265, 275 (1986).

§ 1767. Declaratory summary judgment.

Although many summary judgments are compensatory, summary judgment may be declaratory as well as compensatory. NRCP 56(b); *Ambassador Insurance Co. v. Bozarth*, 94 Nev. 543, 582 P.2d 798 (1978); *Sarkes Tarzian, Inc. v. Nevada Legislature*, 104 Nev. 672, 765 P.2d 1142 (1988); *Town of Pahrump v. County of Nye*, 105 Nev. 227, 773 P.2d 1224 (1989); *Insurance Corp. of America v. Rubin*, 107 Nev. 610, 818 P.2d 389 (1991).

§ 1768. Harmless error.

Failure to comply with the formal, procedural requirements of Rule 56 is subject to the harmless error rule. *Exber, Inc. v. Sletten Construction Co.*, 92 Nev. 721, 558 P.2d 517 (1976).

§ 1769. Sanctions for bad faith affidavit.

Under little used Rule 56(g), attorney fees are allowable when the trial court makes a discretionary finding that an affidavit has been presented in bad faith or solely for the purpose of delay. *Arley v. Liberty Mutual Fire Insurance Co.*, 80 Nev. 5, 388 P.2d 576 (1964).

F. Materials Considered by Court.

§ 1770. In general.

Rule 56(c) allows a motion for summary judgment to be either supported or opposed by the pleadings, discovery, admissions on file and affidavits, if any. In addition, the court may consider any other material that would be admissible under the rules of evidence at trial. 10A Wright & Miller, § 2721, at 5. *But see Chambers By Cochran v. Sanderson*, 107 Nev. 846, 822 P.2d 657 (1991). The reported cases have allowed the following:

A. Depositions on oral examination. NRCP 56(c); *Parman v. Petricciani*, 70 Nev. 427, 272 P.2d 492 (1954); *Osborn v. Richardson-Lovelock, Inc.*, 79 Nev. 71, 378 P.2d 521 (1963); *Adamson v. Bowker*, 85 Nev. 115, 450 P.2d 796 (1969); *Butler v. Bogdanovich*, 101 Nev.

449, 705 P.2d 662 (1985); *May v. G.M.B., Inc.,* 105 Nev. 446, 778 P.2d 424 (1989).

B. Qualifying affidavits. *Lockitch v. Boyer,* 74 Nev. 36, 321 P.2d 254 (1958); *Kellar v. Snowden,* 87 Nev. 488, 489 P.2d 90 (1971); *Richards v. Conklin,* 94 Nev. 84, 575 P.2d 588 (1978); *Schofield v. Copeland Lumber Yards, Inc.,* 101 Nev. 83, 692 P.2d 519 (1985); *Baughman & Turner, Inc. v. Jory,* 102 Nev. 582, 729 P.2d 488 (1986).

C. *Verified* pleadings. *In re Franktown Creek,* 77 Nev. 348, 364 P.2d 1069 (1961); *Dredge Corp. v. Husite Co.,* 78 Nev. 69, 369 P.2d 676, *cert. denied,* 371 U.S. 821, 83 S. Ct. 39, 9 L. Ed. 2d 61 (1962); *May v. G.M.B., Inc.,* 105 Nev. 446, 778 P.2d 424 (1989) (footnote 8).

But not *unverified* pleadings or statements which must be disregarded. NRCP 56(e). *Dredge Corp. v. Husite Co.,* 78 Nev. 69, 369 P.2d 676, *cert. denied,* 371 U.S. 821, 83 S. Ct. 39, 9 L. Ed. 2d 61 (1962); *Scapecchi v. Harold's Club,* 78 Nev. 290, 371 P.2d 815 (1962); *Dzack v. Marshall,* 80 Nev. 345, 393 P.2d 610 (1964); *Western Mercury, Inc. v. Rix Co.,* 84 Nev. 218, 438 P.2d 792 (1968); *contra: Daugherty v. Wabash Life Insurance Co.,* 87 Nev. 32, 482 P.2d 814 (1971).

D. Timely filed interrogatory answers. *Osborn v. Richardson-Lovelock, Inc.,* 79 Nev. 71, 378 P.2d 521 (1963); *Adamson v. Bowker,* 85 Nev. 115, 450 P.2d 796 (1969); *Daugherty v. Wabash Life Insurance Co.,* 87 Nev. 32, 482 P.2d 814 (1971). But the court may disregard tardily filed answers to interrogatories. *Western Mercury, Inc. v. Rix Co.,* 84 Nev. 218, 438 P.2d 792 (1968).

E. Admissions under Rule 36, including those from failure to timely respond. *Dzack v. Marshall,* 80 Nev. 345, 393 P.2d 610 (1964); *Daugherty v. Wabash Life Insurance Co.,* 87 Nev. 32, 482 P.2d 814 (1971); *Graham v. Carson-Tahoe Hospital,* 91 Nev. 609, 540 P.2d 105 (1975). This is true even if the admissions conflict with earlier verified answers to interrogatories. *Wagner v. Carex Investigations & Security, Inc.,* 93 Nev. 627, 572 P.2d 921 (1977).

F. Admissions in pleadings. NRCP 56(c) (*i.e.,* "admissions on file") 28 Fed. Proc. L. Ed. § 62:607 n.65; 10A Wright & Miller, Federal Practice and Procedure § 2722 n.17.

G. Transcript of sworn testimony in another, earlier proceeding. *Catrone v. 105 Casino Corp.,* 82 Nev. 166, 414 P.2d 106 (1966) (preliminary hearing in criminal case).

H. Judicially noticeable facts — even though Rule 56(c) doesn't say so. *Pine v. Leavitt,* 84 Nev. 507, 445 P.2d 942 (1968); *cf. Hampton v. Washoe Co.,* 99 Nev. 819, 672 P.2d 640 (1983).

I. Oral testimony at the summary judgment hearing. *Leggett v. Estate of Leggett,* 88 Nev. 140, 494 P.2d 554 (1972), and NRCP 43(c). But it is arguable that allowing oral testimony to support or oppose a motion for summary judgment (rather than the witnesses' affidavit) undesirably turns the hearing into a "mini trial" and is contrary to the spirit and intent of Rule 56. *See* 53 A.L.R. 4th 527 (1987) and *supra* § 1756.

J. Stipulated facts — even though Rule 56(c) doesn't say so. 28 Fed. Proc. L. Ed. § 62:589 n.29.1.

K. But *not* factual assertions made by the attorneys in their Points and Authorities. *Hampton v. Washoe Co.,* 99 Nev. 819, 672 P.2d 640 (1983).

L. *Certified* documents. *Chambers By Cochran v. Sanderson,* 107 Nev. 846, 822 P.2d 657 (1991). This paternity case held — without citation to authority — that certified blood test results validly supported a motion for summary judgment. The party against whom summary judgment was granted argued that the test results could not support the motion because, although they were certified, they were not in affidavit form. In affirming the summary judgment, the Court said:

Contrary to [the opposing argument], NRCP 56(e) does not mandate that all evidence accompanying a motion for summary judgment be in affidavit form.

The Court did not cite NRCP 56(c) which also governs the documents which may support a motion for summary judgment. Rule 56(e) is limited to the form of affidavits — if affidavits are used.

10A Wright & Miller, § 2723 n.37; 28 Fed. Proc. L. Ed § 62:601 nn.22-24. The only way in which the holding would be good law is if — under the rules of trial evidence — the document would be admissible in evidence without foundation testimony. *Hamm v. Sheriff, Clark County,* 90 Nev. 252, 523 P.2d 1301 (1974).

M. Acknowledgment of counsel at oral argument. *May v. G.M.B., Inc.,* 105 Nev. 446, 778 P.2d 424 (1989). *Cf.* Rule 56(d).

§ 1771. Qualifications for affidavits.

An affidavit (or another under-oath statement) qualifies under Rule 56(e) to support or oppose a motion for summary judgment only to the extent that it meets *all* of the following requirements:

A. Is made on personal knowledge. *Dredge Corp. v. Husite Co.,* 78 Nev. 69, 369 P.2d 676, *cert. denied,* 371 U.S. 821, 83 S. Ct. 39, 9 L. Ed. 2d 61 (1962) (not by corporate attorney on information and belief); *Osborn v. Richardson-Lovelock, Inc.,* 79 Nev. 71, 378 P.2d 521 (1963); *Daugherty v. Wabash Life Insurance Co.,* 87 Nev. 32, 482 P.2d 814 (1971); *Gunlord Corp. v. Bozzano,* 95 Nev. 243, 591 P.2d 1149 (1979); *Bird v. Casa Royale West,* 97 Nev. 67, 624 P.2d 17 (1981); and
B. Sets forth such facts as would be admissible in evidence at trial, under the ordinary rules of trial evidence. *Catrone v. 105 Casino Corp.,* 82 Nev. 166, 414 P.2d 106 (1966); *Adamson v. Bowker,* 85 Nev. 115, 450 P.2d 796 (1969); *Daugherty v. Wabash Life Insurance Co.,* 87 Nev. 32, 482 P.2d 814 (1971); *Collins v. Union Federal Savings & Loan Association,* 99 Nev. 284, 662 P.2d 610 (1983). Under the ordinary rules of evidence, all relevant evidence is admissible unless barred by a particular rule of evidence which is raised by the party seeking to exclude such evidence. If no objection is made, the otherwise applicable rule of evidence is waived. *Whalen v. State,* 100 Nev. 192, 679 P.2d 248 (1984); and
C. Such facts may not be set forth in a *conclusory* manner without factual support in the record; but rather must be stated *specifically.* *Bond v. Stardust,* 82 Nev. 47, 410 P.2d 472 (1966); *Daugherty v.*

Wabash Life Insurance Co., 87 Nev. 32, 482 P.2d 814 (1971); *Gunlord Corp. v. Bozzano,* 95 Nev. 243, 591 P.2d 1149 (1979); *Ma-Gar Mining & Exploration v. Comstock Bank,* 100 Nev. 66, 675 P.2d 992 (1984); *Las Vegas Star Taxi v. St. Paul Fire & Marine Insurance Co.,* 102 Nev. 11, 714 P.2d 562 (1986); *Michaels v. Sudeck,* 107 Nev. 332, 810 P.2d 1212 (1991). *See also Lujan v. National Wildlife Federation,* 497 U.S. 871, 110 S. Ct. 3177, 111 L. Ed. 2d 695 (1990) and *supra* § 1721; and

D. Shows affirmatively that the affiant is competent to testify to the matters stated therein. *Lockhart v. MacLean,* 77 Nev. 210, 361 P.2d 670 (1961) (summary judgment in favor of doctor in medical malpractice action affirmed since affidavit of plaintiff's California expert was rejected on the ground that he was *incompetent* to give an opinion as to the standard of practice in Reno); *Daugherty v. Wabash Life Insurance Co.,* 87 Nev. 32, 482 P.2d 814 (1971); *Saka v. Sahara-Nev. Corp.,* 92 Nev. 703, 558 P.2d 535 (1976); *Gunlord Corp. v. Bozzano,* 95 Nev. 243, 591 P.2d 1149 (1979).

These rules apply to all under-oath statements in support of or opposition to the motion. *Hickman v. Meadow Wood Reno,* 96 Nev. 782, 617 P.2d 871 (1980) (Answers to Interrogatories).

§ 1772. Supporting documents.

Under Rule 56(c) and (e), any documents that are relied upon to support or oppose summary judgment must be:

A. Authenticated (*i.e.,* sworn or certified copies); *Buss v. Consolidated Casinos Corp.,* 82 Nev. 355, 418 P.2d 815 (1966); *Hasmer v. Avayu,* 97 Nev. 584, 636 P.2d 875 (1981); *Collins v. Union Federal Savings & Loan Association,* 99 Nev. 284, 662 P.2d 610 (1983); *Hampton v. Washoe Co.,* 99 Nev. 819, 672 P.2d 640 (1983); *and*

B. Attached to the affidavit or other sworn evidence, or be served therewith. *Daugherty v. Wabash Life Insurance Co.,* 87 Nev. 32, 482 P.2d 814 (1971); *Havas v. Hughes Estate,* 98 Nev. 172, 643 P.2d 1220 (1982).

The rule is mandatory, and a trial court's reliance upon an affidavit which does not comply with the rule may constitute reversible error. *Havas v. Hughes Estate,* 98 Nev. 172, 643 P.2d 1220 (1982). But, uncertified documents may be considered if not challenged, *i.e.,* the authentication requirement may be waived if not objected to. *Collins v. Union Federal Savings & Loan Association,* 99 Nev. 284, 662 P.2d 610 (1983); *Whalen v. State,* 100 Nev. 192, 679 P.2d 248 (1984).

§ 1773. Conflict between a party's verified pleading and deposition.

Where a party's deposition or affidavit conflicts with the earlier averments in that party's verified pleading, in deciding whether a fact issue requiring trial is raised, the trial court should look to the later sworn statement and disregard the verified pleading. *In re Franktown Creek,* 77 Nev. 348, 364 P.2d 1069 (1961); *Smith v. Gabrielli,* 80 Nev. 390, 395 P.2d 325 (1964).

§ 1774. Conflicting sworn statements by the same party.

A "genuine issue of material fact" may *not* be created by conflicting sworn statements of the party against whom summary judgment was entered. Rule 56 expects the fact issue to be created by adversaries. When the record contains conflicting sworn statements (in verified pleadings and/or affidavits) of the same party (who is opposing summary judgment), the court may disregard the ones that are not worthy of belief and enter summary against that party. Nevada law does not promise a trial to one who views the sanctity of an oath so lightly, if preliminary procedures show his case to be unworthy. *Aldabe v. Adams,* 81 Nev. 280, 402 P.2d 34 (1965); *Bank of Las Vegas v. Hoopes,* 84 Nev. 585, 445 P.2d 937 (1968) (applying *Aldabe* to an *acknowledged* satisfaction of debt). *See also Sawyer v. Sugarless Shops, Inc.,* 106 Nev. 265, 792 P.2d 14 (1990).

§ 1775. Entire record at time of submission.

The trial court must consider and decide a motion for summary judgment based upon the entire trial record as it existed at the time of briefing and argument. NRCP 56(c). *Moore v. Moore,* 78 Nev. 186, 370 P.2d 690 (1962); *Adamson v. Bowker,* 85 Nev. 115, 450 P.2d 796 (1969); *Whiston v. McDonald,* 85 Nev. 508, 458 P.2d 107 (1969) (*Collins* dissent); *Zuni Construction Co. v. Great American Insurance Co.,* 86 Nev. 364, 468 P.2d 980 (1970).

It should not consider issues raised by a pleading filed after submission of the motion for decision. *Moore v. Moore,* 78 Nev. 186, 370 P.2d 690 (1962).

§ 1776. No affidavit in support.

Contrary to the rule applicable to the party *opposing* summary judgment (who cannot rest on his pleadings and must come forward with affidavit or other evidence), the party moving for summary judgments may do so "... with or without supporting affidavits...." NRCP 56(a). The rule does *not* require that the motion be *supported* by verified pleading or affidavit. *Tobler & Oliver Construction Co. v. Board of Trustees,* 84 Nev. 438, 442 P.2d 904 (1968) and *Clauson v. Lloyd,* 103 Nev. 432, 743 P.2d 631 (1987).

Rather, the moving party may simply "show" that no fact issue exists and that he is entitled to judgment as a matter of law. NRCP 56(c). Thus, in a products liability case, the defendant may obtain summary judgment by pointing out to the court that the plaintiff has produced no proof that the defendant's product caused any injury to plaintiff. *Celotex Corp. v. Catrett,* 477 U.S. 317, 106 S. Ct. 2548, 91 L. Ed. 2d 265 (1986). *See supra* § 1718.

§ 1777. Amended or supplemental affidavits.

NRCP 56(e) gives the trial court the discretion to permit the amendment or supplementation of affidavits. In view of the harsh nature of summary judgment, the trial court should lean towards allowing the party opposing summary judgment to show the existence of a fact issue by amendment or supplementation, if he can do so, and makes a timely request. *Orcutt v. Miller,* 95 Nev. 408, 595 P.2d 1191 (1979).

§ 1778. Amendment of pleadings.

Rule 15(a) causes a problem, since a summary judgment motion is not a "responsive pleading" for purposes of cutting off the opponent's right to amend his pleading before service of a responsive pleading. 6 Moore's § 56.10. Therefore, a "matter of right" amendment may be made to the opponent's pleading even though a motion for summary judgment is pending. But in order to defeat the motion, the amendment will have to clearly be one of substance and not form. *Adamson v. Bowker,* 85 Nev. 115, 450 P.2d 796 (1969).

If an amendment is made — whether by right or by leave of court — it then becomes a part of the record and must be considered by the court in determining whether a genuine issue of material fact exists. 28 Fed. Proc. L. Ed. § 62:566.

Of course, the court should not consider amendments after submission of the motion. *Moore v. Moore,* 78 Nev. 186, 370 P.2d 690 (1962).

G. Appeal and Review.

§ 1779. In general.

This section addresses direct appeal from summary judgment and order denying summary judgment and review by extraordinary writ. If the Nevada Supreme Court has and accepts jurisdiction, the appellate review is *de novo, i.e.,* the *standards* for review are the same as the standards for decision by the trial court: Whether a genuine issue of material fact existed, assuming evidence most favorable to the non-moving party to be true. *A.L.M.N., Inc. v. Rosoff,* 104 Nev. 274, 757 P.2d 1319 (1988); *Tore, Ltd. v. Church,* 105 Nev. 183, 772 P.2d 1281 (1989); *Bulbman, Inc. v. Nevada Bell,* 108 Nev. 105, 825 P.2d 588 (1992). *See supra* § 1723, *et seq.*

§ 1780. Granted summary judgment.

If a motion for summary judgment is *granted* and a summary *judgment* is entered which adjudicates all of the claims against all of the parties in the action, NRCP 54(b), it is a "final judgment" which is directly appealable to the Nevada Supreme Court. NRCP 54(a) and NRAP 3A(b)(1). But the appeal must be from the judgment rather than the order; *Musso v. Triplett*, 78 Nev. 355, 372 P.2d 687 (1962); *see infra* § 1763; and the judgment must adjudicate all of the claims against all of the parties or it is not a final appealable determination under NRAP 3A(b)(1). *KDI Sylvan Pools, Inc. v. Workman*, 107 Nev. 340, 810 P.2d 1217 (1991).

§ 1781. Order denying summary judgment.

An order *denying* a motion for summary judgment is *not* an appealable order, but is interlocutory in nature. *Smith v. Hamilton*, 70 Nev. 212, 265 P.2d 214 (1953); Dzack v. Marshall, 80 Nev. 345, 393 P.2d 610 (1964); *Sorenson v. Pavlikowski*, 94 Nev. 440, 581 P.2d 851 (1978); *Clark Co. v. Bonanza No. 1*, 96 Nev. 643, 615 P.2d 939 (1980).

§ 1782. — Cross-motions.

The nonappealability rule applies even when there is already an existing, allowable appeal in a cross-motion situation. On cross-motions for summary judgment and cross-appeals, the party against whom summary was entered may appeal the granting of the motion against him, but he may not appeal the failure of the trial court to enter summary judgments in his favor. That is a nonappealable order, even if there is already an existing appeal in which the issues can be raised and decided. *Smith v. Hamilton*, 70 Nev. 212, 265 P.2d 214 (1953). *But see 25 Corporation, Inc. v. Eisenman Chemical*, 101 Nev. 664, 709 P.2d 164 (1985), where the court ruled on a cross-appeal from a failure to enter summary judgment.

§ 1783. Thirty days to appeal.

The thirty-day time limit to appeal from the entry of summary judgment runs from the date of service of notice of entry of judgment. A motion for relief from the summary judgment under NRCP 60(b) does not extend the thirty-day period. *Smilanich v. Bonanza Air Lines*, 72 Nev. 10, 291 P.2d 1053 (1956).

§ 1784. Extraordinary writ review — current law.

Since 1983, orders denying summary judgment have not been reviewable by extraordinary writ. *State Department of Trans. v. Thompson*, 99

Nev. 358, 662 P.2d 1338 (1983); *Clark County Liquor & Gambling Licensing Board v. Clark,* 102 Nev. 654, 730 P.2d 443 (1986).

H. Summary Judgment Bibliography.

73 Am. Jur. 2d, *Summary Judgment,* pp. 719-775
5 Am. Jur. *Trials,* pp. 105-123
27 and 28 Federal Procedure L. Ed. §§ 62:530-62:649
10 and 11 Wright & Miller, *Federal Practice and Procedure* §§ 2711-2742
West Key Numbers: Judgment #'s 178-190 and Fed. Civil Procedure #'s 2461-2559

CHAPTER 18

PRETRIAL CONFERENCES AND MOTIONS IN LIMINE

Authors: Mary Phelps Dugan
         Pat Lundvall
         Arthur E. Mallory

§ 1801. Introduction and scope.

This chapter explains the purpose for the various types of pretrial conferences allowable under the NRCP and amplifies on the scheduling and planning requirements, as well as the subjects appropriate for discussion at pretrial conferences, including the use of motions in limine. It also discusses pretrial memorandums, orders, the imposition of sanctions and traps for the unwary contained in pretrial conferences.

Rule 16 gives the court authority to conduct pretrial conferences in all cases. It also provides authority for a discovery commissioner to conduct scheduling conferences and enter scheduling orders in all cases which have not been designated as complex litigation pursuant to Rule 16.1(f).

NRCP 16(b) begins with the phrase, "[e]xcept in categories of actions exempted by district court rule ...." This language was adopted directly from the federal rule. Although there are no specific exemptions in the Nevada District Court Rules, Rule 2.55 of the Eighth Judicial District Court does specifically provide "All cases not commenced by the filing of a complaint are exempt from the entry of a scheduling order pursuant to NRCP 16(b)." And although the district court rules for several of the other districts have been amended since the addition of NRCP 16.1, there has been no other mention of a definition of exempted cases. It would appear, however, that the practice of the various district courts has been to exclude such cases as guardian and estate proceedings, petitions for writs of habeas corpus, and matters which by their nature are essentially uncontested.

§ 1802. Purpose of pretrial conferences.

The purpose under NRCP 16, and for that matter all of the Nevada Rules of Civil Procedure, is aptly addressed in NRCP 1. It states that the rules in all civil suits, "shall be construed to secure the just, speedy and inexpensive determination of every action." To help ensure that the goal of NRCP 1 is met, Rule 16 authorizes different types of pretrial conferences which may be held separately or be combined, as each may be appropriate.

Four types of pretrial conferences are contemplated under Rule 16:

(1) Scheduling conferences, to be conducted soon after the filing of the complaint;

(2) Case management conferences, to resolve motions or discovery disputes;

(3) Settlement conferences, to be conducted at any time appropriate under the facts of each case; and

(4) Trial management conference, to be conducted shortly before trial.

Through adoption of recent rule changes, the Nevada Supreme Court has expressed its desire that trial judges assume a more active role in the management and control of cases. Utilizing the various types of pretrial conferences that Rule 16 contemplates, the judges are given the ability and the obligation to establish a schedule which will determine the pace at which the case moves, the objectives which the case will attempt to achieve, and the expense involved for resolution of the case. It is hoped this Rule 16 mechanism will assist in settling cases and will provide the method for insuring that those cases which do proceed to trial are tried smoothly and effectively with a minimum of inconvenience to jurors and witnesses and with a minimum of expense to the parties.

Thus, Rule 16(a) specifies the following objectives:

(1) Expediting the disposition of the action;

(2) Establishing early and continuing control so that the case will not be protracted because of lack of management;

(3) Discouraging wasteful pretrial activities;

(4) Improving the quality of the trial through more thorough preparation; and

(5) Facilitating the settlement of the case.

§ 1803. Scheduling and planning.

According to Rule 16(b), the trial judge or discovery commissioner must issue a scheduling order as soon as practical, but in no exception later than 180 days after the filing of the complaint. Therefore, counsel are well advised to keep the 180-day deadline in mind if they plan on filing a motion to have the case designated as complex under NRCP 16.1(f) (*see* § 1607, *supra*), and also, if they schedule a Rule 16 pretrial conference for purposes of providing information to the court to assist the court in drafting its scheduling order. Counsel are also reminded that, according to Rule 16, the scheduling order is not easily modified once it has been issued.

Simultaneously, with the court designating a case as complex, the court must also set a date for a scheduling conference. NRCP 16.1(f). If the court does not set a date for a scheduling conference, the attorneys should request one. This is advisable for at least two reasons. First, Rule 16(b) states that the judge should consult with the attorneys before issuing a scheduling order. Second, if the attorneys do not meet with the judge, they run the risk of a scheduling order being issued without their input. Some attorneys might consider this to be a disadvantage. Though the above is largely self-explanatory, it is contemplated that the scheduling order will not just provide a cut-off date for all discovery. The forty-five-day rule already accomplishes that. Rather, the scheduling order may do such things as establish a date upon which witness lists must be exchanged; it may provide beginning and ending dates for such discovery activities as interrogatories, which ordinarily are sent out early in discovery, and depositions, which are ordinarily taken closer to the trial date; and it may set a date before which no NRCP 56 motion may be filed.

As a scheduling matter, NRCP 16(c) requires that at least one person acting as counsel for each party participating in any pretrial conference "have authority to enter into stipulations and to make admissions regarding all matters that the participants may reasonably anticipate may be discussed." In the ordinary situation, therefore, the trial counsel would be required to personally attend all pretrial conferences and to be well-acquainted with the case at the time of each such conference. Having the authority to act must also be accompanied by sufficient knowledge of the case so the attending counsel may make informed decisions.

NRCP 16(d) deals with the scheduling and attendance requirements of a trial management conference. The rule requires that this conference "be held as close to the time of trial as reasonable under the circumstances ..." and that at least one individual representing each party at trial be present at the conference.

Because it is important for all parties and witnesses to be able to plan and schedule their courtroom appearances, it has becoming increasingly necessary that trial dates be firm. It is incumbent upon the attorneys to plan their discovery and their personal calendars in such a way that they can agree upon a firm trial date at the time the scheduling order is issued. They should, therefore, not ask the court for continuances and under Rule 16, the trial judge should see that continuances are granted only in the most unusual of circumstances. It may be desirable to state this policy in the scheduling order.

§ 1804. — Local rules and practice.

With the advent of the changes in NRCP 16, an issue presented was the extent to which the existing local rules on pretrial conferences were to be applied to every pretrial conference held in a case. Since the advent of NRCP 16.1, the Second, Third, and Eighth and Ninth District Courts have promulgated new local rules. The Second and Eighth District Courts have simply referred to pretrial conferences in the plural, required some pretrial conferences for settlement purposes, or distinctly identified the former pretrial conference as the final pretrial conference. WDCR 6; EDCR 2.67. The Third and Ninth District Court Rules refer to only one pretrial conference, however, there has been no indication of a problem in the case law since the effective date of NRCP 16.1 as it clearly refers to the final pretrial conference held within a few days of the commencement of the trial. TJDCR 4; NJDCR 14. Rules 16 and 16.1 may yet necessitate some revisions of local rules in the future and should be read with that background in mind.

The First, Second, Third, Seventh and Ninth Judicial Districts have adopted local rules dealing with pretrial conferences. The rules adopted by all of the above Districts vary in content and should be carefully studied prior to engaging in pretrial practice before those courts. In general they allow the judge to require a pretrial conference or by motion allow counsel to request a pretrial conference if the motion is filed thirty days prior to the trial date. Generally, where a pretrial conference is held, these local rules also require settlement negotiations, although the Second and Ninth Districts only require settlement negotiations in jury cases. The Second, Seventh and Ninth Judicial Districts also allow the judge, for good cause, to continue the pretrial conference date. Most of the districts with local rules on pretrial conferences also provide that statements made by counsel during the conference are inadmissible except to the extent that they are incorporated into the pretrial order. The one exception among the courts having local rules governing pretrial conferences is the Third Judicial District. In that District, the local rules specifically state that nothing said with respect to either compromise or settlement is later admissible unless the court, for good cause, permits it.

Both the Third and the Eighth Judicial Districts' local rules set forth in considerable detail the topics for consideration at the final pretrial conference, the material which is to be included in the proposed pretrial orders submitted by counsel for each party not later than ten days prior to the pretrial conference, and the precise format which the proposed pretrial order is to follow. These rules also state with specificity that the court may require a pretrial conference. Although Rule 4 of the Third District's local rules does not specifically state that counsel may request a pretrial conference, counsel is free to do so under NRCP 16 and normal motion procedures. Rule 2.68 of the Eighth District local rules seems to clearly indicate that there will be a final pretrial conference.

§ 1805. — Pretrial memorandum.

The content of the pretrial memorandum will vary depending on the subject of the pretrial conference for which the memorandum is being written. NRCP 16(c) lists numerous possible topics which may be designated in the memorandum for consideration at a pretrial conference. Eleven general subjects listed by NRCP 16(c) are the following:

(1) The formulation and simplification of the issues, including the elimination of frivolous claims or defenses;

(2) The necessity or desirability of amendments to the pleadings;

(3) The possibility of obtaining admissions of fact and of documents which will avoid unnecessary proof, stipulations regarding the authenticity of documents, and advance rulings from the court on the admissibility of evidence;

(4) The avoidance of unnecessary proof and of cumulative evidence;

(5) The identification of witnesses and documents, the need and schedule for filing and exchanging pretrial briefs, and the date or dates for further conferences and for trial;

(6) The advisability of referring matters to a master;

(7) The possibility of settlement or the use of extrajudicial procedures to resolve the dispute;

(8) The form and substance of the pretrial order;

(9) The disposition of pending motions;

(10) The need for adopting special procedures for managing potentially difficult or protracted actions that may involve complex issues, multiple parties, difficult legal questions, or unusual proof problems; and

(11) The limitation of the number of expert witnesses.

Rule 16(c) also includes open-ended language stating that a pretrial conference is the proper forum for considering "[s]uch other matters as may aid in the disposition of the action." NRCP 16(c)(12). Thus, the NRCP 16(c) list of specific pretrial subjects is meant only as a guide. All of the listed subjects need not be addressed in any one pretrial conference and some of the listed subjects fit more appropriately in either the early or the late stages of the pretrial period. For instance, NRCP 16(c)(1) addressing "[t]he need for adopting special procedures for managing potentially difficult or protracted actions ..." is a subject which may be addressed more often in the scheduling conference. As each case has its own peculiarities, the court and counsel are invited by the rules to use their collective wisdom and their imagination if necessary in formulating at the scheduling conference the most efficient and effective procedure by which to conduct discovery and any other activities which may be engaged in during the pretrial time frame of the case.

If a pretrial conference is scheduled for case management purposes, such as resolving a single major issue which has developed during discovery, all counsel may be well aware of the issue to be resolved and the notice need not be detailed. However, when a pretrial conference is held for purposes of trial management, the conference should be noticed by a formal order and the order should specify a number of issues which might properly be addressed during the final conference. Also, the whole procedure is benefitted by a meeting between counsel before the trial management conference in order to eliminate issues before the conference. Form 18A, a Pretrial Conference Directive, contains the typical requirements for a pretrial conference held for purposes of trial management. Form 18B is a typical order for a pretrial settlement conference.

§ 1806. Conducting pretrial conferences.

As mentioned above, the format of each pretrial conference will vary depending upon the subjects to be addressed at the conference.

One of the objectives of the early pretrial conferences is to allow the court to become familiar with the case and its peculiar problems. The court is also assisted by information concerning the personal calendars of the attorneys involved in the case. Both scheduling and case management conferences allow the court to schedule the case with a view to prompt determination and to provide adequate time to counsel, taking into consideration their personal schedules. Counsel preparing for pretrial conferences which are held for scheduling purposes should supply the court with all pertinent information so the court may make an appropriate scheduling order. Though a single pretrial conference may in some cases be combined for purposes of both scheduling and case management, in larger cases it might be necessary to hold separate conferences — the first for scheduling purposes and the second for case management purposes.

When a pretrial settlement conference is held, it is recommended that it be conducted by a trial judge other than the one who is scheduled to try the actual case, preferably by a judge experienced in that type of action. Counsel desiring a settlement conference must first obtain permission from the judge who is assigned the case, requesting that he allow them to hold the settlement conference before another judge. The purpose of the settlement judge is to avoid any possible prejudice with the judge presiding at the trial. The parties should submit to whichever judge conducts the settlement conference all information, exhibits and, in some cases, witness's testimony which might significantly affect the value of the case. All parties should also bring their clients to the settlement conference.

Pretrial conferences held shortly before trial should be held for purposes of trial management. Because there is considerable variation in the court rules of each judicial district with regards to these final pretrial conferences, counsel should review local district court rules at least forty-five days before the trial date to find the applicable deadlines for filing a Motion for Pretrial Conference. Also, advance notice is helpful in scheduling a meeting with opposing counsel to prepare for a trial management conference.

At the conference, the judge first reviews the parties' pretrial memorandums. Proposed amendments are discussed and the pleadings are subsequently reshaped. In *Ennis v. Mori,* 80 Nev. 237, 391 P.2d 737 (1964), the defense counsel attempted to amend his answer and plead fraud as an affirmative defense at trial, even though counsel had approved his pleadings at the pretrial conference. The trial court denied the motion to amend. The Supreme Court upheld the trial court, demonstrating that it is within the trial judge's discretion to deny a motion to amend made after the pretrial conference.

At the conference, the parties also discuss the possibility of abandoning or clarifying issues and defenses. The names of the parties, in the caption of the case, are subsequently verified and the superfluous John, Jane and Corporate Does eliminated. Exhibits are reviewed and marked. If the parties stipulate to the admission of exhibits, they are in evidence. Counsel should check with the court regarding the method used by that court for marking exhibits. Some courts require that numbers be used, some require one party to mark exhibits with numbers and opposing party to mark with letters. Any exhibits to which the parties do not stipulate are marked and may be admitted at the trial after further argument.

Witnesses who will testify are also determined. Absent good cause, witnesses not named in the pretrial order cannot be called at trial. Indeed, in *Southern Pacific Co. v. Watkins,* 83 Nev. 471, 435 P.2d 498 (1967), the Nevada Supreme Court held that the trial court did not abuse its discretion in refusing to allow the defendant to call a witness who had not been named during the pretrial conference.

All known motions in limine should be asserted during the trial management conference, and ruled upon at that time. *See* § 1811, *infra.*

Depositions which are to be used in place of testimony at the time of trial should be designated in the pretrial memorandum with any objections listed. The court may rule on the objections during the conference.

Proposed jury instructions should be submitted to the court, each side submitting both unmarked copies and marked copies containing supporting authority. *See* Form 18A, *infra.*

In connection with the trial management conference, counsel should be aware not only that the conference must be attended by attorneys with authority and knowledge sufficient to enable them to enter into stipulations and make admissions on behalf of their clients as required by NRCP 16(c), but also that NRCP 16(d) requires that "[t]he conference shall be attended by at least one of the attorneys who will conduct the trial for each of the parties and by any unrepresented parties." Implicitly, failure to comply with these provisions would constitute a failure to appear at the pretrial conference and would subject the party who has failed to appear, or whose attorney has failed to appear, to a number of potential sanctions. If one of the attorneys is absent, the case may be continued, the offending party may be cited pursuant to the court's contempt powers (i.e., NRCP 16(f)), or the case may even be dismissed. See generally Wilmurth v. First Judicial District Court, 80 Nev. 337, 393 P.2d 302 (1964).

§ 1807. Pretrial order.

Because of the increased number of pretrial conferences under both Rule 16 and Rule 16.1 cases, and because many of these will be held in close proximity to the time of trial, it may become increasingly difficult for the court to write and issue pretrial orders in a timely fashion. Therefore, it is recommended that a court reporter be present at all pretrial conferences so the court may issue its order on the record. The transcript of the order can then be produced and filed either before trial or as needed, the costs for the court reporter to be borne equally between the parties.

As mentioned above, if a trial management pretrial conference is held, the purpose of the order issued pursuant to that conference is to shape and control the course of the trial itself. In Walters v. Nevada Title Guaranty Co., 81 Nev. 231, 401 P.2d 251 (1965), the Supreme Court considered whether a trial court may enter judgment upon an issue framed by the pleadings but not mentioned in a pretrial order. The court echoed the literal language of the rule by stating that as a general proposition a pretrial order controls the subsequent course of a trial and supersedes the pleadings; however, the court concluded under the circumstances of the case, where the order did not refer to a contingent cross-claim, that if error occurred, it was harmless.

§ 1808. Sanctions.

NRCP 16 has been amended to add a new provision dealing with sanctions. Though numerous sanctions were previously allowable under NRCP Rule 37, the new additions in Rule 16(f) provide the courts with greater specificity, in relation to both the possible justifications for sanctions, the individuals who can be sanctioned, and the variety of sanctions which could properly be imposed. Counsel should note that under NRCP 16(f), sanctions may properly be imposed not only for failure to appear at a scheduling or pretrial conference, but also for being "substantially unprepared to participate" or for failure to participate in good faith. Sanctions are easily avoided if counsel prepare for and attend the conferences for which they are noticed, if they participate in good faith at the conferences and if they obey the orders of the court.

§ 1809. Motion in limine defined.

A motion in limine, as used in both civil and criminal procedure, seeks the court's ruling on the admissibility of certain evidence in advance of trial. Historically, the motion in limine has been used as a pretrial device to exclude potentially prejudicial evidence from a jury trial. *See generally Howell, The Use of Motions in Limine in Civil Litigation,* 1977 Ariz. St. L.J. 443 (1977). However, it has been increasingly used to seek the admission of evidence prior to trial. *See, e.g., LeRoy v. Sabena Belgian World Airlines,* 344 F.2d 266 (2d Cir.), *cert. denied,* 382 U.S. 878 (1965).

Perhaps the most unique aspect of the motion is that while no jurisdiction expressly authorizes its use, a vast number of jurisdictions, including Nevada, employ it in civil and criminal motion practice. Annot., 63 A.L.R.3d 311, § 2(a), at 314, § 33(a), at 381 (1975). A number of Nevada civil cases have made reference to motions in limine, but the question of the basis of the court's authority to consider such a motion has never been raised. The Supreme Court has tacitly approved the motion, stating in one case, "[t]he motion in limine should have been granted," *Bull v. McCuskey,* 96 Nev. 706, 712, 615 P.2d 957, 961 (1980), and approving the granting of a motion in limine as within the court's discretionary power to rule on the admissibility of evidence. *State ex rel. Department of Highways v. Nevada Aggregates & Asphalt Co.,* 92 Nev. 370, 376, 551 P.2d 1095, 1098 (1976). At a pretrial conference the court may make "advance rulings ... on the admissibility of evidence" which are, in fact, rulings on motions in limine. NRCP 16(c)(3). In the Second and Eighth Judicial Districts, the use of the motion in limine is specifically authorized. WDCR 5; EDCR 2.47. *See* § 1811, *infra.*

Several courts and noted authors derive the authority for filing motions in limine from: (1) Federal Rule of Evidence 103(c) (Nevada counterpart NRS 47.080), which requests that inadmissible evidence be kept from the hearing of the jury; (2) Federal Rule of Evidence 403 (Nevada counterpart: NRS 48.035(1)); and (3) Federal Rule of Civil Procedure 16 on pretrial conferences. (Nevada counterpart NRCP 16). Howell, *The*

Use of Motions in Limine in Civil Litigation, 1977 Ariz. St. L.J. 443, 445, 453 (1977) (citing treatise and cases).

§ 1810. — Purpose of the motion in limine.

Some of the principal purposes which can be served by an appropriate motion in limine are:

(1) to avoid bringing prejudicial matters before the jury which may result in a mistrial;

(2) to promote a smoother running and more efficient trial by reducing interruptions during trial for arguments (a) involving complex evidentiary questions or (b) dealing with evidence crucial to one or more of the parties that requires more careful consideration;

(3) to provide for a better informed decision based upon previously submitted memoranda of points and authorities along with the arguments of counsel under circumstances that reduce the chances of error; and

(4) to increase the likelihood of settlement, as an advance ruling on evidence bearing on the potential results of the trial allows each party to better evaluate its case prior to the commencement of trial.

See Howell, *The Use of Motions in Limine in Civil Litigation,* 1977 Ariz. St. L.J. 443, 447 (1977).

The motion in limine is not generally intended to address those normal evidentiary questions that do not serve one of the above purposes and that can be expeditiously ruled upon during trial.

§ 1811. — Procedure in using the motion in limine.

Traditionally, the motion in limine is heard prior to jury selection. This avoids any prejudicial effect upon the jury and reduces the obstructiveness of objecting to the introduction of evidence at trial, excusing the jury, arguing outside of the jury's presence, and then reassembling. The motion should be written and submitted with a memorandum of points and authorities pursuant to applicable rules for motions. The local rules for the Second Judicial District set forth the following procedure for filing a motion in limine:

All motions in limine to exclude or admit evidence must be in writing and attached to the trial statement. The court may refuse to consider any oral motion and any motion in limine which is not filed with the trial statement.

WDCR 5. The local rules for the Eighth District prescribe the following procedure:

All motions in limine to exclude or admit evidence must be in writing and noticed for hearing not later than the date and time of the pretrial conference or, if no pretrial conference was set by the court, no later than 7 days before trial. The court may refuse to consider any oral motion in limine and any motion in limine which is not timely noticed.

EDCR 2.47.

In attempting to exclude prejudicial evidence, the movant is advised to request a protective order prohibiting the parties, their counsel, and witnesses from referring to the excluded evidence during trial. This requires a concisely drawn order so that opposing counsel cannot circumvent the purpose of the motion. Nevada has rejected the argument, at least in a criminal case, that a ruling on a motion in limine is only advisory in nature. *Moore v. State,* 96 Nev. 220, 607 P.2d 105 (1980).

Of vital concern to the trial attorney is the necessity of preserving the issue of admissibility of evidence for appeal. For example, in *Daly v. State,* 99 Nev. 564, 665 P.2d 798 (1983), the appellant was charged with sexual assault allegedly perpetrated on his fourteen-year-old stepdaughter. Before trial, the appellant's motion in limine to exclude evidence relating to other acts of misconduct, such as shouting at his daughter, was granted. However, the appellant failed to object to witness testimony during trial that appellant struck his stepdaughter on a number of occasions. The Supreme Court held that "the making of the motion in limine without further objection is not enough to preserve the issue on appeal," and that the appellant waived the issue of trial court error by failing to object to the subject testimony. This result reinforces the advisability of seeking a protective order. *Accord Collins v. Wayne Corp.,* 621 F.2d 777, 785 (5th Cir. 1980).

In Nevada, a ruling on a motion in limine is not final. If a motion in limine to exclude evidence is granted, as in the *Daly* case, the party seeking to admit the evidence can offer proof during the course of the trial that the proffered evidence (in light of the trial record) is relevant, material, and competent. *Deveroux v. State,* 96 Nev. 388, 610 P.2d 722 (1980).

§ 1812. — Use of the motion in limine to seek admission of evidence.

LeRoy v. Sabena Belgian World Airlines, 344 F.2d 266 (2d Cir.), *cert. denied,* 382 U.S. 878 (1965), is a classic case often used by authors to demonstrate how the motion in limine can secure the admission of evidence prior to trial. *See* Howell, *The Use of Motions in Limine in Civil Litigation,* 1977 Ariz. St. L.J. 443 (1977). In *Leroy,* the plaintiff sued an airline for wrongful death stemming from an airplane crash. The plaintiff sought a pretrial ruling on the admissibility of the flight recording transcript of radio transmissions to the aircraft before the crash. The transcript was vital to plaintiff's case, which sought to prove that a navigational error directed the aircraft off its flight path.

To satisfy evidentiary prerequisites for admitting the evidence, the plaintiff established that the transmissions were recorded and kept by the air controller as a business record, that the voices on the tapes originated from the airplane, that the transcript was a proper transcription from the tape, and that the transcript was the best evidence. The transcript was admitted, thus relieving the plaintiff from having to prepare certain ancillary evidence of navigational error for use at trial in case the transcript was ruled inadmissible at trial. This use of a motion in limine to seek the admission of evidence greatly reduced the plaintiff's burden and expense of presenting its case at trial. Moreover, as the opposing party had ample notice to prepare objections to the evidence prior to the in limine hearing, the eventual possibility of trial court error was significantly reduced.

The caveat to the use of motions in limine to admit evidence before trial is that the opposing party will become privy to the proponent's trial strategy.

Form 18A

PRETRIAL CONFERENCE DIRECTIVE

A. Prior to the pretrial conference, the designated trial attorneys for all the parties shall meet together at a convenient time and place for the purpose of arriving at stipulations and agreements, all for the purpose of simplifying the issues to be tried. At this conference between counsel, all exhibits must be exchanged and examined and counsel must also exchange a list of the names and addresses of all witnesses including experts to be called at the trial. The attorneys for each party shall then prepare a joint "Pretrial Memorandum" which shall be filed by the date previously ordered by the Court and as stated above. If agreement cannot be reached, this memorandum can be prepared separately by each counsel and so submitted.

B. The memorandum shall be as concise as possible and shall state the date the conference between the parties was held and cover in numerical order the following items:

1. A list of all claims for relief asserted by each party seeking affirmative relief and a list of all elements thereof.

2. A list of all affirmative defenses.

3. A brief statement of the claimed facts supporting the party's claim or defenses against all other parties.

4. A list of all the exhibits the party preparing the memorandum expects to offer at trial.

5. A specification of any objections the party preparing the memorandum may have to the admissibility of the exhibits of the opposing parties. If no objection is stated, it will be presumed that counsel has no objection to the introduction into evidence of the exhibits exchanged at the meeting between counsel before the pretrial conference.

6. A list of the witnesses and their addresses (including experts) which the party preparing the memorandum intends to call. Failure to list a witness will result in the court's precluding the party from calling that witness. This restriction shall not apply to rebuttal witnesses, the necessity of whose testimony cannot reasonably be anticipated before the time of trial.

7. A brief statement of each principal issue of law which the party preparing the memorandum believes will be contested at the time of trial. This statement shall include with respect to each principal issue of law the position thereof of the party preparing the memorandum.

C. Counsel shall bring to the pretrial conference all exhibits in their possession and an exhibit list for use by the clerk.

D. All subpoenas to hospitals calling for the production of medical records as authorized by NRS 52.325 shall direct the hospital to appear at the time of the pretrial conference instead of the trial.

E. At the pretrial conference, the Court will consider the following subjects:

1. All motions in limine which must have been served and filed not later than 21 days before the pretrial conference.

2. Which depositions the parties desire to use at trial and any objections to the use thereof or to the questions asked therein.

337

3. Applications for leave to amend the pleadings.

4. The simplification of issues.

5. The prospects of settlement.

6. The desirability of trial briefs, dates for filing the same and the legal issues to be contained therein.

7. The marking and admitting of exhibits (including medical records produced by NRS 52.325).

8. Such other matters as may aid in the disposition of the action.

9. Proposed jury instructions.

10. Proposed jury voir dire.

F. The pretrial conference shall be attended by the designated trial attorney. Should the designated trial attorney fail to appear at the pretrial, or to comply with the directions set out above, an ex parte hearing may be held and judgment of dismissal or default or other appropriate judgment entered or sanctions imposed.

Form 18B

DISTRICT COURT
CLARK COUNTY, NEVADA

Plaintiff.	CASE NO.
	DEPARTMENT NO.
vs.	DOCKET
Defendant.	

ORDER FOR PRETRIAL SETTLEMENT CONFERENCE

TO ALL COUNSEL:

IT IS HEREBY ORDERED that a pretrial settlement conference be held on _____ at the hour of _____. Pretrial settlement memorandums must be filed by _____.

Prior to the pretrial settlement conference, the designated trial attorneys for all the parties shall meet together at a convenient time and place for the purpose of arriving at stipulations and agreements, all for the purpose of simplifying the issues to be tried. The attorneys for each party shall then prepare a "Pretrial Settlement Memorandum" which shall be filed by the date previously ordered by the Court and stated above. The memorandum shall be as concise as possible and shall state the date the conference between the parties was held and cover in numerical order the following items:

1. A list of all claims for relief asserted by each party seeking affirmative relief and a list of all elements thereof.

2. A brief statement of the claimed facts supporting the party's claim or defenses against all other parties; a statement of admitted or undisputed facts; and, a statement of remaining issues of fact to be tried.

3. Any amendments required to the pleadings.

4. Any tender of issues in the pleadings that are to be abandoned.

5. A proposal for settlement of the claims or defenses. Rather than comply with this requirement, counsel may submit a confidential letter to the court, in camera, which will not be disclosed without permission of its author.

The pretrial settlement conference shall be attended by the designated trial attorney and a representative of each party who has authority to represent that party in settlement negotiations. Should the designated trial attorney fail to

339

appear, or to comply with the directions set out above, an ex parte hearing may be held and judgment of dismissal or default or other appropriate judgment entered or sanctions imposed.

  DATED this ____ day of _____, 19 ____.

           _____

          J. CHARLES THOMPSON, DISTRICT JUDGE

Form 18C

Case No. ——

Dept. No. ——

IN THE SECOND JUDICIAL DISTRICT COURT OF THE STATE OF NEVADA
IN AND FOR THE COUNTY OF WASHOE

_____

_____

      Plaintiff(s),

vs.   MOTION IN LIMINE NO. 1

_____

_____

      Defendant(s).

_____

Defendant _____, through its attorneys _____, moves this Court for its order *in limine,* before trial and selection of a jury, instructing Plaintiff, its counsel, and all witnesses called on its behalf as follows:

That no evidence may be offered or received relative to _____ and that Plaintiff is precluded from using any pleading, testimony, remarks, questions, or arguments that might inform the jury about _____, on the ground that such evidence is not relevant and that if the evidence is somehow found to be relevant, its probative value is substantially outweighed by the danger of unfair prejudice, confusion of the issues, and misleading the jury.

This motion is brought to Washoe District Court Rule 5. It is based on NRS 48.015 through 48.035, all documents on file with the court in this matter, and the points and authorities and exhibits that follow.

DATED this _____ day of _____, 19__.

_____

          Attorney for _____

POINTS AND AUTHORITIES

Motions in limine have long been recognized as a vehicle by which a party may seek to preclude the introduction of evidence prior to trial to avoid undue prejudice. Determinations about admissibility of evidence are properly "conducted out of the hearing of the jury, to prevent the suggestion of inadmissible evidence." NRS 47.080. In this case, any evidence of _____ must be excluded under NRS 48.025 or, alternatively, under NRS 48.035(1).

Evidence regarding _____ is not relevant for the following reasons:

1)

2)

3)

4)

341

Even if evidence about _____ were found to be relevant, it is inadmissible because its probative value is substantially outweighed by the danger of unfair prejudice, confusion of the issues, and misleading the jury.

For the reasons set forth above, Defendant respectfully requests this Court for its order instructing Plaintiff, its counsel, and witnesses called on its behalf not to mention, refer to, interrogate about, or attempt to convey to the jury in any manner, either directly or indirectly, any information about _____ at the trial of this matter. Defendant further request that this Court instruct Plaintiff, its counsel, and witnesses called on its behalf not to make any reference to this motion or the fact that it has been filed and decided.

DATED this _____ day of _____, 19__.

_____
Attorney for _____

CHAPTER 19

CONSOLIDATION AND SEVERANCE

Author: G. Mark Albright

§ 1901. Introduction and scope.

This chapter covers the types of consolidation that may occur, and the procedures and effects of consolidation. It considers NRCP 42(a) and EDCR 2.50, discusses the various forms of severance, and notes the distinctive features of NRCP 13(i), 14(a), 21 and 42(b).

§ 1902. Consolidation: in general.

The Nevada rule concerning consolidation is embodied in NRCP 42(a) as follows:

> (a) Consolidation. When actions involving a common question of law or fact are pending before the court, it may order a joint hearing or trial of any or all the matters in issue in the actions; it may order all of the actions consolidated; and it may make such orders concerning proceedings therein as may tend to avoid unnecessary costs or delay.

The provisions of NRCP 42(a) and FRCP 42(a) are identical and no Nevada decision appears to distinguish between the federal and state court applications of such rule. Indeed, the Nevada Supreme Court has relied on federal case law when interpreting NRCP 42(a). *See Mikulich v. Carner,* 68 Nev. 161, 228 P.2d 257 (1957).

§ 1903. History, purpose and basis of Rule 42(a).

In Nevada, as in the federal system, consolidation is permitted as a matter of discretion, to avoid unnecessary costs or delays, or as a matter of convenience and economy in administration. *Mikulich, supra.* The court is given broad discretion to determine when consolidation is proper, and the consent of the parties is not required.

In ordering consolidation, usually the affected actions are of a "like nature" as where negligence actions arise out of the same collision, or actions filed by different plaintiffs arise out of the same tort. However, different types of actions may also be consolidated. For example, an action by an insurer to cancel a policy may be consolidated with the action of the insured to recover upon such policy; an action of a landlord for eviction or to forfeit rent may be consolidated with the tenant's action involving deposits and rent; or an action for personal injury may be consolidated with a claim for indemnification.

§ 1904. Types of consolidation.

In Nevada, the term "consolidation" is used in different contexts. One use is where several actions are combined into one, losing their separate identities and becoming a single action. Another use is where several actions are tried together but each retains its separate character. *See Randall v. Salvation Army,* 100 Nev. 466, 686 P.2d 241 (1984).

In *Mikulich, supra,* the Nevada Supreme Court relied on federal cases which have consistently construed FRCP 42(a) consolidation orders providing for the combined trial of two or more cases as "not having the effect of merging the several claims into a single cause." The trial court, in cases tried together, had entered two separate judgments. Consequently, the Nevada Supreme Court held that full payment and satisfaction of one judgment by the defendant did not bar the defendant from appealing a judgment entered for the prevailing plaintiff in the other action. *Id.*

In *Ward v. Sheeline Banking & Trust Co.,* 54 Nev. 442, 22 P.2d 358 (1933), the Nevada Supreme Court indicated that failure to timely oppose a consolidation order can result in a waiver of such an objection. The Court also indicated that where consolidation is not a matter of right, the trial court is vested with discretion to grant or refuse consolidation, subject to reversal only in case of abuse of that discretion.

When determining whether to order consolidation, the trial court should consider if the cases are at different stages of pretrial preparation. Even where two actions involve common questions of law and fact, consolidation may be improper if only one action is ready for trial and the other is in an early discovery phase. *Prudential Insurance Co. of America v. Marine National Exchange Bank,* 55 F.R.D. 436 (E.D. Wis. 1972). In essence, the court must weigh the time, effort, and expense consolidation would save against any inconvenience, delay, or expense that it would cause. *Huene v. United States,* 743 F.2d 703 (9th Cir. 1984). Consolidation may be improper if it results in aligning parties who have conflicting interests, *Dupont v. Southern Pacific Co.*, 366 F.2d 193 (5th Cir. 1966), or if the common issue is not central or material, *Shump v. Balka,* 574 F.2d 1341 (10th Cir. 1978).

§ 1905. Consolidation: procedure.

The local rules of each district should be consulted for the appropriate procedures to implement when filing consolidation motions. In the Eighth District, EDCR 2.50 provides that motions for consolidation of two or more cases must be heard by the judge who was assigned to the case which was first filed. If consolidation is granted, the consolidated case will be heard before the judge who ordered consolidation. Documents filed after the consolidation order must list all case numbers and captions, with the lowest case number appearing first. The court clerk must be provided with sufficient copies of pleadings and motions, etc., for each case number listed. *Id.*

Currently, the local rules published by the First, Second, Third, Seventh and Ninth District Courts have not expressly adopted specific procedures for handling consolidated cases; however, such courts frequently consolidate cases consistent with the procedure contained in EDCR Rule 2.50 (or such districts have only one judge).

§ 1906. Lead counsel and peremptory challenges of jurors or judges.

After ordering consolidation, the court may "make such order concerning proceedings therein as may tend to avoid unnecessary costs or delay." NRCP 42(a). This may include appointing one attorney to act as lead counsel or general counsel to supervise and coordinate the consolidated cases (*e.g.,* schedule pretrial discovery) under compelling circumstances and if no conflict of interest exists. *See, e.g., Feldman v. Hanley,* 49 F.R.D. 48 (S.D.N.Y. 1969).

If there are two or more parties on any side, and their interests are diverse, the court may allow an additional four peremptory juror challenges to the side with multiple parties. NRS 16.040. If the multiple parties on a side cannot agree upon the allocation of the additional challenges, the court will make the allocation. *Id.*

Additionally, each side is entitled to one change of judge by peremptory challenge. SCR 48.1. However, consolidated proceedings under this rule "shall be treated as having only two sides." Consequently, if one of two or more parties on one side files a peremptory challenge, "no other party on that side may file a separate challenge." *Id.*

Even after consolidation, the actions retain their separate identities, and the parties and pleadings in one action do not automatically become parties and pleadings in the other action. *Mikulich, supra.* Thus, consolidated litigants may be excluded from the courtroom as non-party witnesses during certain portions of the joint trial. *Randall v. Salvation Army,* 100 Nev. 466, 686 P.2d 241 (1984). However, the court may treat consolidated actions as one for the purpose of allowing attorneys' fees and witness' fees. 9 Wright & Miller, *Federal Practice and Procedure* § 2385 (1971).

§ 1907. Consolidation: real and personal property taxes

Two other statutory provisions concerning consolidation are found at NRS 361.435 and NRS 361.560. NRS 361.435 provides that a property owner seeking to recover real property taxes paid under protest, where the property is located in more than one county, may "consolidate any of the suits in one action and bring the action in any court of competent jurisdiction in Carson City, Nevada." NRS 361.560 provides that where an owner of personal property appears to have been delinquent in paying taxes on property that is used and operated in more than one county of the state, "the district attorneys of each of such counties or the attorney general may consolidate all civil actions brought against the owner for the recovery of all or any portion of the delinquent taxes in one civil action brought in a court of competent jurisdiction in Carson City, State of Nevada ...."

§ 1908. Consolidation of arbitration proceedings.

The Nevada Supreme Court has approved the consolidation of arbitration proceedings by the trial court where the evidence, witnesses and legal issues are the same, and there is no showing of prejudice. The court found that consolidating such arbitration proceedings avoids the possibility of conflicting awards and avoids the duplication of time, effort, and expense separate proceedings would generate. *Exber, Inc. v. Sletten Construction Co.,* 92 Nev. 721, 558 P.2d 517 (1976). *See also* Cable Belt Conveyors, Inc. v. Alumina Partners of Jamaica, 669 F. Supp. 577 (S.D.N.Y.), *aff'd,* 857 F.2d 1461 (2d Cir.), *cert. denied,* 484 U.S. 855 (1987) (separate arbitration proceedings could lead to inconsistent findings).

§ 1909. Class actions and consolidation.

Consolidation is often closely related to class actions. NRCP 23 includes as one of the grounds for consolidation that "there are questions of law or fact common to the class." This language is similar to the "common question of law or fact" required for consolidation under NRCP 42(a). Consequently, when the prerequisites for class certification are satisfied, several class actions may be consolidated together, *Feldman v.*

Hanley, 49 F.R.D. 48 (S.D.N.Y. 1989), or separate actions may be consolidated together into a single class action. *Goff v. Menke,* 672 F.2d 702 (8th Cir. 1982).

§ 1910. Appellate review.

Orders granting or denying consolidation motions are interlocutory and not appealable absent a Rule 54(b) certification. In *Mallin v. Farmers Insurance Exchange,* 106 Nev. 606, 797 P.2d 978 (1990), the Nevada Supreme Court held that when cases are consolidated by the district court, "they become one case for all appellate purposes." Thus an order which resolves fewer than all of the claims in a consolidated action "is not appealable as a final judgment absent NRCP 54(b) certification from the district court." *Id.* The Court, in *Mallin,* explained that the certification need not contain specific findings of fact itemizing the factors which were relied upon by the Court in certifying its judgment as final. Moreover, such certifications are presumed valid, and will be upheld unless there has been "a gross abuse of discretion." *Id.*

§ 1911. Severance: in general.

The Nevada Rules of Civil Procedure concerning severance are Rules 13(i), 14(a), 21 and 42(b). These rules provide in pertinent part as follows:

RULE 13(i)

(i) Separate Trials: Separate Judgment. If the court orders separate trials as provided in Rule 42(b), judgment on a counterclaim or cross-claim may be rendered in accordance with the terms of Rule 54(b) when the court has jurisdiction so to do, even if the claims of the opposing party have been dismissed or otherwise disposed of.

RULE 14(a)

Any party may move to strike the third-party claim, or for its severance or separate trial.

RULE 21

Misjoinder of parties is not ground for dismissal of an action. Parties may be dropped or added by order of the court on motion of any party or of its own initiative at any stage of the action and on such terms as are just. Any claim against a party may be severed and proceeded with separately.

RULE 42(b)

(b) Separate Trials. The court, in furtherance of convenience or to avoid prejudice, or when separate trials will be conducive to expedition and economy, may order a separate trial of any claim, cross-claim, counterclaim, or third-party claim, or of any separate issue of or any number of claims, cross-claims, counterclaims, third-party claims, or issues, always preserving inviolate the right of trial by jury.

§ 1912. History, purpose and basis of severance rules.

NRCP 42(b) allows separate trials of various claims and issues "in furtherance of convenience, or to avoid prejudice, or when separate trials will be conducive to expedition and economy." Severance is sometimes necessary to prevent embarrassment, delay or expense arising out of the liberal rules allowing joinder of various actions, claims and parties. The matter of ordering separate trials rests largely in the discretion of the trial judge. In addition, the Nevada courts may order a separate trial for any issue, or any number of claims, cross-claims, counterclaims or third-party claims. *Gojack v. Second Judicial District Court,* 95 Nev. 443, 596 P.2d 237 (1979); *see also* NRCP 42(b). The factual questions of judicial convenience and prejudice should be resolved at the trial court level. *Inter-Insurance Bureau v. District Court,* 106 Nev. 197, 788 P.2d 1367 (1990). The trial court's discretion must be applied in such a manner as to preserve inviolate the right of trial by jury. NRCP 42(b). The procedure under NRCP 42(b) for separate trials should be distinguished from severance of claims under NRCP 21. Separate trials under NRCP 42(b) usually result in a single judgment, whereas claims severed under NRCP 21 become independent actions to be tried and adjudicated separately. Essentially, NRCP 42(b) is a counterbalance to the broad joinder provisions contained in NRCP 13, 14, and 18 to 24, which place few restrictions on joinder during the pleadings stage.

§ 1913. Severance or separate trials: procedure.

Any party may move for separate trials or the court may so order on its own motion. Bifurcation of the trial on the issues of liability and damages may be ordered if the two issues are separate and distinct. Where the nature of the injuries has an important bearing on the issue of liability, the Nevada Supreme Court has found bifurcation to be an abuse of discretion. *Verner v. Nevada Power Co.,* 101 Nev. 551, 706 P.2d 147 (1985). In *Verner,* the court found "the issues of liability and damages were inextricably interrelated," and separate trials under NRCP 42(b) was improper. Even where bifurcation is ordered, the Court must, when requested, give the contributory negligence jury instruction pursuant to NRS 41.141. *Verner, supra.*

Although bifurcation of personal injury cases usually saves time, some federal studies indicate that separate trials of liability and damages issues should not be routinely ordered because bifurcation often reduces the instances in which personal injury plaintiffs are successful. 9 Wright & Miller, *Federal Practice and Procedure* § 2390, at 299 (1971). The Advisory Committee to the 1966 amendment of FRCP 42(b) suggested that bifurcation should "be encouraged where experience has demonstrated its worth," but that it is "not to be routinely ordered."

A separate trial may also be ordered where evidence admissible only on a certain issue may prejudice a party on other issues, as where in a single trial the jury would learn that the defendant is insured, and the issues are unrelated. *Larsen v. Powell,* 16 F.R.D. 322 (D. Colo. 1954). However, such prejudice does not come into play where the action is to be heard by the Court rather than a jury. *Organic Chemicals, Inc. v. Carroll Products, Inc.,* 86 F.R.D. 468 (W.D. Mich. 1980). In determining whether one or two trials will best serve the convenience of the parties and the court, avoid prejudice, and minimize expense and delay, the major consideration should be which procedure is more likely to result in a just and final disposition of the litigation. *In re Innotron Diagnostics,* 800 F.2d 1077, 1084 (Fed. Cir. 1986).

Further, Nevada trial courts are given additional authority, aside from that found in NRCP 13(i), 14(a), 21 and 42(b), to control the course and conduct of proceedings before the court. Specifically, NRS 50.115 provides in relevant part:

> 1. The judge shall exercise reasonable control over the mode and order of interrogating witnesses and presenting evidence:
> (a) To make the interrogation and presentation effective for the ascertainment of the truth;
> (b) To avoid needless consumption of time; and
> (c) To protect witnesses from undue harassment or embarrassment.

Accordingly, a trial court is authorized to conduct separate evidentiary hearings on any issue as long as the bifurcation of such issues remains consistent with Nevada's statutory scheme. *See Gojack v. Second Judicial District Court,* 95 Nev. 443, 596 P.2d 237 (1979). However, Nevada trial courts are without jurisdiction to enter a final divorce decree without contemporaneously disposing of any community property. *Id.*

Nevada trial courts may order separate trials of any cross-claim or counterclaim pursuant to NRCP 13(i). An order separating such claims should be issued for the reasons provided in NRCP 42(b). Judgment on the separate claims may be certified as final in accordance with the terms of NRCP 54(b) if the judgment is final as to fewer than all of the claims or parties. Further, NRCP 14(a) provides that any party may move to strike a third-party claim, or for its severance or separate trial. Similarly, any claim against a party may be severed and proceeded upon separately pursuant to NRCP 21.

When separate trials are ordered, the court may stay or postpone discovery of the issues to be tried in the second trial pending completion of the first trial. For example, courts may defer discovery on damages issues until liability is first proven. *In re Master Key Antitrust Litigation,* 70 F.R.D. 23 (D. Conn.), *appeal dismissed,* 528 F.2d 5 (2d Cir. 1975). Different juries may hear the bifurcated liability and damages issues if the issues to be tried are distinct and not interwoven and no injustice would result. *Id.* However, some federal commentators believe the preferred practice is to use the same jury for all issues, even though the trials are conducted at different times. 9 Wright & Miller, *Federal Practice and Procedure* § 2391, at 302 (1971).

§ 1914. Appellate review.

An order granting or denying separate trials is ordinarily not appealable as a final judgment. *Gojack v. Second Judicial District Court,* 95 Nev. 443, 596 P.2d 237 (1979). It is reviewable only upon the entry of a final judgment or order resolving all of the issues, unless a lesser judgment is certified as final under the provisions of NRCP 54(b). Furthermore, any objection to the order must be asserted in the trial court and not be raised for the first time on appeal. *Inter-Insurance Bureau v. District Court,* 106 Nev. 197, 788 P.2d 1367 (1990). A writ of prohibition under NRS 84.320 may be available if the trial court exceeds its jurisdiction. *Gojack, supra.* In applying the principle of NRCP 21, the Nevada Supreme Court has indicated that a misjoinder of parties will not cause reversal in the absence of prejudice. *See Gershenhorn v. Stutz,* 72 Nev. 293, 304 P.2d 395 (1956), *cert. denied,* 354 U.S. 926 (1957).

CHAPTER 20

DISMISSAL OF ACTIONS

Author: Curtis B. Coulter

§ 2001. Introduction and scope.

In the broad sense, dismissal of actions is governed by Rule 41 of the Nevada Rules of Civil Procedure. This chapter discusses voluntary and involuntary dismissals of actions, the procedure for obtaining a dismissal, and the effect of a dismissal under Rule 41. This chapter, however, does not discuss dismissals under NRCP 25(a), for failure to make timely substitution after the death of a party; dismissals for failure to state a claim or for other procedural or pleading defects under NRCP 12; or dismissals under NRCP 37 as a discovery sanction. Dismissal for these grounds are discussed in Chapters 5, 12, 16, and 22 respectively. A dismissal under Rule 41 is the equivalent of a nonsuit or a discontinuance of the action. *See Hough v. Reserve Gold Mining Co.,* 51 Nev. 275, 278, 274 P. 192 (1929).

§ 2002. Voluntary dismissal.

Nevada Rule of Civil Procedure 41(a) governs voluntary dismissals of actions. A voluntary dismissal of an action may, except in the case where a receiver has been appointed (NRCP 66) or in the case of a class action (NRCP 23(e)), may be dismissed by the plaintiff, upon repayment of the defendant's filing fees without the necessity of court order if the notice of dismissal is filed anytime before an adverse party files an answer or responsive pleading. NRCP 41(a)(1)(i). *See, e.g., Federal Savings & Loan Insurance Corp. v. Moss,* 88 Nev. 256, 495 P.2d 616 (1972). Dismissal where no answer or responsive pleading has been filed is a matter of right running to the plaintiff and may not be extinguished or circumscribed by the adversary or the court. *Id.* at 259, 495 P.2d at 618. An action may also be voluntarily dismissed by the filing of a stipulation of dismissal signed by all parties who have appeared in the action. NRCP 41(a)(1)(ii). *Jeep Corp. v. Second Judicial District Court,* 98 Nev. 440, 652 P.2d 1183 (1982) (Stipulation for dismissal filed after trial during pendency of appeal). A voluntary dismissal under NRCP 41(a)(1), unless otherwise stated in the notice of dismissal or stipulation, is a dismissal without prejudice. The practitioner should, however, be cautious because the notice of dismissal also operates as an adjudication on the merits.

An oral stipulation for dismissal may be enforceable if approved by the judge and entered into in open court and appears upon the minutes of the court. *See Prostack v. Lowden,* 90 Nev. 230, 606 P.2d 1099 (1980). Estoppel, however, will not apply in preventing a defendant from asserting the mandatory dismissal rule. *See Great W. Land & Cattle Corp. v. Sixth Judicial District Court ex rel. County of Pershing,* 86 Nev. 282, 467 P.2d 1019 (1970); *Prostack v. Lowden,* 90 Nev. 230, 606 P.2d 1099 (1980).

§ 2003. Dismissal by order of court.

Except as provided above, no action can be dismissed in the plaintiff's insistence except by order of the court and upon such terms and conditions as the court deems proper. The court's order is only reviewable for abuse of discretion. *See Desert Plaza Apartments, Inc. v. Freeman,* 75 Nev. 170, 336 P.2d 771 (1959). Unless otherwise stated, a dismissal under this section, NRCP 41(a)(2) is without prejudice. Any dismissal pursuant to this section must be obtained by motion to the court. Such a motion cannot be heard ex parte. *See Monroe, Ltd. v. Central Telephone Co.,* 91 Nev. 450, 453, 538 P.2d 152, 154 (1975). If a counterclaim has been pled by a defendant prior to the service upon him of the plaintiff's motion to dismiss, the court may not dismiss the plaintiff's action unless the counterclaim can remain pending for independent adjudication by the court.

§ 2004. Voluntary dismissal with pending counterclaim.

Rule 41(a)(2) provides that in actions where a counterclaim has been pled by a defendant prior to the plaintiff's service of the motion to dismiss, the action shall not be dismissed without the defendant's approval unless the counterclaim can remain pending for independent adjudication.

§ 2005. Conditions on voluntary dismissal.

NRCP 41(a)(1) expressly imposes one condition on voluntary dismissal: the plaintiff must repay the defendant's filing fees. Except as may be stated under NRCP 41(a)(2), the court has no power to impose any terms or conditions on the voluntary dismissal of an action. This is because the plaintiff may dismiss the action as a matter of right at anytime before the adverse party files a responsive pleading. NRCP 41(a)(1)(i). The parties who have appeared however, may by stipulation under NRCP 41(a)(1)(ii), set any conditions upon which they enter into the stipulated dismissal.

§ 2006. Effect of voluntary dismissal.

A dismissal as a matter of right or by or stipulation under NRCP 41(a)(1) is without prejudice to the commencement of another action unless otherwise stated in the notice of dismissal or stipulation. There is however one exception, and that is that if the notice of dismissal is "with prejudice" it operates as an adjudication on the merits if the plaintiff has previously dismissed an action in any state or federal court based on or including the same claim. This Rule, however, operates as a matter of right. It does not apply to dismissals by stipulation or dismissals upon motions of the court nor involuntary dismissals. It should also be noted that the *second* "notice of dismissal" not only operates as an adjudication upon the merits, but is a dismissal with prejudice even if the notice states otherwise.

§ 2007. Involuntary dismissal.

As stated in § 20.01 above, this chapter is not an exhaustive overview of every procedure or method for dismissals of actions. Where actions may be dismissed pursuant to Rule 12 for insufficiency of pleading or pleading defects, see Chapter 10, *supra*. Dismissal as a discovery sanction is also addressed in Chapter 16, *supra*.

§ 2008. Dismissal as sanction.

Rule 11 of the Nevada Rules of Civil Procedure states that the signature of an attorney or party constitutes a certificate by that attorney or party that he or she has read the pleading, motion, or other paper; that to the best of his or her knowledge, information and belief, formed after reasonable inquiry under the circumstances obtaining at the time of the signature, that it is well grounded in fact and warranted by existing law or a good faith argument for the extension, modification, or reversal of existing law, and that the pleading or paper was not interposed for any improper purpose such as to harass or to cause unnecessary delay or needless increase in the cost of litigation. The rule further states that if the pleading, motion or paper is signed in violation of Rule 11, the court, upon motion or upon its own initiative, *shall* impose upon the person who signed it, a represented party, or both, an appropriate sanction, which may include an order to pay the other party or parties the amount of the reasonable expenses incurred because of the filing of the pleading, motion or other paper, including a reasonable attorney fee. The sanction under Rule 11 has on at least one occasion been the basis of a dismissal of an action where the complaint was only signed by out-of-state counsel and where there was ample evidence that there was a deliberate violation of the rule. *See Naimo v. Fleming*, 95 Nev. 13, 588 P.2d 1025 (1979).

§ 2009. Involuntary dismissal under Rule 41(b).

Subsection (b) of Rule 41 sets forth two specific grounds for dismissal. An action may be dismissed at the close of the plaintiff's case in chief for failure to prove a prima facie case to support the alleged cause of action. *See Nevada Industrial Development, Inc. v. Benedetti*, 103 Nev. 360, 741 P.2d 802 (1987). This ground for dismissal is also discussed in Chapter 22. Subsection (b) of Rule 41 also permits dismissal at any time "for failure of the plaintiff to comply with these rules or any order of court ...."

§ 2010. Procedure for involuntary dismissal.

Rule 41(b) addresses the involuntary dismissal of an action on the motion of the defendant. If the motion is made during the hearing or trial, notice of the motion is unnecessary and the motion need not be in writing. A defendant may bring a Rule 41(b) motion at the close of the plaintiff's case in chief, but he is not specifically required to do so before presenting evidence himself. *See Warner v. Dixon*, 92 Nev. 677, 679, 558 P.2d 540, 541 (1976). If the motion is made at any time other than in open court, the requirements of Rule 7(b) must be satisfied and the motion must be served as provided in Rule 5.

The district court may grant a motion for involuntary dismissal when it has interpreted the evidence in a light most favorable to the plaintiff and the plaintiff has failed to prove sufficient evidence to support a prima facie case. *See Nevada Industrial Development, Inc. v. Benedetti*, 103 Nev. 360, 741 P.2d 802 (1987); *M & R Investment Co. v. Mandarino*, 103 Nev. 711, 748 P.2d 488 (1987).

§ 2011. Effect of involuntary dismissal.

An involuntary dismissal under Rule 41(b) operates as an adjudication on the merits unless the court otherwise specifies or the dismissal is for lack of jurisdiction, improper venue, or failure to join a necessary party under Rule 19. A dismissal under Rule 41(b) which does not expressly state that it is without prejudice is, by operation of the rule, a dismissal with prejudice. *See Dubin v. Harrell*, 79 Nev. 467, 386 P.2d 729 (1963).

§ 2012. Dismissal of counterclaims, cross-claims and third-party claims.

Subsection (c) of Rule 41 applies to the dismissal of any counterclaim, cross-claim, or third-party claim. It provides that a voluntary dismissal must be made before either a responsive pleading is served or, if there is none, before the introduction of evidence at the trial or hearing. Thus, if (1) a responsive pleading has been filed and served or (2) there is introduction of evidence at the trial or hearing, the counterclaim, cross-claim or third-party claim may only be dismissed by approval of the court pursuant to Rule 41(a)(2). Where a complaint has been filed against two defendants, the voluntary dismissal against one defendant does not affect the cross-claim filed by the other defendant. *Harris v. Shell Development Corp.*, 95 Nev. 348, 594 P.2d 731 (1979).

§ 2013. Costs of a previously-dismissed action.

If a plaintiff who has once dismissed an action in any court and commences another action based upon or including the same claim against the same defendant, the court may order the payment of costs of the action previously dismissed be paid by the pursuing party. The court may further stay the proceedings in the subsequent action until the plaintiff has complied with the court's order regarding the payment of costs.

Rule 41(d) in regard to the payment of costs is, however, left to the discretion of the court. That Rule expressly applies only when the plaintiff has voluntarily dismissed a previous action. It does not apply when the prior dismissal was involuntary. Rule 41(d) also does not apply where the first suit was based on a different claim than that asserted in the second suit. *See Volpert v. Papagna*, 83 Nev. 429, 433 P.2d 533 (1967).

§ 2014. Involuntary dismissal for lack of prosecution.

Rule 41(e) provides that the court in its discretion *may* dismiss any action for want of prosecution upon motion of any party or on the court's own motion after due notice to the parties, whenever the plaintiff has failed for two years after the action is filed to bring such action to trial. Rule 41(e) also provides that any action not brought to trial within five years after the plaintiff has filed the action *shall* be dismissed. This Rule is commonly referred to as the "five-year rule." The parties may, however, stipulate in writing that the five-year period may be extended.

The purpose behind Rule 41(e) is to compel diligence in the prosecution of actions and to prevent unreasonable delays in litigation. *See Hassett v. St. Mary's Hospital Association*, 86 Nev. 900, 478 P.2d 154 (1970); *C.R. Fredrick, Inc. v. Nevada Tax Commission*, 98 Nev. 387, 649 P.2d 1372 (1982). In addition to the specific provisions set forth in Rule 41, the court retains inherent power to dismiss actions for lack of prosecution. *See Harris v. Harris*, 65 Nev. 342, 196 P.2d 402 (1948); *Volpert v. Papagana*, 85 Nev. 437, 456 P.2d 848 (1969). Before the court exercises its inherent power and dismisses an action, it should only do so "after due notice to the parties" as required by Rule 41(e).

For the purpose of this Rule, the mandated time limits commence upon the filing of the claim not upon the filing of a counterclaim. *See Volpert, supra*. Likewise, the five-year rule applies from the date of the filing of the original claim, not the filing of cross-claims, counterclaims or third-party claims. *See United Association of Journeymen & Apprentices of Plumbing & Pipe Fitting Industry v. Manson*, 105 Nev. 816, 783 P.2d 955 (1989).

An action may also be dismissed for want of prosecution if, after judgment is obtained, a motion for new trial has been made and a new trial granted. Such an action shall be dismissed upon motion of any party after due notice to the parties, or by the court on its own initiative if no appeal has been taken, unless the action is brought to trial within three years after the entry of the order granting the new trial. This is an exception to the general "five-year rule" and may also be modified by written stipulation. NRCP 41(e).

§ 2015. Discretionary dismissal by the court.

Under either Rule 41(e) or based upon its inherent powers, the court may in its discretion dismiss any action for want of prosecution whenever plaintiff has failed for two years after an action is filed to bring the action to trial.

In a motion brought to dismiss for failure to prosecute, the burden of proof rests upon the plaintiff to show circumstances excusing the delay and apparent lack of diligence on his part. *Volpert v. Papagana*, 85 Nev. 437, 456 P.2d 848 (1969); *Hassett v. St. Mary's Hospital Association*, 86 Nev. 900, 478 P.2d 154 (1970). As stated in the rule, the motion can only be brought "after due notice to the parties." An ex parte motion for dismissal cannot be heard. *Monroe, Ltd. v. Central Telephone Co.*, 91 Nev. 450, 538 P.2d 152 (1975).

In motioning the court for dismissal for lack of prosecution, prejudice from the delay diligence is presumed. *See Northern Illinois Corp. v.*

Miller, 78 Nev. 213, 370 P.2d 955 (1962). It is the duty of the plaintiff at every stage of the proceeding to expedite his case to final determination. *Thran v. First Judicial District Court ex rel. Ormsby County,* 79 Nev. 176, 380 P.2d 297 (1963).

It is the duty of the plaintiff to show the diligence has been taken in proceeding with the action. *Johnson v. Harber,* 94 Nev. 524, 582 P.2d 800 (1978). A lack of diligence by the plaintiff's attorney is imputed to the client. *See Valente v. First Western Savings & Loan Association,* 90 Nev. 377, 528 P.2d 699 (1974).

In exercising its discretion on a motion to dismiss for lack of prosecution, the court's decision will be upheld absent a gross abuse of discretion. *See Volpert v. Papagana,* 85 Nev. 437, 456 P.2d 848 (1969). Discretion has been held to be abused where a trial date has been obtained and the plaintiffs have diligently pursued their case for approximately one year, even though there had been a previous lack of diligent prosecution. *See Spiegelman v. Gold Dust Texaco,* 91 Nev. 542, 539 P.2d 1216 (1975).

Rule 41(e) does not state whether the involuntary dismissal is with or without prejudice. A plaintiff, however, whose claim for relief has been dismissed for want of prosecution under Rule 41(e) and who has failed to appeal from the dismissal order, may not commence another action against the same defendant on the same claim for relief. *See Dubin v. Harrel,* 79 Nev. 467, 386 P.2d 729 (1963). It is therefore clear that a dismissal under Rule 41(e) precludes a subsequent action based upon the same claim for relief. *Williams v. Jensen,* 81 Nev. 658, 408 P.2d 920 (1965). When the court involuntarily dismisses an action for lack of prosecution, it, when justice so requires, may however dismiss the action without prejudice. *See United Association of Journeymen & Apprentices of Plumbing & Pipe Fitting Industry v. Manson,* 105 Nev. 816, 783 P.2d 955 (1989).

§2016. Mandatory dismissal for lack of prosecution.

Rule 41(e) provides three rules of mandatory dismissal. First, any action which is not brought to trial within five years ("the five-year rule") after it is filed must be dismissed. Second, after judgment, and a motion for new trial is made and granted, the action must be dismissed if it is not brought to trial within three years after the entry of the order granting the new trial. Third, when, after judgment, an appeal has been taken, the judgment reversed, and the matter remanded for a new trial, the action must be dismissed if it is not brought to trial within three years from the date the remittitur is filed by the clerk of the trial court.

A dismissal pursuant to Rule 41(e) may be on motion or by the court's own initiative after notice has been given to the plaintiff. It is essential to show that: (1) the applicable time period has passed; (2) that the action has not been "brought" to trial or pursued with due diligence; and (3) that no written stipulation extending the time has been made.

An action is considered to have been "brought" to trial when a litigant obtains a trial date within the statutory period, appears for trial in good faith, argues motions, and examines jurors. *See Smith v. Timm*, 96 Nev. 197, 606 P.2d 530 (1980). It has also been held for the purpose of complying with Rule 41(e) that an action can be "brought to trial" by calling a witness who testifies. *See Ad-Art, Inc. v. Denison*, 94 Nev. 73, 574 P.2d 1069 (1978); *A French Bouquet Flower Shoppe, Ltd. v. Hubert*, 106 Nev. 1990, 793 P.2d 835 (1990). The witness called upon to testify, however, may not be the opposing counsel. *See Lipitt v. State*, 103 Nev. 412, 734 P.2d 108 (1987). It should also be noted that proceedings before a master do not constitute the bringing of an action to trial within the meaning of Rule 41(e). *Garden Park Townhouse Association v. Homewood Builders, Inc.*, 97 Nev. 630, 637 P.2d 1214 (1981).

Rule 41(e) does not mandate dismissal with prejudice. The court may when justice so requires, dismiss an action without prejudice. *United Association of Journeymen & Apprentices of Plumbing & Pipe Fitting Industry v. Manson*, 105 Nev. 816, 783 P.2d 955 (1989).

§ 2017. Exceptions to mandatory dismissal for want of prosecution.

The only stated exception to mandatory dismissal under Rule 41(e) is a written stipulation extending the specified time limit. Words and conduct do not satisfy the written stipulation requirement. *See Great Western Land & Cattle Corp. v. Sixth Judicial District Court ex rel. County of Pershing*, 86 Nev. 282, 467 P.2d 1019 (1970); *Prostack v. Lowden*, 96 Nev. 230, 606 P.2d 1099 (1980). An oral stipulation, however, may satisfy the written stipulation requirement if entered into in open court, approved by the trial judge, and recorded upon the court minutes. *See Prostack, supra*. No exception to the stipulation rule based upon the conduct of the parties will preclude the mandatory dismissal, even if the defendant is responsible for the delays. *See Thran v. First Judicial District Court ex rel. Ormsby County*, 79 Nev. 176, 380 P.2d 297 (1963).

Although perhaps not properly characterized as exceptions to the rule, the Nevada Supreme Court has identified some circumstances in which an action is not subject to mandatory dismissal, notwithstanding the apparent expiration of the stated time period. The court has held that a period during which the parties to an action are prevented from bringing the action to trial by reason of a stay order is not to be counted in determining whether the five year period has elapsed. *See Boren v. City of North Las Vegas*, 98 Nev. 5, 638 P.2d 404 (1982). The court has also held that the policy considerations which underlie the rule of giving a plaintiff three years to bring a case to trial following a remand for new trial require that the plaintiff have an equal amount of time following a remand which is not for a new trial, but rather for the purpose of concluding trial preparation and bringing the matter to trial in the first instance. *McGinis v. Consolidated Casinos Corp.*, 97 Nev. 31, 623 P.2d 974 (1981). These apparent exceptions seem no less worthy than delays that are caused by referring the matter to a special master.

§2018. Effect of involuntary dismissal under Rule 41(e).

The rule specifically states that "a dismissal under this subdivision (e) is a bar to another action upon the same claim for relief against the same defendant unless the court otherwise provides." Therefore, even though dismissal may be mandatory, the court retains discretion over whether the dismissal is with or without prejudice to a subsequent action on the same claim. *Lindauer v. Allen*, 85 Nev. 430, 456 P.2d 851 (1969); *Lighthouse v. Great Western Land & Cattle Corp.*, 88 Nev. 55, 493 P.2d 296 (1972).

CHAPTER 21

ALTERNATIVE DISPUTE RESOLUTION (ADR)

Authors: Lester H. Berkson
          John R. Hawley
          A. William Maupin

§ 2101. Introduction and scope.

Alternate methods of resolving civil disputes are being adopted and utilized nationwide to reduce the time, expense, and intimidation of traditional litigation. The ADR procedures discussed in this chapter include voluntary arbitration, mediation, and mandatory non-binding court annexed arbitration.

§ 2102. Arbitration by agreement.

The Uniform Arbitration Act, NRS 38.015 *et seq.*, provides the statutory framework for arbitrations conducted by mutual agreement of the parties. Some of the advantages and issues raised by arbitration agreements are:

(1) *Prompt Resolution and Informality*: Although parties consenting to arbitration waive the right to directly proceed with a bench or jury trial, see NRS 38.235 allowing trials "de novo" in district court, they often gain the advantage of a more economical and expeditious resolution of the controversy. Also, the parties may waive their rights to trial by agreement that the arbitration is "binding." The parties are provided an arbitration hearing where the rules of evidence are generally relaxed, a situation that allows them to more fully express underlying concerns. Also, the informality of the proceedings reduces the level of intimidation for lay parties. Most arbitrations can be completed within several months, depending on the schedules of the parties.

(2) *Discovery*: The arbitrator has authority to limit discovery. NRS 38.087. Most arbitrators will limit the taking of depositions and will allow depositions only if a real need is shown and the deposition is cost effective. The emphasis is on the exchange of information. Arbitration does not involve the extensive motion practice prevalent in traditional litigation.

(3) *Decision Maker*: In ordinary litigation, the parties have little or no control over which judge will hear a controversy or over his or her qualifications. In arbitration, the parties are able to control the qualifications and expertise of the arbitrator and, under certain circumstances, may appoint more than one arbitrator to hear the case. For example, it is normal in a construction controversy exceeding $200,000 in claims to have a three-arbitrator panel, consisting of an attorney experienced in construction law, an architect, an engineer, or a contractor. This type of panel is ideal for complicated construction matters because of the specific expertise of its members. The same type of advantage exists in any matter where a special background is beneficial. *E.g.*, securities, mining, and personal injury cases.

(4) *Cost Saving*: The cost of an arbitration is often substantially less than the cost of traditional litigation. The primary savings are effected because arbitration may not involve formal discovery or extensive motion practice, is subject only to limited appeal rights, and provides an accelerated and firm hearing date.

§ 2103. Arbitration agreements.

A binding arbitration agreement may take the form of a contract provision requiring that subsequent disputes be arbitrated, or may be created by an independent agreement to arbitrate entered into after the dispute arises. NRS 38.035.

Arbitration clauses in contracts are generally enforceable except where important considerations of public policy are offended. Notable public policy exceptions to enforceability include arbitration clauses in automobile liability policy provisions governing uninsured motorist coverages (NRS 690 B.017), and clauses in adhesion contracts [see *Obstetrics & Gynecologists v. Pepper*, 101 Nev. 105, 693 P.2d 1259 (1985)]. Where the circumstances show mutual consent, arbitration agreements will be enforced even though not signed by the parties. *Campanelli v. Conservas Altamira, S.A.*, 86 Nev. 838, 477 P.2d 870 (1970). An arbitration agreement may delineate venue, the nature of equitable relief available, the number of arbitrators, qualifications of arbitrator(s), whether punitive damages are awardable, provisions for findings of fact and conclusion of law, time limitations, and limitations on what kinds of controversies are arbitrable. There is a strong public policy in Nevada favoring arbitration, and arbitration agreements will be liberally construed by the court. *Phillips v. Parker*, 106 Nev. 415, 794 P.2d 716 (1990). The parties can provide that the American Arbitration Association (AAA) rules will apply, that some other rules will apply, or that the laws of the State of Nevada or of some other jurisdiction are controlling. *Richardson v. Harris*, 107 Nev. 763, 818 P.2d 1209 (1991), in which Nevada law was applied under a conflicts of law analysis in the absence of a choice-of-law provision.

§ 2104. Motion to compel or stay arbitration.

NRS 38.045 provides the statutory authority for a court hearing to determine whether the controversy must be arbitrated. If the opposing party refuses to proceed with arbitration, the party requesting arbitration may file a petition with the court to obtain a hearing on whether arbitration should proceed. Orders to proceed with arbitration are not appealable and the parties must proceed with arbitration. *Clark County v. Empire Electric, Inc.*, 96 Nev. 18, 604 P.2d 352 (1980). Conversely, a party opposing arbitration may request that the district court stay arbitration proceedings pursuant to NRS 38.045, provided such party has a basis to claim the absence of an arbitration agreement. If the stay is granted, the losing party may take an immediate appeal pursuant to NRS 38.205. In either instance, the court summarily determines the question of arbitrability under the purported arbitration agreement. Going further, the Nevada Supreme Court has ruled that all doubts concerning the arbitrability of a dispute are to be resolved in favor of arbitration. *Exber, Inc. v. Sletton Construction Co.*, 92 Nev. 721, 558 P.2d 517 (1976).

§ 2105. Appointment of arbitrator(s).

The arbitration agreement may provide for the number of arbitrators, method of appointment and qualifications. If the parties cannot agree or an arbitrator appointment fails, the court appoints the arbitrator(s). NRS 38.055.

Where the parties agree to utilize the services of a private arbitration service provider, the provider supplies the parties with a list of potential arbitrators. In the event that the parties do not agree upon the arbitrators provided, the arbitration service provider may, if the parties agree, make an administrative appointment itself from the pool being utilized.

§ 2106. Arbitration hearing.

The arbitration agreement may provide for the location and time and place of the hearing. In the absence of an agreement of the parties, NRS 38.075 allows the arbitrator to appoint a time and place for the hearing. The arbitrator may postpone the hearing at the request of a party for good cause. NRS 38.075. If good cause exists and the arbitrator rejects a postponement, the aggrieved party may later move to vacate the award under NRS 38.145. If a party who has been properly notified fails to appear, the arbitrator(s) can proceed to hear the evidence and make an award. § NRS 38.075.

Under NRS 38.075, the "parties are entitled to be heard, to present evidence material to the controversy and to cross-examine witnesses appearing at the hearing." Because most arbitrators will relax rules of evidence, the primary objections to evidence that are normally recognized involve materiality, reliability, and fundamental fairness. Arbitrators are cautious in excluding evidence because awards may be vacated if the arbitrator has refused to hear evidence "material" to the controversy. NRS 38.145(1)(d).

§ 2107. The award.

The only statutory requirement for an award is that it be in writing and signed by the arbitrator(s). NRS 38.105. If there is more than one arbitrator, the award must be made by majority action of the arbitrators. NRS 38.065. Although not necessarily required, an arbitration agreement may require the award to include findings of fact and conclusions of law, or a memorandum opinion. The award should be dispositive of all claims submitted to the arbitration.

§ 2108. Attorney's fees.

Where the agreement submitted to arbitration provides the authority to award attorney's fees to the successful or prevailing parties, the decision of the arbitrator on the issue may not be overturned by the district court. *See New Shy Clown v. Baldwin*, 103 Nev. 269, 737 P.2d 524 (1987). In the absence of such a provision in the arbitration agreement, attorney's fees incurred during arbitration may not be awarded. *See* NRS 38.125 and *County of Clark v. Blanchard Construction Co.*, 98 Nev. 488, 653 P.2d 1217 (1982). However, fees generated in obtaining judicial confirmation under NRS 38.135 may be awarded by the district court. *See* § 2109, *infra*.

§ 2109. Confirmation of award and judgment.

In the absence of an application to vacate or modify the award, any party may apply within one year to confirm the award. NRS 38.135. Upon confirmation, judgment is entered on the award and is enforced like any other judgment. NRS 38.165.

§ 2110. Application to vacate award.

The grounds for vacating an award are limited to those delineated in NRS 38.145. Judicial review of arbitration awards via applications to vacate are governed by the following principles: (1) whether the party seeking arbitration is asserting a claim which on its face is governed by the contract in question; (2) the award must be based upon the agreement and must be enforced by the courts even if the arbitrator's interpretation of the contract is ambiguous or would differ from the court's interpretation; and (3) the arbitrator's decision is bound only by the scope of the submission. *IBEW Local 396 v. Central Telephone Co.*, 94 Nev. 491, 581 P.2d 865 (1978). Unless the arbitration hearing is reported, or the arbitration agreement requires the arbitrator provide findings, it is difficult to establish grounds for vacation of the award.

An application to vacate an award must be made within ninety days after delivery of the award to the applicant. An exception exists where the award is obtained by fraud, corruption, or other undue means, in which case the application must be made within ninety days after such grounds are known or should have been known. NRS 38.145(2).

An award may not be collaterally attacked via independent action. The aggrieved party must move to vacate under NRS 38.145 and thereafter may appeal pursuant to NRS 38.205. *Williams v. New York Meat & Provisions*, 96 Nev. 1, 604 P.2d 357 (1980).

Because NRS 38.145(1)(b) provides that an award may be vacated where evident partiality or corruption of the arbitrator is shown, it is critical for the arbitrator to make full disclosure of any conflicts or past dealings with the parties, attorneys, or witnesses. Likewise, if an attorney for a party during the course of an arbitration becomes aware of a conflict, the conflict should be revealed to give the arbitrator an opportunity to effect recusal.

§ 2111. Appeal.

NRS 38.205 sets forth the statutory grounds for appeals to the Nevada Supreme Court:

1. An appeal may be taken from:

(a) An order denying an application to compel arbitration made under NRS 38.405;

(b) An order granting an application to stay arbitration made under subsection 2 of NRS 38.045;

(c) An order confirming or denying confirmation of an award;

(d) An order modifying or correcting an award;

(e) An order vacating an award without directing a rehearing; or

(f) A judgment or decree entered pursuant to the provisions of NRS 38.015 to 38.205, inclusive.

2. The appeal shall be taken in the manner and to the same extent as from orders or judgments in a civil action.

Extraordinary writs are inappropriate for review of an order confirming an award. The parties are relegated to an appeal solely on the grounds set forth in NRS 38.205.

§ 2112. Trial in district court.

If the parties have not agreed to "binding" arbitration where trial rights are specifically waived by the participants, any party may request a trial of any or all issues litigated in the arbitration. NRS 38.235 outlines the conditions on such requests which are available in addition to the rights of the parties to have arbitration awards modified, vacated, or confirmed.

§ 2113. Mediation.

Mediation is a process in which a neutral person assists opposing parties in reaching settlement short of actual arbitration or trial. The mediator conducts informal joint and private meetings or "caucuses" with the parties to facilitate an examination of the respective interests, positions, and risks involved in continuing on with the litigation process. Confidentiality during private caucus meetings between a single party and the mediator is strictly protected. NRS 48.109 provides confidentiality safeguards that may be taken by the mediator.

Generally, the mediator will caucus separately with the parties during which confidential information may be disclosed to the mediator. Unless the mediator is given permission, the mediator may not disclose the confidential information to the opposing party. This protects the parties from prejudicial communication of trade information or trial strategy in the event the mediation fails.

In agreeing to mediation, the parties relinquish none of their rights and the mediation conference may be discontinued at any point if any party feels the process is unproductive.

§ 2114. Non-binding mandatory arbitration.

Prior to promulgating the Nevada Arbitration Rules, effective July 1, 1992, the only mandatory scheme for arbitration was found in NRS 38.215. This statute applied to all personal injury and property damage cases (subject to the limitations on the amount in controversy discussed below) arising from the ownership, maintenance, or use of motor vehicles within the State of Nevada. The terms of this provision made the arbitrator's ruling provisionally "binding," subject to the right to modify, confirm, or vacate awards via NRS 38.135, .145 and .155, and subject to a conditional right of trial de novo in district court. *See* NRS 38.235. Effective October 1, 1991, the legislature raised the jurisdictional ceiling for such arbitrations to $25,000. However, as is discussed below, mandatory arbitration of motor vehicle cases under NRS 38.215 will be conducted within the confines of the new court-annexed program of mandatory non-binding arbitration. *See* NAR 3. Although NRS 38.215, effective October 1, 1991, requires that motor vehicle cases where the amount at issue does not exceed $25,000 be arbitrated in accordance with the provisions of NRS Chapter 38, the court rules mandate inclusion of these cases in the court annexed arbitration program. *See Volpert v. Papagna*, 85 Nev. 437, 456 P.2d 848 (1989), and *Lindauer v. Allen*, 85 Nev. 430, 456 P.2d 851 (1969). This was not meant as a rejection of the legislative prerogative; it was meant to fulfill the legislative purpose to streamline litigation, to simplify mandatory arbitration procedures by creating a single system rather than two separate systems, and to apply the more specific and comprehensive sanction provisions contained within the court rules to trials de novo in motor vehicle cases (NRS 38.235 only mandates that accrued costs be paid by the party requesting trial prior to proceeding into district court).

§ 2115. Outline of the court annexed arbitration program and its "enabling" legislation.

Under the Nevada Arbitration Rules, all civil actions filed in district courts on or after July 1, 1992, wherein money damages of $25,000 or less are sought, must be submitted to mandatory non-binding arbitration. The program applies to judicial districts with populations in excess of at least 100,000 and to other districts that adopt local rules implementing all or part of the program. NAR 1. The following categories of cases are exempt from mandatory arbitration: class actions; appeals from courts of limited jurisdiction; probate proceedings; divorce and other domestic relations cases; actions seeking judicial review of administrative decisions; actions concerning title to real property; actions for declaratory relief; actions governed by the provisions of 41A.003 to 41A.069 inclusive (medical malpractice cases); actions presenting significant issues of public policy; actions in which the parties have agreed in writing to submit the controversy to arbitration or other alternate dispute resolution method prior to the accrual of the cause of action; actions seeking equitable or extraordinary relief; damage cases filed in justice courts; and actions where the probable jury award would exceed $25,000, exclusive of interest and costs, and regardless of comparative liability.

All cases involving claims for money damages are presumed to be arbitrable. NAR 3 and 5. To demonstrate, all such cases are automatically subject to arbitration if one of the parties does not seek an exemption from arbitration within twenty days of the filing of the Answer by any party defendant [(NAR 5(A)], or where all parties stipulate in writing to "private" arbitration. The discovery commissioner rules on claims for exemption from the program. NAR 5(B).

In specifically exempted matters other than cases where the exemption is based on the presence of important public policy issues or the monetary value of the case, the claim for exemption is dispensed with by simply designating the category of claimed exemption in the caption. NAR 5(A). Probate and domestic relations matters are automatically exempted as a matter of local court procedure in the Eighth Judicial District because of the letter designation preceding their assigned case numbers. In cases where money damages are sought and arbitrability is contested, the discovery commissioner makes an evaluation of the damage claim which is dispositive of the issue of arbitrability. NAR 5(B).

Because of the due process implications of the discovery commissioner's ruling, any party ultimately aggrieved by the arbitration process may have a complete trial de novo before the bench or before a jury. In this way, the arbitration rules do not conflict with the due process requirements of NRCP 56.

Objections to the decision of the discovery commissioner regarding arbitrability must be filed with the district judge to whom the case is assigned within ten days of service of the discovery commissioner's decision on all parties. NAR 5(B). The court's ruling on this issue is not reviewable. NAR 5(C). The district judge is empowered to impose any sanctions authorized by NRCP 11 against any party who without good cause or justification attempts to remove any matter from the arbitration program. NAR 5(D).

NRCP 16.1 is not applicable to matters subject to the arbitration program except with regard to the types of materials which must be exchanged prior to the arbitration hearing. Thus, the NRCP 16.1 early case conference/reporting requirements are dispensed with. NAR 5(C).

§ 2116. Assignment to the arbitrator (NAR 6).

Parties may stipulate to use any person as an arbitrator, including a person who has not been formally appointed to the established panel of arbitrators. Such stipulations must be made and furnished to the discovery commissioner within twenty days after the filing of any answer of any party defendant and must include an affidavit that is signed and verified by the arbitrator named in the stipulation if the person named is not on the panel of arbitrators. NAR 6(A).

If the parties do not stipulate to use a particular arbitrator or some other alternate method of dispute resolution, the discovery commissioner serves the parties with identical lists of arbitrators selected at random from the Panel. NAR 6(C). In cases involving only two parties, a list of five potential arbitrators is submitted by the discovery commissioner's office. If there are more than two adverse parties, two additional arbitrators per each additional party are added to the list (multiple parties represented by one attorney are considered to be one party for the purpose of this rule). NAR 5(E). Each party has ten days to return the list with no more than two names stricken. If the parties to the arbitration each strike two of the potential arbitrators, the remaining panel member on the list becomes the arbitrator. Otherwise, the discovery commissioner simply appoints an arbitrator from the names not stricken. If none of the parties respond within ten days, the discovery commissioner appoints one of the arbitrators on the list. NAR 6(C)(1)-(4).

If an arbitrator is assigned to a case and additional parties are subsequently added to the action, the additional parties may lodge objections to the arbitrator with the discovery commissioner assigned to the case within ten days of the new party's appearance in the action. NAR 6(F). Such challenges must be for cause. Thus, subsequently added parties are denied the benefit of the peremptory challenge process. NAR 6(F).

Rulings of the discovery commissioner relative to the selection of arbitrators are appealable to district court. District court rulings on these issues are not reviewable.

§ 2117. Qualifications of arbitrators (NAR 7).

Under NAR 7, an arbitrator must have "substantial experience" in his or her area of expertise and shall have engaged in such area of expertise for a period of at least three (3) years. Because Nevada has no certification requirements for specialists, the qualifications are, of necessity, broadly based. The State Bar is required to create and maintain the panel of arbitrators. The program also contemplates the limited use of lay arbitrators in special cases involving construction disputes, accounting disputes and the like. All members of the panel, attorneys and nonattorneys, must complete bar-approved training in resolving disputes and early settlement techniques. Once appointed, no arbitrator may use his or her status on the panel for any advertising purpose.

§ 2118. Authority of the arbitrators (NAR 8).

The arbitrator is empowered to administer oaths or affirmations to witnesses; to relax rules of evidence and procedures to effectuate a speedy and economical resolution of the case without sacrificing a full and fair hearing on the merits; to authorize the parties to obtain subpoenas from the district court clerk to compel the attendance of witnesses and the production of evidence; and to set discovery plans. NAR 8(A) and 11. The clear intent of these rules is to give the arbitrator broad discretion, especially with regard to the types and extent of discovery allowed. The $25,000 limit on awards (NAR 16) provides the primary justification for stringent restrictions on expensive discovery procedures.

The arbitrator's rulings regarding discovery are appealable to the discovery commissioner and then to the district court. NAR 8(B). The discovery commissioner has the discretion to enter stay orders pending final rulings by the district court. NAR 8(B). No right of appeal exists beyond the district court level with regard to disputes originally resolved by the arbitrator.

§ 2119. Stipulations, motions, and restrictions on communications during arbitration (NAR 9 and 10).

Pursuant to NAR 4, the only motions that may be filed with the district court while a matter is in arbitration are dispositive motions or motions permitted under NAR 3(A)(1) for a settlement conference, mediation proceeding, or other appropriate settlement technique. Under NAR 9, after the arbitrator is appointed, all stipulations, motions and other documents relative to the arbitration proceeding must be lodged with the arbitrator. Pleadings that challenge the arbitrator's action are filed with and handled by the discovery commissioner. NAR 8(B).

Neither counsel nor the parties may communicate directly with the arbitrator regarding the merits of the case, "except in the presence of, or with reasonable notice to, all of the other parties." NAR 10. Quite importantly, unless otherwise agreed in writing by all parties, no offer or demand of settlement may be disclosed to the arbitrator prior to the filing of an award.

§ 2120. Discovery (NAR 11).

Within thirty days of the appointment of the arbitrator, the parties must meet in the presence of the arbitrator to confer and exchange documents and lists of witnesses that would otherwise be exchanged pursuant to NRCP 16.1. Thus, while the formalities of NRCP 16.1 such as the early case conference report are dispensed with, other major benefits of the rule are maintained. At this initial meeting, a discovery plan is formulated. It is the clear intent of the rules that formal discovery be limited by the arbitrator to reduce the expense and time of litigation. It is therefore of extreme importance that parties be prepared to articulate and defend their discovery plans at the time of the first meeting with the arbitrator. The discretion of the arbitrator will be upheld absent manifest abuse. Thus, these rules place a substantial burden upon informal investigation by the parties.

§ 2121. Scheduling of hearings (NAR 12).

All arbitrations must be conducted and awards filed no later than six months from the date of the appointment of the arbitrator, unless time is extended pursuant to the rule. The arbitration hearing may be advanced or continued by the arbitrator beyond six months for "good cause." NAR 12(B). Requests for continuances beyond nine months must be submitted to the arbitrator based upon a showing of "unusual circumstances." In cases where a continuance beyond nine months from the arbitrator's appointment is sought, the *arbitrator* must personally apply in writing to the district court for the additional time, up to a maximum of twelve months from the arbitrator's appointment. NAR 12(B). *Consolidated actions are to be heard on the date assigned to the latest case involved.*

§ 2122. Pre-hearing statements (NAR 13).

At least ten days prior to the date of the arbitration hearing, each party must furnish the arbitrator and serve upon all other parties a pre-hearing statement containing a final list of witnesses whom the party intends to call at the hearing and a list of exhibits and documentary evidence anticipated to be introduced. NAR 13(A). The witness list in the pre-hearing statement must include a brief description of the matters about which each witness will testify. Simultaneously with the filing of the pre-hearing statement, each party must make all exhibits and documentary evidence available for copying and inspection by the other parties. NAR 13(A).

Each party must also furnish the arbitrator a copy of all pleadings or other documents contained in the court file that the party deems relevant at least ten days prior to the hearing. NAR 13(C). Parties failing to comply with NAR 13 or any discovery order are precluded from introducing omitted evidence except with permission from the arbitrator upon a showing of "unforeseen and unusual" circumstances.

§ 2123. Conduct of the hearing (NAR 14).

The arbitrator has complete discretion over the conduct of the hearing. NAR 14(A). Any party, at its own expense, may have the hearing reported. NAR 14(B). This is important because severe sanctions are available if a party does not participate in the arbitration proceedings in good faith. *See* NAR 22. A transcript is essential to document good faith participation or the lack thereof. Also, a reporter may be indispensable because of the potential need to impeach a witness in the event the matter goes on to a trial de novo.

§ 2124. Arbitration in the absence of a party (NAR 15).

The arbitrator may conduct the arbitration hearing in the absence of parties who have received notice but fail to appear or obtain a continuance in accordance with NAR 12. However, the arbitrator must require the party actually appearing to submit evidence as may be required for the rendition of the award. Also, based upon the presentation of the appearing party, the arbitrator may offer the absent party an opportunity to present evidence at a subsequent hearing, if necessary. NAR 15. It is therefore within the discretion of the arbitrator to render an award in favor of the absent party, based upon the evidence introduced.

§ 2125. Form and content of the award (NAR 16).

The arbitrator must determine all issues raised by the pleadings, including issues of comparative negligence, if any, damages, if any, and costs. The arbitrator is authorized to award any amount deemed appropriate up to the limit of $25,000, "exclusive of attorney's fees and costs." NAR 16(B). Because a literal reading of the arbitrator's authority in this regard would ostensibly restrict awards of prejudgment interest where prejudgment interest would cause the award to exceed $25,000, and because it was never intended that awards of interest be affected in any way by these rules, it appears that the $25,000 limitation refers only to the substantive award, exclusive of *interest*, costs and attorney fees. Otherwise, smaller damage cases in arbitration would receive full awards of prejudgment interest, while awards at or near $25,000 would have the prejudgment interest component either eliminated or substantially reduced by virtue of the $25,000 limitation. NRS 38.255.3(a) also indicates the $25,000 is exclusive of attorney's fees, interest and costs.

Under NAR 16(D), offers of judgment under NRCP 68 and NRS 17 apply to matters in the program, thus giving parties an opportunity to avoid awards of prejudgment interest and costs, but attorney's fees cannot exceed $3,000. Thus, settlement remains an important factor in arbitrated cases.

The costs and fees of the arbitrator must be paid equally by the parties to the arbitration. NAR 23(C) & 24(C). Disputes regarding the arbitrator's fees and costs are resolved by the discovery commissioner. NAR 23(D) & 24(D). The award of attorney's fees is not expressly covered by the rules and would appear to be dependent upon contract or statute. NAR 16(B) includes the award of costs as an issue to be resolved by the arbitrator. However, as the rules do not provide for filing a cost bill with the arbitrator, it would be wise to have an agreement in the record of the arbitration proceeding as to when and how costs and attorney's fees are to be proven.

NAR 16(B) requires the arbitrator to determine all issues raised by the pleadings. If the issue of attorney's fees is raised by the pleadings, the arbitrator would appear to have the authority to decide the issue and award attorney's fees as a part of the award. NAR 16(D) states attorney's fees may not exceed $3,000, but this limitation is in the paragraph dealing with offers of judgment and the rules are not clear as to whether this limitation applies to other situations. However, a similar $3,000 limitation is found in NAR 20(A) for attorney's fees on trials de novo and it may be that $3,000 is the highest attorney's fee that can be awarded in any situation.

Until a determination has been made by the Supreme Court by rule or decision of the procedure to be used to obtain costs and attorney's fees, the use of a Cost Bill is risky.

Findings of Fact and Conclusions of Law, or a written opinion stating the reasons for the arbitrator's decision, may be prepared at the discretion of the arbitrator.

§ 2126. Filings of awards, requests for trial de novo, and judgments on awards (NAR 17, 18 and 19).

The arbitrator must submit the award within seven (7) days after the conclusion of the hearing. This deadline is modified where post-hearing memoranda are received. In such cases, the arbitrator has thirty days from the receipt of the memoranda to file the award. The filing is made with the discovery commissioner and service is made upon all attorneys of record. NAR 17(A).

The arbitrator may amend his award, but only to correct an obvious error in the record. NAR 17 does not authorize the use of amended awards to change the arbitrator's decision on the merits. These motions should toll the time period within which a request for trial de novo must be filed, or within which the discovery commissioner instructs the clerk to enter judgment.

Parties aggrieved by the arbitrator's award have thirty days following service of the award to file with the District Court Clerk a written request for trial de novo. NAR 18. After the request is filed and served, the trial de novo will be processed in the ordinary course of the district court's business. NAR 21. The failure of a party to defend an arbitrated matter in good faith during arbitration proceedings constitutes a waiver of the right to trial de novo. NAR 22(A). Such issues will be determined by the district judge assigned to the case. The district court is also authorized to issue any sanction authorized by NRCP 11 or 37, if it is determined that any party or attorney has engaged in conduct designed to obstruct, delay, or otherwise adversely affect the arbitration proceedings. NAR 22(B).

§ 2127. Fees and costs for arbitrators (ADR Rules 23 and 24).

Arbitrators are allowed $75 per hour as an hourly fee with a maximum fee of $500. To recover the fee and costs, if any, the arbitrator must submit an itemized bill to the parties within five days of the date of the award. NAR 23 and 24.

As already noted, the fees and costs of the arbitrator are to be borne equally by the parties to the arbitration. NAR 23(C) & 24(C).

§ 2128. Filing.

NAR provides for filing of papers with the district court clerk, with the discovery commissioner and with the arbitrator, and also prohibits or conditions certain filings. Local practice may vary, but NAR would seem to provide as to filing;

With the district court clerk:

Plaintiff's complaint.

Defendant's answer, counterclaims and cross-claims.

Answers and replies to cross-claims and counterclaims.

Summons.

Stipulation to be bound by any arbitration ruling or award. NAR 3(C).

A claimed exemption from the program *if* the initial pleading specifically designates the category of claimed exemption in the caption. NAR 5(A). *See* NRCP 10(A) for form of caption.

Request for trial de novo. NAR 18.

Discovery commissioner's notification of the arbitration award. NAR 19.

Judgment upon the arbitration award. NAR 19.

With the discovery commissioner:

Request to exempt the case from the program. NAR 5(A).

Objections to the discovery commissioner's decision on a claim of exemption. NAR 5(B).

Stipulation to use a private arbitrator with accompanying affidavit. NAR 6(A).

Returned list of arbitrator with no more than two names stricken. NAR 6(C)(1).

Objections to the assigned arbitrator by later parties. NAR 6(F).

Notice of appeal from discovery commissioner's ruling on objection to arbitrator. NAR 6(F).

Any challenge to the authority or action of the arbitrator. NAR 8(B).

Petition to review the discovery commissioner's action upon any challenge to the authority or action of the arbitrator. NAR 8(B).

The arbitrator's award. NAR 17(A).

Disputes regarding the arbitrator's costs. NAR 23(C).

Disputes regarding the arbitrator's fees. NAR 24(D).

With the assigned arbitrator:

During the course of the arbitration, all stipulations, motions and other documents relevant to the arbitration proceeding must be lodged with the arbitrator. NAR 9.

Pre-hearing statement. NAR 13(A).

Prohibited filings:

During the pendency of arbitration proceedings conducted pursuant to NAR, no motion may be filed in with the clerk of the district court except motions that are dispositive of the action or motions made pursuant to NAR 3(A)(1) requesting a settlement conference, mediation proceeding, or other appropriate settlement technique. NAR 4(E).

During the course of the arbitration proceedings, no document other than the motions permitted by NAR 4. NAR 9.

Sealed filings:

The discovery commissioner shall seal any arbitration award if a trial de novo is requested and the award shall not be opened until the jury or judge has decided the trial de novo. NAR 20(A).

CHAPTER 22

TRIALS

Authors: E. Leslie Combs, Jr.
            Allan R. Earl

§ 2201. Introduction and scope.

This chapter concerns matters related to the setting and conduct of a trial, including the presentation of cases from opening statement to final argument and also the charging of the jury. It does not include subjects directly relating to jurors, their selection or conduct. That information is found in Chapter 23, *infra*. Nor does it include rules governing competency of witnesses or admissibility of evidence.

§ 2202. Trial defined.

A generally-accepted definition of a trial is that it is an "examination before a competent tribunal, according to the law of the land, of questions of fact or of law put in issue by pleadings, for the purpose of determining the rights of the parties." *Adams v. Orange County Superior Court,* 345 P.2d 466, 469 (Cal. 1959). A simpler definition is that it is a method by which disputes are resolved after a full hearing on the merits. *See Osborne v. Ninth Judicial District Court,* 654 P.2d 124, 128 (Wyo. 1982).

§ 2203. Setting action for trial: governing rules.

NRCP 40 charges the individual district courts with establishing procedures for setting actions for trial. Actions may be set by three different methods: (1) the court may set an action on its own initiative after notice is given to the parties; (2) a party may request a setting after giving notice to other parties; and (3) actions may be set in any manner deemed expedient by the court. This rule is comparable, although not identical, to Fed. R. Civ. P. 40.

NRCP 65(a)(2) authorizes consolidation of a hearing for a preliminary injunction with a trial on the merits. *See* Chapter 28, *infra.*

Local district court rules generally govern applications for a trial date. Where there is no applicable local rule (in the Fourth, Fifth and Sixth Districts), counsel should comply with the relevant provisions of the District Court Rules (DCR). The district court rules applying to trial settings are as follows: DCR 7; FJDCR 5 and 6; WDCR 4; Rule 2 of the Third and Seventh Districts; EDCR 2.60 and 2.65; NJDCR 4.

Matters related to the court calendar, including the setting of actions for trial, ordinarily fall within the discretion of the local district court. *See Monroe, Ltd. v. Central Telephone Co.,* 91 Nev. 450, 456, 538 P.2d 152 (1975); *Close v. Second Judicial District Court,* 73 Nev. 194, 196, 314 P.2d 379 (1957).

Some cases are entitled to statutory priority in setting the date for trial. For example, the courts must give preference in setting a date for trial of actions involving parties who are seventy years of age or older and parties who are terminally ill. NRS 16.210. Therefore, before counsel set the case for trial a determination should be made as to whether the case is entitled to priority on the court's calendar. If so, counsel should take the appropriate steps, such as a motion for trial preference, to make sure that the case is given the priority to which it is entitled.

§ 2204. — Time for application.

Application to set a matter for trial may be made at some point after the case is determined to be "at issue." Generally, a case is at issue when there is no pleading, as defined in NRCP 7, which remains to be answered. *See, e.g.,* EDCR 2.60(a). The Ninth District additionally requires that discovery has been completed. NJDCR 4.

Plaintiff's counsel must keep in mind NRCP 41 governing dismissal of actions for want of prosecution. *See* Chapter 20, *supra,* on dismissals. Counsel must also consider the normal lead time between the date of application for a trial and the next available date on the trial calendar. *See Monroe, Ltd. v. Central Telephone Co.,* 91 Nev. 450, 538 P.2d 152 (1975); *cf. Maheu v. Eighth Judicial District Court,* 89 Nev. 214, 510 P.2d 627 (1973).

§ 2205. — Jury demand.

A demand for a jury trial may be made at any time after the complaint is filed, but in no event later than the order setting the trial date. NRCP 38.

§ 2206. — Setting and removal in the First District.

Since the court's trial calendar is controlled largely by local rules, the method of setting and removing a trial from the calendar will be discussed for each district.

In the First District, application for a trial setting is made by filing and serving on all parties a notice to appear and set a time for trial. The party making application must give all other parties at least five days' notice of the time to appear. On the date given in the notice, one or more parties may appear before the calendar clerk. A "Trial Date Memo" form provided by the calendar clerk is used to apply for a trial date.

If fewer than all parties are present, the calendar clerk, upon proof of proper notice to the absent parties, must set the action on an available date which is satisfactory to those counsel present. FJDCR 5(B). If the parties cannot agree on an available trial date, the court may set the action on the first available date. FJDCR 5(C).

A party objecting to a trial date may seek relief from the court after giving at least five days' notice to all opponents. FJDCR 5(C).

The First District permits multiple settings of actions on the same date. If a case cannot be heard at the time set because another matter takes precedence, the case may be assigned to another available department for trial on the originally scheduled date. If no department is available, the case is entitled to priority in resetting (except as to criminal matters). FJDCR 5(D).

§ 2207. — Setting and removal in the Second District.

In the Second District, a party may apply for a trial date by filing and serving on all parties a notice to appear and set a time for trial. The party making application must give other parties at least ten days' notice of the date to appear. WDCR 4(5). One or more of the parties must then appear before the department's calendar clerk on the date specified in the notice. If fewer than all parties appear for the setting, the calendar clerk must, upon proof of proper written notice, set the trial for a date agreeable to those who are present. WDCR 4(5).

If counsel cannot agree on a trial date, the court department shall set the case for trial on the first available date. WDCR 4(6).

All disputes concerning calendar settings shall be resolved by each court department. WDCR 4(7).

An "Application for Setting" form, available at the calendar clerk's office, is used to apply for a trial date. After the calendar clerk endorses the date, time and department for which the trial is set, the applicant files the original and serves copies on all parties. WDCR 4(9).

A case may only be removed from the calendar by the consent of the trial judge or chief judge if the trial judge is unavailable. WDCR 4(11).

When a judge sets a matter for trial, counsel must deliver a copy of the order, along with the setting form, to the individual responsible for calendaring cases in each court department. WDCR 4(12). If there are multiple settings, the department shall indicate priority in numerical order on the application.

§ 2208. — Setting and removal in the Third District.

Application for a trial date in the Third District is made by filing with the clerk, and serving on all parties, an application for trial setting. The clerk then places the application for setting on the court's law and motion calendar, for a date at least fourteen days after receipt of the application. The clerk sends questionnaires to each party which must be completed and returned prior to the date scheduled for the setting. On the date of the setting, the court sets the matter for the earliest date that is satisfactory to the court and all parties who responded to the questionnaire. The clerk then notifies the parties of the date set. Third DCR 3(A).

§ 2209. — Setting and removal in the Fourth District.

Application for a trial date is accomplished by motion, requiring at least five days' written notice to opposing parties. The court may also set a matter for trial, on its own motion, after five days' notice is given to all counsel. DCR 7.

§ 2210. — Setting and removal in the Fifth District.

The method for setting trials in the Fifth District is the same as for the Fourth District. *See* DCR 7.

§ 2211. — Setting and removal in the Sixth District.

The method for setting trials in the Sixth District is the same as for the Fourth District. *See* DCR 7.

§ 2212. — Setting and removal in the Seventh District.

The method for setting trials in the Seventh District is the same as for the Third District. *See* Seventh DCR 2(1).

§ 2213. — Setting and removal in the Eighth District.

A case commenced by the filing of a complaint is set for trial by a scheduling order issued from the Discovery Commissioner notifying the trial judge of the earliest available date that the case will be ready for trial. EDCR 2.60(a).

The clerk maintains a file folder for each practicing attorney with a case pending in the Eighth Judicial District. After a trial date is set by the judge, a written notice of the date and time of the trial is placed in the attorney's folder. Each attorney has an obligation to check the folder regularly to be informed of trial dates. EDCR 2.65.

Although the court clerk is required to inform parties in proper person of a pending trial date, counsel would be wise to notify such litigants to avoid risk of oversight.

§ 2214. — Setting and removal in the Ninth District.

After the case conference report is filed, the court clerk issues a setting order and notifies counsel of the date to appear to set the trial date. Counsel may appear or fill out an Information Questionnaire. If fewer than all the parties appear on the date specified, upon proof of proper notice, the calendar clerk will set the matter for trial in accordance with the calendars of the counsel who are present. NJDCR 4(a). If the parties cannot agree on a date, the Judicial Assistant will set the case for the next available date. NJDCR 4(b).

A party who objects to the date set for trial may seek relief by motion, but must do so within ten days after the time of setting. NJDCR 4(c).

If a case settles before trial, all parties have a duty to ensure that the Judicial Assistant and the Judge are notified. The rule specifies that notice be given in writing. NJDCR 4(e).

§ 2215. Settlement before trial.

If a case is settled before its trial date, it is a wise practice either to appear at court and have the stipulation entered in the minutes in the form of an order or to reduce the settlement agreement to writing. No agreement is binding unless such a procedure is followed.

Additionally, it is a generally-recognized rule that an attorney, without specific authority from his client, is prohibited from compromising his client's case. *Van Fleet v. O'Neil*, 44 Nev. 216, 192 P. 384 (1920). It is also important to remember that a settlement involving a minor, regardless of whether or not a complaint has been filed, must be approved by the district court through the use of a formal motion to compromise a minor's claim. NRS 41.200.

Prompt notification of settlement should be given to the judge's chambers and to the calendar clerk; it is important not only to the court's efficient administration but also to other litigants whose cases are set behind the action that settled. See the preceding section on the proper method of removing a case from the calendar in the various districts.

§ 2216. Postponements and continuances.

In Nevada, the term "continuance" is frequently used to refer both to a postponement in starting a trial and to a temporary adjournment in the trial after it has begun.

Statutes applicable to continuances are found in NRS 16.010, 16.020 and 1.310. NRS 16.020(2) specifically governs continuances in actions involving mining claims. In addition, NRS 1.310 authorizes continuances during the legislative session for trials involving attorneys or parties who are members of the legislature.

The procedure for obtaining a continuance is governed largely by local rules discussed below. A close scrutiny of the local rules is required, as they are updated frequently.

Application for a continuance may be by motion or by stipulation. In addition, the court may continue a matter on its own initiative.

Certain of the local rules require client notification when a continuance is sought on the client's behalf. *See, e.g.,* WDCR 13; EDCR 7.30(c). It is always good practice to discuss in advance with clients whether to seek a continuance.

§ 2217. — Motions to continue.

A motion for a continuance is addressed to the discretion of the trial court. *Southern Pacific Transportation Co. v. Fitzgerald,* 94 Nev. 241, 243, 577 P.2d 1234 (1978); *Sheeketski v. Bortoli,* 86 Nev. 704, 708, 475 P.2d 675, 678 (1970).

In all but the Eighth District, DCR 14 appears to control the procedure for seeking a continuance by motion. In the Eighth District, see Rule 7.30.

A motion for a continuance must be supported by affidavit unless exigencies of time prevent it. DCR 14(1). A copy of the affidavit must be served on the opposing party as soon as possible after the moving party becomes aware of the cause for the continuance. DCR 14(4). Amendment or supplementation of the affidavit is not permitted at the time of the hearing. DCR 14(6). Counter-affidavits may be filed in opposition to a continuance. DCR 14(5).

The Second District additionally requires a statement as to whether a continuance has previously been requested or granted and whether counsel seeking a continuance has so advised his or her client. WDCR 13.

See § 2219, *infra,* for affidavits concerning absent witnesses or evidence.

Compliance with the rules on the content of affidavits is mandatory, and a denial of a continuance where the requirements have not been met will generally be upheld. DCR 14(3); *Woodruff v. Woodruff,* 94 Nev. 1, 3, 573 P.2d 206 (1978); *Dodd v. Cowgill,* 85 Nev. 705, 712, 463 P.2d 482 (1969). Defects in a motion or supporting affidavit are waived, however, if not raised in the trial court. *Smith v. Timm,* 96 Nev. 197, 200, 606 P.2d 530 (1980).

If time prevents the filing of an affidavit in support of a continuance, counsel for the moving party must be sworn and testify orally as to the basis for the motion. DCR 14(1). *Bustos v. Sheriff,* 87 Nev. 622, 624, 491 P.2d 1279 (1971) (criminal case involving oral declaration).

Rule 7.30 of the Eighth District is comparable to DCR 14; however, the rule also requires proof of notice to clients when a continuance is sought within thirty days of the trial date, EDCR 7.30(c), and, except in emergencies, at least three days' notice must be given to all opposing parties of a hearing on the motion, which must be held at least one day before trial. EDCR 7.30(f).

§ 2218. — Stipulations to continue.

Generally, even stipulations for continuances must be predicated on a showing of good cause. Several districts require approval of the judge. *See, e.g.,* FJDCR 4(C); EDCR 7.30(f).

The First District requires that the stipulation be in writing and imposes a time restriction, requiring filing at least ten days prior to a jury date or at least five days prior to the start of a bench trial. FJDCR 4(C).

The Second District requires a statement as to whether previous requests for a continuance have been made or granted and whether the parties have been notified of the stipulation. WDCR 13.

A stipulation for continuance in the Third District must be signed by counsel, endorsed by all parties, and filed not less than ten days prior to the trial date. Approval of the judge apparently is not required. Third DCR 5.

§ 2219. — Grounds for continuance.

A continuance should not be sought except for good cause. Absence of an important witness or material evidence are two recognized bases for seeking a continuance. *See, e.g.,* NRS 16.010; DCR 14.

A motion for postponement due to the absence of evidence must be supported by an affidavit showing the materiality of the anticipated evidence and establishing that due diligence was exercised to procure it. The court may require the moving party to state under oath the nature of the evidence which is anticipated. Postponement will be denied if the opposing party either stipulates to the anticipated evidence or shows that it would be inadmissible in any event. NRS 16.010; *O'Neil v. New York & Silver Peak Mining Co.,* 3 Nev. 141, 144 (1867) (stipulation); *Taylor v. Nevada-California-Oregon Railway,* 26 Nev. 415, 426, 69 P. 858 (1902) (inadmissible evidence).

In all districts except the Eighth District, DCR 14 governs the procedure for seeking a continuance based upon the absence of a witness. The motion must be supported by an affidavit setting forth facts which would justify a postponement, including the identity, location and significance of the absent witness and counsel's own lack of culpability as to the circumstances necessitating the continuance. DCR 14(2) specifies the exact requirements for the affidavit. *See* EDCR 7.30(b) for practice in the Eighth District.

A party's failure to exercise diligence in obtaining a pretrial deposition of the absent witness may justify denial of a continuance. *See Thornton v. Malin,* 68 Nev. 263, 229 P.2d 915 (1951). *See also* EDCR 7.30(b)(2). *But see Yori v. Cohn,* 26 Nev. 206, 65 P. 945 (1901); *Beatty v. Sylvester,* 3 Nev. 228 (1867).

Proof that a witness is under subpoena may be an important factor in establishing diligence. See the subsequent section on witnesses and subpoenas.

Other grounds for postponement may require that the party, rather than counsel, affirmatively establish blamelessness for the requested delay in trial. For example, the last minute withdrawal, substitution or engagement of counsel is not by itself justification for a continuance. It must be shown that the party was without fault in the withdrawal or change of attorneys. *Benson v. Benson,* 66 Nev. 94, 98, 204 P.2d 316 (1949); *see also Baer v. Amos J. Walker, Inc.,* 85 Nev. 219, 220, 452 P.2d 916 (1969).

Similarly, the absence of a party or counsel caused by illness is not automatic grounds for a continuance. *See generally Dodd v. Cowgill,* 85 Nev. 705, 463 P.2d 482 (1969).

§ 2220. — Conditions upon granting a continuance.

A party obtaining a continuance must permit the taking of certain depositions to preserve testimony for trial and may be required to pay certain costs as a condition of obtaining the continuance.

Under NRS 16.020, the party obtaining a postponement must permit depositions to be taken of any of the opposing party's witnesses who are then in attendance. The depositions may be used with the same effect as if the witnesses were produced at trial.

NRS 18.070(1) grants discretion to the judge or master to order payment of costs occasioned by postponement of a trial as a condition for granting the postponement. *See also Jacobson v. Stern,* 96 Nev. 56, 605 P.2d 198 (1980); *see generally Luke v. Coffee,* 31 Nev. 165, 101 P. 555 (1909). Entry of judgment as a sanction against a party who failed to pay costs has been upheld. *See Brown v. Warren,* 17 Nev. 417, 30 P. 1078 (1883).

An opponent to a motion for continuance should move for costs as a condition of the continuance. The judge should then require the filing of a memorandum of costs pursuant to NRS 18.

§ 2221. Subpoenas for trial.

It is good practice, and common courtesy, to notify in writing both the client and vital witnesses of their appearance date as far in advance of trial as possible. Early notice allows witnesses to arrange their work schedules and vacations accordingly.

Counsel should ordinarily serve subpoenas on all witnesses in order to guarantee their appearance. In contrast to depositions, no statute or rule requires a party to attend trial unless under subpoena. If a party or other crucial witness fails to attend trial, and is not under subpoena, counsel may be unable to establish good cause for a continuance. (See the preceding section). In other situations where compulsion of the witness to appear is not absolutely necessary, the subpoena may nonetheless help the witness in arranging to miss work or in finding the proper courtroom.

Depositions may be used in place of live testimony. However, if the witness is within the jurisdiction of the court, the party offering the deposition must show that they were unable to procure the attendance of the witness by subpoena. NRCP 32(a)(3).

NRS 50.165 imposes a duty upon a witness, who has been properly served with a subpoena, to appear at the trial at the date and time specified, to bring any specified papers which are under the witness' control, and to remain at trial until either the testimony is closed or the witness is discharged. A witness who is not under subpoena but who is actually present in court or before a judicial officer is charged with the same obligations. NRS 50.165(2).

§ 2222. — Witness fees and allowance.

A witness who is under subpoena is entitled to fees for each day of attendance (as opposed to day of testimony) and an allowance for mileage from the witness' residence. NRS 50.225; *see Lamar v. Urban Renewal Agency*, 84 Nev. 580, 445 P.2d 869 (1968), *overruled on other grounds, Casey v. Williams*, 87 Nev. 137, 482 P.2d 824 (1971). Unless at least one day's fees and mileage allowance have been paid, the witness is not required to appear. NRS 50.225.

Any witness who attends the trial and is sworn is entitled to fees regardless of service of a subpoena. NRS 50.225(2)(b).

An attorney serving in the pending action is not entitled to any fees if called to testify. NRS 50.255.

The amount for fees and mileage for lay witnesses is set in NRS 50.225. The amount of fee to which an expert witness is entitled, when not specifically retained by the party calling the witness, is not set in any rule or statute. However, by analogy to the rules of discovery, counsel should move the court to set a reasonable fee for the expert's testimony. *Cf.* NRCP 26(b)(4)(C)(i) and NRCP 30(h).

A contract to pay for testimony, which makes the right of compensation contingent upon the outcome of the litigation, is void, at least if the witness' only interest in the outcome of litigation is based upon that contract. *Western Cab Co. v. Kellar*, 90 Nev. 240, 244, 245, 523 P.2d 842 (1974).

§ 2223. — Testimony from incarcerated persons.

Securing the testimony of one who is incarcerated either in a state prison or a county jail is controlled by NRS 50.215. A prisoner is under the same compulsion to answer at trial as if under a subpoena. *Maxwell v. Rives*, 11 Nev. 213, 219 (1876). As a practical matter, the testimony of incarcerated witnesses should be procured by deposition pursuant to NRCP 30.

§ 2224. — Issuance of subpoenas.

NRCP 45 governs procedure related to witness subpoenas. The clerk of the court is authorized to issue blank subpoenas which are signed and sealed. Counsel inserts the title of the action and specifies the time and place where the witness is commanded to appear. The subpoena may also direct the witness to bring documents or other physical evidence.

§ 2225. — Service of subpoenas.

Anyone who is eighteen years of age or older, but not a party to the action may serve a subpoena. The sheriff or deputy sheriff is also empowered to serve subpoenas. NRCP 45(c). An attorney may not be permitted to serve a subpoena. *Nevada Cornell Silver Mines, Inc. v. Hankins,* 51 Nev. 420, 279 P. 27 (1929) (the attorney for the plaintiff was not permitted to serve a summons). A subpoena for trial may be served anywhere within the state. NRCP 45(e). Rule 45(c) requires that service be made personally, not through the mail or by delivering to an agent. It is accomplished by showing an original and giving a copy of the subpoena to the person.

Unless the subpoena is issued on behalf of the State of Nevada or its agency, the person under subpoena may require payment in advance of fees and allowable mileage for one day's attendance. NRCP 45(c). (This portion of the rule departs from Fed. R. Civ. P. 45(c), which requires tendering fees and mileage without demand.) As a practical matter, fees and estimated mileage allowance should always be tendered with the subpoena since, under NRS 50.225(2)(a), a person is not obliged to testify unless one day's fees and mileage have been paid.

Proof of service is made by filing either the sheriff's return or the affidavit of any other person making the service.

§ 2226. — Subpoena duces tecum at trial.

A subpoena duces tecum commands a witness to bring to court documents or other tangible things under the witness' control. NRCP 45(b); *see also* NRS 50.165(1). The materials sought should be designated as specifically as possible.

§ 2227. — Sanctions.

Failure to obey a subpoena without a legal excuse may be deemed a contempt of court. NRCP 45(f). If a witness fails to attend trial, a warrant may be issued to the county sheriff to arrest and bring the witness before the court. NRS 50.205. The witness must pay the aggrieved party $100 in addition to all damages sustained because of the failure to attend. NRS 50.195(2).

Refusal to be sworn or to answer, when no legal privilege is invoked, is also punishable as a contempt. NRS 50.195(1); *Maxwell v. Rives,* 11 Nev. 213, 220 (1876). This is true even if the witness is not under subpoena. NRS 50.195(1); *Maxwell, supra.* If the refusing person is a party, the court may strike any pleading or enter a judgment against the party. NRS 50.195(1).

§ 2228. — Relief from a subpoena.

A motion to quash or modify the subpoena, sometimes styled as a "Motion for Protective Order," is the appropriate vehicle to obtain relief from a subpoena. The motion must be made no later than the time of compliance specified on the subpoena. A subpoena duces tecum may be quashed or modified, pursuant to NRCP 45(b), if it is unreasonable or oppressive; it may also be conditionally denied until the reasonable cost of producing materials is advanced by the party serving the subpoena. A motion for relief is also appropriate where the evidence sought is privileged.

§ 2229. — Recovery of witness fees as litigation costs.

Witness fees must be taxed as costs against the losing party upon submission of an affidavit that the fees were actually incurred (unless the court determines that a witness was called without reason or necessity). NRS 50.225(3); 18.005(4). Fees are recoverable even though the witnesses have not yet been paid. NRS 18.110(2). Restrictions on recoverable witness fees are found in NRS 18.005, 18.020, and 50.225(3). NRS 18.110 specifies the requirements for recovering costs.

§ 2230. Order of the trial.

Matters relating to the conduct of a trial are controlled by the court's discretion. *Screen v. Screen,* 76 Nev. 60, 64, 65, 348 P.2d 756 (1960).

The normal order of proceedings for a jury trial is set forth in NRS 16.090. This course of events is mandatory unless the court, for special reasons, orders otherwise:

(1) Before jury voir dire, the parties may either have the pleadings read or they or the court may give a brief explanation of the nature of the case along with the names of prospective witnesses.

(2) The jury is selected and sworn.

(3) After the jury has been selected and sworn, counsel for each side may give an opening statement. (The defense may make an opening statement immediately after the plaintiff's statement or may wait until the start of its own case).

(4) Evidence is presented by the plaintiff and defendant.

(5) Both parties may offer rebuttal evidence (unless the court specifically permits them to offer additional evidence on their case in chief.

(6) If there are multiple parties and separate claims or defenses involving different counsel, the court determines the order of presenting evidence and argument.

(7) The court settles and gives jury instructions. (Additional jury instructions may be given later if necessitated by closing argument).

(8) The parties may give closing arguments. If arguments are given, the plaintiff must give the first argument. The plaintiff is entitled to give the concluding argument.

§ 2231. — Order of evidence.

The taking of evidence is the central part of the trial. The court is charged with the obligation and authority to control the mode and order of taking evidence. The manner of taking evidence should serve the following ends: effectiveness, efficiency, and avoidance of harassment and embarrassment of the witnesses. NRS 50.115(1). The court has discretion to limit the amount of evidence or the number of witnesses. *Couturier v. Couturier,* 76 Nev. 60, 64, 348 P.2d 756 (1960).

The party bearing the burden of proof, ordinarily the plaintiff, presents its case first. *Cf. Truckee River General Electric Co. v. Durham,* 38 Nev. 311, 149 P. 61 (1915) (in eminent domain proceedings, defense may start since it bears burden of proof). Next, the defendant's evidence is presented, and then evidence "in chief" on any counterclaim or cross-claim. The plaintiff may introduce rebuttal evidence, and if there is a counterclaim, any evidence in opposition to it. The defendant may then introduce rebuttal evidence. In cases involving multiple parties, the court directs the order of evidence.

The extent to which a party may anticipate a defense in its case in chief is controlled by the court's discretion. *Gillson v. Price,* 18 Nev. 109, 119, 1 P. 459 (1883); *but see Bailey v. Butner,* 64 Nev. 1, 16, 176 P.2d 226 (1947). The court in its discretion may also permit evidence to be presented out of order; the opposing party must object immediately to the evidence to preserve the issue for appeal. *Warner v. Dillon,* 92 Nev. 677, 679, 558 P.2d 540 (1976).

§ 2232. — Reopening after resting.

Each side rests after having had the opportunity to present its case in chief and to provide rebuttal evidence, if any. Reopening of a case, after resting, may occur at any stage of the proceedings. New or former witnesses may be called, and documentary evidence may be introduced. The adverse party is then given an opportunity for rebuttal.

A party has no right to reopen its case after having rested, but upon motion the court may permit the party to do so. *See Zasucha v. Allen,* 56 Nev. 339, 343, 51 P.2d 1029 (1935). Although the court's decision is discretionary, if an essential element of a case can easily be established by reopening, refusal to do so may constitute abuse of discretion. *See Zasucha v. Allen,* 56 Nev. 339, 343, 51 P.2d 1029 (1935) and *Andolino v. State,* 99 Nev. 345, 662 P.2d 631 (1983).

A party wishing to have its case reopened should be prepared to make an "offer of proof" on the record concerning the value of the anticipated testimony. Failure to do so may constitute waiver of the issue and preclude appellate review. NRS 47.040(b); 47.050; *see Meinhold v. Clark County School District,* 89 Nev. 56, 506 P.2d 420 (1973).

§ 2233. Opening statements.

After the jury has been selected and sworn, counsel for both sides may make opening statements. NRS 16.090(1). Plaintiff's counsel makes the initial statement. Immediately afterward, the defense may make its opening statement or may wait until the presentation of its case.

Generally speaking, an opening statement in a jury trial should never be waived. There may, however, be exceptional circumstances under which the defense chooses either to waive or give only a brief opening statement. Opening statements are more frequently waived in trials to the bench since the pleadings or trial statement should provide sufficient introduction for the court.

§ 2234. — Purpose and scope.

The object of an opening statement is to create a context for the proof a party intends to present and to make it easier for the trier of fact to follow the evidence and witnesses. Generally, the opening statements consist of a brief outline of the evidence which the parties believe they will be able to present.

The statement need not be long to be effective. In fact, it should be as brief as possible. Often, ten to fifteen minutes is ample time and consistent with the jury's attention span. Although the technique of an effective presentation is beyond the scope of this section, counsel should consider providing a thorough but simple outline of the case, including identification of the parties and explanation of any details (such as technical terms) which are important to understanding the case. Sometimes it is necessary to include (and defuse) matters which are potential problems for a party.

Counsel should also consider securing permission to use visual aids and trial exhibits which have been approved in advance by the court. Counsel may wish to make individual copies of key exhibits for each juror to use during testimony. Permission of the court should be obtained in advance, for example, at a pretrial conference.

§ 2235. — Legal sufficiency.

It is important that plaintiff's counsel outline a prima facie case in the opening statement. Although no Nevada decision considers the subject, other jurisdictions have held that failure to state a prima facie case in opening statement might be grounds for dismissal. *See, e.g., Best v. District of Columbia,* 291 U.S. 411, 54 S. Ct. 487, 78 L. Ed. 882 (1934). If an element of a claim is omitted, counsel should be given opportunity to amend the statement. Since such a dismissal ordinarily would not be on the merits, denying the opportunity to amend would only result in the inconvenience of resetting the case. *See Best, supra.*

§ 2236. — Objectionable content.

Opening statements should not be patently argumentative nor should they include other kinds of improper references, including mention of clearly objectionable evidence, allegations which will not be supported by admissible evidence, matters which are subject to a pending motion in limine, or insulting references to opponents. Objectionable remarks may not only be stricken, but if serious enough, may precipitate a mistrial. *Cf. Maxworthy v. Horn Electric Service,* 452 F.2d 1141 (4th Cir. 1972) (good faith test applied in federal court to references to inadmissible evidence or unprovable facts).

§ 2237. Exclusion of witnesses.

Before the taking of evidence, one party will typically move to exclude all witnesses from the courtroom until the time of their actual testimony. The court may also order the exclusion of witnesses on its own motion. NRS 50.155(1).

The rule of exclusion does not apply to the parties or to their attorneys nor does it apply to an officer or employee of any party (other than a natural person) who is designated as its representative. NRS 50.155(2)(a)(b). Anyone else whose presence is shown to be essential to the presentation of either side's case is also excepted from the rule. This exception is sometimes used to permit an expert witness to remain in the courtroom. *See* NRS 50.155(2)(c). Particularly in complex matters, it may be wise for counsel to have an expert in the courtroom in order to listen to testimony and help prepare the attorney for direct or cross-examination. Permission should be obtained through a pretrial conference or a motion in limine.

The court must order the exclusion of witnesses if a request is made by any party. NRS 50.155. Prejudice is presumed from the court's refusal to do so, and the error will not be deemed harmless unless the record reveals that the unsequestered witnesses' testimony was not influenced by the hearing of other testimony. *Cf. Givens v. State,* 99 Nev. 50, 55, 657 P.2d 97 (1983) (criminal case). Violation of the sequestration rule has important implications for retrial since the presumed prejudice will in many cases prevent any future testimony of the tainted witnesses. *See Givens, supra,* 99 Nev. at 56, 657 P.2d at 101.

§ 2238. Taking of evidence.

The most common method of proof is testimonial evidence from in-court witnesses. However, a number of other methods are authorized under the rules and statutes, some having distinct advantages over testimonial evidence. These options include tangible or demonstrative evidence, pleadings, stipulations, judicial notice, presumptions and discovery-generated materials. Methods of proof should be selected on the basis of their availability, efficiency, effectiveness and capacity to stimulate the jurors' interest.

The taking of testimony is governed both by statute and the Rules of Civil Procedure. Chapters 47 through 56 of the NRS set forth the substantive rules of evidence. NRCP 43, substantially similar to FRCP 43, establishes the procedure for taking evidence.

Testimony of witnesses must be taken orally, in open court, unless a statute or rule of procedure permits otherwise. NRCP 43(a). When appropriate, the court may appoint interpreters, set a reasonable fee for the service, and direct the source of the payment. NRCP 43(d). In the Eighth District, an interpreter will be supplied by the court upon 48 hours' notice and tender of the required fees. EDCR 7.80.

Every witness is required to take an oath or affirmation to testify truthfully before giving evidence. NRS 50.035; NRCP 43(b).

Whether witnesses not reasonably disclosed to the opposing party may be precluded from testifying is discussed in Chapter 17, *supra,* on pretrial conferences.

The competency of a witness to testify is determined by the court upon substantive legal principles. *See generally Smith v. State,* 100 Nev. 570, 688 P.2d 326 (1984); *Lanoue v. State,* 99 Nev. 305, 661 P.2d 874 (1983). There is, however, a general presumption that a witness is competent to testify. NRS 50.015. A preliminary examination of either lay or expert witnesses, called voir dire, may be conducted by the opposing party if there appears to be an issue of competency. Some judges require tender of the witness to the court for approval and recognition as an expert witness after foundation questions as to the qualifications of the witnesses.

The judge is empowered to question and even to call witnesses. NRS 50.145. The credibility of a witness, however, is determined by the trier of fact. Thus, once a witness is permitted to testify in a jury trial, the judge may not comment on the witness' credibility to the jury. Nev. Const. Art. 6, § 12; NRS 3.230; *see also Gordon v. Hurtado,* 91 Nev. 641, 541 P.2d 533 (1975).

§ 2239. — Direct examination of witnesses.

Examination by the party calling the witness is called direct examination. The purpose of direct examination is to present, in an understandable fashion, the facts necessary to establish a party's case. Care should be taken that each element of the plaintiff's case is established by the direct examination of one or more witnesses. There must be sufficient proof of facts to support findings of fact in a bench trial or jury instructions in a jury trial. If possible, direct examination should also be sufficiently dramatic and interesting to hold the jury's attention. In preparing for trial, counsel should make a list of witnesses to be called and the facts to which each can testify.

Generally, leading questions (those suggesting their own answers) cannot be used in direct examination without permission of the court. NRS 50.115(3)(a). An important exception to the rule is where a party calls either an adverse party, a witness identified with an adverse party, or a hostile or unwilling witness. NRS 50.115(4).

§ 2240. — Cross-examination of witnesses.

After the direct examination of a witness, opposing parties may cross-examine. Cross-examination may be used to bolster a party's case by emphasizing areas of agreement, confirming the testimony of a party's own witnesses, or establishing the credibility or credentials of a party's witness (particularly an expert) through an opponent's witness. It may also be used to attack the opponent's case by discrediting the opponent's witnesses.

Cross-examination is generally limited to matters introduced on direct examination. NRS 50.115(2). Bias, truthfulness (including a history of certain criminal convictions) and accuracy are considered appropriate subjects for cross-examination even though they are not normally a part of direct examination. NRS 50.115(2); *see also Van Fleet v. O'Neil,* 44 Nev. 216, 192 P. 384 (1920). The court, in its discretion, may permit inquiry into matters which were not raised on direct examination. NRS 50.115(2); *see also Anderson v. Berrum,* 36 Nev. 463, 136 P. 973 (1913).

A party may call an adverse witness in their case in chief and may examine that witness using leading questions. However, the adverse party in cross-examination of that witness may not use leading questions, and the scope of the cross-examination is limited to the evidence elicited in the direct examination. NRS 50.115(2) and (4).

The court has discretion to limit the length of cross-examination. *See Foster v. Bank of America,* 77 Nev. 365, 365 P.2d 313 (1961); *see also Sullivan v. McNeill,* 74 Nev. 339, 331 P.2d 853 (1958). Counsel must inform the court of the basis for extending the examination (*i.e.,* make an offer of proof) in order to preserve an objection to such an order. *See Dyer v. State,* 99 Nev. 422, 663 P.2d 699 (1983).

§ 2241. — Redirect and recross-examination.

The purpose of redirect examination is to rebuild the testimony elicited on direct examination. This may be done by returning to the orderly structure of direct examination, by explaining any apparent inconsistencies, or by pointing out areas of weak attack. Although the scope of redirect is generally limited to matters raised in cross-examination, it may be expanded at the court's discretion.

The opportunity to recross-examine a witness is generally left to the sound discretion of the judge.

§ 2242. — Refreshing the witness' recollection.

Witnesses may use any writing to refresh their recollection. This is particularly useful in examining doctors, police officers and other witnesses whose memory may need refreshing in order to report details accurately.

A common threshold question to obtain use of a writing for these purposes is to ask the witness if he or she can recall the facts without reference to the report.

When a witness uses a report to refresh his or her recollection, the adverse party is entitled to inspect it, to cross-examine the witness from the statement, and to introduce portions of the statement relating to the witness' testimony and credibility. NRS 50.125(1). The court is authorized to excise portions of the statement not relating to the witness' testimony before it is turned over to the adverse party. NRS 50.125(2). Sanctions are provided for failure to produce a requested statement. NRS 50.125(3).

The document used to refresh is generally not admitted into evidence unless admissible under a separate hearsay exception.

§ 2243. — Impeachment of witnesses.

A witness may be impeached by any party, even the party calling the witness. The same witness may be impeached by both sides. NRS 50.075. Several methods of impeachment are discussed below.

Impeaching by evidence of a prior conviction is limited to certain kinds of felonies occurring within the relatively recent past. Counsel should carefully check the statutory requirements for compliance. *See* NRS 50.095. The Courts do not condone the use of cross-examination that insinuates criminal convictions which cannot be proved. *Tomarchio v. State,* 99 Nev. 572 (1983). The best practice is to have an exemplified copy of the judgment of conviction available at trial.

Witnesses may also be impeached by the use of prior inconsistent statements. In Nevada, the statement need not be shown to the witness, nor is counsel required to disclose its contents before questioning the witness. However, upon request, the statement must be shown or disclosed to opposing counsel. NRS 50.135.

Either side may use the deposition testimony of a witness to impeach or contradict the witness' testimony. NRCP 32(a)(1).

Although a party may impeach a witness with a prior contradictory statement, that statement is not admissible as substantive evidence unless either of two conditions is satisfied. First, a prior statement is admissible if it is not hearsay under NRS 51.035. Alternatively, the statement can be admitted into evidence if the witness is given an opportunity to explain or deny it, and opposing counsel is permitted to question the witness on the statement. NRS 50.135(2).

§ 2244. — Documentary or other tangible evidence.

Physical (or demonstrative) evidence provides an almost unlimited source of proof. It includes the following: photographs, films, sound recordings, written instruments, treatises, machinery, the human body and its parts, illustrative tests and experiments, computer-generated graphics, product samples and clothing. Demonstrative evidence is a particularly effective form of proof since it operates directly on the jurors' senses and does not require the intervention of a witness.

Demonstrative evidence may be introduced after it has been authenticated by a witness (unless a statute authorizes introduction by another method). Before introduction (and in most courts, before trial), the evidence is marked (by letter for Defendant or number for Plaintiff) for identification purposes. Other parties may examine it, inquire about its authentication, and challenge its admissibility. This process is called voir dire. The offering party may then move for its introduction, and if no objection is sustained, it becomes part of the evidence.

Where a serious dispute is anticipated as to the admission of tangible evidence, counsel should prepare in advance a memorandum of law or a motion in limine on its admissibility. (See § 2255, *infra*). If the material sought to be admitted is particularly dramatic (*e.g.,* gruesome photographs) it is advisable to keep the materials concealed from the jury until admitted in order to avoid the possibility of a mistrial if the proof is refused. Counsel may request a hearing on the matter outside the presence of the jury.

The jury is entitled to read or examine the exhibit after it is admitted. If not admitted, it retains its identification mark for purposes of appeal. Counsel must make sure that the exhibit is formally admitted into evidence; otherwise, it is not a part of the record for any purpose, including the sustaining of a verdict or judgment. *See Burroughs Corp. v. Century Steel, Inc.,* 99 Nev. 464, 664 P.2d 354 (1983).

§ 2245. — Facts admitted in pleadings.

Facts admitted in pleadings do not require independent proof. *See Richards v. Steele,* 60 Nev. 66, 99 P.2d 641 (1940). NRS 16.090(1) appears to permit a party to read its own pleadings, but does not necessarily mandate, upon request, the reading of an opponent's pleading. In a jury trial, a party seeking to have the opposing party's pleadings read should raise the matter in a pre-trial conference, and enter into a stipulation of admitted facts or request that the court take judicial notice of those facts.

§ 2246. — Stipulations.

Stipulations between the parties as to a fact or facts may substitute for other proof to that effect. *See* Chapter 11, *supra.*

§ 2247. — Judicial notice.

Judicial notice may be taken as to certain matters of fact and matters of law. NRS 47.130, 47.140. If requested by a party, and furnished with the necessary basis, the court must take judicial notice of a matter. NRS 47.150. The court must also take judicial notice of the law of the case as propounded in a prior appeal. *Andolino v. State,* 99 Nev. 346, 662 P.2d 631 (1983).

§ 2248. — Presumptions.

Presumptions allow a fact to be proven by the establishment of certain other foundational facts. A presumption may be rebuttable or conclusive. A rebuttable presumption shifts the burden of proof to the other side to establish that it is more likely than not that the presumed fact does not exist. NRS 47.180. Examples of rebuttable presumptions are found in NRS 47.150. The statutory list of rebuttable presumptions is not exclusive. *Privette v. Faulkner,* 92 Nev. 353, 550 P.2d 404 (1976). A list of conclusive presumptions is found in NRS 47.240. Methods for establishing presumptions are found in NRS 47.190, 47.200, 47.210, 47.220.

§ 2249. — Discovery-generated materials.

Discovery-generated materials, including depositions upon oral examination or written interrogatories, answers to interrogatories, and Rule 36 admissions are excellent sources of proof at trial. A pre-trial conference provides an opportunity for counsel to present to the court the materials sought to be introduced at trial. The court may then resolve any disputes over their use, including the elimination of objectionable parts.

Counsel should file the original discovery documents with the court before they are used. NRCP 5(d). The materials, or excerpts from them, are then read to the jury, or in the case of bench trials, submitted to the court. With approval of the court, counsel may designate a person or persons to read the evidence to the jury.

The procedure for obtaining these materials is discussed in Chapter 16, *supra.*

§ 2250. — Oral and written depositions.

NRCP 32 governs the use of oral and written depositions at trial. The rule is comparable though not identical to Fed. R. Civ. P. 32.

Any deposition may be used by any party to contradict or impeach the deponent as a witness at trial, or for any other purpose permitted by the Nevada Rules of Evidence, NRS Chapters 47-56. NRCP 32(a)(1). Depositions of an adverse party, or in certain instances, its representative (as defined in NRCP 30(b)(6), 31(a) and 32(a)(2), may be used *for any purpose,* and thus may constitute substantive proof regardless of the availability of the deponent to testify at trial.

Any relevant portion of an adverse party's deposition may be read into evidence by the other party during its case in chief.

Depositions of anyone else may be used by any party for any purpose under certain exceptional circumstances, including the witness' death, absence from the forum or inability to testify, the party's inability to serve the witness with a subpoena, or other exigent circumstance. *See* NRCP 32(a)(3).

If only part of a deposition is offered into evidence, an adverse party may demand that other parts of the deposition be introduced as fairness requires. Any other party may also introduce other parts of the deposition if the matters testified to would be admissible during live testimony. NRCP 32(a)(4).

Substitution of parties, in accordance with NRCP 25, does not alter the right to use depositions at trial. NRCP 32(a)(4).

Depositions from a previous action involving the same subject matter between the same parties, their representatives or successors, may be used in a later action. The deposition is admissible as if it were taken in the pending action. NRS 32(a); NRS 51.325.

§ 2251. — Interrogatories.

The use of answers to interrogatories at trial is governed by NRCP 33(b), which is identical to Fed. R. Civ. P. 33(b). Answers to interrogatories may be introduced at trial, subject to the normal rules governing the admissibility of evidence. Parties may introduce answers containing facts or the opinions of a party or the application of law to fact.

§ 2252. — Admissions.

Admissions of a party, made pursuant to NRCP 36, can be particularly useful. Rule 36 is an efficient method for establishing in advance of trial the authenticity of documents or other tangible evidence for admission into evidence. Rule 36(b) (which is identical to Fed. R. Civ. P. 36(b)) provides that any matter admitted is conclusive for the purposes of the pending action only. Upon motion, the court may grant relief from an admission, by allowing it to be withdrawn or amended, if the presentation of the merits of the action would be promoted. To avoid amendment or withdrawal, the opposing party should show that substantial prejudice would result because of reliance on the admission and the inability or expense of procuring alternate proof. *See, e.g., Auto Fair, Inc. v. Spiegelman,* 92 Nev. 656, 557 P.2d 273 (1976).

§ 2253. — Views.

A view is an inspection of premises or tangible property that is the subject matter of litigation or is otherwise related to the action. The purpose of a view is to assist the trier of fact in understanding circumstances or events surrounding an action. *Eikelberger v. State ex rel. Department of Highways,* 83 Nev. 306, 429 P.2d 555 (1967); *see also Love v. Mt. Oddie United Mines Co.,* 43 Nev. 61, 77, 181 P. 133 (1919). Although, strictly speaking, a view is not evidence, it can be an important adjunct to formal proof. *Cf. Albion Consolidated Mining Co. v. Richmond Mining Co.,* 19 Nev. 225, 8 P. 480 (1885) (a model of real property may constitute evidence, but a view is not evidence).

In a jury trial, the court, in its discretion, determines whether a view would be appropriate. *Eikelberger v. State,* 83 Nev. 306, 429 P.2d 555 (1967). The jury is accompanied by a bailiff to the site. The court determines who may speak to the jury about the site. NRS 16.100.

A motion requesting a view should be made before trial and should set forth the reasons that a view would be beneficial and should also establish that the site or other property is substantially unchanged in condition from the time in issue.

Since the view itself is not evidence, counsel procuring a view should arrange to have a court reporter attend the view in order to record testimony of a witness who can point out important matters at the site and indicate for the record what the jurors actually observe. Additionally, the courts should be requested to take judicial notice of matters observed pursuant to NRS 47.130.

§ 2254. Admission and exclusion of evidence.

The trial court has broad discretion in admitting or rejecting offered evidence. Its decision will not be overturned absent a showing of "palpable abuse." *State ex rel. Department of Highways v. Nevada Aggregates & Asphalt Co.,* 92 Nev. 370, 551 P.2d 1095 (1976); *see also Way v. Hayes,* 89 Nev. 375, 513 P.2d 1222 (1973) and *Wickliffe v. Sunrise Hospital,* 101 Nev. 542, 706 P.2d 1383 (1985). Even a clearly erroneous ruling ordinarily will not constitute a ground for reversal (at least in the absence of constitutional considerations), unless a specific objection has been made. *Nevada State Bank v. Snowden,* 85 Nev. 19, 449 P.2d 254 (1969).

§ 2255. Motions in limine and memoranda on admissibility of evidence.

The court should be fully briefed in advance of trial on the major evidentiary disputes that can be anticipated. The method for doing so is a memorandum of law or a motion in limine on the admissibility or exclusion of evidence. A written document is not only likely to be more thorough than oral discussion, but also encourages a more carefully considered decision by the trial court. It also provides a foundation for appellate review of challenged rulings. Motions in limine are discussed at length in Chapter 18, *infra.*

§ 2256. Record of proceedings to preserve review.

All trial proceedings should be properly and completely reported to ensure a basis for later review. Under NRS 3.320, any party or the judge may request reporting of all testimony, objections and rulings. In order to preserve an issue for appeal, the issue must be part of the record of the district court either by way of transcript, order, or otherwise.

When matters are discussed and determined in chambers (or at the bench during a jury trial), it is important for counsel to request reporting if any issue should be preserved for review. *See Carson Ready Mix, Inc. v. First National Bank,* 97 Nev. 474, 635 P.2d 276 (1981). Representations of what occurred, without support in the record, will not preserve the matter for appellate review. *Screen v. Screen,* 82 Nev. 220, 414 P.2d 953 (1966).

Ordinarily at trial the court should rule immediately on evidentiary issues rather than holding its ruling in abeyance. Sometimes counsel must insist upon a timely ruling; otherwise, the issue may be waived. *See Havas v. 105 Casino Corp.,* 82 Nev. 282, 417 P.2d 239 (1966); *see also Silver Dollar Club v. Cosgriff Neon Co.,* 80 Nev. 108, 389 P.2d 923 (1964).

Although it was formerly necessary to make a formal exception to any ruling or order to preserve the matter for appeal, it is now necessary only to inform the court specifically of the action or ruling that is sought. NRCP 46.

Pretrial memoranda or motions in limine are most effective in handling evidentiary disputes. Nevertheless, when evidentiary arguments are made during trial, counsel should cite legal authority as well as any factual basis supporting the position. NRS 47.040; 47.050; *see Patton v. Henrikson,* 79 Nev. 197, 380 P.2d 916 (1963). If an in-court argument is likely to be prejudicial to the jury, counsel should request to have the jury excused. *Patton, supra.*

§ 2257. Offers of proof on excluded evidence.

When an objection to evidence is sustained, the offering party should tender the excluded evidence or make what is otherwise known as an "offer of proof." In jury trials, such offers are generally made outside the presence of the jury. The offer should be made immediately upon denial of the admission of evidence. Usually, upon request of counsel or order of the court, the record is made at the next recess out of the presence of the jury. The procedure involves making a record of the substance of the excluded testimony, its relevancy and other grounds for its admissibility. Most often, a verbal representation by counsel is made setting forth the substance, form and extent of the evidence. Otherwise, a witness is sworn and testifies as to the testimony that has been excluded. If the evidence is a document or other tangible item, it should be marked and offered as evidence. The court may also make a record of the character of the evidence, the form in which it was offered, the basis of the objection and the determination by the court. The same procedure generally applies to bench trials; however, at the request of a party the court must take the entire evidence and have it reported unless it is clearly inadmissible for any purpose. NRS 47.040; 47.050.

Offers of proof should adequately state the legal justification for admitting the evidence; additional grounds generally will not be considered on review. *See El Cortez Hotel, Inc. v. Coburn,* 87 Nev. 209, 484 P.2d 1089 (1971). A legally sufficient offer of proof must also include the substance of the evidence. *Cf. Dyer v. State,* 99 Nev. 422, 663 P.2d 699 (1983) (counsel failed to inform trial court of the substance and significance of additional cross-examination). The actual content is necessary to determine its weight and, therefore, whether error, if any, was prejudicial. *See McCabe v. Pearson,* 89 Nev. 176, 509 P.2d 825 (1973). If an objection to a question is sustained, the offer of proof should include not only the question, but also the answer that would have been elicited. *Alamo Airways, Inc. v. Benum,* 78 Nev. 384, 374 P.2d 684 (1962).

An offer of proof does not correct a failure to tender evidence during the presentation of one's case. *Southern Pacific Transportation Co. v. Fitzgerald,* 94 Nev. 214, 577 P.2d 1234, *rehearing denied,* 94 Nev. 245,

579 P.2d 1251 (1978). Instead, counsel should seek leave of the court to reopen the case.

§ 2258. Opposing evidence.

Failure to object to the admission of evidence usually waives the right to challenge any error. *Southern Pacific Transportation Co. v. Fitzgerald,* 94 Nev. 214, 577 P.2d 1234 (1978).

The two basic methods of opposing evidence during trial are objections and motions to strike. An objection generally is the more effective device, particularly if it is made immediately after a question is asked and before the witness can answer (or immediately upon the offering of evidence). Once objectionable matters are before the jury, even the court's admonishment cannot be expected to remedy the damage. Nevertheless, the court's instruction to disregard the testimony generally is considered to cure the error for purposes of appeal. *See Gotelli v. Cardelli,* 26 Nev. 382, 69 P. 8 (1902).

A motion to strike is made after objectionable evidence is admitted. It is useful where: (1) the moving party failed to establish grounds for objection at the time the evidence was offered; (2) the witness answers in spite of an objection; (3) an improper or objectionable answer is given to a proper question; or (4) it later appears that previously admitted evidence may not properly remain in the record. *See, e.g., Stamps v. State,* 83 Nev. 232, 428 P.2d 188 (1967); *Levine v. Remolif,* 80 Nev. 168, 390 P.2d 718 (1964); *Leport v. Sweeney,* 11 Nev. 387 (1876); *Sharon v. Minnock,* 6 Nev. 377 (1871). A motion to strike may also be coupled effectively with an earlier objection. *See Gordon v. Hurtado,* 91 Nev. 641, 541 P.2d 533 (1975).

Opposition to evidence must be (1) timely, (2) specific, and (3) based upon legally correct grounds. Timeliness of an objection depends upon the particular circumstances. *See* NRCP 46. Once the incompetency of the evidence becomes known to counsel, an objection should be raised immediately. *In re Dumais,* 76 Nev. 409, 356 P.2d 124 (1960) (objection to hearsay, after cross-examination, is too late); *see Sharon, supra.* A later motion to strike may not protect the litigant. *See Hotel Riviera, Inc. v. Short,* 80 Nev. 505, 396 P.2d 855 (1964); *cf. Schwartz v. Schwartz,* 95 Nev. 202, 591 P.2d 1137 (1979) (objection to irrelevant evidence was timely when made as soon as import of evidence became known). Nor will a previous motion in limine, without timely objection at trial, necessarily preserve an objection. *See Daly v. State,* 99 Nev. 564, 665 P.2d 798 (1983); *but see State v. Kallio,* 92 Nev. 665, 557 P.2d 705 (1976).

An objection must be sufficiently specific, factual and legal, to apprise the court of the basis for excluding the offered evidence. A general objection will not support a later challenge to the evidence. *See State v.*

Kallio, supra. For example, merely stating evidence is hearsay may not be sufficiently specific. *See, e.g., State v. Jukich,* 49 Nev. 217, 236, 242 P. 590 (1926); *State v. Murphy,* 9 Nev. 394 (1874).

The reason stated for objecting must also be legally correct. Even if the evidence is not incompetent, its admission will ordinarily be upheld unless the court was informed of a legally correct basis for exclusion. *See Ginnis v. Mapes,* 86 Nev. 408, 470 P.2d 135 (1970). However, an evidentiary ruling which is based upon a general objection or an erroneous reason will be upheld if there is any basis in the law to support it. *Morris v. Morris,* 83 Nev. 412, 432 P.2d 1022 (1967); *see also Hotel Riviera, Inc. v. Torres,* 97 Nev. 339, 632 P.2d 1155 (1981).

§ 2259. Continuing objections.

If an objection is overruled, counsel can avoid disrupting the proceedings and antagonizing the court by asking the court to permit a continuing objection instead of making serial objections.

§ 2260. Limiting instructions.

If evidence is admissible on one aspect of the case, but inadmissible on another, counsel opposing the evidence should immediately request a limiting instruction to minimize prejudice. NRS 47.110; *Southern Pacific Co. v. Watkins,* 83 Nev. 471, 435 P.2d 498 (1967); *Mahan v. Hafen,* 76 Nev. 220, 351 P.2d 617 (1960). The limiting instruction can be given at the time the evidence is received and/or by way of a jury instruction.

§ 2261. Rephrasing objectionable questions.

When an objection to a question is sustained, if the question can be rephrased to be proper, counsel should ask for leave of the court to rephrase it. Obtaining the court's permission will help the attorney to avoid a possible contempt citation for violating a previous order.

§ 2262. Directed verdict or involuntary dismissal.

During trial, two methods exist to test the sufficiency of the evidence to sustain a judgment. A motion for an involuntary dismissal (sometimes referred to as nonsuit) of the plaintiff's case or any claim, pursuant to NRCP 41(b), may be made in either a jury or bench trial. In a jury trial, any party may move for a directed verdict against the opponent's case. NRCP 50(a).

§ 2263. Involuntary dismissal.

NRCP 41(b) governs the procedure for granting an involuntary dismissal. An involuntary dismissal is generally directed toward the plaintiff's case or any of the plaintiff's claims; however, the rules also apply to testing the sufficiency of counterclaims, cross-claims and third-party complaints. *See* NRCP 41(c); *Kline v. Robinson,* 83 Nev. 244, 428 P.2d 190 (1967), *overruled on other grounds, Pease v. Taylor,* 88 Nev. 287, 496 P.2d 757 (1972). Thus, the term "plaintiff," when used within this chapter, also refers to counterclaimants, cross-claimants, and third-party plaintiffs.

§ 2264. — Standard for granting involuntary dismissal.

An involuntary dismissal is warranted if the plaintiff has failed to present a sufficient case based upon the facts and the law. To withstand a motion to dismiss, the plaintiff must produce enough evidence, which if believed, would constitute a prima facie claim for relief. *268 Ltd. v. Sanson,* 97 Nev. 173, 625 P.2d 1173 (1981). Evidence which would otherwise be inadmissible, but is not objected to, is competent to establish a prima facie case. *Lagrange v. Kent,* 83 Nev. 277, 429 P.2d 58 (1967).

In considering a motion to dismiss, the plaintiff's evidence and all reasonable inferences that can be drawn from it must be deemed admitted. The evidence must be interpreted in a light most favorable to the plaintiff. *Combustion Engineering, Inc. v. Peters,* 99 Nev. 329, 661 P.2d 1304 (1983); *El Cortez Hotel, Inc. v. Coburn,* 87 Nev. 209, 484 P.2d 1089 (1971).

§ 2265. — Timing of motion for involuntary dismissal.

A motion for involuntary dismissal of the plaintiff's case or any of the plaintiff's claims can be made after the plaintiff's case is completed. NRCP 41(b). The district court, however, cannot dismiss an action on the merits before the completion of the plaintiff's case. *Taft v. Steinberg,* 97 Nev. 597, 637 P.2d 533 (1981).

§ 2266. — Defendant's right to present evidence.

A defendant does not waive the right to move for involuntary dismissal by calling a witness out of order during the plaintiff's case in chief. *Warner v. Dillon,* 92 Nev. 677, 558 P.2d 540 (1976). Nor does moving for dismissal constitute a waiver of the defendant's right to present evidence in its own behalf. It is possible, however, to waive the right to assert a counterclaim by moving for involuntary dismissal (or directed verdict) of an opposing claim. Thus, counsel should take care to preserve any counterclaim in the event that the motion is granted. *See Gottlieb v. Close,* 81 Nev. 38, 398 P.2d 248 (1965).

§ 2267. — Effect of involuntary dismissal.

With a few exceptions specified in NRCP 41(b), a dismissal under that subsection ordinarily constitutes an adjudication on the merits.

§ 2268. — Effect of a denial.

Denial of a motion to dismiss does not require an entry of a judgment for the plaintiff even if the defendant does not present any additional evidence in its own behalf since the trier of fact is still free to weigh the evidence and assess the credibility of the witnesses. *Cf. Martin v. Ross,* 96 Nev. 916, 620 P.2d 866 (1980) ("involuntary dismissal" was coupled with findings of fact where defense testimony occurred in the plaintiff's case in chief).

§ 2269. Directed verdict.

NRCP 50(a) controls procedure for directing a verdict. A directed verdict, even though so named, does not require the assent or other participation of the jury. It is simply entered as an order by the court.

Unlike a motion under Rule 41(b), a motion for directed verdict may be made by any party, even one having the burden of proof. The defendant may move for a directed verdict after either the plaintiff or defendant has rested; the plaintiff may so move after the defendant's case; and any party may move at the conclusion of all evidence. *See* Chapter 25, *infra.*

§ 2270. — Constitutionality of directed verdict.

Rule 50 has been determined to be constitutional even though it may permit a case to be taken from the jury. *Sobrio v. Cafferata,* 72 Nev. 145, 297 P.2d 828 (1956).

§ 2271. — Standard for granting a directed verdict.

A directed verdict must not be granted if there is evidence to sustain a verdict for the opponent. Stated another way, a directed verdict is appropriate only where any verdict other than the one directed would be wrong as a matter of law. Such a determination requires the establishment of "clear, uncontradicted, self-consistent, and unimpeached evidence." *Sheeketski v. Bortoli,* 86 Nev. 704, 475 P.2d 675 (1970); *see also Mendez v. Brinkerhoff,* 105 Nev. 157, 771 P.2d 163 (1989). The court determines whether there are any issues of fact remaining for the jury. *See Connell v. Carl's Air Conditioning,* 97 Nev. 437, 634 P.2d 673 (1981); *Bliss v. DePrang,* 81 Nev. 599, 407 P.2d 726 (1965). *M & R Investment Co. v. Mandarino,* 103 Nev. 711, 748 P.2d 488 (1987).

The procedure for evaluating the case upon motion for directed verdict is virtually identical to the involuntary dismissal standard. The court must view the evidence and all inferences from the evidence in a light most favorable to the party against whom the motion is directed; it must not weigh the evidence or evaluate the credibility of the witnesses. *Connell v. Carl's Air Conditioning,* 97 Nev. 437, 634 P.2d 673 (1981); *Kline v. Robinson,* 83 Nev. 244, 428 P.2d 190 (1967), *overruled on other grounds, Pease v. Taylor,* 88 Nev. 287, 496 P.2d 757 (1972).

§ 2272. — Directed verdict and judgment n.o.v. compared.

Sufficiency of the evidence to sustain a verdict after it is rendered is tested by a motion for judgment n.o.v. pursuant to NRCP 50(b). *See* Chapter 25, *infra,* on judgments n.o.v.

§ 2273. — Effect of moving, or failing to move, for a directed verdict.

It is no longer necessary in Nevada to move for a directed verdict in order to preserve the right to seek a judgment n.o.v. after trial. Nevertheless, such a motion is important to a later challenge of the judgment on appeal. *See Bill Stremmel Motors, Inc. v. Kerns,* 91 Nev. 110, 531 P.2d 1357 (1975) (issue of sufficiency of the evidence waived where party failed to move for directed verdict, judgment n.o.v. or new trial); *see also Outboard Marine Corp. v. Schupbach,* 93 Nev. 158, 561 P.2d 450 (1977); *but see Avery v. Gilliam,* 97 Nev. 181, 625 P.2d 1166 (1981) ("plain error" or manifest injustice exception to failure to move for directed verdict). *Schwabacher & Co. v. Zobrist,* 102 Nev. 55, 714 P.2d 1003 (1986).

Moving for a directed verdict does not waive the right to present evidence on the movant's behalf. Nor does it waive the right to a jury trial even if all parties request a directed verdict.

§ 2274. Amendments of pleadings to conform to the evidence.

NRCP 15(b) allows amendment of pleadings to conform to the evidence adduced at trial. Amendments may be made at any time during or after trial, even after entry of judgment. The rule permits conformance to the issues which are actually tried; it also permits a party to raise an issue at trial which was not specified in the original pleadings.

Rule 15(b) amendments are more thoroughly discussed in Chapter 8, *supra.* However, it is important here, however, to emphasize that counsel must be very familiar with the pleadings and alert to statements of opposing counsel and evidence as it is received so objections can be made to matters which are irrelevant as outside the scope of pleadings. Otherwise, consent to try new issues may be implied by counsel's failure to object. *See generally Schwartz v. Schwartz,* 95 Nev. 202, 591 P.2d 1137 (1979); *Whiteman v. Brandis,* 78 Nev. 320, 372 P.2d 468 (1962); *Poe v. La Metropolitana Co.,* 76 Nev. 306, 353 P.2d 454 (1960). When an issue is tried by implied consent, it is treated as if it were raised in the pleadings. *Schmidt v. Sadri,* 95 Nev. 702, 601 P.2d 713 (1979).

§ 2275. Jury instructions.

Although the obligation to charge the jury lies with the court, the responsibility for preparing the instructions lies largely with the litigants. Jury instructions are statements of law applicable to the case.

NRS 16.090(6) and 16.110 and NRCP 51 governs the manner of instructing the jury generally. NRCP 51 also governs requests for and objections to proposed instructions. Some districts have local rules establishing the method for preparing and submitting the instructions. *See* FJDCR 10; WDCR 7; Seventh DCR 6; NJDCR 16.

§ 2276. — Time for submitting instructions.

NRCP 51 states that at the close of evidence, or at an earlier time if the court reasonably directs, any party may file requested jury instructions; this rule, however, is modified by local rule and custom. The time for submitting instructions varies among the districts. *See* FJDCR 10 (at start of trial); WDCR 7 (before trial); Rule 6 of the Seventh District (ten days before trial); NJDCR 16 (at start of trial). Instructions that could not have been anticipated at the start of trial may be submitted later.

Although these rules specify a deadline for submitting instructions, an adequately prepared attorney should be able to prepare and submit proposed instructions well in advance of trial. Early submission allows the court an opportunity initially to review the instructions at its convenience and further helps to prepare counsel for presentation of the case.

§ 2277. — Form of requested instructions.

The local rules specify the exact form in which the instructions should be submitted. Generally speaking, requested instructions should be prepared on $8\frac{1}{2}" \times 11"$, non-letterhead pleading paper. There should be no identifying party on the original. The original and one copy is filed with the court. *See* NRS 16.110. Counsel should provide additional copies for each party. The copies, but not the original, should contain legal authority supporting the instruction.

§ 2278. — Settling instructions.

It is very important that a record be made by counsel in lodging objections to the court's giving or refusal to give proposed jury instructions. If no objection to an instruction is made, there is no compliance with Rule 51 and the error is not preserved for appellate consideration. *Wagon Wheel v. Mavrogan,* 78 Nev. 126, 369 P.2d 688 (1962). *See Carson Ready Mix v. First National Bank,* 97 Nev. 474, 635 P.2d 276 (1981). When the record does not contain the objections or exceptions to instructions given or refused, the supreme court will not consider appellant's claim of error with regard to those instructions. *Powers v. Johnson,* 92 Nev. 609, 555 P.2d 1235 (1976); *Shoshone Coca-Cola Bottling Co. v. Dolinski,* 82 Nev. 439, 420 P.2d 855 (1966). *See* §§ 2283 and 2285, *infra.*

If an informal conference to settle jury instructions is held in chambers, it should be followed by a proceeding on the record. The settlement conference instructions should not be held after the jury has been charged, except by stipulation of the parties.

§ 2279. — Time for charging the jury.

Normally, the instructions are read to the jury immediately prior to final arguments. NRCP 51 directs the court to settle instructions before closing arguments, but to charge the jury after the arguments unless either party demands otherwise. However, NRS 16.090 requires the reading of instructions before argument, and this is the procedure commonly followed by the district courts. Both NRCP 51 and NRS 16.090(6) authorize the giving of additional instructions during or after closing arguments if something occurs which requires further instruction. *See also El Cortez Hotel, Inc. v. Coburn,* 87 Nev. 209, 484 P.2d 1089 (1971); *Johnson v. Brown,* 75 Nev. 437, 345 P.2d 754 (1959).

The court may give further instructions or clarification of instructions even after the jury has begun deliberations. NRS 16.140; NRCP 51. Any additional instruction must be given in the presence of, or after notice to, the parties or their counsel. These instructions must be in writing unless the parties agree otherwise.

The jury may take the instructions into the jury room for use during deliberations, NRCP 51.

§ 2280. — Extent of instructions.

The obligations to instruct on general principles of law rest with the trial court. *Nichter v. Edmiston,* 81 Nev. 606, 407 P.2d 721 (1965). Nevertheless, the parties bear the burden of ensuring that the instructions are complete by submitting instructions. Failure to request an instruction generally waives the right to complain about its omission even if there is ample evidence in the record to support it. *See Johns v. McAteer,* 85 Nev. 477, 457 P.2d 212 (1969).

The number of instructions given is discretionary with the court. The court need not give all appropriate requested instructions if they are adequately covered by others that are given. *Duran v. Mueller,* 79 Nev. 453, 386 P.2d 733 (1963); *see also Crown Controls Corp. v. Corella,* 98 Nev. 35, 639 P.2d 555 (1982).

The court must, however, instruct on all theories of a party's case which are supported by evidence and pleadings (assuming that a correct instruction had been tendered). *Combustion Engineering Co. v. Peters,* 99 Nev. 329, 661 P.2d 1304 (1983); *Rocky Mountain Produce Trucking Co. v. Johnson,* 78 Nev. 44, 369 P.2d 198 (1962). Failure to do so is reversible error. *Wickliffe v. Sunrise Hospital,* 104 Nev. 777, 766 P.2d 1322 (1988). Determination of whether there is evidence in the record to support an instruction is a question of law for the court. *See Wickliffe v. Fletcher Jones,* 99 Nev. 353, 661 P.2d 1295 (1983). It has been said that if there is "any evidence" to support a party's theory, an instruction must be given. *See American Casualty Co. v. Propane Sales & Service,* 89 Nev. 398, 513 P.2d 1226 (1973). The theory may be established by a single witness. *Silver Mining Co. v. Fall,* 6 Nev. 116 (1870).

In addition to general ("stock") instructions, parties are entitled to instructions on specific points of law if the point is important and the request is properly made and supported by authority. A special instruction need not be based upon a statute. *Close v. Flanary,* 77 Nev. 87, 109, 360 P.2d 259 (1961). It is reversible error to refuse a special instruction if the general instructions are insufficient for an intelligent decision. *American Casualty, Co., supra.*

§ 2281. — Effect of failure to object.

Objections may be made to the giving or rejection of an instruction. Ordinarily, failure to object at trial to the giving, or failing to give, of any jury instruction waives appellate review of any alleged error. NRCP 51; *Hotel Riviera v. Short,* 80 Nev. 505, 396 P.2d 855 (1964); *Wagon Wheel v. Mavrogan,* 78 Nev. 126, 369 P.2d 688 (1962). This may be so even when the effect of the erroneous instruction is to direct a verdict or to remove the burden of proof. *See, e.g., Fireman's Fund Insurance Co. v. Shawcross,* 84 Nev. 446, 442 P.2d 907 (1968); *Bill Stremmel Motors, Inc. v. Kerns,* 91 Nev. 110, 531 P.2d 1357 (1975).

A rare exception to the rule exists when the reviewing court determines that "plain error" was committed. *See Tidwell v. Clarke,* 84 Nev. 655, 447 P.2d 493 (1968).

§ 2282. — Procedure for objecting.

NRCP 51 requires a specific objection to the giving, or refusal to give, any jury instruction. Counsel must specify both the objectionable matter in an instruction and the grounds for the objection; however, the amount of specificity required will vary according to the circumstances presented. *See, e.g., Otterbeck v. Lamb,* 85 Nev. 456, 456 P.2d 855 (1969); *see also Galloway v. McDonalds Restaurants,* 102 Nev. 534, 728 P.2d 826 (1986); *Tidwell v. Clarke,* 84 Nev. 655, 447 P.2d 493 (1968) (tendering correct statement of law, without further explanation, held sufficient).

The consequences of failing to comply with Rule 51 mandate specific accurate objections to require counsel to correct any erroneous or incomplete statement of law before the jury is instructed. *See Downing v. Marlia,* 82 Nev. 294, 417 P.2d 150 (1966); *Lathrop v. Smith,* 71 Nev. 274, 288 P.2d 212 (1955).

§ 2283. — Objection to an offered instruction.

To apprise the court fully (and to make a good record for appeal), opposition to an offered instruction should include the following: a specific statement of any objectionable language in the instruction; a statement of the grounds for the objection, based upon the evidence presented and the legal foundation required for the instruction; citation to pertinent legal authorities; and tendering, if appropriate, a correct statement of the law. All of this must be presented in a written or oral (reported) form which will be a part of the record. Failure to object, combined with failure to offer a correct instruction, may result in a waiver. *See Ross v. Giacomo,* 97 Nev. 550, 635 P.2d 298 (1981); *see also Alpark Distributing, Inc. v. Poole,* 95 Nev. 605, 600 P.2d 229 (1979).

§ 2284. — Grounds for objection.

An instruction may be objectionable because it is an incorrect statement of the law, *Stevens v. Duxbury,* 97 Nev. 517, 634 P.2d 1212 (1981); or because it is confusing, *Stevens, supra;* or misleading, *Davies v. Butler,* 95 Nev. 763, 602 P.2d 605 (1979); or incomplete, *Davies, supra;* or conflicting, *Wells, Inc. v. Shoemake,* 64 Nev. 57, 72, 177 P.2d 451 (1947).

An instruction may also be objectionable because there is no evidence in the record to support it. *See, e.g., Horvath v. Burt,* 98 Nev. 186, 643 P.2d 1229 (1982); *see also Davies v. Butler,* 95 Nev. 763, 602 P.2d 605 (1979).

It is also objectionable to comment on the evidence by an instruction which unduly emphasizes a fact or theory of one of the parties. *See, e.g., Lightenburger v. Gordon,* 81 Nev. 553, 573-76, 407 P.2d 728 (1965). Such an instruction violates Nevada Constitution, Article 6, Section 12 and NRS 3.230 which proscribe the judge from making factual findings in a jury trial. Similarly, an instruction is improper if it assumes a fact in issue. *Gaudette v. Travis,* 11 Nev. 149 (1876).

If, however, a fact is clearly proved and not disputed, the court may properly take the issue from the jury. *See Northern Nevada Mobile Home Brokers v. Penrod,* 96 Nev. 394, 610 P.2d 724 (1980); *cf. Fennell v.*

Miller, 94 Nev. 528, 583 P.2d 455 (1978) and *Kerr v. Mills,* 87 Nev. 153, 483 P.2d 902 (1971) (admissible factual evidence, as distinguished from conclusions or opinions, that is uncontradicted, unimpeached and not inherently unbelievable must be taken as true by the trier of fact).

In contrast, it is improper for the court to instruct the jury that there is insufficient evidence to support an element of a party's case. If there is no legal issue, then a directed verdict is appropriate. *See Wheeler v. Twin Lakes Riding Stable,* 88 Nev. 485, 500 P.2d 572 (1972). Otherwise, when a factual issue cannot be determined as a matter of law, it must be submitted to the jury. *Daniel, Mann, Johnson & Mendenhall v. Hilton Hotels Corp.,* 98 Nev. 113, 642 P.2d 1086 (1982).

§ 2285. — Objection to a refused instruction.

Objection to the court's refusal to give an offered instruction should include the following: a statement of the proposed instruction; an explanation of the grounds for its use, including its relationship to the evidence or a party's case theory and a statement of its legal foundation, with supporting legal authorities. *Cf. Downing v. Marlia,* 82 Nev. 294, 417 P.2d 150 (1966) (saying instruction is "proper under the evidence" is insufficient). An objection must be in such a written or oral form that it will be part of the record on appeal; otherwise, the objecting party risks waiver. *See Carson Ready Mix, Inc. v. First National Bank,* 97 Nev. 474, 635 P.2d 276 (1981).

§ 2286. — Grounds for reversal.

An objecting party must establish prejudicial effect in order to obtain a reversal for the error in instructions. *See Driscoll v. Erreguible,* 87 Nev. 97, 482 P.2d 291 (1971) and *Mizushima v. Sunset Ranch,* 103 Nev. 259, 737 P.2d 1158 (1987).

If the jury returns a general verdict unaccompanied by special interrogatories and there is a substantial error in instruction on any of the alternative theories of liability or defense, the case must be remanded for a new trial. *Otterbeck v. Lamb,* 85 Nev. 456, 456 P.2d 855 (1969); *but see Galloway v. McDonalds Restaurants,* 102 Nev. 534, 728 P.2d 826 (1986); *Lightenburger v. Gordon,* 81 Nev. 553, 569-76, 407 P.2d 728 (1965) (Thompson, J., concurring). Similarly, the refusal to instruct on a valid claim requires a new trial on that limited issue. *Buck v. Greyhound Lines,* 105 Nev. 756, 783 P.2d 437 (1989).

§ 2287. Closing argument.

After the jury has been instructed, counsel may make closing arguments. The party having the burden of proof is allowed to open and close, and the defending party presents its argument in the interim. NRS 16.090.

§ 2288. — Purpose and scope.

The purpose of closing argument is to motivate the jury to reach a particular verdict. Although the technique of effective argument is beyond the scope of this book, it is important to emphasize that a closing argument is not simply a summation of the evidence; it is an opportunity for the party, through its counsel, to explain to the jury how they should view and weigh the evidence. Because its object is to move the jury toward a particular result, the argument should focus on the highlights of the party's position. A long argument that attempts to respond to every evidentiary dispute is likely not only to confuse and bore, but may be taken as an insult to the jury's intelligence. Like the opening statement, the closing argument should be concise and well-organized.

The argument should be limited to the issues, the evidence and the reasonable inferences which can be drawn from the evidence. Counsel may argue how the facts of the case apply to the law as set forth in the jury instructions.

Visual aids of key instructions may help in explaining how the facts relate to the law. It is also proper to use exhibits that have been admitted into evidence. With the court's permission, other visual aids prepared specifically for closing argument (such as a chart summarizing damages), may be used as well.

§ 2289. — Ethical considerations.

The bounds of permissible argument are governed largely by the rules of ethics. Basic rules of honesty and fair play require that attorneys refrain from unfair attempts to mislead jurors about the facts or a party's position. Counsel should not assert a fact that is not in evidence. SCR 173(5); *Burch v. Southern Pacific Co.*, 32 Nev. 75, 104 P. 225 (1909); *see also Boyd v. Pernicano*, 79 Nev. 356, 385 P.2d 342 (1963).

Facts which are already known to the jury, or are a matter of common knowledge, may be referred to even if not proven at trial. *See, e.g., Hotel Riviera, Inc. v. Short*, 80 Nev. 505, 512, 396 P.2d 885 (1964).

It is improper for plaintiff's counsel to save, until rebuttal, material arguments upon which the plaintiff's case is known to rely. (Counsel is not precluded, however, from rebutting other arguments raised by the opposition.) Obviously, it is impermissible to misquote the law, evidence or opposing counsel's argument.

An attorney should not vouch for the integrity of a client or witness, except to the extent that the evidence bears on the matter. Counsel may properly argue that circumstances support his or her client and not the testimony of opposing witnesses. SCR 173(5); *Hotel Riviera, Inc. v. Short,* 80 Nev. 505, 396 P.2d 855 (1964).

An attorney should not indulge in expressions of personal belief concerning the justice of a cause. SCR 173(5); *see McGuire v. State,* 100 Nev. 153, 677 P.2d 1060 (1984). Counsel may, however, point out facts in evidence which support a witness' version of events. *See Hotel Riviera, Inc. v. Short,* 80 Nev. 505, 396 P.2d 855 (1964).

Counsel should refrain from disparaging personal remarks, including references to idiosyncracies, concerning opposing counsel. *See McGuire v. State,* 100 Nev. 153, 677 P.2d 1060 (1984); *Mahan v. Hafen,* 76 Nev. 220, 351 P.2d 617 (1960); *Riley v. State,* 107 Nev. 205, 808 P.2d 551 (1991).

"Golden Rule" appeals or arguments suggesting that jurors "trade places" with one of the litigants are also improper. *McGuire v. State,* 100 Nev. 153, 677 P.2d 1060 (1984); *Doyle v. State,* 104 Nev. 729, 765 P.2d 1156 (1988); *Howard v. State,* 106 Nev. 713, 800 P.2d 175 (1990).

§ 2290. — Objections to argument.

To protect a client's interests, and to preserve any claim of misconduct, an objection to argument must be timely and specific. It is important to request that closing arguments be reported and transcribed as part of the record. *See Beccard v. Nevada National Bank,* 99 Nev. 63, 657 P.2d 1154 (1983).

A party may be entitled to additional instructions by reason of improper argument. NRS 16.090; NRCP 51; *see also El Cortez Hotel, Inc. v. Coburn,* 87 Nev. 209, 484 P.2d 1089 (1971). However, a jury verdict will not be disturbed where the error is invited by counsel for the complaining party. *See Desert Cab, Inc. v. Marino,* 108 Nev. __, __ P.2d __ (1992).

§ 2291. Attorney conduct.

Trial conduct is under the control of the court, but is governed largely by Supreme Court Rules and basic dictates of etiquette. Proper attorney conduct is that which is consistent with courtesy, honesty and a general sense of fair play.

Respect for the court requires that an attorney be adequately prepared and punctual. If tardiness or absence can be anticipated, the attorney should notify the court as much in advance as possible. Adequate preparation also includes keeping the court fully informed on matters, including settlements and elimination of issues. It also assumes the ability to proceed smoothly and without unnecessary delays during trial.

Respect for the court also requires proper attire and respectful posture while sitting or standing. Counsel should not only stand while the court enters and exits the courtroom, but also when addressing or being addressed by the court. When it is necessary to approach the bench or a witness, or to move in order to hear a witness or see evidence, leave of the court should first be obtained.

Each judge runs his or her court differently. Inquiry should be made prior to trial regarding the court's preference in dealing with witnesses, exhibits, and movement about the courtroom.

Respect for the court also includes proper demeanor toward the judge, opposing counsel, parties and witnesses. Comments, objections and argument should be directed to the judge and not opposing counsel. The judge is properly addressed as, "Your Honor," and referred to as "His/Her Honor" or "Judge [surname]."

Counsel should avoid any display of disparagement or acrimony regarding opposing counsel. *See McGuire v. State,* 100 Nev. 153, 677 P.2d 1060 (1984); *Mahan v. Hafen,* 76 Nev. 220, 351 P.2d 617 (1960); *Riley v. State,* 107 Nev. 205, 808 P.2d 551 (1991). Questions intended to degrade or insult a witness or a party or behavior which is in any other way abusive or inconsiderate is not permissible. *See generally Bull v. McCuskey,* 96 Nev. 706, 615 P.2d 957 (1980); *Yates v. State,* 103 Nev. 200, 734 P.2d 1252 (1987).

In making objections, care should be given not to interrupt a question unless the question is clearly objectionable or there is reasonable ground to believe that the question will disclose improper matter to the jury. It is also obviously improper to interrupt either the argument of opposing counsel or the comments of the judge.

Intentional misquotations of the law, the judge, the testimony of a witness, the contents of a document or the argument of opposing counsel are improper. SCR 172(a). It is also improper to refer to authorities known to have been vacated, repealed, overruled or distinguished, without making a full disclosure. SCR 172(c).

Obviously, intentional disobedience of a trial court ruling constitutes misconduct. SCR 173(3); *see McGuire v. State,* 100 Nev. 153, 677 P.2d 1060 (1984). Violation of the law, as established by appellate decision, may also be misconduct, at least where the attorney knew or should have known about the existence of the law. *McGuire, supra.*

Fairness prohibits lawyers from asking any question which is known to be improper, including those suggesting matters which are known to be inadmissible or untrue. SCR 173(5). Fairness also prohibits an attorney from proposing a stipulation in the presence of the jury unless the attorney knows, or has reason to believe, that opposing counsel will accept the stipulation.

Fairness also imposes limitations on the attorney's interaction with jurors and potential jurors. Before the jury is sworn, a lawyer may investigate prospective jurors to determine if there is a basis for challenge; the investigation, however, must not include either direct or indirect communication with the juror, any member of the juror's family, an employer, or anyone else which might lead to direct or indirect communication with a prospective juror. SCR 176(4). Of course, this prohibition applies to investigators or agents of the parties.

A lawyer has a duty to disclose to the judge and opposing counsel any information regarding any juror's possible interest in the outcome of the litigation. Counsel must also disclose any information suggesting that a juror is acquainted or in any way connected with any of the litigants, prospective witnesses or lawyers in the case (including any lawyer's partner, employee or associate). SCR 176(2).

A lawyer must disclose to the court information concerning improper conduct toward the jury or a jury member.

Before and during trial, counsel should avoid any conversation with a juror on any subject. The lawyer should also avoid any behavior which may be interpreted as an effort toward ingratiation with the jury or any member of the jury. SCR 176(1).

§ 2292. — Consequences of misconduct.

In addition to disciplinary proceedings, the potential consequences of attorney misconduct include mistrial, setting aside the verdict, reversal and even imposition of fines. Cf. McGuire v. State, 100 Nev. 153, 677 P.2d 1060 (1984) (criminal case resulting in reversal and attorney fine); see also Stephens v. Southern Nevada Music Co., 89 Nev. 104, 507 P.2d 138 (1973). Sanctions may be imposed against an attorney who "should have known" his or her behavior was highly improper. McGuire, supra.

Because of the severity of potential sanctions, not to mention the harm to an attorney's reputation, it is always prudent, when possible, to bring problematic areas (i.e., appropriate bounds of questioning) to the court's attention for ruling outside the presence of the jury.

§ 2293. Conduct of the judge.

The judge has a reciprocal duty to behave in a respectful manner toward counsel. The judge should not act in any way which would deter proper presentation of a case or which would prevent the making of a complete and accurate record.

It is particularly important that the judge maintain the appearance of impartiality before the jury. This is so because of the potential influence which the judge could otherwise exert over the jury performance. See generally Peterson v. Silver Peak, 37 Nev. 117, 140 P. 519 (1914).

Although a judge may call or question witnesses, and may even state the evidence to the jury, it is improper for the judge to comment on the weight, character, credibility or probative value of any evidence or witness in a jury trial. Article 6, Section 12 of the Nevada Constitution prohibits the court from charging the jury on factual matters. *See also* NRS 50.145; 3.230; *Gordon v. Hurtado,* 91 Nev. 641, 541 P.2d 533 (1975); and *Barrett v. State,* 105 Nev. 356, 776 P.2d 538 (1989). If the court chooses to state the evidence, the jury must be informed that it is not bound by the judge's characterization of the facts. It is, therefore, improper for the court, in the presence of the jury, to justify its evidentiary rulings based upon witness qualifications or the probative value of the evidence. *Gordon, supra; cf. Peterson v. Silver Peak,* 37 Nev. 117, 140 P. 519 (1914) (improper to state that the evidence will do no harm).

§ 2294. — Relief from judicial misconduct.

If, during any stage of the litigation, a judge manifests actual bias or prejudice, a party may interrupt the proceedings to file a motion for actual bias under NRS 1.230(1) and have a hearing conducted by another judge. NRS 1.230(4). A party may waive the issue of bias if it does not comply timely with the requirements for seeking recusal of the trial judgment pursuant to NRS 1.235. *Brown v. Federal Savings & Loan Insurance Corp.*, 105 Nev. 409, 777 P.2d 361 (1989) and *Nevada Pay TV v. District Court,* 102 Nev. 203, 719 P.2d 797 (1986). *See A Minor v. State,* 86 Nev. 691, 694, 476 P.2d 11 (1970); *State ex rel. Welfare Division v. Eighth Judicial District Court,* 85 Nev. 642, 646 n.2, 462 P.2d 37 (1969).

Judicial misconduct may also be raised on appeal; however, for purposes of review, there must be a sufficient record of misconduct to warrant relief. *See generally Lawler v. First National Bank,* 95 Nev. 196, 576 P.2d 1121 (1978); *Duran v. Mueller,* 79 Nev. 453, 461, 386 P.2d 733 (1963). Counsel must make a specific objection as to the prejudicial effect of judicial misconduct in order to preserve the error for appellate consideration. *Ginnis v. Mapes Hotel Corp.*, 86 Nev. 408, 470 P.2d 135 (1970).

Care should be taken to make an adequate record of misconduct. If the trial transcript does not reflect the misconduct or its full extent (*i.e.,* where the nonverbal misconduct occurs), counsel should consider supplementing the record out of the presence of the jury.

§ 2295. Mistrial.

A mistrial is a termination of a trial prior to a verdict or decision either because a fair or impartial trial has become impossible or because the jury cannot agree on a verdict.

Ordinarily, mistrials are limited to jury actions because a judge presumably is not subject to the same influences that prejudice a jury. *Hui v. State,* 103 Nev. 321, 738 P.2d 892 (1987).

Although mistrials are very rarely granted, a number of situations serve as a basis for such a motion. Misconduct of a litigant, witness, counsel, judge or juror is a ground for a mistrial. *See generally Stephens v. Southern Nevada Music Co.,* 89 Nev. 104, 507 P.2d 138 (1973). A mistrial should also be declared when a person without interest in a suit officiously intermeddles therein. *Lum v. Stinnett,* 87 Nev. 402, 488 P.2d 347 (1971). A mistrial may also result from the withdrawal of a juror prior to verdict if there are no alternates, and counsel are unwilling to stipulate to a lesser number of jurors. For that reason, it is important to have at least one alternate on each jury, and more for longer trials. *See also* NRS 175.061(1); 175.071. *Cf. McKenna v. State,* 96 Nev. 811, 618 P.2d 348 (1980) (substitution of alternate after discharge of juror prevented declaration of mistrial), where juror explained before deliberations that she was not impartial; *but see Williamson v. Sheriff,* 89 Nev. 507, 515 P.2d 1028 (1973) (juror's announcement that she was acquainted with and biased against witness required judge to declare mistrial).

The court may impose attorneys' fees and costs against any party or attorney who, in the judgment of the court, purposely caused a mistrial. NRS 18.070(2).

After a mistrial has been declared, the action may be tried again either immediately or at a time set by the court. NRS 16.150.

§ 2296. Masters.

Nevada law authorizes the appointment of a master or masters to assist the trial court only in actions which present exceptional circumstances. NRCP 53(b). In jury actions, reference to a master may be made only when the issues are complicated. In actions to be tried to the bench, a reference may be made only upon a showing that some exceptional condition requires it. This apparently is true even for accountings and actions involving difficult computations of damages. Reference to a master may be appropriate only when accounting or computation is beyond the competence of the court or where inordinate judicial resources would otherwise be consumed. "Calendar congestion, complex issues of fact and law, and prospectively lengthy trials" do not constitute grounds for reference. *Russell v. Thompson,* 96 Nev. 830, 619 P.2d 537 (1980). (The district judge is not authorized under NRCP 53(b) to refer all issues set forth in the pleadings to a special master, *but see Southern Trust v. K & B Door Co.,* 104 Nev. 504, 763 P.2d 353 (1988). The order may also state the inclusive dates for taking evidence, conducting hearings and filing the master's report. If so empowered by order of the court, a master may require production of evidence, may examine witnesses and parties under oath, and may rule on the admissibility of evidence. Upon request, the master must take and report any excluded evidence, unless the evidence is clearly inadmissible on any grounds or is privileged. NRS 47.050.

Proceedings conducted by a master are governed by 53(d). The rule provides that a master shall set the first meeting for the parties or their attorneys within twenty days from the order of reference. A master has a duty to act with diligence. On notice to the master and all parties, any party may move the trial court for an order to expedite the proceedings and master's report. *Cf. Garden Park Townhouse v. Homewood Builders,* 97 Nev. 630, 637 P.2d 1214 (1981) (involuntary dismissal resulting from master's failure to take testimony (or submit report) within five years from filing of complaint, and three years from reference).

The parties may procure witnesses at a master's proceeding by subpoena as set forth in Rule 45. A witness so subpoenaed is subject to sanctions under NRCP 37 and 45.

§ 2297. — Master's report.

The master must prepare a report to be filed with the court, setting forth the matters determined pursuant to the reference order. In a nonjury action, unless otherwise ordered, the master also files a transcript of the proceedings along with the evidence and exhibits.

In bench trials, the master's findings of fact must be accepted unless clearly erroneous. NRCP 53(e)(2). The court retains authority to accept, reject or modify the findings and may also receive additional evidence or remand the matter to the master.

In jury actions, the master is not permitted to report the evidence; but the master's findings are admissible as evidence and may be read to the jury. NRCP 53(e)(3).

If the parties have stipulated that the master's findings are final, then the court is empowered only to consider questions of law arising from the findings. NRCP 53(e)(4).

CHAPTER 23

THE JURY TRIAL

Author: Kent R. Robison

§ 2301. Introduction and scope.

Jury trials are the glory of the law. It is before juries that the competitive and creative juices flow. In jury trials, the delicate application of forensic psychology blends with a coherent knowledge of law. Jury trials mandate humility, sincerity, resiliency, perseverance, and honesty.

This chapter discusses the mechanics of trial by jury. Techniques of jury trial practice are beyond the scope of this book. However, where necessary, practice suggestions have been included. This chapter concerns matters ranging from one's right to a jury to post-trial jury contact. It is intended to provide the reader with full understanding of the procedures relevant to the jury's existence, function, purpose and problems.

A discussion of the jury's verdict is also included. Proper verdict forms appear in the Nevada Patterned Jury Instructions.

§ 2302. Right to trial by jury.

A jury trial is a constitutional right. Nevada Constitution Article 1, Section 3. This right however is not absolute. The constitutional right of trial by jury has reference to the right as it existed at the time of the adoption of the state Constitution. The court upon motion or of its own initiative can therefore refuse the right to jury on issues for which jury trials are not permitted under the constitution or statutes of the state. A jury cannot be claimed, as a matter of right in a case in equity, or upon an issue solely of law, for those are for a court's determination. Likewise, the legislature has eliminated the right to trial by jury in divorce proceedings, and in requests for extraordinary relief.

If the parties consent, the court may order a jury trial in an action not otherwise triable of right by a jury and the jury's verdict will have the same effect as if trial by jury had been a matter of right. In this regard, however, one must be cautious and should be familiar with *Misty Management Corp. v. First Judicial District Court,* 83 Nev. 253, 428 P.2d 196 (1967). In a "primarily" equitable proceeding where no objections were made to a demand for trial by jury, the verdict was determined on appeal to be "merely advisory to the court."

§ 2303. Advisory jury verdicts.

In an action not triable of right by a jury, the court may upon motion try any issues with an advisory jury. A request for an advisory jury is addressed to the court's discretion. An advisory jury hears the evidence and renders a decision the same as if the matter were triable by jury as a matter of right. Its verdict is merely advisory to the court, and is not binding. The case is then decided by the court. Yet, the economic realities of litigation have made the use of advisory juries rare. When both legal and equitable issues are to be determined in an action, it is permissible for the court, under NRCP 38 and 39(b), to allow the jury to decide the legal issues and to reserve to itself determination of the equitable issues.

§ 2304. Jury demand and waiver of right to jury.

A party can waive its right to jury trial by failing to strictly comply with the requirements of NRCP 38. Waiver can occur as follows:

1. Failing to *file* the jury demand before "entry of the order *first* setting the case for trial." (Emphasis added. NRCP 38(b)).

2. Failing to *serve* the jury demand before "entry of the order *first* setting the case for trial." (Emphasis added. NRCP 38(b)).

3. Failing to deposit when or before the demand is filed with the clerk an amount of money equal to the fees to be paid the trial jurors for their services for the first day of trial (*i.e.,* $120, see NRS 6.150(2)).

Therefore, if a jury is desired, the timing involved in filing and serving the demand and in making the requisite deposit of jury fees is crucial. It is essential to know what constitutes the "order first setting the case for trial" and when the order is "entered." Unfortunately, the setting procedure and timing differs throughout the state. *See* §§ 2206-2214, *supra.*

Notwithstanding the failure of a party to serve and file a demand pursuant to NRCP 38(b), the court in its discretion upon motion may order a trial by jury of any or all issues. NRCP 39(b). *Walton v. Eighth Judicial District Court,* 94 Nev. 690, 586 P.2d 309 (1978).

§ 2305. Form of jury demand.

Any party may demand a jury trial of any issue triable of right by a jury by serving upon the other parties a demand in writing not later than the time of entry of the order setting the case for trial. NRCP 38(b).

The jury demand must be contained in a separate paper filed in accordance with NRCP 5(d). *Walton v. Eighth Judicial District Court,* 94 Nev. 690, 586 P.2d 309 (1978). Accordingly, one cannot rely on any entries on setting forms or other court documents such as the "Request for Trial Setting" which is used in the Eighth District. The demand may specify the issues to be tried by a jury; otherwise, it is deemed a demand for a jury trial of all issues so triable. A simple unqualified jury demand is a demand for jury trial on all issues. If a party has demanded a jury trial for only some of the issues, any other party, within ten days after service of the demand, may serve a demand for trial by jury of any other or all of the issues of fact in the action. Moreover, once a timely and proper demand is filed and served, all parties should be entitled to rely upon the demand, and need not make a separate demand for jury trial.

An interesting question is created when one party demands a jury and then later withdraws the demand or is dismissed from the case before trial. Rule 38(d) provides that a demand for jury can be withdrawn "only with the consent of the parties" or for good cause shown upon such terms and conditions as the court may fix. Accordingly, it appears that a properly filed and served demand may be relied upon by all parties and may not be withdrawn unless all parties consent.

§ 2306. Deposit of fees.

At the time a demand for jury trial is filed, the party so demanding is required to deposit with the clerk an amount of money equal to the fees to be paid the jurors for their services for the first day of trial. NRCP 38(d). All the districts require $120. *See* NRS 6.150. Again, late deposit of fees may constitute a waiver of one's right to jury trial.

§ 2307. Summoning of jurors: Washoe and Clark Counties.

This district court "may by rule of court designate the clerk of the court, one of [its] deputies or another person as a jury commissioner, and may assign to the jury commissioner such administrative duties in connection with trial juries and jurors as the court finds desirable for efficient administration." NRS 6.045(1).

A jury commissioner has been selected in Washoe and Clark Counties. It is their function to estimate the number of trial jurors which will be required for attendance on the district court and to select that number from the "qualified electors" of the county not exempt by law from jury duty, whether registered as voters or not. A qualified elector is simply a person "eligible" to vote, *i.e.*, a resident over eighteen years of age. "The jurors may be selected by [a] computer whenever procedures to assure random selection from computerized lists are established by the jury commissioner." A record must be kept of the name, occupation and address of each person selected. NRS 6.045(2).

The procedure used in Clark and Washoe Counties is similar, but the results differ substantially. In Clark County, the source of potential jurors is the persons who have registered with the drivers license division of the Department of Motor Vehicles. This includes drivers and non-drivers, since many nondrivers seek identification cards from the Department of Motor Vehicles. These names are entered into the County Jury Commissioner's computer. The list of names is updated every six months.

Each week, 3,000 names are randomly selected by the computer, and a jury summons is sent to each person selected. The summons sets forth the qualifications for jurors and "District Court Policy" concerning exemptions. The summons directs the prospective juror to call if any exemption is requested. The exemption is automatically given if requested. These exemptions include financial hardship, inconvenience, and even desire not to serve. As a result, only persons who want to serve report for jury service. Accordingly, approximately 500 of the 3,000 persons that receive the jury summons actually report to the courthouse for jury service.

While Washoe County also used the Department of Motor Vehicles as a source for jurors, only statutory exemptions excuse jurors from jury service. Thus, the venire in Clark County will consist only of jurors who want to serve. In Washoe County the venire will also consist of persons who do not want to serve. It is frequently suggested in trial strategy literature that jurors who want to serve are better jurors for plaintiffs and prosecutors while defense attorneys should prefer antagonistic jurors who do not want to serve. If the literature is accurate, a significant tactical advantage exists for the plaintiff's bar and prosecutors in Clark County.

§ 2308. — Summoning of jurors: other counties.

In counties where there is no jury commissioner, the district court, before the board of county commissioners of the county holds its first regular meeting in each year, and from time to time thereafter as may be required, shall estimate as nearly as possible the number of trial jurors that will be required for attendance on the district court of the county for a period of not more than 1 year, and shall by an order entered in its minutes notify the board of that number of jurors and period. The board at its next regular meeting after receipt of the order shall select from the qualified electors of the county, whether registered or unregistered, not exempt by law from jury duty, such number of qualified electors as the court has estimated to be necessary.

NRS 6.050(1).

The board shall transmit to the county clerk, who shall keep a record thereof in his office, the name, occupation and address of each person so selected.

NRS 6.050(2).

The names so selected shall at the same time be written on separate slips of paper and deposited in a box, to be provided and kept for that purpose and known as the jury box.

NRS 6.060.

When a juror drawn is not summoned or fails to appear, or after appearing is excused by the judge from serving, his name shall be returned to the box to be drawn again. The board of county commissioners shall not select the name of any person whose name was selected the previous year, and who actually served on the jury by attending in court in response to the venire from day to day until excused from further attendance by order of the court, unless there be not enough other suitable jurors in the county to do the required jury duty.

NRS 6.070.

When all the names in the jury box have been exhausted, or there are not enough therein to complete the next panel that may be drawn, the district judge shall certify the same to the board of county commissioners, together with a statement of the number of additional names that will be required, and the board shall thereupon proceed and select such required number of jurors in the manner provided in NRS 6.050 and 6.060, and thereafter trial jurors may be drawn therefrom as before.

NRS 6.080(1).

It shall at all times be in the discretion of the court, with the consent of all parties litigant to the action or actions to be tried thereby, either to draw the names of the jurors from the box or to issue an open venire directed to the sheriff, requiring him to summon, either immediately or for a day fixed, from the citizens of the county, but not from the bystanders, such number of persons having the qualifications of jurors as may be needed. The persons thus summoned shall be as competent trial jurors in all respects as if drawn from the jury box.

NRS 6.080(2).

To constitute a regular panel of trial jurors for the district court in a county in which the board of county commissioners selects jurors on an annual basis, such number of names as the district judge may direct must be drawn from the jury box. The district judge shall make and file with the county clerk an order that a regular panel of trial jurors be drawn, and the number of jurors to be drawn must be named in the order. The drawing must take place in the office of the county clerk, during regular office hours, in the presence of all persons who may choose to witness it. The panel must be drawn by the district judge and clerk, or, if the district judge so directs, by any one of the county commissioners of the county and the clerk. If the district judge directs that the panel be drawn by one of the county commissioners of the county and the clerk, the district judge shall make and file with the clerk an order designating the name of the county commissioner and fixing the number of names to be drawn as trial jurors and the time at which the persons whose names are so drawn are required to attend in court.

NRS 6.090(1).

The drawing must be conducted as follows:

(a) The number to be drawn having been previously determined by the district judge, the box containing the names of the jurors must first be thoroughly shaken. It must then be opened and the district judge and clerk, or one of the county commissioners of the county and the clerk, if the district judge has so ordered, shall alternately draw therefrom one ballot until of nonexempt jurors the number determined upon is obtained.

(b) If the officers drawing the jury deem that the attendance of any juror whose name is drawn cannot be obtained conveniently and inexpensively to the county, by reason of the distance of his residence from the court or other cause, his name may be returned to the box and in its place the name of another juror drawn whose attendance the officers may deem can be obtained conveniently and inexpensively to the county.

(c) A list of the names obtained must be made out and certified by the officers drawing the jury. The list must remain in the clerk's office subject to inspection by any officer or attorney of the court, and the clerk shall immediately issue a venire.

NRS 6.090(2).

§2309. — Serving prospective jurors.

Whenever trial jurors are selected by a jury commissioner, the district judge may direct him to summon and assign to that court the number of qualified jurors he determines to be necessary for the formation of the petit jury. The jurors may be selected by computer whenever procedures to assure random selection from computerized lists have been established by the jury commissioner.

NRS 6.090(3).

Every person named in the venire must be served by the sheriff personally or by the sheriff or the jury commissioner by mailing a summons to the person, commanding him to attend as a juror at a time and place designated therein. Mileage is allowed only for personal service. The postage must be paid by the sheriff or the jury commissioner, as the case may be, and allowed him as other claims against the county. The sheriff shall make return of the venire at least the day before the day named for their appearance, after which the venire is subject to inspection by any officer or attorney of the court.

NRS 6.090(4).

§2310. — Questionnaires.

Before examining jurors, it must be remembered that jury questionnaires have been submitted to the court. The questionnaires contain basic information about the jurors. Pretrial familiarity with this information is valuable and expedites jury selection. Indeed, some practitioners have the jurors' handwriting on the questionnaires analyzed for personality traits. In most judicial districts, the questionnaires are available prior to trial. In the Eighth District, written authorization from the applicable court is required (as a matter of policy) to obtain prior to trial the juror questionnaire. Otherwise, it is provided to counsel the first day of trial immediately prior to jury selection.

§2311. — Juror handbooks.

Another important component of the summoning process is the "jurors' handbook." In the Eighth District, the jurors are given a booklet that contains basic information about the trial process. The trial advocate should be cognizant of the information to which the jurors are first exposed. Knowing what the jurors know about the trial process eliminates inconsistent representations by counsel.

§ 2312. — Juror orientation.

In the Eighth District, each panel of jurors receives an orientation program prior to reporting to the appropriate courtroom. This presentation is made by the jury commissioner, the court administrator, and a judge. Again, the trial advocate should be familiar with this orientation. It is designed to make the jurors more comfortable and reduce their anxiety. Counsel unfamiliar with this process and the information imparted risk making representations inconsistent with those made at the orientation. To maximize one's knowledge of the juror's state of mind, it must be known what, if any, mental preconditioning occurs in the summoning process.

A lawyer's credibility is as important as the credibility of any witness. Since the juror summoning process constitutes the initial "education" of the prospective jurors, a lawyer risks his own credibility if he or she does not receive that same education.

§ 2313. Qualifications of jurors.

Every qualified elector of the state, whether registered or not, who has sufficient knowledge of the English language, and who has not been convicted of treason, felony, or other infamous crime, and who is not rendered incapable by reason of physical or mental infirmity, is a qualified juror of the county in which he resides.

NRS 6.010.

§ 2314. Persons exempt from service as trial jurors.

The following persons are exempt from service as trial jurors, upon satisfactory proof by affidavit or otherwise:

(a) Any federal or state officer.

(b) Any judge, justice of the peace or attorney-at-law.

(c) Any county clerk, recorder, assessor, sheriff, deputy sheriff, constable or police officer.

(d) Any locomotive engineer, locomotive fireman, conductor, brakeman, switchman or engine foreman.

(e) Any officer or correctional officer employed by the department of prisons.

(f) Any employee of the legislature or the legislative counsel bureau while the legislature is in session.

(g) Any physician, optometrist or dentist who is licensed to practice in this state.

(h) All persons of the age of 65 years or over.

NRS 6.020.

Persons entitled to exemptions pursuant to the above criteria may nonetheless waive the exemption and if qualified in other respects serve as trial jurors. *See Otis Elevator Co. v. Reid,* 101 Nev. 515, 706 P.2d 1378 (1985), note 5.

§ 2315. Pretrial investigation of jurors.

The jury is clearly the most important component of a jury trial. Pretrial jury investigation has been the subject of recent attention and abuse. Available in the trial lawyer's arsenal is his or her access to jury studies, jury pools, and investigations. But the line between proper preparation and jury tampering should be clear and distinct.

Trial lawyers can now avail themselves of "jury psychologists" who will assist in jury selection. Indeed, given the proper psychological description of the parties, key witnesses and lawyers, many psychological services claim that a "juror profile" can be furnished describing optimum jurors. These services can also perform jury pools in more publicized civil cases to determine the extent, if any, of pretrial opinions and media-derived notions. Some investigative services promise in-depth evaluations of each juror listed as a prospective juror for the subject trial. It is this type of service and the attendant abuses that have resulted in SCR 176.

SCR 176 provides that before the jury is sworn, a lawyer may investigate prospective jurors to ascertain any basis for challenge, provided that the lawyer or his employees or independent contractor may not, before the commencement of the trial, conduct or authorize any investigation of prospective jurors through any means which are calculated or likely to lead to communications with them of any allegations or factual circumstances relating to the case at issue.

SCR 176 further states that conduct prohibited by the rule includes, but is not limited to, any direct or indirect communication with a prospective juror, a member of the juror's family, an employer, or any other person which may lead to direct or indirect communication with a prospective juror. Common sense must be exercised in any type of pretrial jury analysis. Simply stated, do nothing which could ever be perceived as pretrial juror contact, direct or indirect!

§ 2316. — Ethics and juror contact.

Supreme Court Rule 176 constitutes a comprehensive explanation of what is expected of attorneys and their relationship with the jury.

A member of the state bar should scrupulously abstain from all acts, comments and attitudes calculated to curry favor with any juror, such as fawning, flattery, actual or pretended solicitude for the juror's com-

427

fort or convenience, or the like. Before and during the trial, he or she should avoid conversing or otherwise communicating with a juror on any subject whether pertaining to the case or not. SCR 176(1).

A member of the state bar should disclose to the judge and opposing counsel any information of which he or she is aware that a juror or a prospective juror has or may have any interest, direct or indirect, in the outcome of the case, or is acquainted or connected in any manner with any lawyer in the case or any partner or associate or employee of the lawyer, or with any litigant, or with any person who has appeared or is expected to appear as a witness, unless the judge and opposing counsel have previously been made aware thereof by voir dire examination or otherwise.

SCR 176(2).

Subject to any limitation imposed by law it is a lawyer's right, after the jury has been discharged, to interview the jurors to determine whether their verdict is subject to any legal challenge. The scope of the interview should be restricted and caution should be used to avoid embarrassment to any juror or to influence his action in any subsequent jury service.

SCR 176(3).

Before the jury is sworn to try the cause, a lawyer may investigate the prospective jurors to ascertain any basis for challenge, provided there is no communication with them, direct or indirect, or with any member of their families. SCR 176.

A lawyer should, immediately upon his discovery thereof, make full disclosure to the court of any improper conduct by any person toward the jury or any member thereof. SCR 176.

§ 2317. Jury selection.

In most district courts throughout the state, the lawyers are permitted to participate in the jury selection process by conducting an examination of the prospective jurors. In 1981, the legislature enacted NRS 16.030(6), which states:

The judge shall conduct the initial examination of prospective jurors and the parties or their attorneys are entitled to conduct supplemental examinations which must not be unreasonably restricted.

However, Rule 47(a) of the Nevada Rules of Civil Procedure and Rule 7.70 of the Eighth District Court Rules are in conflict with NRS 16.030(6). Under Rule 47(a) and Rule 7.70, the judge shall conduct the voir dire examination of the jurors. But, upon request of counsel, the trial judge "may permit" counsel to supplement the judge's examination by oral and direct questioning of any of the prospective jurors.

While NRS 16.030(6) prevents the trial judge from unreasonably restricting counsel's voir dire examination of prospective jurors, NRCP

47(a) and EDCR 7.70 preclude attorney examination unless the court permits it in its sound discretion.

The problem of whether the statute prevails over court rule concerning a lawyer's right to conduct reasonable voir dire examination is now resolved. In *Whitlock v. Salmon*, 104 Nev. 24, 752 P.2d 210 (1988), the Nevada Supreme Court found that the purpose of voir dire examination is to determine whether a prospective juror can be fair and impartial. Prohibiting attorney-conducted voir dire altogether "may seriously impede that objective." *Id.* at 212.

Although *Whitlock* permits attorneys to conduct supplemental examinations of prospective jurors, careful preparation and certainly discretion are essential. The court emphasizes that the scope and method of voir dire examination remains within the sound discretion of the district court. The court in *Whitlock* encourages the trial bench not to tolerate "desultory excursions" of unprepared counsel who show little regard for judicial economy.

A civil jury generally consists of eight people. (*See* § 2322, *infra,* for clarification). By stipulation and court order, it may be smaller. Since each side (not party) is entitled to four peremptory challenges, a minimum of sixteen jurors must be allocated to each court conducting a jury trial. Usually twenty-five to thirty are assigned to each courtroom.

The examination may occur in one of two ways, the traditional method or the "Arizona" method. NRS 16.030(3) and (4). Under the traditional method, NRS 16.030(3), the court requires eight names be drawn, and those eight are called to the jury box and examined as to their qualifications. If jurors are removed for cause (NRS 16.050), they are replaced from the remaining prospective jurors and examined. Once the panel is passed for cause, each side is entitled to exercise its peremptory challenges. The plaintiffs' side exercises its first challenge. A replacement is drawn and examined. The defendants then exercise their first challenge, a replacement is drawn and examined. This procedure is followed until all peremptory challenges are used or waived.

The Arizona method set forth in NRS 16.040(4) requires the clerk to draw a number of names to form a panel of prospective jurors equal to the sum of the number of regular jurors and alternative jurors to be selected and the number of peremptory challenges available to the parties. For example, if the court determines to have one alternate juror, nineteen names are drawn and called to the jury box, and all nineteen are examined before any peremptory challenges are made. Since each side has four peremptory challenges, if exercised, eight persons are automatically excused. Each side has one more challenge for the alternate. Accordingly, a total of ten challenges could be exercised leaving a nine-member panel, composed of eight regular jurors and one alternate.

The Arizona method is certainly the preferred method. It is more expedient since all prospective jurors are examined at one time avoiding the repetition of examining jurors called to the jury box after each peremptory challenge is exercised under the traditional method. More important is the fact that the parties do not challenge the jurors in their presence. Once the examination is completed, the jurors are removed from the courtroom and counsel meet in chambers or in the jurors' absence and exercise their challenges outside the presence of the prospective jurors. The jurors eventually selected have no knowledge of which side challenged or excused jurors.

§ 2318. Examination procedure.

Extensive literature exists regarding the strategical considerations of jury selection. This section must by necessity be restricted to the method by which juror examination occurs, but includes some relevant practice suggestions and tactics.

The process and exact procedure followed for jury selection differs somewhat in each court. Generally, the procedure is that the court welcomes the entire panel and they are then given an oath to answer all questions truthfully. Depending on which method is used, a designated number are called randomly by the court clerk to the jury box.

Most judges then conduct an examination consisting of general questions concerning the jurors' experience, qualifications and familiarity with the case, parties and attorneys. Some judges allow the plaintiff's counsel to make a brief introductory remark so the jury has some basic information about the lawsuit prior to answering questions. Some judges expect plaintiff's counsel to introduce the court's staff and describe the respective duties of each staff member during this introductory statement.

After the court's general questions, plaintiff's counsel usually is expected to proceed first with his or her general questions. The better practice is then to allow plaintiff to ask special questions of individual jurors and thereafter permit the defendant to proceed with general questions followed by special questions.

Since the chronology of lawyer participation is not the same in all courts, it behooves the lawyer to familiarize himself or herself with each judge's preference before trial. If one is expected to introduce court personnel, it helps at least to know their names.

In the Eighth District, the following areas of inquiry are not properly within the scope of voir dire examination by counsel:

   (a) Questions already asked by the court or counsel and answered,
   (b) Questions touching upon anticipated instructions on the law,

(c) Questions touching upon the verdict a juror would return when based upon hypothetical facts, and

(d) Questions that are in substance, arguments of the case.

EDCR 7.70.

Once the panel is passed for cause, the peremptory challenges are exercised. Questions have occasionally arisen about the composition of the panel when one side waives challenges. For example, if the plaintiff waives all its challenges and the defendant challenges the twelfth through the fifteenth juror called (under the Arizona method) what combination constitutes the panel? While there is no case authority on point, the better practice is that the *first* eight persons called to the jury box who remain unchallenged constitute the panel. Again, this concern should be clarified prior to the commencement of jury selection and put on the record.

§ 2319. Challenges for cause.

Challenges of prospective jurors for cause are tried by the court. NRS 16.060; *see also Hall v. State,* 89 Nev. 366, 371 n.5, 513 P.2d 1244 (1973). Challenges for cause may be taken under NRS 16.050 on one or more of the following grounds:

(a) "A want of any of the qualifications prescribed by statute (NRS 16.010) to render a person competent as a juror."

(b) "Consanguinity or affinity within the third degree to either party."

(c) "Standing in the relation of debtor and creditor, guardian and ward, master and servant, employer and clerk, or principal and agent, to either party; or being a member of the family of either party or a partner, or united in business with either party; or being security on any bond or obligation for either party." The term "united in business" means any business relationship which would, within the trial court's discretion, "indicate that the juror might be interested, biased, influenced or embarrassed in his [or her] verdict." *Sherman v. Southern Pacific Co.,* 33 Nev. 385, 389, 111 P. 416, 115 P. 909 (1910).

(d) "Having served as a juror or been a witness on a previous trial between the same parties for the same cause of action ...."

(e) Interest on the part of the juror in the subject or result of the action, "except the interest of the juror as a member or citizen of a municipal corporation." It is error to overrule a challenge to a prospective juror who holds stock in a company which is a party to the action where the stockholder is personally liable for a proportionate share of the company's debts. *Fleeson v. Savage Silver Mining Co.,* 3 Nev. 157, 161 (1867).

(f) "Having formed or expressed an unqualified opinion or belief as to the merits of the action, or the main question involved therein; but the reading of newspaper accounts of the subject matter before the court shall not disqualify a juror either for bias or opinion" where there is no expression of an unqualified opinion as to the merits. However, the court does not err in refusing to grant a challenge for cause to a juror where the juror states that he would be able to set aside a previous opinion and keep an open mind. *Snow v. State,* 101 Nev. 439, 705 P.2d 632 (1985), *cert. denied,* 475 U.S. 1031 (1986).

(g) "The existence of a state of mind in the juror evincing enmity against or bias to any party." It is permissible for the court to deny a challenge based upon this ground if a prospective juror, although expressing sympathy for an injured plaintiff in a personal injury action, states on voir dire that he would be able to overcome his feelings of sympathy and render a true and just verdict according to the evidence. *Burch v. Southern Pacific Co.,* 32 Nev. 75, 104 P. 225 (1909).

If a party does not specify one of the statutory grounds in a challenge, but relies only upon a challenge stated in general terms, the court may properly overrule the challenge. *Estes v. Richardson,* 6 Nev. 128 (1870).

As a matter of technique, one must be cautious in attempting to challenge a prospective juror for cause. It must be acknowledged that the prospective juror may be offended or embarrassed by the questions necessary to establish the basis for the challenge, and if the challenge is unsuccessful, one must necessarily use a peremptory challenge. Therefore, if an expression establishing the basis for a challenge for cause is made by a prospective juror, he or she should be thanked for being candid and the advocate should ask the court upon motion to "release" the prospective juror pursuant to NRS 16.050(f) rather than announcing in the juror's presence a "challenge" for cause.

§ 2320. Peremptory challenges.

Each side is entitled to four peremptory challenges of prospective jurors. NRS 16.040(1). "If there are two or more parties on any side and their interests are diverse, the court may allow additional peremptory challenges, [not exceeding four], to the side with the multiple parties." NRS 16.040(2). If one party agrees to allow another party to exercise more than four peremptory challenges, any issue as to the impropriety of the number of such challenges is waived on appeal. *Nurenberger Hercules-Werke v. Virostek,* 107 Nev. 873, 822 P.2d 1100 (1991).

In addition to the peremptory challenges described above, each side is entitled to one peremptory challenge if one or two alternate jurors are to be impanelled, two peremptory challenges if three or four alternate jurors are to be impanelled, and three peremptory challenges if five or six alternate jurors are to be impanelled. These additional peremptory challenges may be used against an alternate juror only, and the other peremptory challenges allowed by law may not be used against an alternate juror. NRCP 47(b).

A peremptory challenge does not enjoy the dignity accorded a challenge for cause. *Frame v. Grisewood*, 81 Nev. 114, 122, 399 P.2d 450, 454 (1965). The legislature may determine whether the right to exercise peremptory challenges shall exist at all, but it cannot abrogate the right to challenge for cause. *Frame, supra.* In view of this fundamental distinction, the trial court is entitled to treat a proposed examination of a prospective juror designed to develop information for the exercise of a peremptory challenge more restrictively than an examination to develop grounds for a challenge for cause.

§ 2321. — Effect of failure to exercise peremptory challenges.

If the court wrongfully denies a challenge of a juror for cause, and the juror is then peremptorily challenged, reversible error may occur if all of the peremptory challenges are exhausted, and there is some objectionable person on the jury who cannot be set aside for cause. *Fleeson v. Savage Silver Mining Co.*, 3 Nev. 157, 163-64 (1867). However, if a party has peremptory challenges left to use, but does not do so, a strong presumption is created that he is fully satisfied with the jury and that it is unobjectionable to him. *Fleeson, supra.*

§ 2322. Numbers of jurors on panel.

There is a conflict between NRCP 48 and NRS 16.030(4) concerning the number of jurors on the panel. NRCP 48 states that the parties may stipulate that the jury consist of "four or eight jurors rather than twelve." On the other hand, NRS 16.030(4) provides that the jury "must consist of eight persons, unless the parties consent to a lesser number," (presumably any number) not lower than four.

To determine if the rule prevails over the statute, the principles set forth in § 2318, *supra,* are applicable. NRCP 48 does not conflict with the state constitution or affect the substantive right to a jury trial. Rather, it merely establishes how many jurors may serve on the panel. Apparently, it can be argued that NRCP 48 prevails over NRS 16.030(4), since the number of jurors may be considered to be a matter of judicial procedure rather than a legislative matter. *See State v. Connery*, 99 Nev. 342, 661 P.2d 1298 (1983); *Volpert v. Papagna*, 85 Nev. 437, 456 P.2d 848 (1969); *Lindauer v. Allen*, 85 Nev. 430, 456 P.2d 851 (1969).

§ 2323. Jury tampering.

In *S. & M. Mining Co. v. Showers*, 6 Nev. 291 (1871), the court set aside a verdict in favor of the defendant because the defendant purchased liquor for the jurors after they had been sworn, but before they had retired to deliberate. In so doing, the court said that the parties are prohibited from intermeddling with the jury, and should keep aloof from the jury during the progress of the trial. *S. & M. Mining Co.*, *supra*, at 302. This rule applies "to any treating of any [juror] at any time after they are sworn, and before they agree upon a verdict; whether once or several times; by design or inadvertently, in the presence of the officer or in his absence; and whether [it] might [be] called or uncalled for by the proprieties of life." *S. & M. Mining Co.*, *supra*, at 302-03.

Subsequently, in *Schissler v. Cheshire*, 7 Nev. 427 (1872), the court declined to set aside a verdict under the rule announced in *Showers*. In *Schissler*, several jurors, while returning from a viewing of a mining claim, were treated to liquor by a witness who was appointed to accompany the jury. The court held that this act of providing liquor did not vitiate the verdict because the witness who supplied the liquor was not shown to have any interest in the outcome of the suit. *Schissler*, *supra*, at 430-31.

In *Carnaghan v. Ward*, 8 Nev. 30 (1872), the court also refused to apply the rule set forth in *Showers* where an attorney for one of the parties obtained a bottle of liniment for a juror who was lame and suffering much pain. The court in *Carnaghan* distinguished that case from *Showers*, noting that the conduct at issue was a mere act of humanity and decency intended to relieve a juror's suffering, while the conduct in *Showers* (purchasing "spiritous liquor" for the jury) was entirely uncalled for by any rule of civility or propriety. *Carnaghan*, *supra*, at 34.

Refusal to set aside a judgment on the ground of jury tampering also occurred in *Hilton Hotels v. Butch Lewis Productions*, 107 Nev. 226, 808 P.2d 919 (1991). The court noted that the trial judge's conclusion that substantial prejudice did not result from the claimed tampering and jury misconduct was within the limits of his judicial discretion and thus would not be disturbed.

§ 2324. Photographing jurors.

On May 30, 1988, the Nevada Supreme Court adopted "Rules on Cameras and Electronic Media Coverage in the Courts," which are set forth in SCR 229-247.

These rules permit, under certain conditions, the photographing and broadcasting of judicial proceedings. However, SCR 238(2) provides that the media may not deliberately photograph the jury or individual jurors. Since cameras in the courtroom are still a sensitive matter, it is important for the trial advocate to be familiar with the rules. Moreover, the jurors should be examined in the jury selection process about their subjective reaction to the fact that the electronic media may record the trial.

SCR 240(1) provides that the judge, in the exercise of his sound discretion, may prohibit the filming or photographing of any participant who does not consent to being filmed or photographed.

§ 2325. Deliberations of jury.

After being charged, the jury is required to retire for deliberation until they reach a verdict or are discharged by the court. The jury must be kept together in a room provided for them, under charge of one or more officers, unless at the discretion of the court they are permitted to go home overnight. "When the jury is kept together, the officer in charge [is required to] keep the jury separate from other persons," and "shall not permit any communication to them, or make any himself, unless by order of the court, except to ask them if they have agreed upon [a] verdict." NRS 16.120(1).

In *Horton v. D.I. Operating Co.*, 84 Nev. 694, 448 P.2d 36 (1968), the court held that jury separation in violation of NRS 16.120(1) did not occur where the foreman and one of the jurors discussed instructions in a hall separating two rooms used by the jury. The court noted that the conversation was audible to the other jurors, did not occur outside of the jurors' quarters, and nothing in the record showed that the conversation improperly influenced the verdict. *Horton, supra*, at 697, 448 P.2d at 38.

§ 2326. Parties' bailiff.

A little known and seldom used trial technique is the use of one's own bailiff. "Each party to [an] action may appoint one or more persons, one of whom on each side is entitled to remain with the officer in charge of the jury, and to be present at all times when any communication is had with any member of the jury except when they are permitted to depart for home overnight, and no communication, either oral or written, may be made to or received from any of the jurors while they are kept together, except in the presence of ... persons selected by the parties." A written communication must not be delivered to the jury until it is read by the persons appointed by the parties. NRS 16.120(2). (*See* § 2325, *supra*).

§ 2327. Jury view.

The court, in its discretion, may allow the jury to view the property which is the subject of the litigation or the place where a material fact occurred. NRS 16.100; *Eikelberger v. State ex rel. Department of High-*

ways, 83 Nev. 306, 429 P.2d 555 (1967). The view is not evidence; it is permitted to enable the jury to more fully appreciate the evidence received during trial. *Eikelberger, supra. See also State v. Merritt,* 66 Nev. 380, 212 P.2d 706 (1949); *Albion Consolidated Mining Co. v. Richmond Mining Co.,* 19 Nev. 225, 8 P. 480 (1885).

When the court permits a jury view, the jury is conducted to the place under the charge of an officer, and the place is shown to the jury by a person appointed by the court for that purpose. NRS 16.100. The person appointed by the court to show the place to the jury is the only person who shall "speak to them on any subject connected with the trial." NRS 16.100.

It is not an abuse of discretion for the court to deny a jury view where there is other evidence presented which gives a clear understanding of the factual pattern involved. *State ex rel. Department of Highways v. Haapanen,* 84 Nev. 722, 448 P.2d 703 (1968).

§ 2328. Jurors' questions during deliberations.

After the jury has retired for deliberation, they may require the bailiff to bring them into court if there is disagreement among them as to any part of the testimony. This is also their option if they desire to be informed of any point of law arising in the cause. Upon the jury being brought into court, the court, in the presence of or after notice to the parties or counsel, may order the court reporter to read the portion of the testimony which they request, or any part thereof, and the court may provide any information requested on the law. NRS 16.140.

The court may not respond to questions propounded by the jury during their deliberations without first notifying the parties. NRS 16.140. It is important to make a record of any response desired that differs from the court's response.

A judge has wide discretion in the manner and extent of his response to a jury's request during deliberation for reading back testimony. *Milu v. State,* 97 Nev. 82, 624 P.2d 494 (1981). *See also* NRS 16.140. Many judges are reluctant to have testimony read back to the jury. It is a tedious time-consuming procedure which often raises more questions than answers. In the Eighth District some courts now use tape recorders instead of, or in addition to, court reporters. This procedure is permitted by NRS 3.380. It is far more convenient and meaningful to "re-play" the testimony (or even arguments) than to have it read from the stenographic notes. Caution is advised. Some have complained that the tape recorders are so sensitive they record counsel-client conversations which occur at counsel table. Screen any tapes to be played to the jury.

§ 2329. Jurors' right to take notes.

Upon retiring for its deliberation, the jury may take with them notes taken by themselves and not by any other person, of the testimony, or other proceedings on the trial. NRS 16.130.

While NRS 175.131 exists as statutory authority for the judge to inform the jury they may take notes in criminal trials, there is no parallel statutory provision for civil trials. However, NRS 16.130 allows jurors in civil trials to take with them upon retiring for deliberation notes of testimony taken by themselves, but none taken by any other person. Presumably, NRS 16.130 serves as the authority for judges permitting jurors to take notes.

If note taking is permitted, the trial attorney should seek an instruction informing the jury that the official record (court reporter's notes) prevails over their notes to the contrary. Strategically, one must also be cognizant of note takers on the jury. If an important point is inaccurately recorded, the entire jury may rely on the notes rather than their collection recollection.

§ 2330. Admonishment of jury.

At each adjournment of the court, whether the jurors are permitted to depart for home overnight or are kept in charge of officers, they must be admonished by the judge or another officer of the court that it is their duty not to: (1) [c]ommunicate among themselves or with any other person concerning their deliberations or any other subject connected with the trial; or (2) Read, watch, or listen to any report of or commentary on the trial or any person connected with the trial by any medium of information, including without limitation newspapers, television and radio.

Section 16.120(3).

§ 2331. Jurors' right to ask questions during trial.

There is a split of authority among the jurisdictions which have considered the question as to the propriety of jurors asking questions during trial. *See* Annot., 31 A.L.R.3d 872 (1970). Some courts have encouraged the practice of jurors asking questions as a means to better enable the jury to understand the facts and issues before it. *Annot., supra* at § 4(a), at 880-81. Other courts have criticized the practice. *Annot., supra* at § 4(b), at 881-82.

To obtain relief by an appellate court on the grounds of improper questioning by a juror, it has been held that there must be an affirmative showing that the improper questioning actually operated to the complaining party's detriment, or that the questioning reflected such prejudicial attitudes as to require reversal. *Annot.,* 31 A.L.R.3d, § 5 and § 6, at 882-83.

It does not appear that the Nevada Supreme Court has directly addressed the propriety of allowing jurors to ask questions during the trial. However, in *Kirkland v. State,* 95 Nev. 83, 590 P.2d 156 (1979), the court held that no prejudice resulted when, after a defense attorney in a criminal trial asked a security guard if he applied pressure to the defendant's arm to gain information, a juror asked, "What has this to do with a robbery?" The court stated that this question was not an improper conversation with fellow jurors or a commentary on the trial, and did not indicate a premature opinion of guilt. *Kirkland, supra,* at 84-85, 590 P.2d at 157. Rather, as noted by the court, the juror simply wanted to know the relevance of the question put to the witness. *Kirkland, supra,* at 85, 590 P.2d at 157.

§ 2332. Polling of jury.

When the verdict is given and is not informal or insufficient, the jury foreman or the clerk shall read it aloud. If the verdict is general, any party may request that the jury be polled. If a poll is requested, the clerk shall call the names of the jurors and ask each "Is this your verdict as read?" If more than one-fourth of the jurors disagree, the jury shall be again sent out; but if no disagreement is expressed, the clerk [records] the verdict in the minutes, the verdict is complete, and the jury [is] discharged from the case.

NRS 16.190.

§ 2333. Number of jurors' votes needed for verdict.

A civil case may be decided by the vote of three-fourths of the jurors. Nev. Const. Art. 1, § 3; *McNally v. Walkowski,* 85 Nev. 696, 462 P.2d 1016 (1969).

There is a split of authority as to whether the same combination of jurors needed for a majority must agree on all issues establishing liability. *See Tillman v. Thomas,* 99 Idaho 569, 585 P.2d 1280 (1978). As stated in *Tillman,* some courts have held that in order to reach a verdict, the same jurors comprising a majority must concur on each issue essential to the outcome of the case. *See, e.g., Earl v. Times-Mirror Co.,* 185 Cal. 165, 196 P. 57 (1921); *Baxter v. Tankersley,* 416 S.W.2d 737 (Ky. 1967); *Clark v. Strain,* 212 Or. 357, 319 P.2d 940 (1958); *Dick v. Heisler,* 184 Wis. 77, 198 N.W. 734 (1924).

Other courts have held that a majority consisting of different jurors on different issues may determine the outcome of a case. *See, e.g., McChristian v. Hooten,* 245 Ark. 1045, 436 S.W.2d 844 (1969); *Ward v. Weekes,* 107 N.J. Super. 351, 258 A.2d 379 (1969); *Naumburg v. Wagner,* 81 N.M. 242, 465 P.2d 521 (1970); *Fields v. Volkswagen of*

America, Inc., 555 P.2d 48 (Okla. 1976). This question has not been decided in Nevada.

§ 2334. Juror consistency in action involving comparative negligence.

Where unanimous vote of jurors is not required, the question arises whether the same jurors who agree on the issue of liability must also be the same jurors who apportion damages in a case involving comparative negligence. In other words, if six out of eight jurors decide that the defendant was negligent and was the proximate cause of the plaintiff's injuries, must those same six jurors also agree on how to apportion the damages among the parties?

The Nevada Supreme Court has not addressed this question. However, in California, it has been held that the same jurors who find liability do not have to be the same jurors who apportion damages. *Juarez v. Los Angeles Superior Court,* 31 Cal. 3d 759, 647 P.2d 128, 183 Cal. Rptr. 852 (1982). In *Juarez,* nine of twelve jurors in a personal injury action agreed that the defendants were negligent and the proximate cause of the plaintiff's injuries. In addition, nine of twelve jurors agreed as to the apportionment of damages under comparative negligence principles. However, the nine jurors who agreed on liability were not the same nine jurors who apportioned the damages. (In California, only nine of twelve jurors' votes are needed to reach a verdict in a civil case).

The California Supreme Court held in *Juarez* that it was permissible, in cases where principles of comparative negligence apply, for jurors who disagree with the majority on the issue of liability to provide votes necessary to decide the issue of how to apportion the damages among the parties.

§ 2335. Post-trial juror contact.

Post-trial juror contact is permissible, provided it is dignified and in accordance with the ethical requirements of the Supreme Court Rules and ABA Code of Professional Conduct. Post-trial juror contact is informative and educational. While the information obtained may serve a technical reinforcement, it must be remembered that the jurors should not be harassed or intimidated in any fashion. To the extent their comments serve as a basis for post-trial procedures, see § 2508, *infra.*

§ 2336. Jury misconduct.

See § 2508, *infra.* For general discussion of Nevada law, see *Stackiewicz v. Nissan Motor Corp.,* 100 Nev. 443, 686 P.2d 925 (1984), and *Hale v. Riverboat Casino, Inc.,* 100 Nev. 299, 682 P.2d 190 (1984).

§ 2337. General verdict.

In a general verdict, the jury finds for either the plaintiff or defendant in general terms. *See, e.g., Nelson v. Smith,* 42 Nev. 302, 310, 176 P. 261 (1918). ("We, the jury find the issues joined in this case in favor of the plaintiffs.")

A general verdict is a finding on all issues in favor of the prevailing party, and it must conform to the evidence and pleadings.

§ 2338. General verdict with written interrogatories.

NRCP 49(b) allows the court to "submit to the jury, together with appropriate forms for a general verdict, written interrogatories upon one or more issues of fact the decision of which is necessary to a verdict."

Three possibilities exist under NRCP 49(b) regarding consistency of answers to interrogatories with the verdict. If the answers and verdict are harmonious, "the court shall direct the entry of the appropriate judgment upon the verdict and answers." NRCP(b). If the answers are "consistent with each other but one or more is inconsistent with the general verdict, the court may direct the entry of judgment in accordance with the answers, ... return the jury for further consideration of its answers and verdict[,] or ... order a new trial." NRCP(b). If "the answers are inconsistent with each other and one or more is likewise inconsistent with the general verdict, the court shall not direct the entry of judgment but may return the jury for further consideration of its answers and verdict or may order a new trial." NRCP(b).

§ 2339. Effect of failure to request that jury answer written interrogatories.

In *Scott v. Chapman,* 71 Nev. 329, 291 P.2d 422 (1955), the jury, upon retiring, was handed a general verdict form with special interrogatories which it was directed to answer. The jury subsequently returned a verdict in favor of the defendant, but did not answer the interrogatories. No objections were made to the jury's failure to answer the interrogatories.

On appeal, the Nevada Supreme Court held that any error resulting from the failure of the jury to answer the special interrogatories was waived in view of the plaintiffs' failure, when the verdict was returned, to call the matter to the attention of the court and request that the jury be directed to answer the interrogatories. *Scott v. Chapman,* 71 Nev. 329, 331, 291 P.2d 422, 423 (1955). In so ruling, the court said that, since counsel for the plaintiffs knew of the provisions of NRCP 49(b), their failure to inquire into the status of the interrogatories indicated an intention not to rely upon any inconsistency or error which the answers to the interrogatories might reveal. *Scott, supra,* at 334, 291 P.2d at 424.

See also Eberhard Manufacturing Co. v. Baldwin, 97 Nev. 271, 628 P.2d 681 (1981).

§ 2340. Special verdict.

"The court may require a jury to return only a special verdict in the form of a special written finding upon each issue of fact." NRCP 49(a). The determination whether to require a special verdict is addressed to the broad discretion of the trial court. *Ross v. Giacomo,* 97 Nev. 550, 555, 635 P.2d 298, 301 (1981).

NRCP 49(a) provides several methods of submitting issues of fact to the jury. The court may (1) "submit written questions susceptible of categorical or other brief answer;" (2) "submit written forms of the several special findings which might properly be made under the pleadings and evidence;" or (3) "use such other method of submitting the issues and requiring the written findings thereon as it deems most appropriate."

If the court decides to use a special verdict, it is desirable for it to notify the parties in advance so they may intelligently prepare requested charges, determine all of the issues that must be submitted, and plan an effective argument.

After the jury reports back to the court on the issues of fact in its special verdict, the court translates those findings into a judgment by applying the law. This procedure leaves to the trial judge the responsibility of applying appropriate legal principles to the facts found by the jury, and the jury need not be instructed concerning the legal principles which the jury will apply to the fact found by them. In translating the jury's findings, the court should literally construe the verdict in order to reach a reasonable interpretation of the jury's intent in view of the evidence presented at trial. *See Cerminara v. California Hotel & Casino,* 104 Nev. 372, 760 P.2d 108 (1988) (although special verdict returned by jury listed "$0" for amount of damages for intentional torts, reasonable interpretation of verdict consistent with evidence was that $5,000 awarded for "total damages" was lump compensatory award which included damages for the intentional torts).

§ 2341. Special verdict: comparative negligence.

NRS 41.141 requires the use of both general and special verdicts in actions involving comparative negligence. If the jury in such an action determines that the plaintiff is entitled to recover, it is required to return: (1) a general verdict indicating "the total amount of damages the plaintiff would be entitled to recover without regard to his comparative negligence;" and (2) "and special verdict indicating the percentage of negligence attributable to each party remaining in the action."

§ 2342. Jury not to be informed of existence or amount of settlement with other defendant.

As amended in 1987, NRS 41.141(3) provides that if a defendant in an action where comparative negligence is asserted as a defense "settles with the plaintiff before the entry of judgment, the comparative negligence of that defendant and the amount of the settlement must not thereafter be admitted into evidence nor considered by the jury. The judge shall deduct the amount of the settlement from the net sum otherwise recoverable by the plaintiff pursuant to the general and special verdicts."

In *Moore v. Brannen*, 106 Nev. 679, 799 P.2d 564 (1990), the court held that the jury also may not be informed of the *fact* of settlement with a co-defendant, since much knowledge may lead to improper speculation.

§ 2343. Clarifying the verdict by jury interrogatory before dismissal.

If the verdict returned by the jury is inconsistent, the parties should seek clarification from the jury before it is dismissed. *Amoroso Construction v. Lazovich & Lazovich*, 107 Nev. 294, 810 P.2d 775 (1991). In *Amoroso Construction*, the verdict returned by the jury awarded damages for breach of contract, *no* damages for fraud, and included an award for punitive damages. Since punitive damages are not permitted solely for breach of contract, the court sent the jury (before its dismissal) an interrogatory asking it to clarify the verdict. The jury explained that it had indeed found liability for fraud, but had included those damages in the award for breach of contract. Thus, an award of punitive damages was proper.

The court, in *Amoroso Construction*, declared that the classification procedure was consistent with *Eberhard Manufacturing Co. v. Baldwin*, 97 Nev. 271, 628 P.2d 681 (1981), and *Novack v. Hoppin*, 77 Nev. 33, 359 P.2d 390 (1961), and that such a procedure should be followed in order to cure inconsistencies and prevent re-trials.

§ 2344. Reconvening the jury to clarify a verdict after dismissal.

In *Sierra Foods v. Williams*, 107 Nev. 574, 816 P.2d 466 (1991), the Nevada Supreme Court held that a trial court has jurisdiction to reconvene an "already-dismissed jury" in order to clarify an apparent inconsistency in a verdict if, at the time it is reconvened, the jury has not yet dispersed and there is no evidence that it has been subjected to outside influences from the time of initial discharge to the time of re-empanelment.

In *Williams*, an error was discovered in the verdict shortly after the jury was excused. The trial judge recalled the jury, which then explained and corrected the verdict. The Supreme Court concluded that, under the circumstances, re-empanelment was proper, explaining:

> In the instant case, the jury had not left the courthouse and remained under the *de facto* control of the court. Further, appellants produced no evidence that the jury was subjected to outside influences from the time of initial discharge. The facts of the instant case thus satisfy the standard developed in [*Newport Fisherman's Supply v. Derecktor*, 569 A.2d 1051 (R.I. 1990) and *Masters v. State*, 344 So. 2d 616 (Fla. App. 1977)]: the exception to the general rule applies when the jury has not yet dispersed or lost its separate identity and when the moving party has presented no proof of outside influence. We conclude that the district court never lost jurisdiction over the jury.

Id. at 576, 816 P.2d at 467.

§ 2345. Special verdict: past damages and future damages/prejudgment interest.

A special verdict which indicates what part of a total verdict is allocated to past damages is required before prejudgment interest may properly be awarded. *Stickler v. Quilici*, 98 Nev. 595, 655 P.2d 527 (1982).

In *Stickler*, the jury returned a general verdict which did not apportion the total award between past and future damages. Prejudgment interest was awarded on the entire verdict. On appeal, the Nevada Supreme Court held that the award of prejudgment interest was erroneous, since interest may not be awarded for any amount representing future damages, and since the verdict failed to distinguish between past and future damages. *Stickler v. Quilici*, 98 Nev. 595, 597, 655 P.2d 527 (1982).

Stickler v. Quilici, 98 Nev. 595, 655 P.2d 527 (1982), was followed in *Jacobson v. Manfredi*, 100 Nev. 226, 679 P.2d 251 (1984) and *Wilkes v. Anderson*, 100 Nev. 433, 683 P.2d 35 (1984). In both of these personal injury cases, the Nevada Supreme Court held that prejudgment interest was improperly allowed on verdicts which did not distinguish between past and future damages. In *Jacobson*, the judgment was modified to include prejudgment interest only on the part of the verdict representing the plaintiff's past medical expenses. In *Wilkes*, a jury verdict in favor of the plaintiff (which had been vacated by a j.n.o.v.) was reinstated, but the matter was remanded to the district court to allow further proceedings on the issue of prejudgment interest.

The rule set forth in *Stickler* was held to be incapable in *Farmers Home Mortgage Insurance Co. v. Fiscus*, 102 Nev. 371, 725 P.2d 234 (1986). In *Farmers Home Mortgage Insurance Co.*, the trial court, after a bench trial, entered judgment in favor of the plaintiff in an action based on the defendant-insurer's breach of contract and breach of the implied covenant of good faith and fair dealing. The judgment included an award of $20,000 representing the plaintiff's damages for mental and emotional distress. Prejudgment interest was awarded on the entire judgment.

On appeal, the defendant argued that *Stickler* precluded the allowance of prejudgment interest on the part of the judgment representing damages for emotional distress, since the judgment did not specify whether the award was for past or future damages. The Nevada Supreme Court rejected this argument. In so doing, the Court noted that, unlike *Stickler,* there was nothing in the record to suggest that future damages were included in the award. Thus, *Stickler* was distinguishable and the award of prejudgment interest was upheld.

In *State v. Eaton,* 101 Nev. 705, 710 P.2d 1370 (1985), the court held that "past damages" subject to the prejudgment interest statute (NRS 17.130(2)) included damages incurred to the date of the jury verdict. However, prejudgment interest may not be awarded on punitive damages. *Ramada Inns Inc. v. Sharp,* 101 Nev. 824, 711 P.2d 1 (1985).

Also, in *Ramadanis v. Stupak,* 104 Nev. 57, 752 P.2d 767 (1988), the court found that where the jury instruction refers only to damages "suffered" and made no reference to future damages, there was no commingling of past and future damages apparent in the jury's verdict, and, therefore, prejudgment interest of the damages awarded was proper. Thus, if the damage instruction refers only to past damages, the special verdict is unnecessary, and prejudgment interest is awardable.

If damages are sustained after the complaint is served but before judgment, prejudgment interest begins to accrue from the date of actual injury. *LTR Stage Lines v. Gray Line Tours,* 106 Nev. 283, 792 P.2d 386 (1990). In 1987, the Nevada Legislature established an adjustable interest rate on judgments. It amended NRS 17.130(2) to provide that a judgment draws interest:

> At a rate equal to the prime rate at the largest bank in Nevada as ascertained by the commissioner of financial institutions on January 1 or July 1, as the case may be, immediately preceding the date of judgment, plus 2 percent. The rate must be adjusted accordingly on each January 1 and July 1 thereafter until the judgment is satisfied.

1987 Nev. Stat., ch. 413, § 1, p. 940.

This adjustable interest rate applies only to causes of action which arise on or after July 1, 1987. 1987 Nev. Stat., ch. 413, § 8, p. 943.

CHAPTER 24

JUDGMENTS

Authors: David R. Grundy
          Michael A. Rosenauer
          Susan Ball Rothe

§ 2401. Introduction and scope.

The subject of judgments is treated extensively in Chapter 17 of the Nevada Revised Statutes as well as in NRCP 54 through 58, 60 and 68. This chapter discusses the nature and effect of offers of judgment, the forms and effect of judgments, as well as the procedure for the entry, modification, assignment and satisfaction of judgments. Also, the various types of judgments, their validity, and actions upon judgments are discussed.

Treated elsewhere in this work are defaults and default judgments (Chapter 10, *supra*), summary judgments (Chapter 17, *supra*), relief from judgments (Chapter 25, *infra*), enforcement of judgments (Chapter 27, *infra*) and declaratory judgments (Chapter 31, *infra*).

§ 2402. Offers of judgment under NRCP 68.

NRCP 68 was adopted as a modified version of Fed. R. Civ. P. 68. NRCP 68, amended in 1987, provides as follows:

At any time more than 10 days before the trial begins, any party may serve upon the adverse party an offer to allow judgment to be entered for the money or property or to the effect specified in the offer, with costs then accrued. If within 10 days after the service of the offer the adverse party serves written notice that the offer is accepted, either party may then file the offer and notice of acceptance together with proof of service thereof and thereupon the clerk shall enter judgment. An offer not accepted shall be deemed withdrawn and evidence thereof is not admissible except in a proceeding to determine costs. If the judgment finally obtained by the offeree is not more favorable than the offer, the offeree shall not recover costs, nor attorneys' fees, but shall pay the costs and attorneys' fees, if any be allowed, of the party making the offer from the time of the offer. The fact that an offer is made but not accepted does not preclude a subsequent offer. When the liability of one party to another has been determined by verdict or order or judgment, but the amount or extent of the liability remains to be determined by further proceedings, the party adjudged liable may make an offer of judgment, which shall have the same effect as an offer made before trial if it is served within a reasonable time not less than 10 days prior to the commencement of hearings to determine the amount or extent of liability.

The principle difference between the Nevada and Federal rules is that Fed. R. Civ. P. 68 does not allow the recovery of attorneys' fees. In certain circumstances, however, a federal court can award attorneys' fees as part of Fed. R. Civ. P. 68, where an underlying substantive statute, which is an issue in the case, defines "costs" to include attorneys' fees. *Marek v. Chesny,* 473 U.S. 1, 105 S. Ct. 3012, 87 L. Ed. 2d 1 (1985). Despite the similarities of NRCP 68 and Fed. R. Civ. P. 68, the Nevada Supreme Court recognized a distinction between the two rules when it noted that NRCP 68 expressly includes attorneys' fees and thereby provides an additional incentive to settle. *See Beattie v. Thomas,* 99 Nev. 579, 668 P.2d 268 (1983), where the Nevada Supreme Court also rejected a United States Supreme Court interpretation of Fed. R. Civ. P. 68.

The purpose of NRCP 68 is to encourage the settlement of litigation, but not to force plaintiffs unfairly to forego legitimate claims. *Beattie v. Thomas,* 99 Nev. 579, 668 P.2d 268 (1983). Even though offers to compromise have been favored in Nevada law since early days of statehood, *Wedekind v. Bell,* 26 Nev. 395, 69 P. 612 (1902), the Nevada Supreme Court has been circumspect in its application of Rule 68. For a defendant to use Rule 68 successfully, great care must be used in planning and executing an offer of judgment. Serious consideration should also be given to making two offers of judgment during the course of litigation: one at the beginning of the case and a second offer of judgment at the conclusion of the discovery.

NRCP 68 applies to class actions even though it is difficult to notify all the members of a class within the ten-day notice period. *Schouweiler v. Yancey Co.,* 101 Nev. 827, 712 P.2d 786 (1985). Because of public policy consideration, the rule does not apply to divorce proceedings, child support cases, or child custody matters. *Leeming v. Leeming,* 87 Nev. 530, 490 P.2d 342 (1971).

§ 2403. — Form.

An offer of judgment must conform to the requirements contained in NRCP 68. An offer to allow judgment to be taken must be formally tendered to the adverse party. *Sherman Gardens Co. v. Longley,* 87 Nev. 558, 491 P.2d 48 (1971).

The rule requires that the party making the offer serve upon the adverse party an offer to allow judgment to be entered "for the money or property or to the effect specified in the offer, with costs then accrued." The offer is not filed at the time of service, but only upon acceptance by the adverse party, after a verdict or judgment, or upon a motion for costs or attorneys' fees. And see *Ramadanis v. Stupak,* 104 Nev. 57, 752 P.2d 767 (1988), where the court, in dicta, stated that separate offers to two plaintiffs conditional upon acceptance by both were invalid.

The rule requires that the party making the offer specify a sum of money, or property, or "to the effect" the offering party will allow judgment to be entered. The offer must be for a definite or ascertainable amount so that the parties can be unequivocally aware of what the offering party is willing to pay for his peace. The offer must specify a definite sum for which judgment may be entered, so that the party can either accept or reject it. If the offer is conditional or indefinite, it is void for the purposes of NRCP 68. *See Stockton Kenworth, Inc. v. Mentzer Detroit Diesel, Inc.,* 101 Nev. 400, 705 P.2d 145 (1985), where the Nevada Supreme Court declined to apply Rule 68 to an offer that included a condition that the plaintiff deliver "good title" to a truck in exchange for $10,000.

Interesting issues are raised when there are multiple plaintiffs and defendants. At least in some circumstances, offers of judgment to or from multiple parties must be apportioned to allow parties to evaluate independently the potential risks and benefits of proceeding to trial. Where there are multiple plaintiffs, a defendant's offers of judgment must be apportioned so that plaintiffs can accept or reject independently. If an unapportional offer is made, it is invalid even if the combined awards at trial are less favorable than the unapportional offer of judgment. *Ramadanis v. Stupak,* 104 Nev. 57, 752 P.2d 767 (1988). In such cases it is impossible to determine that any one plaintiff received a less favorable result than he would have under the offer of compromise.

By the same token, where the offer of judgment is made by multiple plaintiffs, it too must be apportional to be valid. Otherwise, the defendant is deprived of the opportunity to evaluate the likelihood of each plaintiff receiving a more favorable verdict. *Morgan v. DeMille,* 106 Nev. 671, 799 P.2d 561 (1990). In *Morgan,* the court commented upon the importance to the goal of encouraging settlement that the rule be enforced equally as between plaintiffs and defendants.

An offer by one of several defendants who may be jointly and severally liable to plaintiff must exceed the total judgment awarded against joint and several defendants. *Schouweiler v. Yancy Co.,* 101 Nev. 827, 712 P.2d 786 (1985). An offer made by a defendant whose only liability is several, however, should be considered more favorable if that defendant's offer exceeds the portion of the judgment attributable to him.

Joint offers of judgment by joint and several defendants would seem to be acceptable. The court let stand a joint offer in *National Union Fire Insurance Co. v. Pratt & Whitney,* 107 Nev. 535, 815 P.2d 601 (1991), for consideration by the trial court as the date from which attorneys' fees were to be allowed.

The rules requires an offer must be made "with costs then accrued." An offer may be for a specified sum which "includes costs" since defendants would be establishing their total liability. *Fleischer v. August,* 103 Nev. 242, 737 P.2d 518 (1987). By the same token, an offer should judicate whether prejudgment interest or attorney's fees (where recoverable) are to be included or added to the judgment offer.

An ambiguity in an offer of judgment may be explained after service, but before acceptance. An offeree cannot accept an offer adopting terms inconsistent with the written offer of subsequent explanation of those terms by the offeror. *Fleischer v. August*, 103 Nev. 242, 737 P.2d 518 (1987).

However, the Nevada Supreme Court has held that where an offer of judgment fails to comply in a "material aspect" with NRCP 68, it is defective and cannot serve as support for a motion for attorneys' fees and costs. *Wickliffe v. Fletcher Jones of Las Vegas, Inc.*, 99 Nev. 353, 661 P.2d 1295 (1983).

A Rule 68 offer should be made in conjunction with an offer of judgment pursuant to NRS 17.115. Rule 68 does not mention prejudgment interest whereas NRS 17.115 permits the prevailing party to avoid prejudgment interest. The benefits available to the offeror under Rule 68 are limited to the scope of Rule 68 and will not be extended, unless the offer is also made with reference to NRS 17.115. *Ramadanis v. Stupak*, 104 Nev. 57, 752 P.2d 767 (1988). *See also* §§ 2408 and 2409, *infra*.

§ 2404. — Party who may make offer of judgment.

Prior to January 1, 1988, a Rule 68 offer of judgment was available only to "a party defending against a claim." Such parties included defendants, counter-defendants and cross-defendants with respect to the claims being made against them. The Nevada Supreme Court amended Rule 68, effective January 1, 1988, to allow plaintiffs to make offers of judgment. Now that both sides in litigation can avail themselves of the benefits of Rule 68, the Nevada Supreme Court may be more inclined to sustain an award of attorneys' fees to the party entitled thereunder.

§ 2405. — Timing.

An offer of judgment may be served upon the adverse party at any time more than ten days before the trial begins. An offer which is served with insufficient time prior to trial will not afford the offeror the advantages of Rule 68. *Wickliffe v. Fletcher Jones of Las Vegas, Inc.*, 99 Nev. 353, 661 P.2d 1295 (1983). It should be noted that since service must occur "more than ten days" before the trial begins, and since an additional three days must be afforded for service by mail (NRCP 6(e)), an offer of judgment by mail must be served at least fourteen days prior to trial. However, it is suggested that the most prudent method of service is by hand delivery or receipt of copy by the opposing counsel.

In certain instances, an offer of judgment may be made after a trial. Where the liability of one party to another is determined in a bifurcated proceeding (or otherwise by verdict, order or judgment), but damages or the extent of liability remains for a separate proceeding, an offer of judgment may still be made. In such circumstances, the offer of judgment must be served within a reasonable time not less than ten days prior to the damages hearing or subsequent trial, and it shall have the same effect as if made prior to the first trial. NRCP 68.

§ 2406. — Acceptance.

The party receiving service of an offer of judgment accepts the offer by serving written notice to that effect upon the offeror. Either party may then file the offer and notice of acceptance together with proof of service thereof and the clerk shall then enter judgment. Although a formal request to the clerk is not explicitly required by the rule, it is recommended that the request for entry of judgment directed to the clerk be formal and filed in the action.

An offer which is not accepted within ten days after service is deemed automatically withdrawn. An offer is not admissible as evidence in the action except in a proceeding to determine costs or other remedies available after judgment under this rule. However, subsequent offers of judgment may be made after an offer is made but not accepted. NRCP 68.

§ 2407. — Effect of failure to accept.

If an offer is not accepted and the case proceeds to trial, the party who fails to accept the offer may be subject to adverse consequences. Even though the party to whom the offer was directed may receive a favorable verdict or judgment, if the outcome is not more favorable than the terms of the offer of judgment, the offeree shall not recover costs or attorneys' fees. In addition, the offeree shall pay the costs of the offeror and the court, in its discretion, may award attorneys' fees in favor of the offeror incurred from the time of the offer. The award of attorneys' fees is discretionary under the rule, but the court cannot refuse to consider a motion for attorneys' fees on the basis of NRS 18.010 which otherwise limits the availability of attorneys' fees in this state. *Armstrong v. Riggi,* 92 Nev. 280, 549 P.2d 753 (1976). And, if a party is precluded from recovery of attorneys' fees because of an offer of judgment, that party is also foreclosed from recovering fees as a prevailing party under NRS 18.010. *Bowyer v. Taack,* 107 Nev. 625, 817 P.2d 1176 (1991).

In determining if a judgment is "more favorable" than an offer of judgment, the court cannot consider prejudgment interest, costs or attorneys' fees. *Bowyer v. Taack, supra.*

The Nevada Supreme Court has set forth several factors which must be considered by trial courts in determining when and how to exercise their discretion in the award of attorneys' fees after a Rule 68 offer of judgment. Those factors include: (1) whether the plaintiff's claim was brought in good faith; (2) whether the offer of judgment was reasonable and in good faith in both its timing and amount; (3) whether the decision to reject the offer and proceed to trial was grossly unreasonable or in bad faith; and, (4) whether the fees sought by the offeror are reasonable and justified in amount. Before awarding fees, the court should make specific findings that the attorneys' fees sought are reasonable and justified and that the foregoing factors were considered by the court. *Beattie v. Thomas,* 99 Nev. 579, 668 P.2d 268, 274 (1983). Where the court fails to consider these factors, and makes no findings based on evidence that the attorney's fees sought are reasonable and justified, it may be an abuse of discretion for the court to award the full amount of fees requested. The trial court need not decide every factor in favor of its decision; it need only weigh the factors. *National Union Fire Insurance Co. v. Pratt & Whitney,* 107 Nev. 535, 815 P.2d 601 (1991).

In determining whether an offeree acted in "bad faith" or was "unreasonable" in rejecting an offer and proceeding to trial, the Nevada Supreme Court demonstrated its reluctance to assess attorneys' fees against the plaintiffs in *Trustees of Carpenters for Southern Nevada Health & Welfare Trust v. Better Building Co.,* 101 Nev. 742, 710 P.2d 1379 (1985), where the Court noted that the plaintiffs (union trustees) had a fiduciary duty to its union members to collect employer contributions from the defendant. The Nevada Supreme Court held that the lower court did not abuse its discretion in refusing to award attorneys' fees where the plaintiff was unable to obtain essential documents from the defendant until nine months after the offer of judgment had lapsed. Because access to key information is important in determining whether a party was "unreasonable" in rejecting an offer, the offeror should consider tendering an offer of judgment at the conclusion of discovery.

The award of attorneys' fees, in the proper circumstances, is discretionary with the trial court judge and will not be disturbed on appeal unless it appears that the lower court's exercise of discretion was arbitrary or capricious. *Schouweiler v. Yancey Co.,* 101 Nev. 827, 712 P.2d 786 (1985). In determining the amount of attorneys' fees, the amount of the offer of judgment is irrelevant. *See Schouweiler, supra,* 712 P.2d at 790.

The recovery of expert witness fees, is not likely in a Rule 68 offer in light of *Trustees of Carpenters for Southern Nevada Health & Welfare Trust v. Better Building Co.,* 101 Nev. 742, 710 P.2d 1379, 1382 (1985). In that case, the Nevada Supreme Court indicated, by way of dicta, that NRCP 68 should "not be read together" with NRS 17.115 so as to permit the award of expert witness fees in situations where the offer of judgment is tendered under NRCP 68 and not under NRS 17.115.

451

§ 2408. Offer of judgment under NRS 17.115.

After the enactment of the Nevada Rules of Civil Procedure and Rule 68, the Nevada Legislature enacted NRS 17.115. The Nevada Legislature amended NRS 17.115 in 1987 to change the timing of the offer and to include provisions relating to attorney's fees and expert witness fees. NRS 17.115 provides as follows:

1. At any time more than 10 days before trial, either informally or at any pretrial conference presided over by a judge of the court in which the action is pending, any party may serve an offer in writing to allow judgment to be taken in accordance with the terms and conditions stated at that time.

2. If the offer is accepted, the judge of the court in which the action is pending shall enter judgment accordingly.

3. If the offer is not accepted before trial or within 10 days after it is made, whichever occurs first, it shall be deemed withdrawn, and cannot be given in evidence upon the trial.

4. If the party to whom the offer of judgment is made fails to obtain a more favorable judgment, he cannot recover: (a) Interest on the judgment for the period between the time of service of the summons and complaint and the time of entry of the judgment; or, (b) costs or attorney's fees, and the court shall order him to pay to the party who made the offer that party's taxable costs incurred from the date of filing the complaint and may order also a reasonable sum to cover costs of the services of expert witnesses who are not regular employees of any party actually incurred and reasonably necessary in the preparation of the case for trial by the prevailing party, interest on the judgment from the time of the offer to the time of entry of the judgment and reasonable attorney's fees incurred by the party making the offer from the time of the offer.

5. Any taxable costs, attorney's fees and interest which is not derived from an interest-bearing obligation which may have been awarded must not be considered to be part of the judgment when determining whether the judgment was more favorable than the rejected offer.

6. If the attorney of the party for whom the offer of judgment is made is collecting a contingent fee for his services, the amount of any attorney's fees awarded to the party for whom the offer is made must be deducted from that contingent fee.

7. Any judgment entered pursuant to this section shall be deemed a compromise settlement.

In comparison to Rule 68, NRS 17.115 provides additional advantages to the prevailing party relating to prejudgment interest and expert witness fees. To invoke the additional benefits of NRS 17.115, the offer of judgment must be made with reference to this statute. Otherwise, an offer made solely under Rule 68 will be limited to the scope of Rule 68. *Ramadanis v. Stupak,* 104 Nev. 57, 752 P.2d 767 (1988).

Offers under both Rule 68 and NRS 17.115 have been encouraged, however. The court has held that the differences between the rule and the statute will be interpreted harmoniously. An offer made with reference to both will have the advantages of both. *Bowyer v. Taack*, 107 Nev. 625, 817 P.2d 1176 (1991).

§ 2409. — Form.

A statutory offer must be in writing and, like its Rule 68 counterpart, must be served upon the adverse party (but not filed with the court). There is no reason why a properly worded offer may not be made under both Rule 68 and NRS 17.115.

§ 2410. — Availability.

Both the statutory offer of judgment and the Rule 68 offer are available to any party, including plaintiffs, counterclaimants and cross-claimants.

§ 2411. — Timing.

The statutory offer must be served more than ten days before trial and is, in this aspect, exactly like its Rule 68 counterpart.

§ 2412. — Acceptance.

The offeree may accept the offer up to ten days after the offer is made, or prior to trial, whichever occurs first. If the offer is not accepted within those time limits, it is deemed withdrawn and cannot be given in evidence at the trial.

If the offer is accepted, the judge of the court enters judgment in accordance with the terms of the offer. There is no corresponding provision to allow the clerk to enter judgment as is contained in NRCP 68.

§ 2413. — Effect of failure to accept.

If the party to whom an offer is made under this section fails to accept the offer and subsequently fails to obtain a more favorable judgment than the terms contained in the offer, that party cannot recover costs, attorney's fees or any prejudgment interest otherwise allowed by NRS 17.130. In addition, the court shall order him to pay the offeror's taxable costs incurred from the date of the filing of the complaint. In this respect, the statutory offer differs from Rule 68, because the rule only allows costs from the time of the offer rather than the time of filing the complaint. The court may also award a reasonable sum to cover the costs of expert witnesses who are not regular employees of any party, subject to the proviso that the charges were actually incurred and reasonably necessary in the preparation of the case for trial. Reasonable attorney's fees, as well as interest on the judgment from time of offer until entry, may also be awarded by the court. An award of attorneys' fees incurred before the offer is made, however, is invalid. *National Union Fire Insurance v. Pratt & Whitney*, 107 Nev. 535, 815 P.2d 601 (1991). If the court awards attorney's fees, the statute mandates that the attorney must give his client a corresponding credit on his fee when the case is being handled on a contingent fee basis. No such limitation, however, is placed upon attorneys who are retained on other fee arrangements.

The statutory offer contains some guidelines in determining what constitutes a "more favorable judgment." NRS 17.115(5) excludes taxable costs, attorney's fees and interest (which is not derived from an interest-bearing obligation) from calculating the judgment obtained. These same guidelines have been held to apply to Rule 68 offers. *Bowyer v. Taack*, 107 Nev. 625, 817 P.2d 1176 (1991). Despite some differences, both NRS 17.115 and Rule 68 have been held to be nonexclusive and valid in their own right. *Beattie v. Thomas,* 99 Nev. 579, 668 P.2d 268 (1983).

§ 2414. Rendition of judgments in general.

William Blackstone defined judgment as "the sentence of law, pronounced by the court upon the matter contained in the record." *Humboldt Mill & Mining Co. v. Terry,* 11 Nev. 237 (1876). NRCP 54(a) defines judgment as "a decree and any order from which an appeal lies."

The time and place of rendition of judgment had real significance in Nevada prior to the enactment of the Rules of Civil Procedure. As will be seen below, however, the significance of rendition has been largely obviated by NRCP 58, and now the entry of the judgment controls its effectiveness. *See* § 2417, *infra.* The counsel who obtains the judgment must submit the form of the judgment to the clerk or the judge. DCR 21 and EDCR 7.21.

§ 2415. — Elements of rendition: writing.

NRCP 58 and NRS 17.120 *et seq.* generally set forth the elements required of a valid judgment. NRCP 58 provides as follows:

(a) Judgment upon the verdict of a jury. Unless the court otherwise directs, and subject to the provisions of Rule 54(b), judgment upon the verdict of a jury shall be forthwith signed by the clerk and filed. If there is a special verdict or a general verdict accompanied by answers to interrogatories returned by a jury pursuant to Rule 49, the court shall direct the appropriate judgment which shall be forthwith signed by the clerk and filed.

(b) Judgment in other cases. Except as provided in subdivision (a) hereof, and subdivision (b)(1) of Rule 55, all judgments shall be signed by the judge and filed with the clerk.

(c) When judgment entered. The filing with the clerk of a judgment, signed by the judge, or by the clerk, as the case may be, constitutes the entry of such judgment, and no judgment shall be effective for any purpose until the entry of the same, as hereinbefore provided. The entry of the judgment shall not be delayed for the taxing of costs.

(d) Judgment roll. The judgment, as signed and filed, shall constitute the judgment roll.

At one time, the oral pronouncement of a decision in open court was sufficient to constitute the rendition of judgment. *Dillon v. Dillon*, 67 Nev. 428, 220 P.2d 213 (1950). However, NRCP 58 now requires judgments to be in writing and filed with the clerk. *See Fitzharris v. Phillips*, 74 Nev. 371, 333 P.2d 721 (1958), where the Supreme Court also cited the notes of the Advisory Committee on the Rules of Civil Procedure concerning the source and application of Rule 58:

This is a new rule of which subsections (a) and (b) were adapted from Utah, and subsection (c) from New Mexico. It is considered clearer than the federal rule and more desirable than present Nevada law. Under this rule, judgment will become effective, and time will start to run, only when it has been signed and filed with the clerk....

Where a written judgment is inconsistent with minute orders entered by the court or clerk, the written judgment controls. *Bowers v. Edwards*, 79 Nev. 384, 385 P.2d 783 (1963). Similarly, since the court is free to change its decision at any time prior to entry of final judgment, oral pronouncements from the bench, a clerk's minute order, and even an unfiled written order are ineffective for any purposes and cannot be appealed. *Rust v. Clark County School District*, 103 Nev. 686, 747 P.2d 1380 (1987).

§ 2416. — Signing.

A judgment must be signed either by the judge or the clerk of the court. The clerk is authorized, in certain circumstances, to enter judgment by default pursuant to NRCP 55(b)(1). *See* §§ 1011 and 1014, *supra*. The clerk may also enter judgments on jury verdicts, with some exceptions. NRCP 58. The court shall direct the appropriate judgment, which shall be signed by the clerk and filed, where there is a special verdict or general verdict accompanied by answers to interrogatories returned by the jury. NRCP 58(a).

§ 2417. — Filing.

Under NRCP 58(c), no judgment shall be effective for any purpose until it is signed by the judge or by the clerk and filed with the clerk of the court. *Paradise Palms Community Association v. Paradise Homes*, 93 Nev. 488, 568 P.2d 577 (1977); *Fitzharris v. Phillips*, 74 Nev. 371, 333

P.2d 721 (1958). *See also* § 1121, *supra,* where the entry of orders is discussed. The judgment must be filed with the clerk before the judge retires or vacates office. *Fox v. Fox,* 84 Nev. 368, 441 P.2d 678 (1968). *See Lagrange Construction, Inc. v. Del E. Webb Corp.,* 83 Nev. 524, 435 P.2d 515 (1967), where the court stated that filing with the clerk is jurisdictional because of the mandate of NRCP 58(c), even though entry by the clerk is ministerial in nature.

§ 2418. — Time of entry.

At one time, the Nevada statutes required the judges to render written decisions within thirty days of the conclusion of the trial. This rule, however, was not vigorously enforced. In *Schultz v. Provenzano,* 69 Nev. 324, 251 P.2d 294 (1952), the Nevada Supreme Court held that a delay of eleven months did not constitute grounds for reversal. The present rule is that the mere passage of time between the trial and the entry of judgment is not sufficient, in itself, to compel a reversal; the aggrieved party must show that the delay resulted in prejudice in order to reverse the judgment. A delay of four years prior to entry of judgment was not held to constitute prejudice to the losing party where the evidence to support the judgment was a matter of public record rather than human memory. *Anderson v. Richards,* 96 Nev. 318, 608 P.2d 1096 (1980). However, in *Bergendahl v. Davis,* 102 Nev. 258, 720 P.2d 694 (1986), the Supreme Court reversed a judgment that was entered seven years after trial. The court found that the delay resulted in "severe prejudice" to the right to appeal because the court reporter's notes had been destroyed during the seven-year interval.

The Supreme Court has condoned the practice of allowing trial courts, with consent of the parties, to delay the entry of judgment following the trial for the purpose of encouraging settlement. *Heard v. Fisher's & Cobb Sales & Distributors, Inc.,* 88 Nev. 566, 502 P.2d 104 (1972). However, if the parties stipulate to dismiss before the court enters judgment, the court is deprived of jurisdiction to enter a judgment or decision, even though the trial has been concluded. *Jeep Corp. & American Motors Corp. v. Second Judicial District Court,* 98 Nev. 440, 652 P.2d 1183 (1982).

§ 2419. — Entry on the judgment roll.

The judgment, as signed and filed, shall constitute the judgment roll. NRCP 58(d). The Advisory Committee's Note to NRCP 58 points out that the judgment roll, as formerly known, is no longer necessary for appeal or for any purpose. However, reference is made in Rule 58(d) because other statutes refer to the filing of the judgment roll. *See* Advisory Committee Note, NRCP 58, Annotations to Nevada Revised Statutes.

§ 2420. — Entry on the judgment docket.

The clerk of each district court is required by statute to keep a judgment docket. The docket is a book kept in the office of the clerk which reflects the names of judgment debtors, judgment creditors, the nature of the judgment entered, the time of entry of the judgment, whether an appeal was taken, when the appeal was taken, the judgment of the appellate court, whether a satisfaction was made and when that satisfaction of judgment was entered. The judgment docket is kept in alphabetical order by the names of the judgment debtors. NRS 17.160.

Entries must be made in the docket "immediately after filing a judgment." NRS 17.150. The docket is available and open to the public for inspection without charge. NRS 17.170.

§ 2421. Demand for judgment (NRCP 54(c)).

When a claim for relief is asserted, whether as an original claim, counterclaim, third-party claim, etc., the pleading must include a demand for judgment. NRCP 8(a)(2). Notwithstanding NRCP 8(a)(2), the court can grant relief which has not been requested in the pleadings. NRCP 54(c).

The rationale underlying NRCP 54(c) was discussed by the Nevada Supreme Court in *Magill v. Lewis,* 74 Nev. 381, 333 P.2d 717 (1958), where a judgment in favor of the plaintiff was affirmed upon a theory of unjust enrichment, even though the complaint did not mention that theory. The Supreme Court affirmed the judgment on the basis of NRCP 54(c) because the legal theories advanced by counsel are "subordinated to the court's right and duty to grant the relief to which the prevailing party is entitled, whether demanded or not." *Magill, supra, at* 388. The court reasoned that under our "liberalized rules" of pleading, the "judgment is to be based upon what has been proved rather than what has been pleaded." As a result, the prayer for relief may be of assistance in indicating the type of relief to which the plaintiff is entitled, but it is not controlling. *Magill, supra.* Likewise, the award of interest in a collection case for services rendered was upheld by the Nevada Supreme Court pursuant to NRCP 54(c) in *Checker, Inc. v. Zeman,* 86 Nev. 216, 467 P.2d 100 (1970). *See also Smith v. Rahas,* 73 Nev. 301, 318 P.2d 655 (1957), where the Nevada Supreme Court held that reformation of contract is also permissible under NRCP 54(c).

The Nevada Supreme Court has given great deference to NRCP 54(c), even in the face of apparent conflict with NRCP 9(g), which requires that special damages be pleaded with specificity. In *Summa Corp. v. Greenspun,* 96 Nev. 247, 607 P.2d 569 (1980), the Nevada Supreme Court affirmed the award of attorneys' fees as an element of special damages in spite of the fact that the plaintiff did not comply with NRCP

9(g). The court held that NRCP 54(c) "commands" the court to grant relief to which a party is entitled, even if it is not demanded in the pleadings. *See also* § 808, *supra*.

§ 2422. Notice of entry of judgment.

The service of notice that a judgment has been entered is the act which triggers the time periods for the filing of motions for new trials (NRCP 59(b), § 2503, *infra*), motions to alter or amend a judgment (NRCP 59(e), § 2517, *infra*), and, in most instances, the filing of a notice of appeal. Unlike the federal procedure, there is no requirement in Nevada that the court or clerk of court give notice of entry of a judgment. Thus, it is incumbent upon a party, usually the prevailing party, to do so in order to begin the time periods for the above-mentioned motions and appeal.

Caution should be exercised in giving such notice. A simple party should not give more than one notice because the second notice may be deemed to control. *Ross v. Gracome,* 97 Nev. 550, 636 P.2d 298 (1981). However, the parties may not, in an effort to extend the time for appeal by agreement, do so by filing later notices of appeal. *Culinary Workers v. Haugen,* 76 Nev. 424, 357 P.2d 113 (1960). And a subsequent notice by a different party will not serve to extend the time limits after the date established by the first notice of entry of judgment. *Healy v. Volkswagenwerk,* 103 Nev. 329, 741 P.2d 432 (1987).

Not all civil judgments require a notice of entry of judgment for the time period to begin for appeal. *In re Riddle,* 99 Nev. 632, 668 P.2d 290 (1983); *In re Herrmann,* 100 Nev. 1, 677 P.2d 594 (1984); NRS 155.190.

Other than the necessity of beginning the time to run for post-trial motions and notices of appeal, there apparently is no requirement that written notice of entry of a judgment be given. Since a judgment is effective upon filing, execution or other proceedings to enforce a judgment may be commenced immediately upon entry. Thus, the failure to give notice of entry of the judgment does not interfere with its effectiveness.

The Nevada Supreme Court has also allowed minor errors and even technical form violations to exist in notices of entry of judgment without affecting validity. *Culinary & Hotel Service Workers Union Local No. 226 v. Haugen,* 76 Nev. 424, 357 P.2d 113 (1960).

§ 2423. Form and content of judgments.

Sample forms for judgments (jury and nonjury) can be obtained from the Appendix of Forms, NRCP 84. These forms, according to NRCP 84, should be sufficient.

No particular form of judgment is required. The facts of the case need not be cited in the judgment, *Humboldt Mill & Mining Co. v. Terry,* 11

Nev. 237 (1876), although findings of fact and conclusions of law may be required (*see* §2426, *infra*). The judgment shall not contain a recital of the pleadings, the report of a master, or the record of prior proceedings. NRCP 54(a). If the judgment is for any debt, damages or costs, the amount must be computed in dollars and cents, although a judgment may not be considered erroneous for that omission. NRS 17.130(1).

The judgment need not settle all the issues raised in the action, but in order to be a judgment, it must be a determination of issues in the case. *Meyer v. Flood,* 54 Nev. 55, 4 P.2d 305 (1931). Although technical form violations may be disregarded by the Supreme Court, *Pruett v. Caddigan,* 42 Nev. 329, 176 P. 787 (1918), a judgment must be certain in its terms and definite in its requirements. *Ramelli v. Sorgi,* 38 Nev. 552, 149 P. 71, 154 P. 73 (1915). A judgment must fix clearly the rights and liabilities so that a party will readily understand and be capable of performing its terms. "An obscure judgment entry may, however, be construed with reference to the pleadings and record, and, where on the whole record its sense can be clearly ascertained, the judgment will be upheld." *Ellett v. Ellett,* 94 Nev. 34, 573 P.2d 1179 (1978).

§2424. — Rules of construction.

The construction and interpretation of a judgment are questions of law, not of fact; and, the interpreting court may review the entire record in order to harmonize the judgment with the law and facts of the case. *Ormachea v. Ormachea,* 67 Nev. 273, 217 P.2d 355 (1950). Judgments are construed as a whole so as to give effect to every part of the judgment where possible, including any necessary legal implications not expressly set forth. *Aseltine v. Second Judicial District Court,* 57 Nev. 269, 62 P.2d 701 (1936). If any ambiguity exists, the court will adopt the version that renders the judgment "reasonable, effective and conclusive." Although the interpretation of a judgment can not exceed what the language "fairly warrants," the legal effect of the judgment is more important than the express language used. *Ormachea, supra.* Prior to the entry of a final judgment, the district court remains free to reconsider and issue a written judgment different from its oral pronouncement. *Rust v. Clark County School District,* 103 Nev. 686, 747 P.2d 1380 (1987).

Where a trial court is interpreting its own judgment or order, that interpretation is to be given great weight. *Krick v. Krick,* 76 Nev. 52, 348 P.2d 752 (1960). Technical form violations may be disregarded by the court where there is no prejudice to the parties. *Pruett v. Caddigan,* 42 Nev. 329, 176 P. 787 (1918). If a conflict exists between the minute order and the judgment, the judgment controls. *Bowers v. Edwards,* 79 Nev. 384, 385 P.2d 783 (1963).

A judgment must confine itself to the issues presented to the court in the action. Any facts recited or provisions of the judgment which are unrelated to any of the issues raised by the pleadings or presented to the court are to be disregarded. *Perkins v. Sierra Nevada Silver Mining Co.,* 10 Nev. 405 (1876). However, a judgment rendered on a wrong theory will be upheld if the outcome would be correct upon any other theory presented. *Rae v. All American Life & Casualty Co.,* 95 Nev. 920, 605 P.2d 196 (1979).

A motion to alter or amend a judgment can be made pursuant to NRCP 59 and NRCP 60. *See* §§ 2517 and 2518, *infra.* In situations where a judgment is uncertain or vague, the Nevada Supreme Court has noted that motions made under NRCP 59 and NRCP 60 might obviate the need for appellate review. *Ellett v. Ellett,* 94 Nev. 34, 573 P.2d 1179 (1978).

§ 2425. Alternative judgments.

NRS 17.120 provides that in actions to recover the possession of personal property, judgment for the plaintiff may call for the possession of the property or the value of the property if delivery of the property cannot be made. In addition, the judgment may call for damages, if allowed by substantive law. In such actions, the judgment must conform to the statutory requirement by awarding the alternative relief of delivery of the property or its value in case a return cannot be had. *In re Havas,* 78 Nev. 237, 371 P.2d 30 (1962). The judgment cannot, in such actions, award the value alone. *Godfrey v. Gilsdorf,* 86 Nev. 714, 476 P.2d 3 (1970). The failure of the judgment to be in its proper form may render it void, depriving the court or the judgment creditor from acting thereon. *In re Havas, supra.* The court is also empowered to enter alternative judgments in other actions, but such judgments should be carefully drafted. *Ormachea v. Ormachea,* 67 Nev. 273, 217 P.2d 355 (1950).

§ 2426. Findings of fact and conclusions of law (NRCP 52).

NRCP 52(a) requires that the court find the facts specially and state separately its conclusions of law thereon in all actions tried upon the facts where the court sits without a jury or with an advisory jury. Findings and conclusions are also required in granting or refusing interlocutory injunctions. NRCP 52(a). Findings and conclusions are not necessary where cases are disposed of upon motions to dismiss or motions for summary judgment "or any other motion." However, where a hearing is held on such a motion, it is incumbent upon counsel to provide a record of that hearing on appeal. *In re McLean,* 78 Nev. 60, 368 P.2d 872 (1962).

Findings and conclusions are not required for judgment entered by default since these are not "actions tried upon the facts." *Britz v. Consolidated Casinos Corp.,* 87 Nev. 441, 488 P.2d 911 (1971). Where, however, factual issues are determined in default cases, such as where a damage hearing is held after default, findings and conclusions should be prepared. *See* NRCP 55(b)(2).

The findings should sufficiently specify the factual basis for the court's ultimate conclusion and reversible error exists where the court fails to do so. *Lagrange Construction, Inc. v. Del E. Webb Corp.,* 83 Nev. 524, 435 P.2d 515 (1967). For instance, where a detailed itemization of each disputed item of damages is burdensome, the court should at least identify categories of damages and the amounts allocated to each category so that effective review of the propriety of the award is possible. *Bing Construction Co. v. Vasey-Scott Engineering Co.,* 100 Nev. 72, 674 P.2d 1107 (1984). The failure to make a specific finding on a crucial issue of fact may constitute reversible error. Similarly, a simple finding that plaintiff had failed to sustain his burden of proof as to allegations of a complaint is inadequate to fulfill the requirements of NRCP 52(a). *Heidtman v. Nevada Industrial Commission,* 78 Nev. 25, 368 P.2d 763 (1962).

If an opinion or memorandum of decision is filed, it is sufficient if the findings of fact and conclusions of law specifically appear therein. NRCP 52(a). Indeed, where the findings of fact are inadequate, an appellate court may look to the written decision of the trial court to ascertain what matters were considered in determining issues. *Heidtman v. Nevada Industrial Commission,* 78 Nev. 25, 368 P.2d 763 (1962).

§ 2427. — Requirement of completeness.

The trial court is required to find facts and make conclusions upon all issues necessary for a determination of the case. Where an appellate court is unable to determine those issues from the record, the case will be remanded for the entry of such findings and conclusions or a new trial will be ordered. *Luciano v. Diercks,* 97 Nev. 637, 637 P.2d 1219 (1981). However, where the record clearly supports a judgment and where findings may be implied, the failure to make specific findings as to critical issues may not be fatal. *Griffin v. Westergard,* 96 Nev. 627, 615 P.2d 235 (1980); *Gorden v. Gorden,* 93 Nev. 494, 569 P.2d 397 (1977).

Where different theories or claims for relief are pleaded in the alternative, the court need not specify in its findings and conclusions as to which of such theories or claims the decision rests. *Garibaldi Brothers Trucking Co. v. Waldren,* 74 Nev. 42, 321 P.2d 248 (1958).

If a finding of fact is incorrectly designated as a conclusion of law, the Nevada Supreme Court will disregard technical form violations and look to the substance of the lower court's decision in reviewing the case. *Hardy v. First National Bank,* 86 Nev. 921, 478 P.2d 581 (1970).

§ 2428. Interest.

NRS 17.130 sets forth the applicable interest rate to be awarded on a judgment when no rate of interest is provided by contract or otherwise by law. Other statutory provisions that relate to the award of interest are beyond the scope of this work. NRS 17.130 was amended by the Nevada Legislature in 1979, 1981 and, most recently, in 1987. Under the present statute, the judgment draws interest from the time of the service of the summons and complaint until the judgment has been satisfied. The present interest rate is calculated on a sliding scale at a rate equal to the prime rate at the largest bank in Nevada as ascertained by the Commissioner of Financial Institutions on January 1 or July 1, as the case may be, immediately preceding the date of judgment, plus two percent. According to the statute, the rate must be adjusted accordingly on each January 1 and July 1 thereafter until the judgment is satisfied. Judgments for future damages draw interest at the same rate, but only from the time of entry of judgment until it is satisfied.

Prejudgment interest is not allowed on an award of future damages. Therefore, it is the plaintiffs' burden, in cases where both past and future damages are awarded, to require the judgment to specify what portion of the judgment is for future damages. If the plaintiff fails to do so, no prejudgment interest is awardable. *Jacobsen v. Manfredi,* 100 Nev. 226, 679 P.2d 251 (1984); *Stickler v. Quilici,* 98 Nev. 595, 655 P.2d 527 (1982). *See also Ramadanis v. Supak,* 104 Nev. 57, 752 P.2d 767 (1988).

If there is no evidence at trial concerning future damages, the judgment does not have to reflect a division between past and future damages. *See Farmers Home Mutual Insurance Co. v. Fiscus,* 102 Nev. 371, 725 P.2d 234 (1986), where it clearly appeared that all of the damages were "past" damages and prejudgment interest was, therefore, awarded on the entire judgment.

At least in contract cases, prejudgment interest on a damage award is only allowed where the damage award is known or ascertainable at a time prior to entry of judgment, either by references to amounts fixed by the contract, or from established market prices. *Hornwood v. Smith's Food King No. 1,* 107 Nev. 80, 807 P.2d 208 (1991).

Because of the recent amendments to NRS 17.130, whereby the relevant interest rate has been changed, problems have arisen concerning which statute to apply. In *Arnold v. Mt. Wheeler Power Co.,* 101 Nev. 612, 707 P.2d 1137 (1985), the Nevada Supreme Court applied the statute that was in effect at the time the cause of action arose. Since the cause of the action arose in October, 1980, the 1981 amendment to the statute was not applicable because the statutory history of the amendment revealed that it was to apply to causes of action that arose on or after July 1, 1981.

Prejudgment interest, pursuant to NRS 17.130(2), is not recoverable on a punitive damage award. Because the award of punitive damages is not a matter of right and must be determined solely in the discretion of the trier of fact at the time of trial, prejudgment interest pursuant to NRS 17.130(2) is inappropriate. *Ramada Inns, Inc. v. Sharp,* 101 Nev. 824, 711 P.2d 1 (1985).

In the rare instances where parties intended that no interest should be recoverable in an action, prejudgment interest, at least, cannot be included in the judgment. *Jacobsen v. Best Brands, Inc.,* 97 Nev. 390, 632 P.2d 1150 (1981).

Interest, as authorized by NRS 17.130, when the damages were sustained after service of the complaint, but prior to entry of judgment, begins to accrue from the time the damages actually occur if they are sustained after the complaint is served but before judgment, rather than from the date of serving the complaint or from the date of judgment. The date the damages were incurred and the amount of damages must be proven by a preponderance of the evidence. *LTR Stage Lines v. Gray Line Tours,* 106 Nev. 45, 792 P.2d 386 (1990).

§ 2429. Costs.

If costs have been taxed or ascertained at the time of entry of judgment, the clerk shall include in the judgment those amounts. If not, the clerk shall, within two days after costs are taxed or ascertained, insert that amount in a blank to be left in the judgment for that purpose. NRS 18.120. The entry of judgment shall not be delayed for the taxing of costs. NRCP 58(c). The failure of the clerk to insert the amount of plaintiff's cost bill in the judgment, where a memorandum is filed in a timely fashion after entry of judgment, does not render the judgment invalid. *Bailey v. Littell,* 24 Nev. 294, 53 P. 308 (1898).

NRS 18.005, *et seq.,* governs the award of taxable costs to the prevailing party. *See also* § 2229, *supra,* and § 2726, *infra.*

§ 2430. Persons entitled to and subject to judgments: parties.

Before a person or entity can become a judgment debtor, he must be a party to the action. *Brown v. Brown,* 101 Nev. 144, 696 P.2d 999 (1985). In a lawsuit against a partnership, all of the partners should be joined in the action. If fewer than all of the partners are joined as defendants, the plaintiff can still secure a judgment against the partnership. *Smart v. Valencia,* 50 Nev. 359, 261 P. 655 (1927).

Unless a partner is bankrupt, dead or outside the jurisdiction of the court, all partners must be joined in an action against a partnership. If one of the parties is deceased and the decedent's estate is not substituted in the action, the judgment can be enforced against the partnership assets. But, in the event that the partnership property proves insufficient to satisfy the debt, the plaintiff may execute against the separate property of the individual partners, so long as they were properly joined in the action. *Diamond National Corp. v. Thunderbird Hotel, Inc.,* 85 Nev. 271, 454 P.2d 13 (1969). *See also Gearhart v. Pierce Enterprises,* 105 Nev. 517, 779 P.2d 93 (1989).

§ 2431. — Persons other than parties.

Ordinarily, a judgment may be entered only against one who is named as a party and over whom the court has acquired jurisdiction. *Young v. Nevada Title Co.,* 103 Nev. 436, 744 P.2d 902 (1987). Actual service of process or legally-provided substituted service must have occurred. *C.H.A. Venture v. G.C. Wallace Consulting,* 106 Nev. 381, 794 P.2d 707 (1990).

A joint obligor, however, may be summoned after judgment and is bound by the judgment unless he can show the judgment to be invalid that a defense ... has arisen subsequent to the entry of the judgment, or that he is not liable on the obligation upon which the judgment was recovered. NRS 17.030, *et seq.* A person who is found liable under a judgment in this fashion is liable only for the amount of the original judgment remaining unsatisfied as against the defendants originally named and served. NRS 17.080. A judgment may also be amended so as to include previously unnamed parties where, for instance, the assets of a judgment debtor corporation are transferred to another corporation which is the alter ego of the judgment debtor corporation. *Frank McCleary Cattle Co. v. Sewell,* 73 Nev. 279, 317 P.2d 957 (1957).

§ 2432. — Judgments involving multiple claims or multiple parties (NRCP 54(b)).

A judgment should determine all of the issues presented to the court in a given case, unless a specific determination is made under NRCP 54(b). Thus, a court cannot bifurcate a trial and enter a final decree of divorce, reserving the right to determine property issues at a later time. *Gojack v. Second Judicial District Court,* 95 Nev. 443, 596 P.2d 237 (1979). A district court does not have to make findings of fact in order to determine whether there is just reason for delay. *Mallin v. Farmers Insurance Exchange,* 106 Nev. 606, 797 P.2d 978 (1990).

When multiple parties or multiple claims are involved in an action, a judgment is not final unless the rights and liabilities of all of the parties are adjudicated. The district court may, however, direct the entry of a final judgment as to fewer than all of the parties by making an express determination that there is no just reason for delay under NRCP 54(b). The same is true with regard to a case that involves multiple claims. In the absence of such determination, a decision affecting fewer than all of the parties is "subject to revision at any time before the entry of judgment" as to all parties. NRCP 54(b). The failure to obtain a 54(b) certification can result in a significant delay in obtaining appellate review when the remaining case involves other claims. If the 54(b) certification is not obtained, the party seeking appellate review will have to wait until the remaining claims have been resolved before an appeal can be commenced. *Donoghue v. Rosepiler,* 83 Nev. 251, 427 P.2d 956 (1967).

In order to invoke NRCP 54(b), the district court must make a determination that there is "no just reason for delay" in order to create an appealable judgment where there are remaining parties or claims in the pending action. Failure to do so is a jurisdictional defect which will mandate the dismissal of the appeal. *First Western Savings & Loan Association v. Steinberg,* 89 Nev. 582, 517 P.2d 793 (1973). The determinations to be made by the district court in relationship to NRCP 54(b) should not be entered routinely or as an accommodation to counsel. The entry of a 54(b) certification in an ex parte order was looked upon with disfavor by the Nevada Supreme Court in *Knox v. Dick,* 99 Nev. 514, 665 P.2d 267 (1983).

If a right to direct appeal exists under a statute or rule, certification pursuant to NRCP 54(b) is not necessary even if the underlying case continues with remaining parties or claims. *See De Luca Importing Co. v. The Buckingham Corp.,* 90 Nev. 158, 520 P.2d 1365 (1974), where the dismissal of a claim for injunctive relief was appealable pursuant to NRAP 3A(b)(2) and certification under NRCP 54(b) was, therefore, not required, even though other claims remained to be adjudicated. A similar result was rendered in *Lane-Tahoe, Inc. v. Kindred Construction Co.,* 91 Nev. 385, 536 P.2d 491 (1975), where certification pursuant to NRCP 54(b) was not required for the appeal of an order that denied an application to compel arbitration under the Uniform Arbitration Act (NRS 38.045). Since NRS 38.045 expressly provided for a direct appeal, certification under NRCP 54(b) was not necessary even though other claims remained in the litigation.

Certification by the district court does not, in itself, create a right of appeal. For example, the denial of a motion for summary judgment is not a final judgment under NRAP 3A, and the certification of such an order under NRCP 54(b) does not create jurisdiction for the Nevada Supreme Court to entertain the appeal. *See Taylor Construction Co. v. Hilton Hotels Corp.,* 100 Nev. 207, 678 P.2d 1152 (1984).

The Nevada Supreme Court has been very restrictive in its interpretation of what constitutes "one claim for relief" under NRCP 54(b). A compulsory counterclaim, as defined by NRCP 13(a), "arises out of the transaction or occurrence that is the subject matter of the opposing parties' claim." A compulsory counterclaim, by itself, may not be considered

a "separate claim" under NRCP 54(b). *See United States Fidelity &
Guarantee Co. v. Nevada Cement Co.,* 93 Nev. 179, 561 P.2d 1335 (1977),
where the Nevada Supreme Court held that a compulsory counterclaim
for rescission of contract is not a "separate claim for relief" as specified
in NRCP 54(b). Since the compulsory counterclaim for rescission arose
out of the same transaction that was the subject matter of the opposing
parties' claim, certification under 54(b) was improper. *KDI Sylvan Pools,
Inc. v. Workman,* 107 Nev. 340, 810 P.2d 1217 (1991). The Supreme
Court reasoned that if the appeal had been entertained, important as-
pects of the main case would be decided on appeal and would thus become the "law of the case" without a complete adjudication at the district
court level. Likewise, NRCP 54(b) certification is not available in a lawsuit for the recovery of insurance proceeds even if the "losses" are set
forth as separate counts in the complaint. The right to recover insurance
proceeds normally arises out of a single transaction or series of related
transactions and thus constitutes only one claim for relief under NRCP
54(b). *Mid-Century Insurance Co. v. Cherubini,* 95 Nev. 293, 593 P.2d
1068 (1979).

If the district court grants a motion for partial summary judgment on
the issue of liability alone, that determination may not be reviewed on
appeal until a final judgment is rendered. *See Mid-Century Insurance
Co., supra.* If the claims asserted in an action, albeit separate, are so
closely related that this court must necessarily decide important issues
pending below in order to decide the issues appealed, there can be no
finding that there is no just reason for delay and certification of an order
deciding some buy not all of those claims as final is an abuse of the
district court's discretion. *Hallicrafters v. Moore,* 102 Nev. 526, 728 P.2d
441 (1986).

When a district court is asked to certify a judgment based on the
elimination of a party, it should first consider the prejudice to that party
in being forced to wait to bring its appeal. Second, the district court
should consider the prejudice to the parties remaining below if the judgment is certified as final. The standard from *Hallicrafters, supra,* is also
a part of the analysis when dealing with multiple parties. The district
court should weigh the prejudice to the various parties and should certify
a judgment as final in a "parties" case if the prejudice to the eliminated
party would be greater than the prejudice to the parties remaining below. A certification of finality based on the elimination of a party will be
presumed valid and will be upheld by the supreme court absent a gross
abuse of discretion. *Mallin v. Farmers Insurance Exchange, supra.*

Although NRCP 54(b) does not set forth any time limits as to when the
certification should be obtained, the certification should be obtained at
the time the judgment or order is entered. A delay in seeking the certification may not be fatal if there is no prejudice to the other party. *See*

Williams v. City of North Las Vegas, 91 Nev. 622, 541 P.2d 652 (1975), where there was an eighteen-month delay between the dismissal of one of the defendants and the entry of the 54(b) certification. The Nevada Supreme Court held that the granting of the 54(b) certification was not an abuse of discretion by the district court because the defendant could not demonstrate any prejudice and the plaintiff would otherwise have been denied her day in court.

§ 2433. — Judgments against deceased persons.

If a party dies after a verdict or decision upon any issue of fact, but before entry of judgment, the court may nevertheless render judgment. Any such judgment shall become a claim against the estate, but shall not act as a lien on the real property of the deceased party. NRS 17.140. This statute is not inconsistent with NRCP 58(c), which establishes when a judgment becomes effective. NRS 17.140 modifies the common law rule that all proceedings are arrested by the death of a party. The statute preserves the benefits of a cause of action which has ripened into a jury verdict or a decision before the death occurs. *See Koester v. Administrator of the Estate of Koester,* 101 Nev. 68, 693 P.2d 569 (1985).

However, NRS 17.140 does not alter the general rule that requires the substitution of the personal representative before the court enters judgment. If the personal representative is not substituted before the court enters judgment, the judgment is voidable. In certain circumstances, a nunc pro tunc order can be utilized to relate the judgment back to the date of decision (before death) in order to validate an otherwise voidable judgment. *See Koester v. Administrator of the Estate of Koester,* 101 Nev. 68, 693 P.2d 569 (1985), which involved a divorce action.

§ 2434. Judgment lien: recording abstract.

After the entry of judgment by filing with the clerk, the judgment may be recorded in the office of the recorder of any county. Upon recordation of the judgment, it becomes a lien upon the real property of the judgment debtor owned at the time of recording or subsequently acquired thereafter. The lien attaches to the property not exempt from execution in the county where the judgment is recorded. NRS 17.150(2). The recording can be accomplished by filing a certified copy of the judgment or decree. *See* § 2710, *infra.* Where that is unavailable, the judgment creditor may record a transcript of the original docket maintained by the clerk or an abstract of the judgment. If an abstract is recorded, it must contain: (a) the title of the court and cause and the number of the action; (b) the date of entry of the judgment or decree; (c) the names of the judgment debtor and the judgment creditor; (d) the amount of the judgment or decree;

and, (e) where the judgment is entered in the minutes or judgment docket. NRS 17.150(3).

Any judgment entered by a District Court of the State of Nevada or by the United States District Court in and for the District of Nevada may be recorded. NRS 17.150(2). Additionally, judgments rendered by a United States District Court in another state may be recorded where a copy of that judgment is filed with the clerk of the United States District Court for the District of Nevada and further certified by the clerk of that court. *Bennett v. Dunn,* 504 F. Supp. 981 (D. Nev. 1980).

A judgment obtained from justice court becomes a lien only if an abstract in the statutory form is filed with the county recorder. The lien thus acquired only affects real property located in the county in which the abstract is filed. The lien attaches to real property which is owned by the judgment debtor at the time of filing or acquired by him thereafter, until the lien expires. NRS 68.040. The form for a justice court abstract is prescribed by statute. *See* NRS 68.010 and 68.040.

§ 2435. — Effective date of judgment lien.

The lien becomes effective upon recording pursuant to NRS 17.150(2). *Kockos v. Bank of Nevada,* 90 Nev. 140, 520 P.2d 1359 (1974).

§ 2436. — Duration of judgment lien.

NRS 17.150 provides that a judgment lien, once recorded, is effective until the expiration of six years from the date the judgment or decree was docketed unless enforcement of the judgment or decree is stayed on appeal, the judgment is satisfied or the lien is otherwise discharged. The time during which the execution of the judgment is suspended by appeal, action of the court or defendant in effect "tolls" the six-year limitation period.

A judgment lien rendered in a justice court continues for six years, unless the judgment is previously satisfied. NRS 68.040.

A different limitation period is specified in judgments entered in actions for damages as the result of mining claim jumping. NRS 40.190 provides that any such judgment lien continues only for two years.

§ 2437. — Property subject to judgment lien.

The lien described in NRS 17.150 applies to "all the real property of the judgment debtor not exempt from execution in [the county of recording], owned by him at the time, or which he may afterward acquire, until the lien expires."

The statute provides that the lien applies only to property owned by the judgment debtor at the time of recording or acquired thereafter.

Thus, where the judgment debtor holds record title to property, but which title is void due to total failure of consideration, such property is not subject to the lien. *Kockos v. Bank of Nevada,* 90 Nev. 140, 520 P.2d 1359 (1974).

It has also been held that where a judgment debtor redeems his own property pursuant to NRS 21.190 after sale on execution, said property is subject to an existing judgment lien for the amount of any deficiency after the sale. *Kaye v. United Mortgage Co.,* 86 Nev. 183, 466 P.2d 848 (1970). The result is different, however, when the debtor's successor in interest redeems the property. Since there is no judgment against the successor in interest to which a lien can attach, the successor redeems the property free of the lien. This rule promotes the primary purpose of statutory redemption, to wit: forcing the purchaser at execution sale to bid on the property at a price approximating its fair value. *See Kaye, supra.*

§ 2438. — Priority of judgment lien.

A judgment lien, as stated above, attaches at the time of its recording. Thereafter, priorities are determined as in any other lien upon property. *See generally Daly v. Lahontan Mines Co.,* 39 Nev. 14, 151 P. 514, 158 P. 285 (1915); *Persing v. Reno Stock Brokerage Co.,* 30 Nev. 342, 96 P. 1054 (1908). *See also* NRS 108.225, which sets forth the priority of mechanics' and materialmens' liens.

§ 2439. Duration of the right to an action on a judgment.

NRS 11.190(1)(a) provides that an action upon a judgment or decree of any court of the United States or of any state must be commenced within six years or within the renewal thereof. *See* NRS 17.214 (judgments may be renewed for an additional six years); *see also* § 2441, *infra.* This limitation period is subject to the various tolling provisions contained in NRS Chapter 11, such as absence from the state (NRS 11.300) and certain disabilities (NRS 11.250). The six-year statute of limitations for actions upon a judgment to recover arrearages in child support payments begins to run against each installment as it becomes due. *Bongiovi v. Bongiovi,* 94 Nev. 321, 579 P.2d 1246 (1978); *Brown v. Vonsild,* 91 Nev. 646, 541 P.2d 528 (1975). However, in a proceeding to enforce the provisions of a judgment entered in a divorce case, NRS 11.190 was tolled during the infancy of the child. *See Gibbs v. Giles,* 96 Nev. 243, 607 P.2d 118 (1980), where the child pursued the judgment against her father to compel the payment of monies for the establishment of a trust. Because the child was the intended third-party beneficiary of the trust, the statutory period was tolled during the beneficiary's minority pursuant to NRS 11.250.

§ 2440. — Limitation upon execution.

NRS 21.010 mandates that execution upon an existing judgment take place within six years after its entry. Similarly, any writs of execution issued upon a judgment cease to be effective six years after entry of the judgment. *See* Chapter 27, *infra.*

§ 2441. — Revival of judgment.

Prior to the legislature's enactment of NRS 17.214, judgments were not renewed, but were revived by means of a separate, independent action. *See, e.g., Polk v. Tully,* 97 Nev. 27, 623 P.2d 972 (1981). Although no case or statute specifically directs the practitioner to use the NRS 17.214 methodology, *Polk,* when read in concert with NRS 17.214, sends a strong message that the renewal of judgments is more favored than the revival. *See* § 2728. A judgment may be revived by the filing of an independent action within the limitation period established by NRS 11.190. Additionally, a statutory method of renewal of judgments was approved by the 1985 legislature (1985 Nev. Stats. 699-700, NRS 17.214). A judgment may be renewed by the judgment creditor or his successor by filing an affidavit of renewal. The affidavit must be filed with the clerk of the court where judgment is entered within ninety days before the judgment expires by limitation.

The contents of the affidavit are detailed in the statute and include, among other matters, identification of the parties, court and judgment, the amount of the judgment, and the exact amount then due. The affidavit must be served upon the judgment debtor within three days after filing by certified mail, return receipt requested, at the debtor's last known address.

The affidavit renews the judgment for another six years (NRS 11.190(1)) and the renewed judgment may be successively renewed in the same fashion (NRS 17.214(4)). The legislature did not amend the execution limitation of six years to provide explicitly for renewal, although it would defeat the purpose of allowing renewed judgments if execution were not available to enforce a renewed judgment. Prior to the enactment of the renewal statute, a simpler procedure had been approved by the Nevada Supreme Court. *Polk v. Tully,* 97 Nev. 27, 623 P.2d 972 (1981). The continued viability of the revival method under *Polk* is in doubt after adoption of the above-described statutory scheme in 1985. *See* § 2728, *infra.*

§ 2442. Attacking validity of judgments.

The usual mode of challenging the validity of a judgment is by motion for relief from judgment or order under NRCP 60. Such a motion is the preferred procedure in cases involving void judgments. However, an appeal from a void judgment may be considered and acted upon. *Osman v. Cobb,* 77 Nev. 133, 360 P.2d 258 (1961).

A challenge may also be instituted by way of separate action attacking the judgment. *Misty Management Corporation & Triaviation Corp. v. First Judicial District Court,* 83 Nev. 180, 426 P.2d 728 (1967). Such an action, however, must allege that the judgment is void, for instance, on the basis of extrinsic fraud. *Colby v. Colby,* 78 Nev. 150, 369 P.2d 1019 (1962); *Libro v. Walls,* 103 Nev. 540, 746 P.2d 632 (1987). *See also Misty Management Corp., supra,* where the Nevada Supreme Court stated that NRCP 60(b)(3) is not available to challenge a "void" judgment unless the basis of the attack is upon the jurisdiction over the parties or the subject matter, or, where the court was disqualified from acting.

When a judgment is attacked in some fashion other than in the action in which the judgment is entered, the attack is said to be "collateral." *State ex rel. Smith v. Sixth Judicial District Court,* 63 Nev. 249, 167 P.2d 648 (1946). Only void judgments are subject to collateral attack, however, and where the challenge is not based upon the court's jurisdiction to enter judgment, a collateral attack is not allowed. *Bowler v. Leonard,* 70 Nev. 370, 269 P.2d 833 (1954).

An attack on a judgment rendered in this state must be commenced in the judicial district which entered the judgment. One district court cannot generally set aside another district court's order. *State Engineer v. Sustacha,* 108 Nev. 223, 826 P.2d 959 (1992).

A judgment may also be attacked by writ of mandate in the action in which the judgment is entered. The supreme court may order a judgment stricken when it is entered without jurisdiction by the trial court. *Jeep Corp. & American Motors Corp. v. Second Judicial District Court,* 98 Nev. 440, 652 P.2d 1183 (1982); *Dredge Corp. v. Peccole,* 89 Nev. 26, 505 P.2d 290 (1973) (plaintiff never served with order dismissing complaint with prejudice or notice of order of dismissal with prejudice).

Where a losing party has an opportunity to appeal an adverse judgment, but does not do so, it is improper to seek relief pursuant to NRCP 60. The provisions of that rule are not a substitute for a timely appeal. *Misty Management Corp. & Triaviation Corp. v. First Judicial District Court,* 83 Nev. 180, 426 P.2d 728 (1967); *Holiday Inn Downtown v. Barnett,* 103 Nev. 60, 732 P.2d 1376 (1987).

See Chapter 25, *infra,* for a more detailed discussion of the availability of relief from judgment.

§ 2443. — Dependence upon jurisdiction.

Where a judgment is entered by a court which lacks jurisdiction, that judgment is void. *C.H.A. Venture v. G.C. Wallace Consulting Engineers,*

Inc., 106 Nev. 381, 794 P.2d 707 (1990); *Misty Management Corp. & Triaviation Corp. v. First Judicial District Court,* 83 Nev. 180, 426 P.2d 728 (1967). The absence of jurisdiction may be the result of improper activity by the clerk, *Long v. Tighe,* 36 Nev. 129, 133 P. 60 (1913), or by a justice court. *State ex rel. Wood v. Haeger,* 55 Nev. 331, 33 P.2d 753 (1934).

The lack of jurisdiction which may render a judgment void may be jurisdiction over the subject matter, *Fitchett v. Henley,* 31 Nev. 326, 102 P. 865, 104 P. 1060 (1909), or jurisdiction over the person, *La Potin v. La Potin,* 75 Nev. 264, 339 P.2d 123 (1959), *Foster v. Lewis,* 78 Nev. 330, 372 P.2d 679 (1962).

Relief may be had when a court improperly alters a final judgment in excess of its jurisdiction. *Dredge Corp. v. Peccole,* 89 Nev. 26, 505 P.2d 290 (1973). A judgment may also be void where it is entered against or in favor of a party which does not exist or is not subject to suit. *Causey v. Carpenters Southern Nevada Vacation Trust,* 95 Nev. 609, 600 P.2d 244 (1979).

It has been held that a judgment is invalid where it decides issues which are not presented by the pleadings. *Carpenter v. Sixth Judicial District Court,* 59 Nev. 42, 73 P.2d 1310 (1937), or when the court lacks evidence upon which it clearly must have relied upon to come to the conclusion. *Moore v. Moore,* 75 Nev. 189, 336 P.2d 1073 (1959). However, NRCP 15 allows the amendment of pleadings to include issues tried in the case by the express or implied consent of the parties, and such an amendment may be made at any time, even after judgment. *See also* § 2421, *supra.*

Where jurisdiction is present, but irregularities occur in the judgment, the judgment is said to be voidable, meaning that it is valid until modified or set aside. *Smith v. Smith,* 82 Nev. 384, 419 P.2d 295 (1966). A voidable judgment can only be attacked directly in the action in which it was rendered. *See* § 2442, *supra.*

§ 2444. — Presumptions affecting validity.

It is generally recognized that judgments entered by courts of general jurisdiction are presumed to have been entered with jurisdiction and the judgment is presumed to be valid. *Conforte v. Hanna,* 76 Nev. 239, 351 P.2d 612 (1960). No such presumption, however, is afforded judgments of courts of limited jurisdiction. Thus, where the record on appeal from a judgment in a justice's court did not disclose that summons had been served or service had been waived, such judgment was void for want of jurisdiction. *State ex rel. Wood v. Haeger,* 55 Nev. 331, 33 P.2d 753 (1934).

§2445. — Status of record.

Where it appears from the judgment or order that the judgment was entered without jurisdiction, the judgment is void. However, where a jurisdictional defect is technical, for instance where it appears the court lacks jurisdiction because of a defect of proof, but jurisdiction actually exists, the technical defect may be removed after judgment. *Williamson v. Williamson,* 52 Nev. 78, 280 P. 651 (1929).

§2446. — Effect of invalidity.

As indicated earlier, there is a distinction between defects which are jurisdictional and those which render a judgment merely voidable. The difference may be critical. A void judgment may be attacked without limitation to the time limits specified in NRCP 60. *Foster v. Lewis,* 78 Nev. 330, 372 P.2d 679 (1962). A void judgment may be attacked in forums other than the court in which the judgment is entered, *Maheu v. Hughes Tool Co.,* 88 Nev. 592, 503 P.2d 4 (1972), by any person, *Beck v. Curti,* 56 Nev. 72, 45 P.2d 601 (1935).

If a judgment is void, it is void for all purposes and a person cannot be held in contempt for ignoring it. *Daines v. Markoff,* 92 Nev. 582, 555 P.2d 490 (1976). Caution should be advised, however, because if the judgment is held to be only voidable, disobedience may be punished by contempt.

Once a void judgment has been entered, it usually cannot be later validated. Thus, where a judgment was entered after improper service, the subsequent general appearance in the action by the defendant does not "breathe life" into the previously entered void judgment. *Deros v. Stern,* 87 Nev. 148, 483 P.2d 648 (1971).

§2447. Judgments in rem.

A judgment in rem may be distinguished from a judgment in personam in that it is "an adjudication pronounced upon the status [of] some particular thing or subject matter." *Perry v. Edmonds,* 59 Nev. 60, 84 P.2d 711 (1938). Since it affects only property, it is not only binding upon parties and their privies, but also binds strangers to the underlying action. *State v. Central Pacific Railroad,* 10 Nev. 47 (1875).

A judgment in rem is only good to the extent of the amount realized from the specific property seized, actually or symbolically, in the action. *Perry v. Edmonds,* 59 Nev. 60, 84 P.2d 711 (1938). However, where a judgment in rem is entered without jurisdiction, it is no more enforceable than any other type of judgment. *Scorpion Silver Mining Co. v. Marsano,* 10 Nev. 370 (1875).

§ 2448. Judgments by consent.

After an action is commenced, parties are allowed, by stipulation, to consent to the entry of judgment in an action at law. It can be in the form of a settlement of a pending action, particularly when payment of money damages may continue beyond the settlement.

In such cases, the parties may be allowed to stipulate to the terms of the judgment which normally will be approved by the court. Many times a judgment is entered and the parties execute a collateral agreement setting out the methodology for payment. However, the court is obligated to guard against collusion of the parties and not to permit judgment to be entered unless the court is satisfied that a cause of action exists. *Haley v. Eureka County Bank,* 21 Nev. 127, 26 P. 64 (1891).

Although the parties may, within reason, control the terms of the judgment, they cannot by consent confer jurisdiction upon the court which did not otherwise exist. *Finley v. Finley,* 65 Nev. 113, 180 P.2d 334 (1948); *B.F. Hastings & Co. v. Burning Moscow Co.,* 2 Nev. 93 (1866).

Oral settlement agreements, however, do not constitute consent judgments and are not enforceable as such. District Court Rule 16 provides that no agreement or stipulation between the parties is effective unless it is in writing or entered in the court's minutes in the form of an order. *Szilagyi v. Testa,* 99 Nev. 834, 673 P.2d 495 (1983). This rule has been held to preclude the enforcement by motion of oral settlement agreements for which a court record has not been made. *Resnick v. Valente,* 97 Nev. 615, 637 P.2d 1205 (1981).

§ 2449. Judgments by confession.

Nevada statutes allow the entry of judgments by confession. A judgment by confession is one entered without action, either for money due or to become due, or to secure any person against contingent liability on behalf of the defendant, or both. NRS 17.090.

The judgment is entered upon a statement made by the defendant. The statement must be in writing, signed by him and verified by his oath. It must specifically authorize the entry of judgment for a specified sum. If it is for money due or to become due, the statement must concisely set out the facts constituting the liability and show that the sum confessed therefor does not exceed the same. NRS 17.100. If it is for a sum within the jurisdictional limit of the justice court, it may be entered there if specified in the confession. NRS 68.050.

The defendant's statement must be filed with the clerk of the court in which the judgment is sought. A judgment is then entered with the defendant's affidavit attached and an entry made in the judgment docket maintained by the clerk. The costs awardable are limited by statute to $20. NRS 17.110.

If the judgment contains the substance required by the statute, it is sufficient. No particular form is specified or necessary. *Humboldt Mill & Mining Co. v. Terry,* 11 Nev. 237 (1876).

§ 2450. — Authority of confessor.

A judgment by confession may be challenged by questioning the authority of the party confessing judgment, where that party signs in a representative capacity. Thus, where a corporation attorney confesses judgment, his authority may be challenged in the Nevada Supreme Court upon petition for writ of prohibition. *Shelton v. Second Judicial District Court,* 64 Nev. 487, 185 P.2d 320 (1947). Similarly, although the court recognizes that attorneys are normally presumed to have authority to act on behalf of their clients, they are not presumed to have the power to confess judgment unless authority for that purpose is specifically shown. *Golden v. Fifth Judicial District Court,* 31 Nev. 250, 101 P. 1021 (1909).

§ 2451. — Availability.

Certain creditors and potential creditors are precluded by statute from utilizing confessions of judgment. Certain small lenders are precluded from using such devices (NRS 675.350), as are licensed thrift companies (NRS 677.750). Federal Trade Commission rules should also be consulted.

§ 2452. Satisfaction of judgments.

The satisfaction of judgment is governed by statute. NRS 17.200 establishes that satisfaction of a judgment may be entered in the clerk's docket in one of three ways. First, it may be entered upon return of an execution in which satisfaction is indicated. Second, it may be entered upon an acknowledgement of satisfaction filed with the clerk by the judgment creditor or his attorney. Finally, when a judgment is satisfied in a manner other than upon execution, the court may compel a party or his attorney to give acknowledgement of satisfaction or may order the entry of satisfaction without such acknowledgement.

Where a judgment is satisfied but no evidence of such satisfaction appears on the judgment record, a party with knowledge of that satisfaction may not rely upon its absence from the record. Thus, where a former wife, with full knowledge of satisfaction of a judgment obtained by her against her former husband, purchases property at an execution sale which she causes to be held, such a sale may be set aside. *Mauldin v. Mauldin,* 88 Nev. 336, 497 P.2d 886 (1972).

§ 2453. — Satisfaction by payment or otherwise.

Payment of the amount specified in the judgment acts as satisfaction of that judgment. However, judgment may be satisfied in other ways. For instance, where a judgment creditor accepts a note in satisfaction of an existing judgment, after which the debtor defaults upon the note, a new cause of action is created and execution is not available under the original satisfied judgment. *Walker v. Shrake,* 75 Nev. 241, 339 P.2d 124 (1959). A judgment may also be satisfied by agreement between the judgment creditor and the judgment debtor.

§ 2454. — Entry of satisfaction.

Satisfaction must be entered by the clerk in the docket upon the return of an execution which is satisfied. Where a judgment debtor pays a judgment and becomes entitled to satisfaction, he may, by motion, compel the opposing party or his attorney to acknowledge that satisfaction formally. *Arley v. Liberty Mutual Fire Insurance Co.,* 81 Nev. 411, 404 P.2d 426 (1965).

However, the court cannot compel the creditor to acknowledge satisfaction where satisfaction is shown by a return on execution. The order of the court should be directed against the clerk to enter satisfaction of the judgment. *Sweeney v. Hawthorne,* 6 Nev. 129 (1870).

§ 2455. — Effect of satisfaction.

The primary effect of the entry of satisfaction of judgment is that it brings the case to a final and complete close after which an appeal cannot be taken. A party cannot accept the fruits of his judgment or order while at the same time exercise a right to appeal. *Clark County v. Roosevelt Title Insurance Co., Ltd.,* 80 Nev. 303, 393 P.2d 136 (1964). An anomalous situation, and exception to the rule, exists where the case remains on appeal by the defendant and the plaintiff has satisfied his judgment because defendant has not posted a supersedeas bond, or if defendant voluntarily pays the judgment to cut off the accrual of interest. Under these circumstances, the case may not be completely closed and final.

The general rule holds true even where the creditor accepts only part of the benefit of his judgment so long as the portion from which he benefits is connected and dependent upon the remaining portions of the judgment. *Hummel v. Roberts,* 70 Nev. 225, 265 P.2d 219 (1954).

It should be noted, however, that where a defendant is subject to two separate actions arising out of the same incident which are not consolidated and which result in separate judgments for each plaintiff, the defendant may satisfy one judgment and still be free to pursue his appeal from the other. *Mikulich v. Carner,* 68 Nev. 161, 228 P.2d 257 (1951).

The acknowledgement of satisfaction also destroys that party's right to reopen the case to seek additional relief. Thus, where a party neglects to include in the judgment an element of damage to which he might be entitled, and that judgment is satisfied, it may not be reopened to include the omitted award. *Solen v. Virginia & Truckee R.R.,* 15 Nev. 313 (1880).

CHAPTER 25

POST TRIAL MOTIONS

Authors: Ginger R. James
         B. Alan McKissick

§ 2501. Introduction and scope.

This chapter describes only those motions which may be made after trial of the action has occurred and does not include motions for relief from default judgments which are discussed in Chapter 10, *supra*. It considers motions for judgment notwithstanding the verdict (n.o.v.), NRCP 50(b), and for new trial, NRCP 59, emphasizing the time limitations and standards for review in the district court. Motions to correct clerical mistakes in judgments or orders and for relief from final judgments or orders under NRCP 60 are also discussed. The procedure for obtaining a stay of execution after entry of judgment is explained. Finally, material differences between the relevant Nevada Rules of Civil Procedure and the Federal Rules of Civil Procedure are noted.

§ 2502. Motion for judgment notwithstanding the verdict: history, purpose and scope of NRCP 50(b).

It is no longer necessary to make a Rule 50(a) motion for a directed verdict as a condition precedent to a motion for judgment n.o.v. under Rule 50(b). That requirement still exists in federal practice, but was deleted in Nevada in 1971. In federal practice, a motion under Rule 50(a) Fed. R. Civ. Proc., is now known as a motion for judgment as a matter of law, not a motion for a directed verdict.

The purpose of a motion for a directed verdict or for judgment n.o.v. is to test the sufficiency of the evidence to support the verdict. A motion for judgment n.o.v. presents solely a question of law to be determined by the court. *Dudley v. Prime*, 84 Nev. 549, 551, 445 P.2d 31 (1968). The standard for reviewing a judgment n.o.v. is the same as for reviewing a motion for directed verdict. *Twardowski v. Westward Ho Motels, Inc.*, 86 Nev. 784, 786-87, 476 P.2d 946 (1970).

Even though a motion for directed verdict is not necessary to review the sufficiency of the evidence so long as a motion for judgment n.o.v. is timely made, it may be a better practice to first move for directed verdict at the close of the case.

A motion for judgment n.o.v. only applies to a jury verdict. It is well established that a proper ruling upon a Rule 50(b) motion does not violate the constitutional guarantee of a jury trial. *Misty Management Corp. v. First Judicial District Court*, 83 Nev. 180, 183, 426 P.2d 728 (1967).

§ 2503. — Time for motion and appeal: appealability of order.

NRCP 50(b) requires that the motion be made not later than ten days after service of written notice of entry of judgment; the corresponding federal rule requires the motion not later than ten days after entry of judgment. The ten-day period in state practice is extended by three days when the notice of entry of judgment is served by mail. NRCP 6(e). *But see In re Herrmann*, 100 Nev. 1, 677 P.2d 594 (1984) (thirty-day period runs from actual notice of entry of probate order under NRS 155.190). Any untimely motion for judgment n.o.v. will be denied. *Ross v. Giacomo*, 97 Nev. 550, 553, 635 P.2d 298 (1981). The trial court is not permitted to extend the time for moving under Rule 50(b). NRCP 6(b).

The thirty-day time period for appeal is extended by a timely filing of a motion for judgment n.o.v. NRAP 4(a). The thirty-day time limit begins to run from the date of service of entry of the order granting or denying a motion under Rule 50(b). However, an untimely motion for judgment n.o.v. does not toll the thirty-day period in which a notice of appeal must be filed. *Ross v. Giacomo,* 97 Nev. at 553.

§2504. — Standard for review in district court.

"A motion for JNOV may be granted *only* when, ... there can be but one reasonable conclusion as to the proper judgment." *Bates v. Chronister,* 100 Nev. 675, 691 P.2d 865 (1984) (emphasis in original), quoting 5A *Moore's Federal Practice* §50.07[2] (1984). In passing on a motion for judgment n.o.v. the district court may not consider the credibility of witnesses or the weight of evidence, *Air Service Co. v. Sheehan,* 95 Nev. 528, 530, 594 P.2d 1155 (1979); it must review the "evidence and all inferences most favorably to the party against whom the motion is made." *Bliss v. DePrang,* 81 Nev. 599, 601, 407 P.2d 726 (1965); *see also Jeffers v. Bob Kaufman Machinery,* 101 Nev. 684, 707 P.2d 1153 (1985).

A motion for judgment n.o.v. is properly granted when the prevailing party has failed to establish an essential element of his cause of action or defense. Thus, in *Cleveland v. Bally Distributing Co.,* 96 Nev. 552, 612 P.2d 684 (1980), the court upheld the district court's grant of judgment n.o.v. in favor of the defendant because the defendant was found to owe no duty of care to the plaintiff. Alternatively, in *Pruett v. First National Bank,* 89 Nev. 442, 514 P.2d 1186 (1973), *cert. denied,* 415 U.S. 995 (1974), the district court properly set aside a defense verdict where the plaintiff's liquidated damages claim had been established as a matter of law.

Where it is asserted that there are no controverted issues of act upon which reasonable persons could differ, the standard for review becomes "whether the evidence is such that reasonable [persons] would have necessarily reached a different conclusion" than that set forth in the jury verdict. *Drummond v. Mid-West Growers Cooperative,* 91 Nev. 698, 704, 542 P.2d 198 (1975). The motion for judgment n.o.v. will not be granted where there is conflicting evidence presented in regard to material issues of fact. A motion for judgment n.o.v. is properly denied where "there is evidence tending to support the verdict, or where there is a conflict of evidence, so that the jury could properly decide, either way ...." *Dudley v. Prima,* 84 Nev. 549, 551, 445 P.2d 31 (1968), *quoting Ries v. Sanders,* 34 F.R.D. 468, 470 (N.D. Miss. 1964).

In short, a directed verdict or judgment n.o.v. is proper only in instances where the evidence is so overwhelming for one party that any other verdict would be contrary to law. *Bliss, supra.*

§ 2505. Motion for new trial: history, purpose and scope of NRCP 59(a).

The general rule at common law was that a new trial would be granted where an injustice had been done. *Shute v. Big Meadow Investment Co.,* 45 Nev. 99, 102, 198 P. 227 (1921). The grounds for a new trial under NRCP were initially patterned after FRCP 59(a) which included "any of the reasons for which new trials have heretofore been granted." NRCP 59(a) was revised in 1953 to include the existing grounds for new trial in Nevada. The Nevada Supreme Court stated in dictum prior to enactment of the Nevada Rules of Civil Procedure that a trial court has inherent power to grant a new trial for causes other than those enumerated in the statute, but that the additional ground had to be for some cause that was good at common law. *Shute, supra.*

The major difference between federal practice and Nevada practice is that the federal courts may grant a new trial on the ground that the verdict was against the weight of the evidence. In deciding that question, federal judges may weigh the evidence and pass on the credibility of witnesses. Up until 1964, Nevada practice allowed the trial court the same latitude. As a result of Justice Thompson's concurring opinion in *City of Reno v. Van Ermen,* 79 Nev. 369, 381-83, 385 P.2d 345 (1963), "insufficiency of the evidence to sustain a verdict" as a ground for new trial was deleted by the Nevada Supreme Court. Striking of that ground has greatly curtailed the discretion of state trial courts to grant new trials.

Another noteworthy difference between state and federal court practice is that a federal court judge may order a new trial on his own initiative under Fed. R. Civ. P. 59(d), whereas a state court judge may not order a new trial sua sponte. A federal court which grants a new trial on its own initiative must do so within ten days after entry of judgment. However, if a timely motion for new trial has been filed, the federal court may grant the motion for a reason not stated in the motion and is not subject to the ten-day limit under that circumstance, but a state court judge cannot grant a new trial for reasons not stated in a motion.

Nevada's rule concerning harmless error, NRCP 61, sets forth the general standard governing the grant of a new trial.

§ 2506. — Time for motion and appeal: appealability of order granting or denying new trial.

NRCP 59(b) requires that a motion for new trial must be served within ten days after service of written notice of the entry of the judgment. The ten-day period is extended by three days where the notice of entry of judgment is served by mail. NRCP 6(e).

The time for filing a motion for new trial cannot be enlarged by the court. NRCP 6(b). *See also Culinary & Hotel Service Workers Union, Local No. 226 v. Haugen,* 76 Nev. 424, 427, 357 P.2d 113 (1960). If a motion for new trial is not timely made, it must be denied. *Ross v. Giacomo,* 97 Nev. 550, 553, 635 P.2d 298 (1981). An untimely motion for new trial will not toll the thirty-day period in which a notice of appeal must be filed. *Ross, supra. See also* NRAP 4(a).

If the notice of appeal from the judgment is filed first and then a timely motion for new trial is made, the trial court is divested of jurisdiction to rule on the motion for new trial because of the filing of the notice of appeal. If this occurs, the trial court may hear the motion for new trial and, if the trial court is inclined to grant it, may certify to the Nevada Supreme Court its intention. Once the trial court has certified its intention to the Nevada Supreme Court to grant the motion, the moving party must request that the case on appeal be remanded to the trial court. *Huneycutt v. Huneycutt,* 94 Nev. 79, 80, 575 P.2d 585 (1978). Although the district court does not have authority to grant a new trial prior to remand of the appeal, it probably does have authority to deny the motion even though a notice of appeal has been filed. *Layton v. State,* 89 Nev. 252, 254, 510 P.2d 864 (1973), *quoting United States v. Hays,* 454 F.2d 274, 275 (9th Cir. 1972).

In Nevada practice, an order granting or denying a new trial is an appealable order. NRAP 3A(b)(2).

§ 2507. Grounds for new trial: NRCP 59(a)(1) — irregularity in the proceedings or abuse of discretion preventing fair trial.

Two Nevada cases which discuss "irregularity of the proceedings" involved "Mary Carter" agreements between insurance companies for some of the defendants and counsel for the plaintiff. In *Ponderosa Timber & Clearing Co. v. Emrich,* 86 Nev. 625, 627-28, 472 P.2d 358 (1970), the court held that the agreement whereby two of the co-defendants would escape liability pursuant to a hold harmless agreement, if a judgment was entered against all of the defendants in excess of a specified sum, was not an irregularity which would constitute a denial of a fair trial. The opposite result was achieved in *Lum v. Stinnett,* 87 Nev. 402, 488 P.2d 347 (1971), where a similar agreement was entered into and the court held that it was contrary to law and public policy. The court distinguished the two factual situations by stating that in the former case the validity of the agreement was not an issue on appeal since the lower court had ordered a new trial unless the plaintiff disclaimed an interest in one-half of the judgment, which he did. Of significant importance in the latter case was the fact that counsel for the defendant who was not a party to the agreement repeatedly sought the trial court's protection and thus preserved the issue for appeal. *See also Vosburg Equipment v. Zupancic*, 103 Nev. 266, 737 P.2d 522 (1987) (agreement between property damage claimants to equally share costs and attorney's fees in exchange for equal share of recovery did not constitute champerty or maintenance).

In the case of *Pappas v. State*, 104 Nev. 572, 763 P.2d 348 (1988), one of the jurors, who was never instructed to submit questions regarding jury instructions to the trial court for clarification, knocked on the jury room door and explained to the Judge's secretary, who came to the door, that the juror had a question regarding the jury instructions. The secretary instructed the juror to reduce the question to writing and informed the jury that the judge and the attorneys were not presently available. The jury then arrived at a verdict without submitting the question to the trial judge. The Nevada Supreme Court affirmed the trial court's ruling that the jury's course of conduct in this situation did not amount to an irregularity in the proceedings sufficient to support a new trial under Rule 59(a)(1). The Court also noted in *Pappas* that juror affidavits could not be used to support the motion for new trial because such affidavits, "... are inadmissible for proving the jurors' mental processes or the effects of alleged misconduct upon jurors." *Id.*, 104 Nev. at 575.

Only one Nevada civil case exists discussing the trial court's abuse of discretion preventing a fair trial. In *Moore v. Cherry*, 90 Nev. 390, 395, 528 P.2d 1018 (1974), the court held that an abuse of discretion did not occur in dismissing the case where the plaintiff and his attorney disregarded the rules of court. For a more thorough discussion of judicial discretion, see Chapter 29.

§ 2508. — NRCP 59(a)(2): misconduct of the jury or prevailing party.

The ground of misconduct on the part of the jury or a juror has been discussed in Nevada cases in terms of quotient verdicts, conversations between jurors and non-jurors during juror deliberations, an intoxicated juror and use of a juror's affidavit or his testimony to impeach the jury verdict.

In order for the jury to agree on the amount of a verdict, the jurors may each set forth their proposed sum, add all amounts and then divide by the number of jurors, so long as none of the jurors agreed to be bound. *Kaltenborn v. Bakerink*, 80 Nev. 16, 20-21, 388 P.2d 572 (1964).

It is, of course, improper for counsel for either party to speak to jurors during trial or during deliberations. If a motion for new trial is made on the basis of jury misconduct by virtue of impermissible conversations, the record must show that such conversations improperly influenced the verdict of the jury. *Horton v. D.I. Operating Co.*, 84 Nev. 694, 696, 448

P.2d 36 (1968). The alleged misconduct by the juror or prevailing party should be the subject of an objection prior to the jury's verdict, otherwise it will be considered waived. *Jefferes v. Cannon,* 80 Nev. 551, 553-54, 397 P.2d 1 (1964).

If a juror has drunk to an "intoxicated extent," then a new trial may be required. *Curtis v. George Grifall Co.,* 84 Nev. 375, 376, 441 P.2d 680 (1968), *citing Davis v. Cook,* 9 Nev. 134 (1874).

If it is alleged that a juror has made an independent investigation regarding a possible cause of an accident, the district court must decide whether prejudice to the losing party resulted. The question of prejudice is an issue of fact to be determined by the district court and it will not be set aside unless abuse of discretion is manifest. *Stackiewicz v. Nissan Motor Corp.,* 100 Nev. 443, 686 P.2d 925, 931 (1984).

Juror "mention" of insurance coverage or the effect of income taxes upon the award during deliberations is not sufficient to require a new trial predicated on alleged juror misconduct. *Stackiewicz v. Nissan Motor Corp.,* 100 Nev. 443, 686 P.2d 925, 931 (1984).

As a general rule, jurors will not be permitted to impeach their own verdict. *Jeep Corp. v. Murray,* 101 Nev. 640, 708 P.2d 297 (1985). The leading case on the use of juror affidavits and testimony to impeach a jury verdict is *McNally v. Walkowski,* 85 Nev. 696, 462 P.2d 1016 (1969). That case abrogated Lord Mansfield's Rule that a juror's statement could not be admitted to impeach the verdict. A juror's affidavit may be used is "when it is charged that a juror has answered falsely on voir dire about a matter of potential bias or prejudice." *McNally, supra,* at 700, *quoting Department of Public Works & Buildings v. Christensen,* 184 N.E.2d 884, 887 (1962); *see also Walkowski v. McNally,* 87 Nev. 474, 488 P.2d 1164 (1971). To constitute misconduct, the failure of a juror to answer a question touching upon his qualification must amount to an intentional concealment. The misconduct must have improperly influenced the jury or tainted its verdict to justify a new trial. This determination is left to the sound discretion of the trial court. *Hale v. Riverboat Casino, Inc.,* 100 Nev. 299, 682 P.2d 190, 193 (1984). A juror's affidavit may also be used "to show physically what transpired in the jury room," *Pappas v. State,* 104 Nev. 572, 763 P.2d 348 (1988), which must be objective facts "capable of ascertainment by any observer, ..." *Barker v. State,* 95 Nev. 309, 312, 594 P.2d 719 (1979).

It has been held that trial counsel's improper threat of a defamation suit against an adverse witness, accompanied by the trial court's failure to instruct the witness to answer after assuring him that his testimony was absolutely privileged, was sufficient misconduct on the part of the prevailing party to justify a new trial. *Campus Village Shopping Center Trust v. Brown,* 102 Nev. 17, 713 P.2d 566 (1986).

§ 2509. — NRCP 59(a)(3): accident or surprise.

"The grant or denial of a new trial based upon a claim of 'surprise' lies within the sound discretion of the trial court." *Havas v. Haupt,* 94 Nev. 591, 593, 583 P.2d 1094 (1978) (citations omitted). The "surprise" contemplated by this rule "must result from some fact, circumstance, or situation in which a party is placed unexpectedly, to his injury, without any default or negligence of his own, and which ordinary prudence could not have guarded against." *Havas, supra,* at 593.

If a situation occurs on the eve of trial, such as the disappearance of a key witness, which ordinary prudence could not have guarded against, it is incumbent upon the adversely affected party to immediately resolve the dilemma, or at least move for a continuance of the trial. If no action is taken to eliminate or lessen the adverse consequences prior to trial or during the trial, it will not be an abuse of discretion for the trial court to deny a new trial on the basis of accident or surprise.

If evidence is introduced during trial of such a nature to come under this rule, counsel must either object or request an appropriate instruction concerning that evidence during the trial. Counsel cannot decide not to object or request an appropriate instruction and thereafter hope for a favorable jury verdict. Such inaction will preclude a subsequent claim of surprise as a ground for new trial. *Mahan v. Hafen,* 76 Nev. 220, 229, 351 P.2d 617 (1960).

§ 2510. — NRCP 59(a)(4): newly discovered evidence.

A significant difference exists between Nevada state court practice and federal court practice in this area. The Federal Rules of Civil Procedure provide that "newly discovered evidence" is a basis for relief from a judgment under FRCP 60(b). In Nevada, newly discovered evidence is a ground for a motion for new trial under NRCP 59(a), but is not a ground for relief under NRCP 60(b). "This departure from the federal rules was intentionally made in order to preserve the practice theretofore established under the Civil Practice Act." *Horton v. D.I. Operating Co.,* 84 Nev. 694, 698, 448 P.2d 36 (1968).

It is mandatory that the newly discovered evidence used as a basis for new trial be brought to the trial court's attention within ten days after entry of judgment.

The determination of whether or not to grant a new trial based on newly discovered evidence is largely within the discretion of the trial court. *Bramlette v. Titus,* 70 Nev. 305, 312, 267 P.2d 620 (1954). This is one of the limited occasions in which the trial court may balance the weight and credibility of opposing affidavits in passing upon the motion. *Drespel v. Drespel,* 56 Nev. 368, 375, 45 P.2d 792 (1935). Where an important issue is the subject of conflicting affidavits, the moving party may be entitled to an evidentiary hearing. *See Nevada Power v. Fluor Illinois*, 108 Nev. 638, 837 P.2d 1354 (1992) (evidentiary hearing required to determine motion to dismiss as a discovery sanction).

The rule requires that the new evidence could not have, with reasonable diligence, been produced at trial. The litigant must with particularity set forth in his affidavit the acts performed which it is contended constitute reasonable diligence. *Drespel v. Drespel*, 56 Nev. 368, 373-75, 45 P.2d 792 (1935). The conclusions set forth in the affidavit in support of the motion for new trial must be supported by the facts. Mere conclusions which omit a showing of reasonable diligence or facts upon which diligence might be inferred are insufficient.

The type of evidence which the litigant contends is sufficient for grant of a new trial is important. Hearsay is entitled to little, if any, consideration in support of the motion. *Bramlette v. Titus*, 70 Nev. 305, 312, 267 P.2d 620 (1954). Cumulative evidence is also disfavored, particularly if similar evidence was available for admission during trial. *Bramlette, supra.* Impeachment evidence is also disfavored. If impeachment evidence is asserted as a ground for new trial, it must actually impeach and concern a material point in the case. *Pate v. Mead*, 79 Nev. 230, 232 n.3, 381 P.2d 230 n.3 (1963).

§ 2511. — NRCP 59(a)(5): manifest disregard by the jury of the instructions of the court.

The present standard for review of a motion for new trial upon the ground of manifest disregard by the jury of the instructions of the court is whether the trial court or appellate court is able to declare that, "had the jurors properly applied the instructions of the court, it would have been impossible for them to reach the verdict which they reached." *M & R Investment v. Anzalotti*, 105 Nev. 224, 226, 773 P.2d 729 (1989), *quoting Weaver Bros., Ltd. v. Misskelley*, 98 Nev. 232, 234, 645 P.2d 438, 439 (1982). *See also Town & Country Electric v. Hawke*, 100 Nev. 701, 692 P.2d 490 (1984). The court need not determine how the jury reached its conclusion; it needs only to determine whether it was possible for the jury to do so. *M & R Investment v. Anzalotti*, 105 Nev. at 226, *quoting Town & Country Electric v. Hawke*, 100 Nev. at 702.

A motion for new trial under NRCP 59(a)(5) is not the best method for arguing that as a matter of law the litigant is entitled to a verdict in his favor. *Amundsen v. Ohio Brass Co.*, 89 Nev. 378, 381, 513 P.2d 1234 (1973). However, this argument can be made where there is plain error in the record or a showing of manifest injustice. If there is "obvious disregard, by the jury, of the court's instructions resulting in a verdict which is shocking to the conscience of a reasonable man," it will be considered manifest injustice and a new trial will be ordered. *Avery v.*

Gilliam, 97 Nev. 181, 183, 625 P.2d 1166 (1981), *quoting Price v. Sinnott,* 85 Nev. 600, 607, 460 P.2d 837, 841 (1969).

The Nevada Supreme Court has held: "[M]anifest injustice is present when a verdict 'strikes the mind, at first blush, as manifestly and palpably contrary to the evidence.'" *Meyer v. Swain,* 104 Nev. 595, 598, 763 P.2d 337, 339 (1988), *quoting Kroeger Properties v. Silver State Title,* 102 Nev. 112, 715 P.2d 1328 (1986).

The plaintiff in *Van Duzer v. Shoshone Coca Cola Bottling Co.,* 103 Nev. 383, 741 P.2d 811 (1987), a products liability action, succeeded in presenting a prima facie case of strict liability, and the defendants failed to present any evidence negating the elements of this cause of action or supporting its defense of product misuse. The Nevada Supreme Court held the jury's verdict in favor of the defendants could only have resulted from manifest disregard of the jury instructions and held plaintiff was entitled to a new trial.

Since the standard for grant or denial of a motion for new trial on the ground of manifest disregard by the jury of the instructions of the court is very similar to the standard for review of a motion for judgment n.o.v. under Rule 50(b), the better practice is to combine both motions for filing at the same time. If the trial court finds that the jury did disregard its instructions, the judgment n.o.v. should be granted in appropriate cases.

The trial court cannot weigh the evidence or assess the credibility of witnesses in determining whether the jury has manifestly disregarded the jury of the court's instructions. It is an abuse of discretion for the trial court to do so. *Fox v. Cusick,* 91 Nev. 218, 221, 533 P.2d 466 (1975). The court reaffirmed this finding in *Brascia v. Johnson,* 105 Nev. 592, 781 P.2d 765 (1989), where it was held that a trial court is precluded from substituting its own judgment unless the jury erred as a matter of law, and should refrain from granting a new trial if the question concerns only the weight of the evidence.

§ 2512. — Additur.

If a verdict is returned in favor of a plaintiff where liability is clearly established, but the damages awarded are obviously inadequate, the prevailing party should consider a motion for additur or, in the alternative, for a new trial on the issue of damages. There is no specific ground set forth in Rule 59(a) upon which a motion for additur must be based, although it is clearly established that, if it is granted and the increased verdict is not accepted by the defendant, then a new trial may be had.

Additur is not allowed in federal court practice.

The leading case on the trial court's ability to increase a jury award in favor of a plaintiff is *Drummond v. Mid-West Growers Coop.,* 91 Nev. 698, 542 P.2d 198 (1975). It is soundly established in Nevada law that additur does not violate the Nevada constitutional and common-law right of trial by jury. *Drummond, supra* at 711-12.

In order to obtain additur, the plaintiff must establish that the damages awarded by the jury are "clearly inadequate" and that the case is proper for granting a motion for a new trial, unless the defendant consents to an additur set by the court. *Eikelberger v. Tolotti,* 94 Nev. 58, 60-61, 574 P.2d 277 (1978).

If there is substantial conflicting evidence on the issue of liability or an interrelationship between the liability and damage issues, and the jury returns a verdict in favor of the plaintiff which is considered inadequate, additur is not appropriate. *Shere v. Davis,* 95 Nev. 491, 493, 596 P.2d 499 (1979). Thus, additur will only be affirmed on appeal where there is *no* substantial conflict of evidence on the issue of liability.

If the court grants additur or, in the alternative, a new trial limited to the issue of damages, counsel for the defendant must be careful in deciding whether to appeal the court's additur *or* agreeing to a new trial. If an appeal is taken, the appellant is deemed to have made his election and cannot choose a new trial if he loses his appeal concerning the additur issue. *Jacobson v. Manfredi,* 100 Nev. 226 n.4, 679 P.2d 251, 255 n.4 (1984).

§ 2513. — NRCP 59(a)(6): excessive damages appearing to have been given under the influence of passion or prejudice — remittitur.

Rule 59(a)(6) is one of the few grounds for new trial where the trial court is permitted to weigh the evidence and pass on the credibility of witnesses in exercising its discretion.

When a judgment is entered in favor of the plaintiff, the trial court is authorized to order a remittitur or, in the alternative, a new trial if the amount of the reduced verdict is not accepted by the plaintiff. When conflicting evidence on the issue of damages does appear in the record, the trial court has wide discretion to grant remittitur or, in the alternative, new trial based on passion or prejudice of the jury. "However, this is not so when the evidence regarding damage is not in conflict." *Harris v. Zee,* 87 Nev. 309, 312, 486 P.2d 490 (1971).

The mere fact that a compensatory or punitive damage award is large is not conclusive that the verdict was a result of passion or prejudice. *Nevada Cement Co. v. Lemler,* 89 Nev. 447, 453, 514 P.2d 1180 (1973); *Miller v. Schnitzer,* 78 Nev. 301, 308, 371 P.2d 824 (1962). "The order to remit immediately becomes suspect unless the amount awarded by the jury, standing alone, is so excessive as to suggest the intrusion of passion and prejudice upon its deliberations." *Harris, supra.*

A motion for new trial based on alleged passion or prejudice on the part of the jury resulting from improper closing arguments will not be granted unless the conduct giving rise to the jury's alleged passion or prejudice is objected to at trial. *Beccard v. Nevada National Bank*, 99 Nev. 63, 66, 657 P.2d 1154 (1983).

If the trial court refuses to grant a new trial or remit a portion of the award based on the defendant's claim that the damages are excessive and a result of passion or prejudice, the appellate court will be reluctant to substitute its judgment for that of the trier of fact on the issue of damages. *Automatic Merchandisers, Inc. v. Ward*, 98 Nev. 282, 284, 646 P.2d 553 (1982). However, if the appellate court's judicial conscience is shocked by the jury award, it may order a remittitur or, if not accepted, a new trial. *Keller v. Brown*, 101 Nev. 273, 701 P.2d 359 (1985).

If the trial court grants remittitur or, in the alternative, a new trial, and the plaintiff appeals the remittitur, an election will probably be found and the appellant may not later choose to accept a new trial. *See Jacobson v. Manfredi*, 100 Nev. 226 n.4, 679 P.2d 251, 255 n.4 (1984) (election rule applied as to additur).

The Nevada Supreme Court may reduce a judgment on its own initiative irrespective of whether or not a motion under Rule 59(a)(6) was made. When the court does so, it is not technically a "remittitur" unless an option is given to the plaintiff to accept a new trial instead of the reduced judgment. *See, e.g., Kellar v. Brown*, 101 Nev. 273, 701 P.2d 359 (1985) (new trial ordered on issue of punitive damages unless remittitur accepted). The Nevada Supreme Court has reduced judgments where there was no evidentiary support for a portion of an award, *Mort Wallin v. Commercial Cabinet*, 105 Nev. 855, 784 P.2d 954 (1989) and *Sierra Foods v. Williams*, 107 Nev. 574, 816 P.2d 466 (1991), and where the amount awarded by the jury "... is clearly disproportionate to the blameworthiness and harmfulness in the conduct ..." of the defendant. *Republic Insurance Co. v. Hires*, 107 Nev. 317, 322, 810 P.2d 790 (1991).

§ 2514. — NRCP 59(a)(7): error in law occurring at the trial and objected to by the party making the motion.

It is not necessary to move for a new trial pursuant to Rule 59(a)(7) in order to preserve the right to appellate review of an alleged error of law occurring at trial. However, it is critical for purposes of a motion for new trial and appellate review that the alleged error of law be objected to and brought to the trial court's attention. *City of Reno v. Silver State Flying Service*, 84 Nev. 170, 180, 438 P.2d 257 (1968).

Common examples of errors of law occurring during trial involve admission or exclusion of evidence and the giving or failure to give jury instructions. In either event, the aggrieved litigant should have fully

apprised the court of his legal argument prior to the time for a motion for
new trial. It is good practice to renew the claims of legal error on motion
for new trial so that the trial court is allowed an opportunity to correct
the defect before the lengthy process of appellate review.

§ 2515. — Motions for new trial in cases tried to the bench.

Rule 59(a) provides that on a motion for new trial in an action tried
without a jury, the court may open the judgment if one has been entered,
take additional testimony, amend findings of fact and conclusions of law
or make new findings and conclusions, and direct the entry of a new
judgment. All of the grounds set forth in Rule 59(a), except those specifically relating to jury misconduct or manifest disregard by the jury of
instructions, can be utilized as a basis for new trial in a court tried case.

§ 2516. Joinder of motion for new trial with motion for judgment n.o.v.

(a) Relationship between motions under NRCP 50 and motion for
new trial.

Rule 59(b) provides that a motion for a judgment n.o.v. may be joined
with a motion for new trial. When the alternative motion is made, Rule
50(b) provides that, "[if] a verdict was returned the court may allow the
judgment to stand or may reopen the judgment and either order a new
trial or direct the entry of judgment as if the requested verdict had been
directed. If no verdict was returned the court may direct the entry of
judgment as if the requested verdict had been directed or may order a
new trial."

The alternative motion for judgment n.o.v. and for new trial "is a
remedy for the party who lost the verdict. He asks for judgment notwithstanding the verdict and thus contends that he is entitled to judgment as
a matter of law. By the alternative motion, he asks the court to grant
him a new trial if he is wrong in his contention that he is entitled to
judgment. He may ask for a new trial on any of the grounds that would
support a motion for a new trial under Rule 59 and this branch of the
motion is tested by the same standards that would apply if the motion
were made independently under Rule 59." 9 Wright & Miller, *Federal
Practice & Procedure, Civil* § 2539, at 608 (1971).

Rule 50(c)(1) provides that if the motion for judgment n.o.v. is granted,
counsel for the moving party should do everything in his power to assure
the trial court also rules on the alternative motion for new trial "by
determining whether it should be granted if the judgment is thereafter
vacated or reversed," and by specifying "the grounds for granting or
denying the motion for the new trial." *Cerminara v. District Court,* 104

Nev. 663, 765 P.2d 182 (1988), involved a defendant who had filed a motion for judgment notwithstanding the verdict or in the alternative, motion for new trial and/or remittitur. The trial court granted defendant's motion for judgment n.o.v., but failed to rule on the motion for new trial and/or remittitur. When the judgment n.o.v. was later reversed and the original jury verdict reinstated, the court held defendant's failure to object to the fact the district court did not rule on its motion for new trial, and its failure to take action to compel a ruling, suggested that defendant had abandoned its motion, and as such, the district court lacked jurisdiction to entertain the motion for new trial.

§ 2517. Motion to amend or alter judgment under NRCP 59(e).

As stated in *Chiara v. Belaustegui*, 86 Nev. 856, 859, 477 P.2d 857 (1970): "Rule 59(e) provides an opportunity, within a severely limited time, to seek correction at the trial court level of an erroneous order or judgment, thereby initially avoiding the time and expense of appeal. Rule 59(e) provides the remedy that, where the issues have been *litigated* and resolved, a motion may be made to alter or amend a judgment. Such a motion might propose to alter a judgment of dismissal without prejudice to a dismissal with prejudice and vice versa; to include an award of costs; or to change the time and conditions of the payment of a master." (Emphasis in original).

The motion to alter or amend must state with particularity the grounds for it and must set forth the relief or order sought. *United Pacific Insurance Co. v. St. Denis*, 81 Nev. 103, 111, 399 P.2d 135 (1965).

A motion to amend or alter judgment under Rule 59(e) does toll the thirty-day time limit for appeal. *Morrell v. Edwards*, 98 Nev. 91, 93, 640 P.2d 1322, 1324 (1982). NRAP 4(a). If the motion is not served within ten days after service of written notice of entry of judgment, the time for appeal is not tolled. *Morrell, supra.* The ten-day time limit for service of the motion is extended by three days where the notice of entry of judgment is served by mail. NRCP 6(e). The ten-day time limit for serving a motion to alter or amend the judgment cannot be enlarged by the court. NRCP 6(b). A motion to stay execution of judgment under Rule 62(b) will not excuse the untimely filing of a motion to amend the judgment. *Stapp v. Hilton Hotels Corp.*, 108 Nev. 209, 826 P.2d 954 (1992). The ten-day time limit under NRCP 59(e) does not, however, apply to motions for attorney's fees made pursuant to NRS 18.010. *Farmers Insurance Exchange v. Pickering*, 104 Nev. 660, 662, 765 P.2d 181 (1988).

A motion for rehearing does not toll the thirty-day time limit for appeal and will not be construed as a motion to amend. *Alvis v. State*, 99 Nev. 184, 186, 660 P.2d 980 (1983).

A motion to amend or alter judgment in cases tried to the court is also governed by Rule 52.

§ 2518. NRCP 60(a): relief from clerical mistakes in judgments or orders — purpose and scope of NRCP 60(a).

Nevada case law on this subject distinguishes "clerical error" from a "judicial error." A clerical error is a mistake in writing or copying. It is a mistake or omission by a clerk, counsel, judge, or printer which is not the result of the exercise of the judicial function. *Pickett v. Comanche Construction*, 108 Nev. 422, 836 P.2d 42 (1992). "A judicial error, on the other hand, is one made when the court reaches an incorrect result in the intentional exercise of the judicial functions. It occurs when a judge reaches a wrong or incorrect decision in deciding a judicial question." *Marble v. Wright*, 77 Nev. 244, 248, 362 P.2d 265 (1961) (citations omitted).

It is the burden of the moving party to establish that the error was clerical, not judicial. *Alamo Irrigation Co. v. United States*, 81 Nev. 390, 394, 404 P.2d 5 (1965).

Correction of a judgment or order under Rule 60(a) is not the subject of trial court discretion. If the trial court's oversight is an error of judgment, it will be considered a faulty determination of a matter of law, not a clerical error. *Smith v. Epperson*, 72 Nev. 66, 69, 294 P.2d 362 (1956).

If the alleged error contained in the judgment is truly of a clerical nature and subject to correction under Rule 60(a), an order correcting the decree nunc pro tunc is permissible. *State ex rel. Welfare Division v. Vine*, 99 Nev. 278, 284, 662 P.2d 295, *cert. denied*, 104 S. Ct. 413 (1983).

An example of the trial court's proper correction of a judgment under Rule 60(a) is *Channel 13 of Las Vegas, Inc. v. Ettlinger*, 94 Nev. 578, 583 P.2d 1085 (1978), where the complaint contained the correct amount owing but the prayer for relief indicated the wrong amount and the trial court corrected the summary judgment inserting the proper amount. Also, error in computation of a judgment by the trial court was properly corrected in *Kirkpatrick v. Temme*, 98 Nev. 523, 527, 654 P.2d 1011 (1982). However, it was held in *Rodela v. Rodela*, 88 Nev. 134, 494 P.2d 277 (1972), that the failure by the trial court to know the terms of a settlement agreement which it had approved was not a clerical mistake arising from oversight or omission under Rule 60(a).

§ 2519. — Time for relief and appellate court review.

It is well established that clerical errors may be corrected by the court at any time on its own motion or on the motion of any party under Rule 60(a). *Marble v. Wright*, 77 Nev. 244, 248, 362 P.2d 265 (1961). Thus, in

Alamo Irrigation Co. v. United States, 81 Nev. 390, 404 P.2d 5 (1965), a decree which was thirty-six years old was ordered corrected.

An order granting a motion to correct a clerical error is reviewable by the Nevada Supreme Court by way of appeal. It also appears that an order denying a party's motion to correct an ambiguity is reviewable by appeal. *Alamo Irrigation Co. v. United States,* 81 Nev. 390, 394, 404 P.2d 5 (1965). If the court denies that it has jurisdiction to correct a clerical error, mandamus is the appropriate remedy. *Silva v. Second Judicial District Court,* 57 Nev. 468, 66 P.2d 422 (1937).

A motion under Rule 60(a) does not toll the thirty-day time limitation for filing a notice of appeal of a final judgment or order set forth in NRAP 4(a).

Rule 60(a) establishes the procedure for review by the trial court of an order after an appeal has been taken when a party alleges that a clerical mistake exists in the judgment or order.

§ 2520. Relief from judgment or order under NRCP 60(b): history, purpose and scope of NRCP 60(b).

The most significant difference between NRCP 60(b) and Fed. R. Civ. P. 60(b) is that the Nevada rule was revised to delete the additional federal grounds for relief from a final judgment of "(2) newly discovered evidence which by due diligence could not have been discovered in time to move for a new trial ... [and] (6) any other reason justifying relief from the operation of the judgment." FRCP 60(b). The deletion of newly discovered evidence as a ground for relief under Rule 60(b) in Nevada was intentionally made in order to preserve the practice followed in Nevada prior to the adoption of the Nevada Rules of Civil Procedure. *Child v. George Miller, Inc.,* 74 Nev. 223, 225, 327 P.2d 342 (1958).

The litigant may move under Rule 60(b) in the same case in which the final judgment was rendered or may file an independent action for relief. An independent action for relief, as opposed to a motion in the same case, is usually done in cases where fraud or other misconduct is alleged in the prior proceedings. Relief may also be granted in an independent action after the statutory period has run when based on mutual mistake. *Nevada Industrial Development v. Benedetti,* 103 Nev. 360, 741 P.2d 802 (1987). This procedure is more fully detailed in § 1031, *supra* and § 2447, *supra.* Whether relief is requested by motion or independent action, notice must be provided to all parties who may be affected by the relief sought. *Moore v. Moore,* 75 Nev. 189, 193-94, 336 P.2d 1073 (1959).

"The right to bring an independent action for equitable relief is not necessarily barred by res judicata." *Amie v. Amie,* 106 Nev. 541, 796 P.2d 233 (1990). In limited instances, the policies furthered by granting relief under Rule 60(b) outweigh the doctrine of former adjudication.

Nevada Industrial Development v. Benedetti, 103 Nev. at 365. Res judicata will not bar an equitable independent action by an individual who was not a party to the prior proceeding if he demonstrates that he is directly injured or jeopardized by the prior judgment. *Pickett v. Comanche Construction,* 108 Nev. 422, 836 P.2d 42 (1992).

"Motions under Rule 60(b) are addressed to the sound discretion of the trial court and the exercise of discretion by the trial court in granting or denying such motions is not to be disturbed on appeal absent an abuse of discretion." *Heard v. Fisher's & Cobb Sales & Distributors, Inc.,* 88 Nev. 566, 568, 502 P.2d 104 (1972) (citations omitted). Rule 60(b) provides the district court with a discretionary power to relieve the litigant from a final judgment "upon such terms as are just," and that power applies to each ground stated in the rule. *Deros v. Stern,* 87 Nev. 148, 151, 483 P.2d 648 (1971).

However, the discretion of the court is not unlimited. Where equitable relief from a judgment was sought in an independent action on the grounds of mutual mistake as to the amount due, the trial court erred in dismissing the case where the plaintiff had made out a case of mutual mistake and unjust enrichment. *Nevada Industrial Development, Inc. v. Benedetti,* 103 Nev. 360, 741 P.2d 802 (1987).

Rule 60(b) is a remedial statute which should be liberally construed by the district court. *Heard, supra.* However, this policy of liberal construction must be balanced against "the desire to achieve finality in litigation." 11 Wright & Miller, *Federal Practice & Procedure, Civil* § 2857, at 159 (1973). This is particularly so in cases where a trial has occurred and each side was allowed to present its case.

§ 2521. Grounds for relief under NRCP 60(b): mistake, inadvertence, surprise or excusable neglect.

Most of the Nevada case law on the subject of relief under this ground concerns default judgments, discussed in Chapter 10, § 1026, *supra.* However, the court has used the test adopted in *Hotel Last Frontier v. Frontier Properties, Inc.,* 79 Nev. 150, 380 P.2d 293 (1963) (*see* § 1026, *supra*), to set aside more than just default judgments. For example, a judgment that was entered after defendant and his counsel failed to appear for trial was properly set aside for "excusable neglect" in *Passarelli v. J-Mar Development, Inc.,* 102 Nev. 283, 720 P.2d 1221 (1986), where defense counsel's law practice had disintegrated as the result of a psychiatric disorder and the defendant satisfied the test set forth in *Hotel Last Frontier, supra.* In addition to a client's unknown abandonment by counsel, as was the case in *Passarelli,* excusable neglect is also demonstrated where a client fails to act because of a reasonable belief that he or she will be represented, either by counsel or through the actions of another party to the litigation. *Dagher v. Dagher,* 103 Nev. 26, 28, 731 P.2d 1329 (1987) (citations omitted).

In *Culinary & Hotel Service Workers Union, Local No. 226 v. Haugen,* 76 Nev. 424, 357 P.2d 113 (1960), the appellant failed to timely move for a new trial or file a notice of appeal because of an erroneous belief that time had been extended to do so. The court held that misunderstanding was not sufficient for relief under Rule 60(b)(1).

If the litigant moves for relief from a final judgment on the basis of "mistake," the motion will not be granted if the mistake originated, in some respect, from the conduct of the moving party. *Smilanich v. Bonanza Air Lines,* 72 Nev. 212, 214, 298 P.2d 819 (1956).

In *Westside Charter Service v. Gray Line Tours,* 99 Nev. 456, 458-59, 664 P.2d 351 (1983), the alleged lack of notice of the trial setting was insufficient to support the claim of "surprise" for relief under Rule 60(b)(1).

In *Nevada Industrial Development, Inc. v. Benedetti,* 103 Nev. 79, 741 P.2d 802 (1987), the parties stipulated to a judgment of $83,875, both mistakenly believing that represented the principal plus interest due on a promissory note. Some seven months later, the defendant discovered the mistake and filed an independent action for equitable relief. The district court dismissed the action holding that relief was time-barred under NRCP 60(b). The Nevada Supreme Court reversed, holding that the time limitations of NRCP 60(b) have no application to an independent action. The Court also held that the plaintiff in the independent action had made out a prima facie case upon which equitable relief could be granted because any negligence was not "inexcusable" as a matter of law.

In addition to a showing of "mistake, inadvertence, surprise or excusable neglect," a moving party must ordinarily also show a meritorious defense. While the court did eliminate such a showing "where a person has been deprived of property in a manner contrary to the most basic tenets of due process," *Price v. Dunny,* 106 Nev. 100, 104, 787 P.2d 785 (1990), *citing Peralta v. Heights Medical Center, Inc.,* 485 U.S. 80 (1988), the requirement still exists absent due process concerns. *See Kahn v. Orme,* 108 Nev. 510, 835 P.2d 790 (1992).

§ 2522. — Fraud (whether heretofore denominated intrinsic or extrinsic), misrepresentation or other misconduct: fraud upon the court.

Up until 1981, Nevada case law recognized a distinction between extrinsic and intrinsic fraud. Extrinsic fraud was recognized as a basis for relief from a final judgment although intrinsic fraud was not. Numerous Nevada cases discussing the difference between extrinsic and intrinsic fraud no longer apply since the amendment in 1981 of Rule 60(b)(2) to allow relief on the basis of fraud "whether heretofore denominated intrinsic or extrinsic."

The most important consequence of the amendment allowing relief in cases previously denominated intrinsic fraud is that a judgment can now be successfully attacked on the ground that it had been obtained by perjury. 11 Wright & Miller, *Federal Practice & Procedure, Civil* § 2861, at 194 (1973).

The savings clause contained in Rule 60(b) provides that a party may file an independent action for relief from a judgment, order or proceeding for "fraud upon the court." In order to prevail on this ground, the burden is on the moving party to show by clear and convincing evidence that "an unconscionable plan or scheme ... designed to improperly influence the court in its decision" had been perpetrated. *Occhiuto v. Occhiuto*, 97 Nev. 143, 146 n.2, 625 P.2d 568 (1981), *quoting England v. Doyle*, 281 F.2d 304, 309 (9th Cir. 1960).

§ 2523. — The judgment is void.

A motion under Rule 60(b)(3) is different than the other grounds because the district court has no discretion when ruling on it. "Either a judgment is void or it is valid. Determining which it is may well present a difficult question, but when that question is resolved, the court must act accordingly." 11 Wright & Miller, *Federal Practice & Procedure, Civil* § 2862, at 197 (1973).

In *Misty Management Corp. v. First Judicial District Court*, 83 Nev. 180, 183, 426 P.2d 728 (1967), the court held that, even if the trial court incorrectly granted judgment n.o.v., "[a] judgment which is erroneously entered by reason of the trial court's improper view of the proof is not a void judgment within the meaning of Rule 60(b)(3)."

A judgment will be considered void where the district court which rendered it lacked "jurisdiction of the subject matter, or of the parties, or if it acted in a manner inconsistent with due process of law." 11 Wright & Miller, *Federal Practice & Procedure, Civil* § 2862, at 198-200. Thus, in *LaPotin v. LaPotin*, 75 Nev. 264, 266, 339 P.2d 123 (1959), where it was established that the defendant was never served with process, the court never acquired personal jurisdiction and the divorce decree was held void.

In *Dredge Corp. v. Peccole*, 89 Nev. 26, 27, 505 P.2d 290 (1973), the appellate court held that the lower court was without jurisdiction to alter a judgment which had first been entered "without prejudice" to a dismissal "with prejudice" where the defendant did not appeal the dismissal "without prejudice" or by appropriate motion after judgment, attempt to have the court reconsider or amend its determination.

§ 2524. — The judgment has been satisfied, released or discharged.

There are no Nevada cases discussing the ground for relief that the judgment has been satisfied, released, or discharged.

The ground for relief that a prior judgment upon which it is based has been reversed or otherwise vacated, concerns cases where the present judgment is based on the prior judgment as a matter of res judicata or collateral estoppel. 11 Wright & Miller, *Federal Practice & Procedure, Civil* § 2863, at 204 (1973). In *Arley v. Liberty Mutual Fire Insurance Co.*, 85 Nev. 541, 544, 458 P.2d 742 (1969), the court held that a change in judicial view of the applicable law, after a final judgment, is not a basis for vacating a judgment entered before announcement of the change.

§ 2525. — Time for motion.

The reasonable time requirement of Rule 60(b) does not apply when attacking a judgment on the basis that it is void. A motion under all other grounds must be made in a reasonable time. Prejudice to the party opposing the motion and the diligence of the party seeking relief are the main criteria in determining whether the motion is timely.

Motions for relief under clauses (1) and (2) of Rule 60(b) must be made not more than six months after the judgment, order, or proceeding was entered or taken. This six-month period is an extreme time limit. It is possible that the motion will be rejected as untimely even though the six-month period has not elapsed. *See* 11 Wright & Miller, *Federal Practice & Procedure, Civil* § 2866, at 232 (1973) (addressing one-year limitation in federal court practice).

The trial court in *Peterson v. Peterson*, 15 Nev. 133, 771 P.2d 159 (1989), had ruled that the former wife's motion to set aside a judgment and divorce decree based on fraud had not been filed within a reasonable time, even though it had been within the six-month time limit prescribed by NRCP 60(b). The Nevada Supreme Court reversed, noting that the questionable timeliness of the motion was primarily due to the attorney's delay in preparing the motion. The court emphasized that because the purpose of Rule 60(b) is to redress injustices resulting from excusable negligent or the wrongs of an opposing party, the rule should be liberally construed, and held that the lower court's ruling produced harsh results which were inconsistent with the spirit of the rule. *Id.* at 134-35.

This six-month limitation on allegations of fraud is inapplicable to fraud upon the court. *Savage v. Salzmann*, 88 Nev. 193, 195, 495 P.2d 367, 368 (1972). The court in *Murphy v. Murphy*, 103 Nev. 185, 734 P.2d 738 (1987), held that, where the respondent perpetrated fraud upon the court, the appellant was not required to file an independent action to set aside the judgment, but instead could proceed by motion to set aside judgment under NRCP 60(b).

The six-month time limit of Rule 60(b) though has no application to an independent action for equitable relief on the grounds of mutual mistake or fraud. An independent action is, by definition, not a "motion" under Rule 60(b) and, therefore, the only time limitations on such an action are laches and the appropriate statute of limitations. *Nevada Industrial Development, Inc. v. Benedetti,* 103 Nev. 360, 741 P.2d 802 (1987).

§ 2526. — Appellate review.

The filing of a motion for relief from a final judgment or order under Rule 60(b) does not toll the time limitation of thirty days for filing a notice of appeal from such judgment or order. *Smilanich v. Bonanza Air Lines,* 72 Nev. 10, 291 P.2d 1053, *aff'd,* 72 Nev. 212, 298 P.2d 819 (1956).

If a notice of appeal is not filed within thirty days after notice of entry of the judgment and a motion for relief under Rule 60(b) is filed, the district court order denying the motion is appealable, but the appellate court will only review the propriety of the denial of the motion and will not review the underlying judgment itself. *Westside Charter Service v. Gray Line Tours,* 99 Nev. 456, 458, 664 P.2d 351, 352 (1983).

The standard for review on appeal is whether the district court abused its discretion. *Heard v. Fisher's & Cobb Sales & Distributors, Inc.,* 88 Nev. 566, 568, 502 P.2d 104 (1972), except with respect to a judgment which is void, in which case the district court's decision is not discretionary.

A problem exists where an appeal has been filed from the final judgment and, thereafter, one of the parties moves for relief in the district court under Rule 60(b). The procedure to be followed is that the district court may hear the motion and, if it is inclined to grant it, may then certify to the appellate court its intention, in which case a request for remand of the case on appeal can be made by the moving party. *Huneycutt v. Huneycutt,* 94 Nev. 79, 80, 575 P.2d 585 (1978). The district court probably does have the power to deny the motion, after which time a separate appeal may be taken from that denial. *See Layton v. State,* 89 Nev. 252, 510 P.2d 864 (1973) (court had power to deny motion for new trial after notice of appeal).

§ 2527. Stay of proceedings to enforce judgment: stay pending post trial motions.

NRCP 62(a) permits execution immediately upon the entry of the judgment, unless the district court otherwise directs. It is necessary to request a temporary stay of execution, if desired. Counsel for the defendant which has had a judgment rendered against it should immediately request a temporary stay of execution for a period of at least ten days after service of notice of entry of judgment. Such a motion in a jury case can, and should, be made after the jury verdict has been read. In any event, the request for a temporary stay of enforcement should be made prior to the time of entry of judgment.

Rule 62(b) provides that the district court may further stay the execution of any proceedings to enforce a judgment pending the disposition of post trial motions under Rule 50, 52(b), 59 and 60. The filing of a motion for stay of execution does not extend the ten-day time limit for filing post trial motions under those rules. *Stapp v. Hilton Hotels Corp.*, 108 Nev. 209, 826 P.2d 954 (1992). The filing of a post trial motion does not itself stay the judgment.

The district court has wide discretion in granting temporary stays of execution pending the passage of ten days after entry of the judgment, thus giving the defendant time to obtain a supersedeas bond. Wide discretion is also possessed by the district court in staying execution pending the ruling on a post trial motion. Since the ruling on a post trial motion usually will not consume a great amount of time, security in the form of a bond or other collateral is usually not required. However, Rule 62(b) does allow the district court to require security pending a determination on the post trial motion and if counsel for the plaintiff feels that circumstances justify such security, it should be requested.

§ 2528. — Stay of enforcement pending appeal.

After notice of entry of judgment the losing party has thirty days in which to file a notice of appeal. However, under Rule 62(a), the plaintiff may execute on the judgment immediately after it is entered. Therefore, if an appeal is contemplated, a temporary stay of enforcement should be requested under Rule 62(a) for a period of thirty days after entry of the judgment, or for a period of thirty days after the court's order denying post trial motions under Rules 50, 52(b), 59 or 60.

NRAP Rule 8(a) provides that an application for stay of the judgment must ordinarily be made in the first instance in the district court, although under certain conditions prescribed under that rule the Supreme Court may provide such relief. The Nevada Supreme Court has stated that "it is sound policy for the district court to first consider applications for stays." *State ex rel. Public Service Commission v. First Judicial District Court*, 94 Nev. 42, 44 n.1, 574 P.2d 272 (1978).

Pursuant to Rule 62(d), the posting of a supersedeas bond may stay enforcement of a judgment pending appeal. The district court is confronted with two questions in regard to its review of an application for a stay of enforcement of the judgment pending appeal. The first is the issue of the defendant's entitlement to the stay. The second issue concerns the sufficiency and amount of the supersedeas bond. *State ex rel. Public Service Commission v. First Judicial District Court,* 94 Nev. 42, 44-45, 574 P.2d 272 (1978).

The district court has wide discretion in its preliminary decision whether or not to grant the stay. Only in very unusual circumstances will the district court refuse to grant a stay where the defendant is ready and willing to post a supersedeas bond in the amount of the entire judgment plus an additional amount for the estimated amount of post judgment interest which would accrue during the pendency of the appeal. If the district court does refuse this stay, application for the stay can be made to the Nevada Supreme Court under NRAP 8(a).

The district court also has discretion in ruling on the sufficiency and amount of the supersedeas bond. "The purpose of a supersedeas bond is to protect the prevailing party from loss resulting from a stay of execution of the judgment. Thus, a supersedeas bond posted under NRCP 62 should usually be set in an amount that will permit full satisfaction of the judgment. A district court, in its discretion, may provide for a bond in a lesser amount, or may permit security other than a bond, *when unusual circumstances exist and so warrant.*" *McCulloch v. Jenkins,* 99 Nev. 122, 123, 659 P.2d 302, 303 (1983) (emphasis in original). If the district court does decide to accept a bond or other security in an amount less than the full judgment, it must "set forth specific and substantial reasons for so doing in an appropriate order." *McCulloch, supra,* at 124.

If the defendant does not timely file a notice of appeal after entry of the judgment, the judgment is final and the district court cannot thereafter entertain a motion for a stay of execution of the judgment. *Renfro v. Forman,* 99 Nev. 70, 72, 657 P.2d 1151, 1152 (1983).

§ 2529. Motions for attorney's fees.

A. *Grounds for awarding attorney's fees.*

The general rule with respect to awards of attorney's fees is that, in the absence of a statute or contract authorizing such an award, attorney's fees may not be recovered by a party litigant. *Schouweiler v. Yancey Co.,* 101 Nev. 827, 712 P.2d 786 (1985). There are, however, a number of ways for a litigant in Nevada to recover attorney's fees from an opposing party. Both NRS 17.115 and NRCP 68 permit parties to serve written offers of judgment at any time more than ten days before trial. If the offer is rejected and the ultimate judgment is not more favorable than that offered, the party rejecting the offer may be liable for the offering party's attorney's fees incurred from the date the offer was made. (For a thorough discussion of offers of judgment under NRS 17.115 and NRCP 68, see §§ 2402 through 2413, *supra*). Likewise, NRS 18.010 permits the court to award attorney's fees to a prevailing party under two circumstances: (1) when the prevailing party has not recovered more than $20,000, or (2) when the court finds that a claim, counterclaim, cross-claim or third-party complaint or defense of the opposing party was brought without reasonable ground or to harass the prevailing party.

B. Time for moving for attorney's fees.

Rule 68 and the above-cited statutes providing for awards of attorney's fees are silent as to the time limits for moving for attorney's fees. The court in *Farmers Insurance Exchange v. Pickering*, 104 Nev. 660, 765 P.2d 181 (1988), discussed the fact that NRS 18.010 does not specify the time period during which motions for attorney's fees will be entertained. *Pickering* involved a plaintiff who had prevailed in the trial court, but waited until the Nevada Supreme Court had affirmed the lower court's ruling before filing a motion for attorney's fees pursuant to NRS 18.010. The Nevada Supreme Court affirmed the lower court's ruling that the motion was timely, concluding that, absent a specific statutory provision governing the time frame in which a party must request attorney's fees, the timeliness of such request is a matter left to the discretion of the trial court. In reaching this decision, the court noted that plaintiff had been diligent in seeking fees, as his request had been made immediately upon completion of the appellate process, at which time he was assured that he was the prevailing party within the meaning of NRS 18.010(2). The court also noted that defendants had neither alleged nor demonstrated that plaintiff's request for fees following the appeal prejudiced or unfairly surprised appellant.

C. Awards of fees discretionary.

The award of attorney's fees resides within the discretion of the court, and in the absence of a manifest abuse of discretion, the court's decision on the issue will not be overturned. *County of Clark v. Blanchard Construction Co.*, 98 Nev. 48, 653 P.2d 1217 (1982). In *Pandelis Construction Co. v. Jones-Viking Associates*, 103 Nev. 129, 734 P.2d 1236 (1987), a case in which the trial court had denied a request for attorney's fees pursuant to NRS 18.010, the Nevada Supreme Court ruled that a trial judge must state his reasons for refusing to grant a prevailing party's attorney's fees, and that failure to do so constitutes abuse of discretion.

In *Beattie v. Thomas*, 99 Nev. 579, 668 P.2d 268 (1983), the Nevada Supreme Court identified several factors to be carefully evaluated by the trial court in exercising its discretion regarding the allowance of attorney's fees and costs. These factors include the following: (1) whether the plaintiff's claim was brought in good faith, (2) whether the defendant's offer of judgment was reasonable and in good faith in both its timing and amount, (3) whether the plaintiff's decision to reject the offer and proceed to trial was grossly unreasonable or in bad faith, and (4) whether the fees sought by the offeror are a reasonable and justified amount.

D. Amount of attorney's fees awarded.

After a determination is made as to whether fees and costs are to be allowed, the court must determine the reasonable amount to be awarded for attorney's fees. The proper factors to be considered in making this determination are: (1) the qualities of the advocate, *i.e.*, his ability, training, education, experience, professional standing and skill, (2) the character of the work to be done, *i.e.*, its difficulty, intricacy, importance, the time and skill required, the responsibility imposed and the prominence and character of the parties when they affect the importance of the litigation, (3) the work actually performed by the lawyer, *i.e.*, the skill, time and attention given to the work; and (4) the result, *i.e.*, whether the attorney was successful and what benefits were derived. *Schouweiler v. Yancey Co.*, 101 Nev. 827, 712 P.2d 786 (1985) (addressing attorney's fees awarded under NRCP 68).

Although the rule and statutes providing for awards of attorney's fees do not specifically set forth the tender of proof of reasonableness of attorney's fees required, at the very least counsel moving for attorney's fees should provide an affidavit attesting to the reasonableness of his fees and the necessity of work performed on behalf of his client. It is recommended that additional evidence such as time records and billing and payment documents also be attached to a motion for attorney's fees and oftentimes such records are required by the trial court. It is therefore imperative that counsel keep detailed and accurate time records.

§ 2530. Motion to tax costs.

NRS 17.115 provides that if a party does not accept an offer of judgment and then recovers less than that offer at the trial, the party who refused to accept the offer must pay the party who made the offer's taxable costs incurred from the date of filing the complaint. NRCP 68, on the other hand, only provides that the party who did not accept the offer must pay the other party's costs from the time the offer of judgment was made.

In order for a party to be awarded costs, NRS 18.110 requires that the party in whose favor judgment is rendered must file a verified memorandum of costs with the clerk and serve a copy upon the adverse party within five days after the entry of judgment. Within three days after service of a copy of the memorandum, the adverse party may move the court, upon two days' notice, to retax and settle the costs.

NRS 18.005 defines the categories of items which may be recovered as taxable costs under the rule and statutes. In the event a party seeks costs not included in this list, Section 16 of this statute allows "[a]ny other reasonable and necessary expense incurred in connection with the action."

CHAPTER 26

PRE-JUDGMENT REMEDIES

Form 26G. Order directing the issuance of a prejudgment writ of attachment and garnishment.
Form 26H. Writ of attachment.
Form 26I. Third-party claim.
Form 26J. Instructions to the sheriff.
Form 26K. Writ of garnishment.
Form 26L. Ex parte application for order to show cause why collateral should not be taken from the defendants and delivered to plaintiffs.
Form 26M. Affidavit in support of order to show cause why property should not be taken from the defendants and delivered to plaintiffs.
Form 26N. Order to show cause.
Form 26O. Order granting temporary writ of possession.
Form 26P. Temporary writ of possession.
Form 26Q. Thirty-day notice to quit premises.
Form 26R. Five-day notice to pay rent or quit the premises.
Form 26S. Three-day notice to quit pursuant to NRS 40.255(1)(c).
Form 26T. Affidavit of service.
Form 26U. Affidavit of complaint for summary eviction.
Form 26V. Order for summary eviction.
Form 26W-1 Instructions to the constable.
Form 26W-2 Eviction instructions re: lock change.
Form 26X. Complaint for unlawful detainer.
Form 26Y. Ex parte motion for order to show cause why a temporary writ of restitution should not issue.
Form 26Z. Affidavit in support of order to show cause why a temporary writ of restitution should not be issued.
Form 26AA. Order to show cause why a temporary writ of restitution should not issue.
Form 26BB. Order directing issuance of temporary writ of restitution.
Form 26CC. Temporary writ of restitution.
Form 26DD. Notice of execution on writ of execution.
Form 26EE. Writ of restitution.

Author: Phillip S. Aurbach

§ 2601. Introduction and scope.

This chapter focuses on four prejudgment remedies: attachment, garnishment, claim and delivery, and unlawful detainer.

A writ of attachment gives the creditor a prejudgment lien on property which the debtor has in his possession. NRS 31.010. A writ of garnishment gives the creditor a prejudgment lien on property of the debtor in the hands of a third party or obligations of a third party which are owed to the debtor. NRS 31.240. These prejudgment liens give the creditor security for payment of the judgment that he or she may recover. A writ of possession gives possession of personal property to the owner pending trial. NRS 31.840. An unlawful detainer lawsuit requests that a writ of restitution be issued to give possession of real property to the owner or landlord. NRS Chapter 40. The prejudgment remedies of attachment and garnishment must be distinguished from the post-judgment remedies of execution and garnishment, which are addressed in Chapter 27, *infra*. Also not discussed in this chapter is the use of attachment and garnishment to obtain jurisdiction.

§ 2602. Attachment.

The following sections discuss the effect of a writ of attachment, the notice requirements prior to issuance of a writ of attachment, the showing needed prior to issuance, the bond requirement, third-party claims on the property sought to be attached, and discharging the writ.

§ 2603. — Effect of attachment.

A writ of attachment is a prejudgment remedy that places a judicial lien on real or personal property that the debtor has in his possession. NRS 31.010; *Turner v. Dorland,* 89 Nev. 408, 411, 514 P.2d 210 (1973). Once the creditor obtains a judgment, a writ of execution is used to enforce the lien which was obtained by the attachment. NRS 31.140(2). A writ of execution is a post-judgment remedy which is used to obtain a judicial lien on property in the debtor's possession, force a sale of the property, and apply the proceeds of the sale to the judgment. The writ of execution is discussed in Chapter 27, *infra.* If the court orders that a writ of attachment be issued, it is directed toward property of the debtor that is in his possession. The attachment lien is dependant on the sheriff obtaining and retaining actual or constructive possession of the property. NRS 31.060(2); *Nevada Credit Rating Bureau, Inc. v. Williams,* 88 Nev. 601, 606, 503 P.2d 9 (1972) (attachment lien in effect even though sheriff left equipment in debtor's possession where sheriff recorded serial and identification numbers, placed sheriff's seals on it and told debtor not to move any of it); *Beemer v. Seaborn,* 54 Nev. 459, 21, 22 P.2d 356 (1933); *Green v. Hooper,* 41 Nev. 12, 21, 167 P. 23 (1917); *Moresi v. Swift,* 15 Nev. 215, 229 (1880) (constructive possession is sufficient). However, the attachment lien does not follow the property into the hands of third-party transferees. *Hulley v. Chedic,* 22 Nev. 127, 140, 36 P. 783 (1894).

There is a split of authority as to the time that the attachment lien becomes effective. 6 Am. Jur. 2d, *Attachment and Garnishment* 456, at 879-80 (1963). Some courts find that it becomes effective at the time the writ of attachment is placed in the hands of the sheriff. Other courts hold that it is only effective at the time of the levy, *i.e.,* seizure of the property by the sheriff. Nevada courts will probably follow the latter case law since Nevada cases have indicated that the sheriff must have possession of the property to keep the lien in effect. *Hulley v. Chedic,* 22 Nev. 127, 140 P. 783 (1894). The Nevada Supreme Court has held in a garnishment proceeding that a garnishment lien is effective as of the date of service of the writ of garnishment on the garnishee by the sheriff. *Board of Trustees of the Vacation Trust Carpenters Local No. 1780 v. Durable Developers, Inc.,* 102 Nev. 401, 724 P.2d 736 (1986). This issue arises when a court must decide priorities between two creditors who have obtained writs of attachment against the same property. The general

507

rule is that first in time has priority. *See Board of Trustees, supra,* at
415. If there is a priority conflict between a judgment creditor who has
sent a writ of execution to the sheriff and a nonjudgment creditor who
has sent a writ of attachment to the sheriff, NRS 31.140 resolves the
conflict. A writ of attachment has priority over property that has been
subjected to a writ of execution only if the writ of attachment was issued
before the other judgment was recovered. NRS 31.120 restates this rule.

§ 2604. — Obtaining the writ of attachment; the application.

An application for an order directing the clerk to issue a writ of attachment must contain an affidavit reciting specific facts. However, the affidavit may be supplemented by additional evidence at a hearing if one is
required. NRS 31.020. If notice and a hearing are required, NRS 31.024
sets forth the procedure for setting the hearing on the writ. If no notice is
required, the court merely reviews the application and supporting documents. NRS 31.022. Finally, NRS 31.028 lists what must be contained in
the order directing the issuance of the writ.

§ 2605. — Affidavit requirements.

An application to the court for a writ of attachment must be accompanied by an affidavit of the plaintiff or any other person having personal
knowledge of facts constituting at least one of the grounds for attachment. NRS 31.020. Additionally, NRS 31.020 requires that the affidavit
must:

(1) State the nature of the plaintiff's claim and that it is valid;
(2) State the amount that each plaintiff is entitled to recover from
each defendant if there is more than one;
(3) Provide reasonable and clear detail of the facts which establish
the grounds for the attachment;
(4) Describe with reasonable detail the money or property sought to
be attached and its location;
(5) Describe, to the best knowledge and information of the affiant,
the value of the property, less prior liens or encumbrances;
(6) Name third persons upon whom a writ of garnishment in aid of
the writ of attachment will be served, if appropriate;
(7) Attach a copy of a foreign judgment to the affidavit, if such is
involved; and
(8) State, to the best information and belief of the affiant if the
money or property is exempt from execution.

A form Affidavit in Support of an Application for a Writ of Attachment
is included in this chapter as Form 26A. The affidavit has alternative
language that applies to an application with notice as well as an application without notice. As indicated in § 2622, *infra,* the requirements for
issuance of a writ of garnishment are almost identical to those for a writ

of attachment and very often both writs are sought at the same time. Thus, the form also has the garnishment requirements in brackets.

§ 2606. — Notice requirements.

Although an attachment may be obtained at any time after issuance of the summons, there are specific circumstances that must be present before the court has authority to issue a writ of attachment without notice and a hearing. NRS 31.010. These requirements are listed below.

§ 2607. — Obtaining the writ without notice and a hearing.

NRS 31.017 states that writs of attachment may be issued without notice in cases where:

(1) A Nevada resident is suing a nonresident;
(2) The suit is based on a foreign money judgment, is for conversion of personal property, is based on a fraudulent conveyance under NRS Chapter 112 or is for child support under NRS Chapter 130;
(3) The Defendant is about to remove his property from Nevada;
(4) The Defendant is about to pledge, dispose of or conceal property;
(5) The suit is to recover money that the Defendant obtained by embezzlement, forgery, larceny or extortion; and
(6) Jurisdiction is obtained by the attachment.

Procedurally, the court reviews the ex parte motion for an order directing the issuance of the writ and, if appropriate, orders the writ to issue without notice to the defendant. NRS 31.022. A form Ex Parte Motion for Order Directing the Issuance of a Prejudgment Writ of Attachment and Garnishment Without Notice is included in this chapter as Form 26B. NRS 31.045 states that if you request and obtain a writ of attachment without notice, the sheriff must serve the debtor with "Notice of Execution" and a copy of the writ by regular mail at the debtor's last known address, or, if represented by an attorney, at the attorney's office, by the next business day after the day the writ was served. In addition, the clerk of the court is to affix notice on the writ of attachment regarding the time the writ was issued. A Notice of Execution is included in this chapter as Form 26C. As indicated in § 2622, *infra,* the requirements for issuance of a writ of garnishment are almost identical to those for a writ of attachment and very often both writs are sought at the same time. Thus, the form refers to issuance of both writs.

§ 2608. — Obtaining the writ after notice and a hearing.

Notice and hearing are generally required prior to issuance of a prejudgment writ of attachment. This writ may issue in the following cases: unsecured contract actions or secured contract actions where the security has become valueless, or where extraordinary circumstances exist which

justify issuance of the writ because of the improbability of reaching the
debtor's assets by the time a judgment is rendered. NRS 31.013. Procedurally, an Ex Parte Motion for an Order to Show Cause Why a Writ of
Attachment Should Not Issue is submitted to the court along with a
proposed order to show cause. NRS 31.024. A form Ex Parte Motion for
Order to Show Cause Why a Writ of Attachment and Garnishment
Should Not Issue after Notice is included in this chapter as Form 26D.
As indicated in § 2622, *infra,* the requirements for issuance of a writ of
garnishment are almost identical to those of a writ of attachment and
very often both writs are sought at the same time. Thus, the form refers
to the issuance of both writs. In addition to setting the time and place of
the hearing, the order to show cause must contain specific information,
such as when and how the order should be served on the defendant, as
well as advice to the defendant that he has a right to file affidavits or
present evidence at the hearing. Finally, the order must inform the defendant that if he fails to appear he will waive his right to the hearing
and in such case the court may order the clerk to issue a writ of attachment. NRS 31.024. A form Order to Show Cause Why a Writ of Attachment Should Not Issue is included in this chapter as Form 26E. Property
may only be attached if the creditor serves the defendant with notice of
execution, pursuant to the one found in Form 26C of this chapter, at the
time the notice of hearing is served pursuant to NRS 31.013.

§ 2609. — The hearing on the application.

At the hearing, the court may consider affidavits, testimony and other
evidence presented. NRS 31.026. The court must make a determination
of the probable validity of the plaintiff's claim against the defendant in
determining whether to order the clerk to issue the writ of attachment.
NRS 31.026. The hearing is to be conducted without a jury. NRS 31.026.

§ 2610. — Contents of order directing the writ to issue.

NRS 31.028 requires that the order directing the clerk to issue the
writ of attachment must contain the following:

    (1) The grounds for the attachment;
    (2) The fact or reason why the court believes the existence of the
grounds;
    (3) That the plaintiff has alleged a meritorious claim;
    (4) The amount for which the attachment will issue;
    (5) The amount of security which must be given by the plaintiff
before the writ will issue;
    (6) The names of third parties upon whom writs of garnishment in
aid of attachment may be served; and

(7) A reasonably detailed description of money or property to be attached, with the value of that property based upon the evidence or affidavits.

The court may order writs to be issued for the sheriff of different counties. NRS 31.028(7). Two form orders directing the writ of attachment to issue are included in this chapter as Forms 26F and 26G. Form 26F is an order resulting from an Order Directing the Issuance of a Prejudgment Writ of Attachment and Garnishment Without Notice and Form 26G is an Order Directing the Issuance of a Prejudgment Writ of Attachment and Garnishment to Issue after a show cause hearing. As indicated in § 2622, *infra,* the requirements for issuance of a writ of garnishment are almost identical to those of a writ of attachment and very often both writs are sought at the same time. Thus, the forms refer to issuance of both writs.

The court may impose other conditions that must be satisfied prior to ordering the issuance of the writ of attachment, such as foreclosing on real property that is security for the debt. *McMillan v. United Mortgage Co.,* 82 Nev. 117, 412 P.2d 604 (1966).

§ 2611. — Contents of the writ of attachment.

The only statutory requirement for a Writ of Attachment is that it must demand the amount for which the attachment will issue as set forth in the order directing the attachment to issue. NRS 31.028(7). A Writ of Attachment form is included in this chapter as Form 26H. This form refers to property in the hands of a third party. Thus, a Writ of Garnishment must also be issued. *See* Form 26K.

§ 2612. — Written undertaking and bond requirements.

The plaintiff must provide a written undertaking by two or more sureties in a sum not less than the amount claimed by the plaintiff, costs that may be awarded to the defendant and damages which the defendant may sustain, including attorney's fees, if the defendant is successful. *See* NRS 31.030(1). It is the duty of the clerk to require the plaintiff to file the written undertaking before the writ of attachment is issued. NRS 31.030(2). However, the requirement of providing two or more sureties is satisfied by filing one bond under NRS 20.030. If there is a dispute regarding the amount of the property sought to be attached and, consequently, the amount of the undertakings to be provided by the defendant, that value shall be established by not more than three appraisers appointed by the court. *See* NRS 31.190(2).

§ 2613. — Discharge from attachment.

A judgment in favor of a defendant discharges the attachment and the undertaking and any property held by the sheriff, pursuant to the attachment lien, must be returned to the defendant unless there is an appeal. NRS 31.170. If the plaintiff appeals, the court may, upon just terms, stay the dissolution of the writ pending the appeal. NRS 31.170. Thus, the sheriff will retain the property pending the appeal.

The defendant may move for a discharge of the attachment upon his filing an undertaking. NRS 31.180.

The defendant may also challenge the sufficiency of the sureties by filing an exception to the sureties not later than five days after the actual notice of the levy (*i.e.*, secured by the sheriff). If the defendant does take exception to the plaintiff's sureties, the plaintiff has five days to justify the surety to the judge, justice or clerk of the court in which the action is pending. The failure of plaintiff to justify within these time requirements results in the attachment being vacated. NRS 31.030(3).

Other than filing an undertaking, NRS 31.200 lists several other grounds the existence of which will discharge the attachment: that the writ was improperly or improvidently issued; that the property levied upon is exempt from execution or necessary and required by the defendant for the support and maintenance of himself and his family; or that the levy is excessive.

§ 2614. — Claim of exemption.

Exempt assets cannot be attached. *See* NRS 31.020(1)(h) and 31.200. The Nevada legislature has deemed certain assets exempt from execution. *See* Chapter 27, *infra*. Execution is a post-judgment remedy which is also described in more detail in Chapter 27, *infra*. If the sheriff levies on exempt assets, how does a debtor claim his exemption? NRS 21.112 provides a procedure to claim the exemption. However, this statute refers to post-judgment proceedings (execution and garnishment), not to prejudgment attachment or garnishment. It would appear that the debtor should follow the post-judgment procedures. The debtor must, within five days after the levy, *i.e.*, seizure of the assets, serve on both the sheriff and the creditor an affidavit setting forth the claim of exemption. After the debtor claims the exemption, as mentioned above, the sheriff must release the property within five days after the creditor receives a demand from the sheriff for an undertaking equal to double the value of the property. *See* NRS 21.112 for more particulars.

§ 2615. — Third-party claims.

If the property attached belongs to someone else, a third-party claim must be filed. NRS 21.120 and 31.070(1). The claim must be in writing, verified by his (or his agent's) oath and must set out the third party's right to possession. A Third-Party Claim form is included in this chapter as Form 23H. The third-party claim must then be served on the sheriff. The sheriff must release the property if the person who had the writ issued fails, within seven days after written demand, to give the sheriff an undertaking equal to double the value of the property levied upon. However, if the undertaking is given, the sheriff retains possession. Note that the sheriff may demand and exact the undertaking to protect the third party, notwithstanding any defect, informality or insufficiency of the verified claim of a third party served upon him. NRS 31.070(4). Either the third-party claimant or the plaintiff may request a hearing within ten days from service of the third-party claim for the purpose of determining who owns the property. Additionally, there are various notice and time limits that must be followed in NRS 31.070.

A third party may take exception to the surety submitted by the plaintiff within seven days after notice of receipt of the undertaking. NRS 31.070(3). If the exceptions are not taken, the third person shall be deemed to have waived any and all objections to the sufficiency of the sureties.

The Nevada Supreme Court has on more than one occasion enforced the undertaking requirements of the attachment statutes, specifically rejecting other attempts to obtain relief. In *Cooper v. Liebert,* 81 Nev. 341, 402 P.2d 989 (1965), the Nevada Supreme Court held that NRS 31.070 not only applied to attachments of real property as well as personal, but that the provisions of that statute were the exclusive remedy available to third persons whose property had been attached. *See also Romy Hames, Inc. v. McNeil Construction Co.,* 91 Nev. 134, 137, 532 P.2d 602 (1952) (Trial court has jurisdiction over action to determine title to property that was levied upon by a creditor and was also claimed by parties who had unperfected security interests).

The exclusive remedy of the statutory attachment provisions was also discussed by the court in rejecting an attempt to obtain injunctive relief by posting a bond in lesser amount. *Aronoff v. Katleman,* 75 Nev. 424, 345 P.2d 221 (1959).

§ 2616. — Liability of the attaching creditor and the sheriff.

The causes of action for improper attachment are malicious prosecution and abuse of process. Abuse of process is the misuse of regularly issued process and malicious prosecution is the wrongful issuance of process. *Nevada Credit Rating Bureau v. Williams,* 88 Nev. 601, 606, 503 P.2d 9 (1972) (it was abuse of process to attempt to force payment of a debt by attaching all of the debtor's equipment and refusing to release any of it; this was the willful act not proper in the regular conduct of the proceedings).

The sheriff may also be held liable if he is negligent. In the case of *Fireman's Fund Insurance Co. v. Shawcross*, 84 Nev. 446, 442 P.2d 907 (1968), the Nevada Supreme Court held that a sheriff and his deputies could be held liable for their negligence in effecting a discharge of attachment. The Nevada Supreme Court noted, however, that a sheriff who follows the instructions of plaintiff's counsel could not be judged as though he were trained in legal niceties. The sheriff need only exercise the judgment of a person of ordinary care and prudence.

Additionally, an action for wrongful attachment is subject to dismissal as being premature where the underlying action on the debt is still pending at the time the wrongful attachment is filed. *Clarence E. Morris, Inc. v. Vitek*, 85 Nev. 652, 461 P.2d 864 (1969).

§ 2617. — Liability of sureties.

A condition precedent to liability on an undertaking posted by a defendant is the creditor who obtained the judgment to have a writ of execution issued and returned unsatisfied by the sheriff. NRS 31.160. Additionally, only certain expenses may be recovered against the bond. In *Great American Indemnity Co. v. Sweetwater Mining Co.*, 74 Nev. 219, 326 P.2d 1105 (1958), the Nevada Supreme Court explained when expenses are allowed against the surety in an action for damages due to wrongful attachment. If the attachment is defective and subject to being dissolved by virtue of a defect, without regard to the merits of the claim, then the expenses in setting aside that defective attachment are recoverable from the surety on the attachment undertaking. However, if the attachment is not defective but its wrongfulness is due to the lack of the cause of action, then the expenses incurred in prevailing in that action upon the merits are not attributable to the attachment and, therefore, are not recoverable from the surety. *Great American Indemnity Co., supra*, at 222.

The Nevada Supreme Court also held in *Covrig v. Powers*, 74 Nev. 348, 332 P.2d 650 (1958), that, in an action against a surety, the surety cannot attempt to go back to inquire as to whether the attachment was regular or irregular in the underlying action.

Finally, the court in *United Pacific Insurance Co. v. Chism Homes, Inc.*, 102 Nev. 494, 728 P.2d 809 (1986), held that even if there is an incorrect determination of the value of property sought to be released from the attachment lien by the posting of a bond, the bonding company is liable to pay the full amount of the bond up to the amount of the judgment. In this case, it was undisputed that $75,000 was the net value of the property attached (market value minus encumbrances) instead of

$600,000 which had been previously set by appraisal. The surety was liable on the full $600,000 bond that was ordered to be posted.

§ 2618. — Instructions to the sheriff.

The writ of attachment directs the sheriff to attach by levying on the property, *i.e.*, seizing it and safely keeping the property within his county. The sheriff is to seize only as much nonexempt property as may be needed to satisfy the amount demanded by the writ of attachment. The sheriff must be given instructions relative to what to do. Instructions to the Sheriff form are included in this chapter as Form 26J.

The sheriff attaches various property as follows:

(1) Real property is attached by leaving a copy of the writ with an occupant or, if no occupant, by posting a copy of the writ in a conspicuous place on the property and recording a copy of the writ, together with a description of the property that is the subject of the attachment. NRS 31.060(1). If the property is vacant land, it is a good idea to give the sheriff a parcel map and directions to the property;

(2) Personal property is attached by taking it into the immediate custody of the sheriff or by placing a keeper in charge of the property or business. NRS 31.060(2). The plaintiff is required to prepay the expense of the movers, storage facilities and keeper during the period of attachment. By order of court or consent, the defendant may continue to operate in the ordinary course of his business if sales are for cash and the proceeds are paid to the keeper under the writ of attachment;

(3) A mobile home, as defined in NRS 40.215, is attached by the posting of a copy of the writ in a conspicuous place on the mobile home, by taking the mobile home into immediate custody, or having a keeper in charge of the mobile home for a maximum of two days. NRS 31.060(3). Again, the plaintiff is required to prepay the expenses of the keeper. The defendant may continue to occupy the home during the two-day period; and

(4) NRS 31.060(4) provides that the debts and credits and other property in the possession or under the control of persons other than the defendant must be attached by service of a writ of garnishment.

The plaintiff is required to deposit with the sheriff a sum of money sufficient to pay for the expenses of taking and safely keeping personal property that is easily transportable for a period not to exceed thirty days. NRS 31.065(1). If further detention is required, the sheriff may make written demand upon the plaintiff or the plaintiff's attorney for further deposits for additional periods not to exceed thirty days each. NRS 31.065(2). If plaintiff fails to pay that money when demanded, the sheriff shall notify the defendant within five days after the funds for storing are no longer available and shall release the property to the person from whom it was taken. NRS 31.065(3).

After the sheriff has served the writ of attachment or has attempted to do so, the sheriff shall return the writ of attachment within twenty days after its receipt, with a certificate of his proceeding. The "return" contains the date, time and place of each levy upon real or personal property with a full inventory of the personal property attached and a description of real property attached. *See* NRS 31.110. Many times the attorney that caused the writ to be issued never knows that the sheriff has filed such a "return." Thus, it is good practice to include a request in the "Instructions to Sheriff" that the sheriff send a copy of the return to the attaching creditor's attorney.

§ 2619. — Sale of attached property and satisfaction of judgment.

The provisions regarding sale of attached property are set forth in NRS 31.120 to 31.150. Perishable goods are to be sold by the sheriff in the manner ordered by the court. NRS 31.120. Otherwise, the property attached is retained by the sheriff to answer any judgment that may be recovered in the action. NRS 31.120. Debts and credits attached may be collected, if that can be accomplished without suit. NRS 31.120.

The court may order such property to be sold in the same manner as under an execution, with the proceeds to be deposited in the court pending the judgment. NRS 31.130.

If the plaintiff recovers a judgment, the sheriff shall satisfy that judgment out of the property attached. This shall be accomplished by paying the plaintiff the proceeds of all prejudgment sales. If any balance remains due, a writ of execution must be issued on the judgment and the sheriff then sells as much of the property as is necessary to satisfy the balance of the judgment. NRS 31.140. If the property attached does not sufficiently satisfy the judgment, after deducting the fees of the attachment, then the sheriff shall proceed to collect the proceeds of any debts or credits upon execution as in any other case. Alternatively, if the judgment has been paid and the sheriff still retains the property, the sheriff shall, upon reasonable demand, deliver that property and any proceeds to the defendant. NRS 31.150.

§ 2620. Garnishment.

The following sections discuss the effect and time when a writ of garnishment may issue, the application and affidavit requirements prior to issuance of the writ, issuance and contents of the writ of garnishment, and the liability of the garnishee.

§ 2621. — Effect of garnishment and time for issuance.

A writ of garnishment causes the money, credits, effects, debts, choses in action or other personal property of the defendant in the possession of third persons to be held as security for a judgment the plaintiff may recover in a suit against the defendant. NRS 31.060(4). *See also* NRS 31.240. The writ of garnishment may issue at the time a writ of attachment is issued or at any time thereafter. NRS 31.240. However, the party seeking garnishment occupies the same position against the garnishee as the defendant or debtor. *Board of Trustees of Vacation Trust Carpenters Local No. 1780 v. Durable Developers, Inc.*, 102 Nev. 401, 724 P.2d 736 (1986) (garnishor is subject to all defenses garnishee has against the defendant, including the right of setoff); *Valley Bank v. Dobson*, 97 Nev. 276, 629 P.2d 229 (1981) (a husband's profit sharing retirement account is not subject to garnishment for child support and alimony since the husband did not have access to the funds being held by the garnishee). If the garnishee's obligation to the debtor is contingent and might never become due, then that obligation may not be garnished. *Craig v. Margrave*, 84 Nev. 638, 446 P.2d 653 (1968); *Margrave v. Craig*, 92 Nev. 760, 558 P.2d 623 (1976). The obligation may be attached if it is merely subject to a lien rather than a contingency that might not occur. *Grouse Creek Ranches v. Budget Financial Corp.*, 87 Nev. 419, 488 P.2d 917 (1971).

§ 2622. — Application and affidavit requirements.

The application for the writ of garnishment must be made by affidavit, stating that the named garnishee is the employer of the defendant or is indebted to or has property in his possession that belongs to the defendant and that such property is not exempt from execution. NRS 31.249. The affidavit may be and usually is contained in an application for a writ of attachment since the grounds and procedure for a writ of garnishment are identical to those for a writ of attachment. NRS 31.249. The application for writ of garnishment is thus identical to the application for writ of attachment with the exception that the affidavit in support of the application must contain an additional line stating that the garnishee owes the debtor money or has property of his. If the named garnishee is subject to more than one writ of garnishment regarding the defendant, the court shall determine both the priority and the method of satisfying the claims, except if the writ of garnishment is to satisfy a judgment for the collection of child support, it must be given first priority. NRS 31.249(5). Forms 26A through 26G included in this chapter request issuance of both writs.

§ 2623. — Issuance and contents of writ of garnishment.

NRS 31.260 states that the writ of garnishment is to be issued by the sheriff and must contain the names of the court, the parties, and the name and address of the plaintiff's attorney or the plaintiff's address. Additionally, the writ must be directed to the garnishee defendant and require such person to file an answer to certain garnishment interrogatories within twenty days. The writ must also notify the garnishee that a judgment will be entered against him if he does not answer the garnishment interrogatories. NRS 31.290 contains interrogatories that may be contained in the writ. A creditor may want to include additional interrogatories, if necessary. A Writ of Garnishment form is included in this chapter as Form 26K.

§ 2624. — Liability of the garnishee.

Service of the writ of garnishment and tender of the garnishee's $5.00 fee pursuant to NRS 31.270 gives the court personal jurisdiction over the garnishee. NRS 31.280. Thus, if he fails to answer the garnishment interrogatories within twenty days after service as required in NRS 31.260, a default judgment may be rendered against the garnishee. NRS 31.320.

If the garnishee answers the interrogatories within the twenty days, he must do so by way of affidavit and the creditor can reply by filing an affidavit traversing the garnishee's answer, in whole or part, with information charging the garnishee with liability under Chapter 31. NRS 31.330. The matter is then tried as any other civil issue. NRS 31.340. If the garnishee answers that no funds are owed the debtor and if the creditor fails to traverse this answer, the creditor is deemed to have accepted the answer as true and no judgment can be obtained against the garnishee. NRS 31.330. *Board of Trustees of Vacation Trust Carpenters Local No. 1780 v. Durable Developers, Inc.,* 102 Nev. 401, 724 P.2d 736 (1986); *Grouse Creek Ranches v. Budget Financial Corp.,* 87 Nev. 419, 488 P.2d 917 (1971); *Petri v. Sheriff,* 87 Nev. 579, 552, 491 P.2d 43 (1921).

If the garnishee answers that he has property of the debtor, the creditor can apply to have it delivered to the sheriff pending judgment. NRS 31.300(1). If the property in the hands of the garnishee is subject to a lien to secure an obligation of the debtor to the garnishee, the creditor can pay off the lien and have the property delivered to the sheriff. NRS 31.400. If the garnishee answers that he has money or a debt owed to the debtor, the creditor can apply for a judgment in favor of the debtor for the use of the creditor against the garnishee. NRS 31.300(2). Such a judgment against the garnishee relieves him of any liability to the debtor. NRS 31.370. The garnishee's liability is reduced by any sums that can be set off against the amount due the debtor. NRS 31.360.

If the garnishee indicates in his answer that he is the employer of the defendant, the writ of garnishment served on the garnishee continues for 120 days or until the amount demanded in the writ is recovered, whichever occurs first. NRS 31.296. In addition to the $5.00 fee required by NRS 31.270, a garnishee is entitled to a fee from the plaintiff of $3.00 per pay period from each withholding made off the defendant's earnings. This amount is not to exceed the $12.00 per month and does not apply to the first pay period in which the defendant's earnings are garnished.

It is unlawful for an employer to discharge an employee because he is required to withhold the employee's earnings pursuant to a writ of attachment. NRS 31.298. However, if the defendant is terminated for some other reason, before the writ of garnishment is satisfied, the employer is liable only for the amount of disposable earnings subject to garnishment earned by the defendant but not yet paid. NRS 31.296(3).

If an employer refuses to withhold the defendant's earnings as demanded in a writ of garnishment or knowingly misrepresents the defendant's earnings, he may be ordered by the court to appear and show cause why he should not be subject to penalties. If the court finds the employer's excuses to be without legal justification, he will be ordered to pay the plaintiff the amount of arrearages caused by the employer's refusal to withhold or his misrepresentation of the defendant's earnings. Additionally, the employer may be ordered by the court to pay punitive damages to the plaintiff, in an amount not to exceed $1,000, for each pay period the employer withheld the defendant's earnings or misrepresented them. NRS 31.297.

§ 2625. Claim and delivery.

The remedy of claim and delivery affords a plaintiff an opportunity to obtain possession of personal property at the time of issuing a summons or at any time before the answer to the complaint. NRS 31.840 *et seq.* The wording of NRS 31.840 appears to preclude the use of claim and delivery after an answer is filed.

Generally, this remedy is used by a party whose property is wrongfully held by another party. Often the remedy is used by secured creditors to obtain immediate possession of the security or collateral after the debtor has defaulted. Similarly, a supplier who has not been paid for goods that have already been delivered may use the remedy of claim and delivery to reclaim the delivered goods.

In *Adelson, Inc. v. Young Electric Sign Co.,* 76 Nev. 367, 355 P.2d 173 (1960), a plaintiff had sought to replevy a neon display sign or, in the alternative, the reasonable value of the sign that had been leased to the defendant. The Nevada Supreme Court denied the relief sought and affirmed the lower court judgment stating that "[h]ad plaintiff elected to do so, it could have recovered possession of the sign prior to judgment through the provisional remedy of claim and delivery." NRCP 64, NRS 31.840. *Adelson, Inc., supra,* at 372.

Another case in which a party failed to recognize its remedy under the claim and delivery status is *Ewing v. Fahey,* 86 Nev. 604, 472 P.2d 347 (1970). The plaintiffs initiated the action in district court alleging conversion of their automobile by the Ewings, doing business as Ewing Brothers Automobile Body. The Ewings obtained possession of the Fahey's vehicle in 1966 under a garagemen's lien for work performed in 1965. The Ewings held the vehicle for two years before selling it to satisfy the lien. The Nevada Supreme Court reversed a judgment for the plaintiff, indicating that there was no time limit under the garagemen's lien statute for sale. The Supreme Court also stated that a debtor could seek possession of property retained by a lienholder by claim and delivery under NRS 31.840. However, the Nevada Supreme Court, in a more recent case, indicated that a creditor should not retain property for very long without selling it if the property may decrease in value because of the delay. *Royal West Airways v. Valley Bank,* 103 Nev. 652, 242 P.2d 895 (1982).

As the above-cited cases indicate, counsel should be aware of the remedy of claim and delivery to protect clients whose property is wrongfully detained. While a party may not be able to recover the loss of use of that property, an action seeking claim and delivery for the immediate possession of the property may restore possession of the property.

§ 2626. — General discussion of procedure.

An action should be commenced by the filing of a complaint seeking immediate possession of the property in question, together with damages. To trigger the claim and delivery relief, the plaintiff should then file an application for claim and delivery by writ of possession. An Ex Parte Application for Order to Show Cause Why Collateral Should Not Be Taken from the Defendants and Delivered to the Plaintiffs form is included in this chapter as Form 26L. The application should be supported by the affidavit of the client, explaining why that party is entitled to immediate possession. An Affidavit in Support of Order to Show Cause Why Property Should Not be Taken from the Defendants and Delivered to Plaintiffs form is included in this chapter as Form 26M. Counsel should then obtain an order to show cause, scheduling the matter for hearing upon at least ten days' notice to the adverse party. An Order to Show Cause form is included in this chapter as Form 26N.

§ 2627. — Time for claim and delivery.

NRS 31.840 provides that a plaintiff in an action to recover personal property may, at the time of issuing the summons or before the answer is due, claim the delivery of such property pursuant to NRS 31.840 to 31.950.

§ 2628. — Application for claim and delivery by writ of possession with supporting affidavit.

Upon filing the complaint and issuing the summons or before the answer is due, the plaintiff seeking possession of personal property should file an application for claim and delivery supported by an affidavit of the client or other person having knowledge of the facts supporting the request for relief. The requirements for the affidavit supporting the claim delivery are contained in NRS 31.850. In order to meet the requirements of NRS 31.850, the affidavit supporting the application for claim and delivery must show:

    (1) That the plaintiff is the owner of the property claimed or is lawfully entitled to the possession thereof;
    (2) That the property is wrongfully detained by the defendant;
    (3) The alleged cause of the detention;
    (4) That the [property] has not been taken for a tax, assessment or fine pursuant to a statute, or seized under an execution or an attachment against the property; and
    (5) The actual value of the property.

See Form 26M.

NRS 31.863(2) requires a plaintiff who successfully obtains a writ of possession to post a bond equal to double the value of the property to protect the defendant. However, no bond is required if there is reasonable cause to believe that the plaintiff is a secured party. Therefore, if the applicant is a secured party, as defined in NRS 104.9105 *et seq.*, the affidavit should additionally include a statement of facts establishing the applicant's secured creditor status.

§ 2629. — Order to show cause requirements.

After the application and affidavit are filed requesting a claim delivery, an order to show cause should be issued pursuant to NRS 31.853. The complaint and application for claim and delivery with supporting affidavit may be filed at the same time the summons is issued. Copies of those pleadings may then be attached to the original order to show cause and delivered to the district court judge who has been assigned the action. The court or clerk scheduling the hearing should be requested to schedule the order to show cause hearing on a date which will afford plaintiff's counsel time sufficient to provide ten days' notice to the defendant. NRS 31.853(1).

Under NRS 31.853, the order to show cause should be directed to the defendant to show cause why the property should not be taken from him and delivered to the plaintiff. Such order shall:

(1) Fix the date and time for hearing, which shall be no sooner than 10 days from the issuance of the order;

(2) Inform the defendant that he may file affidavits on his behalf with the court and may appear and present testimony at the hearing or that he may file a written undertaking prior to the hearing pursuant to NRS 31.890;

(3) Inform the defendant that, if he fails to appear, the plaintiff will apply to the court for a writ of possession; and

(4) Require service of the affidavit and order on the defendant and fix the time and manner within which such service shall be made, which shall be by personal service or such other service as the court may determine to be reasonably calculated to afford notice of the proceeding to the defendant.

See Form 26N.

§ 2630. — Service of process.

The plaintiff may serve the defendant with a complaint, application for claim and delivery, affidavit of the plaintiff, order to show cause, and the original summons at one time. The affidavit of service can be modified to indicate that the defendant was served with the application, the affidavit and the order to show cause, in addition to the complaint.

§ 2631. — Hearing procedure.

As required by NRS 31.853, the order to show cause informs the defendant that he may file affidavits on his behalf and may appear and present testimony at the hearing. The party that signs the affidavit in support of the application for claim and delivery or a person with knowledge of the facts alleged in the complaint should be present with original documentation. The defendant may also appear and present evidence.

At the hearing, the court must make a preliminary determination as to which party, with reasonable probability, is entitled to possession and use of the property pending final adjudication. NRS 31.863(1). An Order Granting Temporary Writ of Possession form is included in this chapter as Form 26O.

§ 2632. — Written undertaking and bond provisions.

As with the extraordinary remedies of attachment and garnishment, written undertakings are required by the party obtaining a prejudgment writ of possession or by the party seeking to stay that relief. NRS 31.863(2) indicates that the writ of possession shall not issue until the plaintiff has filed a written undertaking executed by two or more court approved sureties to the effect that they are bound to the defendant for double the value of the property, as determined by the court, for the return of the property to the defendant if that relief is ordered, and for payment of any sums recovered by the defendant against the plaintiff. *See* 2628, *supra*.

Within two days after service of the writ, the defendant may give notice to the sheriff that he excepts to the sufficiency of the sureties, otherwise he is deemed to have waived any such objection. After an exception by the defendant, the surety shall justify on notice in the same manner as upon bail on arrest. NRS 31.880. The sheriff shall be responsible for the sufficiency of the sureties until the objection is either waived or until justified. If the defendant excepts to the sureties, he cannot immediately reclaim the property by filing undertakings for the benefit of the plaintiff. NRS 31.890.

After the writ is issued, but before delivery of the property to the plaintiff, a defendant may retain the property by filing sureties, if the defendant has not objected to the plaintiff's sureties. NRS 31.890. The defendant must file an undertaking by two court-approved sureties to the effect that they are bound in double the value of the property, as stated in the plaintiff's affidavit, for the delivery of that property to the plaintiff, if delivery is adjudged. If the return of the property is not required by the defendant filing the undertakings within five days after service of the writ of possession and undertaking on the defendant, the property shall be delivered to the plaintiff subject to claims of third parties. The defendant's sureties shall justify before the judge or clerk in the same manner as upon bail and arrest upon notice to the plaintiff of not less than two and not more than five days. Upon that justification, the sheriff shall deliver the property to the defendant. The sheriff is responsible for the defendant's sureties unless they are justified or waived. NRS 31.900.

§2633. — Third-party claims.

If a third-party claims title or a right of possession to the property taken by the sheriff pursuant to a writ of claim and delivery, that party may file an affidavit stating the grounds for such title or right of possession with the court and serve the sheriff. NRS 31.940(1). If so, the sheriff is not bound to keep the property or deliver it to the plaintiff unless the plaintiff, pursuant to demand of the sheriff, indemnifies the sheriff against such claim. This is done by an undertaking of two sureties accompanied by affidavits that such sureties are each worth double the value of the property as specified in the affidavit of the plaintiff, above any debts and liabilities, exclusive of property exempt from execution. The title to such property shall be determined in the same manner as provided for third-party claims after levy under a writ of execution or attachment. *See* NRS 31.070 regarding third-party claims to attach property and NRS 31.350 regarding third-party claims to garnished property. A Third-Party Claim is included in this chapter as Form 26I.

§ 2634. — Writ of possession and relief ordered.

NRS 31.866 provides that the writ of possession shall be directed to the sheriff in whose jurisdiction the property is located, describing both the specific property to be seized and its probable location. The writ shall direct the levying officer to seize the property and retain it in his custody. A Temporary Writ of Possession form is included in this chapter as Form 26P. Copies of the written undertaking of the plaintiff shall be attached to the writ which shall inform the defendant that he has the right to take exception to the sureties or to file a written undertaking for redelivery as provided in NRS 31.890.

If an additional location for the property must be provided, the plaintiff shall submit an additional affidavit upon probable cause and file it with the court. The writ of possession may then be endorsed by the court, without further notice, to direct the levying officer to search for the property at that other location. *See* NRS 31.866(2).

§ 2635. — When the writ of possession may be issued without hearing.

In very limited cases, a writ of possession may be issued without notice to the defendant. NRS 31.856. The writ may be issued prior to the hearing if the plaintiff's affidavit or presentation of other evidence establishes reasonable cause to believe the probability of any one of the following:

(1) That the defendant gained possession of the property by the commission of a criminal act forbidden by Chapter 205 of NRS, such as burglary, larceny, buying or receiving stolen goods, embezzlement, extortion, or fraud;

(2) The property possessed by the defendant consists of negotiable instruments or credit cards; or

(3) The property sought to be returned is either perishable and will perish before the hearing can be had or, by reason of threatened action by the holder, such property is in immediate danger of destruction, serious harm, concealment or removal from the state, or sale to an innocent purchaser.

If the writ of possession does not issue prior to a hearing, the defendant or other person from whom possession has been taken may apply to the court for an order shortening the time for the hearing. The court may, upon application, shorten the time for the hearing and direct the matter to be heard on not less than forty-eight hours' notice to the plaintiff. NRS 31.856(2). Even though a writ may issue without a hearing pursuant to NRS 31.856, no such writ of possession may issue until the plaintiff has filed with the court the written undertaking required by NRS 31.863. *See also* NRS 31.856(3).

§ 2636. Unlawful detainer: obtaining possession of real property.

If you need help regaining possession of real property or a mobile home, and if you can prove that the person in possession is guilty of an unlawful detainer, that is, remaining in possession of real property or a mobile home after proper notice to vacate, there are two prejudgment remedies available to assist you to regain possession: summary eviction or a writ of restitution. The following sections discuss the definition of an unlawful detainer, the notices that must be served on the tenant, when the Court has authority to issue a summary eviction order, and the effect of an eviction. Additionally, the writ of restitution is discussed, including the showing needed prior to the issuance of a prejudgment, temporary writ of restitution, the bond requirements, the judgment that is ultimately rendered, and to what extent an appeal is available. The following sections do not discuss the landlord/tenant relationship as it deals with landlords with over five dwelling units (NRS Chapter 118A) or termination of a rental agreement relating to mobile home parks (NRS Chapter 118B). Also, the following sections do not deal with obtaining possession of public lands (NRS Chapter 326).

§ 2637. — Unlawful detainer defined.

NRS 40.220 states that possession of real property can only be taken away from someone "in cases where entry is given by law" and in a peaceable manner. Obviously if a tenant or someone in possession of real property leaves, you can retake possession based on their abandonment. *See* NRS 118A.330(4)(b) relative to residential abandonment. Whether the tenant has abandoned is a question of fact. The landlord has a duty to relet the premises and if he does, the rental agreement terminates and the tenant is liable only for damages resulting from the abandonment. NRS 118.175. If the landlord fails to make reasonable efforts to rent the premises at a fair value or if the landlord accepts the abandonment as a surrender of the premises, the rental agreement is terminated as of the date the landlord receives notice of the abandonment. NRS 118.175. NRS Chapter 40 provides two prejudgment remedies to regain possession if it can proven that a person in possession is guilty of an unlawful detainer: summary eviction and a temporary writ of restitution. NRS 40.250

through 40.255 define the circumstances that must first be proven prior to obtaining these remedies:

(1) Remaining in possession after the lease term expires. NRS 40.250.

(2) Remaining in possession after receiving a seven-day, thirty-day or five-day notice to quit the premises when the tenant has leased the property on a week to week, month to month or at will basis, respectively. NRS 40.251. A Thirty-Day Notice to Quit Premises form is included as Form 26Q.

(3) Remaining in possession and not paying rent for five days (ten days if it is a mobile home lot) after service of written notice requiring the tenant to pay rent or get out. NRS 40.2512. A Five-Day Notice form is included as Form 23R. The Notice to Pay Rent or Quit does not need to specify the default in the payment of rent. *Gasser v. Jet Craft, Ltd.*, 87 Nev. 376, 380, 487 P.2d 346 (1971) (at a minimum, the Five-Day Notice must demand payment of rent to be effective); *Volpert v. Papagna*, 83 Nev. 429, 433, P.2d 533 (1967) (five-day notice which contained a reservation of rights to pursue additional rents was not void).

(4) Remaining in possession for three days after service of a Three-Day Notice to Quit based on the tenant's improper assignment, sublease, waste, unlawful business on the premises or creating a nuisance. NRS 40.2514.

(5) Remaining in possession for five days after service of a written notice requiring alternatively performance of obligations in a lease other than payment of rent or surrender of the premises. NRS 40.2516.

(6) Although not technically defined as an unlawful detainer, a writ of restitution is available to regain possession of real property or a mobile home where it has been sold under an execution sale or foreclosed under a deed of trust or mortgage if a three-day notice to quit is served on the possessor of the property after the sale or foreclosure. NRS 40.255. A Three-Day Notice to Quit form is included as Form 26S.

§ 2638. — The notices.

The notices required to place a tenant in a position of being guilty of an unlawful detainer are more than conditions precedent to the remedies; they are jurisdictional. *Gasser v. Jet Craft, Ltd.*, 87 Nev. 376, 379, 487 P.2d 346 (1971); *Aikins v. Andrews*, 91 Nev. 746, 748, 542 P.2d 734 (1975) (The five-day notice provision of NRS 40.250(1)(e) cannot be waived or neglected). The notice must be specific since an uncertain notice will be considered defective. *Gasser, supra,* at 380; *Roberts v. Second Judicial District Court,* 43 Nev. 332, 185 P. 1067 (1920). The notices must be from all co-lessors or with authority from all co-lessors. *American Fence, Inc. v. Wham,* 95 Nev. 788, 791, 603 P.2d 274 (1979). The landlord cannot by contract or other agreement shorten these notice periods. NRS 40.252(1). NRS 40.280 provides strict requirements relating to service of the notice to quit. Proof of service is a condition precedent to obtaining an order to remove the tenant. NRS 40.280(3). The proof of service must contain, in addition to an affidavit of service, "[a] statement, signed by the tenant and a witness, acknowledging that the tenant received the notice on a specified date," NRS 40.280(3)(a), or endorsement of the sheriff, constable or other process server stating the time and manner of service. NRS 40.280(3)(c). A copy of an adequate Affidavit of Service is included as Form 26T.

§ 2639. — The summary eviction remedy.

The summary eviction procedure can be used in two circumstances: unlawful detainer based on nonpayment of rent or, in certain cases, if there is an unlawful detainer on any other grounds.

If the basis of the unlawful detainer is the nonpayment of rent, NRS Chapter 40.253 provides a remedy called "summary eviction." First, the landlord must serve the tenant with a five-day notice to pay rent or quit the premises. NRS 40.253(1). If the tenant does not comply with the Five-Day Notice required by NRS 40.253(1), the landlord or his agent files an affidavit with the court of the township wherein the dwelling, apartment, mobile home or commercial premises is located. Where damages claimed do not exceed $5000 or where no damages are claimed, a summary eviction case begins in Justice Court. NJCRCP Rule 102. *See* NRS 4.370(1)(g).

The landlord's affidavit must contain specific information required by NRS 40.253(2)(a). A landlord's Affidavit of Complaint for Summary Eviction is included as Form 23U. If the tenant, within the five-day period, files an affidavit contesting the Five-Day Notice on the grounds he has paid or tendered the rent, the Justice Court schedules a summary eviction hearing and notifies both the landlord and tenant of the time and place of the hearing pursuant to NRS 40.253(3). The eviction hearing is informal since the intent is to "dispense fair and speedy justice." NJCRCP 105. If the tenant fails to file an affidavit, or the court finds there is no legal defense to the alleged unlawful detainer based upon nonpayment of rent, the court has authority pursuant to NRS 40.253(3) to issue a summary order for removal of the tenant or providing for nonadmittance of the tenant. NJCRCP 103. Justice courts may not award sanctions or attorneys fees in the summary eviction proceedings if there is no finding of an unlawful detainer. *Gibby's, Inc. v. Aylett,* 96 Nev. 678, 615 P.2d 949 (1980). An Order for Summary Eviction is included as Form 26V. Two sets of Instructions to the Constable are included as Forms 26W-1 and 26W-2, eviction instructions and instructions relative to changing the locks. This order cannot be issued until proof of service of the Five-Day Notice is filed with the court. NRS 40.280(3). This is usually filed with the landlord's affidavit mentioned above. If the court finds a legal defense, the court is required by NRS 40.253(3) to require any further proceedings to be conducted pursuant to NRS 40.290 through 40.420. A tenant may file a motion with the court, on a form provided by the court clerk, to dispute the amount of costs claimed by the landlord for the inventory, moving and storage of personal property left on the premises. The motion must be filed within twenty days after the summary order for removal of the tenant, the abandonment of the property by the tenant, or within twenty days after the tenant has vacated or been removed from the premises and a copy of the charges has been either requested by or provided to the tenant. NRS 40.253(4). Upon the tenant's filing of the motion, the court shall schedule a hearing which must be held within ten days after the filing of the motion. NRS 40.253(5). The court affixes the date of the hearing to the motion and orders a copy to be served upon the landlord. At the hearing, the court may determine the costs claimed by the landlord pursuant to the procedure required by NRS 118A.460 for disposing of personal property abandoned or left on the premises. The court may also order the release of the tenant's property if no charges are due or upon payment of the charges determined to be due. None of this applies to the tenant of a mobile home lot or a recreational vehicle lot in this state, other than an area designated as a recreational vehicle lot which is rented or held out for rent to accommodate a recreational vehicle for less than three months. NRS 40.253(6). These sections require a complaint alleging an unlawful detainer and a trial thereon. Many times the tenant's defense to the summary eviction proceedings is that there are repairs that the landlord has not made and the tenant does not want to pay rent until the landlord fixes them. However, this not a valid defense unless the tenant gave a fourteen-day notice to the landlord of the tenant's intent to pay for a repair and the landlord failed to make the repair. If the tenant gives the correct notice, the tenant may pay for the expense and deduct the amount paid from the rent pursuant to NRS 118A.360(1).

If the basis of the unlawful detainer is something other than nonpayment of rent, and if the tenant's dwelling is subject to the provisions in NRS Chapter 118A (landlord must own five or more dwelling units), or the tenant is in a mobile home, NRS 40.254 gives the landlord the option to utilize the summary eviction procedure. However, the Five-Day Notice and the landlord's affidavit must contain additional facts. The Five-Day Notice must advise the tenant that he or she can contest the Five-Day Notice by filing an affidavit stating he or she is not guilty of an unlawful detainer instead of an affidavit stating merely that the tenant has paid or tendered the rent as required by NRS 40.253(1). Additionally, the affidavit of the landlord must state when the tenancy began, the term of the tenancy, when the tenancy terminated, the date when the tenant became subject to the provision of NRS 40.251 to 40.2516, together with supporting facts and a statement that the claim for relief was authorized by law.

§ 2640. — Effect of eviction.

When a landlord seeks to oust the defaulting tenant, he or she has made an election to declare the lease terminated. *Lynn v. Ingalls,* 100 Nev. 115, 118, 676 P.2d 797 (1984). However, the issuance of the summary eviction order does not preclude the landlord's suit for damages, nor an action by the tenant for any damages or other relief to which the tenant may be entitled. NRS 40.253(3). Additionally, it should be noted that no subtenants need to be made parties defendant in any proceedings, nor are any proceedings abated as a result of the nonjoinder of any party defendant. NRS 40.290. All persons who enter under the tenant after commencement of the action are bound by the judgment as if they were parties. NRS 40.290.

§ 2641. — The writ of restitution.

If the remedy of summary eviction is not available because the unlawful detainer is not based on nonpayment of rent, or if the court finds a valid prima facie defense to the payment of rent, the proceedings must proceed by way of complaint seeking a writ of restitution. NRS 40.300 sets forth the required contents of the complaint. The complaint must set forth the facts on which the landlord seeks to recover, describe the premises with a reasonable certainty, and describe the unlawful detainer. Prior to 1989, the complaint had to be filed in Justice Court. *K.J.B., Inc. v. Second Judicial District Court,* 103 Nev. 473, 745 P.2d 700 (1987) (Justice Court has exclusive jurisdiction over unlawful detainer actions). However, in 1989, NRS 40.253 was amended and now allows an application to the Justice Court in which the premises are located or to the District Court in which the premises are located, whichever has jurisdiction over the amount of damages claimed. Presently under NRS 4.370, Justice Court has jurisdiction only if the sum claimed, exclusive of interest, does not exceed $5,000. Thus, the District Court has jurisdiction over unlawful detainer actions when damages exceed $5,000. Nevada Constitution Article 6, § 6 (District courts shall have original jurisdiction in all cases excluded by law from the original jurisdiction of justices' courts).

If the basis of the unlawful detainer is the nonpayment of rent, which it can be if the summary eviction proceedings were unsuccessful or avoided, the complaint must state the amount of such rental arrearages. NRS 40.300(1). It is important to note that subsection (2) of NRS 40.300 allows the court to enter an order modifying the summons to shorten the time within which the tenant is required to appear and defend the action. A Complaint for Unlawful Detainer form based on a person remaining in possession of real property after a trust deed foreclosure sale is included as Form 26X. NRS 40.300(3) provides a summary, prejudgment proceeding for the issuance of a temporary writ of restitution. This remedy allows you to obtain temporary possession of the premises after the complaint is filed but before trial. In most cases where the unlawful detainer is not based on nonpayment of rent, this will be the summary procedure used to remove the tenant. An Ex Parte Motion for Order to Show Cause Why a Temporary Writ of Restitution Should Not Issue, an Affidavit in Support thereof, Order to Show Cause Why a Temporary Writ of Restitution Should Not Issue, an Order Granting the Issuance of a Temporary Writ of Restitution, and a Temporary Writ of Restitution are all included as Forms 26Y, 26Z, 26AA, 26BB, and 26CC respectively. A bond must be posted by the landlord. NRS 40.300(3)(c). It is important to note that if proper demand is made by one of the parties, the issues of fact of the trial "shall" be tried by a jury. NRS 40.310. Amendments to the complaint to conform to proof are statutorily required to be made freely. NRS 40.330. It should be noted that NRS 40.370 requires that this complaint be verified as well as the answer. However, the failure to verify is waived by the defendants filing an answer. *Musso v. Triplett,* 78 Nev. 355, 372 P.2d 687 (1962).

§ 2642. — Notice of execution on writ of restitution.

A writ of restitution may be executed only if the sheriff serves the debtor with "Notice of the Execution" and a copy of the writ by regular mail at his last known address, or if represented by an attorney, at the attorney's office. NRS 40.425. The service must be mailed by the next business day after the day the writ of execution was served. A copy of a Notice of Writ of Execution and a Writ of Restitution can be found in Forms 26DD and 26EE in this chapter. The notice must describe the types of property exempt from execution and explain the procedure for claiming those exemptions. In addition, the court clerk is to attach the notice of the writ at the time the writ is issued.

§ 2643. — Judgment, damages and enforcement.

NRS 40.360(1) states that if there is a judgment in favor of the landlord, then "judgment shall be entered for restitution of the premises" and if the unlawful detainer proceedings are based upon the neglect or failure to perform any condition or covenant of the lease or after default and payment of rent, the judgment "shall also declare the forfeiture of such lease...." NRS 40.360(2) also requires the court to assess the damages occasioned by the plaintiff as a result of the unlawful detainer. A problem arises when the damages exceed $5,000, the jurisdictional limit of Justice Court. NRS 40.360(2) requires the Justice Court to render judgment relative to damages, but in 1989, NRS 40.253 was amended to allow either the justice court or the district court to have jurisdiction depending on whichever has jurisdiction over the property and the amount of damage. However, the justice court does still have exclusive jurisdiction if the amount claimed as damages does not exceed $5,000. NRS 40.360(3) provides an automatic stay of enforcement of the court's order granting a permanent writ of restitution. No execution on the judgment can be issued until five days after entry of the judgment. This allows any tenant, subtenant or mortgagee or other interested party to pay the amount of the judgment and costs and restore the tenant to his estate. NRS 40.360(3).

§ 2644. — Appeal.

Although NJCRCP 106 precludes an appeal from a summary eviction order, NRS 40.380 allows either party to appeal from the unlawful detainer judgment within ten days. *Gibby's, Inc. v. Aylett,* 96 Nev. 678, 615 P.2d 949 (1980). The tenant's appeal does not stay execution of the judgment unless he files an undertaking with the court in an amount not less than twice the judgment and costs. If such an undertaking is filed, then further proceedings in the case are stayed. NRS 40.380.

Form 26A

E. S. CHOIR, ESQ.
E. S. CHOIR, LTD.
State Bar No. 0000
324 South Avenue
Las Vegas, Nevada 89101
Attorneys for Plaintiff

DISTRICT COURT
CLARK COUNTY, NEVADA

JOHN DOE,

    Plaintiff,

vs.

FRED SMITH, DOES I through X,
inclusive,

    Defendants.

CASE NO. A123456
DEPT. NO. VI
DOCKET NO. K

Date:_____

Time:_____

AFFIDAVIT OF JOHN DOE

STATE OF NEVADA   )
) ss:
COUNTY OF CLARK   )

JOHN DOE, being first duly sworn, deposes and says:

1. That I am the Plaintiff herein and I have a valid claim for relief for breach of contract, fraud, embezzlement, and conversion.

2. I believe that I am entitled to recover from Fred Smith at least the sum of $252,231.91.

3. There exist grounds for attachment and garnishment without notice under Nevada law since the Defendant and I were equal partners and he embezzled partnership profits for his own use. Our agreement required him to pay my share of the profits directly to me. Since the Defendant has embezzled and converted partnership profits to his own use and because I believe that the Defendant has been disposing of or concealing his property by transfers to his friends and relatives to avoid my collection efforts, his assets should be attached and/or garnished pending final resolution by this Court.

4. There exist grounds for attachment and garnishment with notice under Nevada law since our partnership agreement required Defendant Fred Smith to pay my share of the profits directly to me and the Defendant's obligation to pay profits to me was not secured by a mortgage, lien or pledge upon any real or personal property situated in the State of Nevada.]

5. Attached hereto, labeled Exhibit 1 and incorporated herein by this reference is a list of property which describes in reasonable detail the property sought to be attached and garnished. Its present location is Nevada Title, 333 South Rancho Drive, Las Vegas, Nevada.

6. To the best of Affiant's information and belief, the value of the property to be attached and garnished less any prior liens or encumbrances is $252,231.91.

7. There are no third persons upon whom a writ of garnishment in aid of the writ of attachment will be served. [The third persons upon whom a writ of garnishment in aid of the writ of attachment will be served are Nevada Title.]

8. This is not an action upon a foreign judgment, therefore, a copy of such a judgment is not attached hereto.

9. To the best information and belief of the Affiant, the property listed on Exhibit 1 hereto is currently being held and in the possession of [Nevada Title] and is not exempt from execution under Nevada Law.

10. That I have read all of the allegations in my Complaint on file herein and all of the allegations contained therein are true and correct to the best of my knowledge and belief. [Use this paragraph only if the complaint is not verified.]

_____

JOHN DOE

SUBSCRIBED AND SWORN to before me
this _____ day of _____, 19____.

_____

NOTARY PUBLIC in and for
said County and State

Form 26B

E. S. CHOIR, ESQ.
E. S. CHOIR, LTD.
State Bar No. 0000
324 South Avenue
Las Vegas, Nevada 89101
Attorneys for Plaintiff

DISTRICT COURT

CLARK COUNTY, NEVADA

JOHN DOE,	CASE NO. A123456
	DEPT. NO. VI
Plaintiff,	DOCKET NO. K
vs.	
FRED SMITH, DOES I through X,	Date:_____
inclusive,	Time:_____
Defendants.	

EX PARTE MOTION FOR ORDER DIRECTING THE ISSUANCE OF A PREJUDGMENT WRIT OF ATTACHMENT AND GARNISHMENT WITHOUT NOTICE

Plaintiff moves the Court without notice and hearing pursuant to NRS Chapter 31, for an Order Directing the Issuance of a Prejudgment Writ of Attachment and Garnishment without Notice.

This Motion is made and based upon the following Points and Authorities and the Affidavit of JOHN DOE attached hereto.

DATED this _____ day of _____, 19____.

E. S. CHOIR, LTD.

By: _____
E. S. CHOIR, Esq.
Nevada Bar No. 0000
324 South Avenue
Las Vegas, Nevada 89101
Attorneys for Plaintiff

POINTS AND AUTHORITIES

I. NRS CHAPTER 31 GIVES THIS COURT AUTHORITY TO ORDER THE CLERK TO ISSUE A WRIT OF ATTACHMENT AND GARNISHMENT WITHOUT NOTICE AND HEARING UPON SHOWING OF AN ACTION BASED UPON EMBEZZLEMENT OR CONVERSION.

NRS 31.010 (*When attachment may issue*) states:

The plaintiff at the time of issuing the summons, or at any time thereafter, may apply to the court for an order directing the clerk to issue a writ of attachment and thereby cause the property of the defendant to be attached as security for the satisfaction of any judgment that may be recovered, unless the defendant gives security to pay such judgment as provided in this chapter.

NRS 31.017 (*Grounds for attachment without notice*) states:

The court may order the writ of attachment issued without notice to the defendant only in the following cases:

    1. [resident v. nonresident] ...
    2. [foreign judgment] ...
    3. In an action for the recovery of the value of personal property, where such personal property is owned by the plaintiff and has been taken or converted by the defendant without the consent of the plaintiff.
    4. In an action by a resident of this state, where the defendant is about to remove his money or property, or any part thereof, from this state, and the defendant's property which may remain within this state, if any, will be insufficient to satisfy plaintiff's claim ...
    5. [Defendant about to conceal or dispose of property] ...
    6. In an action for the recovery of money or property, or the proceeds thereof, obtained from the plaintiff by the defendant through embezzlement, forgery, larceny or extortion.
    7. [fraudulent conveyance] ...
    8. [uniform reciprocal enforcement] ...
    9. [jurisdiction by attachment] ..."

NRS 31.020 (*Contents of Affidavit for Attachment*) states:

    1. All applications to the court for an order directing the clerk to issue a writ of attachment without notice to the defendant shall be accompanied by the affidavit of the plaintiff or any other person having personal knowledge of the facts constituting one or more of the grounds for attachment, which affidavit or affidavits shall:

    (a) Set forth clearly the nature of the plaintiff's claim for relief and that the same is valid.

    (b) Set forth the amount which the affiant believes the plaintiff is entitled to recover from the defendant, and if there is more than one plaintiff or more than one defendant, the amount the affiant believes each plaintiff is entitled to recover or the amount that the plaintiff is entitled to recover from each defendant.

    (c) Describe in reasonable and clear detail all the facts which show the existence of any one of the grounds for an attachment without notice to the defendant.

    (d) Describe in reasonable detail the money or property sought to be attached and the location thereof if known.

(e) If the property sought to be attached is other than money, set forth to the best knowledge and information of the affiant, the value of such property less any prior liens or encumbrances.

(f) Name all third persons upon whom a writ of garnishment in aid of the writ of attachment will be served.

(g) In an action upon a foreign judgment attach a copy of the judgment to the affidavit for attachment as an exhibit.

(h) State whether to the best information and belief of the affiant, the money or property sought to be attached is exempt from execution.

NRS 31.022 (*Procedure when notice, hearing not required*) states:

"The court shall, without delay, examine the plaintiff's application and affidavit and receive additional evidence if necessary, and shall order the clerk to issue a writ of attachment without notice to the defendant if:

1. The plaintiff's affidavit, alone or as supplemented by additional evidence, meets the requirements of subsection 1 of NRS 31.020; and
2. The court determines, specifically, that there exist one or more grounds for attachment without notice as indicted in such affidavit or by additional evidence."

NRS 31.240 (*When garnishment may issue*) states that:

At the time of the order directing a writ of attachment to issue or at any time thereafter, the court may order that a writ of garnishment issue ....

NRS 31.249 (*Grounds for garnishment*) states that a court may order a writ of garnishment to issue in the order directing the clerk to issue a writ of attachment and it further states in subsection 2(b) that a writ of garnishment may issue upon an affidavit filed on behalf of the Plaintiff stating that the affiant is informed and believes that the named garnishee is indebted to or has property in his possession or under his control belonging to the Defendant and that such indebtedness or property is to the best of the knowledge and belief of the affiant not by law exempt from execution.

The attached Affidavit of the Plaintiff meets the requirements of NRS 31.020(2) since it sets forth (a) the nature of Plaintiff's valid claim for relief, (b) the amount Plaintiff is entitled to recover from each Defendant, (c) the grounds for the attachment, (d) the location and description of the property to be attached, (e) the value of the property less any prior liens or encumbrances, (f) the name of all third persons upon whom a writ of garnishment in aid of the attachment will be served, (g) whether this is an action on a foreign judgment, and (h) whether the property sought to be attached is exempt from execution. Additionally, the affidavit meets the requirements of NRS 31.249 relative to issuance of a writ of garnishment since it states that to affiant's knowledge and belief the garnishee is indebted to or has property in his possession or under his control belonging to the Defendant.

536

Therefore, Plaintiff requests that this Court enter an Order directing the Clerk to issue a Writ of Attachment and a Writ of Garnishment Without Notice.

E. S. CHOIR, LTD.

By: _____

E. S. CHOIR, Esq.
Nevada Bar No. 0000
324 South Avenue
Las Vegas, Nevada 89101
Attorneys for Plaintiff

Form 26C

JUSTICE COURT, LAS VEGAS TOWNSHIP

CLARK COUNTY, NEVADA

JOHN DOE,   CASE NO. A123456

    Plaintiff,

    vs.

FRED SMITH, DOES I through X,
inclusive,

    Defendants.

NOTICE OF EXECUTION

TO: FRED SMITH:

YOUR PROPERTY IS BEING ATTACHED OR YOUR WAGES ARE BEING GARNISHED

Plaintiff alleges that you owe him money. He has begun the procedure to collect that money. To secure satisfaction of judgment the court has ordered the garnishment of your wages, bank account or other personal property held by third persons or the taking of money or other property in your possession.

Certain benefits and property owned by you may be exempt from execution and may not be taken from you. The following is a partial list of exemptions:

1. Payments received under the Social Security Act.

2. Payments for benefits or the return of contributions under the public employees' retirement system.

3. Payments for public assistance granted through the welfare division of the department of human resources.

4. Proceeds from a policy of life insurance.

5. Payments of benefits under a program of industrial insurance.

6. Payments received as unemployment compensation.

7. Veteran's benefits.

8. A homestead in a dwelling or a mobile home, not to exceed $95,000, unless the judgment is for a medical bill, in which case all of the primary dwelling, including a mobile or manufactured home, may be exempt.

9. A vehicle, if your equity in the vehicle is less than $1,500.

10. Seventy-five percent of the take-home pay for any pay period, unless the weekly take-home pay is less than 30 times the federal minimum wage, in which case the entire amount may be exempt.

11. Money, not to exceed $100,000 in present value, held for retirement pursuant to certain arrangements or plans meeting the requirements for qualified arrangements or plans of sections 401 et seq. of the Internal Revenue Code (26 U.S.C. 401 et seq.).

12. A vehicle for use by you or your dependent which is specially equipped or modified to provide mobility for a person with a permanent disability.

13. A prosthesis or any equipment prescribed by a physician or dentist for you or your dependent.

These exemptions may not apply in certain cases such as proceedings to enforce a judgment for support of a child or a judgment of foreclosure on a mechanic's lien. You should consult an attorney immediately to assist you in determining whether your property or money is exempt from execution. If you cannot afford an attorney, you may be eligible for assistance through _____ (name of organization in county providing legal services to the indigent or elderly persons).

GIVEN UNDER MY HAND this ____ day of _____, 19__.

_____
JUSTICE OF THE PEACE

Submitted by:
E. S. CHOIR, LTD.

By: _____
E. S. CHOIR, Esq.
324 South Avenue
Las Vegas, Nevada 89101
Attorneys for Plaintiff

Form 26D

E. S. CHOIR, ESQ.
E. S. CHOIR, LTD.
State Bar No. 0000
324 South Avenue
Las Vegas, Nevada 89101
Attorneys for Plaintiff

DISTRICT COURT
CLARK COUNTY, NEVADA

JOHN DOE,	CASE NO. A123456
	DEPT. NO. VI
Plaintiff,	DOCKET NO. K
vs.	
FRED SMITH, DOES I through X,	Date:_____
inclusive,	Time:_____
Defendants.	

**EX PARTE MOTION FOR ORDER TO SHOW CAUSE WHY
PREJUDGMENT WRIT OF ATTACHMENT AND GARNISHMENT
SHOULD NOT ISSUE AFTER NOTICE**

Plaintiff moves the Court, pursuant to NRS Chapter 31, for an Order to Show Cause why an Order for Prejudgment Attachment and Garnishment should not issue.

This Motion is made and based upon the following Points and Authorities and the Affidavit of JOHN DOE filed herewith.

DATED this _____ day of _____, 19____.

E. S. CHOIR, LTD.

By: _____
E. S. CHOIR, Esq.
Nevada Bar No. 0000
324 South Avenue
Las Vegas, Nevada 89101
Attorneys for Plaintiff

POINTS AND AUTHORITIES

I. NRS CHAPTER 31 GIVES THIS COURT AUTHORITY TO ORDER THE DEFENDANT TO SHOW CAUSE WHY AN ORDER FOR ATTACHMENT AND GARNISHMENT SHOULD NOT ISSUE SINCE PLAINTIFF'S CAUSE OF ACTION IS BASED UPON AN UNSECURED CONTRACT.

NRS 31.010 (*When Attachment May Issue*) states:

The plaintiff at the time of issuing the summons, or at any time thereafter, may apply to the court for an order directing the clerk to issue a writ of attachment and thereby cause the property of the defendant to be attached as security for the satisfaction of any judgment that may be recovered, unless the defendant gives security to pay such judgment as provided in this chapter.

NRS 31.013 (*Grounds for Attachment with Notice*) states:

The court may after notice and hearing, order the clerk to issue a writ of attachment in the following cases:

　1. In an action upon ... a contract, express or implied, for the direct payment of money:

　　(a) If the ... contract is not secured by mortgage, lien or pledge upon real or personal property situated in this state ....

NRS 31.020 (*Affidavit for attachment: Contents*) states:

　1. All applications to the court for an order directing the clerk to issue a writ of attachment without notice to the defendant shall be accompanied by the affidavit of the plaintiff or any other person having personal knowledge of the facts constituting one or more of the grounds for attachment, which affidavit or affidavits shall:

　　(a) Set forth clearly the nature of the plaintiff's claim for relief and that the same is valid.
　　(b) Set forth the amount which the affiant believes the plaintiff is entitled to recover from the defendant, and if there is more than one plaintiff or more than one defendant, the amount the affiant believes each plaintiff is entitled to recover or the amount that the plaintiff is entitled to recover from each defendant.
　　(c) Describe in reasonable and clear detail all the facts which show the existence of any one of the grounds for an attachment without notice to the defendant.
　　(d) Describe in reasonable detail the money or property sought to be attached and the location thereof if known.
　　(e) If the property sought to be attached is other than money, set forth to the best knowledge and information of the affiant, the value of such property less any prior liens or encumbrances.
　　(f) Name all third persons upon whom a writ of garnishment in aid of the writ of attachment will be served.
　　(g) In an action upon a foreign judgment attach a copy of the judgment to the affidavit for attachment as an exhibit.
　　(h) State whether, to the best information and belief of the affiant, the money or property sought to be attached is exempt from execution.

　2. All applications to the court for an order directing the clerk to issue a writ of attachment with notice to the defendant shall be accompanied by an affidavit setting forth the item required by subsection 1, except that such affidavit may show the existence of any one of the grounds for attachment with notice.

NRS 31.024 (*Contents of Order to Show Cause re: Attachment*) states:

If the plaintiff's application is for an order directing the clerk to issue a writ of attachment after notice and hearing, and the plaintiff's affidavit, alone or as supplemented by additional evidence received by the court, meets the requirements of subsection 2 of NRS 31.020, the court shall issue an order directed to the debtor to show cause why the order for attachment should not be issued. Such order shall:

1. Fix the date and time for hearing on the order, which shall not be set sooner than 3 days after the service of the order.
2. Direct the time within which service of the order shall be made upon the defendant or his attorney.
3. Fix the manner in which service of the order shall be made, which may be personal service upon the defendant or service upon his attorney. If such service cannot be made, service may be by publication or in such manner as the court determines is reasonably calculated to afford notice to the defendant under the circumstances set forth in the plaintiff's affidavit.
4. State that the debtor has the right to file affidavits on his behalf and may appear personally or by way of an attorney, and present testimony on his behalf at the time of hearing.
5. State that if the defendant fails to appear he shall be deemed to have waived his right to the hearing and that in such case the court may order the clerk to issue a writ of attachment.

NRS 31.240 (*When Garnishment May Issue*) states that:

At the time of the order directing a writ of attachment to issue or at any time thereafter, the court may order that a writ of garnishment issue ....

NRS 31.249 (*Grounds for Garnishment*) states that a court may order a writ of garnishment to issue in the order directing the clerk to issue a writ of attachment and it further states in subsection 2(b) that a writ of garnishment may issue upon an affidavit filed on behalf of the Plaintiff stating that the affiant is informed and believes that the named garnishee is indebted to or has property in his possession or under his control belonging to the Defendant and that such indebtedness or property is to the best of the knowledge and belief of the affiant not by law exempt from execution.

The attached Affidavit of the Plaintiff meets the requirements of NRS 31.020(2) since it sets forth (a) the nature of Plaintiff's valid claim for relief, (b) the amount Plaintiff is entitled to recover from each Defendant, (c) the grounds for attachment, (d) the location and description of the property to be attached, (e) the value of the property less any prior liens or encumbrances, (f) the name of all third persons upon whom a writ of garnishment in aid of the attachment will be served, (g) whether this is an action on a foreign judgment, and (h) whether the property sought to be attached is exempt from execution. Additionally, the affidavit meets the requirements of NRS 31.249 relative to issuance of a writ of garnishment since it states that to affiant's knowledge and belief the garnishee is indebted to or has property in his possession or under his control belonging to the Defendant.

Therefore, Plaintiff requests that an Order to Show Cause be entered requiring the Defendant to appear and show cause why a Writ of Attachment and a Writ of Garnishment should not issue.

E. S. CHOIR, LTD.

By: _____

E. S. CHOIR, Esq.
Nevada Bar No. 0000
324 South Avenue
Las Vegas, Nevada 89101
Attorneys for Plaintiff

Form 26E

E. S. CHOIR, ESQ.
E. S. CHOIR, LTD.
State Bar No. 0000
324 South Avenue
Las Vegas, Nevada 89101
Attorneys for Plaintiff

DISTRICT COURT

CLARK COUNTY, NEVADA

JOHN DOE,	CASE NO. A123456
	DEPT. NO. VI
Plaintiff,	DOCKET NO. K
vs.	
FRED SMITH, DOES I through X,	Date:_____
inclusive,	Time:_____
Defendants.	

ORDER TO SHOW CAUSE

The Court having considered the Ex Parte Motion of Plaintiff for an Order to Show Cause why an Order for Attachment and Garnishment should not Issue, together with the Affidavit of John Doe in support thereof, and good cause appearing therefor,

IT IS HEREBY ORDERED that Defendant appear on _____, 19____ at 9:00 o'clock a.m. in Department VI, of the Eighth Judicial District Court of the State of Nevada in and for the County of Clark, and show cause, if any, why an Order for Issuance of Prejudgment Writ of Attachment and Garnishment should not issue as prayed for, and

IT IS FURTHER ORDERED that this Order be served personally upon said Defendant or his attorney no later than _____, 19____, and

IT IS FURTHER ORDERED that Defendant has the right to file affidavits on his behalf and may appear personally or by way of an attorney, and present testimony on his behalf at the time of hearing, and

IT IS FURTHER ORDERED that if the Defendant fails to appear, he shall be deemed to have waived his right to the hearing and that in such case the Court may order the Clerk to issue the Writ of Attachment and Writ of Garnishment.

DATED this _____ day of _____, 19____.

_____
DISTRICT COURT JUDGE

Submitted by:
E. S. CHOIR, LTD.

By: _____
    E. S. CHOIR, Esq.
    324 South Avenue
    Las Vegas, Nevada 89101
    Attorneys for Plaintiff

Form 26F

E. S. CHOIR, ESQ.
E. S. CHOIR, LTD.
State Bar No. 0000
324 South Avenue
Las Vegas, Nevada 89101
Attorneys for Plaintiff

DISTRICT COURT

CLARK COUNTY, NEVADA

JOHN DOE,	CASE NO. A123456
	DEPT. NO. VI
Plaintiff,	DOCKET NO. K
vs.	
FRED SMITH, DOES I through X,	Date:_____
inclusive,	Time:_____
Defendants.	

ORDER DIRECTING THE ISSUANCE OF A PREJUDGMENT WRIT OF ATTACHMENT AND GARNISHMENT WITHOUT NOTICE

After consideration of Plaintiff's Ex Parte Notion for Writ of Attachment and Writ of Garnishment to Issue Without Notice, Plaintiff's Affidavit attached hereto as well as Plaintiff's Complaint on file herein the Court being fully advised in the premises and good cause appearing therefor, and the Court making the following findings:

1. That the action in question appears to be one in which attachment without notice may be allowed because said action is brought pursuant to NRS 31.017(3) and (6).

2. The facts and reasons why these grounds exist are Plaintiff 's allegations and the supporting affidavits which show that Defendant, Fred Smith, received approximately $500,000.00 in profits which were not disclosed to Plaintiff; that Plaintiff was entitled to the direct payment of one-half of these profits based on their equal partnership and Defendant received Plaintiff's one-half and appropriated Plaintiff's one-half ($252,231.91) for himself and in a manner other than that for which it was given to Defendant.

3. Having reviewed the Complaint of Plaintiff and the documents on file herein, it appears that the Plaintiff has alleged a meritorious claim for relief.

4. The amount for which the attachment and garnishment will issue in this action is the sum of TWO HUNDRED FIFTY-TWO THOUSAND TWO HUNDRED THIRTY-ONE AND 91/100 DOLLARS.

5. Prior to attachment, a written undertaking on the part of Plaintiff payable in lawful money of the United States in a sum of $252,231.91 shall be given before the Writs herein will issue.

6. The names of all third persons upon whom writs of garnishment in aid of attachment may be served are Nevada Title.

7. The property to be attached and garnished herein is properly described as follows: obligations, or funds, due Defendant from Nevada Title, 333 South Rancho Drive, Las Vegas, Nevada. The value of the foregoing property based upon the Affidavit of JOHN DOE is the sum of TWO HUNDRED FIFTY-TWO THOUSAND TWO HUNDRED THIRTY-ONE AND 91/100 DOLLARS ($252,231.91).

IT IS, THEREFORE, ORDERED that a Writ of Attachment and Writ of Garnishment in this action be issued in the amount of $252,231.91 against the property of Defendant FRED SMITH, described above, upon the posting of a Surety by Plaintiff in the amount of $252,231.91.

DATED this ——————— day of ——————, 19——.

_____
DISTRICT COURT JUDGE

Submitted by:
E. S. CHOIR, LTD.

By: _____
    E. S. CHOIR, Esq.
    324 South Avenue
    Las Vegas, Nevada 89101
    Attorneys for Plaintiff

Form 26G

E. S. CHOIR, ESQ.
E. S. CHOIR, LTD.
State Bar No. 0000
324 South Avenue
Las Vegas, Nevada 89101
Attorneys for Plaintiff

DISTRICT COURT

CLARK COUNTY, NEVADA

JOHN DOE,	CASE NO. A123456
	DEPT. NO. VI
Plaintiff,	DOCKET NO. K
vs.	
FRED SMITH, DOES I through X, inclusive,	Date:_____
	Time:_____
Defendants.	

ORDER DIRECTING THE ISSUANCE OF A PREJUDGMENT WRIT OF ATTACHMENT AND GARNISHMENT

A hearing having been held on the _____ day of _____, 19____, on this Court's Order to Show Cause Why an Order Directing a Prejudgment Writ of Attachment and Writ of Garnishment should not Issue and the Court having considered the Defendants' opposition thereto and the pleadings, papers and documents on file herein and the Court being otherwise fully advised in the premises and good cause appearing therefor, the Court makes the following findings:

1. The grounds for the attachment and garnishment which have been relied on in issuing this order are the Plaintiff's allegations relating to his cause of action for the direct payment of money which was not previously secured by a lien on real or personal property.

2. The facts and reasons why these grounds exist are Plaintiff's allegations and the supporting affidavits which show that Defendant, Fred Smith, received approximately $500,000.00 in profits which were not disclosed to Plaintiff; that Plaintiff was entitled to the direct payment of one-half of these profits based on their equal partnership and Defendant received Plaintiff's one-half and appropriated Plaintiff's one-half ($252,231.91) for himself and in a manner other than that for which it was given to Defendant.

3. Having reviewed the Complaint of Plaintiff and the documents on file herein, it appears that the Plaintiff has alleged a meritorious claim for relief.

4. The amount for which the attachment and garnishment will issue in this action is the sum of TWO HUNDRED FIFTY-TWO THOUSAND TWO HUN-DRED THIRTY-ONE AND 91/100 DOLLARS ($252,231.91).

5. Prior to attachment, a written undertaking on the part of Plaintiff payable in lawful money of the United States in a sum of $252,231.91 shall be given before the Writs herein will issue.

6. The names of all third persons upon whom writs of garnishment in aid of attachment may be served are Nevada Title.

7. The property to be attached and garnished herein is properly described as follows: obligations, or funds, due Defendant from Nevada Title, 333 South Rancho Drive, Las Vegas, Nevada. The value of the foregoing property based upon the Affidavit of JOHN DOE is the sum of TWO HUNDRED FIFTY-TWO THOUSAND TWO HUNDRED THIRTY-ONE AND 91/100 DOLLARS ($252,231.91).

IT IS THEREFORE, ORDERED that a Writ of Attachment and Writ of Garnishment in this action be issued in the amount of $252,231.91 against the property of Defendant FRED SMITH, described above, upon the posting of a Surety by Plaintiff in the amount of $252,231.91.

DATED this ———— day of ———— 19——.

————————————————————
DISTRICT COURT JUDGE

Submitted by:
E. S. CHOIR, LTD.

By: ————————————————————

    E. S. CHOIR, Esq.
    324 South Avenue
    Las Vegas, Nevada 89101
    Attorneys for Plaintiff

Form 26H

E. S. CHOIR, ESQ.
E. S. CHOIR, LTD.
State Bar No. 0000
324 South Avenue
Las Vegas, Nevada 89101
Attorneys for Plaintiff

DISTRICT COURT

CLARK COUNTY, NEVADA

JOHN DOE,

     Plaintiff,

   vs.

FRED SMITH, DOES I through X, inclusive,

     Defendants.

CASE NO. A123456
DEPT. NO. VI
DOCKET NO. K

Date:_____

Time:_____

WRIT OF ATTACHMENT

THE STATE OF NEVADA TO THE SHERIFF OF CLARK COUNTY, GREETINGS:

YOU ARE HEREBY COMMANDED to attach and safely keep the property of the Defendant in order to satisfy the Plaintiff's demand of $252,231.91 exclusive of interest and costs.

The property to be attached, which is not exempt from execution and the value of which does not exceed the Plaintiff's demand, is described as follows: The obligation or funds due Defendant from Nevada Title, 333 South Rancho Drive, Las Vegas, Nevada.

If the Defendant shall give you security in lawful money of the United States or by posting a bond or by the undertaking of at least two sufficient sureties in an amount equal to the lesser of the Plaintiff's demand exclusive of costs or the value of the property levied upon, then you shall accept such bond or undertaking in lieu of attaching the aforesaid property. You are required to serve and return this Writ and with the results of your levy endorsed thereon, and within 20 days from the day you receive it, return it to the Clerk of the Court with a copy to the party at whose direction it was issued. Issued at direction of:

E. S. CHOIR, ESQ.

By: _____
E. S. CHOIR, Esq.
Nevada Bar No. 0000
324 South Avenue
Las Vegas, Nevada 89101
Attorneys for Plaintiff

JOHN MORAN, Sheriff of Clark County

By: _____
    Deputy   Date
    309 South Third Street, Suite 230
    Las Vegas, Nevada 89101

I HEREBY CERTIFY that this is a true and correct copy of the original Writ of Attachment.

JOHN MORAN, Sheriff of Clark County

By: _____

      Deputy   Date

I HEREBY CERTIFY that I have this date served this Writ of Attachment on the ____ day of _____, 19____ by:

____ (a) taking into my possession the following described property to be held in my custody until further order of this Court:

_____

_____

_____

____ (b) posting a copy of this Writ of Attachment upon the real property set forth herein by affixing a copy of this Writ to the improvement thereon or upon the property if unimproved and by delivering a copy of this Writ on the ____ day of _____, 19__ to the County Recorder to be recorded.

____ (c) serving on the ____ day of _____, 19__ at ____ .m. o'clock a Writ of Garnishment in aid of this Writ of Attachment on _____, Clark County, Nevada. A true and correct copy of said Writ of Garnishment is attached hereto.

____ (d) returning this Writ of Attachment unsatisfied.

JOHN MORAN, Sheriff of Clark County

By: _____

      Deputy   Date

Form 26I

E. S. CHOIR, ESQ.
E. S. CHOIR, LTD.
State Bar No. 0000
324 South Avenue
Las Vegas, Nevada 89101
Attorneys for Plaintiff

DISTRICT COURT
CLARK COUNTY, NEVADA

JOHN DOE,	CASE NO. A123456
	DEPT. NO. VI
Plaintiff,	DOCKET NO. K
vs.	
FRED SMITH, DOES I through X, inclusive,	Date:_____
	Time:_____
Defendants.	

THIRD-PARTY CLAIM

TO: JOHN MORAN, Sheriff of Clark County, State of Nevada
YOU ARE HEREBY NOTIFIED that a certain 1966 15′ Sears Boat, with 45-horsepower motor and 2-wheel Sears trailer, Title No. J129453, which you levied on pursuant to a Writ of Execution as the property of FRED SMITH, belongs to U. S. CREDIT UNION; that its interest therein is that of legal owner as secured party on a promissory note and Security Agreement dated December 21, 1986.
DATED this _____ day of _____, 19__.

U. S. CREDIT UNION
SAM SIMMONS
Assistant Manager

STATE OF NEVADA	)
	) ss:
COUNTY OF CLARK	)

SAM SIMMONS, being first duly sworn, deposes and says:
That he is the Assistant Manager of U. S. CREDIT UNION, the Third-Party Claimant in the above-entitled action; that he has read the foregoing Third-Party Claim, knows the contents thereof and that the same is true to the best of his knowledge except as to those facts therein stated upon information and belief and as to those facts, he believes them to be true.

SAM SIMMONS, Assistant Manager
U. S. CREDIT UNION

SUBSCRIBED and SWORN to before me
this ____ day of _____, 19__.

_____

Notary Public in and for said
County and State

    RECEIPT OF COPY of the foregoing Third-Party Claim is hereby acknowl-
edged this ____ day of ____, 19__.

_____

        JOHN MORAN, Sheriff
        SMITH & JONES

       _____

        Attorneys for Third-Party Claimant
        100 Las Vegas Blvd. South
        Las Vegas, Nevada 89101

Form 26J

INSTRUCTIONS TO THE SHERIFF

CLARK COUNTY, NEVADA

JOHN DOE,

    Plaintiff,

  vs.

FRED SMITH, DOES I through X, inclusive,

    Defendants.

CASE NO. A123456
DEPT. NO. VI
DOCKET NO. K

Date:_____

Time:_____

_____ DISTRICT _____   _____ A 123456 _____

_____ JOHN MORAN _____ $_____

SHERIFF OF THE COUNTY OF CLARK   Storage Deposit or Fees Collected

You are hereby instructed to levy by virtue of the accompanying Writ, in the above-entitled suit, by following below instructions:

_____ Serve Writ of Garnishment and Writ of Attachment upon: _____

_____ Nevada Title, 333 Rancho Road, Las Vegas, Nevada _____

_____

_____

It is hereby acknowledged that vague or otherwise unenforceable instructions shall not be processed and will be returned to *the preparer for redrafting.* Bench Warrants must include DOB, and Social Security Number. Instructions to execute on vehicles must include VIN#, make, model, year, Lic. # and color. All other personal or real property attached or executed upon must have complete description. Advance money deposit is required with all instructions on property to be placed in storage or in custody of a keeper (NRS 31.065). Incomplete or unsigned instructions will not be accepted for service.

_____ DATE _____   SIGNATURE OF ATTORNEY OR LITIGANT

_____ E. S. CHOIR, LTD. _____   324 South Avenue, Las Vegas, Nevada
Type or Print Name and Business   Address

Form 26K

E. S. CHOIR, ESQ.
E. S. CHOIR, LTD.
State Bar No. 0000
324 South Avenue
Las Vegas, Nevada 89101
Attorneys for Plaintiff

DISTRICT COURT

CLARK COUNTY, NEVADA

JOHN DOE,

    Plaintiff,

vs.

FRED SMITH, DOES I through X, inclusive,

    Defendants.

CASE NO. A123456
DEPT. NO. VI
DOCKET NO. K

Date:_____

Time:_____

WRIT OF GARNISHMENT

THE STATE OF NEVADA TO: NEVADA TITLE, Garnishee

You are hereby notified that you are attached as garnishee in the above-entitled action and you are commanded not to pay any debt from yourself to Fred Smith, Defendant, and that you must retain possession and control of all personal property, money, credits, debts, effects and choses in action of said Defendant in order that the same may be dealt with according to law; where such property consists of wages, salaries, commissions or bonuses the amount you shall retain shall be in accordance with 15 U.S. Code 1673 and Nevada Revised Statutes 31.295; Plaintiff believes that you have property, money, credits, debts, effects and choses in action in your hands and under your custody and control belonging to said Defendant described as: Escrow Proceeds

_____

YOU ARE REQUIRED within 20 days from the date of service of this Writ of Garnishment to answer the interrogatories set forth herein and to return your answers to the office of the Sheriff or Constable which has issued this Writ of Garnishment. In case of your failure to answer the interrogatories within 20 days, a judgment by default in the amount due the Plaintiff may be entered against you.

YOU ARE FURTHER REQUIRED to serve a copy of your answers to the Writ of Garnishment on Plaintiff's attorney whose address appears below. Issued at direction of:

E. S. CHOIR, ESQ.

By: _____

E. S. CHOIR, Esq.
Nevada Bar No. 0000
324 South Avenue
Las Vegas, Nevada 89101
Attorneys for Plaintiff

JOHN MORAN, Sheriff of Clark County

By: _____

Deputy   Date
309 South Third Street
Suite 230
Las Vegas, Nevada 89101

STATE OF NEVADA   )
) ss:
COUNTY OF CLARK   )

The undersigned, being duly sworn, states that I received the within Writ of Garnishment on the ____ day of _____, 19__ and personally served the same on the ____ day of _____, 19__ by showing the original Writ of Garnishment, informing of the contents and delivering and leaving a copy, along with the statutory fee of $5, with _____ at _____, County of Clark, State of Nevada.

_____
Deputy Sheriff

INTERROGATORIES TO BE ANSWERED BY THE GARNISHEE UNDER OATH:

1. Are you in any manner indebted to the Defendant Fred Smith, either in property or money, and is the debt now due? If not due, when is the debt to become due? State fully all particulars.

Answer:_____
_____
_____
_____

2. Did you have in your possession, in your charge or under your control, on the date the Writ of Garnishment was served upon you any money, property, effects, goods, chattels, rights, credits or choses in action of the Defendant or either of them, or in which Defendant is interested? If so, state its value and state fully all particulars.

Answer:_____
_____
_____
_____

3. Do you know of any debts owing to the Defendant, whether due or not due, or any money, property, effects, goods, chattels, rights, credits or choses in action, belonging to the Defendant, or in which Defendant is interested, and now in the possession or under the control of others? If so, state particulars.

Answer:_____
_____

4. State your correct name and address, or the name and address of your attorney upon whom written notice of further proceedings in this action may be served.

Answer:_____

_____

_____

_____

Garnishee

STATE OF NEVADA   )
) ss:
COUNTY OF CLARK   )

I, _____, do solemnly swear (or affirm) that the answers to the foregoing interrogatories subscribed by me are true.

Garnishee

SUBSCRIBED and SWORN to before me
this ____ day of _____, 19__.

_____
Notary Public in and for said
County and State.

Form 26L

E. S. CHOIR, ESQ.
E. S. CHOIR, LTD.
State Bar No. 0000
324 South Avenue
Las Vegas, Nevada 89101
Attorneys for Plaintiff

DISTRICT COURT
CLARK COUNTY, NEVADA

JOHN DOE,	CASE NO. A123456
	DEPT. NO. VI
Plaintiff,	DOCKET NO. K
vs.	
FRED SMITH, DOES I through X,	Date:_____
inclusive,	Time:_____
Defendants.	

EX PARTE APPLICATION FOR ORDER TO SHOW CAUSE WHY COLLATERAL SHOULD NOT BE TAKEN FROM THE DEFENDANTS AND DELIVERED TO PLAINTIFFS

Plaintiffs ALFRED SMITH and JOANNE SMITH, by and through their attorney, E. S. Choir of the law firm of E. S. CHOIR, LTD., move this Court for an Order to Show Cause Why the Property Should not be Taken from the Defendants and Delivered to Plaintiffs since Plaintiffs have a security interest in said property and Defendants have defaulted in their payments on the underlying obligation. This Application is based upon the pleadings, papers and documents on file herein, the Points and Authorities attached hereto.

DATED this ____ day of _____, 19__.

E. S. CHOIR, LTD.

By: _____

E. S. CHOIR, Esq.
Nevada Bar No. 0000
324 South Avenue
Las Vegas, Nevada 89101
Attorneys for Plaintiff

POINTS AND AUTHORITIES

I. THIS COURT HAS AUTHORITY TO ENTER AN ORDER TO SHOW CAUSE WHY PROPERTY SHOULD NOT BE TAKEN FROM THE DEFENDANTS AND GIVEN TO THE PLAINTIFFS WHEN IT IS SHOWN BY AFFIDAVIT THAT PLAINTIFFS ARE LAWFULLY ENTITLED TO THE PROPERTY, THE PROPERTY IS BEING WRONGFULLY DE-

TAINED BY THE DEFENDANTS, THE CAUSE OF THE DETENTION
OF THE PROPERTY, THAT THE PROPERTY HAS NOT BEEN PREVI-
OUSLY SEIZED, AND THE ACTUAL VALUE OF THE PROPERTY.

NRS 31.850 states:

Where a delivery is claimed, an affidavit shall be made by the plaintiff, or by
someone in his behalf and filed with the court showing:

1. That the plaintiff is the owner of the property claimed (particularly
describing it), or is lawfully entitled to the possession thereof.
2. That the property is wrongfully detained by the defendant.
3. The alleged cause of the detention thereof according to his best knowledge and information and belief.
4. That the same has not been taken for a tax, assessment or fine pursuant to a statute, or seized under an execution or an attachment against the
property of the plaintiff, or, if so seized, that it is by statute exempt from
such seizure.
5. The actual value of the property.

NRS 31.853 states:

The court shall promptly examine the affidavit, and if it is satisfied that it
meets the requirements of NRS 31.850, shall issue an order directed to the
defendant to show cause why the property should not be taken from the defendant and delivered to the plaintiff. Such order shall:
1. Fix the date and time for the hearing thereon, which shall be no sooner
than 10 days from the date of issuance of the order.
2. Inform the defendant that he may file affidavits on his behalf with the
court and may appear and present testimony on his behalf at the hearing, or
that he may, at or prior to such hearing, file with the court a written undertaking to stay delivery of the property pursuant to NRS 31.890.
3. Inform the defendant that if he fails to appear, the plaintiff will apply
to the court for a writ of possession.
4. Require service of the affidavit and order upon the defendant, and fix
the time and manner within which such service shall be made, which shall
be by personal service or in such other manner as the court may determine to
be reasonably calculated to afford notice of the proceeding to the defendant
under the circumstances appearing from the affidavit.

As indicated in the affidavit filed herewith and incorporated herein by this
reference, the requirements of NRS 31.850 have been met and, thus, this Court is
authorized pursuant to NRS 31.853 to issue an appropriate Order to Show Cause.

E. S. CHOIR, LTD.

By: _____

E. S. CHOIR, Esq.
Nevada Bar No. 0000
324 South Avenue
Las Vegas, Nevada 89101
Attorneys for Plaintiff

559

Form 26M

E. S. CHOIR, ESQ.
E. S. CHOIR, LTD.
State Bar No. 0000
324 South Avenue
Las Vegas, Nevada 89101
Attorneys for Plaintiff

DISTRICT COURT

CLARK COUNTY, NEVADA

JOHN DOE,	CASE NO. A123456
Plaintiff,	DEPT. NO. VI DOCKET NO. K

vs.

FRED SMITH, DOES I through X, inclusive,

Date:_____
Time:_____

Defendants.

AFFIDAVIT IN SUPPORT OF ORDER TO SHOW CAUSE WHY PROPERTY SHOULD NOT BE TAKEN FROM THE DEFENDANTS AND DELIVERED TO PLAINTIFFS

STATE OF NEVADA)
) ss:
COUNTY OF CLARK)

ALFRED SMITH, being first duly sworn, deposes and says that he has personal knowledge and is competent to testify to the following facts:

1. That I am one of the Plaintiffs in the above-entitled matter.

2. Attached hereto as Exhibit 1 is a Promissory Note and a Security Agreement, a copy of which is attached hereto as Exhibit 2, granting Plaintiffs a security interest in the collateral described in Exhibit 3 attached hereto. Defendant BRENT JONES has defaulted under his Note and Security Agreement by not making payments thereunder.

3. Therefore, I am lawfully entitled to possession of the collateral described in Exhibit 3.

4. Said property is being wrongfully detained by the Defendants since demand has been made for their return pursuant to the Security Agreement and they have failed to deliver said property to me.

5. To the best of my knowledge, information and belief, they have no grounds to continue detaining and keeping possession of the property.

6. The above-mentioned property has not been taken for a tax, assessment or fine pursuant to a statute, or seized under an execution or an attachment against my property to the best of my knowledge or belief.

7. The actual value of the property is listed in Exhibit 3 attached hereto.

8. I am a secured creditor of the Defendants as defined in Chapter 104 of the NRS.

_____

ALFRED SMITH

SUBSCRIBED and SWORN to before me
this ____ day of _____, 19 ____.

_____
Notary Public in and for said
County and State

Form 26N

E. S. CHOIR, ESQ.
E. S. CHOIR, LTD.
State Bar No. 0000
324 South Avenue
Las Vegas, Nevada 89101
Attorneys for Plaintiff

DISTRICT COURT

CLARK COUNTY, NEVADA

JOHN DOE,

    Plaintiff,

    vs.

FRED SMITH, DOES I through X, inclusive,

    Defendants.

CASE NO. A123456
DEPT. NO. VI
DOCKET NO. K

Date:_____

Time:_____

ORDER TO SHOW CAUSE

TO: BRENT JONES and XYZ, INC., Defendants:

The Court having examined the Complaint and Affidavit in Support of Order to Show Cause on file herein and finding that the Affidavit and Complaint meet the requirements of the Nevada Revised Statutes and the Court being fully advised in the premises and good cause appearing; therefore,

IT IS HEREBY ORDERED that you are to appear in Department VI of the above-entitled Court at the hour of 9:00 o'clock a.m. on the _____ day of _____, 19__, and show cause why the property described in said Complaint and Affidavit should not be taken from you and delivered to the Plaintiffs;

IT IS FURTHER ORDERED that you may file affidavits on your behalf with the Court and you may appear and present testimony on your behalf at the hearing, or you may, at or prior to the hearing, file with the Court a written undertaking to stay delivery of the property pursuant to NRS 31.890;

IT IS FURTHER ORDERED that if you fail to appear, the Plaintiff will apply to the Court for a Writ of Possession;

IT IS FURTHER ORDERED that this Order and the Affidavit in support of this Order shall be served upon the Defendants pursuant to NRCP Rule 4(d) by service of a true copy thereof pursuant to said rule no later than two (2) days prior to the above-mentioned hearing date.

DATED this _____ day of _____, 19__.

_____
DISTRICT COURT JUDGE

Submitted by:

E. S. CHOIR, LTD.

By: _____

    E. S. CHOIR, Esq.
    324 South Avenue
    Las Vegas, Nevada 89101
    Attorneys for Plaintiff

Form 260

E. S. CHOIR, ESQ.
E. S. CHOIR, LTD.
State Bar No. 0000
324 South Avenue
Las Vegas, Nevada 89101
Attorneys for Plaintiff

DISTRICT COURT

CLARK COUNTY, NEVADA

JOHN DOE,	CASE NO. A123456
	DEPT. NO. VI
Plaintiff,	DOCKET NO. K
vs.	
FRED SMITH, DOES I through X,	Date:_____
inclusive,	Time:_____
Defendants.	

ORDER GRANTING TEMPORARY WRIT OF POSSESSION

Plaintiffs ALFRED SMITH and JOANNE SMITH's Order to Show Cause Why a Writ of Possession should not issue having come on for hearing in Department VI of the Eighth Judicial District Court on the ____ day of _____ 19__, and the Defendants having been personally served with the Summons, Complaint, Application for Order to Show Cause, Affidavit in Support thereof, and the Order to Show Cause, the Plaintiffs being represented by E. S. Choir of the law firm of E. S. CHOIR, LTD., and there being no opposition to the Order to Show Cause, the court finding: (1) that there is a reasonable probability that Plaintiffs are entitled to possession, use and disposition of the property pending final adjudication of the parties' claims; (2) that this is an appropriate action for issuance of a temporary writ of possession; and (3) that no bond shall be required for the issuance of the writ of possession since there is reasonable cause to believe the Plaintiffs are a secured party pursuant to NRS Chapter 104 and the Court being otherwise fully advised in the premises and good cause appearing; therefore

IT IS HEREBY ORDERED that the Plaintiffs should have the right to possession of the following collateral described in Exhibit A attached hereto, and that the Defendants be ordered to deliver possession of said collateral to Plaintiffs forthwith;

IT IS FURTHER ORDERED that a temporary writ of possession be issued and the Sheriff of Clark County, Nevada, shall take into custody the above-described property possessed by the Defendants wherever said property may be located in the County of Clark, State of Nevada; and

IT IS FURTHER ORDERED that the Sheriff shall deliver said property to Plaintiffs ALFRED SMITH and JOANNE SMITH.

DATED this _____ day of _____ 19__.

_____
                           DISTRICT COURT JUDGE

Submitted by:

E. S. CHOIR, LTD.

By: _____

    E. S. CHOIR, Esq.
    324 South Avenue
    Las Vegas, Nevada 89101
    Attorneys for Plaintiff

Form 26P

E. S. CHOIR, ESQ.
E. S. CHOIR, LTD.
State Bar No. 0000
324 South Avenue
Las Vegas, Nevada 89101
Attorneys for Plaintiff

DISTRICT COURT

CLARK COUNTY, NEVADA

JOHN DOE,	CASE NO. A123456
	DEPT. NO. VI
Plaintiff,	DOCKET NO. K
vs.	
FRED SMITH, DOES I through X,	Date:_____
inclusive,	Time:_____
Defendants.	

TEMPORARY WRIT OF POSSESSION

TO: THE SHERIFF OF CLARK COUNTY, NEVADA, GREETINGS

WHEREAS, the above-named Plaintiffs are entitled to a temporary writ of possession to recover the possession of personal property hereinafter described pursuant to an Order from this Court dated the _____ day of _____ 19__.

NOW, THEREFORE, in the name of the State of Nevada, you are hereby commanded and directed to seize and take from the possession of the Defendants, or its agents, and retain in your custody the personal property listed on the exhibit attached hereto and incorporated herein by this reference which there is probable cause to believe will be found at _____, Las Vegas, Nevada.

You are further commanded and directed to keep said property in a secure place, and deliver said property to Plaintiffs, upon receiving your lawful fees for taking and necessary expenses for keeping the same.

You are further commanded and directed to return this Writ of Possession, with your proceedings endorsed thereon, to the Clerk of the above-entitled Court within twenty (20) days of taking possession of said personal property. Defendants have the right to file a written undertaking for the redelivery of such property in accordance with NRS 31.890.

WITNESS my hand and the seal of this Court this _____ day of _____ 19__.

CLERK OF THE COURT
By: _____
Deputy Clerk

566

Submitted by:

E. S. CHOIR, LTD.

By:_____

    E. S. CHOIR, Esq.
    324 South Avenue
    Las Vegas, Nevada 89101
    Attorneys for Plaintiff

Form 26Q

THIRTY-DAY NOTICE TO QUIT PREMISES

[NRS 40.251(1)(b)]

TO: FRED SMITH; and
TO: ANY SUBTENANTS OF THE PREMISES DESCRIBED BELOW:

PLEASE TAKE NOTICE that your month-to-month tenancy at the above premises is hereby terminated. You must vacate within thirty (30) days from the date of service of this Notice the premises commonly described as 3000 Spencer Avenue, Las Vegas, Nevada and more particularly described as:

LOT TWENTY-TWO (22) IN BLOCK FOURTEEN (14) OF RESUBDIVISION OF LOT 12 IN BLOCK 10 OF PARADISE PARKS UNIT NO. 4, AS SHOWN BY MAP THEREOF ON FILE IN BOOK 21 OF PLATS, PAGE 27, IN THE OFFICE OF THE COUNTY RECORDER OF CLARK COUNTY, NEVADA.

You will be guilty of an unlawful detainer unless you vacate the premises within said period of time.

JOHN DOE

By: E. S. CHOIR, LTD., His Attorneys in Fact

By: _____

E. S. CHOIR, Esq.
Nevada Bar No. 0000
324 South Avenue
Las Vegas, Nevada 89101
Attorneys for Plaintiff

Form 26R

FIVE-DAY NOTICE TO PAY RENT OR QUIT THE PREMISES

TO: Tenant: FRED SMITH, 3000 Spencer Avenue, Las Vegas, Nevada;

Or any subtenants of the above-named person or any persons in possession of the above-mentioned property.

PLEASE TAKE NOTICE that demand is hereby made upon you pursuant to Sections 40.250 and 40.253 of the Nevada Revised Statutes to either pay rent [in the sum of] or in the alternative to surrender the premises at or before noon of the fifth day after receipt of this Notice.

PLEASE BE ADVISED that you have the right to contest this Notice by filing within five (5) days an Affidavit with the Justice of the Peace that you have tendered payment or are not in default of payment of said rent or are not otherwise guilty of an unlawful detainer.

PLEASE BE FURTHER ADVISED that in addition to seeking an order evicting you for your noncompliance with this notice, the undersigned landlord intends to hold you liable for the balance of your rent obligation under your lease notwithstanding these eviction proceedings and notwithstanding any subsequent attempt to mitigate these damages by the landlord's reletting the premises.

OWNER/LANDLORD

By: E. S. CHOIR, LTD., its Attorneys

By: _____

E. S. CHOIR, Esq.
Nevada Bar No. 0000
324 South Avenue
Las Vegas, Nevada 89101
Attorneys for Plaintiff

Form 26S

THREE-DAY NOTICE TO QUIT PURSUANT TO NRS 40.255(1)(c)

NAME OF ORIGINAL OBLIGOR(S): FRED SMITH
ADDRESS: 3000 Spencer Avenue, Las Vegas, Nevada

WHEREAS, the above-mentioned original obligors signed a promissory note secured by a Deed of Trust encumbering the property located at the address stated above and legally described as:

LOT TWENTY-TWO (22) IN BLOCK FOURTEEN (14) OF RESUBDIVISION OF LOT 12 IN BLOCK 10 OF PARADISE PARKS UNIT NO. 4, AS SHOWN BY MAP THEREOF ON FILE IN BOOK 21 OF PLATS, PAGE 27, IN THE OFFICE OF THE COUNTY RECORDER OF CLARK COUNTY, NEVADA.

WHEREAS, by virtue of the default of the above-mentioned original obligors under the terms of said note and Deed of Trust, foreclosure proceedings were initiated against said property, and

WHEREAS, JOHN DOE has become the owner and has perfected his title to said property pursuant to a Trustee's Deed recorded on the 2nd day of April, 1987, as Instrument No. 123456 in Book No. 0001 of the Clark County, Nevada Recorder's Office.

THEREFORE, YOU AND ALL OTHERS IN POSSESSION OF THE ABOVE PREMISES ARE HEREBY notified that pursuant to NRS 40.255(1)(c), you shall vacate the aforesaid premises within three (3) days from the date of service of this notice upon you. You are further notified that if you fail to comply with this demand, legal proceedings will be brought against you for recovery of possession of those premises and for costs accrued together with attorney's fees.

DATED this ____ day of _____, 19____.

OWNER/LANDLORD

Form 26T

E. S. CHOIR, ESQ.
E. S. CHOIR, LTD.
State Bar No. 0000
324 South Avenue
Las Vegas, Nevada 89101
Attorneys for Plaintiff

DISTRICT COURT

CLARK COUNTY, NEVADA

JOHN DOE,	CASE NO. A123456
	DEPT. NO. VI
Plaintiff,	DOCKET NO. K
vs.	
FRED SMITH, DOES I through X,	Date:_____
inclusive,	Time:_____
Defendants.	

AFFIDAVIT OF SERVICE

STATE OF NEVADA   )
) ss:
COUNTY OF CLARK   )

_____, being first duly sworn, deposes and says that the attached notice was served upon the tenant on the ____ day of _____, 19____, in accordance with NRS 40.280 by:

I acknowledge I received this Notice to Quit on the ____ day of _____, 19____ (Tenant). I acknowledge I witnessed the tenant received this Notice to Quit on the ____ day of _____, 19__, (Name of Witness).

Personally delivering a copy to the above-mentioned tenant personally in the presence of a witness at Las Vegas, Nevada. (Name of Witness).

Delivering a copy to a person of suitable age or discretion at the above-mentioned tenant's (residence) (place of business) *and* mailing a copy to said tenant(s) place of residence or business at _____, Las Vegas, Nevada.

Posting a copy in a conspicuous place on the leased property *and* also delivering a copy to the person residing there if someone was present *and* mailing a copy to said tenant(s) at the place where the property is situated, _____, Las Vegas, Nevada.

SUBSCRIBED and SWORN to before me
this _____ day of _____, 19 ____.

_____

Notary Public in and for said
County and State

Form 26U

JUSTICE COURT, LAS VEGAS TOWNSHIP
CLARK COUNTY, NEVADA

JOHN DOE,   CASE NO. A123456

    Plaintiff,

  vs.

FRED SMITH, DOES I through X,
inclusive,

    Defendants.

AFFIDAVIT OF COMPLAINT FOR SUMMARY EVICTION

STATE OF NEVADA   )
) ss:
COUNTY OF CLARK   )

    E. S. CHOIR, being first duly sworn, states:

1. He is (the landlord) (the landlord's duly appointed agent), at the premises located at 3000 Spencer Avenue, Las Vegas, Nevada, situated within Las Vegas Township, Clark County, Nevada.

2. The tenancy commenced on April 2, 1987. The amount of periodic rent is $620 per month. The tenant paid a rent deposit of $0, a security deposit of $0 and a cleaning deposit of $0.

3. Rental payments became delinquent on April 2, 1987, and the tenant has remained in possession without paying rent since that date. The amount of rent claimed due and delinquent is $620.

4. On the third day of May, 1987, a written notice to the tenant was served on the tenant in accordance with NRS 40.280, a copy of the notice with the proof of service is attached to this Affidavit.

5. The tenant (did) (did not) sign a rental agreement. (If tenant signed a rental agreement, you must attach a copy to this Affidavit).

6. Affiant requests that the Court enter an Order for the summary eviction of the tenant from the premises and that the Constable of Las Vegas Township, or the Sheriff of Clark County be ordered to remove the tenant within twenty-four (24) hours after receipt of Court Order.

                                _____

                                Affiant

SUBSCRIBED and SWORN to before me this ____ day of _____, 19 ____.

_____
Notary Public in and for said
County and State

Form 26V

JUSTICE COURT, LAS VEGAS TOWNSHIP

CLARK COUNTY, NEVADA

JOHN DOE,   CASE NO. A123456

    Plaintiff,

    vs.

FRED SMITH, DOES I through X,
inclusive,

    Defendants.

ORDER FOR SUMMARY EVICTION

The Plaintiff-landlord having applied by affidavit for an order seeking summary eviction of the above-named Defendant-tenant, and it appearing from the record on file herein that the statutory Five-Day Notice to Quit the premises, or in the alternative, for payment of the rent in the amount therein claimed has been served upon the above-named Defendant-tenant requiring either payment or the surrender of the premises by noon within five days, or ten days if the premises is a mobile home lot, following the date of service and it further appearing that said Defendant-tenant is in default of payment and still unlawfully detains and withholds the premises, good cause therefore, it is hereby:

ORDERED, that the Constable of Las Vegas Township or the Sheriff of Clark County within twenty-four (24) hours after receipt of this Order, using all necessary force as may be required, is hereby authorized to enter upon the premises known generally as: 3000 Spencer Avenue, Las Vegas Nevada, located in Las Vegas Township, Clark County, Nevada and to summarily remove the Defendant-tenant from the property.

_____   _____
Date   JUSTICE OF THE PEACE

Form 26W-1

JUSTICE COURT, LAS VEGAS TOWNSHIP
CLARK COUNTY, NEVADA

JOHN DOE,   CASE NO. A123456

    Plaintiff,

  vs.

FRED SMITH, DOES I through X,
inclusive,

    Defendants.

INSTRUCTIONS TO THE CONSTABLE

YOU ARE HEREBY INSTRUCTED TO LEVY ON THE FOLLOWING:

WAGES: _____

_____

AMOUNT PAID: (   ) _____

_____

BANK: _____

_____

AMOUNT PAID: (   ) _____

_____

PROPERTY: _____

_____

AMOUNT PAID: (   ) _____

_____

EVICTIONS: 3000 Spencer Avenue, Las Vegas, Nevada ____

_____

OTHER: _____

_____

_____

Plaintiff
Phone No.: 555-5555

Form 26W-2

JUSTICE COURT, LAS VEGAS TOWNSHIP

CLARK COUNTY, NEVADA

JOHN DOE,   CASE NO. A123456

    Plaintiff,

    vs.

FRED SMITH, DOES I through X,
inclusive,

    Defendants.

EVICTION INSTRUCTIONS RE: LOCK CHANGE

To secure property at the time of eviction locks must be changed, lock boxes or slip keys used. All entrances must be secured prior to Court Seals being placed on the property.

Please answer all questions below and sign:

    Does landlord or agent wish to be present during eviction? Yes_____ No_____
    Will landlord or agent provide for lock change? Yes_____ No_____
If answer is "Yes" to either question please provide the name and phone number of authorized person to call for lock change between the hours of 8:00 a.m. and 10:00 a.m.

E. S. Choir, Esq. (702) 555-5555
Name and Phone Number

In the event that the landlord or agent cannot be contacted I hereby authorize the Constable's Office to contact a locksmith and have the locksmith open property for inspection and then to secure property and have the locksmith bill me accordingly, and I guarantee payment in full to said locksmith.

_____
Signature

COURTS NOTATION:

Form 26X

JUSTICE COURT, LAS VEGAS TOWNSHIP

CLARK COUNTY, NEVADA

JOHN DOE,   CASE NO. A123456

Plaintiff,

vs.

FRED SMITH, DOES I through X,
inclusive,

Defendants.

COMPLAINT FOR UNLAWFUL DETAINER

Plaintiff, by and through his attorneys, E. S. CHOIR, LTD., allege as follows:

1. Defendant FRED SMITH is and at all times mentioned herein was a resident of the State of Nevada, County of Clark.

2. That the true names and capacities, whether individual, corporate, associate or otherwise of Defendant named herein as DOES I through V, inclusive, are unknown to Plaintiffs who therefore sues said Defendants by such fictitious names and Plaintiff will ask leave to amend this Complaint to show their true names and capacities when the same have been ascertained. Plaintiffs believe that each Defendant named as a DOE is negligent or responsible in some manner for the events herein referred to and caused damages proximately thereby to Plaintiffs as herein alleged.

3. Plaintiff is and has been since the 2nd day of April, 1987, the owner entitled to the possession of real property located at 3000 Spencer Avenue, Las Vegas, Nevada and more particularly described as:

LOT TWENTY-TWO (22) IN BLOCK FOURTEEN (14) OF RESUBDIVISION OF LOT 12 IN BLOCK 10 OF PARADISE PARKS UNIT NO. 4, AS SHOWN BY MAP THEREOF ON FILE IN BOOK 21 OF PLATS, PAGE 27, IN THE OFFICE OF THE COUNTY RECORDER OF CLARK COUNTY, NEVADA.

4. Defendant is guilty of unlawful detainer based on the following events:

a. Plaintiff became the owner of said property by virtue of a Trustee's Deed after a properly conducted Trustee's foreclosure sale pursuant to a power of sale contained in a Deed of Trust executed by Defendant. A copy of the Trustee's Deed is attached hereto, labeled Exhibit 1 and incorporated herein by this reference.

b. Proper notice to quit pursuant to NRS 40.225(1)(c) was given to the Defendant and said notice was properly served pursuant to NRS 40.280. A copy of the Affidavit of Service and Notice to Quit is attached hereto, labeled Exhibit 2 and incorporated herein by this reference.

c. Defendant, since the date of the Notice to Quit, has continued in possession of the premises without the consent of the Plaintiff and more than three (3) days have elapsed since service of said notice on Defendants.

5. All owners of the property join in the Notice to Quit and these eviction proceedings.

577

6. Therefore, Plaintiff is entitled to removal of Defendant by the issuance and service of a temporary and permanent writ of restitution pursuant to NRS Chapter 40.

7. The fair and reasonable value of said property is $20.00 per day for each and every day since the day of the above-mentioned Trustee's Deed upon foreclosure and Plaintiff will be damaged in said sum until such time as Defendants quit the premises and surrender possession thereof to Plaintiff.

8. It has become necessary for Plaintiff to engage the services of an attorney to commence this action and Plaintiff is, therefore, entitled to reasonable attorney's fees and costs as damages.

WHEREFORE, Plaintiff prays for judgment as follows:

1. That the Court grant Plaintiff's request for a temporary and permanent writ of restitution and a temporary and permanent judgment for restitution of the premises.

2. For damages in the sum of $20.00 per day from the day of foreclosure until such date as defendant shall quit possession of the premises to the Plaintiff.

3. For reasonable attorney's fees;

4. For costs of suit; and

5. For such other and further relief as the Court may deem just and proper in the premises.

E. S. CHOIR, LTD.

By:_____

E. S. CHOIR, Esq.
Nevada Bar No. 0000
324 South Avenue
Las Vegas, Nevada 89101

VERIFICATION

STATE OF NEVADA   )
) ss:
COUNTY OF CLARK   )

E. S. CHOIR, being first duly sworn, deposes and says that he is the attorney for the Plaintiff herein and that he makes this verification for the reason that the Plaintiff and each of them are without the County of Clark, State of Nevada; that he has read the above and foregoing Complaint for Unlawful Detainer and knows the contents thereof and that he is informed and believes and upon the basis of such information and belief alleges the same to be true.

_____
E. S. CHOIR

SUBSCRIBED and SWORN to before me this ____ day of _____ 19____.

_____
Notary Public in and for said
County and State.

Form 26Y

JUSTICE COURT, LAS VEGAS TOWNSHIP
CLARK COUNTY, NEVADA

JOHN DOE,   CASE NO. A123456

    Plaintiff,

vs.

FRED SMITH, DOES I through X,
inclusive,

    Defendants.

EX PARTE MOTION FOR ORDER TO SHOW CAUSE WHY A TEMPORARY WRIT OF RESTITUTION SHOULD NOT ISSUE

Plaintiff, by and through his attorneys, E. S. CHOIR, LTD., applies to this Court for an Order to Show Cause Why a Temporary Writ of Restitution Should Not Issue. This Motion is based upon the pleadings, papers and documents on file herein, the Points and Authorities attached hereto, the evidence presented and the argument of counsel at the time of hearing.

DATED this ____ day of _____ 19__.

                       E. S. CHOIR, LTD.

                       By:_____

                       E. S. CHOIR, Esq.
                       Nevada Bar No. 0000
                       324 South Avenue
                       Las Vegas, Nevada 89101
                       Attorneys for Plaintiff

POINTS AND AUTHORITIES

I. THIS COURT HAS AUTHORITY TO ENTER AN ORDER DIRECTING THE DEFENDANT TO SHOW CAUSE WHY A TEMPORARY WRIT OF RESTITUTION SHALL NOT BE ISSUED REMOVING THE DEFENDANT FROM THE PREMISES.

NRS 40.300(3) states:

At any time after the filing of the complaint and issuance of summons, the court, upon application therefor, may issue a temporary writ of restitution; provided:

(a) That the temporary writ of restitution shall not issue ex parte but only after the issuance and service of an order to show cause why a temporary writ of restitution shall not be issued and after the defendant has been given an opportunity to oppose the issuance of a temporary writ of restitution.

(b) That the temporary writ of restitution shall not issue until the court has had an opportunity to ascertain the facts sufficiently to enable it to estimate the probable loss to the defendant and fix the amount of a bond to indemnify the party or parties against whom the temporary writ may be issued.

(c) that the temporary writ of restitution shall not issue until there has been filed with the approval of the court a good and sufficient bond of indemnification in the amount fixed by the court.

As indicated in the verified Complaint on file herein and the Affidavit filed herewith, the Plaintiff is entitled to an Order to Show Cause Why a Temporary Writ of Restitution Should Not Issue where, as here, the property has been sold under a power of sale granted to the trustee of a deed of trust, title under such sale has been perfected in the Plaintiff, proper notice to quit pursuant to NRS 40.255(1)(c) has been given the Defendant and Defendant refuses to vacate the premises.

E. S. CHOIR, LTD.

By:_____

E. S. CHOIR, Esq.
Nevada Bar No. 0000
324 South Avenue
Las Vegas, Nevada 89101
Attorneys for Plaintiff

Form 26Z

JUSTICE COURT, LAS VEGAS TOWNSHIP

CLARK COUNTY, NEVADA

JOHN DOE,   CASE NO. A123456

    Plaintiff,

    vs.

FRED SMITH, DOES I through X,
inclusive,

    Defendants.

**AFFIDAVIT IN SUPPORT OF ORDER TO SHOW CAUSE WHY
A TEMPORARY WRIT OF RESTITUTION SHOULD NOT BE
ISSUED**

STATE OF NEVADA   )
) ss:
COUNTY OF CLARK   )

    E. S. CHOIR, being first duly sworn, deposes and says that he has been informed and is competent to testify the following facts:

    1. That he is one of the attorneys for the Plaintiff in the above-entitled matter.

    2. Plaintiff is and has been since the 2nd day of April, 1987, the sole owner entitled to the possession of real property located at 3000 Spencer Avenue, Las Vegas, Nevada, and more particularly described as:

    LOT TWENTY-TWO (22) IN BLOCK FOURTEEN (14) OF RESUBDIVISION OF LOT 12 IN BLOCK 10 OF PARADISE PARKS UNIT NO. 4, AS SHOWN BY MAP THEREOF ON FILE IN BOOK 21 OF PLATS, PAGE 27, IN THE OFFICE OF THE COUNTY RECORDER OF CLARK COUNTY, NEVADA.

    3. Plaintiff became the owner of said property by virtue of a Trustee's Deed after a properly conducted Trustee's foreclosure sale pursuant to a power of sale contained in a Deed of Trust executed by Attorneys Equity Corporation. A copy of the Trustee's Deed is attached to the Complaint filed herein.

    4. Proper notice pursuant to NRS 40.255(1)(c) was given to Defendant and said notice was properly served pursuant to NRS 40.280. A copy of the Affidavit of Service and Notice to Quit is also attached to the Complaint filed herein.

    5. Defendant has, since the date of the Notice to Quit, continued in possession of the premises without the consent of the Plaintiff, and more than three (3) days have elapsed since service of said notice on Defendant.

    6. All owners of the property have joined in the Notice to Quit and these eviction proceedings.

    7. Therefore, Plaintiff is entitled to removal of Defendant by the issuance and service of a temporary and permanent writ of restitution pursuant to NRS Chapter 40.

8. The undersigned is informed and believes the fair and reasonable value of said property is $20.00 per day for each and every day since the day of the foreclosure, and Plaintiff will be damaged in said sum until such time as Defendant quits the premises and surrenders possession thereof to Plaintiff.

_____
E. S. CHOIR, Esq.

SUBSCRIBED and SWORN to before
me this _____ day of _____, 19__.

_____
Notary Public in and for said
County and State

Form 26AA

JUSTICE COURT, LAS VEGAS TOWNSHIP
CLARK COUNTY, NEVADA

JOHN DOE,   CASE NO. A123456

    Plaintiff,

vs.

FRED SMITH, DOES I through X,
inclusive,

    Defendants.

ORDER TO SHOW CAUSE WHY A TEMPORARY WRIT
OF RESTITUTION SHOULD NOT ISSUE

TO: FRED SMITH, Defendant; and
TO: All tenants or occupants of the premises located at 3000 Spencer Avenue,
    Las Vegas, Nevada:

WHEREAS, on the ____ day of _____ 19__, a verified complaint for unlawful detainer was filed in the above-entitled Court initiating these proceedings, summons issued thereon, and

WHEREAS, the Court has reviewed the verified complaint and the exhibits attached thereto, the application for order to show cause and supporting affidavit and good cause has been shown for a hearing on whether a temporary writ of restitution should issue;

NOW, THEREFORE, YOU, AND EACH OF YOU SERVED WITH A COPY OF THIS ORDER, ARE HEREBY ORDERED to appear before the above-entitled Court in Department No. __ thereof at Las Vegas, Nevada, on the ____ day of _____ 19__, at the hour of _____ o'clock a.m. of said day to show cause, if you have any, why a temporary writ of restitution should not be issued forthwith granting the Plaintiff herein the immediate right to possession of that certain properties commonly described as 3000 Spencer Avenue, Las Vegas, Nevada, and more particularly described in the Complaint on file herein.

IT IS FURTHER ORDERED that this Order to Show Cause shall be served upon the Defendant together with a copy of the Summons and Complaint and the hearing shall be based on these pleadings, papers and documents on file herein.

DATED this ____ day of _____, 19__.

                                 JUSTICE OF THE PEACE

Submitted by:

E. S. CHOIR, LTD.
By: _____
    E. S. CHOIR, Esq.
    324 South Avenue
    Las Vegas, Nevada 89101
    Attorneys for Plaintiff

Form 26BB

JUSTICE COURT, LAS VEGAS TOWNSHIP

CLARK COUNTY, NEVADA

JOHN DOE,   CASE NO. A123456

    Plaintiff,

vs.

FRED SMITH, DOES I through X,
inclusive,

    Defendants.

ORDER DIRECTING ISSUANCE OF TEMPORARY WRIT OF RESTITUTION

This matter having regularly come on for hearing on the ＿＿ day of ＿＿＿＿＿＿, 19＿, at the hour of ＿＿＿＿＿ a.m., in the above-entitled Court to inquire into the Defendant's unlawful possession and holding over of premises in Clark County, Nevada, commonly described as 3000 Spencer Avenue, Las Vegas, Nevada, and more particularly described as:

LOT TWENTY-TWO (22) IN BLOCK FOURTEEN (14) OF RESUBDIVISION OF LOT 12 IN BLOCK 10 OF PARADISE PARKS UNIT NO. 4, AS SHOWN BY MAP THEREOF ON FILE IN BOOK 21 OF PLATS, PAGE 27, IN THE OFFICE OF THE COUNTY RECORDER OF CLARK COUNTY, NEVADA.

with the Defendant present and with the Plaintiff represented by E. S. CHOIR, LTD., and after an opportunity to sufficiently review the facts and after due consideration by the Court that Plaintiff has presented a prima facie case of Defendant's unlawful detainer and is, therefore, entitled to temporary restitution of the above premises, and further the Court has determined that an estimate of the probable loss to the Defendant resulting from issuance of the temporary writ of restitution is $＿＿＿＿＿, and it appearing from the evidence, pleadings, papers and documents on file herein that the Defendant was properly served with an Order to Show Cause Why a Temporary Writ of Restitution Should Not Issue and it appearing that the Plaintiff is entitled to temporary restitution of the above premises.

IT IS HEREBY ORDERED that a Temporary Writ of Restitution may issue upon Plaintiff filing a good and sufficient bond of indemnification in favor of Defendant in the sum of $＿＿＿＿＿.

GIVEN UNDER MY HAND this ＿＿ day of ＿＿＿＿＿, 19＿.

_____
JUSTICE OF THE PEACE

Submitted by:

E. S. CHOIR, LTD.

By: _____
     E. S. CHOIR, Esq.
     324 South Avenue
     Las Vegas, Nevada 89101
     Attorneys for Plaintiff

Form 26CC

JUSTICE COURT, LAS VEGAS TOWNSHIP
CLARK COUNTY, NEVADA

JOHN DOE,   CASE NO. A123456

    Plaintiff,

    vs.

FRED SMITH, DOES I through X,
inclusive,

    Defendants.

TEMPORARY WRIT OF RESTITUTION

TO: THE SHERIFF OR CONSTABLE OF THE COUNTY OF CLARK, STATE
OF NEVADA, GREETINGS:

WHEREAS, upon request by the Plaintiff, this Court held a hearing before me,
a Justice of the Peace for the above-mentioned County, on the ____ day of
_____, 19__, in Department No. __ at ____ o'clock a.m., to inquire into the
Defendant's unlawful possession and holding over of premises in Clark County,
Nevada, commonly described as 3000 Spencer Avenue, Las Vegas, Nevada, and
more particularly described as:

LOT TWENTY-TWO (22) IN BLOCK FOURTEEN (14) OF RESUBDIVISION
OF LOT 12 IN BLOCK 10 OF PARADISE PARKS UNIT NO. 4, AS SHOWN
BY MAP THEREOF ON FILE IN BOOK 21 OF PLATS, PAGE 27, IN THE
OFFICE OF THE COUNTY RECORDER OF CLARK COUNTY, NEVADA.

with the Defendant present and with the Plaintiff represented by E. S. CHOIR,
LTD., and after the Court concluding that Plaintiff should have temporary restitution of the above premises;

    YOU ARE THEREFORE COMMANDED to take with you the force of the
County, if necessary, and cause the said Defendant and any subtenants to be
immediately removed from the above-mentioned premises by the ____ day of
_____, 19__, at 5:00 p.m. and allow the Plaintiff to have peaceable restitu-
tion of the same. You are also commanded to make return hereof within thirty
(30) days of this date.

    GIVEN UNDER MY HAND this ____ day of _____, 19__.

                                    _____
                                    JUSTICE OF THE PEACE

Submitted by:

E. S. CHOIR, LTD.

By:_____

E. S. CHOIR, Esq.
324 South Avenue
Las Vegas, Nevada 89101
Attorneys for Plaintiff

Form 26DD

JUSTICE COURT, LAS VEGAS TOWNSHIP

CLARK COUNTY, NEVADA

JOHN DOE,   CASE NO. A123456

    Plaintiff,

vs.

FRED SMITH, DOES I through X,
inclusive,

    Defendants.

**NOTICE OF EXECUTION ON
WRIT OF RESTITUTION**

Plaintiff, John Doe, alleges that you are in unlawful possession of property. Plaintiff has initiated court proceedings to recover a judgment against you and to have restitution of the premises.

Certain benefits and property owned by you may be exempt from these proceedings and may, under certain circumstances, not be taken from you. The following is a partial list of exemptions:

1. Payments received under the Social Security Act.

2. Payments for benefits or the return of contributions under the public employees' retirement system.

3. Payments for public assistance granted through the welfare division of the department of human resources.

4. Proceeds from a policy of life insurance.

5. Payments of benefits under a program of industrial insurance.

6. Payments received as unemployment compensation.

7. Veterans' benefits.

8. A homestead in a dwelling or a mobile home, not to exceed $95,000, unless the judgment is for a medical bill, in which case all of the primary dwelling, including a mobile or manufactured home, may be exempt.

9. A vehicle, if your equity in the vehicle is less than $1,500.

10. Seventy-five percent of the take-home pay for any pay period, unless the weekly take-home pay is less than 30 times the federal minimum wage, in which case the entire amount may be exempt.

11. Money, not to exceed $100,000 in present value, held for retirement pursuant to certain arrangements or plans meeting the requirements for qualified arrangements or plans of sections 401 et seq. of the Internal Revenue Code (26 U.S.C. 401 et seq.).

12. A vehicle for use by you or your dependent which is specially equipped or modified to provide mobility for a person with a permanent disability.

13. A prosthesis or any equipment prescribed by a physician or dentist for you or your dependent.

These exemptions may not apply in certain cases such as a proceeding to enforce a judgment for support of a person or a judgment of foreclosure on a mechanic's lien. You should consult an attorney immediately to assist you in determining whether your property or money is exempt from execution. If you cannot afford an attorney, you may be eligible for assistance through (*name of organization in county providing legal services to the indigent or elderly persons*).

If you believe that the money or property taken from you is exempt or necessary for the support of you or your family, you must file with the clerk of the court on a form provided by the clerk a notarized affidavit claiming the exemption. A copy of the affidavit must be served upon the sheriff and the creditor within 8 days after this Notice of Execution is mailed. The property must be returned to you within 5 days after you file the affidavit unless the creditor files a motion for a hearing to determine the issue of exemption. If this happens, a hearing will be held to determine whether the property or money is exempt. The hearing must be held within 10 days after the motion for a hearing is filed.

Form 26EE

JUSTICE COURT, LAS VEGAS TOWNSHIP

CLARK COUNTY, NEVADA

JOHN DOE,   CASE NO. A123456

    Plaintiff,

  vs.

FRED SMITH, DOES I through X,   Date:_____
inclusive,   Time:_____

    Defendants.

WRIT OF RESTITUTION

TO: THE SHERIFF OR CONSTABLE OF THE COUNTY OF CLARK, STATE OF NEVADA, GREETINGS:

WHEREAS, A.B., of the County of Clark, at a court of inquiry of an unlawful holding over of (*lands*) (*tenements*) (*a mobile home*), and other possessions, held at my office (stating the place), in the county aforesaid, on the _____ day of _____ 19__, before me, a justice of the peace for the county aforesaid, by the consideration of the court, has recovered judgment against C.D., to have restitution of (*here describe the premises as in the complaint*). You are therefore commanded, that taking with you the force of the county, if necessary, you cause C.D. to be immediately removed for the premises, and A.B. to have peaceable restitution of the premises. You are also commanded that of the goods and chattels of C.D., within said county, which are not exempt from execution, you cause to be made the sum of $_____ for the Plaintiff, together with the costs of suit endorsed hereon, and make return of this Writ within 30 days after this date. Given under my hand, this _____ day of _____ 19__.

    GIVEN UNDER MY HAND this _____ day of _____ 19__.

                     _____

                        JUSTICE OF THE PEACE

Submitted by:

E. S. CHOIR, LTD.

By:_____

    E. S. CHOIR, Esq.
    324 South Avenue
    Las Vegas, Nevada 89101
    Attorneys for Plaintiff

CHAPTER 27

ENFORCEMENT OF JUDGMENTS

Author: Todd Touton

§ 2701. Introduction and scope.

This chapter discusses enforcement of judgments, the property against which judgments may be enforced, the methods and procedures of enforcement, the revival of judgments and the enforcement of foreign judgments. This chapter deals mainly with NRS Chapters 17, 21 and 22 with reference to other applicable statutes and case law.

A chronology of an execution appears at the end of this chapter. Forms are included for:

27A. Stipulation and Confession of Judgment.
27B. Stipulation and Order for Judgment.
27C. Writ of Execution.
27D. Instructions to Sheriff to Seize, Post and Sell Personal Property; Instructions to Sheriff to Seize and Sell Real Property.
27E. Motion for Supplementary Proceedings.
27F. Order for Supplementary Proceedings.
27G. Ex Parte Motion for Order Allowing Examination of Judgment Debtor.
27H. Order Allowing Examination of Judgment Debtor.
27I. Motion for Order for Delivery of Stock Certificates.
27J. Affidavit.
27K. Order for Delivery of Stock Certificates.
27L. Motion for Order to Charge Partner's Interest, Appoint Receiver and Direct Sale of Defendant's Partnership Interest.
27M. Affidavit in Support of Charging Order.
27N. Order Charging Partner's Interest.
27O. Satisfaction of Judgment.

§ 2702. Initial considerations.

Obtaining a judgment for a client is a useless act unless the client can enforce that judgment. Enforcement will frequently require as much, if not more, skill and imagination as was required to obtain the judgment. Therefore, before commencing a lawsuit, both the attorney and the client must consider and appreciate the enforceability of a potential judgment. In considering the enforceability of a judgment, the attorney and client will require knowledge of the debtor's financial condition, or a willingness to take the risk that they can enforce the judgment. Sometimes the debtor will agree to make payments. In such cases, if suit has not been filed, consider drafting a stipulation and confession of judgment for the debtor to sign. (See Form 27A). If suit has been filed, consider drafting a stipulation that will allow the debtor to make payments, but provide that the creditor can obtain a judgment if there is a default. (See Form 27B). After obtaining a judgment, the attorney and client must reevaluate the debtor's financial condition. Questions which must be considered include:

1. Is the debtor willing and able to pay the judgment? If so, enforcement is no problem. Simply ask for payment.

2. Is the debtor willing to pay the judgment but presently unable to do so? In such a case, consider reasonable arrangements for an installment payment plan or deferred lump sum payment, as well as possible security for such deferred payment arrangements. Be aware that debtors often transfer assets to friends and relatives during negotiations for deferred payments. If a creditor does not receive security in exchange for his promise not to execute, the creditor takes a risk that the debtor will transfer assets during the reprieve created by a deferred payment plan.

3. Is the debtor able to pay the judgment but unwilling to do so? This situation creates the need for the procedures reviewed in this chapter.

4. Has enforcement of the judgment been stayed? If so, a judgment creditor may not enforce the judgment until the stay has been removed. *See* § 2733, *infra.*

5. Has the debtor filed a petition in bankruptcy? Again, if so, enforcement of the judgment is automatically stayed under § 362 of the Bankruptcy Code.

6. If the judgment requires the judgment debtor to perform a specific act which the judgment debtor fails to perform, the court may order someone else to perform the act. Additionally, if the act requires the judgment debtor to convey property, the court may enter a judgment which conveys the property to the appropriate party without any further action by the judgment debtor. (NRCP 70 and NJRCP 70).

§ 2703. Locating the debtor's assets.

Judgments are enforced against the debtor's assets. Consequently, to satisfy the judgment, a creditor must locate adequate and available assets. Sources of information include:

1. *The client and the client's records.* The client may possess information such as the debtor's financial statement, credit applications, tax returns, bank account identification, real or personal property holdings, employment, all of which may identify the nature and the location of the debtor's assets.

2. *Trial material.* Discovery or trial material may contain information concerning the debtor's assets.

3. *County Assessor.* Records maintained by county assessors will reflect property assessed to the debtor. Most assessors will respond to letters or telephone calls and will give the detail their office has with respect to the debtor's property. Reviewing prior years' assessments can also reveal transfers of property the debtor may have made.

4. *County Recorder.* The County Recorder's Office will show transactions or property holdings of the debtor. Lawyers, skilled assistants, title companies and abstractors can make such searches. In the rural counties, personnel in the recorder's office may be willing to make such

searches. Items to locate include deeds of trust in which the debtor may be a beneficiary, deeds in which the debtor is grantor or grantee, limited partnership certificates in which the debtor may be shown as a partner, trust agreements, contracts, mechanics liens and other miscellaneous items. All of the indexes in the recorder's office should be searched.

5. *Uniform Commercial Code Filings.* Records maintained by the Secretary of State and the County Recorders will show whether Financing Statements (UCC-1's) have been filed for a particular debtor, both as debtor and as secured party. Copies of Financing Statements may be obtained by sending a Request for Information (UCC-3) form to the appropriate office and paying the required fee. The information available in Financing Statements may provide additional information relating to the nature and location of assets.

6. *Motor Vehicle Department.* Information describing motor vehicles registered to the debtor may be obtained from the Department of Vehicles by submitting standard forms available from the Department of Motor Vehicles. Mobile homes are no longer licensed by the Department of Motor Vehicles. Instead, the Manufactured Housing Division issues ownership certificates. (NRS 489.501). Accordingly, inquiries concerning the ownership of mobile homes must now be submitted to that division of government in Carson City. Keep in mind, however, that mobile homes can be exempt from execution. NRS 21.090.1(m) and NRS 21.095.

7. *Other Suits.* Check the county and federal clerk's records to see if the debtor is a party to any other litigation. The debtor may have a claim against another person that can be garnished. Additionally, another attorney may have collected a judgment against the debtor, and may be able to provide information concerning the debtor's assets. A divorce action in which the debtor is a party can be an excellent source of property information.

8. *Bankruptcy Court.* Check with the clerk of the bankruptcy court to see if the debtor is in a bankruptcy proceeding which will stay any further enforcement action pursuant to 11 U.S.C. § 362.

9. *On-line Data Bases.* Various on-line information services are now available including Information America, Global (covering secretary of states' records in over 30 states), Duns Business Records Plus and Asset Locator, Data Resources (which includes Nevada State Contractors' Board's records and business license records in the Southern Nevada area), and Data Times (providing access to newspaper articles). More services of this kind are sure to come.

§ 2704. The importance of names and adding names.

Assets of the debtor may be indexed, registered or titled under many variations of the debtor's name, while other persons may also have names similar to the debtor. To aid enforcement of the judgment, the complaint and the judgment should name the debtor by all names by which the debtor may be known. The complaint and judgment should also identify the nature of the debtor if the debtor is a corporation, partnership, or other entity. Rule 17(b) of the Nevada Rules of Civil Procedure makes it unnecessary to allege or prove the capacity of a party unless capacity is put in issue by a responsive pleading. However, if a judgment is to be enforced, the judgment should state whether the debtor is a corporation, partnership, or the like so the assets of the correct entity can be seized when enforcing the judgment. If the debtor is a partnership or other association, each member should also be named as a defendant to facilitate the enforcement of the judgment against the members' assets.

§ 2705. Associations.

NRS 12.110 permits associates to be sued by a common name, but the judgment binds only the property owned by the association. NRS 14.060 sets forth the procedure to be followed in obtaining and enforcing judgment where two or more defendants are sued on a common debt but fewer than all associates are served. The property of any individual associate is subject to the judgment only if the individual associate has been made a party to the action by being named and served as an individual.

§ 2706. — Adding names as judgment debtors.

If a plaintiff obtains a judgment against less than all those jointly liable on an obligation, NRS 17.030-17.080 provides a post-judgment procedure for adding the previously unnamed parties as judgment debtors. However, the reference in NRS 17.030 to NRS 14.060 may imply that this procedure may be used only if the party to be added as a judgment debtor was originally named as a defendant but not served. If the party to be added was not so named, a motion to amend the complaint by adding the additional name might be necessary. These complications demonstrate the importance of naming all potential debtors in the complaint before judgment is entered. *See* the discussion respecting names in Chapter 5, *supra.*

In *Frank McCleary Cattle Co. v. Sewell,* 73 Nev. 279, 317 P.2d 957 (1957), the Nevada Supreme Court allowed a corporation to be added as a judgment debtor by motion made after judgment had been entered on the basis that the corporation was the alter ego of the judgment debtor. Before adding additional parties as judgment debtors, due process requires that notice and a hearing be afforded to such persons. *Nicoladze v. First National Bank,* 94 Nev. 377, 580 P.2d 1391 (1978).

§ 2707. — Fictitious name certificate.

The county clerk's office maintains a record of any fictitious name certificates in the name of the debtor. Ficticious firm names may lead to identifying others who could be liable.

§ 2708. — Partnerships as defendants.

A judgment against "John Smith and Richard Roe, dba Smith and Roe, a partnership" is *not* a judgment against the partnership. The phrase "dba Smith and Roe" has been held to be only a description of John Smith and Richard Roe and not a naming of the partnership as a defendant. *Potts v. Whitson,* 52 Cal. App. 2d 199, 125 P.2d 947 (1942); *see also Diamond National Corp. v. Thunderbird Hotel,* 85 Nev. 271, 434 P.2d 13 (1969); *see* Chapter 5, *supra.* The correct naming of the defendants would be "John Smith, Richard Roe, and Smith and Roe, a partnership of John Smith and Richard Roe." If the partnership is liable for the debt, the judgment should be entered against the partnership as well as against the individual partners because a judgment against the partners but *not* against the partnership is not enforceable against partnership assets. NRS 87.250. *See* § 2723, *infra.*

§ 2709. Fair debt collection practices.

The enforcement of judgments usually requires the seizing of another's money or property. A judgment creditor must exercise caution to ensure that the assets seized belong to the debtor. While lawyers are presently not subject to NRS Chapter 649 which regulates collection agencies, a recent amendment has brought lawyers within the provisions of the Federal Fair Debt Collection Practices Act, 15 U.S.C. § 1692. The provisions of this act deal with collection of consumer debts. Thus, lawyers should not engage in the following collection practices, which are prohibited by either state or federal law:

1. Use subterfuge, pretense or deceptive means.
2. Attempt to collect more than is due.
3. Harass a debtor's employer.
4. Communicate with a debtor represented by an attorney, which is also prohibited by rules of ethics.
5. Communicate with the debtor other than between 8:00 a.m. and 9:00 p.m.
6. Communicate with the debtor at the debtor's place of employment if it is known the employer prohibits such communications.
7. Threaten of use of violence or other criminal means.
8. Use obscene or profane language.
9. Threaten to take any action that cannot legally be taken or is not intended to be taken. Threatening criminal prosecution if a debt is not

paid may constitute the crime of "compounding" prohibited by NRS 199.290.

Lawyers should be aware that demand letters to collect "consumer" debts and to collect legal fees due the attorney are acts that fall within this federal legislation. Therefore, lawyers should review U.S.C. § 692g(a), relating to the content of such demand letters. Demand letters must advise the debtor of how much is owed and the name of the creditor. Additionally, the letter must inform the debtor that the debt will be assumed valid unless the debtor disputes the debt within thirty days. The letter must also state that if the debtor disputes the debt within the thirty-day period, the attorney will obtain verification of the debt and mail it to the debtor. The careful practitioner will review this statute in detail prior to mailing the garden variety demand letter.

§ 2710. Recording judgment.

A certified copy of a judgment, abstract of judgment, or transcript of the original docket of a judgment rendered by a court sitting in Nevada may be recorded with the county recorder of any county. When so recorded, the judgment becomes a lien upon all real property of the debtor, not exempt from execution, which the debtor then has or thereafter acquires. The lien continues for a period of six years from the date of entry of judgment. If the judgment is entered by the justice's court, a lien is created only by recording an abstract of the judgment. NRS 68.040. A form for such an abstract can be found at NRS 68.010.

Unless there is a compelling reason not to do so, judgments should be promptly recorded in all cases and in all counties in which the debtor has or may acquire real property. Recording the judgment creates a judgment lien against the debtor's real property, and should be done as early as possible, since other liens may also be filed against the property.

There is *no* provision in Nevada law for recording a foreign judgment, and doing so is a useless act. Foreign judgments must first be made a Nevada judgment. Only the judgment of the Nevada court will create a lien when recorded. *See* discussion of Uniform Enforcement or Judgment Act, § 2731, *infra*.

If the debtor has no property when the Nevada judgment is recorded, the judgment becomes a lien upon any real property the debtor later acquires in the county in which the judgment is recorded. NRS 17.150(2).

§ 2711. Exemptions.

State and federal law exempt various types of property from execution.

The most important exemption in Nevada is the $95,000 homestead exemption provided by NRS 115.010. Two or more tenants in common may each declare a homestead. NRS 115.030. The statutes do not refer to the rights of joint tenants, but husband and wife may claim only one homestead. NRS 115.010(1). Either spouse may declare the homestead and bind the other in that selection. *In re Landy*, 58 B.R. 104 (D. Nev. 1986). A homestead cannot be claimed on partnership property. NRS 87.250. In Nevada, a homestead is effective even if declared after judgment but before the execution sale is completed or after a bankruptcy petition is filed. *Massey Ferguson, Inc. v. Childress,* 89 Nev. 272, 510 P.2d 1358 (1972); *Myers v. Matley,* 318 U.S. 622, 63 S. Ct. 780, 87 L. Ed. 1043 (1943) (a pre-Bankruptcy Code case). If the creditor believes the debtor's interest in the homestead property is worth more than $95,000, the creditor must follow the procedure set forth in NRS 115.050, and obtain a court order before holding an execution sale. The statute appears to require that execution be issued against the property as a prerequisite to using the procedure set forth in of the statute.

A judicial exception to the homestead protection was announced in *Breedlove v. Breedlove,* 100 Nev. 133, 691 P.2d 426 (1984). The court held a homestead declaration by a husband and his second wife did not protect their home against execution on a debt for child support owed to a former wife.

When exempt property, other than a homestead, is levied on, the debtor must claim the property is exempt by following the procedure provided in NRS 21.116. Except for the homestead exemption, Nevada has no procedure for determining exemptions in advance of levy.

Other property exempt from execution is listed in NRS 21.090, and include:

(a) Private libraries not to exceed $1,500 in value, and all family pictures and keepsakes.

(b) Necessary household goods, as defined in 16 CFR § 444.1(i) as that section existed on January 1, 1987, and yard equipment, not to exceed $3,000 in value, belonging to the judgment debtor to be selected by him.

(c) Farm trucks, farm stock, farm tools, farm equipment, supplies and seed not to exceed $4,500 in value, belonging to the judgment debtor to be selected by him.

(d) Professional libraries, office equipment, office supplies and the tools, instruments and materials used to carry on the trade of the judgment debtor for the support of himself and his family not to exceed $4,500 in value.

(e) The cabin or dwelling of a miner or prospector, his cars, implements and appliances necessary for carrying on any mining operations and his mining claim actually worked by him, not exceeding $4,500 in total value.

(f) Except as otherwise provided in paragraph (o), one vehicle if the judgment debtor's equity does not exceed $1,500 or the creditor is paid an amount equal to any excess above that equity.

(g) For any pay period, 75 percent of the disposable earnings of a judgment debtor during that period, or for each week of the period 30 times the minimum hourly wage prescribed by section 6(a)(1) of the federal Fair Labor Standards Act of 1938 and in effect at the time the earnings are payable, whichever is greater. Except as otherwise provided in paragraph (n), the exemption provided in this paragraph does not apply in the case of any order of a court of competent jurisdiction for the support of any person, any order of a court of bankruptcy or of any debt due for any state or federal tax. As used in this paragraph, "disposable earnings" means that part of the earnings of a judgment debtor remaining after the deduction from those earnings of any amounts required by law, to be withheld.

(h) All fire engines, hooks and ladders, with the carts, trucks and carriages, hose, buckets, implements and apparatus thereunto appertaining, and all furniture and uniforms of any fire company or department organized under the laws of this state.

(i) All arms, uniforms and accouterments required by law to be kept by any person, and also one gun, to be selected by the debtor.

(j) All courthouses, jails, public offices and buildings, lots, grounds and personal property, the fixtures, furniture, books, papers and appurtenances belonging and pertaining to the courthouse, jail and public offices belonging to any county of this state, all cemeteries, public squares, parks and places, public buildings, town halls, markets, buildings for the use of the fire departments and military organizations, and the lots and grounds thereto belonging and appertaining, owned or held by any town or incorporated city, or dedicated by the town or city to health, ornament or public use, or for the use of any fire or military company organized under the laws of this state and all lots, buildings and other school property owned by a school district and devoted to public school purposes.

(k) All money, benefits, privileges or immunities accruing or in any manner growing out of any life insurance, if the annual premium paid does not exceed $1,000. If the premium exceeds that amount, a like exemption exists which bears the same proportion to the money, benefits, privileges and immunities so accruing or growing out of the insurance that the $1,000 bears to the whole annual premium paid.

(l) The homestead as provided for by law.

(m) The dwelling of the judgment debtor occupied as a home for himself and family, where the amount of equity held by the judgment debtor in the home does not exceed $95,000 in value and the dwelling is situated upon lands not owned by him.

(n) All property in this state of the judgment debtor where the judgment is in favor of any state for failure to pay that state's income tax on benefits received from a pension or other retirement plan.

(o) Any vehicle owned by the judgment debtor for use by him or his dependent that is equipped or modified to provide mobility for a person with a permanent disability.

(p) Any prosthesis or equipment prescribed by a physician or dentist for the judgment debtor or a dependent of the debtor.

(q) Money, not to exceed $100,000 in present value, held in:

(1) An individual retirement arrangement which conforms with the applicable limitations and requirements of 26 U.S.C. § 408;

(2) A written simplified employee pension plan which conforms with the applicable limitations and requirements of 26 U.S.C. § 408;

(3) A cash or deferred arrangement which is a qualified plan pursuant to the Internal Revenue Code; and

(4) A trust forming part of a stock bonus, pension or profit-sharing plan which is a qualified plan pursuant to § 401 *et seq.* of the Internal Revenue Code (26 U.S.C. § 401 *et seq.*).

The following types of income are also exempt: Industrial insurance compensation, NRS 616.550; unemployment compensation, NRS 612.710; welfare assistance, NRS 422.291; some life insurance proceeds, NRS 687B.260; public employees' retirement benefits, NRS 286.670; and Social Security benefits, even after receipt. 42 U.S.C. § 407. The following types of property are also exempt: collections of mineral ores, art curiosities, and paleontological remains that are catalogued and arranged for public view. NRS 21.100. A special exemption exists for a judgment debtor's primary dwelling if execution is sought upon a judgment for a medical bill. NRS 21.095.

While funds payable by the federal government to private individuals are not exempt from execution, the federal government will not honor a state court execution. Thus, a creditor with a state court judgment cannot seize the wages of a federal employee until the wages have been paid. 30 Am. Jur. 2d *Executions* § 814; *see also Brockelman v. Brockelman,* 478 F. Supp. 141 (D. Kan. 1979); *but see* 42 U.S.C. § 659 as to an exception in child support and alimony cases.

A creditor may not levy on the interest of a beneficiary of a spendthrift trust or certain court trusts to enforce a judgment against the beneficiary. NRS 21.080(2).

§ 2712. The writ of execution.

Judgments of Nevada district courts are enforced by writs of execution. NRS 21.020.

An execution may immediately issue on a state court judgment [NRCP 62(a) and NJRCP 62(a)] unless the court grants a stay or unless the appellant posts a supersedeas bond. NRCP 62(d). If the bond is posted, it only stays writs from being issued after it is filed. NRCP 62(d). Writs that were issued prior to filing the bond may proceed. *See* 4 Am. Jur. 2d *Appeal and Error* § 372 (1962). An execution will not be issued on a federal court judgment until ten days after entry of the judgment. FRCP 62(a). Such writs may be issued for six years following entry of the judgment but cease to be effective six years after the entry of the judgment. NRS 21.010. Similar provisions apply to judgments of justice's courts (NRS 70.010-70.050). Judgments of federal courts are enforced in accordance with state law. FRCP 69. The form of a writ of execution is provided in NRS 21.025 and is included as Form 27C, *supra.*

Execution on the writ may now occur only if the sheriff serves the judgment debtor with a notice of the writ which describes Nevada exemptions and the procedure for claiming those exemptions. NRS 21.075. The notice must be served by regular mail the next business day after the writ is served. NRS 21.076.

Death of the judgment debtor or creditor does not prevent enforcement of the judgment. NRS 21.060. A sale may be held on a writ of execution that was levied upon the deceased's property during his lifetime. If the writ was not levied during the decedent's lifetime, a writ cannot be issued after his death. Instead, a claim must be filed in the estate. NRS 147.210. An attorney cannot represent a deceased client; substitution of a representative of the deceased party must be made in order for the court to have subject matter jurisdiction. *Walker v. Burkham*, 68 Nev. 250, 229 P.2d 158 (1951).

The clerk of the court in which the judgment was entered issues the execution. The execution is directed to the sheriff of the county in which the execution is to be levied. Executions may be issued at the same time to different counties. NRS 21.070.

A writ of execution may not be issued on a judgment against an estate, unless foreclosing a lien. NRS 147.200.

Do *not* use forms from other states. Writs obtained on forms from other states (for example, writs of execution or preliminary writs, such as a writ of possession in claim and delivery under NRS 31.866) may not track Nevada law. You may not be able to levy on the desired assets, and you may possibly expose your client to liability.

§ 2713. Levy of writ of execution.

All property and property rights not exempt from execution are subject to execution. NRS 21.080(1). The writ is executed by the sheriff levying, *i.e.*, seizing money of the debtor and paying it to the judgment creditor or seizing property of the debtor, selling it and paying the proceeds to the judgment creditor. NRS 21.110.

As a matter of practice, the levying officer (sheriff, constable or federal marshall) will not make any search for property or any determination of what asset to levy on. Therefore, the levying officer must be given written instructions clearly describing the asset to be levied on, the location of the asset, and the name and address of the person having custody of the asset. If a motor vehicle is to be levied on, the levying officer must be given the license number of the vehicle. Most sheriffs will verify the ownership of the vehicle with the Department of Motor Vehicles and will refuse to seize the vehicle if the judgment debtor is not shown as the registered owner. *See* Form 27D for instructions to the sheriff for levy of a writ of execution on personal property. These forms can usually be obtained from the clerk's office.

If property is seized and must be sold, the sale must be conducted in accordance with NRS 21.130. The sale cannot proceed unless notice of the sale has been properly given to the judgment debtor. NRS 21.130(2). The civil department of the sheriffs' offices will require the judgment creditor's attorney to prepare the necessary documents, to wit: the notice of sale, affidavit of posting, certificate of sale, and sheriff's deed. In every case, the judgment creditor's attorney must stay in touch with the sheriff's office to make sure the levy and sale are made properly and timely.

§ 2714. Attachment and garnishment: garnishment in aid of execution.

Property or claims that have been attached or garnished as a prejudgment remedy can only be applied to the judgment through levy of a writ of execution after judgment. *See* Chapter 26, *supra,* for a further discussion of garnishment.

Garnishment is also available to aid in the enforcement of a writ of execution. NRS 21.120. Counsel using a writ of garnishment in aid of execution should closely study the garnishment statutes. NRS 31.240 to 31.460. *See* Chapter 26, *supra.* Note that garnishment in aid of execution requires notice be given to the judgment debtor.

In the event the garnishee wrongfully fails to acknowledge possession of property owned by the debtor in the garnishment interrogatory answers, an affidavit in traverse may be filed. *See* NRS 31.330. Issues created upon traverse proceed to trial and special provisions are made for recovery of costs and fees. NRS 31.340.

§ 2715. Levy on going business.

The sheriff may place a keeper in a going business to receive all proceeds of the business. NRS 21.118 (dealing with execution). NRS 31.060(2)(b) (dealing with attachment). The creditor must prepay the expense of such keeper to the sheriff.

§ 2716. Receiver.

A receiver may be appointed to aid in the enforcement or collection of a judgment. NRS 32.010. A receiver can receive the funds of a going business, among other things. *See* Chapter 28, *infra.*

§ 2717. Execution sales.

Sections 21.130 through 21.190 set forth the procedure for conducting execution sales. A buyer purchasing property at an execution sale receives only that interest in the property that the judgment debtor has. NRS 21.170; 21.190; *Allison Steel Mfg. Co. v. Bentonite,* 86 Nev. 494,

471 P.2d 666 (1970). If the buyer is the judgment creditor, he will have to pay the sheriff's fees and costs in cash, but will otherwise credit the amount owed to him against the judgment. You should note that NRS 248.275(2) allows the sheriff to collect a commission for receiving or paying over money on execution or process where real or personal property has been levied on, advertised, or sold. The levying creditor's attorney should be at the sale and make sure this item of cost is included in any bid from buyers because the sheriff's bill for this commission is usually sent fourteen to thirty days after the sale.

If a purchaser of real property is evicted because of irregularities in the sale, NRS 21.260 provides the procedure for setting aside the sale and restoring the parties to the status quo.

NRS 21.130 provides the manner of giving notice of execution sales. Notice to the judgment debtor is required for all types of property. NRS 21.074. This notice must be served by the sheriff by regular mail the day after "the writ was served" (presumably meaning the day after the levy). NRS 21.076. The sheriff serves this notice by regular mail.

§ 2718. Right of redemption.

Unless the real property interest levied on consists of a leasehold for an unexpired term of less than two years, NRS 21.190-21.250 provide a one-year right of redemption. The judgment debtor can either redeem the property or can sell his or her right of redemption to another, who may thereafter redeem the property. NRS 21.200. The right of redemption of real property is exercised by paying to the purchaser the amount of the purchase price plus interest, together with taxes, assessments, and payments made by the purchaser towards liens created prior to the purchase, less rents and profits received. NRS 21.210; NRS 21.250.

However, the judgment creditor's rights following redemption differ depending on whether the judgment debtor or a successor in interest redeems the property. When a judgment debtor redeems property, he or she reacquires the same title and interest he or she previously possessed. Therefore, if a deficiency still exists, a lien for the deficiency once again attaches to the property as though no execution had taken place. A judgment creditor would then be able to execute upon the property a second time to satisfy the deficiency. If, on the other hand, a successor in interest redeems the property, a lien for any deficiency that might exist does not attach to the property. The successor in interest takes the property free and clear of the judgment creditor's lien. The difference in result serves one of the primary purposes of statutory redemption: It forces the purchaser of real property at an execution sale to bid a price approximating its fair value. *Kaye v. United Mortgage Co.*, 86 Nev. 183, 466 P.2d 848 (1970).

Hence, a judgment creditor who purchases the property at a price considerably below either the true value of the property or his judgment, risks losing any additional benefit from the property and even his judgment, if a successor in interest redeems the property. Consequently, the judgment creditor is well advised to bid either close to the true value of the debtor's interest or the full amount of the judgment, whichever is less.

In order to evaluate the value of the debtor's interest in the property, a creditor should obtain a title report on the property, determine the amount of taxes and other liens upon the property, attempt to determine the price at which the property was most recently sold, and otherwise make a sensible determination of the amount to bid on the property.

There is no right of redemption of personal property.

Redemption must be made within one year following the execution sale (NRS 21.210), but if redemption is prevented or delayed by mutual mistake, fraud or other reasons recognized in equity, redemption may be permitted after the one-year period. *Pace v. Malonea,* 79 Nev. 365, 385 P.2d 353 (1963).

§ 2719. Supplementary proceedings: debtor's examination.

NRS 21.270 to 21.340 provide for proceedings by which the debtor and third persons may be required to testify before a judge, master, or an attorney representing the judgment creditor regarding the debtor's assets. Under these provisions, orders can be entered requiring the debtor to apply designated assets to the judgment under threat of contempt. The procedures contemplated by these statutes vary in the different local practices. Forms 27E and 27F are used for supplementary proceedings before a master. Forms 27G and 27H are used to require the debtor to testify about his assets before the judge. In the past, many judges had the debtor sworn in open court and then sent to an open room, such as a jury room, to answer the creditor's attorney's questions. Now the debtor may be required to appear before the creditor's attorney.

The discovery procedures afforded by the Nevada Rules of Civil Procedure are available to aid in the enforcement of judgments and executions. NRCP 69. However, the sanctions available under these rules are not effective after judgment except as to witnesses. Of course NRCP 45 therefore permits use of subpoenas and the sanction of contempt.

An intense and well-prepared examination of the judgment debtor on supplementary proceedings may be used by counsel to reach an agreement, made from the witness stand, for installment payment or some other arrangement for satisfaction of the judgment. A good checklist for examining debtors is located in Interrogatory Forms 1, 2, Earnings, Income and Assets, *Bender's Forms of Discovery,* Vol. 5 (1979).

The statutes authorizing supplementary proceedings do not authorize, nor do any other statutes authorize, an order directing the sheriff to enter the judgment debtor's premises to search for or seize property to be sold on execution. *Luciano v. Marshall,* 95 Nev. 276, 593 P.2d 751 (1979).

No judgment debtor can be required to appear for an examination outside of the county in which he resides. NRS 21.270. There is no such limitation, however, against debtors of the judgment debtors sought to be examined. NRS 21.300; NRS 21.330.

§ 2720. Bank accounts.

Bank accounts can be seized by a writ of garnishment in aid of execution, since it is property of the debtor in the bank's possession.

Service on a bank will seize only that property and those deposits in the branch served. No mechanism exists for serving all branches of a bank by serving the head or main office. A judgment creditor must serve each branch separately. NRS 31.291.

§ 2721. Intangibles.

Intangible property interests can be levied against and sold under execution just like physical property. The standard form garnishment interrogatories specifically refer to "choses in action," and therefore if the judgment debtor has pending claims against a third party, the defendant can be garnished with respect to any potential obligation upon that claim. More directly, the claim (subject to certain exceptions for non-assignable or personal claims) can be executed upon, sold and thereafter extinguished by the buyer. *GPA, Inc. v. Humana, Inc.,* No. 20377 (Nev. Sept. 14, 1990), cited in *Humana v. GPA, Inc. (In re GPA, Inc.),* BK-S-89-2384, Adv. No. 89-175 (D. Nev. 1992).

§ 2722. Stock certificates.

Stock certificates ordinarily must be taken into possession by the sheriff in order for the levy to be valid. Procedures now exist to levy on uncertificated securities by notice given to the issuer and the debtor. NRS 104.8317(7). Judgment creditors may obtain court orders to aid in acquiring possession of certificates. NRS 104.8317 and 21.080. However, in *Searchlight Development, Inc. v. Martello,* 84 Nev. 102, 437 P.2d 86 (1968), the court found a sheriff's sale of stock to be valid as against a party claiming to be a prior assignee of the stock where the stock certificates had not been delivered to the assignee at the time of the assignment. The decision failed to state whether the sheriff had obtained possession of the certificates prior to the sale.

If the court or master determines ownership of stock certificates supplementary proceedings, it can order the judgment debtor to deliver the certificates to the sheriff for sale. Otherwise, judgment creditors can usually obtain an order for such delivery by motion supported with an affidavit showing ownership of the shares. Any such order should be sent to the stock transfer agent a copy of any such order to guard against improper transfers. (*See* Forms 27I, 27J and 27K for a motion, affidavit and order to obtain possession of stock certificate).

§ 2723. Partnership interests.

Partnership property is not subject to levy for a judgment entered against one or more of the partners but not against the partnership. NRS 87.250. However, a "partner's interest" in a partnership is subject to sale through the procedure of a charging order. NRS 87.280. Section 87.260 of the Nevada Revised Statutes defines a "partner's interest" as the partner's share of the profits and surplus. Therefore, the sale of a "partner's interest" will only include the partner's rights in profits and surplus. *See Tupper v. Kroc,* 88 Nev. 146, 494 P.2d 1275 (1972). The sale of a "partner's interest" would exclude a partner's right to participate in the management of the partnership, his right to specific partnership property, and, unless capital is regarded as a part of profits and surplus, would also exclude the partner's right to capital he contributed. However, NRS 87.280, which authorizes a partnership charging order, also authorizes the court, at the time the charging order is entered, to:

> then or later appoint a receiver of his share of the profits, and of any other money due or to fall due to him in respect of the partnership, and make all other orders, directions, accounts and inquiries which the debtor partner might have made, or which the circumstances of the case may require.

The language authorizing the appointment of a receiver may be broad enough to include capital and management. A receiver so appointed could, if the partnership articles so authorize, terminate the partnership or take such other action as the debtor partner might have taken to obtain funds to pay the judgment. *Tupper v. Kroc,* 88 Nev. 146, 494 P.2d 1275 (1972), indicates that a receiver appointed under NRS 87.280 may exercise the debtor's management rights.

A creditor may obtain a charging order by a motion supported with an affidavit showing the existence of the partnership interest. A copy of the charging order and of the notice of sale of the interest should be served on all partners. Often this will result in voluntary payment of the judgment if the value of the partnership interest so warrants. *See* Forms 27L, 27M and 27N for a motion, affidavit and order for a partnership charging order.

A limited partnership's assets may include the obligation of partners to pay contributions to the partnership. NRS 88.475. Limited partners are not ordinarily liable to partnership creditors unless they permitted creditors to believe they were general partners. NRS 88.430.

§2724. Fraudulent transfers.

Prior to July 1, 1987, fraudulent transfers within the Uniform Fraudulent Conveyance Act, NRS 112.010 to 112.130 could be ignored and levy made as if the transfer had not taken place. NRS 112.100. However, the 1987 legislature repealed the Uniform Fraudulent Conveyance Act and enacted the Uniform Fraudulent Transfer Act. Section 9 of the new act provides that court authorization is required prior to a judgment creditor levying on the asset so transferred. As to the liability of corporate directors, officers and shareholders as transferees, see NRS 78.625 and 78.225.

If the fraudulent transferor has died, his estate has an obligation to recover the fraudulent conveyance for the benefit of the creditors. NRS 143.150.

If a judgment against a corporation cannot be enforced because of a lack of corporate assets, a judgment creditor may inquire into corporate transactions during supplementary proceedings to determine if a remedy is available against some third party.

§2725. Interest.

The judgment should state the rate of interest continuing to accrue and the amount or items of the judgment upon which the interest is to be computed, as well as the date interest commences. *See* Chapter 24, *supra,* for an extended discussion of interest allowed in judgments.

§2726. Costs.

Many of the costs of collecting a judgment can be collected as a part of the judgment. NRS 18.160 sets forth the items that can be collected on a post judgment memorandum of costs; NRS 18.170 and 18.180 set forth the procedure to be used to recover additional costs not taxable by memo in a motion.

§2727. Satisfaction.

The judgment creditor has an obligation to acknowledge satisfaction of a judgment in a writing filed with the county clerk. The obligation to acknowledge satisfaction of a judgment also extends to the creditor's attorney, unless his authority has been revoked. NRS 17.200. A certified copy of the satisfaction of judgment may be recorded with the county recorder to show the termination of the lien created by the previously recorded judgment. However, there is no obligation on the part of the judgment creditor to cause such a recording. (*See* Form 270 for a satisfaction of judgment).

§ 2728. Reviving judgments.

Prior to 1985 Nevada had no statutory procedure for reviving or extending a judgment past the six-year effective period. Judgment creditors were required to start a new action on the judgment before the six-year period expired. Further, a complaint in the original action to revive the judgment was probably subject to the requirement that leave of court be obtained. *Polk v. Tully,* 97 Nev. 27, 623 P.2d 972 (1981). In the *Polk* case, a summons was issued and served on the judgment debtor together with the complaint and, other than the complaint being in the original case, was handled as if the new complaint commenced an entirely new action. The *Polk* procedure is not recommended. It is much safer to file a new case. Service of the summons and complaint will have to be made on the judgment debtor defendant.

Some courts have entered orders granting motions to renew a judgment, but this procedure is not authorized by rule, statute or case law.

The 1985 legislature enacted NRS 17.214 to provide a statutory procedure for renewing judgments. The legislation did not expressly prohibit renewing the judgment by a separate action, as was the previous practice. Whether a Nevada Court will hold that NRS 17.214 is the exclusive procedure for renewing judgments has not yet been determined. The careful attorney will use the NRS Chapter 17 procedure. Please note that NRS 17.214 requires the renewal procedure be commenced within ninety days before the judgment expires. Prior to the ninety days, a separate action should be employed.

§ 2729. Bankruptcy.

When a debtor files a petition for relief under the United States Bankruptcy Code, an immediate and automatic stay precludes any further attempt to enforce a judgment against the debtor. 11 U.S.C. § 362. However, bankruptcy can be a blessing for creditors in certain kinds of cases. Bankruptcy stops the creditor's race for judgment and execution, and permits complete examination of the debtor's financial affairs, including the discovery of fraudulent conveyances and the prevention of subsequent transfers of assets.

§ 2730. Third-party claims.

If a third party claims a right to property levied on by a judgment creditor under a writ of execution, the parties follow the same procedure used to deal with third-party claims on writs of attachment. NRS 21.120(2). Note that notice of the writ of garnishment is now required in the same manner and form as notices of execution. NRS 21.120(1). This procedure is found in NRS 31.070, and requires that the sheriff release the property unless the judgment creditor posts a bond in an amount double the value of the property levied on within seven days after written demand by the sheriff. This creates a difficult situation for the creditor who often lacks sufficient knowledge of the ownership of the property. This statute applies to real property as well as personalty. *Cooper v. Liebert,* 81 Nev. 341, 402 P.2d 989 (1965). The creditor's problems are compounded by the decision in *Wantz v. Redfield,* 74 Nev. 196, 326 P.2d 413 (1958), which held that a false third-party claim and receipt of the property by the third party was not a conversion and did not render the third-party liable to the levying creditor. However, in a later case citing the *Wantz* case, the court held that failure of the judgment creditor to post the bond following the making of the third-party claim merely gave possession to the third-party pending the court's determination of title. *Kulik v. Albers, Inc.,* 91 Nev. 134, 532 P.2d 603 (1975).

NRS 31.070(5) gives the creditor a right to a hearing on the third-party claim on ten days' notice. However, the right may be hollow if the third party has departed with the property or the court does not quickly hear the claim.

§ 2731. Foreign judgments.

A judgment of a United States Court sitting outside Nevada cannot be enforced without becoming a judgment of the United States Court sitting in Nevada. The judgment when final is easily made a judgment of the United States District Court sitting in Nevada by filing a certified copy of the judgment with the clerk of the United States District Court in Nevada. 28 U.S.C. § 1963. The clerk will then issue a writ of execution. As noted at § 2710, *supra,* recording a foreign judgment will not create a judgment lien; the foreign judgment must first be made a judgment of a Nevada court. Once entered, the judgment of the Nevada court can then be recorded.

Nevada has adopted the Uniform Enforcement of Foreign Judgments Act, NRS 17.330-17.400, which provides a shortened procedure for making a judgment of a federal court or other state court a Nevada judgment. The act also preserves the right to bring an independent action in Nevada on the foreign judgment if desired. NRS 17.390. An independent action should be considered if the prejudgment remedies of attachment or garnishment are appropriate. If diversity of citizenship exists and the amount involved exceeds $50,000, the independent action could be brought in the United States District Court in Nevada. The judgment of another state could thus be made a federal judgment enforceable in other states by registration.

Please note that a federal judgment that has been appealed cannot be filed with the clerk of another federal court until the appeal has been terminated. Thus, a judgment of a federal court outside of Nevada cannot be filed with the clerk of the federal court in Nevada for enforcement in Nevada until the appeal has concluded. However, there is no prohibition against filing suit in a Nevada state court on the foreign federal judgment that is under appeal. In this fashion the judgment could be enforced in Nevada even while on appeal, unless, of course, a stay order has been entered.

The procedure under the Uniform Enforcement of Foreign Judgments Act is as follows: The creditor must file an exemplified (not merely certified) copy of the foreign judgment with the clerk. It may be filed in any district court in Nevada. NRS 17.350. At the time of filing, the judgment creditor must also file an affidavit stating: (1) the name and last known post office address of both the judgment debtor and the judgment creditor; (2) that the foreign judgment is valid and enforceable; and (3) the extent to which the foreign judgment has been satisfied. NRS 17.360(1). If the creditor records a certified copy of the filed, foreign judgment, does it become a lien on real property? NRS Chapter 17 only forbids execution or other process from issuing for thirty days. Process is a writ or summons in the course of a judicial proceeding. See NRS 10.055 and 28.060. Thus, recording a certified copy of the filed, foreign judgment is not precluded by the language of NRS Chapter 17. The judgment creditor must also file a notice of filing. Copies of the notice, affidavit and exemplified foreign judgment are then served by mailing the same by certified mail, return receipt requested, to the judgment debtor and his attorney of record, if any, to the last known address of each. NRS 17.360(2).

After mailing the notice of filing, the judgment creditor may not obtain execution or other process for enforcement for a period of thirty days. NRS 17.360(3). However, the judgment creditor could, if he felt it appropriate under the circumstances of the case, obtain an ex parte writ of attachment. NRS 31.017(2).

Meanwhile, the judgment debtor may seek a stay of enforcement of the foreign judgment, providing: (1) an appeal is pending or will be taken from the foreign judgment; (2) a court of competent jurisdiction has previously entered a stay of execution; or (3) there are grounds upon which enforcement of the judgment could be stayed if the same judgment had been entered in Nevada. If the debtor proceeds under either of the first two grounds, he must show that he has furnished security for satisfaction of the judgment as required by the law of the sister state issuing the judgment. If he proceeds under the third ground, the court will require as a condition for stay that he post security for satisfaction of the judgment. NRS 17.380.

Once the thirty-day period has expired, the judgment creditor can enforce the foreign judgment in the same manner as enforcing a Nevada judgment. However, the exemplified judgment, once filed, is also subject to being set aside if grounds to set it aside exist under Nevada law. NRS 17.350.

§ 2732. Contempt and arrest.

Disobedience of an order of the master or court in supplementary proceedings is contempt. NRS 21.340. Disobedience of a subpoena or a court order directing attendance at supplementary proceedings is also contempt. NRS 22.010(3)-(4).

A court may issue a bench warrant for the arrest of a person guilty of contempt. NRS 22.040. The person guilty of contempt may be imprisoned until he performs the ordered act, if it is within his power to perform. NRS 22.110. If there is danger of the person absconding, NRS 21.280 also authorizes the arrest of a person to bring the person to court on supplementary proceedings.

Arrests may also be used in civil cases in certain limited actions involving fraudulent conduct or concealment of assets. NRS 31.470-31.550.

However, any arrest in a civil case must be approached with caution because of the very real danger of claims of false arrest and false imprisonment if the arrests are not absolutely correct. Additionally, claims of professional negligence could be brought against the attorney who represented the party causing the arrest.

In any cases where an arrest warrant could be issued, the party to be arrested should first be served by the sheriff with an order to show cause. This order, issued by the court, should direct the party to show cause why he should not be held in contempt on such grounds as may exist, and should also advise the person that if he fails to appear as ordered, a bench warrant for his arrest may be issued and that he may be arrested and imprisoned. If the party responds to the order to show cause, the entire matter can be heard by the court. If the party does not respond, a bench warrant can then be issued for the party's failure to respond to the order to show cause, thus bypassing any defects that may exist in the earlier proceedings. The proposed order to show cause should be first issued and served upon the judgment debtor. This process will take a little time and effort, but following this procedure will avoid many possibly serious problems.

CHRONOLOGY OF AN EXECUTION

1. Judgment entered.

2. Judgment enforceable if not stayed.

3. Judgment creditor records the judgment in each county in which the judgment debtor may own real property.

4. Judgment creditor initiates supplementary proceedings by:

a. Filing ex parte motion for order for supplementary proceedings and for appointment of a master to conduct the proceedings.
b. Obtaining ex parte order for supplementary proceedings.
c. Serving order upon judgment debtor and subpoenaing any desired witnesses and documents. Service should be made by the sheriff.
d. Conducting the supplementary examination.
e. Master makes his report to the court.

5. Judgment creditor causes a writ of execution to be levied by:

a. Preparing the form of the writ with all blanks filled in.
b. Having the writ signed by the clerk.
c. Delivering the original writ and several copies to the sheriff of the county in which the asset is located.
d. Giving written instructions to the sheriff containing the description and location of the property to be levied on.
e. Asking the sheriff to serve a writ of garnishment with the writ of execution if that is desired.
f. Giving notice of the execution.
g. Checking with the sheriff's office to determine the sheriff's progress and to determine the date and location of any sale.
h. Checking the sheriff's notice of any sale and the posting and publication of the notice.
i. Determining what to bid at the sale.
j. Attending and bidding at the sale.
k. If the purchaser, obtaining the sheriff's certificate of the sale.
l. Obtaining the proceeds of the sale from the sheriff.
m. Checking to see that the sheriff makes his written return of the sale and files the original writ of execution with the return attached with the clerk.
n. Starting the execution process again if the judgment has not been satisfied.

§ 2733. Stay of execution.

A stay of execution may be obtained in three ways: NRCP 62(a), NRCP 62(d) or NRAP 8. Rule 62(a) states that execution or other enforcement proceedings may begin immediately upon entry of the judgment unless the court directs otherwise on condition of posting security. The unsuccessful litigant should immediately request a stay pursuant to Rule 62(a) for the purpose of staying enforcement proceedings while the client attempts to obtain a supersedeas bond pursuant to Rule 62(d), attempts to obtain other security, or makes a motion for stay pending appeal pursuant to NRAP 8. The Nevada Supreme Court in *McCulloch v. Jeakins,* 99 Nev. 122, 659 P.2d 302 (1983), reversed a stay that was granted by the trial court since no supersedeas bond or other security was required. The

Court held that the bond or security in an amount less than the judgment may be ordered if there are unusual circumstances such as financial inability to post a supersedeas bond. If unusual circumstances exist, the court must set forth specific and substantial reasons for its order allowing the judgment debtor to post a bond or security in an amount less than the judgment. As a practical matter, the motion for stay should also request that the court set the amount of bond or other security that must be posted. EDCR 7.10 prohibits, except in emergencies, applications for such relief to any judge other than the judge who tried the matter.

When a supersedeas bond or other security is posted, all enforcement proceedings are stayed. Rule 62(d). What if the sheriff serves a writ of execution prior to the filing of the supersedeas bond? The common law rule is that any execution served prior to filing of a supersedeas bond may proceed. 4 Am. Jur. 2d, *Appeal and Error* § 372 (1962). NRS 1.030 states that unless superseded by statute or the Nevada Constitution, the common law applies in Nevada. Thus, an astute attorney will make a motion for stay as soon as possible after entry of judgment. Counsel should consider an oral motion for stay when the judge renders his decision. Although the Nevada Supreme Court is empowered to enter a stay order pursuant to NRAP 8, a motion to the Nevada Supreme Court will be denied unless counsel has previously requested such relief from the trial court.

Form 27A

DISTRICT COURT

CLARK COUNTY, NEVADA

JOHN DOE,

      Plaintiff,

vs.

FRED SMITH,   ) CASE NO.
) DEPT. NO.
      Defendant.) DOCKET NO.

STIPULATION AND CONFESSION OF JUDGMENT
(Prior to Suit)

DATE: _____ N/A _____
TIME: _____ N/A _____

1. FRED SMITH does hereby agree, stipulate, confess and authorize the entry of judgment against him in the sum of $50,000 plus interest at the rate of twelve percent (12%) per year from the date of entry and costs if and in the event he does not fully pay the above-mentioned sum pursuant to the payment schedule described below. Any payments received by Plaintiff prior to default of the below payment schedule shall be filed as partial satisfaction of this judgment.

2. This agreement, stipulation, confession and authorization for the entry of judgment is for a debt justly due to Plaintiff which arose from accrued attorney's fees for legal services rendered to Defendant Fred Smith prior to and during the lawsuit entitled Doe vs. Smith filed in the United States District Court for the District of Nevada. After consultation with independent counsel, Defendant Fred Smith expressly stipulates and agrees that the above-mentioned sum is a reasonable fee for the previously agreed upon fees earned by John Doe and these fees are presently due and owing.

3. Payment Schedule: Fred Smith shall deliver to Plaintiff the sum of $_____ by certified check made payable to Plaintiff on or before December 1, 1987. Fred Smith shall also deliver to Plaintiff the sum of $_____ by certified check made payable to Plaintiff on or before December 10, 1987. Each payment shall first be applied to the outstanding interest obligation with the remainder applied to the unpaid principal amount. If, and in the event Plaintiff does not receive the above-mentioned payments pursuant to the above-mentioned payment schedule, Fred Smith expressly agrees that upon the filing of this Stipulation and Confession of Judgment with the above Court, judgment may be entered against him by the Clerk of this Court as outlined above.

DATED this _____ day of October, 1987.

JOHN DOE
Address _____

FRED SMITH
Address: _____

_____

_____

STATE OF NEVADA   )
) ss:
COUNTY OF CLARK   )

FRED SMITH, being first duly sworn, deposes and says: That he is the person who executed the foregoing agreement, stipulation, confession and authorization and knows the contents thereof and the facts stated therein are understood by him and are true of his own knowledge.

_____

SUBSCRIBED and SWORN to before me
this _____ day of June, 1987.

_____
Notary Public in and for said
County and State

Form 27B

DISTRICT COURT

CLARK COUNTY, NEVADA

JOHN DOE,   )
)
            Plaintiff,   )
)
vs.   )
)
FRED SMITH,   )   CASE NO.
)   DEPT. NO.
            Defendant.   )   DOCKET NO.
_____)

STIPULATION AND ORDER FOR JUDGMENT

DATE: N/A
TIME: N/A

IT IS HEREBY STIPULATED by and between the parties by and through their respective counsel as follows:

1. Plaintiff is owed $8,188.67. Defendant disputes this amount. To settle this dispute, Plaintiff will waive all interest, attorney's fees and costs and accept payments of $500 per month, including interest, at the rate of eleven percent (11%) per year accruing on a balance of $6,000 which Defendant admits is presently due and owing to Plaintiff.

2. In consideration of the payment schedule mentioned herein, Plaintiff agrees not to pursue further action herein.

3. The first payment shall be due within five (5) days of execution of this Stipulation with monthly payments due on the same day of each successive month until the December, 1986, payment when the remaining unpaid principal and interest balance shall be entirely due and payable. Each payment shall be made by cashier's check or money order and delivered to the Plaintiff at the following address: E. S. Choir, 324 South Avenue, Las Vegas, Nevada 89101.

4. If Defendant fails to pay five days after written notice is mailed to Defendant's attorney at the address listed below, then on the sixth day, an ex parte judgment may be obtained with no further notice to the Defendant or his attorney for the sum of $8,188.67 plus interest at the rate of twelve percent (12%) per year from the 17th day of September, 1985, the date of filing the Complaint, minus any payments made by Defendant which payments shall first be applied to unpaid interest, then principal.

5. The judgment shall contain reasonable attorney's fees as set by the court, costs and prejudgment interest as mentioned above and the judgment shall accrue interest at the legal rate until all of said sums are satisfied. Each payment shall first be applied to the outstanding interest and then to the judgment which shall contain costs, fees and principal.

616

6. Defendant expressly waives findings of fact and conclusions of law in the above-mentioned judgment.

7. Upon payment in full, Defendant shall prepare and deliver to Plaintiff's attorney a stipulation dismissing this action with prejudice.

8. That trial in this matter presently set for June 16, 1986, be vacated.

DATED this _____ day of April, 1986.

E. S. CHOIR, LTD.   SMITH AND JONES

By _____   By _____

     E. S. Choir   Charles Jones

     Attorneys for Plaintiff   Attorneys for Defendant

     324 South Avenue   100 Las Vegas Blvd. South

     Las Vegas, Nevada 89101   Las Vegas, Nevada 89101

IT IS SO ORDERED this _____ day of April, 1986.

_____

                 DISTRICT COURT JUDGE

Form 27C

District Court
CLARK COUNTY, NEVADA

JOHN DOE,

                         Plaintiff,

—vs—

    FRED SMITH,

                        Defendant.

Case No. __A 123456__

Dept. No. __V__

Docket No. __H__

WRIT OF EXECUTION
XX Earnings   ☐ Other Property
☐ Earnings, Order of Support

THE STATE OF NEVADA TO THE SHERIFF OF CLARK COUNTY, GREETINGS:

On _____July 1._____, 19 _87_ a judgment, upon which there is due in United States Currency the following amounts, was entered in this action in favor of __Plaintiff JOHN DOE__ as judgment creditor and against ___Defendant FRED SMITH___ as judgment debtor. Interest and costs have accrued in the amounts shown. Any satisfaction has been credited first against total accrued interest and costs leaving the following net balance which sum bears interest at _legal_ % per annum, $ _.43_ per day from issuance of this writ to date of levy and to which sum must be added all commissions and costs of executing this Writ.

JUDGMENT BALANCE		AMOUNTS TO BE COLLECTED BY LEVY	
Principal	$1,000.00	NET BALANCE	$1,349.14
Pre-judgment Interest	-0-	Fee this Writ	
Attorney's fee	200.00	Garnishment fee	
Costs	106.00	Mileage	
JUDGMENT TOTAL	1,306.00	Levy fee	
Accrued Costs	-0-	Advertising	
Accrued Interest	43.14	Storage	
Less Satisfaction	-0-	Interest from	
		Date of Issuance	
NET BALANCE	$1,349.14	SUB-TOTAL	
		Commission	
		TOTAL LEVY	

NOW, THEREFORE, you are commanded to satisfy the judgment for the total amount due out of the following described personal property and if sufficient personal property cannot be found, then out of the following described real property:

_____
_____
_____
_____
_____

(See reverse side for exemptions which may apply)

ENFORCEMENT OF JUDGMENTS

EXEMPTIONS WHICH APPLY TO THIS LEVY
(Check appropriate paragraph and complete as necessary)

☐ Property Other Than Wages. The exemption set forth in NRS 21.090 or in other applicable Federal Statutes may apply. Consult an attorney.

☒ Earnings
The amount subject to garnishment and this writ shall not exceed for any one pay period the lessor of:
A. 25% of the disposable earnings due the judgment debtor for the pay period, or
B. the difference between the disposable earnings for the period and $100.50 per week for each week of the pay period.

☐ Earnings (Judgment or Order for Support)
A Judgment was entered for amounts due under a decree or order entered on _____, 19____, by the _____ for the support of _____ for the period from _____, 19____, through _____, 19____, in ____ installments of $_____ .

The amount of disposable earnings subject to garnishment and this writ shall not exceed for any one pay period: (check appropriate box)
☐ a maximum of 50 percent of the disposable earnings of such judgment debtor who is supporting a spouse or dependent child other than the dependent named above;
☐ a maximum of 60 percent of the disposable earnings of such judgment debtor who is not supporting a spouse or dependent child other than the dependent named above;
☐ plus an additional 5 percent of the disposable earnings of such judgment debtor if and to extent that the judgment is for support due for a period of time more than 12 weeks prior to the beginning of the work period of the judgment debtor during which the levy is made upon the disposable earnings.

NOTE: Disposable earnings are defined as gross earnings less deductions for Federal Income Tax Withholding, Federal Social Security Tax and Withholding for any State, County or City Taxes.

You are required to return this Writ from date of issuance not less than 10 days or more than 60 days with the results of your levy endorsed thereon.

Issued at direction of:

_____

E. S. Choir
Attorney for Plaintiff
324 South Avenue
Las Vegas, Nevada   89101 .

I hereby certify that I have this date returned the foregoing Writ of Execution with the results of the levy endorsed thereon.

JOHN MORAN, SHERIFF CLARK COUNTY

By: _____
    DEPUTY   Date

LORETTA BOWMAN, CLERK OF COURT

By: _____
    DEPUTY CLERK   Date

RETURN

_____ not satisfied
_____ satisfied in sum of $_____
_____ costs retained $_____
_____ commission retained $_____
_____ costs incurred $_____
_____ commission incurred $_____
_____ costs received $_____

REMITTED TO
JUDGMENT CREDITOR $_____

619

Form 27D

INSTRUCTIONS TO THE SHERIFF
CLARK COUNTY, NEVADA

JOHN DOE,
_____

_____
Plaintiff,
         vs.

FRED SMITH,
_____

_____
Defendant.

_____District_____	_____A 123456_____
Court (District, Justice, Municipal, Other)	Case No.
_____John Moran_____	$____200.00____
SHERIFF OF THE COUNTY OF CLARK	Storage Deposit or Fees Collected

You are hereby instructed to **levy, post and sell** by virtue of the accompanying Writ, in the above entitled suit, by following below instructions:

1. Levy, i.e. Seize the property listed on the Writ of Execution delivered to you with these instructions by taking the property into your possession and storing it until sale. The property is located at the Flamingo Hilton Parking lot either in the south side under ground parking, the High Rise tower, or the employee parking lot.

2. Post Notice of Sheriff's sale of Personal Property in three (3) public places in Las Vegas, NV, County of Clark not less than 5 nor more than 10 days before the sale.

3. Sell the personal property described in said Notice of Sheriff's Sale to the highest bidder on the _____ day of September, 1984, at the hour of 10:00 a.m. at Quality Towing, 1701 Western Avenue, Las Vegas, County of Clark Nevada.

Description: 1980 Volkswagon Van, License TBV 291, Color - Two tone, brown over white, VIN 22922136083

It is hereby acknowledged that vague or otherwise unenforceable instructions shall not be processed and will be returned to *the preparer for redrafting*. Bench Warrants must include DOB, and Social Security Number. Instructions to execute on vehicles must include VIN #, make, model, year, Lic. # and color. All other personal or real property attached or executed upon must have complete description. Advance money deposit is required with all instructions on property to be placed in storage or in custody of a keeper (NRS 31.065). Incomplete or unsigned instructions will not be accepted for service.

_____	_____E. S. CHOIR_____
Date	Signature of Attorney or Litigant
_____E. S. CHOIR, LTD._____	324 South Avenue, Las Vegas, NV 89101
Type or Print Name and Business	Address Telephone

8-34 Rev. 7-83

620

Form 27E

DISTRICT COURT
CLARK COUNTY, NEVADA

JOHN DOE,
 	
     Plaintiff,
 	
vs.
 	
FRED SMITH,
 	
     Defendant.
	)
	)
	)
	)
	)
	)
	) CASE NO.
	) DEPT. NO.
	) DOCKET NO.
	)

MOTION FOR SUPPLEMENTARY PROCEEDINGS

DATE:_____
TIME:_____

Plaintiff moves the court for an order requiring the defendant to appear before _____ as master herein at the time and place to be set by the court for examination supplementary to execution upon the ground that a judgment has been entered herein in favor of plaintiff and against defendant which remains unsatisfied and that the defendant is a resident of the County of Clark, in which county the supplementary proceedings are to be held.

DATED this _____ day of October, 1987.

E. S. CHOIR, LTD.

By: _____
     E. S. CHOIR
     Attorneys for Plaintiff
     324 South Avenue
     Las Vegas, Nevada 89101

POINTS AND AUTHORITIES

Judgment has been previously entered herein in favor of plaintiff and against defendant. The judgment remains unsatisfied, no satisfaction of the judgment having been made herein. NRS 21.270 authorizes the entry of the order requested by the foregoing motion.

621

DATED this ⎯⎯⎯⎯⎯⎯ day of October, 1987.

E. S. CHOIR, LTD.

By: ⎯⎯⎯⎯⎯⎯⎯⎯⎯⎯⎯⎯⎯⎯⎯⎯⎯⎯⎯⎯
     E. S. CHOIR
     Attorneys for Plaintiff
     324 South Avenue
     Las Vegas, Nevada 89101

Form 27F

DISTRICT COURT

CLARK COUNTY, NEVADA

JOHN DOE,   )
)
    Plaintiff,   )
)
vs.   )
)
FRED SMITH,   ) CASE NO.
) DEPT. NO.
    Defendant.) DOCKET NO.
_____)

ORDER FOR SUPPLEMENTARY PROCEEDINGS

DATE:_____
TIME:_____

Upon the motion for plaintiff and good cause appearing therefore, the defendant above-named is hereby ordered to appear before _____ herewith appointed master herein, for proceedings supplementary to execution, on the _____ day of _____, 19_____, at _____ o'clock ____.m. in Room _____ of the _____, County of Clark, State of Nevada to them and there answer upon oath concerning the property of the defendant and for such other proceedings as may there occur consistent with proceedings supplementary to execution.

DATED this _____ day of October, 1987.

_____
DISTRICT COURT CLERK

Submitted by,
E. S. CHOIR, LTD.

By: _____
    E. S. CHOIR
    Attorneys for Plaintiff
    324 South Avenue
    Las Vegas, Nevada 89101

Form 27G

DISTRICT COURT

CLARK COUNTY, NEVADA

JOHN DOE,	)
	)
Plaintiff,	)
	)
vs.	)
	)
FRED SMITH,	) CASE NO.
	) DEPT. NO.
Defendant.	) DOCKET NO.
_____	)

**EX PARTE MOTION FOR ORDER ALLOWING EXAMINATION
OF JUDGMENT DEBTOR**

DATE:_____
TIME:_____

Plaintiff John Doe, by and through his attorneys E. S. CHOIR, LTD., moves this Court for an Order requiring the above-named Defendant to appear before this Court and answer questions upon oath regarding his property.

This Motion is based upon the Points and Authorities attached hereto, the pleadings and papers on file herein and the argument of counsel at the hearing of this Motion.

DATED this _____ day of October, 1987.

E. S. CHOIR, LTD.

By: _____
E. S. CHOIR
Attorneys for Plaintiff
324 South Avenue
Las Vegas, Nevada 89101

POINTS AND AUTHORITIES

NRS 21.270 states:

A judgment creditor, at any time after the judgment is entered, is entitled to an order from the judge of the court requiring the judgment debtor to appear and answer upon oath concerning his property, before the judge or a master appointed by him at a time and place specified in the order, but no judgment debtor may be required to appear before a judge or master outside the county in which he resides when proceedings are taken under the provisions of this chapter.

624

Therefore, since a Judgment has been entered against the Defendant, a copy of which is attached hereto, labeled Exhibit 1 and incorporated herein by this reference, Plaintiff is entitled to an Order requiring the Defendant to appear before this Court to answer questions under oath regarding his property.

Form 27H

DISTRICT COURT

CLARK COUNTY, NEVADA

JOHN DOE,   )
)
      Plaintiff,   )
)
vs.   )
)
FRED SMITH,   )   CASE NO.
)   DEPT. NO.
      Defendant.   )   DOCKET NO.
_____)

ORDER ALLOWING EXAMINATION
OF JUDGMENT DEBTOR

DATE:_____
TIME:_____

It appearing to the Court by the Ex Parte Motion for Order Allowing Examination of Judgment Debtor that Judgment was entered against Defendant on September 14, 1985, and renewed by this Court's order on July 23, 1987, and good cause otherwise appearing, it is hereby

ORDERED that the Judgment Debtor, FRED SMITH, Defendant in the above action, is ordered to appear before the above entitled Court in Department V thereof, on the _____ day of _____, 1987, at the hour of 9:00 a.m., and on such further days as the Court shall name, to testify under oath concerning his property, and said Judgment Debtor is hereby forbidden in the meantime from disposing of any property not exempt from execution.

Failure to appear at the time and place stated above will result in a bench warrant being issued for your arrest.

DATED this _____ day of October, 1987.

_____
DISTRICT COURT JUDGE

Submitted by,
E. S. CHOIR, LTD.

By: _____

    E. S. CHOIR
    Attorneys for Plaintiff
    324 South Avenue
    Las Vegas, Nevada 89101

Form 27I

DISTRICT COURT

CLARK COUNTY, NEVADA

JOHN DOE,	)
	)
Plaintiff,	)
	)
vs.	)
	)
FRED SMITH,	) CASE NO.
	) DEPT. NO.
Defendant.	) DOCKET NO.
_____	)

**MOTION FOR ORDER FOR DELIVERY
OF STOCK CERTIFICATES**

DATE:_____
TIME:_____

Plaintiff moves the court for an order requiring the defendant to deliver to the Sheriff of Clark County, Nevada, for levy and sale pursuant to Writ of Execution issued or to be issued herein all stock certificates of the defendant in _____ Corporation upon the ground that the defendant is the owner of said stock certificates and that the same cannot be levied upon until in the possession of the Sheriff, that judgment has been previously entered herein in favor of plaintiff and against defendant, which judgment remains unsatisfied, and that plaintiff is entitled to have the Sheriff sell said certificates upon execution and apply the proceeds towards the satisfaction of said judgment.

DATED this _____ day of October, 1987.

E. S. CHOIR, LTD.

By: _____
E. S. CHOIR
Attorneys for Plaintiff
324 South Avenue
Las Vegas, Nevada 89101

POINTS AND AUTHORITIES

As is shown by the affidavit of plaintiff submitted herewith, defendant is the owner of stock certificates in _____ Corporation. As the securities in question are certificated, NRS 104.8317 and NRS 21.080 prohibit the levy or sale of such certificates in satisfaction of the judgment entered herein until the certificates have been taken into possession by the Sheriff and further authorize the court to issue orders assisting the Sheriff to obtain such possession.

627

DATED this ＿＿＿＿＿＿ day of October, 1987.

E. S. CHOIR, LTD.

By: ＿＿＿＿＿＿＿＿＿＿＿＿＿＿＿＿＿

E. S. CHOIR
Attorneys for Plaintiff
324 South Avenue
Las Vegas, Nevada 89101

Form 27J

DISTRICT COURT

CLARK COUNTY, NEVADA

JOHN DOE,
 	
      Plaintiff,
 	
vs.
 	
FRED SMITH,
 	
      Defendant.
	)
	)
	)
	)
	)
	)
	) CASE NO.
	) DEPT. NO.
	) DOCKET NO.
	)

AFFIDAVIT

DATE:_____
TIME:_____

STATE OF NEVADA   )
) ss:
COUNTY OF CLARK   )

_____, being first duly sworn, deposes and says:

1. That he is the plaintiff above-named.
2. That defendant is the owner of stock certificates in _____ Corporation.
3. That the judgment previously entered herein in favor of plaintiff and against defendant remains unsatisfied.

_____
JOHN DOE

SUBSCRIBED and SWORN to before me
this _____ day of October, 1987.

_____
Notary Public in and for said
County and State

Form 27K

DISTRICT COURT

CLARK COUNTY, NEVADA

JOHN DOE,
 	
    Plaintiff,
 	
vs.
 	
FRED SMITH,
 	
    Defendant.
	)
	)
	)
	)
	)
	)
	) CASE NO.
	) DEPT. NO.
	) DOCKET NO.
	)

ORDER FOR DELIVERY OF STOCK CERTIFICATES

DATE:_____
TIME:_____

Upon the motion and affidavit of plaintiff and good cause appearing therefor, defendant is herewith ordered and directed to immediately deliver to the Sheriff of Clark County, Nevada, all stock certificates which the defendant owns in _____ Corporation, which certificates shall then be sold by the Sheriff pursuant to a Writ of Execution issued or to be issued herein. The defendant shall not make any disposition of said certificates following receipt of this order other than to deliver the same to said Sheriff pursuant hereto.

DATED this _____ day of October, 1987.

_____
DISTRICT COURT JUDGE

Submitted by,
E. S. CHOIR, LTD.

By: _____
    E. S. CHOIR
    Attorneys for Plaintiff
    324 South Avenue
    Las Vegas, Nevada 89101

Form 27L

DISTRICT COURT
CLARK COUNTY, NEVADA

JOHN DOE,   )
)
      Plaintiff,   )
)
vs.   )
)
FRED SMITH,   ) CASE NO.
) DEPT. NO.
      Defendant.   ) DOCKET NO.
_____)

NOTICE OF MOTION AND MOTION FOR ORDER TO CHARGE PARTNERS INTEREST, APPOINT RECEIVER AND DIRECT SALE OF DEFENDANT'S PARTNERSHIP INTEREST

DATE:_____
TIME:_____

TO: FRED SMITH, Defendant; and
TO: CHARLES MORE, ESQ., his attorney:

PLEASE TAKE NOTICE that on the _____ day of November, 1987, at the hour of 9:00 a.m., or as soon thereafter as counsel may be heard in the above-mentioned Department of the Eighth Judicial District Court, County of Clark, City of Las Vegas, located in the Clark County Courthouse, 200 South Third Street, Las Vegas, Nevada, Plaintiff by and through its attorney E. S. Choir of the law firm of E. S. CHOIR, LTD., will move this court for an order charging the interest of Defendant as a partner in the partnership known as Sunrise Company, a Nevada partnership, with payment of the unsatisfied judgment against Defendant that was made and entered in this action and appointing a receiver with the necessary powers to collect Defendant's share of profits and of any other monies due to him from the partnership and giving the receiver the necessary powers to make all directions, accounts and inquiries that the Defendant could make, or that the circumstances of the case may require, and an order directing said interest in the partnership to be sold on the grounds set forth in the attached Points and Authorities, the pleadings, papers and documents on file herein and the argument of counsel and evidence presented at the hearing of this Motion.

DATED this _____ day of October, 1987.

E. S. CHOIR, LTD.

By: _____

    E. S. CHOIR
    Attorneys for Plaintiff
    324 South Avenue
    Las Vegas, Nevada 89101

POINTS AND AUTHORITIES

I. THIS COURT HAS AUTHORITY TO ENTER A CHARGING ORDER, APPOINT A RECEIVER AND ORDER THE SALE OF THE PARTNERSHIP INTEREST.

NRS 87.280 states:

1. On due application to a competent court by any judgment creditor of a partner, the court which entered the judgment, order or decree, or any other court, may charge the interest of the debtor partner with payment of the unsatisfied amount of such judgment debt with interest thereon; and may then or later appoint a receiver of his share of the profits, and of any other money due or to fall due to him in respect of the partnership, and make all other orders, directions, accounts and inquiries which the debtor partner might have made, or which the circumstances of the case may require.

2. The interest charged may be redeemed at any time before foreclosure, or in case of a sale being directed by the court may be purchased without thereby causing a dissolution:

(a) With separate property, by any one or more of the partners, or,

(b) With partnership property, by any one or more of the partners with the consent of all the partners whose interests are not so charged or sold.

3. Nothing in this chapter shall be held to deprive a partner of his right, if any, under the exemption laws, as regards his interest in the partnership.

The Nevada Supreme Court, in *Tupper v. Kroc,* 88 Nev. 146, 153, 494 P.2d 1275 (1972), held that pursuant to NRS 87.280(1), the District Court has authority to enter a charging order, appoint a receiver, and direct the sheriff of Clark County to sell the Defendant's interest in the partnership which is subject to the charging order. Plaintiff suggests that the sale by the sheriff of the partnership interest be conducted pursuant to NRS 21.130(2) which states:

2. *Other personal property.* In case of other personal property, by posting a similar notice in 3 public places of the township or city where the sale is to take place, not less than 5 nor more than 10 days before sale, and, in case of sale on execution issuing out of a district court, by the publication of a copy of the notice in a newspaper, if there be one in the county, at least twice, the first publication being not less than 10 days before date of sale.

Form 27M

DISTRICT COURT

CLARK COUNTY, NEVADA

JOHN DOE,	)
	)
Plaintiff,	)
	)
vs.	)
	)
FRED SMITH,	) CASE NO.
	) DEPT. NO.
Defendant.	) DOCKET NO.
_____	)

AFFIDAVIT IN SUPPORT OF CHARGING ORDER

DATE:_____
TIME:_____

STATE OF NEVADA	)
	) ss:
COUNTY OF CLARK	)

_____, being first duly sworn, deposes and says:

1. That he is the plaintiff above named.
2. That the judgment earlier entered herein in favor of plaintiff and against defendant remains unsatisfied.
3. That defendant is a partner in _____ Partnership.

_____
JOHN DOE

SUBSCRIBED and SWORN to before me
this _____ day of October, 1987.

_____
Notary Public in and for said
County and State

Form 27N

DISTRICT COURT

CLARK COUNTY, NEVADA

JOHN DOE,	)
	)
Plaintiff,	)
	)
vs.	)
	)
FRED SMITH,	) CASE NO.
	) DEPT. NO.
Defendant.	) DOCKET NO.
	)

ORDER CHARGING PARTNER'S INTEREST

DATE:_____

TIME:_____

Plaintiff's Motion for Order to Charge Partner's Interest, Appoint Receiver and Direct Sale of Defendant's Partnership Interest having come on for hearing on the _____ day of _____, 1987, with the Plaintiff appearing by and through his attorney E. S. Choir of the law firm of E. S. CHOIR, LTD., and the Court being fully advised in the premises and good cause appearing, therefore,

IT IS HEREBY ORDERED as follows:

1. That Plaintiff's Motion is hereby granted and that a charging order charging Defendant's interest in the Sunrise Company be entered;

2. That Plaintiff shall be appointed as receiver; and

3. That the sale be conducted on the after notice pursuant to NRS 21.130(2).

DATED this _____ day of October, 1987.

_____

DISTRICT COURT JUDGE

Submitted by,
E. S. CHOIR, LTD.

By: _____

    E. S. CHOIR
    Attorneys for Plaintiff
    324 South Avenue
    Las Vegas, Nevada 89101

Form 270

DISTRICT COURT
CLARK COUNTY, NEVADA

JOHN DOE,	)
	)
Plaintiff,	)
	)
vs.	)
	)
FRED SMITH,	) CASE NO.
	) DEPT. NO.
Defendant.	) DOCKET NO.
	)

SATISFACTION OF JUDGMENT

DATE: _____N/A_____
TIME: _____N/A_____

FOR AND IN CONSIDERATION of the sum of $42,000.00 (FORTY-TWO THOUSAND AND 00/100 DOLLARS) received from the Defendant by E. S. Choir as attorneys for Plaintiff, full satisfaction is hereby acknowledged of the Judgment entered in said action on 26th day of June, 1985, in favor of Plaintiff and against Defendant for the sum of $47,018.00, together with interest thereon at the rate of 12% per annum from August 24, 1984, and I do hereby authorize and direct the clerk of the above entitled Court to enter satisfaction of record of said Judgment.

DATED this _____ day of October, 1987.

E. S. CHOIR, LTD.

By: _____

E. S. CHOIR
Attorneys for Plaintiff
324 South Avenue
Las Vegas, Nevada 89101

STATE OF NEVADA	)
	) ss:
COUNTY OF CLARK	)

E. S. CHOIR has acknowledged to me that he is the attorney for the Plaintiff herein, has authority to acknowledge satisfaction of judgment as indicated above and that he executed the above Satisfaction of Judgment.

_____
Notary Public in and for said
County and State

CHAPTER 28

INJUNCTIVE RELIEF

Authors: Jean Parraguirre
Michael E. Pavlakis

§ 2801. Introduction and scope.

NRCP 65 sets forth the general procedure for obtaining injunctive relief. This chapter describes that procedure, citing the Nevada cases which have construed the rule. Where no Nevada authority exists, counsel should consult federal cases construing Fed. R. Civ. P. 65.

NRCP 65(f) states that Rule 65 is not applicable to "suits for divorce, alimony, separate maintenance or custody of children. In such suits, the court may make prohibitive or mandatory orders, with or without notice or bond, as may be just." These remedies are beyond the scope of this chapter. NRS 33.020, NRS 125.050 and local rules of practice (*e.g.,* EDCR 5.20) should be consulted in such cases. NRCP 65 does apply to all other civil actions even though injunctive relief is specifically authorized by statute.

It is beyond the scope of this chapter to detail all the circumstances wherein injunctive relief may be granted or denied. Traditional principles of equity jurisdiction should be consulted in every case. The more common prerequisites to injunctive relief are covered, however. Also, the more important Nevada cases are cited by subject matter.

Remedies for a wrongful injunction are discussed in § 2816, *infra,* and NRCP 65.1, the motion procedure for recovery against the security, is covered in § 2817, *infra.* Since NRCP 65.1 is applicable to any bond posted in a civil case, the procedure outlined in § 2817, *infra* may be used in situations other than a recovery against the security for a wrongful injunction.

§ 2802. Nature of remedy, definitions and principles of general application.

Article 6, section 6 of the Nevada Constitution specifically grants the district courts power to issue writs of injunction. Injunctive relief is exclusively an equitable remedy. *Sherman v. Clark,* 4 Nev. 138 (1868). An order granting such relief is an in personam order directed to a party (or in certain cases to a nonparty) forbidding certain conduct, permitting certain acts, or requiring that certain things be performed. The granting, refusing, or dissolving of injunctions or restraining orders is a matter of discretion. *Coronet Homes, Inc. v. Mylan,* 84 Nev. 435, 442 P.2d 901 (1968); *Thorn v. Sweeney,* 12 Nev. 251 (1877). Additionally, a party seeking the equitable remedy of injunctive relief must itself do equity. *Overhead Door Co. v. Overhead Door Corp.,* 103 Nev. 126, 734 P.2d 1233 (1987).

NRCP 65 recognizes three kinds of injunctive orders: (1) temporary restraining orders, (2) preliminary injunctions and (3) permanent injunctions. A temporary restraining order is an order granting injunctive relief issued on an emergency basis, valid only for a limited period of time — until the court can hear the matter at a motion for preliminary injunction. In circumstances of extreme urgency, a temporary restraining order may be granted ex parte if the requirements of NRCP 65(b) are met. A preliminary injunction, sometimes called an interlocutory injunction, may issue only after notice and an opportunity to be heard. It is interlocutory in nature because it preserves the status quo until the final determination of the respective claims of the litigants. A permanent injunction is the final injunction issued at the conclusion of the case.

The permanent injunction decree is not necessarily permanent in the sense that it can neither be modified nor dissolved; it is permanent only in the sense that it is intended as a final solution to the dispute rather than as a temporary or emergency one. No security need be posted upon the entry of a permanent injunction.

Where the party sought to be restrained is afforded sufficient notice to file affidavits or present evidence in opposition to an application for a temporary restraining order, the granting of the application should be termed a preliminary injunction. *See* § 2803, *infra.* Courts and counsel sometimes misname such orders. The distinction is important because while a preliminary injunction is an appealable order, a temporary restraining order granted without notice will expire in fifteen days (if not extended) and is not appealable. *See Sugarman Co. v. Morse Brothers,* 50 Nev. 191, 255 P. 1010 (1927).

A restraining order or injunction is binding only upon the parties to the action, their officers, agents, servants, employees, and attorneys, and upon those persons in active concert or participation with them who receive actual notice of the order by personal service or otherwise. NRCP 65(d). An act violating an injunction is valid unless the party that obtained the injunction properly attacks the validity of the act. *All Minerals Corp. v. Kunkle,* 105 Nev. 835, 784 P.2d 2 (1990). Only a party to the suit can move to dissolve an injunction. *State ex rel Garaventa Land & Livestock Co. v. Second Judicial District Court,* 61 Nev. 350, 128 P.2d 266 (1942).

As a matter of form, most injunctions forbid some conduct. These are called prohibitory injunctions. Occasionally, injunctions are issued requiring some affirmative act rather than forbidding it. These affirmative orders are called mandatory injunctions. At one time the use of mandatory injunctions fell into disfavor with the courts. Today such reluctance has disappeared. Mandatory injunctions are sanctioned to accomplish the restoration of the status quo. *Leonard v. Stoebling,* 102 Nev. 543, 728 P.2d 1358 (1986). Indeed the form and wording of injunctions is seldom important since an injunction prohibitory in form may operate in substance to compel a positive act either as a logical or practical necessity. *City of Reno v. Matley,* 79 Nev. 49, 378 P.2d 256 (1963).

Injunctive relief is an extremely powerful remedy. It can become an instrument of some danger in a free society. Frequently time does not permit a full hearing before a temporary restraining order is signed. Preliminary injunctions are often granted before the defendant has even filed a responsive pleading or before the parties have had the opportunity to conduct discovery. The judge must be extremely careful to ensure that traditional notions of fair play and substantial justice are not forgotten. The unusual requirements of Rule 65 exist in order that the judge considering injunctive relief be as fully educated on the subject as possible, within the amount of time permitted, before exercising this awesome power of restraint.

§ 2803. Temporary restraining orders.

As indicated in § 2802, *supra,* the purpose of a temporary restraining order is to prevent irreparable harm *temporarily,* that is, until the parties can be heard on a motion for a preliminary injunction. Of course one or more of the grounds for granting injunctive relief must exist. *See* § 2808, *infra.* Except under special circumstances, *see* § 2809, *infra,* the applicant must demonstrate that irreparable injury will occur before a hearing on a motion for a preliminary injunction can be held. *See* § 2809, *infra.* Plaintiff must also show a "reasonable probability" of success on the merits. *See* § 2811, *infra.*

Temporary restraining orders may be granted with or without notice. Where the party sought to be restrained is afforded sufficient written or oral notice to file affidavits or present evidence, the order granting the application should be a preliminary injunction. By its terms, Rule 65(b) does not apply to temporary restraining orders entered with notice. The better reasoned federal cases require, however, that the duration of such an order not exceed fifteen days (unless extended), and a hearing on an application for a preliminary injunction be conducted as though the order was entered without notice. If the court indicates that it is entering a temporary restraining order (after notice has been given) rather than a preliminary injunction, counsel will be wise to comply with all the requirements of Rule 65(b).

In the Eighth District, no temporary restraining order may be granted unless coupled with an order fixing the time for hearing a motion for preliminary injunction. EDCR 2.10(b).

A temporary restraining order may be granted without notice to the adverse party or his attorney only if: "(1) it clearly appears from specific facts shown by affidavit or by the verified complaint that immediate and irreparable injury, loss, or damage will result to the applicant before the adverse party or his attorney can be heard in opposition; and (2) the applicant's attorney certifies to the court in writing the efforts, if any, which have been made to give the notice and the reasons supporting his claim that notice should not be required." NRCP 65(b). *See State ex rel. Friedman v. Eighth Judicial District Court,* 81 Nev. 131, 399 P.2d 632 (1965); *Farnow v. Department 1 of Eighth Judicial District Court,* 64 Nev. 109, 178 P.2d 371 (1947).

If the temporary restraining order is granted ex parte, without notice to the defendant, the judge will have heard only the plaintiff's side of the story and even that will be in an abbreviated form, usually by way of affidavit or verified complaint. The defendant will not have had an opportunity to either attack the plaintiff's claim or set forth his own side of the story. The temporary restraining order without notice, therefore, is potentially a most dangerous instrument. If possible and reasonable, the court should require the applicant to give notice before considering the application. In the final analysis, courts should be reluctant to issue a temporary restraining order without notice unless the plaintiff makes a showing of a need for relief so compelling that the conduct sought to be restrained will be performed if any notice is given.

There are special requirements in the form of every order granting injunctive relief. *See* § 2807, *infra.* In addition, "[e]very temporary restraining order granted without notice shall be endorsed with the date and hour of issuance; shall be filed forthwith in the clerk's office and entered of record; shall define the injury and state why it is irreparable and why the order was granted without notice ...." NRCP 65(b). Written notice of the entry of the order should be given not later than the end of the next judicial day. DCR 17(1).

Before the temporary restraining order is even *filed,* security must be posted or the order is void. *See* § 2806, *infra.*

When notice can be given prior to the entry of a temporary restraining order, the court may direct the applicant to give reasonable oral notice. The length of the notice will vary depending upon the urgency of the circumstances, from a few minutes to many days. In the exercise of its equitable powers, the court could insist upon written notice if the interval will be more than twenty-four hours.

If the temporary restraining order is entered without notice, it expires

> by its terms within such time after entry, not to exceed 15 days, as the court fixes, unless within the time so fixed the order, for good cause shown, is extended for a like period or unless the party against whom the order is directed consents that it may be extended for a longer period. The reasons for the extension shall be entered of record. NRCP 65(b).

This provision precludes an indefinite temporary restraining order. The order must be reviewed by the court within fifteen days. While it may be extended by the court for up to an additional fifteen days, it clearly cannot be extended indefinitely and the court must consider the matter at a hearing on plaintiff's application for a preliminary injunction within the original fifteen days or within an extension authorized by the rule. While no Nevada law exists on this point, some federal cases have held that the original term of the temporary restraining order plus one extension for a like period is the longest that a temporary restraining order can be operative. *See* Comment, *The Duration of Temporary Restraining Orders in Federal Court,* 12 U. Balt. L. Rev. 276 (1983). Under the federal rule, the term of a temporary restraining order is ten days which may be extended for a like period once. If Nevada adopts this construction of the federal rule, a temporary restraining order in Nevada will be valid only for thirty days unless extended by consent of the parties.

When a temporary restraining order is granted without notice, the application for a preliminary injunction is entitled to priority on the court's calendar.

> In case a temporary restraining order is granted without notice, the motion for a preliminary injunction shall be set down for hearing at the earliest possible time and takes precedence of all matters except older matters of the same character; and when the motion comes on for hearing the party who obtained the temporary restraining order shall proceed with the application for preliminary injunction and, if he does not do so, the court shall dissolve the temporary restraining order. NRCP 65(b).

A party against whom a temporary restraining order has issued without notice is entitled to be heard on an emergency basis.

On 2 days' notice to the party who obtained the temporary restraining order without notice or on such shorter notice to that party as the court may prescribe, the adverse party may appear and move its dissolution or modification and in that event the court shall proceed to hear and determine such motion as expeditiously as the ends of justice require. NRCP 65(b).

The rule does not indicate how notice of a motion to dissolve the temporary restraining order should be given. Telephonic notice might be sufficient, depending upon the circumstances. Should the court decide on such an application that the temporary restraining order without notice was granted improvidently, the court should dissolve the temporary restraining order and set the matter for hearing on a motion for preliminary injunction.

§ 2804. Preliminary injunctions.

A preliminary injunction to preserve the status quo is normally available upon a showing that the party seeking it enjoys a reasonable probability of success on the merits and that the defendant's conduct, if allowed to continue, will result in irreparable harm for which compensatory damage is an inadequate remedy. *Pickett v. Comanche Construction Co.*, 108 Nev. 422, 836 P.2d 42 (1992); *Dixon v. Thatcher*, 103 Nev. 414, 742 P.2d 1029 (1987). *See* §§ 2808-2812, *infra*. Sometimes referred to as an interlocutory injunction, a preliminary injunction is usually granted on an emergency basis after notice before trial. It is designed to protect the applicant from irreparable injury and to preserve the status quo pending final judgment. *Ottenheimer v. Real Estate Division*, 91 Nev. 338, 535 P.2d 1284 (1975); *Memory Gardens of Las Vegas, Inc. v. Pet Ponderosa Memorial Gardens, Inc.*, 88 Nev 1, 492 P.2d 123 (1972). *Berryman v. International Brotherhood of Electrical Workers*, 82 Nev. 277, 416 P.2d 387 (1966).

Generally, the grant or denial of a preliminary injunction is a question addressed to the discretion of the district court. *Number One Rent-A-Car v. Ramada Inns, Inc.*, 94 Nev. 779, 587 P.2d 1329 (1978); *Boyes v. Valley Bank*, 101 Nev. 287, 701 P.2d 1008 (1985). Because such injunctive relief is not available in the absence of actual or threatened injury, loss or damage, the party seeking the preliminary injunction must prove the "reasonable probability" that real injury will occur before a trial on the merits can be held. *Berryman v. International Brotherhood of Electrical Workers*, 82 Nev. 277, 416 P.2d 387 (1966); *Sherman v. Clark*, 4 Nev. 138 (1868). Public officers can only be enjoined from acts that exceed their authority or unlawful acts. *City Council of Reno v. Reno Newspapers, Inc.,* 105 Nev. 886, 784 P.2d 974 (1989).

No preliminary injunction may issue without notice to the adverse party. NRCP 65(a)(1). While that rule does not indicate the amount of notice that should be given, NRCP 6(d) requires five days' notice unless a different period is fixed by order of the court. Of course, local rules must also be complied with also. In the Eighth District, a motion for preliminary injunction must be made upon the notice required by EDCR 2.20 unless an order fixes a shorter notice. *See* EDCR 2.10.

The hearing on the motion for a preliminary injunction may be relatively informal. Like any other pre-trial motion, the court may decide the motion on the affidavits or may permit testimony. Absent testimony or exhibits establishing the material allegations of the complaint, an application for injunctive relief should be denied. *Coronet Homes, Inc. v. Mylan,* 84 Nev. 435, 442 P.2d 901 (1968).

Either before or after the commencement of the hearing of an application for a preliminary injunction, the court may order the trial of the action on the merits to be advanced and consolidated with the hearing of the application. NRCP 65(a)(2); *see* § 2805, *infra.*

Special requirements exist for the form of every order granting injunctive relief. Section 2807, *infra,* should be consulted before a preliminary injunction is drafted.

Before the preliminary injunction is *filed,* security must be posted or the order will be void. *See* § 2806, *infra.*

A preliminary injunction may be modified at any time whenever the ends of justice require such action. *Hansen v. Edwards,* 83 Nev. 189, 426 P.2d 792 (1967).

§ 2805. Advancement of the trial on the merits.

"Before or after the commencement of the hearing of an application for a preliminary injunction, the court may order the trial of the action on the merits to be advanced and consolidated with the hearing of the application." NRCP 65(a)(2). The rule is clear that either party may request consolidation and the court may order it on its own initiative. While a written motion to consolidate is permissible, it is not required. Service of a written motion will solve most problems of notice, however.

It is important that the parties be afforded some notice of the court's intention to consolidate the trial of the action with the hearing on the application for a preliminary injunction. In *Zupancic v. Sierra Vista Recreation, Inc.,* 97 Nev. 187, 625 P.2d 1177 (1981), the Supreme Court considered the issue of when the trial court must give notice to the parties before ordering consolidation. In that case, following the presentation of evidence at the hearing on the motion for a preliminary injunction, the trial court consolidated the hearing with the trial on the merits and entered a final decree. In affirming the trial court, the Supreme Court stated:

> We agree with those cases standing for the proposition that the preferred manner of consolidation would include advance notice to the parties, but the mere fact that a party may be surprised that his day in court has arrived is alone not a sufficient basis for reversal; prejudice must also be shown....
> This burden properly rests upon the appellant Zupancic, who must show that the consolidation affected his "substantial rights" ....
> *Zupancic, supra,* 97 Nev. at 191, 625 P.2d at 1180.

Advancing the trial of the action to the time of the application for the preliminary injunction will frequently save a great deal of time. Many suits requesting injunctive relief can be decided on a single issue without substantial discovery. However, it is an abuse of discretion for the district court to enter a permanent injunction without first conducting a "full and fair evidentiary hearing." *Housewright v. Simmons,* 102 Nev. 610, 729 P.2d 499 (1986), *overruled on other grounds, Las Vegas Novelty, Inc. v. Fernandez,* 106 Nev. 113, 787 P.2d 772 (1990).

Even if consolidation is not ordered, any evidence received at the hearing on the application for the preliminary injunction must be transcribed and will become a part of the record and need not be repeated at the time of the trial. *See* NRCP 65(a)(2).

If counsel intends to request a jury trial, the demand should be filed before an order of consolidation. *See Memory Gardens of Las Vegas, Inc. v. Bunker Brothers Mortuary, Inc.,* 91 Nev. 344, 535 P.2d 1293 (1975).

§ 2806. Security.

NRCP 65(c) provides:

> No restraining order or preliminary injunction shall issue except upon the giving of security by the applicant, in such sum as the court deems proper, for the payment of such costs and damages as may be incurred or suffered by any party who is found to have been wrongfully enjoined or restrained. No such security shall be required of the State or of an officer or agency thereof.

Security was required by statute prior to the adoption of the Nevada Rules of Civil Procedure in 1953. *Shelton v. Second Judicial District Court,* 64 Nev. 487, 185 P.2d 320 (1947), construing that earlier statute, held that "[w]here a bond is required by a statute before the issuance of an injunction, it must be exacted or the order will be absolutely void." Shelton, *supra* at 484. In *State ex rel. Friedman v. Eighth Judicial District Court,* 81 Nev. 131, 399 P.2d 632 (1965), the supreme court reaffirmed the holding of Shelton and applied it to the provisions of NRCP 65(c). The Nevada Supreme Court has consistently held that an order granting a temporary restraining order must contain a provision for a bond. If no provision for bond has been made, the order is void. *State ex rel. Hersh v. First Judicial District Court,* 86 Nev. 73, 464 P.2d 783 (1970); *Brunzell Construction Co. v. Harrah's Club,* 81 Nev. 414, 404 P.2d 902 (1965).

The court in *Friedman* also quoted from *State ex rel. Culinary Workers Union, Local No. 226 v. Eighth Judicial District Court,* 66 Nev. 166, 207 P.2d 990 (1949), where, inter alia, the court stated, "The law requires that the bond be filed *before* the order is made, and the fact that the bond was procured about the time the order was issued and was later filed under a nunc pro tunc order does not cure the defect." *State ex rel. Culinary Workers Union, Local No. 226, supra,* at 183 (emphasis added). Therefore, the security should be posted with the clerk of the court before the signed temporary restraining order or preliminary injunction is filed.

The amount of the security to be required is left to the sound discretion of the court. The purpose of the security is to enable the restrained or enjoined party to secure indemnification for his losses in the event it is determined that he was wrongfully enjoined or restrained. In determining the amount of the security to be ordered, the court should consider the potential for loss in the event that the court later determines that the restraint is unlawful, including a reasonable attorney's fee which the defendant may have to incur to dissolve the injunction.

Upon application, the court may increase the amount of the security during the pendency of the injunction. *Tracy v. Capozzi,* 98 Nev. 120, 642 P.2d 591 (1982).

Sections 2816 and 2817, *infra* describe the procedure for obtaining a recovery against the bond for wrongful injunction.

§ 2807. Form of order.

Every temporary restraining order, every preliminary injunction and every permanent injunction "shall set forth the reasons for its issuance; shall be specific in terms; shall describe in reasonable detail, and not by reference to the complaint or other document, the act or acts sought to be restrained ...." NRCP 65(d). Compliance with these requirements is necessary for proper review on appeal. Injunctive orders not complying with the rule will be carefully scrutinized. Any temporary restraining order or preliminary injunction issued by a trial judge in Nevada is *void,* not merely voidable, where the order lacks both a statement of reasons and fails to describe the acts to be restrained with adequate specificity. However, where only the statement of reasons is lacking, this does not necessarily invalidate a permanent injunction if the reasons for the injunction are readily apparent elsewhere in the record and are sufficiently clear to permit meaningful appellate review. *Las Vegas Novelty, Inc. v.*

Fernandez, 106 Nev. 113, 787 P.2d 772 (1990). The distinction between "void" and "voidable" is important because a void order may be violated with impunity, without fear of sanctions, whereas a voidable order must first be set aside.

The requirement that the order be specific in its terms and describe in reasonable detail the act or acts sought to be restrained is important for another reason. It should be so clear and certain that a party may readily know what he is being restrained from doing and that he disregards it at his peril. *Kress v. Corey,* 65 Nev. 1, 189 P.2d 352 (1948). In *Maheu v. Hughes Tool Co.,* 88 Nev. 592, 503 P.2d 4 (1972), the court found a preliminary injunction vague and ambiguous, thus rendering the order void, where the order required the defendant to return to the plaintiff "all books, documents, records and communications of plaintiff or pertaining directly or indirectly to the business operations or affairs of plaintiff, including all copies or other reproductions of same, and all other property belonging to plaintiff, as may be in the possession, custody or control of defendants directly or indirectly," *Maheu, supra* at 594 (emphasis omitted). Accordingly, counsel should exercise extreme caution in preparing temporary restraining orders and injunctions.

A temporary restraining order granted pursuant to NRCP 65(b) must also be: (1) endorsed with the date and hour of issuance (this is usually filled in by the judge in a blank left at the conclusion of the form of order prepared by the applicant); (2) filed forthwith in the clerk's office and entered of record (or filed with the judge if the office of the clerk is closed); (3) define the injury and state why it is irreparable and why the order was granted without notice. An order that fails to meet any of these requirements would be void. *See State ex rel. Friedman v. Eighth Judicial District Court,* 81 Nev. 131, 399 P.2d 632 (1965).

A motion for a preliminary injunction must accompany an application for a temporary restraining order if the latter is issued ex parte. *State ex rel. Friedman v. Eighth Judicial District Court,* 81 Nev. 131, 399 P.2d 632 (1965).

In the Eighth District, a temporary restraining order must fix the time within which the restraining order, all pleadings, affidavits and briefs in support of the restraining order, and the motion for preliminary injunction shall be served upon the adverse party, and the time for filing the opposition, counter-affidavits and briefs. EDCR 2.10(c). No temporary restraining order may be granted unless coupled with an order fixing the time for hearing a motion for preliminary injunction. EDCR 2.10(b).

§ 2808. Considerations in granting injunctive relief.

An infinite number of possible cases exist where a court might be authorized to enter a temporary restraining order or grant injunctive relief. Each case is different and the facts must be examined in light of any applicable case authority or statute authorizing such relief. General principles of equity must always be considered. Rule 65 does not affect the substantive principles governing the availability of injunctive relief.

NRS 33.010 outlines, generally, the basic considerations that are involved in deciding whether to grant injunctive relief:

> An injunction may be granted in the following cases:
> 1. When it shall appear by the complaint that the plaintiff is entitled to the relief demanded, and such relief or any part thereof consists in restraining the commission or continuance of the act complained of, either for a limited period or perpetually.
> 2. When it shall appear by the complaint or affidavit that the commission or continuance of some act, during the litigation, would produce great or irreparable injury to the plaintiff.
> 3. When it shall appear, during the litigation, that the defendant is doing or threatens, or is about to do, or is procuring or suffering to be done, some act in violation of the plaintiff's rights respecting the subject of the action, and tending to render the judgment ineffectual.

While no precise burden of proof must be met by a party seeking injunctive relief, analysis of the cases reveals four factors, either individually or collectively, which courts most often discuss: (1) the threat of irreparable harm; (2) the relative interests of the parties; (3) plaintiff's likelihood of success on the merits; and (4) the interest of the public. The first and third considerations are most often cited. *E.g., Sobol v. Capital Management Consultants, Inc.,* 102 Nev. 444, 726 P.2d 335 (1986). "A preliminary injunction is available upon a showing that the party seeking it enjoys a reasonable probability of success on the merits and that the defendant's conduct, if allowed to continue, will result in irreparable harm for which compensatory damages is an inadequate remedy." All four considerations are discussed in §§ 2809, 2810, 2811 and 2812, *infra.* Section 2813 lists many Nevada cases by subject matter to aid the court or counsel in determining whether the facts of a particular case warrant the granting of an application for injunctive relief.

§ 2809. — Threat of irreparable injury.

In the early case of *Champion v. Sessions,* 1 Nev. 478 (1865), Chief Justice Lewis said,

> when a complete and adequate remedy can be had at law, it is settled that a court of equity will not interfere; but on the other hand, if the injury is likely to be irreparable, or if the defendant be insolvent, equity will always interpose its power to protect a person from a threatened injury.

Champion, supra, at 483. The writ will not issue upon the bare possibility of injury or upon any unsubstantial or unreasonable apprehension of it. *Sherman v. Clark,* 4 Nev. 138 (1868). Further, an injunction ordinarily will not redress wrongs already committed. *Sherman, supra; see also Berryman v. International Brotherhood of Electrical Workers,* 82 Nev. 277, 416 P.2d 387 (1966).

Cases involving completed acts are diverse. However, several cases have approved injunctions granted for the purpose of restoring the parties to status quo even though the damage appears to have been done. *Memory Gardens of Las Vegas, Inc. v. Pet Ponderosa Memorial Gardens, Inc.,* 88 Nev. 1, 492 P.2d 123 (1972) (mandatory injunction requiring landlord to restore use of water supply to pet cemetery after grass was dead); *City of Reno v. Matley,* 79 Nev. 49, 378 P.2d 256 (1963) (mandatory injunction requiring city to reconstruct roadway with access to abutting properties).

If the plaintiff has an adequate remedy at law, the harm is not "irreparable." *Number One Rent-A-Car v. Ramada Inns, Inc.,* 94 Nev. 779, 587 P.2d 1329 (1978); *State ex rel. Mongolo v. Second Judicial District Court,* 46 Nev. 410, 211 P. 105 (1923). In *Conley v. Chedic,* 6 Nev. 222 (1870), the court stated:

> Equity will not take jurisdiction or interpose its powers when there is a full, complete and adequate remedy in the ordinary course of law; that is, when the wrong complained of may be fully compensated in damages, which can easily be ascertained, and it is not shown that a judgment at law cannot be satisfied by execution. *Conley, supra,* at 224.

On the other hand, if the adequacy of the remedy at law is unclear, injunctive relief should be granted. *Ripps v. City of Las Vegas,* 72 Nev. 135, 297 P.2d 258 (1956) (city was restrained from demolishing unsafe building while lessees sought to prove that landlord could repair the premises and avoid demolition). Further, the existence of a remedy at law will not preclude an injunction where the equitable remedy is "far superior" to the legal remedy. *Nevada Escrow Service v. Crockett,* 91 Nev. 201, 533 P.2d 471 (1975) (foreclosure of trust deeds would be enjoined until issue of payment was resolved). Also, the existence of a legal remedy will not preclude an injunction where the damages are difficult to calculate. *Harmon v. Tanner Motor Tours of Nevada, Ltd.,* 79 Nev. 4, 377 P.2d 622 (1963) (mandatory injunction requiring Board of County Commissioners to execute contract awarding exclusive franchise where "the legal remedy is deemed inadequate primarily because of the difficulty in fairly determining damage").

One need not demonstrate irreparable injury if vested property rights are to be enforced. *Gladstone v. Gregory,* 95 Nev. 474, 596 P.2d 491 (1979) (enforcing restrictive covenant by ordering plaintiff's neighbor to remove second story structure). Indeed, the loss of real property rights generally results in irreparable harm. *Dixon v. Thatcher,* 103 Nev. 414,

742 P.2d 1029 (1987); *Dickstein v. Williams,* 93 Nev. 605, 571 P.2d 1169 (1977) (enforcing restrictive covenant by requiring removal of home addition); and *Leonard v. Stoebling,* 102 Nev. 534, 728 P.2d 1308 (1986) (view from home is unique asset; injunction issued to preserve view).

The requirement that plaintiff show irreparable injury is also relaxed when plaintiff's water supply is endangered. *Czipott v. Fleigh,* 87 Nev. 496, 489 P.2d 681 (1971); *Robison v. Bate,* 78 Nev. 501, 376 P.2d 763 (1962).

Prospective loss of employment is regarded as an irreparable injury. *Ottenheimer v. Real Estate Division,* 91 Nev. 338, 535 P.2d 1284 (1975). Furthermore, equity will restrain the publication of false and defamatory communications where the restraint is essential to preserve a business. *Guion v. Terra Marketing of Nevada, Inc.,* 90 Nev. 237, 523 P.2d 847 (1974).

The legislature has authorized the granting of injunctive relief under certain circumstances. For example, personal property may be protected by restraining order pending a hearing on an order to show cause why a writ of possession should not issue. NRS 31.859. An injunction will prevent the grazing of livestock on certain federal lands. NRS 565.270. These statutes are sufficient authority for the granting of injunctive relief without a showing of irreparable harm. *Nevada Real Estate Commission v. Ressel,* 72 Nev. 79, 81, 294 P.2d 1115 (1956) ("Where the statute provides for injunctive relief, no invasion of a property right need be shown, as the statute effects an enlargement of the equity powers of the court"); *see also Itcaina v. Marble,* 56 Nev. 420, 55 P.2d 625, 630 (1936) ("It is well settled that the state, in the exercise of its police powers, may authorize courts of equity in proper cases to prohibit by injunction the violation of the provisions of an act of the legislature, though no property right is involved."); *Terrie v. City of Las Vegas,* 96 Nev. 912, 620 P.2d 864 (1980) (an injunction is a proper remedy when there is a zoning violation); *Smith v. City of Las Vegas,* 80 Nev. 220, 391 P.2d 505 (1964) (a city may enjoin a violation of a zoning ordinance).

§ 2810. — Weighing the relative interests of the parties.

The granting, refusing or dissolving of injunctions or restraining orders is a matter of discretion. *Coronet Homes, Inc. v. Mylan,* 84 Nev. 435, 442 P.2d 901 (1968). Probably the most important consideration of the trial judge in deciding how to exercise that discretion is the relative interests of the parties — how much damage will the plaintiff really suffer if the restraint is denied versus the hardship to the defendant if it is granted. *Home Finance Co. v. Balcom,* 61 Nev. 301, 127 P.2d 389 (1942). *See also Ottenheimer v. Real Estate Division,* 91 Nev. 338, 535 P.2d 1284 (1975) where, without deciding the constitutionality of a statute which required subdivision salesmen to be licensed real estate brokers or salesmen, the supreme court stated: "we note that denying a preliminary injunction would force appellants to leave established intrinsically lawful employment, thereby sustaining substantial irreparable injury if the legislation is indeed unconstitutional. By comparison, maintaining the status quo pending final judgment will impose small burden on the state." *But see Gladstone v. Gregory*, 95 Nev. 474, 596 P.2d 491 (1979) (equitable principle of relative hardship is not available to a party who proceeds with knowledge that he is acting contrary to the vested rights of another).

§ 2811. — Plaintiff's likelihood of success.

While the issue is not always addressed in the cases, a temporary restraining order or preliminary injunction to preserve the status quo clearly is available only upon a showing that the party seeking it enjoys a "reasonable probability" of success on the merits. *Christensen v. Chromalloy American Corp.*, 99 Nev. 34, 656 P.2d 844 (1983); *Republic Entertainment, Inc. v. Clark County Liquor & Gaming Licensing Board*, 99 Nev. 811, 672 P.2d 634 (1983); *Number One Rent-A-Car v. Ramada Inns, Inc.*, 94 Nev. 779, 587 P.2d 1329 (1978); *Dixon v. Thatcher*, 103 Nev. 414, 742 P.2d 1029 (1987).

§ 2812. — The interest of the public.

Occasionally, the public will have an interest in the outcome of private litigation and the court may consider that interest in granting or in refusing to grant injunctive relief. *Ellis v. McDaniel*, 95 Nev. 455, 596 P.2d 222 (1979) (a post-employment restrictive covenant contained in the employment agreement of a physician would not be enforced where the services of the physician were needed in a rural area. "[T]he public interest in retaining the services of the specialist is greater than the interest in protecting the integrity of the contract provision to its outer limits.").

§ 2813. — Nevada cases.

The following list of Nevada cases is designed to aid counsel's search in locating authority for or against the granting of injunctive relief. The cases are listed by subject matter. Since the circumstances of each case are different, no indication is given as to whether or not the injunctive relief requested was granted.

1. Administrative Proceedings.

State v. Glusman, 98 Nev. 412, 651 P.2d 639 (1982); *Cummings v. City of Las Vegas*, 88 Nev. 479, 499 P.2d 650 (1972); *Eagle Thrifty*

Drugs & Market, Inc. v. Hunter Lake P.T.A., 85 Nev. 162, 451 P.2d 713 (1969); *State Gaming Control Board v. Eighth Judicial District Court,* 82 Nev. 38, 409 P.2d 974 (1966); *Public Service Commission v. Eighth Judicial District Court,* 61 Nev. 245, 123 P.2d 237 (1942); *Lakeside Community Hospital, Inc. v. Levenson,* 101 Nev. 777, 710 P.2d 727 (1985).

2. Advertising.

Coronet Homes, Inc. v. Mylan, 84 Nev. 435, 442 P.2d 901 (1968).

3. Arrest.

Cummings v. City of Las Vegas, 88 Nev. 479, 499 P.2d 650 (1972).

4. Attachment.

Aronoff v. Katleman, 75 Nev. 424, 345 P.2d 221 (1959).

5. Business Interference.

Sobol v. Capital Management Consultants, Inc., 102 Nev. 444, 726 P.2d 335 (1986).

6. Covenant Not to Compete.

Las Vegas Novelty, Inc. v. Fernandez, 106 Nev. 113, 787 P.2d 772 (1990); *Ellis v. McDaniel,* 95 Nev. 455, 596 P.2d 222 (1979); *Hansen v. Edwards,* 83 Nev. 189, 426 P.2d 792 (1967).

7. Criminal Proceedings.

Sheriff of Lander County v. Nevada National Bank, 90 Nev. 90, 518 P.2d 602 (1974); *Cummings v. City of Las Vegas,* 88 Nev. 479, 499 P.2d 650 (1972).

8. Defamation.

Guion v. Terra Marketing of Nevada, Inc., 90 Nev. 237, 523 P.2d 847 (1974); *Coronet Homes, Inc. v. Mylan,* 84 Nev. 435, 442 P.2d 901 (1968).

9. Distributorship.

Overhead Door Co. v. Overhead Door Corp., 103 Nev. 126, 734 P.2d 1233 (1987); *DeLuca Importing Co. v. Buckingham Corp.,* 90 Nev. 158, 520 P.2d 1365 (1974).

10. Elections.

Caine v. Robbins, 61 Nev. 416, 131 P.2d 516 (1942); *Cirac v. Lander County,* 95 Nev. 723, 602 P.2d 1012 (1979); *Lauritzen v. Casady,* 70 Nev. 136, 261 P.2d 145 (1953).

11. Employment.

Ottenheimer v. Real Estate Division, 91 Nev. 338, 535 P.2d 1284 (1975).

12. Enforcement of Judgments.

Franklin v. Bartsas Realty, Inc., 95 Nev. 559, 598 P.2d 1147 (1979).

13. False Statement.

Guion v. Terra Marketing of Nevada, Inc., 90 Nev. 237, 523 P.2d 847 (1974); *Coronet Homes, Inc. v. Mylan,* 84 Nev. 435, 442 P.2d 901 (1968); *Landex, Inc. v. State ex rel. List,* 94 Nev. 469, 582 P.2d 786 (1978).

14. Foreclosure.

Pickett v. Comanche Construction, Inc., 108 Nev. 422, 836 P.2d 42 (1992); *Dixon v. Thatcher,* 103 Nev. 414, 742 P.2d 1029 (1987); *Boyes v. Valley Bank of Nevada,* 101 Nev. 287, 701 P.2d 1008 (1985); *Nevada Escrow Service, Inc. v. Crockett,* 91 Nev. 201, 533 P.2d 471 (1975); *Mahaffey v. Investor's National Security Co.,* 103 Nev. 615, 747 P.2d 890 (1987).

15. Franchise.

DeLuca Importing Co. v. Buckingham Corp., 90 Nev. 158, 520 P.2d 1365 (1974); *Harmon v. Tanner Motor Tours of Nevada, Inc.,* 79 Nev. 4, 377 P.2d 622 (1963); *Dixon v. Thatcher,* 103 Nev. 414, 742 P.2d 1029 (1987).

16. Gaming.

State of Nevada v. Glusman, 98 Nev. 412, 651 P.2d 639 (1982); *State Gaming Control Board v. Eighth Judicial District Court,* 82 Nev. 38, 409 P.2d 974 (1966).

17. Intra-Union Dispute.

Berryman v. International Brotherhood of Electrical Workers, 82 Nev. 277, 416 P.2d 387 (1966).

18. Judgment.

Franklin v. Bartsas Realty, Inc., 95 Nev. 559, 598 P.2d 1147 (1979).

19. Judicial Proceedings.

Walker v. Walker, 84 Nev. 118, 437 P.2d 91 (1968); *Brunzell Construction Co. v. Harrah's Club,* 81 Nev. 414, 404 P.2d 902 (1965).

20. Labor Dispute.

International Union of Operating Engineers, Local No. 3 v. Bing Construction Co., 90 Nev. 183, 521 P.2d 1231 (1974); *Vegas Franchises, Ltd. v. Culinary Workers Union, Local No. 226,* 83 Nev. 236, 427 P.2d 959 (1967); *State ex rel. Culinary Workers Union, Local No. 226 v. Eighth Judicial District Court,* 66 Nev. 166, 207 P.2d 990 (1949).

21. Litigation.

Walker v. Walker, 84 Nev. 118, 437 P.2d 91 (1968); *Brunzell Construction Co. v. Harrah's Club,* 81 Nev. 414, 404 P.2d 902 (1965).

22. Mining.

All Minerals Corp. v. Kunkle, 105 Nev. 835, 784 P.2d 2 (1989); *Christensen v. Chromalloy American Corp.,* 99 Nev. 34, 656 P.2d 844 (1983).

23. Multiple Lawsuits.

Memory Gardens of Las Vegas, Inc. v. Pet Ponderosa Memorial Gardens, Inc., 88 Nev. 1, 492 P.2d 123 (1972); *Home Finance Co. v. Balcom,* 61 Nev. 301, 127 P.2d 389 (1942).

24. Open Meeting Law.

City Council of Reno v. Reno Newspapers, Inc., 105 Nev. 886, 784 P.2d 974 (1989).

25. Physician Staff Privileges.

Lakeside Community Hospital, Inc. v. Levenson, 101 Nev. 777, 710 P.2d 727 (1985).

26. Picketing.

International Union of Operating Engineers, Local No. 3 v. Bing Construction Co., 90 Nev. 183, 521 P.2d 1231 (1974); *Vegas Franchise, Ltd. v. Culinary Workers Union, Local No. 226,* 83 Nev. 236, 427 P.2d 959 (1967); *State ex rel. Culinary Workers Union, Local No. 226 v. Eighth Judicial District Court,* 66 Nev. 166, 207 P.2d 990 (1949).

27. Post-Employment Covenant.

Las Vegas Novelty, Inc. v. Fernandez, 106 Nev. 113, 787 P.2d 772 (1990); *Hansen v. Edwards,* 83 Nev. 189, 426 P.2d 792 (1967); *Ellis v. McDaniel,* 95 Nev. 455, 596 P.2d 222 (1979).

28. Promissory Note.

Aronoff v. Katleman, 75 Nev. 424, 345 P.2d 221 (1959).

29. Public Demolition.

Ripps v. City of Las Vegas, 72 Nev. 135, 297 P.2d 258 (1956).

30. Public Sale by Tax Assessor.

Johnson v. Wells Fargo & Co., 6 Nev. 224 (1870).

31. Public Safety.

Ripps v. City of Las Vegas, 72 Nev. 135, 297 P.2d 258 (1956).

32. Public Service Commission.

Public Service Commission v. Eighth Judicial District Court, 61 Nev. 245, 123 P.2d 237 (1942).

33. Restrictive Covenant.

Gladstone v. Gregory, 95 Nev. 474, 596 P.2d 491 (1979); *Dickstein v. Williams,* 93 Nev. 605, 571 P.2d 1169 (1977); *City of Reno v. Matley,* 79 Nev. 49, 378 P.2d 256 (1963).

34. Search Warrant.

Sheriff of Lander County v. Nevada National Bank, 90 Nev. 90, 518 P.2d 602 (1974).

35. Tax Sale.

Johnson v. Wells Fargo & Co., 6 Nev. 224 (1870).

36. Tort.

Guion v. Terra Marketing of Nevada, Inc., 90 Nev. 237, 523 P.2d 847 (1974).

37. Trade Name.

Sobol v. Capital Management Consultants, Inc., 102 Nev. 444, 726 P.2d 335 (1986).

38. Trespass.

Cook v. Maremont-Holland Co., 75 Nev. 380, 344 P.2d 198 (1959); *Parkinson v. Winniman,* 75 Nev. 405, 344 P.2d 677 (1959); *State ex rel. Mongolo v. Second Judicial District Court,* 46 Nev. 410, 211 P. 105 (1923); *Thorn v. Sweeney,* 12 Nev. 251 (1877); *Champion v. Sessions,* 1 Nev. 478 (1865).

39. Violation of Law.

Nevada Real Estate Commission v. Ressel, 72 Nev. 79, 294 P.2d 1115 (1956); *Itcaina v. Marble,* 56 Nev. 420, 55 P.2d 625 (1936).

40. Water.

Memory Gardens of Las Vegas, Inc. v. Pet Ponderosa Memorial Gardens, Inc., 88 Nev. 1, 492 P.2d 123 (1972); *Czipott v. Fleigh,* 87 Nev. 496, 489 P.2d 681 (1971); *Robison v. Bate,* 78 Nev. 501, 376 P.2d 763 (1962).

41. Zoning.

Eagle Thrifty Drugs & Markets, Inc. v. Hunter Lake P.T.A., 85 Nev. 162, 451 P.2d 713 (1969); *Terrie v. City of Las Vegas,* 96 Nev. 912, 620 P.2d 864 (1980); *Smith v. City of Las Vegas,* 80 Nev. 220, 391 P.2d 505 (1964).

§2814. Appellate review.

An order granting or refusing to grant or dissolving or refusing to dissolve an injunction is an appealable order. NRAP 3A(b)(2). The trial court need not comply with NRCP 54(b) and direct the entry of a final judgment as to that issue. *DeLuca Importing Co. v. Buckingham Corp.,* 90 Nev. 158, 520 P.2d 1365 (1974). Attacking a preliminary injunction by petition for a writ of prohibition is procedurally incorrect. *Ellis v. McDaniel,* 95 Nev. 455, 596 P.2d 222 (1979) (original proceeding in prohibition was treated as an appeal).

An order granting or refusing to grant a temporary restraining order is not an appealable order. If the circumstances warrant, however, the supreme court may consider the propriety of a temporary restraining order in an original proceeding for a writ of certiorari or, alternatively, for a writ of prohibition. *See State ex rel. Friedman v. Eighth Judicial District Court,* 81 Nev. 131, 399 P.2d 632 (1965) (without indicating whether the court was granting certiorari or prohibition, a temporary restraining order entered without bond was held void and ordered vacated).

Only a party to the action can move to dissolve an injunction. Therefore, if a nonparty is adversely affected by the restraint, an original proceeding in certiorari is the appropriate remedy. *Garaventa v. Second Judicial District Court,* 61 Nev. 350, 128 P.2d 266 (1942).

Certiorari also is available to review the restraint if the district court was without jurisdiction. *State Gaming Control Board v. Eighth Judicial District Court,* 82 Nev. 38, 409 P.2d 974 (1966) (district court is without jurisdiction to stay hearing before the Nevada Gaming Commission).

§2815. Enforcement of injunctions.

Temporary restraining orders, preliminary injunctions and permanent injunctions are binding only upon the parties to the action, their officers, agents, servants, employees and attorneys and upon those persons in active concert or participation with them who receive actual notice of the order by personal service or otherwise. NRCP 65(d).

Disobedience or resistance to any order including an injunction constitutes a contempt of court. NRS 22.010. *Phillips v. Welch,* 12 Nev. 158 (1877). A district court can enforce an injunction by subsequent contempt proceedings. *City Council of Reno v. Reno Newspapers, Inc.,* 105 Nev. 886, 784 P.2d 974 (1989). Contempt proceedings are also available against nonparties who are otherwise bound to obey the restraint. *Ahlers v. Thomas,* 24 Nev. 407, 56 P. 93 (1899).

§ 2816. Wrongful injunctions.

Any injunctive restraint is "wrongful" and a recovery on the security posted is permissible if such restraint is later dissolved — "regardless of the good or bad faith of the complainant in seeking the restraint." *Tracy v. Capozzi,* 98 Nev. 120, 642 P.2d 591 (1982). Generally, the claim against the surety does not accrue until the court finally determines that the plaintiff was not entitled to the restraining order or injunction. A final determination may take the form of an order dismissing the suit, a total or partial dissolution of the injunction, or a determination that there has been a failure to carry the burden of proof at the hearing on the preliminary injunction. *Aetna Casualty & Surety Co. v. Bell,* 95 Nev. 822, 603 P.2d 692 (1979); *Glen Falls Insurance Co. v. First National Bank,* 83 Nev. 196, 427 P.2d 1 (1967). Refusal to grant a preliminary injunction constitutes a determination that the original restraining order was wrongful and should have been dissolved even if it expired by its own terms. *Glen Falls Insurance Co. v. First National Bank,* 83 Nev. 196, 427 P.2d 1 (1967). A voluntary dismissal of the injunction suit by the plaintiff is also regarded as a final determination that the plaintiff was not entitled to the injunction unless the dismissal is by mutual agreement of the parties. If the party against whom the injunction was granted stipulates to dismiss the case, he waives his rights under the bond and cannot afterward maintain a claim for wrongful injunction. *Aetna Casualty & Surety Co. v. Bell,* 95 Nev. 822, 603 P.2d 692 (1979).

Absent a showing that the plaintiff obtained the temporary restraining order or preliminary injunction maliciously or in bad faith, the defendant's recovery for wrongful injunction is limited to the amount of the bond. *Tracy v. Capozzi,* 98 Nev. 120, 642 P.2d 591 (1982). In the event the defendant feels the bond is inadequate, he may move for an increase in that bond. *See Tracy, supra.*

The damages recoverable for wrongful injunction include the costs and expenses which may have been incurred or suffered by the party found to have been wrongfully enjoined or restrained. This includes a reasonable attorney's fee, the amount of which is discretionary with the trial court, for dissolving the restraint or for preventing a preliminary injunction from issuing after a temporary restraining order was granted. *See Artistic Hair Dressers, Inc. v. Levy,* 87 Nev. 313, 486 P.2d 482 (1971); *Glen Falls Insurance Co. v. First National Bank,* 83 Nev. 196, 427 P.2d 1 (1967).

§2817. Proceedings against surety.

NRCP 65.1 provides a uniform procedure for enforcing the liability of a surety on a bond, including temporary restraining order and preliminary injunction bonds. The method is cumulative, and an independent action is always available.

The simple summary procedure found in NRCP 65.1 for the enforcement of the sureties' liability commences with the filing of a motion in the action wherein the security was posted. The rule provides that each surety on such a bond "submits himself to the jurisdiction of the court and irrevocably appoints the clerk of the court as his agent upon whom any papers affecting his liability on the bond or undertaking may be served." NRCP 65.1. The motion and such notice of motion as the court may prescribe may be served on the sureties or may be served on the clerk of the court who shall forthwith mail copies to the sureties "if their addresses are known." NRCP 65.1. The rule is silent as to the method of service when service upon the clerk is not utilized but it would seem clear that compliance with Rule 5 and particularly NRCP 5(b) would suffice.

CHAPTER 29

A PRACTICAL GUIDE TO JUDICIAL DISCRETION

Author: Rex A. Jemison

§ 2901. Judicial discretion defined.

The term "judicial discretion" produces confusion because discretion means to act with restraint, but it can also mean to act without restraint. *See* Smithburn, *Judicial Discretion* 3-4 (2d ed. 1991). If one examines standard legal sources in search of a definition for "judicial discretion," one would find widely divergent and contradictory descriptions. The Supreme Court of Nevada made the following comment in *Goodman v. Goodman,* 68 Nev. 484, 487, 236 P.2d 305, 306 (1951): "Few legal terms are subject to a wider diversification of definition and construction." In Smithburn, *Judicial Discretion, supra,* at 3-12, the author notes that authorities have provided the following divergent definitions:

(1) Judicial discretion allows a court to do as it pleases.

(2) Judicial discretion is a mixed question of law and fact. Once the factual issue has been decided, there is a rule of law which governs.

(3) Judicial discretion is the power of a court to decide a matter according to the personal judgment of the court.

(4) Judicial discretion is that area of law in which there is no established right or wrong answer. The court is free to select from two or more "correct" answers.

(5) Judicial discretion involves a balancing of conflicting rights and equities in a complex factual situation.

The definition of judicial discretion must be broad enough to encompass all of these facets. If all of these descriptions are true, and they are, then judicial discretion must be defined as the *process* by which a judge decides a matter when there is no established rule which governs the particular question in a particular factual setting.

There are as many types of judicial discretion as there are circumstances in which there is a legal problem with no established solution. The nature of each form of judicial discretion is governed by the particular reasons, in a given case, for the absence of a fixed rule.

§ 2902. Type I — Absolute discretion.

At one end of the spectrum is absolute discretion. The reason for the non-existence of a fixed rule is that the court has an absolute power of choice. This power may come from statute, rule, precedent or the inherent powers of the court. In Type I discretion, the court can literally do as it pleases. Whether a court has absolute discretion depends entirely upon whether the proposed exercise of discretion affects the substantial rights of a party. No court is ever granted the power to do as it pleases when substantial rights of a party are at stake. This type of discretion only exists when no substantial rights of the parties are involved. For example, a court has absolute discretion to grant or deny a request for a particular verdict form under FRCP 49. The court can exercise this discretion "for any reason or no reason whatever." *Skidmore v. Baltimore & Ohio Railway,* 167 F.2d 54 (2d Cir. 1948). This broad discretion is granted because courts do not consider that the form of a verdict affects any substantial right of the parties.

In matters of calendaring, procedure, and courtroom behavior, the judge is granted great power because these matters do not ordinarily involve the substantial rights of a party. The moment substantial rights become involved, the court may not do as it pleases but must endeavor to reach a correct resolution of the problem.

The existence of absolute discretion cannot be determined by mere reference to the subject matter. For example, in a particular circumstance, an order granting a continuance may not affect the substantial rights of a party while an order denying a continuance may affect substantial rights. It is necessary to examine the effect of the particular proposed order in the particular factual setting.

§ 2903. Type II — No discretion.

At the opposite end of the spectrum is the second reason for the absence of a rule which governs the problem. No rule of law can be stated because the matter is not an issue of law, but rather a mixed question of law and fact. This type of discretion involves a circumstance in which there is a rule of law which governs the matter once the factual portion of the problem has been decided. Type II does not involve discretion at all in the sense of the power of choice. Once the factual portion of the issue has been resolved, then there is a rule of law which must be followed.

This form of judicial discretion can be likened to a miniature court-tried case within the confines of a jury trial. The law directs the burden of proof, the factual issue to be decided, and the result upon deciding the factual issue. There are two circumstances in which this type of discretion exists: (a) where there is a rule of law which applies subject to a *single* factual issue; and (b) where there is a rule of law which applies subject to several factors but, in the particular case, *all* the factors favor the same party. In these circumstances there is no discretion at all.

For example, there is a *single* factual issue which governs the determination of whether an expert may testify. The court inquires as to whether all of the following factors are present:

(1) The subject matter is a proper one for expert testimony;
(2) The witness has the minimum qualifications as an expert; and
(3) The witness has enough facts to state an opinion.

If the court finds all these factors are present, the court must allow the testimony. If the court finds that any one of the factors is missing, the court must disallow the testimony. No power of choice is granted to the trial judge. Discretion here is the discernment of the course prescribed by law. In *Goodman v. Goodman, supra,* the court relied upon the following quotation by Mr. Justice Marshall in *Osborn v. Bank of the United States,* 22 U.S. (9 Wheat.) 738, 866, 6 L. Ed. 204, 234 (1824):

> Judicial power, as contradistinguished from the power of the laws, has no existence. Courts are the mere instruments of the law, and can will nothing. When they are said to exercise a discretion, it is a mere legal discretion, a discretion to be exercised in discerning the course prescribed by law; and, when that is discerned, it is the duty of the court to follow it. Judicial power is never exercised for the purpose of giving effect to the will of the judge; always for the purpose of giving effect to the will of the legislature; or, in other words, to the will of the law.

The other circumstance in which a court has no discretion is when there are multiple factors to be considered, but all of the factors favor one party. In *Fabbi v. First National Bank,* 62 Nev. 405, 414, 153 P.2d 122 (1944), the Supreme Court of Nevada stated:

> What amounts to such abuse has been aptly defined in *State ex rel. Merritt v. Superior Court for Kitsap County,* 147 Wash. 690, 267 P. 503, 505: "When the evidence is clear, unconflicting in the essentials, and points unerringly to one result, to refuse to follow it is what the law denominates an abuse of discretion, such as justifies this court in taking cognizance of the matter."

§ 2904. Type III — Personal judgment.

It often happens that after all the factual issues have been decided, there still is no established rule which governs the circumstance. There are three reasons for this void:

(1) *Leeway discretion.* The trial judge is granted leeway to adopt any reasonable solution to a new and novel issue, pending the development of the law to the point that a generally accepted rule emerges. *United States v. Criden,* 648 F.2d 814 (3d Cir. 1981). It is important to recognize,

661

however, that leeway discretion is temporary and ceases to exist when the appellate court makes a decision to adopt a rule.

Professor Rosenberg describes this type of discretion as follows:

An area of trial court discretion is a pasture in which the trial judge can roam and graze freely rendering rulings his appellate betters might not have made, unless and until the higher court fences off a corner of the pasture by announcing that a rule of law covers the situation and has been violated. Until that occurs, the trial judge, wielding discretionary power, need not be right by appellate court lights in order to be upheld. Even if the appellate judges disagree with his call, they will defer to him.

Rosenberg, *Judicial Discretion: Discretion of the Trial Court Viewed From Above,* 22 Syracuse L. Rev. 635, 650 (1971).

In *People v. Tally,* 301 N.W.2d 809 (Mich. 1981), the court explained how leeway discretion may change into a rule of law:

Discretion is lodged in a judge in areas where "hard and fast" rules have not yet developed. This, of course, does not mean that once the common law labels a particular type of decision discretionary that it will remain so forever. After courts gain experience with the considerations involved in a particular type of decision, a "hard and fast" rule may develop. Repeated encounters with a particular type of question, at first labeled discretionary, may over time lead to a rule or at least to a more specific list of considerations to be weighed by the judge and to that extent limit his discretion.

(2) *Balancing discretion.* It sometimes happens that some of the factors to be considered in exercising discretion will favor one party while other factors will favor the other party. Under these circumstances the trial judge is required to balance the conflicting rights and equities between the two parties.

(3) *Complex discretion.* It sometimes happens that the factual circumstances presented are so complex and so unique that no rule could ever exist.

The trial judge employs the same methodology in solving all the foregoing problems. The court will apply its personal judgment, but this is a very different concept than the one involved in Type I — Absolute discretion. The trial judge applies the logic of the entire legal system to obtain a reasonable solution to the problem. The procedure was described by Justice Cardozo in a series of lectures collected in *The Nature of Judicial Process* 141 (1921). There Justice Cardozo spoke about the nature of judicial discretion:

The judge, even when he is free, is still not wholly free. He is not to innovate at pleasure. He is not a knight-errant roaming at will in pursuit of his own idea of beauty or of goodness. He is to draw his inspiration from consecrated principles. He is not to yield to spasmodic sentiment, to vague and unregulated benevolence. He is to exercise a discretion informed by tradition, methodized by analogy, disciplined by system, and subordinated to "the primordial necessity of order in the social life." Wide enough in all conscience in the field of discretion that remains.

This process is very familiar to lawyers. It is the same technique which is utilized by the bar applicant in answering a question when the applicant does not know the answer. The applicant calls upon his or her knowledge of the problem solving techniques which constitute the law. The applicant calls upon the logic of the legal system to provide a reasonable solution to the particular question presented. The applicant does not rely upon his or her eccentric view of the law, but rather the techniques which are learned in the study of the law. A court acts properly within its discretion when it employs these same techniques to resolve Type III judicial discretion issues.

§ 2905. Abuse of discretion.

An error in the exercise of judicial discretion is called an abuse of discretion. There are five stages to the exercise of judicial discretion and error can exist at any one of the stages.

(1) The failure to exercise discretion when required is an abuse of discretion. *Massey v. Sunrise Hospital,* 102 Nev. 367, 724 P.2d 208 (1986).

(2) A court abuses its discretion when it makes a factual finding which is not supported by substantial evidence and is clearly erroneous. This is the same standard which is applied to findings of fact made by the trial court in a court tried case. *Real Estate Division v. Jones,* 98 Nev. 260, 645 P.2d 1371 (1982).

(3) An abuse of discretion can be an error of law in determining the factors which govern discretion. *Franklin v. Bartsas Realty, Inc.,* 95 Nev. 559, 598 P.2d 1147 (1979).

(4) The court can err in the exercise of personal judgment and does so when no reasonable judge could reach such a conclusion under the particular circumstances.

In *Delno v. Market Street Railway,* 124 F.2d 965, 967 (9th Cir. 1942), the court explained that discretion is abused:

when the judicial action is arbitrary, fanciful or unreasonable, which is another way of saying that discretion is abused only where no reasonable man would take the view adopted by the trial court. If reasonable men could differ as to the propriety of the action taken by the trial court, then it cannot be said that the trial court abused its discretion.

A court does not abuse its discretion when the court reaches a result which could be found by a reasonable judge. *Goodman v. Goodman, supra.*

(5) The court can abuse its discretion by failing to provide a statement of reasons which will facilitate reasonable appellate review. In *Jones v. Jones,* 86 Nev. 879, 478 P.2d 148 (1970), *overruled on other grounds, Mays v. Todaro,* 97 Nev. 195, 626 P.2d 260 (1981), the Nevada Supreme Court held that it was an abuse of discretion for a trial judge to fail to provide a statement of reasons for the exercise of discretion in denying an award of attorneys fees under NRS 18.010(3)(a).

> We think he should have stated his reasons, to enable this court to undertake a reasonable review. In that sense he violated his discretion. *Iske v. Metropolitan Utilities District of Omaha,* 157 N.W.2d 887 (Neb. 1968).

This rule was followed in *Lyon v. Walker Boudwin Construction Co.,* 88 Nev. 646, 503 P.2d 1219 (1972), and again in *Pandelis Construction v. Jones-Viking Associates,* 103 Nev. 129, 734 P.2d 1236 (1987). Thus far, this rule has only been applied to discretion in awarding attorney's fees under NRS 18.010. However, the logic of these cases would seem to apply to other areas of discretion, and it is submitted that a trial judge should provide a statement of reasons explaining the exercise of judicial discretion when all of the following factors exist:

(1) The exercise of discretion involves a matter of importance.

(2) A statement of reasons is necessary to reasonable appellate review.

(3) A statement of reasons could be provided without unduly delaying the trial of the case.

(4) A statement of reasons has been requested.

The circumstances in which a court can find an abuse of discretion were enumerated in *Johnson v. United States,* 398 A.2d 354, 366-67 (D.C. App. 1979):

> No hard and fast rule can indicate in each case whether reversal is appropriate. Although no list can hope to be exhaustive, we cannot enumerate some of the factors that might be relevant in deciding whether the trial court's error warrants reversal. If the error in the discretionary determination jeopardized the fairness of the proceeding as a whole, or if the error had a possibly substantial impact upon the outcome, the case should be reversed. *Tinsley v. United States,* D.C. App. 1976, 368 A.2d 531; *Koppal v. Travelers Indemnity Co.,* D.C. App., 297 A.2d 337, 339 (1972). Similarly, if the court failed to undertake a required factual inquiry or if it ignored an apparent deficiency in the record, reversal is appropriate. *Pollock v. Brown,* D.C. App., 395 A.2d 50 (1978); *Farrell v. United States,* D.C. App., 391 A.2d 755 (1978). Even though the specific harm of the error might not be cognizable, the failure to inquire for the record deeply enough into the immediate problem suggests that the trial court did not exercise its judgment properly. For much the same reason reversal should follow if it is discerned that the trial court did not recognize its capacity to

exercise discretion or did not purport to exercise it. *Berryman v. United States, supra; (Bradford) Brown v. United States, supra.* So, too, reversal may follow when the trial court purports to exercise discretion that it does not have. *Cf. Hall v. Watwood,* D.C. App., 289 A.2d 626 (1972). Further, if the trial court's decision is supported by improper reasons, reasons that are not founded in the record, or reasons which contravene the policies meant to guide the trial court's discretion or the purposes for which the determination was committed to the trial court's discretion, reversal likely is called for. *Gaither v. United States, supra.*

When the trial court's error is not so extreme as to require reversal by itself — as, for example, when the record is thin but not barren, or the reasoning is weak but not insubstantial — the reviewing court must weigh the severity of the error against the importance of the determination in the whole proceeding and the possibility for prejudice as a whole. *See, e.g., Morris v. United States, supra,* at 1352-53. The "right to be wrong without incurring reversal," Rosenberg, *Judicial Discretion, supra,* at 637, is not absolute.

In sum, the appellate court makes two distinct classes of inquiries when reviewing a trial court's exercise of discretion. It must determine, first, whether the exercise of discretion was in error and, if so, whether the impact of that error requires reversal. It is when both these inquiries are answered in the affirmative that we hold that the trial court "abused" its discretion.

CHAPTER 30

RECEIVERS

Authors: Craig Demetris
         Douglas A. Emerick
         Rew R. Goodenow
         Cecilia L. Rosenauer

§ 3001. Introduction and scope.

The purpose of this chapter is to outline the context in which a receiver may be appointed and the Nevada statutory bases for appointment. This chapter also outlines the mechanism of appointment, the powers, duties and liabilities of the receiver, representation of creditors in a receivership, fees, and appeals. This chapter focuses on Nevada state law, with reference to the federal procedural rules. The federal statutory bases for appointment are not discussed.

A receivership is an ancillary remedy used to preserve the value of assets pending the outcome of the principal case. *Johnson v. Steel, Inc.,* 100 Nev. 181, 183, 678 P.2d 676, 678 (1984). The receivership proceeding does not determine substantive rights between the parties, but is merely a means of preserving the status quo.

A receiver is an officer of the court who exercises duties in the interests of all parties to the litigation as the court may direct. *Lynn v. Ingalls,* 100 Nev. 115, 120, 676 P.2d 797 (1984); *Jones v. Free,* 83 Nev. 31, 37, 422 P.2d 551 (1967); *Bowler v. Leonard,* 70 Nev. 370, 382, 269 P.2d 833 (1954); *Gottwals v. Manske,* 60 Nev. 76, 82, 99 P.2d 645 (1940). A receiver is also a "fiduciary" as that term is defined in NRS

667

162.020(1)(b), the Uniform Fiduciaries Act. A receiver is a neutral person between the parties to a cause, appointed by the court to receive and preserve the property or fund which is the subject of litigation. A receiver is appointed when it does not seem reasonable to the court that either party to the litigation should hold or control the property or fund. *Bowler v. Leonard,* 70 Nev. 370, 382, 269 P.2d 833 (1954). The statutory authorization for the appointment of a receiver is found at NRS 32.010, NRS 78.347, NRS 90.640, NRS 106.025, NRS 107.100, NRS 645B.160 and NRS 645A.150. Additional statutory bases for the appointment of a receiver are discussed in § 3003. For further information, see 39 Nevada Digest 14021-14070; 82 Federal Practice Digest, Receivers, 710-30 (4th ed. 1992); 45 Pac. Digest, Receivers, 165-84 (1992); 65 Am. Jur. 2d 841-1005 & 66 Am. Jur. 2d 1-292; 75 CJS 644-1104, Receivers; Clarke on Receivers (3d ed. 1959). In addition, the Local Rules of Practice for the District of Nevada ("LR"), Rule 210, N.R.C.P. 66 and F.R.C.P. 66 should be consulted.

§ 3002. Nature and purpose of remedy and comparison with federal bankruptcy law.

A court is empowered to appoint a receiver under many statutorily authorized circumstances, as discussed in § 3003. For example, a receiver may be appointed when a business has been mismanaged or to collect rents generated from real property under a deed of trust. However, the remedy is flexible and can be fashioned in the context of many additional disputes.

The additional protections available under federal bankruptcy law should be considered in seeking the appointment of a receiver. The purpose of this section is to outline briefly the advantages peculiar to bankruptcy that are not available in a state or federal receivership. In general, the choice of options should rest on the goals of the entity under consideration. If the entity is to be liquidated or reorganized, bankruptcy should be more seriously considered. If the entity does not require restructuring of debt or liquidation, but only temporary measures, such as controlling mismanagement, a state or federal court receivership should be more seriously considered. This discussion is not an exhaustive comparison of the two bodies of law or an exposition of all the advantages or disadvantages of either. Rather, this section highlights the unique characteristics of bankruptcy law as compared to receiverships.

a. The automatic stay.

The primary advantage in bankruptcy for both individuals and business entities is the automatic stay in bankruptcy, 11 U.S.C. § 362(a), which enjoins any action against the debtor or the property of the debtor's estate. As a general rule, acts in violation of the automatic stay are void. *Kalb v. Feuerstein*, 308 U.S. 433, 60 S. Ct. 1343, 84 L. Ed. 370 (1940); *In re Schwartz*, 954 F.2d 569 (9th Cir. 1992); *In re Shamblin*, 890 F.2d 123 (9th Cir. 1989); *In re Stringer*, 847 F.2d 549, 551 (9th Cir. 1988); *Morgan Guaranty Trust Co. of New York v. American Savings & Loan Association*, 804 F.2d 1487 (9th Cir. 1986), *cert. denied*, 482 U.S. 929, 107 S. Ct. 3213, 96 L. Ed. 2d 700 (1989); *In re Sambo's Restaurant, Inc.*, 754 F.2d 811, 816 (9th Cir. 1985). Willful violation of the automatic stay may be grounds for the imposition of sanctions, which may include actual and punitive damages. 11 U.S.C. § 362(h). Protection of the automatic stay is frequently sought to enjoin loss of property through foreclosure, litigation, or execution of adverse judgments, or to obtain relief from the financial pressures that force a debtor into bankruptcy.

Although an order appointing a receiver may contain language similar to that contained in 11 U.S.C. § 362(a), the effect of this language is not as broad as the automatic stay in bankruptcy. By filing a petition in bankruptcy, a debtor instantly invokes the protections of the automatic stay by operation of law and without further process or order of the bankruptcy court. In the context of a receivership, the court may enjoin certain actions. For example, the state court may enjoin a creditor from levying on, or proceeding to exercise any lien rights or other claim on property under the receiver's possession and control. *See Mack v. Second Judicial District Court*, 50 Nev. 318, 258 P. 289 (1927); *Gottwals v. Manske*, 60 Nev. 76, 99 P.2d 645 (1940); *cf. State ex rel. Nenzel v. Second Judicial District Court*, 49 Nev. 145, 241 P. 317 (1925). However, the injunction is prospective in nature and the party seeking this protection must affirmatively apply for and receive it. The remedy is not automatic and may take too much time.

b. Avoiding powers under bankruptcy law.

The second primary advantage to bankruptcy is the avoiding powers granted under the bankruptcy code at 11 U.S.C. §§ 547 and 548. Section 547 allows the trustee or the debtor in possession to set aside "preferential transfers," those transfers made by a debtor to a creditor that allow the creditor to receive greater satisfaction than would be available in bankruptcy. This section, in conjunction with 11 U.S.C. § 550, has been interpreted to allow a debtor to set aside the payments made to a creditor within one year prior to bankruptcy, when those payments benefitted the debtor's insider guarantor. *Levit v. Ingersoll Rand Financial Corp. (In re Deprezio)*, 874 F.2d 1186 (7th Cir. 1989); *In re C-L Cartage Co.*, 899 F.2d 1490 (6th Cir. 1990); *In re Robinson Brothers Drilling, Inc.*, 97 Bankr. 77 (W.D. Okla. 1988), *aff'd*, 892 F.2d 850 (10th Cir. 1989).

Section 548 of the bankruptcy code allows the debtor in possession or the trustee to set aside a transfer of property that was made within one year of bankruptcy if the transfer was made with actual intent to hinder, delay or defraud creditors, or if the transfer was one for which the debtor received less than reasonably equivalent value.

Moreover, the so-called "strong-arm" provision of bankruptcy law allows a debtor in possession or trustee to set aside certain transactions pursuant to state law. 11 U.S.C § 544(b).

Under the Nevada Uniform Fraudulent Transfers Act, only creditors have standing to avoid fraudulent transfers. NRS 112.210. The power of the debtor to avoid such transfers pursuant to state law in bankruptcy court may be a persuasive reason to seek the protection of bankruptcy law, as a receiver would not enjoy this power to set aside a transfer of property on behalf of a creditor. Moreover, state law does not have a provision analogous to § 547 of the bankruptcy code.

c. The discharge of debts.

A third fundamental advantage to bankruptcy law, which only applies to individuals, is the entry of the discharge in bankruptcy. 11 U.S.C. § 727(a)(1). The discharge is at the heart of the fresh start provisions of the code and may be denied if the debtor conducts himself in a manner that is inconsistent with the protections of bankruptcy law, for example, if he conveys assets to hinder, delay or defraud creditors, conceals or destroys records, lies under oath or refuses to obey an order of the court. 11 U.S.C. § 727(a)(2)-(9). The discharge of particular debts may also be denied under the conditions specified in 11 U.S.C. § 523. A receivership proceeding does not absolve the personal liability of an individual as pervasively as the discharge in bankruptcy.

A multiplicity of additional concerns should affect the decision to seek appointment of a receiver as opposed to seeking the protection of bankruptcy law. These include the following nonexhaustive examples:

d. Who may be a debtor.

A railroad company, a domestic or foreign insurance company, bank, savings and loan, credit union, homestead association or industrial bank may not be a debtor under Title 11. 11 U.S.C. § 109(b).

e. Standing of a corporation.

In the case of corporate disputes, the required resolution of the board of directors that is necessary to file a voluntary bankruptcy petition may not be readily obtained. The required number of creditors who are able and willing to file an involuntary petition against a debtor in bankruptcy may not be available. 11 U.S.C. § 303(b).

In contrast, any stockholder of ten percent (10%) of the outstanding and issued stock of a corporation has standing to petition for appointment of a receiver. *Transcontinental Oil Co. v. Free*, 80 Nev. 207, 391 P.2d 317 (1964).

f. Bad faith dismissal.

Disputes between members of a closely-held corporation that do not involve bona fide disputes with more than one creditor may render a bankruptcy filing in bad faith and subject to dismissal.

g. Various procedural considerations.

Bankruptcy court offers nationwide service of process, obviating the personal jurisdictional issues that may arise in Nevada state court if a receiver must sue a nonresident person or entity. Proximity to the state or bankruptcy court and the congestion of their respective dockets may be important considerations for rural receivership proceedings.

h. Management's role in bankruptcy.

The role of the management of the debtor under a chapter 11 reorganization as the debtor in possession, with the attendant duties of reporting to the court and acting as a fiduciary for the benefit of creditors, may affect the decision of filing for bankruptcy. The alternative of a receivership as a temporary solution without the obligations for management that would arise in bankruptcy may be more attractive.

Bankruptcy also offers the option of having an independent examiner appointed to review the debtor's business practices.

i. Costs.

The costs of bankruptcy include filing fees, fees to file certain motions, and fees to bring adversary proceedings in bankruptcy court. In addition, the costs of administering a chapter 11 estate are high, a reflection of statutorily mandated reporting requirements to the bankruptcy court, quarterly fees to the office of the United States Trustee, and legal fees in defending creditors' actions and taking the case through confirmation of a plan of reorganization. In addition, consideration should be given to the negative impact on a business or on individual credit that is inherent when bankruptcy is chosen. All of these costs should be compared to those of a receivership.

j. Liquidation.

If the board of directors elects to liquidate a business, they remain personally involved in the liquidation process and are jointly and severally liable for the debts of the corporation to the extent of the amount of money or property of the corporation. NRS 78.595. If the board of directors elects to liquidate through bankruptcy, a trustee in bankruptcy is appointed, who assumes the responsibility of the liquidation process. 11 U.S.C. § 704.

In the context of a partnership, the winding up by the partners themselves or by a receiver does not affect the personal liability of the partners for the unsatisfied claims, absent specific agreement. NRS 87.360.

§ 3003. Appointment of a receiver

a. Statutory authority.

The appointment of a receiver is controlled by statute. *State ex rel. Nenzel v. Second Judicial District Court,* 49 Nev. 145, 155, 241 P. 317 (1925). If the statutory requirements are not met, the court lacks jurisdiction to appoint a receiver. *Shelton v. District Court,* 64 Nev. 487, 494, 185 P.2d 320 (1947).

(i). General statutory grounds, NRS 32.010.

Numerous statutes authorize the appointment of receivers in specific situations. The basic "catch-all" statute, however, authorizing the appointment of a receiver in nearly all situations is found in NRS 32.010. Subsection (1) of that statute deals with vendors who seek to set aside a fraudulent purchase of property, or creditors who wish to subject a particular property or fund to the creditor's claim. NRS 32.010(1) also deals with disputes between partners, where one claims an ownership interest in the property or proceeds belonging to the enterprise and can prove that such property or fund is in danger of being lost, removed or materially injured.

Subsection (2) of NRS 32.010 gives mortgagees of either real or personal property a right to seek the appointment of a receiver when insufficient equity exists to discharge the mortgage debt. The issues regarding such situations are more fully addressed in this section at (a)(iv).

Subsections (3) and (4) of NRS 32.010 provide for the appointment of a receiver in post-judgment proceedings, *e.g.,* when it is necessary "to carry the judgment into effect," or to assist "in the aid of execution."

Subsection (5) authorizes the appointment of a receiver in a case where a corporation has been dissolved, or is insolvent, or is in imminent danger of insolvency, or has forfeited its corporate rights. In addition to this statute, other statutes also authorize the appointment of a receiver to manage a corporation, discussed in this section at (a)(ii).

Section (6) of NRS 32.010 contains a "catch-all" phrase wherein the court may, in its discretion, appoint receivers in all other cases which have previously been authorized by the "usages of the courts of equity."

NRS 32.010 was borrowed from the California code. In *State ex rel. Nenzel v. Second Judicial District Court,* 49 Nev. 145, 156, 241 P. 317 (1925), the court stated that the California decisions construing a similar statute would be given "great weight" in Nevada.

NRS 32.010 has been used to allow relief where other equitable remedies provided by law may not be sufficient because, without a receiver, the final judgment of the court may become meaningless. For example, *Bowler v. Leonard,* 70 Nev. 370, 269 P.2d 833 (1954) involved a lawsuit that could have been filed under the claim and delivery statute. The plaintiff and the defendant had conflicting claims to the ownership of a specific herd of cattle. Prior to the filing, the defendant had possession of the cattle. The court held that it was proper for the district court to appoint a receiver to take possession of the cattle, and to safeguard and manage the herd pending the outcome of the litigation to determine the proper ownership. *See also Kraemer v. Kraemer,* 79 Nev. 287, 382 P.2d 394 (1963).

In addition, a receiver may be appointed on general equitable grounds, pursuant to NRS 32.010(6). *Kraemer* was a divorce action in which the wife contended that her husband and an associate were guilty of a conspiracy to defraud her. The supreme court affirmed the appointment of a receiver, even though the wife did not ultimately prevail on her fraud claim.

(ii). Corporations.

In addition to NRS 32.010(5), three statutes authorize a court to appoint a receiver to manage a corporation: NRS 78.600, 78.630 and 78.650.

NRS 78.600 applies where the corporation has become "dissolved or ceased to exist in any manner whatever." In such instances, either a shareholder or creditor of the corporation can apply to the court for the appointment of a receiver.

Pursuant to NRS 78.600, in cases where a corporation is already a party to litigation and, during the course of the litigation, the corporation has sold all of its assets or has otherwise become dissolved, the court would continue with the pending litigation and appoint either a receiver or the members of the last board of directors to act as "trustees" of the corporation to conclude the litigation. The trustees or receiver would have the authority to "collect the debts and property due and belonging to the corporation with power to prosecute and defend, in the name of the corporation." NRS 78.600. In such circumstances, the party bringing suit should serve and file with the court a "suggestion of corporate dissolution." *Kelly Broadcasting Co. v. Sovereign Broadcasting, Inc.,* 96 Nev. 188, 606 P.2d 1089 (1980); *Pierce Co. v. Sherman Gardens Co.,* 82 Nev. 395, 419 P.2d 781 (1966). There is no time limit for bringing a motion to substitute the new trustees or receiver of the corporation following a suggestion of corporate dissolution. *See* NRS 78.695.

Under NRS 78.630, a receiver may be appointed to manage a corporation in a case where the corporation: (1) is about to become insolvent; or (2) has suspended its ordinary business for want of funds; or (3) has been and is conducting its business at a great loss and in a manner that is greatly prejudicial to the interests of its stockholders and creditors. Under such circumstances, NRS 78.630 provides that a creditor holding ten percent of the outstanding indebtedness of the corporation, or a stockholder holding ten percent of the outstanding stock of the corporation may bring a complaint and apply to the district court for the appointment of a receiver in addition to a "writ of injunction." NRS 78.630(1); *International Life Underwriters, Inc. v. District Court,* 61 Nev. 42, 48, 113 P.2d 616 (1941).

However, NRS 78.630, 78.635 and 78.640 do not apply to complaints which are brought to dissolve a corporation. *International Life Underwriters, Inc. v. District Court,* 61 Nev. 42, 48, 113 P.2d 616 (1941).

In the context of corporate dissolution, NRS 78.650 provides the authority to appoint a receiver. NRS 78.650 sets forth ten separate grounds, any one of which may justify the court in appointing a receiver for the purpose of winding up the corporation's affairs. *Transcontinental Oil Co. v. Free,* 80 Nev. 207, 391 P.2d 317 (1964). The only parties entitled to bring such a complaint for relief under NRS 78.650, however, are stockholders who own at least ten percent of the issued and outstanding capital stock of the corporation.

NRS 78.650 provides that a receiver may be appointed on the following ten grounds:

1. The corporation has willfully violated its charter. *Peri-Gil Corp. v. Sutton,* 84 Nev. 406, 410-11, 442 P.2d 35 (1968).

2. Directors of the corporation have been guilty of fraud or collusion or gross mismanagement in the control of the corporation's affairs. *State ex rel. Hersh v. District Court,* 86 Nev. 73, 79, 464 P.2d 783 (1970).

3. The directors have been guilty of misfeasance, malfeasance, or nonfeasance. *See State ex rel. Hersh v. First Judicial District Court,* 86 Nev. 73, 79, 464 P.2d 783 (1970).

4. The corporation is unable to conduct the business or to conserve its assets by reason of the act, neglect, or refusal to function of any of the directors of the corporation. *Nishon's, Inc. v. Kendigian*, 91 Nev. 504, 506, 538 P.2d 580 (1975).

5. The assets of the corporation are in danger of waste, sacrifice, or loss through attachment, foreclosure, litigation, or otherwise.

6. The corporation has abandoned its business. *See Nishon's, Inc. v. Kendigian*, 91 Nev. 504, 538 P.2d 580 (1975) (management effectively abandoned its business). *Foster v. Arata*, 74 Nev. 143, 158, 325 P.2d 759 (1958).

7. The corporation has not proceeded diligently to wind up its affairs or distribute its assets in a reasonable time.

8. The corporation has become insolvent.

9. The corporation, although solvent, is, for any cause, not able to pay its debts or other obligations as they mature.

10. The corporation is not able to resume its business with safety to the public. *Transcontinental Oil Co. v. Free*, 80 Nev. 207, 211, 391 P.2d 317 (1964); *International Life Underwriters, Inc. v. District Court*, 61 Nev. 42, 50, 113 P.2d 616 (1941).

(iii). Partnerships.

The only statutory basis for the appointment of a receiver involving a partnership dispute between the various partners is found in NRS 32.010(1). In the context of a partnership, the courts have taken a very liberal approach towards the appointment of a receiver in the case where one partner is shown to be guilty of oppressive action against another partner. *Sugarman Co. v. Morse Brothers*, 50 Nev. 191, 200-01, 255 P. 1010 (1927). The law of receivership applicable to corporations does not control in a partnership receivership proceeding. *Sugarman Co.*, 50 Nev. at 200; *State ex rel. Hatch v. Ninth Judicial District Court*, 50 Nev. 282, 286, 257 P. 831 (1927); *see also Maynard v. Railey*, 2 Nev. 313 (1866).

(iv). Mortgagees.

NRS 32.010(2) provides the general statutory framework for a mortgagee to seek the appointment of a receiver. That statute encompasses both real and personal property. *See Martin v. Duncan Automobile Co.*, 50 Nev. 91, 252 P. 322 (1927) (appointment of receiver in context of Article 9 security interest).

Other statutory provisions also authorize the appointment of a receiver in the case of a mortgage instrument concerning real property. NRS 106.025 contains numerous covenants that may be adopted into a mortgage instrument. Covenant 11 of NRS 106.025 expressly provides for the consent of the mortgagor to appointment of a receiver.

675

NRS 107.100 authorizes a court to appoint a receiver when the mortgagor has executed a deed of trust. Unlike NRS 106.025, however, there is no statutory authorization to obtain the appointment of a receiver without notice to the trustor.

The grounds for the appointment of a receiver under NRS 107.100 closely parallel the grounds for the appointment of a receiver under NRS 32.010. Under both statutes, the beneficiary of a deed of trust must show that the real property subject to the deed of trust is in danger of being wasted, or that the income from such property is in danger of being lost, or that the value of the property is insufficient to discharge the mortgage debt.

The equities may weigh strongly in favor of the appointment of a receiver to collect rents generated by property that is encumbered by more than one deed of trust, particularly in order to protect the interests of junior lienholders or when the equity in the property is eroding. Moreover, the appointment of a receiver is appropriate where the value of the property is insufficient to pay encumbrances, the mortgagor threatens to destroy the property, commits waste or colludes with tenants to divert rents. *Hyman v. Kelly*, 1 Nev. 148, 151 (1865).

If the security document contains an absolute assignment of rents provision, the secured party may enforce the provision, even if the security is not impaired. *See In re Charles D. Stapp of Nevada, Inc. v. Fishman*, 641 F.2d 737 (9th Cir. 1981); *cf. First Western Financial Corp. v. Vegas Continental*, 100 Nev. 710, 692 P.2d 1279 (1984).

(v). Miscellaneous statutory provisions.

In addition to the foregoing statutes, numerous other statutes authorize the appointment of a receiver, listed below, which have been infrequently interpreted by the Nevada supreme court:

    (1) In aid of execution — NRS 21.240.

    (2) Non-profit corporation/association — NRS 82.456 and 82.471.

    (3) Violation of securities laws — NRS 90.640.

    (4) Divorce judgments that have been difficult to enforce — NRS 125.240.

    (5) Housing authority impaired — NRS 315.520.

    (6) Escrow company's operation impaired — NRS 645A.150.

    (7) Mortgage company's operation impaired — NRS 645B.160.

    (8) Savings and loan association impaired — NRS 673.499.

    (9) Installment loan company impaired — NRS 675.430.

    (10) Thrift company impaired — NRS 677.530.

    (11) Credit union dissolved — NRS 678.830.

    (12) Insurance company operation impaired — NRS 696B.140 and NRS 696B.350.

(13) A supplier of water or sewer service impaired — NRS 704.681.

(14) Unlawful detainer action — *Lynn v. Ingalls,* 100 Nev. 115, 119, 676 P.2d 797 (1984); *Johnston v. DeLay,* 63 Nev. 1, 14, 158 P.2d 547 (1945).

b. The Complaint and Petition for Appointment.

After the complaint is filed to commence the action, the party seeking the appointment must file a "petition" stating sufficient facts to justify the appointment. *State ex rel. Nenzel v. Second Judicial District Court,* 49 Nev. 145, 157, 241 P. 317 (1925). In the petition, the applicant must clearly identify the relationship of the applicant to the proposed receivership estate and give the court a factual explanation why a receiver should be appointed.

The appointment of a receiver is to a considerable extent a matter resting in the discretion of the court, to be governed by all the circumstances in the case. *Bowler v. Leonard,* 70 Nev. 370, 383, 269 P.2d 833 (1954). The applicant must satisfy the same criteria for obtaining injunctive relief, including the demonstration of reasonable probability of success on the merits. *Hines v. Plante,* 99 Nev. 259, 262, 661 P.2d 880 (1983). In the absence of such reasonable probability, the application for a receivership may be denied. *Charmicor, Inc. v. Bradshaw Finance Co.,* 92 Nev. 310, 313, 550 P.2d 413 (1976). The applicant must also show that legal remedies are inadequate. *State ex rel. Nenzel v. Second Judicial District Court,* 49 Nev. 145, 160, 241 P. 317 (1925). For example, the applicant should show that the receivership is necessary to preserve assets or preserve the status quo. Denial of an application to appoint a receiver does not impact the merits of the underlying action. *Johnson v. Steele, Inc.,* 100 Nev. 181, 183, 678 P.2d 676, 678 (1984).

c. Qualifications of receiver.

The applicant should propose a receiver who is neutral and disinterested. *Lynn v. Ingalls,* 100 Nev. 115, 120, 676 P.2d 797 (1984); *Bowler v. Leonard,* 70 Nev. 370, 382, 269 P.2d 833 (1954). In proposing a receiver, the applicant should tailor the choice of receiver to the type of property the receiver is being asked to manage. For example, the receiver for businesses involved in highly technical or specialized fields should be at least acquainted with the operation of that type of business. As a practical matter, the petition should include an affidavit or resume from the proposed receiver setting forth his or her qualifications.

As an officer of the court, the receiver must be of sufficient integrity and knowledge to respond to the court's direction regardless of his or her relation to the appointing party. The attorneys involved in the litigation may not act as a receiver in that litigation. *Peri-Gil Corp. v. Sutton,* 84

Nev. 406, 412, 442 P.2d 35 (1968); LR 210-6. Under rare circumstances, a party to the litigation has been appointed receiver. *Kraemer v. Kraemer,* 79 Nev. 287, 293, 382 P.2d 394 (1963).

NRS 78.650(4) provides that a director of the corporation who has not been guilty of any negligence in bringing about the placement of the corporation into receivership shall be given preferential treatment, in either the appointment of the receiver or the nomination of the receiver. That preferential treatment, however, is not binding upon the court. In *Peri-Gil Corp. v. Sutton,* 84 Nev. 406, 411, 442 P.2d 35 (1968), the court held that non-negligent directors have only a preferred right, or an "advisory right," to be heard as to their qualifications. A non-negligent director does not have a right to veto some other nomination of a receiver or dictate to the court who shall be the receiver.

In the case of a partnership, no statute gives one party preference over another party regarding the appointment of a receiver. Moreover, the law of receiverships regarding corporations has no application to partnerships. *Sugarman Co. v. Morse Brothers,* 50, Nev. 191, 199-200, 255 P.2d 1010 (1927). Therefore, a non-negligent partner may not use NRS 78.650(4) by analogy to secure the preferred right to nominate a receiver. However, under NRS 87.370, a partner who has not been guilty of any act causing a dissolution of the partnership has the right to wind down the affairs of the partnership. Therefore, an innocent partner may argue a preferred right of nomination over a culpable partner.

No statute requires that the moving party provide a bond to secure against damages. *Bowler v. Leonard,* 70 Nev. 370, 386, 269 P.2d 833 (1954). The court may require security for the appointment of a receiver and the amount of security is left to the discretion of the court. *Id.* at 386-87; *Kraemer v. Kraemer,* 79 Nev. 287, 293, 382 P.2d 394 (1963). The bond is not required to protect parties from damages which may result from the appointment. Rather, the bond is required to protect parties from injury resulting from an action of the receiver outside of his or her court granted authority. *Clark on Receivers,* Vol. 1, Para. 119 (3d ed. 1959). The receiver must file a satisfactory final account and report to the court in order to be discharged and have the bond exonerated. *Kraemer,* 79 Nev. at 294.

d. Ex parte appointment and order to show cause.

In addition to filing the complaint and petition, the party seeking the appointment must also request a hearing on an order to show cause. The order to show cause hearing is an evidentiary hearing and the applicant has the burden of proof.

It is, however, possible to have a receiver appointed on an ex parte basis. The applicant must be prepared to show that the delay resulting from giving notice to the adverse parties would defeat the rights of the complainant, or that it would result in great injury to him. *Maynard v. Railey,* 2 Nev. 313, 317 (1866).

After the appointment of a temporary receiver, the applicant must also set and notice a hearing on the appointment of a permanent receiver. In this regard, the procedure is similar to the entry of a preliminary injunction following the issuance of a temporary restraining order pursuant to NRCP 65. Counsel should consult with that rule and case law interpreting it when seeking ex parte appointment.

The legislative authorization for the ex parte appointment of a receiver with respect to real estate mortgages is found at NRS 106.025, covenant 11. No statute specifically allows for the ex parte appointment of a receiver under a deed of trust. However, many security documents contain consent clauses authorizing a creditor to seek ex parte appointment of a receiver. *See* § 3003 *supra*, at (a)(iv).

No statute or case specifically authorizes appointment of a corporate receiver on an ex parte basis. *State v. Wilder,* 34 Nev. 94, 123, 116 P. 595 (1911). NRS 78.650 requires at least five days' notice to the corporation of the show cause hearing. The court may direct a longer or shorter period of time for such notice. In *Hettel v. District Court,* 30 Nev. 382, 388, 96 P. 1062 (1908), the court held that notice to the stockholders and directors was required before entertaining an application for appointment of a permanent receiver, one who will wind up a corporation that has been judicially dissolved. Careful examination should be made of the cases construing that statute. *See, e.g., International Life Underwriters, Inc. v. District Court,* 61 Nev. 42, 113 P.2d 616 (1941); *Shelton v. District Court,* 64 Nev. 487, 185 P.2d 320 (1947); *Golden v. District Court,* 31 Nev. 250, 101 P. 1021 (1909).

In contrast to the notice requirements for appointment of a permanent receiver, a temporary receiver, one who is appointed pending a judicial dissolution of a corporation, may be appointed on five days' notice to the resident agent pursuant to NRS 78.630. *State ex rel. Hersh v. District Court,* 86 Nev. 73, 78, 464 P.2d 783 (1970).

e. Venue.

Both NRS 78.630 and 78.650 require that a petition to appoint be made to the district court in the county where the corporation has its principal office or principal place of business. *Flournoy v. McKinnon Ford Sales,* 90 Nev. 119, 520 P.2d 600 (1970).

§ 3004. Defenses to the appointment of a receiver.

As stated above, the appointment of a receiver is addressed to the sound discretion of the trial court. *Bowler v. Leonard,* 70 Nev. 370, 383,

269 P.2d 833 (1954). Although the supreme court affirmed the appointment of a receiver in *Bowler*, the court characterized the remedy as "harsh" and "extreme," to be "used sparingly" in the interests of justice. *Id.* at 388. If the desired outcome may be achieved by some other method, case law dictates that method be used. *Hines v. Plante*, 99 Nev. 259, 261, 661 P.2d 880 (1983).

In opposing a receivership, the goal is to demonstrate to the court an alternative and equally efficient method of achieving the purpose for which the receivership is sought. For example, an "oversight receiver," who merely oversees the income and expenses without actually taking possession of the property may be sufficient. In other cases, a "keeper" or a lockbox procedure may suffice. In any event, opposition to the appointment of a receivership should be creative and flexible.

To obtain the appointment of a receiver, the plaintiff must satisfy the same equitable criteria as that required for injunctive relief. *Hines v. Plante*, 99 Nev. 259, 262, 661 P.2d 880 (1983). If, for example, the applicant cannot demonstrate a reasonable probability of success on the merits, the application for a receivership will be denied. *Charmicor, Inc. v. Bradshaw Finance Co.*, 92 Nev. 310, 313, 550 P.2d 413 (1976); *Hines*, 99 Nev. at 262. Similarly, the petition for appointment of a receiver will also fail if the defendant can demonstrate that legal remedies are adequate. *State ex rel. Nenzel v. Second Judicial District Court*, 49 Nev. 145, 160, 241 P. 317 (1925).

Other barriers may preclude appointment of a receiver. For example, the appointment of a receiver must be "ancillary to" or "in aid of" the action and not the sole claim for relief. Thus, in *State ex rel. Nenzel v. Second Judicial District Court*, 49 Nev. 145, 241 P. 317 (1925), the court denied an application for a receiver because the complaint sought no relief other than the appointment.

Defense against the appointment of a receiver can be made on the bases that a receiver is potentially costly and can greatly add to the expense of litigation; the receivership impinges upon the ability of principals to conduct business and may endanger the viability of the business; and on the ground that the receivership may impose a substantial administrative burden on the court. *Hines v. Plante*, 99 Nev. 259, 261, 661 P.2d 880 (1983).

In the context of a corporate receivership, allegations and proof of applicant's ten percent ownership in a corporation are jurisdictional. *Searchlight Development, Inc. v. Martella*, 84 Nev. 102, 109, 437 P.2d 86 (1968); *see Transcontinental Oil Co. v. Free*, 80 Nev. 207, 209-10, 391 P.2d 317 (1964) (allegation may be supplied by amended pleading without depriving court of jurisdiction). Pursuant to NRS 78.630, a petitioning creditor must allege and prove that the creditor represents ten percent of the outstanding indebtedness of the corporation.

§3005. Duties and liabilities of the receiver.

Many of the receiver's powers and duties are prescribed by statutes, as in the case of corporations — NRS 78.635, 78.640, 78.645, 78.655-78.715 — or some other enabling statute authorizing the appointment of a receiver over a specific institution or enterprise, such as a savings and loan company or thrift company. NRS 677.530 and NRS 673.497. There are no statutes, however, addressing the powers and duties of a receiver in those cases where the receiver is appointed under NRS 32.010 or NRS 106.025, such as in partnership disputes or mortgage defaults. Therefore, the receiver's powers and duties arise from case law and are usually set forth in the order appointing the receiver. The proposed order appointing the receiver should include all potential acts which a receiver might be called upon to take.

a. Duty to control and take possession of property.

The primary function of the receiver is to take possession of and to manage the assets of the receivership estate. The receiver does not ordinarily have title to the property. *See, e.g.,* NRS 78.665; *Lynn v. Ingalls,* 100 Nev. 115, 120, 676 P.2d 797 (1984). No one may interfere, however, with the receiver's right to possession in the absence of a court order. *Gottwals v. Manske,* 60 Nev. 76, 83, 99 P.2d 645 (1940). The receiver must seek a court order authorizing the sale of property.

The federal rules require the deposit of funds received by the receiver into a depository designated by the court in an account entitled Receiver's Account, together with the name of the action. Local Rule 210-8. The receiver must post a bond in an amount to be determined by the court. Local Rule 210-9. The United States District Court Local Rules further provide that in all respects not governed by the state statutes or applicable local rules, receivership estates are to be administered in a similar manner to chapter 11 bankruptcy cases. Local Rule 210-11. While the local rules of Nevada state courts do not contain a similar mandate, a similar procedure should be followed.

See §3007, *infra* for a discussion of the presentation of claims.

b. Right to reject contracts and compromise claims.

A receiver may reject contracts that are deemed detrimental to the receivership estate. *See Jones v. Free,* 83 Nev. 31, 39, 422 P.2d 551 (1967). However, rejection of a contract merely relieves the receiver from performing. The contracting parties remain bound by the terms of the contract. *See Sterling Builders, Inc. v. Furman,* 80 Nev. 543, 550, 396 P.2d. 850 (1964).

The receiver may also compromise claims and litigation. *Jones,* 83 Nev. at 38.

c. The right to sue and be sued.

A receiver may hire an attorney during the administration of the receivership estate. *See F.C. Mortimer v. Pacific States Savings & Loan Co.,* 62 Nev. 142, 147 P.2d 552 (1943). The receiver has the right to prosecute lawsuits against parties to the litigation and against strangers to the receivership litigation. *State ex rel. Cameron v. Second Judicial District Court,* 48 Nev. 198, 203, 228 P. 617 (1924). Additionally, the receiver may be sued in his official capacity by third parties seeking recovery from the assets of the receivership.

Although the receiver is a neutral party in disputes regarding competing interests among creditors in the receivership estate, the receiver may deviate from neutrality to serve the best interests of the estate or to prevent interference with administration of the receiver's duties. *See State ex rel. Cameron v. Second Judicial District Court,* 48 Nev. 198, 203, 228 P. 617 (1924); *Esmeralda County v. Wildes,* 36 Nev. 526, 532, 137 P. 400 (1913) (receiver may appeal from judgment that affects estate as a whole).

d. Limitations on receiver's powers.

The powers of a receiver are limited to those conferred by statute, by the provisions of the order of appointment, or other customs and practices of equity. *Bowler v. Leonard,* 70 Nev. 370, 383, 269 P.2d 833 (1954). If a question arises as to the receiver's authority, the proper procedure is to seek instruction from the appointing court or amendment of an existing order. *Gottwals v. Manske,* 60 Nev. 76, 83, 99 P.2d 645 (1940).

A receiver is not authorized to sell, transfer or encumber receivership property without a court order. *See Gottwals v. Manske,* 60 Nev. 76, 82, 99 P.2d 645 (1940). The receiver must resist the levy against receivership property and must hold the property pending instructions from the court. *Id.* at 83.

§ 3006. Representing the receiver.

If the receiver distributes property without a court order, the receiver and his attorney can be held in contempt of court and the receiver may be held personally liable. *Gottwals v. Manske,* 60 Nev. 76, 83, 99 P.2d 645 (1940). Counsel should advise the receiver to monitor employees, to collect accurate information upon which decisions are based, and to seek court approval of all actions. The motion to the court should be noticed to all creditors and should include candid and complete disclosures to the court of all relevant facts.

Although Nevada law is silent with respect to this issue, other courts have held that a receiver enjoys a qualified, derived judicial immunity for acts performed within the course and scope of this authority. *New Alaska Development Corp. v. Guetschow*, 869 F.2d 1298 (9th Cir. 1989); *Property Management Investments, Inc. v. Lewis*, 752 F.2d 599 (11th Cir. 1985); *Brewer v. Hill*, 453 F. Supp. 67 (N.D. Tex. 1978); *see Receiver's Personal Liability for Negligence in Failing to Care for or Maintain Property in Receivership*, 20 A.L.R.3d 967. In *Alaska Development*, the court of appeals compared the liability of a receiver to that of a trustee in bankruptcy, citing two cases in which bankruptcy trustees have been held liable for intentional or negligent actions outside the scope of their authority.

Thus, by analogy to the personal liability of a bankruptcy trustee, a receiver has broad immunity when acting within the scope of authority granted by the appointing court and pursuant to court order. *See Mullis v. United States Bankruptcy Court*, 828 F.2d 1385 (9th Cir. 1987). However, a receiver would not be immune from liability arising from his or her intentional or negligent violations of duties imposed by law. *See In re Cochise College Park, Inc.*, 703 F.2d 1339 (9th Cir. 1983). A receiver has the duty to treat all creditors fairly and to exercise the care and diligence that an ordinarily prudent person would under similar circumstances. For example, failure to maintain fire insurance on property that was burned, causing loss to the owners and lessee, could render the receiver liable in both his personal and his official capacity. *149 Clinton Ave. North, Inc. v. Grassi*, 382 N.Y.S.2d 185 (App. Div. 1976); *Citibank, N.A. v. TTP Realty Corp.*, 417 N.Y.S.2d 691 (App. Div. 1979). A receiver would have the obligation not to act out of self-interest or out of the interest of the persons employed by the receiver, even if in good faith. *Mosser v. Darrow*, 341 U.S. 267 (1951). Qualified judicial immunity may be contingent upon candid disclosure of relevant circumstances and obtaining court approval before acting. *See In re San Juan Hotel Corp.*, 847 F.2d 931 (1st Cir. 1989); *Bennett v. Williams*, 892 F.2d 822 (9th Cir. 1989). An erroneous judgment may serve as the basis for liability if the receiver knows or should have known that he was violating his duty. *See In re Rigden*, 795 F.2d 727 (9th Cir. 1986).

On the other hand, if the receiver's liability arises solely from acts within the ambit of the receiver's official duty, the doctrine of derived judicial immunity should shield the receiver from personal liability. *See Lonneker Farms, Inc. v. Klobucher*, 804 F.2d 1096 (9th Cir. 1986).

If the receiver continues to operate a business, the order appointing the receiver should contain specific authority to conduct the business and specific instructions with respect to the operations. Prudence and case law dictate that a receiver should not operate a business under the prospect of a continuing loss. *R.J. Reynolds v. Jones*, 54 F.2d 329 (8th Cir. 1931). Incurring debts beyond the ability of the receivership property to pay and without court approval may subject the receiver to personal liability for the amount of the debts. *Haines v. Buckeye Wheel Co.*, 224 F. 289 (6th Cir. 1985). Pursuant to 28 U.S.C. § 959(a), receivers "may be sued, without leave of the court appointing them, with respect to any of their acts or transactions in carrying on business connected with such property." A receiver appointed in federal court "shall manage and operate the property in his possession as such trustee, receiver or manager according to the laws of the State in which such property is situated, in the same manner that the owner or the possessor thereof would be bound to do if in possession thereof." 28 U.S.C. § 959(b).

The receiver and counsel for the receiver have independent and equal priority claims against the receivership estate for their fees and costs, which are entitled to priority as part of the cost of administering the receivership. *Gordon v. Como Consolidated Mining Co.*, 55 Nev. 13, 15, 23 P.2d 372 (1933); *see F.C. Mortimer v. Pacific States Savings & Loan Co.*, 62 Nev. 142, 146-47, 141 P.2d 552 (1943). In a receivership for a corporation, NRS 78.705 specifically provides for the recovery of compensation for the services of the receiver and all of the costs and expenses connected with the administration of the estate. Moreover, receivership proceedings shall be paid "first" out of the assets of the corporation. NRS 78.705. *See also Right of a Receiver Who is an Attorney to Employ Another Attorney at the Expense of the Estate*, 62 A.L.R. 1536. The party defending against the wrongful appointment of a receiver may be awarded attorneys' fees. *See Warren v. DeLong*, 59 Nev. 481, 494, 97 P.2d 792 (1940).

Compensation is measured by the reasonable value of services rendered and is within the discretion of the trial court. *F.C. Mortimer v. Pacific States Savings & Loan Co.*, 62 Nev. 147, 158, 145 P.2d 733 (1944). In *Mortimer*, the court considered the value of the property; the practical benefits to the estate; the labor and skill required; and the degree of activity, integrity and dispatch of the receiver's work.

Fees may not be awarded ex parte, but only after a noticed hearing. *F.C. Mortimer v. Pacific States Savings & Loan Co.*, 62 Nev. 147, 159, 145 P.2d 733 (1944).

The receiver's fees and other costs and expenses are paid out of the general receivership estate, rather than out of any special assets awarded to a particular party, implying that all parties to the litigation share in the cost of the receivership, regardless of any fault or culpability by the various parties associated with the litigation. The expenses of the receivership may not be recovered as a cost of litigation. NRS 18.010; *see McKenzie v. Coslett*, 28 Nev. 220, 221, 80 P. 1070 (1905).

§ 3007. Representing claimants.

Under NRS 78.675, creditors must present their claims within six months from the date of appointment of the receiver for a corporation, if the court has not ordered that the claims be filed sooner. Failure to file a claim bars the claimant from participating in the distribution of the assets of a corporation. NRS 78.675. As a practical matter, claimant's counsel should notify the receiver and counsel of the claimant's interest and file a request for notice of all actions in the proceeding. Similarly, counsel for claimant should review the court file to determine the last day for filing claims and should ensure that a timely and complete claim, including all invoices and other proof of indebtedness, is filed with the court.

Immediately upon the expiration of the time fixed for the filing of claims, in a corporate receivership, NRS 78.685(1) requires the clerk of the district court to notify the receiver of the filing of claims. The receiver is then to inspect the claims and to notify each claimant of the receiver's decision to accept or reject the claim within thirty days. Pursuant to NRS 78.685(1), the receiver may require creditors whose claims are disputed to submit to an examination under oath or affirmation. If the receiver denies a claim, NRS 78.685(2) provides that the claimant may appeal to the district court within thirty days. Former NRS 78.685 allowed a claimant to demand a jury trial on the claim. This statute was repealed in 1991.

In non-corporate receivership proceedings, the procedure is much less well defined. Although the local rules for the United States District Court for the District of Nevada provide that the receiver must give all creditors notice of all hearings, the Nevada state district courts do not have a similar rule, suggesting that intervention pursuant to NRCP 24 may be the most effective mechanism to monitor the proceedings and protect the claimant's interest. Local Rule 210-5 (1992).

Under NRS 78.720, employees have a lien upon the assets of the corporation for wages not exceeding $1,000 earned within the three months preceding insolvency or dissolution of a corporation. Chapter 78 also prescribes the priority of administrative claims and the method of distribution to creditors, the only context in which a lien or priority against the receivership estate is statutorily created. In the case of a partnership that was placed in receivership, partial payments to a creditor did not discharge the individual partners from further obligations. *Sterling Builders, Inc. v. Fuhrman*, 80 Nev. 543, 550, 396 P.2d 850 (1964).

Any dividend which remains unclaimed for seven years reverts to the general fund of the estate. NRS 32.020. The funds are then paid to costs and expenses of the administration and to a new dividend distributed to creditors whose claims have been allowed but not paid in full, and the balance is presumed to be abandoned pursuant to NRS 120A.210. Although the statute does not define dividend, it appears to encompass any payments to be made to creditors.

§ 3008. Winding up a receivership.

During the pendency of the corporate receivership, NRS 78.670 requires the receiver to file an inventory, list of debts, and report every three months. Before distribution, the assets of the insolvent corporation are first used to pay reasonable compensation to the receiver, the costs and expenses of the administration of the receivership and the cost of the proceedings in the court. NRS 78.705. After the payment of these administrative expenses, secured creditors are paid to the extent of their priority, and unsecured creditors are to be paid in proportion to the amount of their respective debts, except mortgage and judgment creditors "when the judgment has not been by confession for the purpose of preferring creditors." NRS 78.710. The surplus funds, if any, are distributed to stockholders. *Id.*

The corporate statutes do not discuss the procedure for winding up a receivership in any greater depth and neither Chapter 32 nor Chapter 107 provides any guidance on winding up receiverships. However, NRCP 66 requires that "an action where a receiver has been appointed may not be dismissed except by order of the court." Prudent practice dictates that the receiver apply to the court for an order authorizing final distribution, file a final report and obtain an order dismissing the receivership and discharging the receiver. All potentially interested parties should be provided notice of the final report and the request for distribution. The United States District Court Local Rules provide that a receiver may not be dismissed except by leave of court and on notice to all parties. Local Rule 210-10.

§ 3009. Appeals.

a. Appealable orders.

An aggrieved party does not have the right to appeal a judgment or order except as expressly granted by statute or rule. NRAP 3A(a); *Alper v. Posin,* 77 Nev. 328, 330, 363 P.2d 502 (1961). Appeal may be taken from an order appointing or refusing to appoint a receiver, or vacating or refusing to vacate an order appointing a receiver. NRAP 3A(b)(2). The order of final distribution may be appealed. *Martin & Co. v. Kirby,* 34 Nev. 205, 215, 117 P. 2 (1911). However, interlocutory orders approving actions and decisions made by a receiver during the ordinary course of administration may not be appealed. For example, an order confirming the sale of certain receivership assets is not appealable. *Alper,* 77 Nev. at

330. Similarly, an order approving a compromise of claims arising out of a joint venture agreement is not appealable, unless the order also finally terminates the litigation. *Jones v. Free*, 89 Nev. 31, 35, 422 P.2d 551 (1967).

In the absence of a right to appeal, extraordinary relief may be available in the form of a petition for a writ of certiorari when the district court exceeds its jurisdiction, NRS 34.020 *et seq.*, a petition for writ of mandamus to compel the performance of an act, NRS 34.150 *et seq.*, or a petition for writ of prohibition to prohibit the proceedings, NRS 34.320 *et seq.* In the federal forum, the All Writs Statute, 28 U.S.C. § 1651, may provide extraordinary relief in the absence of a remedy at law accompanied by damage or prejudice to a petitioner that may not be correctable on appeal. *Cf. In re Allen*, 896 F.2d 416, 419-20 (9th Cir. 1990); *The Oregonian Publishing Co. v. U.S. District Court for the District of Oregon*, 920 F.2d 1462, 1464 (9th Cir. 1990).

b. Standing.

The general rule of standing that a party who has appeared or intervened and has an interest to be protected on appeal should apply with equal force to appellate litigation arising from receivership proceedings. Thus, a state regulatory agency may appeal an award of fees in a receivership case even though the state would not be entitled to share in a distribution of assets that would otherwise be available if the fees were not paid. *State v. Wildes,* 37 Nev. 55, 139 P. 505 (1914). A creditor who is dissatisfied with the final account and order of distribution has standing to appeal. *Cf. State ex rel. Cameron v. Second Judicial District Court,* 48 Nev. 198, 203, 228 P. 617 (1924). Officers and directors of a corporation have standing to appeal. *Jones v. Free,* 89 Nev. 31, 36, 422 P.2d 551 (1967). The receiver has standing to appeal a judgment that affects the interests of the estate as a whole, but lacks standing in a dispute between creditors as to right to distribution of receivership funds. *Esmeralda County v. Wildes,* 36 Nev. 526, 532, 137 P. 400 (1913). Counsel for a receiver has standing to appeal an order awarding attorney's fees. *F.C. Mortimer v. Pacific States Savings & Loan Co.,* 62 Nev. 142, 146-47, 141 P.2d 552 (1943).

c. Time within which to appeal.

The time within which to file a notice of appeal is governed by NRAP 4. The notice of appeal from an order concerning the appointment of a receiver must be filed within thirty days after the date of service of written notice of entry of the order. *See Maitia v. Allied Land & Live Stock Co.,* 49 Nev. 451, 465, 248 P. 893 (1926). An appeal from an order appointing a receiver that was not taken until after the entry of final judgment is untimely.

d. Standard of review on appeal.

The decision to appoint a receiver rests on the sound discretion of the trial court. The standard of review of an order appointing or refusing to appoint a receiver will not be disturbed on appeal in the absence of a clear abuse of that discretion. *Nishon's, Inc. v. Kendigian,* 91 Nev. 504, 505, 538 P.2d 580 (1975); *Peri-Gil Corp. v. Sutton,* 84 Nev. 406, 411, 442 P.2d 35 (1968); *Bowler v. Leonard,* 70 Nev. 370, 383, 269 P.2d 833 (1954).

An award of fees for the receiver and counsel is within the discretion of the trial court and is reviewed for abuse of discretion. *F.C. Mortimer v. Pacific States Savings & Loan Co.,* 62 Nev. 147, 158, 145 P.2d 733 (1944).

Form 30A

Case No.
Dept. No.

IN THE _____ JUDICIAL DISTRICT COURT OF THE
STATE OF NEVADA
IN AND FOR THE COUNTY OF _____

_____,

     Plaintiff,

                               CLAIM FOR RELIEF

v.

_____,

     Defendant.
_____/

(Receiver)

IA.

NRS § 32.010 provides that a receiver may be appointed in an action by a creditor to subject any property.

IB.

NRS § 78.630 provides that a receiver may be appointed for a corporation whenever it shall become insolvent or shall suspend its ordinary business for want of funds to carry on the same, or if its business has been and is being conducted at a great loss and greatly prejudicial to the interest of its creditors or stockholders, on application of any creditor's holding 10% of the outstanding debt or stockholders owing 10% of the outstanding capital stock entitled to vote.

II.

Plaintiff has interests in _____'s real and personal property, which interests are entitled to protection during the pendency of these proceedings.

III.

The appointment of a receiver during the pendency of these proceedings is necessary to conserve, preserve, protect and administer _____'s assets in which Plaintiff has an interest and to administer the final disposition of _____'s assets and the distribution of the proceeds thereof.

IV.

If a receiver is not appointed to preserve and protect _____'s assets and to ultimately administer the disposition of said assets and the distribution of

689

the sale proceeds, _____'s assets are likely to suffer economic loss, waste and/or injury.

V.

The appointment of a receiver is appropriate under the circumstances of the present case under the authority of NRS § 32.010 _____ [NRS 78.622].

WHEREFORE, Plaintiff prays for relief as follows:

1. For a joint and several judgment against _____ [debtor] for damages suffered by Plaintiff in an amount in excess of $_____, the exact amount of which is to be proven at the trial in this matter;

2. For an order appointing a receiver of _____'s assets including, but not limited to, the personal property and real property described on Exhibits "_____" and "_____," hereto, for the purpose of conserving, preserving, protecting, administering and ultimately disposing of _____'s assets and distributing the proceeds thereof;

3. For an order authorizing the receiver to _____ [manage] [liquidate] _____'s assets;

4. That any proceeds of the assets be applied in payment of the amounts due to Plaintiff;

5. For an order requiring that all persons claiming an interest in the assets be noticed;

6. For an order authorizing the receiver to pay to Plaintiff the amount of _____ as interim compensation required by _____;

7. For an award of reasonable attorney's fee incurred in connection with the prosecution of this action;

8. For costs of suit; and

9. For such other and further relief as this Court deems just and proper in the premises.

DATED: This _____ day of _____, 1992.

By: _____
Attorneys for Plaintiff

Form 30B

Case No.

Dept. No.

IN THE _____ JUDICIAL DISTRICT COURT OF THE
STATE OF NEVADA
IN AND FOR THE COUNTY OF _____

_____,

Plaintiff,

v.

APPLICATION BY RECEIVER
FOR ORDER REQUIRING
PRESENTATION AND FILING CLAIMS

_____,

Defendant.

_____/

COMES NOW, _____, the court-appointed Receiver for
[_____ business name]'s assets and makes application to the court as
follows:

1. Under the provisions of this court's order dated _____ appointing
_____ as receiver of _____, a defendant herein, _____ is
charged with the duty, among others, of paying the debts and liabilities of said
defendant.

2. In order for the receiver to discharge its aforesaid duty, it is necessary that
this court enter an order setting a time for the filing of claims, specifying the
form and manner in which said claims shall be filed, and setting forth the manner in which such order shall be published and notice thereof otherwise given to
the known creditors of said defendant.

3. _____ recommends that claimants should be required to state in
their claims their name, address, and telephone number; the amount of the
claim; the priority status, if any, claimed; and the nature and value of any
security held by them.

WHEREFORE, [_____ name of receiver] prays that this court enter an
order directing all persons having claims or demands against _____, a
defendant herein, to file such claims in this cause and furnish copies thereof to
[business] within such time and in such form and manner as the court may
direct, and that this court also instruct _____ as to the manner of publishing and giving notice of such order.

DATED this _____ day of _____, 1992.

By _____
Attorney for Receiver

Form 30C

Case No.

Dept. No.

IN THE _____ JUDICIAL DISTRICT COURT OF THE
STATE OF NEVADA
IN AND FOR THE COUNTY OF _____

_____,

Plaintiff,

v.

ORDER REQUIRING
PRESENTATION AND FILING
OF CLAIMS

_____,

Defendant.

_____ /

The petition of _____, the court-appointed receiver herein, for an order requiring the presentation and filing of claims having been filed and submitted to this court for consideration and for good cause shown,

IT IS HEREBY ORDERED that all persons, firms, or corporations having claims or demands against _____, a defendant herein, are required, on or before to file the same in this proceeding and serve a copy thereof on receiver herein, _____ [address of receiver] or _____ [receiver's attorney and address] under penalty of having said claims disallowed by this court if not timely filed;

IT IS FURTHER ORDERED that said claims or demands shall be verified or supported by affidavit, and shall set out the amount and nature of any security or lien held by the claimant, or to which claimant is or may be entitled, and shall also state any claim to preference or priority in payment from the assets in the hands of the receiver or earnings therefrom;

IT IS FURTHER ORDERED that the receiver shall publish a notice setting forth the contents of this order once a week for two successive weeks in a newspaper published and of general circulation in _____ County, and shall also give notice by mail, prior to the expiration of the time for filing claims, to all creditors and claimants of whose names and addresses it may be informed;

IT IS ALSO ORDERED that the receiver shall, as soon as convenient after _____, file with the court a list of all such claims as have been presented to it.

DATED: This _____ day of _____, 1992.

_____
DISTRICT JUDGE

Form 30D

Case No.

Dept. No.

IN THE _____ JUDICIAL DISTRICT COURT OF THE
STATE OF NEVADA
IN AND FOR THE COUNTY OF _____

_____,

     Plaintiff,

v.

                            ORDER APPROVING FIRST
                            REPORT OF RECEIVER

_____,

     Defendant.

_____/

The First Report of the Receiver for the period ending _____ having been presented to the Court, the hearing having been duly noticed and the Court having reviewed the report and arguments of counsel, and good cause appearing therefor,

IT IS HEREBY ORDERED that the First Report of Receiver for the period ending _____, together with the transactions and actions taken by the Receiver as set forth in the report, together with all disbursements of funds and accountings by the Receiver during said period of time, are hereby approved.

DATED this _____ day of _____, 1992.

_____
DISTRICT JUDGE

693

Form 30E

Case No.

Dept. No.

IN THE _____ JUDICIAL DISTRICT COURT OF THE
STATE OF NEVADA
IN AND FOR THE COUNTY OF _____

_____,

Plaintiff,

v.   FIRST REPORT OF RECEIVER

_____,

Defendant.

_____/

COMES NOW _____ [name of receiver], the court-appointed Receiver in the above-entitled action, pursuant to Order of this Court dated _____, and hereby submits the following report for the period ending _____.

The Receiver, in connection with this report, also requests the Court to enter an Order approving said report and the actions and transactions implemented by the Receiver, for said period as outlined hereafter.

Attached hereto and marked Exhibit "A" is a Memorandum to the undersigned counsel from _____ [receiver] which summarizes the operating results of _____ [name of business] and the Receiver's actions and accountings through _____ [date]. Attached hereto and marked Exhibit "B" is the operating statement and Balance Sheet for the company for the period ending _____ [date].

In addition to the transactions referred to in the report, the receiver has also _____.

In accordance with the above, the Receiver hereby requests the Court, after a noticed hearing, to approve the First Report of Receiver for the period ending _____ [date], the operating statement and Balance Sheet for the period ending _____ [date], together with the actions, accounts and transactions taken by the Receiver during said period.

DATED: This _____ day of _____, 1992.

By _____
Attorney for Receiver

Form 30F

Case No.

Dept. No.

    IN THE _____ JUDICIAL DISTRICT COURT OF THE
STATE OF NEVADA
IN AND FOR THE COUNTY OF _____

_____,

        Plaintiff,

                              PROOF OF CLAIM

v.

_____,

        Defendant.
_____/

    Pursuant to the Order of this Court, filed _____ [date], _____ [claimant(s)], by and through _____ attorney, hereby submit(s) the following claim in the above-entitled action.

    Pursuant to the agreement held by and between claimant and _____ [debtor's name], _____ [debtor's name] is presently indebted to claimant as follows:

    1. _____

    2. Ongoing amounts accrue from and after _____ in the amount of _____ ($_____) per _____ [month(s)] together with any late fees and any charges.

    The agreement is attached hereto as Exhibit 1.

    Claimant also incorporates into said claim all costs and expenses incurred to date and thereafter in the collection of all rental amounts due as well as any action needed to recover possession of the premises.

    Claimant further submits that said claim is secured based upon statutory lien rights held by claimant over the property and assets located on the premises to the extent of any unpaid rent and any expenses incurred in collecting same.

    Claimant finally submits that said claim is a priority claim based upon the legal relationship of Claimant to Defendant, as evidenced by _____.

    Respectfully submitted this _____ day of _____, 1992.

                         _____

                         Attorney for Creditor
                         _____ [name of creditor]

VERIFICATION

STATE OF NEVADA   )
                         : ss.

COUNTY OF _____   )

_____, being first duly sworn, under penalty of perjury, deposes and says:

That _____ (s)he is agent for _____, Claimant in the above-referenced action; that _____ (s)he read the attached Proof of Claim and knows the contents thereof; that the same is true of _____ (her)/his own knowledge except for those matters therein contained which are stated upon information and belief and as for those matters _____ (s)he believes them to be true.

I declare under the penalty of perjury that the assertions contained in this Verification are true and correct.

Executed in _____, Nevada, this _____ day of _____, 1992.

_____

_____ [name]

SUBSCRIBED and SWORN to before me
this _____ day of _____, 1992.

_____

NOTARY PUBLIC

Form 30G

Case No.

Dept. No.

IN THE _____ JUDICIAL DISTRICT COURT OF THE
STATE OF NEVADA
IN AND FOR THE COUNTY OF _____

_____,

      Plaintiff,

                             NOTICE OF APPOINTMENT

v.   OF RECEIVER

_____,

      Defendant.

_____/

NOTICE IS HEREBY GIVEN that _____ [name and address] was appointed by the court as Receiver for all of _____ [name of business]'s assets on _____, pursuant to NRS 32.010.

DATED: This _____ day of _____, 1992.

                                By _____
                                      Attorney for Receiver

Form 30H

Case No.

Dept. No.

IN THE _____ JUDICIAL DISTRICT COURT OF THE
STATE OF NEVADA
IN AND FOR THE COUNTY OF _____

_____,
     Plaintiff,

v.

_____,
     Defendant.
_____/

MOTION BY _____ [creditor]
TO INTERVENE AS A
DEFENDANT

_____ [creditor] moves for leave to intervene as of right under NRCP 24(a)(2) as a defendant in this action, for the purpose of _____. The Plaintiff has filed a motion for appointment of receiver, and the hearing on that motion has been set for the _____ day of _____, 1992, at __ .m. _____ [creditor] requests that this motion to intervene be granted so that it may participate in the hearing upon the motion of appointment of receiver.

This motion is made and based upon the pleadings and papers on file herein, and on the following points and authorities.

DATED: This _____ day of _____, 1992.

By: _____
Attorneys for _____

POINTS AND AUTHORITIES

As interpreted by the courts, Rule 24(a)(2) requires an application to satisfy a four-part test:
(1) the applicant's motion must be timely;
(2) the applicant must assert an interest relating to the property or transaction which is the subject of the action;
(3) the applicant must be so situated that without intervention the disposition of the action may, as a practical matter, impair or impede his ability to protect that interest; and
(4) the applicant's interest must be inadequately represented by the other parties.

Sagebrush Rebellion, Inc. v. Watt, 713 F.2d 525, 527 (9th Cir. 1983), *citing Smith v. Pangilinan*, 651 F.2d 1320, 1323-24 (9th Cir. 1981). The rule must be liberally construed in favor of intervention. *Sagebrush*, 713 F.2d at 527.

The first requirement, timeliness, is complied with where the applicant moves for intervention at a very early stage of the proceedings; as is the case here where the complaint was filed less than one month ago. *See Alaniz v. Tille Lewis Foods*,

572 F.2d 657, 659 (9th Cir.) (per curiam), *cert. denied*, 439 U.S. 837, 99 S. Ct. 123, 58 L. Ed. 2d 134 (1978).

_____ [creditor] meets the second requirement because _____.

The third requirement is closely related and involves an interdependent analysis with the second requirement. *Pacific Mutual Life Insurance Co. v. American National Bank*, 110 F.R.D. 272, 277 (N.D. Ill. 1986). _____ [creditor]'s interest *may* be impaired by appointment of a receiver, because _____.

Thus, _____'s property interest *may* be impaired or impeded by actions taken in this lawsuit. *See, e.g., County of Fresno v. Andrus*, 622 F.2d at 438 (farmers may intervene where their participation in governmental excess land sales may be impaired by challenge to lack of rulemaking procedures of the Secretary of Interior); *Pacific Mutual Life Insurance Co. v. American National Bank*, 110 F.R.D. at 277 (limited partners may intervene in suit to foreclose on partnership property).

The fourth requirement involves a minimal showing that the applicant's interest may not be adequately represented by the existing parties. *Smith v. Pangilinan*, 651 F.2d at 1325. _____ [creditor]'s interests are clearly adverse to both plaintiff and defendant _____. The present parties will not protect [creditor]'s interest, and they will not make those arguments that [creditor] makes in the attached pleading or at other stages of this action. *County of Fresno v. Andrus*, 622 F.2d 436, 439 (9th Cir. 1980).

Unless the Court summarily grants this motion, _____ requests a hearing pursuant to _____ which it is entitled to receive according to due process requirements. [D]ue process requires that proposed intervenors be provided a hearing prior to a ruling on their motions to intervene. *Jones v. Caddo Parish School Board*, 704 F.2d 206, 222 (5th Cir. 1983).

[Creditor] meets the standards set forth in NRCP 24(a)(2), and the Court should allow [creditor] to intervene as of right.

DATED: This _____ day of _____, 1992.

By: _____

Attorneys for _____

Form 30I

Case No.

Dept. No.

IN THE _____ JUDICIAL DISTRICT COURT OF THE
STATE OF NEVADA
IN AND FOR THE COUNTY OF _____

_____,

    Plaintiff,

v.

    LIMITED OPPOSITION TO
    APPOINTMENT OF RECEIVER

_____,

    Defendant.

Defendant _____, through _____ its/their counsel, _____ of _____, submit _____ this Limited Opposition to this court for appointment of receiver. _____ agrees, generally, that a receiver should be appointed to conserve, preserve, protect and administer _____'s assets and to continue the operation of _____'s business and ultimately dispose of said assets and distribute the proceeds thereof in accordance with further orders of this court. The receiver shall be appointed only to manage the assets of _____ and must post a bond in an amount sufficient to indemnify Defendant _____ acquiescence to the appointment of a receiver is not to constitute an admission of any facts, claims or any liability with respect to this lawsuit or the factual matters provided in the Application for Appointment of Receiver filed by _____. Further, _____'s general agreement with the appointment of a receiver shall not be construed as a waiver of _____'s rights, including without limitation, the right to contest any actions or inactions of the receiver.

DATED: This _____ day of _____, 1992.

                           _____

                           Attorneys for _____

Form 30J

Case No.

Dept. No.

IN THE _____ JUDICIAL DISTRICT COURT OF THE
STATE OF NEVADA
IN AND FOR THE COUNTY OF _____

_____,

Plaintiff,

                                           ORDER APPOINTING

v.   RECEIVER

_____,

Defendant.
_____/

This matter came before the Court the _____ day of _____, 1992, upon an Application for Appointment of Receiver filed herein on the _____ day of _____, by Plaintiff for the appointment of a receiver for all of _____'s ("_____") assets under the authority of NRS § [32.010] [78.635]. Personal appearances were made by _____ on behalf of Plaintiff, _____ on behalf of _____ [debtor] and _____ on behalf of _____, the proposed receiver. The Court has reviewed the Application of Receiver, the Affidavit of _____ in Support of Application for Receiver, and the Verified Complaint filed herein. The Court, after hearing the arguments of counsel and being fully apprised of the premises, finds and concludes that: The appointment of a receiver is necessary to conserve, preserve, protect and administer _____'s assets and to continue to operate _____'s business until said receiver can dispose of the assets; and it would be in the best interest of _____, its estate and its creditors to appoint a receiver for _____'s assets.

NOW, THEREFORE, for good cause appearing,

IT IS HEREBY ORDERED that:

1. _____ be, and hereby is, appointed the receiver of all of _____'s assets utilized in connection with _____ operations including, but not limited to, the real and personal property set forth on Exhibit "A," hereto, which appointment shall become effective at _____ ___.m., on the _____ day of _____, 1992.

2. _____, as receiver, may:

(a) Conserve, preserve and administer _____'s assets,

(b) Manage and operate _____'s business,

(c) Enter into an Exclusive Listing Agreement with _____ to sell _____'s assets,

3. _____, its [stockholders, owners, partners, joint venturers,] employees and agents shall cooperate with the receiver in the operation and sale of _____'s business;

701

4. Except as provided herein, _____, its _____ [stockholders, owners, partners, joint venturers], managers, employees and agents are prohibited and enjoined from:

(a) Collecting any debts due to _____, except as may be requested by the receiver,

(b) Paying out, assigning, selling, conveying, transferring, encumbering, or delivering any of _____'s assets to any other person;

5. _____'s other creditors and any other third parties are prohibited and enjoined from instituting or carrying forward any suit or any other action to enforce claims against _____'s assets so long as the receivership is in place;

6. _____ may serve as receiver _____ with/without the need of filing or posting a bond;

7. _____ may be reimbursed for its key personnel's time at the rate of $_____ per hour, subject to final approval by this Court, and for its out-of-pocket costs from the receivership estate; and

8. _____ may employ counsel and other professionals necessary to receivership, which counsel and other professionals may be paid from the receivership estate subject to the final approval of this court.

9. From _____ __.m., _____, and until _____ [time], _____, its _____ [stockholders, owners, partners, joint venturers], employees and agents shall not:

(a) Pay any debts, obligations or expenses owned by _____ or relating to its radio stations unless _____ shall first have submitted a list of operating expenses it intends to pay to Plaintiff's counsel, _____, and the Plaintiff shall have approved such expenditures, which approval shall be granted or denied within thirty-six (36) hours of _____'s submission of its list to Plaintiff's counsel;

(b) Compromise or negotiate compromises with any of its creditors for the payment of any amounts due to _____. Any amounts which may be paid to _____ by its creditors shall be segregated and _____ shall provide Plaintiff and the receiver with a full accounting of any payments made or monies received between _____ and _____;

(c) Enter into any contracts with any third parties for any purpose except as may be permitted by this Court; and

(d) Pay out, assign, sell, convey, transfer, encumber, or deliver any of _____'s assets to any person or entity.

10. Any other actions pending against _____ in the _____ Judicial District Court of the State of Nevada shall be consolidated with these proceedings.

DATED: This _____ day of _____, 1992.

_____
DISTRICT JUDGE

Form 30K

Case No.

Dept. No.

IN THE _____ JUDICIAL DISTRICT COURT OF THE
STATE OF NEVADA
IN AND FOR THE COUNTY OF _____

_____,

    Plaintiff,

v.

_____,

    Defendant.

APPLICATION FOR
APPOINTMENT OF RECEIVER

Plaintiff, by and through its counsel, _____, hereby applies to this Court for the appointment of a receiver for all of _____'s ("_____") assets under the authority of NRS § _____ [32.010] [78.635].

_____'s assets which would be subject to the receivership would include, but not be limited to, _____'s interests in the real and personal property described in Exhibit "A" attached hereto. The receiver should be appointed to conserve, preserve, protect and administer _____'s assets, to continue the operation of _____'s business, and to ultimately dispose of said assets and distribute the proceeds thereof in accordance with the further orders of this Court. Plaintiff respectively requests that _____ be appointed receiver due to its expertise and knowledge of _____ operations and management, _____ valuation, and _____ regulations and procedures affecting _____ and the _____ industry. Inasmuch as NRS § _____ [32.010] [78.635 et seq.] does not require the posting of a bond by receivers, it is respectfully requested that _____ be appointed as receiver without the requirement of posting a bond.

Plaintiff believes that the appointment of a receiver in this matter to allow it to conserve, preserve, protect and administer _____'s assets and to run _____'s _____ and business until the assets can be disposed of and the proceeds thereof distributed is in the best interest of _____'s estate and its creditors.

Based on the Verified Complaint on file herein, the Affidavit of _____ filed contemporaneously herewith, and the points and authorities which immediately follow, Plaintiff respectfully requests that this Court enter an order:

1. Appointing _____ as the receiver of all of _____'s assets utilized in connection with its business including, but not limited to, the real and personal property set forth on Exhibit "A," hereto;

2. Authorizing _____ as a receiver, to:

    (a) Conserve, preserve, protect and administer _____'s assets,

    (b) Manage and operate _____'s business,

    (c) Enter into an Exclusive Listing agreement to sell _____'s assets,

(d) Dispose of _____'s assets and distribute the sales proceeds as directed by this Court, and

(e) Borrow such sums as may be necessary to continue to operate _____'s business if necessary, pledge _____'s assets as collateral to secure the repayment of any such loans;

3. Directing that _____, its joint ventures, employees and agents shall cooperate with the receiver in the operation and sale of _____'s business;

4. Prohibiting _____, its joint ventures, managers, employees and agents from:

(a) Collecting any debts or demands due to _____, except as may be requested by the receiver,

(b) Paying out, assigning, selling, conveying, transferring, encumbering, or delivering any of _____'s assets to any other person;

5. Prohibiting _____'s other creditors and any other third parties from instituting or carrying forward any suits or any other actions to enforce claims against _____'s assets so long as the receivership is in place;

6. Directing that _____ may serve as receiver without the need of filing or posting a bond;

7. Authorizing _____ to be reimbursed for its key personnel's time at the rate of $_____ per hour, subject to final approval by this Court, and for its out-of-pocket costs from the receivership estate; and

8. Authorizing _____ to employ counsel and other professionals necessary to the receivership, which counsel and other professionals may be paid from the receivership estate subject to the final approval of this Court.

DATED: This _____ day of _____, 1992.

By: _____
    Attorneys for Plaintiff

POINTS AND AUTHORITIES

_____ [NRS § 32.010 provides, in pertinent part, that a receiver may be appointed by the Court in which an action is pending by a creditor to subject any property or fund to his claim where it is shown that the property or fund is in danger of being lost, removed or materially injured. Additionally, NRS § 32.010 provides that a receiver may be appointed in all other cases where receivers have heretofore been appointed by courts of equity.] or [NRS 78.635 provides that] The Verified Complaint on file herein alleges that:

1. _____ [Plaintiff has perfected security interests in all of _____'s property used in connection with its operation of its business]; or [Plaintiff owns 10% of _____'s issued and outstanding voting stock]; or [_____ owes Plaintiff _____ which is 10% or more of _____'s outstanding debt];

2. _____ [_____ has been unable to meet the financial and other non-financial obligations owing to Plaintiff in accordance with _____'s agreement with Plaintiff ("_____ Agreement")]; or [_____'s business has been mismanaged to the Plaintiff's detriment as follows];

3. The appointment of a receiver is necessary to conserve, preserve, protect and administer _____'s assets and to allow the receiver to ultimately dispose of _____'s assets and distribute the proceeds thereof.

_____'s defaults of its obligations owing to Plaintiff include the failure of _____ to pay _____. The amounts of the defaulted payments are $_____.

_____'s defaults of its obligations owing to Plaintiff under the _____ Agreement evidence an inability on _____'s part to pay its obligations to its creditors as they become due. Under such circumstances, the likelihood of economic loss or injury to _____'s assets, including its goodwill and reputation in the community, is great.

Filed contemporaneously herewith is an affidavit of _____, which indicated that the current value of the assets is _____, which sum is much less than the amount owed to the Plaintiff. If Plaintiff were simply to take over _____'s assets, without the receiver's expertise, the value of _____'s assets would decline.

In order to effectively conserve, preserve and protect _____'s assets, it will be necessary for the receiver to continue to operate _____'s business, to borrow operating capital and to employ legal counsel and other professionals. Ultimately, a sale of _____'s assets would be the best solution to the present dilemma and, for that reason, it would be in the best interests of the receivership estate to allow the receiver to enter into a brokerage agreement for the sale of _____'s assets. Attached hereto as Exhibit "B" is a form listing agreement which is fairly standard in the industry and which the receiver desires to execute in order to allow _____ [business] to sell _____'s assets on the receiver's behalf. Plaintiff requests that the receiver be allowed to enter into the brokerage agreement with _____ [business]. Finally, if the receiver is to effectively conserve and preserve _____'s assets, it must be free from interference by _____'s _____ [stockholders, owners, partners, joint ventures], managers, employees, and agents and from the actions of creditors or other third party attempting to collect or seize _____'s assets.

For the reasons hereinabove set forth, Plaintiff respectfully requests this Court to enter an order:

1. Appointing _____ as the receiver of all of _____'s assets utilized in connection with its operations including, but not limited to, the real and personal property set forth on Exhibit "A" hereto;

2. Authorizing _____ as receiver to:
(a) conserve, preserve, protect and administer _____'s assets,
(b) Manage and operate _____'s business,
(c) Enter into an Exclusive Listing Agreement with _____ [business] to sell _____'s assets,
(d) Dispose of _____'s assets and distribute the sales proceeds as directed by this Court, and
(e) Borrow such sums as may be necessary to continue to operate _____'s business if necessary, to pledge _____'s assets as collateral to secure the repayment of any such loans;

3. Directing that _____, its _____ [stockholders, owners, partners, joint ventures], employees, and agents shall cooperate with the receiver in the operation and sale of _____'s business;

4. Prohibiting _____, its _____ [stockholders, owners, partners, joint ventures], managers, employees and agents from:

  (a) collecting any debts or demands due to _____, except as may be requested by the receiver,

  (b) Paying out, assigning, selling, conveying, transferring, encumbering, or delivering any of _____'s assets to any other person;

5. Prohibiting _____'s other creditors and any other third parties from instituting or carrying forward any suits or any other actions to enforce claims against _____'s assets so long as the receivership is in place;

6. Directing that _____ may serve as receiver without the need of filing or posting a bond;

7. Authorizing _____ to be reimbursed for its key personnel's time at the rate of $_____ per hour, subject to final approval by this Court, and for its out-of-pocket costs from the receivership estate; and

8. Authorizing _____ to employ counsel and other professionals necessary to the receivership, which counsel and other professionals may be paid from the receivership estate subject to the final approval of this Court.

DATED: This _____ day of _____, 1992.

By: _____

Attorneys for Plaintiff

CHAPTER 31

DECLARATORY JUDGMENTS

Author: Steven B. Glade

§ 3101. Introduction and scope.

Nevada enacted the Uniform Declaratory Judgments Act, NRS 30.010, *et seq.*, in 1929. This chapter summarizes the Nevada Supreme Court's interpretation of that statute and the requirements which must be satisfied to obtain declaratory relief in Nevada. Nevada's Judicial Confirmation Law, NRS 43.010, *et seq.*, and other specific grants of declaratory power are also discussed briefly.

§ 3102. Declaratory relief defined.

A declaratory judgment is "an authoritative judicial statement of the [legal] relationships between parties to a controversy. It does not itself, however, have any direct coercive effect." *Developments — Declaratory Judgments,* 62 Harv. L. Rev. 787 (1949). Unlike a judgment for damages or an injunction, a declaratory judgment compels no affirmative or prohibitory conduct. *Aronoff v. Katleman,* 75 Nev. 424, 345 P.2d 221 (1959). However, the edicts of a declaratory judgment may be enforced upon a recalcitrant party by application for the supplemental relief necessary to give effect to the declaration. NRS 30.100.

According to Professor Edwin Borchard, who is cited with approval in *Kress v. Corey,* 65 Nev. 1, 189 P.2d 352 (1948), declaratory relief "admits to judicial cognizance an entirely new group of interests, including aggrieved persons who, being prospective defendants to ordinary actions, were not theretofore perceived by the law until they were sued. They were not allowed to initiate proceedings." *Kress, supra,* 65 Nev. at 38. At common law, the courts awaited consummation of a legal wrong before affording a remedy. Although it attempted to escape the common law's rigidity, equity was hemmed in by a host of rigid requirements growing out of case law which fettered the discretion of the courts, leaving many genuinely desperate persons beyond the reach of equity jurisdiction. *See* Borchard, *The Next Step Beyond Equity — The Declaratory Action,* 13 U. Chi. L. Rev. 145 (1945), cited in *Kress, supra.*

The remedial policies served by the declaratory judgment are described in *Kress v. Corey,* 65 Nev. 1, 189 P.2d 352 (1948):

> It was a defect of the judicial procedure which developed under the common law that the doors of the courts were invitingly opened to a plaintiff whose legal rights had already been violated, but were rigidly closed upon a party who did not wish to violate the rights of another nor to have his own rights violated, thus compelling him, where a controversy arose with his fellow, to run the risk of a violation of his fellow's rights or to wait until the anticipated wrong had been done to himself before an adjudication of their differences could be obtained. Thus was a penalty placed upon the party who wished to act lawfully and in good faith which the statute providing for declaratory relief has gone far to remove. *Kress, supra,* at 35-36 [*quoting Tolle v. Struve,* 124 Cal. App. 263, 12 P.2d 61, 64 (1932).]

Thus, declaratory relief can be prophylactic, operating in anticipation of an otherwise harmful change of the *status quo.* An action for a declaratory judgment may be brought not only by a person who desires to enforce the legal status quo, but also by one who hopes to change the legal status quo without danger of penalty.

However, the Uniform Declaratory Judgments Act

> ... does not establish a new cause of action or grant jurisdiction to the court when it would not otherwise exist. [Citation omitted.] Instead, the Act merely authorizes a new form of relief, which in some cases will provide a fuller and more adequate remedy than that which existed under common law.

Builders Association of Northern Nevada v. City of Reno, 105 Nev. 368, 776 P.2d 1234, 1234 (1989). Thus, the Uniform Declaratory Judgments Act was held not to raise a private cause of action to enforce a statutory scheme governing the cost of building permits, where the statute itself created no private remedy and delegated responsibility for enforcement to a state agency. *Builders Association of North Nevada v. City of Reno, supra.*

Neither is declaratory relief appropriate to review questions of administrative discretion. *Prudential Insurance Co. v. Insurance Commissioner,* 82 Nev. 1, 409 P.2d 248 (1966). For example, a district court was without jurisdiction to entertain an action for declaratory relief which sought collateral review of decisions of the joint medicolegal screening panel concerning the admissibility or sufficiency of documents presented to it; the panel's decisions on such questions clearly involved its administrative discretion. *Phelps v. Second Judicial District Court,* 106 Nev. 917, 803 P.2d 1101, 1103 (1990).

Declaratory relief actions to review interlocutory decisions of state agencies are also inappropriate, particularly where such actions frustrate the legislature's purpose of relegating certain matters to a state agency for speedy resolution. *Public Service Commission v. Eighth Judicial District Court,* 107 Nev. Adv. Op. 113, 818 P.2d 396 (1991), where the Nevada Supreme Court also said,

> "It is well-settled that courts will not entertain a declaratory judgment action if there is pending, at the time of the commencement of the action for declaratory relief, another action or proceeding to which the same persons are parties and in which the same issues may be adjudicated." *Haas & Haynie Corp. v. Pacific Millwork Supply,* 2 Haw. App. 132, 134, 627 P.2d 291, 293 (1981). Further, a court will refuse to consider a complaint for declaratory relief if a special statutory remedy has been provided. *See Nelson v. Knight,* 254 Or. 370, 460 P.2d 355 (1969). A separate action for declaratory judgment is not an appropriate method of testing defenses in a pending action, *see Ratley v. Sheriff's Civil Service BD, Etc.,* 7 Kan. App. 2d 638, 646 P.2d 1133 (1982), nor is it a substitute for statutory avenues of judgment and appellate review.

Public Service Commission, supra, 818 P.2d at 399.

§ 3103. Requirements for declaratory relief under the Uniform Act.

The attitude of the Nevada Supreme Court toward the declaratory judgment has changed markedly over the years. The Uniform Act was enthusiastically embraced in *Kress v. Corey,* 65 Nev. 2, 189 P.2d 352 (1948), the first Nevada Supreme Court opinion to address a party's right to seek declaratory relief under the Act. The court lauded the statute's remedial purposes and aligned itself with other jurisdictions entertaining "a broader and more liberal concept" of its applicability, while expressly rejecting case law which restricted the availability of declaratory relief. However, subsequent opinions of the court placed a number of important restrictions upon the availability of declaratory relief which are discussed below.

NRS 30.040 affords declaratory relief to "[a]ny person interested under a deed, will, written contract or other writings constituting a contract, or whose rights, status or other legal relations are affected by a statute, municipal ordinance, contract or franchise ...."

A contract may be construed either before or after its breach. NRS 30.050. NRS 30.060 affords declaratory relief in specified areas to a defined class of persons interested in the administration of a trust or estate. It is significant, however, that the particular uses of declaratory relief listed in NRS 30.040 through 30.060 are not exclusive (NRS 30.070) and do not limit the broad, general power conferred on Nevada courts by NRS 30.030 to "declare rights, status and other legal relations" whenever appropriate.

In *Kress v. Corey*, 65 Nev. 2, 189 P.2d 352 (1948), the court set forth the following requirements necessary to qualify for a declaratory judgment:

> The requisite precedent facts or conditions which the courts generally hold must exist in order that declaratory relief may be obtained may be summarized as follows: (1) there must exist a *justiciable controversy;* that is to say, a controversy in which a claim of right is asserted against one who has an interest in contesting it; (2) the controversy must be between persons whose *interests are adverse;* (3) the party seeking declaratory relief must have a legal interest in the controversy, that is to say, a *legally protectible interest;* and (4) the issue involved in the controversy must be *ripe for judicial determination.* Kress, supra at 26. (Emphasis added.)

This four-pronged test has since provided grounds for narrowing the availability of declaratory relief in Nevada.

§ 3104. — A "justiciable controversy."

In *Cox v. Glenbrook Co.*, 78 Nev. 254, 371 P.2d 647 (1962), the definition of a "justiciable controversy" was narrowed. The parties sought a declaration of the rights conferred by an easement. The plaintiff complained that the defendant's plan to use the easement for a ten-year residential project threatened the rustic beauty of plaintiff's property. The trial court essentially forbade the development. The Nevada Supreme Court modified the trial court's declaration insofar as it dealt with future circumstances:

> [E]very judgment following a trial upon the merits must be based upon the evidence presented; it cannot be based upon an assumption made *before* the facts are known or have come into existence.
> ....
> [F]actual circumstances which may arise in the future cannot be fairly determined now. As to this phase of the case we are asked to make a hypothetical adjudication, where there is presently no justiciable controversy, and where the existence of a controversy is dependent upon the happening of future events. [Citation omitted.] A declaratory judgment should deal with a present, ascertained or ascertainable state of facts.... Cox, supra at 266-68.

In *Colby v. Colby*, 78 Nev. 150, 369 P.2d 1019 (1962), no justiciable controversy was found to exist between a divorced couple, where the ex-husband filed a declaratory action to vacate an earlier Nevada divorce decree. The court recognized that under NRS 30.030, a declaration "shall have the force and effect of a final judgment or decree." Such a final decree had already been entered in the earlier divorce action. Therefore, "a justiciable issue as to the parties' marital status in Nevada does not now exist." *Colby, supra,* at 156.

However, in *El Capitan Club v. Fireman's Fund Insurance Co.,* 89 Nev. 65, 506 P.2d 426 (1973), the trial judge, in the exercise of his discretion, dismissed a declaratory judgment action between an insured and its insurance carrier as premature, since no judgment had been recovered against the insured by injured persons whose claims might eventually be paid by the insurance carrier. The Nevada Supreme Court held that the dismissal was an abuse of discretion and that the action was not premature, referring to the frequent use of declaratory judgments in insurance litigation in other jurisdictions.

§ 3105. — Adverse interests.

The requirement that adverse interests be presented to the court before declaratory relief may be granted is related to the requirement that there be an actual controversy. Adverse interests must be competing interests and not merely a controversy with reference to oneself. *Planned Parenthood Association v. Fitzpatrick,* 401 F. Supp. 554 (D. Penn. 1975). In *Phelps v. Second Judicial District Court,* 106 Nev. 917, 803 P.2d 1101 (1990), the plaintiff failed to name the persons most interested in the dispute as defendants, naming instead state agencies who were neutral in the dispute. Noting the absence of adverse interests, the Nevada Supreme Court said, "The district court was certainly without authority to declare the alleged rights of the [persons] who were not parties to the action before it." 803 P.2d at 1102.

§ 3106. — A "legally protectible interest."

In *Wells v. Bank of Nevada,* 90 Nev. 192, 522 P.2d 1014 (1974), the Nevada Supreme Court narrowly defined what constitutes a "legally protectible interest" worthy of protection by declaratory relief. The administrator of an estate sought a declaration of the validity of a contract between the decedent and his family corporation which set out the terms on which the corporation could reacquire the decedent's stock after his death. The decedent's heirs appear to have counterclaimed for a declaration that the contract was invalid. Although disposition of the stock would greatly affect the size of their inheritance, the court held that the heirs had no legally protectible interest in the contract within the meaning of NRS 30.040 and NRS 30.130, since they were not parties to the contract. Rejecting the heirs' argument that the contract "affected" their claim to the stock in the practical and real sense, the court stated:

> The [Uniform] Act ... is directed only to those who enjoy a legal interest in the agreement under scrutiny. [Citations omitted.] As

noted, the complaining heirs have no rights, duties or obligations under the … agreement and thus do not have standing as interested
persons to challenge the contract in a declaratory judgment action.
Wells v. Bank of Nevada, supra at 197-98.

This opinion narrows the category of persons who can obtain a declaration of rights in a contract. The court tested the heirs' interest in the
controversy only under NRS 30.040, which enumerates the specific uses
of the declaratory power suggested by the Uniform Act. The court ignored the broader grant of general declaratory power raised by NRS
30.030, under which the court might have taken cognizance of the heirs'
very tangible interest in the controversy surrounding the contract.

In *Phelps v. Second Judicial District Court,* 106 Nev. 917, 803 P.2d
1101 (1990), the Nevada Supreme Court held that the district court had
not declared "any right, status or legal relation" (as authorized by NRS
30.030) when it entered a declaration that a medical expert's affidavit
was not appropriate for the joint medicolegal screening panel to consider.
The Nevada Supreme Court reasoned the actions of the panel "do not
involve the substantial right of any party to a medical malpractice action," because the panel's determination "simply affects the burdens of
the parties with respect to the payment of attorney's fees if the matter
proceeds to trial …." 803 P.2d at 1103. Nor is a merely conditional
privilege not to disclose a trade secret sufficiently substantial to qualify
as a "right, status or other legal relation" appropriate for a court's declaratory power. *Public Service Commission v. Eighth Judicial District
Court,* 107 Nev. Adv. Op. 113, 818 P.2d 396 (1991).

§ 3107. — Ripeness.

Closely related to the requirement that the controversy be presently
justiciable is the requirement that the issue be "ripe" for judicial determination. In *Colby v. Colby,* 78 Nev. 150, 369 P.2d 1019 (1962), the
Nevada Supreme Court held that an action seeking a declaration of the
marital status of the parties was no longer ripe years after the default
divorce decree was entered. In *Cox v. Glenbrook Co.,* 78 Nev. 254, 371
P.2d 647 (1962), an action seeking a declaration of the rights of the
parties based upon factual circumstances which had not yet arisen was
held to be premature and not yet ripe for judicial intervention.

If a party can show that harm is likely to occur in the future, then a
ripe case or controversy may exist, but litigated matters must present an
existing controversy and not merely the prospect of a future problem.
Resnick v. Nevada Gaming Commission, 104 Nev. 60, 752 P.2d 229, 231
(1988), where the Nevada Commission's refusal to turn over investigative materials to an applicant for a gaming license, so that the applicant

could better prepare for his licensing hearing, did not present a controversy ripe for judicial determination.

§ 3108. Declaratory relief is discretionary.

A court may deny declaratory relief in the exercise of its discretion. *El Capitan Club v. Fireman's Fund Insurance Co.*, 89 Nev. 65, 506 P.2d 426 (1973).

NRS 30.080 permits a court to refuse to render a declaratory judgment if the judgment would not terminate the uncertainty or the controversy which gives rise to the proceedings.

In *El Capitan Club, supra*, the court adopted the following test for determining whether the declaratory power should defer to another remedy:

> "It is only where the court believes that [1] *more* effective relief can and should be obtained by another procedure and that for that reason [2] a declaration will not serve a useful purpose, that it is justified in refusing a declaration because of the availability of another remedy." *Jones v. Robertson*, 180 P.2d 929, 933 (Cal. App. 1947) [Citing Borchard, *Declaratory Judgments*, 2d Ed., at 302-03.]
>
> ....
>
> [I]t must clearly appear that [3] the asserted alternative remedies are available to the plaintiff seeking the declaratory relief, and that such remedies are [4] speedy and [5] adequate or as well suited to the plaintiff's needs as is declaratory relief. *El Capitan Club, supra*, 89 Nev. at 69-70 (Numerals interlineated.)

Discretion to entertain a declaratory judgment action may be influenced if the declaratory action is used for the purpose of anticipating and prematurely deciding an issue which properly should be resolved in another action. For example, certain factual issues in a declaratory action between an insured and his insurance carrier to test the coverage afforded by his policy might be identical to fact issues which the insured will later face in a liability action brought against him by injured third persons. In *El Capitan Club, supra*, Fireman's Fund successfully moved the trial court to dismiss a declaratory judgment action brought by its insured to determine whether Fireman's insurance policy covered an accident. Fireman's argued below that the requested declaration would necessarily decide issues which would arise in subsequent liability actions against the insured. Reversing, the Nevada Supreme Court balanced the beneficial results of an early determination of the coverage issue against the likelihood that identical issues would crop up in the later actions. The balance favored the declaratory judgment action. *See also Neumann v. Standard Fire Insurance*, 101 Nev. 206, 699 P.2d 101 (1985); *National Fire Insurance v. Reno's Executive Air*, 100 Nev. 360,

682 P.2d 1380 (1984); and *Insurance Corporation of America v. Rubin,* 107 Nev. Adv. Op. 102, 818 P.2d 389 (1991).

Failure to join a person having or claiming an interest in a controversy which would be affected by the desired declaration may lead to dismissal of the action. NRS 30.130. Where it is infeasible to join all interested parties in one action, equity's concern to avoid a multiplicity of suits will influence the exercise of the court's discretion. *Kress v. Corey,* 65 Nev. 1, 189 P.2d 352 (1948).

When a genuine controversy is presented concerning the meaning of an ordinance or statute, the court may be obligated to determine the question of construction. In *Prudential Insurance Co. v. Insurance Commissioner,* 82 Nev. 1, 409 P.2d 248 (1966), where the meaning of a statute taxing the insurance industry was questioned, the court stated:

> If the law is unclear or obscure, a court, when asked, must seek out and proclaim its meaning. Declaratory relief is tailored for that purpose. NRS 30.040 authorizes a declaratory action to "have determined any question of construction...arising under the statute." *Prudential Insurance Co., supra* at 5.

§ 3109. Declaratory relief in tandem with other remedies.

Because declaratory relief is not of itself coercive, it may be sought in conjunction with other appropriate remedies. Declaratory relief is "not intended to be exclusive or extraordinary, but alternative and optional." *El Capitan Club v. Fireman's Fund Insurance Co.,* 89 Nev. 65, 506 P.2d 426 (1973). Declaratory relief is available "whether or not further relief is or could be claimed." NRS 30.030.

An injunction has been held to be a proper provisional remedy in a proceeding to obtain a declaratory judgment. *Sievers v. Zenoff,* 94 Nev. 53, 573 P.2d 1190 (1978); *Nevada Management Co. v. Jack,* 75 Nev. 232, 338 P.2d 71 (1959).

The equitable device of interpleader is often a useful aid to a declaratory judgment action, where rights to make or receive payments are in doubt. *Kress v. Corey,* 65 Nev. 1, 189 P.2d 352 (1948).

§ 3110. Availability of jury trial.

NRCP 57 makes available in an action for declaratory relief all of the procedural devices available in any other civil action under the Nevada Rules of Civil Procedure. The right to a jury trial of fact issues is unimpaired. NRS 30.110. A declaratory judgment action enjoys some preference over other civil actions, in that "[t]he court may order a speedy hearing of an action for a declaratory judgment and may advance it on its calendar." NRCP 57.

§3111. Procedure and parties.

Although the Nevada Rules of Civil Procedure govern actions for a declaratory judgment, a party should plead his right to a declaration with more specificity than required by the "notice pleading" concept of NRCP 8. Declaratory relief may be requested by complaint, by counterclaim, or by any other pleading permitted under NRCP 7.

Failure to join a person having or claiming an interest in a controversy which would be affected by the desired declaration may lead to dismissal of the action. NRS 30.130.

Declaratory judgment actions may be maintained by a proper class pursuant to NRCP 23. *Prudential Insurance Co. v. Insurance Commissioner,* 82 Nev. 1, 409 P.2d 248 (1966).

§3112. Restraints on news media.

NRS 30.170 provides for a declaration of the validity of any trial judge's order which prohibits the news media from reporting or broadcasting a trial or other judicial proceedings. The right to petition for the declaration is vested in the news media. Such petitions are to be advanced on court dockets. NRS 30.170(2). The conclusion of the trial in which the reporter's rights were hampered does not render the petition for a declaration moot because of the "insecurity with respect to constitutional rights" raised by an order affecting freedom of the press. NRS 30.170(3).

§3113. Nevada gaming commission.

NRS 463.343 vests the Nevada Gaming Commission, the Gaming Control Board and gaming licensees with the right to seek a declaration "of any question of construction or validity" of the Nevada Gaming Control Act (NRS 463.010, *et seq.*), or of regulations promulgated by the Gaming Commission. No right is vested in a person or entity which is not licensed by the Gaming Commission and the statute expressly forbids granting injunctive relief to an unlicensed person or others adversely affected by actions of the Gaming Commission. NRS 463.343(5); *State v. Glusman,* 98 Nev. 412, 651 P.2d 639 (1982).

§3114. Constitutionality of ordinance or statute.

A declaratory action may not be filed initially in the Nevada Supreme Court, *Beko v. Kelly,* 78 Nev. 489, 376 P.2d 429 (1962), except where the requested declaration is included in a petition for a writ of mandamus to challenge the constitutionality of a statute or ordinance, *Tam v. Colton,* 94 Nev. 452, 581 P.2d 447 (1978). Where the validity of a statute or ordinance is attacked on constitutional grounds, a copy of the complaint

715

must be served on the Nevada Attorney General, although he or she need not be made a party. NRS 30.130; *City of Reno v. Saibini,* 83 Nev. 315, 429 P.2d 559 (1967).

§ 3115. The Judicial Confirmation Law and other special grants of declaratory power.

Enacted in 1969, Nevada's Judicial Confirmation Law, NRS 43.010 through 43.170, is based on the legislature's finding that "[a]n early judicial examination into and determination of the validity of any power, instrument, act or project of any municipality promotes the health ... and welfare of the people of this state." NRS 43.020(1). The Act therefore vests the "governing body" of any state, county or local agency with the right to petition the courts for a declaration of the validity of virtually any action or project, whether only proposed or already taken. NRS 43.060-43.100. The court takes jurisdiction "in the nature of a proceeding in rem" over the action or project. NRS 43.110. Venue is proper in the county in which the act or project has been, or is about to be, undertaken. NRS 43.100(1). Interested parties are to be notified by publication. NRS 43.120.

The Judicial Confirmation Law does not confer an action upon a private citizen who seeks to invalidate a governmental act or project. Private citizens are relegated to the remedies of the Uniform Act (see NRS 30.040), although under the Judicial Confirmation Law, private citizens who are interested in a government agency's act or project "may appear and move to dismiss or answer the petition." NRS 43.130(1). Failure to thus intervene after notice by publication constitutes a confession of the government agency's petition. NRS 43.140(2).

The Nevada Rules of Civil Procedure apply to petitions under the Judicial Confirmation Law. Petitions under the Law "shall be advanced as a matter of immediate public interest and concern, and be heard at the earliest practicable moment." NRS 43.160.

CHAPTER 32

NEVADA BOND AND LIEN LAW

Author: Richard M. Trachok, II

§ 3201. Introduction and summary.

Prime contractors or their subcontractors are not required to post bid, payment, or performance bonds on privately financed projects. Owners and contractors are free to provide bonding requirements, if any, in their contracts.

Nevada's "Little Miller Act" statute provides for payment and performance bonds on public work projects. Nevada Revised Statutes, Chapter 339. For public projects in excess of $20,000, the statute requires that prime contractors furnish both performance bonds and payment bonds, each in an amount to be fixed by the contracting body, but not less than fifty percent of the contract amount. Payment bonds on Nevada public works projects must protect and benefit all claimants supplying labor or materials to the prime contractor or any of his subcontractors.

Every person who performs labor upon or furnishes material of the value of $50 or more in improving real property is granted mechanic's lien rights. Nevada's mechanic's lien statute is codified at Nevada Revised Statutes §§ 108.221-108.246 ("Lien Law"). No mechanic's lien rights are afforded contractors on public works jobs. *Gill v. Paysee*, 48 Nev. 12, 19, 226 P. 302, 305 (1924). There is a question of whether a mechanic's lien can be attached to property owned by a quasi-public agency, such as an independent airport authority on property not necessary for performing governmental functions. An example would be an air cargo facility to be leased to third-party private commercial interests. The Nevada Supreme Court has not addressed this particular issue, although it has stated that a lien cannot be attached to a public building.

§ 3202. Bond law — general concepts.

The construction surety bond relationship is a tripartite relationship. Each construction surety bond has an obligee which is either an owner or

717

a general contractor, an obligor which is usually the general contractor or subcontractor and its surety.

The surety contract must be in writing and signed by the surety against whom one is making a bond claim. The rights and obligations of the parties vary depending upon the terms of the bond. The bond agreement is treated in the same way as are other contracts. Provided that the minimum statutory requirements are satisfied, the express language of the bond controls and liability may not be imposed beyond the express contractual terms. *Carson Opera House Association v. Miller,* 16 Nev. 327, 334 (1881); *Adelson v. Wilson & Co.,* 81 Nev. 15, 21, 398 P.2d 106, 109 (1965). If the statutory requirements are not included in the bond, the Court will include them, the terms of the contract notwithstanding. The general rules of contractual construction in interpreting the surety contract are applied by the Nevada Supreme Court. *Royal Indemnity Co. v. Special Service Supply Co.,* 82 Nev. 148, 151, 413 P.2d 500, 502 (1966).

§ 3203. Bid bonds.

Nevada law does not require that prime contractors furnish bid bonds on either public or private projects. When required by the contract documents, a bid bond typically guarantees the owner that the lowest, responsive, responsible bidder will enter into the contract upon which it bids. The bid bond provides a penal sum in a set amount in the event the contractor refuses to enter into the contract after an award is made. As with other types of bonds, the rights and liabilities of the parties are set forth in the terms of the bond.

In order for the owner to recover under a bid bond, the bidder must be the lowest, responsive, responsible bidder. If a bidder has made a clerical error in its bid which entitles it to withdraw its bid, 190 Op. Att'y Gen. 41, then both the contractor and its bid bond surety may be able to avoid liability. If a bidder's bid is not responsive because it failed to conform to the requirements set forth in the instructions to bidder provided by the contracting body, then the bidder and its bid bond surety may also be able to avoid liability.

§ 3204. Performance bonds.

Chapter 339 of the Nevada Revised Statutes requires the prime contractor, on public projects in excess of $20,000, to furnish a performance bond of not less than fifty percent of the amount of the prime contract. The contracting body determines the amount of the bond, which amount is set forth in the bid documents. NRS 339.025(1)(a). The term "contracting body" as defined in NRS Chapter 339 is very broad and includes: "the state, county, city, town, school district, or any public agency of the state or its political subdivisions which has authority to contract for the construction, alteration, or repair of any public building or other public work or public improvement." NRS 339.015(2). Chapter 339 expressly provides that Performance Bonds shall be solely for the protection of the "contracting body" which awarded the contract. NRS 339.025(1)(a).

The limitation period within which suit must be brought to enforce a performance bond is generally set forth in the terms of the bond. Unless otherwise provided, the limitation period is that for written contracts which in Nevada is six years.

§ 3205. Payment bonds.

On publicly-financed projects, prime contractors are required to furnish a payment bond of not less than fifty percent of the prime contract amount on projects in excess of $20,000; the amount of the bond is fixed by the contracting body in the contract documents. NRS 339.025(1)(b). Since Nevada's bond law is based in large part upon the federal Miller Act, 40 U.S.C. § 270a *et seq.*, it can be interpreted by reference to Miller Act decisions. Nevada law requires that payment bonds afford coverage to claimants supplying labor or materials to the prime contractor to whom the contract was awarded, or to any of his "subcontractors." NRS 339.025.

It is imperative that claimants under a payment bond strictly comply with the notice requirements set forth in Chapter 339. Under Chapter 339, a claimant with no direct contractual relationship with the prime contractor must *serve* on the prime contractor, *within thirty days of first supplying the materials or labor,* a written notice which must include "the nature of the materials being furnished or to be furnished, or the labor performed or to be performed, and identifying the person contracting for such labor or materials and the site for the performance for such labor or materials." NRS 339.035(2)(a).

It should be noted that the statutory language requires that the labor or material supplier *serve* the written notice on the prime contractor. Whether this requires personal service or service by certified or registered mail has yet to be decided by the Nevada Supreme Court. No other similar type of "notice" provision under Nevada's lien or bond law requires personal service. It is anticipated that service by certified or registered mail would be sufficient. *Capriotti, Lemon & Associates v. Johnson Service Co.,* 84 Nev. 318, 440 P.2d 386 (1968).

Service of the notice after thirty days have elapsed since the first supplying of labor or materials will not invalidate the bond claim. Recovery, however, will be limited to labor or material supplied within the thirty days prior to service of the notice. *AMFAC Distribution Corp. v. Housing Authority,* 100 Nev. 573, 576, 688 P.2d 318, 320 (1984). Failure to give the required notice will render any claim against the bond invalid. *Capriotti, Lemon & Associates v. Johnson Service Co.,* 84 Nev. 318, 321, 440 P.2d 386, 388 (1968).

All claimants who have no direct contract with the prime contractor are required to give a written notice to the prime contractor within ninety days from the date on which the claimant performed the last of the labor or furnished the last of the materials for which it claims payment. This notice must state with substantial accuracy the amount claimed and the name of the person for whom the work was performed or to whom the material was supplied. NRS 339.035(2)(b). Service of the notice by registered or certified mail, postage pre-paid, in an envelope addressed to the contractor at any place where its office is regularly maintained for the transaction of business is required to perfect the claim. NRS 339.035(2)(b).

Those claimants who have a direct contract with the prime contractor are not required to provide either notice required by Chapter 339.

An action may not be brought upon a payment bond by any party before the expiration of ninety days after the day on which the claimant performed the last of its labor or furnished the last of its materials for which it claims payment. NRS 339.035(1).

All actions on the payment bond must be brought within one year from the date on which the claimant performed the last of the labor or furnished the last of the materials. NRS 339.055(2). The statute specifically limits recovery to the contract amount for labor and materials furnished.

§ 3206. Lien law — general concepts.

A mechanic's lien is a form of security device in which the contractor obtains an interest in or an encumbrance against the real property improved. Because the holder of a mechanic's lien is vested with a real property interest superior to that of the owner of the property, the notice and other procedural requirements must be strictly followed. *Fisher Brothers v. Harrah Realty Co.,* 92 Nev. 65, 67, 545 P.2d 203, 204 (1976). A mechanic's lien attaches only to private construction projects. In some special instances, a mechanic's lien may attach to certain property owned by quasi-public agencies where the property and the improvement thereon is not being used for governmental functions. *See* discussion above at § 3201.

§ 3207. Basic provisions.

Unlike some other states, Nevada's mechanic's lien statutes apply to "every person who performs labor upon or furnishes material the value of $50.00 or more to be used in the construction, alteration or repair" of any improvement upon real property. NRS 108.222(1). The use of the word "person" is meant to be broadly interpreted and is not restricted to only contractors and subcontractors. Every contractor, subcontractor, architect, builder, or other person engaged in works of improvement upon real property is afforded mechanic's lien rights. NRS 108.222.

It is sufficient that the work of improvement was provided to the real property in question. It is immaterial whether or not the land was benefitted by the improvements. *Richmond Machine Co. v. Bennett,* 48 Nev. 286, 292, 229 P. 1098, 1099 (1924). A mechanic's lien will not attach to real property if the improvements in question, such as trade fixtures, are intended to be removed at some time in the future without damaging the real property. *Reno Electric Works, Inc. v. Ward,* 51 Nev. 291, 299, 274 P. 196, 197 (1929).

Resort to a mechanic's lien is not restricted to contractors and suppliers, but also extends to designers such as architects and engineers drawing plans and supervising construction of the works of improvement. *Paterson v. Condos,* 55 Nev. 134, 143, 28 P.2d 499, 501 (1934). Coverage also extends to those who provide landscaping, irrigation systems, grading or to one who "otherwise improves the lot or tract of land, or the street in front of or adjoining it." NRS 108.223. The land subject to the mechanic's lien includes "the land occupied by any building or other superstructure, railroad, tramway, toll road, canal, water ditch, flume, aqueduct or reservoir, bridge or fence, together with a convenient space about the same, or so much as may be required for the convenient use and occupation thereof." NRS 108.224.

It is not necessary that the work of improvement be provided pursuant to a contract. It is sufficient that the labor or materials were provided at the instance or request of the owner and the labor or materials were incorporated in the work of improvement. Where the labor or materials were provided pursuant to a contract, the lien attaches in the amount of the unpaid contract price. NRS 108.222(1)(a). In the absence of a contract, the lien attaches in an amount equal to the fair market value of the labor performed or materials supplied or rented, including a reasonable allowance for overhead and profit. NRS 108.222(1)(b).

In Nevada, a properly noticed and recorded mechanic's lien will have priority over any "lien, mortgage or other encumbrance which may have attached subsequent to the time when the building, improvement or structure was commenced, work done, or materials were commenced to be furnished." NRS 108.225(1)(a). Work done on the site must be more than surveying, drafting architectural plans, and soil testing. *Aladdin Heating Corp. v. Trustees of the Central States,* 93 Nev. 257, 260, 563 P.2d 82 (1977). Soil engineering studies which included trenching and drilling of wells was recently held not to be sufficient "work done" to place prospective lenders on notice. *Nevada National Bank v. Snyder,* 108 Nev. Adv. Op. 26 (1992). What is required is "work done" on the site such as to put a prospective lender on notice that actual development of the property had begun.

The priority date for a mechanic's lien is the date upon which actual physical work was commenced on the site so as to put third parties on notice of the commencement of the work of improvement. *Aladdin Heating Corp. v. Trustees of the Central States,* 93 Nev. 257, 260, 563 P.2d 82, 84 (1977). For instance, drawing of plans would not constitute work on the site to establish priority. There must be visible signs of construction to inform prospective lenders inspecting the premises that liens could be attached. *Aladdin, supra, e.g.,* the placing of survey stakes should be sufficient to constitute actual notice of the commencement of work. The priority of all lien claimants providing labor or materials on the project relates back to the date of the first work being performed on the site. NRS 108.225. This poses a significant problem for lenders and their title insurers where the date of recording of the deed of trust or security instrument is subsequent to the commencement of work on the site as all suppliers of labor or materials, including the landscape contractor, will have a priority over any lien or mortgage recorded thereafter.

§ 3208. Lien law notice requirements.

The notice and recording requirements of the lien law must be strictly followed if the lien claimant expects to receive the protection provided therein. The Nevada Supreme Court has only recently considered cases where a notice requirement was not strictly followed. *Board of Trustees v. Durable Developers, Inc.,*102 Nev. 401, 410, 724 P.2d 736, 743 (1986); *Fondren v. K/L Complex Ltd.,* 106 Nev. 705, 708-10, 800 P.2d 719, 720-22 (1990). These cases are limited to those instances where actual notice by the owner was clearly established. These recent decisions notwithstanding, failure to strictly follow the notice requirements is ill-advised as these cases can easily be limited to their facts.

Since the mechanic's lien can result in the claimant selling the property at foreclosure, it is only fair and reasonable that, save and except for those contractors or suppliers with whom the owner has a direct contract, all suppliers of labor or material must promptly provide the owner with written notice thereof. This enables the owner to make whatever arrangements necessary to ensure that these parties are paid.

Every subcontractor or material supplier save and except one who supplies only labor to the project or a contractor or material supplier who "contracts directly with an owner" must, within thirty-one days of first supplying materials, deliver in person or serve by certified mail a written notice upon the owner or reputed owner of the property. NRS 108.245. The issue of whether a contractor who supplies only labor needs to supply the pre-lien notice has not been brought before the Nevada Court. It is sufficient to serve either the owner of record or the owner listed on the building permit. The notice shall be in substantially the following form:

NOTICE TO OWNER OF MATERIALS SUPPLIED OR WORK OR SERVICES PERFORMED

To:_____
(Owner's name and address)
The undersigned notifies you that he has supplied materials or performed work or services as follows:

_____

(General description of materials, work or services and anticipated total value) for improvement of real property identified as (property description or street address) under contract with (general contractor or subcontractor). This is not a notice that the undersigned has not been or does not expect to be paid, but a notice required by law that the undersigned may, at a future date, claim a lien as provided by law against the property if the undersigned is not paid.

(Claimant)

NRS 108.245. The contract or material supplier should also serve a copy of the notice upon the prime contractor. NRS 108.245(1).

Failure to provide this notice will invalidate the claim of a lien. If the pre-lien notice is served subsequent to the thirty-one-day period, the contractor's lien rights can be perfected for all labor or materials supplied to the project thirty-one days prior to the actual service of the notice. *See AMFAC Distribution Corp. v. Housing Authority,* 100 Nev. 573, 576, 688 P.2d 318, 320 (1984). Although *AMFAC* was decided under Nev. Rev. Stat. Chapter 339, it is expected that its rationale would be applied to the lien statute. Any labor or material supplied prior to this thirty-one-day period will not be included in the lien.

All suppliers of labor or material must, before the lapse of ninety days from the completion of the work of improvement or the last delivery of labor or materials, whichever is later, record their notice of claim of lien with the county recorder in the county where the project is located. NRS 108.226. In the event a notice of completion is recorded by the owner, the lien claimant must record the lien within forty days of recording of the notice. NRS 108.226(2). The notice of lien must contain the following information:

(a) A statement of his demand after deducting all just credits and offsets;
(b) The name of the owner or reputed owner if known;

(c) The name of the person by whom he was employed or to whom he furnished the material;

(d) A statement of the terms, time given and conditions of his contract (it is sufficient to incorporate the contract in the lien claim or simply state the payment terms); and

(e) A description of the property to be charged with the lien sufficient for identification. NRS 108.226.

There must be strict compliance with the provisions of this section. Failure to record the lien within the period set forth will cause the lien to be rendered invalid. The section, as it pertains to the contents of the lien, will be liberally construed and substantial compliance is all that is required. *Turner v. Dewco Services,* 87 Nev. 14, 16, 473 P.2d 462 (1971). Subsequent amendments to the claim of lien will be freely allowed, even during the trial. *Holtzman v. Bennett,* 48 Nev. 274, 279, 229 P. 1095, 1096 (1924).

The claim of lien, once filed, must be served upon the record owner within thirty days after the recording of the lien. NRS 108.227. The lien may be personally served upon the owner if he can be located or if personal service is not possible by posting a copy of the lien upon the property and mailing a copy of the lien to the record owner at the place where the property is situated. NRS 108.227. In the event of multiple record owners, service on any single one is sufficient to satisfy the statute. NRS 108.227. Failure to effectuate service on a record owner within this thirty-day period will invalidate the lien. *Fisher Brothers v. Harrah Realty Co.,* 92 Nev. 65, 67, 545 P.2d 203, 204 (1976). It is highly advisable to obtain a preliminary title report from a local title company prior to recording the lien in order to determine the identities of the record owners.

In the event that a claim of lien is recorded against two or more buildings or "other improvements" owned by the same person, the lien claimant must designate the amount due to him on each of such buildings or "other improvement." NRS 108.231. While failure to allocate or apportion the amount owed pursuant to this section will not invalidate the lien, it will subordinate it to other liens or "creditors having liens by judgment or otherwise." *Schultz v. King,* 68 Nev. 207, 213-14, 228 P.2d 401, 404 (1951).

Suit to foreclose the lien must be filed thirty days after the recording of the lien but prior to the lapse of six months of recording the lien in a court of competent jurisdiction. NRS 108.233; NRS 108.244. This six-month period may be extended an additional six months provided a written agreement between the owner and lien claimant extending the same is recorded with the county recorder prior to the expiration of the original six-month period. NRS 108.233. No extension will be granted if it tends to delay or postpone collection of the claims. NRS 108.233. In the event of an arbitration clause in the contract, it is necessary to file suit to foreclose the lien, then stay the proceedings and commence the arbitration. *Lane-Tahoe, Inc. v. Kindred Construction Co.,* 91 Nev. 385, 390, 536 P.2d 491, 494 (1975). In the event a petition in bankruptcy is filed within the six-month period prior to the filing of suit to foreclose on the lien, the period in which the lien claimant must file suit is stayed until notice of termination of the automatic stay. *Depner Architects & Planner, Inc. v. Nevada National Bank,* 104 Nev. 560, 563, 763 P.2d 1141, 1142 (1988). Suit must be filed within thirty days of notice of termination of the stay. *Depner, supra.*

A contractor, in its suit to foreclose on the lien, may recover the contract amount "after deducting all claims of other parties for work done and material furnished." NRS 108.235. The lien claimants' personal claim against the party with whom he contracted is not affected by a suit to foreclose the lien. NRS 108.238. The lien claimant *may* be entitled to interest on his claim at the prime interest rate of the largest Nevada bank plus 2% commencing the date the payment was found to have been due. NRS 108.237(2). The court is required, however, to award attorney's fees to the lien claimant. NRS 108.237(3).

Contemporaneously, with the filing of the lawsuit, the lien claimant must record a notice of pendency of the action (lis pendens) with the county recorder in the county where the project is located. NRS 108.239(2)(a). The lien claimant must also publish a notice of the suit to foreclose the lien once a week for three successive weeks in one newspaper within the county where the project is located. NRS 108.239(2)(b). A copy of the notice must also be served on the other lienholders of record. NRS 108.239(3). All other parties claiming a lien on the property must serve upon the lien claimant within ten days of the last publication of the notice their statements of fact constituting their lien. NRS 108.239(2)(b). The service of the statement of facts constituting a lien operates as a joinder in the lien foreclosure action.

§ 3209. Lien priority.

At the trial the court shall declare the rank or class of each lien. The priorities of the liens will be as follows:

First: All labor whether performed at the instance or direction of the owner, subcontractor or the original contract.

Second: Material suppliers.

Third: The subcontractors, architects and engineers, if such architects and engineers have performed their services, in whole or in part, under contract with the general contractor.

Fourth: The original contractors, architects and engineers, if such architects and engineers have not performed their services in whole or in part, under contract with the general contractor, and all persons other than original contractors, subcontractors, architects and engineers.

NRS 108.236. If the court rules in favor of the lien claimants, it will order the property sold to satisfy the liens. NRS 108.239(6).

A lien may be released at any time upon the posting of a surety bond in the amount of 150% of the lien claim, such amount to include an estimate of attorney's fees and costs. NRS 108.2413-108.2425.

§ 3210. Remedies of the owner.

The owner can assert contractual defenses against any lien claimant with whom it has contracted. The owner may also assert contractual defenses such as defective performance or defective materials against other lien claimants. The owner, in the case where the property has been leased and the lessee is effectuating the works of improvement, may record a notice of non-responsibility within three days after he has obtained knowledge of the commencement of the work of improvement. NRS 108.234. The notice must state that the owner will not be responsible for any such improvements. In the event a notice of non-responsibility is recorded within the time required, the lien claimants will have no rights against the owner's interest in the property. Their claim will be limited to the lessee's rights in and to the property.

CHAPTER 33

GUARDIANSHIPS

Author: Patricia A. Trent

§ 3301. Introduction.

In the initial interview with a client who seeks the appointment as guardian for another, explore all possible alternatives to guardianship and discuss what specific, recent behavior has indicated an inability on the part of the proposed ward to make financial or personal decisions. Verify where the proposed ward currently lives and what changes may be appropriate in the future so as to provide the least restrictive environment in light of the ward's financial means. Request information concerning the ward such as, the names and addresses of the ward's next-of-kin, the ward's date of birth, the name and address of the ward's physician, the ward's physical and mental condition, the location, value and type of assets and income received by the ward, ongoing expenses and obligations of the ward, the ward's prior life-style and prior course of dealing with relatives and friends, and the location of and the terms contained in original documents such as wills, living wills, and powers of attorney.

727

In drafting the guardianship application, reference should be made to NRS Chapter 159, a summary of which is referenced in this discussion in a sequence which will hopefully serve as a guide for the attorney in counseling a future guardian as to the legal requirements and expectations that arise when a guardianship appointment is secured. Form 33A, entitled "Guardian's Acknowledgment," should be executed by the proposed guardian as it may later serve as verification that duties and responsibilities were discussed with the client. At the same time, it can function as a reference guide for the client in the future management of the ward's affairs.

Once appointed, the guardian should be encouraged to communicate to the attorney any changes in the ward's physical or financial needs that may be so significant as to warrant court consideration. The line of communication between the attorney and guardian is of utmost importance in this type of proceeding because, in most cases, the guardianship will remain active until a minor attains the age of majority or an adult ward dies.

§ 3302. Jurisdiction.

The court has jurisdiction, pursuant to NRS 159.035, to appoint (a) guardians of the person, (b) guardians of the estate, or (c) guardians of the person and estate for resident adult or minor wards. Should the proposed ward be a nonresident but be physically present in this state or, should the nonresident ward have property within this state, the court also has jurisdiction to appoint a guardian to manage the ward's personal affairs or property.

§ 3303. Functions.

The function of a guardian for the person of an incompetent adult or minor ward is to see to his or her care, maintenance, education, and support. See NRS 159.079. The function of a guardian for the estate of an incompetent adult or minor ward is to serve, manage, and dispose of the estate according to law in providing care and maintenance to the ward and to others to whom the ward owes the duty of support. See NRS 159.083. The guardian assumes no personal liability on written or oral contracts entered into for or on behalf of the ward when acting within the guardian's authority. See NRS 159.099.

§ 3304. Qualifications.

A person may qualify as a guardian pursuant to NRS 159.059 unless that person is an incompetent, a minor, a convicted felon, an attorney during the term of disbarment or suspension from the practice of law, or a nonresident who has not associated with and filed an application for his or her co-appointment with a Nevada resident or a banking corporation doing business in this state. Factors in determining preferences in appointment are set forth in NRS 159.061. They include a request in a written instrument executed by an adult or a minor over the age of fourteen years. If the ward's will contains a nomination of a guardian, the nominee will also be afforded a priority. Finally, those related by blood or marriage have a preference, however, it may not be absolute. In a minor guardianship action, the "parental preference" may yield to a petitioner whose appointment would better serve the welfare of the child. *See Fisher v. Fisher,* 99 Nev. 762, 670 P.2d 572 (1983).

Consideration of a guardian's custodial rights over a minor who was the subject of a pending adoption proceeding was discussed in the case of *Mendive v. Third Judicial District Court,* 70 Nev. 51, 253 P.2d 884 (1953). Further, a recent amendment to NRS 159.044 includes a reference to NRS 127.045 which addresses adoption proceedings and the need for a natural mother's consent and investigation prior to petitioning for the appointment of a guardian if the petitioner is not related to the minor within the third degree of consanguinity.

§ 3305. Types of guardianships.

The types of guardianships and factors to consider in seeking an appointment as guardian are as follows:

1. *Minor guardianship.* This type of guardianship is generally prompted by a situation affecting a person under the age of eighteen who (1) has experienced the loss of his parents or a circumstance affecting the parents' ability to care for a minor, or (2) is expecting an influx of money from an insurance company, an inheritance, or some other form of benefit. If the minor is over the age of fourteen, a written consent or open court approval by the minor will enable the court to appoint a guardian without the issuance of a citation. NRS 159.049(2). An example of a minor's consent form is referenced as Form 33B.

2. *Adult ward guardianship.* An adult ward guardianship is usually prompted by a determination that a need exists to aid a person who cannot manage his property, take care of himself, or authorize medical treatment due to advanced age, mental illness, mental deficiency, disease or any other cause. *See* NRS 159.019.

3. *Special guardianship.* This type of guardianship is appropriate when the need arises to aid a person of limited capacity who can make some but not all of the decisions necessary for the management of his property and his own care. NRS 159.054(2) provides that the order resulting from the petition for appointment should include a specification of the powers and duties of the special guardian. This type of

guardianship should be limited to cases involving a unique set of problems requiring very specific attention. *See also* NRS 159.0795 and 159.0801.

4. *Temporary guardianship.* A temporary guardianship is generally prompted by an emergency situation involving an immediate risk of financial loss, a risk of physical harm, or a need for medical attention that the proposed ward lacks the capacity to respond to or authorize. *See* NRS 159.052. A good faith attempt must be made to notify the persons referenced in NRS 159.047(2). Temporary appointments expire in ten days and, within that time, a hearing must be conducted to determine the necessity to extend the temporary guardianship for a period not to exceed thirty days or until a general or special guardian is appointed, whichever occurs first. *See* Form 33C, Petition for Appointment of Temporary Guardian, and Form 33D, Order Appointing Temporary Guardian.

5. *Summary guardianship.* NRS 159.201 provides, in pertinent part, for the dispensing of annual accountings and all other proceedings if the value of the ward's property does not exceed $3,000. While this statute appears in the termination section of the guardianship chapter, its application can be useful in situations where, for example, a handicapped child attains the age of majority and his or her property consists solely of monthly income which will be expended as it is received for living expenses. Once a guardianship has been established, a petition may be filed by the guardian seeking the designation of a "summary guardianship" which thereafter will relieve the guardian from expending additional attorneys' fees and effort in the filing of future redundant accountings that reflect little or no assets on hand from year to year. *See* Form 33E, Petition for Summary Guardianship. In other instances, when the ward's property, after payment of debts, does not exceed $3,000, the guardian may petition the court for a summary guardianship by liquidating the property and establishing an investment fund consistent with NRS 159.117 to be held intact pending final instructions from the court.

§ 3306. Steps to appointment as guardian.

The petition for appointment of guardian should include the allegations outlined in NRS 159.044. Those relatives who are to be included in the petition within the second degree of consanguinity include spouses, adult children, parents, siblings, grandparents and grandchildren. *See* Form 33F, Petition for Appointment of Guardian. When seeking the appointment over two or more wards who are related, such as siblings, parent and child or husband and wife, one petition and bond can be filed pursuant to NRS 159.057, however, the guardian must keep separate accounts in the management of each ward's affairs.

An order similar to that which appears on Form 33G should accompany the filing of the petition which instructs the clerk to issue a citation directing the ward, any person having the care, custody and control of the ward, and all other interested persons, to appear and show cause why a guardian should not be appointed. If a petitioner is the recipient of a written nomination of a minor over the age of fourteen, is the custodial parent of a minor, or is a foreign guardian of a non-resident ward who can present an authenticated copy of the evidence of his appointment and letters, the court may appoint a guardian without requiring a citation pursuant to NRS 159.049.

The citation should include the statements outlined in NRS 159.048 and should be issued. *See* Form 33H, Citation to Appear and Show Cause (adult wards). The citation should be served upon the ward, representatives of any institution in which the ward is receiving care, the ward's spouse, and any adult children. If none exist, the citation should be directed to parents and siblings. NRS 159.047(2). *See* Form 33I, Citation to Appear and Show Cause (minor wards), which should be served upon a minor over the age of fourteen, the minor's parents, and any institutional representative caring for the minor. An affidavit of mailing must be filed evidencing service by certified mail with a return receipt requested as outlined in NRS 159.0475 at least twenty days prior to the hearing. If service cannot be accomplished by certified mail, then a due diligence affidavit should be prepared so as to secure an order for service by publication as outlined in NRCP4(e).

Arrangements should be made for the presence of the proposed ward at the hearing as mandated by NRS 159.0535 or a statement from the ward's doctor may be submitted which explains why the ward's presence should be excused for good cause. *See* Form 33J, Affidavit of Attending Physician.

Prepare the order containing the terms outlined in NRS 159.055(2) and, before letters of guardianship are issued, serve the ward with a copy of the Order Appointing Guardian personally or by mail as directed by NRS 159.074. *See* Form 33K.

Arrange for the execution and filing of a bond pursuant to NRS 159.065 unless the ward has no assets, the guardian of the estate is a banking corporation, or the guardian is appointed in a will which waives the bonding requirement for the guardian. In order to keep the value of the bond within the range of the approximate amount the guardian anticipates expending during a specific time frame, it is possible to block the value of those liquid assets which are on deposit with a bank or other type of repository that exceed the amount the guardian wishes to control. *See* Form 33M, Acknowledgment of Blocked Account, which should be filed evidencing that the account or investment is blocked. Should the amount of property that comes within the guardian's control vary from the amount of the bond that has been posted, the court may increase or decrease the bond amount pursuant to NRS 159.067. At the time of the guardian's appointment, great care should be taken to advise the client that the bond is posted to ensure the faithful performance of duties associated with the collection and management of the ward's property coming into the guardian's possession. *See Deegan v. Deegan,* 22 Nev. 185, 37 P. 360 (1894).

Finally, after the guardian has taken the official oath and subscribed his name thereon in the presence of the court clerk or any notary public, the Letters of Guardianship should be issued and filed. *See* Form 33L. If there are a number of investments or agencies in need of verification of guardianship authority, prepare an adequate number of copies to be certified at the time the letters of guardianship are issued to avoid delay and added expense after the original letters of guardianship are filed.

§ 3307. Guardianship duties.

The guardian of the estate must file a verified inventory and appraisement of all of the ward's property pursuant to NRS 159.085 and supplement the same within thirty days after additional property comes into the guardian's possession or knowledge. *See* Form 33N.

Should real property be situated in a county other than the county in which the guardian is appointed, the guardian must record in each of those counties a certified copy of the order of appointment within sixty days as mandated by NRS 159.087. Should the property be encumbered, it may be prudent to record a request for notice of default pursuant to NRS 107.090 in all such counties, including the county in which the guardian is appointed.

The guardian of the person is to file a report regarding the condition of the ward and the actions taken by the guardian annually within sixty days from the anniversary date of his appointment. *See* NRS 159.081. The report does not require a notice for hearing, as no court order approving the same is required.

Other duties assumed by a guardian are specifically set forth in the following statutes: (a) take possession of the ward's property (NRS 159.089); (b) discover the ward's assets in the possession of others (159.091); (c) collect obligations due the ward (NRS 159.093); (d) represent the ward in legal proceedings (NRS 159.095); (e) void invalid contracts and transactions of the ward (NRS 159.097); (f) exercise rights under a ward's stock ownership (NRS 159.101); and (g) approve or defend claims of creditors filed against the ward's estate (NRS 159.103).

§ 3308. Authorization questions and management decisions.

Specific actions as outlined in NRS 159.113 require prior court authority. To ensure the guardian's understanding of this and other responsibilities associated with a guardianship administration, utilize Form 33A, Guardian's Acknowledgment. Notice of proposed actions should be given to interested individuals in accordance with the requirements of NRS 159.115.

For guidance in investing the property of the ward, see NRS 159.117; for continuing a ward's business, see NRS 159.119; for borrowing money, see NRS 159.121; for completing the execution of contracts, see NRS 159.123; and for making gifts from the ward's estate, see NRS 159.125.

For sales of real and personal property, be mindful of the additional step required in guardianship administrations to first obtain court authority to sell the ward's property pursuant to NRS 159.113(f), giving reasons in the petition which would justify the guardian's action in so doing. *See* Form 33O, Petition for Authorization to Sell Real Property. Once the guardian is authorized to sell the ward's real property, NRS 159.134 directs that the completion of the guardianship's sale of real property be accomplished in the same manner as real property sales are finalized in estate proceedings pursuant to NRS 148.060, NRS 148.080 and NRS 148.400.

Petitions for advice and instructions may be addressed to the court pursuant to NRS 159.169 when questions arise concerning the administration of the ward's estate, the priority of paying claims, the propriety of making disbursements, elections to take under a will of a deceased spouse, the exercising of insurance rights or the propriety of exercising property rights. Matters such as these, or questions of a similar nature, may require the issuance of citation directed to any party who may be adversely affected by the proposed action at least twenty days prior to the hearing on the petition. *See* NRS 159.169(3).

§ 3309. Accountings.

A verified account should be prepared by the guardian referencing the time frame covered, cash receipts and disbursements, claims and actions taken thereon, changes in the ward's property, and other information necessary to show the condition of the ward's affairs. *See* NRS 159.179 and Form 33P, First Account and Report of Guardian and Petition for Fees.

The rendering of an account and the notification of the same to those who are interested in the ward's affairs can serve to raise concerns on behalf of others who may be naturally interested in the ward's welfare. However, the case of *In re Walker,* 74 Nev. 230, 327 P.2d 344 (1958), held that the intermeddling of one who is not legally appointed to represent the ward's interests will be considered assistance which the court may accept or reject in determining whether to approve the accounting.

The time frames for the rendering of an accounting are outlined in NRS 159.177. The first annual account is due within sixty days after the anniversary date of the guardian's appointment, within thirty days after the guardian's removal, within ninety days after termination of the guardianship, or at such other time as the court may order.

Should the guardian receive any Veterans' Administration benefits on behalf of the ward, be mindful of the notice requirements of NRS 160.100 which provides for notice to be given to the Veterans' Administration not less than fifteen days prior to the date fixed for the hearing on the accounting, unlike the normal ten-day notice for hearings on most petitions and accountings as required by NRS 155.020.

Information concerning the manner of giving notice for hearing on account and the persons entitled thereto is outlined in NRS 159.115. *See* Form 33Q, Notice of Hearing.

Reasonable compensation for the guardian is based upon similar services performed for persons who are not under a legal disability. Pursuant to the authority granted in NRS 159.183, the guardian may incur reasonable expenses in retaining attorneys, accountants, appraisers and other professionals. However, in a case decided under a former statute, *Sarman v. Goldwater,* 80 Nev. 536, 396 P.2d 847 (1964), the court noted that a guardian is personally obligated to pay for counsel's services; if the services are deemed necessary and if the charge is reasonable, a guardian will then be given credit for that expense at the time of the accounting.

§ 3310. Removal, termination and discharge.

The court may remove a guardian if he has failed to perform his duties, mismanaged the estate, become disqualified or incapable of performing his duties, or if the best interests of the ward would be served by the appointment of another guardian. *See* NRS 159.185. Acting upon a petition filed by the ward or other interested person(s), or upon its own motion, the court may order the issuance of a citation directing persons to appear and show cause why the guardian should not be removed.

Should a guardian die, resign, or be removed, NRS 159.187 provides that a successor guardian may be appointed upon the court's own motion or upon a petition filed by any interested person. The successor guardian may be appointed in the same manner and subject to the same requirements as required for an original appointment.

NRS 159.1905 provides the means by which the ward or another interested person may modify or terminate an existing guardianship. In such a case, the court may appoint an attorney to represent the ward. Petitions seeking to modify a guardianship have been considered by the court in light of its duty to promote the best interests of a child. *See Daly v. Morse,* 99 Nev. 532, 665 P.2d 797 (1983); *Mendive v. Third Judicial District Court,* 70 Nev. 51, 253 P.2d 884 (1953). Factors mandating the termination of a guardianship include the court's finding that the guardianship is no longer necessary, a minor ward's attainment of the age of majority, or the death of an adult ward. *See* NRS 159.191.

Pursuant to NRS 159.193, a guardian may perform duties and retain the property of a ward in winding up the guardianship affairs for no more than ninety days after termination or until an executor or administrator is appointed to represent the ward's estate. The manner in which the guardian is to manage the payment of creditor's claims after the death of the ward is outlined in NRS 159.195.

If property remaining in the ward's gross estate, less encumbrances, does not exceed $25,000, the court may authorize the guardian to distribute the estate in the manner authorized by NRS 146.070, or if the gross value does not exceed $10,000, distribution can be made as authorized by NRS 146.080. Otherwise, the guardian should deliver the ward's property to the executor or administrator and obtain a receipt therefor. *See* NRS 159.197.

Upon the filing of receipts and a showing of compliance in winding up the guardianship affairs, the court will enter an order discharging the guardian and exonerating the bond. *See* NRS 159.199 and Form 33R, Final Discharge. In order to stop ongoing premium expenses and to obtain any refund that may be forthcoming, a copy of the final discharge should be forwarded to the bonding company.

Form 33A

GUARDIAN'S ACKNOWLEDGMENT

The undersigned does hereby certify that he has reviewed the responsibilities that a guardian must assume which include, but are not necessarily limited to, the following:

I. PURPOSE: One who is appointed to serve as guardian for the person and estate of another thereafter acts in a fiduciary capacity, meaning great confidence and trust is reposed in the guardian and the guardian must act with a high degree of good faith. The purpose of a guardianship includes the following:

a. To protect, preserve, and manage the ward's assets;

b. To supply the ward with proper care (including food, shelter, clothing and necessities), maintenance, support and education (including training for a profession, if applicable);

c. To supply the ward with surgical, dental, psychiatric, psychological, hygienic or other care & treatment, if needed.

II. GUARDIAN'S DUTIES:

a. If issuance of letters of guardianship was conditioned upon the posting of a bond, the face amount of that bond should approximate the amount of those liquid assets and income that come within the guardian's control. Should there be a variation of the amount within the guardian's possession, counsel should be informed of such increase or decrease so that arrangements can be made to adjust the bond amount accordingly.

b. The guardian should collect the ward's assets, establish separate accounts and, when establishing bank accounts or holding property on behalf of the ward, title designations should read: "_____, guardian of the person and estate of _____." The guardian may not utilize any guardianship funds for his personal benefit or commingle guardianship funds with his own funds.

c. The guardian may, without prior approval of the court, invest the ward's funds in FDIC insured savings accounts in any bank or savings and loan institution, interest bearing obligations of or guaranteed by the United States or the United States Postal Service, or interest bearing general obligations of any county, city or school district of Nevada, the State of Nevada, or Federal National Mortgage Association.

d. The guardian must file an inventory and appraisement setting forth the description and valuation of the income and assets which comprise the ward's estate within sixty (60) days after letters of guardianship have issued.

e. The guardian must file accounts with the court every year, within sixty (60) days from the anniversary date when letters of guardianship issued, setting forth the amounts received on behalf of the ward, the amounts disbursed on behalf of the ward, and the balance of the ward's estate which the guardian continues to hold. Keep precise and accurate records of all funds received and disbursed for the ward's benefit, along with the source of all receipts and the purpose of all disbursements. This duty includes, but is not limited to, balancing the guardianship checkbook and ensuring that all records are clear, legible, and consistent with the figures referenced on all bank statements.

f. The guardian must ensure that all of the ward's income is reported to the IRS and that all allowable deductions and credits appear on the ward's tax returns which must be filed timely.

III. PRIOR APPROVAL: The filing of an application to the court may be necessary should the guardian take action in certain situations. Some of the acts which require prior court approval include, but are not limited to, the following:

a. Investing the ward's assets in any manner other than those outlined in Section II above.

b. Continuing a business of the ward.

c. Borrowing money for the ward.

d. Entering into contracts or completing the performance of contracts for the ward.

e. Making gifts from the ward's estate or making expenditures for the ward's relatives.

f. Selling, leasing, placing into any trust or surrendering any property of the ward.

g. Exchanging or partitioning the ward's property.

h. Obtaining advice, instructions and approval of any other proposed act of the guardian relating to the ward's property.

i. Authorizing major medical or dental treatment.

j. Exercising or releasing power of the ward as donee of a power of appointment.

k. Changing the state of residence or domicile of the ward.

l. Making expenditures on behalf of the ward for purposes other than providing the ward with food, clothing, shelter and other incidental necessities.

m. Removing the ward's money or property from the State of Nevada.

The guardian understands that he should seek the advice and assistance of counsel if a question arises concerning contemplated acts which may require court approval to ensure full compliance with the laws of the State of Nevada.

The guardian acknowledges that he has reviewed the foregoing and agrees to comply with the rules set forth herein.

DATED this _____ day of _____, 19____.

_____

Form 33B

MINOR'S CONSENT TO GUARDIANSHIP

I, (state minor's name), do hereby consent to the appointment of (state petitioner's name), as guardian of my person and estate, and I hereby request that this Honorable Court allow Letters of Guardianship to issue to (state petitioner's name), forthwith.

DATED this _____ day of _____, 19____.

_____

Form 33C

PETITION FOR APPOINTMENT OF TEMPORARY GUARDIAN

COMES NOW, the Petitioner, _____, whose petition respectfully represents the following to this Honorable Court:

1. That Petitioner is the (state relationship of petitioner to the proposed ward), and is a resident of Clark County, Nevada, his address being

_____.

2. That the proposed ward is a resident of Clark County, Nevada and is currently receiving care and treatment at (state name and address of convalescent facility or, if the proposed ward resides at home, state home address).

3. Petitioner is informed and believes and in reliance thereon alleges that the proposed ward is _____ years of age, his date of birth being

_____.

4. Petitioner is informed and believes and in reliance thereon alleges that the proposed ward owns assets and receives income as follows: (set forth assets owned by the ward and their values, along with income that the ward may receive monthly, quarterly, etc.).

5. Petitioner is informed and believes and in reliance thereon alleges that the proposed ward suffers from (state ward's physical and mental condition), as a result of which he is unable to provide for his own needs, treatment and maintenance. Further, Petitioner alleges that a temporary guardian must be appointed for the benefit of the ward due to the following circumstances: (set forth the reasons for which a temporary guardianship is sought).

6. Petitioner is informed and believes and in reliance thereon alleges that the proposed ward has the following relatives: (state names, addresses and relationships of the ward's relatives within the second degree of consanguinity).

7. Petitioner would request that a bond be posted in the sum of $_____.

8. That your Petitioner is competent and capable of acting as the Temporary Guardian of the person and estate of (insert ward's name), and hereby consents to act in this capacity. That the name of the person for whom Temporary Letters of Guardianship in this matter are requested is (insert petitioner's name), your Petitioner herein, whose address is set forth above.

WHEREFORE, Petitioner prays as follows:

1. That this Honorable Court enter its Order appointing him to act as Temporary Guardian of the person and estate of the proposed ward, and that Temporary Letters of Guardianship issue to him upon his taking the oath of office as required by law, and posting a bond in the sum of $_____.

2. That a hearing be held within ten (10) days in order to determine the need to extend this temporary guardianship proceeding.

3. For such other and further relief as the Court may deem just and proper in the premises.

_____
Petitioner

(VERIFICATION REQUIRED)

Form 33D

ORDER APPOINTING TEMPORARY GUARDIAN

Upon review of the verified Petition for Appointment of Temporary Guardian submitted by (state petitioner's name and his relationship to the adult ward), requesting that he be appointed to act as Temporary Guardian of the person and estate of (insert ward's name), an adult ward, and the Court having considered the same and good cause appearing therefor,

NOW, THEREFORE, IT IS HEREBY ORDERED that the said (insert petitioner's name) be, and he is hereby appointed to act as Temporary Guardian of the person and estate of (insert ward's name), a resident of this State, and that Temporary Letters of Guardianship shall issue to him upon his taking the oath of office as required by law, and posting a bond in the sum of $_____; and it is

FURTHER ORDERED that (insert petitioner's name) shall have the power and authority to preserve the person and property of the said adult ward and protect the same from injury; and it is

FURTHER ORDERED that a hearing of this matter shall be held on ____ *_____, the _____ day of _____, 19____ at the hour of _____ o'clock __ m. of said day, in Department No. _____ of the above-entitled Court, at which time a determination shall be made concerning the necessity to extend this temporary guardianship proceeding.

DATED and DONE this _____ day of _____, 19____.

_____
DISTRICT JUDGE

Submitted by:

*(Reference a hearing date which falls within 10 days of the execution of this order).

Form 33E

PETITION FOR SUMMARY GUARDIANSHIP

COMES NOW, the Petitioner, (insert petitioner's name), whose Petition respectfully represents the following to this Honorable Court:

1. That your Petitioner is the duly appointed, qualified and acting Guardian of the person and estate of (insert ward's name), an adult ward, having been appointed to act in this capacity on the _____ day of _____, 19____, at which time Letters of Guardianship were duly issued to him.

2. That Petitioner has filed herein an Inventory and Record of Value setting forth the total value of the ward's guardianship estate at $_____.

3. That all monthly income received for the benefit of the adult ward is forwarded directly to the facility where the adult ward is receiving care and treatment. Therefore, the assets remaining in Petitioner's possession after satisfying the costs and expenses incident to the ward's care do not exceed the sum of $3,000.

4. Inasmuch as the remaining funds in Petitioner's possession after payment of expenses incident to the ward's care, treatment and maintenance do not exceed $3,000, it is requested that this guardianship be administered under a summary proceeding, by virtue of which the requirement of filing annual accountings with the court would be waived.

WHEREFORE, Petitioner prays that this Honorable Court enter its Order directing that this guardianship matter be administered under a summary proceeding, thereby dispensing with the requirement of filing annual accountings.

(VERIFICATION REQUIRED)

Form 33F

PETITION FOR APPOINTMENT OF GUARDIAN

COMES NOW, the Petitioner, _____, whose petition respectfully represents the following to this Honorable Court:

1. That Petitioner is the (state relationship of petitioner to the proposed ward), and is a resident of Clark County, Nevada, his address being
_____.

2. That the proposed ward is a resident of Clark County, Nevada and is currently receiving care and treatment at (state name and address of convalescent facility or, if the proposed ward resides at home, state home address).

3. Petitioner is informed and believes and in reliance thereon alleges that the proposed ward is _____ years of age, his date of birth being _____.

4. Petitioner is informed and believes and in reliance thereon alleges that the proposed ward owns assets and receives income as follows: (set forth assets owned by the ward and their values, along with income that the ward may receive monthly, quarterly, etc.).

5. Petitioner is informed and believes and in reliance thereon alleges that the proposed ward suffers from (state ward's physical and mental condition), as a result of which he is unable to provide for his own needs, treatment and maintenance.

6. Petitioner is informed and believes and in reliance thereon alleges that the proposed ward has the following relatives: (state names, addresses and relationships of the ward's relatives within the second degree of consanguinity).

7. Petitioner would request that a bond be posted in the sum of $_____.

8. That your Petitioner is competent and capable of acting as Guardian of the person and estate of (insert ward's name), and hereby consents to act in this capacity. That the name of the person for whom Letters of Guardianship in this matter are requested is (insert petitioner's name), your Petitioner herein, whose address is set forth above.

WHEREFORE, Petitioner prays as follows:

1. That this Honorable Court enter its Order to Issue Citation, directing that a time and place be set for hearing this petition; that a citation be issued by the clerk of the court to the said proposed ward, and other interested persons, requiring him to appear at the date, time and place specified therein and show cause, if any, why petitioner should not be appointed to act as guardian of the person and estate of the adult ward.

2. That upon the hearing of this matter, Letters of Guardianship issue to your petitioner upon his taking the oath of office as required by law, and posting a bond in the sum of $_____.

3. For such other and further relief as to the court may deem just and proper in the premises.

(VERIFICATION REQUIRED)

Form 33G

ORDER TO ISSUE CITATION

Upon review of the verified Petition for Appointment of Guardian submitted by (insert petitioner's name), in which the above-named Petitioner alleged that the adult ward (insert ward's name) is unable to manage his personal and financial affairs and that the need exists for the appointment of a Guardian for the person and estate of (insert ward's name) in order to assist the proposed ward, the Court having considered the same and good cause appearing therefor,

NOW, THEREFORE, IT IS HEREBY ORDERED that the Clerk of this Court shall issue a Citation directed to (insert ward's name), and any person having the care, custody, and control of the said (insert ward's name), and all other interested parties, requiring them to appear at the date and time specified therein to show cause, if any they have, why (insert petitioner's name) should not be appointed to act as Guardian of the person and estate of (insert ward's name); and it is

FURTHER ORDERED that this Citation shall be directed to the persons hereinabove named not less than twenty (20) days prior to the date set for the hearing of said petition.

DATED and DONE this _____ day of _____, 19_____.

_____
DISTRICT JUDGE

Submitted by:

Form 33H

CITATION TO APPEAR AND SHOW CAUSE (ADULT WARDS)

Date of Hearing:
Time of Hearing:

TO: THE PEOPLE OF THE STATE OF NEVADA; and

TO: (insert ward's name), and any person having the care, custody and control of the said (insert ward's name):

YOU ARE HEREBY CITED and required to appear before a Judge of this Court at the date, time and place specified below and to show cause, if any, why you, (state ward's name), should not be declared to be incompetent to manage your person and estate and to further show cause, if any, why (insert petitioner's name), should not be appointed to act as Guardian of your person and estate.

YOU ARE NOTIFIED that a Guardian will have the management and control of your person and estate. You have a right to oppose this Petition at the hearing and a right to be represented by an attorney, who may be appointed by the Court if you are unable to retain one.

THIS CITATION is based upon the verified Petition for Appointment of Guardian filed by (insert petitioner's name), and upon order of this Court.

DATE AND TIME OF COURT APPEARANCE

—————————, ——————— o'clock ———.m.

———————————————, 19— in Department ———— of the Eighth Judicial District Court of the State of Nevada, in and for the County of Clark

Clark County Courthouse
200 South Third Street
Las Vegas, Nevada 89155

DATED this ——————— day of ———————————, 19———.

———————————————————, Clerk

By: ———————————————————
          Deputy Clerk

Form 33I

CITATION TO APPEAR AND SHOW CAUSE (MINOR WARDS)

TO: THE PEOPLE OF THE STATE OF NEVADA; and
TO: (insert minor's name), and any person having the care, custody and control of the said (insert minor's name):

YOU ARE HEREBY CITED and required to appear before a Judge of this Court at the date, time and place specified below and to show cause, if any, why the minor (state child's name) should not be declared to be in need of the appointment of a guardian for his person and/or estate and to further show cause, if any, why (insert petitioner's name) should not be appointed to act as Guardian of the minor's person and estate.

YOU ARE NOTIFIED that a Guardian will have the management and control of the minor's person and estate. The minor has a right to oppose this Petition at the hearing and a right to be represented by an attorney, who may be appointed by the Court if he is unable to retain one.

THIS CITATION is based upon the verified Petition for Appointment of Guardian filed by (insert petitioner's name), and upon order of this Court.

PLEASE NOTE that only the minor and the petitioner need to appear at the scheduled hearing unless you wish to enter an objection.

DATE AND TIME OF COURT APPEARANCE

_____, _____ o'clock ____.m.
_____, 19__ in Department ____ of the Eighth Judicial District Court of the State of Nevada, in and for the
County of Clark
Clark County Courthouse
200 South Third Street
Las Vegas, Nevada 89155
DATED this ____ day of _____, 19____.

_____, Clerk

By: _____
Deputy Clerk

Form 33J

AFFIDAVIT OF ATTENDING PHYSICIAN

STATE OF NEVADA   )

                                      :   ss:

COUNTY OF CLARK   )

_____, M.D. being first duly sworn according to law, deposes and says:

I am the attending physician for (insert ward's name) and I am familiar with his condition and diagnosis.

I state that (insert ward's name) will be unable to attend the hearing scheduled for _____, 19____, at which time a guardian may be appointed for my patient due to the following reasons: (set forth reasons that ward cannot be present).

For the above and foregoing reasons, I respectfully request that this Honorable Court excuse the presence of (insert ward's name) at the scheduled hearing.

Under the penalty of perjury, I declare the foregoing to be true and correct.

_____

(If this affidavit is signed under the penalty of perjury, it need not be notarized. If the physician's office is willing to prepare the excuse on office letterhead which explains the ward's condition and which requests that the ward's presence be excused, a letter will suffice).

Form 33K

ORDER APPOINTING GUARDIAN

This matter having come on regularly for hearing on this date upon the verified Petition for Appointment of Guardian filed by (insert petitioner's name), the court having considered this matter and having found that the allegations contained in the verified petition are true and correct, good cause appearing therefor,

NOW, THEREFORE, IT IS HEREBY ORDERED AND DETERMINED that (insert ward's name), a resident of Clark County, Nevada, is incompetent to manage his person and estate; and it is

FURTHER ORDERED that (insert petitioner's name) be, and he is hereby appointed to act as Guardian of the person and estate of (insert ward's name), and that Letters of Guardianship shall issue to the said (insert petitioner's name), upon his taking the oath of office as required by law, and posting a bond in the sum of $_____; and it is

FURTHER ORDERED that (insert petitioner's name) shall have the power and authority as may be necessary in order to conserve and protect the person and property of the adult ward from injury; and it is

FURTHER ORDERED that a copy of this order shall be served upon the adult ward.

DATED and DONE this _____ day of _____, 19____.

_____
DISTRICT JUDGE

Petitioner's Name
Petitioner's Address
Petitioner's Phone Number
Attorney's Name
Attorney's Address
Attorney's Phone Number

Form 33L

LETTERS OF GUARDIANSHIP

On the _____ day of _____, 19___, an order of the court was entered appointing _____ as general guardian of [ ] the estate, [ ] the person of the above-named ward a(n) [ ] minor [ ] adult. The named guardian, having duly qualified, is authorized to act and has the authority and shall perform the duties of such guardian.

In testimony of which, I have this date issued these Letters and affixed the seal of the court.

_____, Clerk of Court

By: _____

Deputy Clerk   Date

OATH

I, _____, residing at _____, whose mailing address is _____, (state mailing address if different from residence), solemnly affirm that I will faithfully perform according to law duties of guardian and that any matters stated in any petition or paper filed with the Court are true of my own knowledge or if any matters are stated on information or belief, I believe them to be true.

_____

Guardian

SUBSCRIBED and AFFIRMED to before me this _____ day of _____, 19___.

LORETTA BOWMAN, Clerk of Court

By: _____

Deputy Clerk

(OR)

_____

NOTARY PUBLIC

County of: _____

State of: _____

Form 33M

ACKNOWLEDGMENT OF BLOCKED ACCOUNT

_____, (insert name of banking institution) does hereby acknowledge that an account has been established with said institution, number _____, said account being titled as follows: (set forth the manner in which the account is titled).

_____, (insert name of banking institution) further acknowledges and understands that this account shall be blocked, and no funds in said account can be removed by the Guardian without first presenting a court order authorizing such action.

_____, (insert name of banking institution) acknowledges receipt of a copy of the Order Appointing Guardian entered on _____.

DATED this _____ day of _____, 19____.

_____
Signature of representative

Form 33N

INVENTORY AND APPRAISEMENT

STATE OF NEVADA	)
	: ss:
COUNTY OF CLARK	)

I, (insert guardian's name), Guardian of the person and estate of the above-named adult ward, do solemnly swear that the accompanying Inventory contains a true and correct statement of all of the property owned by the adult ward at the time of the appointment which has come to my knowledge or possession; it states the fair market value of the property as of such date and its nature as separate or community, and it discloses the type and amount of all encumbrances relating to each item.

_____

SUBSCRIBED and SWORN to before me
this _____ day of _____, 19____.

_____
NOTARY PUBLIC

INVENTORY

Asset Description	Asset Value	Encumbrance	*Ward's Interest	Value of Interest
1. USA bank account	$10,000	-00-	S = 100%	$10,000
2. Residence-111 Main Street	$100,000	$20,000	C = 50%	$40,000

*Designate nature of interest and percentage of ownership; (C) = community; (S) = separate

OATH OF APPRAISER

STATE OF NEVADA	)
	: ss:
COUNTY OF _____	)

I, the undersigned, appraiser of the guardianship estate of the above-named adult ward, solemnly affirm that I will truly, honestly and impartially appraise the inventory of the guardianship estate to the best of my knowledge and ability.

_____
                                                Appraiser

SUBSCRIBED and AFFIRMED to before me
this _____ day of _____, 19____.

_____
NOTARY PUBLIC

APPRAISAL

I, the undersigned appraiser of the guardianship estate of the above-named adult ward, hereby certify that items _____ of the inventory of the guardianship estate have been examined by me and that I appraise these items on the inventory at the value shown opposite thereof for a total sum of _____ Dollars, ($_____).

_____
Appraiser   Date

RECORD OF VALUE

I hereby certify that the property described herein is property where there is no reasonable doubt as to value and is believed to be equal in value to money in the amount set opposite each respective item, and that the net value of the whole of the inventoried estate for the adult ward is in the sum of $_____.

_____
Guardian

(VERIFICATION REQUIRED)

Form 330

PETITION FOR AUTHORIZATION TO SELL REAL PROPERTY

COMES NOW, the Petitioner, (insert petitioner's name), whose Petition respectfully represents the following to this Honorable Court:

1. That Petitioner is the duly appointed, qualified and acting Guardian of the person and estate of (insert ward's name), an adult ward, having been appointed to act in this capacity on the _____ day of _____, 19____, at which time Letters of Guardianship were duly issued to him.

2. That the ward owns the real property located at (insert property address, city, county and state), which Petitioner is seeking authority to sell at this time.

3. That the adult ward is no longer residing in his residence, but is currently receiving care and treatment at (insert name and address of facility where the ward is receiving treatment).

4. Because of the ward's condition, it is highly unlikely that he will be returning to his residence. Therefore, said residence is vacant at this time, and is in danger of being targeted for vandalism.

5. Further, the proceeds realized from the sale of the ward's residence will benefit the adult ward in that funds will come into Petitioner's possession which can be utilized to defray the costs and expenses associated with the ward's care, treatment and maintenance.

WHEREFORE, Petitioner prays that this Honorable Court grant him the authority to sell the ward's real property at this time.

(VERIFICATION REQUIRED)

Form 33P

FIRST ACCOUNT AND REPORT OF GUARDIAN
AND PETITION FOR FEES

(Insert guardian's name), Guardian of the person and estate of the above-named adult ward, now presents to this Honorable Court his First Account and Report of Guardian, along with a verified Petition for Fees, and respectfully represents the following to this Honorable Court:

1. SUMMARY OF ACCOUNT. Petitioner alleges that he should be charged and credited for this accounting period which covers _____ through _____ as follows:

CHARGES

Amount of Inventory:	$
Receipts:	$
Gains on Sales:	$
Total charges:	$
u1440 CREDITS	
Disbursements:	$
Losses on Sales:	$
Other Credits:	$
Assets on Hand:	$
Total credits:	$

2. That Petitioner was appointed to act as Guardian of the person and estate of (insert ward's name) due to the ward's inability to manage his personal and financial affairs. Petitioner reports to the court that the ward's condition remains unchanged and, therefore, the necessity to continue this guardianship exists.

3. That Petitioner has rendered services in connection with this guardianship matter including, but not limited to, marshaling all of the assets of the ward's guardianship estate and inventorying the same, insuring that all costs and expenses associated with the ward's care, treatment and maintenance have been satisfied timely, executing all legal documents and pleadings required to date, along with other services which served to benefit the adult ward. Therefore, Petitioner alleges that the sum of $_____ is a reasonable fee to compensate him for these services.

4. That the law firm of (insert firm name) has rendered services in connection with this guardianship matter including, but not limited to, preparing and filing all documentation necessary to secure Petitioner's appointment as guardian of the ward's person and estate, preparing and filing the guardianship inventory, preparing and filing this instant account and report and all documentation relative hereto. Petitioner alleges that the sum of $_____ is a reasonable fee to compensate said law firm for these services.

WHEREFORE, Petitioner prays as follows:

1. That the foregoing First Account and Report of Guardian be settled, allowed and approved, and all actions taken by the Petitioner as set forth herein be ratified and approved.

2. That this Honorable Court authorize and direct your Petitioner to pay the fees as requested herein.

3. For such other and further relief as to the Court may deem just and proper in the premises.

(VERIFICATION REQUIRED)

Form 33Q

NOTICE OF HEARING

NOTICE IS HEREBY GIVEN to all persons interested in the guardianship of the person and estate of the above-named adult ward that _____, the _____ day of _____, 19____ at the hour of _____ o'clock ___.m. of said day, in the Courtroom of the above-entitled Court, in the City of _____, County of _____, State of _____, is hereby set as the time and place by the Court for the hearing on the (insert name of the petition to be heard by the Court), filed by (insert petitioner's name), at which time all persons interested in said matter are notified then and there to appear and show cause, if any they have, why said petition should not be granted. Reference is hereby by made to said petition, on file herein, for further particulars. YOU DO NOT NEED TO APPEAR UNLESS YOU WISH TO FILE AN OBJECTION.

DATED this _____ day of _____, 19____.

_____, Clerk

By: _____

Deputy Clerk

Form 33R

FINAL DISCHARGE

(Insert guardian's name), Guardian of the person and estate of the above-named adult ward having performed all of the acts lawfully required of him under Decree of Distribution herein, now on motion of counsel for the said Guardian.

IT IS HEREBY ORDERED that the said Guardian has fully and faithfully discharged the duties of his trust; that he has fully and faithfully discharged the duties and responsibilities as such Guardian and that his Letters of Guardianship are hereby vacated and the said Guardian and his sureties are hereby released from any liability to be hereinafter incurred.

DATED and DONE this _____ day of _____, 19____.

_____
DISTRICT JUDGE

Submitted by:

CHAPTER 34

ESTATES OF DECEASED PERSONS

Form 34K. Affidavit of mailing.
Form 34L. Order admitting will to probate and issuing letters testamentary.
Form 34M. Order for probate of estate, for issuance of letters testamentary, and for summary administration of estate.
Form 34N. Order appointing administrator in summary administration.
Form 34O. Letters of administration.
Form 34P. Letters of administration with will annexed.
Form 34Q. Letters testamentary.
Form 34R. Statement of permanent address.
Form 34S. Notice to creditors.
Form 34T. Notice to creditors by mail.
Form 34U. Proof of mailing notice to creditors.
Form 34V. Inventory, appraisement and record of value.
Form 34W. Return of sale of real property and petition for approval and confirmation of sale.
Form 34X. Renunciation and nomination.
Form 34Y. Order settling first and final account, for approval of attorneys' fees, and for decree of final distribution.
Form 34Z. Report of [executor or administrator] pursuant to NRS 143.035 and petition for approval.
Form 34AA. Receipt of distribution.
Form 34BB. Decree of discharge.
Form 34CC. Affidavit terminating joint tenancy.
Form 34DD. Transfer by affidavit.
Form 34EE. Order confirming sale of real property.
Form 34FF. Petition for confirmation of sale of real property.
Form 34GG. Disclaimer of interest in property.

Authors: Robert E. Armstrong
Henry W. Cavallera
James P. Pace

§ 3401. Scope of chapter.

The scope of this chapter is limited to the estates of deceased persons. It does not include tax planning techniques or how to avoid probate. This chapter discusses the administration of estates as a court procedure required to transfer property from a decedent to either his beneficiaries under a will or to his heirs if he died intestate. It also discusses the responsibilities of the executor/administrator in concluding the decedent's tax responsibilities to the Internal Revenue Service.

The administration of the estates of deceased persons is one of the most detailed legal procedures, and a minor forgotten detail can cause endless problems. The attorney should carefully read Title 12 of the Nevada Revised Statutes and the applicable local district rules. The attorney also should use the checklists in the appendix by putting a copy of the appropriate checklist in each new probate file. The appendix also includes the printed forms used in the Eighth Judicial District and additional forms for general use throughout the state.

§ 3402. Introduction to probate.

A. *Introduction*: Under Nevada law, probate of the decedent's will and administration of the decedent's estate are required to transfer legal title to property left by the decedent to heirs and devisees whose equitable title is subject to administration. The Supreme Court of Nevada identified the two primary purposes of estate administration as first, to preserve the estate until distribution can be made, and second, to pay the decedent's debts. *In re Delaney's Estate,* 41 Nev. 384 (1918). At death, the person or entity named in the decedent's will as executor is the legal representative of the deceased even before letters testamentary are issued. *Milner v. Dudrey,* 77 Nev. 256 (1961). The extent and nature of probate administration and court procedures depend upon the gross value of the decedent's probate estate left in the State of Nevada. Title 12 of the Nevada Revised Statutes recognizes several routes for estate administration depending on the decedent's circumstances:

1. Regular Administration: Probate Estate Exceeding $100,000;
2. Summary Administration: Probate Estate over $25,000 and up to $100,000 (NRS 145);
3. Estate Set Aside: Probate Estate of $25,000 or less; To Spouse and/or Child (NRS 146.070); and
4. Estates of $10,000 or less in personalty (NRS 146.080).

B. *Assets of the Probate Estate*: Assets in which the decedent owned at the time of his death are included in the inventory of the decedent's estate. These assets generally include property held individually in fee as a tenant in common, one-half of community property and any separate property. Assets generally excluded from the probate inventory and consequently not controlled by the provisions of the decedent's will (other than for payment of taxes) include life insurance proceeds naming persons other than the decedent's estate as beneficiary, retirement plan benefits, annuity contracts, and property held as joint tenants with rights of survivorship, as community property with rights of survivorship, or in trust. The definitions of separate property and community property are provided at NRS 123.130 and 123.220, respectively. Each spouse has the power to dispose by will of one-half of the community property of the marriage. *See* NRS 123.250.

C. *Practice Considerations*: Upon notification of the decedent's death, the attorney should consider the following preliminary actions:

1. locate will, determine who the executor is, notify executor, determine decedent's domicile, lodge will with appropriate district court, and obtain death certificate;
2. determine if decedent made an anatomical gift;
3. prepare letter to executor advising him of his duties and responsibilities, especially in the marshalling of assets and payment of claims. *See* § 3435;

4. assemble checklists provided by State Bar of Nevada for administration of estate; prepare tax checklists;

5. arrange to meet with the decedent's immediate relatives as soon as it is convenient and request addresses for notices;

6. advise members of family to maintain records for expenditures of money for funeral and cemetery arrangements;

7. advise executor to safeguard assets (*e.g.*, locking home, cancel charge cards, changing mail, care of pets and perishable property, and of maintaining insurance coverage);

8. advise relatives and business associates against attempting to enter decedent's safe deposit box or removal of decedent's property before inventory;

9. obtain all necessary facts concerning decedent's assets and surviving close relatives;

10. when appropriate, attempt to reach a clear understanding with family as to the probable duration and cost of the estate administration and document such discussions in writing, preferably signed by those present;

11. consider use of disclaimers;

12. prepare probate papers and verify court records to make sure no prior will is on file;

13. consider obtaining court order for authority to continue investments and operation of business;

14. open estate savings and checking account or consider use of bank as custodian, or appointment of executor/administrator;

15. conduct a thorough search of decedent's home and place of business for secreted assets and photograph items of significant value; and

16. refer to Appendix 11 for taxation responsibilities of executor or administrator.

§ 3403. Preparation and formalities of wills.

A. *Capacity*: NRS 133.020 — Testator or testatrix must be at least age eighteen and of sound mind. Married women may dispose of their separate property and one-half of any community property. NRS 133.030; NRS 123.250. *See Estate of Hegarty,* 46 Nev. 321 (1923).

B. *Execution*: NRS 133.040 — Except for nuncupative wills and valid holographic wills, wills must be in writing, signed by the testator or by some person in his presence and by his expressed direction, and attested by at least two competent witnesses subscribing their names to the will in the presence of the testator. As a practical matter, witnesses should be over age eighteen, independent, and unrelated to the testator. A devise to a subscribing witness is void unless two other competent subscribing witnesses are provided. *See* NRS 133.060; *Howard Hughes Medical Institute v. Galvin, infra.*

C. *Reference to Unattached List*: NRS 133.045 — A will may refer to a written statement or list which disposes of personal tangible property not otherwise specifically disposed of by will. Such list is effective if it meets the statutory requirements of NRS 133.045.

D. *Self-proving Affidavits*: NRS 133.050 — A sworn statement signed by subscribing witnesses to the will before a notary or officer authorized to administer oaths will be accepted by the court in lieu of personal testimony of witness. *See* statutory form provided at NRS 133.050.

E. *Foreign Execution*: NRS 133.080 — If a will is written and subscribed by the testator in the mode prescribed by either the law of the state where executed or testator's domicile, it is legally effective under Nevada law.

F. *Holographic Wills*: NRS 133.090 — Handwritten wills are valid if entirely written, dated, and signed by testator who is over age eighteen and of sound mind. *See Kanable v. Birch,* 86 Nev. 559 (1970) (question on date did not preclude probate of holographic will); *Dahlgren v. First National Bank of Nevada,* 94 Nev. 388 (1978) (holographic document not probated). The Eighth District requires, and in other districts good practice suggests, that a typewritten copy of the holographic will be attached to the petition for probate. EDCR 4.40.

G. *Nuncupative Wills*: NRS 133.100 — Verbal wills must be made in the presence of two witnesses whom testator requested to bear witness to his will during a last sickness of the testator. Nuncupative wills are only effective for estate of $1,000 or less.

H. *Revocation of Wills*:

1. By subsequent marriage — NRS 133.110. *See Leggett v. Estate of Leggett,* 88 Nev. 140 (1972) (mention in will enough to preclude widow from asserting NRS 133.110); *Horton v. Keating,* 91 Nev. 318 (1975).

2. By subsequent divorce — NRS 133.115. *See DeMarts v. Slama,* 91 Nev. 603 (1975) (Supreme Court would not retroactively apply statute to disinherit ex-wife); *Todora v. Todora,* 92 Nev. 566 (1976); *Reisterer v. Dietmeier,* 98 Nev. 279 (1982).

3. By physical destruction or subsequent will — NRS 133.120;

4. By subsequent agreement — NRS 133.140; and

5. Property passing by will goes subject to mortgage — NRS 133.150.

Revocation of a later will usually does not revive earlier will. *See Shepard v. Gebo,* 77 Nev. 226 (1961) (revocation of earlier holographic will by codicil); NRS 133.130.

I. *Construction of Wills*:

1. Pretermitted Heirs:

a. NRS 133.160 — When a child is born after his parent's will was made, and the will does not provide for the child, the child inherits as though the testator had died intestate, unless it is apparent from the will that the testator intentionally omitted to provide for the child. *See generally Barringer v. Gunderson,* 81 Nev. 288 (1965).

b. NRS 133.170 — When the testator does not provide for a child or a deceased child's issue, it is presumed that the omission was intentional.

c. NRS 133.190 — If a pretermitted heir had an equal proportion of the testator's estate bestowed upon him in the testator's lifetime by way of advancement, he takes nothing under the foregoing provisions.

J. *Death of Devisee Prior to Testator*: NRS 133.200 — When an estate is devised or bequeathed to a child or other relation who dies before the testator, the devisee's or legatee's lineal descendants take the estate as the devisee or legatee would have done had he survived the testator, absent provision in the will to the contrary. *See Gianoli v. Gabaccia,* 82 Nev. 108 (1966) (effect of anti-lapse statute on void bequests).

§ 3404. Succession and intestacy.

A. *Community Property*: NRS 123.250 — Upon the death of either husband or wife:

1. An undivided one-half interest in the community property is the property of the surviving spouse and becomes his or her sole separate property.
2. The remaining interest is subject to the decedent's testamentary disposition. In the absence thereof, this property goes to the surviving spouse, and is the only portion subject to administration under the provisions of Title 12.
3. NRS 134.010 — Upon either spouse's death, community property vests as provided in NRS 123.250, *supra.*

B. *Separate Property*: The laws of intestate succession as to separate property are set forth in NRS 134.030 through NRS 134.110, providing for distribution to decedent's heirs according to their various degrees of relationship to the decedent. *See Pate v. Mead,* 79 Nev. 230 (1963) (half brother and half sister inherit in lieu of decedent's wife's heirs); *see also Barringer v. Gunderson, supra; Horton v. Keating, supra.*

C. *Escheat*: NRS 134.120 — If the decedent is not survived by a spouse or other kindred, the estate escheats to the state for educational purposes.

D. *Murderers*: NRS 134.130 — A person convicted of murdering the decedent cannot succeed to any portion of the estate, but the portion to which he would have been entitled goes to other heirs.

E. *Right of Representation (Per Stirpes)*: NRS 134.140 — Inheritance by right of representation occurs when the descendants of a deceased heir take the same share of an estate that their parent would have taken if living. Posthumous children are treated as living at the death of their parents.

F. *Kindred of Half Blood*: NRS 134.160 — Kindred of the half blood inherit equally with those of the whole blood in the same degree, unless the inheritance comes to the intestate by descent, devise or gift from one of his or her ancestors, in which case all those who are not of the blood of the ancestor are excluded.

G. *Adopted Children*: NRS 134.190 — An adopted child and his adoptive parents and their relatives inherit identically to naturally related persons.

H. *Intestacy by Both Spouses*: NRS 134.210 — When one spouse dies intestate leaving heirs and the other spouse subsequently dies without heirs, the estate of the latter vests in heirs of his or her spouse. *See Pate v. Mead, supra.*

I. *Aliens*: NRS 134.230 — The rights of aliens not residing within the United States or its territories to take property descent or inheritance, either under a will or by intestacy, depend in each case upon the existence of a reciprocal right of U.S. citizens to take property from the country of which the alien is an inhabitant or citizen. The burden of proof is on the alien to establish that the reciprocal rights exist. If reciprocity does not exist, and no heirs other than the aliens are found eligible to inherit, the property escheats to the State of Nevada. These statutory sections are subject to constitutional challenge due to their intrusion on federal jurisdiction in foreign relations. *Zschering v. Miller,* 389 U.S. 434 (1968).

§ 3405. Uniform Simultaneous Death Act.

A. *The "Act"*: NRS 135.020 — Where the title to property or its devolution depends upon priority of death and there is not sufficient evidence that the persons died other than simultaneously, each person's property is disposed of as if he had survived, except as otherwise provided in the Act.

B. *Joint Tenants*: NRS 135.040 — Where joint tenants die simultaneously, their property is distributed one-half as if one had survived, and the other half as if the other had survived.

C. *Insurance Policies*: NRS 135.050 — Where the insured and beneficiary of a life or accident policy die simultaneously, the proceeds of the policy are distributed as if the insured had survived the beneficiary.

D. *Community Property*: NRS 135.060 — Where husband and wife die simultaneously, leaving community property, one-half of the community property is distributed as if the husband had survived, and the other one-half is distributed as if the wife had survived, except in the case of insurance policies as provided in NRS 135.050, *supra.*

E. *Scope*: NRS 135.070 — This chapter does not apply to the distribution of the property of a person who died before March 9, 1949.

F. *Contrary Distribution By Will*: NRS 135.080 — This Act does not apply where a will, living trust, deed or contract of insurance provides for property distribution different from the Act's provisions.

§ 3406. Disclaimers.

Beneficiaries of the estate should be made aware of their right to disclaim all or a part of their potential interest in the estate. The requirements for a disclaimer are set forth in NRS 120.010 through NRS 120.090. The federal requirements for disclaimers are at IRC S2518. Beneficiaries should also be informed that the disclaimer must be made within nine months of the decedent's death.

§ 3407. Anatomical gifts.

Anyone competent to execute a will may give all or any part of his or her body for any one or more of the purposes specified in the Uniform Anatomical Gift Act. NRS 451.500 through NRS 451.590.

§ 3408. — Transfer of personal property not exceeding $10,000.

NRS 146.080 provides for transfer of personal property not exceeding $10,000 in value. This may be done forty days after decedent's death without any court proceeding. An affidavit must be prepared by the person who is entitled to the estate, which meets the requirements of NRS 146.080. *See* Form 34DD, *infra*. Anyone who receives such an affidavit is entitled to rely on it and is immune from civil liability for actions taken in reliance. NRS 146.080(4).

§ 3409. — Setting aside estates not exceeding $25,000.

If the net value of an estate does not exceed $25,000, the estate may be set aside without probate or administration of the estate to the surviving spouse or children after directing such payments as the court deems necessary. If there is no spouse or children, certain creditors have priority. NRS 146.070(2). Any encumbrances against any property are deducted from the value of the property to determine whether or not this section may be used. *See* Form 34C.

The notice requirements differ from the regular administration of estates in that under NRS 146.070(4) the notice must include a statement that a prayer for setting aside the estate to the spouse or child or children is included in the petition. All proceedings under NRS 146.070 must be by verified petition.

§ 3410. Vesting of homestead and family allowances.

A. *Vesting of the homestead*: If a homestead was selected by a husband and wife during their marriage and recorded while both were living, it vests on the death of either spouse in the survivor subject to NRS 115.060.2.

765

A homestead, even if not selected, may be set apart for a limited period of time for the decedent's family. The period for which property is set apart must be set forth in the court order and may not exceed the life of the surviving spouse or the minority of the decedent's children, whichever is longer.

B. *Family allowances*: If the whole property exempt by law is set apart and is not sufficient for the support of the surviving spouse or the children, the court may make allowance out of the estate which is necessary for the maintenance of the family during the settlement of the estate. NRS 146.030.

Family allowances are in preference to all other charges, except funeral expenses, expenses of the last illness, and expenses of administration. NRS 146.040.

The court has discretion to make the appropriate allocation among the persons who would be entitled to a family allowance. *French v. French,* 91 Nev. 248, 533 P.2d 1357 (1975).

The court cannot make the family allowance out of general assets in lieu of exempt assets. General assets can only be utilized for the support of the family when the exempt assets are insufficient. *Hunter v. Downs,* 53 Nev. 132 (1931).

§ 3411. Appointment of attorneys to represent minors or absent heirs.

The court has authority to appoint counsel to represent minors and nonresidents. NRS 136.200.

§ 3412. Jurisdiction and venue.

For a Nevada court to take jurisdiction of a decedent's estate, the decedent must have been a resident of Nevada or have left property within the State of Nevada. *Failkoff v. Nevil,* 80 Nev. 232, 234, 391 P.2d 740 (1964). NRS 136.010 governs the jurisdiction and venue for estate proceedings of both resident and nonresident decedents.

A. *Resident Decedents*: Wills must be proved and letters testamentary granted in the district court in the county where the decedent was a resident when he died, regardless of where he died. The same holds true in intestate administration. The district court of the county where the decedent was a resident has exclusive jurisdiction of his estate, even though there may be assets in other counties. NRS 136.010(1).

B. *Nonresident Decedents*: The estate of a nonresident decedent may be settled in the district court of any county where any part of the estate is located. The district court to which application is first made has exclusive jurisdiction of a nonresident's estate. NRS 136.010(2).

C. *Limitations on Exclusive Jurisdiction*: With respect to a resident decedent, the district court in the county of the decedent's residence has exclusive jurisdiction over the administration of any real property within the State of Nevada and any personal property, both tangible and intangible. With respect to a nonresident decedent, the district court only has jurisdiction to administer real or personal property within the State of Nevada. If a Nevada resident dies with real property situated in another state, it is necessary to commence an ancillary proceeding in that jurisdiction to administer that portion of the decedent's estate, as each state has exclusive jurisdiction over the transfer and descent of real estate within its limits. *In re Forney's Estate,* 43 Nev. 227, 233, 184 P. 206 (1919). If the foreign jurisdiction has adopted the Uniform Probate Code, the transfer of the real property in that state may not require the appointment of another personal representative. The attorney should review the statutes of the state in which the real property is located.

D. *Determine Residency*: Because of Nevada's proximity to California and presence of mobile residents, it is important to make sure the decedent is properly determined to be a resident of Nevada, otherwise California tax authorities will attempt to recharacterize borderline decedents as residents of California.

§3413. Custody of wills, copies, foreign wills.

A. *Delivery of Will*: Any person possessing a will must deliver it to the clerk of the district court which has jurisdiction of the case, or to the named executor, within thirty days after learning of the testator's death. NRS 136.050(1). Any person named executor or executrix must, within thirty days after the death of the testator, or within thirty days after knowledge of such naming, present the will to the district court, if such will is in his or her possession. NRS 136.050(2).

B. *Compelling Production of Will*: Any person failing to deliver a will in accordance with NRS 136.050(1) or (2) without reasonable cause is liable to every interested person for any consequential damages. NRS 136.050(3). The court has the authority to issue an order requiring that a person produce a will. NRS 136.060(1). NRS 136.060(2) gives the judge the authority to make all other necessary orders in chambers to enforce production of the will.

C. *Copies*: If the will is detained in a court of any other state, county or jurisdiction, and cannot be produced for probate in Nevada, a copy of the will may be admitted to probate in Nevada in lieu of the original will and have the same force and effect as if the original were produced. NRS 136.180(1).

§ 3414. Petition for probate of will.

A. *Who May Petition*: Any executor, devisee, or legatee named in a will, or any other person interested in the estate, may petition the court to have the will proved at any time after the testator's death. NRS 136.070(1). All petitions for the probate of a will and the issuance of letters must be signed by the petitioning party or the attorney for the petitioner. NRS 136.100. In the Eighth District the petition must be verified. EDCR 4.14.

B. *Contents of Petition*: The contents of a petition for probate of a will and issuance of letters are governed by NRS 136.090, which provides that the petition must state the following:

1. The jurisdictional facts (death, residence and/or the existence of property within Nevada);
2. Whether the person named as the executor consents to act or renounces his right to letters testamentary;
3. The names, ages and residence of the heirs, next of kin, devisees and legatees of the decedent, and the relationship of the heirs and next of kin to the decedent so far as known to the petitioner;
4. The character and estimated value of the property of the estate; and
5. The name of the person for whom letters testamentary are prayed.

See Form 34A. In the Eighth District, see also EDCR 4.14 and 4.40.
No defect of form or in the statement of jurisdictional facts voids the probate of a will. NRS 136.090(2).

C. *Contents of Petition for Summary Administration*: NRS 146.020 governs estates subject to summary administration (estates in which the gross value does not exceed $100,000). In addition to the requirements set forth above, the petition seeking summary administration additionally must contain:

1. A specific description of all of the decedent's property;
2. A list of all liens and encumbrances of record at the date of his death; and
3. An estimate of value of the property.

See Form 34B. In the Eighth District, see also EDCR 4.14 and 4.40.

§ 3415. — Notice of hearing and proof of notice.

A. *Notice of Hearing*: Notice of a hearing on a petition for probate of a will and issuance of letters must be given in accordance with NRS 155.020 to the heirs of the testator, devisees, and legatees named in the will and all persons named as executors who are not petitioning. The notice must state the fact of filing the petition, that letters testamentary are sought, and the time for proving the will. NRS 136.100(2); *see* the statutory form set forth in NRS 155.020(3) and also Forms 34H, 34I, and 34J. Notice to heirs and other interested parties must be given by registered or certified mail, postage prepaid, at least ten days prior to the date set for hearing. Each notice must be addressed to the intended recipient at his last known address, receipt for delivery requested. NRS 155.020(1)(a) (incorporating NRS 155.010). Notice is given to the public by publication on three dates prior to the hearing. If the newspaper is published more than once a week, there must be at least ten days from the first to the last date of publication, including both the first and the last days. NRS 155.020(b).

If someone other than a named executor presents a petition for probate or if it is presented by one of several named executors, a citation must issue and be served upon the executors not joining in the petition, if they are residents of the county. The citation must be served at least five days before the hearing. NRS 136.120.

B. *Proof of Notice*: At the hearing on the petition for probate of the will and issuance of letters, proof must be made by affidavit or otherwise to the satisfaction of the court that proper notice has been given. NRS 136.140. Proof is normally made by the filing of a certificate of the mailing of the notices and the returned receipts of the registered or certified letters, and by the filing of an affidavit of publication of the notice.

§ 3416. — Hearing and proof of will.

A. *Written Will Accompanied by Self-Proving Affidavit*: NRS 133.050 provides a procedure pursuant to which the attesting witnesses to a will may make an affidavit before any person authorized to administer oaths in or out of the State of Nevada, stating such facts as they would be required to testify to in court to prove a will. The court must accept a self-proving affidavit as if it had been taken before the court. NRS 133.050(1). Therefore, no further proof of the will is necessary if the will contains a self-proving affidavit. Given the potential difficulty associated with locating witnesses to a will, self-proving affidavits should always be obtained when the will is executed by the testator.

B. *Written Will Not Containing Self-Proving Affidavit*: If the will does not contain a self-proving affidavit in the form prescribed by NRS 133.050, the will must be proved by the testimony of the subscribing witnesses showing that the will was executed in all particulars as required by law, and that the testator or testatrix was of sound mind at the time of its execution. All witnesses who appear are sworn and testify orally. NRS 136.140(2). The court is empowered to issue subpoenas to the subscribing witnesses to a will if they reside in the county. NRS 136.130.

If no person appears to contest the probate of the will, the court may admit it to the probate on the testimony of only one of the subscribing witnesses. NRS 136.150. If the witness resides more than twenty-five miles from the court, the ex parte affidavit of the witness stating the facts which the witnesses would testify to must be received in evidence, and have the same force and effect as if the witness was present and testified orally. NRS 136.150(2).

To alleviate the necessity for oral testimony at the hearing on the proof of the will, an attesting witness may, after the testator's death, make an affidavit stating the facts required to prove the will. The affidavit, when written on the will or if that is impracticable, on some paper attached to the will, must be accepted by the court as if it were taken before the court. NRS 136.160(1).

If one or more of the subscribing witnesses, at the time the will is offered for probate, are in the armed forces, dead, or mentally or physically incapable of testifying or otherwise unavailable, the court may admit the will to probate upon the oral or deposition testimony of at least two credible disinterested witnesses that the signature on the will is in the handwriting of the person whose will it purports to be, or upon sufficient proof of the handwriting. NRS 136.170.

C. *Proof of Will by Copy*: If a will is detained beyond the jurisdiction of the state and cannot be produced for probate in Nevada, the court may authorize a photographic copy of the will to be presented to the subscribing witness for his examination in court, or by affidavit and proved as though it were an original will. NRS 136.180.

D. *Foreign Wills*: If a will was duly probated outside Nevada, a certified copy of the will and the probate thereof when proved to the court's satisfaction, have the same force and effect as the original probate of a domestic will. NRS 136.260.

E. *Holographic Will*: A holographic (handwritten) will may be proved in the same manner as other probate writings. NRS 136.190. In the Eighth District, if the will is holographic, a typewritten copy of the document must also accompany the petition. EDCR 4.40.

F. *Nuncupative Will*: A nuncupative (oral) will must be reduced to writing within thirty days after it was spoken and offered for proof within six months after the testamentary words were spoken. NRS 136.080.

G. *Translation of Will in Foreign Language*: If the will is in a foreign language, the court shall certify a correct translation of the will into English and the certified translation will be recorded in lieu of the original. NRS 136.210.

§ 3417. — Lost or destroyed wills.

If a will is lost by accident or destroyed by fraud without the testator's knowledge, the court may take proof of the execution and the validity of the will. NRS 136.230.

The petition for the probate of a lost or destroyed will must state, or be accompanied by a written statement of the testamentary words, or their substance. If the will is established, its provisions must be set forth in the order admitting the will to probate. NRS 136.240(1). The testimony of each witness must be reduced to writing, signed and filed. This testimony is admissible in evidence in any contest of the will, if a witness has died or is permanently removed from the state. NRS 136.240(2).

No will can be proved as a lost or destroyed will unless it is proved to have existed at the testator's death, or shown to have been fraudulently destroyed in the testator's lifetime, and its provisions are clearly and distinctly proved by at least two credible witnesses. NRS 136.240(3). The two witnesses must be able to testify from their personal knowledge, even though NRS 51.105(2) otherwise makes hearsay evidence admissible regarding the execution, revocation, identification, or terms of the declarant's will. *Howard Hughes Medical Institute v. Gavin,* 96 Nev. 905, 908, 621 P.2d 489 (1980).

At common law, when an executed will cannot be found after the testator's death, there is a strong presumption that the testator revoked it by destruction. NRS 136.240(3) codifies the common-law rule and places the burden of overcoming the presumption on the proponent of the lost or destroyed will. *In re Estate of Irvine v. Doyle,* 101 Nev. 698, 703, 710 P.2d 1366 (1985). The court in *Irvine* held that the words "in existence" and "fraudulently destroyed" taken together convey the legislative intent to require the proponent of a lost or destroyed will to prove that the testator did not revoke the lost or destroyed will during his lifetime. The question of whether a will is revoked is a matter to be decided by the trier of fact. *Estate of Irvine, supra.*

§ 3418. Appointment of the personal representative of the estate — executors and administrators.

Executors and administrators are personal representatives who administer decedents' estates. Provisions governing the appointment of executors and administrators with the will annexed are found in Chapter 138 of the Nevada Revised Statutes.

An executor is appointed to administer an estate by designation in the decedent's will. An executor's authority is generally established upon the issuance of "Letters Testamentary."

An administrator is appointed by the court to administer an estate when the decedent dies intestate. The authority of an administrator to act is established upon the issuance of "Letters of Administration."

An administrator with will annexed is a personal representative who is granted the authority by the court to administer the estate where the decedent has failed to name an executor under the will or where the named executor fails to serve and does not appoint a substitute executor. An administrator with will annexed is at times referred to as an administrator c.t.a., from the Latin — Cum Testamento Annexo.

§ 3419. — Appointment of executors and administrators with the will annexed.

NRS 138.020 defines the eligibility of persons to serve as executors by excluding persons who are not competent to serve. The statute provides that a person is not competent to serve as executor if, at the time the will is probated, the person:

a. is under the age of majority;
b. has been convicted of a felony;
c. upon proof is shown to have been adjudicated incompetent to execute the duties of an executor because of drunkenness, improvidence or want of integrity or understanding; or
d. is a banking corporation whose principal place of business is not in Nevada, unless it associates as co-executor a banking corporation whose principal place of business is in Nevada. An out-of-state banking corporation is, however, competent to appoint a substitute executor under NRS 138.045 without forming this association, but any natural persons so appointed must be a resident of Nevada. NRS 138.020(d).

The statutory eligibility requirements do not preclude a nonresident individual from being named as executor. The courts give a testator the absolute right to select the executor of his choice so long as the selection is not contrary to statutory limitations. *See generally Foley v. Silvagni,* 76 Nev. 93, 349 P.2d 1062 (1960). Any interested person may file written objections to the granting of Letters Testamentary to the person named in the will. NRS 138.060.

No person has any powers as an executor until properly and fully qualified, except that funeral charges may be paid and necessary measures may be taken to preserve the estate before Letters are issued. NRS 138.010.

Named executors and alternate executors who are unwilling or unable to undertake or to continue the administration of the estate may appoint a substitute or co-executor who must also be qualified to serve as an executor under NRS 138.020. This substitute or co-executor is, upon appointment, entitled to Letters Testamentary as though named in the will. NRS 138.045.

§ 3420. — Miscellaneous provisions.

Chapter 138 of the Nevada Revised Statutes contains several miscellaneous provisions which give substantive and procedural guidance on authorization and appointment of executors in varying situations and contexts.

A. *Executor Not Specifically Named May Be Appointed*: When the terms of a will reflect a testator's intent to administer the estate through any person as an executor although that person was not named, that person is entitled to Letters Testamentary as though named as executor in the will. NRS 138.040.

B. *Failure to Appoint All Named Executors*: When the court does not appoint all the persons who were named as executors, those who are appointed have the same authority to perform every act and discharge every trust required by the will, and the acts of those who are appointed are effective for every purpose. NRS 138.080.

C. *Successor Executors to Corporate Executors*: Letters may be issued to corporations or associations which are successors by consolidation, merger or other succession provided for by law or to qualified, authorized corporate executors. NRS 138.050.

D. *Executor of an Executor*: No executor of the will of an executor is authorized to administer the estate of the first testator, except that on the death of the sole or surviving executor, letters of administration with the will annexed of the estate of the first testator will be issued. NRS 138.070.

E. *Marriage*: The authority or appointment of an executrix is not affected or extinguished by the fact of her marriage. NRS 138.020.

§ 3421. — Administrators with will annexed and order of their appointment.

Administrators c.t.a. "Cum Testamento Annexo" have the same authority as a named qualified executor except that a discretionary power conferred on the executor under the will is not conferred on the administrator c.t.a. The order of priority to rights of Letters for administrators c.t.a. is the same order of priority established for appointed administrators under NRS 139.040, except that as to foreign letters, a person who is interested in the will has priority of appointment as administrator c.t.a. over a disinterested person. NRS 138.090. The administrator c.t.a. must be a resident of the State of Nevada.

§ 3422. — Special administrators.

The provisions of Chapter 140 of the Nevada Revised Statutes pertain to special administrators. Special administrators, as the name implies, are generally appointed in situations where an executor or administrator has not yet been appointed, and exigencies make it necessary to take prompt actions to marshall assets or otherwise preserve the estate or some interest it may have.

A. *Appointment*: Special administrators are appointed by a district court judge. The special administrator is appointed for an interim pending the appointment of an executor or administrator. Causes for appointment are: delays in granting Letters Testamentary or Letters of Administration; irregular grants of Letters; when no petition is filed for Letters; when an executor or administrator dies or is suspended or removed, and circumstances require immediate appointment of a personal representative; when insufficient bond is filed; and in any other proper case. NRS 140.010.

The appointment of a special administrator may be made ex parte in chambers, or upon such notice as the court deems reasonable. The appointment is made by minutes or order signed and filed, which specifies the powers to be exercised by the special administrator. Upon entry of the order and giving of bond, if any, fixed by the judge, the clerk issues Special Letters of Administration to the person appointed. A certified copy of the Court Order is attached to the letters. Preference in the appointments of special administrators is given to those entitled to Letters Testamentary of Letters of Administration. No appeal from the appointment is allowed under the terms of the statute. NRS 140.020.

B. *Oath and Bond*: Special administrators must give a bond and take the usual oath prescribed for executors and administrators. NRS 140.030.

C. *Duties*: A special administrator has mandatory powers and duties to marshall and preserve (for the executor or administrator to be appointed) all personalty including goods, chattels, debts of the decedent, and income, rents, issues, profits, claims and demands of the estate, and to take charge and manage the real property and protect it from damage, waste and injury. NRS 140.040(1).

A special administrator also has permissive powers and duties, which include filing, maintaining or defending suits or other legal proceedings for all necessary purposes, selling perishable property of the estate without prior court order, borrowing money, leasing or mortgaging or executing a deed of trust on real property, and exercising other powers as may have been granted in the order of appointment. NRS 140.040(2).

The special administrator is not liable in an action on a claim and the special administrator cannot pay any claim against the deceased other than claims involving wrongful death, personal injury or property damage where the estate has no assets other than a policy of liability insurance. NRS 140.040.

The Nevada Supreme Court has construed the permissive power to commence a suit under NRS 140.040(2)(a) as authorizing a special administrator to bring a wrongful death action even though the order of appointment did not specifically authorize that lawsuit. *Nevada Paving, Inc. v. Callahan*, 83 Nev. 208, 427 P.2d 383 (1967). Consistent with the statutory provision that a special administrator's primary duty is to take possession and to preserve the decedent's property, a special administrator has authority to maintain any action necessary to recover estate property and may also be required to defend any claim against the decedent for which the estate is not liable. *Bodine v. Stinson,* 85 Nev. 657, 461 P.2d 868 (1969).

A special administrator (or anyone interested in the estate) may petition for an order authorizing the payment of interest due to a creditor of the estate (under a mortgage, lien, or deed of trust to secure the payment of money) where there is a "danger" that the creditor may enforce his claim and there is equity in the property involved. An order granted in this situation may also direct that interest be paid as it becomes due. Such an order remains in effect and covers future interest to be paid unless and until set aside or modified by the court upon petition and notice. NRS 140.050.

D. *Appointment With Powers of General Administration*: When a special administrator is appointed pending determination of a will contest brought before probate or involving an appeal from an order appointing, suspending or removing an executor or administrator, the special administrator has the same powers, duties and obligations as a general administrator. Letters of Administration issued to the special administrator in these instances are required to recite that the special administrator is appointed with the powers of the general administrator. If a will contest is initiated before probate after the special administrator has been appointed, the court shall order that the special administrator has the additional powers, duties and obligations of a general administrator and require the special administrator to give whatever additional bond the court deems proper. This order is not appealable. NRS 140.060.

E. *Termination of Powers*: The powers of the special administrator cease upon the grant of Letters Testamentary or Letters of Administration. The special administrator is then required to deliver immediately to the executor or administrator all of the decedent's property held by the special administrator. The successor to the special administrator is empowered to prosecute to final judgment any suit commenced by the special administrator. NRS 140.070.

The special administrator is also required to render an accounting of the proceeding (under oath), just as any other administrator is required to do. However, if a special administrator is appointed as the succeeding general personal representative, then this required accounting may be included in the first accounting of the successor general administrator or executor. NRS 140.080.

§ 3423. Administration of estates.

In general, when a decedent dies intestate, the property of his estate will pass to his heirs in the manner provided in the statutes for descent and distribution in NRS 124.040 to 134.120. The administrator of the estate is entitled to take possession of the estate and administer it according to the procedures set forth in Chapter 143. The administrator must be appointed by the court pursuant to the statutory framework set forth in Chapter 139.

§ 3424. — Competency and priority.

As a general rule, any individual is entitled to letters of administration un'ess they are under the age of majority; have been convicted of a felony; have been adjudged incompetent to execute the duties of trust; or are not a resident of the State of Nevada. NRS 139.010. The qualifications are not discriminatory as to gender and a woman may be appointed administratrix. Her authority is not affected by her marital status. NRS 139.020. A decedent's surviving partner may be appointed administrator of the estate, but only if there is no objection by any person interested in the estate. NRS 139.030. Administration of an intestate person's estate may be granted to one or more qualified persons, and the right to letters of administration will be granted in the following order of priority:

1. The surviving husband or wife;
2. The children;
3. The father or the mother;
4. The brother or the sister;
5. The grandchildren;
6. Any other of the kindred entitled to share in the distribution of the estate;
7. Creditors who acquired claims during the decedent's lifetime;
8. A public administrator;
9. Any of the kindred not enumerated above, within the fourth degree of consanguinity;
10. Any person or persons legally competent.

The persons set forth above are entitled to appointment if they are a resident of Nevada or a banking corporation whose principal place of business is in the State of Nevada. NRS 139.040(2). The persons set forth above are entitled to nominate a resident of the State of Nevada or a qualified banking corporation for appointment rather than accept the appointment, and the nominee has the same priority as his nominator. NRS 139.040(2)(b). NRS 139.050 states that "[a]dministration may be granted to one or more competent persons, although not otherwise entitled to the same, at the written request of the person entitled, filed in this court."

NRS 139.040(2)(b) provides that the persons set forth in 139.040(1) are entitled to nominate a resident for appointment "whether or not the nominator is a resident of the State of Nevada" and the priority which the nominator transfers to the nominee is "independent of the residency or corporate qualification of the nominator."

When there are several persons equally entitled to the administration of the estate, the order of priority favors relatives of the whole blood over those of the half blood. NRS 139.060. In addition, when there are several persons equally entitled to the administration, the court may, in its discretion, grant letters to one or more of them. NRS 139.070. Notwithstanding the order of priority, Letters of Administration may be granted to an applicant who has less priority when others having better rights fail to claim the issuance of letters to themselves. NRS 139.080.

§ 3425. — Petition for letters of administration.

A petition for Letters of Administration must be written, signed by the applicant or his counsel, and filed with the clerk of the court. In addition, the petition must state: jurisdictional facts; the names, ages and post office addresses of the heirs of the decedent and their relationship to the decedent; and the character and estimated value of the property of the estate. NRS 139.090(1); EDCR 4.14. *See* Form 34D. A defect of form in the statement of jurisdictional facts will not void an order appointing an administrator in any subsequent proceeding. NRS 139.090(2).

The court clerk sets the petition for Letters of Administration for hearing, and notice must be given to the heirs of the decedent named in the petition as provided in NRS 155.020. The notice must state the fact of the filing of the petition, the object, and the time for hearing. NRS 139.100; *see* the statutory form set forth in NRS 155.020 and also Form 34I. Any person interested may contest the application by filing a written opposition on the ground of the incompetency of the applicant, or may assert his own right to the administration and pray that letters be issued to himself. NRS 139.110.

Before Letters of Administration are granted, certain facts must be proved by evidence of the applicant or others. In particular, the fact of death, that the decedent died intestate, and that notice has been given as required in this chapter, must all be demonstrated to the court. In addition, the court may examine the applicant or any other person concerning the time, place and manner of death, the place of decedent's residence at the time, the character and value of his property, and whether or not the decedent left any will. Also, the court may compel any person to attend as a witness for that purpose. NRS 139.120. *See* Form 34N for an order appointing a general administrator(trix).

§ 3426. — Revocation of letters.

If Letters of Administration have been granted to any person other than the surviving husband or wife, or his or her nominee, the child, father, mother, brother or sister of the intestate, then the Letters of Administration may be revoked by any one of those persons just listed. Such person or persons must present to the district court a petition praying for the revocation and that the Letters of Administration be issued to him. NRS 139.140.

When a petition for revocation is filed, the clerk gives notice and issues a citation to the administrator to appear and answer the petition at the time appointed for the hearing. NRS 139.150(1). At the time appointed for hearing, the court takes evidence upon the petition, and if the right of the applicant is established and he is competent, Letters of Administration will be granted to him and the letters of the former administrator revoked. A surviving spouse or his or her nominee, is entitled to assert a prior right and to revoke the Letters of Administration of the former administrator pursuant to NRS 139.150. In addition, a child, parent, brother or sister of the intestate may assert prior right over any other relatives to revoke Letters of Administration pursuant to NRS 139.150. NRS 139.160.

In the final analysis, it is within the discretion of the court to refuse to grant Letters of Administration, as provided in this chapter, to any person or to any nominee who had actual notice of the first application and an opportunity to contest it. NRS 139.170.

A. *Changes in administration may occur for various reasons.*

1. *Incapacity of All Executors, Administrators*: NRS 141.070 — If all executors or administrators die, are unable to serve, or are removed from office, the court must order letters of administration c.t.a., or otherwise, to be issued to persons entitled, in the same manner as directed in relation to original letters of administration ("c.t.a." — abbreviation of the Latin phrase "Cum Testamento Annexo").

2. *Resignation, Suspension and Removal*: NRS 141.080 — An executor or administrator may resign at any time by writing filed in court, to take effect upon settlement of his accounts.

a. The Court may then revoke the letters and appoint an administrator, general or special, or c.t.a. in the same manner as is directed in relation to original letters of administration.

b. NRS 141.090 — If a District Judge believes, from his or her own knowledge or from credible information, that the representative has done any of the five things listed in this section, he shall suspend the powers until the matter can be investigated.

c. NRS 141.100 — A special administrator may be appointed during period of suspension.

d. NRS 141.110 — When a suspension has been made, the clerk must issue a citation for removal. Citation must be served as provided by NRCP for service of civil process. If the representative cannot be found or has left the state, the citation may be served on attorney of record, and the court has jurisdiction to proceed as if citation has been personally served on the representative.

e. NRS 141.140 — If the representative is removed, acts prior to this removal are valid. A successor may be appointed without again proving the deceased's death and residence. *See* NRS 141.150.

3. *Ancillary Proceeding — Foreign Wills*: NRS 136.260 — A will admitted to probate outside of Nevada may be admitted in the proper court of any county in this state in which the testator left any estate according to the following procedures:

a. A copy of the will and the probate thereof, duly certified, is presented by the executor, his nominee, or by any other person interested in the will, with a petition for probate.

b. The will is filed and a time set for hearing.

c. The notice must be given as on a petition for probate of a domestic will.

d. If probate is not required by the laws of the foreign jurisdiction, a duly certified copy of the will, with the certificate of the legal custodian of the original will that it is a true copy, and that the will has become operative by the laws of that jurisdiction, is presented by the executor, his nominee, or other interested person to the proper court in this state.

§ 3427. — Order, oath, bonds and letters.

Upon admission of a will to probate and appointment of an executor, or the court's order appointing an administrator of an estate, the court will order that Letters Testamentary (in the case of an executor), or Letters of Administration (in the case of the appointment of an administrator) be issued. As to the order admitting a will to probate and for issuance of letters, see Form 34L. No person has any power as an executor in the state until he qualifies, except that, before letters are issued, he may pay funeral charges and take necessary measures for preservation of the estate. NRS 138.010.

Letters Testamentary, Letters of Administration with the will annexed, and Letters of Administration are signed by the clerk and are under seal of the court. NRS 141.010. A form for Letters Testamentary is set forth in NRS 141.020, a form for Letters of Administration with the will annexed is set forth in NRS 141.020, a form for Letters of Administration with the will annexed is set forth in NRS 141.030, and a form for Letters of Administration is set forth in NRS 141.040. *See also* Form 34Q as to the issuance of Letters Testamentary; Form 34P as to Letters of Administration with the will annexed and Form 34O as to general and special Letters of Administration.

Every executor or administrator must take and subscribe (and file with the clerk) an oath for the faithful performance of his duties. NRS 142.010.

The oath of a corporation or banking corporation must be taken and subscribed by one of the officers listed in NRS 142.010(2).

The requirement of a bond is discretionary with the court. NRS 142.020(1). If a bond is required, letters may not be issued until the bond is posted with the court. Bonds are not required in the following cases:

1. Where bond is waived in the will, but the court is not bound by such waiver. NRS 142.070.

2. A banking corporation or trust company doing business in this state is not required to furnish bond unless specifically ordered by the court. NRS 141.020(6).

3. In counties having a population of 100,000 or more, the public administrator posts an official bond of $100,000, and need not post bond in individual estates unless the estate exceeds $25,000 in total assets. NRS 253.040.

Pursuant to NRS 142.020, where a bond is required for an executor or administrator, it may be either:

1. A property bond, with two or more sureties to be approved by the District Judge; or

2. A surety bond by a company duly qualified to act as sole surety within this state.

Personal assets of an estate may be deposited with a domestic banking or trust corporation, subject to withdrawal only upon court order and the bond of the representative may be reduced accordingly. NRS 142.020(5). This is often referred to as a "blocked account."

Upon the sale of real property, the expected proceeds of the sale are treated as personal property, and the bond must be increased accordingly. NRS 142.020(2).

At the hearing on the petition for probate or appointment of an administrator and for issuance of letters, the attorney for the personal representative should be prepared to recommend to the court the amount of the bond if one is required. Corporate sureties are available for bonding purposes through local insurance agencies. Upon completion of administration of the estate, the court's order should discharge the personal representative and his sureties from all liability thereafter incurred.

§ 3428. Will contests.

A. *Pre-Probate*: At any time prior to the hearing on the petition for probate of a will, any interested person, including the attorney general or a devisee or legatee under a former will, may contest the will by filing a written opposition to its probate. Upon such a filing, a citation is issued directed to the decedent's heirs and to all persons interested in the will, including minors and incompetents, requiring them to plead to the contest within thirty days after service of the citation. Service of the citation shall be made either personally or by publication as provided by the Nevada Rules of Civil Procedure for the service of summonses in civil actions.

Any person served with a citation may raise any defense or objection to the will contest by motion as provided by the Nevada Rules of Civil Procedure. If the motion is granted, the contestant has ten days to amend his contest. If the motion is denied, the petitioner and any other interested persons have ten days after receipt of notice of the denial to jointly or separately answer the will contest. All time periods may be extended by the court. NRS 137.010.

B. *Post-Probate*: Subsequent to the admission of a will to probate, any interested person other than a person who had actual notice of a previous contest may, within three months after the admission of a will to probate, contest the will by filing a verified petition for revocation of the probate of the will. NRS 137.080.

A will contest dismissed without prejudice does not constitute a contest for the purposes of this statute. However, a contest which is concluded by a court-approved settlement does constitute a will contest and the provisions of NRS 137.080 apply to it. *Melvin v. Farmer*, 93 Nev. 166, 561 P.2d 455 (1977). The statute of limitations set forth in NRS 137.080 will be tolled when the failure to contest a will within the statutory time limit is the result of extrinsic fraud. *Fullerton v. Rogers*, 101 Nev. 306, 701 P.2d 1020 (1985). Failure to contest the will within the time specified in NRS 137.080 renders conclusive the probate of the will. NRS 137.120. However, the failure to contest a will does not preclude the subsequent probate of a will executed later in time than the one admitted to probate. NRS 137.130.

§ 3429. — Grounds for contesting a will.

A will may be contested upon any of the following grounds:

1. The decedent's incompetency to make a last will;
2. The decedent was under duress, menace, fraud or undue influence when he executed the will. Influence exerted in the making of a will becomes undue only when it prevents the will from being truly the testator's act. *In re Hegarty's Estate*, 46 Nev. 321, 212 P. 1040 (1923);
3. The will was not duly executed or attested; or
4. Any other question substantially affecting the validity of the will. NRS 137.020.

§ 3430. — Procedure in pre-probate will contest.

The contestant in a will contest case is the plaintiff and the petitioner is the defendant. NRS 137.020.

Either party may demand a jury trial of any issue of fact. NRS 137.020. The status of a contestant as an interested person and, therefore, his standing to contest the will may be determined by the court in a preliminary hearing without a jury unless the ultimate issues in the litigation are inextricably interwoven with the standing issues such that their determination would also serve to determine the ultimate factual issues in the litigation. *Close v. Flanary,* 75 Nev. 255, 339 P.2d 379 (1959).

Testimony as to the testator's declarations made while executing the will are admissible insofar as they relate to the testator's intention, state of mind, feelings, competency, or the existence or nonexistence of duress or undue influence. NRS 137.030.

All subscribing witnesses who are present in the county must be produced and examined, or their deaths, absences or insanities must be shown to the court. If none of the subscribing witnesses reside in the county, the court may admit testimony of other witnesses to prove the due execution of the will and may admit proof of the handwriting of the testator and of any of the subscribing witnesses. NRS 137.040.

The jury must return a special verdict on the issues submitted to it. NRS 137.050.

Costs are to be awarded pursuant to the provisions of Chapter 18 of Nevada Revised Statutes. NRS 137.020. NRS 18.020(4) governs awards of costs in a pre-probate will contest. Costs will be allowed against any party against whom judgment is rendered rather than be charged against the estate pursuant to NRS 18.090. *Gavin v. Rhoden,* 97 Nev. 147, 625 P.2d 571 (1981).

§ 3431. — Procedure for will contest after the will has been admitted to probate.

After the filing of the verified petition, a citation is issued directed to the executor of the will, or the administrator with the will annexed, and to all devisees and legatees and to all of the heirs including the personal representatives of any such persons who are dead, directing them to plead to the contest within thirty days after the citation was served. NRS 137.090.

The proceedings and trial in a post-probate will contest are conducted in the same manner as a contest made before admission of the will to probate. Upon a finding that the will is invalid or not the last will of the testator, the court will revoke the probate of the will and Letters Testamentary. Powers of the executor or administrator with the will annexed terminate when revoked. The executor or administrator is not liable for any act done in good faith previous to revocation. NRS 137.100.

The contestant must pay all costs if the probate is not revoked. If the contestant is successful, costs are paid by the party opposing the revocation or out of the estate, as directed by the court. NRS 137.110.

§3432. Changes in executors and administrators.

For the sake of easy reference, executors, administrators and the like are referred to below as "personal representative," unless it is necessary to distinguish in what capacity the personal representative serves.

A. *Resignation*: A personal representative may resign his appointment at any time by filing a written resignation with the district court. The resignation takes effect upon the settlement of the accounts of the personal representative. The court may, because of any delay in settlement of the accounts or for any other good cause, revoke the letters of the personal representative at any time after the written resignation is filed with the court. The court may then appoint an administrator, either special or general, or an administrator with the will annexed. The resigning personal representative, as well as any sureties on his bond, remains liable for his acts until he has delivered all of the estate to the person whom the court appoints to receive it. NRS 141.080.

B. *Suspension*: A District Judge may, by entering an order upon the minutes of the court, suspend the power of any personal representative whenever the District Judge has reason to believe from his own knowledge, or from any credible information, that the personal representative: (1) wasted, converted, or mismanaged, or is about to waste or convert estate property; (2) has committed or is about to commit any wrong or fraud on the estate; (3) has become incompetent; (4) has wrongfully neglected the estate; or (5) has unreasonably delayed the performance of any necessary acts. NRS 141.090.

The District Court may, if the condition of the estate requires it, appoint a special administrator for the estate during the suspension of the personal representative. NRS 141.100.

When a suspension has been made, the clerk of the court must issue a citation requiring the personal representative to appear before the court to show cause why the letters should not be revoked. The citation is served as provided by the Nevada Rules of Civil Procedure for service of process, or, if the personal representative has absconded, concealed himself, or left the state, a citation may be served on his attorney. NRS 141.110.

At the show cause hearing any person may appear and file written allegations why the personal representative should be removed. NRS 141.120. If the personal representative fails to appear at the hearing, or if the court is satisfied that good grounds exist for removal, the letters of the personal representative shall be revoked. The court may grant new Letters of Administration as required. NRS 141.130. The court may compel the personal representative to appear and testify at the hearing and may commit the personal representative to jail for refusal to do so. NRS 141.130.

All acts of the personal representative prior to the revocation of the letters are valid. NRS 141.130.

After the resignation or removal of a personal representative, a successor may be appointed without the necessity of proving the decedent's death and residence. NRS 141.150.

§ 3433. Incapacity of the personal representative.

When there is more than one personal representative of an estate and one of them dies, becomes insane, is convicted of a felony, or otherwise becomes incapable of executing his duties, or has his letters revoked, the remaining personal representatives proceed with their duties and complete the administration of the estate. NRS 141.060. When all personal representatives of an estate die or otherwise become incapable of executing the trust, or have their letters revoked, NRS 141.070 directs the District Court to issue Letters of Administration with the will annexed, or otherwise, to the surviving spouse, next of kin or others, in the same manner as the issuance of original letters. NRS 141.070.

§ 3434. Subsequent probate of will after letters of administration on grounds of intestacy.

If a will is admitted to probate after Letters of Administration were issued on the grounds of intestacy, the Letters of Administration will be revoked. The administrator must render an accounting of his administration within the time the court directs. The executor or administrator with the will annexed may sue to collect all property of the estate and may prosecute any suit commenced by or against the administrator prior to the revocation of the administrator's letters. NRS 141.050.

§ 3435. Powers and duties of executors and administrators.

A personal representative, in addition to whatever powers may be granted by will, has the following general statutory powers:

1. To take possession of all of the decedent's property, real or personal, and to the rents and profits from the real property until distribution or until the estate is closed. NRS 143.020.

2. To take into possession all of the decedent's estate, real or personal, except as exempted by law. NRS 143.030.

3. To collect all debts due the decedent or his estate. NRS 143.030.

4. To have the decedent's interest in a partnership liquidated within a reasonable time and to compel an accounting from the surviving partner. NRS 143.040.

5. To continue the decedent's business. NRS 143.050.

6. To sue and to be sued. NRS 143.060.

7. To institute actions for conversion or trespass. NRS 143.070.

8. To institute actions on the bond of a former personal representative. NRS 143.090.

9. To institute actions for conversion before Letters Testamentary or Letters of Administration are granted. NRS 143.100.

10. To require an accounting by one holding assets of the estate for the personal representative. NRS 143.130.

11. To discharge, compromise or renew obligations due the estate. NRS 143.140.

12. To sue for and to recover for the benefit of creditors assets fraudulently conveyed by the decedent in his lifetime upon a creditor's application and payment of litigation expenses. NRS 143.150 and 143.160.

13. To make deposits and investments of the estate's money without approval of the court in:

a. United States Treasury notes, bills or bonds;

b. Negotiable commercial paper, not exceeding 180 days maturity, of prime quality as defined by a nationally recognized organization which rates such securities;

c. Bankers' acceptances;

d. Savings accounts or certificates of deposit in national banks, banks chartered by the State of Nevada, federal savings and loan associations or savings and loan associations chartered by the State of Nevada; or

e. Any other investment in which a personal representative is authorized by law or by a will to invest moneys or funds under his control.

NRS 143.175.

14. To make loans, advances of credit, and other investments insured by the Federal Housing Administrator. NRS 143.180.

15. To invest in farm loan bonds and other obligations issued by federal land banks and for cooperatives. NRS 143.185.

16. To hold stock in the name of a nominee, although the personal representative is personally liable for any loss to the estate resulting from any act of the nominee in connection with the stock. NRS 143.187.

§ 3436. Authority of multiple personal representatives.

When there are two personal representatives, the acts of one alone are valid if the other personal representative is absent from the state or is under a legal disability. When there are more than two personal representatives, the acts of a majority shall control. NRS 143.010.

§ 3437. Report of estate proceedings.

The personal representative must use reasonable diligence in performing his duties in pursuing the administration of the estate. Every personal representative in charge of an estate which has not been closed must file with the district court a report explaining why the estate has not been closed:

  1. Within six months after his appointment, where no federal estate tax return is required to be filed for the estate; or
  2. Within 18 months after his appointment, where a federal estate tax return is required to be filed for the estate.

NRS 143.035.

§ 3438. Filing of permanent address of personal representative with clerk.

Prior to the issuance of any letters, the personal representative is required to file with the county clerk in which the administration of the estate is pending, a written statement containing his name and permanent address which may be changed by filing a written statement of the new address with the county clerk. NRS 143.190.

§ 3439. Substituted service of process of personal representative.

The county clerk of the county in which the administration of the estate is pending is automatically appointed as the personal representative's true and lawful attorney, upon whom all legal process in any action or proceeding against the personal representative may be served, with the same legal force and effect as if served upon the personal representative personally within the State of Nevada. NRS 143.190.

§ 3440. Purchase of estate property.

A personal representative cannot directly or indirectly purchase any property of the estate he represents. NRS 143.170. If an attorney for a personal representative intends to purchase estate property, he should first review SCR 158(1).

§ 3441. Inventory and appraisement.

An inventory is the public record of all of the property that the decedent owned or had an interest in at death which is subject to probate administration. The inventory serves a critical role in the estate administration process because: (i) the personal representative is accountable to the District Court, the creditors, and the beneficiaries for estate assets; (ii) the District Court determines the amount of bond required by the personal representative or distributee, the family allowance and homestead, whether summary administration is appropriate, necessity of probate sales; (iii) the Internal Revenue Service reviews probate records in auditing an estate and determining tax obligations; and (iv) creditors and beneficiaries are interested in the nature and extent of the inventory to determine the appropriate course of action. The personal representative is required to make and to return to the court within sixty (60) days after his appointment, unless extended by the court, a true inventory and appraisement or record of value of all assets of the decedent's estate which he possesses or of which he is aware. NRS 144.010.

Practice Point The personal representative should engage the services of a competent appraiser as early as possible in the estate process due to their sometimes limited availability, the increased complexity of appraisals in general and the short statutory inventory filing period. Where a federal estate tax return is required, an experienced appraiser or appraisers who have been previously qualified as an expert in court should be considered in evaluating unique estate assets. Because of complex valuations, pending sale negotiations and determination of final federal estate tax values after audit, the personal representative sometimes chooses to delay filing the inventory by requesting court extensions unless discontented or contesting parties are present.

§ 3442. — Contents of inventory.

The inventory is required to include all of the estate of the decedent subject to the court's jurisdiction, and must contain:

(a) All of the estate of the deceased, real and personal.

(b) A statement of all debts, partnerships, and other interests, bonds, mortgages, notes, and other securities for the payment of money, belonging to the deceased, specifying the name of the debtor in each security, the date, the sum originally payable, the endorsements thereon, if any, with their dates, and the sum which, in the judgment of the appraiser, may be collectible on each debt, interest or security.

In addition, the inventory must show:

(a) So far as can be ascertained, what portion of the estate is community property and what portion is the separate property of the deceased.

(b) An account of all moneys belonging to the deceased which the personal representative possesses. NRS 144.040.

Practice Point The inventory is typically set forth in the same order as given in the Federal Estate Tax Return Form 706 (*e.g.*, real estate, stocks and bonds, mortgages, notes and cash, insurance, miscellaneous property) with the same detail as set forth in such form (*e.g.*, item numbers, complete legal descriptions, unit value, and aggregate date of death values) and the same methods of valuation as reflected on such return. The personal representative should include interest, dividends, refunds, rents, and other items that may be accrued, but unpaid at the decedent's death. It is not uncommon to reflect miscellaneous used furniture, furnishings and personal effects in one lump sum due to the unlimited market or value for such items unless such property is reasonably capable of being sold secondhand (*e.g.*, antiques, coin collections, autos, and sporting goods). A copy of the inventory should be provided to each party requesting special notice.

§ 3443. — Appraisement or record of value.

The personal representative may engage a qualified and disinterested appraiser to ascertain, as of the date of the decedent's death, the fair market value of an asset, where the value is subject to reasonable doubt. Different appraisers may be engaged to appraise different kinds of assets in the estate. An appraiser is entitled to reasonable compensation and may be paid by the personal representative out of the estate at any time after completion of the appraisal. If there is no reasonable doubt about the value of an asset, such as cash, bank accounts, or life insurance, the personal representative must file a verified record of value in lieu of the appraisal of the asset. NRS 144.020.

Prior to executing his duties, an appraiser is required to take an oath that he will truly, honestly, and impartially appraise the property for which he has been retained according to the best of his knowledge and ability. An appraiser who directly or indirectly purchases any property of an estate which he has appraised, without full disclosure to and approval by the court, is guilty of a misdemeanor, and the sale is void. NRS 144.030.

§ 3444. — Oath of personal representative.

The personal representative is required to swear that the inventory truly states all of the estate which has come into his possession or of which he has knowledge, all moneys belonging to the decedent, and of all just claims of the decedent against the personal representative. This oath is endorsed upon or annexed to the inventory. NRS 144.070.

§3445. — Failure to file inventory.

If the personal representative does not file the inventory within the time prescribed or such further time as the court may allow, the court may, upon such notice as it may prescribe, revoke the letters of the personal representative. NRS 144.080.

§3446. — Supplemental inventory.

Whenever any property not mentioned in the inventory comes to the possession or knowledge of the personal representative, he must file a supplemental inventory within twenty days after its discovery. The supplemental inventory is filed in the same manner as the original inventory. NRS 144.090.

§3447. Presentation and payment of creditor's claims.

Creditors' claims upon an estate are superior to the rights of the heirs or beneficiaries of the estate. The debts and charges of an estate are paid in the following order:

(a) Funeral expenses;
(b) The expenses of last sickness;
(c) Family allowance;
(d) Debts having preference by laws of the United States;
(e) Wages to the extent of $600 of each employee of the decedent, for work done or personal services rendered within three months prior to the employer's death. If there is insufficient money with which to pay such labor claims in full, the money available must be distributed among the claimants in proportion to their respective claims;
(f) Judgments rendered against the deceased in his lifetime, and mortgages in order of their date. The preference given to a mortgage extends only to the proceeds of the property mortgaged. If the proceeds of the property are insufficient to pay the mortgage, the unsatisfied part must be classed with the other demands against the estate; and
(g) All other demands against the estate.

NRS 150.220.

All claims of a preferred class must be paid fully before any creditor of a lower priority class is paid. If the estate is insufficient to pay all the debts of any one class, each creditor of that class must be paid in proportion to his claim. NRS 150.240(2). If the claim is not due, or is contingent or disputed, the amount of the claim must be paid into the court, to be paid over to the holder when and if he becomes entitled to payment.

The personal representative must publish the notice to creditors and mail, registered or certified mail, return receipt requested, a copy of the notice to those creditors whose names and addresses are readily ascertainable and who have not already filed a claim. NRS 147.010 and 155.020.

Practice Point To ascertain the decedent's creditors, the personal representative should consider reviewing the decedent's personal papers, mail, checking accounts, and public records and should consider interviewing friends, relatives and business associates. Proof that the personal representative took reasonable steps to ascertain creditors should be preserved so that a defense can be established to untimely filed creditor's claims.

In the general administration of an estate, the creditors must file their claims within ninety days after the mailing of the required notice, or within ninety days after the first publication of the notice specified in NRS 147.010.

In the summary administration of an estate as provided in NRS 145.060, the creditors must file their claim within sixty days after the mailing of the required notices, or within sixty days after the first publication of the notice.

The notice to creditors in both summary and general administrations must be in substantially the form set forth in NRS 155.020(4).

A copy of the notice with the affidavit of publication must be filed with the clerk of the court. If the notice is mailed, the proof of mailing must be filed with the clerk of the court. NRS 147.020. If notice is improper, the statute of limitations period will not begin running. Until the statute runs, the personal representative cannot safely satisfy claims that have been brought to his attention and legacies without risking personal liability to creditors later presenting claims.

The caption of the petition for letters testamentary or for letters of administration should set forth all names by which the decedent was known so that the notice to creditors will be sufficient notice to creditors who may have known the decedent by other than his legal name. Notice given in the married name of the decedent who was a nurse-anesthetist was held to be insufficient notice to those who knew her under her professional name. *Kotecki v. Augusztiny,* 87 Nev. 393, 487 P.2d 925 (1971). The notice was not sufficient even though it was given in the form allowed by statute. For example, if Osborne J. Jones was commonly known as Bud Jones, then the caption of the pleading should be given as follows: "In the Matter of the Estate of Osborne J. Jones, also known as Bud Jones, deceased."

§ 3448. — Limit of time for filing of claims.

If a claim is not filed with the clerk within the ninety-day period, the claim is to be forever barred. When a creditor by affidavit or by other proof satisfactory to the court establishes that he did not have notice as provided by NRS 155.020, then the creditor may file his claim at any time before the filing of the final account. NRS 147.040.

In the case of the summary administration of an estate, the time limit for filing of creditor's claims is shortened to sixty days. NRS 145.060.

The claim statute is intended to provide for the efficient and expedient administration of estates and applies to all contingent and noncontingent claims and to all resident and nonresident claimants. *Continental Coffee Co. v. Estate of Clark,* 84 Nev. 208, 438 P.2d 818 (1968).

To come within the claim statute, a claim must be against property constituting an asset of the decedent's estate, and the claim, if successfully prosecuted, must diminish the estate. If not, then the claim does not fall within the claims bar statute. *Bell Brand Ranches, Inc. v. First National Bank,* 91 Nev. 88, 531 P.2d 471 (1975). A claim for the recovery of property held by the decedent in trust does not fall within the claims bar statute since the property is not an estate asset, and its recovery does not diminish the estate. *Minors & Absent Heirs v. First National Bank,* 95 Nev. 146, 590 P.2d 1164 (1979); *Reed v. Sixth Judicial District Court,* 75 Nev. 338, 341 P.2d 100 (1959).

The trial judge has discretion upon good cause shown to allow or disallow the filing of a late claim. Knowledge of the decedent's death or any knowledge of the estate proceedings, coupled with failure to act after such knowledge, are enough to support the lower court's discretion in denying a late filing. *Continental Coffee Co. v. Estate of Clark, supra.* However, under NRS 155.020(4) which requires mailing notice to creditors known to the personal representative, the failure to mail notice would probably allow a creditor to avoid termination of his claim even though he knew of the decedent's death.

§3449. — Actions pending by or against a decedent.

If an action was pending against an individual when he died, the plaintiff in that action must file a timely claim with the clerk. When an action has not proceeded to final judgment, and where, within the time allowed for the filing of a claim, the personal representative of a deceased party is substituted in the decedent's place in the pending litigation, the statutory requirement for filing a timely claim is satisfied. *Carl Needham, Inc. v. Camilleri,* 91 Nev. 235, 533 P.2d 765 (1975).

As a general rule, the personal representative of a decedent must be substituted as a party before the estate of the decedent can be affected by any judgment. NRS 17.140 does not alter the rule that before a court may issue an order or judgment against or for a deceased party, the personal representative must be substituted. *Koester v. Administrator of Estate of Koester,* 101 Nev. 68, 693 P.2d 569 (1985). Personal representatives and creditors should be vigilant to the implications of NRCP 25(a)(1), prescribing the substitution of deceased parties. When plaintiff died and no motion for substitution was made within ninety days after plaintiff's death was suggested upon the record as required by NRCP 25(a)(1), the action must "be dismissed as to the deceased party." *Bennett v. Topping,* 102 Nev. 151, 717 P.2d 44 (1986).

§ 3450. — Form of creditor's claim.

Every claim exceeding $250 filed with the clerk must be supported by the affidavit of the creditor that:

(a) The amount is justly due or if the claim is not yet due, that the amount is a just demand and will be due on a particular day;

(b) No payments have been made which are not credited;

(c) There are no offsets to the knowledge of the claimant or other affiant;

(d) Sets forth the creditor's mailing address;

(e) In the event a claim is not made by a creditor, the reasons why the claim is not made by the creditor must be set forth in the affidavit;

(f) The oath to the creditor's affidavit may be taken before any person authorized to administer oaths;

(g) The amount of interest must be computed and included in the statement of the claim and the rate of interest determined.

For good cause shown, the court may allow a defective claim or affidavit to be corrected or amended upon application made prior to the filing of the final account.

A copy of any written instrument upon which a claim is founded must be attached to the statement of the claim. A copy of any lien upon which a claim is based such as a mortgage, deed of trust, or judgment must be attached to the statement of the claim. NRS 147.080.

A creditor's claim does not have to be set forth with the particularity of a pleading, but the claim should contain sufficient information to enable the personal representative to act advisedly upon it and to apprise the personal representative of the amount of the claim. When there is a possibility that the claim will be contested, the creditor's attorney should consider preparing the claim with the particularity of a pleading to avoid later objections the claim varies from the complaint subsequently filed. In addition, the creditor's attorney should send a courtesy file-stamped copy of the claim to counsel for the personal representative. The creditor's attorney also should file a request for special notice as provided by NRS 155.030 so as to be able to monitor the future administration of the estate. Where the decedent was a settlor of a nontestamentary trust, the trustee thereof may cause publication of a notice to creditors in the manner specified in NRS 155.020. NRS 164.025.

§ 3451. — Allowance or rejection of claim.

Within fifteen days after the time for filing claims has expired, the personal representative must examine all claims filed and note his allowance or rejection of the claim either by dating and endorsing the filed claim indicating allowance or rejection, or dating, endorsing and filing a notice of allowance or rejection. Within five days after the claim examination period, the personal representative must present all allowed claims to the district judge for his approval or rejection. NRS 147.110(2). If the personal representative does not allow or reject a claim within the fifteen-day period, or does not file a notice of allowance or rejection, the claim is deemed rejected but may be allowed at any time before the filing of the final account. NRS 147.110. In the case of the summary administration of an estate, the personal representative must examine all claims filed and note his allowance or rejection within ten days after the time for filing claims has expired. NRS 145.060(1).

The personal representative cannot allow a claim which is barred by the statute of limitations. NRS 147.090. A creditor who timely complies with the claim statute, however, is protected against the general statute of limitations. *Brown v. Eiguren,* 97 Nev. 251, 628 P.2d 199 (1981).

All approved claims become acknowledged debts of the estate and are paid in the due course of administration. NRS 147.120.

The "deemed rejected" provision of NRS 147.110(3) is directed primarily to the conduct of the personal representative rather than to any duty on the part of the creditor. Nonaction by a personal representative in an estate proceeding is not sufficient to trigger the running of the applicable sixty-day period requiring the creditor to file suit within that time period. NRS 147.130(1). Subsection 3 of NRS 147.110 (or in the case of summary administration, NRS 145.060(1)) merely provides that if the personal representative does not act upon the claim within the applicable ten- or fifteen-day period, the claim shall be deemed rejected and the creditor may, thereafter, commence an action to recover his claim in the district court. *Wells v. Bank of Nevada,* 87 Nev. 145, 483 P.2d 205 (1971); and *Brown v. Eiguren,* 97 Nev. 251, 628 P.2d 199 (1981).

The time within which an action must be commenced to collect on a rejected claim does not begin to run until the claim has been actually rejected. *Brown v. Eiguren, supra.*

The personal representative must immediately notify a creditor whose claim is wholly or partially rejected. The creditor has sixty days after receiving notice of rejection to sue the personal representative in the proper court, whether the claim is due or not, or the claim is forever barred. To avoid dispute regarding whether the rejection notice was properly given, written notice of the rejection of the claim must be given personally to the creditor by registered or certified mail, return receipt requested, and forwarded to the creditor's address as shown on the claim form. *See* NRS 147.130(1). As to what is the "proper court" for suit, creditors should be aware of the effect of the decision of *Bergeron v. Loeb,* 100 Nev. 54, 675 P.2d 397 (1984).

The time during which there is a vacancy in the administration of an estate is excluded from the limitations provided by Title 12. NRS 147.140.

Filing a claim is not a necessary prerequisite to the bringing of an action to foreclose a lien against property of the estate where all recourse against any other property of the estate is expressly waived in the complaint. *Reed v. Sixth Judicial District Court,* 175 Nev. 338, 341 P.2d 100 (1959).

If a personal representative doubts the correctness of a claim, then he and the creditor may enter into an agreement to refer the matter in controversy to some disinterested person approved by the court who shall act as a master in reference to the claim. NRS 147.170.

After the time for the presentation of claims has expired, the personal representative, with the approval of the court, may compromise any claim against the estate or any suit brought against the personal representative. To obtain court approval, the personal representative is required to file a petition for compromise showing the advantage to the estate of the compromise. Notice of the hearing of the petition is required to be given for the period and in the manner set forth in NRS 155.010. NRS 147.180(3).

If a creditor who has a partially allowed claim refuses to accept the allowed amount and successfully recovers a greater amount, the creditor will be entitled to costs. The personal representative is personally liable for costs rendered as part of a judgment for a creditor and may recover such costs against the estate unless defense of the claim was without cause. NRS 147.190.

§ 3452. — Payment of claims.

A judgment rendered against a personal representative upon any claim for money against the estate establishes the claim as if the personal representative had allowed it. The judgment is paid in the due course of administration. A certified copy of the judgment must be filed in the estate proceedings, and the creditor may not execute upon the judgment. The judgment does not create any lien upon the estate property or give the judgment creditor any payment priority except for a judgment of foreclosure of a lien. NRS 147.200.

A creditor who obtained a judgment against a decedent in his lifetime may not execute upon it after his death. A certified copy of the judgment shall be attached to the statement of the judgment creditor and filed with the clerk. The filed judgment will be acted upon as any other claim. NRS 147.210.

Unless a different rate applies by contract or otherwise, all claims paid bear interest from the date of filing at the largest bank of Nevada's prime rate plus two percent. The rate is determined on January 1st and July 1st, whichever immediately precedes the date of filing, and adjusted on these dates thereafter until the claim is fully paid. NRS 147.220.

§ 3453. Circumstances permitting a sale of estate assets.

The sale of estate property will be warranted and permitted when it is necessary "to pay debts, legacies, family allowance, or expenses" of the estate. NRS 148.050. Such sale also is authorized when it is demonstrated to be "for the advantage, benefit, and best interests of the estate and those interested therein." NRS 148.050. In addition, the sale of estate property will be justified when the personal representative is directed by the will to sell any property of the estate. NRS 148.090. If the sale of estate property is otherwise warranted, but the personal representative of the estate neglects or refuses to sell the property, any person interested in the property may petition the court for an order requiring the personal representative to sell. NRS 148.090.

When it is determined that estate assets are to be sold, there is no priority between personal and real property, and the property may be sold either at public auction or private sale. NRS 148.050. The personal representative has discretion as to which property to sell first; however, the personal representative's discretion is limited by the ordering rules of NRS 148.010 and 148.020.

§ 3454. Determination of assets to be sold.

The ordering rules of Chapter 148 apply in two different circumstances. If the testator provided in his will for the payment of debts, expenses of administration, or family allowance, then NRS 148.010 mandates that payment of the expenses must be made from estate assets in the following order:

First, the personal representative must look to the will and satisfy expenses from property which the testator designated be sold for this purpose. Second, if the property designated under the will is insufficient to satisfy these expenses, then any estate property which is not disposed of by the will, *i.e.*, the intestate property of the estate, must be appropriated. Third, if the property specified above is insufficient to satisfy the estate expenses, then property given to residuary legatees and devisees must be appropriated. Fourth, if there are insufficient assets from the above sources to meet the estate expenses, then all other property devised and bequeathed is liable for estate expenses, but only in proportion to the value or amount of the devises or legacies. Specific devises and legacies, however, are exempt from this liability if necessary to effectuate the testator's intent and the estate has other sufficient assets.

When estate assets must be sold to pay legacies, the order of resort is as follows:

First, where the will expressly designates certain property to be used for legacy, it will be appropriated and sold by the estate. Second, if no property is expressly designated, then the intestate property of the estate will be applied to satisfy the legacy. Third, if the above property does not satisfy the legacy, then property which is devised or bequeathed to a residuary legatee will be appropriated. NRS 148.020.

§ 3455. Abatement and contribution.

When property available for distribution among the beneficiaries under the will is insufficient to satisfy all of the legacies contemplated by the testator, the gifts under the instrument will "abate" as set forth above. Pursuant to NRS 148.010 and 148.020, a residuary legacy may be reduced to pay debts or expenses of the estate and to pay general and specific legacies. Further, general legacies and devises may be reduced to pay debts or expenses, but such reduction shall be in proportion to the value or amount of the other legacies or devises. NRS 148.010. This proportional reduction is also mandated by NRS 148.030 and 148.040, which requires that "all the devisees and legatees must contribute according to their respective interests to the devisee or legatee whose devise or legacy has been sold." In other words, other devisees or legatees are required to contribute and reserve from their distributive share such pro rata amounts as the court determines. In addition to specific devises and legacies being exempt from abatement if it appears necessary to effectuate the testator's intention, abatement also will take place only between legacies of that class, and legacies to a spouse or to kindred are chargeable only after legacies to persons not related to the testator. NRS 148.030.

§ 3456. Procedural requirements.

In general, in addition to determining which estate property may be sold, the personal representative also must satisfy procedural requirements, including notice of the sale, method of sale and confirmation of the sale by the court.

(a) *Notice of Sale.* In general, a notice of sale is required for both real and personal property. The notice must include the time and place of the sale and a brief description of the property to be sold. NRS 148.190; NRS 148.220.

(b) *Real Property*. In the case of public auctions of real property, notice of the time and place of sale of the property must be published in the newspaper three times, each publication one week apart, beginning two weeks before the day of the sale. In addition, the newspaper in which the publication is made must be published in the county in which the land lies, if there is one; otherwise, the court may direct another paper in which the publication must be made.

In the case of the private sale, the notice must state a place where bids or offers will be received and the day on or after which the sale will be made. The notice must be published within the same time limits for public auctions; however, the publication requirement can be modified, shortening the time of notice by court order. NRS 148.240.

In the case of a sale of real property the value of which does not exceed $500, the personal representative may post a notice of the time and place of sale in three of the most public places of the county in which the land lies in lieu of publication.

The notice requirements under NRS 148.220 serves two purposes. One purpose is to advertise the sale to potential bidders to promote competitive estate sales. The second purpose is to serve constructive notice to all heirs so that they may have the opportunity to contest the sale. *Sarman v. First Judicial District Court*, 99 Nev. 201, 660 P.2d 990 (1983). The advertising requirement does not go to jurisdiction, but the lack of sufficient notice to the heirs may prevent the court from gaining jurisdiction, especially where the decedent dies intestate and not all heirs are known to the personal representative. Nevertheless, lack of compliance with NRS 148.220 will not necessarily deprive the court of jurisdiction to enter an order confirming the sale if notice of the confirmation hearing is sent to all of the beneficiaries of the estate. *Sarman, supra*.

(c) *Personal Property*. In general, the personal representative may sell personal property of the estate only after he has published notice of the time and place of sale and a brief description of the property to be sold. Publication must occur at least ten days before the sale in one or more issues of a newspaper published in the county where the proceedings are pending, or if there is no such newspaper, in one having general circulation in the county.

(d) *Exceptions*. Under certain circumstances, the notice requirement may be waived. For example, if the property is perishable or depreciating, then the personal property may be sold without notice. NRS 148.170. In the case of stocks and bonds, the court may shorten or dispense with notice. NRS 148.180. Where the will authorizes or directs the executor to sell the property, notice is not even required. NRS 148.080.

§ 3457. Performance of sale.

The procedures required for the sale of estate property depend on the type of assets being sold. In general, the statutes set forth limitations on the time, place and manner in which the transaction must be performed.

(a) *Real Property.* In the case of real property, the realty must be sold at a private sale or public auction. A sale at public auction must be made between the hours of 9:00 a.m. and the setting of the sun on the same day in the county in which the land lies. The sale must occur on the day named in the notice, unless the sale was postponed by the personal representative who deemed it in the best interest of all persons concerned. In case of a postponement, notice of postponement must be given by a public declaration at the time and place first appointed for the sale, and the postponement may not exceed three months from the time first appointed for the sale. NRS 148.230.

In the case of a private sale of real property, the sale must take place after the date of first publication of the notice, on or after the day set forth in the notice for sale of property, but such sale must not be made more than a year thereafter. NRS 148.240(1). The bids or offers must be written and may be left either at the place designated in the notice, delivered to the personal representative personally, or filed in the office of the clerk of the court where the proceedings are pending. The bid may be delivered at any time after the first publication or posting of the notice but before the making of the sale. NRS 148.240(2).

(b) *Personal Property.* Public sales of personal property must be made in a public place, such as the courthouse or the residence of the decedent, or another place designated by the personal representative. Unless the court orders otherwise, no sale may be made of any personal property which is not present at the time of sale. In the absence of any provision allowing postponement of a public sale of personal property, such property must be sold on the date set forth in the notice. NRS 148.190.

Practice Point If the estate contains real property that will likely be sold during the administration, early publication of the notice of sale under NRS 148.220 avoids delays when a credible offer is made. Wills often contain specific authorization to the personal representative to sell probate property with or without notice and conduct either a public or private sale.

Although there is no statutory provision setting forth guidelines for a private sale of personal property, a private sale must be in the estate's best interest. NRS 148.050. *A-Mark Coin Co. v. Estate of Redfield,* 94 Nev. 495, 582 P.2d 359 (1978), the Supreme Court upheld the lower court's decision vacating its prior order permitting a private sale of personal property when the lower court found that a public sale was in the best interest of and the greatest benefit to the estate. In determining the estate's best interests, a court may exercise its best discretion on the facts. *Katleman v. Katleman,* 79 Nev. 330, 269 P.2d 257 (1954).

(c) *Credit Sales.* Both personal and real property may be sold for either cash or upon credit. In the case of real property, the personal representative must take a promissory note from the purchaser for the unpaid purchase price which is secured by a mortgage or deed of trust on the property. NRS 148.290(1). The mortgage or deed of trust may contain a provision for release of part of the property if the court approves the provision. NRS 148.290(2).

A sale of personal property upon credit must include not less than twenty-five percent of the purchase price being paid in cash at the time of the sale. In addition, the personal representative must take a note from the purchaser for the balance of the purchase money, secured with a pledge or chattel mortgage on the personal property sold. Alternatively, the personal representative may enter into a conditional sale contract under which title is retained until the balance of the purchase price is paid. The terms of the note and pledge or chattel mortgage or contract must be approved by the court at the time of the confirmation of sale. NRS 148.200.

(d) *Stocks, Bonds and Other Interests.* The sale of stocks and bonds must be made pursuant to a court order fixing the sale terms and conditions. When the minimum selling price is fixed by the court or when the securities are to be sold upon an established stock or bond exchange, no notice of sale is required. NRS 148.180. Partnership interests, an interest in personal property pledged or choses in action are sold in the same manner as other personal property. NRS 148.210. In the case of a partnership interest, the personal representative is not entitled to sell specific partnership property. Only the deceased partner's interest in the partnership, namely, the same share of profits and surplus which the partner held during his lifetime, may be sold. *Balaban v. Bank of Nevada,* 86 Nev. 862, 477 P.2d 860 (1970).

(e) *Perishable, Depreciable and Other "Necessary" Property.* Perishable property and other personal property which will depreciate or lose value if not sold promptly may be sold without notice and title passes without confirmation. In addition, personal property which must be sold to provide the family allowance, pending the receipt of other sufficient funds, may also be sold without notice. The personal representative will remain responsible for the actual value of this property unless, after making a sworn return and upon a proper showing, the court approves of the sale. NRS 148.170. Thus, the personal representative has great flexibility when disposing of perishable, depreciable or other necessary property; however, he must satisfy the court that it is within the estate's best interests. *See A-Mark Coin Co. v. Estate of Redfield,* 94 Nev. 495, 582 P.2d 359 (1978).

§ 3458. Contracts to purchase real property.

A contract for the purchase of real property in the decedent's estate may be sold in the same manner as real property owned by the estate. NRS 148.330. In addition to meeting the sale requirements, the purchaser of the property must execute a bond indemnifying the personal representative and the beneficiaries entitled to the decedent's interest in the contract. NRS 148.340. The bond may be waived. NRS 148.340(3).

§ 3459. Mining property.

In order to sell mining property of a decedent's estate, the personal representative must file a verified petition describing the property in question, stating the terms and general conditions of the proposed agreement or option, showing the advantages possible to the estate, and pray for an order authorizing or directing its execution. There must be a hearing on the petition and notice must be given for the period and in the manner provided in NRS 155.010. NRS 148.360.

§ 3460. Confirmation.

As a general rule, all sales of estate property must be reported to and confirmed by the court before title to the property passes. NRS 148.060. The verified report and a petition for confirmation of the sale must be made within thirty days after the sale. NRS 148.060. Although the sale occurs at the noticed time, title to the property does not become vested in the purchaser until the court confirms the sale. The purpose of the delayed vesting is to ensure that the sale of property is either necessary or for the benefit, advantage and best interest of the estate. *Katleman v. Katleman,* 70 Nev. 330, 269 P.2d 257 (1954). "The primary issue in each case is ... what is for the best interest of the estate." *Katleman, supra.*

To determine if a sale is in the best interest of the estate, any person interested in the estate may file written objections to the confirmation of a sale, and he is entitled to be heard and produce witnesses in support of his objections. The most common objections are whether notice of the sale was proper and whether the property was sold for a fair price. For this reason, courts on occasion will ask if there are any other bidders for the property at the confirmation hearing and the order of confirmation will not be issued until it is proved to the court's satisfaction that notice of the sale conformed to the statutory requirements. *Katleman v. Katleman,* 70 Nev. 330, 269 P.2d 257 (1954).

§ 3461. — Confirmation of sale of real property.

In the case of real property, there are additional statutory requirements which must be satisfied before the court will confirm the sale. In particular, no sale of real property at a private sale will be confirmed by the court unless the court is satisfied that the property was sold for fair market value. NRS 148.260. In order to determine the fair market value of the property, there must have been an appraisal within one year of the time of the sale or a new appraisal must be made before the sale or confirmation. NRS 148.260. In addition, the court must examine whether the sale was necessary or whether it was made to the advantage, benefit and interest of the estate. NRS 148.270. This analysis is made by examining the "return," *i.e.*, the verified report, required to be made pursuant to NRS 148.060, and various witnesses in relation to the sale.

Practice Point The personal representative should be prepared for overbids for estate property. The agreement of sale for estate property should expressly provide that the sale is subject to court confirmation and possible overbid by third parties. At the confirmation hearing, it is essential to readily determine the creditworthiness of the overbidder and bind such party to a written agreement and earnest money deposit. If several parties expressed interest in the estate property to be sold, the personal representative should consider providing interested parties a courtesy copy of the confirmation hearing notice.

The court will not confirm the sale and direct conveyances to be executed until it finds the following:

    (1) good reason existed for the sale;
    (2) the sale was legally made and fairly conducted;
    (3) an appraisal was presented pursuant to N.R.S. 148.260; and
    (4) a higher bid may not be obtained.

If the court receives a written offer which exceeds the bid in the return by at least five percent if the bid is not more than $100,000, or by at least $5,000 if the bid is $100,000 or more and the bid is made by a responsible person and complies with all provisions of the law, then the court may vacate the old sale, accept the offer and confirm the sale to that person, order a new sale, or conduct a public auction in open court. NRS 148.270.

§ 3462. — Confirmation of sale of personal property.

As a general rule, confirmation is required for personal property. Even though there are no statutory requirements that good reason be demonstrated in the confirmation hearing, courts will consider all objections and hear supporting witnesses to determine whether the sale was made in the estate's best interest. NRS 148.050. *Katleman v. Katleman,* 70 Nev. 330, 269 P.2d 257 (1954).

Many exceptions exist to the general requirements for confirmation of the sale of personal property. For example, when perishable or depreciating property is sold, title passes without confirmation. NRS 148.170. In addition, stocks and bonds may be sold upon obtaining a court order and thereafter title passes without confirmation. Furthermore, the court may shorten the time for notice or dispense with it entirely. NRS 148.180.

In the case of summary administration of estates, when the gross value of the estate does not exceed $100,000, the court may order summary administration dispensing with all regular proceedings and further notices, including the necessity of confirmation. NRS 145.040; NRS 145.050(1)(a).

§ 3463. — Confirmation of sale of mining property.

Even though the sale of mining property requires a court order authorizing the sale, the personal representative of the estate must still make a return to the court and petition for a confirmation of the sale. NRS 148.400. A court order confirming the transaction must be made in the same manner as the sale of any real property. NRS 148.400.

§ 3464. — Post-confirmation procedure.

After confirmation of the sale of real property, a conveyance must be executed by the personal representative to the purchaser. The conveyance must refer to the order confirming the sale and directing its execution. A certified copy of the confirmation order must be recorded in the office of the recorder in the county in which the land lies. If the conveyance was made in conformity with all the requirements set forth above, all right, title and interest of the decedent in the premises are transferred retroactively from the time of his death. NRS 148.280.

In the case of real or personal property subject to a mortgage, deed of trust, or other lien, the purchase money must be applied to satisfy these claims. NRS 148.130. The purchase money must be applied to the lien claims without delay. The amounts required to pay these claims, including interest and any other lawful costs and charges involved in the transaction, may be paid to the clerk of the court. The clerk will pay the lien claimants without delay and return the surplus, if any, to the personal representative, unless for good cause shown the court otherwise directs. NRS 148.140.

If the purchaser does not comply with the sale terms after the confirmation, the court (after notice to the purchaser) may vacate the confirmation order and order a resale of property. If the amount realized on the resale does not cover the bid and expenses of the previous sale, the original purchaser is liable to the estate for the deficiency. NRS 148.300. When the court finds that there has been neglect or refusal to perform by a purchaser in a sale subject to NRS 148.300, the court may order the personal representative to hold the earnest money deposit until resale and determination of the statutory deficiency. *Regent International v. Lear,* 97 Nev. 617, 621, 637 P.2d 1207 (1981). However, forfeiture without determination of the statutory deficiency is inappropriate and will warrant reversal. *Regent International, supra.*

Any person interested in the estate who suffers damage as a result of neglect or misconduct of the personal representative in relation to any sale, is entitled to recover damages in an action upon the personal bond. NRS 148.100.

§ 3465. Borrowing money and mortgaging property.

A personal representative may borrow money in order to pay: (a) the debts of the decedent; (b) legacies; (c) expenses; (d) charges of administration; or (e) to pay, reduce, extend, or renew some security interest, lien, mortgage, or deed of trust already existing upon property of the estate. Such loans may be either unsecured or secured by the real or personal property of the decedent. A personal representative also has authority to borrow money in order to improve, utilize, operate, or preserve any property of the estate consisting of an undivided fractional interest. NRS 149.010.

To obtain the necessary orders authorizing any loans or mortgages, the personal representative must first file a verified petition showing:

(a) The particular purpose(s) for which the order is sought;
(b) The necessity for or advantage to accrue from the order;
(c) The amount of money proposed to be raised, if any;
(d) The rate of interest to be paid;
(e) The length of time the note or notes are to run;
(f) A general description of the property proposed to be mortgaged or subjected to such deed of trust, security agreement or other lien.

Notice of the hearing of this petition must be given as provided by NRS 149.020.

Upon approval of the petition, a certified copy of the order must be recorded in the office of the county recorder of each county where the land (or any portion of of it) lies that is affected by the order. NRS 149.030.

§ 3466. Leases.

A personal representative may lease any real property of the decedent upon court approval. NRS 149.060.

To obtain the necessary approval, the personal representative is required to file a verified petition showing the advantage of the lease, a general description of the property proposed to be leased, and the term, rental and general conditions of the proposed lease. Notice of the hearing of this petition must conform to NRS 149.070.

A certified copy of the order authorizing the lease is required to be recorded in the office of the county recorder of each county in which the leased land (or any portion of it) lies. NRS 149.080.

A personal representative may lease real property without a court order when the tenancy is from month to month or for a term not to exceed one year. NRS 149.100.

§ 3467. Conveyance to complete contract.

If a person who is bound by written contract to convey any real property or to transfer any personal property dies before making the conveyance or transfer, and the decedent, if living, might have been compelled to make the conveyance or transfer, the court may authorize and direct the personal representative to convey or transfer the property. NRS 149.110.

The personal representative or the person claiming to be entitled to the conveyance or transfer may file with the clerk of the court a verified petition setting forth the facts upon which the claim to convey or to transfer is predicated. Notice of the hearing of this petition must conform to NRS 149.120.

If the transaction relates to real property, a certified copy of the order must be recorded with any deed in the office of the county recorder of each county where the land or any portion of it lies. NRS 149.130.

§ 3468. Exchange of property.

Upon the petition of the personal representative or of any person interested in the estate, the court may authorize an exchange of estate property for other property, provided the exchange is to the estate's advantage. NRS 149.150. Notice of the hearing of this petition must conform to NRS 149.150.

§ 3469. Accountings.

When the estate is ready to be closed or a first accounting is mandated by NRS 150.090, the personal representative and counsel should review the progress to date of the probate administration, complete pending matters, and attend to matters that may have been overlooked. At this point, a review of a master checklist which integrates statutory dates and critical probate functions is suggested. The following should be performed at this time so counsel can draft a thorough accounting and petition for distribution: A review of filed creditor claims; the inventory and appraisement; the Revised Uniform Income and Principal Act (NRS 164.140 to 164.370, inclusive) ("RUIPA") as it relates to matters of the estate; preliminary distributions; sales of real and personal property; leases, mortgages, and exchanges; federal and state estate tax matters; federal income tax matters; ancillary probates; the decedent's will and its plan of distribution; fees and commissions; notices; preparation of conveyances and receipts.

The first accounting must be filed within thirty days (30) after the judge has acted on creditors' claims. *See* NRS 150.090. This filing deadline is twenty (20) days after the time for filing creditors' claims has expired where no creditors' claims have been filed, or later, if the judge delays action on a particular claim. *See* NRS 147.110.

For estates that will undergo prolonged administration, it is recommended that accountings be performed at least annually in order to afford the personal representative protection under NRS 150.210 and to run the statute of limitations period.

The account should be itemized, showing the amount of money received and expended by the personal representative; the amount of claims filed against the estate; the name of all claimants; the claims rejected and all other matters necessary to show the condition of estate affairs. *See* NRS 150.090(2).

An accounting should be prepared in order to properly disclose the condition of the affairs of the estate. Nevada has not adopted the Uniform Fiduciary Accounting Principles and Model Account Formats promulgated by the American Law Institute. *See Fiduciary Accounting Guide*, 1990 Revision, Robert Whitman, Lawrence J. Kramer. A summary of account generally called a "Charge and Discharge Statement" is the principal format used for accounting and appears as follows:

SUMMARY OF ACCOUNT

CHARGES Amount of inventory and
appraisement _____
After discovered assets _____
Receipts of income during
account period (Schedule A) _____
Gains on sales (Schedule B) _____
Other charges (Schedule C) _____
Total charges
$ _____

CREDITS Disbursements during
accounting period (Schedule
D) _____

SUMMARY OF ACCOUNT

Losses on sales (Schedule E)	_____
Other credits (property distribution) (Schedule F)	_____
Property on hand (Schedule G)	_____
Total credits	
	$ _____

When all estate property has been sold or there are sufficient funds in hand to pay all debts due the estate, and the estate is in proper condition to be closed, the executor shall render a final account and pray for settlement of the administration.

Where an estate has beneficiaries other than individual residuary beneficiaries, a breakdown between principal charges/credits and income charges/credits in accordance with RUIPA is advisable in order to properly account among specific and general legatees, income beneficiaries, residuary beneficiaries and remaindermen. The cash basis method of accounting is the basis of the accounting, but the personal representative should consider disclosing liabilities of the estate (such as taxes) that are typically not reflected on a cash basis accounting. Specific authority should be requested in the accounting to pay creditors' claims in accordance with NRS 150.240 and be ordered consistent with the creditors' claims, respective order of preference as set forth in NRS 150.220. Specific notice requirements need to be followed and represented to the court at the hearing. *See* NRS 150.160 and 155.020.

To document the representative's disbursements, the executor is required to produce vouchers and file them with the court. *See* NRS 150.150. Canceled checks on an estate bank account generally satisfy the voucher requirement. Filing of vouchers with the court can be avoided by use of an accountant's report or a corporate executor.

The personal representative should maintain a reserve against a final distribution of the estate to cover additional costs and expenses (*e.g.,* shipping, additional accounting and attorney's fees).

§ 3470. Fees and administration expenses.

§ 3471. — Attorneys' fees.

NRS 150.060 governs compensation of attorneys involved in estate administration. Unlike commissions to personal representatives, the statute does not provide a fixed fee schedule. The amount of compensation must be agreed upon between the personal representative and the attorney, subject to court approval, after the application, notice and a hearing. The application must contain specific and detailed information supporting the compensation requested, including references to time and hours; nature and extent of services rendered; claimed ordinary and extraordinary services; complexity of the work required; and other relevant information. Attorneys for minors, absent or nonresident heirs are entitled to compensation primarily out of the estate of the distributee they represent unless the services performed are deemed to benefit the entire estate.

§ 3472. — Personal representative fees.

Where no compensation is provided by will, a fixed percentage schedule is provided in NRS 150.020. For the first $15,000, the rate is four percent; for the next $85,000, the rate is three percent; for all above $100,000, the rate is two percent. Further allowances may be made as the court deems just and reasonable for extraordinary services. Examples of possible extraordinary services include: management, sales or mortgages of real or personal property, contested or litigated claims against the estate, the adjustment and payment of extensive or complicated estate taxes, litigation in regard to property of the estate, carrying on of the decedent's business pursuant to an order of the court, and other litigation or special services as may be necessary for the executor to prosecute, defend or perform. Like attorney fees, allowance on commissions may be made anytime after the issuance of letters upon application and hearing before the court.

§ 3473. — Administrative expenses.

The executor is allowed all necessary expenses in the care and management, as well as settlement, of the estate, and for his services. *See* NRS 150.010.

§ 3474. Closing of estates.

Once the time has passed for the running of creditors' claims in general or summary administration, the estate is in a position to close, or at least for the personal representative to make a partial distribution of the estate.

§ 3475. — Partial distribution.

Partial distribution can only be made after the lapse of three months from the issuance of the letters. The personal representative or a person entitled to share in an estate may petition for distribution of a legacy, devise or share or any portion thereof. The court may require a bond from the distributees or may dispense with the bond. NRS 151.010. After the time has run for creditors' claims, the court's main concern in making a partial distribution is that there is no injury to estate creditors. NRS 151.040. Partial distribution is often made because the amount of estate taxes has not been determined or there are certain properties that should be sold before final distribution can be made. There may be other reasons, such as a lawsuit, that the estate cannot be closed although there are sufficient monies to protect the plaintiff/creditor in the lawsuit should plaintiff/creditor prevail.

§ 3476. — Final distribution.

The personal representative should prepare a final account in any petition for final distribution. NRS 151.080 and 151.100. The personal representative should keep in mind Chapter 377B of the Nevada Revised Statutes, which provides that the personal representative is responsible for the payment of estate taxes to the State of Nevada. Counsel is referred to that chapter to determine what is due to the State of Nevada and to the United States Government. The calculation of those taxes is beyond the scope of this chapter and the personal representative should either retain an accountant or request the estate's attorney prepare the estate tax returns along with the income tax returns prior and after the death of the deceased, if any are necessary.

§ 3477. — Receipts.

A receipt for each distributee must be prepared by the personal representative and signed by the distributee before the personal representative may obtain a final discharge. The personal representative should prepare receipts for fees paid to himself and should obtain a receipt from the attorney for payment of the attorney's fees and costs paid. When cash is distributed by check, the distributee often fails to sign the receipt. The attorney should then file with the court a copy of the negotiated check which will evidence receipt of payment to that distributee. A supplemental accounting may be required if there is additional income before final distribution can be made. NRS 151.100.

§ 3478. — Discharge.

When the estate has been fully administered (*i.e.,* when assets have been distributed, claims and expenses have been paid, all the receipts are filed with the court, and, if necessary, a supplemental accounting filed with the court), the personal representative is in a position to petition the court for a decree of discharge. The decree releases the personal representative from further obligations to the estate unless an appeal is timely taken by a party in interest. *See generally* NRS 151.230. A supplemental accounting may be required but in most cases the judge will waive the notice requirement. Once the final discharge is obtained, any bond that was posted is exonerated.

§ 3479. Probate commissioner.

In the Eighth Judicial District Court, the office of probate commissioner administers the filing and processing of probate matters within the court system under the supervision of the probate judge. The probate commissioner prepares an approved list each week of probate matters which can be heard without further testimony or appearance. *See* EDCR 4.14. The Second Judicial District Court has assigned experienced court staff to oversee the filing and processing of probate matters in that district, but no formal local rule has been adopted.

§ 3480. Appeals.

Generally, appeals from probate court orders and decrees must be taken to the Supreme Court within thirty (30) days after their entry. NRS 155.190. Appealable orders and decrees include granting or revoking letters testamentary or letters of administration; admitting a will to probate or revocation of a probate; setting aside an estate claimed to be less than $25,000 in value; setting apart a homestead or property claimed to be exempt from execution; granting or modifying a family allowance; directing or authorizing the sale or conveyance or confirming the sale of property; settling an account of an executor, administrator or trustee; instructing or appointing a trustee; instructing or directing an administrator or executor; directing or allowing the payment of a debt, claim, legacy or attorney's fee; determining heirship; distributing property; and refusing to make an order in matters discussed above or any decision wherein the amount of controversy equals or exceeds, exclusive of costs, $1,000.

> ***Practice Point* The appeal period from probate orders and decrees differs from general jurisdiction appeals which is generally within thirty days after service of written notice of entry of judgment or order from which the appeal is taken. *See* NRAP 4(a).**

§ 3481. Testamentary trusts.

§ 3482. — Definition.

Although not specifically defined by Nevada statute, a testamentary trust is a fiduciary relationship created under the terms of a decedent's last will and testament between the testator, a trustee who is entrusted with the title to and management of assets comprising a trust estate for a term of years or a lifetime or series of lifetimes and a beneficiary or beneficiaries. The testamentary trust typically comes into existence upon the distribution of the testator's probate estate.

§ 3483. — Purposes.

Because of the presence of numerous tax advantages available to a decedent's estate, a definitive creditor's claims statute, a definitive period in which to contest provisions of a testamentary plan, a desire to avoid the cost and formalities necessary to create inter vivos trusts and a desire for ongoing court supervision due to family or business reasons, some testators select the use of a testamentary trust. The tax advantages generally include: (i) the application of throwback rules; (ii) the I.R.C. § 642(c) set-aside contribution deduction; (iii) higher personal exemption of an estate; (iv) the I.R.C. § 267 loss disallowance rule application to trusts; (v) the potential acceleration of deferred tax installments under T. Reg. § 20.6166A-3(e) on funding a sub-trust compared to funding a testamentary trust under a will; (vi) estates are not required to distribute income to a surviving spouse until after estate administration under T. Reg. § 20.2056(b)-5(f)(9); (vii) estate is not required to pay estimated income taxes of a period of two years; (viii) the ability of an estate to select a fiscal year; (ix) the separate share rule applies only to trusts; (x) potential loss of the selection on stock held by a revocable trust; (xi) gifting out of revocable trusts requires careful planning to avoid inclusion of the gift back into gross estate for estate tax purposes; (xii) a grantor trust may not qualify to own I.R.C. § 1244 stock and the grantor is prevented from taking the ordinary loss deduction; and (xiii) I.R.C. § 1239(b) related party rules applies to trusts. Testamentary trusts can be utilized to achieve many of the same estate tax planning results that inter vivos trusts are set up to accomplish.

§ 3484. — Creation.

NRS 163.002 to NRS 163.009 set forth requirements for the creation and validity of trusts, including testamentary trusts. In order to have a legally valid and enforceable testamentary trust under Nevada law, several elements must be present, including:

(a) A testamentary transfer of property by the owner to another person as trustee. NRS 163.002(3). Typically, a testamentary trust is set forth in the last will of a decedent domiciled in Nevada at his death which has been duly admitted to probate under NRS Chapter 136.

(b) The settlor/testator properly manifests an intention to create a trust; and there is trust property. NRS 163.003.

(c) A trust may be created for any purpose that is not illegal or against public policy. NRS 163.004(1).

(d) No consideration is required to create a testamentary trust. NRS 163.005.

(e) A trust, other than a charitable trust, is created only if there is a beneficiary. NRS 163.006.

Property is transferred from an estate to a testamentary trust by an order for distribution of estate assets to the trust under NRS Chapter 151, coupled with a proper delivery or conveyance of estate assets into the possession or name of the trustee of the testamentary trust. The existence of a trustee qualified to act as a testamentary must be confirmed by the court pursuant to NRS 164.010(2). Testamentary trust situs may be moved from one jurisdiction to another. NRS 164.130.

§ 3485. Trustee's appointment, duties and powers.

§ 3486. — Appointment.

The appointment of a trustee is commenced either by petition of the person named in the will or by a beneficiary of the trust to the district court in which the will was probated. NRS 164.010(2). Following consideration of the petition, the court is in a position to confirm the appointment of the trustee and continue in rem jurisdiction over the trust. NRS 153.020(1).

§ 3487. — Instructions.

Unless the will is carefully drafted or in the event of unanticipated events or cautious fiduciaries, the trustee will have to resort to petitioning the court for instructions in the administration of the trust, construction of the trust instrument, or at a final account. NRS 153.040 and 164.030. Ensuing court orders must be appealed within thirty days of the entry of the order. *See supra* § 3480.

§ 3488. — Standard of care.

The trustee's standard of care under Nevada law is that which men of prudence, discretion, and intelligence exercise in the management of their own affairs, except in regard to speculation. NRS 164.050(1). The 1989 Nevada Legislature added a standard of review for the propriety of a particular trust investment which insulates the fiduciary from isolated bad investments. NRS 164.050(2). In *Charleson v. Hardesty,* 839 P.2d 1303 (Nev. 1992), the Nevada Supreme Court found that the attorney for the trustee owed the trust beneficiaries a duty of care and fiduciary duties.

§ 3489. — Powers.

The trustee is vested with the following statutory powers:

(a) To acquire and retain every kind of property. NRS 164.050(1).

(b) To make certain FHA loans and invest in farm loan bonds. NRS 164.060 and 164.065.

(c) To establish and maintain common trust funds if fiduciary is a bank or qualified trust company. *See* NRS 164.080.

(d) To sell, convey or encumber property unless restricted by deed or conveyance. *See* NRS 164.067.

(e) Such other powers expressed in the instrument or statutory enumerated powers incorporated by reference into the instrument. *See* NRS 163.260 to 163.410, inclusive.

(f) Vote corporate stock by proxy. *See* NRS 163.080.

(g) To hold corporate stock in nominee form. *See* NRS 163.090.

(h) To withhold property from distribution. *See* NRS 162.280.

§ 3490. — Prohibited acts.

A trustee may not engage in the following activities without express authority in the trust instrument:

(a) Lending of trust funds to trustee or affiliated individuals or entities. *See* NRS 163.030.

(b) Buying of trust assets or selling of trust assets to trustee or affiliated individuals or entities except with the approval of and accounting to the district court. *See* NRS 163.050.

(c) Sales between trusts with same trustee. *See* NRS 163.060.

(d) Purchase of corporate trustee's own stock or securities. *See* NRS 163.070.

(e) Other acts which are breaches of trust and loyalty under the common law.

§ 3491. — Bonds.

Unlike the specific statutory authority for bonds in the case of estate administration, there is no express requirement for initial testamentary trustees obtaining a bond. The district court has authority to require bonds of trustees who are filling a vacancy. *See* NRS 153.120. Generally, a properly drafted will waives the bond requirement for both executors and trustees unless special circumstances dictate use of a bond.

§ 3492. Inventory, accounting and compensation.

§ 3493. — Inventory.

Within seventy-five days of taking possession of trust property, a duly confirmed testamentary trustee is required to file an inventory under oath with the clerk of the district court where the will was admitted to probate. *See* NRS 165.030. The inventory is required to be valued at market value at the time it became subject to the trust, but a testamentary trustee has the discretion to use final federal estate tax values. *See* NRS 164.180.

§3494. — Accounts.

Within seventy-five days of the conclusion of the first year after the trustee filed his inventory or at the trustee's election, within seventy-five days of the conclusion of the trust's first fiscal year, and thereafter within thirty days after the conclusion of each yearly period, the trustee is required to file an account under oath setting forth with particularity certain matters required by statute. *See* NRS 165.040(1); *see also* NRS 153.020 and 153.030. A corporate trustee is not required to file intermediate accounts, but is required to file a final account which summarizes the same matters that would have been covered in the intermediate accounts. Within ten days of filing the account, the trustee is required to give notice to each known beneficiary by personal service or by registered or certified mail of the filing of the account and a summary of the account with an offer to provide a full account if no hearing is held. *See* NRS 165.070. Any beneficiary or trustee may petition the court for hearing on the account and the trustee is required to apply to the district court for hearing on every third intermediate account to approve all unapproved prior accounts. The notice must contain a statement concerning the amount of commissions and fees requested by the trustee and any other fees to be allowed. Vouchers for trust expenditures are required to be produced in court unless the account is accompanied by a report of a qualified accountant. A corporate trustee is not required to file any vouchers with the district court. Upon approval of an account by the district court, the trustee is relieved of further liability unless appeal is taken within thirty days or the account is reopened for mistake more than one year after its approval unless fraud is found.

§3495. — Revised Uniform Principal and Income Act.

Unless otherwise provided in the will, the RUIPA as defined in §3469 applies to any receipt or expense received or incurred by the trust. *See* NRS 164.140 to 164.370, inclusive. Generally, the provisions of RUIPA will govern proper accounting of credits and charges between income and principal which is of critical importance especially when the income beneficiary and remainderman are not the same.

§3496. — Compensation.

On the settlement of each account of a trustee, the court will allow the trustee's proper expenses and such compensation for services as the court may deem just and proper. The court can apportion fees between co-trustees and set a yearly compensation for each trustee in a set amount or pursuant to a standard fee schedule until further order of the court. *See* NRS 153.070. An attorney for the trust is entitled to receive reason-

813

able compensation for services rendered to the trustee in preparation and presentation of accounts. *See* NRS 165.210(2).

§ 3497. Trust termination.

§ 3498. — Distribution of residue.

At the expiration of a term of years, a lifetime, a fixed date, or upon the exercise of a trustee's discretion under the terms of the will, the trustee is required to prepare a final account and petition for distribution of residue of the trust estate. *See* NRS 153.060, 165.050, and 165.080.

§ 3499. — Rule against perpetuities.

Nevada has adopted the Uniform Statutory Rule Against Perpetuities which generally requires a nonvested property to vest or terminate no later than twenty-one years after the death of a natural person then alive; or the interest either vests or terminates ninety years after its creation. *See* NRS 111.105 to 111.1039. The court is empowered to reform a disposition in the manner that most closely approximates the transferor's manifested plan of distribution. *See* NRS 111.1035.

Form 34A

Case No.
Dept. No.

IN THE _____ JUDICIAL DISTRICT COURT OF THE STATE
OF NEVADA
IN AND FOR THE COUNTY OF _____

IN THE MATTER OF THE ESTATE OF)
)
_____,   ) PETITION FOR PROBATE
) OF WILL AND FOR ISSUANCE
Deceased.   ) OF LETTERS TESTAMENTARY
_____)

_____ (the "Petitioner") hereby petitions the Court to admit the Decedent's Will to probate and to issue to Petitioner Letters Testamentary. In support of the Petition, the Petitioner states as follows:

1. Jurisdiction.

_____ (the "Decedent"), died on _____, in _____, _____ County, Nevada. The Decedent, at the time of his/her death, was a resident of _____ County, Nevada, and left an estate in the State of Nevada subject to probate administration.

2. Will.

The Decedent left a Will dated _____, which Petitioner is informed and believes, and on that basis alleges, is the last Will of the Decedent. On _____, Petitioner caused the original Will to be filed with the Clerk of this Court as provided by law, and the Will will be presented to the Court for probate at the time of the hearing on this Petition.

The Petitioner is informed and believes and on that basis alleges, that the Decedent's Will was duly executed in all particulars as required by law, and at the time of execution of the Will, the Decedent was of sound mind, over the age of eighteen (18) years and was not acting under duress or undue influence.

3. Description of Estate.

Petitioner is informed and believes that the Decedent's estate, subject to probate administration in the State of Nevada, consists of real and personal property with an estimated total gross value in excess of _____ Dollars ($_____).

4. Heirs, Next of Kin, Devisees, and Legatees.

The names, addresses, and residences of the heirs, next of kin, devisees, and legatees of the Decedent, as far as known to the Petitioner, are as follows:

Name and Address	Age	Relationship

5. Qualification of Petitioner.

Petitioner is named in the Will to act as Executor, and he/she hereby consents to act as such. Petitioner is over the age of majority and is otherwise qualified to act as Executor.

6. Petitioner's Address.

Petitioner's permanent address is _____.

7. Petitioner's Bond.

Article _____ of Decedent's Will dated _____, provides that "no bond shall be required of any Executor appointed in this Will."

BASED UPON THE FOREGOING, Petitioner respectfully requests that the Court issue the following orders:

A. That the Decedent's Will dated _____ be admitted to probate;

B. That Letters Testamentary be issued to Petitioner without bond; and

C. That such other and further orders be issued by the Court as the Court deems proper.

Dated this ____ day of _____, 19__.

_____
PETITIONER

APPROVED:

By _____

VERIFICATION

_____, being first duly sworn under penalty of perjury, states the following: That he/she is the Petitioner herein; that he/she has read the foregoing Petition and knows the contents thereof, and that the contents are true of his/her own knowledge, except for those matters stated on information and belief, and as to those matters he/she believes them to be true.

_____

Subscribed and sworn to before me
this ____ day of _____, 19__.

_____
Notary Public

Form 34B

CASE NO.
DEPT. NO.

IN THE _____ JUDICIAL DISTRICT COURT OF THE STATE
OF NEVADA
IN AND FOR THE COUNTY OF _____

IN THE MATTER OF THE ESTATE OF)	PETITION FOR PROBATE OF
)	ESTATE, FOR ISSUANCE OF
_____,)	LETTERS TESTAMENTARY,
)	AND FOR SUMMARY
Deceased.)	ADMINISTRATION OF
_____)	ESTATE

_____ hereby presents Petition for Probate of Estate, For Issuance of Letters Testamentary, and for Summary Administration of Estate, and in support of this Petition, Petitioner respectfully states the following:

1. _____, Deceased (hereafter referred to as the "Decedent"), died on _____, 19__, in _____, _____ County, Nevada.

2. At the time of death, Decedent was a resident of _____, _____ County, Nevada, and left an estate in the State of Nevada subject to probate administration.

3. The Decedent left a Will dated _____, 19__. Petitioner has filed this Will with the Clerk of the above-entitled Court as provided by law, and a true and correct copy of the Will is attached hereto as Exhibit "A," and by this reference is incorporated herein. The Petitioner is informed and believes, and based upon that belief, alleges, that the Decedent's Will of _____, 19__, is the Last Will of the Decedent.

4. The names, relationships, ages and residences of the heirs, next of kin, devisees, and legatees of the Decedent so far as are known to Petitioner are as follows:

Name:	Address:	Relationship/Age:

5. Petitioner is informed and believes that the estimated value of the Decedent's estate subject to probate administration in the State of Nevada is less than One Hundred Thousand Dollars ($100,000). The specific description and the estimated value of all of the property of the Decedent which is otherwise subject to probate administration are as follows:

Description:	Approximate Value:

817

TOTAL

6. At the date of the Decedent's death, as far as known to the Petitioner, there were no liens or encumbrances of record against the Decedent's property, however, there were certain debts and obligations owed by the Decedent.

7. In Paragraph _____ of the Will attached hereto as Exhibit "A," the Decedent nominates your Petitioner to serve as Executor of the Decedent's Will, and the Decedent further directs that no bond or other security for the faithful performance of duties in the office of Executor be required of his Executor.

8. Petitioner is over the age of majority and is otherwise qualified, and consents to act as Executor of the above-entitled estate.

9. Petitioner requests that the Court dispense with the requirement of a bond pursuant to the request of the Decedent set forth in Paragraph _____ of his/her Will, attached hereto as Exhibit "A."

10. Since the gross value of the Decedent's estate known to Petitioner which is subject to probate administration does not exceed One Hundred Thousand Dollars ($100,000), the estate should be subject to summary administration as provided in Chapter 145 of the Nevada Revised Statutes.

BASED UPON THE FOREGOING, Petitioner respectfully requests that the Court issue the following orders:

A. That the Court admit the Will of the Decedent, dated _____, 19__ to probate.

B. That Letters Testamentary be issued to Petitioner to serve without bond.

C. That if the Court finds the gross value of the Decedent's estate does not exceed One Hundred Thousand Dollars ($100,000), that the estate be entitled to summary administration as provided in Chapter 145 of the Nevada Revised Statutes, dispensing with all regular proceedings and notices, except for the Notice to Creditors, the notice of appointment of the Executor and Notice of Application for Attorneys' Fees, and providing that an Inventory, Appraisement and Record of Value be made and returned to the Court.

D. That such other and further orders be made as the Court considers proper.

DATED this _____ day of _____, 19__.

_____

APPROVED:

By_____

STATE OF _____   )

                        : ss.

COUNTY OF _____   )

_____, being first duly sworn, declares under penalty of perjury as follows: I am the Petitioner in the above-entitled action; I have read the foregoing Petition for Probate of Estate and for Issuance of Letters Testamentary, and for Summary Administration of Estate and know the contents thereof. The Petition is true of my own knowledge, except as to those matters that are stated on information and belief, and as to those matters, I believe them to be true.

DATED this _____ day of _____, 19__.

_____

Subscribed and sworn to before me
this _____ day of _____, 19____.

_____
NOTARY PUBLIC

Form 34C

CASE NO.
DEPT. NO.

IN THE _____ JUDICIAL DISTRICT COURT OF THE STATE
OF NEVADA
IN AND FOR THE COUNTY OF _____

IN THE MATTER OF THE ESTATE OF	)
	)
————,	) PETITION TO SET ASIDE THE
	) ESTATE OF
Deceased.	) WITHOUT ADMINISTRATION
	)

Petitioner hereby petitions the Court for an Order setting aside the Estate of _____, Deceased, without administration. In support of this Petition, Petitioner respectfully states the following:

1. The Petitioner is a resident of, _____, Nevada, and is the _____ of _____, Deceased, hereafter referred to as the "Decedent."

2. The Decedent died in _____, _____, Nevada on _____, 19__.

3. At the time of death, the Decedent was a resident of _____, Nevada, and left an estate in Nevada consisting of personal property.

4. The Decedent left no spouse, however, the Decedent left _____ (__) children at the time of death.

5. The Decedent left a Will dated _____, 19__, which has been filed with the Clerk of the Court. The Petitioner is informed and believes, and on that basis alleges, that the Decedent's Will dated _____, 19__, is the Last Will of the Decedent.

6. The Will of the Decedent dated _____, 19__, was properly executed by the Decedent, and at the time of the execution of the Will, the Decedent was over the age of eighteen (18) years, was of sound mind, and was not acting under duress, menace, fraud, or undue influence, and was in every other respect competent to dispose of his/her estate by Will. The Will contains an affidavit of the attesting witnesses, in which the witnesses swear to the due execution of the Will and such additional facts as they would otherwise be required to testify to in Court to prove the validity of the Will.

7. Under the terms of the Will, all of the Decedent's jewelry, clothing, household furniture and furnishings, personal automobiles, and other tangible articles of a personal nature are to be distributed to the Decedent's children in equal shares if the children survive the Decedent for thirty (30) days. The balance of the Decedent's probate estate is to be distributed in equal shares to the Decedent's children who survive the Decedent for ninety (90) days.

8. The names, relationships, ages, and residences of the Decedent's heirs, devisees, and legatees are as follows:

Relationship/

Name: Address: Age:

_____

_____

_____

The specific description and the estimated value of all of the property of the Decedent which is otherwise subject to probate administration are as follows:

Description: Value:

_____

_____

10. At the date of the Decedent's death, there were no liens or encumbrances of record affecting the Decedent's property.

11. Petitioner is informed and believes, and on that basis alleges, that all debts of the Decedent and the Decedent's estate have been paid in full. Under the terms of the Decedent's Will, the Petitioner, as Executor, is authorized to pay all liabilities of the Decedent and the Decedent's estate. Petitioner agrees to pay or have paid from the Decedent's estate all liabilities of the Decedent and the Decedent's estate, if any, that may be subsequently discovered or incurred.

BASED UPON THE ABOVE, the Petitioner alleges good cause has been shown, and, pursuant to Section 146.070 of the Nevada Revised Statutes, the Petitioner respectfully requests that if the Court finds the total gross value of the Decedent's estate does not exceed the sum of Twenty-Five Thousand Dollars ($25,000), the Decedent's entire estate be assigned and set apart as follows:

A. All jewelry, clothing, and other miscellaneous personal effects to, in equal shares;

B. The balance of the estate to, in equal shares.

DATED this _____ day of _____, 19__.

_____

                                        Petitioner

STATE OF NEVADA   )
                         : ss.
COUNTY OF WASHOE   )

_____, being first duly sworn, declares under penalty of perjury as follows:

I am the Petitioner in the above-entitled action. I have read the foregoing Petition to Set Aside the Estate Without Administration, and know the contents thereof. The Petition is true of my own knowledge except as to those matters that are stated on information and belief, and as to those matters, I believe them to be true.

DATED this _____ day of _____, 19__.

_____

Subscribed and sworn to before me
this _____ day of _____, 19__.

_____

Notary Public

Form 34D

CASE NO.
DEPT. NO.

IN THE _____ JUDICIAL DISTRICT COURT OF THE STATE
OF NEVADA
IN AND FOR THE COUNTY OF _____

IN THE MATTER OF THE ESTATE OF	)
	) PETITION FOR LETTERS
_____,	) OF ADMINISTRATION AND
	) SUMMARY ADMINISTRATION
Deceased.	)
	)

The Petition of _____, a resident of Reno, Washoe County, Nevada, respectfully shows:

1. That _____ died intestate on or about the _____ day of _____, 19__, in _____, _____, and was at the date of death a resident of _____, _____.

2. That said decedent left an estate consisting of certain real and personal property situate in the County of _____, State of Nevada, in an amount in excess of $_____, but less than $_____; in particular, the decedent's estate consists of the following:

_____	Value $_____
_____	Value $_____
TOTAL	$_____

3. That there are no liens or encumbrances on the decedent's estate as of the decedent's date of death. (If there are, list them here.)

4. That due search and inquiry have been made to ascertain whether said decedent left any Last Will and Testament, but none has been found, and that according to the best knowledge, information and belief of Petitioner, said decedent died intestate.

5. The Petitioner is advised and believes and therefore alleges that the names, ages and addresses of the decedent's heirs, and their relationship to the decedent are as follows:

_____, (relationship), (age)
address

_____, (relationship), (age)
address

6. That the Petitioner is (explain the relationship between the decedent and the Petitioner and the reason why the Petitioner should be appointed administrator). (Discuss bond here).

7. That the value of this estate does not exceed $100,000, and, pursuant to NRS 145.040, the same should be administered under summary administration; and that pursuant to NRS 145.040(1), all regular proceedings and notices should be dispensed with, except for the notice of the petition for the issuance of letters

of administration, the notice to creditors and notice of application for attorneys' fees.

WHEREFORE, Petitioner respectfully requests that a time be appointed for hearing this petition after due notice thereof has been given as prescribed by law, and that upon said hearing and the proofs being adduced,

1. That letters of administration of said estate may be issued to Petitioner to serve as Administrator without bond (OR, after posting a bond in the amount of $_____).

2. That upon the hearing thereof if the Court finds that the total value of said estate does not exceed the sum of $100,000, the same may be administered under summary administration.

3. That all regular proceedings and notices be dispensed with, except for the notice of the petition for issuance of letters of administration, the notice to creditors and notice of application for attorney's fees, and an inventory and appraisement or record of value shall be made and returned to the Court.

4. That all other necessary and proper orders may be made in the premises.

DATED this _____ day of _____, 19__.

_____

Name of Attorney
Address of Attorney

Under penalties of perjury, the undersigned declares that he/she is the Petitioner named in the foregoing Petition for Letters of Administration and for Summary Administration, and knows the contents thereof; that the pleading is true of his/her own knowledge except as to those matters stated upon information and belief, and that as to such matters, he/she believes it to be true.

_____

(Name of Petitioner)

Form 34E

CASE NO.
DEPT. NO.

IN THE _____ JUDICIAL DISTRICT COURT OF THE STATE
OF NEVADA
IN AND FOR THE COUNTY OF _____

IN THE MATTER OF THE ESTATE OF)
)
_____,) PETITION TO SELL STOCKS
)
Deceased.)
_____)

_____, the Executor of the estate of _____, Deceased, hereby petitions this Court for the authority to sell stocks. In support of this Petition, Petitioner alleges the following:

1. _____, Deceased, (hereafter referred to as the "Decedent"), died on _____, 19__ in _____, Nevada.

2. On _____, 19__, the Will of the Decedent was admitted to probate, and Letters Testamentary were issued to Petitioner.

3. The Will of the Decedent, dated _____, 19__, directs that the Decedent's estate be distributed between _____ (__) of the Decedent's beneficiaries.

4. The inventory, appraisement, and record of value for this estate was filed with this Court on _____, 19__.

5. In order for Petitioner to prepare the First and Final Accounting and Petition for Distribution of the above-referenced estate, and to finally distribute the assets of the estate to the _____ (__) beneficiaries, it is necessary for Petitioner to reduce the above-referenced stock to cash.

6. Petitioner requests that the Court dispense with notice of sale of the stock as the securities are all to be sold upon established stock exchanges. Petitioner will employ the services of _____ to sell the stocks referred to in paragraph 4 on an established stock exchange.

Based upon the foregoing, Petitioner respectfully requests that the Court issue the following orders:

A. That Petitioner be allowed to sell, upon an established stock exchange, each of the securities listed in paragraph 4 of this Petition;

B. That the Court dispense with notice of sale; and

C. For such other and further relief as the Court deems just and proper.

DATED this _____ day of _____, 19__.

_____

APPROVED:

By _____

STATE OF NEVADA   )
) ss.

COUNTY OF _____   )

_____, being first duly sworn, deposes and says under penalty of perjury as follows:

That _____ is the Executor of the Estate of _____, Deceased;

That _____ has read the foregoing Petition to Sell Stocks and knows the contents thereof;

That the same is true of _____ own knowledge except as to those matters therein stated on information and belief, and as to those matters believes them to be true.

DATED this _____ day of _____, 19__.

_____

Subscribed and sworn to before me
this _____ day of _____, 19__.

_____
NOTARY PUBLIC

Form 34F

CASE NO.
DEPT. NO.

IN THE _____ JUDICIAL DISTRICT COURT OF THE STATE
OF NEVADA
IN AND FOR THE COUNTY OF _____

IN THE MATTER OF THE ESTATE OF	) PETITION FOR SETTLEMENT OF
	) FIRST AND FINAL ACCOUNT,
_____,	) FOR APPROVAL OF ATTORNEYS'
	) FEES, AND FOR DECREE
Deceased.	) OF FINAL DISTRIBUTION
	)

_____, the Executor of the estate of _____, Deceased, hereby petitions this Court for the settlement of the first and final account, which is submitted with this Petition, for approval of attorneys' fees, and for a decree of final distribution of the estate. In support of this Petition, Petitioner alleges the following:

1. _____, Deceased, hereafter referred to as "Decedent," died on _____, 19__, in _____, Nevada. The Decedent, at the time of death, was a resident of _____, Nevada.

2. The Decedent died testate and on _____, 19__, _____ Will was admitted to probate and Letters Testamentary were issued to Petitioner, who thereupon duly qualified as Executor and who has acted in that capacity since that date.

3. Petitioner caused to be duly published a Notice to Creditors as required by law, and the first publication of that Notice occurred on _____, 19__. Proof of publication of said Notice has been filed herein, and the time for presentment of claims has expired. No claims were filed against the estate. (If claims were filed, list claimant and amount.)

4. An Inventory and Appraisement and Record of Value of the estate was filed on _____4, 19__, showing the value of the estate to be _____ Dollars ($_____). The Inventory and Appraisement and Record of Value lists all of the assets of the Decedent's estate which are known to Petitioner and which have come into his/her possession.

5. As of _____, 19__, Petitioner is chargeable with, and is entitled to, the credits for the amount set forth in the Summary of Account attached hereto as Exhibit "A," and incorporated herein by reference. The remaining property on hand at _____, 19__, as summarized in Schedule C of the attached Exhibit "A," consists of cash totalling _____ Dollars ($_____).

6. The final federal income tax return of the Decedent for 19__ has been prepared and filed, and reflected a refund to the estate in the amount of _____ Dollars ($_____), which has now been received by the Executor. A federal estate tax return is not required for the estate. A federal fiduciary income tax return will be required for the estate, and the Petitioner agrees to assume the responsibility for filing that return and paying any tax that may be due thereon.

826

7. Petitioner is entitled to a statutory executor's commission in accordance with NRS 155.020, upon the whole amount of the personal estate accounted for by _____. The total estate accounted for by the Petitioner is the sum of _____ Dollars ($_____). Based upon that figure, the Petitioner is entitled to a statutory executor's commission in the amount of _____ Dollars ($_____), computed as follows:

Amount of Personal Estate: Amount:

                    TOTAL $_____

Petitioner requests that the Court ratify, confirm and approve the Petitioner's statutory executor's fee in the amount of _____ Dollars ($_____).

8. The law firm _____ has rendered valuable and necessary legal services to Petitioner for the benefit of the estate during the course of the administration. The law firm has submitted to the Petitioner, and has attached to this Petition as Exhibit "B," an itemization of its time incurred in connection with the estate. The law firm of _____ is entitled to reasonable compensation for the services performed, and Petitioner and the law firm have agreed that the sum of _____ Dollars ($_____) is a reasonable fee for the services. Petitioner and the law firm of _____ have agreed to the payment of this amount, and Petitioner requests the Court to approve and authorize the payment of the sum of _____ Dollars ($_____) to the law firm of _____ for the payment of the legal fees, plus the additional payment of any costs advanced by the law firm on behalf of the estate. Those costs advanced to date total _____ Dollars ($_____) as reflected in Exhibit "B."

9. Pursuant to Paragraph _____ of the Will of the Decedent, Decedent's estate is to be distributed as follows:

10. Petitioner requests that, after the payment of the Petitioner's statutory executor's fee, the fee of _____, the attorneys' fees and costs, and the closing expenses, that the balance of the estate be distributed in accordance with the provisions of the Decedent's Will as discussed in this Petition.

Based upon the foregoing, Petitioner requests that the Court order the following:

A. The administration of the estate be closed without any further accounting;

B. The First and Final Account of Petitioner as Executor of the Decedent's estate be settled, allowed, and approved as filed;

C. All of the acts and transactions of the Petitioner as Executor, as disclosed in the First and Final Account, be confirmed and approved;

D. Petitioner be authorized and directed to pay the sum of _____ Dollars ($_____) to Petitioner as a statutory executor's commission in accordance with NRS 155.020;

E. Petitioner be authorized and directed to pay the sum of _____ Dollars ($_____) to the law firm of _____ as reasonable fees for legal services rendered in connection with the administration of the estate, plus the sum of _____ Dollars ($_____) which is required to reimburse the law firm for costs advanced on behalf of the estate;

F. For such other orders as the Court deems just and proper.

DATED this _____ day of _____, 19__.

_____
Executor

APPROVED:

By_____
   Attorneys for Petitioners

STATE OF NEVADA   )
                          :   ss.
COUNTY OF _____   )

I, _____, being first duly sworn, state under penalty of perjury as follows:
I am the Executor of the estate of _____, Deceased. I have read the foregoing Petition for Settlement of First and Final Account, for Approval of Attorneys'
Fees and for Decree of Final Distribution, and know its contents. The Petition is
true of my own knowledge, except as to those matters that are stated on information and belief, and as to those matters, I believe them to be true.

The First and Final Account contains a full statement of all charges against
me and of all the credits to which I am entitled on account of the estate for the
period stated in the account.

_____

Subscribed and sworn to before me
this _____ day of _____, 19__.

_____
NOTARY PUBLIC

Form 34G

Case No.
Dept. No.

IN THE _____ JUDICIAL DISTRICT COURT OF THE STATE
OF NEVADA
IN AND FOR THE COUNTY OF _____

IN THE MATTER OF THE ESTATE OF)
)
_____,   ) APPLICATION FOR ALLOWANCE
) OF ATTORNEYS' FEES
        Deceased.   )
)
_____)

Pursuant to NRS § 150.060, _____, Esq. of the law firm of _____, the attorneys for the Administrator of the estate of _____, Deceased, hereby requests the Court approve the payment of _____ Dollars ($_____) as attorneys' fees for legal services rendered and costs advanced in connection with the administration of the estate. In support of this application, applicant states the following:

1. An itemized statement containing a description of all services rendered by the members of the firm of _____, including itemized statements of the time and hours expended by each attorney, is attached hereto as Exhibit "A."

2. The law firm of _____ has rendered legal services to the Administrator including the preparation of all pleadings and other legal documents required in the probate proceeding, attendance and representation of the Administrator at all probate hearings, and assisting the Administrator in preparation of the final accounting for the estate.

BASED UPON THE ABOVE, the applicant requests that the Court approve the sum of _____ Dollars ($_____) as a reasonable fee for legal services rendered and costs advanced in connection with the administration of the estate and that the Court authorize and direct payment of _____ Dollars ($_____) to the law firm of _____ to be paid by _____, Administrator.

DATED this _____ day of _____, 19___.

By_____
Attorney for Administrator

AGREED UPON AND APPROVED BY
THE ESTATE OF _____
DECEASED

By_____
Administrator With Will Annexed

829

Form 34H

Case No.
Dept. No.

IN THE _____ JUDICIAL DISTRICT COURT OF THE STATE
OF NEVADA
IN AND FOR THE COUNTY OF _____

IN THE MATTER OF THE ESTATE OF   )
)
_____,   ) NOTICE OF HEARING
) (Set Aside)
       Deceased.   )
_____)

NOTICE IS HEREBY GIVEN that _____ has filed in this Court a Petition for Letters of Administration and Summary Administration of the estate of _____, deceased, and a hearing has been set for _____, the _____ day of _____, 19__, at 9:00 a.m., in Department No. ____, at the Courthouse of the above-entitled Court, in the City of _____, County of _____, State of Nevada. All persons interested in the estate are notified to appear and show cause why the petition should not be granted.

DATED this _____ day of _____, 19__.

_____, CLERK

By_____
Deputy Clerk

Form 34I

Case No.
Dept. No.

IN THE ———— JUDICIAL DISTRICT COURT OF THE STATE
OF NEVADA
IN AND FOR THE COUNTY OF ————

IN THE MATTER OF THE ESTATE OF   )
)
————,   )   <u>NOTICE OF HEARING</u>
)   (Administration)
Deceased.   )
———————————————)

NOTICE IS HEREBY GIVEN that ———— has filed in this Court a Petition for Letters of Administration and Summary Administration of the estate of ————, deceased, and a hearing has been set for ————, the ———— day of ————, 19—, at 9:00 a.m., in Department No. ——, at the Courthouse of the above-entitled Court, in the City of ————, County of ————, State of Nevada. All persons interested in the estate are notified to appear and show cause why the petition should not be granted.

DATED this ———— day of ————, 19—.

————————————, CLERK

By————————————
Deputy Clerk

Form 34J

Case No.
Dept. No.

IN THE _____ JUDICIAL DISTRICT COURT OF THE STATE
OF NEVADA
IN AND FOR THE COUNTY OF _____

IN THE MATTER OF THE ESTATE OF)	
)	
_____,)	NOTICE OF HEARING
)	(Petition for Settlement
Deceased.)	and Fees)
_____)	

NOTICE IS HEREBY GIVEN that _____ and _____ have filed with the Clerk of the above-entitled Court a Petition to _____ in the above-referenced estate, and a hearing has been set for _____, the _____ day of _____, 19__, at ____ a.m. at the Courthouse in _____, Nevada.

All persons interested in the estate are notified then and there to appear and show cause, if any they have, why the prayer of the Petition should not be granted. Reference is made to the Petition for further particulars.

At the hearing referred to above, the Court will be requested to approve the payment of the sum of $_____ to the law firm of _____ for legal services rendered, together with the sum of $_____ for costs advanced by the law firm of _____ in connection with the administration of the estate. Any person interested in the estate may file objections to the approval of these fees and objections will be considered at the hearing.

Reference is made to the Petition for further particulars.

DATED this _____ day of _____, 19__.

Clerk of the Court
By_____
Deputy Clerk

Form 34K

Case No.
Dept. No.

IN THE _____ JUDICIAL DISTRICT COURT OF THE STATE
OF NEVADA
IN AND FOR THE COUNTY OF _____

IN THE MATTER OF THE ESTATE OF	)	
	)	
_____,	)	AFFIDAVIT OF MAILING
	)	
Deceased.	)	
	)	

STATE OF NEVADA	)	
	)	ss.
COUNTY OF _____	)	

I, _____, do hereby swear under penalty of perjury that the assertions of this affidavit are true:

That affiant is, and was when the herein described mailing took place, a citizen of the United States, over twenty-one years of age, and not a party to, nor interested in, the within matter; that on the _____ day of _____, 19__, affiant deposited in the Post Office at Reno, Nevada, copies of the within filed Notice of Hearing in this estate matter, enclosed in sealed envelopes upon which first-class postage was fully prepaid, certified mail, return receipt requested, addressed to the following:

_____

_____.

That there is regular communication by mail between the place of mailing and the place so addressed.

_____

Subscribed and sworn to before me
this _____ day of _____, 19__.

_____
Notary Public

Form 34L

Case No.
Dept. No.

IN THE _____ JUDICIAL DISTRICT COURT OF THE STATE
OF NEVADA
IN AND FOR THE COUNTY OF _____

IN THE MATTER OF THE ESTATE OF)
)
_____,   ) ORDER ADMITTING WILL TO
) PROBATE AND ISSUING
          Deceased.   ) LETTERS TESTAMENTARY
)

The verified Petition of _____ for probate of the Will of the Decedent and for issuance of Letters Testamentary came on regularly for hearing this day. No person appeared to contest the Petition. Upon proof duly made to the satisfaction of the Court, the Court now finds as follows:

1. All notices of the hearing have been duly given as required by law.

2. _____, died on _____, and, at the time of his/her death, was a resident of _____, _____ County, Nevada. The Decedent left an estate in the State of Nevada subject to probate administration.

3. The Decedent left a Will dated _____. The Will has been filed with the Clerk of this Court, as provided by law.

4. The Decedent's Will dated _____ was duly executed in all particulars as required by law, and at the time of the execution of this Will, the Decedent was of sound mind, over the age of eighteen (18) years, and was not acting under undue influence or duress.

5. The Will of the Decedent appoints _____ as Executor thereof, and _____ has consented to act as Executor. The Will provides that no bond shall be required of _____. _____ is qualified for and entitled to Letters Testamentary pursuant to the laws of the State of Nevada.

6. The facts of the Petition having been found to be true, and good cause appearing, the Court now grants the Petition as follows:

A. IT IS HEREBY ORDERED that the Will of the Decedent dated _____ be admitted to probate as Decedent's last Will.

B. IT IS FURTHER ORDERED that _____ be appointed Executor, to serve without bond, and that Letters Testamentary be issued to him/her after taking the oath required by law.

Dated this _____ day of _____, 19__.

                                        _____
                                            District Judge

Form 34M

CASE NO.
DEPT. NO.

IN THE _____ JUDICIAL DISTRICT COURT OF THE STATE
OF NEVADA
IN AND FOR THE COUNTY OF _____

IN THE MATTER OF THE ESTATE OF)	ORDER FOR PROBATE OF
)	ESTATE, FOR ISSUANCE OF
_____,)	LETTERS TESTAMENTARY, AND
)	FOR SUMMARY ADMINISTRA-
Deceased.)	TION OF ESTATE
_____)	

The verified Petition of _____ for probate of estate, for issuance of Letters Testamentary, and for _____ administration of estate came on for hearing this day. No person appeared to contest the Petition. Upon proof duly made to the satisfaction of the Court, the Court now finds as follows:

1. All notices of the hearing have been duly given as required by law.

2. _____, Deceased (hereinafter referred to as the "Decedent") died on _____, 19__, in _____, _____ County, _____. The Decedent left an estate in the State of Nevada subject to probate administration.

3. The Decedent left a Will dated _____, 19__. The Decedent's Will has been filed with the Clerk of this Court as provided by law, and the Court finds that the Will of the Decedent dated _____, 19__ is the Last Will of Decedent.

4. The Will of the Decedent names _____ to serve as Executor of the Decedent's estate, and further directs that no bond or other security for the faithful performance of duties in the office of Executor be required of the Decedent's Executor.

5. The Petitioner, _____, is qualified for and entitled to Letters Testamentary pursuant to the laws of the State of Nevada. The Court finds that no bond shall be required of the Petitioner.

6. The gross value of the Decedent's estate which is subject to probate administration does not exceed One Hundred Thousand Dollars ($100,000), and thus the estate is subject to summary administration as provided in Chapter 145 of the Nevada Revised Statutes. The facts of the Petition having been found to be true, and good cause appearing, the Court now grants the Petition as follows:

A. It is hereby ordered that _____ be appointed Executor of the Decedent's estate, to serve without bond, and that Letters Testamentary be issued to _____ after taking the oath required by law.

B. It is further ordered that the estate be entitled to summary administration as provided in Chapter 145 of the Nevada Revised Statutes, dispensing with all regular proceedings and notices, except for the notice to creditors of the appointment of the Executor and notice of application for attorneys' fees and providing that an inventory, appraisement and record of value be made and returned to the Court.

DATED this _____ day of _____, 19___.

_____
DISTRICT JUDGE

Form 34N

Case No.
Dept. No.

IN THE _____ JUDICIAL DISTRICT COURT OF THE STATE
OF NEVADA
IN AND FOR THE COUNTY OF _____

IN THE MATTER OF THE ESTATE OF)
)
_____,   ) ORDER APPOINTING
) ADMINISTRATOR IN SUMMARY
     Deceased.   ) ADMINISTRATION
)

  The Petitioner, _____, having filed herein with the Clerk of the Court
his/her Petition for Letters of Administration and Summary Administration. The
time for the hearing on the Petition was set for the _____ day of
_____, 19__, and notice of the hearing has been duly given as required
by law, and the court having heard the evidence finds that the facts alleged in
the petition are true and correct and that the Petition ought to be granted;
  IT IS THEREFORE ORDERED AND DETERMINED BY THE COURT that
_____ died intestate on the _____ day of _____, 19__, and at
the time of his/her death was a resident of the County of _____, State of
Nevada; that said Decedent left certain personal property located within the
State of Nevada of a value in excess of $25,000 but less than $100,000; that no
federal estate tax return will be required to be filed for this estate; that this
estate be administered under summary administration with all regular proceedings and notices being dispensed with, except for Notice to Creditors and of the
appointment of the Administrator and Notice of Application for Attorney's Fees;
and that an Inventory and Appraisement or Record of value be made and returned to the Court.
  IT IS FURTHER ORDERED that _____ be appointed as Administrator of
the estate and that Letters of Administration be issued to him/her upon his/her
taking the oath required by law and giving bond in the sum of $_____.
  DATED this _____ day of _____, 19__.

             _____

              DISTRICT JUDGE

Form 340

Case No.
Dept. No.

IN THE _____ JUDICIAL DISTRICT COURT OF THE STATE
OF NEVADA
IN AND FOR THE COUNTY OF _____

IN THE MATTER OF THE ESTATE OF)
)
_____,   ) LETTERS OF ADMINISTRATION
)
           Deceased.   )
_____)

STATE OF NEVADA   )
                        : ss.
COUNTY OF _____   )

This is to certify that by an order of the above-named Court and entered on the
____ day of _____, 19__, _____ was appointed Administrator of
the estate of _____, deceased, by virtue of which these letters are issued this
____ day of _____, 19__, he/she having duly qualified witness my
official signature, with the seal of the Court affixed.

                                  WITNESS, _____, Clerk of the
                                  Judicial District Court of the State
                                  of Nevada, in and for the County of
                                  _____, with the seal thereof
                                  affixed, this ____ day of
                                  _____, 19__.

                                  By Order of the Court.
                                  _____, Clerk

                                  By_____
                                  Deputy Clerk

OFFICIAL OATH

I, _____, do solemnly affirm that I will faithfully perform according to law
all the duties of the office of Administrator of the estate of _____.

                                  _____

Subscribed and affirmed to before me
this ____ day of _____, 19__.
_____, Clerk
By_____
     Deputy Clerk

OR

_____
Notary Public
County of _____
State of _____

Code 1905

Form 34P

Case No.
Dept. No.

IN THE _____ JUDICIAL DISTRICT COURT OF THE STATE
OF NEVADA
IN AND FOR THE COUNTY OF _____

IN THE MATTER OF THE ESTATE OF)
)
_____,   ) LETTERS OF ADMINISTRATION
) WITH WILL ANNEXED
          Deceased.   )
_____)

STATE OF NEVADA   )
                       : ss.
COUNTY OF _____   )

The last Will of _____, deceased, having been admitted to probate in our Court, _____ was by our said court, on the _____ day of _____, 19__, duly appointed as Administrator with the Will annexed, and who, having duly qualified as such, is hereby authorized to act by virtue thereof in testimony whereof, I have officially signed these letters and affixed hereto the seal of the court, this _____ day of _____, 19__.

_____, Clerk

By_____
Deputy Clerk

OFFICIAL OATH

I, _____, do solemnly affirm that I will faithfully perform according to law all the duties of the office of Administrator of the estate of _____.

_____

Subscribed and affirmed to before me
this _____ day of _____, 19__.
_____, Clerk

By_____
Deputy Clerk

OR

_____
Notary Public
County of _____
State of _____

Form 34Q

Case No.
Dept. No.

IN THE _____ JUDICIAL DISTRICT COURT OF THE STATE
OF NEVADA
IN AND FOR THE COUNTY OF _____

IN THE MATTER OF THE ESTATE OF)
)
_____,   ) LETTERS TESTAMENTARY
)
        Deceased.   )
_____)

STATE OF NEVADA   )
                   : ss.
COUNTY OF _____)

    The Last Will of _____, deceased, having been duly admitted to probate in
our Court, _____ who is named therein, was, by our Court on the _____
day of _____, 19__, duly appointed Executor, who, having qualified as such,
is hereby authorized to act by virtue thereof. In testimony whereof, I have officially signed these letters and affixed hereto the Seal of said Court, this
_____ day of _____, 19__.

                                    By Order of the Court
                                  Clerk of the Court
                                  By_____
                                     Deputy Clerk

OFFICIAL OATH

    I do solemnly affirm that I will faithfully perform according to law all the
duties of the office of Executor of the estate of _____.

                                By_____

Subscribed and affirmed to before me
this _____ day of _____, 19__.
_____ Clerk

By _____
    Deputy Clerk

OR

_____

Notary Public
County of _____
State of _____

Form 34R

Case No.
Dept. No.

IN THE _____ JUDICIAL DISTRICT COURT OF THE STATE
OF NEVADA
IN AND FOR THE COUNTY OF _____

IN THE MATTER OF THE ESTATE OF)
)
_____,   ) STATEMENT OF
) PERMANENT ADDRESS
             Deceased.   )
_____)

_____, was appointed by this Court as Executor of the above-entitled estate
on _____, 19__.
The name and address of the Executor are as follows:

NAME: PERMANENT ADDRESS:

_____

_____.

Form 34S

Case No.
Dept. No.

IN THE _____ JUDICIAL DISTRICT COURT OF THE STATE
OF NEVADA
IN AND FOR THE COUNTY OF _____

IN THE MATTER OF THE ESTATE OF)
)
————,) NOTICE TO CREDITORS
)
Deceased.)
_____)

 NOTICE IS HEREBY GIVEN that the undersigned has been duly appointed
and qualified by the above-entitled Court on the _____ day of
_____, 19__, as Executor of the estate of _____, deceased.
 All creditors having claims against said estate are required to file the same,
with the proper vouchers attached, with the Clerk of the Court within [sixty (60)
or ninety (90)] days after the first publication of this notice.
 DATED this _____ day of _____, 19__.

                              _____

By _____
 Attorneys for Executor

Form 34T

Case No.
Dept. No.

IN THE _____ JUDICIAL DISTRICT COURT OF THE STATE
OF NEVADA
IN AND FOR THE COUNTY OF _____

IN THE MATTER OF THE ESTATE OF)
)
_____,   ) <u>NOTICE TO CREDITORS</u>
) <u>BY MAIL</u>
       Deceased.   )
_____)

NOTICE IS HEREBY GIVEN that the undersigned has been duly appointed
and qualified by the above-entitled Court on the _____ day of
_____, 19__, as Administrator of the Estate of _____, Deceased.

All creditors having claims against said estate are required to file the same,
with the proper vouchers attached, with the Clerk of the Court within sixty (60)
days of the mailing of this notice.

DATED: _____, 19__.

                               _____
                                (Name of Administrator)

(Name and address of Attorney
for the estate)

Form 34U

Case No.
Dept. No.

IN THE ———— JUDICIAL DISTRICT COURT OF THE STATE
OF NEVADA
IN AND FOR THE COUNTY OF ————

IN THE MATTER OF THE ESTATE OF)	
)	
————,)	PROOF OF MAILING
)	OF NOTICE TO CREDITORS
Deceased.)	
————————————————)	

STATE OF NEVADA   )
) ss:
COUNTY OF ————)

————, does hereby swear under penalty of perjury that the assertions of this affidavit are true:

1. That I am an employee of ————, attorneys for the [Administrator or Executor] in this estate matter.

2. That as required by NRS 147.010 and NRS 155.020, as soon as practicable after the appointment of the [Administrator or Executor] in this estate matter, in addition to publishing the Notice to Creditors, I mailed a copy of the Notice to those creditors whose names and addresses are readily ascertainable and who have not already filed a claim, enclosed in sealed envelopes upon which first-class postage was fully prepaid, addressed to the following:

(Names and addresses of known creditors)

3. That all such mailing of said Notice to Creditors was completed by ————, 19—, and that [sixty (60) or ninety (90)] days from said date is ————, 19—.

DATED: This ———— day of ————, 19—.

———————————————

Subscribed and sworn to before me
this ———— day of ————, 19—.

———————————————
Notary Public

Form 34V

CASE NO.
DEPT. NO.

IN THE _____ JUDICIAL DISTRICT COURT OF THE STATE
OF NEVADA
IN AND FOR THE COUNTY OF _____

IN THE MATTER OF THE ESTATE OF)

_____,   ) INVENTORY, APPRAISEMENT
) AND RECORD

Deceased.   ) OF VALUE

)

STATE OF NEVADA   )
: ss.
COUNTY OF _____)

I, _____, Executor of the estate of _____, Deceased, do solemnly swear that the accompanying Inventory and Appraisement and Record of Value contains a true statement of all of the assets of the estate of the above-named Decedent which have come into my possession or knowledge and of its value as of _____, 19__, the date of death of the Decedent, as determined by appraisers engaged by the Executor for assets as to which there is reasonable doubt as to value, and as determined from the Record of Value of the Executor for assets as to which there is no reasonable doubt as to value, and particularly of all monies belonging to the Decedent. There were no just claims of the Decedent against the Executor as of date of death. All property listed in this inventory is the sole and separate property of the Decedent.

Subscribed and sworn to before me
this _____ day of _____, 19__.

NOTARY PUBLIC

INVENTORY

Item No.   Description   Value

TOTAL

OATH OF APPRAISER

STATE OF NEVADA   )
) ss.
COUNTY OF _____)

I, _____, do solemnly swear that I will truly, honestly and impartially appraise the property of the estate of the above-named Decedent exhibited to me, or called to my attention, according to the best of my knowledge and ability.

_____

Subscribed and sworn to before me
this _____ day of _____, 19__.

_____

NOTARY PUBLIC

APPRAISAL BY SELECTED APPRAISER

I, _____, hereby certify that the property described in Item No. _____ of the foregoing Inventory have been exhibited to me or called to my attention, and that I appraised each such item as of the date of death of the Decedent at the sum set opposite the respective item.

_____

RECORD OF VALUE

I, _____, Executor of the estate of _____, Deceased, hereby certify that the property described in Item No. _____ of the foregoing Inventory is property where there is no reasonable doubt as to value and is equal in value to money in the amount set opposite the respective items, and that the value of the whole of the inventoried estate of the Decedent as recorded is the total sum of.

_____
Executor

STATE OF NEVADA   )
) ss.
COUNTY OF _____   )

_____, being first duly sworn, hereby swears under penalty of perjury that the assertions of this verification are true: That I am the Executor of the estate of _____, Deceased; that I have read the foregoing Record of Value and know the contents thereof; that the same is true of my own knowledge except as to those matters therein stated on information and belief, and as to those matters, I believe them to be true.
    DATED this _____ day of _____, 19__.

_____

Subscribed and sworn to before me
this _____ day of _____, 19__.

_____

NOTARY PUBLIC

Form 34W

CASE NO. _____
DEPT. NO. _____

IN THE _____ JUDICIAL DISTRICT COURT OF THE STATE
OF NEVADA
IN AND FOR THE COUNTY OF _____

IN THE MATTER OF THE ESTATE OF)	
_____,	) RETURN OF SALE OF REAL
	) PROPERTY AND PETITION FOR
	) APPROVAL AND
Deceased.	) CONFIRMATION OF SALE
	)

_____ ("Petitioner"), the Executor of the Will of _____, Deceased, hereby files Return of Sale of Real Property owned by the above-entitled estate and petitions the Court for approval and confirmation of the sale. In support of the Petition, Petitioner states the following:

1. Decedent's Last Will and Testament, dated _____, 19__, was admitted to probate by Order of this Court dated _____, 19__. The Petitioner qualified as Executor of the Decedent's Will and Letters Testamentary were issued to the Petitioner on _____, 19__. At all times since then, the Petitioner has been and now is the Executor of the Will of the Decedent.

2. Article _____, paragraph _____ of the Decedent's Will provides that the Petitioner, as Executor, has the power to sell, with or without notice, at either public or private sale, and to lease any property belonging to the Decedent's estate, subject only to such confirmation of court as may be required by law. Accordingly, the Petitioner, as Executor of the Decedent's estate, has the express power to sell the real property, and, pursuant to NRS 148.220, notice of sale of the real property has been given as required by law.

3. Pursuant to the power of sale, and with notice of sale, Petitioner has agreed to sell at private sale, all right, title, and interest of the estate of _____, Deceased, in the real property to _____ ("Buyer") in accordance with the terms and conditions set forth in the Standard Purchase Agreement and Earnest Money Receipt attached hereto as Exhibit "A," which is incorporated herein by reference. As provided in the agreement, the total sales price is the sum of _____ Dollars ($_____), all of which is to be paid in cash upon the close of escrow. Buyer shall pay _____ Dollars ($_____) as a cash down payment and obtain a new loan of choice in the approximate amount of _____ Dollars ($_____), which loan shall bear interest at no more than percent _____ (__ %) per annum. Buyer's loan shall be for a term of _____ (__) years. The approximate monthly installment paid by the Buyer pursuant to the loan will be the sum of _____ Dollars ($_____), including principal and interest. The agreement further provides that the estate of _____, Deceased, and the Buyer shall share costs of escrow, title insurance and necessary recording fees and document and transfer taxes in accordance with the standard procedure for the sale of real property in _____ County, Nevada. Title to the real property is to

be transferred to Buyer subject to real property taxes and covenants, conditions, restrictions, rights-of-way and easements of record encumbering the real property. The Petitioner is informed and believes the real property is not subject to any liens or encumbrances which secure payment of any monetary obligations. Rents, if any, real property taxes, and other expenses of the real property are to be prorated as of the date of recordation of the deed transferring title to the real property.

4. The above-described real property was appraised by _____, Street, _____, Nevada 895, as of the date of death of the Decedent, _____, 19__, at a fair market value of _____ Dollars ($_____). A copy of the appraisal is attached hereto as Exhibit "B," and incorporated herein by reference. Accordingly, the sales price of _____ Dollars ($_____) is representative of, and not disproportionate to the fair market value of the real property being sold.

5. The Petitioner believes the sale of the real property on the terms described herein will be of advantage, benefit and of interest to the Decedent's estate. The sale of the real property is necessary in order to close the Decedent's estate, and to pay the fees and expenses incurred in the administration of the estate. The real property has been listed for sale with licensed real estate brokers for a substantial period of time and only one other offer has been received for the real property. The prior offer was received from _____, who offered to purchase the real property for the sum of _____ Dollars ($_____); however, completion of the sale pursuant to the offer was contingent, among other things, _____. On _____, 19__, the _____ withdrew their offer to purchase the real property due to the uncertainty of their offer being accepted and the uncertainty regarding the date of closing the transaction. Attached hereto as Exhibit "C," and incorporated herein by reference, is a copy of the withdrawal letter, dated _____, 19__, addressed to _____.

6. Attached hereto as Exhibits "D" and "E," and incorporated herein by reference, are the Affidavits of _____, the Decedent's natural children. Through those affidavits, indicate they are the only other interested parties in the estate of the Decedent, and that they unequivocally give their consent to the Petitioner and Buyer to purchase the real property in question.

7. The sale was legally made and fairly conducted and Petitioner believes that the purchase is not disproportionate to the value of the real property. The sale is necessary in order to close the estate of the Decedent and to pay fees and expenses incurred in the administration of the estate.

8. The Petitioner has entered into a written agreement with _____, a real estate brokerage firm licensed by the State of Nevada, who procured the purchaser for the real property. The agreement provides for payment of a commission equal to _____ percent (__ %) of the selling price of the property to be paid out of the proceeds of the sale of the real property. Petitioner is informed and believes, and on that basis alleges, that a commission of _____ percent (__ %) of the selling price of the real property, the sum of _____ Dollars ($_____), is a fair and reasonable commission to be allowed to _____ for procuring this sale. Petitioner hereby requests that the Court approve and allow a commission of _____ percent (__ %) of the selling price, the sum of _____ Dollars ($_____), as a fair and reasonable commission to be allowed to _____ for procuring the sale.

Based upon the above, the Petitioner requests that the Court enter the following orders:

A. That the Court confirm and approve the sale of the real property to _____ on the terms described herein;

B. That the Court authorize the Petitioner to pay to _____ a commission equal to _____ percent (__ %) of the selling price of the property, the sum of _____ Dollars ($_____), as a fair and reasonable Commission for procuring the sale;

C. That the Petitioner be authorized and directed to take all action and to execute all documents necessary to complete the sale and conveyance of the real property; and

D. For such other and further relief as the Court deems proper.

DATED this _____ day of _____, 19__.

_____
Executor of the Estate of _____,
Deceased

APPROVED:

By_____
Attorneys for Petitioner

STATE OF NEVADA   )
) ss.
COUNTY OF WASHOE   )

_____, being first duly sworn, states under penalty of perjury as follows:

I am the Petitioner in the above-referenced matter; I have read the foregoing Return of Sale of Real Property and Petition for Approval and Confirmation of Sale and know the contents thereof; the same is true to the best of my knowledge, except as to those matters therein stated on information and belief, and as to those matters, I believe them to be true.

_____

Subscribed and sworn to before me
this _____ day of _____, 19__.

_____
NOTARY PUBLIC

Form 34X

Case No.
Dept. No.

IN THE _____ JUDICIAL DISTRICT COURT OF THE STATE
OF NEVADA
IN AND FOR THE COUNTY OF _____

IN THE MATTER OF THE ESTATE OF)
)
_____ ,   )RENUNCIATION AND
)NOMINATION
          Deceased.   )
_____)

The undersigned was named in the Last Will and Testament of _____ dated _____ , as Executor. I wish to renounce my appointment as Executor due to [state reasons].

I hereby nominate _____ of _____ , the _____ (relationship to decedent) of the Decedent, to serve as Executor in my place and stead.

DATED: This _____ day of _____ , 19__.

_____
(Name and address)

Form 34Y

CASE NO.
DEPT. NO.

IN THE _____ JUDICIAL DISTRICT COURT OF THE STATE
OF NEVADA
IN AND FOR THE COUNTY OF _____

IN THE MATTER OF THE ESTATE OF)
) ORDER SETTLING FIRST AND
_____,   ) FINAL ACCOUNT, FOR
) APPROVAL OF ATTORNEYS'
     Deceased.   ) FEES, AND FOR DECREE
_____) OF FINAL DISTRIBUTION

_____, Executor of the Estate of _____, Deceased, having filed Petition for Settlement of First and Final Account, for Approval of Attorneys' Fees, and for Decree of Final Distribution of the Estate, the Petition having come on regularly for hearing earlier this day, and no person having appeared to contest the Petition, the Court now finds as follows:

1. Notice of the Hearing of the Petition has been regularly given as prescribed by law.

2. All acts and transactions of the Executor of the Estate of _____, Deceased, during the period of the account are accurately shown and should be approved, and all of the allegations of the Petition are true. The Account is complete and correct and should be approved as filed.

3. _____ died testate on _____, 19__, in _____, Nevada, and was at the time of death a resident of _____, Nevada.

4. On _____, 19__, _____ was appointed Executor of the Decedent's estate and qualified as such on that date. _____ has been the Executor of the Decedent's estate since that time.

5. Notice to creditors has been given as required by law, the time for filing or presenting claims has expired, and the estate is now in a condition to be closed. No claims have been filed or presented against the estate. All debts of the Decedent and of the estate, and all expenses of administration, except for attorneys' fees and costs and closing expenses, have been paid.

6. A Federal Estate Tax Return is not required for the estate, but a Federal Fiduciary Income Tax Return will be filed for the estate, and the amount of tax reflected as being due on that return will be paid by _____ and _____.

7. Petitioner is entitled to a statutory executor's commission in the amount of $_____.

8. Distribution of the assets of the estate should be ordered as specified below.

BASED UPON THE FOREGOING, the Court hereby orders the following:

A. The administration of the estate of _____, Decedent, is settled, allowed and approved as filed, without any further accounting.

B. The First and Final Account of the Executor is settled, allowed and approved as filed.

C. All acts and transactions of the Executor as disclosed in the First and Final Account are confirmed and approved.

D. The Executor of the estate of _____ is entitled to a statutory executor's fee in the amount of $_____.

E. The Executor is authorized and directed to pay the law firm of _____ the attorneys for the Executor, the sum of _____ Dollars ($_____) as reasonable compensation for legal services rendered during the administration of the estate, together with the sum of _____ Dollars ($_____) for costs advanced to date by the firm in the administration of the estate, plus any additional costs advanced by the law firm on behalf of the estate.

F. All of the remaining assets of the estate, consisting of cash, shall be distributed as follows:

G. Any property interest of the Decedent or of the estate in any other property not now known or discovered shall be distributed to the Decedent's heirs in accordance with the terms and provisions of _____ Will dated _____, 19__.

DATED this _____ day of _____, 19__.

_____
DISTRICT JUDGE

Form 34Z

Case No.
Dept. No.

IN THE _____ JUDICIAL DISTRICT COURT OF THE STATE
OF NEVADA
IN AND FOR THE COUNTY OF _____

IN THE MATTER OF THE ESTATE OF ⟩
⟩
_____, ⟩ REPORT OF [EXECUTOR OR
⟩ ADMINISTRATOR] PURSUANT
Deceased. ⟩ TO NRS 143.035; AND
_____ ⟩ PETITION FOR APPROVAL

Petitioner, _____, [Executor or Administrator] of the Estate of _____,
Deceased, respectfully presents this verified Report and Petition and states:

1. That _____ died on _____, 19__, in _____, County of
_____, State of Nevada.

2. That Petitioner is the duly appointed, qualified and acting [Executor or
Administrator] of the above-entitled estate, [Letters Testamentary or Letters of
Administration] having been issued to (him/her) on _____.

3. That the Decedent left a duly executed Last Will and Testament dated
_____, which constitutes (his/her) Last Will and Testament [or Decedent died
intestate].

4. That Notice to Creditors was duly published in the _____ (Paper) on
_____, _____ and _____, 19__. That [ninety (90) or sixty (60)]
days have elapsed since the first publication of the notice and proof of publication
is on file herein.

5. That all claims which were approved by the [Executor or Administrator]
and allowed and approved by the Court have been paid.

6. That on _____, Petitioner filed an Inventory, Appraisement, and Record
of Value, showing the value of the estate as of the date of death of the Decedent
was $_____.

7. _____ (Explain here why the estate has not been closed and the
anticipated date the estate may be closed.

8. Petitioner has used reasonable diligence in performing (his/her) duties and
in pursuing the administration of the estate.

WHEREFORE, Petitioner requests as follows:

1. That the court determine that the [Executor or Administrator] has used
reasonable diligence in (his/her) administration;

2. That the Court approve every and all acts of the [Executor or Administrator] taken in (his/her) administration of the estate;

3. For such other and further relief as the Court may deem proper.

DATED: This _____ day of _____, 19__.

_____
[Executor or Administrator]

_____

[Attorney for Estate]

Upon penalties of perjury, the undersigned declares that (he/she) is the [Executor or Administrator] named in the foregoing Report and Petition and knows the contents thereof; that the same is true of (his/her) own knowledge, except for those matters stated upon information and belief, and that as to those matters, (he/she) believes it to be true.

_____

[Executor or Administrator]

Form 34AA

Case No.
Dept. No.

IN THE _____ JUDICIAL DISTRICT COURT OF THE STATE
OF NEVADA
IN AND FOR THE COUNTY OF _____

IN THE MATTER OF THE ESTATE OF)
)
_____,   ) RECEIPT OF DISTRIBUTION
)
      Deceased.   )
_____)

_____, of _____, Deceased, hereby acknowledges receipt of the following assets from the estate in accordance with the terms of that certain Order Settling First and Final Account, for Approval of Attorneys' Fees, and for Decree of Final Distribution entered by the above-entitled Court on _____, 19__.

_____

Form 34BB

Case No.
Dept. No.

IN THE _____ JUDICIAL DISTRICT COURT OF THE STATE
OF NEVADA
IN AND FOR THE COUNTY OF _____

IN THE MATTER OF THE ESTATE OF)
)
_____,   ) DECREE OF DISCHARGE
)
       Deceased.   )

_____, Executor of the above-entitled estate, having fully administered the estate, paid all sums of money due from _____ and distributed all of the property of the estate to the persons entitled thereto pursuant to the Order of the Court decreeing the final distribution of the estate, and having performed all acts lawfully required of _____, is hereby released and discharged from all liability hereafter incurred in matters relating to the above-entitled estate. The estate, being completely distributed, is hereby settled and closed, and _____ is discharged as Executor.

DATED this _____ day of _____, 19__.

                                  DISTRICT JUDGE

Form 34CC

AFFIDAVIT TERMINATING JOINT TENANCY

STATE OF NEVADA   )
) ss.

COUNTY OF _____)

_____ does hereby swear under penalty of perjury that the assertions of this affidavit are true, and declares the following:

1. _____ is the surviving spouse of _____, deceased.

2. _____ died in the City of _____, County of _____, State of _____, on _____, 19__. A certified copy of the Death Certificate of _____ is attached to this Affidavit, marked Exhibit "A."

3. On _____, the undersigned and _____ acquired title as joint tenants to a parcel of real property situated in _____ County, _____, by Deed recorded as Document No. _____, Book _____, Page _____, of the Official Records of _____ County, _____. The legal description of the real property is as follows:

4. At the time of death of _____, title to the real property described in paragraph 3. above continued to be held by _____ and _____, as joint tenants. As a result of the death of _____ and the joint tenancy form of title, the real property described in paragraph 3. above is now owned by _____.

Dated this _____ day of _____, 19__.

                                         _____

Subscribed and sworn to before me
this _____ day of _____, 19__.

_____

Notary Public

Form 34DD

Case NO.
Dept. NO.

IN THE ———— JUDICIAL DISTRICT COURT OF THE STATE
OF NEVADA
IN AND FOR THE COUNTY OF ————

IN THE MATTER OF THE ESTATE OF)
)
————,   ) TRANSFER BY AFFIDAVIT
)
         Deceased.   )

STATE OF ————)
                : ss.
COUNTY OF ————)

————, being first duly sworn, upon oath says:

That ———— is the (spouse, child, brother, sister, sole beneficiary) under the Last Will and Testament (attached hereto as Exhibit "A") of ————, Deceased, who died in the County of ————, State of ————, on the ———— day of ————, 19—, leaving an estate in the County of ————, State of Nevada, which is not real property nor a lien thereon, of a gross value of less than $10,000, consisting of the following, to wit:

That ———— has the right, pursuant to the provisions of NRS 146.080 to succeed to said property of said decedent, and to have any evidence of interest, indebtedness or right transferred to ———— by (person, representative corporation or body, owing the money, or having custody of such property, or acting as registrar or transfer agent of such evidences of interest).

That at least forty (40) days have elapsed since the date of death of Decedent.

That no application or petition for the appointment of a personal representative is pending or has been granted in any jurisdiction.

That all debts of Decedent, including funeral and burial expenses, have been paid or provided for.

That affiant has given written notice, by personal service or by certified mail, identifying his claim and describing the property claimed, to every person whose right to succeed to the Decedent's property is equal or superior to that of affiant, and that at least ten (10) days have elapsed since the notice was served or mailed.

That affiant is personally entitled to full payment or delivery of the property claimed or is entitled to payment or delivery on behalf of and with the written authority of all other successors who have an interest in the property.

I, ————, do hereby swear under penalty of perjury that the assertions of this affidavit are true.

Dated this ———— day of ————, 19—.

————————————

Subscribed and sworn to before me
this _____ day of _____, 19__.

_____
NOTARY PUBLIC

Form 34EE

CASE NO.
DEPT NO.

IN THE _____ JUDICIAL DISTRICT COURT OF THE STATE
OF NEVADA
IN AND FOR THE COUNTY OF _____

IN THE MATTER OF THE ESTATE OF)
)
_____,   ) ORDER CONFIRMING SALE
) OF REAL PROPERTY
        Deceased.   )
_____)

The verified Return of Sale and Petition of _____, the Administrator of the Estate of _____, Deceased, for the confirmation of the sale of a parcel of real property located at _____, _____ County, _____, came on regularly for hearing on _____. The sale for which approval and confirmation was requested was to _____. The sales price of the real property was _____ Dollars ($_____), all of which was to be payable in cash at the close of escrow. In attendance were _____, Esq., counsel for the Administrator, _____ [buyer-1], and _____, Esq., counsel for _____ [buyer-1], _____ [buyer-2], and _____, Esq., counsel for _____ [buyer-2]. During the hearing, _____ [buyer-1] submitted a written offer in the amount of _____ Dollars ($_____). Thereafter, the Court conducted a public auction in open court pursuant to NRS 148.270.3. Several bids were received with a final bid from _____ of _____ Dollars ($_____), which was accepted by the Court.

On proof duly made to the satisfaction of the Court, the Court now finds the following:

1. Notice of the hearing was given as required by law. An Affidavit of Mailing was previously filed with the Clerk of the Court.

2. A Notice of Sale was published in the manner required by NRS 148.220. An Affidavit of Publication was previously filed with the Court.

3. _____ [buyer-2] are responsible persons. The written offer submitted by _____ in the amount of _____ Dollars ($_____) exceeded by more than _____ Dollars ($_____) the sales price for the sale sought to be confirmed, as required by NRS 148.270.3. Accordingly, the Court vacated the sale to _____ [buyer-1], pursuant to NRS 148.702.2.

4. Since Notice of Sale was properly published, notice of the hearing was properly given, and all interested parties were present at the hearing, the Court conducted a public auction in open court pursuant to NRS 148.270.3.

5. The successful bidder in open court was _____. His/her bid of _____ Dollars ($_____) was the highest bid received. The entire sales price is payable in cash at the close of escrow. Title to the real property is to be transferred subject to the lien for real property taxes and covenants, conditions, restrictions, rights-of-way, and easements of record encumbering the real property. Proceeds

of the sale will be used to fully pay the existing Deed of Trust on the real property in favor of _____ [bank]. Rents, if any, real property taxes and other expenses of the real property are to be prorated as of the close of escrow. The estate is to be responsible for payment of the premium of a policy of title insurance insuring Buyer's title to the real property for one-half ($^1/_2$) of all escrow fees and other normal closing costs. The terms for the sale of the real property, other than increasing the sales price to _____ Dollars ($_____), are evidenced by a Standard Purchase Agreement and Earnest Money Receipt, together with two (_____) Addendums thereto, each dated _____, copies of which are attached to the Return and Petition as Exhibit "A."

6. The real property sold is commonly described as _____, _____ County, _____. The legal description of the real property is as follows:

_____

_____

The real property being sold includes all tenements, hereditaments, and appurtenances of the real property, the rents, issues, and profits thereof, and all fixtures located on the real property.

7. The real property was appraised within one (1) year of the sale at _____ Dollars ($_____). The bid by _____ at the appraised value is representative of and not disproportionate to the value of the property being sold.

8. The real property was the personal residence of the Decedent, who left no surviving spouse and no issue. Accordingly, the sale is for the advantage, benefit and in the best interest of the estate and those interested therein.

BASED UPON THE ABOVE, the Court hereby orders the following:

A. The sale to _____ [buyer-1] for the sales price of _____ Dollars ($_____) is vacated.

B. The bid received in open court from _____ [buyer-2] in the amount of _____ Dollars ($_____), all payable in cash, is accepted and confirmed.

C. The Petitioner is ordered to complete the sale in accordance with the terms described herein and the additional terms described in the Standard Purchase Agreement and Earnest Money Receipt, together with the addendums thereto, each dated _____, copies of which are attached to the Return and Petition as Exhibit "A."

D. Upon the close of escrow for the sale, the Petitioner shall execute and deliver to the buyer a deed conveying all of the right, title, and interest of the estate in the real property.

DATED this _____ day of _____, 19__.

_____

DISTRICT JUDGE

Form 34FF

CASE NO.
DEPT. NO.

IN THE _____ JUDICIAL DISTRICT COURT OF THE STATE
OF NEVADA
IN AND FOR THE COUNTY OF _____

IN THE MATTER OF THE ESTATE OF)
)
_____,   ) PETITION FOR CONFIRMATION
) OF SALE OF REAL PROPERTY
             Deceased.   )
_____)

_____ (the "Petitioner"), the Administrator of the Estate of _____, Deceased (the "Decedent"), hereby petitions the Court for confirmation of the sale of a parcel of real property. In support of the Petition, Petitioner states the following:

I

Petitioner has agreed, subject to Court confirmation, to sell to _____, a single/married man/woman, as his/her sole and separate property, the real property owned by the estate which is located at _____, _____ County, _____, the legal description of which is as follows:

_____

_____

_____

The real property described above is hereafter referred to as the "Real Property."
The Agreement for the sale of the Real Property provides for a sales price of _____ Dollars ($_____), all of which is payable in cash at the close of escrow. The escrow is to close within ten (10) days following Court confirmation of the sale. A copy of the Standard Purchase Agreement and Earnest Money Receipt, together with an amendment thereto, are attached hereto as Exhibit "A."

II

The Real Property was appraised by _____ as of _____, for _____ Dollars ($_____). A copy of the Appraisal Report of _____ dated _____, is attached hereto as Exhibit "B."

III

Although the sales price of _____ Dollars ($_____) is less than the appraised value, because no real estate brokerage commission is to be paid on the proposed sale, the sales price of _____ Dollars ($_____) is approximately equal to what the estate would realize if the Real Property were sold at its appraised value and a _____ percent (__ %) brokerage fee were payable by the estate.

IV

The Real Property was the personal residence of the Decedent. The Decedent was not married and left no issue. The Petitioner, the sole heir of the estate, believes that the sale of the Real Property is for the advantage, benefit and in the best interests of the state and of himself/herself.

Based upon the above, Petitioner requests that the Court order the following:

A. That the sale of the Real Property to _____ for the total sales price of _____ Dollars ($_____), payable in cash, be confirmed;

B. That Petitioner be ordered to consummate the sale pursuant to the terms of the Standard Purchase Agreement and Earnest Money Receipt, and amendment thereof, which is attached hereto as Exhibit "A"; and

C. That Petitioner be authorized and directed to execute and deliver a deed conveying title to the Real Property to _____.

DATED this _____ day of _____, 19__.

Address:
ADMINISTRATOR

APPROVED:

By _____

Attorneys for Petitioner

VERIFICATION

STATE OF _____)
) ss.
COUNTY OF _____)

_____, being first duly sworn, deposes and says, that he/she is the Petitioner herein; that he/she has read the foregoing Petition and knows the contents thereof, and the same is true of his/her own knowledge, except as to those matters therein stated on information and belief, and as to such matters he/she believes them to be true.

Subscribed and sworn to before me this _____ day of _____, 19__.

_____

Notary Public

Form 34GG

Case No.
Dept. No.

IN THE _____ JUDICIAL DISTRICT COURT OF THE STATE
OF NEVADA
IN AND FOR THE COUNTY OF _____

IN THE MATTER OF THE ESTATE OF)

)

_____,   ) DISCLAIMER OF INTEREST
) IN PROPERTY

          Deceased.   )

_____)

STATE OF NEVADA   )
) ss.
COUNTY OF _____)

I, _____, a widow, of _____, County, Nevada, do hereby absolutely disclaim and renounce without conditions or reservations of any kind all right, title, and interest that I am entitled to as surviving joint tenant by right of survivorship, and under the laws of intestate succession (NRS 184 et seq.) to any separate or community property interest inuring to the undersigned by reason of the death of my late husband, _____, who died intestate, in the following described property:

_____

_____

_____

My disclaimer is irrevocable and unequivocal, and constitutes a complete and unqualified refusal to accept such property. This disclaimer shall be interpreted to qualify as a disclaimer under Chapter 120 of the Nevada Revised Statutes. The undersigned reserves and retains her undivided one-half ($1/2$) interest in the above-described property as joint tenant which interest existed prior to her husband's death. This disclaimer is intended to cover only those property interests that she would succeed to by reason of her husband's death.

DATED this _____ day of _____, 19__.

_____, Beneficiary

STATE OF NEVADA   )
) ss.
COUNTY OF _____)

On this _____ day of _____, 19__, personally appeared before me, a Notary Public, _____, known to me to be the person who executed the foregoing document, and acknowledged to me that she executed the same for the purposes set forth therein.

_____
NOTARY PUBLIC

Form 34GG NEVADA CIVIL PRACTICE

ACKNOWLEDGMENT OF DELIVERY

I hereby acknowledge delivery to me of the above disclaimer of interest in property on the ———— day of ——————, 19— at Reno, Nevada.

————————————————,
Administrator of the Estate
of ————————————————

EXTRAORDINARY WRITS

Author: Stanley W. Parry

§ 3501. Introduction and scope.

At common law, a writ was an order issued from a court requiring the performance of a specified act or giving authority to have it done. Chapter 34 of the Nevada Revised Statutes provide for four writs: Certiorari; Mandamus; Prohibition; and Habeas Corpus. These writs are sometimes designated as extraordinary writs. Chapter 35 of the Nevada Revised Statutes provides for a proceeding in Quo Warranto.

This chapter will discuss the writs of certiorari, mandamus and prohibition, and a proceeding in quo warranto. Mandamus, certiorari and prohibition all have a common element. Each of these writs allows a superior court to review the acts of an inferior court, tribunal, board or officer to determine whether they have properly performed their official or public duties as imposed by such laws and rules and regulations that govern that body. A proceeding in quo warranto is related to the writs of mandamus, certiorari and prohibition in that it allows the court to determine the legality and appropriateness of the use of a public franchise or office and other related matters. This chapter does not discuss writs of habeas corpus.

§ 3502. Writ of certiorari: nature of remedy, definitions and principles of general application.

Certiorari is a writ which may be issued by the supreme court, a district court, or a judge of the district court when an inferior tribunal, board or officer has exceeded its jurisdiction while exercising its respective judicial functions.

Certiorari can be distinguished from other remedies in that it does not serve to correct errors of law or fact which are not jurisdictional in their nature. Proceedings in certiorari are of an appellate nature, although they are not pursued in the ordinary and technical form of an appeal, *Leonard v. Peacock,* 8 Nev. 157 (1873), cited in *Dixon v. Second Judicial District Court,* 43 Nev. 159, 163, 183 P. 312 (1919), nor will certiorari lie if the right of appeal exists. *State ex rel. Schumacher v. First Judicial District Court,* 77 Nev. 408, 365 P.2d 646 (1961). The practioner in this area should note that, in addition to the writ of certiorari, a writ of mandamus has also been approved as a vehicle to review administrative action of a local governmental body in the absence of a right of direct appeal. *Compare, e.g., Washington v. Clark County Liquor & Gaming Board,* 100 Nev. 425, 683 P.2d 31 (1984), *and City Council of Reno v. Travelers Hotel, Inc.,* 100 Nev. 436, 683 P.2d 960 (1984); *see also* discussion in § 3506, *infra.*

The test for determining if a party is entitled to a writ of certiorari is whether it is a party in form or in substance to the proceedings sought to be reviewed, so that its interests have been concluded by determination in the proceedings. *Electrical Products Corp. v. Second Judicial District Court,* 55 Nev. 8, 23 P.2d 501 (1933), cited in *State ex rel. Garaventa Land & Livestock Co. v. Second Judicial District Court,* 61 Nev. 350, 352, 128 P.2d 266 (1942). A person is not entitled to a writ of certiorari if they are not beneficially interested in the proceedings even though they are a party to the proceedings. *Electrical Prods. Corp. v. Second Judicial District Court.*

While NRS 34.090 provides that review upon a writ of certiorari shall not be extended further than to determine whether the inferior tribunal, board, or officer has regularly pursued the authority of such tribunal, board or officer, the expression "has regularly pursued its authority" does not authorize inquiry into any irregularity or question beyond that of jurisdiction. *Phillips v. Welch,* 12 Nev. 158 (1877), cited in *State ex rel. Fletcher v. Osburn,* 24 Nev. 187, 190, 51 P. 837 (1898), *State ex rel. Hinkley v. Sixth Judicial District Court,* 53 Nev. 343, 355, 1 P.2d 105

(1931), *Goicoechea v. Fourth Judicial District Court,* 96 Nev. 287, 289, 607 P.2d 1140, 1141 (1980).

There are three essential elements that must be present for the issuance of a writ of certiorari: (1) excess of jurisdiction; (2) absence of a right of direct appeal; and (3) lack of a plain, speedy and adequate remedy. In the absence of any one of these elements, a writ will not be issued. *Mack v. District Court,* 50 Nev. 318, 258 P. 289 (1927), cited in *Iveson v. Second Judicial District Court,* 66 Nev. 145, 156, 206 P.2d 755 (1949), *State ex rel. Shumacher v. First Judicial District Court,* 77 Nev. 408, 409, 365 P.2d 646 (1961), *Franklin v. Eighth Judicial District Court,* 85 Nev. 401, 403, 455 P.2d 919 (1969), *State v. Second Judicial District Court,* 85 Nev. 381, 383, 455 P.2d 923, 925 (1969).

When a writ of certiorari has been sought after the lapse of the time for appeal, the writ will not issue. *Chapman v. Justice Court,* 29 Nev. 154, 86 P. 552, 99 P. 1077 (1906), *In re Wixom,* 12 Nev. 219 (1877).

§ 3503. — Form, content and procedure in applying for a writ of certiorari.

The particular issue for which review is being requested will be the determining factor in selecting the form and content of the application for a writ of certiorari. NRS 34.030 provides, "The application shall be made on affidavit by the party beneficially interested, and the court or judge to whom the application is made may require a notice of the application to be given to the adverse party, or may grant an order to show cause why it should not be allowed, or may grant the writ without further notice."

The rules governing proceedings in certiorari are those provisions of the Nevada Rules of Civil Procedure and Rule 21 of the Nevada Rules of Appellate Procedure relative to new trials, and appeals from the district court, except so far as they are inconsistent with NRS 34.010 to 34.120, inclusive. NRS 34.130.

Application for a writ of certiorari should comply with all applicable rules and in addition should set forth all relevant facts which would support the issuance of a writ. The application should contain the following insofar as is practicable: (1) a statement of the facts necessary to understand the issues presented by the application; (2) a statement of the issues presented and of the relief sought; (3) a statement of the reasons why the writ should issue; and (4) copies of any orders or opinions or parts of the record which may be essential to understanding the matters set forth in the petition.

A copy of the record for which review is sought should be attached to the application. The applicant should clearly point out the claims of error as they appear in the record. In addition to the foregoing, the applicant should also show that an appeal does not exist nor are there any plain, speedy and adequate remedies.

§ 3504. — Representative cases of writ of certiorari: successful.

Certiorari obtained where respondent's arrest of petitioner was found to be premature. *Braham v. Fourth Judicial District Court,* 103 Nev. 644, 747 P.2d 1390 (1987).

Court found that respondent court should have granted certiorari to review termination of employee by housing authority. *Watson v. Housing Authority,* 97 Nev. 240, 627 P.2d 405 (1981).

Respondent court was found to be without jurisdiction to stay an administrative proceeding initiated by the State Gaming Control Board. *State Gaming Control Board v. Eighth Judicial District Court,* 82 Nev. 38, 409 P.2d 974 (1966).

Writ granted to party beneficially interested even though they were a stranger to the record. *State ex rel. Garaventa Land & Livestock Co. v. Second Judicial District Court,* 61 Nev. 350, 128 P.2d 266 (1942).

Respondent court was found to have no authority to entertain petition asking for a determination of the relative water rights of users of the Humboldt River. *Ruddell v. Sixth Judicial District Court,* 54 Nev. 363, 17 P.2d 693 (1933).

§ 3505. — Unsuccessful.

Court found that certiorari would not lie to review ministerial action of board of county commissioners. *State ex rel. Casady v. Lauritzen,* 70 Nev. 134, 260 P.2d 783 (1953).

Application to review the constitutionality of a statute which was not jurisdictional in its nature was not reviewable under certiorari. *Mack v. District Court,* 50 Nev. 318, 258 P. 289 (1927).

Application to review an order made in the exercise of legislative, not judicial, function was dismissed. *DeGiovanni v. Public Service Commission,* 45 Nev. 74, 197 P. 582 (1921).

Application for review of order for alimony pendente lite in divorce action found not reviewable when court has complete jurisdiction to make and enforce, during the pendency of the action, all orders for alimony. *Kapp v. Seventh Judicial District Court,* 32 Nev. 264, 107 P. 95 (1910).

Application for review of city council resolutions providing for raising money upon the credit of the city dismissed as being legislative and not judicial in nature. *State ex rel. Fletcher v. Osburn,* 24 Nev. 187, 51 P. 837 (1898).

Application for review of lower court finding of contempt dismissed where court was found to be exercising powers within its jurisdiction. *Phillips v. Welch,* 12 Nev. 158 (1877).

§ 3506. Writ of mandamus: nature of remedy, definitions and principles of general application.

A writ of mandamus may be issued by the supreme court or a district court "to compel the performance of an act" of an inferior state tribunal, corporation, board or person. NRS 34.160. It enjoins the inferior body or person to affirmatively act in a manner which the law already compels the body or person to act. *State ex rel. Piper v. Gracey,* 11 Nev. 223, 233 (1876). The issuance of a writ of mandamus to compel an officer of the state must be for a duty resulting from the office and required by law. *State ex rel. McGuire v. Waterman,* 5 Nev. 323 (1869). Where the official duty is one which is continuing until performed, the writ to perform the duty will lie against the incumbent in office, regardless of the fact that his predecessor in office should have performed the duty. *State ex rel. Haviland v. Bonnifield,* 37 Nev. 44, 138 P. 906 (1914).

The mandamus is never granted in anticipation of an omission of duty but only after actual default. *State ex rel. Piper v. Gracey,* 11 Nev. 223, 233-34 (1876). Though it is true that proceedings in mandamus to direct an action of an individual or board are not of an appellate nature — but are original actions in and of themselves — the issuance of the writ to a lower court is an exercise of appellate jurisdiction. *See, e.g., State v. Babayan,* 106 Nev. 155, 162, 787 P.2d 805, 810 (1990).

Before a writ of mandamus will be issued, certain requirements must be met. First, the act required to be performed must be a duty resulting from the office and required by law. *State ex rel. McGuire v. Waterman,* 5 Nev. 323 (1869). It also must appear that the defendant has it in his power to perform the duty required of him, and that the writ will have a beneficial effect to the applying party. *Id.* The writ of mandamus does not lie to correct errors where an action has been taken, but lies to compel a party to exercise its judgment and render a decision where a failure of justice would otherwise result from a delay or refusal to act.

Mandamus should not be used unless the usual and ordinary remedies failed to afford adequate relief, *and* without it there would be a failure of justice. *State v. Storey County,* 22 Nev. 263, 264, 38 P. 668 (1895), cited in *Abel v. Eggers,* 36 Nev. 372, 381, 136 P. 100 (1913).

The case law interpreting writs of mandamus in Nevada has arguably expanded the scope of this writ. Writs of mandamus have developed into an acceptable proceeding to challenge the decisions of local governmental bodies. Because Chapter 233B of the NRS only provides for judicial review of the administrative decisions of state agencies, a petition for writ of mandamus has become the preferred method for judicial review of local governmental actions. The courts have found that where there is not substantial evidence to support a local governmental body's decision, there is an abuse of discretion and the courts have the power to interfere with the actions of the body's decision through a writ of mandamus. *Nova Horizon, Inc. v. City Council of Reno,* 105 Nev. 92, 769 P.2d 721 (1989); *State ex rel. Johns v. Gragson,* 89 Nev. 478, 515 P.2d 65 (1973); *Henderson v. Henderson Auto Wrecking,* 77 Nev. 118, 359 P.2d 743 (1961).

Where a writ of mandamus is used to review the actions of an inferior board, the court will not conduct a hearing de novo. The reviewing court examines the record below to determine whether there is substantial evidence to support the decision of the board. The reviewing court shall not substitute its judgment of the facts for that of the inferior board. *City Council of Reno v. Traveler's Hotel,* 100 Nev. 436, 683 P.2d 960 (1984).

Since mandamus is remedial in nature, the scope of mandamus is wide, applying in numerous instances. [For representative Nevada cases wherein mandamus was granted, see § 3508.]

§ 3507. — Form, content and procedure in applying for a writ of mandamus.

The Nevada Rules of Civil Procedure apply to writs of mandamus. NRS 34.300. NRS 34.310 provides, "The provisions of the Nevada Rules of Civil Procedure and Nevada Rules of Appellate Procedure relative to new trials in, and appeals from, the district court, except so far as they are inconsistent with the provisions of NRS 34.150 to 34.290 [covering mandamus], inclusive, apply to the proceedings mentioned in NRS 34.150 to 34.290, inclusive."

NRS 34.190 provides that a writ of mandamus must be either alternative or peremptory. It provides that the alternative writ should state the allegation against the party to whom it is directed and should command such party at a designated time to perform the required act or show the court why such act has not been performed. It also provides that the peremptory writ should be similar to the alternative writ with the omission of the show cause language and inserting a return day.

In the Eighth Judicial District Court, Local Rule 2.15 should be noted. This rule sets forth a procedure for petitions for judicial review other than pursuant to the Nevada Administrative Procedure Act. It is unclear whether this rule applies to writs of mandamus. To the extent a writ of mandamus is used as a petition for judicial review in the Eighth Judicial District Court, Local Rule 2.15 should be consulted.

NRAP 21 provides that a petition for a writ of mandamus should be filed with the clerk of the supreme court. The petition should contain the following: (1) a statement of the facts necessary to understand the issues presented by the application; (2) a statement of the issues presented and of the relief sought; (3) a statement of the reasons why the writ should issue; and (4) copies of any orders or opinions or parts of the record which may be essential to understanding the matter as set forth in the petition.

The statute requires that the writ of mandamus be accompanied by an affidavit of the party beneficially interested (though a verified petition need not be accompanied by an affidavit, *State ex rel. Sears v. Wright,* 10 Nev. 167 (1875), cited in *Poulos v. Eighth Judicial District Court,* 98 Nev. 453, 454 n.1, 652 P.2d 1177, 1177 n.1 (1982)), and such an affidavit must be sufficient enough to support the issuance of the writ. *State ex rel. Piper v. Gracey,* 11 Nev. 223, 233 (1876), cited in *Flanigan v. Burritt,* 41 Nev. 504, 507, 173 P. 352 (1918). The petition or affidavit accompanying the writ is required to be answered by the respondent. *Gulbranson v. City of Sparks,* 89 Nev. 93, 95, 506 P.2d 1264, 1265-66 (1973). In addition to the foregoing, proof of service on the respondent judge or judges and on all parties to the action in the trial court must also be attached to the petition.

Once the Nevada Supreme Court has received the petition, it may immediately upon review deny the petition. If, however, it decides that the petition warrants further review, it may issue an order setting a time in which the respondents shall answer against the issuance of the writ. After that date has been reached, the supreme court will review the arguments and either issue or deny the writ at its discretion.

The court may also, in its discretion, order that the question brought by the writ be tried before a jury, and postpone the argument until such trial can be had and the verdict certified to the court. NRS 34.220.

§ 3508. — Representative cases of writ of mandamus: successful.

Directing the state controller to release monies sufficient to pay statutorily mandated pay raises. *State of Nevada Employees Association v. Daines,* 108 Nev. 15, 824 P.2d 276 (1992).

Setting aside an order quashing service of process. *Welburn v. Eighth Judicial District Court,* 107 Nev. 105, 806 P.2d 1045 (1991).

Mandating that the lower court had exceeded its jurisdiction when it ordered a competent defendant to submit to the administration of drugs. *Ford v. Second Judicial District Court,* 97 Nev. 578, 635 P.2d 578 (1981).

Requiring a city council to grant an application for zone change. *Nova Horizon, Inc. v. City Council of Reno,* 105 Nev. 92, 769 P.2d 721 (1989).

Requiring city to issue business license and certificate of occupancy for apartments owned by construction lender following foreclosure on the builder. *City of Reno v. Nevada First Thrift,* 100 Nev. 483, 686 P.2d 231 (1984).

Compelling the zoning administrator to "sign-off" the zoning requirements of the county. *Board of Clark County Commissioners v. Excite Corporation,* 98 Nev. 153, 643 P.2d 1209 (1982).

Ordering department of prisons to apply good time credits to reduce minimum sentences which prisoners had to serve before becoming eligible for parole. *Demosthenes v. Williams,* 97 Nev. 611, 637 P.2d 1203 (1981).

Directing city clerk to issue a call for special election. *Cleland v. Eighth Judicial District Court,* 92 Nev. 454, 552 P.2d 488 (1976).

Compelling reclassification of property by board of city commissioners following a tie vote by the board on the application for reclassification. *Board of Commissioners of Las Vegas v. Dayton Development Co.,* 91 Nev. 71, 530 P.2d 1187 (1975).

Directing State Personnel Advisory Commission to dissolve its stay of a hearing officer's reinstatement order. *Nevada State Personnel Division v. Haskins,* 90 Nev. 425, 529 P.2d 795 (1974).

§ 3509. — Unsuccessful.

Petitioning for a writ to compel a lower court to vacate an order quashing service of process. *MGM Grand, Inc. v. Eighth Judicial District Court,* 107 Nev. 65, 807 P.2d 201 (1991).

Seeking a writ compelling the Nevada Gaming Commission to order the Gaming Board to provide to the applicant an investigative report upon which the Board based its decision to deny a gaming license. *Resnick v. Nevada Gaming Commission,* 104 Nev. 60, 752 P.2d 229 (1988).

Requesting a writ directing Public Service Commission not to re-open a case (for evidence purposes) involving a gas bill. *Southwest Gas v. Lear,* 101 Nev. 120, 693 P.2d 1264 (1985).

Requesting a writ to compel a justice court to grant a jury trial. *Carrell v. Justice's Court of Reno,* 95 Nev. 402, 663 P.2d 697 (1983).

Petitioning for a writ to compel a school board to reinstate a teacher who had voluntarily submitted her resignation. *Carson City School District v. Burnsen,* 96 Nev. 314, 608 P.2d 507 (1980).

Seeking writ to order city council to issue a pawnshop license where the city council denied a pawnshop license based upon the fact of the applicant's majority shareholder's lengthy criminal record. *Mills v. City of Henderson,* 95 Nev. 550, 598 P.2d 635 (1979).

Seeking writ to compel county board of supervisors to award an unsuccessful bidder a contract to install and operate an outdoor billboard sign. *Faust v. Donrey Media Group,* 95 Nev. 235, 591 P.2d 1152 (1979).

Seeking writ to require board of regents' acceptance of his declaration of candidacy. *Tam v. Colton,* 94 Nev. 452, 581 P.2d 447 (1978).

Seeking writ to compel the board of county commissioners to reinstate a revoked liquor license when the conditions of the liquor license were violated. *Kochendorfer v. Board of County Commissioners of Douglas County,* 93 Nev. 419, 566 P.2d 1131 (1977).

Seeking writ to review a district court's discovery order. *Clark County Liquor & Gaming Board v. Clark,* 102 Nev. 654, 730 P.2d 443 (1986).

§ 3510. Writ of prohibition: nature of remedy, definitions and principles of general application.

NRS 34.320 defines the writ of prohibition as, "the counterpart of the writ of mandate. It arrests the proceedings of any tribunal, corporation, board or person exercising judicial functions, when such proceedings are without or in excess of the jurisdiction of such tribunal, corporation, board or person." A writ of prohibition does not serve to correct errors; its purpose is to prevent courts from transcending the limits of their jurisdiction in the exercise of judicial but not ministerial power. *Low v. Crown Point Mining Co.,* 2 Nev. 75 (1866), cited in *O'Brien v. Trousdale,* 41 Nev. 90, 99, 167 P. 1007 (1917), *Walser v. Moran,* 42 Nev. 111, 120, 173 P. 1149, 180 P. 492 (1918), *State ex rel. Marshall v. Down,* 58 Nev. 54, 57, 68 P.2d 567 (1937). Its object is to restrain inferior courts from acting without authority of law in cases where wrong, damage, and injustice are likely to follow from such action. *Walcott v. Wells,* 21 Nev. 47, 24 P. 367 (1890), cited in *Bell v. First Judicial District Court,* 28 Nev. 280, 294, 81 P. 875 (1905), *Turner v. Langan,* 29 Nev. 281, 284, 88 P. 1088 (1907), *Silver Peak Mines v. Second Judicial District Court,* 33 Nev. 97, 116, 110 P. 503 (1910), *O'Brien v. Trousdale, supra.*

The writ of prohibition is an extraordinary remedy that is usually only issued in cases of extreme necessity where usurpation or abuse of power is likely to follow and other remedies of law are not available. It is not a corrective remedy, but rather a preventative measure.

The writ of prohibition may be issued only by the supreme court when no plain, speedy and adequate remedy of law is available. While a writ of prohibition is most often used to restrain courts or judicial tribunals, it can also be used to restrain persons in other classes who are exercising or attempting to exercise judicial or quasi-judicial functions beyond their powers. *See State ex rel. Schloss v. Stevens,* 34 Nev. 146, 116 P. 605 (1911).

In order to obtain the issuance of a writ of prohibition, a petitioner must show the following: (1) that a tribunal, corporation, board or person is about to exercise a judicial or quasi-judicial function; (2) that the exercise of such power is not authorized by law; and (3) that the exercise of such power will result in an injury for which there is no plain, speedy and adequate remedy of law.

§ 3511. — Form, content and procedure in applying for a writ of prohibition.

NRAP 21 provides that a petition for a writ of prohibition should be filed with the clerk of the supreme court. The petition should contain the following: (1) a statement of the facts necessary to understand the issues presented by the application; (2) a statement of the issues presented and of the relief sought; (3) a statement of the reasons why the writ should issue; and (4) copies of any orders or opinions or parts of the record which may be essential to understanding the matter as set forth in the petition. In addition to the foregoing, proof of service on the respondent judge or judges and on all parties to the action in the trial court must also be attached to the petition.

Once the supreme court has received the petition, it may immediately upon review deny the petition. If, however, it decides that the petition warrants further review, it may issue an order setting a time in which the respondents shall answer against the issuance of the writ. After that date has been reached, the supreme court will review the arguments and either issue or deny the writ at its discretion.

§ 3512. — Representative cases of writ of prohibition: successful.

In suit alleging conspiracy to deny a plaintiff employment because of his non-union status, lower court issued summary judgment in favor of all defendants except local union. Court found that union, as separate and distinct entity from local union member, was not accountable for misconduct of one of its local union members, and writ was issued to halt further proceedings against it. *Bair v. Berry,* 86 Nev. 26, 464 P.2d 469 (1970).

Prohibition issued to prevent punishment for contempt for alleged violation of void order and to prevent court from appointing a receiver where order of appointment was void. *State ex rel. Nenzel v. District Court,* 49 Nev. 145, 241 P. 317 (1925).

Writ issued where state court could not exercise jurisdiction of a given controversy which was arguably subject to the prohibitions or protections of the National Labor Relations Act. *Hutchby v. Second Judicial District Court,* 81 Nev. 489, 406 P.2d 710 (1965).

Writ issued where district court was without jurisdiction to grant judicial review of a complaint filed by a business, where such complaint requested that letter sent by director of Public Service Commission's Division of Consumer Relations to business's attorney be set aside as unreasonable, since the letter was not a judicially reviewable "order of the commission," and since business did not exhaust its available administrative remedies. *Gray Line Tours v. Eighth Judicial District Court,* 99 Nev. 124, 659 P.2d 304 (1983).

Writ issued to district court prohibiting original jurisdiction over land-lord-tenant disputes for possession of lands and tenements, since original jurisdiction vested exclusively in justice courts. *K.J.B., Inc. v. Second Judicial District Court,* 103 Nev. 473, 745 P.2d 700 (1987).

Writ issued prohibiting district court from considering late filed water rights exceptions, since the statutory notice requirements are mandatory, requiring strict compliance, and district court was therefore without jurisdiction. *G. & M. Properties v. Second Judicial District Court,* 95 Nev. 301, 594 P.2d 714 (1979).

§ 3513. — Unsuccessful.

Petition seeking to preclude the pronouncement of judgment and imposition of a sentence upon a jury verdict finding petitioner guilty of criminal trespass based upon the premise that the justice of the peace was without jurisdiction to pronounce judgment and impose sentence because the cited statute did not embrace the circumstances of petitioner's case was denied. *Scott v. Justices' Court,* 84 Nev. 9, 435 P.2d 747 (1968).

Petition to prohibit respondent from placing the name of candidate convicted of an offense involving moral turpitude upon the official ballot to be voted on at ensuing election was denied. *State ex rel. Conklin v. Buckingham,* 59 Nev. 36, 84 P.2d 49 (1938).

Petitioner not entitled to writ in light of availability of remedy of appeal from district court order confirming lease-sale to third party and that petitioner's rights and properties would not be further prejudiced by court action which he sought to prevent. *Diotallevi v. Second Judicial District Court,* 93 Nev. 633, 572 P.2d 214 (1977).

§ 3514. — Quo warranto: nature of remedy, definitions and principles of general application.

The legislature has provided that an action in the nature of quo warranto will lie in the following instances:

(1) Against a person who usurps, intrudes into, or unlawfully holds or exercises, a public office, civil or military, except the office of assemblyman or state senator, or a franchise within this state, of an officer in a corporation created by the authority of this state.
(2) Against a public officer, civil or military, except the office of assemblyman or state senator, who does or suffers an act which, by the provisions of law, works a forfeiture of his office.
(3) Against an association of persons who act as a corporation within this state without being legally incorporated.

NRS 35.010. Accordingly, quo warranto is used to determine the legality and appropriateness of the exercise or use of a public franchise or office and to determine the constitutionality of an act of a public officer or franchise without authority of law. *State ex rel. Fletcher v. Osburn,* 24 Nev. 187, 51 P. 837 (1898).

Quo warranto provides the exclusive method for challenging a person's right to hold a public office. A court of equity does not have the jurisdiction to determine rights to an office or validity of an election since such questions can be adequately determined in a court of law by a writ of quo warranto. *Johnson v. Horton,* 63 F.2d 950 (9th Cir. 1933). Quo warranto only lies for the usurping of a public office, but not to challenge a position held at the will and pleasure of another. *State ex rel. Ryan v. Cronan,* 23 Nev. 437, 49 P. 41 (1897), cited in *State ex rel. Mathews v. Murray,* 70 Nev. 116, 120, 258 P.2d 982 (1953).

When a person entitled to be declared elected as a director of a corporation institutes an action in quo warranto, and the director against whom such action is taken is ousted, such person may at any time (within one year after the date of the judgment) bring an action against the person ousted and recover the damages he sustained by reason of such usurpation. NRS 35.140.

§ 3515. — Form, content and procedure in applying for a writ of quo warranto.

Proceedings in quo warranto are civil in nature, and are thus governed by the NRCP. The recognized motions on pleadings (*e.g.,* motions to quash, strike, for a more definite statement, failure to state a claim, etc.) are available in quo warranto.

The action in quo warranto must be brought in the name of the state by the attorney general. NRS 35.030. Private counsel may pursue the action with permission of the attorney general if the attorney general determines that it is "impracticable, uneconomical or could constitute a conflict of interest" for the attorney general to actually do the work. NRS 41.03435. If the attorney general refuses to bring such action, the court may, upon application of the relator and after review of the attorney general's decision not to bring the action, allow an individual to initiate the proceeding in the name of the state upon his own relation. *State ex rel. McMillan v. Sadler,* 25 Nev. 131, 59 P. 284 (1899), cited in *State ex rel. Holland v. City of Reno,* 70 Nev. 167, 170, 262 P.2d 953 (1953), *sub nom. on reh'g, State ex rel. Matthews v. City of Reno,* 71 Nev. 208, 285 P.2d 551 (1955).

Because quo warranto necessarily involves matters of public interest, that is, of wrongs done to the state, the state is the true party in interest rather than the relator. However, allegations that the relator has some right to the office or franchise, or would otherwise have a right to sue, must appear on the application for quo warranto. The state is retained as the formal party out of a historical consideration for the origin of the proceeding. *State ex rel. Holland v. City of Reno,* 70 Nev. 167, 262 P.2d 953 (1953); *State ex rel. City of Reno v. Reno Traction Co.,* 41 Nev. 405, 171 P. 375 (1918).

An appeal may be taken from final judgment in a quo warranto action, but if the judgment ousts the defendant, then there is no stay of execution or proceedings pending such an appeal. NRS 35.270.

§ 3516. — Representative cases of writ of quo warranto: successful.

Ousting persons appointed to the Board of Regents of the University of Nevada by the Legislature, where the vacancies could only be appointed by the governor as directed by the state constitution. *State ex rel. Dickerson v. Elwell,* 73 Nev. 187, 313 P.2d 796 (1957).

Ousting from the office of district attorney of the county the acting district attorney, who had been appointed by original district attorney who had taken military leave, but whose term of office had expired. *State ex rel. Blaisdell v. Conklin,* 62 Nev. 370, 151 P.2d 626 (1944).

Invalidating the appointment of school board trustees, where school district was formed covering portions of two counties and general school law provided that the county having the greater number of children was entitled to appoint two trustees while the other county was entitled to only appoint one, but appointed two anyway. *State ex rel. Schulz v. Sweeney,* 24 Nev. 350, 55 P. 88 (1898).

Quo warranto issued where respondent was not entitled to hold office as ex officio state librarian. Respondent's right to hold office of lieutenant governor after failure to file bond required by statute and conditioned upon his performance of duties as ex officio librarian could not be pronounced vacant. Court could only declare that office of state librarian was forfeited because respondent's right to office of lieutenant governor did not depend upon performance of his duties as state librarian or upon his compliance with statutes concerning bond required of him as librarian. *State ex rel. Davenport v. Laughton,* 19 Nev. 202, 8 P. 344 (1885).

§ 3517. — Unsuccessful.

Writ of quo warranto was denied without prejudice to renewal at later date where factual grounds relied upon by respondent did not appear on the face of the complaint nor were exhibits attached thereto. *State ex rel. Holland v. City of Reno,* 70 Nev. 167, 262 P.2d 953 (1953).

Quo warranto denied in attempt to oust director of Driver's License Division of State Public Service Commission, as position was determined to not be a public office because it had not been created nor were the duties attached thereto, prescribed by law. *State ex rel. Mathews v. Murray,* 70 Nev. 116, 258 P.2d 982 (1953).

Quo warranto did not lie to oust county commissioner appointed by legislature in time of emergency or special occasion calling for extraordinary action. *State ex rel. Wichman v. Gerbig,* 55 Nev. 46, 24 P.2d 313 (1933).

Where action in quo warranto was filed against the incumbent of an office for the sole purpose of having a judicial determination as to who possessed the power of appointment to such office, writ was denied as there was no actual controversy between the parties. *State ex rel. Alexander v. McCullough,* 20 Nev. 154, 18 P. 756 (1888).

Form 35A

DISTRICT COURT

CLARK COUNTY, NEVADA

Petitioners,	))) CASE NO:) DEPT NO:) DOCKET:))))) Hearing Date:) Hearing Time:)
Respondents.	

PETITION FOR WRIT OF MANDATE

Pursuant to NRS 34.150 *et seq.,* Petitioners hereby petition this Court for the issuance of a Writ of Mandate directing Respondents to ...

This Petition is brought on the following grounds:

1.

2.

3.

4. Petitioners have suffered significant damages as a result of the actions of the Respondents.

5. A Writ of Mandate is proper to compel the performance of acts by Respondents from the offices held by Respondents and to determine damages to be awarded to the Petitioners.

6. Petitioners have no plain, speedy, or adequate remedy at law to compel the Respondents to perform their duty.

7. Petitioner's request for a Writ of Mandate is necessary in order to compel Respondents to comply with the dictates of their offices, to prevent further harm and injury to Petitioners and to compensate Petitioners for their damages.

8. This Petition is made and based upon the Exhibits attached hereto, the Affidavits appended hereto, and the Memorandum of Point and Authorities filed herewith.

WHEREFORE, Petitioners request that this Court:

1. Issue a Writ of Mandate compelling the Respondents to ...

2. Award costs, interest, attorneys fees and such other remedies as may be appropriate.

DATED this _____ day of _____, 19____.

Law Firm

VERIFICATION

Form 35B

DISTRICT COURT

CLARK COUNTY, NEVADA

	)	
	)	
	)	CASE NO.
Petitioners,	)	DEPT NO:
	)	DOCKET:
	)	
	)	
	)	
	)	
	)	Hearing Date:
Respondents.	)	Hearing Time:
	)	

MEMORANDUM OF POINTS AND AUTHORITIES IN SUPPORT OF PETITION FOR WRIT OF MANDATE

STATEMENT OF FACTS

I.

A WRIT OF MANDATE SHOULD ISSUE TO COMPEL A MUNICIPAL BODY TO DO WHAT THE LAW REQUIRES

A party is entitled to a writ of mandate when a tribunal such as the Board has failed to legally and properly discharge its obligations under state statute. NRS 34.160 provides in pertinent part as follows:

> The writ may be issued by the supreme court, a district court or a judge of the district court to compel the performance of an act which the law especially enjoins as a duty resulting from an office, trust or station;
> . . . .

The Nevada Supreme Court has ruled that a writ of mandate will issue to enforce the performance of an act which the law requires as a duty resulting from an office. *Marlette Lake Company v. Sawyer*, 79 Nev. 334, 335-36, 383 P.2d 369 (1963). *See also State ex rel. Nevada Building Authority v. Hancock*, 86 Nev. 310, 313, 468 P.2d 333 (1970).

882

II.

CONCLUSION

Petitioners respectfully request that this Court issue a writ of mandate directing Respondents to ...

DATED this _____ day of _____, 19____.

Law Firm

Form 35C

AFFIDAVIT OF

STATE OF NEVADA   )
) ss:
COUNTY OF CLARK   )

_____, being first duly sworn, deposes and says:
1.
2.
3.
4. Further affiant sayeth naught.
DATED this _____ day of _____, 19____.

_____

SUBSCRIBED AND SWORN TO before me
this ____ day of _____, 19____.

_____
NOTARY PUBLIC

Form 35D

DISTRICT COURT

CLARK COUNTY, NEVADA

Petitioners,	))) CASE NO:) DEPT NO:) DOCKET:))))) Hearing Date:
Respondents.	) Hearing Time:)

ORDER THAT ALTERNATIVE WRIT OF MANDATE ISSUE

The Court having read and reviewed the verified Petition for Writ of Mandate filed herein by Petitioner, the Affidavits appended thereto and the Memorandum of Points and Authorities in support thereof, it appearing to the Court that Petitioner has no plain, speedy and adequate remedy in the ordinary course of law, the Court being fully advised in the premises and good cause appearing,

IT IS HEREBY ORDERED that an Alternative Writ of Mandate issue herein, directing Respondents to ...

DATED this ____ day of _____, 19____.

_____
DISTRICT COURT JUDGE

Submitted by:
Law Firm

Form 35E

DISTRICT COURT

CLARK COUNTY, NEVADA

Petitioners,	))) CASE NO:) DEPT NO:) DOCKET:))))
Respondents.	) Hearing Date:) Hearing Time:)

ALTERNATIVE WRIT OF MANDATE

TO:

GREETINGS:

   WHEREAS, Petitioners in the above-entitled action having duly filed herein its Petition for Writ of Mandate, it appearing to the above-entitled Court that an Alternative Writ of Mandate should issue and that said Petitioner has no other plain, speedy or adequate remedy in the ordinary course of law, now therefore,

   YOU ARE HEREBY COMMANDED to ...

   WITNESS THE HONORABLE _____, Judge of the District Court of the State of Nevada, and attested by my hand and seal this _____ day of _____, 19__.

Clerk of the Court

By: _____

Deputy Clerk

Submitted by:

Law Firm

Form 35F

DISTRICT COURT

CLARK COUNTY, NEVADA

	)	
	)	
	)	CASE NO:
Petitioners,	)	DEPT NO:
	)	DOCKET:
	)	
	)	
	)	
	)	
	)	Hearing Date:
Respondents.	)	Hearing Time:
	)	

ORDER THAT PERMANENT WRIT OF MANDATE ISSUE

The Court having read and reviewed the verified Petition for Writ of Mandate filed herein by Petitioner, the Affidavits appended thereto and the Memorandum of Points and Authorities in support thereof, it appearing to the Court that Petitioner has no plain, speedy and adequate remedy in the ordinary course of law, the Court being fully advised in the premises and good cause appearing,

IT IS HEREBY ORDERED that a Permanent Writ of Mandate issue herein, directing Respondents to ...

DATED this _____ day of _____, 19__.

_____
DISTRICT COURT JUDGE

Submitted by:
Law Firm

Form 35G

DISTRICT COURT

CLARK COUNTY, NEVADA

Petitioners,	))) CASE NO:) DEPT NO:) DOCKET:))))) Hearing Date:
Respondents.	) Hearing Time:)

PERMANENT WRIT OF MANDATE

TO:

WHEREAS, Petitioners in the above-entitled action having duly filed herein their Petition for Writ of Mandate, the parties having filed Points and Authorities in support of their positions and the Court having heard argument, and it appearing to the said Court that a permanent Writ of Mandate should issue and that said Petitioner has no other plain, speedy or adequate remedy in the ordinary course of law, and the Court having issued an order directing the issuance of a Permanent Writ of Mandate, now therefore,

YOU ARE HEREBY COMMANDED on or before the _____ day of _____, 19__, to ...

WITNESS THE HONORABLE _____, Judge of the District Court of the State of Nevada, and attested by my hand and seal this ____ day of _____, 19__.

Clerk of the Court

By: _____
Deputy Clerk

Submitted by:
Law Firm

INDEX

A

ABUSE OF PROCESS.
Attachment.
  Cause of action for improper
    attachment, §2616.

ACTIONS.
Abatement of actions, §312.
Bonds, surety.
  Nonresident costs bond, §311.
Class actions, §522.
Classification of actions, §303.
Commencement of action, §304.
  Premature commencement, §305.
Common law.
  Distinction between common law and
    statutory actions, §303.
  Forms of action under common law,
    §302.
Conditions precedent, §306.
  Demand, §308.
  Excuses for nonperformance, §309.
  Notice, §307.
  Pleading performance of conditions
    precedent, §310.
Consolidation of actions, §§1901 to 1910.
  See CONSOLIDATION OF ACTIONS.
Derivative actions by shareholders, §523.
Dismissal of actions.
  See DISMISSAL OF ACTIONS.
Ex contractu and ex delicto actions.
  Distinction, §303.
Form of action, §302.
Generally, §301.
In personam and in rem actions.
  Distinction, §303.
Judgments.
  Duration of right to action on judgment.
    Generally, §2439.
    Limitation upon execution, §2440.
    Revival of judgment, §2441.
Legal and equitable actions.
  Distinction, §303.
Nonresidents.
  Costs bond, §311.
Notice.
  Condition precedent to bringing action,
    §307.

ACTIONS—Cont'd
Parties, §§501 to 525.
  See PARTIES.
Removal, §§701 to 712.
  See REMOVAL OF ACTIONS.
Severance of actions, §§1901, 1911 to
  1914.
  See SEVERANCE OF ACTIONS.
Shareholders' derivative actions, §523.
Splitting causes of action, §313.
Survival of actions, §312.
Venue, §§601 to 624.
  See VENUE.

ADDITUR, §2512.

ADMINISTRATORS OF ESTATES.
General provisions.
  See EXECUTORS AND
    ADMINISTRATORS.

ADMISSIONS.
Requests for admission.
  Pretrial discovery, §1632.
Trial.
  Use of party admissions, §2252.

ADOPTION.
Decedents' estates.
  Inheritance by adopted children, §3404.

ADR, §§2101 to 2128.
See ALTERNATIVE DISPUTE
  RESOLUTION.

AFFIDAVITS.
Attachment.
  Application for writ, §2605.
  Form, Form 26A.
Claim and delivery.
  Application to be filed with supporting
    affidavit, §2628.
Continuances.
  Motions for continuance.
    Affidavit in support, §2217.
Default judgments.
  Form of affidavit in support of entry of,
    Form 10E.
Garnishment.
  Application for writ, §2622.
Judges.
  Disqualification procedure, §211.

889

ATTORNEYS AT LAW—Cont'd

Service of process.
  Documents to be served on attorney, §219.
Substitution, §218.
Trial.
  Closing argument, §§2287 to 2290.
  Conduct at trial, §2291.
    Consequences of misconduct, §2292.
  Opening statements, §§2233 to 2236.
Withdrawal, §218.
  Rights and duties on, §220.
    Return of files, §221.

ATTORNEYS' FEES.

Alternative dispute resolution.
  Arbitration by agreement, §2108.
Decedents' estates.
  See ATTORNEYS AT LAW.
Default judgments, §1021.
Injunctions.
  Wrongful injunction, §2816.
Liens for, §222.
Motions for, §2529.

B

BANKRUPTCY.

Enforcement of judgments, §2728.

BIFURCATION OF TRIAL.

Severance of actions generally, §§1901, 1911 to 1914.
  See SEVERANCE OF ACTIONS.

BONDS, SURETY.

Actions.
  Nonresident costs bond, §311.
Attachment.
  Liability of sureties, §2617.
  Written undertaking and bond requirements, §2612.
Bid bonds.
  Contractors, §3203.
Claim and delivery.
  Written undertaking and bond provisions, §2632.
Contractors.
  Bid bonds, §3203.
  Generally, §§3201, 3202.
  Payment bonds, §3205.
  Performance bonds, §3204.
Costs.
  Nonresident costs bond, §311.
Executors and administrators, §3427.
  Special administrators, §3422.

BONDS, SURETY—Cont'd

Guardians, §3306.
  Acknowledgment of blocked account, §3306.
  Form, Form 33M.
  Winding up of guardianship affairs.
    Exoneration of bond, §3310.
Injunctions.
  Proceedings against surety, §2817.
  Security requirements, §2806.
  Wrongful injunctions.
    Recovery limited to amount of bond, §2816.
Removal of actions.
  Procedure after removal, §711.
Testamentary trusts.
  Trustee, §3491.

BURDEN OF PROOF.

Discovery.
  Attorney work product.
    Burden on party seeking, §1616.
Summary judgment.
  Initial burden, §§1717, 1718.
  Quantum of proof, §1722.
  Shift of burden to opposing party, §1719.
    Cannot rest on pleadings, §§1720, 1721.

C

CALIFORNIA LAW.

Sources of Nevada law, §110.

CERTIORARI.

Application for writ, §3503.
Distinguished from other remedies, §3502.
Essential elements required for issuance, §3502.
Injunctions.
  Review of orders, §2814.
Nature of remedy, §3502.
Receivers.
  Extraordinary relief when court exceeds jurisdiction, §3009.
Representative cases.
  Successful applications, §3504.
  Unsuccessful applications, §3505.

CHANGE OF VENUE.

See VENUE.

CHILD CUSTODY.

Venue, §604.

CLAIM AND DELIVERY.

Affidavits.
  Application to be filed with supporting affidavit, §2628.

CLAIM AND DELIVERY—Cont'd

Application for, §2628.

    Hearing on, §2631.

        Issuance of writ of possession without hearing, §2635.

Bonds, surety.

    Written undertaking and bond provisions, §2632.

Commencement of action, §2626.

Complaints.

    Filing of complaint, §2626.

Forms.

    Order to show cause, Form 26N.

    Affidavit in support, Form 26M.

    Application for, Form 26L.

    Temporary writ of possession, Form 26P.

    Order granting, Form 26O.

Generally, §§2601, 2625.

Order to show cause, §2629.

Forms, Forms 26L to 26N.

Service of process, §2630.

Third-party claims, §2633.

Time for, §2627.

Writ of possession, §2634.

Application for claim and delivery by writ of possession. See within this heading, "Application for."

    Forms.

        Temporary writ of possession, Form 26P.

        Order granting, Form 26O.

    Issuance without hearing, §2635.

CLAIMS AGAINST THE STATE.

Parties.

    Capacity of governmental agencies to sue or be sued, §512.

CLASS ACTIONS, §522.

Consolidation of actions, §1909.

COMMON LAW.

Actions.

    Distinction between common law and statutory actions, §303.

    Forms of action under common law, §302.

Sources of Nevada law, §103.

COMMUNITY PROPERTY, §3404.

Simultaneous death act, §3405.

COMPARATIVE NEGLIGENCE.

Jury.

    Juror consistency in action involving comparative negligence, §2334.

    Settlement with other defendant.

        Jury not to be informed of existence or amount, §2342.

    Special verdict, §2341.

COMPLAINTS.

Answers, §§1301 to 1306.

Claim and delivery.

    Filing of complaint, §2626.

Commencement of civil action, §304.

Default.

    Amended complaint upon default. Effect, §1004.

Receivers.

    Commencement of appointment procedure, §3003.

Third-party practice.

    Time for filing third-party complaint, §1502.

Types of pleadings, §802.

Unlawful detainer.

    Form, Form 26X.

CONFLICTS OF INTEREST.

Attorneys at law, §224.

CONSOLIDATION OF ACTIONS.

Appeals.

    Review of order granting or denying motion, §1910.

Arbitration proceedings, §1908.

Attorneys at law.

    Lead counsel.

        Appointment, §1906.

Class actions, §1909.

Generally, §§1901, 1902.

History of rule, §1903.

Judges.

    Challenges of judges, §1906.

Jury.

    Challenges of jurors, §1906.

Lead counsel.

    Appointment, §1906.

Motions, §1905.

Procedure, §1905.

Property taxes.

    Recovery of taxes paid under protest on property located in more than one county, §1907.

Purpose of rule, §1903.

Types of consolidation, §1904.

CONTEMPT.

Executions.

    Disobedience of orders in supplementary proceedings, §2732.

Inherent jurisdiction of courts, §412.

Injunctions.

    Disobedience or resistance to order, §2815.

Receivers.

    Distribution of property without court order, §3006.

CONTEMPT—Cont'd
Subpoenas.
Failure to obey subpoena, §2227.
Witnesses.
Failure to obey subpoena, §2227.

CONTEST OF WILLS, §§3428 to 3431.
See WILLS.

CONTINUANCES.
Affidavits.
Motions for continuance.
Affidavit in support, §2217.
Conditions upon granting of, §2220.
Generally, §2216.
Grounds, §2219.
Motions, §2217.
Stipulations, §2218.

CONTRACTORS.
Bonds, surety.
Bid bonds, §3203.
Generally, §§3201, 3202.
Payment bonds, §3205.
Performance bonds, §3204.
Liens.
Mechanics' liens, §§3201, 3206 to 3210.
See MECHANICS' LIENS.

CONTRACTS.
Executors and administrators.
Conveyances to complete contract,
§3467.
Venue.
Performance in place other than
residence, §604.

CONTRIBUTION.
Third-party practice.
Substantive law bases for third-party
claims, §1504.

CORPORATIONS.
Parties.
Capacity to sue or be sued, §513.
Receivers.
Appointment to manage corporation,
§3003.
Defenses against, §3004.
Claims.
Filing with receiver, §3007.
Winding up receivership, §3008.
Service of process.
Methods of service on.
Foreign corporations, §908.
Venue.
Residence, §608.

COSTS.
Alternative dispute resolution.
Mandatory non-binding court annexed
arbitration.
Fees and costs of arbitrators, §2127.
Bonds, surety.
Nonresident costs bond, §311.
Default judgments, §1021.
Memorandum of costs and
disbursements.
Form, Form 10G.
Dismissal of actions.
Previously-dismissed action, §2013.
Enforcement of judgments, §2726.
Injunctions.
Wrongful injunctions, §2816.
Judgments.
Inclusion in judgments, §2429.
Mistrial.
Imposition against party who has caused
mistrial, §2295.
Motion to tax costs, §2530.

COUNTERCLAIMS.
Answers.
Amendments to add counterclaims,
§1405.
Compulsory counterclaims, §1403.
Dismissal, §2012.
Voluntary dismissal of action with
pending counterclaim, §2004.
Generally, §1401.
Judgments.
Separate judgments, §1410.
Limitation of actions, §1411.
Parties.
Who may plead a cross-demand, §1406.
Permissive counterclaims, §1402.
Replies.
Generally, §1301.
Time for, §1302.
Types of pleadings, §802.
Separate trials and judgments, §1410.
Service of process, §1404.
State of Nevada.
Counterclaims against, §1407.
Statute of limitations, §1411.
Third-party defendants, §1506.
Trial.
Separate trials, §1410.

COUNTIES.
Service of process.
Methods of service on, §912.
Venue.
Actions by or against counties, §604.

CCURT SYSTEM.
Composition, §215.

DECLARATORY JUDGMENTS
—Cont'd
Nature of declaratory relief, §3102.
Nevada gaming commission.
Right to seek declarations, §3113.
News media.
Restraints on news media, §3112.
Other remedies.
Seeking in tandem with, §3109.
Parties to proceedings, §3111.
Requirements under uniform act.
Adverse interests, §3105.
Generally, §3103.
Justiciable controversy, §3104.
Legally protectible interest, §3106.
Ripeness, §3107.
Ripeness.
Requirements under uniform act, §3107.
Rules of civil procedure.
Applicability to proceedings, §3111.
Judicial confirmation law, §3115.
Special grants of declaratory power, §3115.
Summary judgment, §1767.
Uniform act, §3101.
Requirements for declaratory relief under, §§3103 to 3107.

DEFAULT.
Application for default, §1008.
Complaints.
Amended complaint upon default.
Effect, §1004.
Entry of default, §1003.
Amendment of complaint after default entered.
Effect, §1004.
Application for, §1008.
Form, Form 10B.
Default against any party, §1005.
Entry as a sanction, §1007.
Failure to plead or otherwise defend, §1006.
Failure to plead or otherwise defend.
Entry of default for, §1006.
Form of default, Form 10C.
Generally, §§1001, 1002.
Judgments by default, §1009.
Affidavit in support of entry of default judgment.
Form, Form 10E.
Appearance, §1013.
Appearances which may inure to benefit of codefendants, §1033.
Notice and hearing, §§1018, 1019.
Application for, §1010.
Form, Form 10D.

DEFAULT—Cont'd
Judgments by default—Cont'd
Attorneys' fees, §1021.
Clerk of court.
Entry of judgment by, §1011.
Costs, §1021.
Memorandum of costs and disbursements.
Form, Form 10G.
Court.
Entry of default judgment by, §1014.
Discovery.
Sanctions for failure to make discovery, §1637.
Form of default judgment, Form 10F.
Generally, §1009.
Infants and incompetents, §§1015, 1016.
Military service.
Defendants in, §§1015, 1017.
Setting aside default judgment, §§1022, 1025.
Defendant not personally served, §1032.
Fraud, misrepresentation or other misconduct, §1028.
Independent actions to set aside, §1031.
Meritorious defense requirement, §1024.
Mistake, inadvertence, surprise or excusable neglect, §§1026, 1027.
Satisfaction or release of judgment, §1030.
Void judgment, §1029.
State of Nevada.
Default judgment against state, §1020.
Sum certain, §1012.
Notice.
Appearance by defaulting party.
Notice of application for default judgment, §§1018, 1019.
Intent to take default.
Form, Form 10A.
Setting aside default judgments. See within this heading, "Judgments by default."

DEFENSES.
Answers.
Affirmative defenses, §1306.
Failure to join a party under Rule 19.
Raising by motion, §1209.
Failure to state a claim.
Raising by motion, §1210.

DEFENSES—Cont'd
Mechanics' liens.
  Owners' assertion of contractual
    defenses, §3210.
Motions.
  Defensive motions generally, §§1201 to
    1213.
  See MOTIONS.
Pleadings.
  Affirmative defenses, §806.
  Raising defenses by denials, §805.
Receivers.
  Opposition to appointment of receiver,
    §3004.
Summary judgment.
  Absence of clearly established defense.
    Denial of summary judgment in favor
      of defendant, §1737.
Third-party practice, §1505.

DEPOSITIONS.
Before action, §1628.
Before trial.
  Generally, §1624.
  Oral deposition, §1625.
  Out-of-state depositions, §1627.
  Written depositions, §1626.
Pending appeal, §1628.
Quashing service of process.
  Depositions upon motion to quash,
    §1205.
Trial.
  Before trial, §§1624 to 1627.
  Use in place of live testimony, §2221.
  Use of depositions, §2250.

DIRECTED VERDICT.
Constitutionality, §2270.
Generally, §§2262, 2269.
Judgment n.o.v. compared, §2272.
Motions, §2269.
  Effect of moving or failing to move,
    §2273.
Standard for granting, §2271.

DISCOVERY.
Additional discovery.
  Attorney work product, §1615.
    Burden on party seeking discovery,
      §1616.
  Frequency and extent of use, §1611.
  Generally, §1609.
  Insurance agreements, §1614.
  Nonprivileged matters, §1613.
  Purpose, §1610.
  Relevant matters, §1612.
  Scope, §1610.
  Timings, §1611.
  Trial preparation, §1615.

DISCOVERY—Cont'd
Alternative dispute resolution.
  Mandatory non-binding court annexed
    arbitration, §2120.
Attorney work product, §1615.
Case conferences.
  Mandatory discovery at early case
    conferences. See within this
    heading, "Mandatory discovery at
    early case conferences."
Default judgments.
  Sanctions for failure to make discovery,
    §1637.
Discovery commissioners, §1608.
Dismissal of actions.
  Sanctions for failure to make discovery,
    §1637.
Entry upon land for inspection.
  Pretrial discovery, §1630.
Expert witnesses.
  Expert witnesses expected to be used at
    trial, §1619.
  Expert witnesses neither specially
    retained nor consulted, §1622.
  Expert witnesses not expected to be
    used at trial, §1620.
  Expert witnesses not specially retained
    but informally consulted in
    preparation for trial, §1621.
  Fees of expert witness, §1623.
  Generally, §1618.
Failure to make discovery.
  Sanctions, §1637.
Filing of discovery requests and responses,
  §1636.
Generally, §1601.
Insurance.
  Liability insurance agreements, §1614.
Interrogatories.
  Pretrial discovery, §1629.
Mandatory discovery at early case
  conferences, §1603.
  Case conference disputes, §1606.
  Case conference reports, §1605.
  Complex litigation, §1607.
  Discovery exchange, §1604.
  Generally, §1602.
Motions.
  Use of discovery at hearing of motions,
    §1636.
Orders.
  Protective orders, §1633.
Physical and mental examinations.
  Pretrial discovery, §1631.
Privileges.
  Additional discovery.
    Nonprivileged matters, §1613.

900

E

ENGLISH COMMON LAW.
Primary sources of Nevada law, §103.

ESCHEAT.
Decedents' estates, §3404.

ETHICS.
Attorneys at law.
  Establishment of ethical standards,
    §217.
Judges.
  Establishment of ethical standards,
    §215.
Jury.
  Pretrial investigation of jurors, §2316.

EVICTION.
Unlawful detainer generally, §§2601, 2636
  to 2644.
  See UNLAWFUL DETAINER.

EVIDENCE.
Admission of evidence at trial.
  Exclusion, §2254.
    Offers of proof on excluded evidence,
      §2257.
  Generally, §2254.
  Limiting instructions, §2260.
  Motions in limine and memoranda on
    admissibility, §2255.
  Motions to strike, §2258.
  Objections, §2258.
    Continuing objections, §2259.
    Record of proceedings to preserve
      review, §2256.
    Rephrasing of objectionable questions,
      §2261.
Amendment of pleadings to conform to the
  evidence, §§814, 2274.
Discovery.
  See DISCOVERY.
Motions in limine.
  Admissibility disputes, §2255.
  Use to seek admission of evidence,
    §1812.
Newly discovered evidence.
  Grounds for new trial, §2510.
New trial.
  Grounds for new trial.
    Newly discovered evidence, §2510.
Subpoenas.
  See SUBPOENAS.
Taking of evidence at trial, §2238.
  Admissions, §2252.
  Depositions, §2250.
  Discovery-generated materials, §2248.
  Documentary or other tangible evidence,
    §2244.

EVIDENCE—Cont'd
Taking of evidence at trial—Cont'd
  Examination of witnesses, §§2239 to
    2243.
  Facts admitted in pleadings, §2245.
  Interrogatories, §2251.
  Judicial notice, §2247.
  Presumptions, §2248.
  Stipulations, §2246.
  Views, §§2253, 2327.
Witnesses.
  General provisions.
    See WITNESSES.
  Subpoenas, §§2221 to 2229.
    See SUBPOENAS.

EXECUTIONS.
Arrest.
  Fraudulent conduct or concealment of
    assets, §2732.
Attachment.
  Property or claims attached as
    prejudgment remedy, §2714.
Contempt.
  Disobedience of orders in supplementary
    proceedings, §2732.
Exemptions, §2711.
Forms.
  Instructions to sheriff, Form 27D.
  Partner's interest.
    Charging order, Form 27N.
      Affidavit in support of, Form 27M.
      Motion for, Form 27L.
  Stock certificates.
    Affidavit, Form 27J.
    Order for delivery of, Form 27K.
    Motion for, Form 27I.
  Supplementary proceedings.
    Examination of judgment debtor.
      Ex parte order for motion allowing,
        Form 27G.
      Order allowing, Form 27H.
      Motion for, Form 27E.
      Order for, Form 27F.
  Writ of execution, Form 27C.
Fraudulent transfers, §2724.
Garnishment.
  Bank accounts.
    Seizure by writ of attachment in aid
      of execution, §2720.
  Garnishment in aid of execution, §2714.
    Bank accounts may be seized by,
      §2720.
  Property or claims garnished as
    prejudgment remedy, §2714.
Homestead exemption, §2711.
Intangible property interest.
  Levy against and sale, §2721.

901

FORMS—Cont'd

Attachment—Cont'd

Ex parte motion for order to show cause why prejudgment writ of attachment and garnishment should not issue after notice, Form 26D.

Instructions to sheriff, Form 26J.

Notice of execution, Form 26C.

Order directing issuance of prejudgment writ of attachment and garnishment, Form 26G.

Without notice, Form 26F.

Order to show cause, Form 26E.

Third-party claim, Form 26I.

Writ of attachment, Form 26H.

Change of venue.

Affidavit in support of motion for change of venue, Form 6C.

Change of venue as matter of right, Forms 6D, 6E.

Discretionary change of venue, Form 6F.

Demand for mandatory change of venue, Form 6A.

Motion for change of venue, Form 6B.

Order changing venue, Form 6G.

Claim and delivery.

Order to show cause, Form 26N.

Affidavit in support, Form 26M.

Application for, Form 26L.

Temporary writ of possession, Form 26P.

Order granting, Form 26O.

Decedents' estates.

Affidavit of mailing, Form 34K.

Affidavit terminating joint tenancy, Form 34CC.

Claims of creditors.

Notice to creditors, Forms 34S, 34T.

Proof of mailing, Form 34U.

Discharge of executor.

Decree of discharge, Form 34BB.

Disclaimer of interest in property, Form 34GG.

Inventory and appraisement and record of value, Form 34V.

Letters of administration, Form 34O.

Letters of administration with will annexed, Form 34P.

Letters testamentary, Form 34Q.

Notice of hearings, Forms 34H to 34J.

Order admitting will to probate and issuing letters testamentary, Form 34L.

Order appointing administrator in summary administration, Form 34N.

FORMS—Cont'd

Decedents' estates—Cont'd

Order for probate of estate, for issuance of letters testamentary and summary administration of estate, Form 34M.

Order settling first and final account, for approval of attorneys' fees and decree of final distribution, Form 34Y.

Petition for probate of estate, for issuance of letters testamentary and for summary administration of estate, Form 34B.

Petition for probate of will and for issuance of letters testamentary, Form 34A.

Petition for settlement of first and final account, for approval of attorneys' fees and for decree of final distribution, Form 34F.

Petitions for letters of administration and summary administration, Form 34D.

Petition to sell stocks, Form 34E.

Petition to set aside estate without administration, Form 34C.

Receipt of distribution, Form 34AA.

Renunciation of appointment as executor, Form 34X.

Report of executor or administrator, Form 34Z.

Return of sale of real property and petition for approval and confirmation of sale, Form 34W.

Sale of estate assets.

Confirmation of sale of real property. Order confirming, Form 34EE.

Petition for, Form 34FF.

Statement of permanent address, Form 34R.

Transfer by affidavit, Form 34DD.

Default, Form 10C.

Application for entry of default, Form 10B.

Judgments by default, Form 10F.

Affidavit in support of entry of default judgment, Form 10E.

Application for default judgment, Form 10D.

Memorandum of costs and disbursements, Form 10G.

Notice of intent to take default, Form 10A.

Enforcement of judgments.

Executions. See within this heading, "Executions."

FORMS—Cont'd

Removal of actions.
Notice of removal, Forms 7A, 7B, 7D.
Joinder in notice of removal of civil action, Form 7C.
Satisfaction of judgment, Form 27O.
Unlawful detainer.
Complaint for unlawful detainer, Form 26X.
Notice.
Affidavit of service, Form 26T.
Five-day notice to pay rent or quit premises, Form 26R.
Thirty-day notice to quit premises, Form 26Q.
Three-day notice to quit, Form 26S.
Summary eviction.
Affidavit of complaint, Form 26U.
Instructions, Forms 26W-1, 26W-2.
Order for, Form 26V.
Writ of restitution, Form 26EE.
Notice of execution on writ of restitution, Form 26DD.
Temporary writ of restitution, Form 26CC.
Ex parte motion for order to show cause why temporary writ of restitution should not issue, Form 26Y.
Order directing issuance, Form 26BB.
Order to show cause why temporary writ of restitution should not issue, Form 26AA.
Affidavit in support, Form 26Z.

FORUM NON CONVENIENS.

Dismissal for, §621.
Factors for application of doctrine, §622.
Mandamus as remedy for denial of motion, §623.

FRAUD.

Enforcement of judgments.
Fraudulent transfers, §2724.
Executions.
Arrest.
Fraudulent conduct or concealment of assets, §2732.
Pleading special matters, §808.
Relief from judgment or order.
Grounds, §2522.

FRIVOLOUS PLEADINGS.

Attorney's signature as certification that pleading well grounded, §812.

G

GAMING COMMISSION.

Declaratory judgments.
Right to seek declarations, §3113.

GARNISHMENT.

Affidavits.
Application for writ, §2622.
Application for writ.
Affidavit, §2622.
Contents of writ, §2623.
Effect, §2621.
Executions.
Bank accounts.
Seizure by writ of attachment in aid of execution, §2720.
Garnishment in aid of execution, §2714.
Bank accounts may be seized by, §2720.
Property or claims garnished as prejudgment remedy, §2714.
Form of writ, Form 26K.
Generally, §§2601, 2620.
Issuance of writ, §2623.
Liability of garnishee, §2624.
Time for issuance, §2621.

GUARDIAN AD LITEM.

Parties.
Infants or incompetents, §511.

GUARDIANS.

Accountings, §3309.
First account and report of guardian and petition for fees, Form 33P.
Adult ward guardianships, §3305.
Appointment.
Citation to appear and show cause, §3306.
Adult ward.
Form, Form 33H.
Minor ward.
Form, Form 33I.
Order to issue citation.
Form, Form 33G.
Jurisdiction, §3302.
Letters of guardianship, §3306.
Form, Form 33L.
Order appointing guardian, §3306.
Form, Form 33K.
Temporary guardian, Form 33D.
Petition, §3306.
Form, Form 33F.
Summary guardianship, Form 33E.
Temporary guardian, Form 33C.

LIMITED LIABILITY COMPANIES.
Parties.
  Capacity to sue or be sued, §514.
Service of process.
  Methods of service on, §910.

LONG-ARM STATUTE, §914.

M

MAIL.
Service of process.
  Pleading subsequent to complaint, §919.

MALICIOUS PROSECUTION.
Attachment.
  Cause of action for improper
    attachment, §2616.

MANDAMUS.
Application for writ, §3507.
Forms.
  Affidavit, Form 35C.
  Alternative writ of mandate, Form 35E.
  Order that alternative writ of
    mandate issue, Form 35D.
  Permanent writ of mandate, Form 35G.
  Order that permanent writ of
    mandate issue, Form 35F.
  Petition for writ of mandate, Form 35A.
  Memorandum of points and
    authorities in support of, Form
    35B.
Forum non conveniens.
  Remedy for denial of motion for
    dismissal, §623.
Nature of remedy, §3506.
Receivers.
  Petition to compel performance of act,
    §3009.
Representative cases.
  Successful applications, §3508.
  Unsuccessful applications, §3509.
Requirements for issuance of writ, §3506.
Scope of writ, §3506.

MASTERS, §2296.
Reports, §2297.

MECHANICS' LIENS.
Applicability of statute, §§3201, 3207.
Defenses.
  Owners' assertion of contractual
    defenses, §3210.
Generally, §§3201, 3206, 3207.
Notice.
  Owner.
    Notice of non-responsibility, §3210.
  Statutory requirements as to notice and
    recording, §3208.

MECHANICS' LIENS—Cont'd
Owners' remedies, §3210.
Priority, §§3207, 3209.
Recordation.
  Statutory requirements, §3208.

MEDIATION, §2113.

MILITARY SERVICE.
Default judgments.
  Defendants in military service, §§1015,
    1017.

MINORS.
Default judgments against infants and
  incompetents, §§1015, 1016.
Guardians.
  General provisions, §§3301 to 3310.
  See GUARDIANS.
Parties.
  Capacity to sue or be sued, §511.
Service of process.
  Methods of service on, §911.

MISTRIAL, §2295.

MORTGAGES.
Executors and administrators.
  Property of estate, §3465.
Receivers.
  Procedure for mortgagee to seek
    appointment of receiver, §3003.

MOTIONS.
Affidavits, §1107.
  Contents of affidavits, §1108.
  Defective affidavits, §1109.
  Service of notice of motion.
    Forms of affidavit of service, Forms
      11G, 11H.
  Summary judgment.
    Form of defendant's affidavit in
      support of motion of summary
      judgment, Form 11C.
Alternative dispute resolution.
  Arbitration by agreement.
    Motion to compel or stay arbitration,
      §2104.
  Mandatory non-binding court annexed
    arbitration.
    Motions during arbitration, §2119.
Amendment or alteration of judgment,
  §2517.
Change of venue.
  Demand and motion.
    See VENUE.
Clerical mistakes in judgments or orders.
  Relief from, §§2518, 2519.
Clerk's authority to grant motion, §1127.
Consolidation of actions, §1905.
Contents, §1104.

RECEIVERS—Cont'd
Forms—Cont'd
Claims.
Order requiring presentation and filing of claims, Form 30C.
Application by receiver for, Form 30B.
Proof of claim, Form 30F.
First report of receiver, Form 30E.
Order approving, Form 30D.
Intervention.
Motion by creditor to intervene as defendant, Form 30H.
Generally, §3001.
Intervention.
Motion by creditor to intervene as defendant.
Form, Form 30H.
Liabilities, §§3005, 3006.
Mandamus.
Petition to compel performance of act, §3009.
Mortgages.
Procedure for mortgagee to seek appointment of receiver, §3003.
Nature of remedy, §§3001, 3002.
Orders.
Forms.
Order appointing receiver, Form 30J.
Order approving first report of receiver, Form 30D.
Order requiring presentation and filing of claims, Form 30C.
Partnerships.
Appointment of receiver involving partnership disputes, §3003.
Powers, §3005.
Prohibition, writ of.
Petition to prohibit proceedings, §3009.
Property.
Distribution without court order.
Contempt, §3006.
Duty to control and take possession, §3005.
Qualifications, §3003.
Reports.
First report of receiver.
Form, Form 30E.
Order approving.
Form, Form 30D.
Venue.
Appointment proceedings, §3003.
Winding up receivership, §3008.

RECUSAL.
Voluntary recusal by judge, §205.

RELIEF FROM JUDGMENT OR ORDER.
Motion for.
Appellate review, §2526.
Grounds for relief.
Fraud, §2522.
Misrepresentation or other misconduct, §2522.
Mistake, inadvertence, surprise or excusable neglect, §2521.
Satisfaction, release or discharge of judgment, §2524.
Void judgment, §2523.
History of rule, §2520.
Purpose and scope of rule, §2520.
Time for motion, §2525.

REMITTITUR, §2513.

REMOVAL OF ACTIONS.
Bonds, surety.
Procedure after removal, §711.
Defendant.
Right of removal as belonging to, §707.
Determination of desirability of removal.
Factors, §708.
Diversity removal, §704.
Federal claim removal, §705.
Generally, §701.
Joinder.
Forms.
Joinder in notice of removal of civil action, Form 7C.
Jury.
Procedure after removal, §711.
Nonremovable cases, §706.
Notice.
Filing of notice of removal, §709.
Time for, §710.
Forms, Forms 7A, 7B, 7D.
Joinder in notice of removal of civil action, Form 7C.
Procedure, §709.
Post-removal procedure, §711.
Remand, §712.
Removable cases, §703.
Statutes permitting, §702.

REVISED UNIFORM PRINCIPAL AND INCOME ACT.
Testamentary trusts.
Applicability of act, §3495.

RULE AGAINST PERPETUITIES.
Testamentary trusts, §3499.

S

SATISFACTION OF JUDGMENTS.
Effect, §2455.
Entry of satisfaction, §2454.
Generally, §2452.
How satisfied, §2453.
Payment, §2453.

SEPARATE TRIALS.
Severance of actions generally, §§1901, 1911 to 1914.
See SEVERANCE OF ACTIONS.

SERVICE OF PROCESS.
Affidavits.
Return of service, §918.
Attorneys at law.
Documents to be served on attorney, §219.
Authority to serve process, §904.
Claim and delivery, §2630.
Corporations.
Methods of service on.
Domestic corporations, §907.
Foreign corporations, §908.
Counterclaims, §1404.
Counties.
Methods of service on, §912.
District courts.
Challenging district court's decision on, §922.
Executors and administrators.
Substituted service, §3439.
Generally, §901.
Guardians.
Order appointing guardian.
Service on ward, §3306.
Service on wards, §911.
Incompetent persons.
Service on, §911.
Issuance of process, §902.
Jury.
Summoning jurors.
Serving prospective jurors, §2309.
Limitation of actions.
Tolling period, §921.
Limited liability companies.
Methods of service on, §910.
Long-arm statute, §914.
Mail.
Pleading subsequent to complaint, §919.
Methods of service, §905.
Corporations.
Domestic corporations, §907.
Foreign corporations, §908.
Counties and municipalities, §912.
Limited liability companies, §910.

SERVICE OF PROCESS—Cont'd
Methods of service—Cont'd
Limited partnerships, §909.
Minors, incompetent persons and wards, §911.
Personal service, §906.
Substituted service, §913.
Publication, §913.
Minors.
Methods of service on, §911.
Motions.
Motion to quash service of process, §§1203 to 1206.
Notice of motion, §1105.
Affidavit of service.
Forms, Forms 11G, 11H.
Certificates of service.
Forms, Forms 11D, 11E.
Receipt of copy.
Form, Form 11F.
Motor vehicle operators, §915.
Municipalities.
Methods of service on, §912.
Orders, §1122.
Partnerships.
Limited partnerships.
Service on, §909.
Personal service, §906.
Substituted service, §913.
Pleading subsequent to complaint, §919.
Products liability, §916.
Prohibition, writ of.
Challenging district court's decision on service, §922.
Publication, §913.
Quashing service of process.
Motion to quash, §§1203 to 1206.
Return of service, §918.
Statutory service, §913.
Subpoenas, §2225.
Third-party practice, §917.
Time for, §§903, 920.
Wills.
Contests.
Pre-probate.
Citation, §3428.

SETTLEMENT BEFORE TRIAL, §2215.

SEVERANCE OF ACTIONS.
Appeals.
Review of order granting or denying separate trials, §1914.
Generally, §§1901, 1911.
History of rules, §1912.
Motions, §1913.
Procedure, §1913.

THIRD-PARTY PRACTICE—Cont'd
Time for filing third-party complaint,
§1502.
Warranty.
Substantive law bases for third-party
claims, §1504.
When assertion of third-party claim
appropriate, §1503.

TRIAL.
Admissions.
Use of party admissions, §2252.
Attorneys at law.
Closing argument, §§2287 to 2290.
Conduct at trial, §2291.
Consequences of misconduct, §2292.
Opening statements, §§2233 to 2236.
Bifurcation of trial.
Severance of actions generally, §§1901,
1911 to 1914.
See SEVERANCE OF ACTIONS.
Closing argument.
Ethical considerations, §2289.
Generally, §2287.
Objections to argument, §2290.
Purpose, §2288.
Scope, §2288.
Continuances, §§2216 to 2220.
See CONTINUANCES.
Counterclaims.
Separate trials, §1410.
Defined, §2202.
Depositions.
Before trial, §§1624 to 1627.
Use in place of live testimony, §2221.
Use of depositions, §2250.
Directed verdict, §§2262, 2269 to 2273.
See DIRECTED VERDICT.
Discovery.
Use at trial, §§1636, 2249.
Evidence.
Admission of evidence.
Exclusion, §2254.
Offers of proof on excluded evidence,
§2257.
Generally, §2254.
Limiting instructions, §2260.
Motions in limine and memoranda on
admissibility, §2255.
Motions to strike, §2258.
Objections, §2258.
Continuing objections, §2259.
Record of proceedings to preserve
review, §2256.
Rephrasing objectionable questions,
§2261.
Taking of evidence at trial.
Admissions, §2252.

TRIAL—Cont'd
Evidence—Cont'd
Taking of evidence at trial—Cont'd
Depositions, §2250.
Discovery-generated materials, §2249.
Documentary or other tangible
evidence, §2244.
Examination of witnesses, §§2239 to
2243.
Facts admitted in pleadings, §2245.
Generally, §2238.
Interrogatories, §2251.
Judicial notice, §2247.
Presumptions, §2248.
Stipulations, §2246.
Views, §§2253, 2327.
Generally, §2201.
Instructions to jury, §§2275 to 2286.
See JURY INSTRUCTIONS.
Interrogatories.
Use of answers to interrogatories, §2251.
Involuntary dismissal.
Motion at trial, §§2262 to 2268.
See DISMISSAL OF ACTIONS.
Judges.
Conduct of judge, §2293.
Relief from judicial misconduct, §2294.
Judgments.
Declaratory judgments, §§3101 to 3115.
See DECLARATORY JUDGMENTS.
General provisions, §§2401 to 2455.
See JUDGMENTS.
Offer of judgment, §§2402 to 2413.
See OFFER OF JUDGMENT.
Jury.
General provisions, §§2301 to 2345.
See JURY.
Instructions to jury, §§2275 to 2286.
See JURY INSTRUCTIONS.
Mistrial, §2295.
Opening statements.
Generally, §2233.
Legal sufficiency, §2235.
Objectionable content, §2236.
Purpose, §2234.
Scope, §2234.
Order of trial, §2230.
Reopening after resting, §2232.
Taking of evidence, §2231.
Pretrial conference, §§1801 to 1808.
See PRETRIAL CONFERENCE.
Reopening after resting, §2232.
Setting action for trial.
Application for.
Time, §2204.
Eighth district, §2213.
Fifth district, §2210.

5375